hydro- [Gk. *hydor,* water; now, confusingly, pertaining either to water or to hydrogen]: hydrogen, dehydration, hydraulic, carbohydrate, hydrolytic

hyper- [Gk. *hyper,* over, above, more than]: hyperacidity, hyperthyroid, hypertonic

hypo- [Gk. *hypo,* under, below, beneath, less than]: hypochondria, hypocotyl, hypodermic, hypoglycemia, hypothalamus, hypothesis, hypotonic

in-, im- [L. *in,* in]: imprinting, inbreeding, instinct, insulin

inter- [L. *inter,* between, among, together, during]: interaction, interbreed, intercellular, intercostal

intra-, intro- [L. *intra,* within]: intracellular, intrauterine, intravenous, introduced

-itis [L., Gk. *-itis,* inflammation of]: arthritis, bronchitis, dermatitis

leuko-, leuco- [Gk. *leukos,* white]: leukocyte, leukemia, leukoplast, leukocytosis

-logue, -logy [Gk. *-logos,* word, language, type of speech]: analogue (analogy), homologue (homology), dialogue

-logy [Gk. *-logia,* the study of, from *logos,* word]: anthropology, biology, cytology, embryology

-lysis, lys-, lyso-, -lyze, -lyte [Gk. *lysis,* a loosening, dissolution]: lyse, lysogeny, paralysis, hydrolysis, analysis, catalysis, catalytic

macro- [Gk. *makro-,* now "great," "large"]: macrocyte, macromolecule, macronucleus, macrophage

mega-, megalo-, -megaly [Gk. *megas,* large, great, powerful]: megaspore, megaton, acromegaly

-mere, -mer, mero- [Gk. *meros,* part]: blastomere, centromere, chromomere, polymer

meso-, mes- [Gk. *mesos,* middle, in the middle]: mesentery, mesoderm, mesophyll, Mesozoic

meta-, met- [Gk. *meta,* after, beyond; now often denoting change]: metabolism, metastasis, Metazoa

micro- [Gk. *mikros,* small]: microbe, micrometer, micronucleus, micropyle, microscope

myo- [Gk. *mys,* mouse, muscle]: myocardial, myocardium, myoglobin, myosin

neuro- [Gk. *neuron,* nerve sinew, tendon]: neurasthenia, neuroanatomy, neuroblast, neuron, neurotransmitter,

oligo- [Gk. *oligos,* few, little]: Oligocene, oligochaete, oligotrophic

-oma [Gk. *-oma,* tumor, swelling]: carcinoma, glaucoma, hematoma, lipoma, sarcoma

oo- [GK, *oion,* egg]: oogenesis, oogonium, oophyte

-osis [Gk. *-osis,* a state of being, condition]: arteriosclerosis, cirrhosis, halitosis

osteo-, oss- [Gk. *osteon,* bone; L. *os, ossa,* bone]: ossification, ossified, Osteichthys, osteoblast, periosteum

para- [Gk. *para-,* alongside of, beside, beyond]: paradigm, paralysis, paremedic, parasite

patho-, -pathy, -path [Gk. *pathos,* suffering; now often disease or the treatment of disease]: pathogen, pathology, pathological

peri- [Gk. *peri,* around]: pericardial, pericarp, pericycle, periosteum, photoperiod, peritoneum

phago-, -phage [Gk. *phagein,* to eat]: phagocyte, phagocytosis, bacteriophage

plasm-, -plasm, -plast, -plasty [Gk. *plasm,* something molded or formed; Gk. *plassein,* to form or mold]: plasma, plasma membrane, plasmid, plasmolysis, cytoplasm, nucleoplasm, chloroplast, chromoplast, protoplast, dermoplasty

-pod [Gk. *pod,* foot]: cephalopod, gastropod, pseudopod

poly- [Gk, *poly-, polys,* many]: polychaete, polydactyly, polygenic, polymer, polypeptide

-rrhea [Gr. *rhoia,* flow]: amenorrhea, diarrhea, gonorrhea

septi-, -sepsis, -septic [Gk. *septicos,* rotten, infected]: septic, septicemia, aseptic, antiseptic

-some, somat- [Gk. *soma,* body; Gk. *somat-,* of the body]: chromosome, ribosome

-stat,-stasis, stato- [Gk. *stasis,* stand]: metastasis, thermostat, electrostatic, hydrostatic

stoma-, stomato-, -stome [Gk. *stoma,* mouth, opening]: stoma, cyclostome, deuterostome, protostome

sym-, syn- [Gk. *syn,* with, together]: symbiont, symbiosis, symmetry, synapsis, synchrony

taxo-, -taxis [Gk. *taxis,* to arrange, put in order; now often referring to ordered movement]: taxonomy, chemotaxis, geotaxis, phototaxis

tomo-, -tome, -tomy [Gk. *tome,* a cutting; Gk. *tomos,* slice]: atom [you can't cut it], anatomy, lobotomy, appendectomy

tropho-, -troph, -trophy [Gk. *trophe,* nutrition]: trophic level, trophoblast, atrophy, autotroph, heterotroph

trop-, tropo-, -tropy, -tropism [Gk. *tropos,* to turn, to turn toward]: tropism, tropical, entropy, geotropism, phototropism

ur-, -uria [Gk. *ouron,* urine]: uracil, urea, ureter, phenylketonuria

uro-, -uran [Gk. *oura,* tail]: urochordate, anuran

BIOSPHERE

BIOSPHERE

The Realm of Life

SECOND EDITION

ROBERT A. WALLACE
UNIVERSITY OF FLORIDA

JACK L. KING

GERALD P. SANDERS

SCOTT, FORESMAN AND COMPANY
GLENVIEW, ILLINOIS
BOSTON
LONDON

Library of Congress Cataloging-in-Publication Data

Wallace, Robert A.
  Biosphere : the realm of life.
  Bibliography: p.
  Includes index.
  1. Biology.   I. King, Jack L., 1934–
II. Sanders, Gerald P.   III. Title. [DNLM: 1. Biology.
QH 308.2 W193b]
QH308.2.W355 1987   574   87-16671
ISBN O-673-16717-8

123456—VHJ—939291908988

For those people who have been
so important, interesting, or simply outrageous
(They can sort themselves out):

**Jim Cook, Jack May,
Russell Hurd, Martha Lott,
Charlie Wilson,
and Yvonne Carrejo**
(wherever she is)

RAW

To Rachel, Aaron, and Mary

GPS

PREFACE

For some reason it is more difficult to write a preface for this second edition than it was for the first. This seems to be because, in introducing this new version of what was a very successful book, we feel compelled to cite our "improvements." We would like to think this is unnecessary because each time we finish a project, we believe it simply cannot be improved in any way whatsoever. The reality is that by the day it's printed we would like to change it. Perhaps we've learned new things and, possibly, better ways to present them. Maybe new data are out or someone has made a startling discovery. In any case, we find little rest because we indeed believe we *can* improve on whatever we've done, and reworking our next edition is the way to do it.

Not only do we have changes *we* would like to make, but our colleagues often have changes *they* would like us to make. Some of these reach us as unsolicited (and usually appreciated) informal notes and letters. But we also seek out suggestions. And so we are deluged by reams of reviews that we sort through, looking for common themes, unusual suggestions, and new information and better ways to present it. For this edition we also formed "focus groups" consisting of diverse specialists familiar with all areas of biology. Their selection of topics was partly free-form, partly orchestrated, and the results always forced a careful reexamination of what we had done and what we hoped to do.

Many of the changes thus came about in a rather formal, straightforward way. But other changes were made much more unobtrusively, without clear authorship. Authors must live with their books, and by living with them, we subtly change them (and to an unsettling degree, they change us). So this edition is different from the first, including our learning aids.

PEDAGOGY

One of the most striking changes we've made is the addition of spot summaries set off from the chapter text by a colored background. Those students not entirely acquainted with the rigors of science, we believe, will appreciate these brief pauses to summarize the major preceding idea. We've also added to our review questions, small quizzes that can be used as a kind of yardstick as the reader goes along. (Following each review question the page number on which the answer can be found is in parentheses.)

Reviewers liked our emphasis on the derivation of scientific terminology. We retained this feature in this edition, along with the biological lexicon inside the front cover.

There has also been favorable reaction to our essays. We've carefully revised those that appear in this edition, and we've added some new ones, such as Essay 29.1: Asteroids and the Great Extinctions.

We've retained the pedagogical features of the previous edition, which include an end-of-chapter list of boldfaced key terms and chapter summary expanded to now include main and subordinate heads. The glossary has been completely revised and expanded to reflect the extensive revision the text has undergone, as has the list of suggested readings.

CONTENT

We've changed the first chapter to include introductions to science and its methods and to highlight some of the broad themes in biology, particularly unity and diversity. We've also extensively reworked following sections on chemistry and energetics to make them clearer and simpler without sacrificing the major points.

The detail on chemiosmosis in the respiration and photosynthesis chapters is well-presented with very good support from the new text figures. Highly mechanistic processes such as photosynthesis have all-new art that puts the processes in a cellular perspective. Each step is clearly and cleanly outlined.

Some areas of biology change faster than others (a clavicle is a clavicle, but the Central Dogma is not so dogmatic after all). One of the fastest-changing areas in biology, indeed, falls within the realm of molecular biology and so we've extensively updated sections on DNA, RNA, eukaryote gene organization, and recombinant DNA technology to reflect current technology and applications. Two chapters in the genetics unit were reordered. You will also find brief discussions of genetic engineering throughout the book.

Since evolution is the central theme of this book (indeed, of all biology), we have revised and extended much of this material. We not only directly approach the subject in three chapters, beginning with the general principles of Darwinian evolution, but we also interweave principles of evolution throughout the book.

Again, in our discussions of the various animal systems we describe humans, but in each case we first review principles of comparative biology, covering both invertebrates and vertebrates. This format enables us to underscore, again, the evolutionary theme.

One of the most pressing topics in biology (if not history) is AIDS. We have considered, therefore, not only the disease itself, but the interface between recombinant DNA and immunology in an effort to more clearly show the fundamental nature of the problem. Accordingly, you will find a brand new chapter on immunology where we have outlined the workings of this amazingly complex system.

Scientists who are content experts were engaged to review each chapter in galleys, along with art and captions, to ensure the highest degree of accuracy. Between first and second draft, each chapter was reviewed by six content experts.

These sorts of changes are easy to describe. They're right there in black and white. But other changes are not.

THE NEW LOOK

We are very pleased at the attention the publisher has given to color, and to the general appearance of the book. The art, design and layout of the new edition painstakingly involved a remarkable integration of pedagogical and esthetic approaches. The labelling on every piece of art in the revision was carefully checked to make sure that it is both accurate and a good correlation with the text.

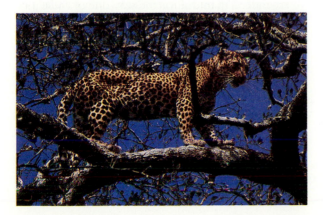

One more point should be made regarding "color". We firmly believe that writing style, itself, can create its own rich spectrum. So we have chosen not to dampen it with academic piety. We have chosen, instead, to let the story be told. In essence, we have tried to let biology live in these pages. It is a tale of mystery, drama, intrigue, disappointment, surprise and, often, humor and spirit. It's a good story, as you will see.

SUPPLEMENTS

With this edition we present an all-new laboratory manual. It contains over 30 experiments carefully coordinated with BIOSPHERE, and each experiment has been field-tested by faculty and students to ensure that it works.

We also provide a new instructor's manual and test bank. The test bank is available on DIPLOMA— Scott, Foresman's electronic classroom management system. In addition, the instructor's manual will have a series of transparency masters, enabling you to use BIOSPHERE's art for testing or review.

A new study guide has been prepared for this edition of BIOSPHERE. In addition to the review exercises for each chapter, there are 100 genetics problems and answers. Etymologies, retained on the inside front cover of the book's new edition, are reinforced in a section of the study guide. Especially difficult topics like respiration and photosynthesis are developed as concept maps. There will also be more informal exercises like word games.

Finally, approximately 175 of the color diagrams and photographs from our new edition will be reproduced as transparencies and slides. These have been relabelled in larger boldface type, allowing students even in the back of the room to see the labels. There will be micrographs included in the package, and each will have line art rendered to it. The art in our new edition of BIOSPHERE has received a great deal of attention—about 25% of the art and photos are new or revised, and the art retained from the previous edition has been carefully relabeled, and color has been added. Thus, these supplements should be very helpful.

ACKNOWLEDGEMENTS

Textbook publishing has changed a great deal over the past several years. It has become, in effect, much more complex and competitive. Each year seems to bring a host of innovations in development, pedagogy, and presentation. So each year, an ever more dedicated and sophisticated group of people are involved in shaping our projects. We would like to acknowldge some of those movers and shapers.

First and foremost we are grateful for our long and productive association with our friend Jim Levy. As general manager of the college publishing division, Jim has sustained a vision of the possible and has unfailingly helped us make it a reality. It's good to know he's there.

Our editor-in-chief Dick Welna has again guided us through the whitewater, often quietly and behind the scenes. He has been involved at almost every level, and the result is clear evidence of his effectiveness.

Jack Pritchard, science and math editor, has a way of worrying his way to success. He constantly seems to be fidgeting with and fine-tuning each project until suddenly it emerges as a clear winner. We're glad to have had the chance to work with him again.

Even the best books can only reach the readers with the dedicated support of the people who work at the interface. Here, we are proud to have Carl Tyson as director of marketing. Carl not only gets the book to the reader in a most effective manner but also actually helps develop the appearance of the book, giving his people the best possible product to work with.

The sales themselves are in the hands of Ben Whitney, national sales manager, whose motivational and managerial skills have led to a remarkable ascension in a tough business. With the merging of the Little-Brown staff with Scott, Foresman's, Ben is handling one of the best sales groups in publishing.

George Duda, marketing manager, pride of the Ukraine, is quite simply the best we've ever worked with. We often have the eerie feeling he knows more about our books than we do. But, considering his success, we don't mind that small embarrassment.

We are again grateful for the help of Art Director Barbara Schneider. She knows her end of the business as few others do, and her discerning eye, determination, and intelligence have led us through technical and esthetic mazes time and again.

This book is largely the product of the hands-on efforts of CRACOM Corp., led by President Craig Cuddeback. He has put together a group of talented professionals with that greatest of virtues, common sense.

Among the CRACOM people we would like to thank is Susan Dust Schapper, director of project development. She can not only outrun us, but she has those organizational skills that, indeed, make things run smoother for everyone.

We had the good fortune to work on a daily basis with Suzanne King Hagan, our developmental editor, who put aside a successful career in science writing to try her hand at managing textbooks. Suzanne is one of those editors with the disconcerting habit of finding all those skeletons you thought you had safely buried. When we weren't driving her up the wall, she effectively managed this project from start to completion. We are grateful.

Art and production director, Peggy Norman, had the enormous task of putting the pieces of all this together and making them fit. In a real sense she is responsible for what you see here. She directed a talented and diverse group of people through the book's development.

We are extremely pleased with the art. For this we can thank Nadine Sokol, artist and art coordinator. Nadine made those long afternoons poring over sketches not so bad after all. The artists who worked with her are Kevin A. Sommerville and Sarah Woodward, among the most talented people in the business. Art was also provided by the artists at Precision Graphics.

Mary Espenschied, project editor, is a delight to work with. She knows her business and finds ways around the inevitable problems. Production design itself was handled competently by Jeanne Genz and Jeanne Gulledge. Linda Lehmann, production assistant, worked closely with all on the many details of the production process. We also think editorial assistants Joy Moore and Kathleen Jenkins for their conscientious efforts with the manuscript.

Photographs and ancillaries were in the hands of Jean Carey-Brendle, Suzanne Hagan, and Bess Arends. Nina Page, of Scott, Foresman, provided substantial support with the photo research. The look of the book is largely due to Diane Beasley, who was responsible for book and cover design. Nelle Garrecht was our copyeditor and indexer, and Judy Ahlers our proofreader.

There are many thankless jobs in publishing, but we are indeed thankful for the way one of these jobs has been done. Jayne Austin, with help from Rob Austin and Harry Austin, diligently prepared our outstanding glossary, one of our most important aids to study.

In addition, our thanks go to Cheryl Jeffrey, whose constant attention to detail made the second draft literally come together.

We want to thank everyone for a job well done.

Robert A. Wallace
Gerald P. Sanders

REVIEWERS

The authors and publishers would like to express their appreciation to a number of biologists who have greatly assisted in the development of this book. Biology is a diverse and evolving discipline, and we owe a great deal to the specialists who reviewed our material.

David W. Aldridge
North Carolina A&T University

Robert Andersen
De Paul University

Julia L. Basham
Shawnee State University

Richard W. Baumann
Brigham Young University

Judith E. Bramble
Washington University, St. Louis

Bruce W. Burkhart
Rio Hondo College

Craig A. Busack
University of Mississippi

Herbert J. Cash
Okaloosa-Walton Junior College

Paul A. Catalano
Lakeland Community College

Billy G. Cumbie
University of Missouri, Columbia

Patrick J. Dailey
Lewis & Clark Community College

Robert F. Edwards
St. Louis Community College, Florissant Valley

Lynn J. Fancher
College of DuPage

Richard F. Firenze
Broome Community College

Lawrence D. Friedman
University of Missouri, St. Louis

Robert Gillespie
St. Louis Community College, Meramec

Fred A. Hopper
New Mexico Highlands University

Richard L. Klotz
SUNY, College at Cortland

Captain Robert C. Kull, Jr.
United States Air Force Academy

W. Joseph Leverich
St. Louis University

Shaun M. McEllin
New Mexico Highlands University

Nancy R. Parker
Southern Illinois University, Edwardsville

Gary B. Peterson
South Dakota State University

William G. Raschi
Bucknell University

Rodney A. Rogers
Drake University

Major George I. Shields
United States Air Force Academy

Gerald Summers
University of Missouri, Columbia

William J. Tietjen
Lindenwood College

Jack T. Tomlinson
San Francisco State University

Leonard S. Vincent
Georgia Southern College

Bailey Ward
University of Mississippi

Douglas Wikum
University of Wisconsin-Stout

Hubert Y. Yamamoto
Minneapolis Community College

Contents In Brief

CONTENTS

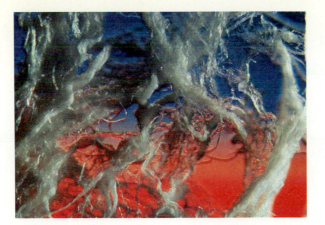

BIOSPHERE

I

SCIENCE AND THE ONGOING FLOW OF LIFE

I

SCIENCE AND ITS DESCENT

The old man was clearly wrong. Any educated person of his time could easily point out the error in his logic—and he was a heretic as well. The Church taught that all the heavenly bodies revolved around a central, unmoving earth. Galileo Galilei, however, believed in a bold new idea that had been put forth by the Polish astronomer, Copernicus, the idea that the earth and the planets revolved around the sun. The churchmen hadn't stopped Galileo from teaching Copernicus' *heliocentric theory,* as long as it was presented as merely an interesting idea; but Galileo had overstepped those bounds. His mistake was in trying to prove the theory with his own astronomical observations.

Now, in 1633, as he stood before the court of the Papal Inquisition in Rome, his bald head was bowed in forced obedience, humiliation, and rage. He was 69 years old (Figure 1.1).

Recant! he was ordered. The Inquisitors handed him a sheet of paper on which were written the words that he was required to say: that he "objured, cursed, and detested" his erroneous claim that the earth moved around the sun. Galileo reluctantly mouthed the words. He was given a prison sentence anyway, based on a forged document purporting to show that he had previously been expressly forbidden to publish his ideas. Later his sentence was to be commuted to lifelong house arrest. As he left the tribunal, Galileo was heard to mutter, "Nonetheless, it moves."

GALILEO AND THE ROOTS OF SCIENCE

What had been Galileo's error? First, he had confronted the powerful Church. But he had also chosen an unaccepted method of attempting to establish truth.

The scholars of the Middle Ages had developed a method for determining truth that was based on the teachings of Aristotle, heavily interpreted by medieval theologians such as Aquinas and Abélard. This was the formal method of deductive reasoning known as *Aristotelian logic.* In Aristotelian logic, one starts with a few established truths and deduces from them other, less obvious truths. The chain of reasoning is presented in the form of a **syllogism,** of the *"if . . . then . . . therefore"* variety that we will encounter shortly in our discussion of deductive reasoning. The formal proofs of plane geometry are the finest products of this approach. The Church, which controlled the schools and the universities, still taught in Gali-

leo's time that Aristotelian logic was the only acceptable method of determining truth. In particular, the philosophers taught that the senses were not to be trusted. Galileo nevertheless was trying to determine truth through observation, by looking through a telescope.

> Galileo's approach was to confirm or test ideas through prediction and further observation, basic elements of today's scientific methodology.

Observation? Why? Observation was clearly unnecessary, he was told, because observation depends on our senses, and our senses can mislead us. Only rigorous, abstract logic could rise above the meaningless distractions of the imperfect, rough-and-tumble world to reveal underlying truths. Or so said the educated men of the time.

Two accepted truths of the time were that *the heavens are perfect,* and *the moon is in the heavens.* It followed, then, that *the moon is perfect.* Another supposedly self-evident truth was that *a sphere is the only perfect shape.* From this it followed that the moon must be a perfect sphere. The problem was that Galileo, using the telescope he helped develop, saw imperfections on the moon—jagged craters and lofty mountains. He had begged the members of the Papal court to look through his telescope and see the imperfections for themselves, but they refused. The craters and mountains were not there, and that was that.

But Galileo persisted. The old man belonged to the coming modern age, not the fading medieval age that still held the minds of the Church philosophers.

Galileo had spent his life devising ways of measuring and weighing things. He measured the speed of sound and had even attempted to measure the speed of light; he measured the speed and acceleration of falling weights. He applied mathematics to the real world, boldly proclaiming that "the book of Nature is written in mathematical characters."

Galileo had been a convinced Copernican since his youth, although he had kept his belief a secret to avoid ridicule. However, with his reliable telescope, he believed he saw a way to test the Copernican theory so that others would realize the truth of it. This notion alone put him on the road to modern science. He could make a prediction based on the heliocentric (sun-centered) theory. (A **prediction** is a statement concerning something that is going to happen or that has already happened but has yet been observed.) With a prediction the Copernican theory became *testable.* For example, Galileo could predict that if the earth and planets revolved around the sun, the planet Venus should have phases like those of the moon; that is, it should always be illuminated on the side facing the sun. Here was a prediction that could be tested through new observations.

Over several years Galileo pointed his long, thin telescope toward Venus and maintained careful records. He found that the planet was, in fact, illuminated on the side that, according to Copernican calculations, should be facing the sun. Because of his observations, Galileo thought he had proved the heliocentric theory.

However, the religious inquisitors and scholars were of another mind; their formal training stood squarely in the way. They could understand Galileo's argument only if they put it into the form of one of their own syllogisms.

1. If the planets and the earth circle the sun, Venus should have phases like those of the moon.
2. Venus does have phases like those of the moon.
3. Therefore, the planets and the earth circle the sun.

Phrased this way, the inquisitors could see that the problem lay in the observation (No. 2). By the conventions of Aristotelian logic, this was clearly a classic example of erroneous, faulty, and invalid reasoning! Obviously, the old man, with his strange machines and cantankerous spirit, simply did not understand how real science was done. They noted that other explanations could just as easily account for Galileo's assertions. Some said that one could just as well argue:

1. If the world is an illusion designed to deceive us, Venus should have phases like those of the moon.
2. Venus does have phases like those of the moon.
3. Therefore, the world is an illusion designed to deceive us.

This line of reasoning was actually more acceptable than that offered by Galileo. The idea of an illusory world had been taught by many of the early philosophers (who, though living in an illusory world, were usually on time for dinner just the same). By comparison, the idea that the earth revolves around the sun was much more difficult to accept. It violated both philosophy *and* common sense (as much as the senses were not to be trusted, they clearly seemed to indicate the sun arcing across the sky over the unmoving land).

Part of the Church's problem was that, years before, its leaders had unknowingly asked for trouble. They had told Galileo that he could publish a book on his ideas if he also stated that the Copernican theory was merely an unproved idea. The problem was this: When Galileo's book was completed, the required provision was there, but his arguments for the Copernican theory were so strong that they made the dictated conclusion of the Church look weak and foolish. Galileo's real crime was not in disagreeing with the Church over whether the sun or the earth was at the center of the universe but in daring to test the real world with a new and dangerous tool. His crime was being a scientist.

Actually, the refusal of the Papal court to look through Galileo's telescope was a credit to their own intellectual integrity. However, they were fighting a doomed battle. They kept Galileo under house arrest until his death eight years later, but in the end the world became convinced of the validity of the heliocentric theory. Today the Church agrees that the earth revolves around the sun.

How did the world become convinced? By the same kind of evidence and reasoning that Galileo had offered. Measurement after measurement supported the theory that the earth and the planets revolve around the sun. Prediction after prediction had been tested and had supported the Copernican hypothesis. Today the guidance and navigational systems of space probes are based on incredibly precise predictions of where each planet will be at any given point in time (Figure 1.2). Perhaps the astronomers and engineers were deceived; the world may yet turn out to be an illusion, but for now we are convinced that it is not. We are convinced, not by formalized proofs, but by the sheer weight of evidence based on observation. Galileo's way of looking for truth—hopelessly flawed by 17th century standards—has been called many things, among them the **scientific method.**

SCIENTIFIC METHOD

In its broadest sense the scientific method might be described as the way one gets at the truth or, as one prominent scientist put it, "doing one's damnedest with one's mind, no matter what." Nonetheless, even in our free-wheeling world, there are rules to getting at the truth, and some methods are held in greater esteem than others. The two methods that have been used for the last hundred years or so are **inductive reasoning** and **deductive reasoning** (Table 1.1).

Inductive Reasoning

Inductive reasoning involves reaching a conclusion based on observations; it moves from the specific to the general. For example, Galileo made a number of specific observations, and from these he drew a general truth regarding the relationship of the earth and the heavens. He *induced* this truth from the available evidence.

FIGURE 1.2 Galileo's theories began the kind of astronomy that would one day contribute to space exploration.

TABLE 1.1   An Example of Inductive and Deductive Reasoning

Inductive Reasoning

Observation: Coral atolls usually consist of a circle of islands.
Observation: Coral atolls form from the deposits of living animals.
Observation: Coral animals without direct access to fresh seawater tend to die.
Observation: The interior of an atoll seems to consist of sunken coral.
Generality: Coral atolls are formed as coral animals secrete deposits. The animals in the center, lacking nutrient-laden water, die and sink. This leaves a ring that, in turn, breaks apart to form a circle of islands.

Deductive Reasoning

Generality: Coral atolls form as coral animals secrete deposits. Animals in the center, lacking nutrient-laden water, die, and sink. This leaves a ring that, in turn, breaks apart to form a circle of islands.
Deduction: Coral atolls will have a sunken center.
Deduction: Coral animals need contact with fresh seawater.
Deduction: Seawater contains something that coral animals need.
Deduction: Coral atolls comprised of more nearly complete rings of land are probably recently formed.

Deductive Reasoning

Unlike the inductive process, deductive reasoning involves drawing specific conclusions from some larger assumption. It leads from the general to the specific, that is, from a broad idea to one or more specific statements. Deductive reasoning leads logically to predictions, which are often described as a form of "if . . . then" reasoning. As Galileo considered the heliocentric theory of Copernicus, he might have thought, "*If* the planets revolve about the sun, *then* Venus should have illuminated phases as we see in the moon." He would have been using deductive reasoning, and the "if" part of his proposition would have been phrased as a **hypothesis.**

Inductive reasoning begins with specific observations and leads to the formulation of general hypotheses. By contrast, **deductive reasoning,** a verifying or testing process, begins with a hypothesis and leads to specific predictions, which can then be tested.

Hypothesis, Theory, and Law

A hypothesis is a provisional conjecture that can be used to form predictions, which can then be tested. If what was predicted does, in fact, come about, we can say that the new observation is *consistent* with the hypothesis and thus supports it; the observation increases our confidence in the likelihood that the hypothesis is true. The hypothesis passes a test that *it might have failed.* On the other hand, if the predicted event is not observed, the new findings are *inconsistent* with the hypothesis, and thus weaken or even destroy it. At the very least, the original hypothesis may have to be reformulated to take account of the new observation.

Einstein's thinking on relativity led to the hypothesis that light is bent by gravity. One resulting prediction was that the apparent position of a distant star would change when a closer, massive star came between it and the earth; that is, the light would be bent by the gravity of the massive star. Soon after this prediction was made, there was an opportunity to test it. Special observatories were set up. The moment came; the astronomers' photographic plates were analyzed and, sure enough, light had been bent just as Einstein had predicted. Thus the hypothesis was supported, but still it was not *proved.* In fact,

Einstein's theory of relativity remains unproved to this day, although it has passed a great number of such tests. Although it is now generally accepted by physicists, it is still subject to further testing and might be disproved or modified in the future.

A scientific observation (or a thousand scientific observations) can support a hypothesis but cannot prove it to be true. On the other hand, a single, repeatable observation can prove a hypothesis to be false.

Some hypotheses generate predictions that are more difficult to test, such as the prediction that continued cigarette smoking causes lung cancer. As the tobacco industry is quick to point out, there are both healthy octogenarian smokers and young, cancer-stricken abstainers. Therefore the hypothesis must be modified to state that cigarette smoking has a *significant tendency* to cause lung cancer. Such a hypothesis can be tested only by using massive numbers of subjects and sophisticated statistical analysis to show that the connection does or does not exist.

Hypotheses are accepted or rejected on the basis of data obtained through experiments or observations as suggested by **predictions.**

As a hypothesis gains weight by the sheer accumulation of evidence, the statement may finally enter the realm of **theory.** A theory is an explanation of nature that enjoys considerably more supporting evidence than does a hypothesis. Ideally, such evidence represents the results of testing a variety of predictions through many experiments or observations. The difference between a hypothesis and a theory is more a matter of confidence than anything else.

As more and more evidence comes in that is consistent with a given theory, it becomes virtually (but not quite) irrefutable and is called a **law.** Laws enjoy more confidence than theories and, in fact, seem to withstand any kind of testing we can invent. Examples are the law of gravity and the laws of thermodynamics, both very lofty, universal statements from physics. Biology is notoriously short on laws because life is by nature shifty, elusive and hard to define. Although biology has its "laws" (such as Mendel's laws and the Hardy-Weinberg law) biological statements wear their titles provisionally and uneasily. Most are based on mathematical descriptions rather than simple observation.

Experiment

Scientists are curious souls and one of their favorite tools is the experiment. Because their reputations as well as their conclusions depend on the nature of their experiments, they carry them out according to time-tested and accepted rules.

The "rules" say that an experiment should begin with a hypothesis. In fact, an experiment often can be considered a contrived situation that tests a hypothesis.

Let's consider an example based on events of recent history. Birdwatchers noticed that many of the eggs in a certain area were failing to hatch. They notified an esteemed biologist in the area and he found the problem to be even greater than was originally believed. One of his first questions was, "Have the conditions in the area recently changed in some way, thereby causing the eggs to fail?" He found that the eggs stopped hatching about the time that foresters began spraying the area with herbicides (plant-killing agents) causing trees to drop their leaves, creating fire-breaks, barren strips that impede the progress of forest fires. His hypothesis therefore became, "The herbicides are somehow killing the eggs." His first prediction was, "If the foresters stop using the herbicide, the eggs will begin to hatch again."

However, the foresters had problems of their own and they refused to cooperate, so the biologist had to devise another testable hypothesis. The new hypothesis became, "If I treat normal, healthy eggs with the herbicide, the eggs will not hatch." He now had the hypothesis and the experimental design. However, the weather had also changed about the time the foresters began spraying, and the days during this period had been unusually warm. The question then became, was the herbicide killing the eggs, or was the warm weather the cause? To separate any two possibly contributing factors, the scientist must hold one of them constant while varying the other.

In the laboratory, the biologist incubated three batches of eggs. The first was cared for under what would be normal conditions in the wild. The conditions for the second batch duplicated those of the first except that the air in the incubator was warmed to duplicate the unusually warm weather at the time.

The third group was incubated normally, except that the air in the incubator contained about the same level of herbicide as the air surrounding failed nests in the wild. The scientist found that the first and second group hatched normally, but the third group failed completely; none of the eggs exposed to the herbicide hatched. He concluded that the herbicide was killing the eggs.

This is obviously a rather simple experiment with rather predictable results. However, there was a twist: The scientist had to rule out the effects of hot weather. This was done by heating one group of eggs without adding herbicide and by maintaining a second group of eggs at the normal incubation temperature while adding herbicide. In this experiment the added heat and herbicide are called **variables.** A variable is the nonconstant part of the experiment that may be responsible for the observed results. The constant part of the experiment (here, the eggs that are incubated under normal conditions) is called the **control.**

In this experiment, if all three groups of eggs had hatched normally, the next step would be to change the variables so that the eggs were subjected to heat and herbicide simultaneously. Experimental design can indeed become complicated, but our example illustrates how the process is started.

What we described here is a **controlled experiment.** There may be many variations in such experiments, but the principle is the same. A number of subjects are randomly divided into two (or more) groups, and each group is treated exactly the same in all respects except one, which becomes the variable. The group subjected to the variable is called the **experimental group.** The others comprise the **control group,** the group to which the treated subject is compared as the results are analyzed. Since only one factor is varied at a time, we can find reliable answers to a question. For example, if we want to find out why a cake will not rise, we should not use less flour, turn down the oven, and add more eggs all at the same time. We have to alter each condition individually. Figure 1.3 illustrates a more complex experiment.

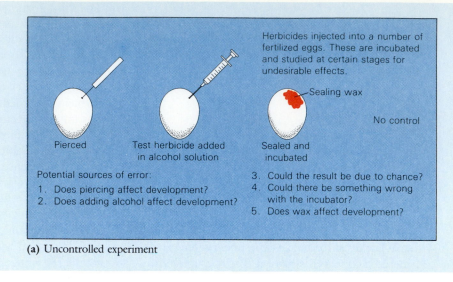

FIGURE 1.3 An experiment intended to determine the effect of an herbicide (plant killer) on bird development prior to its use on plants. **(a)** The experiment contains several sources of potential errors. To correct for such errors, a controlled experiment must be devised. In the controlled experiment **(b)** the results of the three groups are compared, and the results point to the effects of the herbicide.

Herbicides injected into a number of fertilized eggs. These are incubated and studied at certain stages for undesirable effects.

Pierced

Test herbicide added in alcohol solution

Sealing wax

No control

Sealed and incubated

Potential sources of error:

1. Does piercing affect development?
2. Does adding alcohol affect development?
3. Could the result be due to chance?
4. Could there be something wrong with the incubator?
5. Does wax affect development?

(a) Uncontrolled experiment

ESSAY 1.1 HOW SCIENTISTS SPREAD THE NEWS

The process of scientific discovery knows no unbreakable rules and is dominated by intuitive, creative eccentrics "doing one's damnedest with one's mind, no matter what." The conventions of communication among scientists, however, are as formal and intricate as an English country dance. It is not enough just to unravel the universe's little secrets. If new discoveries are to be taken seriously by other scientists, certain rigid criteria must be met. This means, among other things, that the experiments must be done right. Often, as it happens, the discovery comes first, not infrequently by (educated) accident. Still, before the new finding can be published and accepted, the experiment must be repeated and verified according to accepted procedures.

New findings are almost always communicated through a formal **scientific paper** or **journal article.** Scientists may write books, book reviews, and review articles, but these are all based on the all-important research articles. The article may appear in any one of several

thousand **scientific journals**—usually one devoted to the narrow specialty of the investigator. The most important new findings may appear in a journal of general interest to all scientists, such as *Science* or *Nature.*

In either case, the article will not be published until it has undergone the scrutiny of the journal's editor and of two or three anonymous volunteer referees. This is one of the extensive safeguards of formal science. The referee system, however, is not without drawbacks. The most important new ideas in science are those that break with established paradigms (world views) to permit fresh, unfamiliar perceptions, but referees may not be ready for fresh, unfamiliar ideas. Many of the most important landmark papers in any scientific field have had to withstand an initial rejection by suspicious referees. Of course, these referees have also prevented the publication of innumerable allegedly grand ideas and supposed paradigm shifts that were, in fact, pure hokum.

Scientific papers are frequently

presented as lectures, usually illustrated with slides, given at scientific meetings. Scientists attend these meetings to exchange news and, often **preprints**—photocopied manuscripts that have not yet been published. (Preprints are also sent through the mail by the hundreds, but they are supposedly privileged communications between friends and are *not* to be formally cited.) The papers presented at a scientific meeting sometimes are published together in a **symposium volume.**

A standard scientific article consists of six parts: the abstract or summary; introduction; methods and materials; results; discussion; and literature cited. The **Abstract** includes the principal finding, or conclusion, of the experiment being reported. A reader can rapidly skim through a whole pile of journals, reading just the titles and abstracts and delving into the rest of an article only if the abstract seems interesting.

A short **Introduction** reviews any previous relevant work and explains the reasons for proposing

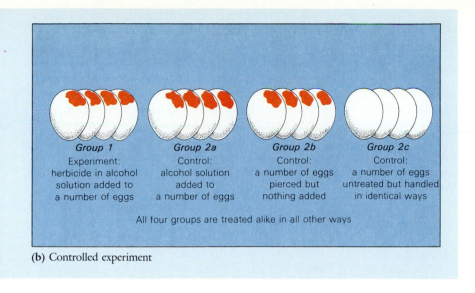

Group 1
Experiment:
herbicide in alcohol
solution added to
a number of eggs

Group 2a
Control:
alcohol solution
added to
a number of eggs

Group 2b
Control:
a number of eggs
pierced but
nothing added

Group 2c
Control:
a number of eggs
untreated but handled
in identical ways

All four groups are treated alike in all other ways

(b) Controlled experiment

the hypothesis that is to be tested. The writing style here, as throughout the article, is usually quite impersonal—maddeningly impersonal to anyone not thoroughly familiar with scientific presentation. One usually learns very little about the investigator's actual thought processes, hunches, dreams, or lucky accidents by reading scientific journals. The experiments themselves are the focus of scientific writing.

The **Methods and materials** section tells exactly how the experiment was conducted. It is written with enough detail and clarity that anyone who is sufficiently interested can repeat the experiment. Repeatability is the only guarantee that the findings are legitimate.

The **Results** section is the key part of most papers. It includes the observations made and experimental data compiled, along with any statistical analysis required to clarify the data. The investigator must accumulate enough data until it becomes extremely unlikely that the results could be due to chance. If the

investigator cannot show this, no reputable journal will publish the paper, and other scientists won't take the results seriously.

In the **Discussion** section, the author may be a little less formal and can even indulge in speculation, comparisons, and suggestions for future research. Here ambiguities in the data can be accounted for and potential objections explored, and persuasion and argument are allowed. After all, it doesn't do much good to make a new discovery if you can't convince the rest of the world. To a surprising degree—given the austere formality and pretended impartiality that good scientific manners demand—the ultimate impact of a work of science depends on the skillful presentation of ideas, on the ability to be interesting, and on just plain good writing. Good writing will not make a dull experiment interesting or render an unimportant discovery important; still, our greatest scientists have often been not only great experimentalists and theorists, but great writers as well.

Some papers end with a **summa-**

ry that condenses the primary question and the findings. Every scientific paper is sprinkled with numerous parenthetical notes or reference numbers referring the reader to the **Literature Cited,** a list of other journal articles that concludes the presentation. Each item on the list includes the name of the author or authors, year of publication, journal title, volume, and page number, and, sometimes, the title of the cited work. These references alert the reader to other important work in the field, in case he or she wishes to pursue the subject. Just as importantly, they give credit to workers who have made previous contributions. The first person to make a discovery has an eternal claim on all who follow. All humans hunger for recognition, appreciation, approval, and understanding from their peers, and most take pleasure in giving recognition where recognition is due. The formality of scientific citation is a humble acknowledgment that science is a cumulative, cooperative, and, above all, human venture.

THE WORKINGS OF SCIENCE

Reductionists and Synthesists

Reducing any problem to its simplest level and studying single factors at this level is called **reductionism.** Scientists who subscribe to this approach are called **reductionists.** They often make the best experimenters because they are interested in solving single aspects of one problem at a time. Sometimes this powerful principle is itself described as being "the" scientific method, but the reductionist approach, as valuable as it is, is only one way of doing science.

In every scientific field there are not only reductionists, but also **synthesists.** These people tend to take the available information (often from a variety of sources) and try to formulate some sort of grand, encompassing principle. These are the "big picture" people. Any active scientist can be either a reductionist or a synthesist at different times, of course. The synthesists tend to be theorists who operate by induction, developing theories that can then be tested through deductive reasoning. Theorists and synthesists generate new ways of looking at old observations (an "old" observation being anything that has already been published). A grand idea or theory usually is formulated from a large body of seemingly unrelated data, often with the stimulus of some new, at first inexplicable, finding. Copernicus was one such theorist; Einstein was another.

Revolutions and Paradigms

The sorts of questions scientists ask and the way they go about answering them depend on a set of encompassing views called paradigms. A paradigm is a general, accepted, and internally consistent view of the world. When an existing paradigm is replaced, the effect may be shattering to the scientific community, and the replacement may meet with stiff resistance. We saw this in the case of the Copernican revolution: Galileo's critics really could not understand the point he was trying to make. Others were all too aware of what the acceptance of Galileo's arguments would mean, and they were determined that Galileo fail in order to preserve the current paradigm.

Major scientific revolutions have played havoc with accepted paradigms, and there have been a number of such revolutions. Physics has seen two major revolutions in thought—relativity and quantum mechanics—in just this century. In the 20th century the science of geology was rocked to its foundations by the idea of continental drift. What is a major paradigm change in one field of science may create only a minor ripple of change in another field. Physicists were only mildly affected by the consequences of the new paradigm in geology, and neither group had to reorganize its thinking as a result of biology's evolutionary paradigm the **theory of evolution,** presented by Charles Darwin.

All of the great "-ologies" of science are artificial contructs. They were devised, in part, so that scientists could deal with narrowly defined tasks. A geologist might think, "I like rocks, and at least I have some hope of being successful in understanding them as long as I don't have to deal with cats." If the biologists, on the other hand, who deal with living things, were to try to explain why the earth's cats live where they do, they would have to include the geologist's paradigm of continental drift in their thinking.

Since the role of science is to explain the natural world—all of it—scientists have had to talk increasingly to each other and to carefully monitor the revolutions and developing paradigms of their colleagues in other areas.

Vitalism and Mechanism

In the 17th and 18th centuries, two quite different notions developed regarding the nature of life: **vitalism** and **mechanism.** Vitalism maintained that living organisms have special properties and are governed by special laws that are not applicable to inanimate objects or to the chemistry of nonliving substances. These special properties have been termed **vital forces.** What is the difference between a man and a corpse, it was argued, except for the presence or absence of a vital force? Unfortunately, because the "vital force" hypotheses were usually untestable, they haven't been subject to the sorts of investigations that comprise "good science."

The other school of thought was **mechanism,** the notion that a living body is a machine, subject to physical and chemical laws and depending only on those laws. Understand the laws and you will understand life, it was held, for life has no laws of its own.

The notoriously unromantic mechanistic view was slow in taking hold. However, a new focus in the ongoing controversy arose in the 19th century over the question of **spontaneous generation.** Historically, vitalists believed that the unexplained rise of molds, bacteria, and even maggots in rotting foods could be attributed to spontaneous generation by the material itself; in other words, life was being created

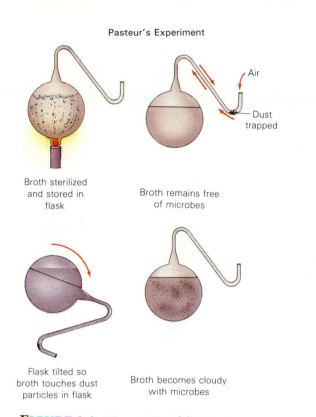

Pasteur's Experiment

Broth sterilized
and stored in
flask

Air

Dust
trapped

Broth remains free
of microbes

Flask tilted so
broth touches dust
particles in flask

Broth becomes cloudy
with microbes

FIGURE 1.4 The question of the spontaneous generation of life has a long history in science. On June 22, 1864, the idea was dealt a fatal blow. Louis Pasteur, the brilliant French biologist, was convinced that decay bacteria were simply carried from place to place by air currents and did not arise spontaneously. He also knew from past experiments that by boiling a rich broth and sealing the container he could preserve the contents indefinitely. His chief antagonist, F. A. Pouchet, quite logically pointed out that without the presence of air—which is essential to life—spontaneous generation could not occur. Pasteur met the challenge. He created a flask in which broth could be sterilized by boiling and air safely admitted. The question of spontaneous generation was laid to rest.

by the "vital forces" of nature. However, the noted scientist Louis Pasteur showed that some food-spoiling organisms simply grew from preexisting life present in the form of dormant but living "spores" (Figure 1.4). Biologists are now convinced that under today's conditions life arises only from preexisting life (called the **biogenetic law;** see Chapter 4). The key term is "today," since life must have originated spontaneously at least once, but under far different circumstances (see Chapter 20).

THE UNITY AND DIVERSITY OF LIFE

One very basic observation in biology is that there are fundamental similarities among very different kinds of living things. This "unity of life" is manifest in numerous ways. For example, the genetic mechanisms of all living things are remarkably similar. Inherited traits are passed along in much the same way in such diverse groups as bacteria, dandelions, and real lions. All living things tend to use similar sorts of molecules as food and to shuffle them along very similar sorts of routes as they are drained of their energy. That energy is then used in very similar ways. These sorts of similarities suggest a rather narrow range in the chemical makeup of quite diverse species.

We also find that the membranes covering the cells of living things are likely to be quite similar from one group to the next. A shark searching the ocean floor has cells bounded by membranes that are similar to those surrounding the cells of a desert mouse. If one were to examine the cells of a shark and a mouse, one would find similar tiny structures within the cells. Most of the life on this planet bears many of the common stamps that suggest relatedness. The notion of relatedness, of course, implies common ancestry. Even very different forms of life on the planet today may well be descended from the same distant ancestor. (The more related the life forms, the less distant the ancestor.) This notion is, of course, the central idea of evolution. We can define evolution simply as gradual change in living things over time. Living things change as they adapt to an ever-changing environment and through these adaptive changes, new species constantly arise. We will return to this central theme of biology again and again.

The Unity and Characteristics of Life

Examples of unity in life abound at all levels and are often referred to as the characteristics of life. Actually, any fundamental statement about life should begin with a definition, but life is notoriously difficult to define. It's much easier to list and describe its characteristics, but in its totality, the list ends up defining life. Let's consider this with a more formal listing (Figure 1.5):

(a) *Life is highly organized.* Nearly everything alive is organized on the cellular principle; that is, organisms are comprised of one or more cells. Across the spectrum of life, cells have many com-

FIGURE 1.5 (a) Organization is the catch-word of life. Even seemingly simple organisms such as the radiolaria are highly organized. The radiolarian skeleton is essentially of glass and its sculptured appearance is testimony to how beautifully complex life forms can become. (b) Life must exist in a steady state, within rather narrow limits and many forms have devised remarkable ways of regulating their internal environments. These bumblebees are vigorously fanning the nest, a common practice among bees when temperatures rise. (c) Life takes in and uses energy in order to retain its own highly organized state. Most energy enters the living realm through photosynthesis in green plants. (d) All organisms respond to their surroundings, but some living things are often extraordinarily responsive to external stimuli. The chameleon's lightning "tongue-flick" is a response to the presence of a moth.

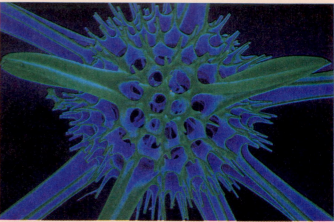

(a)

(b)

(c)

(d)

(e)

(f)

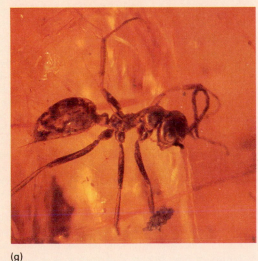

(g)

(e) Living things reproduce in an endless variety of ways. The aphid (*above left*) is giving birth to live offspring, generally considered an attribute of "higher" life forms. The embryos of some terrestrial vertebrates develop in a protective egg as did this emerging gavial (*above right*). (f) Living things adapt to their environment in quite surprising ways. For instance, chimpanzees (*left*) are known to make and use simple tools. The chimp carefully strips a slender stem off its leaves and uses it to gently probe a termite's nest. The stick is carefully withdrawn and any clinging termites are eaten. When not soaring through majestic mountain passes, these bald eagles (*right*) pass the time freeloading in a garbage dump located on Adak Island in the Aleutians. Such visits occur on a regular basis when the usual food supplies become scarce. (g) Life evolves. Much of what we understand about evolution comes from the study of fossils, but the fossil record is notoriously incomplete, especially in providing clues to transitional organisms—extinct forms representing steps in the evolution of today's lines. This fossil insect is a rare and exciting find, a transition species representing a stage in the evolution of ants from waspy ancestors. Its head, eyes, abdomen, and sting are typical of wasps, but its thorax (middle body) and waist are decidedly antlike, while its antennas have characteristics of both insects.

plex molecules and highly regimented chemical processes in common. The same key molecules and reactions are present in nearly all life forms.

(b) *Life requires a constant input of energy and raw materials.* Maintaining a highly ordered state is costly. Much of the material and energy initially entering the living realm is captured by **autotrophs,** plants and plantlike organisms that use the sun's energy and simple molecules. **Heterotrophs** feed on autotrophs, using the autotrophs' valuable, hard-won molecules as a source of energy and building materials for their own purposes. Energy thus passes from one life form to the next.

(c) *Life has a strong homeostatic quality.* **Homeostasis** is the maintenance of a "steady state," a state of chemical and physical constancy in the face of changes in surroundings. The maintenance of such a steady state requires a sensitivity and appropriate response to even minute changes.

(d) *Life makes many short-term responses to stimuli in the surroundings.* Common examples of stimuli are light, heat, cold, sound, movement, touch, and, of course, other organisms. The ability to respond to stimuli is essential to all other aspects of life and is fundamental to maintaining homeostasis. The total pattern of response made by organisms is known as *behavior.*

(e) *Life reproduces itself.* Perhaps the most obvious and unique characteristic of life is its overwhelming focus on reproduction. Perpetuation is the key to survival. All of the chemical and physical qualities that characterize and define each life form are replicated and preserved in new generations of cells and individuals.

(f) *Life adapts through evolution.* The physical, chemical, and behavioral characteristics of life change. Living things constantly adapt to an ever-changing environment. Such adaptations are the products of evolution through natural selection. Evolution is possible only because of myriad variations that exist within each species. Such variations are minute hereditary changes that arise through spontaneous mutations, each to face the test of natural selection. Those changes that pass are preserved, becoming the newest adaptations.

Life is organized, requires energy and materials, has a homeostatic quality, responds to stimuli, reproduces, and evolves.

Biological Diversity and the Wider View of Life

Although common threads run through the realm of life, one is particularly struck with life's great diversity. Evolution has been described as *descent with modification.* The "descent" implies a certain unity, and the "modification" has produced the diversity of life. The diversity, as we will see, is largely due to the great winnowing effects of natural selection. The opportunism of life has allowed the environment to shuffle, massage, enhance, and eliminate various traits of living things in such a way as to take advantage of whatever opportunities the environment affords. As life has probed every nook and cranny of our planet, each habitat has placed certain demands on its denizens, and as life has changed to meet these demands, variation has increased.

We should add that a knowledge of the unity and diversity of life has quite useful applications. For example, when we realize just how a four-chambered heart functions in birds and mammals, we can draw conclusions about how the human heart operates. In fact, medical research has taken advantage of the critical similarities between humans and other animals. (All sorts of animals serve as guinea pigs that, in turn, serve as cheap, expendable humans.) Most modern techniques in heart surgery were first performed on dogs, pigs or baboons—species with structural similarities to ours. Fish and reptiles have different metabolic and circulatory needs, and their hearts have taken developmental routes quite different from our own (Figure 1.6).

Common themes in diverse forms of life suggest common descent.

Of all the sciences, biology is, perhaps, the least subject to rigid laws. It has a fascinating and frustrating element of unpredictability, perhaps even unruliness. Part of the reason lies in the constantly changing realm of life—always shifting, adapting, and modulating. Part of the problem (with apologies to our philosopher friends) also must lie in the phenomenology of biological explanations. Phenomenology encompasses the notion of the interpretation of observations, and biology is an interpretive science. Just as bread is flavored by the peculiar flora of the baker's own hands, so the essence of the biologist enters into his or her own explanations of the world of life. The biologist also has the problem of an eye trying to see itself because, after all, we are indeed a part of the realm of life.

FIGURE 1.6 The hearts of vertebrates reveal certain structural and functional similarities, yet an inescapable trend over time—a progressive evolutionary change—is seen when the hearts are arranged in a series from the simplest to the most complex. The earliest vertebrates were the fishes, with their two-chambered hearts. Most amphibians and all reptiles are air breathers, using the lungs for gas exchange. The hearts of these cold-blooded amphibians and reptiles are mainly three-chambered, a condition that persisted over millions of years. Birds and mammals have evolved as warmblooded creatures who are able to survive quite well in the coldest terrestrial environments. Part of their adaptive success can be attributed to the four-chambered heart, which meets the increased oxygen demands of an elevated metabolic rate.

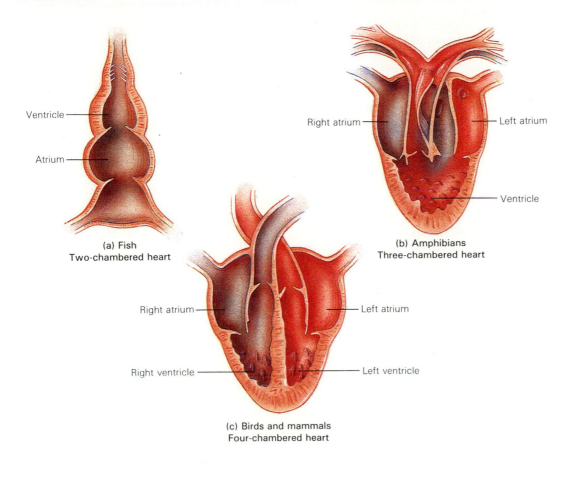

(a) Fish
Two-chambered heart

(b) Amphibians
Three-chambered heart

(c) Birds and mammals
Four-chambered heart

SUMMARY

GALILEO AND THE ROOTS OF SCIENCE

Although others in his time searched for truth through Aristotelian logic, Galileo tested ideas through prediction and observation. Religious inquisitors disputed Galileo's findings because his methods threatened established dogma.

SCIENTIFIC METHOD

Truth can be sought through both inductive and deductive reasoning.

Inductive Reasoning/Deductive Reasoning

With inductive reasoning, specific observations lead to larger generalizations, whereas in deductive reasoning, generalizations give rise to predictions and conclusions.

Hypothesis, Theory, and Law

Hypotheses are provisional explanations. To be useful, they must be testable. While hypotheses cannot be proved (only supported), they can be disproved. Tested and supported ideas may become theories. Where confidence is extremely strong, theories rise to the level of laws.

Controlled experiments are often designed for testing hypotheses. Subjects are arranged into variable and control groups. The variable is treated in the experimental manner while the control represents the normal condition.

THE WORKINGS OF SCIENCE

Reductionist scientists work with single, often minute, aspects of a problem. Synthesists use information from many sources to formulate grand, new schemes.

Revolutions and Paradigms

When new, major ideas or paradigms arise in science, they often meet strong resistance from more traditional forces. Examples of paradigms include evolution through natural selection, continental drift, and relativity.

Vitalism and Mechanism

Whereas vitalism is the notion that vague "vital forces" are responsible for biological functions, mechanism is the conviction that all biological phenomena can be explained through chemical and physical laws. A vitalistic belief known as spontaneous generation (life continually arising from inanimate materials), was disproved in the 19th century, replaced by the biogenetic law.

THE UNITY AND DIVERSITY OF LIFE

Fundamental similarities or commonalities in organisms, the so-called, unifying themes, are seen at all levels, from molecules onward and include both structure and function.

The Unity and Characteristics of Life

Common, unifying characteristics include: complex molecular organization, uptake and utilization of energy, maintenance of a homeostatic (steady) state, response to stimuli, reproduction, and adaptation.

KEY TERMS

---

syllogism	law	reductionism
scientific method	controlled experiment	synthesist
inductive reasoning	experimental group	vitalism
deductive reasoning	control group	mechanism
theory	variable	biogenetic law

REVIEW QUESTIONS

---

1 Compare Galileo's approach to problem solving with the more traditional Aristotelian approach of his day. (p. 3)

2 Explain why the Church was so opposed to the manner in which Galileo reached conclusions. Why was the Copernican theory itself opposed so vehemently? (p. 4)

3 Using examples, distinguish between deductive and inductive reasoning. Discuss the status of each type in science today. (pp. 4-6)

4 What is a hypothesis? What characteristic must a hypothesis have if it is to be a useful part of the scientific method? (p. 6)

5 In general, how do hypotheses, theories, and laws differ in science? (p. 6)

6 Why is it essential that a large number of subjects be used in controlled experiments? Why are controls critical? Distinguish between a control and a variable. (p. 7)

7 Using examples, compare the contributions of synthesists and reductionists. (p. 8)

8 What is a paradigm in science? How do people generally react to such proposals? (p. 8)

9 Using spontaneous generation as an example, distinguish between vitalism and mechanism. (pp. 10–11)

10 List six life characteristics shared by all organisms. (pp. 11–14)

11 Briefly suggest why diversity arises in spite of the unifying characteristics of life. (p. 14)

Since biology is the study of life, it can occupy the attentions of all sorts of scientists. Some wear muddy boots and ask where ducks go. In fact, biology was once almost the exclusive domain of people out tromping around in the woods and fields, telling us about the natural history of the world. But new faces, new ideas, and new techniques have brought other kinds of scientists into the world of biology. Some deal with numbers and are fascinated by odds. Others generate fascinating figures on computer screens to tell us how an organism grows, or how two species might interact. Among the most welcome of modern biologists, too, are those who can tell us about the most fundamental properties of living things—the chemistry of life. We will find that a great deal depends on the behavior of the chemicals that make up life.

2

THE BASIC CHEMISTRY OF LIFE

THE ELEMENTS

Chemists would start by defining elements, atoms, and molecules. An **element** is a substance that cannot be divided into simpler substances by chemical means. There are 92 naturally occurring elements (and 11 more that have been made in the laboratory). Of the naturally occurring elements, just six—*S*ulfur, *P*hosphorus, *O*xygen, *N*itrogen, *C*arbon, and *H*ydrogen—make up about 99% of living matter. Notice that these initials spell SPONCH.

The smallest unit of any element is the **atom** (*atom* is Greek for "indivisible"). Should the atoms of an element be broken down by some means, they would no longer be representative of the element.

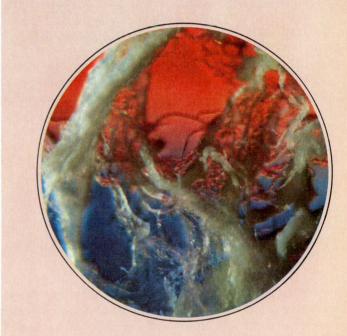

Each of the different **elements** contains fundamental parts called **atoms,** units that cannot be chemically subdivided.

ATOMS AND THEIR STRUCTURE

Let's begin our look at atomic structure by noting that atoms consist of three principal particles, **protons, neutrons,** and **electrons.** Protons and neutrons form a large, dense cluster known as the **nucleus.** Both protons and neutrons are much more massive than electrons, making up most of what is called the **atomic mass.** (If you weigh 150 pounds, your body is made up of about one ounce of electrons and about 149 pounds, 15 ounces of protons and neutrons.*) Protons have positive electrical charges, whereas neutrons have no charge.

The electrons, comparatively minute particles, are found outside the nucleus, traveling in paths known as **orbitals.**† Each tiny electron has a negative charge equal to the proton's positive charge. Since *like* charges repel each other and *unlike* charges attract, the positively charged protons tend to hold the negatively charged electrons and, under the most stable conditions, the electrons remain in their orbitals. If the number of electrons equals the number of protons, the atom is electrically balanced and bears no net charge.

The smallest and lightest atom, hydrogen, consists of a single proton with one electron revolving around it. Since the number of protons in the nucleus determines its **atomic number,** we say that the atomic number of hydrogen is *1*. The largest and heaviest naturally occurring atom is uranium-238, the nucleus of which contains 92 protons and 146 neutrons (Figure 2.1). The atomic number of uranium-238 is 92; its mass is 238 (92 + 146). (The atomic numbers of the six SPONCH elements are 16, 15, 8, 7, 6, and 1, respectively. Notice that the letters are arranged in order of decreasing atomic number.) Table 2.1 lists the atomic numbers and atomic masses of SPONCH and some other elements that are important to life.

Atoms consist of a **nucleus** of positively charged **protons** and uncharged **neutrons.** Negative **electrons** travel in orbitals outside the nucleus. The number of protons determines the **atomic number** and defines the element.

Isotopes

The number protons in an atom (its atomic number) is constant, but the number of neutrons in an element often varies. Atoms with the same atomic number but different atomic masses are called **isotopes.** Carbon-14 is an isotope of carbon-12; likewise, uranium-238 is an isotope of uranium-235.

Of the more than 320 known natural isotopes, about 60 are unstable, or **radioactive.** In addition, about 200 more radioactive isotopes, or **radioisotopes,** have been created in the laboratory. *Unstable*

refers to an isotope's tendency to spontaneously disintegrate, or decay, releasing radiation in some form—either as a subatomic particle, a highly energetic photon (gamma ray), or some combination of these. In the process of decay, the radioactive isotope usually changes from one element to another. (Such a change is brought about by variations in the number of protons in the nucleus.) The new element may or may not be radioactive.

The time required for half of the atoms of any radioactive material to decay is its **half-life.** Half-lives can vary considerably and depend on which isotope of which element is being considered. Most naturally occurring radioisotopes are extremely durable; some half-lives are billions of years long. Uranium-238 has a half-life of about 4.5 billion years, during which half of the atoms decay to form an isotope of lead called lead-206. By contrast, some artificial radioisotopes have a fleeting half-life of only seconds.

Isotopes are atoms of one element that have different numbers of neutrons in their nuclei.

The longer-lived isotopes often are used in determining the age of fossil-bearing strata from the earth's crust. In medicine radioisotopes are used to destroy cancer-ridden tissues (Figure 2.2). Especially since World War II and the advent of nuclear weapons, scientists have been vitally interested in the destructive effects of radiation.

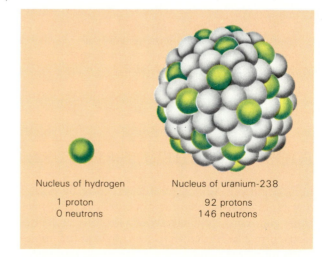

Nucleus of hydrogen

1 proton
0 neutrons

Nucleus of uranium-238

92 protons
146 neutrons

FIGURE 2.1   The lightest and heaviest atomic nuclei. The atomic mass of uranium is approximately 238 times that of hydrogen.

---

*Mass should not be confused with *weight*. *Weight* is the force of gravity pulling on a body. On the surface of the earth, however, the weight of an object (measured in grams, for example) is equal to its mass (also measured in grams).

†Orbitals can have any of a number of three dimensional shapes and can be considered as the space in which an electron is found 99% of a given time.

TABLE 2.1   Some of the Elements Essential to the Processes of Life

Element	Symbol	Atomic Number	Atomic Mass	Example of Role in Biology
Calcium	Ca	20	40.1	Bone formation, muscle contraction
Carbon	C	6	12.0	Component of all organic molecules
Chlorine	Cl	17	35.5	Digestion (as HCl); photosynthesis
Cobalt	Co	27	58.9	Component of vitamin B_{12}
Copper	Cu	29	63.5	Component of oxygen-carrying pigment in mollusks
Fluorine	F	9	19.0	Development of tooth enamel
Hydrogen	H	1	1.0	Component of water and of all organic molecules
Iodine	I	53	126.9	Component of thyroid hormone
Iron	Fe	26	55.8	Component of hemoglobin, oxygen-carrying pigment of many animals
Magnesium	Mg	12	24.3	Component of chlorophyll, the photosynthetic pigment; essential to some enzyme action
Manganese	Mn	25	54.9	Essential to some enzyme action
Molybdenum	Mo	42	95.9	Essential to some enzyme action
Nitrogen	N	7	14.0	Component of all proteins and nucleic acids
Oxygen	O	8	16.0	Essential to aerobic respiration; constituent of water and nearly all organic molecules
Phosphorus	P	15	31.0	High-energy bond of ATP
Potassium	K	19	39.1	Generation of nerve impulses
Selenium	Se	34	79.0	Essential to some enzyme action
Silicon	Si	14	28.1	Component of diatom shells, walls of arteries, and grass leaves
Sodium	Na	11	23.0	Component of body fluids; nerve conduction
Sulfur	S	16	32.1	Component of most proteins
Vanadium	V	23	50.9	Oxygen transport in tunicates
Zinc	Zn	30	65.4	Essential to some enzyme action

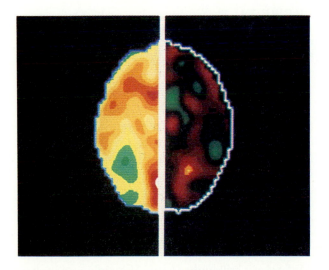

FIGURE 2.2 Medical use of radioactive tracers can pinpoint abnormalities in body structure or function. Here a PET scan of the brain of a patient who received an infusion of a radioactive substance illuminates an abnormality in blood flow to his brain. This patient, later diagnosed as suffering from panic disorder, had an asymmetry of blood flow (right greater than left) in a specific region of the brain.

Shorter-lived radioisotopes are used as tracers to determine the role of certain chemicals in living cells. This is possible because their chemical behavior is identical to nonradioactive atoms. The radioactive isotopes, however, can be traced by their telltale radiation as they move through living systems. Tracking radioisotopes of carbon, phosphorus, and hydrogen has helped unlock the secrets of photosynthesis, the process whereby plants use sunlight energy to convert carbon dioxide and water into sugars. The use of radioactive phosphorus, hydrogen, and indirectly, sulfur, has been vital in determining the structure and function of DNA, the gigantic molecule that determines inheritance.

Depicting the Atom

An atom is too small to be seen, even with the most powerful electron microscope; therefore, much of what we know is derived deductively from circumstantial evidence. In spite of our information, though, depicting an atom has proved to be a major

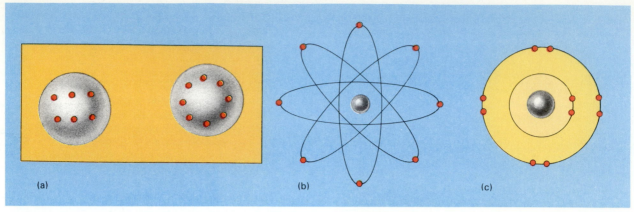

FIGURE 2.3 Three models of atomic structure. **(a)** The "watermelon" model, an attempt to show that atoms contain electrons (depicted as the seed). **(b)** A later model showing electrons orbiting around a central nucleus, much as planets orbit around the sun. **(c)** The concentric circles of the Bohr atom, indicating energy levels or electron shells; here, also, the electrons are depicted as moving around a central nucleus in flat, circular orbits.

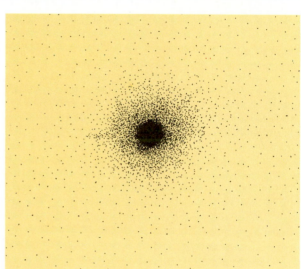

FIGURE 2.4 Electron density cloud model of hydrogen with its one electron. The density of the dots indicates the expected frequency of the electron in that region over a given period of time.

problem because any diagram is bound to be simplistic. Some notions of how atoms must look have been with us a long time, and most have been proved to be completely wrong, but in their time, they were useful (Figure 2.3).

Atoms are still diagramed in a number of ways. Each is useful in its own way, depending on the point of the discussion. For example, the orbitals that we have shown as lines can also be depicted as hazy clouds indicating where there is a certain probability that an electron *might* be at any given point in time. These are called **electron cloud models** (Figure 2.4). In such depictions the orbitals may appear hazy and indistinct, but they have definite shapes, each a precise distance from the nucleus.

Atoms are sometimes described in terms of a model developed by the great physicist, Niels Bohr. In the **Bohr atom,** the nucleus is shown being circled by electrons (much as the planets circle the sun). Bohr's model suggests that electrons move in a single plane, but this is not the case. Electrons can and do move in any plane and at various distances from the nucleus. The distance of a given electron from the nucleus is directly proportional to its energy level. Those electrons with the lowest energy levels are found closest to the nucleus; those with greater energy levels are found further out.

Energy levels and shells.   Scientists have known for some time that there are several distinct energy levels at which the electrons of any element may be found. Such energy levels are also known as **energy shells.** The first (innermost) and lowest energy shell contains a maximum of two electrons. The second shell can hold as many as eight electrons, as can the third (we'll call this the "two, eight and eight rule"). The electrons in the second shell are at a higher energy level than those of the first, and those in the third are at a still higher level. Although even higher electron energy levels exist (and these hold more than eight electrons), we will be primarily interested in the lighter elements in which electrons occupy only the three innermost energy levels. We will see that when the shells are filled with their maximum number of electrons they tend to be stable and nonreactive.

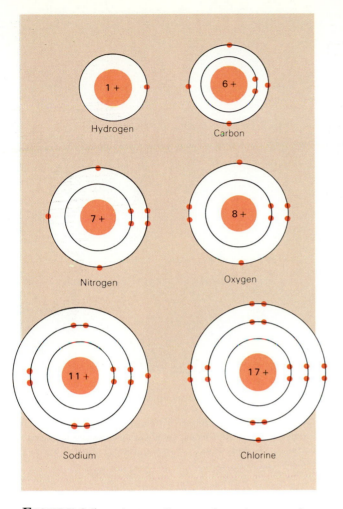

FIGURE 2.5 Bohr atom diagrams of several common elements. Note the regular progression in which the first, second, and third electron shells are filled.

Atoms fill their shells from the innermost shell outward (Figure 2.5). For example, hydrogen's one electron occurs in the first shell, as do the two electrons of helium. Nitrogen (atomic number 7) fills its inner shell with the usual two electrons, and its other five partially fill the second shell. With its 17 electrons, chlorine nearly fills three shells, which contain two, eight, and seven electrons, respectively. The arrangement of electrons and energy levels in the SPONCH elements are given in Table 2.2.

Electrons exist in **shells** at specific distances from the nucleus according to their energy levels. The *maximum* number of electrons in the first shell is 2, in the second, 8, and in the third, 8.

TABLE 2.2 Electron Arrangements of SPONCH and Other Selected Elements

Element	Atomic Number	Electrons in Each Shell		
		First Shell	Second Shell	Third Shell
		(2)	(8)	(8)
Hydrogen	1	1	0	0
Helium	2	2	0	0
Carbon	6	2	4	0
Nitrogen	7	2	5	0
Oxygen	8	2	6	0
Sodium	11	2	8	1
Phosphorus	15	2	8	5
Sulfur	16	2	8	6
Chlorine	17	2	8	7
Argon	18	2	8	8

Electrons can move from one shell to the next in either direction if their energy level is increased or decreased by the amount required. In addition, if an electron in the outer shell is sufficiently energized, it can escape the atom completely.

This is all fascinating stuff, but one might wonder, what does all this have to do with biology? A great deal, it turns out. For example, it is the shifting of electrons energized by the sun, which makes it possible for plants to make the food that supports nearly all forms of life on the earth (see Chapter 7).

MOLECULES AND COMPOUNDS

SPONCH atoms are almost never found singly; nor are the atoms of most other elements. In fact, atoms may be joined in all sorts of combinations to form **molecules.** A molecule is two or more chemically joined atoms.

Consider a simple molecule, atmospheric oxygen. Oxygen in the air does not exist as single atoms. Instead, two oxygen atoms join to form molecular oxygen. Atomic oxygen is written as O, whereas molecular oxygen is O_2, the subscript indicating that two oxygen atoms are joined chemically. Gaseous nitrogen in the air is designated N_2 for the same reason. Three such molecules would be written $3N_2$.

Many molecules consist of different elements. A **compound** contains more than one element, occurring in fixed proportions. For instance, sodium chloride (NaCl)—common table salt—always has equal proportions of sodium and chloride atoms. Water (H_2O) contains twice as much hydrogen as oxygen. Some molecules of interest to biologists may consist of thousands or even millions of atoms. We will encounter some of these in Chapter 3.

As atoms join to form molecules, their orbitals may change shape, and shape can be very important in terms of how molecules interact. Figure 2.5 shows electron orbitals of a simple molecule, methane gas (CH_4). The four hydrogen atoms center on the carbon atom. Note that their orbitals project outward in different directions, each the farthest possible distance from the others. The four tips of a methane molecule form the corners of a perfect **tetrahedron** (Figure 2.6). A number of molecules have this shape.

Molecules are two or more atoms chemically combined. **Compounds** consist of more different elements in specific proportions.

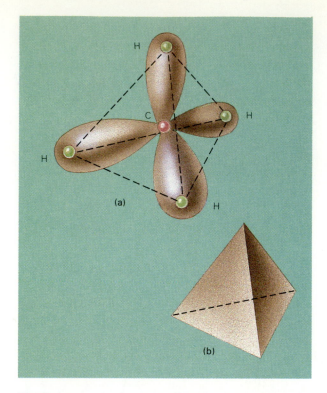

FIGURE 2.6 The electron orbitals of atoms assume different shapes when molecules form. In methane (CH_4), the carbon's outer shell electrons pair with four hydrogen electrons forming pear-shaped orbitals. The imaginary (*dashed*) lines, connecting the hydrogen nuclei as shown, take the form of a tetrahedron.

INTERACTION AND SHIFTING ENERGY

Characteristics that cause atoms to interact with other atoms, that is, to undergo **chemical reactions,** are called **energetic tendencies.** Although they are simple, they form the basis of all life functions—including whatever is going on in your mind this instant and gives you the strength to scratch your head as you ponder a sentence like this. The three basic energetic tendencies that contribute to chemical reactions are:

1. Negative and positive charges of atoms and molecules tend to balance, usually simply by equalizing the numbers of protons and electrons.
2. Electrons within atoms and molecules tend to pair.
3. Electron shells of atoms and molecules tend to become filled.

These three principles are called energetic tendencies because to counteract or violate them requires a known and precise amount of energy. It takes a certain amount of energy to remove an electron from a balanced atom or to remove one electron from an electron pair. Such violations permit chemical changes—changes such as the formation, disruption, and interaction of molecules, the sorts of changes that permit life.

The different energetic tendencies of an atom are sometimes in conflict. For example, the tendency of an atom to balance its electrical charges usually leaves the outer shell unfilled, and when the outer shell is filled, the protons and electrons are usually not in balance.* Oxygen, for example, has eight protons. Thus, it is balanced when it has eight electrons. But note that after the first shell is filled with two electrons, there are only six electrons left for the next shell, although eight are required. Therefore, the outer shell of a charge-balanced oxygen atom lacks two electrons. If the oxygen atom were to fill its outer shell with electrons, it would have 10 electrons and only eight protons, thereby losing the balance between protons and electrons. How are competing energetic tendencies accommodated? Chemical reactions often involve a compromise.

*Atoms that simultaneously fill all three energetic tendencies include the *noble gases*—helium, argon, neon, krypton, xenon, and radon. Noble gas elements are electrostatically balanced; they have even numbers of electrons and full electron shells. Because they rarely participate in chemical reactions, they have few roles in living systems.

CHEMICAL BONDS

An atom can fill its outer shell in one of three ways: (1) it can gain electrons from another atom; (2) it can lose all of the electrons in its outer shell to another atom, exposing the underlying filled shell; or (3) it can share electrons with another atom. In this case a new orbital shape forms, involving the interacting atoms (see Figure 2.6). In either case the result will be a new union through the formation of a **chemical bond.**

The Ionic Bond

Let's first see how atoms can gain or lose electrons (Figure 2.7). Sodium (Na) has 11 protons. It also has 11 electrons: two in the first shell, eight in the second shell, and only one in the third: the outer shell is seven electrons short (see Table 2.2 and Figure 2.3). It is not energetically possible for an atom (in this case, sodium) to gain seven electrons, but if it can lose one electron, then the full second shell will become the outer shell, and its shell requirements will be met. Chlorine (Cl) has 17 protons and 17 electrons. Thus its third shell has seven electrons—one short. Also, one of the seven in that outer shell is an unpaired electron. Chlorine, therefore, can complete two of its three energetic tendencies by accepting just one more electron.

Because of their particular structures, sodium and chlorine react easily and swiftly. In this reaction, sodium is called an **electron donor,** and chlorine, an **electron acceptor.** In its pure state, each element is a deadly chemical, but together, they form table salt (NaCl).

In the process of filling their outer shells, both become ionized, that is, electrostatically unbalanced forming **ions.** (An ion is any atom or molecule that has a net electrical charge, either negative or positive.) The sodium now has only 10 electrons and 11 protons, so it now has a net positive charge of $+1$. Chlorine now has 18 electrons and only 17 protons; it takes on a net negative charge of -1.

Because of the opposite charges on the ionized sodium and chlorine, they are attracted to each other. They join through an **ionic bond** to form sodium chloride (NaCl), or table salt (Figure 2.8). Ionic bonding is common in the chemical world.

> **I**onic bonds form by electrostatic attractions between positive and negative ions that develop when atoms lose or gain electrons.

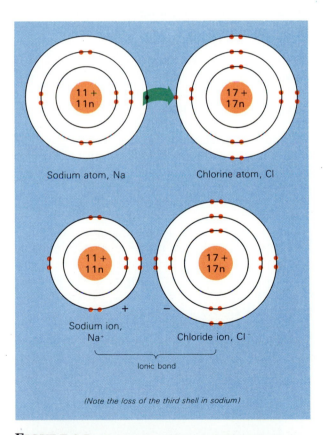

Sodium atom, Na

Chlorine atom, Cl

Sodium ion, Na⁺

Chloride ion, Cl⁻

Ionic bond

(Note the loss of the third shell in sodium)

FIGURE 2.7 The loss of an electron renders sodium positive while the gain of an electron by chlorine renders it negative, and the two form ions. The resulting electrostatic attraction between the two ions is called an ionic bond.

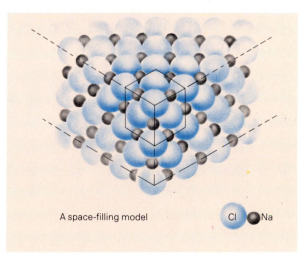

A space-filling model   Cl   Na

FIGURE 2.8 Sodium chloride forms crystals of indeterminate size rather than discrete individual molecules. The crystal can grow from microscopic proportions to gigantic size.

Ions and life. Ions commonly form in the watery fluids of living things. Examples include the simple ions of hydrogen (H^+), calcium (Ca^{2+}), potassium (K^+), and magnesium (Mg^{2+}) as well as more complex ions, such as the phosphate ion ($H_2PO_4^-$), the ammonium ion (NH_4^+), and the sulfate ion (SO_4^{2+}). Carbon, one of the most important elements of life, as we will see, often forms complex molecules with ionized side groups. As you might expect, these charged particles are quite active in living systems and often help with vital functions.

The Covalent Bond: Sharing Electrons

Another way an atom can fill its outer electron shell is by sharing electrons with other atoms. Two atoms sharing electrons form what is called a **covalent bond.**

Consider hydrogen gas (H_2), formed from two hydrogen atoms. Each atom comprises one proton and one electron. Since electrons tend to travel in pairs, the two hydrogen atoms can pool their single electrons and satisfy this requirement. The shared pair of electrons form a new **molecular orbital** that includes both atomic nuclei. In this way, not only are the two electrons paired, but also both atoms satisfy the requirement of their electron shell. Furthermore, they still maintain the balance between protons and electrons (Figure 2.9).

> **C**ovalent bonds form when electrons are shared between two or more atoms.

HYDROGEN BONDS AND THE PECULIAR QUALITIES OF WATER

We are generally aware that water is necessary for life, but we may not know that much of its magic lies in its peculiar molecular bonding. (You may recall that hopes for discovering life on Mars faded when interplanetary probes failed to find significant amounts of water there. Let's see why this finding bred such discouragement.)

The Molecular Structure of Water

A water molecule is made up of two hydrogen atoms covalently bonded to one oxygen atom. All three atoms fill their outer shells by sharing electrons. The two hydrogen atoms and one oxygen atom have, among them, 10 protons and 10 electrons; the internal charges of water are balanced.

The four electron pairs in the outer shell of the oxygen atom move in orbitals with the same tetrahedral shape that we saw in methane. In the water molecule, however, only two of the four molecular orbitals surround the hydrogen nuclei; the other two do not (Figure 2.10). This makes the water molecule strangely and magnificently lopsided. Furthermore, the hydrogen nuclei enclosed by the two orbitals give these orbitals a slight positive charge relative to the other two orbitals. This means that although the positive and negative charges of the molecule are balanced numerically, they are not evenly distributed—the water molecule is *polar*. In essence, a water molecule has a positive side and a negative side. This simple configuration had a great deal to do with the appearance of life on this planet.

FIGURE 2.9 **(a)** Two hydrogen atoms share their lone, unpaired, electrons, forming a covalent bond as H_2 gas. **(b)** The white areas in the photo indicate where electrons may be found at any particular moment in time. (Photograph from *Chemistry*, by Linus Pauling and Peter Pauling. Copyright © by W. H. Freeman and Company. All rights reserved.)

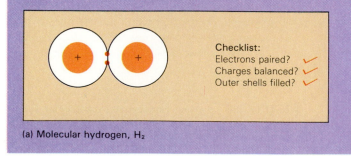

Checklist:
Electrons paired? ✓
Charges balanced? ✓
Outer shells filled? ✓

(a) Molecular hydrogen, H_2

(b)

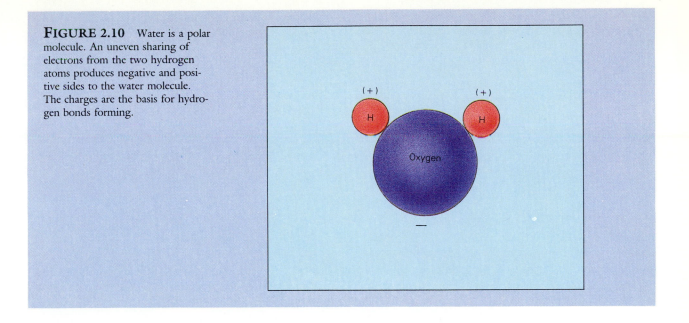

FIGURE 2.10 Water is a polar molecule. An uneven sharing of electrons from the two hydrogen atoms produces negative and positive sides to the water molecule. The charges are the basis for hydrogen bonds forming.

The hydrogen bond. Because water molecules are polar, with positive and negative regions, they interact with each other. The positive region of one water molecule forms a weak, very temporary attraction for the negative region of another. This weak attraction is called a **hydrogen bond.** Hydrogen bonds break and reform with dazzling speed, giving water many of its peculiar characteristics. For instance, despite the weakness of individual hydrogen bonds, their sheer number causes water molecules to cling with surprising tenacity. This stickiness produces **cohesion** (the attraction between molecules of a single substance). So, we see that some of the magic of the hydrogen bond lies in its very weakness.

Water temperature and life. One of the most important qualities of water is its temperature stability. Whoever was watching the proverbial pot that gave rise to the adage was probably amazed by the enormous amount of heat necessary to raise the temperature of water.

Specific heat is the amount of heat required to raise the temperature of a substance to some specified amount. If that substance is water, the specific heat is very high. Raising the temperature of water just 1°C requires 33 times as much energy as is required to produce a similar temperature rise in lead. Why should water be so difficult to heat? Keep in mind that as a substance absorbs energy, its molecules move much faster, and its temperature rises. Water's resistance to increased molecular motion is a product of its countless hydrogen bonds that reform, linking the molecules in place as fast as the bonds are broken. Even when heat is applied to water, no temperature rise occurs until the energy within its hydrogen bonds is exceeded. How is this important to life?

The resistance of water to changing temperatures means that creatures composed largely of water, like ourselves, have a certain built-in temperature stability. It also means that organisms that live in water are buffered to some degree by the resistance of water to changes in temperature.

Anyone living near the seacoast knows that the weather there is much milder—cooler in the summer and warmer in the winter—than the weather of communities only a few miles inland. The sea serves as a great heat reservoir, absorbing heat in summer and releasing it in winter.

Water also freezes slowly because ice is a crystal (Figure 2.11), and the busy water molecules are likely to shift before they can fuse into the regular structure that identifies any crystal. As water cools, its molecules move closer, and it becomes heavier. Thus cooling surface water in a lake sinks, as expected. Its density is greatest at 4°C. As it cools further, its density decreases, reaching its minimum in the open molecular lattice called *ice*. Since ice represents water in a lighter configuration, it forms only on the lake surface, which makes skating much more pleasurable.

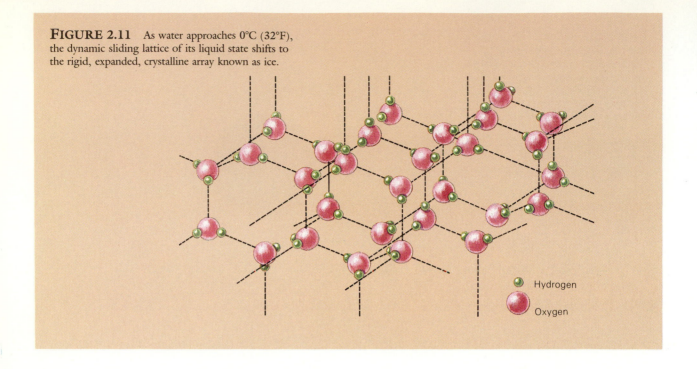

FIGURE 2.11 As water approaches 0°C (32°F), the dynamic sliding lattice of its liquid state shifts to the rigid, expanded, crystalline array known as ice.

Hydrogen

Oxygen

Water the solvent. Water is well known as a cleaning agent, partly because it is not expensive and partly because it is one of the best solvents known. Water's properties as a solvent lie, once again, in its polarity. Because of the imbalance of its charges, it has an affinity for a number of substances, such as salt (NaCl), with its positive and negative parts, and sugars, with their own areas of positive and negative charges. Any substance that interacts readily with water is described as **hydrophilic** (water-loving).

Ionic compounds such as sodium chloride dissolve in water by **dissociating** or **ionizing** (that is, by separating into ions), with water molecules clustering around the resulting ions (Figure 2.12). This happens because negative chloride ions attract the positive parts of polar water molecules; and positive sodium ions attract the negative parts of the water molecules. The same applies to the many other ions that form in our bodies. Other molecules, such as sugar, may be electrostatically balanced, but they may also be polar, with slightly negative and slightly positive regions. Therefore, water will form hydrogen bonds with the appropriate regions of polar molecules, which is why sugar dissolves almost as readily as salt. Such qualities of water are important to living things because delicate internal balances require that many kinds of molecules be easily transported in fluids.

Water's temperature stability (high **specific heat**) and properties as a solvent are products of its polar nature and hydrogen bonding.

Nonpolar molecules, those lacking charged regions—such as oils, petroleum products, and certain fats—do not interact with the charged areas of water and, therefore, they do not dissolve. Instead, the affinity of water molecules for each other causes the excluded molecules to cluster into their own masses. That's why you have to keep shaking Italian dressing.

The behavior of nonpolar molecules in water is called **hydrophobic** interaction. Hydrophobic means "fear of water" or, in this case, "avoidance of water." Hydrophobic interactions account for the fairly strong apparent attraction between nonpolar molecules, or between the nonpolar portions of molecules, that occurs in the presence of water. For example, if melted chicken fat (or any liquid fat or oil) is mixed with water, the fat will join into globules and the globules will merge. Although it may look as though the fat molecules are attracting each other, in reality they are simply being *excluded by the water*. Water molecules, as we've seen, have a strong attraction for each other and for other polar molecules, but

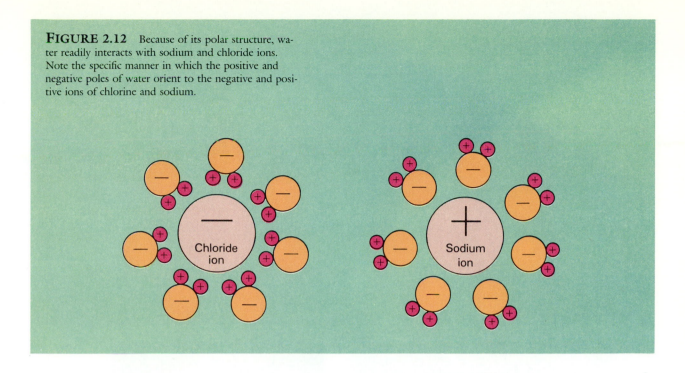

FIGURE 2.12 Because of its polar structure, water readily interacts with sodium and chloride ions. Note the specific manner in which the positive and negative poles of water orient to the negative and positive ions of chlorine and sodium.

they have no attraction for the nonpolar molecules of chicken fat.

Water, Acids, Bases, and the pH Scale

Most of the chemical reactions of life take place in watery solutions, and their specific reactions are strongly influenced by whether the solution is acidic, basic, or neutral.

Acids, as you might know, have a sour taste (such as the citric acid of lemons or the acetic acid of vinegar) and are corrosive. Some are extremely reactive and dangerous. The acid present in your car battery is quite potent and will even produce holes in the seat of your new jeans should you sit in the wrong place while working on your engine. **Bases,** or **alkalis,** as basic substances are known, have a slippery consistency like soap. Some bases, such as oven cleaner, household ammonia, and drain cleaner, are pungent and can also be dangerous.

Pure water is **neutral,** neither acidic nor basic. Although nearly every molecule of pure water is in its molecular form (H_2O), a very minute portion (one molecule in about 550 million) dissociates spontaneously, forming positively charged hydrogen ions (H^+) and negatively charged hydroxide ions (OH^-). (Hydrogen ions are actually just protons.) The ionized particles quickly rejoin to form H_2O, even as other molecules dissociate. A solution increases in acidity when the number of H^+ exceeds the number of OH^-; basicity (or alkalinity) increases with a rise in OH^-. Correspondingly, any substance that releases hydrogen ions when it ionizes in water is an acid, and any substance that releases hydroxide ions when it ionizes in water is a base.

Vinegar, a dilute solution of acetic acid, has a high hydrogen ion content, although not as high as the sulfuric acid of car batteries. Drain openers and oven cleaners also have a very high hydroxide ion content.

An example of a reaction that increases acidity is: HCl (hydrochloric acid) $\longleftrightarrow H^+ + Cl^-$. (Note that the chloride ion has no effect on acidity.)

A reaction that increases basicity is NH_4OH (ammonium hydroxide) $\longleftrightarrow NH_4^+ + OH^-$. (Note that the ammonium ion has no effect on alkalinity.)

Acidity is measured on the **pH scale,** a measure of hydrogen-ion concentration. The scale extends from pH 1 to pH 14, with the strongest acids assigned the lowest numbers (pH 1 or 2) and the strongest bases, the highest pH numbers (pH 13 or 14). The pH 7 refers to the neutral condition found in pure water (see Table 2.3 and Figure 2.13). Note that the pH scale is deceiving. It is not linear, as it might appear; it is *logarithmic*. Therefore, an increase or decrease of one pH number actually represents a tenfold increase or decrease in hydrogen ions.

FIGURE 2.13 Some common foodstuffs of highly varying pH levels.

TABLE 2.3 pH Values of Common Solutions

Molar Concentration of Hydrogen Ions*	pH	Example
$1.0 = 10^{-0}$	0	Concentrated nitric acid
$0.1 = 10^{-1}$	1	Gastric juice
$0.01 = 10^{-2}$	2	Coca-Cola
$0.001 = 10^{-3}$	3	Vinegar
$0.000001 = 10^{-6}$	6	Saliva
$0.0000001 = 10^{-7}$	7	Distilled water
$0.00000001 = 10^{-8}$	8	Sea water
$0.00000000000001 = 10^{-14}$	14	Drain opener

*Note: the scale extends below pH1, where some highly concentrated acids occur.

SUMMARY

THE ELEMENTS

Elements are substances that cannot be chemically simplified. The most common to life are sulfur, phosphorus, oxygen, nitrogen, carbon, and hydrogen (SPONCH). The basic units of elements are atoms.

ATOMS AND THEIR STRUCTURE

Atomic nuclei contain positively charged protons and uncharged neutrons, which together comprise atomic mass. Much smaller, negatively charged electrons travel in orbits outside the nucleus. The atoms in each element have a specific number of protons, which is also the atomic number.

Isotopes

Atoms with the same atomic number but different numbers of neutrons are called isotopes. Radioisotopes emit energy and mass as they break down into simpler elements. The rate of decay is measured in half-lives. Some are used as tracers in research and medicine.

Depicting the Atom

Electrons occur at distinct energy levels or shells, whose distance from the nucleus is in direct proportion to their energy. Shells fill from the innermost out, according to the "two, eight, and eight rule." Those with unfilled outer shells are reactive.

MOLECULES AND COMPOUNDS

Molecules are chemical combinations of two or more atoms. When two or more different elements are involved, such combinations are compounds.

INTERACTION AND SHIFTING ENERGY

The energetic tendencies leading to bond formation include: balancing electrical charges, pairing of electrons, and the filling of outer shells. Competition among these tendencies leads to compromises that become chemical bonds.

CHEMICAL BONDS

Ionic Bonds

In the formation of ionic bonds, electrons move from electron donors to electron acceptors. The loss or gain of electrons produces oppositely charged ions. The resulting electrostatic attraction is an ionic bond. Ions readily separate again in water.

The Covalent Bond: Sharing Electrons

Covalent bonds are formed as elements share electrons and form new molecular orbitals.

HYDROGEN BONDS AND THE PECULIAR QUALITIES OF WATER

The hydrogen bond accounts for many of the characteristics of water.

The Molecular Structure of Water

In water, two hydrogens are covalently bonded to one oxygen. Because of unequal sharing of hydrogen electrons, water molecules have a slight positive and a negative region. The oppositely charged regions of adjacent water molecules attract each other, forming weak hydrogen bonds. The numerous bonds holding water together account for a property called cohesion.

Because of its hydrogen bonds, water has high specific heat: it has greater resistance to temperature changes than most substances. This makes it a favorable environment for life.

As liquid water cools, its density increases, reaching its maximum at 4°C. As ice forms, water becomes much lighter.

Water is a good solvent because its charged regions interact with ions and other polar substances. Water repels nonpolar (uncharged) substances, which form isolated clusters.

Water, Acids, Bases, and the pH Scale

Pure water is neutral, neither acidic nor basic. The presence of hydrogen ions (H^+) in excess of hydroxide ions (OH^-) in water constitutes an acid. The presence of an excess of hydroxide ions characterizes a base or alkalai. A pH scale of 1 to 14 is used to describe the number of hydrogen ions relative to hydroxide ions. Acids range from pH 0 to 7, with the lowest numbers representing the strongest acids. Pure water is pH 7. Bases range from above 7, the highest numbers representing the strongest bases.

KEY TERMS

element	isotope	electron donor	ionizing
proton	electron cloud model	electron acceptor	hydrophobic
neutron	energy shell	ionic bond	acid
electron	molecule	covalent bond	base
atomic mass	compound	specific heat	alkali
orbital	chemical reaction	hydrophilic	neutral
atomic number	energetic tendency	dissociation	pH scale

REVIEW QUESTIONS

1 Define an element and list the six that are most common to life. (p. 17)

2 Name the three principal particles making up atoms, state where they are found and any charges they may have. Explain how they relate to atomic mass and number. (pp. 17–18)

3 List the number of protons, neutrons, and electrons in the following elements. Copper: number 29, atomic mass 64. Iodine: number 53, atomic mass 127. Mercury: number 80, atomic mass 201. (pp. 17–18)

4 In what way do the isotopes of an element differ from each other? Mention two uses for radioisotopes. (pp. 18–19)

5 Using the Bohr model and applying the shell-filling rules, prepare drawings of atoms of the following elements: Helium (no. 2), Oxygen (no. 8), Chlorine (no. 17). (pp. 20–21)

6 Clearly distinguish between the terms *molecule* and *compound* and cite examples of each. (pp. 21–22)

7 List the energetic tendencies of atoms and briefly explain how they may be in conflict. Name two elements in which these conflicts do not exist. (p. 22)

8 Using Bohr models of sodium (no. 11) and chlorine (no. 17), illustrate the formation of an ionic bond between the two. Carry out the same task with atoms of hydrogen (no. 1) and chlorine (no. 17), and with atoms of magnesium (no. 12) and chlorine. (p. 23)

10 Explain how the behavior of electrons differs in the formation of ionic and covalent bonds. (pp. 23–24)

11 Draw a simple model of the water molecule, show its charged regions, and describe the manner in which several molecules interact through water hydrogen bonding. (pp. 24–25)

12 Explain how the presence of hydrogen bonds accounts for the great resistance of water to temperature change. Why is this quality important to life? (p. 25)

13 Describe the relationship between temperature and density in water. Include the two critical temperatures in a body of water. (p. 25)

14 What characteristic of water makes it such a good solvent? Describe the behavior of ionic compounds in water. (p. 27)

15 Explain in terms of hydrogen and hydroxide ions, how solutions become neutral, acidic, or basic. Relate the strength of acids and bases to the pH scale. (p. 27)

Our planet can be viewed as an essentially hostile place, its very nature disruptive to the processes of life. In a sense, life exists not because of the earth's benevolence, but in spite of its constant dangers and frustrations. How has life managed to survive in such a place? Largely because it has developed ways to manipulate its molecules. The molecules of life are able to interact with each other in ways to evade, ignore, conquer, and even use the hostile elements that otherwise would threaten their critical and precise organization.

We are here, in large part, because of such seemingly mundane factors as the number of electrons surrounding the nucleus of an element called carbon. We are here because chemical bonds store energy. We are here because some molecules have fatty tails that hate water. We are composed of molecules and we owe our existence to their precise and predictable behavior. Clearly, then, if we are to understand this improbable thing called life, we need to learn about its tiny constituents, the molecules.

CARBON: BACKBONE OF THE MOLECULES OF LIFE

Carbon is a fascinating molecule that has prompted chemists, not known for their poetry, to refer to its "magic." (We will assume that learning about its specific properties in no way diminishes its magic.) Carbon is found in just about every molecule important to living things. In fact, it is the backbone, or framework, upon which organisms build a range of essential molecules. It is important not only because it can form covalent bonds, but also because it forms four covalent bonds at once.

Carbon is quite versatile in the way it forms bonds. It can form four single covalent bonds with hydrogen four to become methane sharing an electron with each. It also can form double bonds, in which two pairs of electrons are shared with another atom. Carbon dioxide, in fact, contains two sets of double bonds, with the carbon in the middle and double-bonded oxygens on either side: $O=C=O$. Carbon can even form triple bonds, as it does in deadly hydrogen cyanide: $H—C\equiv N$. (Note that each line between atoms represents one pair of shared electrons, a common way of representing covalent bonds in chemistry.)

Carbon atoms can also be linked to form long chains; they can form rings, chains of rings, and a whole range of other complex structures. There seems to be no limit to how large an organic (carbon-

3

THE MOLECULES OF LIFE

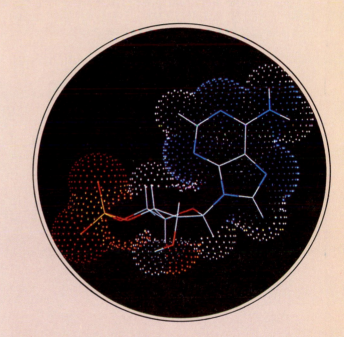

bearing) molecule can be (some contain 50 billion atoms).

Most such large molecules are **polymers,** comprised of chains of repeating units. They often obey the familiar rules pertaining to small molecules, which makes their behavior easier to describe and predict. Most of the important **macromolecules** ("large molecule") of life fall into one of four classes: carbohydrates, lipids, proteins, and nucleic acids.

CARBOHYDRATES

Carbohydrates are common to foods such as fruits, grains, and potatoes; they are also often the prime ingredient of snack (junk) foods because they are relatively easy to acquire and process. For the same reason, carbohydrates comprise a disproportionate share of the diet of the poor. There are several classes of carbohydrates, the most familiar being sugars and starches. Carbohydrates get their name from their chief elements, carbon, hydrogen, and oxygen ("ate" refers to oxygen). The empirical formula (a chemical "common denominator") of all carbohydrates is $(CH_2O)_n$ (the n simply refers to an indefinite number). There may be as few as three carbons in a carbohydrate, or the molecule may be a giant macromolecule known as a **polysaccharide** ("many sugars") that contains literally thousands of carbon atoms. Even these giants are typically comprised of identical, repeating subunits called **monosaccharides** ("single sugars") or **simple sugars.**

Monosaccharides: Simple Sugars

Monosaccharides may have from three to eight carbon atoms, but by far the most familiar is the six-carbon sugar, **glucose** (also called **dextrose**) (Figure 3.1). Glucose units are linked to form most of the large polysaccharides. In addition to its role as a

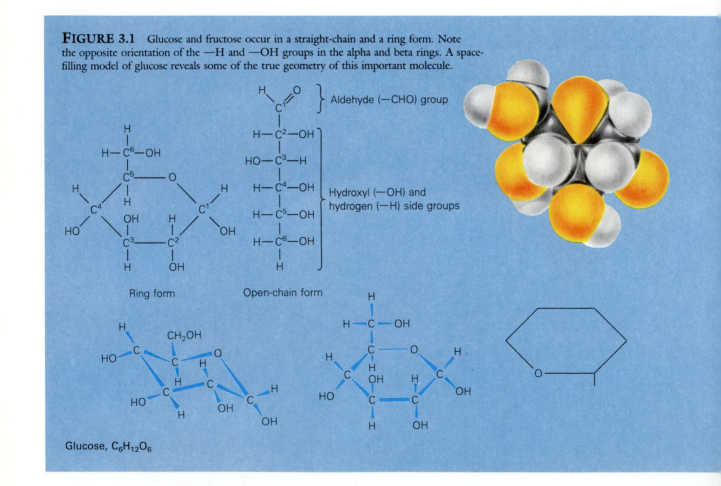

FIGURE 3.1 Glucose and fructose occur in a straight-chain and a ring form. Note the opposite orientation of the —H and —OH groups in the alpha and beta rings. A space-filling model of glucose reveals some of the true geometry of this important molecule.

building block of polysaccharides, glucose is an important energy source for metabolically active cells. Other important six-carbon simple sugars are **fructose,** a common sugar of grapes and other fruits, and **galactose,** found in milk. Incidentally, all three of the six-carbon sugars have the same chemical formula, $C_6H_{12}O_6$, but they differ in geometry.

Other monosaccharides critical to life are the **pentose** sugars with five carbons. Two of these, **ribose** and **deoxyribose,** are constituents of the huge genetic molecules called DNA and RNA, which we'll get to later in the chapter. A third, **ribulose,** is found chiefly in plants and is a key reactant in the formation of glucose.

Glucose, the principal monosaccharide (see Figure 3.1), can take on a straight chain or a closed ring configuration. Extending from its carbon backbone are three types of side groups: hydrogen (—H), **hydroxyl** (—OH), and **aldehyde** (—CHO). Note also that glucose occurs in both **alpha** and **beta** forms, which differ only in the orientation of one of the hydroxyl groups. All of these factors become important as we consider how the subunits are linked to form disaccharides and polysaccharides.

Monosaccharides occur as small chains and rings. Among the most common are glucose, fructose, ribose, and deoxyribose.

Disaccharides: Linking the Monosaccharides

Logically enough, two monosaccharides covalently bonded become a **disaccharide** ("two sugars"). There are several common examples. Two glucose molecules join to form the disaccharide **maltose.** Fructose and glucose, when covalently linked, form **sucrose,** common table sugar. **Galactose,** when linked to glucose, forms **lactose,** or milk sugar. (If you suffer from lactose intolerance, it is this sugar that causes your distress after eating milk products.)

Simple sugars are linked through a process known as **dehydration linkage,** which is one of the most common chemical reactions of life. As part of its name indicates, dehydration synthesis involves the removal of water. A look at the two reacting glucose subunits in Figure 3.2 shows us where the water

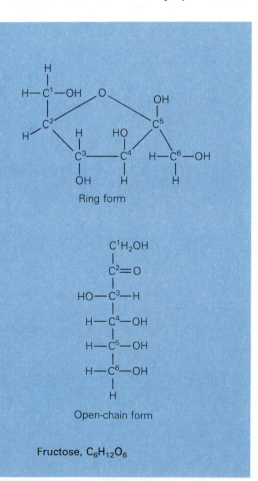

Ring form

Open-chain form

Fructose, $C_6H_{12}O_6$

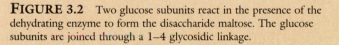

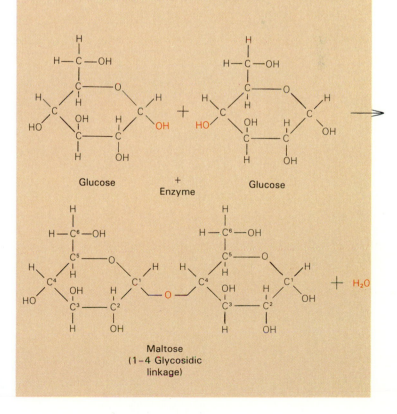

FIGURE 3.2 Two glucose subunits react in the presence of the dehydrating enzyme to form the disaccharide maltose. The glucose subunits are joined through a 1–4 glycosidic linkage.

Glucose
+
Enzyme

Glucose

Maltose
(1–4 Glycosidic linkage)

comes from. In two adjacent hydroxyl groups, one gives up a hydrogen, the other gives up a hydroxyl group, and a molecule of water is released. This frees some electrons, and a new covalent bond forms between the number 1 and 4 carbons of the two glucose molecules. (The carbons of simple sugars are numbered.) The new bond is called **1–4 glycosidic linkage.** A polysaccharide such as a starch will contain many 1–4 glycosidic linkages. When we digest carbohydrates and other foods, this bond is broken in a process called **hydrolytic cleavage** (see Chapter 6). As it is broken, a molecule of water is split to restore the lost hydrogen and hydroxyl groups. Life can be logical.

Dehydration linkages and cleavages do not occur spontaneously but require the presence of special active proteins called **enzymes.** Enzymes have catalytic properties, which means that they promote chemical reactions (see Chapter 6).

Monosaccharides such as glucose are joined through **dehydration synthesis,** during which water is enzymatically removed and **glycosidic linkages** form.

Polysaccharides: the Larger Carbohydrates

Polysaccharides ("many sugars") are long chains of monosaccharides. The simplest polysaccharides are polymers of glucose, joined by dehydration linkages. Such polysaccharides include starches such as **amylose** and **amylopectin** (storage products in plants), and **cellulose,** a carbohydrate that lends strength to plants. Animals also assemble polysaccharides such as **glycogen** (animal starch) and **chitin,** a major structural material in some animal groups. Starches are important storage materials because their energy is so readily available (Figure 3.3). Starches traditionally have formed a large part of our diet. Even today, the diets of most primitive tribes are made up principally of starchy plants.

Cellulose is a principal constituent in plant cell walls. Like starch, it is composed of long chains of glucose molecules. However, there are important differences between the two that are based on whether alpha or beta glucose units are used in the polymer (see Figure 3.1). Because of these differences, starch is fairly soluble, although cellulose is not. Cellulose has great tensile strength that starch lacks; starch is easily digested, but cellulose is completely indigest-

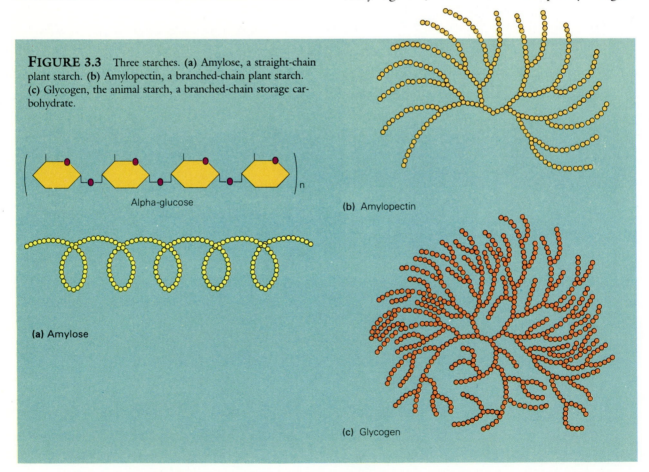

FIGURE 3.3   Three starches. **(a)** Amylose, a straight-chain plant starch. **(b)** Amylopectin, a branched-chain plant starch. **(c)** Glycogen, the animal starch, a branched-chain storage carbohydrate.

Alpha-glucose

(a) Amylose

(b) Amylopectin

(c) Glycogen

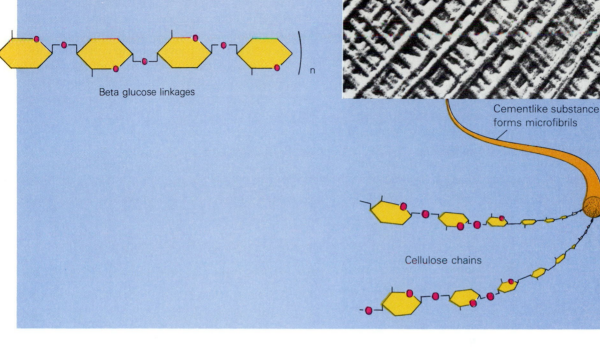

FIGURE 3.4 Cellulose, a structural polysaccharide, is formed from numerous beta glucose subunits. Cellulose chains embedded in cementlike secreted substances form lengthy microfibrils that can be readily resolved by the electron microscope. Their laminated arrangement explains the great strength of plant cell walls.

Beta glucose linkages

Cementlike substance forms microfibrils

Cellulose chains

ible to almost all organisms. Figure 3.4 shows the structure of cellulose and its organization into plant fibers.

Chitin is one of the major materials of the exoskeletons (outer coverings) of arthropods, the group that includes insects, lobsters, and crabs. Although chitin is soft and leathery, it can harden when impregnated with calcium carbonate or certain proteins. Chitin is similar in many ways to cellulose, except that the basic unit is not glucose, but a similar molecule that contains nitrogen. It is indigestible to most animals. Curiously, chitin is also found in the cell walls of fungi.

LIPIDS

The **lipids** are a diverse group of molecules, defined not by their structure but by their insolubility. Although they cannot be dissolved in water, they are soluble in nonpolar (uncharged) solvents such as ether and chloroform. Lipids may be very small, or large and complex, or polymers of simple repeating subunits. They function as energy-storage reservoirs,

insulators, lubricants, and even as hormones. They are also an important part of the membranes that surround cells. Lipids include animal fats, vegetable oils, waxes, steroids, and an interesting group called the **phospholipids.** Your own brain (as perhaps people have told you) consists largely of fat—more accurately, it contains large amounts of fat-soluble phospholipids.

Triglycerides and Their Subunits

Animal fats (such as beef tallow) and vegetable oils (such as corn oil) are familiar lipids. Generally, the two are distinguishable because fats are solid at room temperature, whereas oils are liquid. At the animal's own normal body temperature, however, fats are usually liquid.

Both fats and oils are **triglycerides**—compounds with three **fatty acid chains** covalently bonded to one molecule of **glycerol.** Triglycerides are important as storage lipids.

Glycerol is a small three-carbon molecule with three hydroxyl (—OH) side groups. Glycerol provides the base, or the backbone, for all triglycerides. The differences among various triglycerides depend on what kinds of fatty acid chains are attached to that backbone. These chains can be of different lengths, but the most common are even-numbered chains of 14, 16, 18, or 20 carbons. A fatty acid molecule consists of a **hydrocarbon chain** with a **carboxyl group** (—COOH) at one end (Figure 3.5). When in solution, carboxyl groups ionize, yielding a proton (H^+); thus they are acidic.

A fatty acid can be **saturated** with hydrogen (able to hold no more) or it can be **unsaturated** (capable of accepting additional hydrogen atoms) (Figure 3.5). Health advocates have long urged us to use unsaturated fats in our diet, although recent research has caused some scientists to question this. In general, plant triglycerides are likely to be more unsaturated than are those found in animal fat.

Triglycerides are produced through dehydration linkages (Figure 3.6), which means that, as each fatty acid joins the glycerol, a molecule of water is released.

Triglycerides contain a great deal of stored energy. In fact, they yield about twice as much energy per gram dry weight as do carbohydrates or protein. Plants store triglycerides in seeds, and animals may build up fat as reserves to be used in lean seasons ahead.

Humans also tend to store fat under their skin and around their internal organs. The tendency to build fat reserves may have been advantageous to our hunting ancestors, but improvements in agriculture, food storage, and efficient transportation have largely exempted us from the rigors of seasonal food depletion. Still, many of us seem to be taking no chances.

Triglycerides are the common animal fats and vegetable oils. Each molecule contains three fatty acid chains covalently bonded to one glycerol.

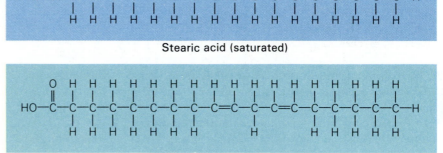

FIGURE 3.5 Stearic acid, an animal fatty acid, contains the maximum number of hydrogen groups possible so it is saturated. Linoleic acid, a plant fatty acid, is unsaturated. Since there is more than one double bond, the term *polyunsaturated* is used.

Stearic acid (saturated)

Linoleic acid (polyunsaturated)

FIGURE 3.6 Triglyceride synthesis. Triglycerides such as animal fats consist of a backbone of glycerol joined to three fatty acids by dehydration linkages. Note the three water molecules that form in the process.

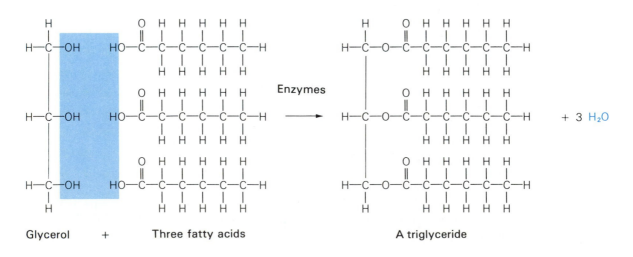

Glycerol + Three fatty acids → A triglyceride + 3 H_2O

Phospholipids

Phospholipids are structurally similar to the triglycerides; however, the two differ in one important respect. Although triglycerides contain three fatty acids covalently linked to one glycerol, phospholipids contain only two fatty acids. In place of the third is a negatively charged phosphate group that forms a link between the glycerol and one of several types of end groups. In cell membranes, for instance, the end group is usually choline, a nitrogen-containing, positively charged group. Because of their charged groups, phospholipids are polar or **hydrophilic** ("water-loving") molecules. This means that the end of the molecule that has the phosphate group can dissolve in water and can also form ionic bonds with certain other charged molecules. The end of the phospholipid with the fatty acid chains is uncharged, **hydrophobic,** and nonpolar. Because of this peculiar arrangement of charges, phospholipids placed in water form spherical clumps, the nonpolar "tails" pointing in and the polar phosphate "heads" pointing out (Figure 3.7).

> **P**hospholipids, constituents of membranes, consist of two fatty acid chains, a glycerol, and a charged phosphate group to which various charged end groups are attached.

Molecules that have polar (water-soluble) parts and nonpolar (lipid-soluble) parts can simultaneously form hydrogen bonds with water and hydrophobic ("water-fearing") interactions with nonpolar substances. For example, laundry detergents consist of molecules with long nonpolar hydrocarbon tails and ionized heads. In practical terms, the hydrocarbon tail forms hydrophobic interactions with gravy on shirts, while the ionized head forms strong bonds with water. Thus the detergent-gravy complex dissolves into the water.

Lecithin, a natural detergent, is a phospholipid of egg yolk. Like laundry detergent, it can dissolve fat in water to some degree. In fact, the lecithin in egg yolk forms a bridge between salad oil and vinegar. The result is mayonnaise.

The dual personality of phospholipids makes them excellent building materials for the membranes of living cells. As we will see in Chapter 4, these membranes are made up of two layers of phospholipids, along with several types of protein. Their nonpolar, fatty acid tails point in toward one another, forming a water-resistant core. Their charged phosphate heads face out, where they interact with charged regions of proteins (Figure 3.8).

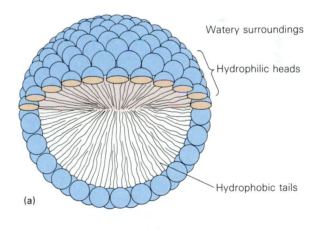

Watery surroundings

Hydrophilic heads

Hydrophobic tails

(a)

FIGURE 3.7 (a) Phospholipids dispersed in water tend to aggregate with their fatty-acid tails clumped together by hydrophobic interaction. Their charged polar heads interact with water. (b) The structure of a phospholipid from a cell membrane.

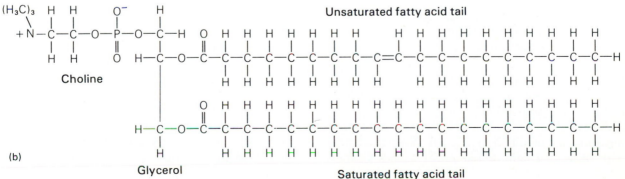

Phosphate group

Unsaturated fatty acid tail

Choline

Glycerol

Saturated fatty acid tail

(b)

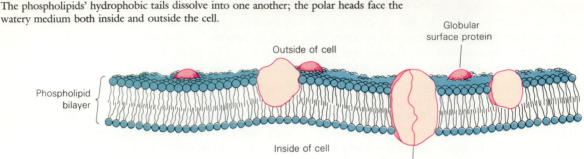

FIGURE 3.8 Phospholipids and proteins are the principal components of most cell membranes. The phospholipids' hydrophobic tails dissolve into one another; the polar heads face the watery medium both inside and outside the cell.

Outside of cell

Globular surface protein

Phospholipid bilayer

Inside of cell

Transmembranal protein

Other Important Lipids

Other lipids include **waxes** and a peculiar group called the **steroids.** Waxes contain one fatty acid, but instead of being bound to glycerol, it is bound to a long-chain molecule with a single hydroxyl group. Because waxes have powerful water-repellent properties, they are common in organisms that must conserve water. Insect bodies generally are covered by a waxy layer, and many plants—especially those in drier areas—have waxy leaves.

Steroids are structurally quite different from fatty acids, but since they are either partly or wholly hydrophobic, they fall within the lipid category. All steroids have a basic structure of four interlocking rings. The differences in their biochemical activities are a function of the side groups that protrude from the rings. Some steroids are very hydrophobic, some less so. We will see later that many of those regulatory chemicals circulating in the blood, the ones called hormones, are steroids, including those influencing sex.

We are all aware of something called **cholesterol** because food manufacturers don't hesitate to boast that their products are cholesterol free. But why should we care? Cholesterol, we are told, creates arterial plaques, abnormal thickenings of the walls of arteries, which can raise blood pressure dangerously (Figure 3.9). It cannot be denied that people with high levels of cholesterol in the blood have a greater risk of some circulatory disease.

However, recent findings suggest that cholesterol is not all bad. We need it for a number of vital functions, such as the development of cell membranes. Blood cholesterol—in the form of *high-density lipoproteins*—is actually beneficial in warding off bacterial disease. Also, *bile salts,* which are necessary for fat digestion, are modified cholesterol. When irradiated with ultraviolet light, cholesterol becomes vitamin

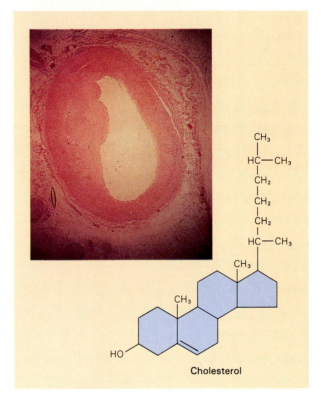

FIGURE 3.9 Cholesterol and arterial disease. Accumulation of cholesterol in plaques on the interior of arteries greatly reduces the inside diameter of the artery and increases the pressure of the blood flowing through it.

Cholesterol

D, which is necessary for normal bone growth. The human sex hormones—as well as the material that gives lustre to your hair—start out as cholesterol. Sports physicians now suspect that women runners need cholesterol to maintain normal menstrual periods.

To summarize, lipids are important in cell construction; they are also able to store great amounts of energy. As waxes, they help both plants and animals to conserve water. They even contribute to those vital chemical messengers called hormones.

PROTEINS

Proteins are huge, twisted, and fascinating molecules with a great variety of roles in the pageant of life. As you might suspect of any molecule with such important and varied responsibilities, there are many kinds of proteins.

Proteins can function as structural molecules, as food reserves, and even as hormones (just as can carbohydrates and lipids). Some proteins form enzymes, vital chemical catalysts that speed up certain chemical reactions in the cell; still others make movement possible. A vast army of protein antibodies help the body to fight off infections. One unique protein found in an Antarctic fish acts as an antifreeze.

Like the simpler carbohydrates and lipids, even these giants have a consistent and understandable organization. All proteins are essentially long chains of simple **amino acids.**

Amino Acids

There are about 20 different naturally occurring amino acids used in the assembly of proteins. Like the subunits of carbohydrates and lipids, amino acids form proteins through covalent dehydration linkages. There are about 150,000 different proteins in the human body alone, all of which function in important ways. No matter how complex they are, proteins are all formed from 20 or so different amino acids. (But then all of the elegantly arranged words in this book are formed from only 26 letters.)

The 20 amino acids clearly differ from each other, but they all have a few critical traits in common (Table 3.1). For example, every amino acid has at least one **carboxyl group** and at least one **amino group** (Figure 3.10). The presence of the two groups causes amino acids to behave in an interesting way in water. The carboxyl and amino groups become ionized, taking on a negative and positive charge, respectively. That is, the carboxyl group loses a proton (H^+) (becoming $-CHO^-$), and the amino group gains a proton (becoming $-NH_3^+$). (By the way, the release of a proton identifies the carboxyl group as an *acid*; the gaining of a proton identifies the amino group as a *base*.)

Each amino acid has one carbon atom (the alpha carbon) linking the carboxyl and amino groups. Attached to one side is a hydrogen atom, and to the other, making up the remainder of the amino acid, is what is called an **R group**. The "R" is simply shorthand for any of the 20 side groups that make one amino acid different from the next (see Table 3.1).

> The 20 or so **amino acids** are short carbon chains containing an **amino group**, a **carboxyl** (acid) **group,** and an **R group** unique to each.

The covalent bond between two amino acids in a protein is called a **peptide bond,** so called because the enzyme **pepsin** breaks this bond in the process of digesting proteins. The bond is formed by a dehydration reaction; thus the formation of each peptide bond yields one molecule of water (Figure 3.11).

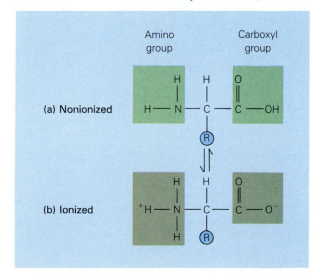

FIGURE 3.10 All amino acids have an amino group, a carboxyl group, and an R group. It is the R group that is different among the many amino acids. Note the non-ionized form **(a)** and the ionized form **(b).**

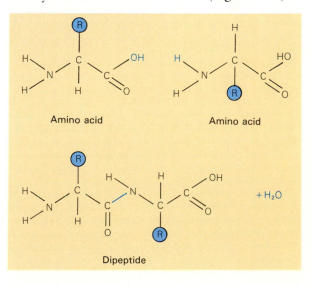

FIGURE 3.11 Amino acids are joined by peptide bonds (dehydration linkages) between adjacent amino and carboxyl groups. Shown here is a simple dipeptide, but the same process accounts for polypeptides.

TABLE 3.1   Amino Acids* Commonly Found in Proteins

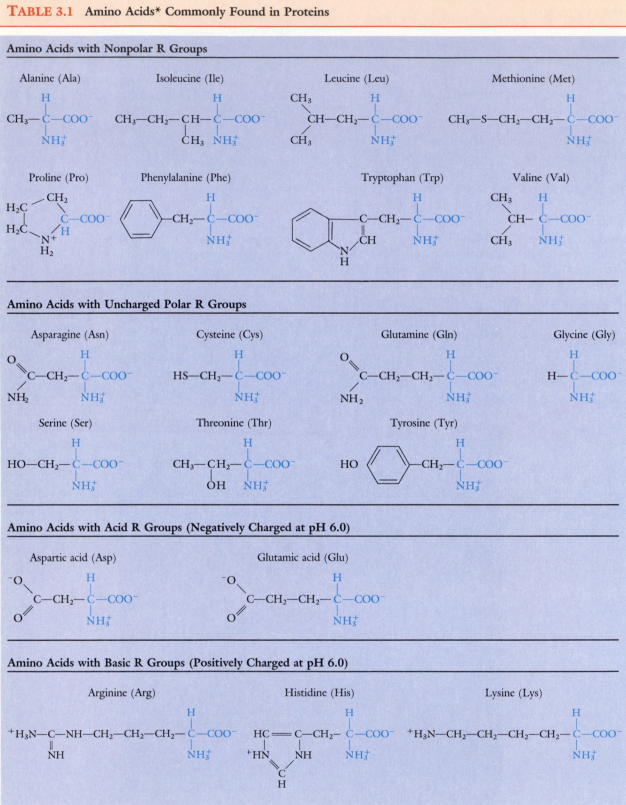

Amino Acids with Nonpolar R Groups

Alanine (Ala) Isoleucine (Ile) Leucine (Leu) Methionine (Met)

Proline (Pro) Phenylalanine (Phe) Tryptophan (Trp) Valine (Val)

Amino Acids with Uncharged Polar R Groups

Asparagine (Asn) Cysteine (Cys) Glutamine (Gln) Glycine (Gly)

Serine (Ser) Threonine (Thr) Tyrosine (Tyr)

Amino Acids with Acid R Groups (Negatively Charged at pH 6.0)

Aspartic acid (Asp) Glutamic acid (Glu)

Amino Acids with Basic R Groups (Positively Charged at pH 6.0)

Arginine (Arg) Histidine (His) Lysine (Lys)

*The portion of the amino acid that is common to all is colored. Note that some of the amino acids contain more than one amino or acid group, giving them greater basic or acid qualities than the others. Cysteine contains a sulfur-hydrogen group at its *R*-terminal. This has special importance in determining the shapes of proteins. The abbreviations given in parentheses are used for convenience in writing protein formulas.

Protein Organization

Joining two amino acids to form a **dipeptide** is a first step in the formation of **polypeptides,** long chains of amino acids that, when they reach a certain length and arrangement, become proteins. Actually, proteins can have as many as four levels of structure (Figure 3.12). The first, or **primary level,** is the arrangement of amino acids into a simple, linear polypeptide. The **secondary level** forms as a result of hydrogen bond attractions between amino acids that may twist the chain into a right-handed coil, which biochemists call an **alpha helix.** In other instances, the secondary level of the polypeptide forms "pleated sheets," characteristic of structural protein such as keratin, the main component of hair, nails, claws, hooves, and skin (see Chapter 31). The contractile filaments of muscle are also a form of fibrous protein.

FIGURE 3.12   Proteins may have four levels of structure. The primary level **(a)** is determined by the amino acid number, content, and order, forming the polypeptide. In the secondary level **(b)** the polypeptide forms a coiling alpha helix. The tertiary level **(c)** characteristic of globular proteins, occurs when the helix becomes folded in highly specific ways. Such folding is seen in myoglobin, an oxygen-carrying pigment occurring in muscles. The quaternary level of organization is characterized by two or more polypeptides joined by cross bridges. Hemoglobin **(d)** has two alpha and two beta polypeptide chains along with four iron-containing heme groups.

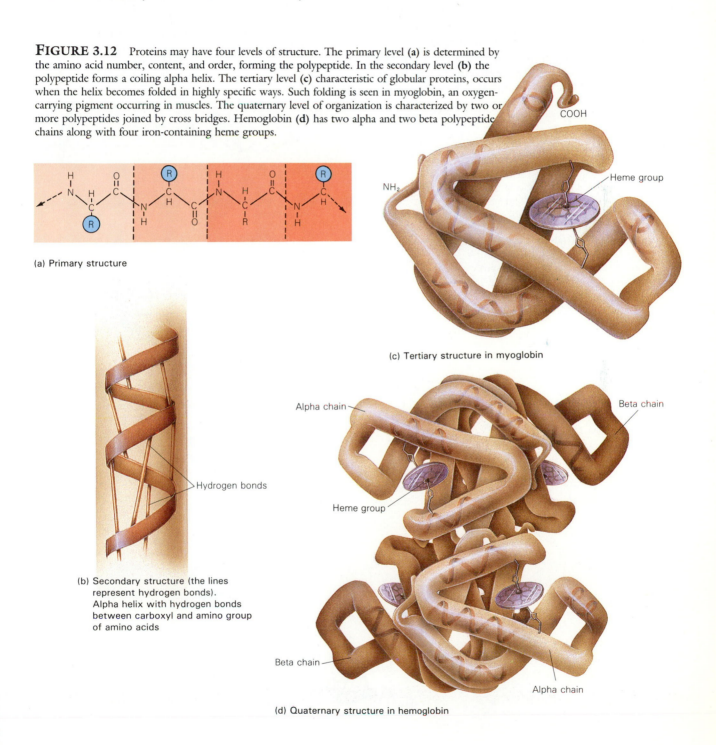

(a) Primary structure

(c) Tertiary structure in myoglobin

(b) Secondary structure (the lines represent hydrogen bonds). Alpha helix with hydrogen bonds between carboxyl and amino group of amino acids

(d) Quaternary structure in hemoglobin

In the **tertiary** (third) level of protein structure, polypeptide coils commonly undergo an elaborate but highly specific folding. An important part of the tertiary level involves the formation of new covalent bonds called **disulfide linkages** (linkages between molecules of certain sulfur-containing amino acids; see cysteine in Table 3.1). Proteins with the tertiary level of organization are often globular (roughly spherical). Examples include the egg-white protein, albumin, enzymes (see Chapter 6), and hemoglobin, the familiar, oxygen-carrying, blood protein.

A fourth or **quaternary structure** occurs when two or more polypeptides become linked. Included are the larger proteins such as enzymes and hemoglobin. Hemoglobin, a giant among globular proteins,

contains four polypeptides. Each polypeptide has one iron atom incorporated in a ring of nitrogen called a **heme group** (hence the name, *hemo*globin). It is the heme group that transports oxygen in the blood (which explains why iron is essential in the diet). Proteins with special groups such as heme are called **conjugated proteins.**

Proteins may have four levels of structure, the amino acid chain, the coiled polypeptide, the folded protein, and the folded protein containing two or more polypeptides.

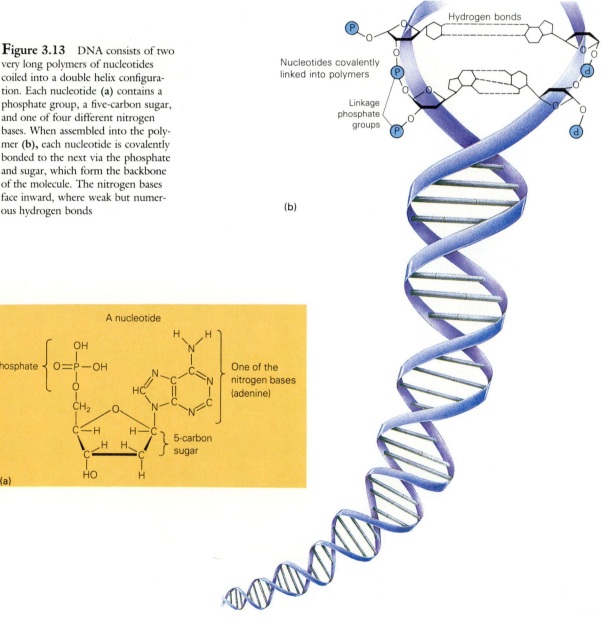

Figure 3.13 DNA consists of two very long polymers of nucleotides coiled into a double helix configuration. Each nucleotide (a) contains a phosphate group, a five-carbon sugar, and one of four different nitrogen bases. When assembled into the polymer (b), each nucleotide is covalently bonded to the next via the phosphate and sugar, which form the backbone of the molecule. The nitrogen bases face inward, where weak but numerous hydrogen bonds

NUCLEIC ACIDS: RNA AND DNA

Our final category in the molecules of life includes the **nucleic acids, RNA (ribonucleic acid)** and **DNA (deoxyribonucleic acid),** the largest of all biological macromolecules. In most organisms, the hereditary units called genes are composed of DNA. DNA molecules are immensely long polymers.

As in all of the large molecules of life, DNA and RNA are composed of repeated subunits, in this instance known as **nucleotides.** Nucleotides contain a five-carbon sugar, a phosphate group, and one of five different ringlike **nitrogen bases** (Figure 3.13a). Despite the immense length of nucleic acids, the organization of their nucleotides is surprisingly simple. In fact, it was DNA's deceptive simplicity that, until the early 1950s, kept biologists in the dark as to the chemical nature of the gene. Although proteins can contain as many as 20 different amino acid subunits, there are only four different subunits (nucleotides) in DNA and four in RNA. These nucleotides are very much alike in most ways.

In the assembly of a DNA polymer, the nucleotides are linked, one atop the other, into two opposing strands. The two strands are wound around each other in such a way as to form the well-known **double helix** (Figure 3.13b). In the assembly of RNA, nucleotides are also linked one atop the other, but because the finished polymer is single stranded, the helix does not form.

> **N**ucleic acids include **DNA** and **RNA,** long polymers of **nucleotides,** each of which contains one of five **nitrogen bases,** a pentose sugar, and a phosphate.

SUMMARY

CARBON: BACKBONE OF THE MOLECULES OF LIFE

Carbon forms the structural backbone for important molecules of life including carbohydrates, lipids, proteins, and nucleic acids. Carbon atoms join other carbon atoms through single and double bonds. They form chains, rings, and chains of rings.

CARBOHYDRATES

Carbohydrates, including sugars and starches, are common constituents of foods. They contain carbon, hydrogen, and oxygen in a $1:2:1$ ratio, occurring as monosaccharides, disaccharides, and polysaccharides.

Monosaccharides: Simple Sugars

Glucose, a common six-carbon monosaccharide, is the structural unit of many polysaccharides. It contains hydrogen, hydroxyl, and aldehyde side groups. Other important simple sugars are six-carbon fructose, galactose, and five-carbon ribose and deoxyribose.

Disaccharides: Linking the Monosaccharides

The linking of monosaccharides into disaccharides such as maltose and sucrose occurs through dehydration synthesis, an enzyme-mediated process in which —OH and —H groups are removed and water is formed. Hydrolysis, the opposite process, utilizes water in the splitting (digestion) of disaccharides, restoring the —OH and —H groups.

Polysaccharides: the Larger Carbohydrates

The most common polysaccharides—starches, glycogen, and cellulose—are lengthy polymers of glucose. While the first two contain alpha glucose and are readily digestible, cellulose contains beta glucose and is indigestible to most organisms. The building blocks of chitin, a polysaccharide common to arthropod exoskeletons, are nitrogen sugars.

LIPIDS

Lipids include fats, oils, waxes, steroids, and phospholipids.

Triglycerides and their subunits

Triglycerides—animal fats and plant oils—contain glycerol with three fatty acid chains attached. They join through dehydration synthesis. A fatty acid is a hydrocarbon chain containing a carboxyl (acid) group. Fatty acids vary in length and may be saturated (maximum hydrogen present) or unsaturated (less than the maximum number of hydrogens present).

Phospholipids

Phospholipids, major components of cell membranes, consist of glycerol, two fatty acid chains, and a charged phosphate-containing variable group such as choline. The charged heads are hydrophilic, attracting water, while the tails are hydrophobic, rejecting it. In living membranes the tails form an oily core.

Other Important Lipids

Waxes are used chiefly in waterproofing. Steroids are utilized in the lipoproteins of blood, in bile salts, vitamin D, and some hormones.

PROTEINS

Proteins are used as structural molecules, enzymes, antibodies, and hormones. Their structural units, or building blocks, are amino acids.

Amino Acids

The various kinds of proteins differ in their amino acid content. There are 20 or so different amino acids, each with at least one carboxyl (acidic) group and at least one amino (basic) group. One amino acid differs from the next in its R group. Amino acids join through dehydration synthesis in which covalent, peptide bonds are formed.

Protein Organization

Proteins may have four levels of organization: The primary level includes the kinds of amino acids used and their arrangement in the polypeptide. The secondary level includes alpha coiling formed through hydrogen bonding between amino acids. The tertiary level is a folding produced by disulfide linkages between sulfur-containing amino acids. The quaternary level is reached when two or more folded polypeptides become cross-linked by disulfide bonds.

NUCLEIC ACIDS: RNA AND DNA

DNA and RNA are polymers consisting of structural units called nucleotides. Nucleotides are made up of a phosphate group, a five-carbon sugar, and one of five nitrogen bases. The DNA molecule contains two chains of nucleotides that twist into a double helix. RNA forms a single strand. DNA contains the hereditary units, or genes, while RNA carries out the genetic instructions.

KEY TERMS

polymer	lactose	glycerol	dipeptide
macromolecule	dehydration synthesis	hydrocarbon chain	polypeptide
monosaccharide	polysaccharide	carboxyl group	alpha helix
glucose	cellulose	saturated fatty acid	disulfide linkage
dextrose	glycogen	unsaturated fatty acid	heme group
pentose sugars	amylose	hydrophilic	conjugated protein
deoxyribose	amylopectin	steroid	nucleic acid
ribose	chitin	cholesterol	ribonucleic acid
disaccharide	lipid	amino acid	deoxyribonucleic acid
maltose	phospholipid	R group	nucleotide
sucrose	triglyceride	peptide bond	nitrogen base
galactose	fatty acid	pepsin	double helix

REVIEW QUESTIONS

1 List three six-carbon and two five-carbon monosaccharides. Write the formulas for the following side groups: hydrogen, hydroxyl, and aldehyde. (pp. 32–33)

2 Name and describe the process through which monosaccharides are joined to form disaccharides and polysaccharides. What is the new covalent bond called? (pp. 33–34)

3 List three polysaccharides found in plants and two found in animals. What purposes does each serve? (pp. 34–35)

4 List the components of a triglyceride and name the process through which they become linked. (pp. 35–36)

5 State two or three ways in which the many kinds of triglycerides differ from each other. (p. 36)

6 Draw a simple model of a phospholipid, showing the fatty acid tails and variable phosphate group. (p. 37)

7 Using a simple drawing, illustrate the assembly of phospholipids into a membrane. Which regions are hydrophobic? Hydrophilic? (p. 38)

8 Describe the structure of a steroid and list three important uses. (p. 38)

9 Write the structural formula for a generalized amino acid, labelling the following: carboxyl group, amino group, alpha carbon, R group. How does one kind of amino acid differ from another? (pp. 39–40)

10 Explain the four levels of protein structure. Name a protein with all four levels present. (pp. 41–42)

11 Describe the general appearance of DNA. List the parts of its structural unit and explain how the five kinds differ from each other. (p. 43)

12 What is the role of DNA? (p. 43)

Robert Hooke realized that he had a problem. He had just been appointed Curator of Experiments for the prestigious Royal Society of London, and one of his first tasks was to devise some sort of demonstration for the next weekly meeting. He wanted something that would enlighten, entertain, and impress. He also wanted to make the Society members aware of his own abilities. Neither would be easy. The problem was, these were some of the brightest, crustiest, most argumentative, skeptical, and jaded people in all of 17th-century England—the elite of British science.

Hooke considered a number of possibilities, working and fretting until he struck upon a solution. Obviously, he had to show them something new, and the most exciting new technology of his day was curved and polished glass. He would demonstrate the lens.

The scientific world was buzzing with talk of lenses. With their ability to magnify, they revealed an entirely new world. Things no one had suspected existed were suddenly visible. Through new eyes, people could again see things long forgotten. With a pair of lenses held in a frame, people who had been nearly blind were able to see again—a miracle come true. Old men who had been unable to read had their books and letters returned to them. Of course, magnification by lenses was not a new idea. Earlier in the century, Galileo had pointed a lens toward the sky and had drawn some conclusions, as well as the wrath of the Church. Hooke, however, had a different intellectual appetite. He wanted to see things that were too small to be seen without a lens. He was so fascinated with the idea of using the lens to explore the world of the miniscule that he built his own microscope, one of the first in the world (Figure 4.1).

Obviously, it is difficult to impress people if you're standing on *their* turf; but microscopy was *Hooke's* turf. So he decided to use his lens in some novel way. But what should he arrange for them? What would they like to see? Maybe cork. Cork was a mystery, appearing to be solid, yet able to float. Perhaps it was not so solid after all. Hooke aimed his microscope at a cork, and what do you think he saw? Wrong. He saw nothing, because microscopes do not work very well with reflected light. So with a penknife he cut a very thin sliver of cork from the bottom, and shined a bright light upward through it. This time, what he saw puzzled him and was sufficiently interesting to please the Society members. Hooke wrote that the cork sliver seemed to be composed of "little boxes." These, he surmised, were full of air, accounting for the ability of corks to float.

4

THE STRUCTURE AND FUNCTION OF CELLS

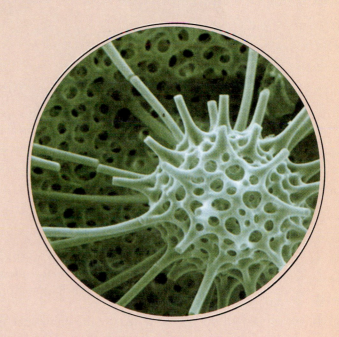

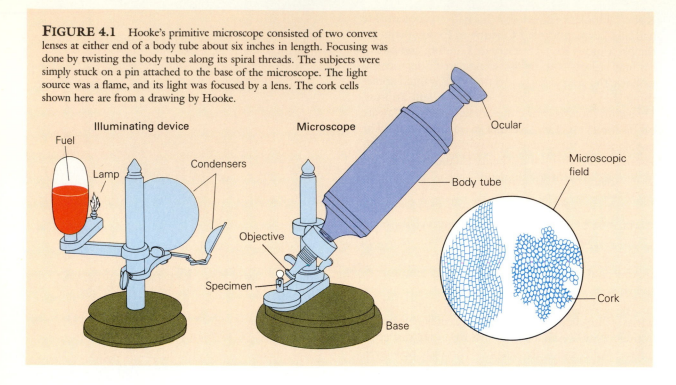

FIGURE 4.1   Hooke's primitive microscope consisted of two convex lenses at either end of a body tube about six inches in length. Focusing was done by twisting the body tube along its spiral threads. The subjects were simply stuck on a pin attached to the base of the microscope. The light source was a flame, and its light was focused by a lens. The cork cells shown here are from a drawing by Hooke.

Hooke called the little boxes *cells* because they reminded him of the rows of monks' cells in a monastery. And from this modest beginning, a new scientific field was born.

CELL THEORY

The birth, however, was slow. What was one to do with such knowledge? The group that week was pleased, but a full century would pass before the scientific world would understand the importance of Hooke's cells.

One of the first to try to use the knowledge was the German naturalist Lorenza Oken, who focused his primitive microscope on just about everything he could think of. Finally, in 1805, he wrote, "All organic beings originate from and consist of vesicles or cells." This simple statement became known as the **cell theory.** Then, in 1838, two other Germans, the botanist Matthias Jakob Schleiden and the zoologist Theodor Schwann, independently published the conclusion that all living things are composed of cells. (Schleiden and Schwann usually get the credit for the idea, even today.) Almost 20 years later, another German, Rudolf Virchow, added the statement, "omnis cellula e cellula." Anything written in Latin is, of course, very important—even if it only

means "all cells come from cells." That was, in fact, not a bad try based on the available data. Today, the idea is known as the **biogenetic law.**

Biology being biology, there are exceptions, (see Essay 4.1) but let's ignore the rigors of science for a moment. Microscopes are fun. Once Hooke had described his little boxes, the art of microscopy blossomed. Everyone in science wanted a microscope. And nothing—literally nothing—remained sacred. Everything was a fair target. Curious souls were anxious to be the first, the very first to see . . . whatever. At first, most of these efforts were prompted by sheer curiosity. In time, however, the more serious among them used microscopes to answer questions. They noticed certain common themes and differences. They began to make generalizations. For example, they suggested that although organisms may be vastly different, certain cells and tissues could be nearly identical. They noted that muscle, nerve, and reproductive cells in most animal species are quite similar. Thus people began to think of cells in terms of function.

> The **cell theory** states that organisms are composed of cells. The **biogenetic law** states that all cells come from preexisting cells.

Life on our small planet presents few opportunities for those who like tidy categories. There are few pigeonholes in the real world of adaptive, changing, opportunistic life. In fact, life is so diverse that there are exceptions to virtually every rule. (This is probably among the most reputable of the rules.) Exceptions to the cell theory are found, for example, in the kingdom Protista, the so-called single-celled creatures. (If they are cells, they are large cells.) These are sometimes large enough to be visible to the naked eye. The length of one common protist, the *Paramecium,* may reach 0.3 mm, and even it is dwarfed by another single-celled organism, the giant amoeba, whose length often measures 5 mm (about 3/16 of an inch). These giant single-celled organisms are 50 times longer than the typical animal cell. Protists are constructed along very different lines than are the cells of multicellular organisms. Because of this, some scientists prefer the term *acellular* when describing the protists. The implication is that they are not single-celled organisms, and that they simply are not organized along cellular principles. There are also organisms such as some flatworms and some fungi that undergo a strange sort of division in which the nucleus may divide, perhaps many times, but the total cell does not. The result is a very large "cell" with many nuclei.

At the other end of the size spectrum, far too small to be seen with the light microscope, are the viruses. Viruses are believed to be the smallest living things, although many scientists do not consider them to be alive.

Viruses lack most cell-associated traits, so perhaps they shouldn't be compared with cells. Structurally, they are very simple, consisting of a protein container with a supply of enzymes surrounding a core of genes. In essence, they are self-reproducing, capable of making more self-reproducing material.

Although the cell theory applies quite well to most organisms, life has a disconcerting way of not allowing easy generalizations. We can see that some forms of life have found it advantageous to take another route. The result is the vast array of life on this planet.

What is a Cell?

Cells are minute, highly organized, living units, surrounded by membranes, and containing a variety of tiny structures, each with a specific role. Biologists distinguish two principal types of cells, those of **prokaryotes** and **eukaryotes.** The first group includes bacteria, very simple, single-celled forms of life that have little visible, internal structure, although they may be biochemically complex. Bacteria make up a kingdom known as Monera (Table 4.1). We will come back to the prokaryotes later in the chapter.

The other group, the eukaryotes, includes all other cellular life. Eukaryotes are distributed into four kingdoms: Protista, Fungi, Plantae, and Animalia. Like prokaryotes, many protists are single celled. In the larger, multicellular organisms, similar cells cluster into **tissues,** which, when grouped together, become **organs** that carry on specific tasks. Organs form **systems** or organ systems which are responsible for major body functions.

Cells carry out virtually all the processes that make life possible (Table 4.2). Thus it should be no surprise to learn that they are complex. Eukaryotic cells contain numerous membrane–surrounded **organelles** ("little organs"), each with a separate role in carrying out life processes. In most cases we know what that role is, but in a few, we still aren't sure.

We do know that certain organelles specialize in synthesizing complex molecules such as proteins. Others convert food stored in the cell into energy, and still others store waste products, either permanently or temporarily. Some organelles may transport materials to the membrane, where they can be released to the outside. Later we will see that almost all cellular activities are directed by yet another membrane-bounded organelle, the cell nucleus.

> **Prokaryotic cells** have little visible internal structure, whereas those of **eukaryotes** have complex, membrane-bounded organelles. Both carry out the fundamental life processes.

Cell Size

Can cells be seen with the naked eye? They can if the naked eye can see a chicken egg yolk, which is a single cell, but most are far too small to be seen without some sort of magnification. It is very difficult to generalize about cell size and shape because there are so

TABLE 4.1 The Kingdoms of Life: A Preview

The earth's millions of species are organized into five major groupings known as kingdoms. Assignments to such kingdoms are made on the basis of similarities in structure and function, and biochemical similarities, which, to the biologist, indicate evolutionary relatedness.

Kingdom	Examples	Major Characteristics
		Prokaryotes
Monera	Bacteria	Single cells, often in colonies; little internal organization; circular; naked DNA
		Eukaryotes
Protista	Protozoans and algae	Both single-celled and multicellular; colonies, many photosynthetic
Fungi	Molds, mushrooms, smuts, rusts	Multicellular; simple tubular body form; elaborate reproductive structures; heterotrophs
Plantae	Mosses, ferns, cone-bearers, and flowering plants	Multicellular; photosynthetic; well-developed tissues, organs, and systems
Animalia	All invertebrate and vertebrates from sponges to grasshoppers and from fish to humans	Multicellular; well-developed tissues, organs, and organ systems; heterotrophs

TABLE 4.2 Key Functions in the Cell

The cell functions are those life processes that are essential to most cells and organisms.

Transport:	the passive and active movement of materials across membranes into and out of the cell
Synthesis:	enzyme-directed manufacture of substances such as protein, carbohydrates, and lipids
Secretion:	the release through the plasma membrane of wastes and special substances synthesized in the cell
Digestion:	the chemical breakdown of foods or other materials by enzymes, usually through hydrolysis (addition of water)
Reproduction:	in the cell, division into two: preparatory events include the copying of all genetic information (DNA)
Assimilation:	the incorporation into the cell proper of materials taken in
Energy transformation:	the formation of useful, energy-rich molecules called ATP (adenosine triphosphate) from light energy, simple inorganic molecules, or food
Movement:	movement in or of the cell through changes in contractile fibers, cell shape, or by active bending of whiplike organelles
Response:	organized response to stimuli from other cells or the environment

many kinds of cells, each specialized for a particular function. For example, there are cells invisible to the human eye that are over a meter long, such as the nerve cells in a giraffe's leg, but they are still too fine to be seen. Most plant and animal cells are about 90 micrometers (μm) long. Almost none are smaller than 10 μm in diameter, and only a few are larger than 100 μm. A micrometer is one millionth of a meter (see Table 4.3). To give you an idea of the size of such cells, about fifty 10-micrometer cells set end-to-end would reach across the period at the end of this sentence. Plant cells tend to be somewhat larger than animal cells, perhaps because they contain water-filled cavities called **vacuoles.** In general, the amount of cytoplasm (living material) in the two types of cells is about the same.

Confronted with such information, biologists are likely to wonder what determines cell size. Why are most of them so small? Why do they first go through a rapid growth phase, then slow down as some critical size is reached, divide in half, and start over? One way to phrase the question is to ask what is the advantage of having small cells.

The surface-volume hypothesis. The generally accepted explanation for the small size of cells is that size strongly affects the ratio of the surface area to the volume. Specifically, smaller cells have larger surface areas in proportion to their volume.

In biology there always seems to be a next question. This time the next question is, why is a large surface area necessary? The answer centers on the fact

TABLE 4.3   A Comparison of Some Cell and Cell Structure Dimensions

The range of cell size is enormous, extending from the bacterium to the meter-long nerve cell, a difference of about a millionfold. Yet most plant and animal cells are about 90 micrometers (µm) across. The smallest known cells, those of *Mycoplasma*, sometimes are not visible through the light microscope. Viruses can be seen only with an electron microscope.

Abbreviations used in table: m = meter; mm = millimeter = 0.001 (10^{-3}) meter; µm = micrometer = 0.000001 (10^{-6}) meter; nm = nanometer = 0.000000001 (10^{-9}) meter. (See also the metric table inside the back cover.)

Human eye	1 meter	Some nerve cells
	100 mm	Ostrich egg
		Hen's egg
	10 mm	
	1 mm	Frog's egg
		Diameter of squid giant nerve cell
Light microscope	100 µm	Human egg
		Ameba
		Human hair
		Human smooth muscle cell
		Human bone cell
		Human liver cell
	10 µm	Human milk-secreting cell
		Human red blood cell
		Chloroplast
		Nucleus of human liver cell
		Mitochondrion (length)
		Bacterium (*E. coli*)
	1 µm	Diameter of human nerve cell process
		Lysosomes
		Mycoplasma
Electron microscope		Cilium (diameter)
		Centriole
	100 nm	Large virus
		Nuclear pore
		Microtubule
		Ribosome
	10 nm	Cell membranes, including plasma membrane (thickness)
		Microfilaments
		Globular protein
		Diameter of DNA double helix
	1 nm	Diameter of protein α-helix
		Amino acid
	0.1 nm	Diameter of hydrogen atom

that the surface area of cells is covered by a regulatory membrane. The larger the membrane relative to the cell's interior, the greater the regulation over the cell's composition, especially since the membrane regulates what enters and leaves the cell. Oxygen and nutrients enter the cell easily, and other materials such as wastes, are quickly expelled.

A large membrane covering a small cell ensures that the material within is never far from the cell's exterior and, therefore, the cell is more likely to be able to carry on transport in an efficient manner (Figure 4.2).

> The **surface-volume hypothesis** proposes that the small size of most cells relates to the need for a relatively large membrane surface area. As volume decreases, surface area increases relative to the volume.

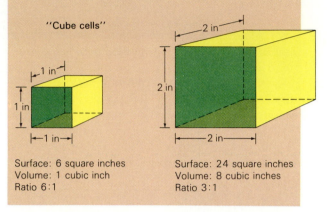

FIGURE 4.2 Surface-to-volume ratio. In two bodies of similar shape, the larger one has more volume for its surface area. If the bodies depend on materials moving through the covering surface, the smaller body will be at an advantage since it has a comparatively large surface area to service its interior.

"Cube cells"

Surface: 6 square inches
Volume: 1 cubic inch
Ratio 6:1

Surface: 24 square inches
Volume: 8 cubic inches
Ratio 3:1

Another reason cells are small is that the vital chemical reactions of life depend to a large degree on the random colliding of molecules within the cells. The likelihood of such critical interactions is increased if the molecules are enclosed in tiny cells.

The question then arises: Why aren't cells even smaller? No one really knows, but biochemists suggest that the lower limits to cell size may be restricted simply by the size of critical macromolecules such as enzymes, proteins, DNA, and RNA. Cells must have certain numbers of these giant molecules, and there must be room for them. The smallest known cells are those of bacteria known as *Mycoplasmas*, which range in size from 0.1 to 0.3 μm (micrometer). Laid out side by side, it could take as many as 1,000 of these bacteria to reach across the period at the end of this sentence.

A Look at Cell Diversity

Cells come in many different sizes and shapes, and each has its own limits and abilities. This is not surprising, since we would not expect the cells of a carrot to be identical to those of a clam, or those of a muscle the same as those of a nerve (Figure 4.3).

Cells with different appearances may also behave differently. For example, some are highly irritable—that is, they respond quickly to environmental changes. Some can contract, others secrete fluids, and still others have long tails and can swim. Such variety indicates the great advantage of multicellularity: **specialization.** A many-celled organism living in a complex environment is better equipped to meet different demands if it has different kinds of cells, each with its own special abilities. Imagine the advantage of having some cells that can react to light, others that can distinguish pain, and others that can contract and therefore move you toward the light and away from the pain. From the perspective of evolution, we could expect groups of cells to become highly specialized for very specific functions, increasingly adapting the organisms they comprise to better exist in a competitive world.

CELL STRUCTURE

Now that we have some idea of the size and variation of cells, let's take a closer look at their structure. For convenience, we have grouped the structures of the eukaryotic cell according to their functions. We'll begin with the cell surface. Figure 4.4 shows a composite view of plant and animal cells.

Support and Transport

Plasma Membrane

The plasma membrane is simply the membrane that surrounds each cell. Now let's see if "simply" is a good choice of words. We learned earlier that the basic function of the membrane is to control the movement of materials into and out of the cell. It should be obvious, since the processes of life must be tightly regulated, that the plasma membrane must be selective about what it allows to pass in and out. It must freely accept some substances and utterly reject others. It may do this passively, like a sleeping gatekeeper, as it does with water and gases; or it may take an active part in transporting materials, alertly and with great discrimination using cellular energy to force other more reluctant substances across. Because of such discrimination plasma membranes are described as **selectively permeable** (see Chapter 5).

The two major components of the plasma membrane are proteins and phospholipids. The phospholipids exist in a double layer, with all the uncharged fatty acid tails directed inward. Under the electron microscope, the membranes look like two dark lines separated by a clear area about 5 nm wide.

Fluid mosaic model. It has been possible to deduce the structure of the cell membrane by pulling together everything known about it and developing a model that accounts for all the facts. It is called the **fluid mosaic model** (described by S.J. Singer). In this model (Figure 4.5a) the phospholipids are visualized as small spheres composed of glycerol, phosphate, and perhaps other organic groups. Each head has two hydrocarbon tails that point inward.

This arrangement forms a hydrophilic ("water-loving") surface that interacts readily with charged substances. The tails, however, are nonpolar or uncharged and cling, forming a more-or-less oily hydrophobic ("water-fearing") core (see Chapters 2 and 3).

Specific proteins are associated with the plasma membrane. Large proteins completely penetrate the bilipid layer; some are involved in transport, and others are enzymes. Smaller proteins may be confined to only the inner or outer lipid layers. Those on the outer side may interact with hormones and other messengers reaching the cell, or they may help cells recognize others of their type. Proteins associated

FIGURE 4.3 Diversity in plant and animal cells. These cells from multicellular organisms are each well adapted to a specific role. (Plant cell photograph courtesy Carolina Biological Supply.)

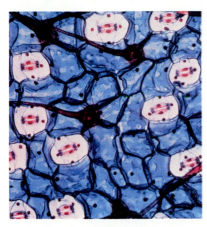
Leaf epidermis cells (covering)

Compact bone cells (support)

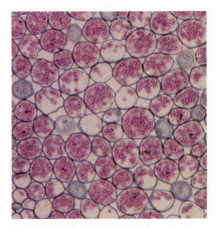
Plant root cells (storage)

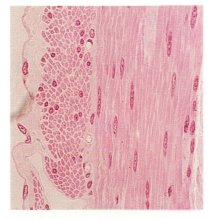
Smooth muscle cells (movement)

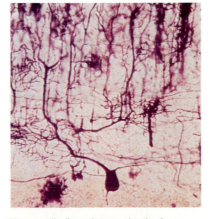
Nerve cells (impulse conduction)

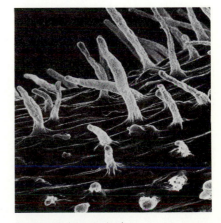
Root hairs (absorption)

FIGURE 4.4 Representative plant and animal cells.

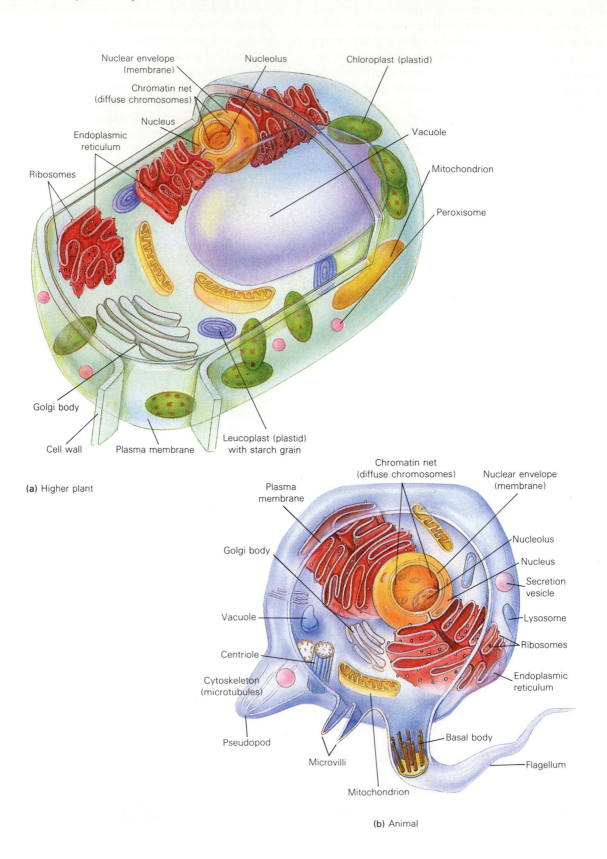

Nuclear envelope (membrane)

Chromatin net (diffuse chromosomes)

Nucleus

Endoplasmic reticulum

Ribosomes

Nucleolus

Chloroplast (plastid)

Vacuole

Mitochondrion

Peroxisome

Golgi body

Cell wall

Plasma membrane

Leucoplast (plastid) with starch grain

(a) Higher plant

Chromatin net (diffuse chromosomes)

Nuclear envelope (membrane)

Plasma membrane

Golgi body

Vacuole

Centriole

Cytoskeleton (microtubules)

Pseudopod

Microvilli

Mitochondrion

Nucleolus

Nucleus

Secretion vesicle

Lysosome

Ribosomes

Endoplasmic reticulum

Basal body

Flagellum

(b) Animal

only with the inner side of the plasma membrane may interact with slender **microfilaments** and **microtubules,** cytoplasmic structures important to cell shape and movement (see Figure 4.4).

The fluid mosaic model is supported by freeze-fracture preparations (Figure 4.5b and c). When frozen cells split precisely between the tails of phospholipids, the membrane proteins remain on one of the surfaces, while the other surface is pitted with indentations where the proteins had been.

Special molecules of the membrane surface. The membrane is composed not only of phospholipid and protein, but also carbohydrates and lipids that, with certain proteins, form **glycoproteins** (sugar proteins) and **lipoproteins.** Other carbohydrates may form part of the outer plasma membrane in ways that are not well understood but that may influence how cells interact with each other.

Let's return to a point just mentioned: cells apparently recognize one another on the basis of the car-bohydrates and proteins of the membrane. That recognition is important in many processes. Cells must be sensitive to foreign cells to build immunity against them. Also, as an embryo develops, recognition of various cell types assists in the coordinated and orderly development of the different body parts. One startling experiment shows the remarkable ability of cells types to recognize each other. If cells from different tissues are mixed together and allowed to grow on a nutrient medium, the cells will slowly begin to move about until each has found others of its own type. The result is distinct masses of specific tissue types. Such specificity of cell membranes plays a part in blood groupings, cancer defense, and the rejection of transplanted organs.

Plant Cell Wall

One of the most obvious structures in all plant cells is the **cell wall,** a rigid, nonliving layer just outside the plasma membrane and composed primarily of cellulose and other polymers (see Figure 3.4). Cell walls

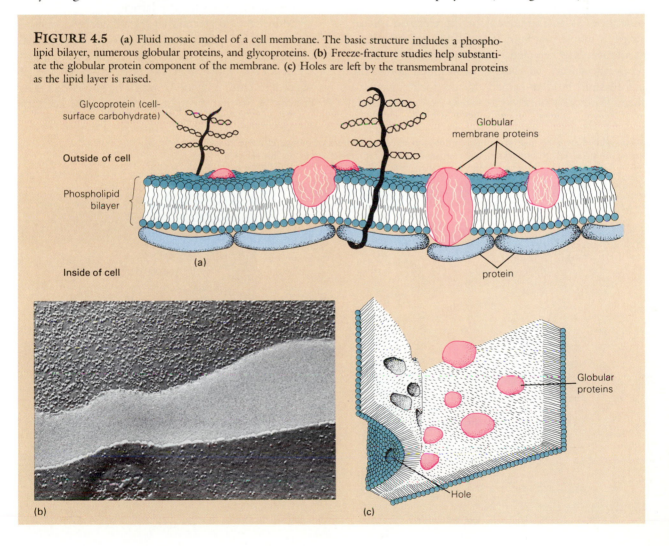

FIGURE 4.5 (a) Fluid mosaic model of a cell membrane. The basic structure includes a phospholipid bilayer, numerous globular proteins, and glycoproteins. (b) Freeze-fracture studies help substantiate the globular protein component of the membrane. (c) Holes are left by the transmembranal proteins as the lipid layer is raised.

Glycoprotein (cell-surface carbohydrate)

Outside of cell

Phospholipid bilayer

Inside of cell

(a)

Globular membrane proteins

protein

Globular proteins

Hole

(b)

(c)

are composed of tiny fibers (microfibrils) of cellulose chains arranged in layers. Each layer lies at an angle with respect to the one below it, forming a laminated, strong, and porous covering for the cell. Its basic structure is strengthened as it becomes impregnated with hardening substances such as pectin.

Other substances may be added to the cellulose and pectin matrix, depending on the function of the cell. For example, **lignin** is continually secreted into the cellulose of cells in the stems of woody plants, forming a hard, thick, decay-resistant wall. **Suberin,** a waxy substance, is secreted into the outer layer of some plant cells, forming a protective, waterproof layer. The cells of the upper surface of leaves, on the other hand, are waterproofed by another waxy secretion called **cutin.**

Microtrabecular Lattice: Skeleton of the Cell

Cytology is clearly one of those areas in which new knowledge depends heavily on advances in technology. For example, by the early 1900s, those cell structures visible through the light microscope had been described. With the advent of the electron microscope, a whole new dimension of the cell, its **ultrastructure,** was revealed. Even with the new microscope, however, we didn't know much about the cytoplasmic fluid in which the organelles seem to float. We could only vaguely refer to "cytoplasmic matrix" or "ground substance," labels that seemed to convey information, but actually didn't. The problem was that cells had to be sliced into ultrathin sections to permit the electrons from the electron microscope to pass through, and this procedure demolished any finer structures within the matrix that might have been present.

With the development of the high-voltage electron microscope (see Essay 4.2) it became possible to obtain a three-dimensional view of the whole cell without slicing it. In this way, an entirely new realm of cytoplasmic detail has been revealed. Cytologists are now studying a fascinating and peculiar structural network that has been dubbed the **microtrabecular lattice** (Figure 4.6).

The microtrabecular lattice appears as a mazelike network of hollow fibers, extending throughout the cell, connecting and suspending the organelles in a kind of three-dimensional web. Researchers are already hard at work unlocking the secrets of this grand network, and have proposed both structural and metabolic roles for the lattice.

Some have suggested that certain enzymes may be suspended in a delicate framework. The spatial arrangement of these enzymes might increase the efficiency of those that operate in some special sequence. Thus, enzyme B would be suspended near enzyme A, so that it might more easily interact with

FIGURE 4.6 The microtrabecular lattice is an extensive network of tubular elements that extends throughout the cell. Note that the major organelles of the cell are suspended in this lattice.

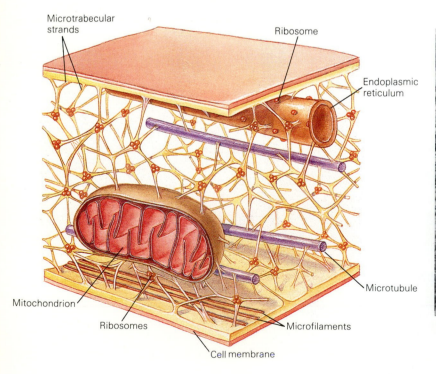
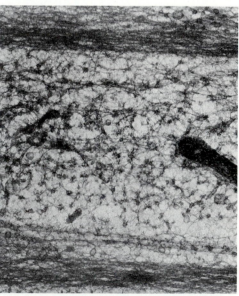

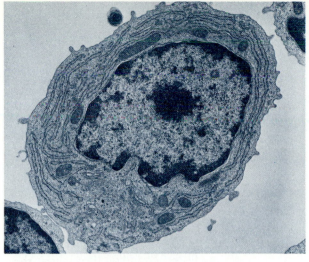

(a)

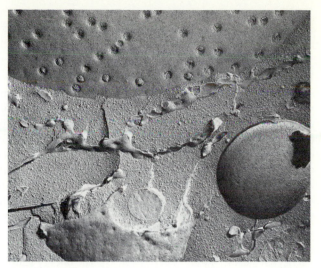

(b)

FIGURE 4.7 Electron microscopic study of the nucleus. **(a)** The nucleus is the large central sphere with its dark-staining chromatids spread about. The dark body is a nucleolus, a synthesis and storage site for ribosomal RNA. **(b)** In the freeze-fracture preparation, the outer nuclear membrane has been pulled away, revealing numerous nuclear pores.

the products of A. Enzyme C would be near B, and so forth. Such a structural organization presumably would be much more efficient than purely random enzyme movement through the cell, long believed to be the way in which enzymes encounter the molecules with which they interact.

> Structures of physical support include the rigid plant cell wall and a complex, weblike, **microtrabecular lattice.**

We have taken a brief look at the plasma membrane, the cell wall, and the microtrabecular lattice. The remaining structures of the cell are the organelles.

Cell Control: The Nucleus

The nucleus is not easily described because of the complexity of its functions. To begin, we should note that the nucleus is the most prominent organelle of the cell. It was also one of the first structures to be seen inside the cell. In fact, the word *nucleus* ("kernel") was first used in 1831, about the time of the development of the cell theory.

The nucleus has two vital functions: *reproduction* and *control*. The first involves preserving the hereditary information and copying it when it is to be passed along to new generations of cells. The hereditary information, encoded in immensely long DNA

molecules, is subdivided into genes, which are passed from generation to generation.

The nucleus also uses its repository of genes to direct virtually everything the cell does. This controlling function is accomplished by the action of enzymes, hormones, and other active molecules, which are synthesized as directed by the nucleus when the need arises. The genes do their controlling through the molecules they specify. We will look further into control by genes later (see Chapters 9, 14, and 15).

Nuclear DNA and its closely associated protein **histone** is called **chromatin,** so named because it readily absorbs color from dyes or stains (Figure 4.7a). Individual DNA molecules and their associated proteins are known as **chromosomes** ("colored bodies"). The number of chromosomes varies greatly in different species. During cell reproduction (**cell division**) the chromosomes—in a highly coiled state and quite visible—take on a sausagelike appearance. At other times, they are spread out and difficult to see except with the electron microscope (see Chapter 9). Most of the time there is little visible structure in the nucleus.

The nucleus is bound by a double membrane called the **nuclear envelope.** It consists of two tightly adjoined membranes, each of which is formed from the familiar lipid-protein bilayers. The two membranes pinch together in scattered places over the nuclear surface to form **nuclear pores** (Figure 4.7b). The word "pore" implies hole, but these are merely

Cytologists, the biologists who study cells, use an arsenal of highly sophisticated devices and precise techniques in their efforts to develop exact descriptions of cells. Their most venerable tool is the direct descendant of Hooke's primitive apparatus. It is the *compound light microscope* (see the illustration). Developed in the 19th century, it is still very useful and marvelously precise, but it is limited by the nature of the energy it uses: light. Any two objects closer together than 250 nanometers (nm) merge as a single, blurred image, because of the properties of visible light. The limitations of any microscope are, therefore, defined as *resolving power*—the ability to distinguish close objects as being separate from one another. In practice, this limitation is half the wavelength of visible light.

Fortunately, we need no longer be limited by the resolving powers of the light microscope. We now have the *transmission electron microscope* (TEM). This remarkable tool was conceived in the early part of the 20th century, but was not perfected until the 1950s. With the TEM, electrons—not light—are the energy source. The electrons are emitted from a heated coil and are focused so that they pass through the object. The electrons' great advantage is that their oscillations (wavelengths) are substantially smaller than the wavelengths of light. They can pass between the most finely separated objects in the cell. As they pass through matter of different densities, they cast an image on a screen or photographic film. The magic of the TEM lies in the fact that its resolving power is practically unlimited as far as cells are concerned. The TEM can magnify an object up to 1 million times. In more understandable terms, consider that the finest light microscopes can produce clear outline images of a single bacterium whereas the TEM can produce a detailed image of its inner structure.

Despite its great advantages the TEM initially met strong resistance among traditional cytologists because the preparation of cells for the TEM involves extremely harsh, dis-

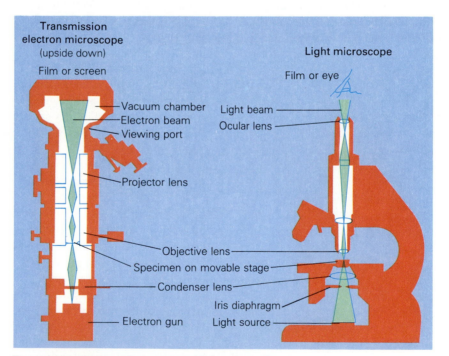

Transmission electron microscope and light microscope.

ruptive steps that could easily alter the material so drastically that no one could be sure of what he or she was actually seeing. (Since that time, the structures identified have been verified in many ways.)

To prepare a cell for the TEM, bits of tissue are "fixed" by permeating them with heavy metal salts that solidify the cell's protein. If the material to be viewed is tiny, as are virus particles, the metallic salts are sprayed on at an angle in what is known as *shadow-casting* (see the illustration). This treatment increases the tendency of cell structures to absorb electrons, making their images darker and sharper.

One of the early techniques has continued to yield particularly valuable information. The technique is called *freeze-fracturing*. Quick-freezing the tissue produces natural fracture lines wherever two lipid regions meet. Because of this, membrane-bound structures within cells become clearly visible (see photograph).

Today an entire family of electron microscopes has emerged, each demanding its own sophisticated techniques. The *scanning electron microscope* (SEM), has produced rather startling three-dimensional images of whole subjects. A shower of electrons sweeps back and forth across the subject, and electrons are scattered in different ways from the subject's surface. They land on image-producing plates, where they are detected and analyzed electronically.

An even newer way to probe the incredible and unseen sea of minutiae around us is the *high-voltage electron microscope*. Its penetrating power is so great—1 million volts—that it is not even necessary to slice the cell in order to see inside it. This three-story-high tool also produces three-dimensional images, revealing incredible details not visible even with the best standard electron microscopy techniques. Only a few of these gigantic microscopes exist at present, and there is a long line of cytologists—eager to probe more deeply into the world of the cell—awaiting their turn to use them.

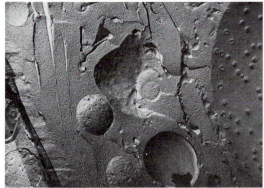

Freeze fracture showing nuclear membrane *(right).*

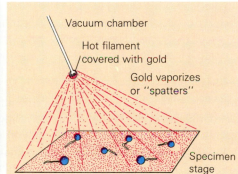

Vacuum chamber

Hot filament covered with gold

Gold vaporizes or "spatters"

Specimen stage

Heavy metal shadow casting.

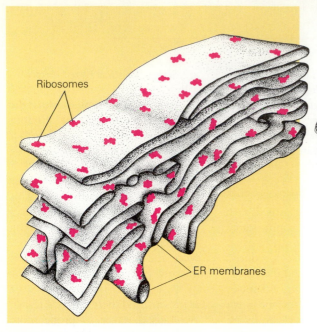

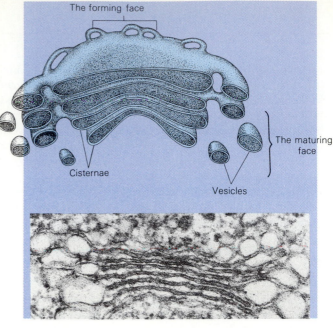

FIGURE 4.8 The rough endoplasmic reticulum (ER) consists of parallel rows of membranes surrounding deep channels. The small round bodies along the ER membranes are ribosomes.

FIGURE 4.9 In this electron microscope view, Golgi bodies appear as flattened stacks of membranes. The three-dimensional drawing suggests the function of the bodies. Note that the flattened membranous sacs seem to fill at either end and "bud off," forming vesicles.

indentations that are filled with special proteins that permit a controlled passage of materials. The pores apparently connect the nucleoplasm and the cytoplasm. Such complex pores are essential, since through them very large molecules can pass from the nucleus to the cytoplasm.

Many nuclei include dark, prominent bodies known as **nucleoli** ("little nuclei"). Nucleoli are rich in the nucleic acid RNA and have the specific task of assembling a special kind of RNA found in small, round structures called **ribosomes,** which we will consider in more detail later.

Organelles of Cell Synthesis, Storage, Digestion, and Secretion

Endoplasmic reticulum. The **endoplasmic reticulum,** or **ER,** is a complex membrane system that takes up a large part of the cytoplasm of eukaryotic cells, particularly those involved in the synthesis of proteins (Figure 4.8). Parts of highly folded ER are known to connect directly to the outer membrane of the nuclear envelope (see Figure 4.4). The ER is involved primarily in the synthesis, modification, and transport of substances produced by the cell.

There are two types of ER: rough and smooth. Rough ER gets its name from the ribosomes that ap-

pear tightly adhered to one side of the membrane, making it look like coarse sandpaper (Figure 4.8). The channels are formed by two sheets of this "sandpaper" lying side-by-side, their rough surfaces out. Rough endoplasmic reticulum is common in cells that manufacture proteins to be secreted outside the cell.

Smooth ER lacks ribosomes, and is found primarily in cells that synthesize, secrete, and/or store carbohydrates, steroid hormones, lipids, or other nonprotein products. A great deal of smooth endoplasmic reticulum is found in the cells of the testis, oil glands of the skin, and some hormone-producing gland cells.

The Golgi bodies. In 1898, Camillo Golgi, an Italian cytologist, discovered that when cells were treated with silver salts, certain peculiar structures appeared in the cytoplasm. The "reticular apparatuses" he described had not been noticed previously, and they didn't show up with any other stains. For the next 50 years cytologists argued over whether **Golgi bodies** were really cell structures or just artifacts caused by the silver treatment.

The electron microscope came to the rescue by showing that Golgi bodies are indeed real (Figure 4.9). Furthermore, they have a characteristic structure, regardless of the kind of cell they are found in.

They are a stack of flattened, membranous sacs, or **cisternae,** lying close to the nucleus. Each Golgi body contains a **forming face,** stacked cisternae, and a **maturing face.** This is a highly dynamic organelle, its membrane area continually forming and diminishing.

Golgi bodies continue some of the chemical functions of the endoplasmic reticulum. Material-laden transport vesicles bud off the ER and fuse with the forming face of nearby Golgi sacs. Within the Golgi bodies the materials are sorted, modified, and packaged in various ways. For instance, powerful proteolytic enzymes are safely isolated for future use in tough **storage vesicles** called **lysosomes.** Other substances enter **secretion vesicles,** spherical containers that periodically break away from the maturing face and move to the plasma membrane where the vesicles fuse with the membrane and the substances carried are released, or secreted, outside the cell.

> Protein synthesis occurs on **ribosomes,** followed by modifications made in the **endoplasmic reticulum** and **Golgi bodies.** Golgi materials enter **vesicles** for secretion or **lysosomes** for storage.

Lysosomes.   Lysosomes are roughly spherical, membrane-bound sacs (Figure 4.10) that contain powerful digestive enzymes, synthesized and packaged by the Golgi apparatus. If these digestive enzymes were released into the cell's cytoplasm, they would quickly digest the cell. Christian de Duve, who first described lysosomes, called them "suicide bags." His poetic fancy was not entirely unwarranted, since lysosomes sometimes do destroy the cells that bear them. However, this is not necessarily disruptive to the organism. Cell death is a normal part of embryonic development. For example, as the fingers form from paddlelike tissue, the cells between them must die and disappear. In addition, lysosomes may rupture and release their deadly enzymes into a superfluous cell or one that is not functioning well. Lysosomes may also aid in digestion within the cell by releasing enzymes into food-containing vacuoles (see below) where digestion can safely occur.

Peroxisomes.   Peroxisomes are small subcellular bodies, surrounded by membranes and found in a great variety of organisms, including plants and animals. (In animals, they are most common in liver and kidney cells.) Peroxisomes appear as very dense bodies with a peculiar crystalline core, somewhat resem-

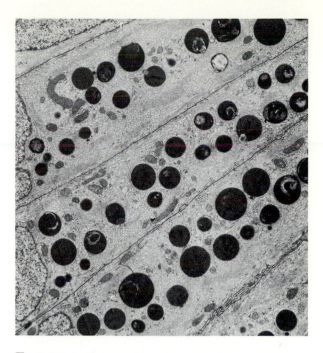

FIGURE 4.10   Lysosomes—the dark spheres in these cells—are storage bodies for powerful hydrolytic enzymes. Hence, their membranes are exceptionally strong.

bling a cross-section through a honeycomb. The peroxisomes contain enzymes that, like those of the lysosomes, are important in certain chemical reactions. For example, the enzymes of peroxisomes are known to break down hydrogen peroxide into oxygen and water, protecting cells from its corrosive effect.

Vacuoles.   The term **vacuole** means "empty cavity" in Latin. In cytology, however, the term refers to a membrane-bound body with little or no inner structure. Of course, vacuoles are not empty; they hold something, but that something can vary widely, depending on the cell and the organism.

Plant cells generally have more and larger vacuoles than animal cells. In fact, the vacuoles of many types of plant cells dominate the central part of the cell, crowding the other organelles against the cell wall (see Figure 4.3).

The fluids within a plant vacuole may be solutions that include inorganic salts, organic acids, atmospheric gases, sugars, pigments, or any of several other materials. Sometimes the vacuoles are filled with a colorful sap containing blue, red, or purple pigments, some of which will grace the petals of flowers. Some plants store poisonous compounds in vacuoles. It has been suggested that this stored material helps protect the plant against grazing animals.

Figure 4.11 summarizes some of the interrelation-

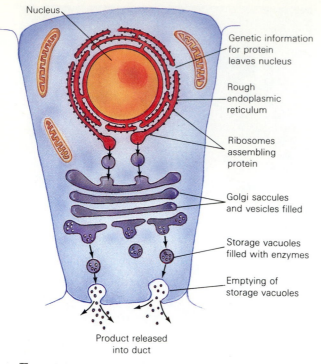

Nucleus

Genetic information for protein leaves nucleus

Rough endoplasmic reticulum

Ribosomes assembling protein

Golgi saccules and vesicles filled

Storage vacuoles filled with enzymes

Emptying of storage vacuoles

Product released into duct

FIGURE 4.11 Activity in a specialized secretory cell suggests a functional relationship among several organelles. Synthesis of the protein secretory product is governed by genetic instructions from the nucleus that are carried out along ribosomes bound to the endoplasmic reticulum. Polypeptides entering the lumen of the rough ER undergo modification there but do not reach the finished protein state until acted upon by enzymes in the Golgi body. Note the transport vesicles budding from the rough ER and joining the forming face of the Golgi. Note also the secretion vesicles budding from the maturing face of the outermost cisterna.

ships among the membrane-bound organelles of the cell.

Cell Energy

Chloroplasts. The **chloroplasts** of plants are large, green, round or oval organelles, easily seen through the light microscope. Most obvious in leaf cells, they are also present in all photosynthetic eukaryotes. (*Photosynthesis* is the process by which plants make food by using the energy of light.)

Like the nucleus, chloroplasts are surrounded by a two-layered membrane. Inside the double membrane are layers of flattened, membranous disks known as **thylakoids,** which contain green, light-capturing pigments called chlorophylls and carotenoids. A stack of the thylakoids is known as a **granum** (plural, *grana*). There are many grana in a chloroplast, each of which is connected to its neighbors by membranous extensions called **lamellae.** The clear fluid area surrounding the grana and lamellae is the **stroma** (Figure 4.12).

Obviously, the chloroplast is a complex, highly organized structure. As a general rule, there is a close relationship between the structure and function of an organelle. In this case, the intricate process of photosynthesis depends so much on the chloroplast structure that if the structure is altered, the process cannot continue.

Chloroplasts are actually specialized **plastids,** plant organelles that include **leukoplasts,** (starch storage bodies) and **chromoplasts** (pigmented bodies that lend their colors to flowers, fruits, and autumn leaves).

Mitochondria. Mitochondria (singular, *mitochondrion*) are complex, energy-producing organelles that are found in every eukaryotic cell. Unlike chloroplasts that use light as an energy source, mitochondria obtain energy from the chemical bonds in foods. Like chloroplasts, mitochondria are enclosed in double membranes; however, mitochondria are much smaller than chloroplasts, partly because the latter usually are somewhat spherical, whereas mitochondria tend to be long (Figure 4.13a). In electron micrographs a mitochondrion usually appears as an oval structure, with the inner membrane folded, with shelflike extensions reaching into the organelle's interior.

The folds of the inner mitochondrial membrane are known as **cristae,** and they greatly increase the inner surface area of the organelle. This is important since most of the mitochondrion's biochemical work is done on the cristae, as we will see in later chapters.

Although mitochondria are found in all eukaryotic cells, there are more in some cells than in others. This should be expected since mitochondria are involved in metabolism and since some cells are more metabolically active than others. For example, mitochondria are abundant in muscle cells.

Cell Movement

Microtubules and microfilaments. Microtubules, as the name implies, are very tiny tubes (Figure 4.14). They not only help maintain the shape of the cell, but also for some, they are important to movement. We knew about them long before we knew of the microtrabecular lattice, but now it is assumed the two work together to maintain the cell's shape. Microtubules are also important parts of centrioles, cilia, and flagella—all organelles involved in certain types of cell movement.

Microtubules are made up of a common protein called **tubulin.** Each tubulin molecule consists of two spheres of slightly different polypeptides linked

FIGURE 4.12 Chloroplasts. **(a)** Chloroplasts in an intact plant cell appear as numerous minute, green spheres. **(b)** At low electron microscope magnification, the inner structure becomes visible. The dark, neat stacks consist of thylakoids, each stack forming a granum. **(c)** This three-dimensional drawing shows a cross-sectional view of a chloroplast, with its stacks of disklike thylakoids.

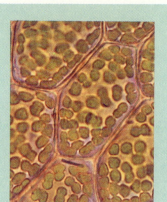

(a) Plant cells with chloroplasts

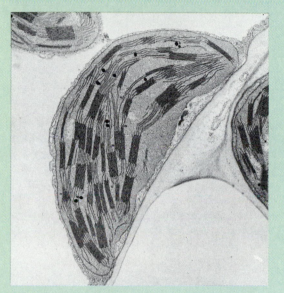

(b) Chloroplast

(c) Cross-section of a chloroplast

Stroma

Double outer membrane

Thylakoid

Lamella

Granum

FIGURE 4.13 The mitochondrion, a site of energy transformation in the cell. **(a)** In thin sections such as this, the long tubular mitochondria appear as irregular ellipses and circles. **(b)** Each has two membranes. The inner one folds repeatedly to form cristae. The F1 particles are sites of ATP synthesis.

(a)

(b)

Outer membrane

Outer compartment

Inner membrane

Crista

F1 particles

Matrix (inner compartment)

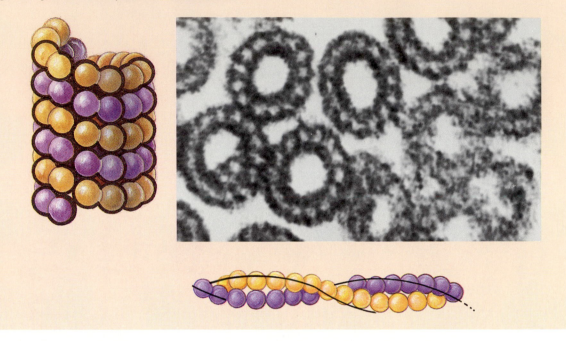

FIGURE 4.14 Microtubules **(a)** appear as long rods which, in cross-section, **(b)** are found to be hollow. The tubes consist of spherical units of the globular protein tubulin. **(c)** Microfilaments also contain globular proteins, but they form a twisted filament.

together into a figure-eight shape. In the microtubule, the tiny figure-eights join in a regular way to form a hollow tube. Microtubules have the remarkable ability to assemble quickly when needed and, just as quickly, to disintegrate when they are no longer required.

Microfilaments are also important in the cytoskeleton and in many structures of movement, such as animal muscle. The microfilament consists of a double strand of the globular protein, **actin,** with each strand wound about the other in the helical conformation so common in protein. We will come to actin again where vertebrate muscle is taken up in Chapter 31.

Cilia and flagella. **Cilia** and **flagella** are fine, hairlike, movable projections extending from the surfaces of some cells. Both the cilia and flagella appear, superficially, to be outside of the cell, but the cell membrane actually protrudes, covering each of them.

Structurally, the cilia and flagella are almost identical to one another, differing only in length, numbers per cell, and patterns of motion. Cilia are short, numerous, and move in a characteristic rowing pattern (Figure 4.15). The cilia of all eukaryotes that have cilia—from protists to humans—are identical in size, structure, and movement. Flagella are more

variable, but they are always long, fewer in number, and move by undulation (in waves). Both cilia and flagella serve to move the cell through its environment or to move the fluid of the environment past the surface of the cell.

In cross-section, a cilium or a flagellum is seen to consist of a regular array of microtubules. Two microtubules run down the center of the shaft and are surrounded by nine additional pairs of microtubules. This universal arrangement is called the "nine-plus-two" pattern. The microtubules in each pair are connected by short arms, and the bending movements of the cilium or flagellum are the result of coordinated sliding movements between microtubule pairs.

Basal bodies. Beneath each cilium or flagellum, in the cytoplasm of the cell, is a **basal body.** The two central microtubules do not extend into the basal body. The nine paired microtubules do, and each pair is joined by yet a third short microtubule; in cross section, therefore, the basal body shows a ring of nine triplets of microtubules (Figure 4.16a), called the "nine-plus-zero" arrangement.

Centrioles and spindle fibers. **Centrioles** have the same appearance, in cross-section, as basal bodies, but centrioles are found deep within the cyto-

FIGURE 4.15   Patterns of motion. Cilia **(a)** move some single-celled organisms by a highly coordinated rowing action. Flagella **(b)** can move in a variety of ways. An undulating flagellum pushes or pulls the cell body through the medium. Various combinations can produce wildly spinning and gyrating movements.

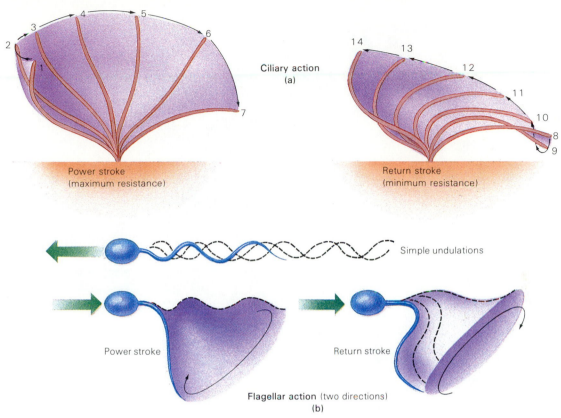

Ciliary action
(a)

Power stroke
(maximum resistance)

Return stroke
(minimum resistance)

Simple undulations

Power stroke

Return stroke

Flagellar action (two directions)
(b)

FIGURE 4.16   Three-dimensional view of a cilium as reconstructed through electron microscopy. **(a)** The longitudinal view reveals the lengthy microtubules that extend to an anchoring base called the basal body. **(b and c)** The cross-section reveals the nine-plus-two arrangement of microtubule pairs.

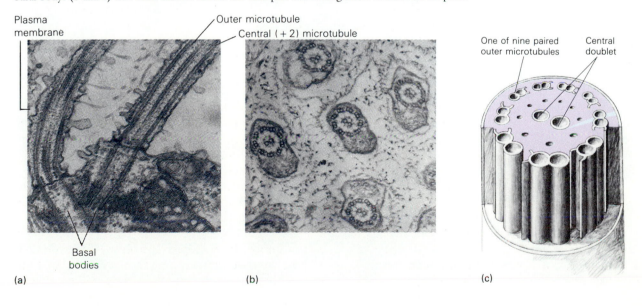

Plasma membrane

Outer microtubule

Central (+2) microtubule

One of nine paired outer microtubules

Central doublet

Basal bodies

(a)

(b)

(c)

FIGURE 4.17 Centrioles. A thin section seen by the electron microscope across the central axis of one of the centriole's paired bodies. Note the nine sets of triplet microtubules.

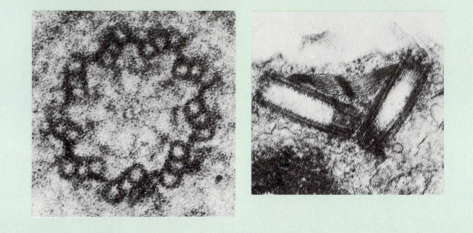

FIGURE 4.18 Prokaryotes lack the membrane-surrounded organelles of eukaryotes. Nevertheless, all life functions, including self-replication, occur in these simpler cells.

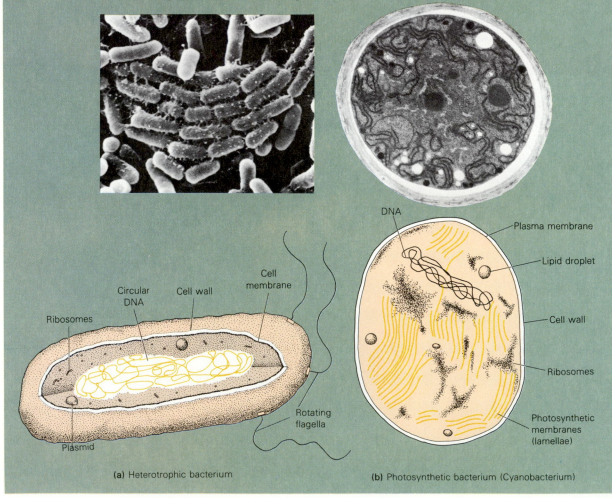

(a) Heterotrophic bacterium

(b) Photosynthetic bacterium (Cyanobacterium)

Feature	Prokaryotic Cell	Higher Plant Cell	Animal Cell
Plasma membrane	External only (two, separated by periplasmic space)	External and internal	External and internal
Supporting structure	None seen	Protein cytoskeleton	Protein cytoskeleton
Nuclear envelope	Absent	Present	Present
Chromosomes	Single, circular, DNA only	Multiple, linear, complexed with protein	Multiple, linear, complexed with protein
Membrane-bound organelles	Absent except for mesosome	Many, including mitochondria, large vacuoles, and chloroplasts	Many, including mitochondria, lysosomes
Endoplasmic reticulum	Absent	Present	Present
Ribosomes	Smaller, free	Larger, some membrane-bound	Larger, some membrane-bound
Cell wall	Peptidoglycan or protein	Cellulose	None
Flagella or cilia (when present)	Tubular, rotating	Never present*	Microtubular (nine-plus-two pattern)
Ability to engulf solid matter	Absent	Absent*	Present, extensive movable membranes
Centrioles	Absent	Absent*	Present

*Although absent in most seed plants, these features are found in more primitive plants. Apparently they have been lost in the course of evolutionary change.

plasm and have a very different function. They are thought to organize the microtubules called **spindle fibers** that serve to separate chromosomes during cell division (Figure 4.17). Each centriole actually consists of two short "nine-plus-zero" cylinders, held somehow at right angles to one another.

The cells of higher plants have no cilia, flagella, basal bodies, or centrioles. They manage to organize their chromosome-separating fibers perfectly well all the same.

THE PROKARYOTIC CELL: A DIFFERENT MATTER

Now let's consider simpler kinds of cells, the kinds believed to be more similar to the ancestral types. These are the prokaryotic cells. Prokaryotes ("before the nucleus") have a simpler cellular organization than do the eukaryotes, but since they are represented solely by single-celled bacteria, this should not be unexpected. The prokaryotes are particularly interesting because they are believed to be similar to the earliest forms of cellular life on Earth, the forms that probably gave rise to today's life.

Characteristics of the Prokaryotic Cell

The prokaryotes are unquestionably cellular, but in most instances their cells are smaller and quite unlike those of eukaryotes. Like plant cells, they are surrounded by a cell wall, but the walls of the two groups are of quite different chemical composition. Also, the organelles of the prokaryote cell are not likely to be surrounded by membranes, and there is no nucleus. The DNA (genetic material) of a eukaryotic cell is found in numerous linear, protein-rich chromosomes whereas the genetic material of a prokaryotic cell forms a single, continuous circular chromosome of nearly naked (protein-free) DNA. The long DNA molecule thus is connected at the two ends to form a loop. Many bacteria have smaller loops of DNA called **plasmids** (see Chapter 16). Some prokaryotes have flagella, but these, too, are quite different structurally from those of the eukaryotes. To illustrate, prokaryotic flagella do not contain microtubules, but, instead, are rigid and tubular. What's more, they rotate. This may be the only rotary structure in any form of life. There are other differences between prokaryotes and eukaryotes (Figure 4.18), some of which we will mention later, but we can already see just how distinctive the prokaryotes are. Table 4.4 compares prokaryotes to plant and animal cells.

SUMMARY

The term *cell* was first applied to life by Robert Hooke when he described the microscopic structure of cork.

CELL THEORY

The cell theory proposes that living organisms are composed of cells. It was suggested by Oken but formally proposed by Schleiden and Schwann in 1838. The biogenetic law, added by Virchow, states that cells arise only from preexisting cells.

What is a Cell?

Cells are the organizational units of life, capable of carrying out the life processes. Two fundamental kinds occur: prokaryotic—(bacterial, of Kingdom Monera) and eukaryotic—(from Kingdoms Protista, Fungi, Plantae, and Animalia). In multicellular organisms, similar cells join to form tissues, which in turn contribute to organs and organ systems.

CELL SIZE

While cells range greatly in size, most plant and animal cells are about 90 μm (micrometers) in diameter. Since the relative membrane area does not increase as fast as volume, a small size favors efficient membranal transport. Cells have a lower limit set by the size of their macromolcules.

A LOOK AT CELL DIVERSITY

Cells in multicellular organisms undergo specialization whereupon each is suited for a specific task.

CELL STRUCTURE

Support and Transport

The plasma membrane surrounding the cell is selectively permeable, favoring the entry and exit of certain substances. In accordance with the fluid mosaic model, it contains a double layer of phospholipids and a number of dispersed proteins and other molecules. The outer surfaces are polar and hydrophilic, while the core is hydrophobic. Some proteins pass through the membrane, others penetrate part way or perch on the surface. The proteins have enzymatic, transport, and cell recognition functions.

The plant cell wall consists of layered microfibrils of cellulose, impregnated with strengthening materials. The microtrabecular lattice is a cytoplasmic network of hollow fibers that support many organelles and enzyme systems.

Cell Control: The Nucleus

The nucleus is a prominent sphere surrounded by the nuclear envelope (two membranes). Nuclear pores permit substances to cross the nuclear envelope. The nucleus contains DNA, organized into genes. Its two roles are reproduction—(copying and passing the genes to new cells) and control—(directing cell activity by specifying the formation of enzymes). DNA plus associated proteins make up the chromatin, organized into chromosomes. Dark-staining regions called nucleoli are sites where the RNA of ribosomes is assembled.

Organelles of Cell Synthesis, Storage, Digestion, and Secretion

An extensive membranous channel, the endoplasmic reticulum (ER), is the site of synthesis and transport. Rough ER (RER) gets its name from the presence of numerous protein-synthesizing bodies called ribosomes. The synthesis of various other substances occurs in the smooth ER (SER).

Golgi bodies consist of flattened, membranous sacs and rounded vesicles. They form continuously from sections of endoplasmic reticulum that contain newly synthesized proteins ready for further chemical modification. Some Golgi bodies secrete their contents outside the cell. Others later carry on chemical reactions within the cell.

Lysosomes, former Golgi vesicles, are tough sacs containing hydrolytic enzymes to be used in digestion.

Peroxisomes are crystalline bodies containing enzymes that break down hydrogen peroxide.

Vacuoles are simple membranous containers that hold many substances, including water, salts, acids, sugars, foods, and pigments.

Cell Energy

Chloroplasts are complex membranous organelles that contain chlorophyll pigments. They capture light energy and use it for making foods. Mitochondria are membranous bodies that contain enzyme systems and mechanisms for transferring chemical energy from foods to a form that is useful to the cell.

Cell Movement

Microtubules and microfilaments are responsible for cell movement. Microtubules occur in cilia and flagella where their coordinated movement causes the required rowing and undulating motion. Microfilaments are associated with cytoplasmic movement and muscle contraction. While cilia and flagella have a 9 + 2 doublet arrangement of microtubules, they originate from basal bodies that have a 9 + 2 triplet microtubular arrangement. Centrioles, organizers of spindle fibers, are paired versions of basal bodies.

THE PROKARYOTIC CELL: A DIFFERENT MATTER

Prokaryotes (bacteria), lack membrane-bound organelles, have cell walls of peptidoglycan or protein, circular DNA that lacks protein, and rigid, tubular flagella that rotate.

KEY TERMS

cell theory
biogenetic law
prokaryote
eukaryote
tissue
organ
system
organelles
surface-volume hypothesis
specialization
selective permeability
plasma membrane
fluid mosaic model
glycoprotein
lipoprotein

cell wall
lignin
suberin
ultrastructure
microtrabecular lattice
histone
chromatin
chromosomes
nuclear envelope
nuclear pore
nucleolus
ribosomes
endoplasmic reticulum
Golgi bodies

cisternae
forming face
maturing face
storage vesicle
lysosome
secretion vesicle
peroxisome
vacuole
chloroplast
thylakoid
granum
lamella
stroma
plastid

leukoplast
chromoplast
mitochrondria
crista
microtubule
tubulin
microfilament
actin
cilia
flagella
basal body
centriole
spindle fibers
plasmid

REVIEW QUESTIONS

1 Summarize the propositions of the cell theory and biogenetic law. Name the chief contributors of each. (p. 46)

2 Clearly distinguish between the terms cell, tissue, organ, organ system, and organelle. In what type of organism are tissues and organs seen? (p. 47)

3 Summarize the size range of cells—the largest and smallest. What dimensions are seen in most animal and plant cells? (pp. 47–50)

4 Suggest two advantages to small cell size. Explain the peculiar relationship between cell surface area and volume. (pp. 48–50)

5 Explain how selective permeability contributes to the principal role of the plasma membrane. (p. 51)

6 Prepare a simplified drawing of the cell membrane showing the arrangement of the phospholipids and proteins. Add a glycoprotein and a glycolipid. (p. 53)

7 Which groups of organisms produce cell walls? Describe how cellulose is used in the formation of such walls. (pp. 54–55)

8 Describe the arrangement of the microtrabecular lattice and list its main functions. (p. 54)

9 List and briefly explain the two functions of the nucleus. (p. 55)

10 Briefly discuss the organization of a chromosome. At which times are the chromosomes most visible? Least visible? (p. 55)

11 Describe the arrangement of the two types of endoplasmic reticulum. In what materials does each specialize? (p. 58)

12 Describe the Golgi body. Explain what goes on in the forming and maturing faces. (pp. 58–59)

13 Explain why de Duve thought of lysosomes as "suicide bags." (p. 59)

14 List several substances carried or stored in plant vacuoles. (p. 59)

15 What is the relationship between the ribosome, rough ER, Golgi body, lysosome, and secretion vesicle? (p. 60)

16 Prepare a simple illustration of a chloroplast, labelling the outer membrane, stroma, grana, lamellae, and thylakoids. (pp. 60–61)

17 What special function does the chloroplast have? In what organisms are these bodies seen? (pp. 60–61)

18 What is the specialized function of the mitochondrion? (p. 60)

19 Describe the general shape and organization of the mitochondria. What are two ways in which the inner membrane is very special? (p. 60)

20 Briefly describe the structure of the microtubule. List three organelles in which they are seen. (p. 60)

21 What special functions do cilia and flagella have? Compare their movement. (p. 62)

22 Compare the microtubular arrangement in cilia, flagella, basal bodies, and centrioles. (p. 62)

23 List five ways in which cells of prokaryotes differ from those of eukaryotes. (p. 65)

5

CELL TRANSPORT

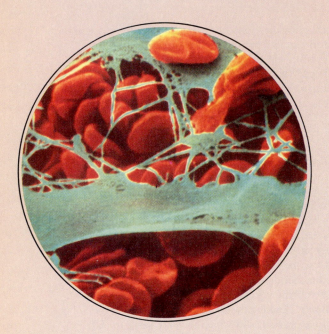

The cell is a lively thing. Inside, in its roiling fluids, the business of life goes on with astonishing precision and swiftness. Molecules are bound and released, ions ebb and flow, chemicals appear and disappear in a constantly shifting scenario. All this is made possible, in large part, by the precise movement of materials in and out of cells and from one cell to another. Such materials must cross the **plasma membrane** which, as we will see, is exquisitely adapted to its function of accepting some substances while rejecting others. The membrane performs its gate-keeper tasks in a variety of ways that generally fall within two categories: (1) **passive transport** and (2) **active transport.**

The two categories involve very different energy sources. One is energy-costly to the cell; the other is not. In passive transport thermal (heat) energy of the cellular environment provides all of the energy, much of it quite random. Active transport, however, requires the cell to do work, and it costs something in terms of the cell's precious energy reserves.

Passive transport makes use of thermal (heat) energy and is free to the cell, whereas **active transport** is powered by the cell's energy reserves.

PASSIVE TRANSPORT

Passive transport includes four distinct kinds of movement, none of which requires an energy expenditure on the part of the cell. The four processes are diffusion, facilitated diffusion, bulk flow, and osmosis.

Diffusion

Diffusion is the *net* movement* of ions or molecules from regions of higher concentration to regions of lower concentration (down a **concentration** or **diffusion gradient**). In biological systems, it is an especially important way for ions and small molecules to get around. Diffusion enables substances to cross cell membranes and to move within the cytoplasm.

Diffusion occurs because the molecules of any liquid or gas move constantly and randomly, bumping into each other and rebounding into new paths. The warmer the gas or liquid is, the faster its molecules

---

*In a system with random movement, particles may move in any direction. If more particles move in one direction more than in any other, there is said to be a *net* movement in that direction.

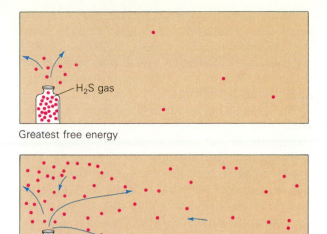

Greatest free energy

H₂S gas

Gradient established

Free energy dissipating

Equilibrium:
no free energy, no net movement in any direction

FIGURE 5.1 Diffusion of a gas. A container of hydrogen sulfide (H₂S) has been uncorked in one corner of a room. Molecular motion is in all directions, but the greatest movement in any direction is toward areas where there are fewer molecules of H₂S.

move. The movement of individual molecules is still random, but heat accelerates the net movement of those molecules, always in accord with the same physical principles—from the region of higher concentration to regions of lower concentration. This net movement continues until the distribution of molecules is random. Once the molecules are randomly dispersed, there will be no further net movement in any direction. Diffusion, then, is a random process: Molecules move away from an area of higher concentration by their own thermal energy until equilibrium is reached (Figure 5.1).

Diffusion is the net movement of molecules and ions from regions of their greater concentration to regions of their lesser concentration.

The rate at which ions and molecules diffuse depends on many factors but principal among these are heat, the steepness of the diffusion gradient (difference in concentration from one end of the system to the other), and the size of the particles in motion.

Diffusion and the plasma membrane.   In living systems other factors influence diffusion. Cells are surrounded by membranes that have specific chemical and physical properties that determine the membrane's **permeability** to various substances. Permeability refers to the tendency of a membrane to allow specific kinds of molecules and ions to cross. The permeability of the plasma membrane, then, depends on both its own characteristics and those of the substances in transit. Such membranes are often described as **selectively permeable.**

The plasma membrane's permeability depends in large part on its physical makeup. Recall that in the fluid mosaic model (see Figure 4.5) the membrane is basically a bilayer of phospholipids interrupted in places by surface and transmembranal proteins and other molecules. The charged heads and uncharged tails of the phospholipids result in the two sides of the molecule bearing polar charges (positive and negative). Sandwiched between these charged layers is an oily, nonpolar, core layer. Because of the polar nature of the membrane, the electrical charges of molecules and ions are critical to their passage across the membrane. Nonpolar molecules such as oil-soluble steroids (sex hormones, for example) readily cross the phospholipid bilayer, as do gases such as oxygen, carbon dioxide, and nitrogen, which are nonpolar and relatively small.

Ionized particles cross at different rates. For example, the membranes of red blood cells more readily accept positive ions than negative ions. Further, singly charged ions cross the membrane more easily than do doubly charged ones.

Although water is decidedly polar, it readily crosses all plasma membranes. This has long represented an enigma to cell biologists who theorized that plasma membranes must have protein-lined pores. Such pores would indeed account for the membrane's permeability. But electron microscopic studies haven't revealed any such pores, and experiments with both protein-free artificial membranes and living cells with little protein in the membrane reveal that water crosses both with ease. Since there is no way that water can be pumped by active transport, scientists are still left wondering how water crosses plasma membranes so easily.

Membranes from various tissues differ considerably in their permeability. Even within the same tissues, permeability to various solutes can change. For example, kidney cells can alter their permeability to water according to the body's need to conserve water (see Chapter 36).

> Factors influencing diffusion rates include temperature, steepness of the concentration gradient, particle size, presence or absence of electrical charges, and general membrane characteristics.

Facilitated diffusion. **Facilitated diffusion** is similar to simple diffusion in that it is passive, it involves thermal energy, and molecules follow the usual diffusion gradient (from high concentration to low). However, it differs from simple diffusion in that the movement of selected molecules is significantly accelerated by carriers known as **permeases.** Permeases are believed to be enzymes that are permanently embedded in the plasma membrane, but just how they work remains a mystery.

Water Potential and Bulk Flow

The development of life on this planet is intimately associated with the abundance of a simple molecule, H_2O. Water is, indeed, important to both the development and sustenance of life. So you can imagine that in the various life forms, evolution has provided adaptations for moving it around, shifting it to places where it will be of greatest advantage.

Water potential is simply the tendency of water to move from one place to another. The rule is that water moves from regions of higher to regions of lower potential. This "potential for movement" is influenced by such commonplace forces as gravity and pressure as well as the more subtle effects, such as **solute concentration.** (A solute, you may recall, is any substance that is in solution in a solvent such as water or other liquid. Salt and sugar are common solutes.)

The simplest example of water potential is seen in a dam. A great deal of water can accumulate behind a dam where the water level is higher than that in the river bed below. Thus, the dammed river has a great water potential. (The potential of that water will become quite clear if the dam should give way.) Simple pressure can also increase water potential. A mechanical pump forcing water up into a storage tank increases the tendency for that water to move downward.

The movement of water by such forces is often referred to as **bulk flow.** Bulk flow, the mass movement of fluids and solutes, moves all molecules in the same direction. (Diffusion, you'll recall, involves random movement, but with the *net* movement of molecules along a gradient.)

Bulk flow is important biologically for a number of reasons. For instance, bulk flow is behind blood movement in our own circulatory systems. Our pumping heart and elastic arteries increase the bulk flow. In plants, bulk flow moves sap through the tubular elements that comprise the food transport system. In this case, water potential is increased by the high solute concentration at the source of the sap flow, which leads to the inward movement of water (see Chapter 25).

> Water moves from areas of higher **water potential** to areas of lower. Water potential can be influenced by gravity, pressure, and solute concentration. The movement of water in one direction is called **bulk flow.**

Osmosis: A Special Case

Osmosis is a word that has been borrowed from science and then twisted and misused beyond recognition. The next time you hear the word in casual conversation, ask the speaker to define it. You will probably make a lifelong friend if you smirk, look around the room, and say, "Wrong! Osmosis is the diffusion of water across membranes, from an area of greater water potential (greater water concentration) to one of lesser potential (lesser water concentration)." Go on by saying, "You see, when two solutions are separated by a selectively permeable membrane—that is, a membrane that allows only water to pass—the net movement of water will be from the solution with the greater concentration of water molecules, through the membrane, to the solution with the lesser concentration of water molecules. Keep in mind also that the concentration of water molecules is *lower* on the side of the membrane that contains the *higher* solute concentrations. Further, it doesn't really make any difference what kind of ion or molecule is in solution; it could be sugar, amino acids, or any other soluble substance. The water moves only according to the relative number of water molecules on either side of the membrane" (Figure 5.2). By now, of course, everyone will probably have left.

But in case anyone should stay around, you should be prepared to answer questions, since osmosis is a very simple principle that, at first, may seem hard to understand. For example, someone might ask how

FIGURE 5.2 In a demonstration of osmosis, a thistle tube containing a 3% sugar solution and covered with a selectively permeable membrane is immersed in distilled water. The membrane will permit water, but not the sugar to cross. As expected, water moves *down its concentration gradient*, crossing the membrane and entering the sugar solution.

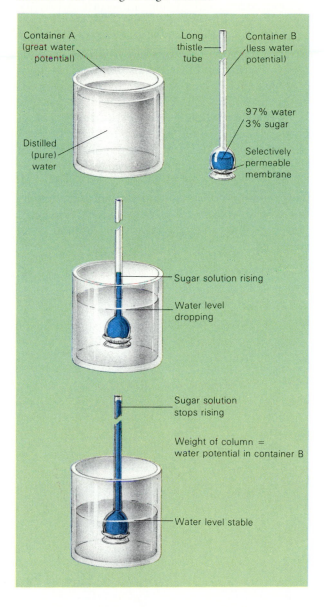

Container A (great water potential)

Long thistle tube

Container B (less water potential)

Distilled (pure) water

97% water 3% sugar

Selectively permeable membrane

Sugar solution rising

Water level dropping

Sugar solution stops rising

Weight of column = water potential in container B

Water level stable

long does osmosis go on? Theoretically, it continues until the water potential (water concentration) on both sides of the membrane is equal. This equilibrium rarely occurs between cells and their surrounding fluids, however. Metabolism demands constant change, and there is a constant ebb and flow of molecules across any living membrane. In the system shown in Figure 5.2, equilibrium can never be reached because the solutes cannot cross the membrane. Of course, this means that there will always be greater water potential on the side with the distilled water.

Osmosis does not simply continue until one side goes dry, because forces other than solute concentration can influence the process. For example, in the tube shown in Figure 5.2 the sheer weight of the rising column of solute will become so heavy that it will exert a counterforce equaling the water potential of the distilled water. The net movement of water will then stop. At this point we are able to measure **osmotic pressure,** the amount of force necessary to equal the water potential. One of the clearest examples of the effects of osmotic pressure in nature occurs in plants, as we will see next.

Osmosis is the movement of water across selectively permeable membranes from higher to lower water potential.

Turgor and wilting. The large central vacuoles of certain plant cells contain water and various solutes called **cell sap.** Each vacuole is surrounded by a selectively permeable membrane and so is subject to osmosis. When the concentration of water outside the cell is greater than that in the vacuole, water enters by osmosis, which causes the vacuole to swell, pressing the rest of the cell contents against the cell wall. Animal cells lack walls and will simply swell and burst. But the plant cell wall is extremely strong, so it holds. As the size of the vacuole continues to increase, it meets increased resistance until, finally, the pressures are equalized and no more water can enter. This special kind of osmotic pressure from within the cell is called **turgor pressure.** Turgor pressure is the force that holds leaves and soft stems of plants erect. Should turgor pressure decrease because of a reduction of water within the plant's vacuoles, the result is **wilting.**

Cells and solute conditions: tonicity. The osmotic environment of cells is described in terms of **tonicity.** For example, environmental conditions are **isotonic** (*iso,* same; *tonic,* tension) when the relative concentrations of water and solutes on either side of the plasma membrane are equal, which, of course, means the water potential is equal. In isotonic systems there is no net movement of water molecules across a membrane.

On the other hand, when the water outside a cell contains less solute than does the water inside (meaning the water potential outside is greater), the environment is called **hypotonic** (*hypo,* low). Cells immersed in hypotonic solutions tend to swell. For example, blood cells in tap water will swell and rupture, leaving limp "ghosts" of their membranes.

When the water outside the cell contains more solutes than that on the inside (resulting in the water potential outside being lower), the condition is called **hypertonic** (*hyper*, over). Cells in a hypertonic solution tend to lose water. Note that the terms "isotonic," "hypotonic," and "hypertonic" refer to the relative solute concentration in water surrounding the cell or organism (Figure 5.3).

Organisms make constant use of the osmotic mechanism, taking in or releasing water and shifting it from cell to cell as needed. While there is no known mechanism for actively transporting water, cells can and do actively transport solutes, and where solutes go, water follows. For example, plants can increase the uptake of water into the root by first actively transporting mineral ions into the root cells. This sets up the desired water potential gradient, and water flows in through osmosis. Similarly, in our own kidneys and those of other water-conserving mammals, the active transport of sodium and chloride ions across the plasma membranes of certain cells sets up the osmotic conditions needed for reclaiming water that would otherwise escape in the urine.

ACTIVE TRANSPORT

Since life is such a delicate and constantly adjusting process, it is not surprising to find cells moving, shifting, adding, and expelling molecules. Accumulations of some molecule often occur inside or outside a cell. For example, mammalian red blood cells work against the concentration gradient to move sodium ions out and accumulate potassium ions. Similarly, many marine fish expel sodium ions from salt-secreting glands in their gills (chloride ions follow passively). They must work against a powerful concentration gradient, because the sea is saltier than their blood. So simple an act as moving molecules against a concentration gradient might crudely be compared to rolling boulders uphill. Work must be done, and work requires the expenditure of energy. This is why this type of movement is called **active transport.** Let's see how molecules are shifted around at an energy cost.

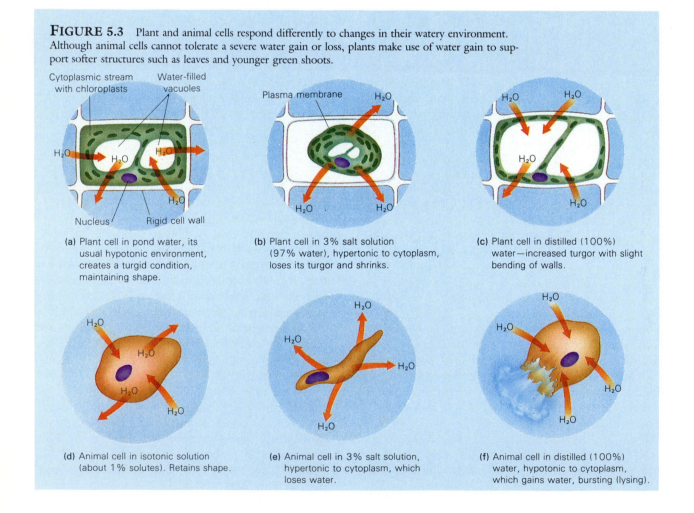

FIGURE 5.3 Plant and animal cells respond differently to changes in their watery environment. Although animal cells cannot tolerate a severe water gain or loss, plants make use of water gain to support softer structures such as leaves and younger green shoots.

Cytoplasmic stream with chloroplasts
Water-filled vacuoles
H_2O
Nucleus
Rigid cell wall

Plasma membrane
H_2O

H_2O

(a) Plant cell in pond water, its usual hypotonic environment, creates a turgid condition, maintaining shape.

(b) Plant cell in 3% salt solution (97% water), hypertonic to cytoplasm, loses its turgor and shrinks.

(c) Plant cell in distilled (100%) water—increased turgor with slight bending of walls.

(d) Animal cell in isotonic solution (about 1% solutes). Retains shape.

(e) Animal cell in 3% salt solution, hypertonic to cytoplasm, which loses water.

(f) Animal cell in distilled (100%) water, hypotonic to cytoplasm, which gains water, bursting (lysing).

FIGURE 5.4 In a model of the membranal sodium-potassium ion exchange pump, each cycle begins with (a) three sodium ions being taken up from the cell cytoplasm and two potassium ions being expelled into the cell cytoplasm. With the sodium sites filled, ATP provides the energy (b) for a change in shape to occur in the carrier, permitting the three sodium ions (c) to be dumped outside. The cycle then repeats (d), and eventually, the two ions develop opposite concentration gradients (e).

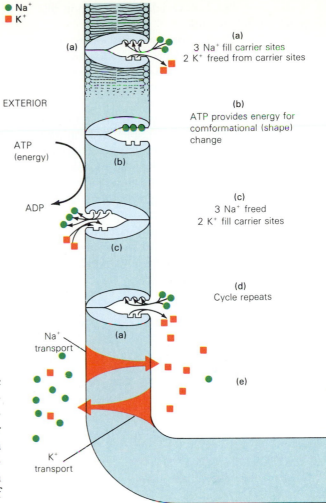

- Na$^+$
- K$^+$

(a)

(a)
3 Na$^+$ fill carrier sites
2 K$^+$ freed from carrier sites

EXTERIOR

(b)
ATP provides energy for comformational (shape) change

ATP (energy)

(b)

ADP

(c)
3 Na$^+$ freed
2 K$^+$ fill carrier sites

(c)

(d)
Cycle repeats

Na$^+$ transport

(a)

(e)

K$^+$ transport

Membrane Pumps

We really don't understand many aspects of active transport, although we do know that some substances are carried across membranes against a gradient by proteins embedded in the membranes. For instance, many cells have **sodium-potassium ion exchange pumps,** membranal carriers that alternately bring in potassium ions and usher out sodium ions. Such pumps are found in a number of kinds of cells, such as those of the nerves and kidneys. They are powered by a special energy-storing molecule called adenosine triphosphate (ATP) (see Chapter 6). For each molecule of ATP expended, the cell captures two potassium ions and ejects three sodium ions, thus creating steep gradients of the two ions. Although much remains to be learned about such pumps, the general principle is described in Figure 5.4.

Active transport mechanisms, such as ion exchange pumps, were once perceived as being rather unusual, but research has revealed that active transport is probably common in most membranes. Researchers have also discovered calcium pumps and special **proton pumps.** The latter function in making new ATP (see Chapter 6).

Membrane pumps, composed of proteins and powered by ATP, transfer substances across plasma membranes against the diffusion gradient.

Endocytosis and Exocytosis

Some forms of active transport are very active. In some animal cells and in many protists one can actually see materials entering and leaving the cell. If the material is being brought into the cell, the process is called **endocytosis** ("inside the vessel"); if the material is being expelled, the process is called **exocytosis** ("outside the vessel"). In both cases the membrane behaves similarly (see the discussion of the Golgi body in Chapter 4).

Endocytosis includes two slightly different processes, **phagocytosis** ("cell eating"), in which solid materials are involved, and **pinocytosis** ("cell drinking"), in which the substances taken in are in solution. Pinocytosis is commonly observed in the walls of animal capillaries where bulk materials are moved in and out of the bloodstream. Materials entering capillary cells through pinocytosis are taken in via channels called **pinocytic vesicles** which, upon filling, pinch off into vacuoles.

Endocytosis and exocytosis were first observed in the feeding of single-celled protists called amebas. When an ameba (also, amoeba) contacts a food particle (often another protist), phagocytosis begins as its complex outer membrane buckles inward, taking on a cuplike appearance and trapping the particle or prey. The cup then pinches off completely, forming a membranous sac called a **food vacuole.** Digestive enzymes from lysosomes enter the food vacuole, and the contents are broken down. The digested products then diffuse into the surrounding cytoplasm, leaving behind undigested residues.

The ameba's digestive wastes are eliminated through exocytosis. In a reversal of the endocytic events, the waste-laden vacuole fuses with the plasma membrane, and the wastes are expelled (Figure 5.5). In addition to helping the ameba get rid of what it no longer needs, exocytosis is also a mechanism commonly used in cell secretion (see Chapter 4).

Phagocytosis is common not only in protists but also in simple invertebrate animals, including sponges, jellyfish, and flatworms. In vertebrates it is the mechanism by which white blood cells engulf invading microorganisms and clean up the debris from dead cells (Figure 5.6).

In **endocytosis** the membrane admits a substance by forming a vacuole around it; in **exocytosis** substances are expelled through the fusion of a vacuole with the plasma membrane.

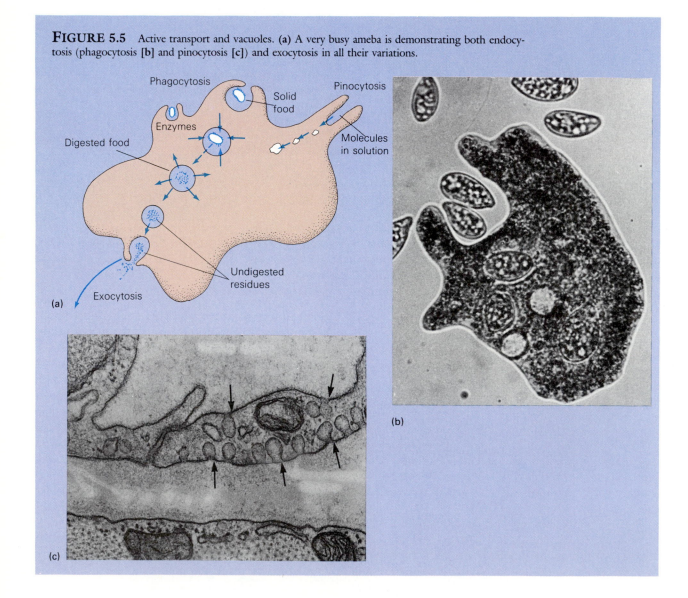

FIGURE 5.5 Active transport and vacuoles. **(a)** A very busy ameba is demonstrating both endocytosis (phagocytosis **[b]** and pinocytosis **[c]**) and exocytosis in all their variations.

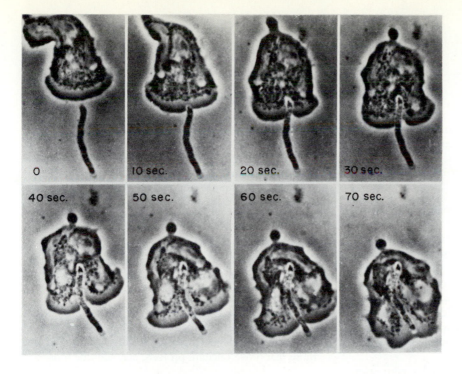

FIGURE 5.6 White cells, known as phagocytes because of their phagocytic activity, roam the body attacking invading bacteria. Here, streptococci (beadlike bacterial cells) are being engulfed.

0   10 sec.   20 sec.   30 sec.
40 sec.   50 sec.   60 sec.   70 sec.

DIRECT TRANSPORT BETWEEN CELLS

One problem in describing cellular processes piecemeal, as we are doing, is that it gives an artificial impression of simplicity. For example, it may seem that cells are isolated entities that simply shift for themselves and maintain independence from surrounding cells. This may be true for one-celled creatures, but for other organisms it is not. In multicellular organisms the cytoplasm of adjacent cells is often in direct contact through special passages, such as the **gap junctions** of animal cells or the **plasmodesmata** of plants. Their presence, of course, facilitates intercellular transport (between cells) and increases the efficiency of cellular coordination.

Such cellular passages were once thought to exist in only a few kinds of cells, but they have been found in so many tissues that they are now believed to be the rule rather than the exception. For example, gap junctions are found in human tissues from the heart, epithelial linings, liver, urinary bladder, pancreas, and kidneys. Their presence in heart tissue is believed to help speed impulses that bring about contraction of that tireless organ. Plasmodesmata are also widespread, occurring commonly in leaf cells, sugar-transporting tissues, and root tip cells.

The openings between cells are formed quite differently in animals and plants. The gap junctions of animals are formed by clusters of protein arranged in circles that surround minute cytoplasmic channels,

and, like elaborate rivets, they firmly hold adjacent membranes together. The plasmodesmata of plants are long, slender, cytoplasmic extensions that pass from cell to cell through membrane-lined pores in adjacent cell walls. In some instances **desmotubules,** slender elements of the endoplasmic reticulum, also pass through the pores.

> **Gap junctions** and **plasmodesmata** are cytoplasmic connections between animal and plant cells, respectively, that greatly facilitate cell-to-cell transport.

The constant influx of essential substances and exodus of manufactured products and wastes are critical aspects of cell function. We have seen a number of such processes at work, but they are actually only a fraction of the processes involved in cell transport. In later discussions we will find, for instance, that the membranes surrounding certain protists are important not only in feeding but also in forcefully regulating the cell's water content. We'll also learn that vertebrate cells have highly specialized receptors that bind with chemical messengers, prompting a cascade of chemical responses (Chapter 35). In addition, we will learn of one of life's most fundamental membrane responses in our discussion of the surprisingly active participation of the egg membrane when nudged and prodded by a lashing sperm (Chapter 42). The stage for such discussions, however, has been set by what we've seen here.

SUMMARY

PASSIVE TRANSPORT

Passive transport is the movement of substances across the plasma membrane without an investment of the cell's own energy. It is based on random movement caused by heat. Passive transport includes diffusion, facilitated diffusion, bulk flow, and osmosis.

Diffusion

Diffusion is the net movement of molecules *down* their concentration gradient, from regions of higher to regions of lower concentration, until randomness is reached. Diffusion rates depend upon heat, concentration gradient, particle size, and charge.

Plasma membranes are selectively permeable, admitting some substances freely, slowing the passage of some, and rejecting others. Small uncharged particles such as gases cross readily, while charged particles may be slowed. With some important exceptions membranes readily admit water.

In facilitated diffusion, carriers known as permeases speed selected molecules and ions down the usual concentration gradient.

Water Potential and Bulk Flow

Water potential—the tendency of water to move—is affected by gravity, pressure, and solute concentration. Bulk flow is the massive movement of water in one direction, from greater to lesser water potential.

Osmosis: A Special Case

Osmosis is the diffusion of water *across a membrane* from areas of greater to areas of lesser water potential. In osmosis, water potential is determined by the amount of solute inside or outside a membrane. Osmosis continues until it is blocked by counterforces, such as gravity and osmotic pressure (also turgor pressure). The terms *isotonic, hypotonic,* and *hypertonic* refer to equal, low, and high solute concentrations. Hypotonic solutions have high water potential, while hypertonic solutions have low water potential.

Organisms create useful osmotic gradients that encourage the movement of water where needed. They do this through the selective, active transport of solutes.

ACTIVE TRANSPORT

In active transport, the cell's energy is used to move substances against the natural concentration gradient.

Membrane Pumps

The best known membrane pump, the sodium-potassium ion exchange pump, uses ATP energy to eject sodium ions and take in potassium ions. Other pumps include those that move calcium, protons, and chloride ions.

Endocytosis and Exocytosis

In endocytosis, segments of membrane actively trap materials and move them into the cell. The intake of solids is phagocytosis, while that of fluids is pinocytosis. Protists phagocytize food, forming food vacuoles in which digestion occurs. Digestive residues are carried to the membrane and expelled through exocytosis.

DIRECT TRANSPORT BETWEEN CELLS

Gap junctions and plasmodesmata form passages between cells in animals and plants respectively. The passages greatly facilitate transport and communication in many kinds of tissues.

KEY TERMS

diffusion	water potential	proton pump
plasma membrane	solute concentration	endocytosis
passive transport	bulk flow	exocytosis
active transport	osmotic pressure	phagocytosis
concentration gradient	turgor pressure	pinocytosis
diffusion gradient	wilting	pinocytic vesicle
permeable	hypotonic	food vacuole
facilitated diffusion	hypertonic	gap junction
permease	sodium-potassium exchange pump	plasmodesmata

REVIEW QUESTIONS

1 Explain how the source of energy differs in passive and active transport. (p. 68)

2 Explain the physical basis for molecular movement. How can such movement have a net direction? At what point does diffusion cease? (pp. 68–69)

3 List three factors that affect the rate of diffusion outside cells. (pp. 69–70)

4 List several characteristics of the plasma membrane that might affect the passage of molecules or ions? (pp. 69–70)

5 Why is it that small, nonpolar molecules pass so readily through the phospholipid layers of the membrane? (p. 69)

6 List three factors that affect water potential. How does water potential affect the direction in which water moves? (p. 70)

7 How does bulk flow differ from diffusion? (p. 70)

8 Using the following terms, write a concise definition of osmosis: water potential, solute concentration, plasma membrane, diffusion. (pp. 70–71)

9 Contrast the effects of hypertonic and hypotonic solutions on plant and animal cells. In what way do plants rely on turgor pressure? (pp. 71–72)

10 Why is it important for biologists to maintain cultures of cells or tissues in an isotonic solution? (p. 71)

11 List two ways in which one could determine whether active transport was going on. (p. 72)

12 Summarize the steps followed in a complete cycle of the sodium-potassium ion exchange pump. Where, in our own bodies, are such pumps located? (p. 73)

13 Explain the role played by the plasma membrane in endocytosis. Contrast the way solids and fluids are taken in through endocytosis and name the processes. (pp. 73–74)

14 What happens to the plasma membrane when exocytosis occurs? Of what value is exocytosis to an ameba? (p. 74)

15 Briefly describe the structure of gap junctions and plasmodesmata and explain how they are important to animals and plants. (p. 75)

6

ENERGY AND THE CELL

We humans often seem to enjoy maligning ourselves, being particularly fond of stressing our unusual savagery. But if humans did not walk the earth, would the planet be a gentler place? Probably not. After all, *life demands energy,* and many living things must derive energy from other living things. The problem is, if an organism wishes to harvest the energy stored in another organism's body, that body must be disrupted, hurt, and, very likely, killed. The unending search for energy can indeed be brutal. Those organisms seeking energy and those avoiding being exploited have developed many ways to carry out these tasks. Dainty plants growing silently on a flower-strewn hillside may relentlessly engage in a battle for survival as they compete for the sun's rays and the earth's minerals. Yet after they have been blessed by the sun and are able to manufacture food, they must often yield that sequestered energy to some casual grazer. In turn, the grazers are likely to fall prey to some sharp-toothed carnivore seeking the energy held in the grazers' bodies (Figure 6.1), energy previously derived from those hillside plants. Eventually, though, even muscular creatures with sharp teeth answer the ultimate call, and the energy they once stored becomes the salvation of small microbes as they break down a ponderous corpse.

We will return to flow of energy through food chains in later chapters. Here our interest is in the energy itself.

ENERGY

The energy is needed because, in this world, matter tends to become disorganized. We see this in a rotting corpse beside the road. That body once had been a rabbit, highly organized in the fashion of rabbits. Now, though, its molecules are being broken down and scattered in a final disorganization.

Life can only exist when molecules resist that tendency and remain organized. The organization, though, is only possible with the expenditure of energy. In a nutshell, this is why any consideration of life must involve the nature of energy.

What are the characteristics of energy? How does it behave? The concept of energy is extremely elusive, but we can begin with a simple definition: **Energy** is the ability to do work. Work, as physicists tell us, is the movement of mass against an opposing force. This work, this energy expenditure, keeps the processes of life organized.

FIGURE 6.1 A grizzly and a young cougar fight over an elk kill. Energy is passed from one organism to the next, usually through dramatic predator-prey interactions.

FIGURE 6.2 As water passes through the dam and falls to a lower level, its potential energy becomes kinetic energy—energy in motion. At this stage, its kinetic energy turns electrical generators, transforming mechanical energy into electrical energy. In turn, electrical energy will be transformed into light, heat, and other forms of energy.

Potential and Kinetic Energy

Energy essentially exists in two states, **potential energy** (also **free energy**) and **kinetic energy** (Figure 6.2). Potential energy is stored: it is not doing anything. For example, a huge boulder may rest on a hill above a house. This boulder represents a considerable store of potential energy (although the homeowner may describe the situation differently, especially if the house is paid for). The boulder may have gained its potential energy long ago as it was raised by some great, geological upheaval.

Should the soil around the boulder give way, we would quickly learn that kinetic energy is energy in motion. As the boulder rolled down the hill, its pathway of destruction would attest to its potential energy being transformed into kinetic energy.

> **P**otential (or **free**) **energy** is energy yet to be released. **Kinetic energy** is energy being released or in motion.

The behavior of energy has been expressed in highly reliable, time-tested observations known as the **laws of thermodynamics.** These physical principles apply equally to the living and nonliving worlds.

THE LAWS OF THERMODYNAMICS

Living systems involve matter and chemical processes, and the laws of physics and chemistry are as valid in living systems as anywhere else. Two of the laws of thermodynamics are essential to our understanding the incredibly complex, delicate, and sensitive processes of life.

The First Law

The first law of thermodynamics states that *energy can neither be created nor destroyed.* This means, simply, that the total amount of energy in a "closed" system remains constant. A closed system is one in which matter and energy can neither enter nor leave. Closed systems are really theoretical abstracts, but perhaps we can understand the idea behind such systems by considering the planet Earth. The earth receives energy from the sun and radiates some energy back into space. The total energy on the planet may remain relatively constant, so that the earth is in a *steady state*. But it is a dynamic steady state. All activity occurs because energy can change from one kind to another, it can be stored and released, and it ebbs and flows in countless directions, changing the face of the planet.

Energy can change in a number of ways. To illustrate, energy is locked in the chemical bonds of gasoline. When the fuel combines with oxygen and a spark inside an engine, the gasoline's chemical bond energy is transformed into the energy of heat, noise, and motion. That is, the potential energy of gasoline becomes kinetic energy expressed as heat. The sudden release of heat expands gases in the cylinder, forcing a piston to move a shaft that causes the machine to roll over your foot. When this happens, certain energy shifts may occur in your own body, and the sound you generate (and later regret) represents chemical energy that was changed to the mechanical energy of vibrating air we know as noise. Once released, much of the energy in such an engine (or in you) is dissipated as useless heat, which brings us to the next law.

The Second Law

The second law of thermodynamics is sometimes called the **law of entropy.** It states that *the free energy in any closed system constantly decreases.* Expressed another way, systems tend to become more random and disorganized as time goes on.

The two laws make it clear that organized systems—those with a complex molecular nature and great amounts of free energy—change, in time, to a simpler, more disordered or randomized molecular state with less free energy (Figure 6.3). The tendency toward disorganization is called entropy.

The concept of entropy can also be illustrated by fuel in an engine. Gasoline molecules are long hydrocarbon chains. They possess both great molecular organization and abundant free energy. As the engine alters those complex molecules, combining them with oxygen and releasing stored energy, those lengthy molecular chains end up as simple carbon dioxide and water, their organization and potential energy depleted. Essentially, the potential energy is dissipated as heat. One can say, then, that both matter and energy have reached a state of maximum entropy. There is no way to convert that heat to useful potential energy again; therefore, the increase in entropy is irreversible. Nevertheless, as we will see, useful work can be accomplished as entropy is increased.

FIGURE 6.3 When an organism dies, its molecular organization and the free energy state yield to the inexorable second law of thermodynamics. Entropy increases as the remains yield to the unpleasantries of decay.

Thermodynamics and the Delicate Processes of Life

Now we will see how work can be accomplished as free energy is lost and entropy increases. (Since we will be discussing the processes of life, we will refer to potential energy as free energy.) Every movement we make, every thought we generate, and every chemical reaction within our cells, involve a quiet shift in energy states and a measurable loss of free energy.

A biologically vital application derives from the second law, although it may be evident to you by now. *Transfers of energy in life—shifts from one kind of energy to another or from one organism to another—are never completely efficient; with every transfer some energy is lost.* For this reason, the myriad chemical activities within our own bodies require that considerably more energy be taken in than is necessary to simply carry out the reactions. This is because much of the energy ends up as heat (and so we have warm bodies). The transfer of energy from one group of organisms to the next (from consumed to the consumers, in what ecologists call food chains) is always less than perfect.

The **first** and **second laws of thermodynamics** state that energy in closed systems remains constant, that there is a trend toward randomness or increased **entropy,** and that losses accompany transfers from one form of energy to another.

CHEMICAL REACTIONS AND ENERGY STATES

We sometimes find the laws of thermodynamics at work in startling ways. Consider the case of the airship *Hindenburg,* the most famous of the giant zeppelins, which unfortunately was filled with molecular hydrogen gas. In the 1930s, Germany sent the *Hindenburg* to the United States as a dramatic effort to impress Americans with the Third Reich's technological advances. It did just that. Moments before landing in New Jersey, it exploded (Figure 6.4). The hydrogen gas combined with the molecular oxygen of the atmosphere to produce water. The speed with which the water was produced proved deadly.

Why was the water formed so explosively? Because of energy states. Water (H_2O) is at a lower energy state than an equivalent amount of H_2 and O_2. Thus a mixture of molecular oxygen and hydrogen contains more free chemical energy than does water. When the *Hindenburg* burned, the chemical

FIGURE 6.4   The hydrogen-filled zeppelin the *Hindenburg* exploded in 1937. Hydrogen is so reactive that the smallest spark or flame can provide the impetus needed for a rapid chain reaction.

mix moved to a lower energy state, producing water and releasing the excess energy as heat and light.

The molecular reaction of such a tragedy may be written as

$$2H_2 + O_2 \rightarrow 2H_2O + Energy.$$

Oxygen and hydrogen will combine explosively to produce energy and water, but if you tried to demonstrate the principle by simply mixing oxygen with hydrogen, nothing would happen. Molecular hydrogen and molecular oxygen tend to remain as they are with their outer orbitals nicely filled. What now? Perhaps a spark of intuition.

With a tiny spark, the mixture will blow your hat off. But why doesn't the mixture blow up without the spark? Molecular oxygen and molecular hydrogen do not combine with each other at room temperature because they must first be energized. The atoms making up each molecule must separate and then rejoin violently to be able to react. The spark provides the energy that forces the molecules apart, allowing the reaction. The atoms separated from each other now have free electrons; that is, the electrons are no longer tied up in covalent bonds.

The energy of a tiny spark is all that is necessary to initiate the reaction. Once the first molecules are disrupted, they are able to enter into chemical reactions and release their own free energy. This free energy then provides the energy to separate the atoms of other molecules. The spark sets off a chain reaction and all of the molecules in the system quickly separate.

Any reaction in which energy is released and the products end up with less energy than the reactants is called an **exergonic reaction.** The violent reaction between hydrogen and oxygen is a good example, as is the combustion of gasoline in the engine mentioned earlier. Exergonic reactions also occur as foods are oxidized in mitochondria of cells, thereby releasing the energy stored in their chemical bonds.

In contrast, **endergonic reactions** create products that have more energy than the reactants. Plants carry on endergonic reactions when they join carbon dioxide with water to form sugars. The first law of thermodynamics should alert us that some outside energy source spurs endergonic reactions. For plants, that outside energy source is virtually unlimited: It is sunlight (see Chapter 7).

Exergonic reactions create products that have less energy than reactants (energy is lost). In **endergonic reactions,** products have more energy than the reactants (energy is gained).

Quieter Changes in Energy States

The energy required to break chemical bonds and start a reaction is called **activation energy** (Figure 6.5). Hydrogen and oxygen can combine to form water at room temperature if a spark provides the energy of activation. Such reactions can also proceed by the addition of **catalysts**—substances that speed up chemical reactions but are unchanged by the reactions. Catalysts work by lowering the required activation energy. Hydrogen and oxygen will combine readily if powdered platinum is present. (In the case of this catalyst, the hydrogen first combines with the platinum and then with the oxygen, leaving the platinum in its original state, unchanged by the reactions.)

In biological systems catalysts are highly active proteins called **enzymes.** They are vital to chemical reactions in cells.

ENZYMES: BIOLOGICAL CATALYSTS

In the highly orchestrated interior of a cell, the use of intense heat would be a disruptive way to initiate biochemical processes. Instead, delicate, intricately coordinated, and vulnerable living systems depend on the gentler activity of enzymes. Enzymes, the cat-

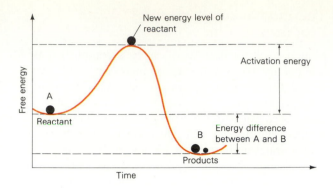

FIGURE 6.5   Activation energy is the energy required to initiate a chemical reaction. The reactant at point *A* will remain inactive until its energy level is raised. At point *B* the products end up at a lower free energy level than the initial reactant.

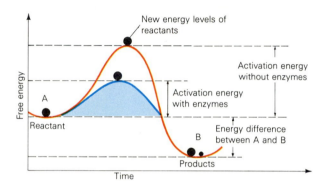

FIGURE 6.6   The graph compares the activation energy requirement for a reaction with and without an enzyme.

alysts of cells, are a special class of biologically active, globular proteins that accelerate biochemical reactions. Many different enzymes comprise any cell's biochemical arsenal, but each enzyme functions in only one kind of reaction. That is, it recognizes and interacts with its own specific **substrate.** In the language of biochemistry, a substrate is simply a substance destined to be chemically altered by an enzyme.

We have now mentioned three important characteristics of enzymes: (1) they are proteins, (2) they are highly specific in their reactions, and (3) they reduce the need for activation energy in bringing about chemical reactions. Figure 6.6 compares the required activation energy with and without the intervention of an enzyme. Let's look further into the factors behind an enzyme's specificity.

Enzymes are biologically-active, highly specific protein **catalysts** that lower **activation energy** requirements and speed reactions.

FIGURE 6.7 Action of a hydrolytic enzyme. **(a)** A substrate entering the active site of an enzyme forms an imperfect fit, held in place chiefly by hydrogen bonds and other subtle forces. A hydrogen bond between two of the enzyme's many amino acids is shown. **(b)** The enzyme, a dynamic molecule, changes shape slightly, placing stress on the substrate at key points and cleaving it into products 1 and 2 (P_1 and P_2). Simultaneously, a hydrogen atom from one of the amino acids joins newly formed P_1, leading to the formation of a temporary enzyme-substrate (ES) bond between P_2 and the affected amino acid. Next, water enters, **(c)** the temporary ES bond breaks, and hydrogen from the water satisfies the enzyme while the —OH group joins P_2. P_2 is released as the enzyme resumes its inactive shape.

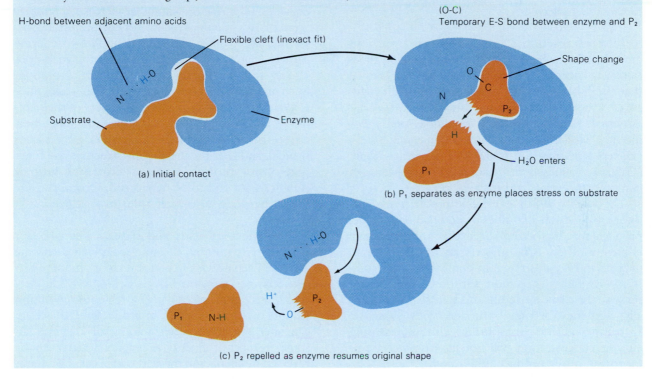

(a) Initial contact

(b) P_1 separates as enzyme places stress on substrate

(c) P_2 repelled as enzyme resumes original shape

A Matter of Shape

The difference between one kind of enzyme and another, and the reason each fits only one kind of substrate, is largely a matter of shape. More specifically, the important differences are in the shape of the enzyme's **active site.** The active site, a crucial part of any enzyme, is a groove or depression on the protein's surface that will hold the substrate. The active site closely matches the molecular configuration of only one kind of substrate. Should the wrong substance collide with the active site of an enzyme, there will be no interaction. Such specificity, as you can imagine, is an important factor in coordinating the cell's chemical activity.

Actually, the fit between active site and substrate is not exact, a fact that partially explains how some enzymes may do their work. According to the **induced fit hypothesis,** as a substrate molecule binds to its corresponding active site, the areas of the

substrate that do not precisely fit are stressed. This weakens some bonds and increases their likelihood of interacting with other substances.

When an enzyme is joined by its substrate, the newly formed complex is appropriately named the **enzyme-substrate (ES) complex.** After an enzyme has done its work, the emerging product or products drift away. The enzyme, unchanged by the reaction, is immediately available for more work. Figure 6.7 illustrates the action of a hydrolytic enzyme, one that uses water as it shears the chemical bonds of the substrate.

The **induced-fit hypothesis** maintains that shape changes in a hydrolytic enzyme's **active sites** place physical stress on the substrate, aiding the formation of the product.

Characteristics of Enzyme Action

Although enzymes obviously play a pivotal role in directing the activities of the cell, they are far from autonomous. Rather, their work is influenced by many factors. Some are simply the conditions in their surroundings, but others act as intricate control mechanisms. Let's look at some of the factors that can influence the speed and efficiency of these remarkable molecules.

Rate of reaction. Enzyme-catalyzed reactions are fast; they generally occur about a million times faster than uncatalyzed reactions. It may have seemed that the process is a bit ponderous—matching, fitting, stressing, interacting, breaking away—but enzymatic molecules work at incredible speeds. For instance, *catalase* (enzyme names often end in "-ase") can repeat its reaction 600,000 times each second. (Catalase, found in peroxisomes, breaks hydrogen peroxide into water and oxygen.)

The rate at which enzymatic products are produced depends on a number of factors. For example, products may be formed faster when more substrate is present. There is no mystery about this, since an enzyme and its substrate join purely by chance collision. Naturally, when more substrate molecules are present, the chances of collision increase. But eventually, enzymes become saturated with substrate. Increasing substrate even further without increasing enzyme concentration will not increase the rate of formation of the product (Figure 6.8).

When the substrate concentration is very low, not only will product formation be slowed, but also, in some instances, the reactions can be reversed, with the product now forming the original reactants. However, such reversibility is not possible if the energy level of the products is substantially lower than that of the reactants or if the products enter other reactions or if they escape.

The effect of heat. Heat initiates chemical reactions, and it may also affect the functioning of enzymes. As a rule of thumb, an increase in temperature of 10°C doubles the rate of chemical reactions. Furthermore, the rule generally applies to enzyme activity (Figure 6.9). The effect of heat in such cases is easy to understand. *Heat* is molecular motion. Such an increase in the movement of substrate molecules and enzyme increases the chances of their collision. Of course, there is a limit to how much heat can be added to any system; enzymes are made of protein, and heat can destroy the structure and function of any protein. Enzymes altered by heat or chemicals are said to be **denatured.** Obviously, any shape change in an enzyme ruins its specificity.

The effect of acids and bases. The pH (see Chapter 2) within a cell can also influence enzyme activity. Each enzyme operates at an optimum pH. A few enzymes perform best in strongly acidic surroundings but most require a more neutral condition (Figure 6.10). Apparently, improper levels of acidity can alter the very specific folding of enzymes. In some instances, an enzyme's actions can even be reversed by changes in the acidity of a cell. For example, the same enzyme that helps synthesize glycogen from glucose at a high pH will reverse the process at a low pH, breaking glycogen down to glucose.

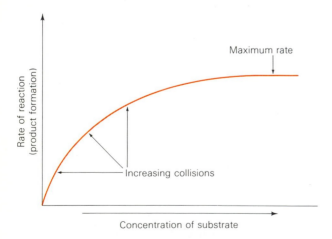

FIGURE 6.8 This shows the rate of reaction when the quantity of enzyme remains constant while the concentration of substrate is increased.

Enzyme reactions rates are affected by enzyme and substrate concentrations, temperature, and pH. Enzymes are **denatured** by harsh chemicals and excessive heat.

Teams of enzymes: metabolic pathways. Any enzymatic reaction is likely to be only one simple link in a long sequence of reactions that keep the cell alive and functioning. This sequence is called a **metabolic pathway.** In such chains, each product becomes the starting material for the next reaction. Clearly, such an interdependent system must be very organized.

Some metabolic pathways involve the breakdown of large, complex molecules. Such processes are called **catabolic.** Pathways that build large molecules by joining smaller ones are called **anabolic.**

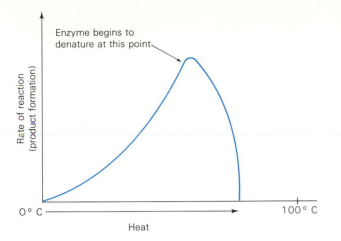

FIGURE 6.9 As thermal energy (heat) is added to an enzyme-substrate mixture, the rate of the reaction increases. However, heat can also denature an enzyme, altering its properties and rendering it inactive.

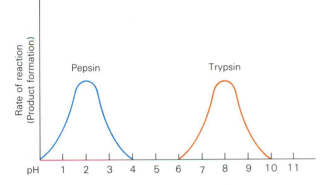

FIGURE 6.10 Enzymes are sensitive to pH. Pepsin, the protein-digesting enzyme of the stomach, is inactive in all but fairly strong acidic conditions (low pH). Trypsin, a protein-digesting enzyme of the small intestine, requires a slightly alkaline environment. Most enzymes work optimally at near-neutral (pH 7) conditions.

Enzymes and cofactors. Many enzymes are assisted in their work by agents known as **cofactors,** which are ions or molecules that must be associated with an enzyme in order for the enzyme to function properly. Cofactors include inorganic ions such as iron (Fe^{2+}), manganese (Mn^{2+}) and zinc (Zn^{2+}). Others are complex organic molecules known as **coenzymes,** many of which are actually modified vitamins.

Calmodulin/calcium ion activation. Biochemists have discovered a remarkable mechanism for the activation of certain enzymes, particularly those that catalyze phosphorylation reactions in the cell. The system involves calcium ions (Ca^{2+}) and the protein **calmodulin.** Although calcium's many cell-activating roles have been known for years, the associated role of calmodulin, a linking agent, is only now being clarified.

Calmodulin is a small protein containing 148 amino acids. Each molecule has four minute pockets; each pocket can hold an activating calcium ion. In its calcium-activated form, calmodulin unites with a number of enzymes that are themselves important links in cell activity. In such unions, calmodulin is thought to alter the shape of the enzyme, changing it to an active form. Such diverse cell activities as muscle contraction, endocytosis and exocytosis, ciliary motion, cell division, glycogen metabolism, the transfer of nerve impulses from cell to cell, and even fertilization all involve enzymes mobilized by calcium-activated calmodulin. This protein is present in all eukaryotic cells, from simple protists to those of plants and humans.

Allosteric sites and enzyme control. Enzymes are controlled in a number of subtle ways. In addition to its active site, an enzyme may have an **allosteric site.** When this second binding site is filled, the shape of the enzyme's primary active site is changed; the enzyme will no longer bind to its usual substrate. The allosteric site is sometimes specific for one of the enzyme's products that subsequently lodges there. In this way, as a product accumulates, the allosteric sites will fill, inhibiting more enzymes. Often, enzymes with allosteric sites will be part of a team of enzymes that act sequentially on the same substrate (Figure 6.11). It is important to know that a molecule doesn't permanently bind to the allosteric site. As soon as the unbound product molecules becomes scarce—used up or enzymatically altered to a new product—the inhibitory effect is lost, and the enzyme can again act.

The operation of the allosteric site is an example of an important biological regulation called **negative feedback.** We will consider it in detail later, but the concept bears mentioning here. In negative feedback, the product of an action inhibits the action that produced it in the first place. As the amount of product increases, the enzyme is inhibited from producing more product. Such regulatory mechanisms are elegant in that they are both simple and automatic.

We are all aware that cells must have energy to do their work. So now we will be introduced to a fascinating molecule called adenosine triphosphate (ATP). This simple molecule is intimately involved with the cell's ability to carry out its tasks.

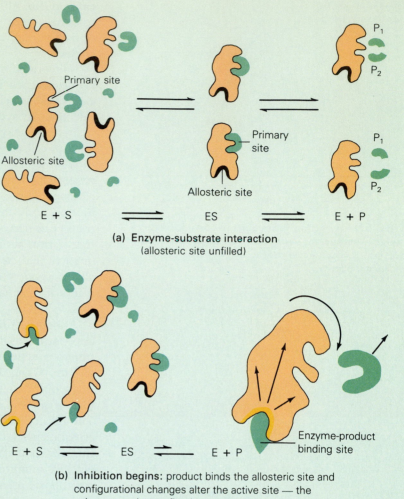

FIGURE 6.11 Some enzymes have two different binding sites. The primary site binds with the substrate molecule as usual **(a)**, but the second (allosteric) site can bind with a small product molecule. When the allosteric site becomes occupied **(b)**, the shape of the enzyme changes enough to render it incapable of forming an enzyme-substrate complex. When products (P_1 and P_2) are used up in other reactions, the enzyme will once again be free to carry out its role in the cell.

(a) Enzyme-substrate interaction
(allosteric site unfilled)

E + S   ES   E + P

Primary site

Allosteric site

Primary site

Allosteric site

P_1

P_2

P_1

P_2

(b) Inhibition begins: product binds the allosteric site and configurational changes alter the active site — the substrate no longer fits the enzyme

E + S   ES   E + P

Enzyme-product binding site

ATP: THE ENERGY CURRENCY OF THE CELL

Adenosine triphosphate (ATP) has been called the cell's "energy currency," because it can be "spent" to get things done. The more energy that is required, the more ATP must be used.

ATP is particularly interesting because it is used by all forms of life; it is a nearly universal molecule of energy transfer. Energy produced in photosynthesis or respiration is stored in ATP. When that energy is needed, it is released by ATP. You may recall that cells can store energy in molecules such as carbohydrates, lipids, and proteins. But before energy can be retrieved from such molecules, it must first be transferred to ATP.

To illustrate the activity of ATP in our daily lives, consider this: *The average adult male uses about 190 kilograms (419 lbs) of ATP each day of his life!* Since few of us even weigh 190 kilos, we obviously don't have that much ATP on hand. In fact, our bodies contain only about 50 grams (1.8 oz) of ATP at any time. This means that this small amount must recycle furiously, making possible the recharging of spent ATP.

Structure of ATP

The secret of ATP's abilities lies in its structure (Figure 6.12). The molecule consists of three parts. The most obvious part is a double ring of carbon and nitrogen called **adenine.** In addition to adenine, each ATP molecule contains a simple, five-carbon sugar called **ribose.** Ribose forms a link between the adenine and three phosphate (triphosphate) units that form a kind of tail. The phosphates are linked together by oxygen atoms.

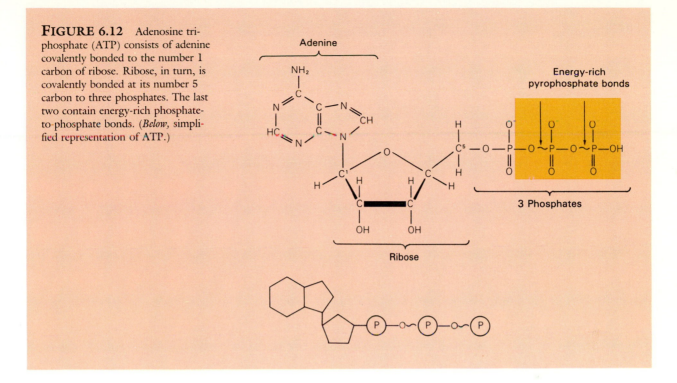

FIGURE 6.12 Adenosine triphosphate (ATP) consists of adenine covalently bonded to the number 1 carbon of ribose. Ribose, in turn, is covalently bonded at its number 5 carbon to three phosphates. The last two contain energy-rich phosphate-to-phosphate bonds. (*Below*, simplified representation of ATP.)

The phosphate-to-phosphate bond. Notice in Figure 6.12 that the phosphates forming ATP's tail are linked by bonds shown as curved lines. These curved lines indicate **high-energy bonds.** Their energy is released when a phosphate bond is broken and the inorganic phosphate ion, P_i, is released. Such bonds can be formed only by enormous energy input, which means that a great deal of energy is released when those bonds are broken. (Specifically, breaking the terminal [outer] phosphate bonds in 1 mole of ATP, yields 7.3 kilocalories of energy*. Yet breaking the bond between sugar and the first phosphate in a mole of ATP yields only 3.4 kilocalories.)

ATP participates in most cellular reactions. Breaking its high-energy bond yields 7.3 kcal of energy/mole.

*A **calorie** (cal) is the energy it takes to raise the temperature of 1 milliliter (ml) of water 1°C. A calorie is 0.001 **kilocalories** (kcal)—the units dieters count. A kilocalorie (or Calorie) is 1000 calories, the energy it takes to raise the temperature of 1 liter of water 1°C. Chemists rarely concern themselves with individual molecules, preferring to think in quantities called "moles." A **mole** of a substance is the combined atomic weights of all its atoms, expressed in grams (gm). Therefore, to calculate 1 mole of glucose ($C_6H_{12}O_6$) we find the atomic weight (mass) of carbon, hydrogen, and oxygen and multiply each by the number of atoms in the molecule. Thus, 1 mole of glucose = $12 \times 6 + 1 \times 12 + 16 \times 6 = 180$ gm (6.3 oz).

ATP and Cellular Chemistry

How does a cell manage to use the energy held in those special, phosphate-to-phosphate bonds of ATP? First, the terminal bond is broken by a simple and familiar process called **hydrolytic cleavage,** or **hydrolysis**—the enzymatic addition of water (see Chapter 3). In this way, the terminal phosphate is removed and replaced by a hydroxyl (—OH), group, changing the ATP to **ADP,** or adenosine *di*phosphate (*di,* "two").

When a high-energy ATP bond is broken, its free energy becomes available for useful work. Unharnessed, that energy would simply escape as heat, but the cell is prepared to avoid this, although some such loss is unavoidable. Frequently, the terminal phosphate and some of its energy are simply transferred to a new substrate in what is called a **phosphorylation reaction.** The new substrate molecule gains some free energy, perhaps increasing its readiness to undergo further change. Typically, the phosphorylated molecule will next enter a **substitution reaction.** The phosphorylated molecule uses its increase in free energy to trade the phosphate for some other useful atom or side group that it could not otherwise accept (Figure 6.13). Such substitution reactions are common in photosynthesis, as we'll see in the next chapter.

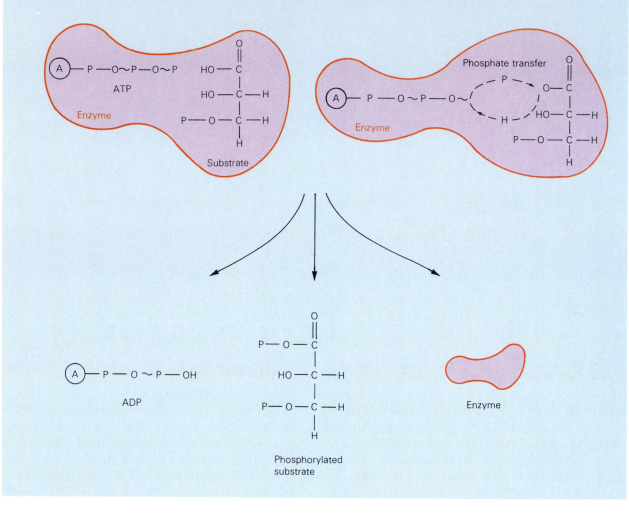

FIGURE 6.13 Interaction between ATP, a substrate molecule, and a phosphorylating enzyme results in transfer of ATP's terminal phosphate to the substrate. The energy of the phosphate molecule increases the free energy in the substrate. It can now enter into cellular reactions.

The ATP Cycle

ATP can lose one phosphate ion (P_i) and become ADP or lose two and become **adenosine monophosphate or AMP.** The ADP or AMP molecules are simply recycled; that is, they regain their phosphate, becoming ATP again, ready to supply the cell's energy.

The problem here is obvious: Because breaking those phosphate bonds *releases* a great deal of energy, making the bonds *requires* a great deal of energy. That energy is made available through two vital processes: cellular respiration and photosynthesis. ATP molecules constantly lose phosphates (releasing energy) and regain them (requiring energy) in one of the most vital cycles of life (Figure 6.14).

ATP commonly phosphorylates substrate, setting it up for additional reactions. Through energy-yielding reactions, ADP is recycled to form ATP.

We have taken a look at two kinds of molecules that are important to cellular energetics—enzymes and ATP. Their roles are closely intertwined, since enzymes are catalysts for chemical reactions and ATP can provide the energy for those reactions. Now let's consider those operating partners of many enzymes, the coenzymes.

FIGURE 6.14 As ATP provides the energy for cellular activities, it becomes ADP and P$_i$. These, in turn, are recycled to energy-transfering organelles where they again become ATP.

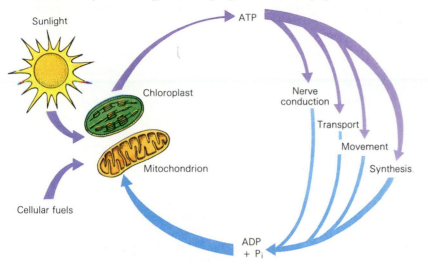

COENZYMES, OXIDATION, AND REDUCTION

In order to understand how high-energy ATP is generated from ADP, we need to know something about the movement of electrons by a special group of cofactors called coenzymes.

Coenzymes work in close association with enzymes and substrate. While there are many kinds of coenzymes, our interest here is in three that are directly involved in making ATP. Two of these are **nicotinamide adenine dinucleotide** (**NAD,** usually pronounced "nad") and **nicotinamide adenine dinucleotide phosphate** (NADP, or "nad-phosphate"). The third is **flavin adenine dinucleotide (FAD).**

Structure of NAD$^+$, NADP$^+$, and FAD

Note in Figure 6.15 that NAD and NADP are chemically similar to ATP: There is a nitrogen base (adenine), two ribose sugars, and a number of phosphates (NADP has one more phosphate than NAD). These molecules also have a nitrogen-containing ring called **nicotinic acid,** which is the chemically active part of these two coenzymes. In FAD, the active group is called **riboflavin.** Both nicotinic acid (also called **niacin**) and riboflavin are derived from B vitamins. In fact, as we go through the role of these coenzymes, you may gain a new respect for vegetables.

Although each of these coenzymes works in its

FIGURE 6.15 The coenzymes NAD$^+$ and NADP$^+$ are very similar, but note the third phosphate of NADP$^+$ (color). The active group is nicotinic acid, shown at the right. As nicotinic acid is reduced, it accepts a hydrogen ion and two electrons.

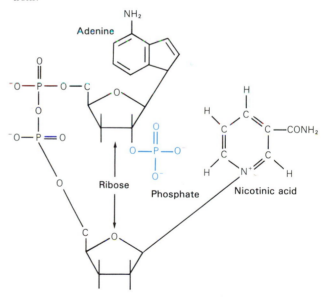

own way, they all do essentially the same thing. Working closely with enzymes, they accept electrons and transfer them to other molecules. Chemically, the removal of electrons or protons (or both, as hydrogen) from substrate is called **oxidation.** The addition of electrons or protons to substrate is called **reduction.** (In a sense, then, biochemically reducing something makes it bigger.)

Oxidation and Reduction by Coenzymes

As oxidizing enzymes strip electrons and protons from a substrate, they pass them to coenzymes. Thus when a substrate loses electrons and protons, a coenzyme gains them: as the substrate is oxidized, the coenzyme is reduced. Coenzymes don't remain reduced very long; they quickly pass their newly acquired electrons and protons to another substrate, thus reducing it. In their oxidized state, the three coenzymes mentioned above are written as NAD^+, $NADP^+$, and FAD. In their reduced state they become $NADH + H^+$, $NADPH + H^+$, and $FADH_2$. Reduced NAD and NADP are often written simply as NADH and NADPH. In their reduced form, NADH and NADPH take in two electrons and one proton (a second proton ends up in the watery medium nearby). $FADH_2$, as its name suggests, takes in two electrons and two protons (the equivalent of two hydrogen atoms).

The reduction of a coenzyme greatly increases its free energy. It becomes "charged" with electrons and protons. These energetic molecules then have the power to shift electrons and protons to some substrate. This ability is critical to cell metabolism, as we'll see.

Let's follow NAD through a complete set of reactions as it goes from the oxidized state to the reduced and back to the oxidized again.

(1) Substrate-A + NAD^+ $\xrightarrow{\text{oxidizing enzyme}}$

Oxidized substrate-A + $NADH + H^+$

(2) Substrate-B + $NADH + H^+$ $\xrightarrow{\text{reducing enzyme}}$

Reduced substrate-B + NAD^+

Oxidized coenzymes NAD^+, $NADP^+$, and FAD are readily reduced by electrons and protons, forming NADH, NADPH, and $FADH_2$. Their reducing power enables them to pass electrons and protons to other substrate.

Reducing Power and Electron Transport Systems

NADH, NADPH, and $FADH_2$ have a great deal of reducing power. They can pass some of this power to a substrate by reducing it. This leaves the substrate more energetic and able to react. These coenzymes, though, can also deliver their electrons and protons to special sites on the membranes of chloroplasts and mitochondria. Here they reduce membrane-bound proteins known as **electron carriers.** Many of the carriers are complex iron-containing proteins called **cytochromes.** Such carriers, arranged in a row across certain membranes, form the **electron transport systems (ETS).**

Members of electron transport systems pass energy-rich electrons from carrier to carrier in a sequence of reductions and oxidations. As electrons move along, their free energy is progressively drained. They finally emerge from the electron transport system in a substantially depleted state (Figure 6.16). So, where does their energy end up? As we'll see, much of the energy ends up in ATP. So let's look at the details of one of life's most vital processes.

Electron transport systems consist of electron carriers, molecules arranged within membranes of chloroplasts or mitochondria, that use the free energy of moving electrons to synthesize ATP.

FORMATION OF ATP IN CELLS

Now that we know something about energy, enzymes, ATP, coenzymes, and electron transport systems, we can look at how cells make ATP. ATP production is cyclic; that is, the phosphorylation of ADP forms ATP, which is then broken back down to ADP. ADP can be "recharged" to ATP in two ways: **substrate-level phosphorylation** and **chemiosmotic phosphorylation.**

Substrate-level phosphorylation is the generation of ATP directly from the chemical bonds of cellular fuels such as glucose. Although this ATP-generating mechanism is commonplace, it delivers far less ATP than chemiosmotic phosphorylation. Substrate-level phosphorylation is thought to be an ancient process, probably used by the earth's first heterotrophic organisms. We will return to the process in Chapter 8; here we will concentrate on chemiosmotic phosphorylation.

Chemiosmosis and Chemiosmotic Phosphorylation

Chemiosmosis is the creation of very steep proton gradients (**chemiosmotic gradients**) between membrane-bound compartments in certain organelles. To form these gradients, immense numbers of protons (hydrogen ions: H^+) are actively transported, or

FIGURE 6.16 The electron transport system. When an electron carrier becomes reduced (gains an electron: A′ B′ C′ D′), its potential energy level is raised considerably. As it reduces the next carrier in the sequence, that carrier's free energy level is also increased, and so on. But because no energy transfer is totally efficient, each transfer results in a loss in free energy of the previous carrier.

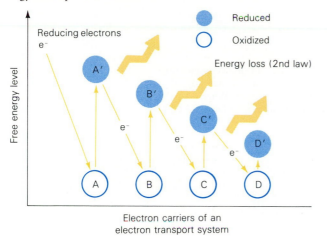

Reduced
Oxidized

Reducing electrons
e⁻

Energy loss (2nd law)

Free energy level

A′
B′
C′
D′

e⁻
e⁻
e⁻

A
B
C
D

Electron carriers of an electron transport system

"pumped," into membrane-surrounded compartments, leaving behind large numbers of hydroxide ions (OH^-). This produces great potential energy, since there is a very strong tendency for the oppositely charged ions to join. The ions will be allowed to rejoin, but in a very special way. The great potential energy of the ions will be gradually released to power enzyme-directed reactions that generate ATP. The use of free energy from the chemiosmotic gradient to form ATP from ADP and P_i is called **chemiosmotic phosphorylation** (Figure 6.17).

Where would one look for such proton-rich compartments in the cell? Since both chloroplasts and mitochondria generate ATP, and since they both have highly membranous inner structures, they represent the most likely places (see Figures 4.12 and 4.13). This becomes clearer when we list the requirements for such a chemiosmotic system.

Chemiosmotic systems require (and mitochondria and chloroplasts provide):

FIGURE 6.17 In 1966, biochemists experimenting with isolated spinach chloroplasts found that ATP synthesis could occur in the absence of light if a proton gradient was artificially produced. In a remarkable experiment, Andre Jagendorf and Ernest Uribe created the proton gradient by first immersing the chloroplasts in an acidic (proton-rich) solution. They quickly raised the pH from 4 to 8, while simultaneously adding ADP and P_i to the medium. The analysis that followed revealed new ATP in the light-free system. The new ATP had to be a product of the contrived proton gradient. The results also suggested that ATP synthesis may not be directly linked to light-driven electron transport. These daring ideas were contrary to those of traditional biochemists, who asserted that ATP formed directly through light-driven electron transport systems.

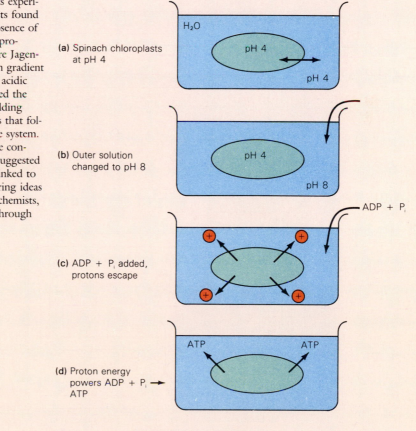

H_2O

(a) Spinach chloroplasts at pH 4

pH 4
pH 4

(b) Outer solution changed to pH 8

pH 4
pH 8

(c) ADP + P_i added, protons escape

ADP + P_i

(d) Proton energy powers ADP + P_i → ATP

ATP
ATP

1. Organelles with their membranes arranged to form inner and outer compartments ("sacs-within-sacs")—precisely how the mitochondria and chloroplasts are organized
2. An inner membrane that is highly *impermeable* to protons—a structural feature of the two organelles

3. Proton pumps embedded in the inner membrane—the electron transport systems of mitochondria and chloroplasts
4. A source of protons and a source of energy to run the proton pumps—oxidation of foods in the mitochondrion; water in the chloroplast

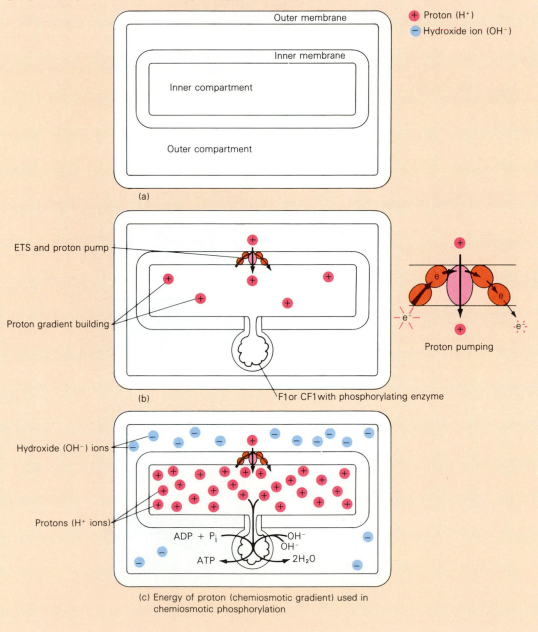

FIGURE 6.18 Chemiosmotic systems require a sac-within-a-sac arrangement of membranes **(a)**, resulting in the formation of two compartments. The inner membrane **(b)** contains the necessary electron transport systems and proton pumps for forming an energy-rich proton gradient. When enough free energy accumulates in the system **(c)**, escaping protons provide the energy needed by F1 or CF1 phosphorylating enzymes to form the high-energy bonds of ATP.

5. Phosphorylating enzyme complexes that can use the free energy of the system to form ATP—the F1 particles of the mitochondrion, and the CF1 particles in the chloroplast.

For a preview of how chemiosmotic systems work, see Figure 6.18.

> The free energy of **chemiosmotic gradients**—massive accumulations of protons in compartments within mitochondria and chloroplasts—is used to make ATP through **chemiosmotic phosphorylation.**

We marvel at the evolution of such complex systems, but in one form or another, they may have been around a long time to be molded by the processes of natural selection. Both mitochondria and chloroplasts are believed to be highly evolved descendants of what were once free-living prokaryotes (bacteria). These ancient, comparatively simple invaders likely employed some form of chemiosmosis as their means of generating ATP. Today's prokaryotes have advanced chemiosmotic systems, so we can't look to them for answers. Interestingly, aerobic (oxygen-using) bacteria simply use their surroundings for their outer compartment, pumping protons out and then letting them back in through phosphorylating enzymes in their plasma membranes. Such bacteria are functionally similar to mitochondria.

Now we will look into some of nature's best-kept secrets—how simple sunlight is used by our green partners to form new chemical bonds in foods, and how cells use the energy in those bonds to form their own ATP.

SUMMARY

ENERGY

Energy passes from organism to organism in food chains. It is defined as the capacity for **work.**

Potential and Kinetic Energy

Potential (free) energy is stored; kinetic energy is in motion. The behavior of energy is expressed by the laws of thermodynamics.

THE LAWS OF THERMODYNAMICS
The First Law

The first law of thermodynamics states that energy can be neither created nor destroyed; within closed systems it remains in a steady state. Energy can change from one form to another (e.g., chemical to heat or light, heat to motion, etc.)

The Second Law

The second law of thermodynamics, or the law of entropy, states that free or potential energy in a system tends to decrease. The state of disorder in a system is its entropy. Heat is the lowest energy form.

Thermodynamics and the Delicate Processes of Life

The second law indicates that each energy transfer is accompanied by a loss, ordinarily in the form of heat.

CHEMICAL REACTIONS AND ENERGY STATES

Hydrogen and oxygen gases react because the two have greater energy than the product, water. Whereas energy must be applied to start the reaction, the subsequent release of energy forms a self-sustaining chain reaction. Reactions that release energy are exergonic, but where the products have greater free energy than the reactants, the reaction is endergonic.

Quieter Changes in Energy States

Reactions generally require substantial activation energy, but in the presence of a catalyst, this energy requirement is greatly reduced. Such catalysts emerge unchanged.

ENZYMES: BIOLOGICAL CATALYSTS

Enzymes are biologically active protein catalysts that reduce the activation energy requirement, thus accelerating cell reactions. Each kind of enzyme reacts only with its own specific substrate.

A Matter of Shape

Molecular structure, particularly the shape of an enzyme's active site, accounts for enzyme-substrate specificity. The induced fit hypothesis maintains that an imperfect fit in the active site aids the reaction by placing physical stress on the substrate. Following the reaction, the product or products leave the site, and the enzyme is ready to act again.

Characteristics of Enzyme Action

Enzyme reaction rates can be increased by the addition of substrate until saturation occurs. Some reactions reverse when substrate levels are low and product levels are high. Heat increases the reaction rate but too much causes denaturation. Most enzymes work best at a neutral pH since they are denatured by strong acids and bases.

Enzymes typically work in teams forming metabolic pathways. Reactions may be anabolic (building molecules) or catabolic (tearing down molecules). Enzymes often require cofactors, inorganic ions or complex organic molecules called coenzymes. Calcium ions join the protein calmodulin, which then activates many kinds of enzymes.

One kind of control system makes use of **allosteric sites** on the enzyme. Excess product fills the site, rendering the enzyme inoperable. As product is depleted, the sites clear and reactions resume. A product controlling its own production is an example of negative feedback control.

ATP: THE ENERGY CURRENCY OF THE CELL

ATP (adenosine triphosphate), the major source of energy in the cell, is produced through energy transfers from foods in cell respiration and through the use of sunlight energy in photosynthesis.

Structure of ATP

ATP contains adenine, ribose sugar and three phosphates. Two of the connecting phosphate linkages are high-energy bonds with nearly twice the energy of other bonds.

ATP and Cellular Chemistry

ATP becomes ADP (adenosine diphosphate) and P_i when its outer high-energy bond is hydrolyzed. In a phosphorylation reaction, the phosphate plus some energy is transferred to substrate, preparing it for further reactions.

The ATP Cycle

After losing both phosphates, ATP becomes AMP (adenosine monophosphate). ADP, AMP, and P_i can be recycled through energy-yielding processes wherein new high-energy bonds are formed, restoring ATP.

COENZYMES, OXIDATION, AND REDUCTION

In the making of ATP, the coenzymes NAD, NADP, and FAD work in close association with enzymes. NAD, NADP, and FAD have oxidation/reduction roles. They become reduced when they take in electrons and/or protons, and they become oxidized when they pass them along. The oxidized forms of the coenzymes are NAD^+, $NADP^+$, and FAD. The reduced forms are NADH ($+ H^+$), NADPH ($+ H^+$), and $FADH_2$. The latter are in a higher energy state.

Reducing Power and Electron Transport Systems

Coenzymes commonly pass their electrons and/or protons to membranal carriers that make up electron transport systems. As electrons pass through such systems, some of their energy is used to form ATP.

FORMATION OF ATP IN CELLS

ATP is produced through substrate level phosphorylation and chemiosmotic phosphorylation. The first occurs through the direct transfer of high-energy phosphate from substrate to ADP, whereas the second occurs at specially structured membranal sites.

Chemiosmosis and Chemiosmotic Phosphorylation

Chemiosmosis is the pumping of protons into membrane-bound compartments. The concentration gradient formed has great free energy, which is used in generating new ATP through chemiosmotic phosphorylation. Chemiosmotic systems have membrane-bound compartments, proton pumps powered by electron transport systems, proton and energy sources, and enzyme complexes (F1 and CF1 particles). Free energy from these systems is used to phosphorylate ADP.

Bacteria carry on chemiosmotic phosphorylation by concentrating protons directly outside the cell and letting them reenter the cell through ADP phosphorylating complexes.

KEY TERMS

energy	induced-fit hypothesis	adenine
potential (free) energy	enzyme-substrate complex (ES)	ribose
kinetic energy	denatured	high-energy bond
laws of thermodynamics	metabolic pathway	calorie
law of entropy	catabolic	mole
exergonic reaction	anabolic	hydrolytic cleavage
endergonic reaction	cofactor	hydrolysis
catalyst	coenzyme	adenosine diphosphate (ADP)
enzyme	calmodulin	phosphorylation reaction
substrate	allosteric site	substitution reaction
activation energy	negative feedback	adenosine monophosphate (AMP)
active site	adenosine triphosphate (ATP)	nicotinamide adenine dinucleotide (NAD)

nicotinamide adenine dinucleotide
  phosphate (NADP)
flavin adenine dinucleotide (FAD)
nicotinic acid (niacin)
riboflavin

oxidation
reduction
electron carriers
cytochrome
electron transport systems (ETS)

substrate-level phosphorylation
chemiosmotic phosphorylation
chemiosmosis
chemiosmotic gradients

REVIEW QUESTIONS

1 State the formal definitions for *energy* and *work*. How do these definitions apply to familiar situations such as moving the limbs, washing down the driveway, and the pumping of blood by the heart. (p. 78)

2 Carefully distinguish between energy that is potential or free and energy that is kinetic. (p. 79)

3 According to the first law of thermodynamics, what happens to energy in a closed system? Is the earth such a system? Explain. (pp. 79–80)

4 Starting with the potential energy of water behind the dam in a hydroelectric facility, suggest a number of energy conversions as that energy is utilized by consumers. In what form does most end up? (pp. 78–79)

5 According to the second law, or law of entropy, what is the fate of the earth? The solar system? The universe? (p. 80)

6 Cite a familiar example of increasing entropy in your surroundings. How might this be reversed? (p. 80)

7 Carefully explain how the second law of thermodynamics applies to energy passing through food chains (reread the chapter introduction). (pp. 78–80)

8 Using the free energy states of hydrogen gas, oxygen gas, and water as a background, explain the chemistry of the *Hindenberg* disaster. (p. 81)

9 Distinguish between exergonic and endergonic reactions. Explain, in light of the first law, how product energy can exceed reactant energy. (p. 82)

10 Fully explain how the presence of a catalyst affects the usual way chemical reactions occur. (p. 82)

11 Briefly discuss the chemical structure, specificity, and value of enzymes. (p. 83)

12 Using the induced-fit hypothesis as a background, explain how a hydrolytic enzyme does its work. (p. 83)

13 Explain why adding more substrate in an enzymatic reaction increases the amount of product, but only up to a point? (p. 84)

14 Why does increasing the temperature around an enzyme increase reaction rate? What limits the use of heat? (p. 84)

15 Explain the organization of enzymes in metabolic pathways. How do catabolic and anabolic pathways differ? (p. 84)

16 Explain how negative feedback works and how it pertains to allosteric enzyme control. (p. 85)

17 Draw a simplified ATP molecule, labelling its three components. Add the high-energy bonds. (p. 86)

18 Compare the energy in ATP's high-energy phosphate bonds with that in its other phosphate bonds. (p. 87)

19 List the two products formed when ATP's terminal phosphate bond is broken. Carry this out another step, with the second phosphate bond being broken. (p. 88)

20 Describe a phosphorylation reaction and explain how this might be used in molecule building. (pp. 87–88)

21 Draw a simple ATP cycle, indicating how ATP is used and how it is regenerated. (p. 88)

22 Carefully define the terms *oxidation* and *reduction*. What is the role of the coenzyme in such reactions? (p. 89)

23 Write the oxidized and reduced forms of the coenzymes NAD, NADP, and FAD. (pp. 89–90)

24 What are electron transport systems? What is the electron energy generally used for? (p. 90)

25 Chemiosmosis involves the concentrating of great numbers of protons in membrane-bound compartments. What does this mean in terms of free energy, and how can such a system be put to use. (pp. 90–91)

26 Keeping the sac-within-a-sac idea in mind, draw your own version of Figures 6.17 and 6.18, illustrating the building of a chemiosmotic gradient and its use in generating ATP. (pp. 91–92)

27 Summarize the five requirements of a chemiosmotic system. (pp. 92–93)

7

PHOTOSYNTHESIS

Recent interest in solar power as an energy source to replace fossil fuels has an almost touching naiveté about it. We seem to view solar power as a new concept. In fact, sunlight has long provided us with our most fundamental source of energy. Such fossil fuels as oil, gas, and coal simply are releasing solar energy stored away in the bodies of long-dead plants and algae. So while we continue to wander in the maze of engineering problems associated with harnessing the sun's energy to produce electricity, perhaps we should turn to the real experts—and the real experts are likely to be green (Figure 7.1).

A great variety of living things on the planet, including green plants and algae, make food from simple molecules such as carbon dioxide and water through a process called **photosynthesis.** This process is powered by the delicate but powerful energy of sunlight. In this chapter we will consider how **autotrophs** ("self-feeders") are able to use something as ethereal as sunlight to manufacture their own nutrients. This happens as the energy of sunlight is captured by certain molecules, such as the chlorophyll of green plants.

OVERVIEW OF PHOTOSYNTHESIS

The energy of sunlight is first used to sharply increase the energy level of certain chlorophyll electrons. Such energy-rich electrons then flow through highly ordered carriers in electron transport systems, powering proton pumps as they go, and finally reducing $NADP^+$ to powerful NADPH. Proton pumps, as we saw in Chapter 6, generate the great free energy of the chemiosmotic systems responsible for forming the energy-rich bonds of ATP. Both ATP and NADPH provide energy that is used to form food (such as glucose) from carbon dioxide and water. (An imaginative biochemist, pondering this delicate electron emission, once philosophized, "Life seems to begin with a little flow of electricity.")

But let's ignore the electrons and energetics for the moment and look at photosynthesis through a time-honored equation. Photosynthesizers use carbon dioxide and water to form glucose, yielding oxygen as a by-product:

$$\underset{\text{carbon dioxide}}{6\,CO_2} + \underset{\text{water}}{12\,H_2O} \xrightarrow[\text{chlorophyll}]{\text{Light}} \underset{\text{glucose}}{C_6H_{12}O_6} +$$

$$\underset{\text{water}}{6\,H_2O} + \underset{\text{oxygen}}{6\,O_2}$$

FIGURE 7.1 Photosynthetic organisms are undoubtedly the dominant forms of life on earth. Nearly all of the earth's creatures depend on their ability to capture the sun's energy.

The equation is a nice overview but hides a great amount of detail. For instance, it is not apparent from the equation that the 12 oxygen atoms (6 O_2) to the right of the arrow come from the water molecules and not from carbon dioxide to the left of the arrow.

The equation also does not show the actual roles of **photons,** discrete packets of sunlight energy that move in a wavelike path. The energy of the photons, when captured by a pigment such as **chlorophyll,** powers the photosynthetic process, generating energy-rich ATP and hydrogen-rich NADPH. Both of these work with teams of enzymes in the glucose-synthesizing pathway.

Also not apparent is the importance of structure to the process. It is no coincidence that the chloroplast is an intricately structured organelle. In fact, its organization is so essential, that we should begin with a closer look at it.

> The "bare-bones" equation for photosynthesis indicates that H_2O and CO_2 react to form glucose, O_2 and H_2O.

THE CHLOROPLAST

Chloroplasts occur in the cells of leaves and green stems of plants and in the cells of algae (Figure 7.2a and b). Recall from Chapters 4 and 6 that chloroplasts are relatively large organelles encasing a watery, protein-rich fluid, the **stroma.** The stroma contains many tiny membrane-bound structures resembling stacks of coins. These are the **grana,** each composed of disklike **thylakoids.** Each thylakoid contains a minute inner compartment known as the **lumen** (the "sac-within-a-sac"; see Chapter 6.) The lumen acts as the proton reservoir in the chloroplast's chemiosmotic system. The membranes that form the thylakoids often extend at intervals as **lamellae,** forming interconnections between neighboring grana.

The clear, watery stroma of the chloroplast contains the enzyme teams responsible for the synthesis of glucose. Thylakoids are responsible for the capture of the light energy needed to drive the process. Embedded in the thylakoid membranes are the light-capturing pigments, organized into the two kinds of **photosystems** described below. Also present are **electron transport systems** and **proton pumps.** They drive chemiosmotic phosphorylation (the charging of ATP) and the reduction of $NADP^+$. The system works well because of the precise organization of the chloroplast: The various sites of chemical activity have an efficient spatial relationship.

> The chemical synthesis of glucose occurs in the **stroma.** Light is captured and put to work in the **thylakoid.**

Photosystems

Photosystems are clusters of light-absorbing pigments and their associated molecules (Figure 7.2c). For example, researchers studying the thylakoids from spinach chloroplasts have found that each cluster, or photosystem, contains about 200 molecules of **chlorophylls** *a* and *b* and about 50 molecules of **carotenoids,** another family of light-absorbing pigments (Figure 7.3). The presence of several kinds of pigments enables the photosystem to absorb light over much of the visible light spectrum (see Essay 7.1).

The energy of the absorbed light is converted to chemical energy in the **reaction center** (Figure 7.2d). This special region consists of one molecule of chlorophyll *a* and a closely associated protein. Since

FIGURE 7.2 (a) Tissues within the leaf contain vast numbers of photosynthetic cells, each with numerous chloroplasts. Within the chloroplasts are membranous grana. Each thylakoid (b) is bound by two complex membranes that are alternately pressed together to form the *lamellae* and bulged outward to form the inner compartments, or *lumina* (singular, *lumen*). Each membrane (c) contains many light-harvesting antennas and associated electron/hydrogen carriers. Note the minute but vital channels in the CF1 particles forming a communication link between the lumen and stroma. An imaginative glance into one light-harvesting antenna (d) reveals numerous molecules of chlorophyll and accessory pigments, whose roles are to capture photons and shunt the captured light energy into a central reaction center.

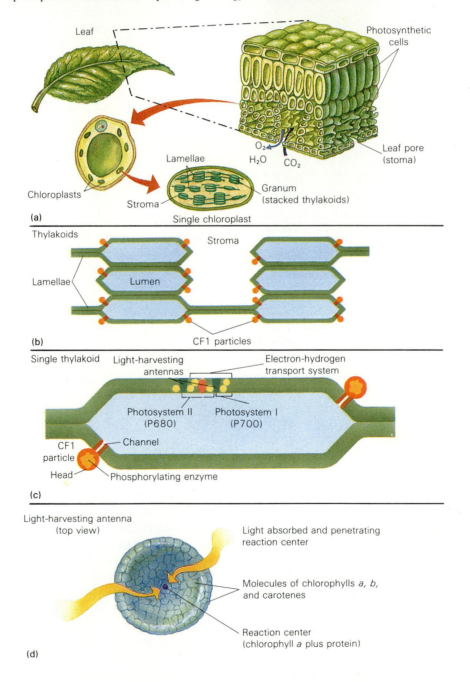

the rest of the pigment cluster only "gathers" light energy, shunting it to the reaction center, it has been aptly named the **light-harvesting antenna.**

> **P**hotosystems contain **chlorophylls a** and **b** and **carotenoids**—light-absorbing pigments organized into a **light-harvesting antenna** and a **reaction center.**

Photosystems I and II. The two photosystems within the thylakoids are designated **photosystem I** and **photosystem II.** Their reaction centers are called **P700** and **P680,** respectively; the numbers refer to slight differences in chlorophyll content that affect the wavelength of maximal light absorption. The paired photosystems are connected by elements of the P680 electron transport system. Photosystem I sometimes occurs alone.

Electron Transport Systems and Proton Pumps

In Chapter 6 we learned that electron transport systems are sequences of carriers within membranes that form pathways for the movement of energy-rich electrons. This energy powers proton pumps. Such pumps actively transport protons into the lumen, thus generating the all-important chemiosmotic gradient. The great free energy established by the isolated protons is then put to work, making ATP.

> **P**hotosystems capture light energy, using it to generate the chemiosmotic gradient, whose free energy powers ATP production in CF1 particles of chloroplasts.

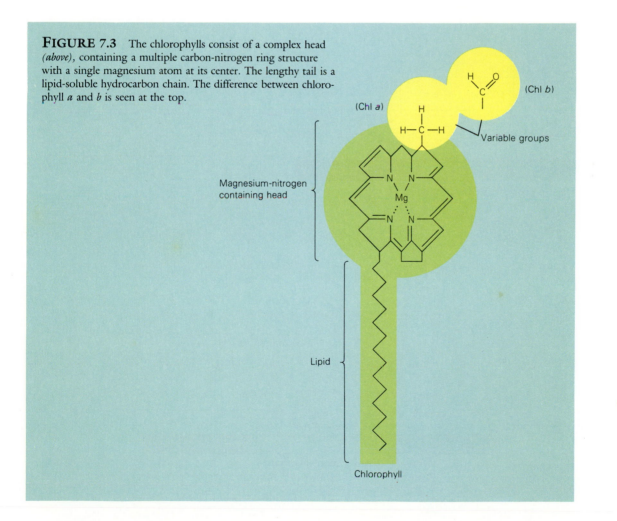

FIGURE 7.3 The chlorophylls consist of a complex head (*above*), containing a multiple carbon-nitrogen ring structure with a single magnesium atom at its center. The lengthy tail is a lipid-soluble hydrocarbon chain. The difference between chlorophyll *a* and *b* is seen at the top.

(Chl *a*)

(Chl *b*)

Variable groups

Magnesium-nitrogen containing head

Lipid

Chlorophyll

The earth is constantly bathed in radiation emanating not only from the sun, but also from a host of other celestial bodies. Part of the radiation that reaches us is **visible light.** Visible light, however, is only part of an **electromagnetic spectrum** that includes (in order of increasing energy) radio waves, microwaves, infrared radiation, visible light, ultraviolet radiation, x-rays, and gamma rays. **(a)** Visible light is visible because it interacts with special pigments (light-absorbing molecules) in our eyes. It also interacts with pigments such as chlorophyll, which are the molecules that absorb the energy of light and provide power for photosynthesis.

Light is very difficult to describe in technical terms. One reason is that it can be considered in two ways: as particles called **photons,** or as waves. Arguments have raged over these two concepts for years. So we will assert that light consists of photons that have a wavelike motion. The energy of any photon is the inverse of its wavelength, which is another way of saying that the shortest waves have the greatest energy.

Infrared light dissipates as heat. Visible light, of course, interacts with the retinas of our eyes, but it also provides the energy that enables green plants to grow. More energetic wavelengths are usually too powerful for most of life to utilize, since they tend to disrupt molecules, especially proteins and DNA. Ultraviolet light (UV), for example, burns our skin and damages the retinas of our eyes. More penetrating radiation, such as the extremely short-waved gamma rays and man-made x-rays, is called **ionizing radiation,** because it can break up the water molecules within cells.

The specific light-absorbing

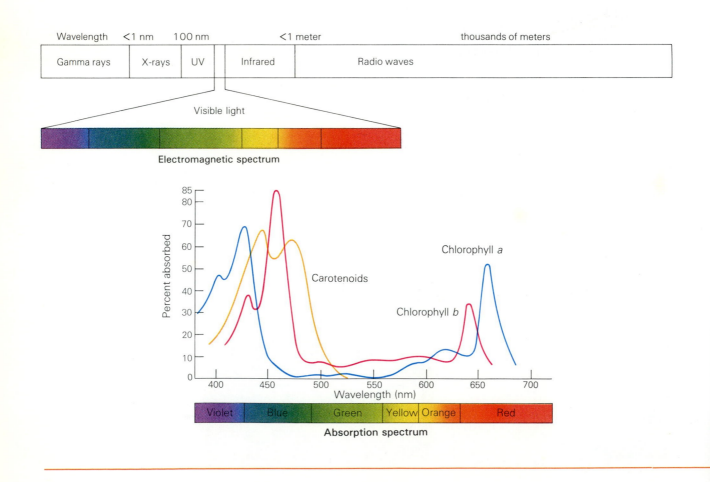

Electromagnetic spectrum

Absorption spectrum

qualities of the chlorophylls and carotenoids can be determined by using a device known as a **spectrophotometer.** First, the pigments are extracted and dissolved in a solution. Next, light of a known wavelength is passed through the solution and measured on the other side. The wavelength of the entering light can be varied to see which wavelength is most absorbed by the solution. Finally, the data are plotted on a graph to form what is called an **absorption spectrum (b).** Note the absorption spectra for chlorophylls *a* and *b* on the graph shown here. The peaks represent light that is maximally absorbed by the pigment; the valleys represent light that passes through. The green and yellow hues are least absorbed. These are the colors that are reflected—the ones that we see when we look at a chlorophyll solution or a leaf.

Certain wavelengths, such as violet-blue and orange-red, are strongly absorbed by chlorophyll. This suggests that these wavelengths participate in the light reactions, but such evidence is circumstantial. It is possible, however, to get more direct evidence. One way is to discover the rate at which some product of photosynthesis is produced when a plant is subjected to monochromatic light (light of one color only). Since photosynthesis produces oxygen, we can measure the rate of photosynthesis by measuring the rate of production of this gas under various wavelengths of light. With these data we can plot what is known as an **action spectrum (c),** which turns out to be very similar to the absorption spectrum. As a result, we can be much more confident in the proposition that the light absorbed by the pigments is the light that drives photosynthesis.

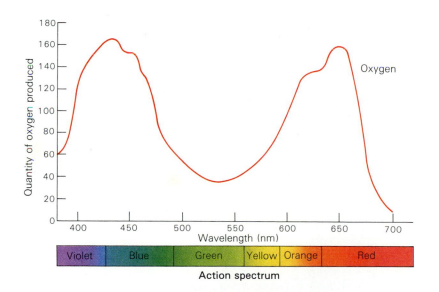

Action spectrum

THE PHOTOSYNTHETIC PROCESS

The notion of gentle sunlight falling peacefully on a green leaf belies the complex activities of photosynthesis that go on inside that leaf. Many of the mysteries of this process remain unsolved, but we do have solid information about much of it. For instance, we know that some reactions require light and that others do not. Thus the process of photosynthesis can be conveniently divided into two parts: the **light reactions** (also called the **light-dependent reactions**) and the **light-independent reactions.** We can consider the light reactions as a way to increase free energy of the system. Light-independent reactions use that free energy to form glucose (Figure 7.4).

THE LIGHT REACTIONS

The increase in free energy made available in the light reactions is used to: (1) build the chemiosmotic or proton gradient, (2) generate ATP, and (3) reduce $NADP^+$ to NADPH.

ATP can be generated in two ways, through **noncyclic photophosphorylation** and **cyclic photophosphorylation** (photo here refers to light driven). We will refer to the two simply as the "noncyclic" and "cyclic" events. The two differ in the route taken by light-activated electrons and in some of the products formed.

Noncyclic Events

The noncyclic events begin as light is absorbed in photosystem II, its energy shunted into the P680 reaction center. This starts a flow of light-activated electrons from chlorophyll a of the reaction center, which passes to the neighboring electron transport system (Figure 7.5).

Once in the electron transport system, energy-rich electrons are passed from carrier to carrier, eventually entering photosystem I. The electron's energy progressively dissipates as it moves along the chain of acceptors. Some of the energy will be used to pump protons across the membrane into the thylakoid lumen. In fact, each light-activated electron enables the proton pump to move one proton across the membrane.

Partially spent electrons from P680 then make their way into P700, which has also been actively absorbing light (see Figure 7.5). Thus the electrons receive a second boost, now reaching their highest energy level yet as they progress through the second

FIGURE 7.4 In a general sense, the light reactions charge the system, increasing its free energy state. The light-independent reactions are essentially downhill, with the decreasing free energy used to accomplish work.

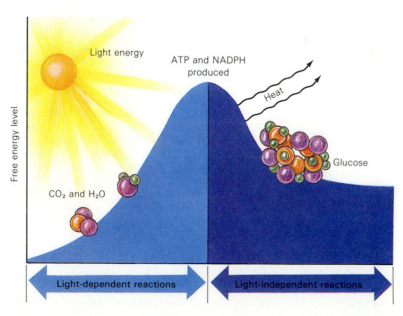

FIGURE 7.5 Building the chemiosmotic gradient: In the noncyclic light reactions, energetic, light-activated electrons begin flowing when photosystem II absorbs light. Water provides the electrons needed to reduce oxidized P680 and, in the same reactions, to donate two protons to the lumen. As electrons flow toward photosystem I, their energy is used to pump protons into the thylakoid lumen. A second boost of light energy in photosystem I provides the free energy to reduce NADP⁺ to NADPH.

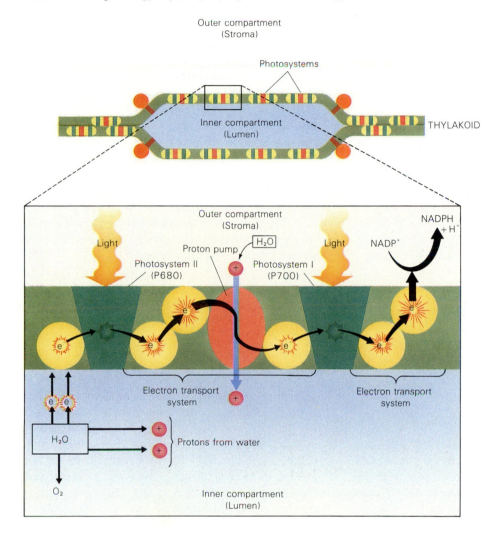

electron transport system. This time, though, as they are passed from carrier to carrier, there will be no proton pumping. Their energy is reserved for one purpose only—the reduction of NADP⁺. At the last stage, two electrons will join NADP⁺, giving it a net negative charge that immediately attracts two protons from the stroma. Thus NADP⁺ is reduced to the highly energetic NADPH.

In the **noncyclic events,** free energy of light-activated electrons from P680 is used to pump protons into the lumen and similar energy from P700 is used to reduce NADP⁺ to NADPH.

Although the electron flow actually began in the P680 reaction center, which might have left the chlorophyll *a* short on electrons, water provides a ready source of new electrons.

The splitting of water. Electrons needed to restore chlorophyll *a* are made available by the splitting of water molecules. This can be represented as:

$$H_2O \longrightarrow 2\ e^- + 2\ H^+ + 1/2\ O_2$$

$$\underset{\text{(2 Oxidized Chl }a)}{2\ Chl\ a^+ + 2e^-} \longrightarrow \underset{\text{(2 Reduced Chl }a)}{2\ Chl\ a}$$

Because two electrons are released in each event, two chlorophyll *a* molecules can be reduced. Splitting the ordinarily stable and resistant water molecule is no easy matter. It is possible only because oxidized chlorophyll *a* in P680 and P700 create a significant "pull" that sets the water-disrupting events in motion. We can look at the electron flow through the photosystems as a "pulling" force as well as a light-driven "push."

In the splitting of water, two protons are released. This is quite important because they are "dumped" directly into the thylakoid lumen, which serves to increase the chemiosmotic gradient.

The other product of the disrupted water molecule is oxygen. Two oxygen atoms join to form molecular oxygen (O_2), a critical gas of the atmosphere. If we balance the noncyclic events in terms of one disrupted water molecule, we can see that for each *two electrons* yielded by water, *four protons* enrich the chemiosmotic gradient ("two pumped and two dumped"), and one highly energetic NADPH molecule is formed. Significantly, two such events provide the earth's animal life with a molecule of oxygen.

In the noncyclic events the splitting of one water molecule yields two electrons to P680, two protons to the lumen, one atom of oxygen, and one NADH molecule.

Cyclic Events

The brief cyclic events involve only photosystem I (the P700 center)—water, photosystem II, and $NADP^+$ are not involved. The excited, light-activated electrons leave the reaction center, pass through part of the electron transport system, and then leave it to follow a special pathway back to P700 again. What does the cyclic process accomplish? As you see in Figure 7.6, each cycling electron reaches the proton pump, powering the transport of one proton into the lumen. The abrupt cyclic process helps to enrich the proton gradient, leading ultimately to the generation of ATP.

Cyclic photophosphorylation by photosystem I was an enigma to biologists for years because it seemed only to duplicate part of the noncyclic process. Most agreed that it was a primitive system, and some theorized that perhaps the cyclic reactions were a form of "photosynthetic engine-idling" that occurred when $NADP^+$ was in short supply or when NADPH simply wasn't needed. But with the development of the chemiosmosis theory, researchers began to see that such a pathway could be useful just for adding protons to the chemiosmotic differential. The idea recently gained strong support when cytologists learned that the elements of photosystem I often occur alone; they are not necessarily physically linked to those of photosystem II as had once been thought. Thus the cyclic process may be far more significant than was once believed.

In the **cyclic events,** each light-activated P700 electron enriches the chemiosmotic gradient by one proton and then cycles back to P700.

Keep in mind that we have considered only the activity in one pair of photosystems. There are many photosystems in the membrane of each thylakoid (see Figure 7.2e), and there are many, many thylakoids in each chloroplast. Consider, further, the numerous chloroplasts in each photosynthetically active leaf cell and the thousands of such cells in a single leaf. (And how many leaves are there on an oak?) Such considerations could seriously alter any idea about plants leading quiet, inactive lives. One might even gain a new, abiding respect for a plate of raw spinach.

FIGURE 7.6 In the cyclic light reactions, energetic, light-activated electrons from photosystem I flow outward from P700, provide the energy for pumping protons into the thylakoid lumen, and cycle back to P700 once again.

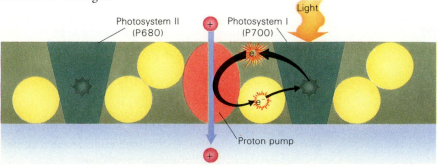

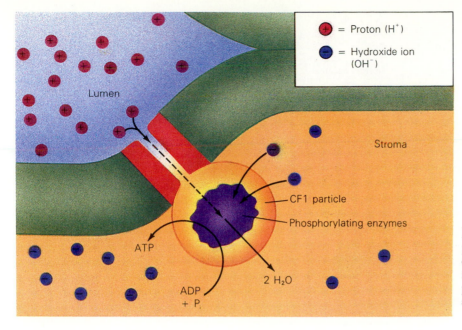

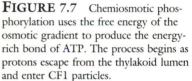

FIGURE 7.7 Chemiosmotic phosphorylation uses the free energy of the osmotic gradient to produce the energy-rich bond of ATP. The process begins as protons escape from the thylakoid lumen and enter CF1 particles.

We have considered various ways that protons can accumulate on one side of a membrane, and we are aware that this gradient serves as an energy source for making ATP. Now let's see just how this happens in the chloroplast.

Chemiosmotic Phosphorylation

The proton concentration in the thylakoid lumen may reach 10,000 times that of the stroma. The protons are joined by chloride ions (Cl^-) to form hydrochloric acid (HCl); the lumen becomes quite acidic. Outside in the stroma the presence of so many hydroxide ions (OH^-) renders this environment very basic. This system has great potential energy: An acid is on one side, a base is on the other, and they have a strong tendency to join. If the system is permitted to go to a lower free energy state—that is, if the protons are permitted to escape and join the hydroxide ions in a controlled manner—the energy of their passage can be harnessed to do work.

There is only one escape route for the sequestered protons: the channels leading into the phosphorylating sites that stud the separating membrane. In the chloroplast these are the CF1 particles, rich in phosphorylating enzymes (Figure 7.7). Energetic protons filing through CF1 particles join hydroxide ions, forming low-energy water and releasing their pent-up energy to new high-energy ATP bonds. It has been calculated that each pair of escaping protons powers the formation of one energy-rich ATP bond.

*F*ree energy of the chemiosmotic gradient is used to form ATP in CF1 particles as escaping protons join hydroxide ions, forming water.

The ATP thus formed in the light reactions, along with the NADPH formed in the noncyclic events will provide the energy and reducing power necessary for the synthesis of glucose in the light-independent reactions out in the stroma. But, before getting into that, let's summarize the main events of the light reactions:

1. Light-activated electrons from P680 pass through the electron transport system and power the transfer of protons into the thylakoid lumen.
2. The missing electrons of chlorophyll *a* of P680 are restored by electrons from the hydrogen of water. The protons of water are released in the lumen, directly increasing the chemiosmotic differential.
3. Electrons passing through photosystem I, along with protons from the stroma, reduce $NADP^+$ to NADPH.
4. Protons passing down the chemiosmotic gradient through the CF1 particles power the phosphorylation of ADP, yielding ATP.

The sequence has been traditionally diagrammed in what is called the **Z-scheme**, shown in Figure 7.8. The elevations along the scheme indicate the relative energy levels of the substances involved.

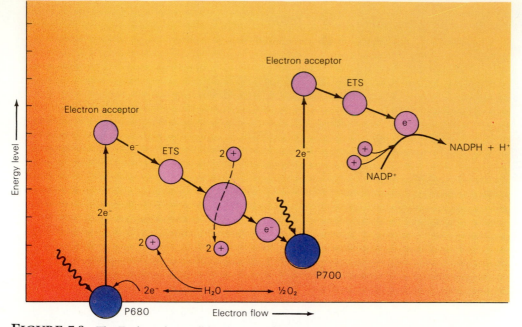

FIGURE 7.8 The Z-scheme is a traditional means of illustrating free-energy levels in the light-dependent reactions. Light-activated electrons from P680 are captured by the first electron acceptor, boosting its energy level considerably. As the electron follows an "energetically downhill" flow, protons are pumped into the thylakoid lumen. A second energy boost provided by P700 raises the free energy level of the next acceptor to the highest in the system, making the reduction of NADP⁺ possible. The numbers of electrons, protons, and NADP molecules involved are based on contributions from one water molecule.

THE LIGHT-INDEPENDENT REACTIONS

The first half of photosynthesis, the light-dependent reactions, produces energy-rich ATP and the powerful reducing agent NADPH. These molecules will provide the energy and hydrogens needed in the light-independent reactions, in which glucose and other carbohydrates are made. This phase of photosynthesis occurs in the watery stroma.

In the light-independent reactions, carbon dioxide finally becomes involved. The events can be summarized as:

$$6\ CO_2 + 12\ NADPH + 12\ H^+ + 18\ ATP + (H_2O)_n \longrightarrow C_6H_{12}O_6\ (glucose) + 12\ NADP^+ + 18\ ADP + 18\ P_i + (H_2O)_n$$

Considerable amounts of ATP and NADPH are used each time a single glucose molecule is formed. The process of incorporating carbon dioxide into glucose is aptly called **carbon dioxide fixation.** The fixing is done by the giant enzyme, **ribulose diphosphate carboxylase (RuDP carboxylase),** which is the most abundant enzyme on earth. Its ability to fix

carbon dioxide represents a vital, unique link between the physical and biological worlds.

Actually, an entire battery of enzymes is involved in glucose production, each catalyzing a specific step. Much of what we know about the process was unveiled by Nobelist Melvin Calvin. Today, the pathway is called the **Calvin cycle** (Figure 7.9). (Note that the reaction numbers in the illustration are those referred to in the text).

> The fixing of CO_2 in the formation of glucose occurs in a multistepped pathway called the **Calvin cycle.**

The Calvin Cycle

The first thing we see in Figure 7.9 is that only one carbon dioxide molecule is involved in each of the cycle's turns. As each carbon dioxide enters the cycle (reaction 1 and inset), it is joined to a five-carbon compound called **ribulose diphosphate (RuDP).** RuDP might be called a "resident molecule" because it cycles continuously.

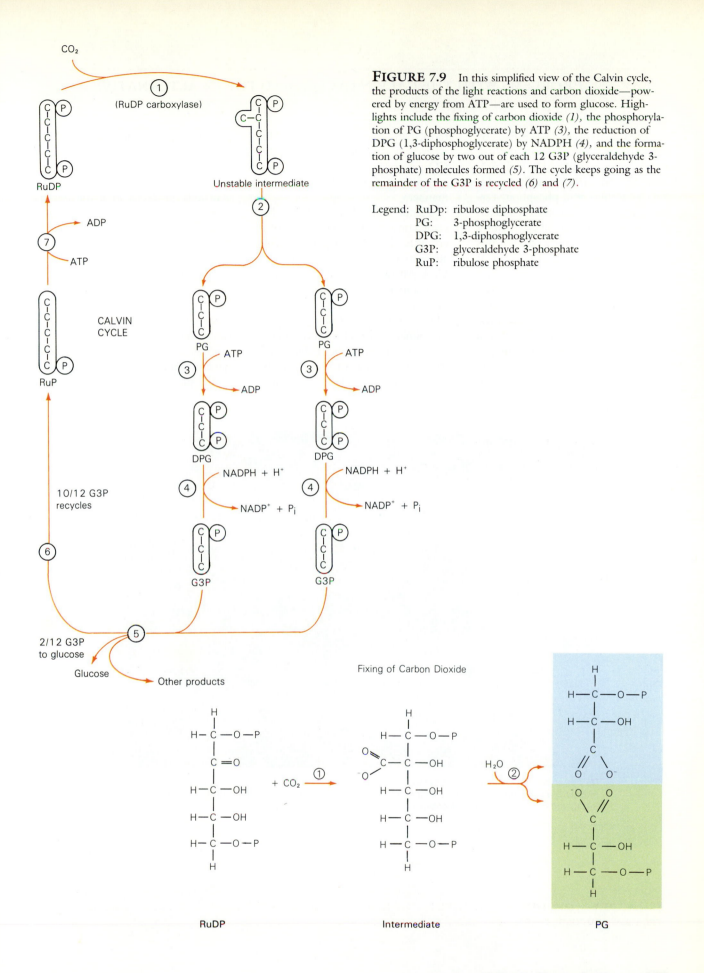

FIGURE 7.9 In this simplified view of the Calvin cycle, the products of the light reactions and carbon dioxide—powered by energy from ATP—are used to form glucose. Highlights include the fixing of carbon dioxide (1), the phosphorylation of PG (phosphoglycerate) by ATP (3), the reduction of DPG (1,3-diphosphoglycerate) by NADPH (4), and the formation of glucose by two out of each 12 G3P (glyceraldehyde 3-phosphate) molecules formed (5). The cycle keeps going as the remainder of the G3P is recycled (6) and (7).

Legend: RuDp: ribulose diphosphate
PG: 3-phosphoglycerate
DPG: 1,3-diphosphoglycerate
G3P: glyceraldehyde 3-phosphate
RuP: ribulose phosphate

In the Calvin cycle, CO_2 is fixed by the giant enzyme, ribulose diphosphate carboxylase (RuDP-carboxylase). The six-carbon product yields two molecules of 3-phosphoglycerate (3PG), a three-carbon product. All plants use the Calvin cycle. But it was discovered in the mid-1960s that some plants first fix CO_2 in an alternative pathway.

Australian researchers M.D. Hatch and C.R. Slack determined that in some plants CO_2 enters the **leaf mesophyll cells** and first joins a substance called **phosphoenol pyruvate (PEP)** to form a four-carbon intermediate. The four-carbon intermediate passes into other cells, where it is acted on by enzymes, and CO_2 is released. The CO_2 then enters the Calvin cycle in the usual manner.

Plants with this capability became known as **C4 plants** (the others were dubbed **C3 plants**). This alternative pathway, the Hatch-Slack pathway, occurs in over 100 genera including Bermuda and crab grasses, corn, and sugar cane **(a).** These plants are well adapted to hot, dry climates where they thrive in the intensely bright sunlight that tends to stunt the growth of C3 plants. Why should this be? Our first clue is

climate, but what does it have to do with the alternative pathway?

The answer lies in the peculiar conditions that arise when photosynthesis proceeds at a maximum rate, perhaps too fast. Intensely lighted conditions trigger a form of biochemical stress known as **photorespiration.** During this process, the CO_2-incorporating enzyme, ribulose diphosphate carboxylase, loses its affinity for CO_2 and starts incorporating O_2 instead. The reactions that follow deplete precious reserves of ATP and NADPH and have no known value to the plant.

C3 plants can survive this trau-

(a) Sugar cane, a C4 plant that thrives in brilliant tropical light, is more efficient at capturing light energy than any other terrestrial plant studied. Sugar cane captures 8% of all photon energy reaching its leaves. The worldwide average is well below 1%.

ma, but if it continues, their metabolism and growth substantially slow. By contrast, photorespiration is virtually absent in C4 plants. C4 plants incorporate CO_2 through the action of an enzyme called **PEP-carboxylase,** which converts phosphoenol pyruvate to four-carbon oxaloacetate. PEP-carboxylase has a much higher affinity for CO_2 than does RuDP-carboxylase, and will bind to it even at very low concentrations. Thus, in spite of its limited quantity, carbon dioxide is rapidly taken up as it enters the leaf, and a steep, inward diffusion gradient is thus established with the surrounding air. C4 plants therefore are much better than C3 plants at capturing carbon dioxide.

The by-product, pyruvate, a three-carbon acid, then recycles to the mesophyll cells. Through this cycle, the plant manages to concentrate CO_2 in the vicinity of the sluggish giant, RuDP-carboxylase, and the Calvin cycle goes on full speed in spite of the climatic conditions.

Whereas C3 plants struggle to grow under the intense illumination of the hot deserts and tropics, C4 plants take advantage of the endless supply of sunlight to grow at a maximum rate. In hot climates Bermuda grass has an advantage as it encroaches on your lawn, threatening to strangle your expensive C3 greenery.

As we see in **(b),** PEP does its magic in the leaf mesophyll cells where its successor, oxaloacetate, is converted to four-carbon **malate.** Malate enters the **bundle sheath cells,** a tissue surrounding the leaf veins. There, at the expense of NADPH, the reactions are reversed, and carbon dioxide is released for uptake into the regular Calvin cycle.

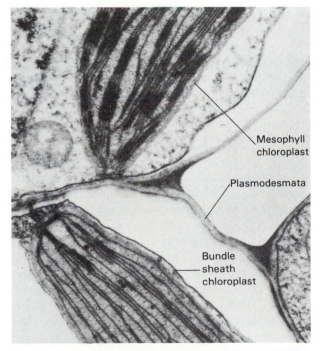

(b) Electron micrograph of green maize chloroplasts. There is a startling difference between C4 bundle-sheath chloroplasts and those of ordinary mesophyll cells. The mesophyll chloroplast *(above)* contains the densely stacked thylakoids that make up the grana. The larger bundle-sheath chloroplast *(below)* lacks grana but maintains the lamellae. The region between is principally the cell wall between the mesophyll and bundle-sheath wall. Tubular plasmodesmata *(upper right)* penetrate the cell wall.

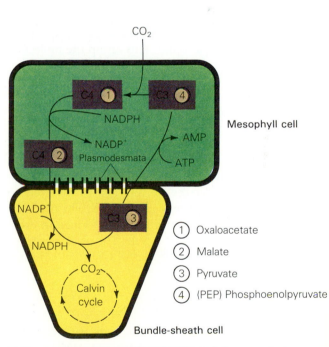

(c) The purpose of this special C4 pathway is to concentrate carbon dioxide in the vicinity of the carboxylating enzyme of the Calvin cycle. This makes it possible for plants to incorporate carbon dioxide rapidly, improving their photosynthetic efficiency.

As carbon dioxide is added to RuDP, the newly forming product (which has never been clearly identified) cleaves simultaneously into two three-carbon molecules of **phosphoglyceric acid** or, more properly, **phosphoglycerate* (PG)** (reaction 2). In reaction 3 the energy of ATP comes into play as two ATP molecules react with the two PG molecules, phosphorylating them to yield two molecules of **1, 3-diphosphoglycerate (DPG)** and two of ADP. Next, two NADPH molecules reduce DPG (reaction 4), forming two molecules of **glyceraldehyde 3-phosphate (G3P; also called phosphoglyceraldehyde or PGAL)** and two of NADP$^+$:

$$2 \text{ DPG} + 2 \text{ NADPH} + \text{H}^+ \longrightarrow$$
$$2 \text{ G3P} + 2 \text{ NADP}^+ + 2 \text{ P}_i$$

> Once CO_2 is fixed, ATP phosphorylates the substrate, NADPH reduces it, and two G3P molecules emerge. G3P can be used to form glucose and other products.

We now see the reason for the previous phosphorylation by ATP. Adding high-energy phosphate to PG created a reactive site. This set up the molecules for the addition of hydrogen, a major step in creating glucose.

Two fates of G3P. With the emergence of G3P, we come to an important branch in the Calvin cycle, one in which the reactions can go in either of two directions. In one case, two molecules of G3P are used to generate one molecule of glucose. In the other, the G3P molecules are returned to the cycle so that more carbon dioxide can be fixed. The two G3P molecules that produce glucose are formed in every sixth complete turn of the cycle. The other five turns simply produce ten molecules of G3P that continue cycling. Thus:

$$12 \text{ G3P (6 turns)} \longrightarrow C_6H_{12}O_6 \text{ (glucose)} +$$
$$10 \text{ G3P back to the cycle}$$

The 10 G3P molecules (five pairs) that continue in the cycle undergo a conversion (reaction 6) to form six five-carbon **ribulose phosphate** (RP) molecules. Next, six more molecules of ATP from the light reactions are invested to change the six RP molecules to six molecules of ribulose diphosphate

(RuDP), our resident molecule (reaction 7). This final reaction permits the cycle to repeat. We can now restate and review the Calvin cycle as:

$$6 \text{ RuDP} + 6 \text{ CO}_2 + 12 \text{ NADPH} + 12 \text{ H}^+ + 18 \text{ ATP} +$$
$$(\text{H}_2\text{O})_n \longrightarrow 6 \text{ RuDP} + C_6H_{12}O_6 \text{ (glucose)} +$$
$$12 \text{ NADP}^+ + 18 \text{ ADP} + 18 \text{ P}_i + (\text{H}_2\text{O})_n$$

> Each yield of glucose requires six turns of the Calvin cycle since the products from five turns are required to keep the cycle going.

This is an interesting cyclic process whereby a renewal of the starting reactant (RuDP) and a yield of glucose are produced with each six turns. The spent ADP and P_i, and the NADP$^+$ (depleted of its reducing power), recycle into the thylakoid where they will again be available for the light-dependent reactions. After their energetic capabilities are restored, both will once again enter the stroma to power the Calvin cycle.

What Does a Plant Do with Its Glucose?

Photosynthesis is a precisely orchestrated sequence of remarkable complexity. Yet it occurs with dazzling speed in the chloroplasts of countless cells. This efficiency results in a great deal of glucose production. What happens to it?

Plants, like animals and most other organisms, use glucose as an energy source; glucose is broken down to elaborate metabolic pathways, and its chemical bond energy is then used to form more ATP (see Chapter 8). But glucose is also important structurally.

In the growing plant, a great deal of glucose is incorporated into cellulose in newly emerging cell walls. Much glucose is stored, as plant cells link the glucose units to form starches. The potato plant, for instance, stores excess starch in swollen underground tubers. Most fruits are sweet because they are laden with sugars. Sugar beets and sugar cane store sucrose, which we use as table sugar, in roots and stems, respectively. Humans are highly dependent on the ability of plants to make and store carbohydrates, one of our primary food sources.

Plants also make other sorts of molecules from the products of the Calvin cycle. For example, G3P is used by most seed plants to fashion a number of lipids and amino acids. Phospholipids are vital to the construction of cell membranes, and triglycerides are stored in great quantities as oils in seeds and grains.

---

*The term "phosphoglyceric acid" refers to the balanced molecule, "phosphoglycerate" refers to the ionized form. Since the ionized form is more common, we will generally use the "-ate" ending when referring to organic acids.

Amino acids are joined to make proteins or are further modified in the formation of nitrogen bases in DNA, RNA, ATP, and coenzymes.

Plants use Calvin cycle products for energy and in the synthesis of cellulose, starches, sugars, lipids, amino acids, and nitrogen bases.

HAVE YOU THANKED A PLANT TODAY?

Nearly all life on this planet depends on capturing the energy radiating from its nearest star. Energy is essential to living things because there is a strong tendency for increases in entropy. Life is highly organized and needs energy to maintain that level of organization.

Deep in the ocean floor there are organisms that derive all of their energy from sulfurous compounds emitted from volcanic vents. Perhaps on other worlds the energy to sustain life comes from different sources, such as heat emanating from the planet's core. But for the majority of life, energy comes from our sun and can be captured only by organisms that are often rudely or cavalierly treated by other species. If plants did not turn solar energy into food, this would be a far, far different place.

Let's add one more parting thought. Photosynthesis is an energetically costly process. Its molecular reactants, water and carbon dioxide, are in a low free-energy state—that is, they are stable—and are quite reluctant to participate in any chemical events. Fortunately for life as we know it, sunlight is plentiful and evolution has provided some organisms with the ability to use it. With this enormous and seemingly inexhaustible energy source, photosynthesizers can power their elaborate biochemical machinery without much concern for fuel economy. In our own energy-hungry world, we have much to learn from plants.

SUMMARY

In photosynthesis, photons of sunlight energy absorbed by chlorophyll generate a flow of energy-rich electrons. They in turn provide the energy needed to establish chemiosmotic systems that generate ATP and to reduce $NADP^+$ to NADPH. Both are subsequently used in forming glucose from carbon dioxide and water.

A simplifed formula for the overall process is:

$$\text{water} + \text{carbon dioxide} \xrightarrow[\text{chlorophyll}]{\text{light}} \text{glucose} + \text{water} + \text{oxygen}$$

THE CHLOROPLAST

The chloroplast provides the required structural organization for photosynthesis. Within is the watery stroma (outer compartment) containing the enzymes for glucose synthesis. Included are numerous grana consisting of light-capturing thylakoids, each enclosing a minute lumen (inner compartment). Thylakoid membranes contain photosystems, electron transport systems, and proton pumps, all used in establishing the chemisomotic gradient and reducing $NADP^+$.

Photosystems

Photosystems I and II contain chlorophylls and carotenoids that act as light-harvesting antennas. They shunt energy into reaction centers designated P700 and P680. Reaction centers release energy-rich electrons.

Electron Transport Systems and Proton Pumps

Light-activated electrons from reaction centers enter electron transport systems where their energy is used to pump protons into the thylakoid lumen.

THE PHOTOSYNTHETIC PROCESS

Light is captured in the light reactions, while glucose is synthesized in the light-independent reactions.

THE LIGHT-DEPENDENT REACTIONS

Light energy provides for building the chemiosmotic gradient, the synthesis of ATP and the reduction of $NADP^+$ to NADPH. The light reactions occur through noncyclic and cyclic events. The use of light energy in forming ATP is called photophosphorylation.

Noncyclic events. Light absorbed in photosystem II produces a flow of electrons into the electron transport system. As they pass to photosystem I, their energy is used for pumping protons into the lumen. Light absorbed in photosystem I provides a new energy boost to electrons, which then pass through a second electron transport system, to $NADP^+$, reducing it to NADPH.

The electrons lost from the P680 reaction center are replaced by those from water, which is split, yielding electrons, protons, and oxygen. The oxygen escapes as O_2, while the protons add directly to the chemiosmotic gradient.

Cyclic events. Light absorbed in photosystem I produces a flow of electrons from P700 that reach the proton pump where their energy is used to transport protons into the lumen. The depleted electrons return to photosystem I. Water and $NADP^+$ are not involved.

Chemiosmotic Phosphorylation

As the chemiosmotic gradient builds, the lumen of each thylakoid becomes acidic and the stroma becomes basic. Protons escape from the lumen through the CF1 particles where their energy is used to form new high-energy bonds between ADP and P_i. The protons join hydroxide groups in the stroma, forming water.

THE LIGHT-INDEPENDENT REACTIONS

With the aid of ATP and NADPH, carbon dioxide entering the stroma is fixed into glucose.

The Calvin Cycle

In the major steps of the Calvin cycle, (a) carbon dioxide combines with ribulose diphosphate, which (b) breaks down to two three-carbon phosphoglycerates (PG). (c) The two PG molecules are joined by ATP forming two molecules of three-carbon 1,3-diphosphoglycerate, which (d) are reduced by NADPH, forming two three-carbon glyceraldehyde-3-phosphate (G3P) molecules.

For every 12 molecules of G3P formed in the Calvin cycle, two are available to form glucose. The remainder recycle, forming ribulose phosphate, which is joined by ATP to form ribulose diphosphate, the starting molecule. ADP, $NADP^+$, and P_i recycle to the light reactions.

WHAT DOES A PLANT DO WITH ITS GLUCOSE?

Uses of glucose include fuel for ATP production and incorporation into cellulose, sugars, and starches. G3P can be converted to amino acids, fatty acids, and nitrogen bases.

HAVE YOU THANKED A PLANT TODAY?

Nearly all life on earth depends on chemical bond energy initially captured by photosynthesizers. Although photosynthesis is energy costly, organisms make common use of the process because sunlight energy is seemingly limitless.

KEY TERMS

photosynthesis
autotroph
photon
chlorophyll
stroma
grana
thylakoid
lumen
lamellae
photosystems
electron transport system
proton pump

chlorophyll *a*
chlorophyll *b*
carotenoid
reaction center
light-harvesting antenna
photosystem I (P700)
photosystem II (P680)
light-dependent reactions
light-independent reactions
noncyclic photophosphorylation
cyclic photophosphorylation

noncyclic events
cyclic events
Z-scheme
carbon dioxide fixation
ribulose diphosphate carboxylase (RuDP carboxylase)
Calvin cycle
phosphoglycerate (PG)
1, 3 diphosphoglycerate (DPG)
glyceraldehyde 3-phosphate (G3P)
phosphoglyceraldehyde (PGAL)
ribulose phosphate

REVIEW QUESTIONS

1 Electricity is often described as a flow of electrons. How is photosynthesis similar? (p. 95)
2 Write a balanced general formula for photosynthesis. Comment on the fate of carbon, hydrogen, and oxygen atoms in each of the reactants. (pp. 96–97)
3 Prepare a simplified illustration of a chloroplast, labelling the following structures and areas: surrounding membrane, stroma, granum, thylakoid, lamellae, lumen. (pp. 97–98)
4 Prepare an illustration of one thylakoid, showing the organization of photosystems I and II, the two electron transport systems, and the proton pump. (pp. 97–98)
5 Explain how the stroma and lumen relate to the sac-within-a-sac analogy of a chemiosmotic system (see Chapter 6). (pp. 97–98)

6 What are the functions of each of the following: chlorophylls and carotenoids, reaction center, electron transport system, proton pump? (pp. 97–99)
7 Summarize the main purposes of the light-dependent reactions. (p. 102)
8 Using your illustration of a thylakoid, add the noncyclic flow of electrons beginning with P680. What two things does this flow accomplish? (pp. 102–104)
9 Explain the role of water in restoring chlorophyll *a* of P680. In what way does the breakdown of each water molecule help increase the free energy of the chemiosmotic gradient? (pp. 103–104)
10 Trace the flow of electrons in the cyclic events of the light reactions. What, precisely, is accomplished by a cyclic flow? (p. 104)

11 The chemiosmotic gradient in a chloroplast is often referred to as a proton gradient, a pH gradient, and an electrical gradient. How can it be all three? (p. 105)

12 Explain how the free energy of the chemiosmotic gradient is put to work forming ATP. A diagram might help. (p. 105)

13 List the three reactants that gather in the stroma for the light-independent reactions. (p. 106)

14 Why is the enzyme RuDP carboxylase thought of as the most abundant enzyme on earth? (p. 106)

15 Explain how carbon dioxide enters the Calvin cycle. What does it join, and what happens immediately afterward? (pp. 106–108)

16 What are the precise roles of ATP and NADPH in the Calvin cycle? What happens to their spent forms, ADP and NADP$^+$? (pp. 107–110)

17 What are the two fates of G3P? What fraction of their number goes to each? (p. 110)

18 From a close look at Figure 7.9, account for the 12 molecules of NADPH and the 18 molecules of ATP required for the net yield of just one molecule of glucose. (p. 107)

19 List five ways in which G3P and glucose are used by the plant. (pp. 110–111)

8

GLYCOLYSIS AND RESPIRATION

As this small planet makes its rounds through space, it is constantly bathed in light from its nearest star. This light literally brings its life-giving energy to earth. This energy maintains organisms' precise and delicately balanced organization despite universal tendencies toward disarray. Living things capture this light energy and store it in the chemical bonds of newly formed molecules such as glucose. This, however, is only half of problem that confronts each living organism. Once the energy is stored, there must be ways of getting it back, releasing it, making it available for life's business. Living things have developed complex and precisely controlled means of releasing this stored energy. Power-laden molecules are handled in elaborate ways, as their energy is gradually drained to support the many processes of life.

Organisms such as plants that can harness the elusive power of sunlight and store it in new chemical bonds are called **photosynthetic autotrophs** (self-feeders). Other kinds of organisms, such as humans, that must rely on the stored energy of autotrophs are called **heterotrophs** (other-feeders). All animals, many protists, all fungi, and a large proportion of bacteria are heterotrophic; they cannot extract energy from light.

Photosynthetic autotrophs use sunlight as a source of energy. **Heterotrophs** obtain their energy from organic substances.

This chapter describes the way cells break down glucose and other cellular fuels, using the potential energy of their chemical bonds to convert ADP to ATP. Glucose metabolism in most organisms involves two major processes, **glycolysis** and **cellular respiration.** (Don't confuse cellular respiration with breathing or gas exchange. Cellular respiration occurs *within* cells.)

Glycolysis, the lysis, or destruction, of glucose, occurs in the fluids of the cytoplasm and is an **anaerobic** process; it *does not require oxygen.* Glycolysis is a prerequisite for cellular respiration. Cellular respiration occurs within the mitochondrion; it *requires oxygen;* thus cell respiration is **aerobic.**

Glycolysis is an **anaerobic** process, not requiring oxygen, whereas **cellular respiration** is an **aerobic,** or oxygen-requiring, process.

You may have heard the old cliche that food is the fuel "burned" by the body. It's a catchy idea but any such one-step process would be disastrous. Cells must use very gradual, multistepped, enzymatically controlled energy transfers for two closely related reasons. First, such transfers must be tightly controlled to avoid unwarranted energy losses. Second, living things hold a great deal of energy within their bodies, and that energy must be released in a stepwise fashion to avoid production of excessive heat. (Were the energy in your body to be released all at once you would be incinerated.)

GLYCOLYSIS

Glycolysis, as we've seen, refers to the destruction of glucose. Let's see just how much destruction really goes on. Upon entering the **glycolytic pathway,** glucose receives an energy boost—two ATP molecules are invested just to get the stable molecule ready to react. Glucose is then broken apart and altered by at least six additional enzymes. Through them it is *phosphorylated, cleaved, oxidized, dephosphorylated,* and *dehydrated.* Note in Figure 8.1 that the most productive reactions of glycolysis are reactions 5 and 8, oxidation and dehydration.

In the oxidation step, hydrogen is transferred to NAD^+, reducing it to NADH (actually NADH + H^+, but we will use the shorter version; see Chapter 6). Reduced coenzymes, you'll recall, have greatly increased energy levels and can perform useful work. Even more significantly, reactions 5 and 8 lead directly to **substrate level phosphorylations,** reactions in which ADP gains a high-energy phosphate directly from the substrate molecule (reactions 6 and 9 and the inset).

Finally, two molecules of a three-carbon acid called **pyruvic acid** (or **pyruvate***, the ionized form) emerge from the glycolytic pathway. These are high-energy molecules, containing most of the free energy originally in the glucose. In fact, they will be used to make as many as 36 ATP molecules in the aerobic phase.

F or each glucose molecule reacting in the **glycolytic pathway,** a net gain of two ATP molecules is made, along with the formation of two NADH molecules and two of **pyruvate.**

---

*Pyruvate is the ionized form of the charge-balanced molecule, pyruvic acid. As mentioned in Chapter 7, we will use the *-ate* ending for organic acids since they are usually ionized in cells.

Note that the glycolytic pathway does not yield much energy (in the form of ATP molecules). Nonetheless, glycolysis is the sole source of energy for many of the earth's anaerobic heterotrophs. Such anaerobes commonly live in airless habitats such as swamps, mucky lake bottoms, wine and beer vats, and even the bowels of animals. Furthermore, in certain circumstances, anaerobic glycolysis is a principal energy-yielding process in vertebrates, including ourselves. Perhaps one reason such an inefficient process is so widespread is because it is so old, having established itself in the early forms of life. Indeed, it is considered to be far more ancient than cellular respiration, perhaps even the earliest metabolic pathway to evolve.

The process of glycolysis can be summarized as:

$$\text{Glucose} + 2\ NAD^+ + 2\ ATP + 2\ P_i + 2\ ADP \longrightarrow$$
$$2\ \text{pyruvate} + 2\ NADH + 2\ H^+ + 4\ ATP$$

You may have noticed that parts of the glycolytic pathway are essentially a reversal of certain parts of the Calvin cycle (see Figure 7.9), in which glucose was the final product, ATP was consumed, and NADPH was oxidized. This "reversed" metabolic pathway is just one of several interesting contrasts between photosynthesis and glucose metabolism.

The pyruvate formed in glycolysis can take any of a number of metabolic pathways, depending on the organism. Although pyruvate is the product of many reactions and alterations, it still has most of the potential energy of glucose, and energy-rich compounds are not to be ignored. Let's first see what happens to pyruvate in aerobic organisms and then look at two common pathways in anaerobes.

CELLULAR RESPIRATION

Following glycolysis in aerobic organisms, the scene shifts from the open cytoplasm to the mazelike interior of the mitochondrion. There, pyruvate and NADH enter the complex processes of cellular respiration wherein most of the cell's ATP is produced. The mitochondrion is a sausagelike organelle with an inner and outer membrane, an arrangement that produces an outer compartment and an inner compartment (a "sac-within-a-sac" organization) (see Figure 4.13). The inner membrane is highly folded into cristae, which greatly increases its surface area. Adequate surface area is quite important since the inner membrane contains numerous electron transport systems (ETS) and proton pumps. In addition, the inner membrane is studded with numerous **F1 particles** containing the vital ATP-forming enzymes.

FIGURE 8.1 (a) In the first three reactions of glycolysis the free energy of glucose is increased at the expense of two ATPs. In reaction 4 the doubly phosphorylated six-carbon product is split into 2 three-carbon fuel molecules. (b) Reaction 5 includes an oxidation (NAD$^+$ is reduced to NADH) and another phosphorylation, destabilizing the three-carbon fuel in preparation for the important event to follow. Then in reaction 6 the first substrate level phosphorylation occurs and two ATPs are gained *(inset)*. (c) The dehydration event in reaction 8 further destabilizes the fuel. Finally, in reaction 9 another substrate level phosphorylation occurs and two more ATPs form *(inset)*.

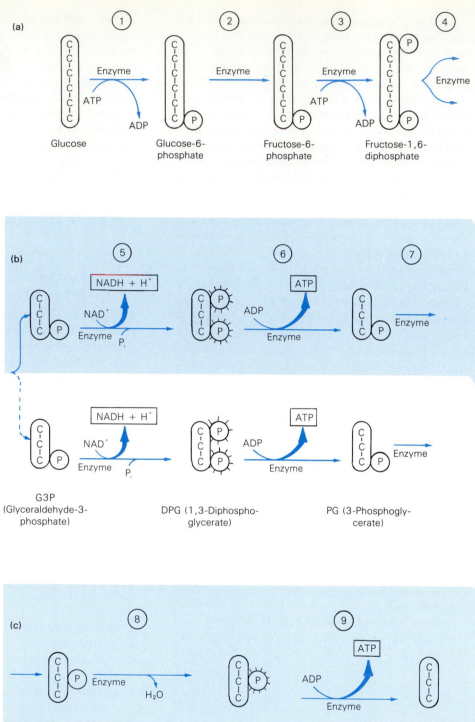

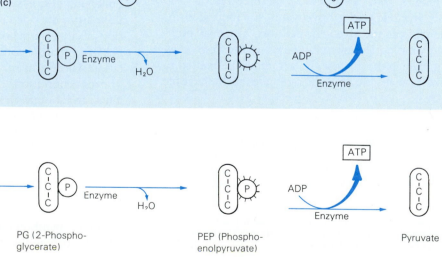

It is apparent that structure and function are quite interdependent in the mitochondrion, just as they are in the chloroplast. (For a preview of mitochondrial organization, see Figure 8.4.)

There are three stages in cellular respiration: the **citric acid cycle, electron transport,** and **chemiosmotic phosphorylation** (Figure 8.2). Cell respiration begins in the mitochondrial inner compartment, the matrix, where energy-rich pyruvate is prepared for the oxidizing reactions of the citric acid cycle.

Citric Acid Cycle

The citric acid cycle was first described in 1937 by the late Oxford biochemist, Sir Hans Krebs. (Hence, it is often called the Krebs cycle.) The pathway begins and ends with a four-carbon acid called **oxaloacetate** (Figure 8.3). So why isn't it called the "oxaloacetic acid cycle?" Aside from the verbal trauma this might generate, Krebs noted that the first new substance formed by the cycle happens to be citrate (the familiar *citric acid* of oranges and lemons). Let's

follow one molecule of pyruvate through the cycle, bearing in mind for bookkeeping purposes that two pyruvate molecules were generated from each molecule of glucose that originally entered glycolysis.

Acetyl-CoA gets the cycle going. Pyruvate readily enters the mitochondrion, but it must be altered before it can enter the citric acid cycle. This alteration includes oxidization and decarboxylation. In other words, it must lose hydrogen and carbon dioxide. The two-carbon fragment that is left (called an acetyl group) then joins a coenzyme called **coenzyme A,** forming a combination called **acetyl-CoA** (see Figure 8.3). The hydrogen that is lost is not wasted; it joins NAD^+ to form energetic NADH.

In the mitochondrion, each pyruvate molecule is converted to **acetyl-CoA** that enters the **citric acid cycle.** One molecule of CO_2 is released and one of NADH forms.

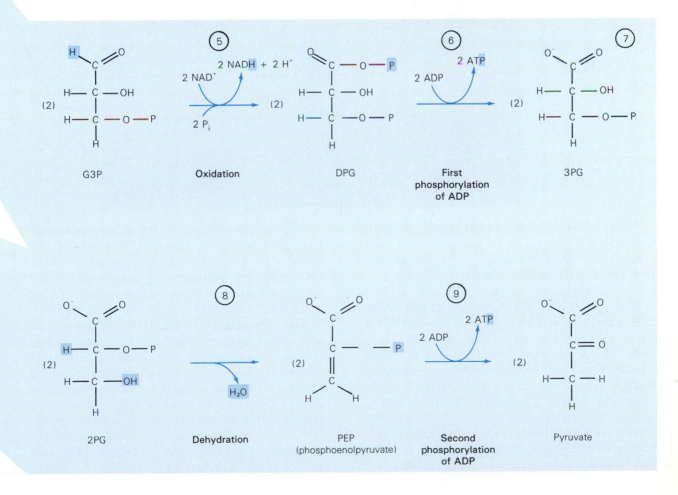

FIGURE 8.2 The major parts of glucose metabolism. Most ATP production in aerobic cells occurs through chemiosmosis.

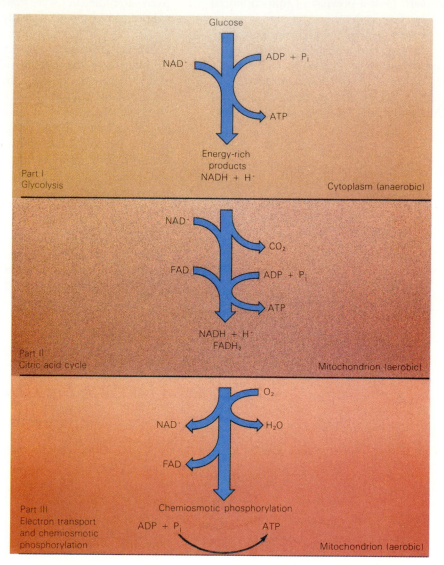

Part I
Glycolysis

Glucose

NAD^+
$ADP + P_i$
ATP

Energy-rich products
$NADH + H^+$

Cytoplasm (anaerobic)

Part II
Citric acid cycle

NAD^+
CO_2
FAD
$ADP + P_i$
ATP

$NADH + H^+$
$FADH_2$

Mitochondrion (aerobic)

Part III
Electron transport and chemiosmotic phosphorylation

O_2
NAD^+
H_2O
FAD

Chemiosmotic phosphorylation
$ADP + P_i$
ATP

Mitochondrion (aerobic)

Now, fully prepared, acetyl-CoA joins oxaloacetate to form six-carbon citrate, whereupon the coenzyme A is released to recycle. (For a look at other fuels entering the citric acid cycle, see Essay 8.1.)

Energy transfers and the release of CO_2. Details of the citric acid cycle are shown in Figure 8.3, but let's make a few important observations. First, each of the 10 major reactions is facilitated by its own specific enzyme. More importantly, energy transfers occur during certain crucial steps. Most are oxidations where NAD^+ is reduced to NADH or FAD is reduced to $FADH_2$ (reactions 4, 6, 8, and 10). Armed with their newly acquired reducing power, both coenzymes will deliver energy-rich electrons and protons to nearby electron transport systems.

Second, with each turn of the cycle one substrate level phosphorylation (reaction 7) generates one molecule of ATP. (Actually, another triphosphate, **GTP [guanine triphosphate]** is generated in the cycle, but it transfers its terminal phosphate to ADP in a second reaction.)

Finally, note where carbon dioxide leaves the citric acid cycle (reactions 5 and 6). This is the carbon dioxide all aerobic cells release during respiration and, incidentally, the same carbon dioxide we are exhaling right now. After the release of two molecules of CO_2, only four-carbon fuels remain. In the final step, four-carbon oxaloacetate is regenerated.

Summing up the citric acid cycle. For each pair of pyruvate molecules completing the acetyl-

FIGURE 8.3 The citric acid cycle involves 10 major reactions, each with its own specific enzyme. In the initial step, four-carbon oxaloacetate joins two-carbon acetyl-CoA to produce 6-carbon citrate. As the cycle turns, two decarboxylations *(reactions 5 and 6)* occur, yielding two carbon dioxides and a 4-carbon product. Four critical oxidation steps *(reactions 4, 6, 8 and 10)* reduce NAD^+ to NADH or FAD to $FADH_2$, the most important products of the cycle (see *inset on reaction 10*). In *reaction 7*, a substrate-level phophorylation occurs, eventually yielding one molecule of ATP. Note the use of guanosine diphosphate (GDP) and guanosine triphosphate (GTP) as intermediates. Finally, in *reaction 10*, oxaloacetate (the only permanent acid in the cycle) emerges, ready to begin again.

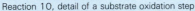

Reaction 10, detail of a substrate oxidation step

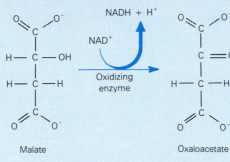

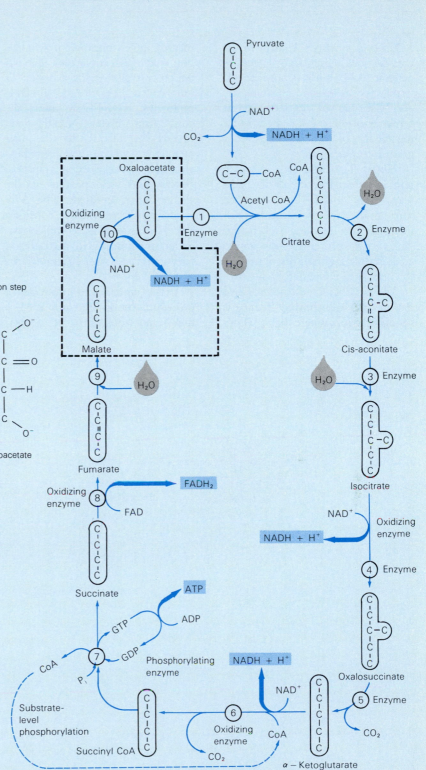

Glucose furnishes much of the energy that living things need to generate ATP, but it is not the only usable fuel. Fats and proteins are also important sources of energy. As a matter of record, fats yield twice the energy of carbohydrates, on a gram-for-gram basis.

However, before fats and proteins can enter the respiratory pathway, they must be simplified through the digestive process. During digestion, fats are broken into fatty acids; proteins, into amino acids. These are then distributed to the cells by the circulatory system.

The fatty acids destined for oxidation are transported into the mitochondrion, where they are frag-mented into a number of two-carbon acetyl-CoA molecules. The latter process also yields a bonus—a number of NADH and $FADH_2$ molecules. Acetyl-CoA enters the citric acid cycle; NADH and $FADH_2$ go directly to the inner membrane, where they contribute electrons to the electron transport systems and yield protons to the chemiosmotic gradient. The ATP yield from fatty acids is considerable. For instance, the complete oxidation of palmitic acid, a 16-carbon fatty acid, yields over 130 molecules of ATP.

If the amino acid products of protein digestion are to be used as fuels, they must first be **deami-nated**—(their amino groups removed). Since the amino groups form ammonia, they must be rapidly eliminated or rendered harmless through additional reactions (see Chapter 36). The useful modification product from the 20 amino acids may differ, with some occurring as pyruvate, others as acetyl-CoA, and still others as the four-carbon acids of the citric acid cycle (diagram).

How much ATP can be derived from amino acid fuels depends on where, after modification, they enter the cycle. The greatest yields of NADH (and $FADH_2$) and ATP, as you might expect, come from those amino acids that are converted to pyruvate.

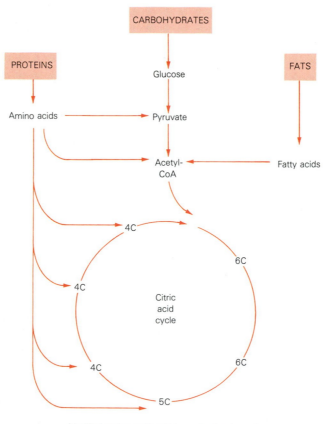

Modified amino acids add to cycle at various places

CoA step and passing through the citric acid cycle, there is a total yield of two molecules of ATP, eight of NADH, and two of $FADH_2$. To obtain a total yield from glucose so far, we add the two molecules of ATP and two of NADH from glycolysis. The total yield so far is four molecules of ATP, 10 of NADH, and two of $FADH_2$. Cytoplasmic NADH cannot enter the mitochondrion because the outer membrane is impermeable to NADH. Instead, its electrons and protons are shuttled in by carriers that reduce mitochondrial NAD^+. The cytoplasmic NAD^+ is left free to recycle, thus keeping glycolysis going. But what about the yield of ATP? Four molecules of ATP seems meager, but that is about to change.

In the citric acid cycle two pyruvate molecules yield eight molecules of NADH, two of $FADH_2$, two of ATP (via GTP), and three of CO_2.

The Electron Transport Systems and Proton Pumping

Once NAD^+ and FAD have been reduced in the citric acid cycle, the final events of cellular respiration can begin. The NADH now crosses the matrix and reduces the first carriers of the electron transport system (Figure 8.4). $FADH_2$ has less reducing power than NADH, so it reduces a carrier further along in the system. Each reduced carrier can use its new reducing power to pass two protons directly into the outer compartment and to shunt two energetic electrons along through the system.

The reduced carriers pass high-energy electrons along from carrier to carrier. Then, at key proton-pumping sites, the electron energy is used to transport more protons across the membrane from the matrix to the outer compartment. Note that this arrangement of compartments is opposite to that of the chloroplast's thylakoid (see Chapter 7). Also notice that the ETS here has three proton pumping sites where each ETS in the thylakoid has only one.

FIGURE 8.4 Chemiosmosis in the mitochondrion. NADH and $FADH_2$ add their hydrogens to the electron transport system at two key sites. In both instances, protons pass across the membrane and energetic electrons pass through the electron transport system. In all, there are three proton-pumping sites available, each of which passes two protons across simultaneously. Each NADH molecule powers three sites, while each $FADH_2$ powers two. Finally, note the fate of energy-depleted electrons (lower right). Each pair of electrons is joined by an oxygen atom and two protons from the matrix, forming water.

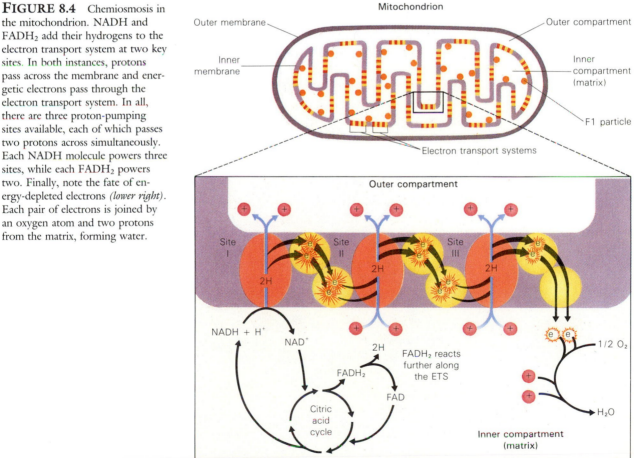

Each NADH molecule accounts for the transfer of six protons into the outer compartment; each FADH$_2$ molecule accounts for four. We will be summing up oxidative respiration soon, whereupon we will equate the number of NADHs and FADH$_2$s and protons pumped with the final generation of ATP.

> Electrons from each molecule of NADH provide energy for pumping six protons into the outer compartment; the less energetic FADH$_2$ molecule provides for four.

We have seen the chemiosmotic system at work in our model (Chapter 6) and in the thylakoids of the chloroplast (Chapter 7), and here the results are similar. But before we move in for a closer look at chemiosmosis in the mitochondrion, let's answer a question that may have occurred to you.

What about the oxygen? Electrons passing through the carriers of the electron transport system reach the last carrier in an energy-depleted condition. This is where oxygen comes in. Specifically, oxygen acts as the final electron acceptor. Oxygen combines with the electrons, along with free protons from the matrix, and water (H$_2$O) forms.

Oxygen, then, in its role of as a final electron acceptor, serves as an electron dump. And that is why we breathe: to provide a receptacle for spent electrons that were once parts of high-energy food molecules.

Chemiosmotic Phosphorylation

The phosphorylation of ADP in the mitochondrion (Figure 8.5) bears a general similarity to the process that occurs in the thylakoid (Figure 7.7). Interestingly, the spatial orientation of the compartments is reversed. Thylakoid protons are transported from an outer to an inner compartment; mitochondrial protons are pumped from an inner to an outer compartment. But the important aspect of chemiosmosis is only that a proton gradient be established. The orientation of the F1 and CF1 channels and enzyme-laden heads or particles, the same in both, indicates that the phosphorylating mechanisms are the same. Once the mitochondrial chemiosmotic gradient is established, and ADP and P$_i$ are present, all that remains is for protons to pass down their gradient through the F1 particles. In these particles, the free energy of the chemiosmotic system is used by phosphorylating enzymes to generate new high-energy ATP bonds.

Cellular respiration in the mitochondrion generates far more ATP than does anaerobic glycolysis: The anaerobic process produces a net gain of only two molecules of ATP per glucose molecule, and the aerobic process nets 36. There is some disagreement over how many escaping protons it takes to make one molecule of ATP, but the consensus is *two*. That is, for every two protons passing through an F1 particle, one ADP is phosphorylated to ATP. The overall yields of coenzyme, proton, and ATP from glucose are shown in Table 8.1.

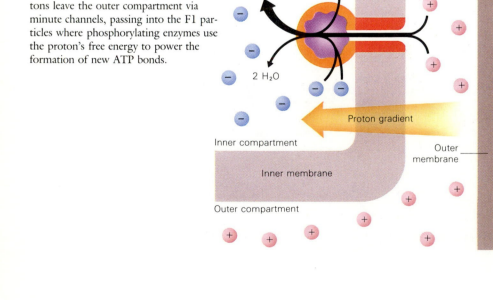

FIGURE 8.5 The phosphorylation of ADP occurs as paired protons pass down the chemiosmotic gradient. Protons leave the outer compartment via minute channels, passing into the F1 particles where phosphorylating enzymes use the proton's free energy to power the formation of new ATP bonds.

ATP   ADP + P$_i$

2 H$_2$O

Proton gradient

Inner compartment

Outer membrane

Inner membrane

Outer compartment

TABLE 8.1 Respiratory Yield: Moles of ATP per Mole of Glucose

Phase	NADH + H$^+$	FADH$_2$	ATP
Glycolysis	2		2
Acetyl CoA	2		
Citric acid cycle	6	2	2
Totals	10	2	4
Proton equivalents	60	8	
ATP equivalents (@ 1 ATP per 2 protons)	30	4	
ATP totals: 38 moles of ATP per mole of glucose	30	4	4

Energy Efficiency in Glycolysis and Cell Respiration

If glucose is completely oxidized experimentally (by burning it and measuring the heat), the energy yield is 680 kcal per mole (see Chapter 6 for an explanation of moles and calories). The caloric value of the terminal energy-rich bonds of ATP is 7.3 kcal per mole. Therefore, the 38 ATP molecules from glycolysis and oxidative respiration represent 277 kcal per mole. These numbers boil down to an ATP efficiency of about 41% ($304/680 = 0.41$; $0.41 \times 100 = 41\%$). All things considered, a fuel efficiency of 41% isn't bad. A well-tuned automobile engine has a fuel efficiency of less than 25%.

What happens to the other 59% of glucose energy? In this instance, 376 kcal of heat is released for each mole of glucose passing through the respiratory mill. The heat eventually escapes from the organism, but in warm-blooded creatures, the heat is not entirely wasted. In fact, heat from respiration is vital in maintaining the constant body temperature that is part of our adaptation to a wide variety of environmental temperatures. (We'll have more to say about this subject in Chapters 36 and 37).

The energy from two protons in the chemiosmotic gradient generates one molecule of ATP. The overall efficiency of glucose metabolism is 41% with the energy difference released as heat.

THE FERMENTATION ALTERNATIVE

We've seen how the glucose molecule is ravaged by glycolysis and how the resulting pyruvate molecules are taken through the equally active citric acid cycle. But this route is not always the destiny of pyruvate. Some pyruvate goes through additional anaerobic reactions in the **fermentation pathways.** There are two major fermentation pathways, and their end-products are quite distinct. In vertebrates and in a number of bacteria the end product is **lactate (lactic acid).** In yeast, it is **ethanol (ethyl alcohol).** In both fermentative pathways, the NADH formed during glycolysis reduces (adds hydrogen to) pyruvate (Figure 8.6). This is a vital step since it frees NAD$^+$, permitting it to recycle and glycolysis to continue.

In the lactate fermentation pathway, pyruvate is reduced by NADH forming **lactate** and freeing NAD$^+$ for recycling.

Alcohol Fermentation and Yeast

The common brewing and baking yeasts and some bacteria use the alcohol fermentation pathway. The yeasts, however, are metabolically quite versatile. They are metabolic "switch-hitters" and can metabolize glucose aerobically as well as anaerobically. When glucose is limited but oxygen is available, yeasts become aerobic. They break down glucose all the way to carbon dioxide and water, just as we do, thus gaining a maximum yield of ATP.

When glucose is abundant, however, yeasts take the simple, anaerobic alternative, even in the presence of oxygen. This seemingly wasteful process enables the yeast to avoid the high metabolic cost of producing the more complex enzyme system needed for oxidative respiration. (In our own energy technology we do the same thing. In spite of its inefficiency and pollution we continue to burn fossil fuels simply because they are cheap and abundant. Only when these fuels become too costly will we extensively develop the technology for harnessing clean energy sources such as sunlight and wind.)

The fermentative activity of yeast is obviously important to the brewer who needs the ethanol, but it is also critical to the baker who uses the gaseous carbon dioxide to make bread rise. The chemical reaction that they are both thankful for is:

$$\text{Pyruvate} + \text{NADH} + \text{H}^+ \longrightarrow$$
$$\text{CO}_2 + \text{Ethyl alcohol} + \text{NAD}^+$$

In the **alcohol fermentation pathway** pyruvate is decarboxylated, yielding CO_2, and reduced by NADH, forming ethyl alcohol. The NAD^+ recycles.

Lactate Fermentation and Muscles

Most people are familiar with the taste of ethyl alcohol, but lactate also has a familiar taste. It is lactate that gives sauerkraut its tangy flavor. (The two products have quite different physiological effects as witnessed by the fact that drivers are not pulled over to be tested for "cabbage-breath.") Lactate also forms in other foods. Lactose (milk sugar), converted to lactate, lends its flavor to buttermilk and yogurt. Essentially, the food and beverage industries make good use of what are really anaerobic waste products. We should keep in mind, though, that from the organism's point of view, the important thing is the recycling of NAD^+.

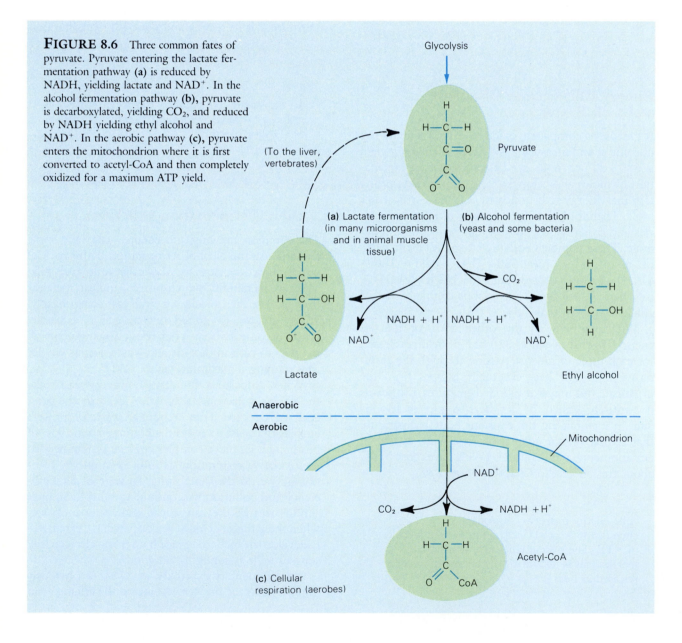

FIGURE 8.6 Three common fates of pyruvate. Pyruvate entering the lactate fermentation pathway **(a)** is reduced by NADH, yielding lactate and NAD^+. In the alcohol fermentation pathway **(b)**, pyruvate is decarboxylated, yielding CO_2, and reduced by NADH yielding ethyl alcohol and NAD^+. In the aerobic pathway **(c)**, pyruvate enters the mitochondrion where it is first converted to acetyl-CoA and then completely oxidized for a maximum ATP yield.

FIGURE 8.7 Nile crocodiles are generally sluggish creatures that can make astonishingly fast charges. However, following such periods of rapid activity the giant reptiles require many hours of inactivity to repay the oxygen debt.

Perhaps of greater interest is the formation of lactic acid by cells in your own body. The formula for the lactate fermentation pathway, starting with pyruvate, is:

$$Pyruvate + NADH + H^+ \longrightarrow Lactate + NAD^+$$

As in the alcohol fermentation pathway, when NADH is oxidized, the NAD^+ formed can recycle to be used again.

In your muscles, aerobic respiration provides adequate ATP during periods of light activity, such as casual strolling. But should you spot the neighbor's pit bull clearing its fence, you may wish to consider a faster gait, say sprinting! Under such conditions the human circulatory system simply cannot provide sufficient oxygen to sustain the sudden new requirement for ATP. So you "go anaerobic," rapidly converting muscle glycogen (animal starch) to glucose and sending the glucose through glycolysis and the simpler and much faster lactate fermentation pathway. In that way you can meet your elevated ATP requirements, at least for a time.

How long a person can rely on glycolysis depends on physical conditioning. Conditioning is partially a matter of how much glycogen is stored and how efficiently the cardiovascular system can deliver oxygen to the muscles. Switching to the anaerobic lactate fermentation pathway can be vital at times, but it has its price—something called an **oxygen debt.** This can be defined as the amount of oxygen (processed through cellular respiration) needed to clear lactate from the muscles, replenish muscle glycogen, and restore the muscles to their former state of readiness.

Oxygen debt builds because with vigorous muscular activity, ATP reserves quickly dwindle, lactate rapidly accumulates in the muscle tissue, and this leads to fatigue. Lactate must be removed from the muscles by transporting it via the bloodstream to the liver where, through a process called **gluconeogenesis,** it is converted back to glucose. The glucose is then returned to the muscles where it is restored to glycogen. Gluconeogenesis is an energy-costly process, requiring six ATP molecules for the conversion of two molecules of lactate to one molecule of glucose. However, from an adaptive point of view, it's worth the price, especially if survival depends on sudden, vigorous movement (as in staying ahead of the pit bull).

Since recovery is essentially an aerobic process, extra oxygen is required. This explains the familiar gasping and panting that follow the sprint. Even a well-conditioned athlete may breathe a bit more heavily for 30 minutes or so after a 100-meter dash. The heavy breathing eventually repays the oxygen debt as muscle glycogen reserves are replenished.

Vigorous muscular activity produces **oxygen debt,** the amount of oxygen that is required in cellular respiration to clear lactate and replenish muscle glycogen.

Interestingly, many smaller animals generate all or most of their muscle ATP aerobically and have no problem with lactate accumulation and oxygen debt. Examples include seemingly tireless migratory birds and small, fast-running mammals. But the great body mass of larger animals does not allow their circulatory systems to keep up with the increased oxygen demands. Nile crocodiles, for instance, are generally sluggish creatures. But when threatened or when stalking prey on land, they can make astonishingly fast charges and can lash their tails about with results that are legendary. Following such outbursts, the giant reptiles must remain still, requiring many hours to repay the oxygen debt (Figure 8.7).

Biochemist Albert Lehninger of Johns Hopkins University muses that an oversized oxygen debt may have cost many a giant dinosaur its life, for following any kind of vigorous activity, it would have had to enter a metabolic stupor when it would have been vulnerable to smaller, sharp-toothed predators. (Shall we add the oxygen-debt hypothesis to the long list of explanations for the extinction of these great beasts?)

Now our look at energetics is complete. We have seen how glucose is produced by autotrophs that use light energy to form this precious commodity. Its great free energy, stored in stable chemical bonds, is then tapped in complex respiratory processes by both autotrophic and heterotrophic cells as they meet the energy requirements of life.

SUMMARY

Photosynthetic autotrophs (plants, algae, and certain bacteria) use light energy and simple inorganic molecules for food-making, whereas heterotrophs (animals, fungi, many protists, and bacteria) rely on organic compounds from plants or other organisms.

The extraction of energy from glucose and other fuels occurs in two ways: an anaerobic, cytoplasmic process called glycolysis and an aerobic, mitochondrial process called cell respiration. Both are multistep metabolic pathways.

GLYCOLYSIS

Glycolysis begins with glucose and includes 10 principal reactions. During the first three, two ATPs are invested, and destabilization begins. In the next two reactions the product is cleaved, oxidized, and phosphorylated (by P_i). In the oxidation step NAD^+ is reduced to NADP.

A substrate level phosphorylation occurs next, as two phosphates are transferred from the fuel to two molecules of ADP, yielding two molecules of ATP. The next two reactions destabilize the fuel once more, and the remaining phosphates are transferred to two molecules of ADP, yielding two more ATPs. The final products of glycolysis are four molecules of ATP, two of NADH, and two of pyruvate. The net yield is two molecules of ATP.

CELLULAR RESPIRATION

Pyruvate, still energy-rich, next enters the mitochondrion where most of the cell's ATP is produced through cell respiration. Several oxidations of the fuel and a substrate level phosphorylation will be followed by electron and proton transport and chemiosmotic phosphorylation.

Citric Acid Cycle

Each pyruvate joins coenzyme A in preliminary reactions that yield carbon dioxide, NADH, and acetyl-CoA. The latter enters the citric acid cycle, joining oxaloacetate to form citric acid. Further reactions in the 10-step cycle yield two more carbon dioxide molecules, one of ATP, and, through four oxidation reactions, three molecules of NADH and one of $FADH_2$.

The Electron Transport Systems and Proton Pumping

Electron transport systems (ETS) in the inner membrane contain three proton pumping sites. Each NADH adds two energy-rich electrons (and two protons) to the first carrier of the ETS, thereby powering the transport of six protons into the outer compartment. Each $FADH_2$ reduces a carrier further along, powering the transport of only four protons into the outer compartment. NAD^+ and FAD recycle. As the electrons complete their transit, they unite with protons and oxygen, forming water.

Chemiosmotic Phosphorylation

Proton pumping creates a steep proton gradient (representing a high free-energy state). The free energy is used to generate ATP as protons pass down their gradient through the F1 particles. There, phosphorylating enzymes join P_i to ADP. Each ATP produced requires the transit of two protons from the outer to the inner compartment.

Energy Efficiency in Glycolysis and Cell Respiration

For each pair of pyruvates entering aerobic cell respiration in the mitochondrion, 36 ATP molecules are generated. The total yield for glucose (including glycolysis) is 38 moles of ATP per mole of glucose, an efficiency of 41%. The remaining energy is given off as heat.

THE FERMENTATION ALTERNATIVE

Ethyl alcohol fermentation and lactate fermentation are two major anaerobic pathways pyruvate may follow. An important aspect of each is the reduction of pyruvate by NADH, which frees NAD^+ for recycling to glycolysis.

Alcohol Fermentation and Yeast

Yeasts can metabolize glucose aerobically as well as anaerobically. In the anaerobic process pyruvate is decarboxylated and reduced, yielding carbon dioxide and ethyl alcohol and freeing NAD^+ for recycling. During baking, the carbon dioxide is essential to the "rise" of bread dough.

Lactate Fermentation and Muscles

The food industry uses lactate from bacterial fermentation to produce a tangy flavor in many foods. The lactate fermentation pathway also occurs in vertebrate muscle. During muscular exertion, vertebrates often rely on anaerobic glycolysis for rapid ATP generation. The end product, pyruvate, is reduced by NADH to lactate, freeing NAD^+

for recycling. The accumulation of lactate produces oxygen debt, whereupon cell respiration must be used in the clearing of lactate and restoration of the muscles. Lactate is transported to the liver where, during gluconeogenesis, ATP is expended to convert lactate back to glucose. Small vertebrates can rely almost entirely on aerobic respiration. Larger vertebrates cannot do this, and fatigue is a common problem.

KEY TERMS

photosynthetic autotroph
heterotroph
glycolysis
cellular respiration
anaerobic
aerobic
glycolytic pathway
substrate level phosphorylation

pyruvate (pyruvic acid)
F1 particles
citric acid cycle
electron transport
chemiosmotic phosphorylation
oxaloacetate
coenzyme A
acetyl-CoA

GTP (guanine triphosphate)
fermentation pathways
lactate (lactic acid)
ethanol (ethyl alcohol)
alcohol fermentation
    pathway
oxygen debt
gluconeogenesis

REVIEW QUESTIONS

1 Compare glycolysis and cell respiration as follows: the site where they occur, the need for oxygen, and the yield of ATP. (See Chapter 7)

2 In general, why are such roundabout means (complex biochemical pathways) used by the cell for extracting energy from its fuels. (p. 115)

3 Briefly summarize the first five steps of glycolysis. What happens to the molecule and how does the reaction lead to a useful energy transfer? (p. 115)

4 Looking closely at the inset (molecular detail) in Figure 8.1, explain how ATP is formed during substrate level phosphorylation. (p. 117)

5 List the final products of glycolysis. What is the net amount of ATP yielded? (pp. 115–116)

6 Develop an illustration of a mitochondrion, labelling the inner and outer membranes and compartments and several F1 particles. (Figure 8.4)

7 Relate the diagram from Question 6 to the "sac-within-a-sac" analogy of a chemiosmotic system (see Chapter 6).

8 Where in the mitochondrion do the following occur: conversion of pyruvate to acetyl-CoA, citric acid cycle, electron transport and proton pumping, chemiosmotic phosphorylation? (pp. 117–122)

9 Summarize the acetyl-CoA step, listing the reactants and products. Which products are of no further value to the cell? (p. 117)

10 Study Figure 8.3 carefully and list the reaction numbers where any of the following occur: decarboxylation, oxidation, phosphorylation, substrate level phosphorylation. (pp. 116–117)

11 State the numbers (per glucose) of ATPs (net) and reduced coenzymes yielded in the following: (a) glycolysis, (b) acetyl-CoA step, (c) citric acid cycle, (d) grand total. (Table 8.1)

12 Prepare an illustration of a mitochondrial electron transport system. Label the electron carriers and proton pumps and indicate the carriers that are reduced by NADH and $FADH_2$. (Figure 8.4)

13 How many protons does the chemiosmotic gradient gain by the action of NADH? $FADH_2$? (pp. 121–122)

14. Oxygen is often described as the final electron acceptor in the mitochondrial electron transport system. Explain. (p. 122)

15 Explain how the free energy of the proton gradient is put to work making ATP. A diagram might be helpful. What is the ratio between protons and ATP? (p. 122)

16 Carry out the calculations that reveal the percent efficiency of glucose metabolism in the cell. (p. 123)

17 Summarize the reactions leading to ethyl alcohol in the alcohol fermentation pathway. Under what conditions do yeasts use this pathway? (pp. 123–124)

18 What organisms besides vertebrates make use of the lactate pathway? How does the food industry make use of these organisms? (pp. 124–125)

19 Under what conditions do our bodies make use of the anaerobic production of ATP? Of what advantage is this? (p. 125)

20 What is oxygen debt and how is it repaid? What makes it possible for small animals to rely heavily on lactate fermentation without fatigue? (p. 125)

9

MITOSIS AND CELL DIVISION

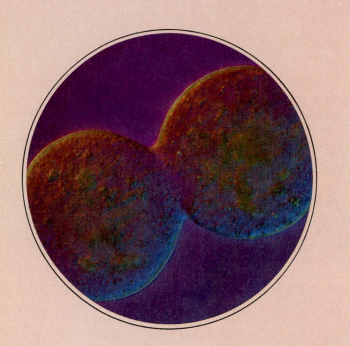

Even as you sit quietly reading this fascinating account, your body is changing at a dazzling rate. Certain cells are being created, others are dying, and still others are being altered. Your body is literally different now from what it was when you started this paragraph. Specifically, you have replaced about 25 million red blood cells; in all, your body's total cell production has been ten times that number. Unless you are still growing, about that same number of cells have died. In this chapter we will see how all those new cells came to be.

Scientists have known for over a century that cells come from other cells, a principle known as the **biogenetic law** (see Chapter 4). In this chapter we will consider just how cells form new cells and how this vitally important process is carried out. Our attention will be focused on the eukaryotic cell. (The prokaryotes divide by a much simpler process, which is described in Chapter 20.)

Essentially, new cells arise when an existing cell divides, forming two new cells. But, one might ask, why does cell division occur at all? A fundamental reason is the relationship between membrane surface area and volume (see Chapter 4). As cell volume increases, the transport functions of the membrane become less efficient. To overcome this problem, hypothetically at least, the cell must divide, thus restoring a more adequate surface-volume relationship. Undoubtedly, other reasons and other signals prompt cell division. In the multicellular organism cell division provides the seemingly countless numbers of cells required for growth and development. In some instances, cell division replaces aging or damaged cells, as occurs in the blood and skin cells.

Cell division is also a means of reproduction for thousands of protists, simple eukaryotic species that increase their numbers by dividing. In addition, sperm and eggs are produced by a special type of cell division (see Chapter 10).

A cell divides to become two cells, and each new cell must have a complete set of identical genes in order to function in an orderly manner. This **genetic continuity** is maintained by preserving the genes from one generation of cells to the next. How is this assured in the nearly countless cell divisions that occur in complex organisms like ourselves?

Two processes, **DNA replication** and **mitosis**, provide for genetic continuity. The first is the orderly, precise copying of the genes encoded in the DNA of chromosomes. The second is the very precise division of the newly formed chromosomes. So, while the first process provides the materials needed, the second assures their faithful division into newly forming **daughter cells.** Only after mitosis has succeeded is the entire cell ready for division. At **cytokinesis,** or actual cell division, the organelles and cell fluids are divided so that the daughter cells are more-or-less identical in these respects.

> DNA **replication** provides duplicates of nuclear DNA. **Mitosis** assures their proper separation before **cytokinesis,** or cell division, occurs.

THE CELL CYCLE AND DNA REPLICATION

The period from one cell division to the next is called the **cell cycle.** As we will see, a lot goes on during this period.

The Cell Cycle

The cell cycle can be divided functionally into two major parts and four subparts. The major parts are **interphase** and **mitosis** (Figure 9.1). Interphase—the period between cell divisions—has three subparts, **G1, S,** and **G2.**

In humans the first part of interphase, **G1** (for **gap-one**), lasts about eight hours. During this time the cell grows to about twice its original size. Growth includes protein synthesis, organelle construction, and storage of materials.

DNA replication occurs in the **S phase.** It is a vital prerequisite for cell division in which each DNA molecule forms a replica of itself. Following DNA replication, **G2** (**gap-two**) begins, a period of renewed protein synthesis in which most of the effort is placed on making *tubulin,* which will later be assembled into numerous microtubules, structures important to chromosome separation.

The duration of the cell cycle can vary tremendously. Newly fertilized sea urchin and frog embryos, for instance, may complete their earliest cell

FIGURE 9.1 Typical cell cycle.

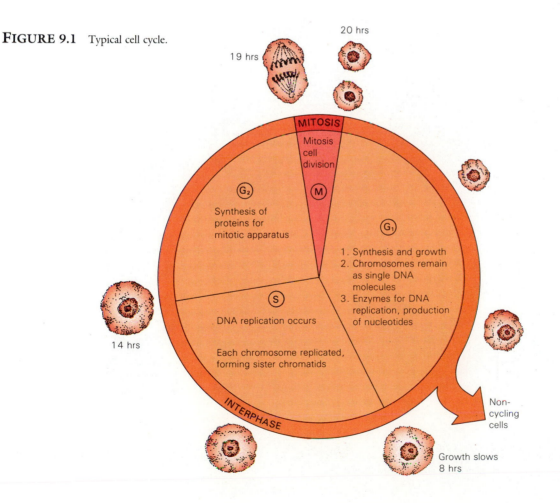

20 hrs

19 hrs

MITOSIS

Mitosis cell division

G₂
Synthesis of proteins for mitotic apparatus

M

G₁
1. Synthesis and growth
2. Chromosomes remain as single DNA molecules
3. Enzymes for DNA replication, production of nucleotides

S
DNA replication occurs

Each chromosome replicated, forming sister chromatids

14 hrs

INTERPHASE

Non-cycling cells

Growth slows 8 hrs

cycles in less than 30 minutes. Certain mouse connective tissues in culture require as long as 22 hours, while root tip cells of the common garden pea spend only 3 hours between divisions. Our own red blood cells live only 120 days. The enormous battery of cells that produce them must undergo 2.5 million cell divisions per second just to keep up. Cells such as those in the muscles, liver, and nerves stop cycling altogether and remain permanently in G1.

G2 completes interphase. The cell is then prepared for mitosis. We will get into mitosis shortly, but first let's see how the important prerequisite of DNA replication is carried out.

> Each cell cycle includes an **interphase,** divided into G1 (growth), S (replication), and G2 (tubulin synthesis). Interphase ends with the **M phase** in which mitosis and cell division occur.

DNA Replication: A Brief Look

DNA is an extremely long, double-stranded polymer consisting of subunits called nucleotides. The two strands are drawn together by numerous hydrogen bonds between adjacent nucleotides. The hydrogen bonds spontaneously wind the two strands into a double helix (Figure 9.2a). Each DNA molecule contains many genes along its length. Each complete molecule, along with its associated protein, is referred to as a **chromosome.**

During DNA replication, a complex of enzymes moves along the double helix, unwinding it at certain places and breaking the hydrogen bonds between the two strands. Where the bonds are broken, the two strands untwist, exposing the individual nitrogen bases (Figure 9.2b). The exposed nucleotides then join with new nucleotides floating free in the nucleoplasm. The additions are not random, however; nucleotides join in a highly specific manner known as **base pairing.** Because of this specificity, base pairing

FIGURE 9.2 DNA replication. (a) enzyme complexes unwind the double helix, breaking its numerous hydrogen bonds and exposing the nitrogen bases. (b) New nucleotides pair and replace the old strand. As the replication enzyme complexes move along, the strands rewind. (c) Eventually two exact replicas of the original DNA emerge.

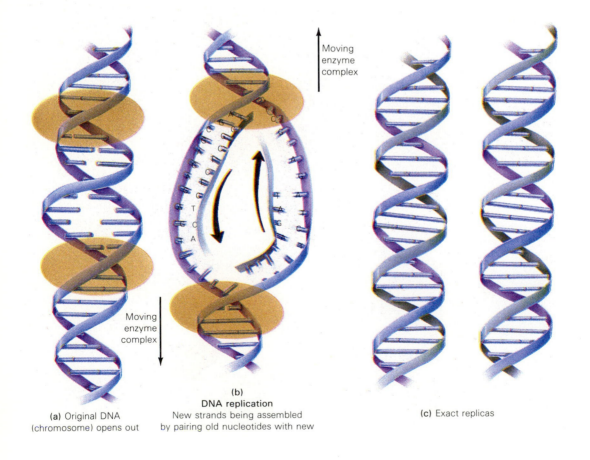

Moving enzyme complex

Moving enzyme complex

**(b)
DNA replication**
New strands being assembled by pairing old nucleotides with new

(a) Original DNA (chromosome) opens out

(c) Exact replicas

FIGURE 9.3 Following replication, a chromosome consists of two chromatids joined at the centromere. The centromere will divide during mitosis, and each chromatid will then be a fully qualified chromosome.

replaces the precise nucleotides that were present before the molecule was unwound and the two DNA strands separated.

In a sense, the DNA molecule is split in half along its length, and each part replaces the half it lost. Newly forming hydrogen bonds then draw the new partners together, and the double helix is restored. In the meantime, the enzyme complex moves ahead, and replication continues along the lengthy molecule. At the completion of the replication process there are now two DNA molecules identical to the first. The details of replication are discussed in Chapter 14.

The newly replicated DNA strands, or **chromatids** as they are called, are bound together at a region known as the **centromere** (Figure 9.3). They are called chromatids only while they are held together by the centromere. During mitosis, the centromere will divide, whereupon each chromatid will become a single, full-fledged chromosome.

The cell has now completed the first requirement for division: it has replicated its DNA. As the cell divides into two daughter cells, each daughter will receive one chromatid from each replicated set. Of course, by then the chromatids will be called chromosomes.

In replication, DNA is unwound, the two strands of nucleotides separated, and matching nucleotides assembled along each strand. The replicas, joined by **centromeres**, are called **chromatids.**

A CLOSER LOOK AT THE CHROMOSOME

Chromatin

Before going on to the mitotic process itself, let's look more closely at the chromosome. First, we should recall that in eukaryotes, the nuclear DNA is bound to protein in a very specific way, forming the brightly staining chromatin. The most abundant protein is histone, which serves as a packaging material, forming globules around which DNA is wound. Other chromosomal proteins are thought to have a gene-controlling function, working in the timely activation and inactivation of specific genes.

In an interphase cell (one not undergoing mitosis), the chromatin is diffuse (spread-out), forming what is called the **chromatin net.** The more diffuse areas represent those in which DNA is active. If nothing else, diffuse chromatin resembles a bundle of yarn subjected to the attention of a demented kitten (Figure 9.4).

Chromosomes are composed of **chromatin,** which is a complex of DNA with its associated proteins. Diffuse chromatin forms a **chromatin net** in the interphase nucleus.

Mitotic Chromosomes

One would be hard pressed to distinguish an individual chromosome in its diffuse state, but as mitosis begins, each separate chromosome will gather itself together, condense, and be quite distinguishable. Then each chromosome becomes attached at intervals to a protein **chromosomal scaffold** that gives shape to the mitotic chromosome. Long loops of the chromosome coil tightly around themselves and hang off the sides of the scaffold like overwound rubber bands. The structure of the tightly condensed chromosome is essentially a system of coils within coils (Essay 9.1).

Mitotic condensation is the ultimate in packaging. The length of DNA double helix in a human X chromosome, one of the larger of our complement of 46 chromosomes per cell, would presumably be about 13 cm (5 in) long if fully stretched out. In its fully coiled and condensed state, however, it is 30,000 times shorter. This tight package can be readily moved about the cell. Without this condensation, mitosis would demand far too much space to be feasible.

FIGURE 9.4 The chromatin net is comprised of diffuse and partially condensed chromatin. DNA must be in a diffuse condition to produce RNA.

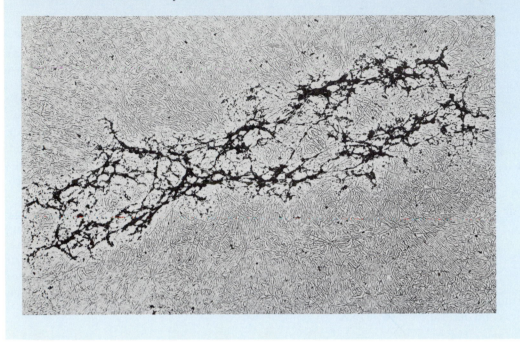

Chromosome Numbers and Pairs

How many chromosomes are in a cell? It depends. Members of each species have a precise number of chromosomes (Table 9.1). For example, human beings have 46, but the lowly ameba has 50, and Rover sleeping at your feet has 78. Essay 9.2 explains how chromosomes are identified and counted by **karyotyping.**

Chromosomes occur in pairs in nearly all human cells and in those of other animals and most plants. That is, for every chromosome (or complete DNA molecule) there is another one virtually identical to it. Pairing of chromosomes is the logical product of sexual reproduction: each parent contributes one member of each pair. Thus, your own paired chromosomes can be traced to your parents, each of whom contributed one member of each pair at the moment of your conception.

Each member of a given pair of chromosomes is called a **homologue** and each has the same linear sequence of genes. However, genes at the same location on homologous chromosomes, although governing the same genetic trait, may not express themselves in an identical manner. For example, although corresponding genes on two homologues may both be responsible for shape of the hair strand, the gene contributed by the father may express itself as straight hair while the gene contributed by the mother expresses itself as curly. The same is true for all genes at the same positions on homologous chromosomes: they may or may not code for the same expression of any given trait.

Cells that contain both homologues of each chromosome pair are termed **diploid,** or **2n** (doubled), cells. Not all cells are diploid. Some have only one homologue from each pair, and these cells are **haploid** or **n** (halved). In humans and other animals, the only haploid cells are **gametes** (sperm and egg cells). Of course, their mission in life is to join during fertilization, producing new individuals whose chromosome state will then be diploid. However, many simpler organisms, particularly protists and fungi, spend much of their life cycle in a haploid state. And the familiar plants, while primarily diploid, have many haploid cells, some of which eventually give rise to gametes.

Chromosomes occur as **homologues** (pairs), each member with the same gene assortment. Cells may be **haploid** or **diploid.**

ESSAY 9.1 THE SUPERCOILED MITOTIC CHROMOSOME

The organization of the mitotic chromosome is mostly a story of coils within coils. *Supercoil* is the term used when the structure that is being coiled already consists of a coil. The condensed chromosome, easily visible through the light microscope, is a supercoil with several levels of organization, each a coil of its own. With the greater magnification (a) the chromosomal arms are seen to consist of a thickened helix. (b) A small segment of this supercoil consists of an incredibly long thread of DNA coiled back and forth into a supercoil. (c) More coiling of the chromosome strand. Here a short length coils back on itself. (d) The nucleosomes: DNA coiled around histone molecules. Structure at this level of organization can be resolved by the electron microscope, but its final helical organization cannot. The familiar DNA helix must be determined using techniques such as X-ray diffraction. (e) The last level of coiling is the double helix of DNA.

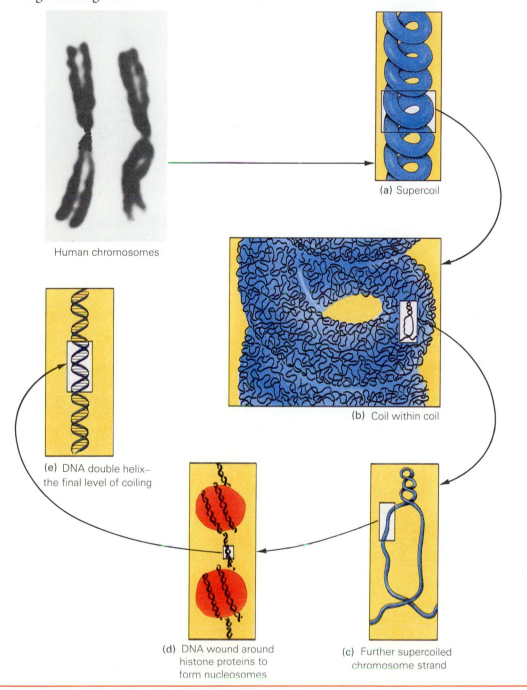

Human chromosomes

(a) Supercoil

(b) Coil within coil

(e) DNA double helix— the final level of coiling

(d) DNA wound around histone proteins to form nucleosomes

(c) Further supercoiled chromosome strand

TABLE 9.1 Chromosome Numbers

There is no apparent significance to chromosome number as far as biologists can determine. Note the variation in some plant and animal species. Plants undergo spontaneous doubling and tripling of chromosome number, so their numbers may vary.

Alligator	32	English holly	40	Opossum	22
Ameba	50	Fruit fly	8	Penicillia	2
Brown bat	44	Garden pea	14	Pheasant	82
Bullfrog	26	Goldfish	94	Pigeon	80, 79
Carrot	18	Grasshopper	24	Planaria	16
Cat	32	Guinea pig	64	Redwood	22
Cattle	60	Horse	64	Rhesus monkey	42
Chicken	78	House fly	12	Rose	14, 21, 28
Chimpanzee	48	Human	46	Sand dollar	52
Corn	20	Hydrae	32	Sea urchin	40
Dog	78	Lettuce	18	Tobacco	48
Earthworm	36	Marijuana	20	Turkey	82
Eel	36	Onion	16, 32	Whitefish	80

MITOSIS

In the last hours of interphase, before the first visible signs of mitosis, DNA replication has been completed and the cell begins to synthesize tubulin. Doubled spheres of tubulin serve as building blocks for slender, hollow microtubules. Microtubules will form the scaffolding upon which mitosis will occur, the delicate, ethereal **spindle.** The spindle will later be involved in the separation of chromatids and movement of chromosomes. The spindle is a prominent structure that functions with great precision during cell division, but is so delicate that it quickly disintegrates if manipulated. The spindle forms anew for each cell cycle and is dismantled after each use. Its appearance is a sign that mitosis is underway.

Mitosis is customarily divided into four phases: **prophase, metaphase, anaphase,** and **telophase.** Because the entire mitotic process is continuous, identifying the end of one phase and the beginning of the next is sometimes arbitrary. Further, mitosis and cell division in animals and plants differ in important ways, as we will see.

Mitosis in Animals

Prophase

Several striking events take place during prophase in animals (Figures 9.5 and 9.6). The chromosomes condense, coil upon coil, and for the first time,

become clearly recognizable bodies. Nucleoli fade from view as does the nuclear envelope. Then the spindle begins to form.

Centrioles and the spindle. Even as the chromosomes condense, the spindle forms in preparation for chromosome movement. At the onset of prophase in animal cells, paired centrioles separate and migrate to opposite sides of the nucleus. Once in place at the **spindle poles,** a surrounding region, the **microtubular organizing center (MOC)** begins to operate, organizing the microtubules into three remarkable structures (Figure 9.6).

The first microtubular structures to form are the **asters** ("stars"), which radiate out from each centriole. Microscopists have watched them for years, but their function remains a mystery. (They may make the surrounding cytoplasm more rigid in preparation for coming events.)

The spindle includes two other types of microtubules. The **continuous spindle fibers** begin their assembly at each organizing center, then extend from both directions across the chromosomes toward the opposite pole. They stop somewhere short of this goal but not before they have slid past each other so that they overlap.

The second type of microtubules, called **centromeric spindle fibers** also extend out from the centrioles, but they link up with the centromeres of the

A **karyotype** is a graphic representation of the chromosomes of any organism in which individual chromosomes are systematically arranged according to size and shape. Each species has its particular karyotype, and so we know the number and kinds of chromosomes found in carrots, fruit flies, and people. Karyotyping in humans is done by a simple and straight-forward method.

A blood sample is drawn and the white cells are separated and transferred to a culture medium. The medium contains not only nutrients, but also chemical agents that first induce mitosis and then stop the process when the chromosomes are at their maximal condensation (the stage at which the chromatids are seen most easily). The cells are then put on microscope slides and stained.

Cells that show all of the individual chromosomes are photographed through a light microscope. A large, glossy print is made from the negative. Because the jumble of chromosomes is difficult to interpret and count, the picture of each chromosome is cut from the photograph. Next, the cut-out images of the chromosomes are sorted by size and shape. The homologous pairs are matched, and the chromosomes are arranged in one or more lines, from the largest to the smallest. Finally, the chromosomal arrangement is mounted with rubber cement. (By convention, pair number 23, the sex chromosomes, is set aside as shown.) This is the karyotype.

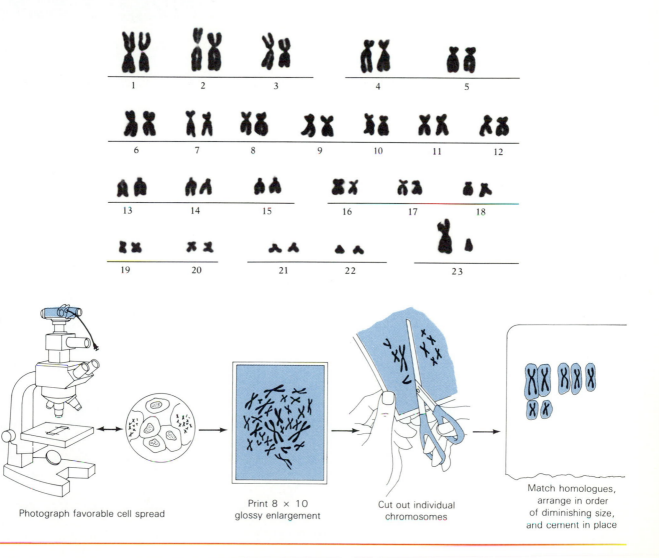

Photograph favorable cell spread

Print 8 × 10 glossy enlargement

Cut out individual chromosomes

Match homologues, arrange in order of diminishing size, and cement in place

FIGURE 9.5 Mitosis in animal cells. (1) The interphase cell reveals little nuclear detail, and the nuclear envelope is intact. (2) In prophase the chromosomes have begun their condensation, and signs of the two asters are present. (3) By metaphase, the two asters are prominent, and the spindle apparatus is clearly visible, extending across the cell. The chromosomes have formed a vertical mass as they line up, forming the metaphase plate. (4) During anaphase, the centromeres divide, and the chromosomes begin their migration to opposite poles. (5) In late telophase, the chromosomes have finished their migration and fade but the most noticeable event is cytokinesis. The line between chromosome masses is a cleavage furrow, typical of animal cells. (Photographs courtesy Carolina Biological Supply.)

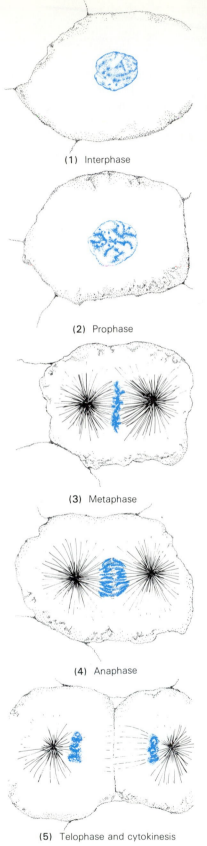

(1) Interphase

(2) Prophase

(3) Metaphase

(4) Anaphase

(5) Telophase and cytokinesis

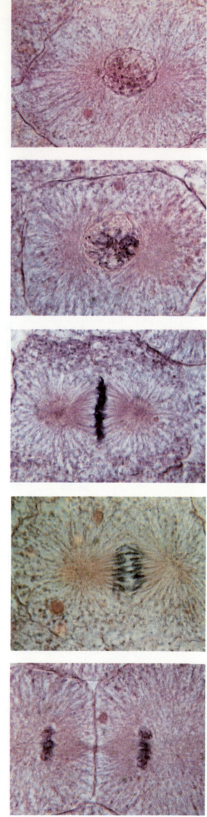

FIGURE 9.6 The mitotic apparatus. We can see here the three ways microtubules are assembled. Some form the aster, while others form the overlapping, continuous spindle fibers; still others form the centromeric spindle fibers that extend from the centrioles to the centromeres.

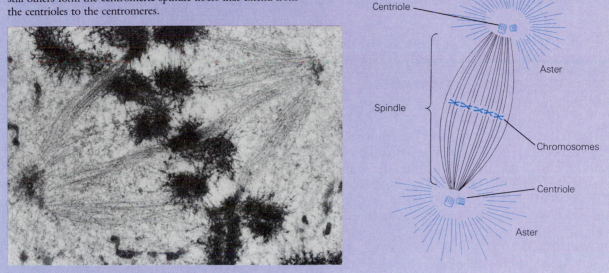

Centriole

Aster

Spindle

Chromosomes

Centriole

Aster

chromosomes. The result is that each centromere is attached to fibers that are joined to each pole. In case you are wondering how the spindle gets through the nuclear membrane, it doesn't. As the spindle is assembled, the nuclear membrane of nearly all eukaryotes is dismantled and disappears.

> Tubulin is organized by the **MOC** into the microtubules that form the **spindle,** composed of **asters, continuous spindle fibers,** and **centromeric spindle fibers.**

Final events of prophase. Once the centromeric spindle fibers have reached out from each pole and attached to the centromeres (much like roping a horse from both sides), the movement of the chromosomes becomes more precise. Now captured by opposing spindle fibers, they are pulled along, finally to line up across the middle of the spindle. There they form a ragged single file that is called the **metaphase plate,** and then metaphase itself begins.

> In **prophase,** the centrioles migrate, the spindle forms, chromosomes condense, the nuclear envelope is dismantled, and chromosomes are drawn to the cell equator.

Metaphase

In metaphase, individual chromatids are easily seen. Although the chromatids lean out in all directions, the centromeres are held in position along the metaphase plate, which can be regarded as the cell's equatorial plane since it lies midway between the poles.

Up to this point, the two chromatids of each chromosome have been held together by a single centromere, and the centromere has been held rigidly in place by the centromeric spindle fibers. The next event, which helps make sense out of previous events, signals the onset of anaphase.

Anaphase

Anaphase is marked by centromere division. When each centromere divides to become two centromeres, the two chromatids are no longer held together—in fact, they are no longer called chromatids. They are now called **daughter chromosomes,** each with its own centromere. Interestingly, centromeres will divide even if the spindle is paralyzed or dissolved by chemical treatment. Biologists now suggest that a centromere is merely a designated region of unreplicated DNA along with replication enzymes. At some unknown signal, the centromere suddenly undergoes replication, permitting the chromatids to separate.

With the division of the centromeres, the identical daughter chromosomes quickly separate. One daughter chromosome moves toward one pole, while its identical counterpart moves toward the other. But with this elegant ballet comes the question: how do the chromosomes move?

In **metaphase** chromosomes pause at the cell equator forming the metaphase plate; in **anaphase** centromeres divide and the chromosomes begin movement to opposite poles.

The spindle and chromosome movement. When the daughter chromosomes separate, the role of the mitotic spindle becomes apparent. The chromosomes are pulled along at their centromeres with the "arms" of the chromosomes trailing behind. Simultaneously, the entire spindle elongates. But how?

Hypothetically, two mechanisms are involved (Figure 9.7). First, the spindle lengthens, so that the opposite poles move apart. Daughter centromeres, being attached to opposite spindle poles, also separate. The overlapping continuous spindle fibers appear to be involved in this spindle lengthening. The mechanism seems to be a form of sliding filament action wherein the continuous spindle fibers actively slide past each other, shortening the zone of overlap.

The second mechanism of chromosome movement in anaphase involves the centromeric spindle fibers, which are able to shorten and to pull on their attached centromeres. The shortening occurs by a process known as **subunit disassembly,** which simply means that the spindle fiber microtubules are broken down piecemeal into their subunit tubulin molecules. As small sections fall away from the spindle, it manages to maintain its linear structure, shortening all the while. As this occurs the shortening fibers somehow remain firmly attached at both ends.

Chromosome movement in anaphase involves both sliding continuous microtubules and the disassembly of centromeric microtubules.

Telophase

Telophase, which begins after the chromosomes have been pulled to their poles, is like prophase in reverse. The chromosomes uncoil, reversing the condensation process. The spindle is disassembled and the nuclear membrane—now actually two nuclear membranes, one around each clump of chromosomes—is reassembled. Nucleoli also reappear. In

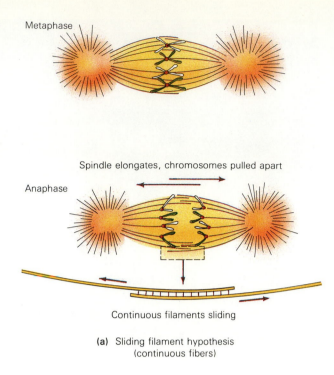

(a) Sliding filament hypothesis (continuous fibers)

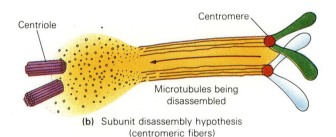

(b) Subunit disassembly hypothesis (centromeric fibers)

FIGURE 9.7 The sliding filament–microtubular disassembly hypothesis suggests that the spindle is elongated as anaphase begins. Elongation is produced as the continuous microtubules, or filaments, "ratchet" past each other. Simultaneously, the centromeric microtubules pull the chromatids along, somehow disassembling themselves in the process.

animals, the centrioles may replicate at this time or later. Telophase also marks the time of actual cell division (cytokinesis).

Cytokinesis in Animals

In animals (and many protists), cytokinesis begins with a furrow along the cell's equator. The furrow eventually becomes a deep groove. Finally, the cell is pinched in two, forming two daughter cells. The entire sequence is often referred to as **cleavage** (Figure 9.8). The **cleavage furrow** is produced by contracting rings of actin microfilaments that are just under the plasma membrane.

Mitosis in Plants

Plants, as we have indicated from time to time, do things differently. As you see in Figure 9.9, the events of plant mitosis are similar to those of mitosis in animal cells. Note, however, the absence of centrioles and asters. In fact, the absence of centrioles has caused many biologists to doubt their specific role in mitosis, since the plant spindle apparatus forms quite well without them, and mitosis goes on according to schedule. This difference has not been satisfactorily explained.

Cytokinesis in Plants

Cytokinesis in plants must occur within the confines of a cell wall. Because the wall is rigid, cleavage cannot occur. Thus the plant cell simply produces a new wall between the telophase nuclei.

The new wall begins with the formation of a number of tiny vesicles originating from Golgi bodies (see Chapter 4), which form in the plane of the metaphase plate. The vesicles fuse to form a **cell plate,** which extends to the original cell wall. The cell plate fills with pectin, a carbohydrate, to form the **middle lamella.** This is a gummy layer that will come to lie between the mature cell walls of adjacent plant cells. New plasma membranes assemble over the middle lamella, and cellulose is deposited through the membrane of each daughter cell, forming a new **primary cell wall** (Figure 9.10).

Cytokinesis in animals occurs when microfilaments form a **cleavage furrow,** pinching the cell in half. In plants a **cell plate** forms, followed by a **middle lamella** and **primary cell wall.**

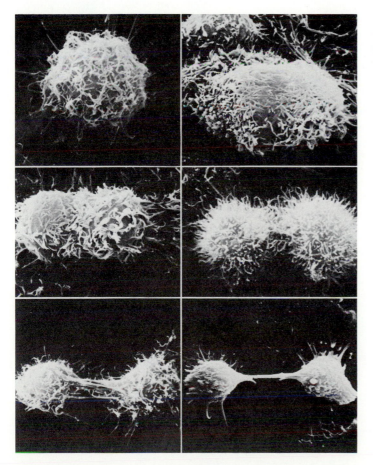

FIGURE 9.8 Cytokinesis in an animal cell. From *Scanning Electron Microscopy in Biology: A Student's Atlas on Biological Organization,* by R. G. Kessel and C. Y. Shih. Copyright © 1974-Springer-Verlag.)

FIGURE 9.9 Mitosis and cytokinesis in plant cells. Little activity is apparent in interphase (1), but in prophase (2) the chromosomes are clearly visible. Note the absence of centrioles and asters. The spindle is visible at metaphase (3), where the chromosomes align to form the metaphase plate. The centromeres divide, and the chromosomes move apart as usual during anaphase (4). During telophase (5) there is no cleavage furrow, but a new cell wall develops between the new daughter cells as the events of mitosis end.

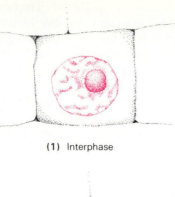
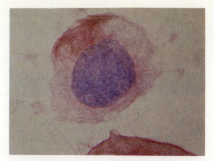

(1) Interphase

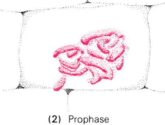
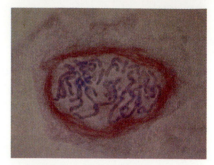

(2) Prophase

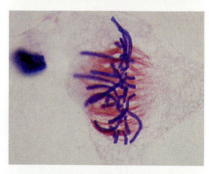

(3) Metaphase

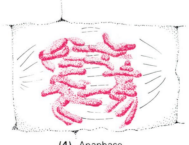

(4) Anaphase

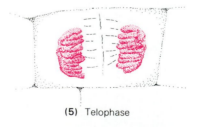
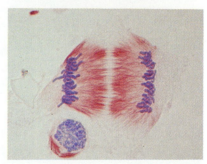

(5) Telophase

FIGURE 9.10 In plants cytokinesis begins as a new cell wall is constructed between daughter cells. Cytoplasmic division is first seen as the formation of vesicles at the middle of the cell. These coalesce and extend across the cell, forming the cell plate. The completed plate is known as the middle lamella, from which the primary cell wall will emerge.

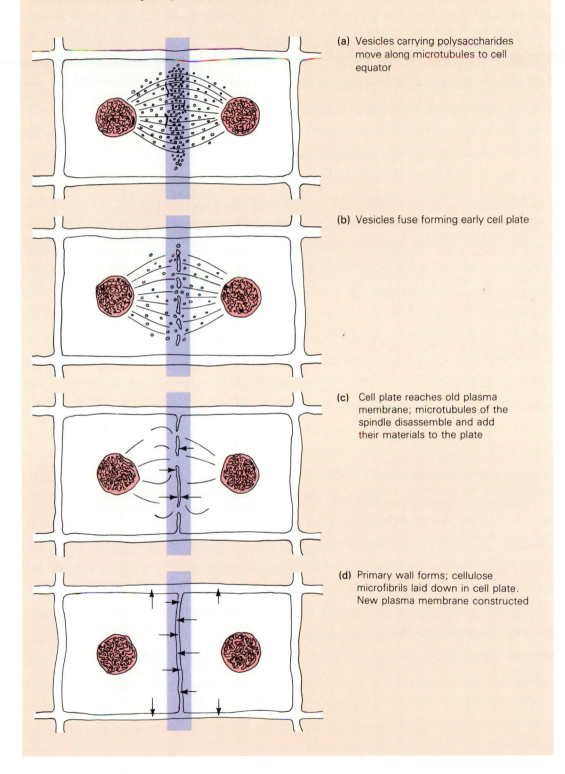

(a) Vesicles carrying polysaccharides move along microtubules to cell equator

(b) Vesicles fuse forming early cell plate

(c) Cell plate reaches old plasma membrane; microtubules of the spindle disassemble and add their materials to the plate

(d) Primary wall forms; cellulose microfibrils laid down in cell plate. New plasma membrane constructed

SUMMING UP CELL DIVISION

Cell division involves two distinct parts—mitosis and cytokinesis. The primary objective of mitosis is to divide the products of DNA replication—the chromatids—equally between the two daughter cells. Mitosis is followed by cytokinesis, which involves a less precise division of cytoplasm. Its mechanisms differ greatly in plants and animals, but in both the results are the same: one cell gives rise to two.

The primary function of mitosis in single-celled eukaryotes is reproduction. In multicellular organisms mitosis is principally involved in growth and repair. Mitosis in multicellular organisms begins at conception, and from then on provides a continuous supply of cells to be molded into the embryo's structures. In animals, mitosis continues rapidly until maturity, after which it occurs much less frequently, except in areas where cells can be expected to wear out quickly. Since plants grow throughout their life spans, new cells are continuously needed for that growth, and mitosis occurs at a relatively constant rate.

SUMMARY

Cell division permits cells to remain small, establishing a favorable cytoplasm-to-membrane relationship. It also permits organized growth and development to occur in multicellular organisms, replaces aging or damaged cells, provides for sperm and egg, and is a means of reproduction in protists. Genetic continuity is provided by DNA replication—chromosome copying and mitosis—the organized division of replicas. Mitosis is followed by cytokinesis (cytoplasmic division).

THE CELL CYCLE AND DNA REPLICATION
The Cell Cycle
Interphase is divided into G1 (growth), S (DNA replication), and G2 (chiefly tubulin synthesis) phases. Interphase is followed by the M Phase (mitosis) and then cytokinesis.

DNA Replication: A Brief Look
In replication, the DNA molecule is unwound from its helix, and sections of its two strands (the nucleotide polymers) are separated. Through the use of base-pairing, new matching nucleotide strands are then assembled. Two identical molecules emerge. While they are attached at the centromere they are called chromatids. When separation occurs, they become chromosomes.

A CLOSER LOOK AT THE CHROMOSOME
Chromatin
Chromosomes are made up of DNA molecules and proteins, forming chromatin. In the interphase nucleus, chromatin in a highly diffuse state forms the chromatin net.

Mitotic Chromosomes
In early mitosis, chromosomes condense along a chromosomal scaffold, forming coils upon coils and becoming readily visible. The condensed form aids in separation during mitosis.

Chromosome Numbers and Pairs
Chromosome numbers vary among species. Chromosomes in most cells occur as homologues (pair members), a contribution from each parent at conception. Each gene along a chromosome has a matching gene on the homologous chromosome. The two genes may vary in their specific expression. While most cells in animals are diploid (all homologues present), gametes are haploid (one homologue from each pair present). The diploid condition is restored at fertilization.

MITOSIS
The tubulin synthesized in G2 will be assembled into microtubules that make up the spindle upon which chromosomes move. Mitosis consists of four phases: prophase, metaphase, anaphase, and telophase.

Mitosis in Animals
Prophase. In early prophase, the centrioles migrate, chromosomes condense, nucleoli fade, the nuclear membrane is dismantled, and the spindle appears. The spindle's three parts originate in the microtubular organizing centers (MOC) around the centrioles. Asters radiate in all directions, continuous spindle fibers from each MOC pass outward and overlap, and centromeric spindle fibers from each side attach to centromeres. In prophase, the chromosomes are moved to a central region forming the metaphase plate.

Metaphase/Anaphase. At metaphase the chromosomes pause at the plate, each centromere attached to opposing centromeric spindle fibers. At anaphase, the centromeres divide and the chromatids separate, moving to opposite poles. Movement is believed to occur through (a) an active sliding mechanism between overlapping continuous fibers and (b) through the shortening of centromeric spindle fibers.

Telophase. In telophase, the chromosomes uncoil, the spindle breaks down, nuclear membrane and nucleoli reappear, and centrioles may replicate.

Cytokinesis in Animals

In animal cells cytokinesis (cleavage), the contraction of microfilaments, forms a deepening cleavage furrow, dividing the cell.

Mitosis in Plants/Cytokinesis in Plants

Although centrioles are absent in most plants, spindle formation and chromosome movement are similar to that of animals. Cytokinesis occurs through the establishment of new cell walls. Vesicles form a cell plate, which takes in pectin, establishing a middle lamella. With the deposition of cellulose, a primary cell wall emerges.

KEY TERMS

biogenetic law	chromatid	telophase
genetic continuity	centromere	spindle pole
DNA replication	chromatin	microtubular organizing center (MOC)
mitosis	chromatin net	aster
daughter cells	chromosomal scaffold	continuous spindle fiber
cytokinesis	karotyping	centromeric spindle fiber
cell cycle	homologue	metaphase plate
interphase	diploid (2n)	daughter chromosome
G1 (gap-one)	haploid (n)	subunit disassembly
S phase	gamete	cleavage
G2 (gap-two)	spindle	cleavage furrow
M phase	prophase	cell plate
chromosome	metaphase	middle lamella
base pairing	anaphase	primary cell wall

REVIEW QUESTIONS

1 List five important purposes for cell division. (p. 128)

2 List the three subparts of interphase and describe the activity in each. List three examples of cells that do not cycle. In what part of the cell cycle do such cells remain? (pp. 129–130)

3 Using simple diagrams of DNA, explain how replication occurs. What assures that the two emerging molecules are exact replicas? (pp. 130–131)

4 What is the composition of chromatin? The chromatin net? Why is the diffuse state necessary? (p. 131)

5 Describe the organization of a mitotic chromosome. Why is such a compact organization necessary? (p. 131)

6 Compare the chromosome number in every fifth species listed in Table 9.1. What is the significance of the chromosome number? (p. 134)

7 What are homologous chromosomes? What event in the life of an organism brings homologous chromosomes together? (p. 132)

8 Where in humans would one find cells with the diploid number of chromosomes? The haploid number? (p. 132)

9 Name the spindle protein and describe its organization into spindle fibers. What is another name for spindle fiber? (p. 134)

10 List five changes that occur in the cell at the onset of mitotic prophase. (pp. 134, 137)

11 Describe the arrangement in the cell of the asters, continuous spindle fibers, and centromeric spindle fibers. (pp. 134, 137)

12 Briefly describe the attachment of the centromeric spindle on each chromosome along the metaphase plate. What is the effect of such an attachment when anaphase begins? (p. 137)

13 Summarize the two mechanisms that account for the migration of chromosomes from the metaphase plate. (p. 138)

14 List five events associated with telophase. (p. 138)

15 What is cytokinesis? Explain how it occurs in animals. (p. 138)

16 What effect, if any, does the absence of centrioles in higher plants have on mitosis? What problem does this seem to introduce? (p. 139)

17 List the events surrounding cytokinesis in plants. What factors make plant cytokinesis different from animal cytokinesis? (p. 139)

10

MEIOSIS AND SHUFFLING CHROMOSOMES

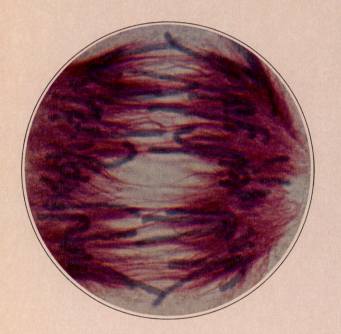

As we live out our lives on this planet, whether climbing the earth's great peaks or "meditating" in a hammock, our bodies are undergoing constant changes as, each instant, millions of cells die, while new ones take their place. But while our cells are in rapid turnover, our bodies maintain a remarkable constancy. The constancy is due, of course, to the precise mechanisms of mitosis that ensure the similarity of cells descended from a single line. However, some cells—those that give rise to **gametes,** that is, to eggs and sperm—produce daughter cells that are not alike. (The odds that two sperm or two eggs will be genetically identical have been calculated at 13 billion to one.) The process by which such genetically diverse cells arise is called **meiosis** (an orderly cell division by which chromosome numbers are halved, resulting in one homologue in each daughter cell).

MEIOSIS: AN OVERVIEW

A cell going through meiosis produces daughter cells that have only half the number of chromosomes that were in the original cell. The chromosomes themselves have also undergone genetic changes. From these haploid, or "halved," cells eggs and sperm (and spores in plants) are formed. This should not be surprising if you think about it. Eggs and sperm combine their genetic material at fertilization, forming **zygotes** (fertilized eggs). If the normal complement of chromosomes were added together at each occasion, the number of chromosomes in each new generation would double. Obviously that wouldn't do.

The basic process of meiosis is outlined in Figure 10.1. (We have simplified the scheme by showing only two pairs of homologous chromosomes, rather than our own 23, and by omitting such complications as crossing over, which is discussed later in this chapter.) As we see, meiosis consists of two divisions, wherein each diploid meiotic cell eventually produces four haploid daughter cells. (Recall from Chapter 9 that *diploid* cells contain both homologues of each chromosome pair, whereas *haploid* cells contain only one homologue of each pair. Thus a diploid human cell has 46 chromosomes, or 23 pairs, and a haploid human gamete has 23 unpaired chromosomes.)

A cell designated for meiosis will require two divisions (without replication between) to become haploid. The first division is aptly termed **meiosis I,** and the second division, **meiosis II.** In meiosis the chromosomes are distributed in a manner uniquely different from mitosis.

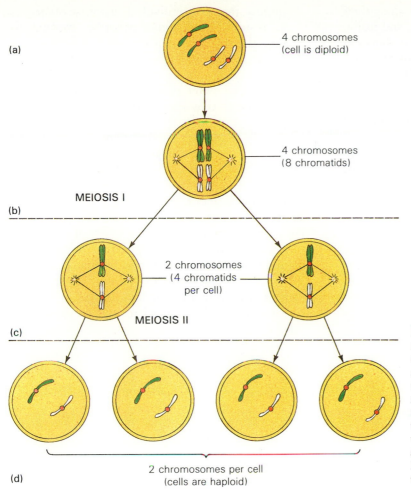

(a)

4 chromosomes
(cell is diploid)

4 chromosomes
(8 chromatids)

MEIOSIS I

(b)

2 chromosomes
(4 chromatids
per cell)

MEIOSIS II

(c)

(d)

2 chromosomes per cell
(cells are haploid)

FIGURE 10.1 (a) The chromosomes replicate, and at the start of meiosis (b) eight chromatids are present. (c) The first of two successive meiotic divisions then occurs. Note that the centromeres do not divide, and pair members have separated. Each daughter cell receives a member from each pair. (d) With the second meiotic division, centromeres divide and daughter cells receive two chromosomes per cell. This means they are now haploid (compare these to the diploid cell at the top).

Meiosis requires two divisions, **meiosis I** and **meiosis II,** to reduce the chromosome number from diploid to haploid.

Comparing Meiosis and Mitosis

Meiosis and mitosis have enough in common to cause us to confuse one with the other, at least at first, but they also have some crucial differences. We just mentioned that meiosis requires two divisions during which one diploid cell becomes four haploid cells. There are also more subtle but equally critical differences. For instance, although centromeres normally divide in anaphase of mitosis, *they do not divide in meiosis I.* Instead, *the homologous chromosomes (the pair members) separate,* each moving to an opposite pole and each still containing two chromatids. *It is not until the second division, meiosis II, that the centromeres divide,* finally permitting the chromatids to sep-

arate and move apart as daughter chromosomes. (See Figure 10.1c and d.)

Meiosis also differs from mitosis in that meiotic cells experience **genetic recombination,** that is, they have a different association of genes from that present in the original cell.

Unlike mitosis, in meiosis I, centromeres remain intact, and homologous chromosomes become separated.

Genetic Recombination

In mitotic cells homologous chromosomes go through countless rounds of replication and separation while remaining completely apart from each other. In meiosis, however, homologues of paternal and maternal origin not only recognize each other but become intimately associated, intertwining, and actually fusing together at various places along their length. During **synapsis,** as the pairing and fusing process is known, a form of genetic recombination called **crossing over** occurs. During crossing over, homologous chromatids exchange equivalent segments of DNA. Simply put, they swap genes (or portions of genes). The homologues then separate, but by then each chromatid contains a new mix of genes.

We will look into the details later, but to gain some perspective on what this means, consider this. Homologues, members of chromosome pairs, were first brought together when sperm and egg united in fertilization. Then throughout the millions of replications and mitotic cell divisions that followed, the original genes on each parental chromosome were faithfully copied and retained. But during meiosis many chromosomes exchanged genes, thus becoming genetically unique. So, *Mitosis provides for genetic continuity and helps to assure the emergence of genetically identical daughters; meiosis dictates that daughter cells will be genetically different.*

In **prophase I** of meiosis, homologues synapse and genes are exchanged between chromatids through **crossing over,** a form of **genetic recombination.**

What possible purpose could such unexpected events serve? What good is crossing over? Briefly, it results in new combinations of genes in the gametes, the sperm and eggs. In turn, more varied gametes lead to greater genetic variation, or diversity, among the offspring of a population. For the most part genetic variation is adaptive; it promotes survival in a constantly changing environment. If we human beings as a population were genetically alike and something changed, say a deadly new viral strain arose, we'd all be dead. But since we are genetically different, there is a better chance that some of us would survive, and the survivors would pass their fortuitous genes on to offspring who could also fight off the new virus. (Considering the threat of AIDS today, the example is not entirely academic.)

In summary, the differences between meiosis and mitosis are:
1. Mitosis requires one division; meiosis requires two.
2. In mitosis the chromosome number is retained, but in cells emerging from meiosis the number is halved.
3. Although centromeres divide in anaphase of

mitosis, they do not divide in anaphase of meiosis I. Instead, homologues separate, moving to opposite sides of the cell.
4. In mitosis homologues remain aloof, but in meiosis, they synapse; crossing over occurs.
5. Mitotic daughter cells are genetically identical, but meiotic cells are genetically diverse.

MEIOSIS I: THE FIRST DIVISION

During the usual cell cycle, a cell preparing for mitosis grows, replicates its DNA, and forms spindle protein. The same thing happens to a cell preparing for meiosis. Because of DNA replication, a human cell entering the first prophase of meiosis is a G2 cell with 92 DNA molecules. In the "halving" arithmetic of meiosis, decreasing from 92 to 23 requires two steps (cell divisions) (92 reduced to 46; 46 reduced to 23).

Prophase I

As the cell enters **prophase I,** the chromosomes begin to condense, just as we would expect. But in meiosis, the process occurs with agonizing slowness (Figure 10.2a). We are eventually able to detect the long, spindly chromosomes as they first begin to shorten, but we may also see that they are moving—almost as if searching for something. That "something" is each other. Each chromosome must find its counterpart, its homologue. The meiotic cell nucleus slowly begins to roll or tumble in such a way that the chromosomes within are moved randomly about. When two homologues finally bump into each other in the right way, homologous *regions* of the chromosomes will adhere, side-by-side (Figure 10.2b). The regions of side-by-side fusion grow as the two homologues come together much like the two halves of a zipper.

The structure responsible for this zipperlike pairing is a complex nucleoprotein organelle called the **synaptonemal complex.** It is synthesized on the chromosomes before they actually pair, and forms a bridge between homologues. In some electron micrographs, the synaptonemal complex even looks surprisingly like a zipper (Figure 10.3a).

It is within the synaptonemal complex that crossing over—the actual shuffling of genes—takes place (Figure 10.3b). In human meiosis, there is an average of about 10 exchanges per chromosome pair. How does it happen? The details are still a subject of intense scientific investigation. The most important

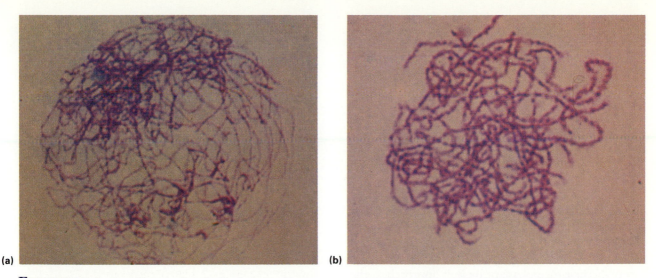

(a)   (b)

FIGURE 10.2   In earliest prophase I of meiosis **(a)** chromosomes only partially condense, appearing as long, spindly strands. Chromosomes begin to move, and homologues find each other and fuse **(b)**, permitting crossing over to occur. (Each strand represents two fused homologues.)

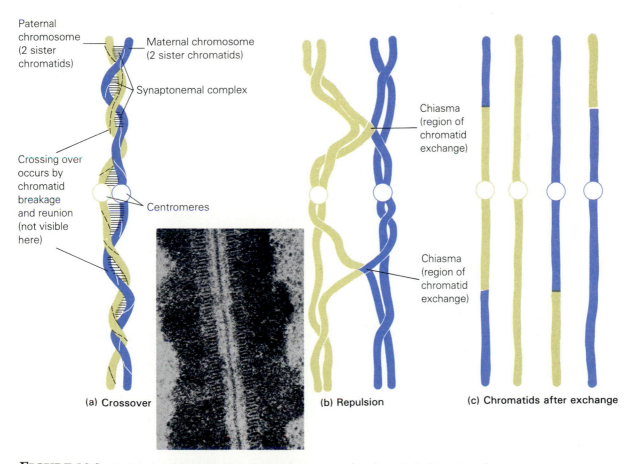

Paternal chromosome (2 sister chromatids)

Maternal chromosome (2 sister chromatids)

Synaptonemal complex

Crossing over occurs by chromatid breakage and reunion (not visible here)

Centromeres

Chiasma (region of chromatid exchange)

Chiasma (region of chromatid exchange)

(a) Crossover   (b) Repulsion   (c) Chromatids after exchange

FIGURE 10.3   Early in prophase I, **(a)** homologous chromosomes fuse through the formation of a zipperlike synaptonemal complex. In this state, crossing over occurs. Following synapsis **(b)**, repulsion occurs, and the four chromatids are clearly visible. Clinging regions form X-shaped chiasmata that will mark crossover regions. The four emerging chromatids **(c)** have undergone genetic recombination.

thing to realize about crossing over is that it is in no way an accident or a byproduct of other processes. It is such an important process that at least 50 genes and their enzymes are responsible for seeing that it happens.

After crossing over, things begin to happen a bit more rapidly. The chromosomes continue to shorten and condense, and then at some point the synaptonemal complex breaks down. The homologues lose their affinity for each other, and they move apart in a process appropriately called **repulsion.**

Repulsion doesn't occur as completely as it might because the homologues persist in clinging together at scattered points called **chiasmata** (singular, *chiasma*). They mark the places where crossing over had taken place earlier (Figure 10.3b).

As the first metaphase of meiosis approaches, the chiasmata slide to the ends of the chromosomes, much like a ring being pulled off two napkins. Finally, the chromosomes are joined only at their tips. They continue to touch for this last moment as they move together to the metaphase plate where they prepare to be separated forever.

The **synaptonemal complex** permits synapsis and crossing over, following which it breaks down; chromatid **repulsion** occurs, and the resulting **chiasmata** mark the crossovers.

Metaphase I and Anaphase I

At **metaphase I,** when the chromosomes form the metaphase plate, there is a brief pause in activity. Then the last of the clinging homologues completely disengage and **anaphase I** begins. But as emphasized, unlike what happens during mitotic anaphase, *the centromeres do not divide.* Instead, sister chromatids remain joined and move together, with homologues drawn toward opposite poles of the cell. Let's be sure this is clear. In the language of genetics, pair members become segregated, they end up at opposite sides of the cell, and, following cytokinesis, they end up in different cells. This cannot be a random process; *it must be pair members that separate in anaphase I.* Any other kind of separation would mean that the daughter cells would end up with some genes missing and extra copies of other genes. Both situations can be lethal.

How is the precision of anaphase I guaranteed? What assures that all homologues move in opposite directions? The answer brings up yet another difference between meiosis and mitosis. Recall that in mitosis (see Figure 9.7), each individual chromo-some received centromeric spindle fibers from both poles. Not so in meiosis I. At metaphase I of meiosis, each pair member receives only one set of centromeric spindle fibers, and these are from the pole opposite those received by the other pair member (Figure 10.4). This arrangement guarantees the segregation of homologous chromosomes in anaphase I. Once the chromosomes have gathered at their respective poles, telophase I begins.

Opposing centromeric spindle fiber attachments and resistant centromeres assure the precise segregation of all homologues during **anaphase I.**

Telophase I

Telophase I is similar to mitotic telophase. The chromosomes uncoil (sometimes only partially), the nuclear membrane forms around them, centrioles replicate, and cytokinesis occurs. Of course, the daughter cells are unlike any produced by mitosis, since chromosome pairs no longer exist. Remember, the maternal and paternal homologues were separated forever at the metaphase plate.

After telophase I, the daughter cells enter their **meiotic interphase,** the period before the second stage of meiosis begins. In this interphase there is *no DNA replication,* so the chromosomes entering meiosis II will appear exactly as they did at the end of meiosis I. Each chromosome will be composed of two recombined chromatids still attached by a centromere.

MEIOSIS II

Meiosis II is a bit easier to follow since it proceeds much as does mitosis (see Figure 10.1). Both daughter cells from meiosis I enter **prophase II** (with a few exceptions). At this stage, the centromeric spindle fibers from each pole attach to either side of the chromosomal centromeres, just as they do in mitosis. The chromosomes then line up on the metaphase II plate in preparation for being separated. The centromeres finally divide as **anaphase II** begins, and the chromatids, now daughter chromosomes, are drawn to opposite poles. Following **telophase II** the two daughters of meiosis I divide into four cells.

The final four daughter cells of meiosis each contain half the chromosome number of the original cell.

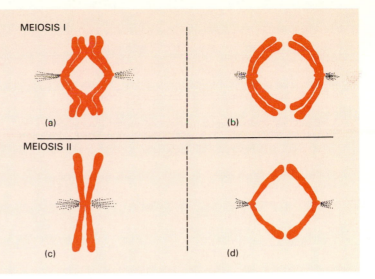

FIGURE 10.4 The arrangement of centromeric spindle fibers explains how homologues become segregated during meiosis I and how chromatids finally separate during meiosis II. In anaphase I **(a)**, the spindle fibers that attach to each homologue *originate at opposite poles*. When the pulling occurs, homologues become separated and end up segregated in the two daughter cells. In anaphase II **(b)**, as in mitosis, centromeric spindle fibers attach to *each side of each chromosome*. When the pull occurs, the centromeres divide and the chromatids separate.

MEIOSIS I

(a)

(b)

MEIOSIS II

(c)

(d)

They are now haploid. In addition, each is unique, its chromosomes bearing a different combination of genes from those of the original cell. Figure 10.5 makes a final comparison between mitosis and meiosis.

> In **anaphase II,** centromeres divide, and sister chromatids are pulled to opposite poles. Following **telophase II,** four haploid cells emerge.

Although we have emphasized the precision of meiosis, you shouldn't be surprised to learn that such a complex mechanism sometimes fails. Errors in chromosome and chromatid separation do occur. For example, the centromeres may not release the chromosomes, and one cell will end up short one chromosome while the other has an extra one. Should such an abnormal gamete enter into fertilization and the embryo survive, the results are usually tragic. Such an error, known as **nondisjunction,** occurs all too frequently in our own meiotic mechanisms (Essay 10.1).

WHERE MEIOSIS TAKES PLACE

In multicellular organisms, meiosis usually takes place in the **germinal tissues.** In animals, the organs in which germinal tissues are found are the **ovaries** (in females) and the **testes** (in males). In flowering plants, the equivalent structures are the flower's **ovaries** and **anthers.** Curiously, the germinal tissues of animals begin to form early, while the individual is

still an embryo. Flowering plants, however, maintain regions of uncommitted tissues, which begin to change following an environmental cue, some breaking out of the usual cycling and developing into the floral parts.

Meiosis in Humans

In humans, as well as most other animals, the gonads (ovaries and testes) are formed during embryonic development. In males, the germinal tissue forms the lining of the long, highly coiled tubules that make up most of the mass of the testes. However, once these tissues are formed, activity ceases until puberty—when the cells begin dividing again. Some of the new cells produced in these divisions will begin to undergo meiosis, while others continue with mitosis, forming a ready reserve supply (for future sperm). Male meiosis, or **spermatogenesis,** holds no surprises. In each complete meiotic event, four haploid cells are formed. Each of these will become a sperm. However, meiosis in females is quite different (Figure 10.6).

> **Spermatogenesis**—meiosis in males—is ongoing in humans from puberty to old age with each event resulting in four potential haploid sperm.

Meiosis in women. In women (and in females of other vertebrate species as well), the cells in the ovaries that will give rise to eggs take a somewhat unexpected developmental route. Meiosis in females, or **oogenesis,** is well under way during the embryonic stage. In fact, a newborn girl already has all the

FIGURE 10.5 Comparison of mitosis and meiosis. The differences between mitosis and meiosis become apparent when they are compared stepwise.

At *metaphase*, the alignments are also different. Mitotic chromosomes align randomly with the spindle fibers attached on both sides. In meiotic metaphase I, attachments form on one side only.

At mitotic *anaphase*, the centromeres divide and chromatids separate, while in anaphase I of meiosis they do not. Sister chromatids remain attached and homologous chromosomes, still doubled, move apart.

Mitosis terminates with *telophase*. The cell enters interphase, and its DNA will be replicated in the S phase. In addition, the manner of division at anaphase ensures that each daughter cell will have the same number of chromosomes as the mother cell. The meiotic daughter will not enter an S phase, and no DNA replication occurs.

In *meiosis*, a second division will occur with centromeres now dividing and sister chromatids (now chromosomes) moving to opposite poles, just as happened in mitosis. Unlike mitosis, however, the four daughter cells will be haploid, with exactly half the chromosome number of the mitotic daughter cells.

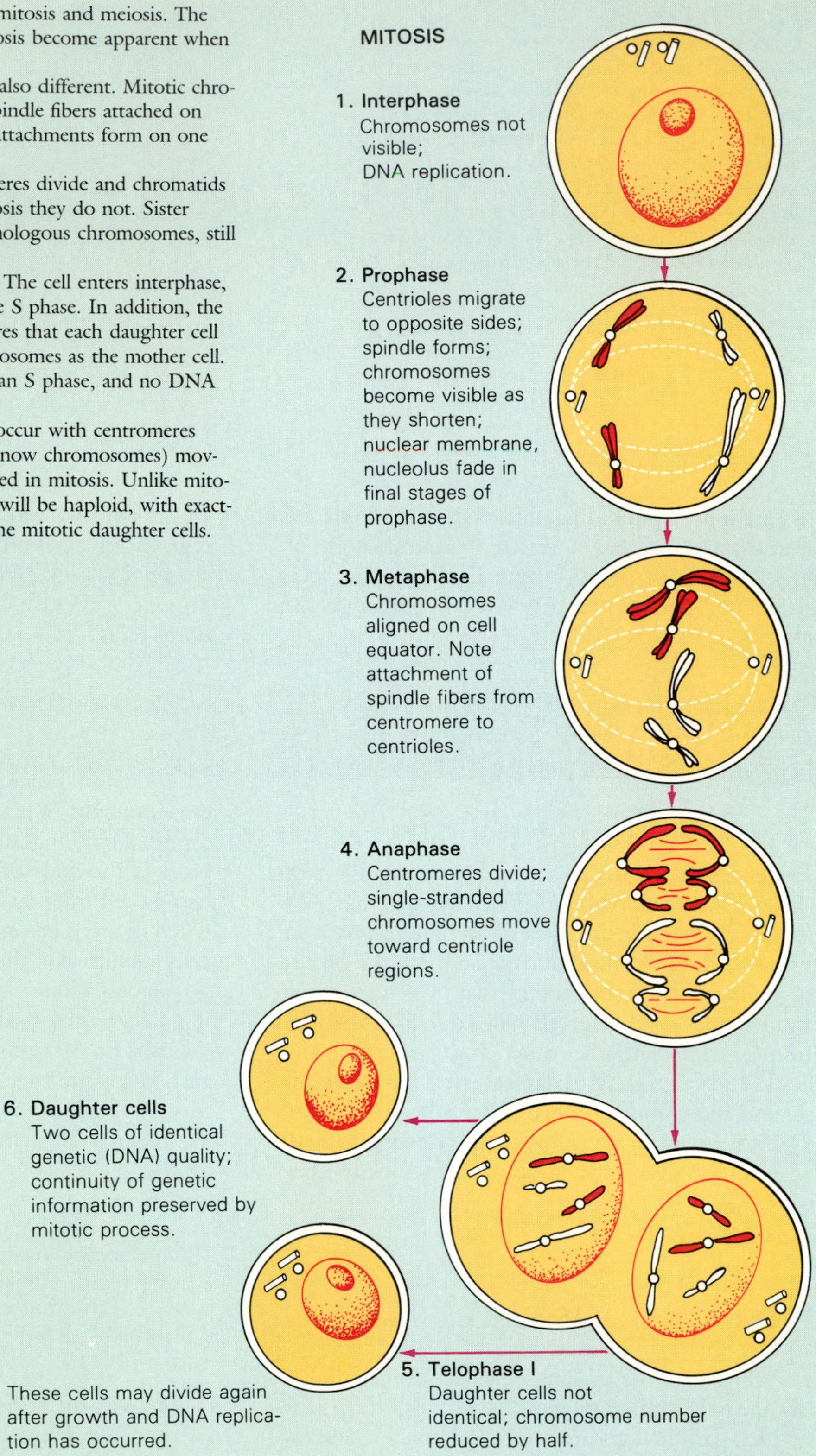

MITOSIS

1. Interphase
Chromosomes not visible; DNA replication.

2. Prophase
Centrioles migrate to opposite sides; spindle forms; chromosomes become visible as they shorten; nuclear membrane, nucleolus fade in final stages of prophase.

3. Metaphase
Chromosomes aligned on cell equator. Note attachment of spindle fibers from centromere to centrioles.

4. Anaphase
Centromeres divide; single-stranded chromosomes move toward centriole regions.

6. Daughter cells
Two cells of identical genetic (DNA) quality; continuity of genetic information preserved by mitotic process.

These cells may divide again after growth and DNA replication has occurred.

5. Telophase I
Daughter cells not identical; chromosome number reduced by half.

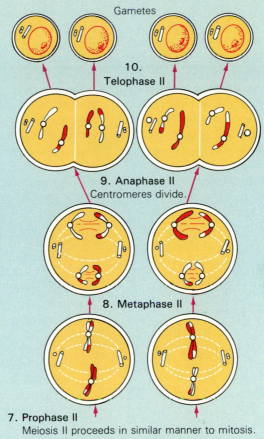

MEIOSIS I

MEIOSIS II

Gametes

1. **Premeiotic Interphase;** DNA replication.

10. **Telophase II**

2. **Prophase I** In the long prophase, homologues pair, crossing-over occurs, and the homologues begin to move apart (shown here).

9. **Anaphase II** Centromeres divide.

3. **Metaphase I** Note different alignment of double-stranded chromosomal pairs at mid-cell; chromosomes held together only at their tips.

8. **Metaphase II**

4. **Anaphase I** Centromeres do not divide; pairs of chromosomes separate.

7. **Prophase II** Meiosis II proceeds in similar manner to mitosis. Note chromosome alignment and centromere division;

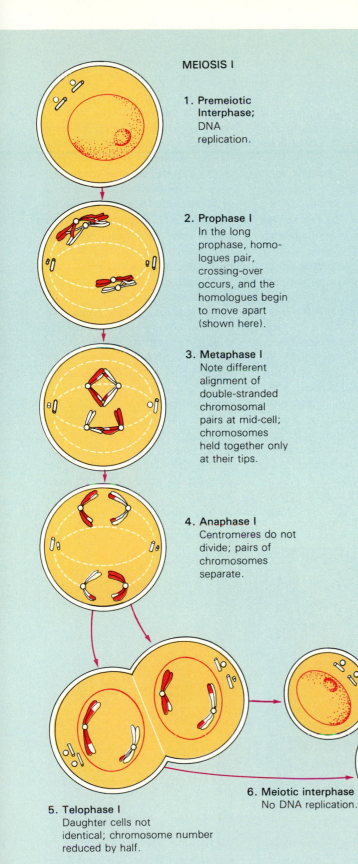

6. **Meiotic interphase** No DNA replication.

5. **Telophase I** Daughter cells not identical; chromosome number reduced by half.

Meiosis is a much more complicated process than mitosis. When you consider the lengthy prophase with all the subphases of chromosome pairing, crossing over, and repulsion, in addition to the presence of two cell divisions, you shouldn't be surprised that frequently something goes wrong. In humans, for instance, about one third of all pregnancies spontaneously abort in the first two or three months. When the expelled embryos can be examined, it turns out that most of them have the wrong number of chromosomes. Failure of the chromosomes to separate correctly at meiosis is termed nondisjunction.

Not all failures of meiosis result in early miscarriage. There are late miscarriages and stillbirths of severely malformed fetuses. Even worse, about one live-born human baby in 200 has the wrong number of chromosomes, accompanied by severe physical and/or mental abnormalities.

About one baby in 600 has three copies of tiny chromosome 21. Such persons may grow into adulthood, but they have all kinds of abnormalities. The syndrome is known both as **trisomy**-21 and **Down syndrome,** after the 19th century physician who first described it. Characteristics of the syndrome are general pudginess, rounded features, and a rounded mouth in particular, an enlarged tongue which often protrudes, and various internal disorders. Often a peculiar fold in the eyelids is seen and in the past this was erroneously equated with the characteristic eye fold of Asians (thus the earlier name "mongoloid"). Trisomy-21 individuals also have a characteristic barklike voice and unusually happy, friendly dispositions. The "happiness" is a true effect of the extra chromosome and not a result of their usually extremely low IQs; those with serious mental impairment are usually, by most indications, miserable.

Trisomy-21 occurs most frequently among babies born to women over 35 years old. At that age the incidence is about 2 per 1000 births. By age 40, this climbs to about 6, and by age 45, 16 children with Down syndrome are born for each 1000 births. The age of the father apparently has little, if any, effect. We can guess that the much-prolonged prophase I of the human oocyte might have something to do with this.

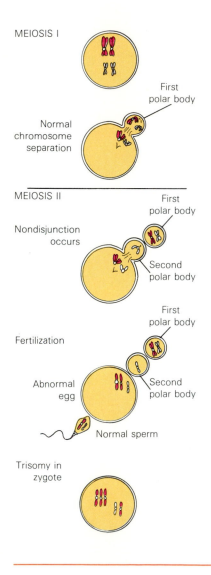

MEIOSIS I

First polar body

Normal chromosome separation

MEIOSIS II

First polar body

Nondisjunction occurs

Second polar body

First polar body

Fertilization

Abnormal egg

Second polar body

Normal sperm

Trisomy in zygote

FIGURE 10.6 Meiosis occurs during spermatogenesis *(right),* as expected, yielding four haploid cells (later becoming sperm); oogenesis, however, *(left)* is different. In both the first and second divisions, the metaphase plate forms to one side of the oocyte. Each complete meiotic event in oogenesis results in the formation of one large ovum and one polar body.

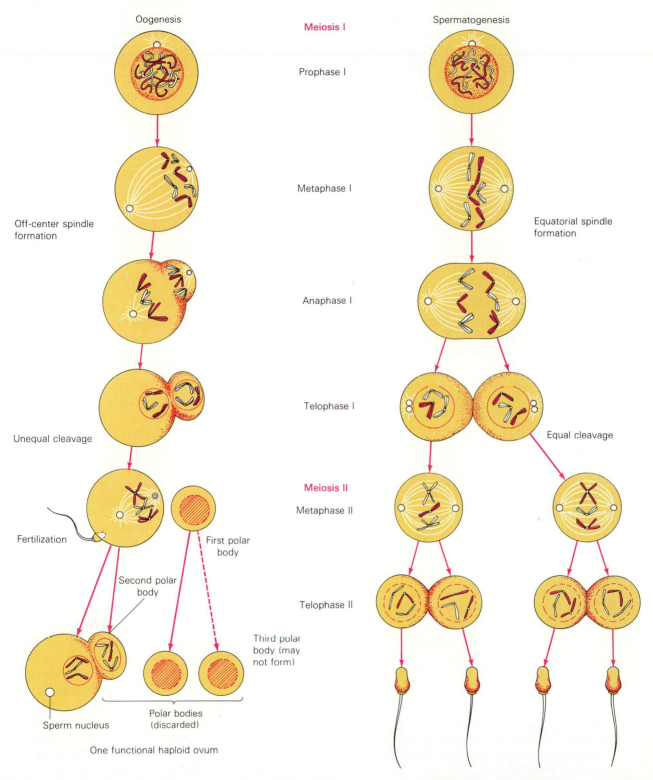

Oogenesis

Meiosis I

Spermatogenesis

Prophase I

Metaphase I

Off-center spindle formation

Equatorial spindle formation

Anaphase I

Telophase I

Unequal cleavage

Equal cleavage

Fertilization

Meiosis II

Metaphase II

First polar body

Second polar body

Telophase II

Third polar body (may not form)

Sperm nucleus

Polar bodies (discarded)

One functional haploid ovum

Four functional, haploid sperm

developing eggs she will ever have; and most are already in prophase I, where they will stay until puberty.

When a girl reaches puberty, one or two **oocytes** (future eggs, or ova) resume meiosis each month, in preparation for **ovulation** (release of the egg from the ovary). This process will be repeated throughout the reproductive life of a woman. Although an infant girl is born with several thousand developing eggs in her ovaries, only about 400 to 500 actually mature. So, although sperm are produced continuously after puberty in men, women are born with all the oocytes they will ever have.

There are other significant differences between meiosis in males and females. Consider numbers of gametes, for instance. We've seen that females are born with several thousand developing or **primary oocytes.** Males, by comparison, produce nearly countless sperm cells, releasing some 300 million with each ejaculation. Further, oocytes are often metabolically active, accumulating great quantities of nutrients, thus becoming far larger than sperm. Even the meiotic arithmetic is different. The end product of meiosis in males is the usual four gametes for each cell going through meiosis, but the result for the same event in females is only one potential egg cell. What happens to the other three cells we have come to expect?

In females, meiosis I results in two cells as expected, but they are far different in size. It seems that the cleavage plane in the female oocyte is off to one side of the cell and even though chromosome separation occurs as expected, one daughter cell gets nearly all of the cytoplasm. The other, much smaller second cell, known as a **polar body,** acts only as a receptacle for half the homologues, an important task, although the cell has no real future. Once produced, polar bodies may or may not divide again.

The larger cell, now called a **secondary oocyte,** enters meiosis II and divides as expected, but again, a highly unequal cytoplasmic division produces a large cell and another polar body. Of course, the large cell becomes the haploid ovum. (Actually, in humans, as in other mammals, meiosis II begins with ovulation, but will not be completed unless fertilization occurs.) Meiosis in females produces only one functional haploid gamete. The two or three polar bodies simply disintegrate.

> **O**ogenesis (meiosis in females), which goes to prophase I in the embryo, resumes at maturity. Each complete event results in one **ovum** and two or three **polar bodies.**

Meiosis in Plants

Gamete production in animals (humans being rather typical examples) is the direct result of meiosis. However, this isn't true in most plants. In flowering plants meiosis in the anthers is followed by mitosis, so that there are two haploid cells in each pollen grain (in such plants, pollen houses the male gamete). However, only one of the two cells in pollen is a potential sperm cell. Another peculiarity of flowering plants is that just before fertilization, the sperm cell will enter mitosis again, producing two sperm. In the ovary of flowering plants, meiosis proceeds as usual, but only one of the haploid products will survive. Rather than becoming an egg, it enters three rounds of mitosis, producing eight nuclei. One produces two, which produce four, which produce eight, only one of which will become an egg cell (see Chapter 23).

Ferns are stranger still. Like a number of nonflowering plants, ferns live double lives. The familiar, graceful plant we admire does not itself engage in sex, although it does carry on meiosis. Its meiotic products, millions of tiny, dust-sized spores containing haploid chromosomes, are carried away by wind and water. Should they find themselves in a favorable situation, the spores will begin to grow and divide, producing tiny (but independent) plants. The primary role of each plant is to produce sperm and egg cells by mitosis. Once fertilization occurs, a new, graceful, but celibate individual will emerge—to produce more spores (see Chapter 22).

> **I**n plants, meiosis results in haploid cells that first increase in number and later form gametes.

Summing Up

What does meiosis accomplish? Meiosis and fertilization are part of a cycle that allows genes to come together to form one individual, and to separate again to form other individuals. The *crossing over* that occurs at meiosis *facilitates evolution* by allowing every gene to be, in a sense, an interchangeable plug-in module, which must survive or fail on its own merits. The merit of meiosis is defined by the advantage it confers on the reproducing organism. Asexual species that have lost the ability to undergo meiosis and fertilization do exist, producing generation after generation of identical descendants, seemingly forever. But, in fact, such species face a relatively short tenure on our small planet. Their sexual relatives, by contrast, adapt—through genetic recombination—to an ever-changing world, and survive time and again to face new challenges.

SUMMARY

MEIOSIS: AN OVERVIEW

Through meiosis, cells become haploid and their chromosomes obtain a mix of parental genes. Meiosis requires two divisions, termed meiosis I and meiosis II.

Comparing Meiosis and Mitosis

(a) Centromeres divide in anaphase of mitosis. They do not divide in anaphase I of meiosis. Instead, homologues separate. (b) In mitosis, homologues remain aloof, and genetic continuity is protected. In meiosis, homologues synapse (fuse), exchanging DNA segments through crossing over.

Crossing over is a form of genetic recombination, a process that increases genetic variability, which, in turn, improves the ability of a population to survive change.

MEIOSIS I: THE FIRST DIVISION

Prophase I

Early in prophase I, homologues synapse, synaptonemal complexes form between homologues, and crossing over occurs. The repulsion of homologues follows, except at crossover points called chiasmata, where they still cling.

Metaphase I and Anaphase I

During prophase I each homologue has received centromeric spindle fibers from an opposite pole. They line up in this fashion on the metaphase plate at metaphase I. The result is that homologues move to opposite poles during anaphase I. Centromeres do not divide.

Telophase I

In telophase I, the chromosomes uncoil, the nuclear membrane and nucleolus reappear, centrioles replicate, and cytokinesis occurs. But there is no DNA replication in the ensuing interphase.

MEIOSIS II

Meiosis II is similar to mitosis, including the attachment of centromeric spindle fibers from each pole to opposite sides of each chromosome. Centromeres divide, and chromatids finally separate. Following telophase II, four haploid cells emerge. Each will carry one homologue from each chromosome pair. Each chromosome will carry a mix of parental genes.

Nondisjunction is the failure of chromosomes to separate properly during meiosis, resulting in gametes that carry abnormal numbers of chromosomes.

WHERE MEIOSIS TAKES PLACE

Meiosis occurs in germinal tissue in the ovaries and testes of animals and in the ovaries and anthers of plants.

Meiosis in Humans

Meiosis in males, called spermatogenesis, occurs in the walls of tubules within the testes. It begins at puberty and each complete meiotic event produces four haploid sperm.

Meiosis in females, called oogenesis, occurs in the germinal tissue of the ovaries. It begins in the embryo, but the oocytes become arrested in prophase I. Meiosis resumes at puberty, occurring in one or two oocytes each month. Cytokinesis in the oocytes is highly uneven with large, functional cells and minute polar bodies forming in both divisions. Because of this, the product of each complete meiotic event is one egg instead of four.

Meiosis in Plants

Meiosis in flowering plants yields haploid cells that later produce gametes through mitosis. Following meiosis in the anther, each haploid product in the anther enters mitosis, forming two cells, one of which will divide again to form two sperm cells.

Following meiosis in the ovary, three of the haploid cells are lost, but the remaining cell undergoes mitosis three times. One of the resulting cells formed becomes the egg.

In ferns, the products of meiosis are haploid aerial spores, some of which, upon germination and development, produce minute, independent plants in which sperm and egg cells form through mitosis.

KEY TERMS

gamete	synatonemal complex	anaphase II	oogenesis
zygote	repulsion	telophase II	oocyte
meiosis I	chiasma	nondisjunction	ovulation
meiosis II	metaphase I	ovary	primary oocyte
genetic recombination	anaphase I	testis	polar body
synapsis	telophase I	anther	secondary oocyte
crossing over	meiotic interphase	spermatogenesis	ovum
prophase I	prophase II		

REVIEW QUESTIONS

1 What is the logic in the "arithmetic" of meiosis. What would happen at fertilization if chromosome reduction did not occur? (p. 144)

2 Is there any special way that pairs of chromosomes are reduced and assigned to gametes during meiosis? Explain. What would happen if the assignment were random? (pp. 145, 148)

3 Explain why it requires two divisions for meiosis to be completed. (p. 144)

4 How does the behavior of centromeres differ between mitosis and meiosis I? (p. 145)

5 Briefly explain synapse and crossing over in meiosis. What effect does crossing over have on the genetic make up of the daughter cells? (pp. 145–146)

6 What is the long-term advantage of genetic recombination in the individuals of a population? (p. 146)

7 Describe the specifics of crossing over. What evidence of crossing over remains after repulsion occurs? (pp. 145–148)

8 With the aid of a drawing, show the specific manner in which centromeric spindle fibers are attached to homologues prior to anaphase I. What effect does this have on their movement during anaphase I? (pp. 148–149)

9 List a fundamental difference between mitotic interphase and interphase between meiosis I and meiosis II. Why would this make sense in meiosis? (p. 148)

10 Describe the attachment of centromeric spindle fibers to each chromosome in metaphase II. How does this affect the behavior of the chromatids in anaphase II? Compare this to the similar events in mitosis. (p. 148)

11 Compare the following aspects of spermatogenesis and oogenesis: site of germinal tissue, time of life in which meiosis begins, size of cells, numbers of gametes. (pp. 149, 154)

12 Develop a diagram illustrating human oogenesis, with emphasis on polar body formation. What is the only purpose of the polar body? (p. 153)

13 In animals, meiosis gives rise directly to gametes. Contrast this to the formation of gametes in plants. (p. 154)

14 Explain the peculiar double life of ferns. Where and how are gametes finally produced? (p. 154)

II

GENETICS AND EVOLUTION
History and Horizons

II

GREGOR MENDEL AND THE FOUNDATIONS OF GENETICS

Charles Darwin was the 19th century's greatest biologist. Even so, he was a terrible geneticist, and most of his ideas about heredity were wrong! Darwin's chief mistake was to accept the only intellectually respectable theory of his day, which was that of *blending inheritance*. According to this theory, the "blood" or hereditary traits of both parents blended in the offspring, just as two colors of ink blend when they are mixed. The blending theory appeared superficially to work reasonably well for some traits—such as height or weight, where there is a continuous gradation of possible values—but it couldn't account for others.

It's always surprising, in hindsight, to recognize the degree to which a strongly held belief will blind its proponents to obvious contradictions. The blending theory would predict that the offspring of a white horse and a black horse should always be gray, and that the original white or black should never reappear if gray horses continued to be bred. In reality, of course, the offspring of a white horse and a black horse are not always gray, and black or white descendants do appear. Something was obviously wrong with the theory, but no one seemed to notice—or if they did, they tried to ignore it.

Darwin had become embroiled in the aftermath of his new book, *On the Origin of Species by Natural Selection* (1859). His most trying problem was to counter the arguments of his sharper critics, who logically pointed out that natural selection and blending inheritance are opposing concepts; any new traits that might arise would be swamped by existing traits and simply be "blended away." Darwin was never able to answer this criticism adequately. But across the Channel, deep in the European continent, a bright and dedicated monk was setting the groundwork for a new revolution by crossing strains of garden peas. He was also answering Darwin's most vexing questions, but Darwin would die ignorant of the monk's work.

The monk Gregor Johann Mendel (Figure 11.1) was a member of an Augustinian order in Brunn, Austria (now a part of Czechoslovakia). Early in his life Mendel began training himself, and he became a rather competent naturalist. To support himself during those early years, he worked as a substitute high school science teacher. The professors at the school, noting his unusual abilities, suggested that he take the rigorous qualifying examination to become a regular member of the high school faculty. Mendel took the test and did reasonably well, but he failed to qualify, so he joined a monastic order.

In 1851 his superiors, confident of his abilities,

FIGURE 11.1 Gregor Johann Mendel (1822–1884) developed the basic laws of heredity.

sent him to the University of Vienna for two years of concentrated study in science and mathematics. There he learned about the infant science of statistics. He was to use this information when he returned to his old hobby of plant breeding. This time, though, he had specific questions in mind and he thought he knew how to go about finding the answers.

MENDEL'S CROSSES

Mendel began by trying to find the effects of crossing different strains of the common garden pea, but he carried out his research with more precision than mere casual curiosity would call for. To begin with, he based it on a very carefully planned series of experiments and, more importantly, he attempted to analyze the results statistically. The use of mathematics to describe biological phenomena was a new concept. Clearly, Mendel's two years at the University of Vienna had not been wasted.

Mendel was able to purchase 34 true-breeding strains of the common garden pea for his experiments. These strains differed from each other in very pronounced ways, so that there could be no problem in identifying the results of a given experiment. Mendel decided to work with seven different pairs of traits:

1. Seed form—round or wrinkled
2. Color of seed contents—yellow or green
3. Color of seed coat—white or gray
4. Color of unripe seed pods—green or yellow
5. Shape of ripe seed pods—inflated or constricted between seeds
6. Length of stem—short (9–18 inches) or long (6–7 feet)
7. Position of flowers—axial (along the stem) or terminal (at the end of the stem)

MENDEL'S FIRST LAW: PAIRED FACTORS AND THEIR SEGREGATION

What we will discuss here is something we already know; the point is that we learned it from Mendel. Remember that in the first meiotic division, homologous chromosomes bearing gene pairs are segregated from each other, one going to each of the two daughter cells (see Chapter 10). Mendel didn't know anything about meiosis or genes—he called genes "factors"—but somehow, he concluded that *factors come in pairs* and that each *goes to a different gamete.* He called this separation **segregation:** the segregation of alternate factors. The concepts of paired factors controlling heredity and their segregation in gametes are two principles included in Mendel's first law. Mendel was truly operating at the frontier of science, with little to go on except his own ample intuition and creativity.

To see how he started, first we must know something about peas. Each pea in a pod is essentially a unique plant, with its own genes and traits, or, in the language of genetics, its own **genotype** and **phenotype.** (The total combination of an organism's genes is called its genotype, and the combination of its visible traits is called its phenotype.) Therefore, the first three traits in Mendel's list of pea traits can be categorized by simply examining the peas in their pods.

Mendel proposed that heredity was controlled by paired factors that segregated when gametes formed and rejoined at fertilization.

TABLE 11.1   Glossary of Genetics Terms

allele	one of two or more alternative forms of a gene (A and a, R and r)	monohybrid cross	a cross in which one pair of alternative alleles is under consideration
dominance	where the expression of one allele masks the expression of its alternative (**round** × **wrinkled** = Round)	phenotype	an individual's visible traits (e.g., **tall, round, green**)
dihybrid	a cross in which two different pairs of alleles are under consideration	progeny testing	determining the genotype of offspring by self-pollinating or inbreeding
factor	an allele	Punnett square	a grid used to record the possibilities in a cross
genotype	the combination of genes producing a trait (e.g., **Tt, RR, gg, Gg**)	recessivity	where an allele's expression is masked by its alternative allele (**wrinkled** × **round** = **round**)
heterozygous	an individual with two alternative forms of a pair of alleles (e.g., **Tt, Rr, Gg**)	segregation	the physical separation of homologous alleles (those on homologous chromosomes) when meiosis occurs
homozygous	an individual with identical alleles for a gene (e.g., **TT, rr, gg, GG**)	test cross	determining the genotype of a dominant individual by crossing it to a recessive (**T?** × **tt**)
independent assortment	where the segregation of one pair of alleles has no effect on the segregation of another		
linked genes	genes situated on the same chromosome	true-breeding	individuals whose offspring are genetically identical to themselves (homozygous)

The Experimental Procedure

Mendel's approach, a novel one at that time, was to cross two **true-breeding** strains that differed in only one characteristic. (True-breeding strains are those that consistently, generation after generation, yield offspring with the same traits.) Mendel began by asking simple questions, such as: What will happen if I cross a true-breeding yellow-seed pea plant with a true-breeding green-seed pea plant?

Pea breeding, by the way, is extremely tedious work. To carry out a cross, Mendel first had to select and plant his seeds, and then wait for them to grow and flower. That gives one plenty of time to read, file one's nails, and practice accents. But later things become a bit more hectic. A garden pea plant, if left alone, generally will self-pollinate, each flower then fertilizing itself (Figure 11.2). In this way, garden peas go on happily producing their own true-breeding kind. But Mendel was interested in crosses. To cross two strains, he had to open the flowers early in their growth and cut off the pollen-producing anthers of particular plants. Then, using a fine brush, he had to transfer pollen from other flowers—a laborious task. The plants selected for the cross would be called the P_1 (first parental) generation and their off-spring the F_1 (first filial) generation. The offspring of the F_1 would be called the F_2, and so on.

F_1 **Generation and the principle of dominance.** When Mendel crossed his original P_1 plants, he found that the characteristics of the two plants didn't blend, as prevailing theory said they should. When plants grown from yellow seeds were crossed with those grown from green seeds, their F_1 offspring did not have yellowish green seeds. Instead, all of them had yellow seeds, indistinguishable from the yellow seeds of the true-breeding parental strain. Mendel termed the trait that appeared in the F_1 generation the **dominant** trait, and he described the one that had failed to appear as the **recessive** trait. The concept of dominance and recessivity is a third principle from Mendel's first law. But Mendel was left with a vexing question. What had happened to the recessive trait?

Dominance is the expression of one factor obscuring the expression of an alternative factor (the recessive).

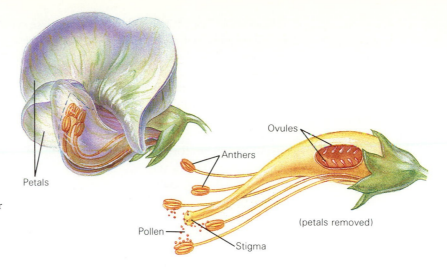

FIGURE 11.2 The unusual petals of the garden pea generally ensure self-pollination. To cross-pollinate a plant, Mendel had to open the young flower and remove the pollen-bearing anthers. Then he transferred pollen from another flower to the stigma (female receptive structure) to accomplish the cross he wanted.

Petals

Ovules

Anthers

(petals removed)

Pollen

Stigma

FIGURE 11.3 In his P_1 generation, Mendel crossed true-breeding yellow peas with true-breeding green peas (**a**). All the seeds in the F_1 generation (**b**) were yellow. These seeds were planted and, when grown, were allowed to self-pollinate, producing an F_2. F_2 seeds included both yellow and green peas (**c**) in a ratio of ¾ to ¼, or 3:1 (**d**).

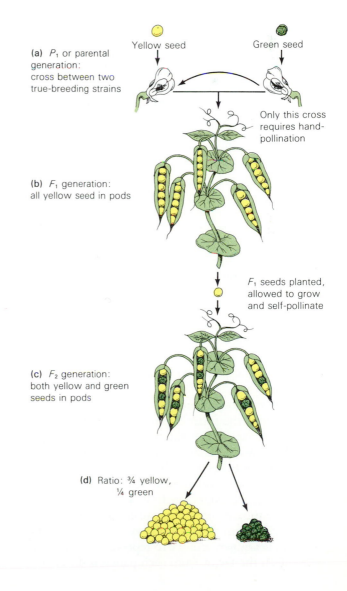

(a) P_1 or parental generation: cross between two true-breeding strains

Yellow seed

Green seed

Only this cross requires hand-pollination

(b) F_1 generation: all yellow seed in pods

F_1 seeds planted, allowed to grow and self-pollinate

(c) F_2 generation: both yellow and green seeds in pods

(d) Ratio: ¾ yellow, ¼ green

Mendel had quite a puzzle on his hands, but he was apparently quite good at puzzles. His next step, a stroke of intuition, was to allow his F_1 plants to self-pollinate. In this second filial generation (the F_2 generation), Mendel found that roughly ¼ of the peas were green and that ¾ were yellow. The recessive trait had reappeared (Figure 11.3)! He repeated the experiment with other pea strains, with comparable results. When he crossed a round pea strain with a wrinkled pea strain, all of the F_1 peas were round; but in the F_2 generation, about ¼ of the peas were wrinkled. The constancy of the ratios did not escape the tenacious Mendel, who was determined to keep tackling the problem until he could make some sense of it.

Two kinds of yellow peas: homozygous and heterozygous. From his experiments thus far Mendel realized that there were two kinds of yellow peas: the true-breeding kind, like the original parent stock, which would grow into plants that would bear only yellow peas; and another type, which—when grown and self-pollinated—would produce pods containing both yellow and green peas. Two kinds of yellow peas: one pure-breeding, one not. Were there also two kinds of green peas? There were not. When green peas were cultivated and allowed to self-pollinate, they always bore only green peas. This kind of experiment is now called **progeny testing.**

And we now call the true-breeding peas **homozygous** and the other kind **heterozygous.** Homozygous means that the organism bears the genes for only one trait (such as green color in peas); heterozygous means that the organism bears genes for different traits, regardless of its appearance. Thus a yellow F_1 or F_2 pea *could* be carrying unexpressed genes for green color.

> In **homozygous** individuals, paired factors are identical, both dominant or both recessive (e.g., TT or tt); in **heterozygous** individuals they are different (e.g., Tt).

Clearly, some factor determining the recessive form was passed down from the true-breeding recessive P_1 parental strain, through the hybrid (offspring of crossbreeding) F_1 generation to the true-breeding recessive F_2 generation; whatever it was, however, it was not being expressed in the F_1 generation. Mendel, at that time the world's only mathematical biologist, thought he could use algebraic symbols to express his dilemma.

He let a capital letter, say **Y,** represent the factor that determines the dominant form, and let a lower-case letter, say **y,** represent the factor that determines the recessive form. The F_1 hybrid, he concluded, must have both factors present, and could be represented as **Yy.** Since there are two parents, Mendel figured that in the hybrid, **Y** comes from one parent and **y** from the other. (If this sounds simplistic, considering what you know about chromosomes, remember that Mendel didn't know about chromosomes.) Using reciprocal crosses, Mendel determined experimentally that it didn't matter which parental strain bore the peas and which provided the pollen.

If heterozygous plants get a **Y** from one parent and a **y** from the other parent, and are symbolized **Yy,** it makes sense that the true-breeding dominant forms get two **Y** factors—one from each parent—and can be symbolized **YY.** In the same way, the true-breeding recessive forms get **y** factors from both parents and can be symbolized **yy.** We can use **YY** to symbolize the *dominant homozygote* (when the factor from each parent is identical), **yy** to symbolize the *recessive homozygote,* and **Yy** to represent the *heterozygote* (when the factor from each parent is different).

Let's use these symbols to take a closer look at Mendel's first crosses.

Mendel had by now deduced:

True-breeding P_1:	**YY**	×	**yy**
F_1 progeny:		All **Yy**	
F_1 inbreeding cross:	**Yy**	×	**Yy**
F_2 progeny:	**YY**	**2Yy**	**yy**

The genotypic ratio expressed in the F_2 is 1:2:1, or

1/4 round (**YY**)	=	Homozygous yellow
1/2 round (**Yy**)	=	Heterozygous yellow
1/4 wrinkled (**yy**)	=	Homozygous green.

What would be the phenotypic (visible) ratios here? Actually, there is a simpler way of representing the results, using what is known as a **Punnett square,** developed by Reginald Crandall Punnett, an early 20th-century fan of Mendel (Figure 11.4). (Some aspects of Mendel's first law can also be illustrated by simply flipping pennies; see Essay 11.1.)

> When heterozygotes are crossed, the phenotypic ratio will be 3:1 and the genotypic ratio, 1:2:1.

Summing Up Mendel's First Law

Mendel's discoveries in the crosses described so far have been brought together into a number of principles that form what we call Mendel's first law (or the law of paired factors and segregation). An expanded form of this law states:
1. Any trait is produced by at least a pair of factors. The pair may be homozygous or heterozygous. These factors segregate during pollen and ovule formation.
2. A gamete receives one of a pair of factors.
3. For each trait, offspring receive only one factor from each parent. If one parent's factors are heterozygous, the offspring has an equal chance of receiving either factor.
4. Where dominance is found, the dominant factor will be expressed over the recessive; the recessive will be expressed only when two recessive factors come together in offspring.

These statements are not in Mendel's words, except for the term *factor* which, in more modern terminology, would be **allele** (one form of a gene). Most of what the first law contains actually is attributable to simple meiosis, but remember that Mendel had no knowledge of that phenomenon. He arrived at his conclusions through sheer logic.

Mendel's first law includes the concepts of paired factors, segregation, chance recombination, and dominance.

Science and Models

We have called Mendel a mathematical biologist not just because he was trained in both mathematics and biology or because he was the first biologist to use statistical analysis in his work, but because of the way he arrived at his conclusions. What does a mathematical biologist do? Usually, he or she starts with a set of observations. In Mendel's case, it was the dominance of one trait in the first generation and the reappearance of the recessive trait in a subsequent generation. Through a mental process involving both intuition and logic, the mathematical biologist then constructs a **model.** The model is an imaginary biological system based on the smallest possible number of assumptions, and it is expected to yield numerical data consistent with past observations. New experiments are then performed to test further predictions of the model. If the new data don't fit the predictions, the model is discarded or adjusted to fit the new observations so that further experiments can be done. A model, then, can be thought of as a biological hypothesis with mathematical predictions.

Models and hypotheses cannot be proved with experimental data. We can only say that the data are *consistent* with the model. Mendel did not prove his first law, but its simplicity and consistent usefulness in verifying predictions enabled him to make and test new predictions. His success came very close to a formal proof, at least as far as he was concerned. However, others were unconvinced until after the discovery of chromosomes and meiosis. Have you noticed how well Mendel's findings fit with what you already know about meiosis? Imagine how elated Mendel would have been if meiosis had been discovered in his own lifetime!

We've mentioned that Mendel extended his crosses to all seven selected traits. How well did his results fit the mathematical model? Table 11.2 shows that in each cross, his results were amazingly close to the 3:1 phenotypic ratio predicted by his models (see Figure 11.4). The closeness between Mendel's expectations and observations did not escape the attention of certain skeptical statisticians. In 1936, R.A. Fisher, a noted statistician and geneticist, concluded that Mendel's data were literally too good to be true. Did the good abbot fudge his data? Or did he see only what he had expected to see, an all-too-human trait? The question has generated great controversy, but we will leave all that to the historians. Whatever the case, Mendel's first law was found to apply to animals as well as plants, and it has held up under the most rigorous scrutiny.

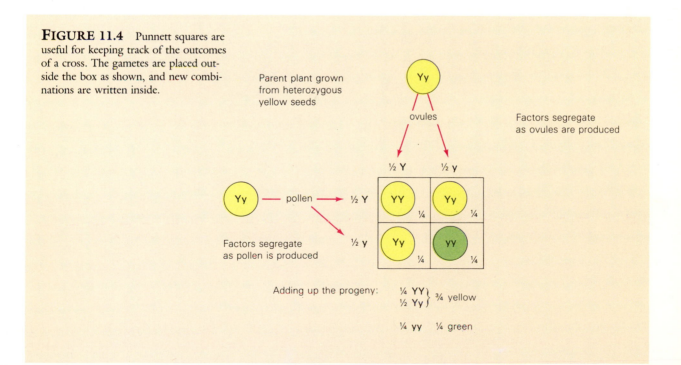

FIGURE 11.4 Punnett squares are useful for keeping track of the outcomes of a cross. The gametes are placed outside the box as shown, and new combinations are written inside.

Suppose someone flips a penny and says, "call it." If the penny is a real one you can assume that there is a statistical probability of 1/2 that the coin is "heads." This can be written in algebra as follows: $P(H) = 1/2$; that is, the probability of heads $= 1/2$. If you didn't know anything about coins and tried to generalize from the single toss, you might assume that coins *always* come up tails. But the more times you toss the coin the closer the number of tails will be to 1/2. That's why a large sample size (large numbers) is better in the statistical game.

Predicting the results of simple Mendelian crosses has a lot in common with flipping coins. For example, we begin Mendelian crosses by determining what types of gametes are possible. Obviously, there's no chance involved when a homozy-gote produces gametes; it's like flipping a two-headed coin. Heterozygous individuals, however, have two different alleles for a trait, say **A** and **a**; an **Aa** individual forms two kinds of gametes, **A** and **a**, in equal numbers. The probability that any given gamete will carry the **A** allele is 1/2. The probability that a gamete will carry **a** is also 1/2. All of Mendelian genetics is based on this 50–50 segregation of alternate alleles.

So far we have only seen how flipping a penny can represent segregation in the gametes. Let's see how it applies to a cross between two gamete-forming individuals. For this you need a partner and two coins. Since each penny has two sides, a head **(H)** and a tail **(T)**, the result of:

$$HT \times HT$$

will be any of four *possible outcomes:*

1. both coins come up heads **(HH)**;
2. both coins come up tails **(TT)**;
3. your coin is *heads,* your partner's is *tails* **(HT)**; or
4. your coin is *tails,* your partner's is *heads* **(TH)**.

All four of these possible outcomes are equally likely; each has a probability of 1/4. Why is this? It's an example of the **multiplicative law of probability,** which states that *the probability of two independent outcomes both occurring is equal to the product of their individual probabilities.* (Independent outcomes are outcomes that don't influence one another; we assume that the way your coin lands has no influence on the way your partner's coin lands, and vice versa.) The law states that

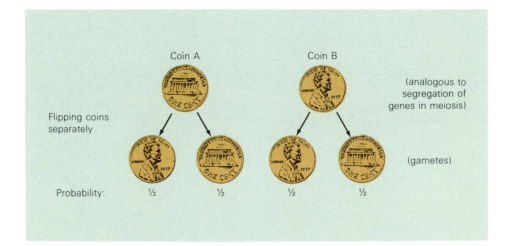

the probability of **HH** equals the probability of your coin landing heads *times* the probability of your partner's penny landing heads, which is 1/2 × 1/2 = 1/4.

The third and fourth possible outcomes are more interesting and can be used to illustrate another law. First, let's see how their probabilities are determined. The probability of:

- your penny landing heads and your partner's landing tails is 1/2 × 1/2 = 1/4;
- your penny landing tails and your partner's landing heads is 1/2 × 1/2 = 1/4.

What is the probability of heterozygous offspring **(Aa)** in our cross? To determine the answer, the probabilities of the last two possible outcomes are simply added together (1/4 + 1/4 = 1/2). There is a 1/2 chance that the two pennies will come up one head and one tail.

This basic law, called the **additive law of probability**, states that *the probability that any one of two (or more) mutually exclusive outcomes will occur, is equal to the sum of their individual probabilities*. Mutually exclusive outcomes means that if one happens, the other can't; for instance, if the outcome is: your coin, *heads;* your partner's coin, *tails;* this excludes the possibility of the outcome being the other way around.

Now, what is the probability that at least one head will be showing? Here, we combine the three mutually exclusive outcomes (1), (3), and (4). The probability that at least one head will come up is 1/4 + 1/4 + 1/4 = 3/4.

The multiplicative and additive laws can be applied to independent assortment, where two or more traits are considered simultaneously (the dihybrid cross). It's like tossing two pennies and two quarters at the same time. If you toss two pennies and two quarters simultaneously, what is the probability of seeing both Lincoln and Washington (at least once each)? The probability of seeing Lincoln is 3/4 (the probability of heads, see the paragraph above); the probability of seeing Washington is also 3/4; the chance of seeing both is 3/4 × 3/4 = 9/16. The chance of seeing Abe and *not* seeing George is 3/4 × 1/4 = 3/16, the same as for seeing George and not Abe; and the probability of seeing neither president is 1/4 × 1/4 = 1/16. Of such simple stuff are Mendelian ratios made.

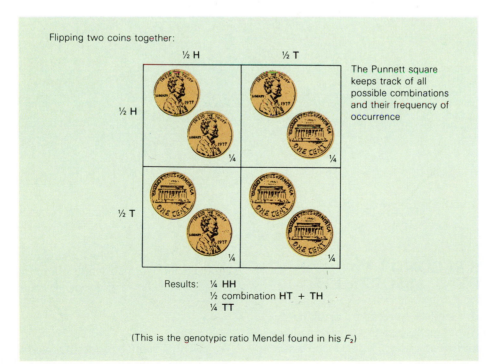

Flipping two coins together:

Results: ¼ **HH**
½ combination **HT** + **TH**
¼ **TT**

The Punnett square keeps track of all possible combinations and their frequency of occurrence

(This is the genotypic ratio Mendel found in his F_2)

TABLE 11.2   Mendel's F_2 Generations

The dominant and recessive traits analyzed by Mendel are shown, along with the results of F_1 and F_2 generations. Note the large numbers he worked with. How does a large sample size (large numbers) improve the validity of the conclusions? How well do his numbers in the last two columns agree with what we would expect in the crosses (see Essay 11.1)? The proportion of the F_2 generation showing recessive forms is in the far-right column.

	Dominant Form	Number in F_2 Generation		Recessive Form	Number in F_2 Generation	Total Examined	Ratio	Proportion of F_2 Generation
	Round seeds	5,474		Wrinkled seeds	1,850	7,324	2.96:1	0.253
	Yellow seeds	6,022		Green seeds	2,001	8,023	3.01:1	0.249
	Gray seed coats	705		White seed coats	224	929	3.15:1	0.241
	Green pods	428		Yellow pods	152	580	2.82:1	0.262
	Inflated pods	882		Constricted pods	299	1,181	2.95:1	0.253
	Long stems	787		Short stems	277	1,064	2.84:1	0.260
	Axial flowers (and fruit)	651		Terminal flowers (and fruit)	207	858	3.14:1	0.241

MENDEL'S SECOND LAW: INDEPENDENT ASSORTMENT

We have noted Mendel's success in breaking his problem down to it smallest parts, that is, studying only one characteristic at a time. His next step was to consider two characteristics at a time. He therefore crossed a true-breeding strain that bore round, yellow peas with another true-breeding strain that bore wrinkled, green peas.

The F_1 offspring (which, remember, could be categorized and counted while still in the pod) were all round and yellow. We can symbolize this as follows:

$$RRYY \times rryy \longrightarrow RrYy$$

We will now begin considering two factors, and from now on we will refer to factors as **alleles,** a more modern term. Allele means a particular form or variant of a gene at a locus. The term **locus** (plural, *loci*), derives from our present knowledge that each gene occupies a specific place, or locus, on the chromosome. **R** and **r** will be symbols for the two alleles of the round-or-wrinkled locus, and **Y** and **y** will be the symbols for the two alleles of the yellow-or-green locus.

Now let's see what happened in the F_2 generation when Mendel crossed plants that were different in two ways (called a **dihybrid cross**) (see Table 11.3). Remember that the F_1 peas were uniformly round and yellow. In the F_2 generation—the offspring of $F_1 \times F_1$ (**RrYy × RrYy**)—Mendel found and classified 556 peas. He was able to divide them into four groups:

315 round and yellow	**R–Y–**	
101 wrinkled and yellow	**rrY–**	
108 round and green	**R–yy**	
32 wrinkled and green	**rryy**	

Note that a total of 133 peas were wrinkled and 140 peas were green. In either case, this comes close to 139, which is ¼ of 556. The dashes mean that either allele could exist there without altering the phenotype.

So about ¼ of the F_2 peas were wrinkled and ¼ were green, while ¾ were round and ¾ were yellow, which demonstrates Mendel's first law in both cases. But the data indicated more than that. Mendel now suspected that the two pairs of contrasting characters were inherited *independently*. Another way of stating this is: the two pairs of alleles illustrate the principle of **independent assortment**. This means that a gamete's receipt of an **R** or an **r** has nothing to do with its receipt of a **Y** or a **y**. How did Mendel arrive at that? He looked at the numbers (Figure 11.5).

> **W**hen all possible combinations of traits appeared in the offspring of his dihybrid crosses, Mendel concluded that when P_1 gametes formed, the two pairs of factors assorted independently.

As Figure 11.5 reveals, two pairs of alleles assort independently, producing four kinds of gametes in both the pollen and the ovules. The chances of any particular combination of alleles occurring in any of the progeny is equal to that of any other combination. Therefore, we have to multiply the four kinds of male gametes by the four kinds of female gametes to predict the outcome of independent assortment. Again, the Punnett square comes to the rescue, helping us keep track of the products.

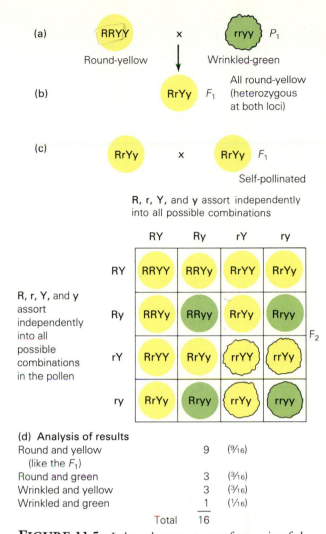

(d) Analysis of results

Round and yellow (like the F_1)	9	(⁹⁄₁₆)
Round and green	3	(³⁄₁₆)
Wrinkled and yellow	3	(³⁄₁₆)
Wrinkled and green	1	(¹⁄₁₆)
Total	16	

FIGURE 11.5 Independent assortment of two pairs of alleles. The scheme illustrates the crosses from P_1 through F_2, using the Punnett square to show the results of the F_1 self-pollinated cross. The traits being considered are round and wrinkled shape and yellow and green color. The F_2 generation comprises four distinct phenotypes, which include every possible color and shape combination. These occur in a 9:3:3:1 ratio.

The 9:3:3:1 Ratio

When Punnett squares are used, the gametes possible from both individuals must be determined first. If two traits are being considered in plants and both individuals being crossed are heterozygous for both traits, there will be four kinds of pollen and four kinds of ovules. Should a parent be homozygous for one of the traits, only two types of gametes will occur. We can use this information to sum up a cross between plants differing in two traits. The phenotypic results are ⁹⁄₁₆, ³⁄₁₆, ³⁄₁₆, and ¹⁄₁₆. These readily convert to the ratio 9:3:3:1, which is as familiar in genetics as $E = mc^2$ is in physics.

TABLE 11.3 Mendel's Predictions and Results for F_2 Phenotype (556 seeds observed)

Phenotype of F_2	Fraction Predicted	Number Predicted Out of 556	Number Actually Observed
Round and yellow	$9/16$	312.75	315
Wrinkled and yellow	$3/16$	104.25	101
Round and green	$3/16$	104.25	108
Wrinkled and green	$1/16$	34.75	32

TABLE 11.4 Mendel's Predictions and Results for the F_2 Genotypes (529 Peas Classified by Progeny Test)

Genotype of F_2	Fraction Expected	Number According to the Hypothesis	Number Actually Observed by Progeny Testing
RRYY	1/16	33	38
RRYy	2/16	66	65
RRyy	1/16	33	35
RrYY	2/16	66	60
RrYy	4/16	132	138
Rryy	2/16	66	67
rrYY	1/16	33	28
rrYy	2/16	66	68
rryy	1/16	33	30

NOTE: Keep in mind that Mendel had to perform a progeny test for each of the 529 F_2 peas in order to learn their genotype. There is no other way to prove the genotype of a heterozygote.

As we see in Table 11.3, when Mendel classified his 556 peas according to the four possible phenotypes and counted the peas in each group, the ratio was remarkably close to $9/16 : 3/16 : 3/16 : 1/16$, as would be expected if two gene loci were segregating independently, each with a $3/4 : 1/4$ phenotypic ratio.

When dihybrid F_1 individuals (heterozygotes) are crossed, the phenotypic ratio will be 9:3:3:1.

But the monk wasn't finished yet. A good scientist is never satisfied with explanations that merely account for observations that have already been made. To be useful an explanation must lead to new predictions that can then be tested. Mendel's theory predicted that when there were four phenotypes in a 9:3:3:1 ratio, there should be a total of nine genotypes in a 1:1:1:1:2:2:2:2:4 ratio. Mendel knew that he could determine the genotypes of his peas by letting them grow to adult plants and examining their progeny; so the 556 peas went into the soil, and Mendel waited another year. 529 of the resulting plants fertilized themselves and produced a new crop of peas, the F_3 generation. Now their genotypes could be determined; the results are shown in Table 11.4. Mendel was elated—his prediction had held.

The Test Cross

Although Mendel had carried out numerous progeny tests for determining whether a dominant individual was homozygous or heterozygous, he soon devised a much simpler procedure, the **test cross**. The subject was simply crossed with a recessive individual. Recessives are always homozygous, so the predictions are straightforward. Let's use the traits round and wrinkled as an example:

1. If the dominant round individual in question is homozygous, then the test cross becomes **RR × rr,** and all of the progeny will be round (**Rr**).
2. If the dominant round individual is heterozygous, then the test cross becomes **Rr × rr,** and, statistically, half the offspring will be heterozygous round (**Rr**) and half will be wrinkled (**rr**).

The test cross is often applied today to test the pedigrees of plants and animals in agriculture (Figure 11.6).

Summing Up Mendel's Second Law

Mendel's own statement of the principle encompassed in his second law, in translation, is as follows:
- The behavior of each pair of differing traits in a hybrid association is independent of all other differences between the two parental plants.

Or, in terms of meiosis:
- The way in which a pair of alleles on one set of homologues segregates during meiosis I has no effect on the way a pair of alleles on another set of homologues segregates.

Another modern version of the principle of independent assortment is:
- If an organism is heterozygous at two or more unlinked loci, each locus will assort independently of the others.

Note that a new word—"unlinked"—has been inserted. This just reminds us that Mendel didn't know everything. Most pairs of gene loci follow his second law, but some don't. The ones that do are called **unlinked,** and the ones that don't are called **linked.** Mendel's second law, as important as it is, is true only some of the time. As you may have guessed, linked genes are genes that are located on the same chromosome so that they are usually passed along together. Linkage will be discussed further in Chapter 12.

The impact of Mendel's laws on science is almost incalculable, yet new ground is broken by dissenters. The source of new ideas in genetics, we'll find, was in the dogged pursuit of exceptions to Mendel's laws.

> The **principle of independent assortment** indicates that the segregation of one pair of factors, or alleles, has no influence over the way any other pair segregates.

THE DECLINE AND REBIRTH OF MENDELIAN GENETICS

In 1866, after seven years of experimentation (at the very time Darwin was pondering the enigma of heredity), Mendel presented his results to a meeting of the Brunn Natural Science Society. His audience of local science buffs sat there politely, probably not understanding a word of what they were hearing. The minutes of the meeting, which still exist, record that not a single question was asked. Instead, the restless audience launched into a discussion of the "hot" topic of the time—Darwin's *Origin of Species.*

Mendel's single paper was published in the society's proceedings the following year and was distributed widely. The learned scientists of the day were just as baffled and uninterested as was Mendel's original audience. Historians have come up with a small, sad, but remarkable piece of information. In Darwin's huge library, which is also still intact, a one-

FIGURE 11.6 The test cross. Sir Beauregard Thickfuzz, a prize ram, will be useful for breeding only as long as we are sure he is homozygous for white wool. White is dominant over black in sheep. To test our prize white ram, we mate it with some homozygous black ewes.

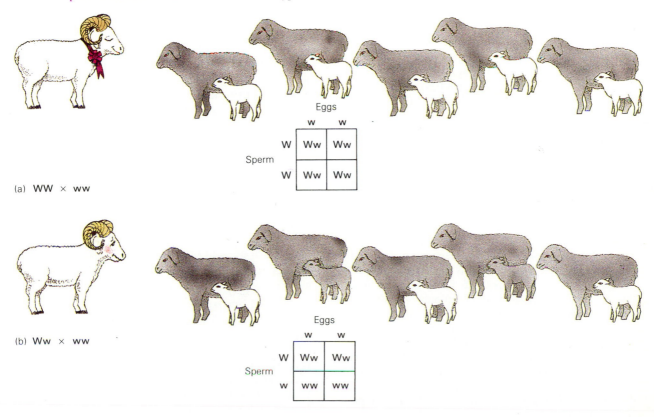

(a) WW × ww

(b) Ww × ww

page account of Mendel's work with peas appears in a German encyclopedia of plant breeding. Some relatively obscure work is described on the facing page, and it is covered with extensive notes in Darwin's handwriting. The page describing Mendel's work is clean. Darwin must have seen the paper that could have clarified his theory of natural selection, saving him years of agony and uncertainty. But even Darwin was not ready for mathematical biology, and he too failed to grasp Mendel's simple but profound ideas.

Mendel's work continued to be ignored until 1900, the year his work was suddenly revived with great fanfare. In that year three biologists in three different countries, each trying to work out the laws of inheritance, searched through the old literature and came up with Mendel's paper. They immediately recognized its importance. Science had changed in 35 years. The 20th century had arrived, and the obscure monk became one of the most famous scientists of all time. But he had been dead for 16 years.

SUMMARY

Because he subscribed to the notion of blending inheritance, Darwin could not successfully explain how new genetic variation arose. This was important in arguing his case for natural selection. Mendel's background in mathematics, particularly elementary statistics, was a significant factor in his success at analyzing his crosses.

MENDEL'S CROSSES

In planning his crosses, Mendel made use of true-breeding strains of peas, each with easily recognized traits. True-breeding pea strains are those whose traits always appear without variation in their offspring.

MENDEL'S FIRST LAW: PAIRED FACTORS AND THEIR SEGREGATION

Part of Mendel's first law, the segregation of alternative factors, can be anticipated through a consideration of genes, homologous chromosomes, and meiosis. Recall that genes occur on chromosomes and each has its counterpart on the homologous chromosome. When homologues separate during meiosis I, gene pairs (Mendel called them factors) must also separate (Mendel used the term segregate), going to opposite daughter cells.

An individual's genotype is the combination of genes it carries, while its phenotype is the outward, commonly visible expression of those genes.

The Experimental Procedure

Mendel began by crossing true-breeding peas differing in one trait. This was his P_1 generation. Because only one of the two traits appeared in the F_1 generation, it was called dominant, while the absent trait was called recessive.

When the F_1 peas self-pollinated, the recessive trait reappeared in the F_2 generation, but in only ¼ of the offspring; the remaining ¾ displayed the dominant trait. Through progeny testing (self-pollinating) of the F_1 generation, Mendel found that some of the dominant individuals were true-breeding, or homozygous, while others were not. The latter were heterozygous (carried both a dominant and a recessive factor). The recessive F_1 individuals were all homozygous. In such crosses, the phenotypic ratio is 3:1, and the genotypic ratio is 1:2:1.

Summing Up Mendel's First Law

Traits are produced by two factors that segregate when pollen and ovules are produced. Chance determines the combination of factors in offspring. Only one dominant factor is required for the dominant trait to appear, but a recessive trait requires two recessive factors.

Science and Models

Mendel's laws are mathematical models or hypotheses. They can be used to make predictions about the outcome of crosses. In testing the model, the results of crosses are compared to the predictions to see whether or not the model is supported by the observations. The amount of support determines whether the hypothesis is to be supported or rejected.

MENDEL'S SECOND LAW: INDEPENDENT ASSORTMENT

By crossing P_1 individuals differing in two traits, Mendel determined that the segregation of factors governing one trait occurred independently of the segregation of factors governing another.

In the cross of round/yellow × wrinkled/green, the F_1 were all round and yellow, the dominant traits. However, four phenotypes appeared in the F_2. The phenotypic ratio was 9:3:3:1.

⁹⁄₁₆ round/yellow
³⁄₁₆ round/green
³⁄₁₆ wrinkled/yellow
¹⁄₁₆ wrinkled/green

The 9:3:3:1 ratio can be predicted in any such cross if Mendel's second law, the law of independent assortment, is applicable.

The 9:3:3:1 Ratio

When the factors **RrYy** segregate (in meiosis) each pollen or ovule will receive one of each kind of factor, and all of the possible combinations will be found in equal numbers. Thus there are:

Four kinds of pollen: **RY, Ry, rY,** and **ry**
Four kinds of ovules: **RY, Ry, rY,** and **ry.**

If all possible combinations of the four kinds of pollen and ovules are taken into account (a Punnett square helps), the result will always be a 9:3:3:1 phenotypic ratio.

When Mendel tested his new model with various combinations of true-breeding peas, it was clearly supported by the results.

The Test Cross

In test crosses, individuals with the dominant phenotype are crossed with recessives to determine whether they are homozygous or heterozygous. The appearance in the offspring of even one recessive establishes heterozygosity.

Summing Up Mendel's Second Law

When pollen or ovules form, the paired factors governing one trait assort independently of the paired factors governing any other trait.

In modern terms, the genes responsible for traits reside at specific loci on chromosomes, and the alternative forms of a gene are called alleles. Where two gene loci occur on different chromosomes, the separation of one pair of alleles in meiosis I has no effect on the separation of any other pair of alleles. However, if two loci are on the same chromosome (linked genes), independent assortment does not apply.

THE DECLINE AND REBIRTH OF MENDELIAN GENETICS

Although they were published in his lifetime, Mendel's findings were largely ignored until after his death. In 1900, his achievements were rediscovered and their importance proclaimed by three independent researchers.

KEY TERMS

segregation	F_1	heterozygous	dihybrid cross
genotype	dominant	Punnett square	independent assortment
phenotype	recessive	allele	test cross
true-breeding	progeny testing	model	unlinked gene
P_1	homozygous	locus	linked gene

REVIEW QUESTIONS

1 Briefly explain why the blending concept opposed rather than supported natural selection. (p. 158)
2 What does the term *pure-breeding* mean? What might have happened had Mendel used heterozygous individuals to start his work? (pp. 159–160)
3 Aside from being a careful and perhaps lucky researcher, what other special qualities did Mendel have that might help account for his success? (pp. 158–159)
4 Part of Mendel's first law actually describes the behavior of one pair of chromosomes in meiosis. To illustrate this, draw a pair of chromosomes as they would appear in prophase I, but add a pair of factors or alleles (say an upper case *A* to one and a lower case *a* to the other), and complete meiosis with successive drawings (review Chapter 10 as necessary).
5 Using Punnett squares as needed, carry out a cross between pure-breeding tall and short pea plants. Then, cross two of the F_1 individuals and determine the F_2. State the phenotypic and genotypic ratios. (pp. 159–160)
6 Carry out a cross between a heterozygous yellow-seeded pea plant and a green-seeded pea plant. State the phenotypic ratio in the offspring. What are the chances (expressed as a fraction) of getting heterozygous offspring in such crosses? (pp. 159–161)
7 An experimenter cross-pollinates two plants bearing red flowers, plants the seeds produced, and in the next generation counts 289 plants with red flowers and 112 with white flowers. What genotypes would you suspect in the parent plants? Test your answer.
8 Assuming that your calculation of the parental genotypes was correct in the cross above (Question 7), what numbers of red and white would you have *expected* in the offspring? Give a logical explanation for the difference between the *expected* and the *observed*?
9 Which method is more efficient for determining the genotype of dominant F_2 offspring, progeny testing or test crossing? Explain your answer. (pp. 162, 168)
10 Briefly explain the term *methematical model*. Explain how such models are used by scientists. (p. 163)
11 Two sets of traits with which Mendel worked were pod shape (inflated versus constricted) and flower location (axial versus terminal). Inflated and axial are dominant. Consider the following cross involving both sets of traits:

Ii Aa × Ii Aa

a List all of the allele combinations possible in the pollen and ovules. (Would they be the same in each?)

b Show the cross using a Punnett square.

c List the phenotypes and their fractions, and then convert this to a phenotypic ratio. (p. 167)

12 Carry out a cross between a pea plant that is homozygous for round seeds and heterozygous for yellow with one that produces wrinkled seeds and is also heterozygous for yellow. State the expected phenotypes of the offspring and their phenotypic ratio. (p. 167)

13 An experimenter carries out a dihybrid cross of pea plants and finds the following in the offspring:

32 have round, yellow seeds

29 have round, green seeds

9 have wrinkled, yellow seeds

11 have wrinkled, green seeds

Working back to the parents, determine their most probable genotypes. Prove your answer. (Begin by considering the total numbers for each trait; e.g., there are 61 round and 20 wrinkled, etc.)

Small but critical differences in the sequence of DNA bases along a chromosome can result in blue or brown eyes, in sick or healthy people, in round or wrinkled peas, and, for that matter, in round or wrinkled people. But the pathway between the DNA in the cell nucleus (the genotype) and the physical characters that can be seen and measured (the phenotype) is often complex and indirect. Genes act through intricate developmental processes that may involve feedback loops, branches, interactions, and built-in corrections. Also, the expression of every gene is influenced by tens of thousands of other genes, as well as by other gene products. Genetic expression also may be influenced, directly or indirectly, by environmental factors.

Mendel frankly attributed his success to his deliberate decision to work only with "factors" that always produced large, dramatic effects with clear and distinct phenotypes. He examined such traits, one or two at a time, in highly inbred, genetically unvarying pure strains. Only in such simple systems could he have worked out his famous ratios. However, not all genetic variation is so simple. Mendel's discoveries were valuable because nearly all genes have proved to be Mendelian in their meiotic behavior and in their transmission from generation to generation—that is, on a genotypic level. But most genetic variation is not Mendelian at the level of the phenotype because of the complexities of development and gene expression that Mendel had so fortuitously avoided.

NORMAL AND ABNORMAL ALLELES

"Normal" alleles are those that have accumulated in the population because they have withstood the rigors of natural selection. Thus, there is a high probability that they are adaptive; that is, in some way they help the organism survive and reproduce. However, we will also see that the simple presence of a gene does not mean that it is adaptive. Common alleles that confer no benefit or harm at all can be passed endlessly through generations. Also, some alleles are harmful. These are generally the result of recent mutations, and they are not in harmony with the rest of the genotype or with the organism's environment.

Geneticists tend to be interested in such abnormal alleles for a variety of reasons. For one thing, they may be able to help people with genetic disabilities, and, through genetic counseling, to help families avoid bringing more children with such disabilities

12

HOW GENES EXPRESS THEMSELVES

into the world. From an academic point of view, abnormal mutant alleles are interesting because they often meet Mendel's requirement of having an easily classified phenotype. This characteristic is very useful in many kinds of genetic studies, such as linkage mapping. But this narrow focus misses most of the real genetic variety of nature. In truth, most genes do not have a single normal or "wild-type" allele, but a whole range of slightly different wild-type alleles, all of which are functional, normal, and adaptive. This falls within the realm of normal genetic variation.

Most of the genetic differences we see in our friends—differences in height, weight, body build, skin color, temperament, facial features, athletic ability, intelligence, and hairiness—are due to normal allelic variation (along with modifying effects by environment). These normal phenotypic differences, which add so much to human interest, seldom show up in the usual Mendelian ratios, although the genes responsible may segregate and assort with faithful Mendelian precision. Even blue and brown eye color, a popular example of Mendelian inheritance in humans, turns out to be quite complex and unpredictable. People do not merely have blue or brown eyes; they may have gray, light blue, deep blue, hazel, flecked, or green eyes. In this chapter we will look beyond Mendel to learn more about how Mendelian genes behave in non-Mendelian ways.

GOING BEYOND MENDEL

The actual expression of genes into phenotypes in natural populations is influenced or determined by many kinds of complications that Mendel deliberately avoided. Whole courses in genetics are devoted to these complications, but we can list the major categories and then give some examples of each. The question might be: Why don't we find Mendel's simple 3:1 ratios everywhere? And the answers are:

1. *Dominance relationships*. Mendel considered only **complete dominance,** in which the effect of one allele completely masks the effect of the other. Actually there is a whole range of ways in which two homologous alleles can interact, producing intermediate effects.
2. *Multiple alleles*. Up to a point, we have considered only two alleles at each gene locus. There actually may be many different functional alleles that can occupy a specific gene locus—and, for that matter, many different kinds of mutants of the same gene.

3. *Gene interactions*. The genes at one locus may affect the phenotypic expression of genes at another locus.
4. *Polygenic inheritance*. Many different gene loci may have an additive effect on the same phenotypic trait, especially if the trait is one that varies continuously, such as height or weight. The phenomenon is called **polygenic inheritance** ("many origins"); many genes interact to determine a single trait.
5. *Other sources of variability*. Also important are environmental interactions (the same genotype may be expressed differently in different environments), sex influences (the same trait may be expressed to different degrees in males and females), and effects of development and aging (some genes begin to exert their effects only in adulthood or old age).

Dominance Relationships: The Interactions Between Homologous Alleles

Mendel's first empirical discovery was *dominance;* in all of his original crosses, one form of the trait (one allele) was completely dominant over the other. He had no idea why this should be, but there it was. Later, when he stopped crossing peas and turned to string beans, he was greatly puzzled by his new discovery of partial dominance and polygenic inheritance.

A diploid organism can have two different alleles at the same locus on homologous chromosomes (that is, in fact, the definition of *heterozygous*). The various ways in which two different alleles interact to form a phenotype are called **dominance relationships.** Recall that the basic advantage of diploidy is that it provides, among other things, a backup system in case one of the genes isn't working properly (see Chapter 10).

What really happens when the gene from one parent and the corresponding gene from the other parent give conflicting directives? Say an allele for blue eyes comes from one parent and an allele for brown eyes comes from the other. What then? Actually, many things can happen, but one of the most common results is that one of the two sets of instructions will appear to be ignored completely. In that case, as we've seen, the other allele is dominant. That's what Mendel observed in the heterozygous pea plants for his seven pairs of contrasting traits.

So far we have given only observations and definitions, not explanations. What *really* happens when two different alleles occur together? How is one suppressed? And how does the organism "choose" between two sets of information?

The inoperative allele. Dominance usually involves one allele fulfilling some biological function while the other allele doesn't do anything. For instance, many genes contain coded instructions for making enzymes. A mutant allele of an enzyme-coding gene may simply code no enzyme, or for a bogus protein with no enzymatic activity. This problem is clearly observed in some rare medical disorders in which the absence of an enzyme can have a severe or even lethal effect. In a relatively benign example, an **albino** organism lacks any one of the enzymes necessary to make melanin, the normal black, red, or brown pigments of animals. Albinos do not receive a functioning gene from either parent, so that their melanin-producing mechanism is defunct: they are recessive homozygotes. Human albinos of the most extreme variety have white hair and pinkish skin (see Figure 18.4); the absence of pigment from the retina and iris makes the eyes appear pink or red, as in albino rabbits. Less severe forms of albinism in which the mutant allele retains a small measure of enzymatic activity may result in the individual having pale yellow hair and pale blue eyes.

Heterozygotes for albinism or other enzyme deficiencies, by contrast, have one working allele and one nonworking allele. They produce only half the normal amount of the enzyme in question, but this is usually enough to produce a normal phenotype.

> In the simplest form of dominance and recessivity, the dominant allele operates normally but the recessive allele is inoperative—it has no recognizable gene product.

Partial dominance. Sometimes the conflicting instructions of two alleles are compromised in what is called **partial dominance**. Partial dominance occurs whenever the phenotype of the heterozygote is somewhere between the two contrasting phenotypes of the two homozygotes.

In snapdragons, a cross between a true-breeding red-flowered strain (say RR) and a true-breeding white-flowered strain (say WW) results in a uniform F_1 generation (RW) in which the flowers are neither red nor white, but pink. This is partial dominance (Figure 12.1).

Codominance. In other cases one homozygote will show one trait, the other homozygote will show

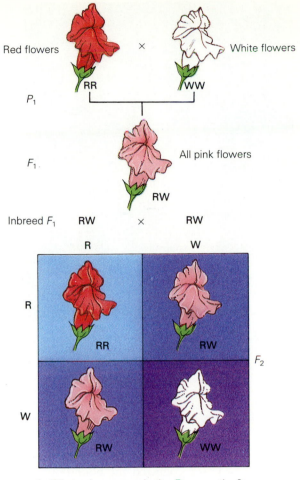

1. What colors appear in the F_2 generation?
2. What is the phenotypic ratio?

FIGURE 12.1 Snapdragons represent a good example of *partial dominance*. When (in the P_1) white-flowered snapdragons are crossed with red-flowered snapdragons, the F_1 offspring are pink, as shown in the first cross. In the second cross, pink heterozygotes have been crossed, resulting in red, pink, and white in the F_2 progeny.

a different phenotypic trait, and the heterozygote will show both traits. The interaction is called **codominance**: there is no compromise as there is in partial dominance, because both alleles are fully expressed (Figure 12.2).

The most familiar example of codominance is found in the human ABO blood group system. One allele, **A,** codes for an enzyme that, in turn, synthesizes a cell-surface sugar called the **A antigen**. Specific antibodies can recognize and bind to this sugar on the surface of human red blood cells. An alternate allele, **B,** codes for an alternate enzyme that, in turn,

FIGURE 12.2 All three-color cats are heterozygous for orange and black coat-color genes. Since both alleles are expressed, three-color cats show codominance for this trait.

synthesizes an alternate cell-surface sugar called the **B antigen.** It too is recognized and bound by an antibody. In heterozygous persons, **AB,** there is neither dominance nor compromise. Both antigens are expressed, and the red blood cells react to both antibodies. Such persons are said to have the blood type AB. (For a look at the Rh blood groups and the incompatibility problem, see Essay 12.1.)

In **partial dominance,** both alleles are partially expressed. In **codominance,** both alleles are completely expressed.

Multiple Alleles

So far we have been looking at traits that are governed by two alternative alleles. However, many traits are the product of **multiple alleles,** three or more allelic forms of one gene. (Keep in mind that in this situation, each individual still receives just one pair of alleles.)

Multiple alleles are of great interest today because of the growth of organ and tissue transplant surgery. A primary requirement for a successful transplant—one that will not be rejected—is that the tissues of

the donor and recipient be as genetically and immunologically compatible as possible. This gets to be quite a problem because some of the genes that create incompatibilities have a great many allelic forms. (One has 12 different allele possibilities and another has more than 20!) Even close matches, however, cannot prevent rejection.

The term **multiple alleles** refers to the presence of three or more allelic forms of the same gene.

The example of multiple alleles we will look at in detail is once again from the ABO blood group system where there are three alleles possible at a single locus. There are several alleles responsible for blood types, with A, B, and O being the most common.

Persons who are homozygous for the **A** allele produce one kind of cell-surface antigen and are said to be **type A.** Persons who are homozygous for the **B** allele produce a different kind of cell-surface antigen and are said to be **type B.** Heterozygotes, **AB,** carry both alleles, producing both kinds of cell-surface antigens, and are said to be **type AB.**

Persons who have neither the A antigen nor the B antigen belong to a fourth type—**type O.** Type O is the most common blood type. It seems that O is a third allele at the same gene locus, one that has neither enzymatic activity. It is recessive when paired with either B or A. With three different possible alleles, there are six different possible genotypes:

Genotype	A Antigen	B Antigen	Blood Type
AA	present	absent	type A
AO	present	absent	type A
BB	absent	present	type B
BO	absent	present	type B
AB	present	present	type AB
OO	absent	absent	type O

Although **A** and **B** are codominant with respect to each other, they are simply dominant with respect to the **O** allele. Note that although there are three alleles of this gene locus in the human species, no one individual can have all three alleles at once. Diploid organisms like ourselves are limited to two at a time.

In the **ABO system,** A and B are codominant to each other and dominant over O.

At one time some women who knew their blood type was Rh negative actually sought out Rh negative men as potential husbands. They did so in an effort to keep from destroying their own children in the womb.

The basis of their concern was that the Rh positive allele (Rh$^+$) is dominant over the Rh negative allele (Rh$^-$). Therefore, when an Rh$^-$ woman is impregnated by an Rh$^+$ man, the baby she carries may be Rh$^+$. If the man is homozygous, this will certainly be the case, but if he is heterozygous, the child has a 50:50 chance of being Rh$^+$. (In either case, the Rh$^+$ baby will definitely be heterozygous.)

There is a certain element of risk in such matings since a serious incompatibility may arise if some of the baby's Rh$^+$ red cells should cross the placenta and enter the mother's bloodstream (or should she receive Rh$^+$ blood in a transfusion.) When this happens, the mother's immune system responds by producing Rh antibodies against the cell-surface antigens carried by the invading red cells. There is little danger to the mother, but should her antibodies cross the placenta, they can begin agglutinating the fetus's red cells causing a severe, even fatal, condition called **erythroblastosis fetalis.** It involves erythrocyte (red blood cell) destruction, which can lead to severe anemia and jaundice.

The problem generally doesn't arise with the first pregnancy, since most blood mixing occurs during delivery, too late for the mother's immune system to react and affect that baby. But in subsequent pregnancies, the sensitized mother's newly formed Rh antibodies can readily cross the placenta, as many useful antibodies do, late in pregnancy. Once in the baby's circulatory system, they begin their deadly role. If the baby survives delivery, a massive blood transfusion may be necessary for its survival.

It is now standard medical practice to treat Rh$^-$ mothers of newborn Rh$^+$ babies with a single injection of Rh antibodies shortly after delivery. The antibodies destroy any of the baby's invading red blood cells before they can trigger the immune response. In the treated mother, the injected antibodies soon dissipate, and subsequent pregnancies are as safe from the Rh incompatibility problem as was the first.

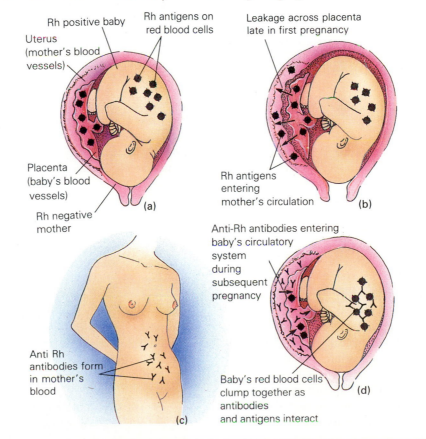

Rh positive baby
Rh antigens on red blood cells
Uterus (mother's blood vessels)
Leakage across placenta late in first pregnancy
Placenta (baby's blood vessels)
Rh negative mother
Rh antigens entering mother's circulation
(a)
(b)
Anti Rh antibodies form in mother's blood
Anti-Rh antibodies entering baby's circulatory system during subsequent pregnancy
Baby's red blood cells clump together as antibodies and antigens interact
(c)
(d)

Blood typing—the determination of an individual's blood type—is simply done. Two drops of the individual's blood are placed on a slide. To one drop is added a small amount of **anti-A antiserum;** to the other drop is added a small amount of **anti-B antiserum.** The antisera interact only with their appropriate antigens: the anti-A antiserum, for instance, will cause type A cells to **agglutinate** (clump). This clumping (not to be confused with clotting, a different process) is readily visible after a few minutes. The anti-B antiserum will clump type B cells, and either antiserum will clump type AB cells. (If neither drop agglutinates, the person is type O (Figure 12.3).

Such information is critical in blood transfusions. Should a mismatch occur, antibodies naturally present in the blood plasma will react with the antigens introduced, and the red blood cells from the transfused blood will agglutinate. Agglutinated blood is dangerous because it can block small blood vessels, possibly causing death.

Why anti-A and anti-B antibodies are naturally present in some of us isn't completely known, but immunologists believe that their formation is stimulated by certain foods that contain carbohydrates similar to the A and B antigens. The immune system of persons with both the A and B antigens (type AB) recognizes the troublesome chemical groups as "friendly"; people with type AB blood do not produce anti-A or anti-B antibodies. Persons with type A blood, as you would expect, produce anti-B antibodies, and persons with type B produce anti-A antibodies. What antibodies, if any, might people with type O produce against such look-alike antigens in their foods? (For a closer look at the immune system at work, see Chapter 39.)

Blood typing is also important for other reasons. Consider the problem of identifying the true father of a child whose paternity is in dispute. Could a man with type O blood father a child with AB blood? Could a man with type AB blood be the parent of a child with type O?

Gene Interactions and Epistasis

When Mendel crossed true-breeding round, yellow peas with true-breeding wrinkled, green peas, the F_2 generation yielded 9/16 round and yellow, 3/16 round and green, 3/16 wrinkled and yellow, and 1/16 wrinkled and green. Such ratios are possible only in straightforward situations in which the genes do not influence each other. When two different gene loci do interact, the tidy 9:3:3:1 ratio doesn't show up. One such example is due to **epistasis,** wherein the

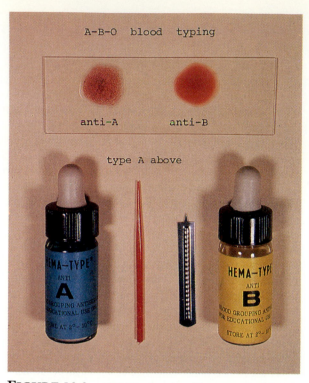

FIGURE 12.3 ABO blood typing. The presence of A and B antigens in blood can be determined in a simple test using anti-A (blue) and anti-B (yellow) antisera. A positive reaction (agglutination) is characterized by a distinct graininess occurring in the mixture.

expression of one gene interferes with or masks the expression of another.

Mouse coat color, for instance, would have driven Mendel up the wall. Consider two gene loci that affect the coat color of mice. In one case, black (**B**) is dominant to brown (**b**). If a true-breeding black strain (**BB**) is crossed with a true-breeding brown strain (**bb**), the F_1 generation will all be heterozygous and black (**Bb**), and the F_2 will show a 3:1 ratio of black to brown. No surprises there.

But at yet another gene locus there is another pair of alleles that can also affect coat color. These are the alleles at the albino locus. The recessive homozygote (**cc**) is a snow-white albino mouse. The dominant homozygote (**CC**) and the heterozygote (**Cc**) have normal pigment, although it can be black or brown, depending on the gene at the first locus. The recessive albino gene (**c**) is defective and does not supply one of the enzymes necessary for the production of pigment.

Now consider a mating between an albino mouse from a true-breeding white strain and a mouse from a true-breeding brown strain. What would you expect? You might *not* expect the litter to be entirely black. But here is one way it could happen.

CCbb (brown) × **ccBB** (white) ⟶ **CcBb** (black)

The dominant **B** alleles were carried by the white strain, completely hidden. In this example of epistasis, the recessive albino genotype is epistatic to the brown/black genotype.

Considering the genotypes of the participants in the cross above, the only possible outcome in the offspring would be **CcBb**. Since there is both an active allele for pigment formation and a dominant color allele present (**C** and **B**), the entire litter is black.

Now consider random crosses among the doubly heterozygous offspring, **CcBb** × **CcBb**. Will the usual 9:3:3:1 ratio appear in the offspring (providing you raise enough of them)? No. The F_2 generation will approximate a 9:3:4 ratio: 9/16 black, 3/16 brown, and ¼ albino. Figure 12.4 confirms that the two gene loci assort independently, just as Mendel would have predicted. But because of epistasis, the last two terms of the 9:3:3:1 ratio are combined to produce the 9:3:4 ratio. After all, once a mouse is albino, it doesn't much matter whether the other gene locus specifies brown or black.

> **E**pistasis is interference by one gene in the expression of another gene.

Polygenic Inheritance

Many of the phenotypic traits that are most important to biologists, and especially to plant and animal breeders, do not fit into "either-or" categories. Instead, these traits occur in a gradient of phenotypes, a situation known as **continuous variation.** Differences among individuals are still caused by different alleles at specific gene loci on chromosomes, and these alleles segregate and assort according to the usual Mendelian laws. But in these cases, many different gene loci will contribute to a single phenotypic trait, with each individual gene having a very small effect. This is called **polygenic inheritance.** Common examples of continuous variation in humans are height, skin color, foot size, nose size, weight at birth, and aspects of intelligence. At first glance, continuous variation may seem to lend belated support to the old notion of blending inheritance, but it can be explained quite satisfactorily in Mendelian terms.

A great many gene loci determine height, but for simplicity we'll assume that height is determined by only three loci. Also, in reality there may be multiple alleles possible at each gene locus, but in our example we'll assume only two alternatives are available: "short" alleles and "tall" alleles.

Now let's assume that the presence of a "tall" allele rather than a "short" allele increases adult height by about 5 cm (2½"). People with only the "short" alleles (six in all) will then grow to be about 160 cm (5'3"), while those with only the "tall" alleles (again, six) grow to 190 cm (6'3"). In the middle, with three short alleles and three tall alleles, are individuals about 175 cm tall (5'9"). Table 12.1 summarizes the seven height categories possible in this model. We've

FIGURE 12.4 This diagram shows the path of two pairs of genes that influence mouse coat color. The B (black) and b (brown) alleles occur at one locus, and the C (color) and c (albino) alleles occur at another locus. The two pairs assort independently in typical Mendelian fashion, but produce strange ratios when heterozygous F_1 are inbred (CcBb × CcBb). The resulting ratio is 9:3:4 because of an epistatic interaction.

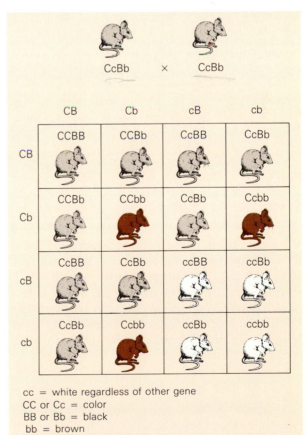

cc = white regardless of other gene
CC or Cc = color
BB or Bb = black
bb = brown

TABLE 12.1 Polygenes Controlling Height: A Model of Three Loci

Genotypes	Number of "Tall" Alleles	Number of "Short" Alleles	Height (cm)	Distribution
AABBCC	6	0	190	1/64 (1.6%)
AaBBCC, AABbCC, AABBCc	5	1	185	6/64 (9.4%)
aaBBCC, AAbbCC, AABBcc, AaBbCC, AaBBCc, AABbCc	4	2	180	15/64 (23.4%)
aaBbCC, aaBBCc, AabbCC, AaBBcc, AaBbCc, AAbbCc, AABbcc	3	3	175	20/64 (31.3%)
aabbCC, aaBBcc, AAbbcc, AaBbcc, AabbCc, aaBbCc	2	4	170	15/64 (23.4%)
aabbCc, aaBbcc, Aabbcc	1	5	165	6/64 (9.4%)
aabbcc	0	6	160	1/64 (1.6%)

added the relative frequencies of the seven predictable height categories in the F_2 generation of a hypothetical cross between a short race and a tall race. Note that the distribution approximates the "bell-shaped curve" (or *normal distribution*) that is, in fact, observed in real populations for adult height and for nearly every other kind of continuous variation. Most people are of intermediate height; few are very tall or very short (Figure 12.5).

Polygenic traits, including height, weight, and body build, are influenced by the collective action of two or more different genes.

Other Sources of Variability

It may have occurred to you that the polygenic model of the genetic control of adult height can't possibly explain everything. For one thing, men (as a group) tend to be taller than women (as a group). And what about diet, general health, and other environmental factors? Modern-day humans are taller than their medieval and 19th-century ancestors (have you noticed how small the suits of armor in museums are?), and young Japanese adults are noticeably taller than their own parents because of rapid improvements in the Japanese standard of living. Furthermore, don't we all get shorter in our old age? We do, indeed. The point is that nongenetic effects have very marked influences on many genetic traits.

Environmental interactions. Environmental interactions may be very direct or very subtle. Let's consider a straightforward example: the Siamese cat. One of the enzymes in its pigmentation pathway has mutated so that it is now sensitive to temperature; the enzyme functions only below a certain temperature. As a result, Siamese cats are darker in their cooler extremities: the nose, ears, tail, and feet (Figure 12.6).

Incomplete penetrance. Incomplete penetrance refers to a condition in which an individual may bear genes for some abnormal condition but may have a normal phenotype anyway. Sometimes a Mendelian dominant gene appears to skip a generation entirely, only to express itself among the offspring of later generations.

For instance, a rare dominant gene in humans causes **polydactyly,** a condition characterized by extra fingers or toes. Occasionally someone will receive the defective gene from a polydactylous parent, but, by chance, will have normal hands and feet. In such a case, fortune has smiled four times and the person would be unaware of carrying the polydactyly gene at all, if it weren't for the fact that about half of his or her children will probably have extra fingers or toes.

Persons who have this dominant gene show variable expression. All four extremities may be affected, with six or seven digits on all hands and feet; or only the feet may be affected; or only the hands; or perhaps only one hand or foot (Figure 12.7). This expression appears to be entirely a matter of chance.

Sex-limited and sex-influenced effects. A dominant gene is known to be responsible for a rare

FIGURE 12.5 Normal distribution. (a) Polygenic genetic traits, when plotted by phenotypes gathered from large samples, tend to form curves approximating the idealized distribution shown here. (b) The accompanying photograph shows a good example. The people are arranged in rows according to height.

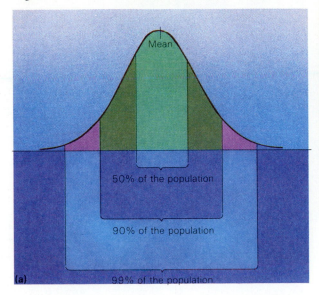

(a)
Mean
50% of the population
90% of the population
99% of the population

(b)

FIGURE 12.6 Coat color in the Siamese cat is an example of the influence of environment on gene expression. Where the skin is coolest, in the extremities, dark pigment is produced in the hair.

type of cancer of the uterus. This is a **sex-limited** trait since, needless to say, it has no influence on men. Still other genetic conditions affect one sex more often, or more severely, and are said to be **sex influenced.** The most common kind of middle-age baldness is an example. It behaves like a dominant in men and a recessive in women. Pyloric stenosis is also sex influenced. It is a serious but correctable problem in newborn babies, in which abnormally thick muscle development restricts the movement of food into the small intestine. It runs in families, but affects five times as many boys as girls.

Variable age of onset. Baldness due to a dominant gene, in addition to being sex influenced, also has a **variable age of onset.** Even among brothers carrying the same dominant gene, one man may lose his top hair in his 20s, while the other loses it in his 40s or even later. A more serious example of a dominant gene with a late, variable age of onset is that for *Huntington's disease.* This disease is characterized by a severe neuromotor condition that begins with subtle personality changes and progresses through tremors and paralysis to death. The dominant gene does not usually begin to show its effects until sometime in adulthood. The average age of onset of symptoms is about 40, but it can begin affecting heterozygous men or women as early as age 15 or as late as age 60. Unfortunately, many victims learn of the defective gene's presence only after they have children.

Many of the more common diseases of old age are believed to have a genetic basis, at least in part. The genes for some "old-age disorders" may be considered to have a delayed and variable age of onset. At some point, it is impossible to tell what is genetic and what is environmental, but we do know this: some folks are old at 40, while others are surprisingly young at 70.

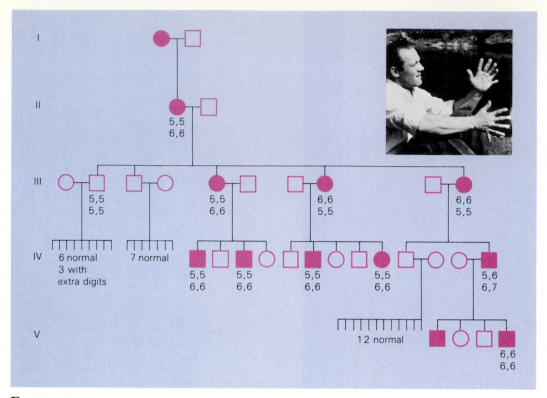

FIGURE 12.7 Polydactyly expresses itself in the development of extra fingers or toes or both. In the family portrayed in the chart, the numbers represent the number of digits on the left and right hands *(top set of figures)* and left and right feet *(bottom set of figures)*. The dominant gene expressed itself in either the hands or feet of every carrier except for the first male in the third generation. Although he was phenotypically normal, three of his children were afflicted. For some reason, his dominant gene did not *penetrate* during his embryological development. (□ = male; ○ = female.)

SUMMARY

NORMAL AND ABNORMAL ALLELES

Normal genes are those that are beneficial or have no detrimental effect. Because of the emphasis on abnormal mutants, the great number of such "wildtype" genes is often ignored. Most familiar human traits are governed by more complex genetic systems than simple Mendelian factors.

GOING BEYOND MENDEL
Dominance Relationships: The Interactions Between Homologous Alleles

Dominance relationships refer to the various ways alleles interact. Simple Mendelian dominance and recessiveness refer to the masking of an inoperative (recessive) allele by a normally functioning (dominant) allele. The enzyme deficiency responsible for the absence of pigment in the albino is an example.

Partial dominance occurs when alternative alleles produce a compromising effect. Pink snapdragons are an example.

In codominance both alternative alleles fully express themselves. People with the A and B blood group allele express both, producing both the A and B red blood cell antigens.

Multiple Alleles

The term multiple alleles applies to genetic traits produced by more than the usual two alternative alleles. In the human ABO blood system, each person carries two alleles from the three alternatives: A, B, and O. Because of codominance between the A and B alleles and recessiveness of the O allele, four phenotypes (A, B, AB and O) and six genotypes (AA, AO, BB, BO, AB, and OO) are possible.

Blood types are identified through the use of two antisera derived from blood sensitized against the A and B antigens of red cells. Blood agglutination (clumping) is a positive reaction. Blood typing is essential prior to transfusion to avoid agglutination, and it is sometimes used to resolve paternity issues.

Gene Interactions and Epistasis

In mouse coat color one allele pair determines black and brown color in the usual Mendelian manner. The dominant form of a second pair of alleles does not affect color, but its recessive form is epistatic; that is, it inhibits the genes for color formation. Both pairs follow Mendel's law of independent assortment, but the epistatic effect results in strange, non-Mendelian phenotypic rations.

Polygenic Inheritance

In polygenic inheritance two or more pairs of alleles contribute to a single phenotypic trait such as human body height. The effect is a gradient of phenotypes called continuous variation. For example, if six pairs of alleles contribute to one trait, seven distinct phenotypes are possible.

Other Sources of Variability

Diet, climate, chance, sex, and age are among the variables that often influence the expression of a trait. For example, better diet increases body height; in cold temperatures Siamese cats get darker; the dominant allele for extra digits randomly skips generations; and sex affects the expression of some traits. Sex-limited traits involve one sex only, whereas sex-influenced traits occur more frequently in one sex. Certain genetic abnormalities only arise later in life.

KEY TERMS

complete dominance	codominance	anti-A antiserum	polydactyly
polygenetic inheritance	A antigen	anti-B antiserum	sex-limited trait
dominance relationship	B antigen	agglutinate	sex-influenced trait
albino	multiple alleles	continuous variation	variable age of onset
partial dominance	ABO system	polygenic inheritance	

REVIEW QUESTIONS

1 Review the terms gene, locus, homologue, allele, dominant, recessive, phenotype and genotype, before answering the questions below (see Table 11.1 and the Glossary).

2 The absence of pigment in albinism, a recessive abnormality, provides us with a fairly clear-cut example of Mendelian dominance and recessiveness. Are people who are heterozygous for albinism visibly affected? Why or why not? What exactly does the recessive allele do? (p. 175)

3 Carefully distinguish between the three forms of dominance: complete dominance, partial dominance, and codominance. (pp. 174–176)

4 In a flower called the four o'clock, a cross between white and red produces pink. What form of dominance is this? Carry out a cross involving a pink- and a white-flowered plant, stating the phenotypic and genotypic ratios. (p. 175)

5 A grower wants to produce a line of pure-breeding pink snapdragons. What advice would you give the person? Explain why. (p. 175)

6 In humans, one of the blood groups involves red cell antigens designated M and N. People test either M positive, N positive, or MN positive. What kind of dominance, if any, is involved here? What phenotypes would you expect to appear in the children of a couple who are both MN positive? State the phenotypic ratio. (pp. 175–176)

7 List the three genetic concepts represented in the genetics of the human ABO blood group. (pp. 175–178)

8 Three alleles, A, B, and O, are responsible for the human ABO blood groups. How many alleles does each person carry? List all of the genotypes and phenotypes possible. (p. 176)

9 Jones, Smith, White, and Doe each claim to be heirs to a fortune left by a wealthy couple who had only one child. The couple's blood types are known to have been AB and A; the father of the type A individual was known to have been type O. Which of the following blood types, if any, are ruled out. Jones: Type AB, Smith: Type O, White: Type B, Doe: Type A.

10 If you were blood type A and were in critical need of a transfusion, but the only donors available were of type O, AB, and B, which would be your safest bet? Explain your choice. Which blood type offers the greatest advantage as far as receiving transfusions is concerned? (pp. 176–177)

11 Carry out this version of the epistatic cross involving mouse coat color: **CcBb** × **ccBb**. State the phenotypic ratio in the offspring. (Remember that **BB** and **Bb** are black and **bb** is brown. Also, where **cc** appears, no pigment is produced.) (pp. 178–179)

13 Careful study of a variety of tomatoes reveals that there are five distinct colors (yellow, orange, light red, dark red, and deep red) present in the ripened fruit. How might the concept of polygenic inheritance be applied here? Assuming that random mating was involved, which color would you expect to be most common? Least common? (pp. 179–180)

14 Considering the tomato color problem in Question 13, carry out the following cross representing random mating in the population: **AaBb** × **AaBb**. Determine the phenotypic ratio of the offspring. Graph the results and describe the shape of the resulting curve.

15 Why is it difficult to accurately predict the appearance of extra fingers and toes in a family carrying the dominant allele for polydactyly? (p. 180)

16 Carefully distinguish between sex-limited and sex-influenced traits. Provide an example of each. (p. 181)

Long, idyllic days of thoughtful puttering in a Moravian monastery once marked the leading edge of the field that would be called genetics. The coming of warm spring days would, year after year, signal new growth, new experiments, and new ideas by the talented abbot, Gregor Mendel. He was almost ignored in those days. Science itself was not ready for him. Other scientists read his work but did not grasp its importance.

Nevertheless, even in Mendel's final years there were rapid improvements in the microscope and in various techniques for studying cells. Biologists were able to watch the puzzling pageant of mitosis and meiosis, wherein those strange, twisted bodies go about their slow dances. They decided that chromosomes must be important, but they had no idea why. The closing years of the 19th century marked a very busy, exciting, and often baffling time for biologists.

The stuff of genes, DNA, was isolated and characterized in Mendel's own lifetime, although a more precise understanding of the chemical nature of the gene was 50 years away. By the first year of the 20th century, the world was at last ready for Mendel. After years of obscurity, Mendel's work was thrust upon 20th-century science. Biologists of the time were keenly interested in heredity, and some were experimenting with plants. It was inevitable that dominance and 3:1 ratios would occur. Then the inevitable happened. Three researchers independently rediscovered the monk's findings, grasping at once the meaning of Mendel's ratios. The Mendelian revival was followed by an era of intense activity, in which 3:1 and 9:3:3:1 ratios dominated the conversations of turn-of-the-century geneticists.

MENDEL AND MEIOSIS

Mendel, we have mentioned, referred to the units of inheritance as factors, or what we now call genes or their alleles. The genes, as you are well aware by now, carry the instructions for producing specific kinds of proteins, among them the various enzymes. The genetic message is encoded in the linear sequence of the DNA nucleotides. One gene follows another, with ample "spacer DNA" between, along this single informational molecule—rather like a series of coded messages in a punched tape.

The phenomenon of pairing and separation of homologous chromosomes in meiosis wasn't worked out until 1900, the year of the rediscovery of Mendel's work. Some microscopists already suspected

13

GENES AND CHROMOSOMES

that chromosomes were the carriers of inheritance; and soon after Mendel's work was republished, Theodor Boveri in Europe and Walter Sutton in America published influential papers pointing out the relationship between Mendelism and meiosis.

It isn't hard to follow their thinking. Suppose a pair of alternate alleles (for instance, **R** and **r**) are carried on a pair of homologous chromosomes. When the homologous chromosomes separate during the first division of meiosis, exactly half of the haploid cells will receive one of the alleles **(R),** and exactly half will get the other **(r).** And that, quite simply, is the physical basis of Mendel's first law.

The interpretation of Mendel's second law—the law of independent assortment—is almost as clear. (Recall from Chapter 11 that the second law involves alelles, or factors, that are located on different chromosome pairs.) Suppose one pair of homologous chromosomes carries one pair of alternate alleles—**R** and **r**—and a second pair of chromosomal homologues carries another pair of alleles—**Y** and **y** (Figure 13.1). When the chromosomes line up on the metaphase plate, either of two things can happen. In one possible way of lining up, the **R**- and **Y**-bearing chromosome will go to one pole of the dividing cell, and the chromosome with **r** and **y** will go to the other

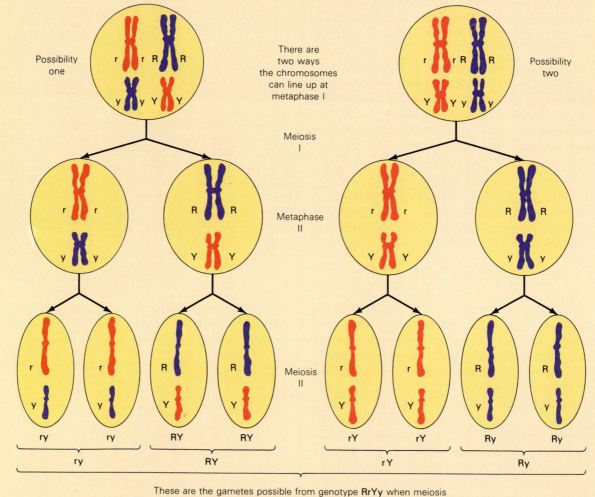

FIGURE 13.1 Mendel's second law, independent assortment, also describes the behavior of chromosomes in meiosis. The cell entering meiosis with two pairs of genes on two different chromosome pairs has two alternatives at metaphase of meiosis I. As each alternative continues through meiosis, there are four equally likely combinations of chromosomes and genes in the gametes.

pole. In the second way of lining up, the chromosome carrying **R** and **y** moves to one pole and the one with **r** and **Y** alleles moves to the other. There is exactly the same chance of one possibility as of the other. The overall result, when many such cells undergo meiosis, is that the genotypes of the haploid cells formed will be RY, Ry, rY, and ry in equal numbers—just as Mendel claimed. (Keep in mind the importance of large numbers in determining probability.)

> The cellular basis for Mendel's principles of segregation and independent assortment is seen in the way homologues align and separate in meiosis.

SEX AND THE CHROMOSOME THEORY OF INHERITANCE

The theory that chromosomes were the carriers of genetic information was strengthened, in the early years of this century, when it was shown that chromosomes could determine sex. In mammals and many insects (including fruit flies), there are two **heteromorphic** ("different shape"), sex-determining chromosomes designated **X** and **Y**. The X and Y sex chromosomes can be readily distinguished from **autosomal chromosomes** by their appearance (Figure 13.2). (**Autosomes** include all chromosomes other than sex chromosomes.) But, even though X and Y chromosomes appear different, they are homologous. This is evident by the fact that they pair with one another during meiosis. (Also see Essay 9.1).

Watching a heteromorphic X and Y chromosome pair segregate during meiosis supported Mendel's principle of segregation (part of the first law), but it was necessary to watch *two* pairs of chromosomes in action to verify independent assortment (his second law). This wasn't long in coming. An insect species was found that had a pair of homologous but heteromorphic *autosomes;* one member of this pair had a big, dark-staining knob of extra chromatin. Tracking the heteromorphic X and Y and the heteromorphic autosomes in the same cell soon established that the pattern of segregation in one pair had nothing to do with segregation in the other pair. Thus the cellular basis of Mendel's second law was established.

In 1910, T. H. Morgan showed that one gene, the

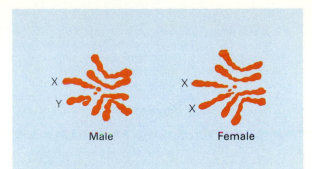

FIGURE 13.2 *Drosophila melanogaster* (the fruit fly) has four pairs of chromosomes. In females, each pair contains identical pair members. In males, however, only three pairs are truly homologous. The fourth pair consists of an X chromosome and a peculiar J-shaped Y chromosome.

one determinant of white eyes in *Drosophila* (the fruit fly), was located on the X chromosome (Figure 13.3). Thus it followed that the trait was not inherited independently of sex, but showed a complex pattern of inheritance known as **sex linkage.** Morgan eventually received the Nobel prize for his achievement.

SEX LINKAGE IN HUMANS

Human males are designated as **XY**. At conception each male receives an X chromosome from his mother and a Y chromosome from his father. Females are designated **XX**. Likewise, at conception every female gets an X chromosome from her mother and another X chromosome from her father.

Since a female has only X chromosomes, every egg she produces must carry an X chromosome. Of course, in males, half of the sperm produced will carry an X chromosome and half will have a Y. The sex of the offspring will depend on whether the fertilizing sperm is X-bearing or Y-bearing. (So now you know who to blame!) Thus an XX combination in the zygote produces a female child and an XY combination, a male.

> In the distribution of sex chromosomes at conception, females receive two X chromosomes, and males an X and a Y chromosome.

Of the two human sex chromosomes X and Y, the X is the more interesting, because it carries thousands of genes that affect all aspects of the phenotype. Also,

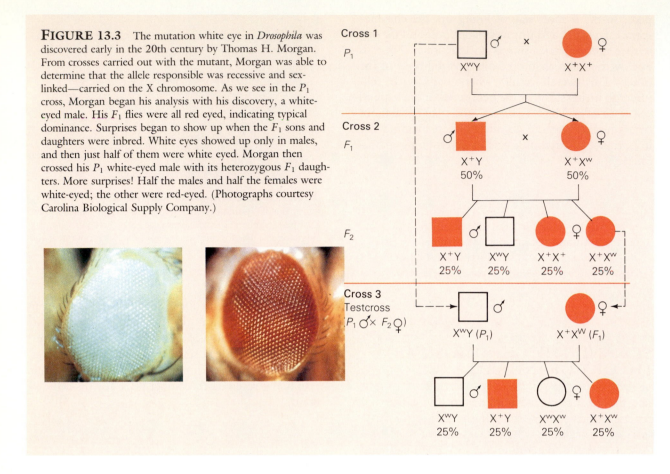

FIGURE 13.3 The mutation white eye in *Drosophila* was discovered early in the 20th century by Thomas H. Morgan. From crosses carried out with the mutant, Morgan was able to determine that the allele responsible was recessive and sex-linked—carried on the X chromosome. As we see in the P_1 cross, Morgan began his analysis with his discovery, a white-eyed male. His F_1 flies were all red eyed, indicating typical dominance. Surprises began to show up when the F_1 sons and daughters were inbred. White eyes showed up only in males, and then just half of them were white eyed. Morgan then crossed his P_1 white-eyed male with its heterozygous F_1 daughters. More surprises! Half the males and half the females were white-eyed; the other were red-eyed. (Photographs courtesy Carolina Biological Supply Company.)

its pattern of inheritance is the more complex, since it is present in both sexes. But before we try to understand the genetics of the X chromosome, we should take a brief look at its smaller partner, the Y chromosome.

The Y Chromosome

The Y chromosome's pattern of inheritance is simplicity itself: it is passed from fathers to sons, period. If you are a man, your Y chromosome was inherited intact from your father, from your father's father, and from your father's father's father and so on, right back to the first mammalian Y chromosome. And unlike all other human chromosomes, the Y chromosome never undergoes crossing over.

In XY species, such as flies and mammals, the Y chromosome is nearly devoid of identifiable genes. The few genes that are present on the Y chromosome include several genes for sperm function. In humans, the Y chromosome also has genes that influence height. In humans and all other mammals, the Y chromosome carries the determinant of sex itself, the **TDF gene.** At about six weeks the TDF gene ("testis

determining factor") in male embryos stimulates development of the testes, which respond by secreting male hormones. Under their influence the male reproductive organs develop. In the absence of male hormone, female structures develop (see Chapter 42).

The X Chromosome and X-linked Genes

In earlier chapters we emphasized that diploid organisms have two copies of every gene—one from the father and one from the mother. This is perfectly true for women, who get two X chromosomes, but it is not true for men. About 10% of all human genes are carried on the X chromosome, and for each of these gene loci, a man (XY) gets one copy from his mother. From his father he gets (in addition to one of each of the 22 human autosomes) only the genetically impoverished Y chromosome.

This means that human males are effectively haploid for approximately 10% of their estimated 40,000 to 50,000 genes. The lone copies of a mother's X-linked genes in her son therefore can be referred to as neither homozygous nor heterozygous; geneticists have coined a special term for them: **hemizygous;** they have no allelic counterparts.

> **A**lthough the X chromosome has thousands of genes, the Y has no matching loci. Thus males are **hemizygous** for X-linked genes.

Both in theoretical terms and in terms of human experience, the implications of this are enormous—especially when it comes to harmful, recessive mutant genes. Diploid organisms usually are protected from the effects of recessive genes since such alleles usually are "covered" and rendered harmless by a normally functioning dominant allele on the homologous chromosome. This protective effect of dominance still works for X-linked recessives, but only in females. If a woman (XX) has received a nonfunctioning, recessive, X-linked allele from one parent, she still has a good chance of receiving a normal dominant allele from the other parent. But when a man (XY) receives a detrimental, recessive, X-linked gene from his mother, it will always be expressed. His Y chromosome will be of no help. (Can males receive X-linked alleles from their fathers?)

This is not to say that women cannot express sex-linked traits. They can and do, but the probability is quite reduced. Men get the dubious distinction of being the ones who are most often affected by X-linked genetic pathologic conditions. The list of these is long and depressing and includes three kinds of muscular dystrophy, two kinds of hemophilia (bleeder's disease), Lesch-Nyhan syndrome, three types of hereditary deafness, pituitary dwarfism, testicular feminization, and several kinds of congenital blindness, in addition to less life-threatening conditions such as color blindness (Figure 13.4). (For a look at a sex-linked disease that has had a substantial effect on history, see Essay 13.1).

> **S**ince males have only one copy of each X-linked gene, those genes will be expressed. Thus recessive, sex-linked traits are far more common in males than in females.

Barr Bodies, Drumsticks, and the Lyon Effect

A simple chromosome study has been used in women's athletic competitions to determine whether a competitor is, in fact, a woman. The lining of the

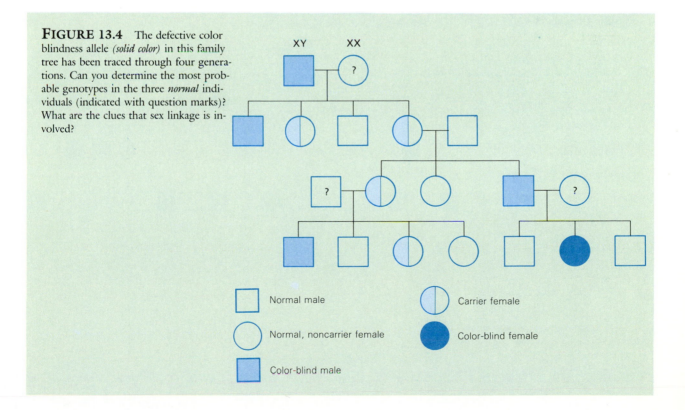

FIGURE 13.4 The defective color blindness allele *(solid color)* in this family tree has been traced through four generations. Can you determine the most probable genotypes in the three *normal* individuals (indicated with question marks)? What are the clues that sex linkage is involved?

☐ Normal male

◯ Normal, noncarrier female

■ Color-blind male

◐ Carrier female

● Color-blind female

Because ruling monarchs consolidated their empires through marriage alliances, hemophilia was transmitted throughout the royal families of Europe. **Hemophilia** is a sex-linked recessive condition in which the blood does not clot properly; any small injury can result in severe bleeding—and if the bleeding cannot be stopped, in death. Hence, it has sometimes been called the *bleeder's disease*.

The hemophilia allele has been traced back as far as Queen Victoria, who was born in 1819. One of her sons, Leopold, Duke of Albany, died of the disease at the age of 31. Apparently, at least two of Victoria's daughters were carriers, since several of their descendants were hemophilic. Hemophilia played an important historical role in Russia during the reign of Nikolas II, the last Czar. The Czarevich, Alexis,

was hemophilic, and his mother, the Czarina, was convinced that the only one who could save her son's life was the monk Rasputin—known as the "mad monk." Through this hold over the reigning family, Rasputin became the real power behind the disintegrating throne.

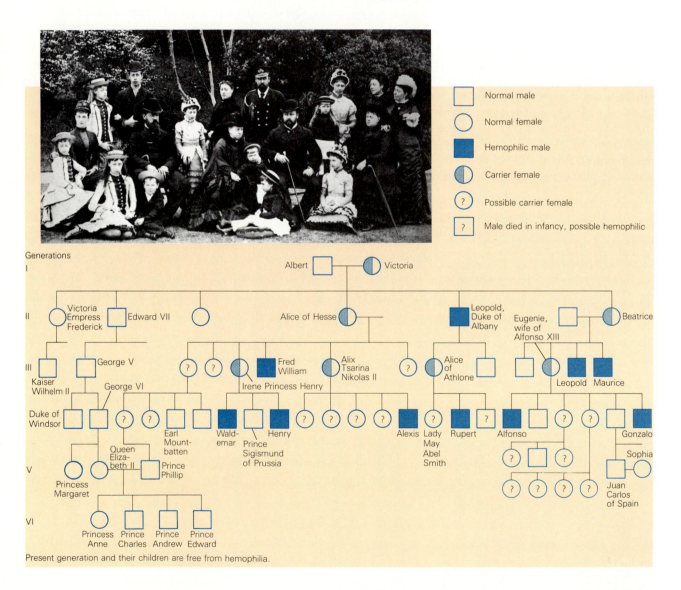

Present generation and their children are free from hemophilia.

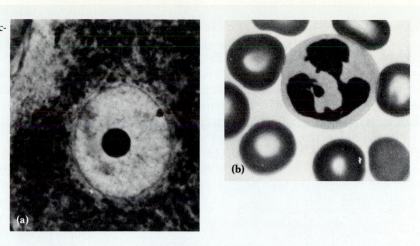

FIGURE 13.5 Condensed and inactive chromatin is seen in the Barr body **(a)** and the drumstick of cells from women **(b)**. Barr bodies are visible in specially stained cells; the drumstick is seen in stained white blood cells.

athlete's mouth is gently scraped and the cells are stained. A quick study of cell nuclei will establish genetic sex (XX or XY). The nucleus in female mouth cells reveals a dark-staining body, the **Barr body,** actually a condensed X chromosome (Figure 13.5a). Barr bodies are absent in normal males.

The condensed X chromosome also can be viewed microscopically in certain white blood cells, where it forms a characteristic projection from the cell nucleus called the **drumstick.** Although the Barr body was named after Murray L. Barr, its discoverer, the drumstick got its name because it reminded someone of a chicken leg (Figure 13.5b).

Why is an X chromosome visible when the other chromosomes are spread out and impossible to detect? Every female cell has twice as many X-linked genes as are present in a male cell. Presumably, there would be a physiological imbalance if both X chromosomes were activated. In any case, evolution has solved the problem through what is called the **Lyon effect** (first discovered by a British geneticist, Mary Lyon). One of the two X chromosomes in each XX cell is permanently deactivated during embryonic development (except for the germ line cells, those that form gametes). Which of the two X chromosomes is inactivated seems to be a matter of chance.

So every tissue in the adult female is a mosaic of cells in which one or the other X chromosome remains condensed and inactive. However, the condensed X is replicated normally and is passed from cell to daughter cell. It is inactive only with regard to metabolic function. For instance, the muscle tissue of women who are heterozygous carriers of X-linked muscular dystrophy is made up of patches of normal muscle and degenerate muscle. The normal cells expand in size and strength, fully compensating for the defective ones, so that such women appear to be normal.

> **F**emales have one permanently condensed X chromosome in each cell (except for oocytes): the **Barr body** in cheek cells and the **drumstick** in certain white cells.

GENE LINKAGE

In science, it has often been said, the answer to one question inevitably gives rise to new questions. This was the case with both Sutton's and Boveri's findings. Both had decided that chromosomes bore hereditary factors and that many such factors (genes) were contained on each chromosome. The problem they encountered, however, was that Mendel's principle of independent assortment didn't work with all genes. This, they decided, was because genes on the same chromosome should stay together during assortment, moving with the chromosomes as part of a **linkage group.** Linkage group came to be defined as any group of genes on the same chromosome.

> **L**inked genes are those that are situated on the same chromosome.

Problems with Mendel's Second Law

The expression of linked genes, of course, would produce exceptions to independent assortment. And soon enough, some exceptions to the second law began to surface. William Bateson and R.C. Punnett, in trying to reconfirm Mendel's findings, for example, got some puzzling results. They started with two sweet pea strains: one with blue flowers (**BB**) and long pollen grains (**LL**), the other with red flowers (**bb**) and round pollen grains (**ll**). The offspring of this cross had blue flowers and long pollen grains, so "blue" and "long" were Mendelian dominants. This is their original cross:

$$\text{BBLL} \times \text{bbll} \rightarrow \text{BbLl}$$

Following Mendel, they tried to reconfirm the law of independent assortment by crossing the double heterozygote **BbLl** back to the double recessive **bbll** parental strain (a test cross):

$$\text{BbLl} \times \text{bbll}$$

According to Mendel's second law, the offspring should have included four different phenotypes, all occurring in equal numbers:

25% BbLl : 25% Bbll : 25% bbLl : 25% bbll
(blue-long) (blue-round) (red-long) (red-round)

However, they didn't get this ratio at all. At this point you might think, "In that case the two genes are linked on the same chromosome." And the phenotypes would therefore be:

50% BbLl : 50% bbll
(blue-long) (red-round)

It turned out though that *neither* prediction held up. Although all four phenotypes showed up in the offspring (blue-long, blue-round, red-long, and red-round), suggesting independent assortment, *the numbers were all wrong*! When the phenotypes were counted, almost all were either blue-long (44%) or red-round (44%). Blue-round and red-long accounted for only 6% each. Bateson and Punnett found themselves confronted by a $7:7:1:1$ ratio (see Table 13.1).

The two Mendel fans were stumped. Such unexpected experimental results require the formulation of new hypotheses, and they couldn't come up with anything that made sense. Bateson and Punnett could only apologetically suggest that somehow the ovules or pollen with the original parental genotypes (blue-long and red-round) had increased in number just prior to fertilization. They recognized this was a lame explanation, but they never did figure out what was happening.

As it happens, the real explanation is even more bizarre than they suggested. The real explanation involves that remarkable process called crossing over, in which homologous chromosomes exchange parts during prophase of meiosis I, forming new allelic combinations and patterns (see Chapter 10). In Bateson and Punnett's time people knew very little about meiosis, and without that information they were hard pressed to explain such aberrant test results. But let's take what we know about meiosis and see what really happened to their sweet peas.

The genes for flower color and pollen shape are linked on the same chromosome, so barring some new phenomenon, only the two P_1 phenotypes, blue-long and red-round, should have shown up. But the blue-round and red-long offspring did show up, albeit only 12% of the time. So 12% of the progeny were the products of allele exchanges between

TABLE 13.1 The Bateson, Punnett Test Cross

Offspring		Expected Frequency		Observed Frequency
Phenotype	Genotype	Hypothesis I*	Hypothesis II†	
Blue, Long	BbLl	25%	50%	44%
Blue, round	Bbll	25%	0	6%
red, Long	bbLl	25%	0	6%
red, round	bbll	25%	50%	44%

*Mendel's independent assortment.
†Sutton's complete linkage.

homologous chromosomes, permitting the new combination of dominant and recessive alleles to appear in the crossover offspring. That is, genetic recombination occurred. But why the odd percentages? The answer can be found in a closer look at crossing over and genetic recombination.

The failure of independent assortment to occur when predicted indicates the presence of gene linkage. When an independent assortment of linked genes appears to have occurred, but with highly irregular ratios in offspring, crossing over is indicated.

GENETIC RECOMBINATION

By way of review, genes linked on the same chromosome are called linkage groups. The formation of new associations of linked genes require the breaking of chemical bonds of the DNA of the two chromosomes and the mutual exchange of DNA segments. Thus, alleles that were once located on different homologous chromosomes end up on the same chromosome. This is the process of crossing over (see Chapter 10). Geneticists today still argue about the molecular details of the process, so it's no wonder the early geneticists had a hard time of it. Amazingly, they worked out the concepts of gene linkage and crossing over using only crosses, test crosses, and progeny counts.

It was confusing at first. Some genes showed much stronger tendencies to remain linked than others, remaining together through generation after generation of test crosses (Figure 13.6). Others, such as Bateson's and Punnett's **B** and **L** and **b** and **l** alleles, regularly broke out of their linked state, with their recombination progeny dependably showing up in the test cross results (Figure 13.7). Still others underwent recombination regularly, but in much smaller frequencies, perhaps a fraction of a percent.

Gene pairs that had very low percentages of recombination were described as *tightly linked,* and those with higher percentages of recombination were described as *loosely linked.* These test cross numbers had none of the appeal of Mendel's wonderfully precise ratios. If the terms "loosely" and "tightly" linked genes sound vague, consider the dilemma of the geneticists of that period. A considerable time would pass before they would be able to equate linkage groups with the linear structure of DNA.

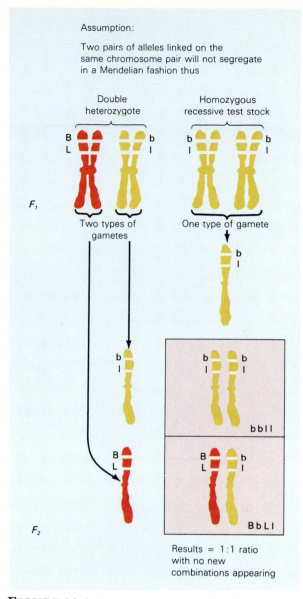

FIGURE 13.6 In this situation, genes **B** and **L** and genes **b** and **l** are permanently linked as though crossing over could not occur. In this test cross, a heterozygous individual is crossed with a homozygous recessive. Since the genes are passed as units, only two phenotypes are possible in the offspring, and these occur in a 1:1 ratio.

The frequency of crossing over increases in direct proportion to the distance between gene loci.

Linkage Groups and Genetic Maps

Working with fruit flies, A. H. Sturtevant eventually reasoned that the more tightly linked gene pairs (those more likely to stay together in crosses) were

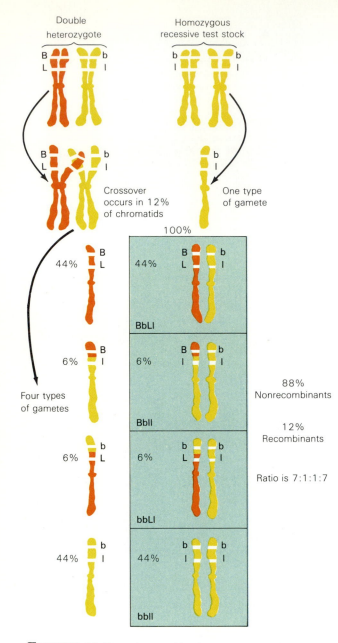

Double heterozygote

Homozygous recessive test stock

B
L

b
l

b
l

b
l

Crossover occurs in 12% of chromatids

One type of gamete

100%

44%

B
L

44%

B
L

b
l

BbLl

6%

B
l

6%

B
l

b
l

Bbll

88% Nonrecombinants

12% Recombinants

Ratio is 7:1:1:7

Four types of gametes

6%

b
L

6%

b
L

b
l

bbLl

44%

b
l

44%

b
l

b
l

bbll

FIGURE 13.7 Let's reconsider the test cross seen in Figure 13.6, this time allowing for a limited amount of crossing over between the two loci. Here, 12% of the chromatids undergo reciprocal exchange between the two genes for flower color and pollen shape. The remaining 88% of the chromatids do not undergo exchange. There are two kinds of *recombinant* chromosomes produced and two kinds of *nonrecombinant* chromosomes produced. Note the 7:1:1:7 ratio.

very close together on a chromosome, while the loosely linked gene pairs (those more likely to separate) were spaced farther apart on the same chromosome. The farther apart two genes were, Sturtevant reasoned, the greater was the chance that the length of chromosome separating them would break and rejoin in a crossover. The idea of genes being beads

on a string, that is, all arranged on a line in any given chromosome, began to win acceptance.

Eventually, some patterns began to emerge. Two mutant genes, *bar eye* and *scalloped wings* in the fruit fly *(Drosophila melanogaster)* were linked. In addition, *Bar eye* and *garnet eye* also were found to be linked. A number of such mutually linked genes formed a linkage group. The inference, as mentioned previously, was that all members of a linkage group were on the same chromosome.

The numbers began to make some sense, too. For instance, in the example given, Bar eye and scalloped wings showed 6% recombination in a test cross; scalloped wings and garnet eye showed 7% recombination; and in another test cross, Bar eye and garnet eye showed just slightly less than 13% recombination progeny. (According to our calculations, 6% plus 7% equals 13%.)

Sturtevant believed that these data meant not only that all three genes were on the same chromosome, but also that they were in a line, with scalloped wings in the middle (Figure 13.8). He made maps of all of the linkage groups, with each "map unit" being equal to 1% recombination. Each site on the gene map was henceforth called a **gene locus,** and a given gene locus could be occupied by one of two or more alleles on homologous chromosomes. Genetic maps eventually were made of all of the *Drosophila* chromosomes and included hundreds of known genes (Figure 13.9). The technique was soon used for other organisms.

Crossover frequencies are used to establish the relative order and distance between gene loci in recombination chromosome maps.

Mapping human genes. It's one thing to perform breeding experiments for gene mapping on fruit flies, but it's another thing when we come to humans. For obvious reasons, human genetics research must be done differently. For example, human genetic maps can be developed from statistical studies, that is, by pooling data from population studies. However, such information, by its nature, is hard won and not entirely reliable.

Recently, however, a new area of research, called **genetic engineering** (see Chapter 16), has yielded ways of mapping human chromosomes. Human cells can be fused with those of other species—typically mouse cells—to form genetic hybrids. As the mouse cells divide, most of the human chromosomes are lost, but by chance some cells retain just one. Such cells are then cloned and many descendants produced. The specific human chromosome is then identified (by size, centromere, and known banding patterns). Finally, the researcher looks for human gene products (such as enzymes). In this way a certain gene—deemed responsible for a certain product—can be located on the human chromosome. More recently, cytologists have learned how to simplify the hybridizing techniques by inserting specific chromosomes or parts of chromosomes into host cells. Through these techniques the specific locations of hundreds of human genes have been reliably determined.

CHROMOSOMAL MUTATIONS AND ABNORMALITIES

Although chromosomes are relatively stable, they are nonetheless subject to wear, tear, and disruptive influences such as heat, radiation, viruses, and harsh chemicals. Any resulting change in the nucleotide sequence is called a **lesion,** and although most lesions are repaired by special DNA repair systems in the nucleus (see Chapter 15), some are not. These permanent changes in DNA are called **mutations.** (The agents causing such a change are called **mutagens.**)

FIGURE 13.8 In recombination mapping, each percent of recombination is equal to one map unit. In this example, the locus of scalloped wing was determined to be between Bar eye and garnet eye, all mutant characters of *Drosophila.* The percent recombined was determined by test crosses between heterozygous individuals and homozygous recessives.

Separate test crosses indicate

13% recombination between bar eye and garnet eye
 7% recombination between garnet eye and scalloped wings
 6% recombination between scalloped wings and bar eye

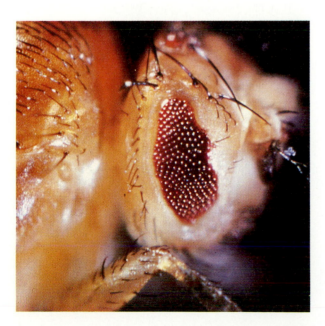

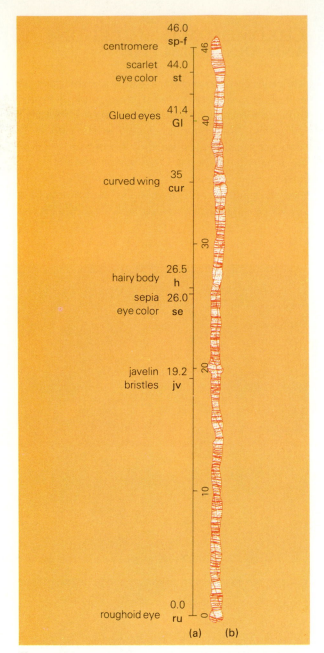

centromere	46.0 sp-f	46
scarlet eye color	44.0 st	
Glued eyes	41.4 Gl	40
curved wing	35 cur	
		30
hairy body	26.5 h	
sepia eye color	26.0 se	
javelin bristles	19.2 jv	20
		10
roughoid eye	0.0 ru	0

(a)　(b)

FIGURE 13.9 Recombination maps (vertical ruler lines with loci indicated) of part of a *Drosophila* chromosome, and reproductions of the actual chromosome. Recombination map distances are seen on the left of the vertical ruler lines, along with the names of mutant traits. The numbers on the right of the vertical lines are the actual loci as visually determined through the study of the distinct bands on the chromosomes themselves.

Although mutations certainly can be significant in the life of a given individual (they cause some forms of cancer), they are genetically important only if they are capable of being passed along to offspring. This means they must occur in gametes or in gamete-producing cells of the gonad.

Although mutations can be limited to individual nucleotide changes or to a small regions of DNA, we are more interested in the gross, large-scale changes in entire portions of chromosomes. Such changes are called **chromosomal mutations.** Again, such abnormalities become especially important when they occur in cells that are destined to enter meiosis and form gametes. You will recall that the early meiotic process, with its highly organized synapsis, crossing over, and repulsion, is quite precise, as is the unique chromosome segregation that follows. It isn't surprising that chromosomal abnormalities can play havoc with such highly orchestrated events.

Chromosomal Mutations

Massive chromosomal mutations involve the breaking of one or more chromosomes and their rejoining in abnormal ways.

Chromosome breakage is not unusual, and most breaks are quickly repaired. Studies of *Drosophila*, the fruit fly, reveal that more than 99.9% of chromosome breaks are successfully repaired. Unfortunately, some breaks are not repaired at all and some are repaired incorrectly.

The potential for repair errors increases when two or more chromosomes break or more than one break occurs in the same chromosome of a cell. In both instances, small fragments, commonly lacking the centromere, are lost when mitosis or meiosis occurs. Where two chromosomes break, fragments from the wrong (nonhomologous) chromosomes may be joined, producing what is called a **translocation.** We will come back to an important example of translocation shortly.

If a chromosome breaks two or more times, a whole segment may be left out in the repair process. The repaired but shortened chromosome is said to have undergone a **deletion.** Needless to say, cells or offspring with deletion chromosomes, should they survive, will not be normal. A very serious abnormality in humans, called cri-du-chat (cat's cry) syndrome, has been traced to a deletion in part of the fifth chromosome. The syndrome includes, in addition to the plaintive mewing voice the name suggests, serious mental retardation, gross facial abnormalities, and motor difficulties.

Another abnormality resulting from a double break is an **inversion:** the middle fragment is turned end-for-end before the repair occurs. Although all of the genes may be intact, an inversion chromosome presents interesting complications when it attempts to pair up with its normal homologue in the next meiotic prophase (Figure 13.10).

Even more exotic is the repair error that results in

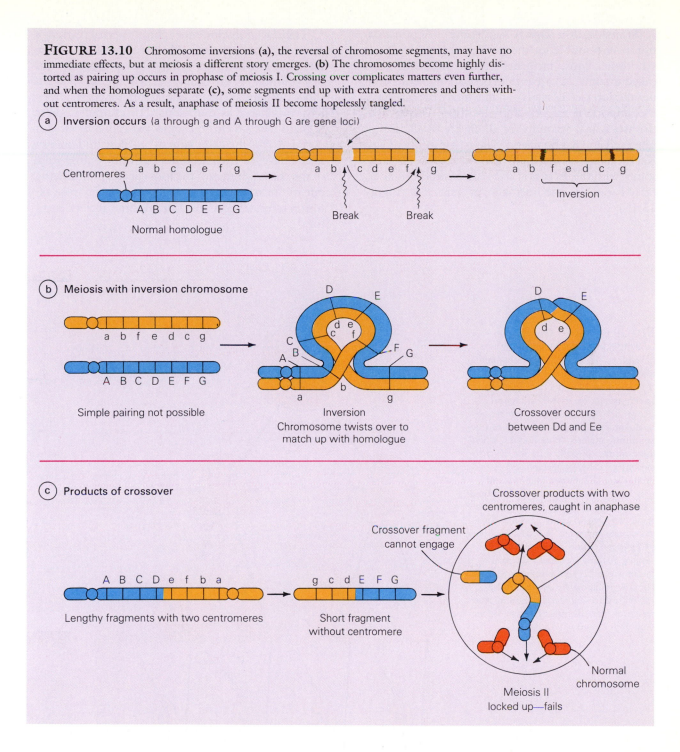

FIGURE 13.10 Chromosome inversions **(a)**, the reversal of chromosome segments, may have no immediate effects, but at meiosis a different story emerges. **(b)** The chromosomes become highly distorted as pairing up occurs in prophase of meiosis I. Crossing over complicates matters even further, and when the homologues separate **(c)**, some segments end up with extra centromeres and others without centromeres. As a result, anaphase of meiosis II become hopelessly tangled.

a Inversion occurs (a through g and A through G are gene loci)

Centromeres
a b c d e f g

Normal homologue
A B C D E F G

a b c d e f g
Break   Break

a b f e d c g
Inversion

b Meiosis with inversion chromosome

a b f e d c g

A B C D E F G

Simple pairing not possible

D   E
C   c d e f
B
A   F G
a   b   g

Inversion
Chromosome twists over to
match up with homologue

D   E
d e

Crossover occurs
between Dd and Ee

c Products of crossover

Crossover products with two
centromeres, caught in anaphase

Crossover fragment
cannot engage

A B C D e f b a

Lengthy fragments with two centromeres

g c d E F G

Short fragment
without centromere

Normal
chromosome

Meiosis II
locked up—fails

a **ring chromosome.** A large chromosome segment, complete with its centromere, has its two sticky ends fused together forming a circle. The genetic effects are variable, depending in part on how vital the lost fragments were. There are reasonably healthy people walking around today with ring chromosomes in every one of their cells. However, ring chromosomes are also associated with hereditary mental retarda-

tion. Ring chromosomes, needless to say, also complicate the early meiotic events.

Because they interfere with synapsis, crossing over, and segregation in meiosis, **chromosomal mutations** result in abnormal gametes and offspring.

Translocation Down syndrome. A translocation is responsible for the hereditary form of Down syndrome. Most incidents of the syndrome (also called trisomy 21) are products of spontaneous nondisjunction (see Essay 10.1), in which maternal age is the important factor. **Translocation Down syndrome,** which accounts for about 2% of all cases, is inherited and has no relationship to the mother's age. Karyotyping of the child reveals normal chromosomes with the exception of an extra chromosome 21 tacked on to one member of pair 14 (Figure 13.11).

Translocations and other chromosomal rearrangements aren't always bad. Most are harmful or lethal, but those rare harmless or beneficial ones are the stuff of evolution. Even closely related species *as a rule* show substantial chromosomal differences that must have originated as mutations. For example, normal humans have 46 chromosomes per cell, but our closest relatives—the chimpanzees, gorillas, and orangutans—have 48 chromosomes per cell. A close study of the chromosomes of the four species indicates that one of our treasured human chromosomes arose as a fusion translocation mutation in some ancient ancestor.

FIGURE 13.11 Translocation Down syndrome is brought about through an inherited chromosomal mutation. The translocation and fusion of chromosomes 14 and 21 are found in a carrier mother (a), but they have no effect on her since the correct number of homologues is present. The problems begin during meiosis in her oocytes, where there are two possible ways for the chromosomes to align in metaphase I (b). From these alignments, four kinds of eggs are possible (c). After fertilization of the oocyte (d), four kinds of zygotes can result (e). One will have a normal chromosome complement. A second will be a 14/21 translocation carrier, just like the mother. A third results in a deletion of chromosome 21, so the embryo will fail. The fourth alternative results in a trisomy, with three number 21 chromosomes present in the offspring. This will be the child with Down syndrome.

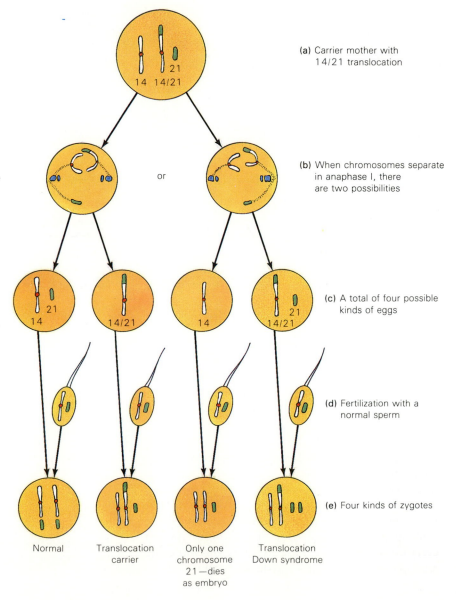

(a) Carrier mother with 14/21 translocation

(b) When chromosomes separate in anaphase I, there are two possibilities

(c) A total of four possible kinds of eggs

(d) Fertilization with a normal sperm

(e) Four kinds of zygotes

Normal   Translocation carrier   Only one chromosome 21—dies as embryo   Translocation Down syndrome

SUMMARY

MENDEL AND MEIOSIS

Although Mendel knew nothing about meiosis, upon the rediscovery of his work, the relationship between his laws and the meiotic process was soon established. In the dihybrid cross **RrYy** × **RrYy** (see Chapter 11), the way alleles combine in the gametes (**RY, Ry, rY, ry**) is explained in the two ways two pairs of chromosomes bearing such alleles align and separate during meiosis I.

SEX AND THE CHROMOSOME THEORY OF INHERITANCE

Sex is chromosomally determined. In many species the sex-determining pair are **heteromorphic,** designated as **X** and **Y.** The **XX** combination produces females, and the **XY** combination, males. Observers tracking two pairs of heteromorphic chromosomes through meiosis were able to relate meiosis to Mendel's laws.

SEX LINKAGE

T. H. Morgan discovered sex-linkage in the fruit fly.

The Y Chromosome

The human Y chromosome carries genes related to sperm function, height, and male sex. The TDF gene stimulates testis development in the early embryo.

The X Chromosome and X-linked Genes

The human X chromosome carries 4000 to 5000 genes that have no counterpart on the Y. Thus all X-linked genes act as dominants in males, a condition called **hemizygous.** Predictably, the frequency of sex-linked abnormalities in males greatly exceeds that in females.

Barr Bodies, Drumsticks, and the Lyon Effect

Female cells can be identified by the presence of a condensed X chromosome (the Barr body in mouth cells and the "drumstick" in certain white blood cells). One of the two X chromosomes in each cell is randomly but permanently deactivated.

GENE LINKAGE

Variations from Mendel's genetic ratios are sometimes due to the presence of **linkage groups**—genes linked together on a single chromosome.

Problems with Mendel's Second Law

A dihybrid P_1 cross carried out by Bateson and Punnett produced the usual F_1 phenotypes. Progeny testing of the F_1 yielded four phenotypes, which might have meant that independent assortment was occurring, but a $7:7:1:1$ ratio emerged instead of the expected $1:1:1:1$. Had the alleles been fully linked, the test cross would have produced a $1:1$ phenotypic ratio. The peculiar results can be explained through crossing over, which, in the Bateson-Punnett cross, occurred in 12% of the meiotic events.

GENETIC RECOMBINATION

Crossing over, a form of genetic recombination, occurs through the exchange of DNA segments between homologous chromosomes. In early studies, genes that crossed over frequently were called loosely linked and those that crossed over frequently, tightly linked.

Linkage Groups and Genetic Maps

Geneticists determined that the frequency of crossover was directly proportional to the distance between gene loci. Using recombination frequencies from fruit fly crosses, Sturtevant developed chromosome maps. They indicated the chromosome on which a given gene locus occurred, the relative order of loci, and their distances from each other.

Genetic engineering techniques have now been applied to human chromosome mapping.

CHROMOSOMAL MUTATIONS AND ABNORMALITIES

Mutagens are agents that damage DNA, creating lesions. Unrepaired lesions become mutations. Should the mutation end up in a gamete, it will be passed on to offspring. Chromosomal muations are large-scale changes in chromosomes.

Chromosomal Mutations

Although most chromosome breakages are correctly repaired, translocations, deletions, inversions, and rings form. Translocations involve the union of nonhomologous chromosomes, while deletions are lost segments. In an inversion, a segment is turned end-for-end before being rejoined. The union of two broken ends form a ring chromosome. All chromosome rearrangements create problems when normal and affected chromosomes pair up or synapse in early meiosis I. Translocation Down syndrome, a hereditary form of trisomy 21, is the product of translocation between chromosomes 21 and 14, resulting in an extra chromosome in the cells of affected individuals.

KEY TERMS

heteromorphic	drumstick	lesion	deletion
TDF gene	linkage group	mutagen	inversion
hemizygous	gene locus	chromosomal mutation	ring chromosome
Barr body	genetic engineering	translocation	translocation Down syndrome
Lyon effect			

REVIEW QUESTIONS

1 Using two pairs of chromosomes with the markers **A** and **a** on one pair and **B** and **b** on the other, carefully illustrate the principle of independent assortment through the events of meiosis. Bear in mind that demonstrating this relationship requires at least two cells going through meiosis. (Why?) (pp. 186–187)

2 Explain why two pairs of heteromorphic chromosomes must be present in meiosis for independent assortment to be observed. (p. 187)

3 How does the appearance of sex chromosomes differ in fruit flies? In humans? (p. 187)

4 What genes does the human Y chromosome carry? Compare this to the human X chromosome. (pp. 188–189)

5 Explain why all alleles on the X chromosomes act as dominants in males. Can females express sex-linked traits at all? Explain. (pp. 188–189)

6 Using the symbols XX and XY to represent female and male sex, suggest why the ratio of sexes in offspring (at birth) is about $1:1$. (Use a Punnett square.)

7 Who can males blame their sex-linked abnormalities on? Is this always true? Explain both answers. (p. 189)

8 Carry out a cross between a color blind man and a color blind carrier (heterozygous) woman. In what fraction of the children should color blindness occur? Are there color blind females? Carrier females? (You might symbolize the cross as **Cc × co,** or **Cc × cY,** just to remind yourself of hemizygosity in the male.)

9 In a family with two male and two female children, one of the boys is color blind, but the rest of the children are normal. List the *most probable* genotypes of the other children and the parents.

10 In a family of six children, there is a hemophilic boy with normal vision, two color blind boys with normal clotting times, two completely normal girls, and one color blind girl with normal clotting time. Determine, as accurately as you can, the genotypes of the parents.

Remember that both abnormalities are sex linked and recessive.

11 What are Barr bodies and drumsticks? What would their absence indicate about the bearer of the cells being studied? (pp. 189, 191)

12 According to the Lyon hypothesis, abnormal X-linked alleles will be active in half of the cells of a carrier woman. Why then do women rarely express sex-linked abnormalities? (p. 191)

13 Review the Bateson-Punnett F_1 test cross, **BbLl × bbll.** Carefully work out the cross so that you can and determine (a) what the results would have been if independent assortment had been at work, (b) what the results would have been had the genes been completely linked, and (c) the precise way the crossover occurred that produced the new combinations seen. (pp. 192–194)

14 Distinguish between the terms "loosely linked" and "tightly linked." How would we explain these ideas today? (pp. 193–194)

15 What is a genetic map? Explain the rationale behind using recombination frequencies to determine gene locus distances in the construction of such maps. (pp. 194–195)

16 Briefly review the method geneticists are now using to isolate and study individual human chromosomes. (pp. 194–195)

17 Define mutation. In what ways are mutations significant to the individual? What must happen before they are significant to a population or species. (pp. 195–196)

18 Using simple diagrams, explain how each of the following chromosomal abnormalities might occur: translocation, deletion, inversion, ring. (pp. 196–197)

19 Using one or two examples, explain how chromosome mutations might affect meiosis. Why is this effect so important? (pp. 196–197)

Mendel and the early Mendelians dealt with genes as abstract entities, but they knew that, at some level, genes must have a physical reality. As William Bateson put it in 1906: "But ever in our thoughts the question rings, what are these units (genes)? How the pack is shuffled and dealt, we are beginning to perceive; but what are they—the cards? Wild and inscrutable the question sounds, but genetic research may answer it yet."

Simply counting kinds of offspring has proved to be a powerful technique for discovering the nature of the gene and how it mutates, recombines, and interacts with other genes. But there are other equally valid ways to study the gene, such as isolating and analyzing both the gene and its products. We are now at the point where we can begin to successfully merge such diverse techniques as progeny counts and biochemistry. Since the inception of molecular biology (the study of genes and gene action at the molecular level), geneticists and molecular biologists have learned more than they expected about the gene. They have learned, for example, that genes have two fundamental functions: to be preserved and transmitted from generation to generation, and to control such biological processes as cell synthesis, development, and even behavior.

In this chapter and the next, we'll review some of the experiments that led to our modern concept of the gene. We'll take a close look at the biochemical structure of the gene and at how genes direct protein synthesis. Finally, we will consider how the genes themselves are controlled and how accidental changes in DNA (mutations) can affect gene function.

Historically, genetics consists of two stories that finally merge: the story of gene function, and the story of gene structure (that is, the chemical stucture of DNA).

14

WHAT IS DNA?

DISCOVERING DNA: THE STUFF OF GENES

It seems incredible, but DNA was isolated and characterized in Mendel's lifetime. In 1869 Johann Friedrich Miescher, a Swiss chemist, first isolated the nuclei of concentrated, dead white blood cells gathered from pus (biologists will look at anything) and then chemically dissolved the nuclear membrane and most of the remaining protein. This left a phosphorus-rich material he called *nuclein*, which we now call **chromatin** (DNA and its associated proteins were discussed in Chapter 9). That same year he also found nuclein in a number of other cell types. He speculated that the material might simply serve as a way for the cell to store phosphate, and he also suggested that it might have something to do with heredity.

By 1889, other European chemists, who had further purified nuclein by removing the last traces of protein, found that they were left with a gummy, acidic substance, which they named **nucleic acid.** Researchers eventually determined that there are two kinds of nucleic acid, which we now call **DNA** (deoxyribonucleic acid) and **RNA** (ribonucleic acid). The researchers of that day, however, had no way of putting their findings into a context that would clarify the basic mechanisms of genetics. But their progress set the stage for later experiments, such as those by A. E. Garrod.

Genes in Metabolic Pathways: An Early Look

In 1908 an English physician, A. E. Garrod, published a book called *Inborn Errors in Metabolism.* Garrod was keenly interested in genetic breakdowns in the biochemical processes of life and had for some time noticed that certain metabolic disorders tended to run in families. A number of these, Garrod believed, were caused by simple, inoperative, recessive alleles, those whose appearance could be predicted through the Mendelian laws. Although the expression of some of the abnormal alleles could be determined by a simple glance at the visible phenotype, others required a chemical analysis of the blood or urine. In such body fluids the recessive genes revealed their failure through the presence of abnormal products.

In **phenylketonuria,** for example, the amino acid phenylalanine accumulates in the blood of newborn infants and, in large amounts, causes severe mental retardation. Garrod suggested that the excess levels of the amino acid were caused by an absence of the enzyme that breaks it down. Furthermore, he suggested that the presence of the enzyme was controlled by a gene. (Phenylketonuria is a rare disease caused by a recessive allele.)

Garrod had shown that genes can act directly on biochemical metabolism by dictating whether specific enzymes are or are not present. In retrospect, this might have helped remove some of the early haziness about the gene concept, but alas, Garrod was ignored in his own time.

Garrod made the connection between genes and enzymes, noting that some inherited metabolic abnormalities could be the result of defective enzymes.

Transformation

In 1928 Fred Griffith, a British bacteriologist, conducted what seemed at first to be an oddball experiment, but it proved to be a classic. He studied the virulence (disease-producing capacity) of two strains of the bacterium from a species that causes pneumonia. One strain was dangerous and the other was harmless. The virulent strain formed a smooth, gummy polysaccharide coating that apparently protected it from the host's defenses. The harmless strain lacked a gummy coat. When grown in the laboratory, the virulent strain produced smooth, glistening colonies, whereas the harmless strain (which lacked the proper enzymes to make a gummy coat) produced rough colonies.

When Griffith injected the dangerous smooth-strain bacteria into mice, the mice died, as expected. When he injected the harmless rough-strain bacteria into other mice, the mice did not die. But then Griffith mixed dead smooth-strain bacteria with live rough-strain bacteria—both of which had earlier proved to be harmless—and injected the mixture into another group of mice. These mice died. What had happened?

Autopsies showed that the dead mice were full of virulent, living, smooth bacteria! Where did they come from? Apparently the genetic material of the harmless, living, rough-strain bacteria had somehow been **transformed** by something in the dead, smooth-strain bacteria, something that made them deadly also. Moreover, the rough-strain's progeny were all smooth (Figure 14.1).

DNA: The Transforming Substance

Sixteen years later, O. T. Avery and his colleagues set out to learn more about transformation. After finding that the phenomenon could take place in test tubes as well as in living mice, they decided to try to discover just what substance was causing it. Various substances derived from the dead smooth bacteria were isolated and purified to see whether they might be the mysterious "transforming substance." In 1944, they finally found it. Avery and his colleagues discovered that purified DNA from the deadly

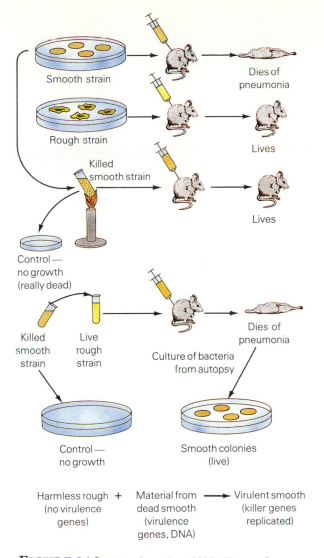

Smooth strain

Dies of pneumonia

Rough strain

Lives

Killed smooth strain

Lives

Control — no growth (really dead)

Killed smooth strain

Live rough strain

Culture of bacteria from autopsy

Dies of pneumonia

Control — no growth

Smooth colonies (live)

Harmless rough (no virulence genes) + Material from dead smooth (virulence genes, DNA) → Virulent smooth (killer genes replicated)

FIGURE 14.1 Transformation (1928). Twenty-five years before the function of DNA was finally resolved, Griffith's experiments clearly laid the groundwork for the idea that DNA was the genetic material.

smooth-strain bacteria could transform a rough-strain pneumococcus bacterium, giving it the ability to synthesize the necessary enzymes for making the protective smooth coat.

Avery determined that DNA was the agent that **transformed** Griffith's harmless rough pneumonococcal strain to a virulent smooth strain.

One Gene, One Enzyme

The slogan "one gene, one enzyme" was an electrifying bit of public relations in its day, 32 years after Garrod's work. It referred to the Nobel Prize-winning studies of George Beadle and Edward Tatum, who once again applied Mendelian analysis to metabolic pathways. But instead of drawing inferences from human abnormalities or from crosses of mutant flies, Beadle and Tatum imaginatively chose what was until then a very unusual experimental organism: the strikingly pink fungus *Neurospora*, relative of the green mold that can ruin oranges. *Neurospora* was to be the first in a series of important microorganisms that would be used in the upstart field of molecular biology.

Beadle and Tatum irradiated (x-rayed) *Neurospora* spores to produce random mutations. They then grew the irradiated spores and screened for biochemical mutations; that is, they looked for strains that could not grow unless certain simple biochemical compounds were added to the nutrient medium (the food on which the fungus was grown). These simple compounds were the metabolites (intermediate products) that are routinely present in biochemical pathways under normal conditions. Their idea was that if a mutant gene was not producing a certain enzyme, then the enzyme's usual product would not be produced and the biochemical pathway would be brought to a lethal halt. The biochemical pathway could be said to be *blocked* at a critical step. Therefore, by adding the product, missing because of the blocked step, the scientist would be able to unblock the pathway, allow it to proceed to completion, and watch the fungus thrive (Figure 14.2).

Once the "nutritional mutants" had been identified, mutant strains of the fungus could be maintained and genetic crosses could be made. All of the enzyme deficiencies turned out to follow the rules of Mendelian genetics; hence the slogan "one gene, one enzyme." Garrod's idea had been rediscovered: biologists now knew that specific genes were responsible for the presence or absence of specific enzymes.

The work of Beadle and Tatum established that genes were responsible for the presence of enzymes in the metabolic pathways of *Neurospora*.

Informational macromolecules. The idea of **informational macromolecules** was beginning to take hold. Certain chromosome-associated molecules obviously contained information that somehow

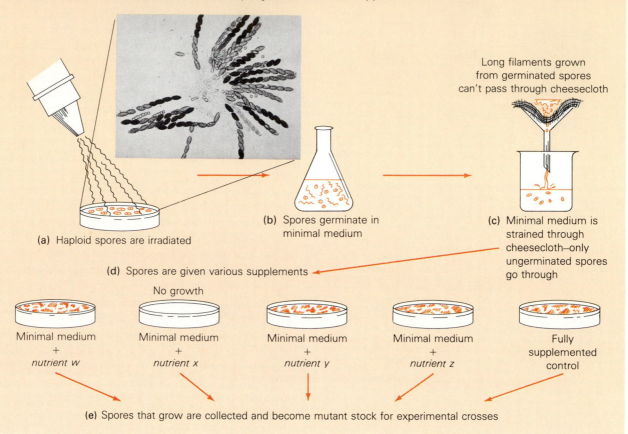

FIGURE 14.2 (a) Beadle and Tatum irradiated *Neurospora* spores, growing them in a minimal medium (b) to isolate nutritional mutants (c). The mutants were then grown in various nutrient combinations (d) and typed according to the nutrients they required in order to live (e).

Long filaments grown from germinated spores can't pass through cheesecloth

(a) Haploid spores are irradiated

(b) Spores germinate in minimal medium

(c) Minimal medium is strained through cheesecloth—only ungerminated spores go through

(d) Spores are given various supplements

No growth

Minimal medium + *nutrient w*

Minimal medium + *nutrient x*

Minimal medium + *nutrient y*

Minimal medium + *nutrient z*

Fully supplemented control

(e) Spores that grow are collected and become mutant stock for experimental crosses

directed the cell's biochemical processes. Avery's work pointed to DNA as being an informational molecule, though most scientists of the day favored proteins. It was not until 1953 that Frederick Sanger was able to analyze precisely the structure of a simple protein—the hormone insulin—and to prove, for the first time, that it had a highly specific, unvarying, linear sequence of amino acids. By this time, the eyes of the scientific community were already beginning to focus on DNA.

Hershey and Chase: The Great Kitchen Blender Experiment

Progress in molecular biology often follows the development of new technology. Given a new tool researchers can expect new information. In this case, the new technology was provided by Fred Waring, a popular band leader of the 1950s. When he was not leading his group in song, he was busy inventing the kitchen blender. The blender, of course, whips food

into a mush. The gourmet cook probably is not interested in the fact that, in so doing, it disrupts cells. But biologists happened to need a good way to disrupt cells, and so they crept away with their kitchen blenders and installed them in their laboratories.

In 1952, Alfred Hershey and Margaret Chase, who had followed Avery's work with interest, performed a crucial experiment. Their work firmly established that DNA was the only genetic material of at least one organism: the **bacteriophage** (or **phage,** for short). The bacteriophage, a virus that attacks bacteria, was a new tool for genetic analysis. If you have ever wondered whether a germ can get sick, you will be glad to learn that it can. It can be infected by a bacteriophage that can even kill it.

The phage resembles a hypodermic needle both in form and function (Figure 14.3). When it touches down on the surface of its bacterial host, tail (needle) first, it pierces the bacterial cell and injects its entire complement of DNA. Then a peculiar thing happens. The phage genes take over the synthesizing machinery of the host cell. The obliging host puts its own ribosomes, enzymes, and ATP to work, making a hundred or so new viral protein coats and viral DNA molecules. The burgeoning new viruses then reward the bacterial host by rupturing its cell, and in the process freeing the new viruses to infect other cells.

It is important to note that only the DNA is injected into the host cell. The original empty protein body stays outside like a discarded overcoat. Hershey and Chase discovered this by growing bacteriophages on bacteria that had been fed radioactive sulfur (^{35}S) and radioactive phosphorus (^{32}P). They knew that proteins contained sulfur and no phosphorus, whereas nucleic acid contained phosphorus and no sulfur; so they had simultaneously and uniquely "tagged" both kinds of molecule (Figure 14.4).

Hershey and Chase infected bacteria with these radioactive bacteriophages and allowed enough time for them to attach themselves and inject their DNA, but not enough time for the production of new bacteriophages. Then they put the mixture into their Waring blender.

The empty viral coats, which were pure protein, were broken loose from the bacterial surfaces and could be separated from them by centrifugation. That is, the whole mixture, consisting of infected bacteria and loose empty viral coats in liquid, was put into a high-speed centrifuge. The whirling force settled the bacterial cells at the bottom of the centrifuge tube, leaving the viral coats suspended in the remaining liquid. All of the radioactive sulfur was found in the liquid with the empty protein coats, and *all of the radioactive phosphorus was found inside the infected bacteria*. Since the infected bacteria could still produce complete, virulent virus particles, Hershey and Chase had shown that all of the genetic information of the tiny organisms resided in its DNA—and only in its DNA.

> Hershey and Chase determined that the hereditary molecule of the bacteriophage was DNA and not protein.

GENE STRUCTURE: CLOSING IN ON DNA

DNA was shown to be the stuff of genes. Attention had at last turned to this key molecule: What was its structure? How was it formed and how did it carry out the work of the gene? How was it able to make precise copies of itself?

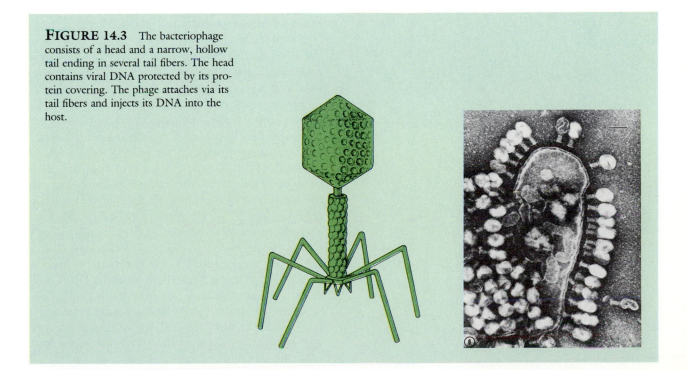

FIGURE 14.3 The bacteriophage consists of a head and a narrow, hollow tail ending in several tail fibers. The head contains viral DNA protected by its protein covering. The phage attaches via its tail fibers and injects its DNA into the host.

Chargaff's Rule

Erwin Chargaff tried to answer such questions with analytical biochemistry. He broke down purified DNA from many sources into its constituents: the four nucleotides of **adenine** (A), **thymine** (T), **guanine** (G), and **cytosine** (C). He carefully measured the exact quantity of each of these four subunits. Up to that time, the four nucleotides A, T, G, and C were believed to exist always in equal amounts. By about 1953, Chargaff reported that it wasn't so; the relative amounts of the four bases varied from species to species. It was therefore clear that not all DNA was alike.

In spite of this, a peculiar pattern emerged in Chargaff's data that came to be known as **Chargaff's rule.** In each species studied, he found that *the amount of adenine was always equal to the amount of thymine, and the amount of guanine was always equal to the amount of cytosine.* There are various ways to state this. In addition to A = T and G = C, one could also state A + G = T + C = 50%. That is, regardless of the source of DNA, exactly half of the nucleotide bases are **purines** (adenine and guanine) and exactly half are **pyrimidines** (thymine and cytosine). We will come back to the significance of this vital finding shortly. Let's just note that his work was being watched very closely by James Watson and Francis Crick in England, who were trying to work out DNA structure. Eventually, they saw the physical relationship behind Chargaff's rule.

> **C**hargaff's rule states that in DNA the quantity of **adenine** equals the quantity of **thymine,** and that of **cytosine** equals that of **guanine.**

FIGURE 14.4 Hershey-Chase experimental procedure. Hershey and Chase were able to grow phage particles that had their DNA labeled with radioactive phosphorus (^{32}P) and their protein coats labeled with radioactive sulfur (^{35}S). They were later able to show that only the phage DNA enters the cell to carry out its genetic activity.

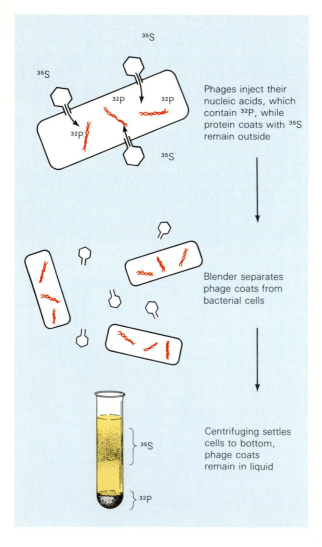

Phages inject their nucleic acids, which contain ^{32}P, while protein coats with ^{35}S remain outside

Blender separates phage coats from bacterial cells

Centrifuging settles cells to bottom, phage coats remain in liquid

Sizing Up the Molecule: X-ray Crystallography

X-ray crystallography is a technique that helps to determine the structure of crystals. It involves shooting a narrow beam of x-rays at a crystal and noting how the rays are diffracted (bent) before reaching a target of photographic film (Figure 14.5).

By the early 1950s, only a few organic substances had been studied this way. DNA was much on everyone's mind, and a few laboratories were beginning to look at DNA crystals.

Among those engaged in such work were Maurice Wilkins and Rosalind Franklin (who died before her work was fully appreciated). Their studies revealed a few repeating distances within the molecules of DNA: 0.34 nm, 2 nm, and 3.4 nm. We'll see what these numbers mean later; at the time they were just mysteries. But Wilkins and Franklin also saw a pattern indicating that DNA was a **helical** (corkscrew-shaped) molecule. Franklin had even argued that there were probably two strands in each molecule of DNA, not one or three. These two workers had the data and had almost figured out what the DNA molecule was like, but they couldn't nail it down. The problem was to be solved by the young researchers James Watson and Francis Crick. They did no crystallography of their own, but relied instead on Wilkins' and Franklin's data.

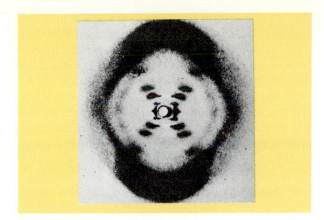

FIGURE 14.5 From the pattern, produced through x-ray crystallography analysis of DNA, Wilkins and Franklin were able to determine its helical form and critical intramolecular distances.

Watson and Crick would finally put it all together for us. They would deduce the structure of DNA. The story is a fascinating one, but since you already know the ending, let's summarize their findings first and then see how they went about unraveling the mystery.

DNA STRUCTURE: A BRIEF LOOK

DNA, we now know, is a **polymer,** that is, a chain of repeating subunits. The repeating subunits are called **deoxynucleotides** or, simply, **nucleotides.** The DNA molecule itself consists of two strands wound around each other in a **double helix,** resembling two wires twisted around each other. Each of the two strands of a DNA molecule is forged of strong covalent bonds between adjacent nucleotides. The two strands are attracted by enormous numbers of hydrogen bonds.

DNA includes two linear chains of **nucleotides** held together by hydrogen bonding and coiled into a double helix.

The DNA Nucleotides

The first diagram below represents one of the four nucleotides of DNA, the adenine nucleotide, as it appears in DNA. The pentagon-shaped portion in

the lower center is **deoxyribose,** a sugar. Attached to the sugar are both a **phosphate ion** and adenine, also called a **nitrogen base.** The five carbons of the sugar molecule have been numbered as usual, but the numbers have primes ['']. Thus the five deoxyribose carbon atoms are numbered 1' (one prime) through 5' (five prime).

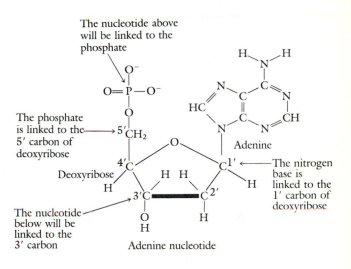

The deoxyribose molecule serves as a link holding the other parts of the DNA molecule. Its important bonding points are the 1', 3', and 5' carbons. The nitrogen bases are always covalently bonded to the 1' carbon of deoxyribose, as shown in the diagram. In free-floating nucleotides, the phosphate is linked to the 5' carbon only; but when the nucleotides are joined to make a strand of DNA, the 5' phosphate of one nucleotide is joined to the 3' carbon of the next nucleotide. The alternating phosphates and sugars form what is called the backbone of the DNA strand; the nucleotide bases hang off the sides of the molecular backbone.

All four of the DNA nucleotides follow this organization, with only the identity of the nitrogen base portion being different. The four DNA bases, as we have seen, are adenine, thymine, guanine, and cytosine (A, T, G, and C, respectively). The purines (guanine and adenine) consist of two attached rings: one ring with five sides and one with six sides, the two rings sharing a common side. The pyrimidines (thymine and cytosine) each consist of a single six-sided ring.

Nucleotides contain **deoxyribose,** covalently bonded to **phosphate** and to one of the four **nitrogen bases.**

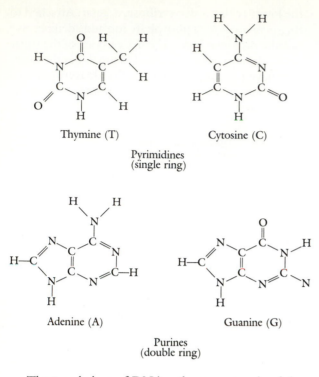

Thymine (T)   Cytosine (C)

Pyrimidines
(single ring)

Adenine (A)   Guanine (G)

Purines
(double ring)

The two halves of DNA—the two strands of the double helix—fit together in an interesting way. But that's Watson and Crick's story; let's return to them and see how they finally figured out the structure of DNA.

WATSON, CRICK, AND THE GREAT SYNTHESIS

Consider first what Watson and Crick knew when they tackled the DNA problem in 1953. They knew: (1) that DNA was a polymer containing great numbers of nucleotides; (2) the chemical structures of the nucleotides; and (3) that the deoxyribose and the phosphate alternated in long chains, with the nucleotide bases hanging off the sides of each chain like signal flags on a single rope. (4) From Wilkins' and Franklin's work they knew that DNA formed some kind of a helix, with three intramolecular distances: 0.34 nm, 2.0 nm, and 3.4 nm. (5) They knew Chargaff's rule: the number of adenines somehow had to equal the number of thymines, and the number of guanines had to equal the number of cytosines. *That* was where everything came together.

The Watson and Crick Model

Watson and Crick's experimentation was based on real models made of wire, sheet metal, and (literally) nuts and bolts. These models were designed to pro-

vide a graphic representation of the DNA molecule and its constituent parts. They began to fiddle with these models, to see how the parts might fit together—sometimes the fingers can grasp what the mind cannot!

Biological intuition and fitting the pieces this way and that seemed to indicate that there might be two strands wrapped around one another, with the phosphate-sugar backbone on the outside and the nucleotide bases inside, facing one another. But how were the bases arranged inside?

Wilkin's and Franklin's numbers began to make sense:

- 2 nm: their molecular model was consistent with the entire double helix being just 2 nm wide.
- 0.34 nm: the nucleotide bases were just about 0.34 nm thick, and perfectly flat. If the bases were stacked one on top of the other, like pennies in a roll, the layers would be 0.34 nm apart.
- 3.4 nm: with a gentle curve to the twisting helix, the double backbone would make one complete turn every 3.4 nm along the axis of the molecule; in other words, there would be exactly ten nucleotide pairs in each helical turn (Figure 14.6).

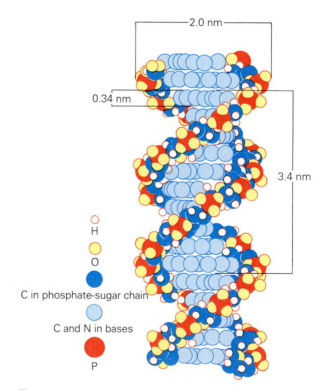

FIGURE 14.6 In the space-fillng model of the DNA double helix we can clearly distinguish the sugar-phosphate backbone of the two intertwining strands. The pairs of nitrogen bases are represented by lines of spheres lying stacked within the helix. Each measurement was determined through x-ray crystallography studies.

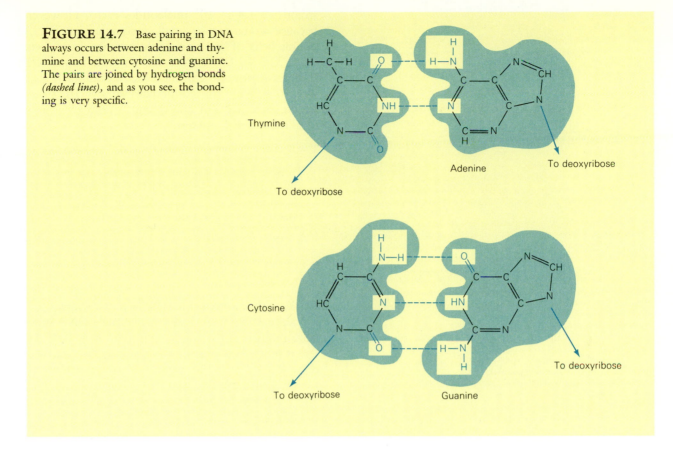

FIGURE 14.7 Base pairing in DNA always occurs between adenine and thymine and between cytosine and guanine. The pairs are joined by hydrogen bonds *(dashed lines)*, and as you see, the bonding is very specific.

Thymine

To deoxyribose

Adenine

To deoxyribose

Cytosine

To deoxyribose

Guanine

To deoxyribose

Putting Chargaff's rule to work. It was Watson who insightfully grasped the true meaning of Chargaff's strange rule. In the sheet metal and wire model, two purines would not fit opposite one another within the 2-nm confines of the double helix; and two pyrimidines would leave a gap. But one purine and one pyrimidine *could* fit opposite one another. Watson saw that adenine (a purine) and thymine (a pyrimidine) in a flat plane would form two hydrogen bonds with one another; guanine (a purine) and cytosine (a pyrimidine) would similarly form three hydrogen bonds in a plane (Figure 14.7). And this was the *only* way the DNA molecule would hold together. Opposite every adenine in one strand there had to be thymine in the other strand; every guanine in the one strand could be firmly hydrogen-bonded to a cytosine in the other strand, and so on. This was the key to DNA structure.

Base pairing. Watson and Crick's discovery of this relationship, called **base pairing,** was their major finding. The linear order of nucleotides in any one strand might seem perfectly arbitrary, but whatever nucleotides were in one strand rigidly fixed the sequence of nucleotides in the other strand. Thus Chargaff's empirical rules suddenly made logical sense: every A with a T, every T with an A, every G with a C, every C with a G. From this belatedly obvious conclusion sprang a whole new era in science, the era of molecular biology.

The paired bases lie perfectly flat and are stacked one on another much like a stack of coins. The thickness of the layers and the molecular distances along the sugar-phosphate backbone produce the characteristic coiling of the molecule. The flat base pairs are not quite aligned with the one below, but are slightly offset, like the steps in a winding staircase.

The two chains of the DNA molecule run in opposite directions. That is, if you pictured a DNA molecule vertically on a page, one of the chains would appear upside-down relative to the other (Figure 14.8). If one strand has its 3′ end at the top of the page and its 5′ end at the bottom of the page, the other strand will have its 5′ end at the top and its 3′ end at the bottom.

DNA molecules can be quite long. The average chromosomal DNA molecule in a human cell nucleus consists of about 140 million nucleotide pairs (two

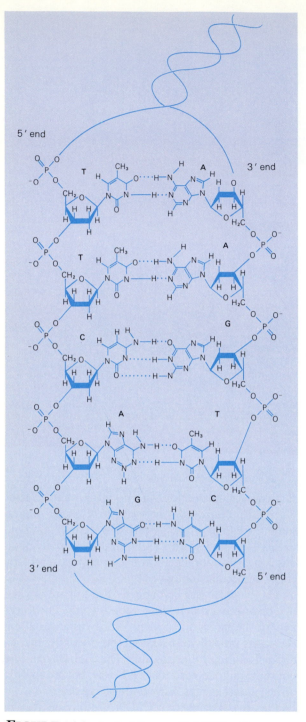

FIGURE 14.8 In the fully assembled DNA polymer, one strand appears upside-down to the other. Note the covalent bonds of the sugar-phosphate backbone and the hydrogen bonds between pairs of bases. In this view the bases have been turned up 45 degrees to show their structure and bonds, but in the actual molecule, only their edges would be seen.

strands of 1.4×10^8 nucleotides each). However, because atoms are so small, a stretched-out DNA double helix of that size would be only about 5 cm long. The 46 DNA molecules in each human cell nucleus (prior to chromosome replication) total some 6.4 billion nucleotide pairs (6.4×10^9 pairs) which, stretched out end-to-end, would measure a little more than 2 meters.

In base pairing a purine in one DNA strand always bonds to a pyrimidine in the other; specifically, adenine opposes thymine and guanine opposes cytosine (A–T, G–C).

Crick Solves the Riddle of DNA Function

Crick, with his great intellectual powers, made the conceptual leap from DNA structure to DNA function. DNA is fairly simple stuff, with only four different subunits arranged in a repetitive way. But how does DNA work? How could it be responsible for the incredibly complex role of the hereditary material? Crick deduced how the perfectly matched strands of DNA could unwind and how each half of the original double helix could direct the synthesis of a new, perfect, identical double helix. He also was among the first to propose that a short sequence of DNA nucleotides along the DNA molecule could somehow specify a single amino acid in the construction of a protein. His mind was forced to race ahead of the available data. How was he to get around the fact that, in eukaryotes, proteins are synthesized *only* in the cytoplasm, while the DNA (which directed the synthesis) occurred *only* in the nucleus? Crick had only the flimsiest of circumstantial evidence with which to work. He knew from the findings of others that a molecule called RNA (explained below) moved from the nucleus to the cytoplasm; perhaps RNA was copied from DNA. Next, he proposed the existence of an "adapter molecule." This molecule, he suggested, could join with a particular amino acid and then be able to recognize a particular RNA sequence, possibly a sequence only three nucleotide pairs long.

Later, as we shall see, something like Crick's adapter molecules were found and were named **transfer RNA (t RNA)**. Before the decade was over, Crick, whose awesome intellect had come to dominate molecular biology, was able to formulate what he called "the central dogma." Let's take a closer look at Crick's bold synthesis.

THE CENTRAL DOGMA

Since we're discussing science, you may be surprised to see the word **dogma.** Dogma usually refers to something that can't be questioned, and the term is usually reserved for matters of religion and politics. In a sense, the only dogma in science is that there can be no dogma—everything and anything can and should be questioned and tested. Crick's term originally was meant as a kind of self-deprecating joke, but it stuck. It is amusing that his idea was so powerful that many people accepted his little joke with not even a raised eyebrow.

In any case, the **central dogma** has been a landmark finding, in spite of the fact that there are, even now, important details to be worked out and intriguing mysteries to be solved. Some of these questions perhaps may never be answered; furthermore, each answer begets new questions. But with the working out of DNA function and the central dogma, the essence of the life process becomes better understood. But we're getting ahead of ourselves. Just what is the central dogma? Simply stated, it is as follows:

1. All DNA is copied from other DNA (a process called **replication**).
2. All RNA is copied from DNA (a process called **transcription**).
3. All proteins are synthesized from RNA in such a way that three sequential RNA nucleotide bases code for (direct the placement of) one amino acid in a protein chain, using a genetic code that is the same for all organisms (a process called **translation**).

Hardly the stuff, it would seem, for an earth-shattering intellectual revolution. Perhaps it seems that way only because the revolution has already happened, and we live in a world where the central dogma is accepted. (There are some interesting exceptions to these three absolute statements, requiring a couple of amendments to the dogma that will be discussed in the next chapter.) Let's restate the central dogma in more general terms.

All *biological information* (here, "information" refers to the coded directions needed for the organism to develop, function, and reproduce) is contained in linear sequences of nucleic acid bases in DNA. It is retained when these sequences are copied into newly synthesized DNA. It is also capable of being copied into ribonucleic acid sequences and uniquely determines the linear sequences of amino acids in protein synthesis. Finally, the linear sequence of amino acids in a protein uniquely determines the

shape and function of the protein itself (see Figure 3.12).

According to the **central dogma,** new DNA is **replicated** from preexisting DNA, RNA is **transcribed** from DNA, and RNA is **translated** into protein.

DNA Replication

You already know that DNA molecules are made by replication, using existing molecules to make new copies. Watson and Crick knew it too, but they had to arrive at this knowledge from raw data and their nuts-and-bolts model of DNA. In fact, they ended their classic 1953 paper by stating, "It has not escaped our notice that the specific pairing we have postulated immediately suggests a possible copying mechanism for the genetic material." Their suggestion was soon shown to be correct.

The complementary pairing of nucleotide bases in DNA suggests the analogy of a positive and a negative photographic film. The same information is present in both; one can make a positive print from a negative and a negative film from a positive. Similarly, a DNA "Watson" strand can be produced from a "Crick" strand (—an "inside joke"; a Watson strand or a Crick strand can be either one of the two halves of a DNA molecule). In DNA replication the Watson and Crick strands unwind, a new Crick strand is produced from the information in the Watson strand, and a new Watson strand is made from the information in the Crick strand. Thus there are two complete DNA molecules where before there was only one. Since each new polymer contains an intact strand and a newly assembled strand, the process is called **semiconservative replication.**

Replication enzymes at work.   Note in Figure 14.9 that the first step in DNA replication is the unwinding of the double helix. This involves breaking the weak hydrogen bonds holding the two strands together. The process requires energy and a special "unwinding enzyme" called **helicase.** Helicase is joined by a second enzyme, **DNA polymerase** to form a large **replication complex.**

After helicase unwinds and opens the DNA polymer, DNA polymerase base-pairs each exposed nucleotide with a new complementary nucleotide, thus generating two new opposing strands. Note also that replication can only proceed from the 5′ to the 3′ direction. The energy comes from ATP and from the nucleotides themselves. Raw nucleotides occur in a nuclear pool as **triphosphate nucleosides.** Like ATP, each has two high-energy bonds available for use in replication.

> Replication complexes containing the enzymes **helicase** and **DNA polymerase** unwind DNA, open it up, and form new opposing strands by base-pairing new nucleotides.

Replication complexes work in pairs, proceeding in both directions along DNA, and forming two Y-shaped **replication forks** (see Figure 14.9). One of new strands being assembled is known as the **leading** or **continuous strand;** the other is the **lagging** or **discontinuous strand.** The names come from the fact that DNA replication must move from the 5′ to the 3′ direction of the original molecule. In the leading strand, nucleotides are added one after another in a smooth, "continuous" manner. But since the other strand runs in the wrong direction, assembly is discontinuous. Nucleotides are first assembled in short sections (in the 5′ to 3′ direction). With the help of another enzyme called **ligase,** the pieces, called **Okazaki fragments** (for their discoverer), are inserted into the lagging strand.

Replication in prokaryotes and eukaryotes. In eukaryotes each of the several chromosomes consists of one very long DNA molecule, with a large number of histone spheres and other proteins (see Essay 9.1). In prokaryotes most or all of the cell's DNA is in a circular, protein-free molecule of DNA. It is not nearly as long as a typical eukaryote DNA molecule. In fact, you have about 1,400 times more DNA per cell than does the average bacterium. As you might expect, these differences affect the way replication is done.

Replication in eukaryotes is not a single event. Numerous replication forks simultaneously produce hundreds of spreading, bubblelike replication events all along each chromosome. Eventually all of the bubbles run into each other and the new replicas emerge. In prokaryotes replication begins at some specified spot in the circular DNA molecule and just two replication forks form. The two travel in opposite directions, eventually backing into each other and completing replication (Figure 14.9).

How does a bacterium get along with just two replication forks? It's a matter of speed. Prokaryotes can add nucleotides at the rate of 1 million per minute. Eukaryotes are infinitely slower, adding only 500 to 5,000 nucleotides per minute. If they used just one replication site, it would require weeks instead of hours for most eukaryotes to complete DNA replication. *Drosophila,* the fruit fly, may be a eukaryote record holder. Using some 50,000 replication sites, its newly fertilized egg can complete replication of the four pairs of chromosomes in about three minutes!

> Replication in prokaryotes is much faster than in eukaryotes: only two replication forks are required in the former, whereas hundreds to thousands are needed in the latter.

NEWER DEVELOPMENTS IN MOLECULAR BIOLOGY

As you can imagine, molecular biologists were not about to enshrine the central dogma and let it go at that. They sat around and admired its elegance for a while, but being the restless souls that they are, they soon began to ask the inevitable questions. Such poking and probing very quickly uncovered exceptions that significantly added to the body of knowledge about genes.

Cytoplasmic DNA

It would somehow be nice if life weren't full of exceptions: if, for example, we occasionally could rely on dogma. But perhaps part of the enchantment of life lies in its subtleties and exceptions. One exception to the notion that genes lie safely within the nucleus was the discovery of **cytoplasmic DNA.** Nearly all DNA does, in fact, reside in the nucleus, but some is cytoplasmic. Specifically, this cytoplasmic DNA is found in the mitochondria and chloroplasts. Both **mitochondrial DNA (mtDNA)** and **chloroplast DNA (cpDNA)** are active, regularly undergoing replication and transcription. Curiously, cytoplasmic DNA, with its *circular form and the absence of histone,* is far more similar to that of viruses and prokaryotes than it is to the DNA in the nearby nucleus. Recent studies of both ribosomal RNA and the ribosomes present in the two organelles reveal that they, too, are similar to those of prokaryotes. (These findings have lent strong support to the symbiosis hypothesis discussed in Chapter 21.)

FIGURE 14.9 During replication the original DNA chain **(a)** is opened by traveling replication complexes **(b)** that unwind the helix, separate the opposing strands, and build two complete strands by base pairing. Note the use of Okazaki fragments in the lagging strand. At the completion of replication **(c)**, each replica will consist of an old and a new strand.

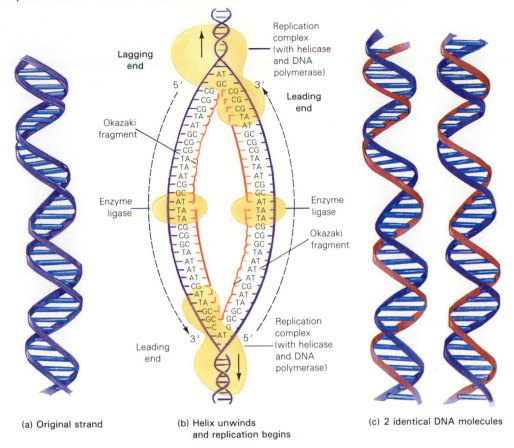

(a) Original strand

(b) Helix unwinds and replication begins

(c) 2 identical DNA molecules

The DNA in mitochondria and chloroplasts does not operate autonomously. For example, in both organelles the DNA requires a number of proteins synthesized by nuclear genes to do its work.

Although the analysis of mitochondrial and chloroplast DNA is recent, our knowledge of the genetic influence of the cytoplasm is not. Since early in this century biologists have known about a peculiar "maternal" influence that seemed to have nothing to do with genes but was related somehow to the egg cytoplasm. The sperm has very little cytoplasm and the egg has a great deal. Logically, any extranuclear inheritance observed had to come principally from the egg since it contributed far more cytoplasm. The intuition and reasoning of the older generation of scientists was right on track. Today we can finally explain such maternal influences as mitochondrial and chloroplast genes at work, and these come primarily from the egg.

The so-called maternal influence of the egg is actually the expression of genes in the **cytoplasmic DNA** of chloroplasts and mitochondria.

Repeated DNA Sequences and Satellite DNA

Recent studies of DNA have revealed a puzzling bit of news. About 30% of all eukaryotic DNA consists of short, repeated sequences of nucleotide bases. There may be millions of such copies in a nucleus. Apparently, though, none of it ever gets translated into RNA, and its presence is therefore a great puzzle.

Even more peculiar is the so-called **satellite DNA,** repeated short sequences consisting almost entirely of base-paired adenine and thymine. It was first discovered during centrifugation studies of the DNA of crabs. (Why crabs? We don't know.) It is called satellite DNA because it appeared as a minor, isolated, or "satellite" band of lightweight DNA in the centrifugation tubes. Neither the repeated sequences nor the satellite DNA has any known function.

Gene Amplification

Recently, it has been discovered that many genes occur several times throughout the eukaryote genome. The condition is called **gene amplification.** Apparently, the product of such genes is needed in great quantities, and this is one way of meeting the cell's needs. For example, there are multiple copies of the genes that transcribe the RNA of ribosomes in the nucleoli of certain oocytes (cells destined to become eggs). It seems that the ribosomal material is needed to produce the vast amounts of proteins needed for the great activity that occurs after fertilization.

> Multiple (repeated) genes make it possible for the cell to produce large quantities of special proteins.

Introns and Exons

With the discovery of a linear sequence of information in DNA came the notion that the entire length of a gene was essential to producing a protein. This notion proved to be wrong. In fact, *most* of the gene is inactive. That is, most of it does not specify the polypeptide or protein for which it is responsible. The parts of the gene that actually code for the polypeptide are called the **expressed sequences,** or **exons.** Those lengthy segments of the gene that do not code for the polypeptide are called **intervening sequences,** or **introns.** Introns, it turns out, are routinely removed from RNA transcripts prior to protein synthesis. We will look further into this phenomenon when we consider the transcription and translation aspects of the central dogma in Chapter 15.

Transposons

In belated recognition of a startling idea, geneticist Barbara McClintock, at age 79, was awarded a Nobel prize for her discovery of the so-called jumping genes of corn. The idea of movable or **transposable genes** had come to her some 30 years earlier as she observed the appearance of "impossible" combinations of traits in her crosses. Their occurrence could be explained only by the movement of genes from one locale to another. Since that time other researchers have learned of such gene mobility in both prokaryotes and eukaryotes.

Transposable genes are known to be responsible for sudden changes in **mating types** in yeasts. Yeasts, like many fungi and protists, have no gender in the usual sense of male sperm and female egg. However, a primitive form of sexual fusion can occur if mutually attractive, biochemically different mating types are present. These are generally designated plus and minus strains. Sudden changes in mating type occur when the gene responsible for one mating type is excised and a copy of the gene specifying the other mating type is copied from its locus and inserted in the empty "slot."

Of great significance to vertebrates is the transposable nature of antibody-producing genes. Human B lymphocytes, for instance, are capable of producing up to a million different antibodies. Even if every human structural gene were dedicated to the task of producing antibodies, we would fall far short of the number needed (the late Jack L. King of the University of California, Santa Barbara, determined that humans have only some 40,000 structural genes). The dilemma was solved when it became known that although only a few hundred genes were actually involved in antibody synthesis, these loci could be excised and rejoined in a seemingly infinite number of ways (see Chapter 39).

Transposons are complete, functional, transposable units. They include one or more genes and special segments called **insertion sequences.** Insertion sequences are nucleotide sequences of 600 to 6,000 base pairs. Insertion is made possible by specific enzymes that recognize the insertion sequence and then splice it into the chromosome. Through the action of such enzymes, not only can genes change loci on chromosomes, but also they can move from a viral genome to a bacterial genome and vice versa. An example of this versatility is the way bacterial species can transfer antibiotic resistance genes from one to the other (see Chapter 16).

> **Transposable genes** are those that move from one chromosomal location to another. Along with **insertion sequences** they form **transposons.**

In the next chapter we will see how DNA carries out its mission in directing protein synthesis. In essence, we will see how genes express themselves.

SUMMARY

DISCOVERING DNA: THE STUFF OF GENES

Mischner isolated DNA in 1869, naming it nuclein and describing its phosphate-rich quality. Its gummy, acidic nature, and the two forms of nucleic acid, DNA and RNA, were described in the late 1800s.

Genes in Metabolic Pathways: An early look

Garrod related inherited metabolic diseases, such as phenylketonuria, to enzyme deficiencies, which he believed had a definite genetic basis.

Transformation/DNA: The Transforming Substance

Griffith found that if live cells from a harmless strain of bacteria were mixed with dead cells of a virulent, pneumonia-causing strain, transformation would occur and the harmless strain would become virulent. Later, Avery repeated the experiment, but used purified DNA instead of dead cells from the virulent source. He determined that the transforming substance was DNA and that DNA had genetic capabilities.

One Gene, One Enzyme

Beadle and Tatum irradiated the fungus, *Neurospora*, creating various nutritionally deficient strains. Each had to be supplied with a specific metabolite to survive. By carrying out crosses among their mutant strains Beadle and Tatum determined that enzyme deficiences had a straightforward Mendelian genetic basis. Thus they established the relationship between genes and enzymes (i.e., a faulty mutant gene produces a faulty useless enzyme).

Hershey and Chase: The Great Kitchen Blender Experiment

Hershey and Chase knew that bacteriophages injected their genes into host bacterial cells. They introduced bacteriophages whose proteins had incorporated radioactive sulfur and whose DNA had incorporated radioactive phosphorus, into bacterial cultures. Allowing time for gene injection, they dislodged the viruses and then determined that it was the DNA (viral genome) that entered the cells whereas the protein (viral coats) remained outside. DNA was again shown to be the genetic material.

GENE STRUCTURE: CLOSING IN ON DNA
Chargaff's Rule

Through a study of nitrogen bases from the DNA of many kinds of cells, Chargaff determined that adenine, thymine, guanine, and cytosine, occur in specific proportions: A = T and G = C (Chargaff's rule). This relates to the fact that purines and pyrimidines always pair in DNA.

Sizing Up the Molecule: X-ray Crystallography

Using a technique called x-ray crystallography, Wilkins and Franklin studied the molecular structure of DNA, making specific measurements and determining that it was helical and double stranded.

DNA STRUCTURE: A BRIEF LOOK

DNA contains two strands of nucleotides attracted by hydrogen bonds and twisted into a double helix.

The DNA Nucleotides

Each nucleotide is made up of deoxyribose (a sugar), a phosphate ion and one of four nitrogen bases. The pyrimidines (thymine and cytosine) are single rings of nitrogen and carbon, whereas the purines (adenine and guanine) are double rings.

WATSON, CRICK AND THE GREAT SYNTHESIS

From the available information on DNA structure, Watson and Crick deducted its molecular structure.

The Watson and Crick Model

In developing their nuts-and-bolts model of DNA, Watson and Crick determined the meaning of x-ray studies: the molecule was 2 nm wide, its base pairs 0.34 nm thick, and a complete turn of the helix, 3.4 nm (10 base pairs). From Chargaff's rule, they derived base-pairing, the idea that each pyrimidine in the DNA chain is opposed by a purine; specifically adenine opposes thymine and guanine opposes cytosine. The bases lie in a flat plane, each hanging off of the sugar-phosphate backbone.

Because of base-pairing, the order of bases in one strand determines the order of bases in the other. Each strand has a 5′ (phosphate) end and a 3′ (deoxyribose) end. Further, one strand is upside down relative to the other. The average human DNA molecule has 140 million base pairs.

Crick Solves the Riddle of DNA Function

Crick reasoned that because of base-pairing, the double strand could unwind and a new strand could be assembled along each of the old. He suggested that RNA was somehow used to carry the genetic message to the cytoplasm where proteins were assembled. He also recognized the need for transfer RNA.

THE CENTRAL DOGMA

The central dogma is the proposal that the principal activities of DNA were replication (duplication of genes), transcription (transcribing of the genetic message into RNA), and translation (using the RNA transcript for assembling amino acids into protein).

DNA Replication

In replication, the double helix unwinds and the strands separate. The order of bases in each strand is followed in assembling a new partner strand. The two DNA molecules formed are replicas of the former DNA molecule. Because the old strands are retained, replication is called semiconservative.

Replication requires a replication complex consisting of the unwinding enzyme (helicase) and the nucleotide assembling enzyme (DNA polymerase). Energy is available from high-energy bonds in the pool of nucleoside triphosphates. Replication complexes proceed in opposite directions forming two replication forks. The assembly of nucleotides occurs in the 5' to 3' direction, a requirement that results in a different means of assembly in the leading and lagging strands.

Eukaryotes form numerous replication forks, carrying on simultaneous replication. Prokaryotes form just two replication forks that travel in opposite directions around the circular chromosome.

NEWER DEVELOPMENTS IN MOLECULAR BIOLOGY

Cytoplasmic DNA

Mitochondria and chloroplasts contain their own genes (mtDNA and cpDNA), although they utilize products of the nuclear genes. This fact supports the symbiosis hypothesis.

Repeated DNA Sequences and Satellite DNA/Gene Amplification

Eukaryotic DNA contains nucleotide sequences of unknown function, including repeated sequences known as satellite DNA. Many genes have multiple copies, called gene amplification, assuring the availability of gene products needed in quantity.

Introns and Exons

Genes contain lengthy nucleotide segments called introns (intervening sequences) that are not translated into protein. They are removed following transcription, leaving only the exons (expressed sequences).

Transposons

Transposable genes or transposons are genes capable of changing loci. For example, the formation of nearly countless antibodies is made possible by the rearrangement of gene segments. Transposons are made up of one or more genes along with insertion sequences that aid in splicing the gene into its new locus.

KEY TERMS

nucleic acid	deoxynucleotide (nucleotide)	lagging (discontinuous) strand
DNA	double helix	ligase
RNA	deoxyribose	Okazaki fragment
transformation	phosphate ion	cytoplasmic DNA
informational macromolecules	base pairing	mitochondrial DNA
bacteriophage	central dogma	chloroplast DNA
adenine	replication	satellite DNA
thymine	transcription	gene amplification
guanine	translation	expressed sequence
cytosine	semiconservative replication	exon
Chargaff's rule	helicase	intervening sequence
purine	DNA polymerase	intron
pyrimidine	replication complex	transposable gene
x-ray crystallography	triphosphate nucleoside	mating type
helical	replication fork	insertion sequence
polymer	leading (continuous) strand	

REVIEW QUESTIONS

1 List two DNA discoveries that were made before the 1900s. (pp. 201–202)
2 Explain how A. E. Garrod made the connection between genes and metabolic disorders such as phenylketonuria. (p. 202)
3 Summarize the observations on transformation made by F. Griffith. How was the transforming substance finally identified? (p. 202)
4 Briefly summarize the experimental methods of Beadle and Tatum and explain what they were able to add to the conclusions and speculations made earlier by Garrod. (pp. 203–204)

5 Describe the bacteriophage and explain how it enters a bacterial cell and how it reproduces. (pp. 204–205)
6 Explain the experimental procedure that led Hershey and Chase to conclude that the genetic material was DNA. Did they prove this to be true of all life? Explain. (pp. 204–205)
7 What did Chargaff find about the amounts of the four nitrogen bases in cells? Did he immediately understand the meaning of these quantities? (p. 206)
8 Summarize the findings of Wilkins and Franklin. What technique did they apply to study DNA? (p. 206)

9 List the molecular subunits of a nucleotide. What is important about the 1′, 3′, and 5′ carbons of the sugar? How does one DNA nucleotide differ from the next? (pp. 207–208)

10 Name the four DNA bases and state whether they are purines or pyrimidines. (pp. 207–208)

11 What did Watson learn about the molecular distances, 2 nm, 0.34 nm, and 34 nm, discovered earlier by Wilkins and Franklin? (p. 208)

12 Explain the specific pairing of bases in DNA. Summarize the intuitive thinking that led Watson to the discovery of base pairing. (p. 209)

13 Describe the arrangement of nucleotide bases along the DNA molecule and the orientation of the two strands. (p. 209)

14 What did the double-stranded structure of DNA and the newly discovered base-pairing principle suggest to Crick about DNA replication? (p. 210)

15 List the three aspects of central dogma. What central life process does number one make possible? (p. 211)

16 Explain how the structure of DNA makes it an informational molecule. (p. 210)

17 Using the following nucleotide sequence, show how DNA replication occurs (ignore the replication complexes):

ATGCCGTTATAATCG
TACGGCAATATTAGC

18 Name the two enzymes of the replication complex and summarize their roles. (p. 211)

19 Suggest a reason why nucleoside triphosphates are used as raw materials for replication. (p. 212)

20 Briefly explain why Okazaki fragments must be used in replication of the lagging strand. How does this differ from replication in the leading strand? (p. 212)

21 Summarize a major difference between prokaryote and eukaryote replication. Suggest a reason for the difference. (p. 212)

22 Where, specifically, is cytoplasmic DNA found, and how does its presence support the symbiosis hypothesis? (pp. 212–213)

23 Characterize the transposon, its general role, and explain how gene rearrangements might be essential to the body's antibody defense mechanism. (p. 214)

15

DNA IN ACTION

We have followed the history of science's long, tedious search for the stuff of heredity. We have seen the search move first in one direction and then another, as various kinds of molecules were proposed and rejected until one remained. We saw it unveiled as DNA and found that the key to its signals to the cell is the sequence of the nucleotides along its length. We have also found how the DNA replicates, and that the precision of the replicating mechanism explains the constancy of the DNA from one generation to the next. So let's now see how this fascinating molecule dictates the business of the cell by directing the synthesis of specific enzymes and other proteins.*

We should keep in mind that the genes control protein synthesis in an indirect manner. Although the protein-specifying code is preserved in DNA, the information in the code works through intermediaries. These intermediaries are molecules of ribonucleic acid (RNA). The genetic message in the DNA is copied on strands of RNA within the nucleus, and these strands then move into the cytoplasm, where they direct protein synthesis. The copying phase, as we have seen, is called transcription, and the synthesis of protein is called translation. We will look at two other aspects of DNA action as well. We will venture into the little-known frontier area of gene control—the activation and deactivation of DNA—and, finally, return to mutations for a look at chemical change on the molecular level.

THE RNA MOLECULE

Right off the bat we can see that DNA and RNA are very similar. Both DNA and RNA are lengthy polymers of nucleotide subunits that are held together by covalent bonds between phosphates and sugars. The nucleotide bases of both extend from the familiar sugar-phosphate backbone like signal flags on a line. But in spite of their fundamental similarity, there are marked differences between them.

1. In RNA, the five-carbon sugar is **ribose** instead of **deoxyribose.** As you see in the molecules shown below, the 2′ carbon of deoxyribose of DNA contains two hydrogen side groups. This same carbon in the ribose of RNA has a single hydrogen side group, but opposing it is a hydroxyl (OH) side group (deoxy refers to less oxygen).

*Note: Actually we will be describing polypeptide synthesis. A protein contains one or more polypeptides and has assumed a final, coiled and folded, functional form (see Chapter 2).

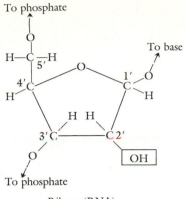

To phosphate

To base

Ribose (RNA)

2. Both RNA and DNA contain adenine (A), guanine (G), and cytosine (C), but the thymine (T) of DNA is replaced in RNA by a base called **uracil** (U). Uracil is structurally very similar to thymine and base-pairs with adenine in the same way:

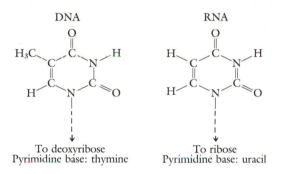

DNA

RNA

To deoxyribose
Pyrimidine base: thymine

To ribose
Pyrimidine base: uracil

3. DNA almost always occurs as a double-stranded helix with a very regular structure. RNA almost always occurs as a single-stranded molecule, and some forms have complex secondary (coiled) and tertiary (folded) structure, twisting and folding on themselves, much as proteins do, forming a precise three-dimensional shape.

4. DNA molecules are typically much longer than RNA molecules. DNA molecules are millions of nucleotides long, whereas the RNA nucleotides number only in the thousands.

5. DNA is more stable than RNA; that is, it is more resistant to chemical breakdown.

6. There are several different classes of RNA molecules, each with different functions, whereas all DNA functions in information storage and transmission.

RNA is a single-stranded molecule that is less stable than DNA. It contains **ribose** rather than deoxyribose and **uracil** rather than thymine.

TRANSCRIPTION: THE SYNTHESIS OF RNA

RNA transcription is at first reminiscent of DNA replication. DNA is unwound and its bases are exposed, just as if it were about to begin replication. Instead of each strand of DNA making a complementary strand, however, one strand lies dormant while short sections of the other act as a template for the formation of RNA. And, as we mentioned, uracil is used instead of thymine in RNA. During RNA synthesis, uracil pairs with DNA's adenine all along the strand being transcribed. After the copying is over, the RNA **transcript** drifts free and the DNA rewinds (Figure 15.1).

Just as the replication complex of DNA synthesis consists of the enzymes helicase and DNA polymerase, transcription is accomplished by a **transcription complex** consisting of helicase and **RNA polymerase.** In eukaryotes the length of DNA along which a single RNA molecule is transcribed is roughly equivalent to a gene.

Transcription begins at special DNA sequences called **promoters.** As soon as the first few bases of an RNA sequence have been formed, the DNA and RNA strands begin to separate, and the growing RNA chain, or transcript, begins to dangle off to the side. The DNA to which it was attached is then free for further transcription. Many RNA molecules can be transcribed in a very brief time from the same DNA transcription unit. This is known as **simultaneous transcription** (Figure 15.2).

Transcription complexes containing **RNA polymerase** open the DNA helix and, using RNA nucleotides, form RNA transcripts along one DNA strand.

THREE KINDS OF RNA

By now we are aware that there are several kinds of RNA. Three of these are of special interest because they are necessary for protein synthesis: **messenger RNA (mRNA), ribosomal RNA (rRNA),** and **transfer RNA (tRNA).** Each has a specific role in the synthesis of enzymes and other proteins. Let's begin with mRNA and see what its message is all about.

FIGURE 15.1 (a) In transcription, the DNA helix unwinds and the double strand opens. RNA polymerase then goes to work base-pairing RNA nucleotides to the transcribing strand of the DNA. (Notice that every A in DNA becomes opposed by a U in the RNA strand. (b) As is often the case, the simultaneous transcription of RNA occurs.

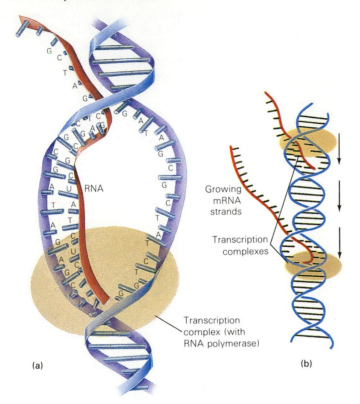

RNA

Growing
mRNA
strands

Transcription
complexes

Transcription
complex (with
RNA polymerase)

(a)

(b)

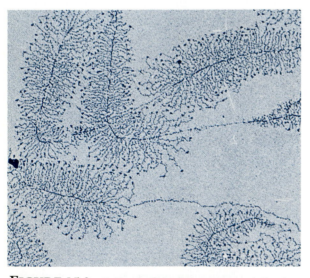

FIGURE 15.2 Evidence of simultaneous transcription is seen in chromosomes from an amphibian egg as the cell builds its protein reserves. The shorter, feathery strands of RNA are just starting, while the longer ones are well along in the transcription process.

Messenger RNA and the Genetic Code

Messenger RNA carries the specific information that has been stored in the sequence of nucleotides in DNA. In DNA that information is coded in the form of nucleotide base sequencing—the linear order in which A, T, C, and G are arranged in DNA strands. The equivalent sequence is copied into RNA, with U replacing T.

RNA processing: introns and exons. Raw mRNA starts out as a transcript, a complete copy of a transcription unit. Before this RNA transcript can be considered mRNA and before it can move out into the cytoplasm, it must undergo **posttranscriptional processing.** Recall that eukaryote genes typically include **introns,** or **intervening sequences** (Chapter 14). Although they are transcribed, they must be removed as RNA is processed. After their removal, the introns are simply disassembled into nucleotides and recycled for further use. What remains are called the **exons,** or **expressed sequences.** They comprise the actual genetic message.

Curiously, introns are not trifling amounts of DNA. For instance, they make up 85% of the DNA in a gene known to code for ovalbumin, a protein of bird eggs. On the average a raw mRNA transcript contains about 50,000 nucleotides, but after processing it is reduced to only 6,000. Some of the clipped-out introns contain as many as 10,000 nucleotides—quite a stretch of RNA. The removal of introns is a precise and complex process: The loss or gain of even a single nucleotide can seriously affect the genetic message, resulting in a useless enzyme or faulty structural protein.

There is no proved advantage to the presence of introns, although biologists are willing to guess. Some biologists think that introns may be adaptive—that they absorb their share of spontaneous chemical change. Thus, some potentially damaging mutations would be actually removed before protein synthesis begins. Other biologists maintain that introns greatly facilitate successful crossing over during meiosis. With the gene effectively divided into many "domains," they say there are simply many more chances for recombination to occur. This helps the species to maintain a certain level of genetic variability.

The processed mRNA contains the coded message that will then undergo **translation.** Recall that translation is the synthesis of protein from the message contained in mRNA. The translated portion of mRNA is preceded by a *5' leading region* and a *3' following region.*

In the processing of raw mRNA transcripts, **introns** are removed and **exons** rejoined to form the final message.

Codons. The message is written in the genetic code. The messenger RNA molecule carries its message in the form of **codons,** which are groups of three nucleotides. Each codon specifies one of the 20 different amino acids commonly found in proteins. For example, the three-nucleotide sequence GAG (guanine-adenine-guanine) is a codon specifying *glutamic acid.* The 64 codons (representing all of the ways in which four kinds of nucleotides can be arranged in a sequence of three) are shown in Table 15.1, together with the amino acids they specify.

TABLE 15.1   The Genetic Code

FIRST LETTER	SECOND LETTER								THIRD LETTER
	U		**C**		**A**		**G**		
U	UUU UUC	Phe	UCU UCC	Ser	UAU UAC	Tyr	UGU UGC	Cys	U C
	UUA UUG	Leu	UCA UCG		UAA UAG	STOP STOP	UGA UGG	STOP Trp	A G
C	CUU CUC CUA CUG	Leu	CCU CCC CCA CCG	Pro	CAU CAC	His	CGU CGC	Arg	U C
					CAA CAG	Gln	CGA CGG		A G
A	AUU AUC AUA	Ile	ACU ACC ACA	Thr	AAU AAC	Asn	AGU AGC	Ser	U C
	AUG	Met	ACG		AAA AAG	Lys	AGA AGG	Arg	A G
G	GUU GUC GUA GUG	Val	GCU GCC GCA GCG	Ala	GAU GAC	Asp	GGU GGC	Gly	U C
					GAA GAG	Glu	GGA GGG		A G

Amino acid abbreviations: alanine, Ala; arginine, Arg; asparagine, Asn; aspartic acid, Asp; cysteine, Cys; glutamic acid, Glu; glutamine, Gln; glycine, Gly; histidine, His; isoleucine, Ile; leucine, Leu; lysine, Lys; methionine, Met; phenylalanine, Phe; proline, Pro; serine, Ser; threonine, Thr; tryptophan, Trp; tyrosine, Tyr; valine, Val.

This is the famous **genetic code,** a major discovery of 20th-century science.

To better understand how the code works, let's consider the **principle of colinearity,** a concept that Francis Crick so elegantly proposed long before much was known about RNA. DNA, RNA, and protein are each linear molecules consisting of repeated subunits, and there is a clear relationship among the units. According to this principle, the linear ordering of nucleotides in DNA specifies the order of codons in mRNA, and the linear ordering of codons in mRNA specifies the linear ordering of amino acids in the protein (Figure 15.3).

> **P**rinciple of colinearity: The linear order of DNA nucleotides corresponds to the order of RNA nucleotides, which determines the amino acid order in polypeptides.

It is now well established which amino acids are specified by which codons, but working out the genetic code required the efforts of some of the best minds in molecular biology and a great deal of painstaking experimental verification. Once the genetic code table was finally worked out, the code proved to be exactly the same for such diverse groups as humans, *Escherichia coli,* and yeast—underscoring the basic relationships and unity of life—and so it was known for decades as the "universal" genetic code. However, it has since been shown that our very own mitochondria use a slightly different genetic code. Furthermore, yeast mitochondria have yet other slightly different codon assignments. So there are several dialects of the genetic language, and the code isn't quite so universal after all.

A closer look at the genetic code. You have probably wondered why there are 64 codons to code for only 20 amino acids. Obviously, some of the amino acids must be coded for by more than one codon. That is indeed the case, and different codons that specify the same amino acid are called **synonymous codons.** As you can see in Table 15.1, most (but not all) synonymous codons come in blocks and differ only in the third position.

Three of the 64 codons do not specify amino acids at all but indicate STOP. These are UAA, UAG, and UGA; they are, in effect, punctuation marks, and translate into "this is where to end the polypeptide." There is also a START codon, AUG; it also specifies the amino acid methionine. This means that all newly synthesized polypeptides have to start with methionine. If a methionine in the first position of a protein doesn't suit the needs of the organism—and apparently it often doesn't—then it will have to be removed enzymatically later on. Since AUG is the only codon for methionine, when it occurs in the middle of a message, it is ignored as a START codon and is simply read as a methionine-specifying codon.

> **T**he information units of the genetic code are the 64 different codons—nucleotide triplets—most representing the 20 different amino acids used in protein.

We've seen that the genetic message is transcribed from DNA into mRNA, which, in turn, carries the encoded message to the cytoplasm for translation. Before we can understand how the sequence of codons in mRNA is translated into a sequence of amino acids in a polypeptide, we must look at the other two types of RNA involved in protein synthesis: ribosomal RNA and transfer RNA.

> **M**ost amino acids are represented by **synonymous codons** (more than one) in the genetic code. Other codons act as **START** and **STOP** punctuation.

FIGURE 15.3 The colinearity concept illustrates the relationship between DNA, mRNA, and protein. The triplet nucleotides of DNA are transcribed into the codons of mRNA, which in turn specify the order and kind of amino acids to be inserted into protein.

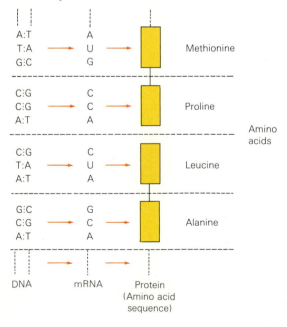

Ribosomal RNA and the Ribosome

Ribosomal RNA (rRNA) occurs in ribosomes. Unlike other RNA, most of it is formed within the nucleolus along lengthy loops of DNA known as **nucleolar organizing regions.** These regions contain multiple copies of the genes carrying the rRNA coding, an example of gene amplification (see Chapter 14).

Two large and two small rRNAs are joined by 75 to 80 special protein molecules forming the ribosome. Ribosomes are the vital organizing centers where messenger RNA and transfer RNA assist in assembling polypeptides. Ribosomes have been likened to gigantic enzyme complexes (or to mobile factory workbenches), but they are like no other molecular complex or cellular organelle in all of life. Recent intense electron microscopic and biochemical studies of the ribosome have begun to clarify their unique structure.

Ribosomes have two distinct parts, a **large subunit** and a **small subunit,** each with its own characteristic shape. The large subunit looks like a cartoon head; the smaller one resembles a wide chin. (Now try looking at Figure 15.4 without thinking of that.)

Each functioning (assembled) ribosome contains several important attachment sites (Figure 15.4). One site holds the lengthy mRNA in a groove formed between the two subunits. Two sites are pockets in which tRNAs with amino acids fit as they are assembled. Another site accommodates **peptidyl transferase,** an enzyme active in linking pairs of amino acids. Finally, there is a mRNA binding site, important to the initial activation of the ribosome.

> Ribosomal RNA, assembled by **nucleolar organizing regions** in nucleoli and joined by proteins, forms the **large** and **small subunits** of **ribosomes.**

Transfer RNA

We've seen that messenger RNA carries the instructions for polypeptide assembly to the cytoplasm and that ribosomal RNA is used in constructing ribosomes, the "traveling workbench" upon which the actual assembly occurs. What, then, is the purpose of transfer RNA, the third member of the RNA triad?

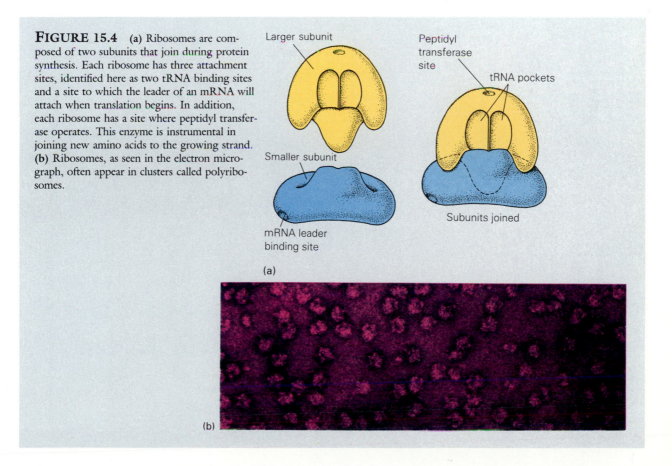

FIGURE 15.4 (a) Ribosomes are composed of two subunits that join during protein synthesis. Each ribosome has three attachment sites, identified here as two tRNA binding sites and a site to which the leader of an mRNA will attach when translation begins. In addition, each ribosome has a site where peptidyl transferase operates. This enzyme is instrumental in joining new amino acids to the growing strand. (b) Ribosomes, as seen in the electron micrograph, often appear in clusters called polyribosomes.

Larger subunit

Smaller subunit

mRNA leader binding site

Peptidyl transferase site

tRNA pockets

Subunits joined

(a)

(b)

Transfer RNA handles a central task in translation, getting the amino acids to the mRNA and ribosome and assuring that they land in the right positions. If you think of messenger RNA as the assembly line and ribosomes as the workbench where workers assemble the product, then perhaps the tRNAs are specialized forklifts, scurrying back and forth between stockroom and assembly line delivering the parts to be assembled. Let's see how all of this really happens in the cell.

Transfer RNA's role in the assembly of the polypeptide can be broken down into three parts:

1. Each tRNA becomes *charged;* that is, it locates and binds its own specific amino acid.
2. Charged tRNAs join binding sites on the ribosome where a polypeptide is being assembled.
3. Charged and bound tRNAs recognize a specific codon in mRNA and insert their amino acids accordingly.

The role of tRNA is to bond to specific amino acids and assist in their assembly into polypeptides on the ribosome.

Transfer RNA: charging and structure. The proper connections between tRNA and specific amino acids are made by charging enzymes. There is a highly specific charging enzyme for each variety of tRNA. Each enzyme has three binding sites, one for the tRNA, a second for the proper amino acid, and a third for ATP. The enzyme uses the energy of ATP to form the bond connecting the amino acid to the tRNA.

Transfer RNA is formed from a linear strand of about 100 nucleotides whose sequence is transcribed from tRNA genes just as mRNA sequences are transcribed from other genes. After tailoring, the strand becomes twisted and folded into a definite three-dimensional shape, forming three "loops" and a "stem." In its finished form the whole molecule takes on sort of an **L** shape (Figure 15.5).

The stem and loops in the final tRNA configuration play individual roles. The **3′ end,** or **CCA stem,** common to all tRNAs is the site of amino acid attachment. A side loop then forms base-pairing attachments to ribosomal RNA in the ribosome. Most interesting is the **anticodon loop,** which contains a three-base sequence known as an **anticodon.**

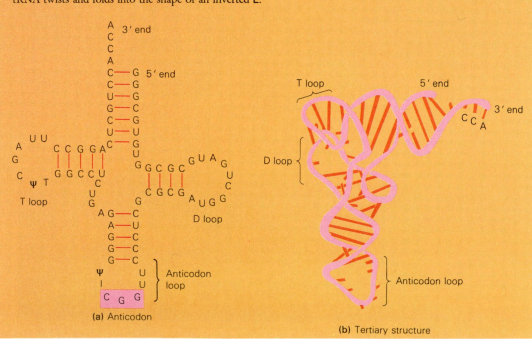

FIGURE 15.5 **(a)** In its secondary form, the nucleotides of tRNA base pair to produce a multilooped figure. The 3′ CCA end is the attachment site for an amino acid, whereas one of the side loops interacts with rRNA on the ribosome. The lower, or anticodon, loop holds three nitrogen bases that pair or match up with codons in mRNA. (ψ = various modified bases.) **(b)** In its final or tertiary form, tRNA twists and folds into the shape of an inverted **L**.

FIGURE 15.6 Glycine-tRNA contains the anticodon CGG, which will pair up with the condon GCC. This is but one step in the translation of genetic code into protein.

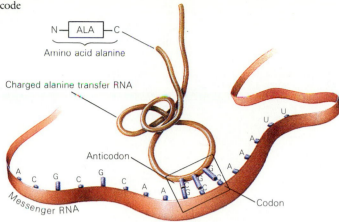

As the name suggests, anticodons "oppose" codons. That is, the three bases of a tRNA anticodon will base-pair with the three bases of a mRNA codon. For example, the mRNA codon GCC (according to the genetic code table) specifies alanine. One of the alanine-specific tRNA molecules has the anticodon CGG, which makes the proper base pairing with GCC (Figure 15.6).

> Charged tRNAs place their amino acids in the correct position by base-pairing their **anticodon** with a matching codon on mRNA.

PROTEIN SYNTHESIS: TRANSLATION OF THE GENETIC MESSAGE

We now have all of the elements needed for a step-by-step description of protein synthesis. The process will be divided into three parts: **initiation, elongation,** and **termination.** These terms refer respectively to the beginning, the middle, and the end of the process.

Initiation

Initiation begins when three elements known as the **initiation complex** are brought together: mRNA (with its AUG START codon), the ribosome, and a charged tRNA molecule (Figure 15.7). Since methionine is always the first amino acid in any protein

being synthesized, this will be a methionine-charged tRNA. Its anticodon—UAC—will match the codon—AUG—on messenger RNA.

All three elements of the initiation complex must be present before the two ribosome subunits can join to form an intact ribosome. When the initiation complex is assembled, the methionine-charged tRNA will occupy the left-hand pocket of the larger ribosome subunit, and the AUG codon of the mRNA will fit into the ribosomal groove. All is now ready for the next step, elongation.

> At **initiation** the two ribosomal subunits combine with mRNA and methionine-charged tRNA.

Elongation

With the initiation complex in place, elongation, the addition of amino acids, can proceed. Recall that the lefthand pocket of the ribosome was occupied by methionine-charged tRNA; the righthand pocket was empty. Below the right pocket, however (as seen in Figure 15.7), was the next mRNA codon waiting for a charged tRNA with a matching anticodon. Many charged tRNA molecules, in random motion, may bounce in and out of the empty pocket, but only one with the correct anticodon will bind. When the match occurs, the righthand pocket will be filled.

Once the second charged tRNA is in place, the two amino acids will join, producing the first of many covalent **peptide bonds.** The enzyme responsible for this event, peptidyl transferase, is integrated into the larger ribosomal subunit. When the peptide

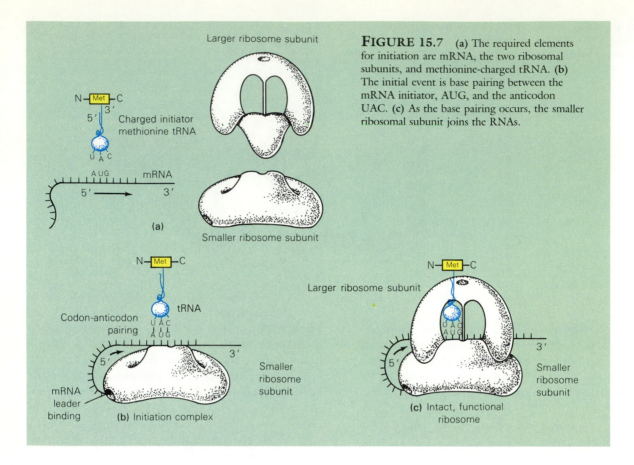

Larger ribosome subunit

N—Met—C

Charged initiator
methionine tRNA

5' 3'

U A C

A UG   mRNA

5'   3'

(a)

Smaller ribosome subunit

FIGURE 15.7 **(a)** The required elements for initiation are mRNA, the two ribosomal subunits, and methionine-charged tRNA. **(b)** The initial event is base pairing between the mRNA initiator, AUG, and the anticodon UAC. **(c)** As the base pairing occurs, the smaller ribosomal subunit joins the RNAs.

N—Met—C

tRNA

Codon-anticodon
pairing   U A C
               A UG

5'   3'

mRNA
leader
binding   **(b)** Initiation complex

Smaller
ribosome
subunit

N—Met—C

Larger ribosome subunit

U A C
A UG

5'   3'

(c) Intact, functional
ribosome

Smaller
ribosome
subunit

linkage has formed, a crucial step called **translocation** can occur.

In translocation the ribosome moves one codon to the right, and in so doing the tRNA in the lefthand pocket, now uncharged, is bumped out by tRNA from the right. The ousted tRNA, once freed, will drift away to be recycled. Emptying of the righthand pocket permits another codon to enter its charged tRNA to pair up, so that the cycle can be repeated. Figure 15.8 picks up the action about half way through elongation. A number of amino acids have been joined to produce the growing polypeptide and yet another is about to be added.

Thus the action continues, with the ribosome clumping along its mRNA in short jumps of one codon at a time. Charged tRNA molecules arrive constantly as the righthand pocket keeps emptying. With every translocation step, the polypeptide grows one amino acid longer. You can see how the ribosome plays its essential role in keeping things organized. By moving along the mRNA strand exactly one codon at a time, it ensures the accurate translation of the code.

All of this may seem a bit complex and tedious, so how long does it take? The fastest time known for the completion of an entire, good-sized polypeptide is six seconds (in *E. coli*).

In **elongation** an amino acid is added to a polypeptide through peptide bonding and the translocation of tRNA from one ribosomal pocket to the other.

Termination: Derailing the Ribosome

As the ribosome moves along its mRNA to the end of the message, it runs into one or another of the three STOP codons: UAA, UAG, or UGA. Sometimes there are double stops (for example, UAAUAG), just to be sure that the ribosome gets the message.

The next step is the termination of the building process. There are no tRNAs with anticodons that correspond to any of the STOP codons. Instead there are specific proteins that move into position when the STOP codon is on the ribosome. There they seem to clog the works and bring about the release of the last tRNA, which is then removed enzymatically from the end of the now-completed polypeptide.

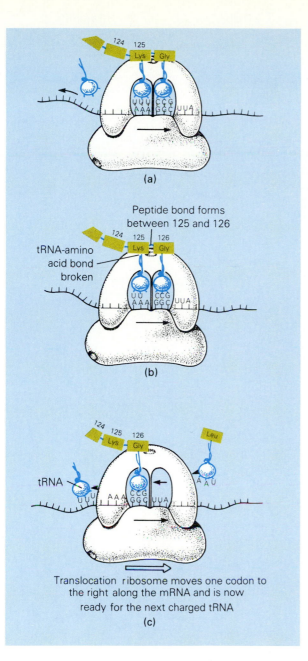

FIGURE 15.8 (a) The activity represents the translation process midway through the synthesis of a polypeptide. The lefthand pocket is occupied by lysine tRNA. Its amino acid, lysine, has already covalently bonded to the growing polypeptide chain. Glycine tRNA has landed in the righthand pocket.
(b) Next, with the aid of the enzyme peptidyl transferase, a covalent bond forms between lysine (125) and glycine (126).
(c) During translocation, the ribosome moves along one codon to the right, bumping lysine-tRNA out as glycine-tRNA occupies the left pocket. The right pocket is again empty. Leucine-tRNA, a newcomer, is about to drop into the empty pocket.

Finally, with no charged tRNAs in place, the ribosome separates into its large and small subunits, which drift away from the messenger to recycle for another run.

The polypeptide, now a free chain of amino acids at the primary level of protein structure, has its own fate. It will automatically form its secondary structure and may join other polypeptides, reaching the tertiary and quaternary levels of protein structure (see Chapter 3). Some will form the enzymes that are the link between the coded genes of DNA and the metabolic activities of the cell. (Figure 15.9 reviews the entire process, including termination.)

> In **termination** a ribosome encounters a stop codon, the ribosomal subunits separate, and the completed polypeptide is released.

Polyribosomes

During active protein synthesis ribosomes generally occur in small clusters, with perhaps two to 10 ribosomes per cluster. Each cluster is called a **polyribosome** (or, sometimes, **polysome**). A polyribosome is actually a strand of messenger RNA with a group of attached ribosomes, like pearls on a string (Figure 15.10). Each ribosome will travel the whole length of the mRNA, from the START codon to the STOP codon, then each will fall apart and drop off, as others assemble at START. Thus several ribosomes can be producing copies of the same protein at the same time, each working on a different portion of the message.

The polyribosomes can be free in the cytoplasm, or they can appear to be bound to the membranes of the endoplasmic reticulum (ER). The bound ribosomes produce proteins that will be secreted by the cell at some later time. Actually the polyribosomes themselves are not directly attached to the membrane, but are held there by the growing polypeptides that are moving into the ER where they will undergo transport and further modification (see Chapter 4). The polypeptides are able to penetrate the ER because their leading ends contain a sequence of peptides that recognize and bind to ER receptor sites.

> Ribosomes often form clusters called **polyribosomes** as they read the same mRNA molecule. Bound ribosomes cluster at special sites on the ER.

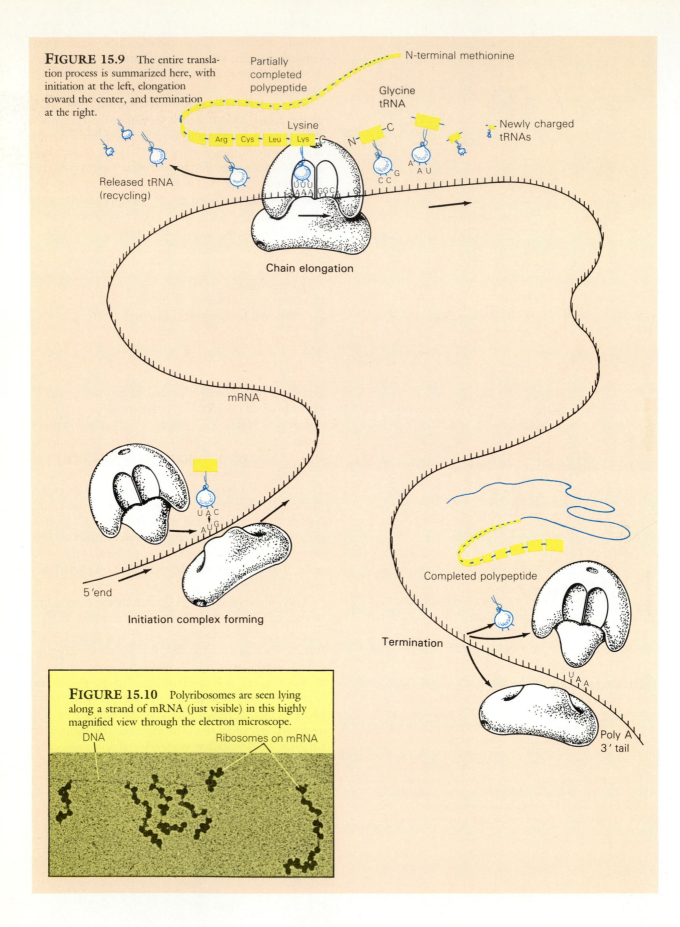

FIGURE 15.9 The entire translation process is summarized here, with initiation at the left, elongation toward the center, and termination at the right.

Partially completed polypeptide

N-terminal methionine

Glycine tRNA

Newly charged tRNAs

Lysine

Arg — Cys — Leu — Lys

N — C

Released tRNA (recycling)

Chain elongation

mRNA

5′ end

Initiation complex forming

Completed polypeptide

Termination

Poly A 3′ tail

FIGURE 15.10 Polyribosomes are seen lying along a strand of mRNA (just visible) in this highly magnified view through the electron microscope.

DNA

Ribosomes on mRNA

MECHANISMS OF GENE CONTROL

Although it has been modified through the years, the central dogma answered many difficult questions. Biologists finally knew the chemical structure of the gene and the basic mechanism by which it expresses its information. But even with all this knowledge, a major question remained. What controls transcription? In other words, how is DNA turned on or off? This question has proven difficult indeed, partly because there are in fact numerous mechanisms. Also, different organisms, it turns out, control their genes in different ways. The mechanisms of gene control in bacteria are best understood, so we must turn once again to our smaller and simpler contemporaries.

Gene Organization and Control in Prokaryotes: The Operon

About the time Crick was putting together the idea of the central dogma, and while molecular biologists were still trying to work out the genetic code and the mechanism of protein synthesis, two French microbiologists were concluding a long experimental program of their own. In 1961 François Jacob and Jacques Monod unveiled their model of bacterial gene organization and control. They called their system, which included a set of genes and the factors that influenced them, the **operon.** Molecular biology suddenly took a huge leap forward.

Inducible enzymes in *E. coli.* Jacob and Monod knew that some of the enzymes of *E. coli* were produced constantly, while other enzymes were under some kind of control. The tiny bacterium could make these enzymes when it needed them and could stop production when it didn't.

For instance, if *E. coli* is grown on a medium that does not contain lactose (milk sugar), it will not bother to produce the specific enzymes that are needed for lactose metabolism. That makes perfectly good sense from the standpoint of evolution and energetics; protein synthesis is energetically expensive, and producing unneeded enzymes would be wasteful. *E. coli* is nothing if not practical.

If these same bacteria are placed into a medium that does contain lactose, they will almost immediately begin to produce enzymes that break the lactose down into its constituents, glucose and galactose. These lactose-metabolizing enzymes are said to be inducible, because their production can be induced, or stimulated, by an appropriate substrate.

It turns out that three enzymes are induced by the presence of lactose. These are *beta galactosidase, galactose permease,* and *thiogalactoside transacetylase;* but Jacob and Monod found it easier to refer to them simply as enzymes *z, y,* and *a,* letters that also refer to the genes that code for the three enzymes. Jacob and Monod's question was an ambitious one: just how did lactose in the medium activate them? That is, how are such genes turned off and on?

The lac operon. The lactose operon, or **lac operon** as it is known, was found to consist of six parts: three enzyme-specifying genes, a regulator gene, and two control segments (Figure 15.11). The enzyme-specifying genes, dubbed *z, y,* and *a,* are located in a row on the *E. coli* chromosome, and all three are transcribed together producing a single mRNA strand containing three complete messages. (Such complex mRNA—called **polycistronic mRNA**—is found only in prokaryotes, never in eukaryotes.) The regulatory gene, sensibly named the **regulator,** produces a **repressor protein** that inhibits functioning in the control segments.

The control segments include the **promoter,** mentioned earlier as a region where RNA transcription begins, along with another segment called the **operator.** The operator lies just ahead of the three enzyme-specifying genes and must be active for those genes to be transcribed. It is the operator that is specifically inactivated by the regulator gene's repressor protein.

> The **lac operon** includes three enzyme-specifying genes, a **regulator gene** that produces a **repressor protein,** the transcription controlling **promoter,** and the **operator.**

The regulator gene is the key to the control process. In all cells, induced or not, it constantly (but slowly) transcribes mRNA. The mRNA codes for a repressor protein, which is produced in very small quantities, about 10 molecules per cell. It is called a repressor protein because it has a high affinity for the operator gene, binding to it and preventing transcription from occurring in the rest of the operon. While the repressor protein is bound to the operator DNA, the RNA polymerase transcription complex cannot move past it. In effect the structural genes are

FIGURE 15.11 (a) Transcription of the genes coding for lactose metabolism are controlled through the lac operon, an inducible system that is only active when lactose is present in the cell. The regulator slowly (1) transcribes mRNA that codes for a repressor protein (2) which, binds the operator (3). This immobilizes RNA polymerase, thus preventing transcription of the enzyme-coding genes z, y, and a (4).

(b) Lactose entering the cell (5) binds to the repressor protein (6), which loses its affinity for the operator. Transcription of genes z, y, and a occurs (7), followed by the assembly of the enzymes by ribosomes (8). The enzymes break down lactose (9), and when it is gone, the repressor protein is freed, once again binding the operator (as in a, above). This shuts down the lac operon.

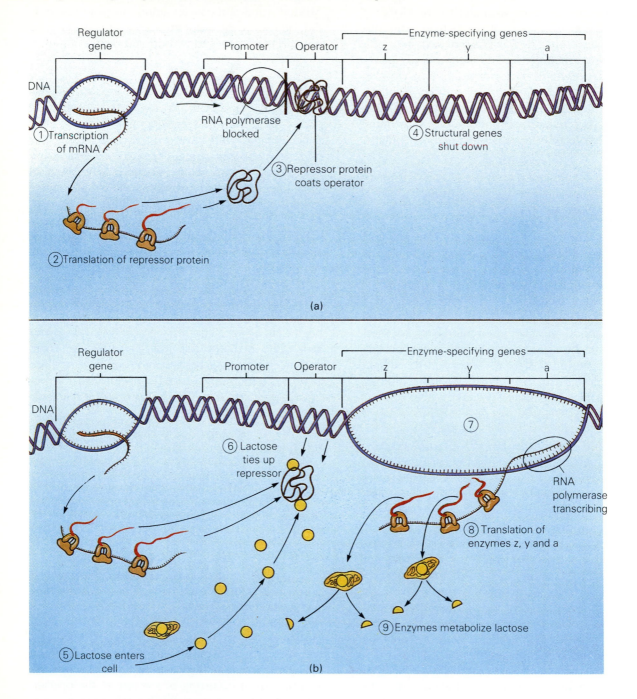

turned off as long as the repressor protein is present and active in the cell.

However, the repressor protein has an even greater affinity for lactose; when lactose molecules are present in the cell, some of them will bind to the 10 repressor protein molecules, rendering them incapable of binding to the operator. Soon the operator gene is free, and the entire unit of transcription becomes operational, transcribing messenger RNA which, in turn, becomes translated on the bacterial ribosomes into the three enzymes. This, then, is the way lactose acts as an inducer of gene action.

Perhaps it will help to consider a fanciful analogy. Suppose RNA polymerase is a train that must run along a DNA track. The repressor protein is an elephant that has a penchant for sitting on the track. However, when peanuts are available, the elephant lumbers off to eat the peanuts, and the train may at last proceed. So the availability of peanuts controls whether the train will run or not.

This scheme leaves us with the problem of shutting the system down again when the enzymes are no longer needed. When the enzymes hydrolyze the lactose molecules into glucose and galactose, the repressor protein (which is still being slowly produced) is free to bind the operator gene. Thus transcription of the three structural genes is shut down again. The lactose operon, and others like it, utilize *negative control;* the inducer molecule, lactose in this case, makes something happen by repressing a repressor.

> In the lac operon, repressor protein blocks transcription unless lactose is present, whereupon the operator is freed and the lactose-metabolizing enzymes are produced.

Other operons. Other operons have been found that function in different ways. For instance, the second operon to which Jacob and Monod turned their attention was the **tryptophan operon,** which controls a series of enzymes that are needed for the synthesis of the amino acid tryptophan. They were interested because tryptophan is always needed by the cell for protein synthesis. They found that the tryptophan operon functions continually *except* when there is ample free tryptophan already in the medium. Again, the adaptive function of such control is obvious: there's no sense in putting cellular resources into making tryptophan when tryptophan is available at no cost.

Jacob and Monod learned that the tryptophan operon is also under negative control: in this case the repressor protein will not bind to its operator unless it first binds to a tryptophan molecule. The tryptophan operon is a **repressible operon** and tryptophan is its repressor.

Many other operons have been discovered since 1961. Alas, each seems to operate according to its own principles. Some operator sequences, for example, have multiple binding sites for repressor molecules, allowing for graduated responses: that is, the gene doesn't necessarily have to be either "turned on" or "turned off," but is, in effect, controlled by a dimmer switch.

Gene Control in Eukaryotes

We know very little about comparable control systems in eukaryotes. For the most part, such gene control systems appear to be quite different from those in bacteria. This is not surprising, considering the complexity of the eukaryotic chromosome. Recall from Chapter 9 that eukaryote DNA is tightly bound to histone-rich nucleosomes. When condensed, DNA is also tightly bound up in several levels of coiling. For this reason, eukaryotic gene activation requires a preliminary phase during which the dense chromatin must be loosened, or "decondensed." Only then can specific gene activating mechanisms be brought to bear.

For many years, cytologists have been able to observe activated regions of eukaryotic DNA in the giant **polytene chromosomes** of the salivary glands in *Drosphila* larvae (Figure 15.12). Polytene chromosomes consist of multiple DNA copies—many sister chromatids lying side by side—with a distinctive, identifiable banding. Active regions are recognized as **chromosome puffs,** "blown out" sections where the individual DNA helix and emerging messenger RNA transcripts are actually visible. In the case of *Drosophila* larvae, the molting hormone **ecdysone** is known to induce the appearance of chromosome puffs.

Another example of gene activation by a hormone is seen in the young chicken. The oviducts of baby chicks have been found to be responsive to the steroid *estrogen,* the female sex hormone. In the presence of estrogen the chick oviduct will begin to produce albumin and other egg-white proteins. Radioactively labeled estrogen molecules have been found to enter the cell, where they are bound by a specific cytoplasmic receptor protein. The protein-steroid complex then passes into the nucleus, where it binds tightly to a nonhistone chromosomal protein. This complex then initiates mRNA transcription through positive control.

FIGURE 15.12 Chromosome puffs, a general loosening and looping of DNA from a region on the giant chromosomes, occur with regularity in fruit fly larvae. These are known to be regions of DNA transcription of RNA. **(a)** Microphotograph of one puff after experimental exposure to the molting hormone, ecdysone. **(b–d)** Puff is diagrammed in increasing magnifications. The granules are thought to be messenger RNA being transcribed.

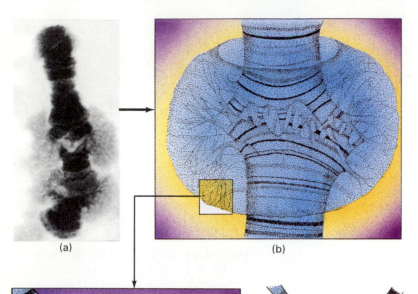

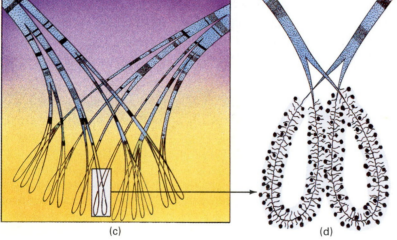

(a)

(b)

(c)

(d)

The steroid-hormone system is similar in some ways to that of a bacterial operon. But even this, the simplest of all known eukaryote gene control systems, is much more complex than the lactose operon. To illustrate, estrogen doesn't induce the synthesis of egg-white proteins in any other kind of chick cell; apparently only the chromosomes of oviduct cells have the specific chromatin receptors. Also, estrogen may have very different effects on different genes and different tissues. For example, it can suppress the synthesis of some proteins as it induces the synthesis of others. Estrogen also has well-documented effects on behavior.

MUTATIONS: ERRORS IN THE GENETIC MESSAGE

DNA is well adapted to its function as a repository of genetic information. One of its adaptations is the resistance to spontaneous, random chemical changes called mutations. Such resistance is vital. After all, each DNA molecule descends from generations of similar molecules that have withstood the relentless process of natural selection. Random changes in these time-tested molecules are not likely to be beneficial to the species. Let's look at the basis for this resistance.

Chemical Stability and DNA Repair Systems

The double helix itself provides a measure of protection, since the encoded nucleotide bases are tucked inside and tightly hydrogen-bonded to one another. Further, in eukaryotes, DNA is tightly bound to protective histone molecules and packaged into beadlike nucleosomes (see Essay 9.1). The most important protection that DNA has against random chemical change, however, is the base-pairing organization itself. The specific ordering of bases in one strand uniquely determines the specific ordering of bases in the other, so that there are actually two copies of the coded information in each DNA molecule. If one strand is accidentally altered by a mutagen such as ultraviolet light or x-rays, the cell is able to throw out the damaged strand and to make a new, perfectly good replacement by using the other strand as a template.

Such spontaneous changes, known as **primary lesions,** are common, but fortunately most primary lesions are quickly corrected by enzyme complexes known as **DNA repair systems** (Figure 15.13). Such repair systems may contain the replication enzymes, DNA polymerase and ligase. Like railroad repair crews, DNA repair systems rove along DNA strands, uncovering irregularities such as broken phosphate bonds and altered or unmatched nucleotide bases. When such irregularities are encountered, segments of perhaps 100 nucleotides are routinely "clipped out," and a new, correct sequence is assembled and inserted. Although repair systems are quite efficient, some lesions escape detection and sometimes repair systems fail entirely. When this happens the primary lesions become heritable mutations.

> **DNA repair systems** locate DNA errors, remove the erroneous strand, and, using DNA polymerase and ligase, assemble and add in a new one.

Mutation at the Molecular Level

We have seen that chromosomal mutations involve entire chromosomes (see Chapter 13). They include losses or gains in chromosomes, as occurs through nondisjunction and translocation, as well as errors in chromosome breakage repair with its wide range of resulting abnormalities.

Mutations involving minor changes in the DNA sequence—ones that geneticists call **point muta-**

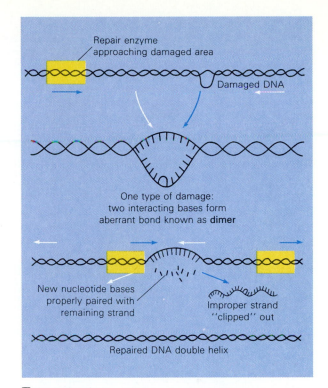

FIGURE 15.13 DNA repair systems. When a damaged portion of DNA is encountered, the faulty section is removed and a new strand is assembled by matching the nucleotide bases in the remaining strand.

tions—are far more subtle and less destructive; they stand a better chance of being passed on from generation to generation. The effects may be neutral or even beneficial. Point mutations fall into three general categories: **base substitutes, insertions,** and **deletions.**

Base substitutions. Single base changes in a protein coding region of DNA change one of the 64 codons to another. Such changes may have no effect at all if the new codon happens to be synonymous to the old (as occurs when the third base of many codons is changed; see Table 15.1). In this instance there would be no change in the protein. Synonymy in the codons has distinct advantages.

Other base substitutions may actually alter the code, causing single amino acid substitutions in the protein product. A change from GAA to GUA, for instance, would mean that glutamic acid is replaced by valine (Figure 15.14). Such a change may produce a **silent mutation,** one with no recognizable effect at all, or the effect could be severely damaging and even lethal.

FIGURE 15.14 A base substitution in DNA can have serious implications. A simple substitution of A (adenine) for T (thymine) in the DNA *(below)* changes the corresponding codon in mRNA from GAA to GUA. Instead of glutamic acid appearing in the corresponding position in the polypeptide, we now see valine. This particular change sets up a chain of events leading to sickle-cell anemia.

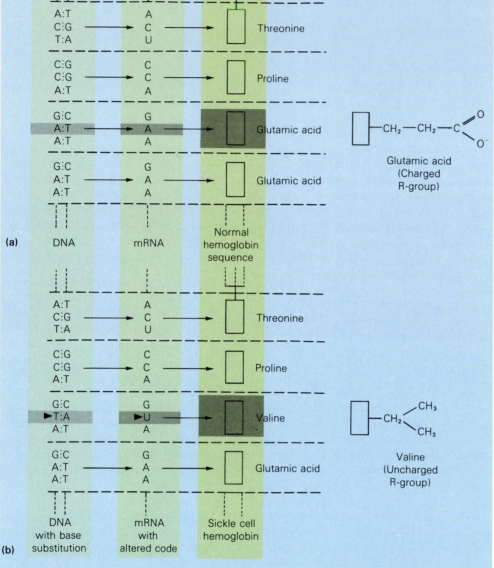

In the genetic disease **sickle cell anemia,** for example, a single base substitution changes glutamic acid to valine in the sixth amino acid of one of the polypeptides of human hemoglobin; this small change causes the molecule to crystalize in the cell. The long, slightly bent crystals distort red blood cells into a sickle shape and also reduce the ability of the hemoglobin to carry oxygen. The damaged cells cause painful and eventually fatal blood clots to form in small blood vessels (see Essay 15.1).

If the new codon caused by a base substitution happens to be one of the three STOP codons, the mutation is called (not surprisingly) a **chain-terminating mutation.** If a ribosome encounters one, it will fall off its mRNA at a new place, resulting in an abnormally short polypeptide. Unless the new STOP codon is very close to the end of the coding sequence, the protein will be totally nonfunctional.

Molecular biologists have aimed the powerful new tools of genetic engineering squarely at hemophilia, the sex-linked blood-clotting abnormality. They have traced some kinds of hemophilia back to newly acquired base substitution mutations. The substitutions result in STOP codons arising randomly in the genetic message specifying certain critical blood-clotting factors.

Insertions and deletions. What would you expect to happen when extra nucleotides are inserted into or deleted from the coding region of a gene? The usual effect of inserting or deleting a single nucleotide is to cause a **frame-shift mutation.** Ribosomes can only read mRNA molecules three nucleotides at a time. Thus if the normal sequence were, say,

$$\text{U}$$
$$\downarrow$$

$$5' \longrightarrow \underline{UGG} \ \underline{GAG} \ \underline{AAA} \ \underline{AAA} \ \underline{UUU} \ \underline{AAG} \longrightarrow 3'$$

Tryp — Glu — Lys — Lys — Phe — Lys

and a U were inserted at the point indicated by the arrow, the new sequence would be translated:

$$5' \longrightarrow \underline{UGU} \ \underline{GGA} \ \underline{GAA} \ \underline{AAA} \ \underline{AUU} \ \underline{UAA} \ G \longrightarrow 3'$$

Cys — Gly — Glu — Lys — Ile — STOP

The translated protein in this instance would have a large number of amino acid changes and would be nonfunctional. Not surprisingly, frame-shift mutations, when homozygous, are usually lethal.

Retroviruses. There is one special class of insertions and deletions that deserves special attention. Biologists have discovered that the DNA of most or all higher organisms is heavily infected by **retroviruses.** Like all viruses they are complete parasites and must infect living cells in order to carry on the ordinary life functions. The retrovirus is special in

that, like the transposable element, it inserts itself randomly into the host chromosome where it may remain for some time. Incidentally, the name, "retrovirus" ("reverse virus"), refers to the peculiar nature of this group. Their chromosome consists entirely of RNA rather than DNA. Upon penetration of the host cell, the virus uses a unique enzyme called **reverse transcriptase** to *transcribe its RNA genes into DNA,* which can then be inserted into the host chromosome. (Note the clear violation of the central dogma: we warned you about dogma in science!) (For more on reverse transcription, see Chapter 20.)

What has this to do with mutation? You can imagine the havoc produced when a retrovirus inserts itself into the middle of a host gene: the gene won't work anymore. What we see is a king-sized insertion.

To the surprise of every geneticist, it has recently been shown that many alleged "point mutations," studied so intently over the past decades, have, in fact, been changes produced by gene-wrecking retroviruses and transposable elements. Included are T. H. Morgan's famous white-eyed fruit fly mutants of 1910 (see Chapter 13). Much more recently, immunologists have determined that the agent of the frightening disease AIDS is a retrovirus. Its gene insertions are invariably lethal since they literally wreck the proper functioning of key lymphocytes in the immune systems. We'll have much more to say about AIDS in Chapters 20 and 39.

We have come a long way since Francis Crick presented the "central dogma" to a bemused world. The euphoria that swept the scientific community in those days, when a surprisingly simple system of genetic coding was first unveiled, has been dampened by the realization that the system is not so simple after all. But the very complexity of life that discourages some people stimulates others. They see the complexity and the variety of life as providing not just challenges but opportunities. Some of the greatest opportunities lie before us now. We are on the verge of being able to manipulate genes, to turn them on, to turn them off, to move them about, and to make them work for us in very critical and specific ways, as we will see in the next chapter.

In 1949 Linus Pauling, the great theoretical chemist, investigated and compared purified hemoglobin (the oxygen-carrying protein of blood cells) from certain sick and healthy persons. The sick people had the genetic disease called sickle cell anemia, which is characterized by strangely misshapen red blood cells that are inefficient at carrying oxygen. Pauling found that the net electrical charge of purified hemoglobin from affected homozygotes (genotype, $H^S H^S$) was slightly different from that of the healthy people (genotype $H^A H^A$). The difference in charge was due to a difference of one amino acid out of 287! Heterozygous carriers of the sickle cell gene (genotype, $H^A H^S$) had both kinds of hemoglobin.

Pauling demonstrated that very small molecular shifts could be responsible for large-scale phenotypic effects. This one small change in an amino acid sequence produces extremely destructive effects and has initiated one of the most intense research efforts in medical history. The condition is generally lethal in homozygotes, since the sickled cells cannot efficiently bind oxygen and they tend to form clots within the blood vessels. The heterozygotes bear both normal and sickled genes, and their blood may have only about 70% of the hemoglobin content of normal blood. For this reason they tend to suffer from anemia.

Sickle cell anemia is most common in east Africa and in Ghana in west Africa. It would seem that its obvious disadvantages would result in its continual decline in the population; however, it persists because of a peculiar biological twist to the story. Persons heterozygous for the condition are highly resistant to malaria, a disease that kills many people who produce only normal hemoglobin. The people with affected cells are protected because the malarial parasite cannot live within these abnormal cells. With natural selection favoring the heterozygotes, it is apparent how the sickled condition is able to persist in the population. In fact, in some of the more severely stricken malarial regions, over 40% of the population are carriers of the sickle cell gene.

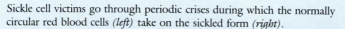

Sickle cell victims go through periodic crises during which the normally circular red blood cells *(left)* take on the sickled form *(right)*.

When subjected to an electrical field (passing through a tray of starch pudding in a procedure called *gel electrophoresis*), sickle cell hemoglobin separates from the normal protein and can be identified in both homozygous (H^SH^S) and heterozygous (H^AH^S) individuals. Note in the analysis that approximately half the hemoglobin of heterozygotes matches hemoglobin of normal (AA) individuals. This indicates that both the normal and sickle cell alleles in heterozygotes are functional. In spite of this, heterozygotes (carriers) rarely suffer the symptoms of sickle-cell anemia.

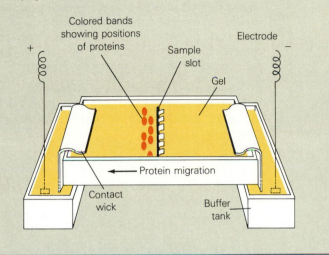

Phenotype	Genotype	Hemoglobin electrophoretic pattern	Hemoglobin types present
		Origin ⟶ +	
Normal	AA		A
Sickle-cell trait	AS		S and A
Sickle-cell anemia	SS		S

SUMMARY

DNA, the molecular substance of genes, directs the cell's activities through the enzymes and other proteins whose structure it determines. It produces these from the nucleus, through RNA intermediaries.

THE RNA MOLECULE

RNA is a single-stranded polymer composed of nucleotides that utilize ribose sugar and the nitrogen base uracil (instead of deoxyribose and thymine, as in DNA).

TRANSCRIPTION: THE SYNTHESIS OF RNA

Transcription is similar to replication, except it occurs along one DNA strand only. Helicase and RNA polymerase make up transcription complexes, several of which may carry on simultaneous transcription along one DNA segment.

THREE KINDS OF RNA

RNA occurs as messenger RNA, ribosomal RNA, and transfer RNA.

Messenger RNA and the Genetic Code

The nucleotide sequence of messenger RNA (mRNA) specifies the amino acids to be incorporated into a newly synthesized protein. Raw transcripts contain a number of intervening sequences (introns) that are removed, leaving only the expressed sequences (exons), the actual coded message. Intervening sequences may be important for nullifying the effects of mutagenic agents and for facilitating crossing over.

The genetic code consists of triplets, three-base sequences of nucleotides called codons, most of which represent amino acids. This coding can be visualized through the **colinearity** principle: DNA, RNA, and protein have similar organization. The linear order of subunits in one dictates the linear order of subunits in the next.

Of the 64 codons possible, one specifies START, three specifiy STOP, and the rest represent amino acids. Nearly all amino acids have synonymous (extra) codons.

Ribosomal RNA and the Ribosome

Ribosomal RNA (rRNA), which is assembled primarily in the nucleolus, joins with protein in the cytoplasm to form ribosomes. Ribosomes contain large and small subunits that unite during protein synthesis. Each has a mRNA groove, two tRNA pockets, and other special sites.

Transfer RNA

Transfer RNAs link to specific amino acids, which they carry to the ribosome for polypeptide assembly. The linkage, called charging, occurs on specific enzymes and utilizes ATP energy. Transfer RNAs have specific anticodons, three-base sequences that match codons on mRNA. This provides a means for correctly inserting amino acids according to the mRNA coding.

PROTEIN SYNTHESIS: TRANSLATION OF THE GENETIC MESSAGE

Initiation

Messenger RNA (with its START codon in position), methionine-charged tRNA, and the large ribosomal subunit form an initiation complex. When it is joined by the smaller ribosomal subunit, translation begins.

Elongation

In polypeptide elongation, both ribosomal pockets are occupied with charged tRNAs. Next, a peptide bond forms joining the two amino acids and permitting translocation to occur. In translocation, the ribosome moves one codon to the right, the tRNA from the right pocket enters the left pocket by bumping out the former occupant. This frees the right pocket for the entry of another charged tRNA.

Termination: Derailing the Ribosome

Upon encountering a STOP codon, termination proteins cause the ribosomal subunits to separate, and the polypeptide is released.

Polyribosomes

Typically, a number of ribosomes, or polysomes, carry on simultaneous translation along one mRNA. Bound ribosomes, those of the rough ER, are held in place by their polypeptide chains, which are themselves directed into ER lumen.

MECHANISMS OF GENE CONTROL

Control mechanisms are responsible for the activation and deactivation of specific genes.

Gene Organization and Control in Prokaryotes: The Operon

Jacob and Monod proposed a mechanism of prokaryote gene control they called the operon. In the inducible lac (lactose) operon, three genes transcribe mRNA that directs the synthesis of lactose-metabolizing enzymes. However, transcription only occurs when lactose is present. Otherwise, the genes are inhibited by repressor protein, a product of the regulator gene, which blocks the promotor by binding with the operator. When lactose is present, it binds the inhibiting protein, and transcription begins. As the enzymes break the lactose down, inhibition begins once more. Repressible operons work in an opposite manner. They actively direct enzyme production unless the enzyme's product is made available from another source, whereupon the system is shut down.

Gene Control in Eukaryotes

Eukaryotic control is complicated by the complex chromosome-protein association, which requires preliminary decondensing. Actively transcribing regions in fruit fly chromosomes occur as chromosome puffs. Some puffs form when the molting hormone ecdysone is present. The hormone estrogen is a known gene activator in chickens.

MUTATIONS: ERRORS IN THE GENETIC MESSAGE

Chemical Stability and DNA Repair Systems

Because the order of nucleotides in one strand of DNA dictates that in the other, the molecule is easily repaired. DNA repair systems detect lesions that are readily removed and replaced by correct nucleotide sequences.

Mutation at the Molecular Level

Point mutations, changes in nucleotide sequences in DNA, include base substitutions, insertions, and deletions. Substitutions have no effect if they occur in the third letter in synonymous codons. While some amino acid changes have little effect, others are disastrous. For example, sickle cell anemia results from a single base substitution. Substitutions that result in the early STOP codons wreck the protein. Insertions and deletions produce frame-shift mutations. When translated, all of the amino acids beyond the altered codon are changed, rendering the protein useless.

Retroviruses, such as the agent of AIDS, create gene-wrecking insertions. Using the enzyme reverse transcriptase, retroviruses convert their RNA chromosome to DNA, which they then insert randomly into the host chromosome.

KEY TERMS

ribose	peptidyl transferase	promoter
uracil	3′ end	operator
transcript	CCA stem	tryptophan operon
transcription complex	anticodon loop	repressible operon
RNA polymerase	anticodon	polytene chromosome
messenger RNA (mRNA)	initiation	chromosome puff
ribosomal RNA (rRNA)	elongation	primary lesion
transfer RNA (tRNA)	termination	DNA repair system
posttranscriptional processing	initiation complex	point mutation
intron	peptide bond	base substitution
exon	translocation	insertion
translation	polyribosome	deletion
codon	operon	silent mutation
principle of colinearity	lac operon	sickle cell anemia
synonymous codon	polycistronic mRNA	frame-shift mutation
nucleolar organizing region	regulator	retrovirus
subunit	repressor	reverse transcriptase

REVIEW QUESTIONS

1 List three differences between RNA and DNA—those involving sugars, nitrogen bases, and the polymer itself. (pp. 218–219)

2 Using simple diagrams of DNA and RNA, describe the transcription process. What is simultaneous transcription? (p. 219)

3 What is the role of messenger RNA? Explain why post-transcriptional modification is necessary. In what ways might introns be important to the gene? (p. 220)

4 Describe the basic organization of the genetic code. What makes up a codon? What does a codon represent in protein? (p. 221)

5 In looking at the genetic code table, explain the roles of the codons UAA, UAG, UGA, and AUG. In how many instances are amino acids represented by four codons? What term describes these codons? (p. 221)

6 Where is most of the ribosomal RNA formed? What assures an adequate supply of these vital particles? What general role do ribosomes play in protein synthesis? (p. 223)

7 Explain the organization of the ribosome. Include its molecular composition, its subunits, and its principal external features. (p. 223)

8 The analogy of a factory forklift was used to describe the role of tRNA. Explain this. (pp. 223–224)

9 Describe the events in charging of tRNA. (p. 224)

10 List the three important regions of any tRNA molecule. Explain how a charged tRNA manages to insert its amino acid at right place on the messenger. (p. 225)

11 List the participants that form the initiation complex. What is the last event prior to the start of elongation? (p. 225)

12 Describe the events leading up to elongation. How does translocation occur? What happens to uncharged tRNA? (pp. 225–226)

13 Describe the events that end translation. What happens to the mRNA and ribosomal subunits? (p. 226)

14 Describe the performance of polyribosomes. How is their performance adaptive to the cell? (p. 227)

15 List the five elements of the lac operon and very generally explain what each does. Why is the lac operon termed inducible? (pp. 229, 231)

16 How does the substrate lactose overcome the inhibition state in the lac operon? Once activated, how is the lac operon shut down? (pp. 229, 231)

17 Using the tryptophan operon as an example, explain how enzyme synthesis in a repressible operon is controlled. (p. 231)

18 Review the experiment that suggested a gene-activating role for the hormone estrogen. (p. 232)

19 Summarize the work of DNA repair systems. (p. 233)

20 How does a point mutation differ from a chromosomal mutation? List three types of point mutations. (p. 233)

21 How does codon synonymity provide some protection against base substitution mutations? (p. 233)

22 Explain the mutational basis for the disease sickle cell anemia. (p. 234)

23 What effect does the insertion or deletion of a nucleotide base have on the polypeptide produced? How might this affect an enzyme's performance? (p. 235)

24 Review the manner in which retroviruses insert themselves into host chromosomes. (p. 235)

Some scientists are disturbed—and others elated—by our newly emerging abilities to manipulate genes. The grounds for the disagreement are apparent, considering the possibilities that may lie before us. Few are morally indignant because we can insert rat growth hormone genes into developing fertilized mouse cells to produce giant mice. A mouse would have to be gigantic indeed to bother most people. And probably few would object to our ability to make human hormones out of a bacterial soup. After all, an abundant supply of hormones could solve a number of human problems. People with a number of abnormalities could be made normal. But dare we try not just to bring abnormal people to normality, but to make normal people "better"? Taller? Stronger? Smarter? See the problem? We will shortly take a look at the promise and threat brought about by our expanding ability to manipulate genes, but first let's see how we got to where we are today.

Over the years, different organisms have tended to dominate the study of genetics. First there were Mendel's true-breeding pea plants, followed by the hardy, prolific, and amazingly versatile fruit fly. Later, the cutting edge of genetic research focused on the corn plant, *Zea mays;* next, Beadle and Tatum brought the mold *Neurospora* into the spotlight. Then, in the late 1940s, a surprising organism became in vogue: an invisible microbe. Geneticists began to focus on *Escherichia coli,* the common colon bacterium, and the viruses that infect it.

Perhaps the emergence of *E. coli* should not have been so surprising. After all, the thrust of molecular biology has been to reduce problems to their simplest terms, and bacteria, when all is said and done, are much simpler than fruit flies, corn, or even mold. The viruses that infect bacteria are simpler still, since they consist of only a DNA or RNA molecule, a protein coat, and a few enzymes.

E. coli organisms did, indeed, offer a number of advantages as experimental subjects. Not only were they genetically simple, but also bacterial cells have little internal structure and are easily broken open so that their cellular machinery can be isolated and analyzed biochemically. More importantly, bacteria and viruses can be grown in enormous numbers in very short periods of time—*E. coli* can double in number in 20 minutes—so experiments can be done quickly. Billions of such organisms can be grown in a drop of fluid, so statistical sampling is never a problem, and even very rare events (such as the occurrence of specific mutations) will occur infrequently enough to be detected.

16

FRONTIERS IN MOLECULAR BIOLOGY

GENETIC RECOMBINATION IN BACTERIA

From Mendel's time on, genetic analysis had always depended on genetic recombination, which, it seemed, depended on meiosis and sex. This is the main reason why bacteria such as *E. coli* had originally been of little interest to geneticists: like other biologists, they believed that bacteria were confirmed celibates, capable only of asexual reproduction.

It's true that bacteria, in true prokaryote fashion, have never mastered the processes of meiosis, fertilization, and sexual reproduction that together constitute a crucial aspect of the life cycles of most eukaryotes. But *E. coli* and many other bacteria do exhibit some rudiments of genetic recombination. What passes for sex in bacteria is incomplete, bizarre, and infrequent—*so* infrequent that the odds of its occurrence are about one in a million. Fortunately for the geneticist, however, something that happens to one or two out of a million cells still occurs with dependable frequency when billions of cells are grown and tested.

In 1946, Joshua Lederberg and Edward Tatum (the same Edward Tatum, who, with George Beadle, developed the notion of "one gene, one enzyme") performed an imaginative experiment that provided the first evidence of genetic recombination in bacteria. Following the lead of Tatum's own *Neurospora* research, they chose two mutant bacterial strains that had different enzyme deficiencies. Neither strain, by

itself, could grow on the usual bacterial **minimal medium** (food) that consists of glucose, glycine, and minerals in a jellylike matrix of **agar.** To grow, each **nutritional mutant strain** required the addition of one or more specific metabolites that their own enzymes could not synthesize. In a simple but ingenious experiment, Lederberg and Tatum combined the two strains and spread the mixture on minimal medium agar. They reasoned that any bacteria that could grow on this minimal medium would represent new genetic recombinants: that is, they would be the descendants of bacteria that had somehow managed to combine the *functional* enzyme-specifying genes from both parental strains.

They got their recombinants. Some of the bacteria were indeed able to grow on minimal medium; therefore the two strains had obviously managed to exchange genetic material. But their problems were not over. From the recombination frequencies, they tried to make a genetic map, using the techniques that had proved so useful for fruit flies and corn. They had a terrible time! The worst problem was the strange nature of bacterial "sex" itself. The rules of recombination and crossing over that had been worked out for peas and *Drosophila* clearly did not work for bacteria.

The first evidence of sex and genetic recombination in bacteria came from the nutritional mutants of Lederberg and Tatum.

FIGURE 16.1 The slender sex pilus between the two bacteria of different strains provides a passageway for the transfer of a plasmid.

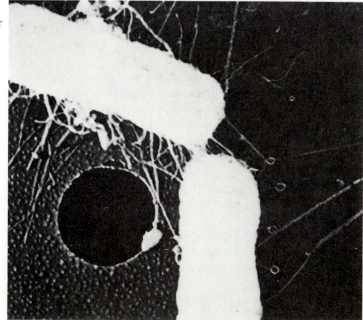

The Sex Life of *E. coli*

Other investigators picked up Lederberg and Tatum's promising lead, and as new data came in, a strange and confusing picture of bacterial sex began to emerge.

First, they discovered that mating occurred through a primitive process called **conjugation,** the fusing of cells and transfer of genes. Second, mating occurred only between different strains—the transfer of genes during conjugation was a one-way process only. Because of this, the two strains were quickly dubbed "male" and "female," perhaps *too* quickly since there were some definite peculiarities. For instance, during conjugation between the two strains, only a *few* genes actually ended up in the recipient or female cell. In other words, only a small amount of actual genetic recombination occurred in each transfer. This is quite different from sex in eukaryotes, where fertilization involves an equal mixing of *two complete genomes* (sets of genes).

However, the strangest discovery by far was one made in the early 1950s by microbiologist William Hayes. Hayes discovered that after conjugation, some "female" cells became *males,* which could mate with other females. Unlike the rare occurrences of regular genetic recombination, as observed by Lederberg and Tatum, this peculiar genetic change occurred regularly, involving about one-third of the offspring. Somehow, sex was catching, and it was quite contagious!

> Hayes found that a one-way transmission of fertility genes from "male" strains to "female" strains changed the recipients to males.

It took some doing, but eventually microbiologists caught on to what was happening in bacterial sex. Since the terms "male" and "female" were not all that appropriate, male cells were subsequently designated F+ cells ("fertility positive") and females, F− cells ("fertility negative"). In *E. coli,* maleness is due to the presence of a tiny genetic element called a **plasmid,** a small circle of DNA independent of the main chromosome and containing only a few genes.

The male-determining plasmid—or **F plasmid** as it became known—includes genes responsible for bacterial conjugation. More specifically, it induces the construction of a small, hollow tube called a **sex pilus** (Figure 16.1) that extends from the F+ cell to the F− cell. When the sex pilus is in place, the circular DNA of the plasmid produces a linear replica; this plasmid replica is transferred to the recipient F− cell

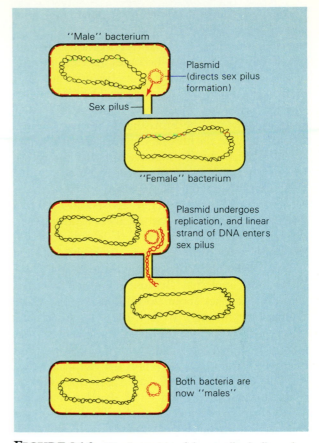

FIGURE 16.2 The formation of the sex pilus is directed by a specific plasmid inside the male cell. The plasmid DNA then replicates, and a copy is sent through the tube. The recipient cell contains the genes for producing a sex pilus and thus becomes a "male."

(Figure 16.2). As you can see, once the F− cell has a copy of the F plasmid, it becomes F+ with all of the male capabilities. Interestingly, also included in the DNA of the plasmid is a gene that makes the recipient cell unreceptive to the advances of any other male cell. So, while sex is catching, it can only be caught once!

> Fertility in the F+ strains of *E. coli* is the product of an **F plasmid** whose genes direct sex pilus construction and subsequent conjugation.

So far, we have explained how conjugation occurs and how new males arise. These aspects of bacterial sex involve only the F plasmid. What about the limited transfer of other genes? For instance, we have yet to learn how genetic recombination involving metabolic genes takes place. How did Lederberg and

Tatum's two nutritional mutants produce nutritionally sufficient offspring?

As it turns out, the F plasmid occasionally—very rarely, but occasionally—becomes inserted into the main circular chromosome of its bacterial host as a linear sequence in the larger circle. The plasmid can show up anywhere in the host chromosome. After such an insertion, the F plasmid DNA is replicated right along with the host DNA, and can be passed on to all of the bacterial progeny. But later, when the plasmid attempts its usual transfer to a susceptible F− bacterium, strange things begin to happen.

First, the F plasmid begins its special round of linear replication, just as it always does when attempting a transfer. But since it is now part of a larger circle, the entire structure—host chromosome and all—attempts to pass through the sex pilus as a linear DNA molecule. Because the chromosome is very long, it takes about 90 minutes for the whole thing to get through. In fact, the sex pilus usually breaks apart before the transfer is completed, so that only part of the host chromosome and only one end of the F plasmid sequence enter the recipient bacterial cell. The recipient cell isn't transformed into an F+ cell, but the bacterial DNA that has made the journey can recombine, through a kind of crossing over, with the main chromosome of the recipient cell (Figure 16.3). This is the principal mechanism by which genetic recombination occurs in bacteria. DNA left over after crossing over takes place is simply dismantled by enzymes.

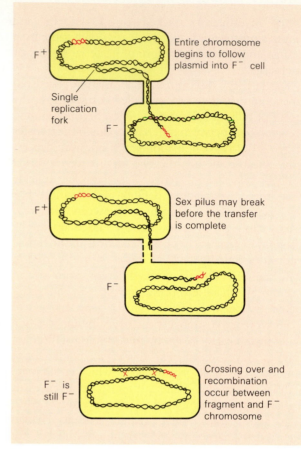

FIGURE 16.3 A portion of the replicated plasmid gene enters the sex pilus, drawing the main chromosome after it. Although some of the F+ cell's genes make it through, the pilus generally breaks before a complete transfer occurs.

Where conjugation follows **F plasmid** insertion, part of the F+ cell's main chromosome is drawn into the F− cell, whereupon crossing over takes place. This is a principal mechanism for sexual recombination in bacteria.

It wasn't long before Hayes and others were able to develop pure strains of bacteria in which *every* individual had the F plasmid integrated into the main chromosome at precisely the same place. Such strains are a thousand times more efficient at transferring bacterial genes than are ordinary F+ bacteria. The new ones were called **Hfr strains,** for "high frequency of recombination."

Hfr strains and bacterial gene mapping. Gene mapping in *E. coli* is done somewhat differently from gene mapping in higher organisms. The breakthrough was pioneered by François Jacob and Elie

Wollman. They noted that when the Hfr strain conjugated, the genes closely behind the leading part of the F plasmid were transferred efficiently, but that the trailing genes made it less frequently since the sex pilus was more likely to break before they made it through. They reasoned that if they could control this process they could discover the linear order of genes on *E. coli* main chromosome. They mixed the Hfr strain with a recipient F− strain and poured the mixture into a number of kitchen blenders. After allowing the bacteria to conjugate for different prescribed lengths of time in each blender, they turned the machines on. This rudely broke apart the mating bacteria.

Jacob and Wollman found that when the genetic transfer was interrupted after just a few minutes, some of the genetic markers would make it across, while others always remained behind. As the periods of mating were extended, more and more markers were transferred and could be recovered in the prog-

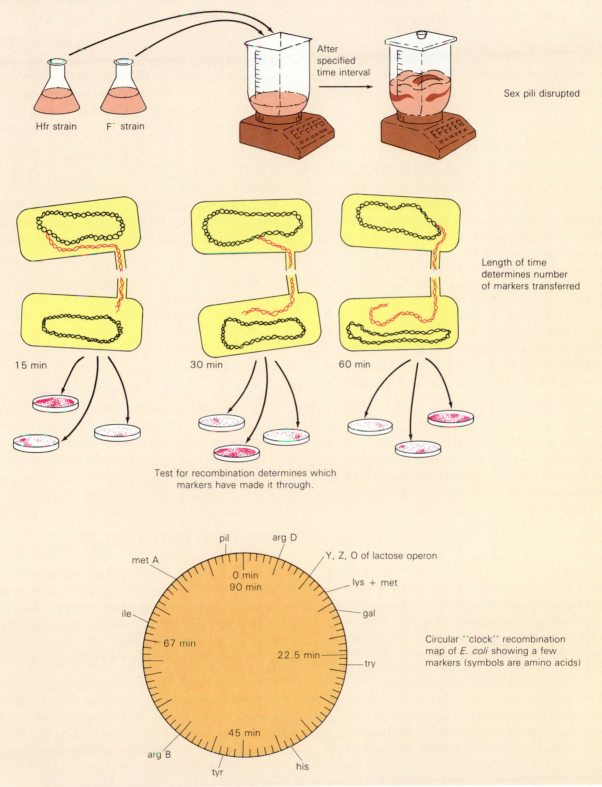

FIGURE 16.4 Jacob and Wollman used Hfr *E. coli* strains to develop recombination maps. The lengthy chromosome transfer was disrupted at increasing time intervals between 0 and 90 minutes in sequential cultures. Then the cells representing each time interval were studied for evidence of genetic recombination.

Hfr strain   F⁻ strain

After specified time interval

Sex pili disrupted

Length of time determines number of markers transferred

15 min   30 min   60 min

Test for recombination determines which markers have made it through.

pil   arg D
met A
0 min
90 min
Y, Z, O of lactose operon
lys + met
ile
gal
67 min
22.5 min
try
45 min
arg B
tyr   his

Circular "clock" recombination map of *E. coli* showing a few markers (symbols are amino acids)

eny. The markers that appeared with greater frequency obviously were nearer the leading end of the length of DNA. The frequency of appearance fell off for those that were more distant. In this way, the gene sequence could be mapped (Figure 16.4).

> Gene mapping is done by varying the time of conjugation in **Hfr strains** and determining which genes of the main chromosome were transferred.

Plasmids and Plasmid Genes

The F plasmid is only one of many kinds of bacterial plasmids that have been discovered. None of the rest can transfer the host's chromosomal genes to other bacteria, but they do have roles in bacterial genetics, with genes of their own. Most have genes for making sex pili, as well as those for coating the cell surface to protect the host (and the plasmid) from infection by other plasmids. In addition, some have genes that protect their hosts (and thus themselves) in other ways. For example, a plasmid is responsible for the deadly toxins produced by the diphtheria bacterium. Other plasmids enable the host cell to fix nitrogen (incorporate N_2 gas from the air into a useful nitrogen compound). Still others induce plant tumors or synthesize insect toxins (each a story of its own).

Some plasmids carry genes that make their hosts resistant to antibiotics. One plasmid, known as the **multiple-resistance plasmid,** endows its host with resistance to six important antibiotics. This plasmid can also be transferred between distantly related species of bacteria. Now that we know this, some mysteries have been cleared up.

Time and again physicians have nearly defeated some bacterial infection with antibiotics, only to find that the same disease erupts again and is no longer susceptible to the same antibiotic. What has happened is that natural selection has been at work, and our very success at battling microbes has given rise to new, more potent strains. The new strains arise through the transfer of multiple-resistance plasmids among surviving bacteria. The drug industry has tried to keep up with the challenge by continually developing new or modified antibiotics.

The widespread use of antibiotics is a controversial issue in health science today because of the resistance phenomenon. Antibiotics are used routinely in livestock feed to accelerate growth rates and to protect against disease, and those antibiotics can be transferred to the carnivorous consumer. In 1984, an article in the *New England Journal of Medicine* reported on 18 cases of bacteria-generated illness traced to hamburger made from cattle that were raised on low doses of antibiotic. An analysis of plasmids in *Salmonella* cultured from the contaminated hamburger revealed that those causing the illness were identical to those growing in the cattle.

Some physicians routinely prescribe antibiotics for all types of minor ailments—in part to guard against secondary infections, but all too often to satisfy their patients' demands that something dramatic be done to end the sniffles. Such indiscriminate use of antibiotics is believed to have selected for monstrous, super-resistant bacterial strains. For instance, some strains of *Salmonella typhimurium*, the agent of salmonellosis, have picked up the multiple-resistance plasmid and show resistance to antibiotics. Salmonellosis is a serious disease with symptoms that include acute inflammation of the digestive tract along with severe diarrhea. With complications, it can be fatal.

> **Multiple-resistance plasmids,** known to move from one bacterial species to another, greatly intensify the problem of antibiotic resistance in pathogens.

Plasmids have recently taken on new significance in molecular biology. Many of the original advances in genetic engineering have involved plasmids. Their small genomes are readily isolated and manipulated, and they are widely used as carriers of spliced genes in recombinant DNA experiments. Let's take a closer look at these advances.

GENETIC ENGINEERING

Molecular biology has become interesting to big business. The reason is simple: there are now opportunities in **genetic engineering,** or the application of some of this technology to practical ends. (Or, in the dim view of some critics, molecular biology is about to be perverted because there are now lucrative opportunities available.)

A new generation of molecular biologists, genetic engineers, we might call them, have learned to manipulate genes with amazing ease. Through the use of the new **recombinant DNA technology (gene sequencing, splicing,** and **cloning)** they can locate and excise any specific segment of DNA from the genes of a cell (including human cells). The segment can then be spliced into a bacterial plasmid or into viruses, which then infect cells. The spliced DNA is then routinely replicated as the cells cycle. Such genes can be collected and stored for future use, or they may be removed again, analyzed for their nucleotide sequences, perhaps altered to some new specification, and once again introduced to a cell. As the cell population grows, the inserted DNA makes its protein product right along with the cells' usual products. Since cells reproduce prolifically, and each cell gives rise to an immense clone (a number of identical descendents), it is easy to retrieve large amounts of specific gene products by chemically extracting them from the descendents of the altered generation.

A growing list of gene products are now regularly harvested, including human insulin, human growth hormone, and several types of human interferon. A very recent addition to the list is a giant protein called **factor VIII,** the critical blood-clotting agent missing from the blood of hemophilia A sufferers. The agent has been available in the past but it was far too costly for many of the afflicted.

Future possibilities of genetic engineering stagger the imagination. For example, we will soon be able to manufacture almost any of the body's molecules easily and cheaply.

> The major techniques of **genetic engineering** are **gene sequencing** (finding the nucleotide sequence), **gene splicing** (combining DNA segments), and **cloning** (producing identical descendents).

Recombinant DNA Technology: How Gene Splicing, Cloning, and Sequencing Are Done

Gene splicing and cloning. Gene splicing depends on the availability of **restriction enzymes,** which are a normal part of the bacterial cell's defenses against the foreign DNA of viruses and plasmids. Restriction enzymes have the ability to cut DNA at specific places along its length. Commercial companies now purify dozens of kinds of restriction enzymes and sell them by the bottle. Each variety recognizes a certain short DNA sequence and cuts wherever it is found along the molecule.

For example, a restriction enzyme called Eco-R1 recognizes the following sequence in double-stranded DNA, and cuts it at a particular place (X stands for any nucleotide):

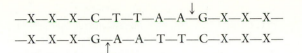

Note that the two strands are not cut directly opposite each other, but that the cuts are offset (*arrows*). This leaves new free ends of complementary, single-stranded DNA:

—X—X—X—C—T—T—A—A—   —G—X—X—X—
—X—X—X—G—   —A—A—T—T—C—X—X—X—

The free, single-stranded ends will recognize and base-pair with one another, given the opportunity and the right conditions. For this reason, they are called **sticky ends.** After such base-pairing, the DNA can be joined again by another enzyme called **ligase.** Specific sequences, such as the one shown above, are found in many life forms. The same restriction enzymes will break any of these. If the DNA of one life form, broken in this way, should encounter the DNA from another life form, the two forms of DNA can join, mixing the genes of two species (Figure 16.5). Do you want an organism that combines bacterial genes with genes from, say, a chicken? It's been done. If you think a genetic cross between a chicken and a bacterium is amusing, you'd better ponder the implications very carefully. Techniques are improving so rapidly that any combination of genes is technically possible.

How are such modified genes introduced into a new generation of cells? The gene splicers' usual trick involves using a restriction enzyme to cut open the circular DNA of a plasmid and then to splice in a fragment of DNA from some other organism. The plasmids with foreign DNA inserts are then allowed to infect susceptible bacteria. As the newly infected bacteria multiply rapidly in their usual fashion, copies of the altered plasmid and its new insert are passed on to all descendents (see Figure 16.5). If the altered bacteria are infused with genes that make human insulin, for example, the bacteria will make human insulin. Because bacteria multiply so rapidly, it isn't long before significant amounts of this hormone can be recovered.

> In gene splicing, specific **restriction enzymes** cleave DNA strands from different sources in a manner that makes their splicing possible. New combinations can then be cloned.

FIGURE 16.5 Through the use of gene splicing techniques, donor DNA from nearly any source can be inserted into a bacterial plasmid where it will be transcribed and translated along with the bacterial DNA. The donor DNA is routinely transcribed and translated in the host cell and eventually its protein product can be collected.

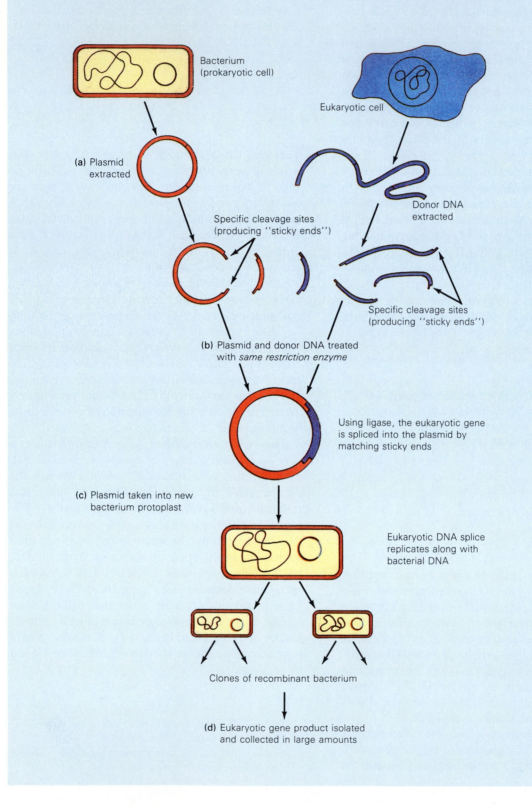

Bacterium (prokaryotic cell)

Eukaryotic cell

(a) Plasmid extracted

Donor DNA extracted

Specific cleavage sites (producing "sticky ends")

Specific cleavage sites (producing "sticky ends")

(b) Plasmid and donor DNA treated with *same restriction enzyme*

Using ligase, the eukaryotic gene is spliced into the plasmid by matching sticky ends

(c) Plasmid taken into new bacterium protoplast

Eukaryotic DNA splice replicates along with bacterial DNA

Clones of recombinant bacterium

(d) Eukaryotic gene product isolated and collected in large amounts

Getting genes from one cell to another (that is, from donor to recipient) has become a highly developed, diversified art in genetic engineering. Bacteria routinely take up nucleic acid fragments (a process called **transformation;** see Chapter 14), so it's no surprise that this capability was used early in the growing field of genetic engineering. Improving the efficiency of this process by removing the bacterial cell wall was simply a way of making the uptake more efficient and dependable. However, this was only one way to enhance the transfer of genetic material between bacteria.

Even before the techniques of gene splicing and cloning were developed, biologists were routinely working with **cell fusion.** They were aware that cultured cells from different sources would fuse when treated with fusing agents (such as a chemical called polyethylene glycol or certain inactivated viruses). Although the fused cell is binucleate for a time, eventually a single nucleus emerges bearing a combination of chromosomes from both parental cells. As we mentioned in Chapter 13, this technique is sometimes used to determine the location of genes along the chromosome. Also, the fused cells can even be from different species.

It's one thing to mix genes, but it's another to insert a *particular* recombinant gene into a eukaryotic cell. Such transformations require quite specific techniques. One such technique involves the recombinant gene hitchhiking a ride on a virus. This is called the **recombinant virus technique** (Figure 16.6a). For instance, engineered hemoglobin genes from a rabbit have been fused to the chromosome of a monkey virus (called SV40) and the virus introduced to monkey cells. The result: monkey cells that produce rabbit hemoglobin! You may ask, who cares? Researchers trying to understand such life-destroying hemoglobin disorders as sickle-cell anemia care.

Mammalian cells, like bacterial cells, may undergo transformation, that is, they may take up bits of DNA from their surroundings. The event occurs on the order of one cell in a million, but because of this tendency it is possible to add specific DNA segments to the mammalian genome. The procedure, called **DNA-mediated gene transfer,** involves mixing the desired gene with DNA molecules and adding calcium ions. The calcium ions bond to the phosphate backbone of DNA forming a precipitate that holds the DNA firmly together.

Again, just one cell in a culture of one million cells will take up the precipitate, but if the population in the culture is vast enough, that's enough to produce a new hybrid cell line, one that has incorporated the desired DNA. In one instance, researchers corrected a hereditary nutritional defect in the cultured cells of mice by introducing a new, functional gene through this method. Of course, there must be a way to separate out those cells that have been appropriately transformed. In the mouse experiment, researchers were able to isolate the few genetically altered cells by withholding the nutrient that the afflicted mouse cells could not metabolize. Since only those with the newly altered gene survived, identifying the altered cells was easy.

There are other, far more direct means of introducing genes. One of these involves **microinjection,** the use of an extraordinarily fine micropipette to pierce a recipient cell nucleus, whereupon the engineered gene is squirted in. The procedure is illustrated in Figure 16.6b.

> Getting engineered genes into cells is done through the use of **transformation, cell fusion, recombinant virus technique,** and **microinjection.**

Gene Sequencing

Gene sequencing techniques permit molecular biologists to determine the exact nucleotide sequence of any piece of DNA or RNA they can isolate—and they can isolate just about any piece they want to. Since 1977, well over 100 mammalian genes have been sequenced. Among these are those coding for insulin, hemoglobin, interferon, and cytochrome *c*. Let's look at a particularly precise method of DNA sequencing.

A selected segment of DNA is cloned in order to produce vast numbers of identical strands. Each strand is then altered so that the usual phosphate group at the 5′ end is replaced by radioactive phosphate (^{32}P). The radioactive phosphate, as we'll see, will act as a marker, making it possible to later identify the 5′ end.

The cloned and marked DNA is then divided into four samples. Each sample is treated chemically in such a way that only one specific nucleotide is removed from each strand. That nucleotide will be an A (adenine) in the first sample, G (guanine) in the second, C (cytosine) in third, and T (thymine) in the fourth. Since only one nucleotide is removed, the procedure breaks each DNA strand into two fragments. But since individual nucleotides are generally repeated many times in even a short DNA chain and nucleotide removal is random, each sample ends up with fragments of many different lengths.

FIGURE 16.6 **(a)** In one common technique of gene introduction, a virus is used as a gene vector (transmitter). The eukaryotic gene of interest is selected from the eukaryote genome and inserted into the viral chromosome. Once introduced, the gene begins to function normally in its new nuclear environment. **(b)** Microinjection involves the use of a micropipette. While the operator observes through the light microscope, the pipette penetrates the cell nucleus and the desired engineered gene is injected.

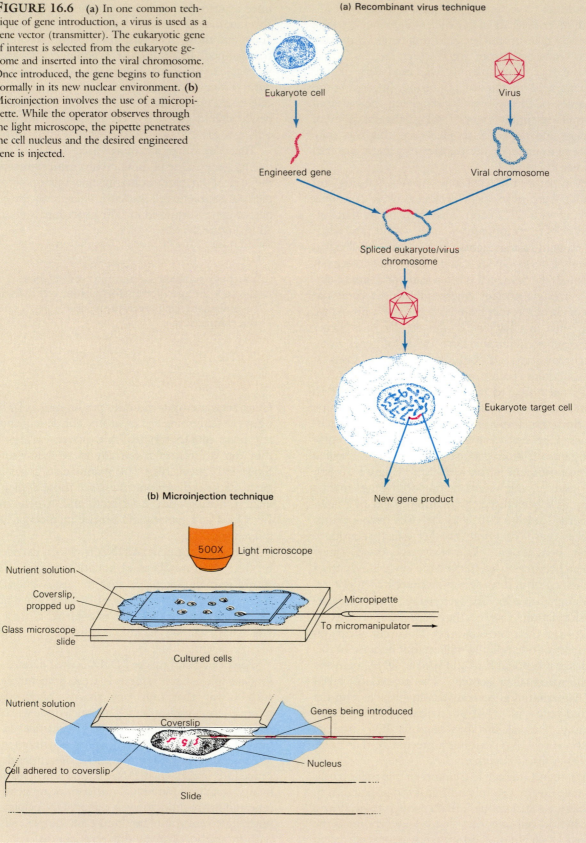

(a) Recombinant virus technique

Eukaryote cell

Virus

Engineered gene

Viral chromosome

Spliced eukaryote/virus chromosome

Eukaryote target cell

New gene product

(b) Microinjection technique

500X Light microscope

Nutrient solution

Coverslip, propped up

Glass microscope slide

Micropipette

To micromanipulator →

Cultured cells

Nutrient solution

Coverslip

Genes being introduced

Nucleus

Cell adhered to coverslip

Slide

For a closer look, let's consider the sample marked "A," the one in which adenine is affected. Although the experimenter wouldn't know this yet, we will assume that the actual order of nucleotides was:

$$^{32}\text{P—TGCACTTGAACGCATGCT}$$

Note the presence of four adenines in the strand. If the treatment removes an A randomly from each of the many identical strands in the A sample, there are four ways in which they will cleave:

$$^{32}\text{P—TGC} \qquad \text{CTTGAACGCATGCT}$$

$$^{32}\text{P—TGCACTTG} \qquad \text{ACGCATGCT}$$

$$^{32}\text{P—TGCACTTGA} \qquad \text{CGCATGCT}$$

$$^{32}\text{P—TGCACTTGAACGC} \qquad \text{TGCT}$$

Note also that in each case only one set of fragments (the ones on the left) contains the radioactive tracer. The others (those on the right) can be ignored. (You've probably noticed that in this procedure, the DNA is single stranded.)

In each sample, a different nucleotide is affected. Next, the samples are subjected to gel electrophoresis, a procedure illustrated in Figure 16.7. The fragmented samples are isolated in their own "lanes," marked A, G, C, and T. They begin to migrate from the top of the lanes. The shortest fragments migrate the longest distance.

Identifying the 5' end of the fragments is possible by the presence of the radioactive phosphorus, which shows up as a dark band. Figure 16.7 explains how the nucleotide sequence is read.

Actually, the process is much more laborious than we have indicated, since DNA strands tend to be quite long. The usual method is to cleave the long DNA polymers with very specific restriction enzymes, separate them, and then repeat the sequencing process with the shorter strands.

Gene sequencing can be an enormously tedious undertaking. As we will see, however, there are shortcuts that can sometimes be applied.

> **G**ene sequencing, determining the nucleotide sequence, can be done by exposing specifically cleaved fragments to **gel electrophoresis.**

Improving DNA sequencing procedures. In addition to the tediousness of gene sequencing another problem inherent to recombinant DNA technology is the nature of the gene itself. If you recall from our discussion of transcription (Chapter 15), genes are not the clean and simple linear messages we once thought them to be. They contain huge intervening sequences of nucleotides that end up being transcribed along with the actual gene. The introns are then clipped out leaving the exons (expressed sequences), the actual protein-specifying message in the highly processed mRNA transcript. Because of the introns, the direct sequencing of DNA produces a much longer version of the gene than is actually translated into protein. In addition, there is no guarantee that the lengthy gene segment being analyzed is complete or that it doesn't contain portions of other genes. There is a way around these problems, a technique genetic engineers have picked up from those peculiar entities called retroviruses.

As we learned in Chapter 15, the genome of the retrovirus exists as single-stranded RNA. When the retrovirus infects a cell, it inserts its genome into the host chromosome. Of course, first it must convert its RNA chromosome into DNA. The virus uses the enzyme reverse transcriptase to assemble a strand of DNA nucleotides along its RNA template. The RNA of the new hybrid strand is then broken down, and an opposing strand of DNA is assembled. The new DNA is inserted into the host chromosome where it behaves as if it belonged there, undergoing round after round of replication.

The potential for using reverse transcriptase to clean up the problems of gene sequencing (and obtaining engineered genes for splicing and cloning) has not escaped the genetic engineers. They now collect mRNA from cell fractions, select the desired strands, and subject it to the action of reverse transcriptase, converting the RNA to DNA. The cleaned-up, intron-free gene can then be cloned. When a sufficient number of copies are available, the gene can be sequenced through the usual techniques.

> **C**lean, intron-free genes can be obtained through reverse transcription, using the retroviral enzyme reverse transcriptase to convert processed mRNA to DNA.

DNA Libraries

The entire base sequences of DNA in bacteriophages, plasmids, polio viruses, and human mitochondria have been determined. They run pages and pages filled with A, T, C, and G; for example, there are exactly 5315 in the case of the first bacteriophage sequence to be discovered. Your own DNA sequence

FIGURE 16.7 In a standard method of gene sequencing, many identical strands of DNA are tagged at their 5′ end with ^{32}P, a radioisotope, and separated into four samples. Each sample is then cleaved at a different specific nucleotide (A, T, G, or C), yielding fragments of many sizes. The samples are then subjected to gel electrophoresis, each in its own lane. Under the influence of an electrical field, the fragments migrate through the gel, the smaller fragments migrating the greatest distances.

To determine the nucleotide sequence in the DNA strand, the operator begins at the bottom of the columns where the shortest fragments cluster. Following the numbers, the operator works upward, back and forth across the lanes, looking for the radioactive tag, which appears as a dark line in the gel (*dashed line*). As the photo reveals, the sequence is recorded simply by writing the letters (A, T, G, C) adjacent to where the nucleotides appear.

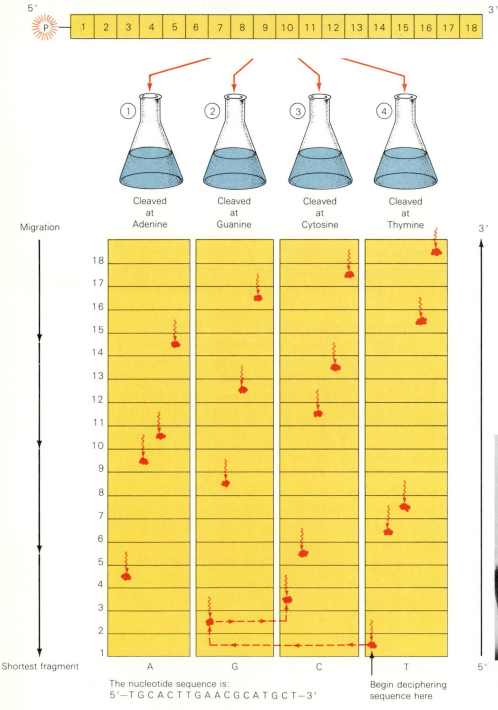

The nucleotide sequence is:
5′—T G C A C T T G A A C G C A T G C T—3′

of some 6.4 billion nucleotide pairs, if it were ever determined, would fill a thousand volumes the size of this one. And, incredible as it sounds, the task is already well underway. Tom Maniatis, a molecular biologist, has chopped human DNA into fragments a few tens of thousands of nucleotides long, has inserted them into the DNA of a bacteriophage, and is maintaining three million separate clones of cultured human DNA. Such a collection is called a **DNA library.**

Nucleic acid hybridization: how DNA libraries are used. What does one do with a DNA library? Simple. One goes there to "borrow" genes. This really isn't as silly as it sounds. After all, a library is simply a collection of sorts, and if one has access to a collection of specific genes, those genes can be retrieved and borrowed for the many uses modern geneticists have for such a special product. It's one thing, of course, to have these special genes; it's another thing to get at them. How does one retrieve precisely the genes needed? In a library, you can follow code numbers from the card catalog, but in recombinant DNA technology things are a bit trickier. You must use a **DNA probe** to locate and retrieve the DNA segment you want. This requires a **hybridization** technique.

First, a DNA library sample in which the gene is known to exist is treated with a strong alkali (pH 13) or is heated to 100°C, since either treatment will cleave hydrogen bonds, rendering all of the molecules single stranded. Then the DNA probe is added. A probe consists of a short, single-stranded sequence of nucleotides, perhaps 30 or so, from a cloned version of the gene. Certain molecules along the probe's length have been replaced with their radioactive counterparts or perhaps dyed with fluorescent dyes so that they can be found later. When the probe encounters a matching sequence of exposed nucleotides, it forms a hybrid, which can then be isolated through autoradiographic techniques.

Such probes have other uses as well. Hybridization techniques can be used to locate a gene among the eukaryotic chromosomes. For instance, probes can be sent into the intact cell nucleus, one in which the DNA has been treated as described above. When the probe has hybridized to its complementary DNA strand, the location is made visible by the radioactive or fluorescent probe. This technique was applied during the successful cloning of the factor VIII blood-clotting gene.

Genetic Engineering: A Social Issue

When the use of plasmids for genetic engineering was introduced by Paul Berg and others in the late 1970s, the possibilities were so dramatic and so bizarre that the new technology immediately spawned a raging controversy. Trouble started when the very people who invented the techniques called for a research moratorium while any possible dangers could be evaluated. Did they say "possible dangers"? The scare was on.

Supporters of the new gene-splicing technology claimed that it held great promise for humanity, and that some of our more pressing problems soon might be solved. They spoke glowingly of cancer cures and of a possible end to all genetic disease. Some even visualized a possible end to hunger with the synthesis of new plants that combine, say, the productivity and photosynthetic efficiency of maize with the nitrogen-fixing ability and protein production of peanuts.

In the minds of genetic engineering proponents, the principal benefit is that scientists like themselves will be able to do more experiments and to learn things faster—and that's nothing to scoff at. There are also more practical benefits, some of which have been realized and some of which are on the horizon. For example, there are thousands of growth hormone–deficient people who, with the help of human growth hormone, can attain normal height. In the past, growth hormone had to be extracted from the pituitary glands of human cadavers and was extremely expensive. Even though the glands of 50 cadavers are needed for only one dose, a few thousand seriously undersized adolescents have been treated to some extent—as well as one man who grew to normal height after having been only four feet tall until the age of 35. Perhaps in the future, no one will have to be any shorter than he or she wants to be. Does that seem to you like a blessing, or like cavalier tampering with nature?

One enormously valuable agricultural feat has already been accomplished: engineered *E. coli* now grows the antigen for hoof-and-mouth disease, making possible a relatively inexpensive vaccine against that costly disease.

Alarmed critics of the new techniques, on the other hand, saw nothing but disaster ahead. Their fears ranged from the possible release of newly created disease organisms—genetic monsters capable of creating uncontrollable plagues—to new kinds of cancer, to constructing new kinds of humans. Nonsensical scare fiction began to appear. Some critics accused the new biologists of "playing God," of messing around with primal forces, or of seeking demonic new power. Politicians tried to capitalize on the scare; the city fathers of Cambridge, Massachusetts passed an ordinance prohibiting recombinant DNA research within the city limits (which include Harvard University and the Massachusetts Institute of

For most of this century, cancer research has focused on viruses as possible cancer-causing agents. Although they have now been ruled out as a major cause of human cancer, virus research may help identify certain human genes that are implicated in at least some cancers.

Researchers discovered that some cancerous cells contain genes that can be incorporated into viruses and then transmitted to normal cells. Once there, they can cause cancer. It has also been discovered that those same genes are actually a normal part of the cell's genome. That is, they occur in normal cells. In normal cells, however, oncogenes, as the cancer-related genes are known, are under tight control.

So far about 20 oncogenes have been identified. Since the hallmark of cancer is uncontrolled cell proliferation, it is not surprising that at least one oncogene functions in normal cell division. Apparently, the division-related gene can be activated inappropriately, or overactivated, causing the rapid and unrestrained growth of cancer cells, which subsequently invade and displace normal tissue.

How does the virus-transported oncogene affect the normal cell? One possibility is that viruses may also pick up and transmit the DNA sequence that can activate uncontrolled cell proliferation. Or it may be that the viruses transmit the oncogenes into healthy cells without also passing along the DNA control segments, those that restrain the gene and keep it from acting inappropriately (as an oncogene). Thus, while viruses themselves are not actually cancer-causing agents, their ability to transport genes and alter their control makes them important accessories.

The mechanism of triggering cancer suggested by viral research could also account for the way that chemical carcinogens (cancer causers) and ultraviolet rays operate. They might stimulate the activity of oncogenes directly, or they might activate the control region of the DNA sequence (the operator gene) that would in turn activate the oncogene. Carcinogens that are able to move around sections of DNA could conceivably shift the oncogene so that it would fall under the control of an operator gene that could activate it.

Such findings are promising, but final answers are not around the corner. For example, the notion of oncogenes as a primary mechanism of cancer is incompatible with the long lapse between exposure to a carcinogen and development of the disease.

Technology). The National Institutes of Health set up rigid guidelines as to what kinds of research were to be allowed and what precautions were to be taken.

Do you see why some people were alarmed? It's possible to put the gene for botulism toxin into *E. coli,* a bacterium that is already adapted for thriving in your gut. It's also possible to clone the entire genome of a cancer-causing virus, or the specific cancer-causing genes. Unlikely, you think? This, too, has been done. That was one of the scare items, but now that it has actually happened, the isolation of cancer-causing genes (oncogenes) has been hailed as the research breakthrough that may lead science to a final understanding of the cancer process and possibly to a dependable cure (Essay 16.1). Not that anyone can afford to be careless: we mustn't forget that the last two minor epidemics of smallpox in Europe—including the very last death ever caused by this virus—were caused by escaped laboratory strains. The deadly smallpox virus, which only two decades ago infected millions of people, is now extinct except for laboratory cultures.

The genetic engineering controversy died down for a time. Interestingly, this happened at about the time gene splicing became big business, with Wall Street taking a lively interest. The City of Cambridge relented, and the NIH guidelines were relaxed. But now the controversy is back and the issues are hotter than ever.

In 1987, the focus was on manufactured human growth hormone. Apparently a considerable amount was stolen, and authorities feared it would soon appear as a "black market" item. Who would be willing to pay exorbitant prices for growth hormones? Obvious candidates might be the people who inject themselves with steroids, ignoring the apparent risks. In modern society, tallness has many rewards other than athletic prowess. Studies clearly reveal that height is a positive factor in social and business success. How far will people go to succeed in our keenly competitive world? You already know the answer. It is abundantly clear that social issues arising from genetic engineering are just beginning to appear.

SUMMARY

Bacteria are experimentally useful because they are relatively simple and increase rapidly enough for rare mutational events to be observed.

GENETIC RECOMBINATION IN BACTERIA

While on rare occasions bacteria exhibit a form of genetic recombination, the usual events of meiosis, gametogenesis, and fertilization do not occur. Lederberg and Tatum detected genetic recombination in nutritional mutants of *Escherichia coli,* the colon bacterium.

The Sex Life of *E. coli*

Early observations indicated that bacteria mate through **conjugation,** but this ability was restricted to certain "male" strains that passed genes to recipient "female" strains. Females then became males. Later it became known that cells of the male strain, designated F+, had a minute chromosome, the F plasmid, which enabled them to produce a tubelike sex pilus through which a copy of the plasmid passed to the F− strain.

Genetic recombination, as observed by Lederberg and Tatum, involved genes on the main chromosome. It was later determined that on rare occasions, the F plasmid inserts there, and then upon replication and conjugation the plasmid replica draws a number of such genes into the F− cell. Genetic recombination in the main chromosome takes place through crossing over.

Hfr strains, those in which plasmid insertion regularly took place, were isolated and observations of genetic recombination greatly facilitated. By controlling the transfer of main chromosome genes, geneticists were able to map the *E. coli* chromosome.

Plasmids and Plasmid Genes

Further study has uncovered the presence of other plasmids including the multiple-resistance plasmid, which confers antibiotic resistance to the bacterial cell. The transfer of such plasmids among strains and even between species has produced many superresistant strains of pathogens. The overuse of antibiotics is blamed for this development. Plasmids are now routinely used in genetic engineering.

GENETIC ENGINEERING

Genetic engineering includes recombinant DNA technology—gene sequencing, splicing, and cloning. Genes can be removed from cells, altered, inserted into other cells, grown, and their products harvested. Products include insulin, interferons, growth hormone, and blood clotting factor VIII.

Recombinant DNA Technology

Specific restriction enzymes are used to excise DNA segments. The cleaving leaves "sticky ends" that can be joined to other DNA segments with matching "sticky ends." Spliced segments can be introduced through transformation, cell fusion, the use of viral transfer agents, and microinjection. Mammalian cells will take in calcium-treated DNA segments in a manner similar to bacterial transformation.

Gene Sequencing

Gene sequencing is detecting the order of nucleotide bases. A central method involves selecting a DNA segment, producing a great many copies through cloning, and incorporating radioactive phosphorus to the 5′ end of each. Next, the treated DNA is divided into four quantities, labelled A, G, C, and T, respectively. Each is treated with a different cleaving enzyme that breaks the strand once at the nucleotide designated in its label. The cleaved segments from each sample are placed in their own electrophoretic column, and the bases at the start of each segment are identified.

In another procedure, selected segments of mRNA are converted to DNA using the enzyme reverse transcriptase. Such DNA segments, free of troublesome introns, can then be cloned and the clean version of the gene sequenced.

DNA Libraries

Spliced and cloned genes are now being maintained in collections called DNA libraries. DNA probes are used to identify desired genes for recovery from the library. Probes are single stranded, radioactive DNA segments whose nucleotide sequence matches part of the gene being sought. The two join through base-pairing, and the gene is then removed for use.

Genetic Engineering: A Social Issue

Because of its unlimited potential for the manipulation of life, genetic engineering is highly controversial. While it holds great promise for treating and eliminating genetic defects and vastly improving agriculture, there are potential applications that are objectionable. Included are the enormous potential for germ warfare and the accidental creation and release of new, drug-resistant pathogens.

KEY TERMS

minimal medium	recombinant DNA technology	recombinant virus technique
nutritional mutant strain	gene sequencing	DNA-mediated gene transfer
conjugation	gene splicing	microinjection
plasmid	cloning	DNA library
F plasmid	factor VIII	DNA probe
Hfr strain	transformation	hybridization
multiple-resistance plasmid	cell fusion	
genetic engineering		

REVIEW QUESTIONS

1 List five experimental organisms that have been used by geneticists in past years. What are several advantages in using bacteria? (p. 241)

2 In what basic way does sexual reproduction in prokaryotes differ from that in most eukaryotes? (Consider both mechanisms and frequency.) (p. 242)

3 How did Lederberg and Tatum determine that two nutritionally deficient strains of bacteria had undergone genetic recombination? Looking ahead, why did their attempts at mapping the bacterial chromosome fail? (p. 242)

4 Describe the peculiar behavior of "male" and "female" bacteria following conjugation. (p. 243)

5 Explain how the discovery of the F plasmid solved the riddle of changing sex in *E. coli*. (p. 243)

6 What did the transfer of the F plasmid have to do with genetic recombination as observed by Lederberg and Tatum? (pp. 243–244)

7 What are Hfr bacterial strains? Explain the techniques involved in mapping the chromosomes in the Hfr strain bacteria. (p. 244)

8 What is a multiple-resistance plasmid? How is it involved in the rise of antibiotic-resistant bacterial strains? How might the indescriminate use of antibiotics have encouraged this? (p. 246)

9 In general, what does the field of genetic engineering encompass? (p. 246)

10 Briefly explain what gene sequencing, splicing, and cloning are. (pp. 246–247)

11 List several important gene products made available through recombinant DNA technology. (p. 247)

12 Explain how two strands of DNA from unrelated organisms are spliced together. (p. 247)

13 How are bacterial plasmids used in recombinant DNA technology? (pp. 247–249)

14 Briefly discuss two or three specific methods used in getting spliced genes into recipient cells. (p. 249)

15 Outline the steps followed in sequencing a DNA strand. (pp. 249, 251)

16 Explain how reverse transcriptase is used in preparing DNA segments for sequencing. What advantage does this hold over the use of DNA segments obtained directly from the cells? (p. 251)

17 Describe the contents of DNA libraries. Of what potential value are such collections? (pp. 251–253)

18 Explain what a DNA probe is and how it is used to recover genes from a DNA library. (p. 253)

19 What real risks are there in the applications of genetic engineering? Suggest several kinds of safeguards needed. (pp. 253–254)

20 What are some of the future benefits from genetic engineering? (pp. 253–254)

During the reign of Queen Victoria, while the French were engaged in a violent and bloody revolution and the United States was rationalizing its legalized slavery, the British were enjoying a period of relative tranquility. The British upper classes were peering down their noses at the unseemly behavior of the foreigners, but mostly they were busy with their horses, hounds, and gardens. They were also setting the stage for world trade. Their ships were everywhere; their military was everywhere, and with it the more adventurous of British scientists were probing, peering, describing, and winning over. Among those young scientists of the day was one Charles Darwin (Figure 17.1).

Young Darwin was a well-bred, well-connected naturalist of great energy and immense curiosity. His social position helped him land a position as naturalist on an extended (he thought overextended) voyage around the world. During the voyage, Darwin saw things that no other British scientist of his time had seen. After his return to England, he put his ideas together and developed a new paradigm that was to shake the intellectual world to its foundations. The new grand scheme sought to explain the diversity of life through a process called **evolution.** Although the concept of evolution did not originate with Darwin, he was the first to provide an overwhelming amount of observational evidence to support it. He was also the first to suggest a mechanism through which evolution might occur.

Evolution has been defined in many ways. For now, though, we can define evolution as changes in lines of living things over time. Although this is a simple definition and should apparently give no one trouble, it gives a lot of people trouble. That's because it can be used to explain how living things are related and how a species can change. (For our purposes, at this point, species can be considered specific kinds of living things, such as pineapples or dogs.) In fact, the theory of evolution has come to imply that all organisms are related to one another by common ancestry and that all forms of life have diverged from a single ancestral form over eons of time (about 3.5 billion years, to be more specific). The result is one grand family tree. The theory suggests that not only are all men our brothers, but that whales, redwoods, lice, and molds are our relatives, too.

Evolution is the process of change over time through which the diverse forms of life have emerged from a common ancestry.

17

PRINCIPLES OF EVOLUTION

FIGURE 17.1 Charles Darwin at age 27, shortly after returning from the voyage of the *Beagle*.

EVOLUTION THROUGH NATURAL SELECTION

Darwin was the first to propose that evolution generally proceeds through a process called **natural selection.** Simply stated, natural selection implies that individuals with traits that better adapt them to a specific environment will survive and outnumber other, less well-suited individuals. Natural selection is based on four observations:

1. *Overproduction*. Organisms commonly produce far greater numbers of offspring than can survive.
2. *Limited resources*. Because of their great reproductive potential, organisms tend to exceed the food supply and other resources needed to sustain them. Thus organisms of the same type must compete with each other for the limited resources. (Darwin called this the "struggle for existence.")
3. *Genetic variation*. Genetic (heritable) variation exists within the populations that make up species. Today we know that such variation originates through continuing genetic mutation.
4. *Survival of the best adapted*. Some variations promote survival better than do others. Individuals with such traits are said to be better adapted to a given environment and will tend to leave more offspring than others. Each generation is thereby made up of the offspring of the most successful reproducers of previous generations. In a sense,

then, *nature selects* which lines of living things will survive and prosper (and reproduce) and which lines will fade and die (Figure 17.2).

Scientists today generally accept the idea of evolution, but as biology has grown more sophisticated, they argue strongly over whether it occurs *primarily* through natural selection. Because of such arguments (which can quickly become rather technical and esoteric), some people, especially those of the creationist persuasion, like to think that there is disagreement over whether evolution occurs. Actually, there is little disagreement about this among most scientists, but there *is* disagreement over *how* it occurs.

> **Natural selection** operates when there is an overproduction of young, genetic variation, and competition for limited resources. Those individuals with advantageous variations will survive in greater numbers and reproduce more of their kind.

The theory of evolution challenged the previously accepted idea that each species was a permanent, fixed entity; that idea had to go. Gone was the idea of *perfection* in nature. Naturalists had always assumed or proclaimed that biological organisms were perfectly adapted to their environments; Darwin showed that the adaptations of nature, no matter how admirable or wonderful, were not perfect but were always open to change and improvement. Gone was the assumption that nature was full, that there was a place for every creature and that every creature was in its place. Gone was the idea of the "balance of nature," the deep-seated, almost mystical belief that all creatures interacted in a harmonious way that ensured that all would prosper. Gone was the idea that some organisms existed for the benefit of others—the lamb for the wolf or the flower for the bee. Swept away, in fact, was the more recent, hard-won conviction that biology, like physics, was governed by fixed laws, and that all of nature was predictable if only the laws were known. In the place of these comforting ideas, Darwin offered only the cold arithmetic of inequality and differences in reproductive success.

There are those who like to say that Darwin's explanations are somehow an attack on an all-wise and all-powerful God. However, Darwin didn't really have anything to say on the subject; an "overseer" was simply unnecessary to the processes he described. Others have noted that religious beliefs, by definition, are unfalsifiable hypotheses and, therefore, are outside of the realm of science.

FIGURE 17.2   The giraffe's neck has long been a source of evolutionary speculation. The neck is apparently a feeding specialization for browsing on lofty tree foliage that is unavailable to most other plant eaters. How did this unusual specialization come about? Applying the principle of natural selection, we can speculate that the giraffe's mammalian ancestors had relatively short necks, and probably had to compete for food and avoid predators along with many similar primitive browsing, hooved herbivores. Variants—mutants with slightly longer necks—probably arose from time to time, but until long necks became important, the variants' impact on the giraffe population was minimal. Certainly, chance favored such variants. The longer-necked giraffes found untapped food sources in the higher branches. Because of their competitive edge, the longer-necked oddities thrived, and thus were able to pass their novel genes on to more descendants than their shorter-necked contemporaries could.

The Sources of Darwin's Ideas

Young Charles Darwin was something of a problem to his wealthy family. He had already failed at medical school and would not be following the footsteps of his father and grandfather, both successful and famous physicians. He had trained for the clergy, but he showed little inclination for ecclesiastical pursuits. It seems that he was most interested in collecting beetles and in gathering rocks. Natural history and amateur geology were acceptable hobbies for a young gentleman, and the family had plenty of money, but Charles was 22 and his father felt that he should have a job.

The opportunity came just before Charles had to decide whether to enter the clergy. Meanwhile, another young, wealthy, and rather more successful man, Captain James Fitzroy of the Royal Navy, needed a companion of his own social class to accompany him aboard the *H.M.S. Beagle* (Figure 17.3) on a five-year expedition around the world (1831–1835). The Captain's companion would have the official position of Naturalist, and was expected to collect and study plants and animals along the way. The position was to be without pay, of course; only gentlemen need apply. One of Darwin's professors had recommended him to Captain Fitzroy, and in time Charles' father agreed to let him go. In retrospect, it was a momentous decision because, as we noted earlier, it was on this voyage that Darwin would begin to develop his ideas on how species changed. Let's follow Darwin and see how the seeds of change were planted in his mind.

The first new continent that the eager and seasick Darwin visited was South America. There Darwin had observed that many distinctly local mammals and birds were doing the same things in the same ways as similar mammals and birds in other parts of the world. For instance, the Pampas grasslands were the home of the mara (Figure 17.4), a mammal that looked like a rabbit and behaved like a rabbit; it was not a rabbit, however, but a rodent related to other South American rodents such as the guinea pig. Why

FIGURE 17.3 The *Beagle* was a small vessel, just under 100 feet in length, but her fearless captain, James Fitzroy, an expert navigator, guided her unerringly through a five-year voyage around the globe.

FIGURE 17.4 The mara, or Patagonian hare *(Dolichotis patagonum)*, a South American rodent that lives much as a rabbit does.

should this be? Other naturalists, if pressed, might have said that the Pampas was the right place for this creature just as Europe was the right place for rabbits. Darwin concluded that there must once have been an empty place in nature, an opportunity for a rabbit or rabbitlike creature to survive and flourish. However, European or North American rabbits had no way to cross the ocean. Thus, their ecological role or **niche,** as it is called by ecologists (see Chapter 47), was exploited by a South American rodent, whose descendants became increasingly adapted, over time, to the grassland habitat—that is, they became increasingly rabbitlike.

In time it became clear to Darwin that *chance* plays a large role in the history of life. He would conclude that evolution depends not only on the chance occurrence of heritable variations on which natural selection could act, but also on such chance events as what kinds of plants and animals were available to exploit opportunities in nature, or what kind of geographic features or barriers would prevent (or facilitate) the spread of living things from one place to another.

Darwin was aware that empty places in nature presented opportunities for animals that chanced to be prepared to exploit them.

The picture became clearer to Darwin as the ship pressed on to a group of bizarre little islands off the coast of Ecuador. The Galápagos Islands rose as volcanos from the Pacific Ocean floor in fairly recent geological times (on average about 100,000 years ago). The animals and plants that live there now apparently are the descendants of a chance assemblage of random migrants that floated or were blown there and found a variety of new opportunities. Each island has unique species of land birds, each adapted to a different and particular way of life. When Darwin collected them, he assumed that they were an unrelated motley collection of blackbirds, finches, and wrens. But later analysis by experts revealed that all of these ecologically very different birds were finches that were rather closely related to one another. It is clear from Darwin's journal that this belated revelation—two years after the *Beagle's* return—was the shock that suddenly opened his mind to the idea of evolution. He realized that all of the Galápagos land birds had probably descended from a pair of mainland finches that had been storm-blown to the islands tens of thousands of years previously. The descendants of these pioneers moved from island to island and eventually diverged into a number of distinct species (Figure 17.5).

Darwin the Experimenter

Some of the implications of Darwinism are easy to test and some are not. The formation of two species from one is a slow process; we can see that it has occurred, but so far no one has been able to make it occur experimentally. Other implications could be tested more readily. As one small example, oceanic islands are inhabited by species that are strictly terrestrial on the mainland. The question arose: if they were not able to cross the water, how did they reach the island?

Perhaps their ancestors floated in or were brought in on the feet or in the crops of migrating birds. Darwin noted that salt is notoriously lethal to land snails; experimentally, however, he found that hibernating land snails could float for weeks in salt water, then later wake up and crawl away. He found viable seeds in the crop of a dead pigeon that had floated for weeks on the sea, and he observed tiny land plants sprouting from the droppings of birds. He suspended a duck's foot in an aquarium, and observed that a variety of freshwater forms immediately clung to the foot and could not be easily dislodged; later they would voluntarily dislodge themselves. He found other organisms and seeds in the mud on the feet of wild ducks and concluded that ducks may be a major,

FIGURE 17.5 Although they are now considered separate species, evidence from many studies clearly indicates that the different kinds of Galápagos finches evolved from a common finch ancestor.

The Galápagos Archipelago includes habitats ranging from dry, lowland deserts to wet, species-rich highlands. The islands are home to a bizarre collection of life, from grazing lizards and giant tortoises to a variety of bird life and shore dwellers. Darwin, who despised the place, was to make it famous because he saw it as an experiment of nature in progress.

(a) Compare the lush vegetation of the Santa Cruz highlands to the more arid regions of the lowlands *(top facing page)*.

(b) The flightless cormorant, *Nannopterum harrisi,* uses its wings to keep its balance as it walks.

(c) Tidal pool and dry terrain near Topocra Bay on Isabela Island.

(e) The swallow-tail gull *(Creagus furcatus)* is a nocturnal bird unique to the Galápagos.

(d) The male frigate bird *(Fregata magnificens)* inflates its chest during sexual display.

(f) Desert vegetation along the coast of Hood Island.

(g) Blue-footed boobies *(Sula nebouxii)* establish pair bonds.

(h) Colorful Sally Lightfoot crabs *(Grapsus grapsus).*

(j) The land iguana, *Conolophus subcristatus,* is an herbivore.

(i) Galápagos tortoises. These are just one of 13 species.

(k) The predatory Galápagos Hawk, *Buteo galapagoensis,* is closely related to vultures.

if unwitting, force in the spread of freshwater species (Figure 17.6). His methods were clearly scientific. First, evidence was accumulated (perhaps preceded by a hunch), and based on the evidence, an explanatory hypothesis was formed. The hypothesis was tested by vigorous experimentation. The species eventually inhabiting an island, it appeared, depended to an astonishing degree on the vagaries of chance dispersal.

EVIDENCE OF EVOLUTION

How good is the evidence supporting the theory of evolution? How well has Darwin's idea held up? Pretty well, it turns out, with some fine tuning by those who followed. Let's consider some of the most powerful supporting evidence for the theory, in particular the fossil record, biogeography, comparative anatomy, and genetic similarity.

The Fossil Record

Darwin is best known as a biologist, but he was also one of the foremost geologists of his time. His interest in rocks and strata and his enthusiasm for digging fossils contributed powerfully to his development of evolutionary theory. In his "geologizing" in South America, he uncovered the fossil remains of an extinct giant armadillo (Figure 17.7). The remains were found deep in ancient rocks, deposited long ago. Above were smaller armadillos of a different

sort, alive and scurrying over the graves of the giants. To Darwin, this suggested change over time. The extinct species, he thought, must have been ancestral to the living species.

Many fossils have been discovered since the time of Charles Darwin, and the known record is now immense. Fortunately for an aging Darwin, one of the most amazing records was uncovered during his lifetime. In 1879, Yale University paleontologist Othniel C. Marsh published a comprehensive study on the evolution of the modern horse, *Equus*. These findings lent considerable credibility to a troubled Darwin, whose book, *The Origin of Species,* published 20 years earlier, had raised a storm of controversy. Thomas Huxley, master debater and Darwin's greatest defender, put these findings to good use in arguing the case of evolution through natural selection.

Saga of the horse. Tracing the origin of the horse has taken paleontologists back some 65 million years to the Eocene epoch of the Cenozoic era (see the geological table, Appendix A). In that distant time lived *Hyracotherium*, a timid, doglike, woodland creature that browsed on the soft parts of plants and literally tiptoed around the forest (like the dog, it had multiple toes and footpads). From this decidely "un-horse-like" creature arose a succession of forms that gradually took on the appearance of a respectable horse (Figure 17.8). The changes represented a continuing adaptation to a new source of energy, grass. Grasses first appeared in the Eocene epoch and began their gradual spread into today's vast grasslands.

FIGURE 17.6 Darwin is best known as a synthesist—one who theorizes about the larger meaning of observations and data—but he was also an excellent reductionist. Among the many smaller issues he investigated was the question of island colonization.

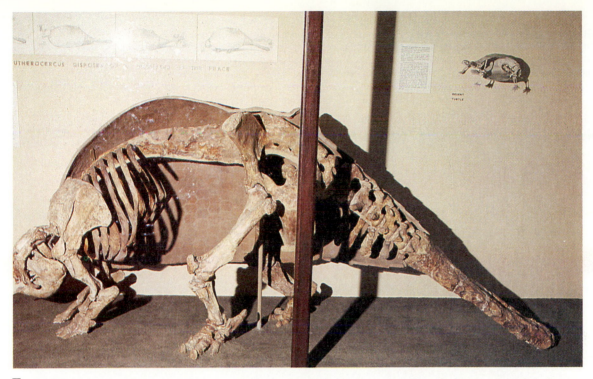

FIGURE 17.7   Fossil of extinct giant armadillo from South America.

Adapting to the grasslands required many changes in the horse's anatomy, not the least of which was in dentition (teeth). Grasses are highly abrasive—feeding requires large incisors for nipping and molars with broad, hardened surfaces for chewing. Of course, as the primitive horses left the forests, predators followed. Because concealment was more difficult in the open spaces, natural selection favored "early warning systems" in the form of long necks and better vision and hearing. It also favored the ability to respond with great speed, thus we see major changes in the lower legs and feet, particularly the consolidation of the toes into the hooved foot.

Punctuated equilibrium versus missing links in the fossil record.   Although the excellent fossil record of the horse provides strong supporting evidence for evolution, it is probably an exception to the rule. A general problem with the fossil record has been the notable lack of transitional forms. If evolution occurs gradually, as Darwin said, the fossils in one layer of rock should gradually give rise to those found in more recent layers. The view of evolution in which one form gradually changes to another, in fact, is called **gradualism.**

Unfortunately, the fossil record does not always support the gradualist view of evolution. Quite often, one form seems to change abruptly to another, in what would be a "geological instant" (that is, perhaps over a few thousand years). Biologists agonized over this problem for perhaps more years than they should have, but a new comprehensive hypothesis finally has been proposed.

The American Museum of Natural History's Niles Eldridge and Harvard's Stephen Jay Gould, may have an answer. They call their idea **punctuated equilibrium.** From their interpretation of the fossil record they contend that species often persist, virtually unchanged, for millions of years and then disappear, suddenly replaced by a new, often similar form. They suggest that evolutionary change probably progresses in fits and starts, following long periods of relative inactivity (thus, the "punctuation marks" in an otherwise equilibrium, or balanced, state). This is a far cry from the traditional gradualist view and one that has raised considerable controversy. We will look further into punctuated equilibrium in Chapter 19.

The fossil record supports evolutionary theory, although change may come about through both **gradualism** and **punctuated equilibrium.**

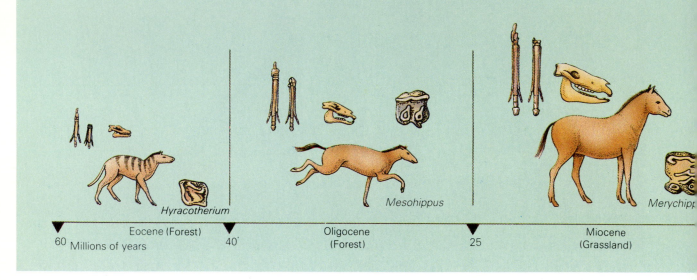

FIGURE 17.8 The reconstruction of the ancestral history of the modern horse reveals changes in size, skull, feet, and teeth. The modern horse may stand 152 cm (60 in) tall at the shoulder, but the first known horse, *Hyracotherium,* was only one-sixth that size (about 11 inches). Adaptations to grassland living began sometime during the Miocene epoch. Note the loss of some toe bones and enlargement of the remainder as the hoof became consolidated. Along with the enlargement of the skull, the teeth enlarged and the hardened enamel surfaces increased (seen here are the upper molars).

Biogeography

The study of the distribution of living things over the earth—**biogeography**—offers another line of supporting evidence for evolution. Why does each geographically isolated region have its own peculiar assemblage of plants and animals? Recall that Darwin noticed that the mara, or Patagonian hare, exists where one would expect rabbits, and it has, in fact, many rabbitlike characteristics. South America, Darwin deduced, doesn't have rabbits because rabbits can't get there. The niche generally occupied by rabbits has been established by a different kind of mammal. Darwin also noticed that remote oceanic islands have few mammals except those that travel well over water, such as bats. With the exception of bats and introduced animals, Australia, an isolated island continent, is populated only by primitive marsupial (pouched) mammals (those lacking a true placenta). Marsupials are rare over the rest of the earth (the opossum is the exception). Since studies of today's marsupials show that they are related to each other, their distribution lends support to the idea that animals are where they are because of their evolutionary history. Related animals are likely to be found in the same area.

> The special traits of organisms in specific geographical regions often suggest a common ancestry and evolutionary history.

Comparative Anatomy: Homology and Analogy

An important source of information about evolutionary relationships comes from the study of **comparative anatomy** in which the structures of modern species are compared. Such studies are particularly useful where the fossil record is too poor to help, but often they just reinforce our interpretation of the fossil record. For instance, studies of the skulls of various vertebrates (animals with backbones) have provided many clues to the evolutionary trends that led to today's representatives. The skeleton abounds with examples. The relatedness of mammals is supported by the fact that all of them, from bats to whales, have exactly seven neck (cervical) vertebrae. Also consider the gill arches: all vertebrate embryos (including humans) have gill arches. Studies of development reveal that although gill arches give rise to gills in fishes, they become highly modified into wholly unrelated structures in other vertebrates (ours become part of the lower jaw, middle ear, larynx, and

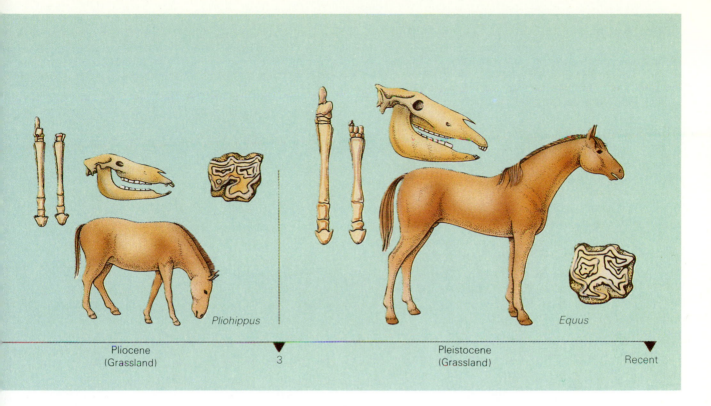

Pliohippus		*Equus*	
Pliocene (Grassland)	3	Pleistocene (Grassland)	Recent

tongue). The study of embryos provides many other evolutionary clues as well (see Chapter 42).

In the comparative study of anatomy it is necessary to distinguish structures that are **homologous** from those that are **analogous.** Homologous structures are those with common origins in the embryo, indicating common evolutionary origin. Actually, though, they may look quite different and may even have taken on different functions. Analogous organs are those that have similar functions and often appear similar, but are unrelated in evolution because they form differently in the embryo. The wings of insects and birds are often cited as examples of analogous structures.

Studies of vertebrate anatomy provide many examples of homologous organs and, along with the fossil record, have given biologists a clear idea about vertebrate evolution. For instance, what inferences can you make from a consideration of the forelimbs of the cat, whale, bat, bird, and horse, and the upper arm of a human (Figure 17.9)? A study of the embryos of these vertebrates reveals that in each case, the limbs emerge from similarly formed limb buds.

A closer look at the whale's anatomy and that of the python presents another slant to the idea of homology. Both lack hind limbs, but tucked away in the body are useless **vestigial** bones that are clearly

remnants of what was once a functional pelvic (hip) girdle. There are even vestigial hindleg bones (Figure 17.10). Both animals are apparently descended from four-legged land dwellers. Vestigial organs are looked upon as rare but welcome records of past evolutionary events.

> **H**omologous structures, those with common origin in the embryo, suggest evolutionary relatedness; **analogous structures,** those that may have the same role, but that lack common embryological origin, do not.

Comparative Biochemistry and Genetic Similarity

Recent evidence from biochemistry and genetic engineering promises to shed more light on evolutionary relationships. Species whose close relationship has been established through some of the traditional means described above also show strong similarity in the arrangement of their amino acid sequences and DNA base sequences. For example, the analysis of amino acid sequences in common proteins has enabled biologists to examine evolutionary change on the molecular level. DNA studies have provided

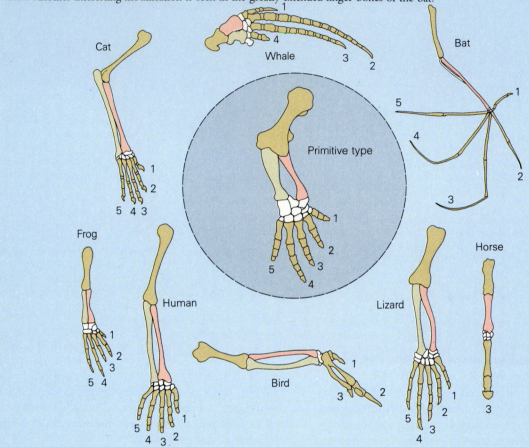

FIGURE 17.9 Homologous structures. The forelimbs of several representative vertebrates are compared here with those of the suggested primitive ancestral type. Since they all have the same embryological origin, they are said to be homologous. The most dramatic changes can be seen in the horse, bird, and whale. In these animals, many individual bones have become smaller and some have even fused. Another interesting modification is seen in the greatly extended finger bones of the bat.

FIGURE 17.10 Vestigial organs (vestiges of the past) in the python include remnant pelvic girdles and hindlimbs. Functionless, remnant organs in humans are numerous and include the infamous appendix and wisdom teeth (both of which cause us miseries), our tailbones (coccyx), ear muscles, and the nipples of males.

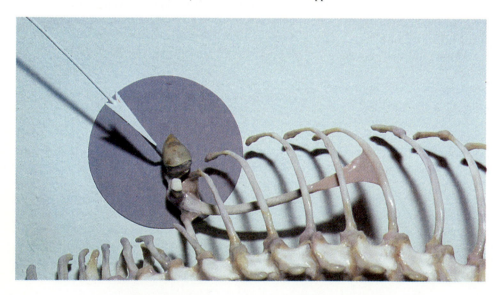

similar but even more fundamental kinds of information. For instance, based on wide-ranging studies of anatomy, behavior, and physiology, chimpanzees and humans have for some time been considered closely related. From the study of human and chimp DNA sequences, there now is little doubt. Such studies have also shown that there are greater differences between humans and orangutans and still greater differences between humans and other primates. We will look into the techniques of comparative DNA and amino acid analysis in Chapter 19.

This thumbnail sketch of evolution has probably left you with questions, some of which simply cannot be answered at present. Some questions that have presented nagging problems for evolutionists are being answered, as we will see shortly. Here, though, we have set the historical framework in which this pivotal theory arose. Our focus has been quite broad and general. However, to get to the basic mechanisms of evolution we must descend from such overviews back to the allele, the hereditary unit itself. There we will learn something of how genetic variation arises and, once in place, how it is tested by the pervasive forces that characterize natural selection.

Evolutionary relationships among organisms can be inferred by amino acid and nucleotide sequencing.

SUMMARY

Charles Darwin developed a new paradigm in which the diversity of life was explained through evolution. Evolution, which means change over time, implies that all organisms have a common line of descent.

EVOLUTION THROUGH NATURAL SELECTION

As a mechanism of evolution, Darwin proposed natural selection. Its four main aspects are overproduction of young, limited resources, genetic variation, and survival of the best adapted.

In accepting evolution we discard such notions as perfection in nature, fixed or unchanging species, and balance and harmony in nature.

The Sources of Darwin's Ideas

Darwin's observations during his voyage on the *Beagle* and his studies afterward convinced him that life underwent change or evolution. He recognized the uniqueness of animals on other continents and was greatly impressed by past geological events and the presence of unique fossil life. The puzzle of the Galápagos finches played a central role in his developing the concept of natural selection.

Darwin the Experimenter

In addition to his observations, Darwin developed experiments to test his ideas. Included were several that provided important clues to island colonization.

EVIDENCE OF EVOLUTION
The Fossil Record

The most compelling evidence for evolution is the fossil record. The fossil history of the horse can be traced throughout the Cenozoic era. Changes in its feet and limbs and dentition reveal ongoing adaptations to the newly emerging grasslands.

The frequent absence of transitional forms in the fossil record has led some paleontologists away from the idea of gradualism and toward punctuated equilibrium. The latter proposes that long periods of evolutionary inactivity (equilibrium) lead to brief but far-reaching episodes of extinction and change (punctuation). In these periods new species arise and rapidly replace existing species.

Biogeography

The uniqueness of animal groups in different geographic regions supports the idea that each group had its own line of descent from a common ancestor. Thus its members are more closely related to each other than to other such groups.

Comparative Anatomy: Homology and Analogy

Evidence of common ancestry is seen in homologous structures. For instance, the limbs in various vertebrates appear quite different and have different specializations. Yet common features are usually still visible, and when the development of each is compared in the embryo, they are seen to have similar origin. Analogous structures, such as bird and insect wings, differ in developmental origin, thus are not a sign of common evolutionary origin. Vestigial organs are convincing signs of past evolution.

Comparative Biochemistry and Genetic Similarity

The techniques of DNA and amino acid sequencing permit biologists to examine evolutionary events at the molecular level. In general, such studies support older theories and conclusions.

KEY TERMS

evolution   punctuated equilibrium   homologous
natural selection   biogeography   analogous
niche   comparative anatomy   vestigial
gradualism

REVIEW QUESTIONS

1 Although Darwinian concept of evolution represents a paradigm, others before him proposed the idea. Why is he given so much credit? (p. 257)

2 Evolution means change, but it is more than that. What inescapable conclusion does the idea also embrace? (p. 257)

3 Why was the concept of natural selection so important to Darwin's theory of evolution? (p. 258)

4 List the four main aspects of natural selection and explain how each fits into the whole concept. (p. 258)

5 What is the status of the evolution concept among scientists today? What part of Darwin's thesis remains controversial? (p. 258)

6 List three specific beliefs about nature that were challenged by Darwin's ideas. With what specific aspect of most religions does evolution most seriously conflict? (p. 258)

7 Specifically, what inferences on evolution did Darwin draw from his observations of the mara? (pp. 259–260)

8 What was Darwin challenging when he came to believe that chance was responsible for much of what he observed? Explain. (p. 258)

9 Of what importance were the Galápagos finches to Darwin's emerging theory? (p. 261)

10 List several proposals about colonization that Darwin tested through experimentation. (p. 261)

11 In general, how does the fossil record support the concept of evolution? (p. 264)

12 Review highlights in the fossil history of the horse. What general adaptive trends do the fossils suggest? (pp. 264–265)

13 Briefly discuss the idea of punctuated equilibrium. What prompted its development? (p. 265)

14 What is there about the geographical distribution of animals that supports the idea of common ancestry? (p. 266)

15 Carefully distinguish between analogous and homologous structures. Which indicates common ancestry? (pp. 266–267)

16 Considering forelimb structure and function in the horse, bat, bird, and cat, why would anyone conclude that these animals have common ancestry? In what way do embryos provide help with this? (pp. 266–267)

17 Considering, again, the limb structure of various vertebrates, what might the limbs of the common ancestor of today's vertebrates have looked like? (pp. 266–267)

18 What is a vestigial organ? How do such organs support the idea of evolution? (p. 267)

19 What is DNA or amino acid sequencing about? How might such sequences provide clues to past evolutionary events? (pp. 267–269)

Living things reproduce; at least living things today are the offspring of predecessors that reproduced, and among those offspring we will always find variation. Look your little brother directly in the eye and you might develop a new appreciation for this principle. Biologically, the differences between you and him may be your parents' way of ensuring that at least one of you will be able to cope with the unpredictable world in which you find yourselves. One of you is simply likely to be more suited than the other to whatever environment might arise. But keep in mind that there are biological implications of the differences between you and him. For instance, your little brother's close-set eyes, receding chin, prominent brow, sloping forehead, and the tendency to snort may interfere with his success in the world of fraternities. But his unusually long arms may prove beneficial if things should change so that climbing and throwing became more important. The prevailing environment, then, can "select," or favor, the traits of one of you over the other. The process, as described in the last chapter, is called **natural selection.** It is distinguished from **artificial selection,** the process by which a breeder chooses which traits to perpetuate in his stock. A cattle rancher, for example, might wish to breed only those cows that yield more beef (Figure 18.1).

In *The Origin of Species,* Charles Darwin used the example of artificial selection as an analogy to natural selection. Even though artificial selection involves human intervention and often human whim, it certainly shows how radically the phenotype can be altered in a short time.

THE POPULATION AND HOW IT EVOLVES

Evolution is defined as descent with modification. It involves the principle that *genes* evolve: that is, they persist and yet their frequencies* in the population change. But we should keep in mind that *populations* also evolve. That is, the characteristics of a population change over time, usually for the good. And, of course, *species* evolve. These are referred to as **levels of evolution.** Here we will be concerned with evolution at the population level.

*The term *frequency*, which is fundamental to population genetics, refers to a proportion or fraction of the *whole*. Accordingly, frequencies are expressed in numbers 0 through 1 only. For example, if there are 40,000 people in a town and 10,000 refuse to eat meat, the frequency of vegetarians will be 10,000/40,000 (or ¼, or 0.25).

18

EVOLUTION IN POPULATIONS

FIGURE 18.1 Today's cattle are the result of generations of intense artificial selection. The longhorn *(left)* was a rangy beast, tough and well suited to the spare western grassland. It was very similar to its wild ancestors. The Hereford *(right)* is the result of breeding for maximum beef yield.

A **population** is a group of interbreeding individuals of a single species. All of the alleles found in such a population make up the **gene pool.** Most human gene pools today are complex and highly varied because of their size and because of the constant flow of new individuals in and out. However, even among humans, if the gene pool is small and new input is discouraged, variation is much more limited (Figure 18.2). As certain alleles in a population increase or decrease, the character of the gene pool changes. Such changes represent the first stirrings of evolution at work. We'll begin with a few fundamental ideas in **population genetics,** the study of allele behavior in populations.

The Hardy-Weinberg Law and Populations in Equilibrium

G. H. Hardy, an eminent mathematician, had few professional interests in common with R. C. Punnett, the young Mendelian geneticist, but they frequently met for lunch or tea at the faculty club of Cambridge University. One day in 1908 Punnett was telling his colleague about a small problem in genetics. Someone had noted that there was a rare dominant gene for abnormally short fingers, while the allele for normal fingers was recessive. In view of the famous 3:1 Mendelian ratio, shouldn't short fingers become more and more common with each generation, until no one in Britain had normal fingers at all? Punnett didn't think this argument was correct, but he couldn't explain why.

Hardy thought the problem was simple enough, and wrote a few equations on his napkin. He showed that the relative numbers of people with normal fingers and people with short fingers ought to stay the same for generation after generation, *as long as there were no outside forces—such as natural selection—to change them.*

Punnett was excited. He was amazed that his friend had solved so complex a puzzle so casually and wanted to have the idea published (on something besides a napkin) as soon as possible. But Hardy was reluctant. He felt that the idea was so simple and obvious that he didn't want to have his name associated with it and risk his reputation as one of the great mathematical minds of the day. But Punnett prevailed, and the relationship between genotypes and phenotypes in populations quickly became known as *Hardy's law.* As fate would have it, Hardy, who was indeed one of the great mathematical minds of the day, is now best known for his reluctant contribution to biology.

In Germany, Hardy's law was known as *Weinberg's law,* since it had been discovered independently by a German physician by that name. Weinberg, in fact, published his version within weeks of the publication of Hardy's short paper. Eventually the concept became known as the **Hardy-Weinberg law,** and it is now the basis of the population genetics of

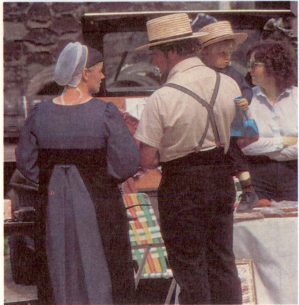

FIGURE 18.2 The degree of variability in a human population depends, to a great extent, on its size and whether new input is restricted. In the larger population, new members are constantly incorporated, adding their varied alleles to the gene pool. In smaller, more restricted populations, such as the Amish, membership from the outside is strongly discouraged. As a result, variability is limited and certain alleles may occur in much higher frequencies than is usual. For instance, in the general population, the frequency of the allele causing a rare form of dwarfism that affects just the lower legs and lower arms is only 1/1000, but among the Amish in Lancaster County, Pennsylvania, the frequency is 1/14.

sexual organisms. Later, it was discovered that both had been scooped by an American, W. E. Castle, who had published a neglected paper on the relationship in 1903. Some people now refer to the Castle, Hardy, Weinberg law, but we will follow convention and also neglect our compatriot for now.

> Hardy, Weinberg, and Castle showed mathematically that in the absence of outside influences, the frequency of an allele in the population will not change.

Genetic equilibrium: an implication of the Hardy-Weinberg principle. To rephrase the problem of the Mendelians, let's consider human eye color. Although the genetics of eye color isn't well understood (several gene loci are thought to be involved), we will ignore the complications and note that the allele for brown eyes is dominant over the allele for blue. So why are blue eyes still around?

From basic Mendelian genetics we know what happens in a cross between a homozygous blue-eyed person and a homozygous brown-eyed person. But in population genetics, we must consider not just one cross, but large numbers of matings and all their outcomes taken together. Imagine thousands of blue-eyed homozygotes (**bb**) mating with thousands of brown-eyed homozygotes (**BB**). The several thousand children resulting from such festivity will all be brown-eyed, since all the offspring will be **Bb** heterozygotes. Blue eyes have disappeared, as feared by the early Mendelians.

Now imagine that all these genetically identical F_1 heterozygotes grow up, choose mates, and manage to reproduce. Now it becomes apparent that the blue-eye alleles didn't disappear after all. In fact, about one fourth of their children will have blue eyes. Now if we let the F_2 generation grow up and choose mates, things start to get complicated.

But why? They weren't so complicated in Mendel's pea plants, which were entirely self-fertilizing. But humans are not self-fertilizing. And, despite songs and poems to the contrary, we can assume that people don't care all that much about blue or brown eyes, but will essentially mate at random in so far as eye color goes. So let's take a look at our F_2 generation. We find blue-eyed males, blue-eyed females, brown-eyed males, and brown-eyed females. And, in fact, there are two kinds of brown-eyed individuals of each sex—homozygotes and heterozygotes. We end up with six genetically distinct kinds of humans in our population: three genotypes of males and three genotypes of females. This means that there can now be *nine* kinds of matings.

We will let these types wander off into the sunset and begin pairing off. In due time the F_3 generation will appear. When we look them over we see that once again one-fourth of the children will be blue-eyed and three-fourths will be brown-eyed (Figure 18.3). And so it will continue for generation after generation.

We see, then, that the gene for blue eyes didn't disappear at all. What did happen? Since the heterozygotes harbored hidden blue-eyed genes, the actual frequency of the blue-eyed allele remained at 50%, just as at the start. The idea is, whether genes are expressed in homozygotes or hidden in heterozygotes, they are distinct physical entities that don't just go away without some reason. In the language of population genetics, eye color and the alleles for finger length are in **genetic equilibrium.** The crux of the Hardy-Weinberg law, then, is that barring selection or other biasing factors we will consider shortly, in randomly mating populations, allele frequencies do not change.

A population whose frequency of alleles remains the same for generation after generation is said to be in **genetic equilibrium.**

An Algebraic Equivalent

In the example above, the two alleles start out at the same frequency—half **B** and half **b.** The Hardy-Weinberg law also works in populations in which the alleles have different frequencies. For those burning with a fierce love of mathematics, let's put it into algebra. First, let p be the allele frequency of allele **B,** while q is the allele frequency of allele **b.** If there are only two of these alleles:

$$p + q = 1$$

The expression above—the frequency of alleles—can be expanded to take in the genotype frequencies. We do this by considering all possible ways in which the **B** and **b** alleles can combine in a population: Males have two kinds of alleles, **B** + **b,** and females have the same two kinds, **B** + **b,** so all of the possible matings can be represented as:

$$\mathbf{B} + \mathbf{b} \times \mathbf{B} + \mathbf{b}, \text{ or } (\mathbf{B} + \mathbf{b})^2$$
$$(\mathbf{B} + \mathbf{b})^2 = \mathbf{B}^2 + 2\mathbf{Bb} + \mathbf{b}^2$$

The expression, $p + q = 1$ represents the allele frequencies, translating to "the frequency of the dominant allele and the frequency of the recessive allele must add up to 1 (or all)."

FIGURE 18.3 Random mating in F_2 individuals where the genotypes are **BB, Bb,** and **bb,** and the phenotypic ratio is 1/4, 1/2, and 1/4, occurs in nine possible ways. The frequency of the two alleles was the same in the P_1, F_1 and F_2 generations. Is the frequency the same in the F_3 generation?

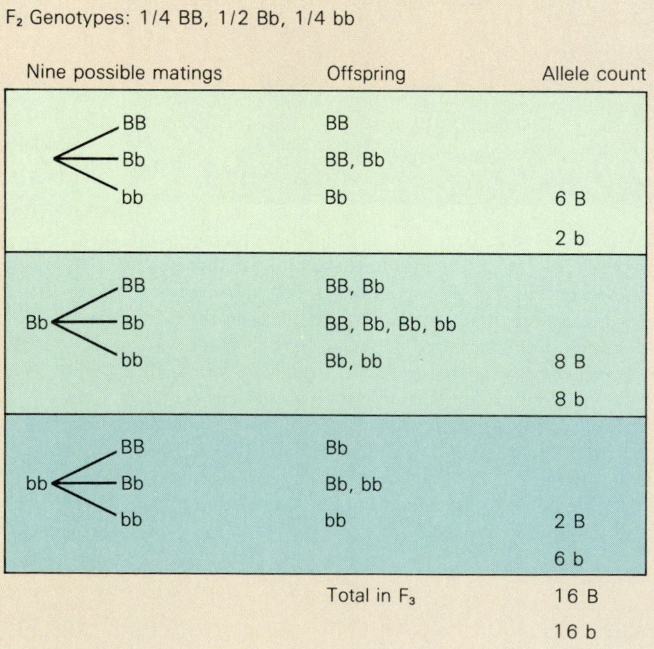

F₂ Genotypes: 1/4 BB, 1/2 Bb, 1/4 bb

Nine possible matings	Offspring	Allele count
BB → BB, Bb, bb	BB; BB, Bb; Bb	6 B; 2 b
Bb → BB, Bb, bb	BB, Bb; BB, Bb, Bb, bb; Bb, bb	8 B; 8 b
bb → BB, Bb, bb	Bb; Bb, bb; bb	2 B; 6 b
Total in F₃		16 B; 16 b

This might be more familiar to you if we expressed it as **BB + 2Bb + bb.** Actually, expressing the genotype frequencies this way is appropriate only when the alleles have the same frequency. In actual population studies, this is highly unlikely. So let's return to our use of p and q, letters that represent, respectively, the actual frequency of the dominant and recessive allele:

$$p + q = 1 \text{ (all alleles)}$$

or,

$$(p + q)^2 = 1 \text{ (all matings)}$$

and, finally

$$p^2 + 2pq + q^2 = 1 \text{ (all genotypes)}.$$

The latter expression is often called the Hardy-Weinberg formula.

The Hardy-Weinberg formula tells us that we can find the frequency (proportion) of the homozygous dominant individuals in a population by squaring the frequency of the dominant allele (p).

Similarly, we can find the frequency of the recessive individuals by squaring the frequency of the recessive allele (q).

Finding the frequency or proportion of heterozygotes is a little different. To do this, we multiply the frequency of the dominant and recessive alleles and then multiply that answer by 2. (If you have forgotten where the 2 comes from, see Essay 11.1.)

All of this begins to make considerably more sense when the Hardy-Weinberg formula is applied to real life examples, so let's have a look at albinism in human populations.

> The expression, $p^2 + 2pq + q^2 = 1$ represents genotype frequencies, translating to: "the frequency of the dominant individuals plus that of the heterozygotes and the recessive individuals must add up to 1 (or all)."

Albinism: people and the algebraic equivalent. The Hardy-Weinberg law is not just a mathematical exercise. It has implications that could affect such diverse areas as politics, law, and sociology. For example, if we know the prevalence in the population of persons affected with a recessive condition such as albinism—the absence of normal melanin pigment (Figure 18.4)—we can predict, within limits, the probability that a normal couple will have an albino baby. Here's how this would work. Normal skin and eye pigment in humans is dominant over the albino condition; thus albinism is associated with a recessive allele, **a.** Normal pigmentation is associated with the

FIGURE 18.4 In homozygous individuals the recessive alleles for albinism reveal themselves through the absence of colored pigments in the hair, skin, and eyes.

corresponding dominant allele **A.** The homozygous recessive genotype (**aa**) occurs in about one of every 20,000 people. According to the Hardy-Weinberg law, this frequency would be given by q^2, so

$$q^2 = 1/20,000.$$

The frequency of the allele **a** has to be the square root of this, or:

$$q = \sqrt{1/20,000} = 1/141.$$

The frequency of the dominant allele **A** would then be $p = 1 - q$, or

$$p = 1 - 1/141 = 140/141.$$

The heterozygous condition **Aa** would occur in the population with a frequency of $2pq$:

$$2pq = 2 \times 140/141 \times 1/141 = 1/70,$$

or about 1.4%. Therefore, about one person in 70 is a *carrier* for this fairly rare condition. Since 1/70 of 20,000 is 280, about 280 people are heterozygous carriers (**Aa**) for every homozygous, affected albino (**aa**).

Earlier we asked about the chances of a normal couple having an albino baby. In this population the chances are 1 out of 19,600. We determine this by first recognizing that the man and woman must both be heterozygous, and secondly, by applying the multiplicative law (see Essay 11.1). The chances of getting heterozygotes together in our randomly mating population is 1/70 times 1/70, or 1/4900. Since the probability of such a mating (**Aa** × **Aa**) producing an albino child (**aa**) is 1/4, we must multiply again: 1/4900 × 1/4 = 1/19,600.

We might note that there are actually several different kinds of albinism, due to different mutant alleles at different gene loci. That makes this kind of analysis very difficult unless the initial diagnosis is completely accurate; for the Hardy-Weinberg law to be of use, only one gene locus at a time can be considered.

> **O**nce the proportion of homozygous recessive individuals is known, all of the values of the Hardy-Weinberg formula (p, q, p^2, $2pq$, and q^2) can be derived.

A closer look at the model. If it has occurred to you that mathematical models are often a little short on realism, you're right. In fact, the Hardy-Weinberg law has a number of stringent restrictions:

1. Mating must be completely random.
2. There can be no migration either into or out of the population.
3. The alleles in question must segregate according to Mendel's first law. This eliminates, for example, sex-linked alleles.
4. The simple model applies only to loci that have two alleles (or two classes of alleles). (If multiple alleles are under consideration, more complex forms of the Hardy-Weinberg law must be used.)
5. The model is valid only within single, interbreeding populations.
6. The expectations are exact only if the population and the sample are infinitely large.

Of these restrictions, the last is the least realistic, since no populations and no samples are infinitely large. But statisticians are willing to assume that smaller samples are representative of an infinite population.

Obviously, it's easy to violate the assumptions of the Hardy-Weinberg law. So is it of any real use? What happens when the assumptions of the Hardy-Weinberg law are violated? For many purposes, the Hardy-Weinberg predictions are the most useful when they don't come true. There are many conditions in natural populations that will give rise to departures from Hardy-Weinberg expectations. These departures themselves are interesting and can sometimes tell us such things as how much mutation, natural selection, or plain random change may be going on. These, of course, are the primary forces of evolution. The only way evolution can proceed is through such events; thus a population *out of equilibrium* is immediately interesting.

Looking at the population from a much broader perspective, let's note that the gene pool is the reservoir of genetic information of any population. This pool, though, should not be likened to a still pond. Its apparent stillness is deceptive; these waters change. As some flows over the dam to be lost, new genetic waters join the pool through myriad tributaries. The point is that although some gene pools change slowly and others change rapidly, they do change. Let's see now how the gene frequencies in such a pool can change and what this means in the evolution of living things.

There are three major forces that can change gene frequencies: **natural selection, mutation,** and **genetic drift.** None of these forces acts alone, but together they direct the course of evolution.

> **H**ardy-Weinberg model populations require a fully random mix of alleles as the population reproduces. Populations subjected to natural selection *do not* meet this expectation.

NATURAL SELECTION

Natural selection can act in rather extreme ways, as in the case of certain **lethal** alleles. Lethal genes can kill you outright. Thus, the death removes the individual (and the allele) from the gene pool. Let's consider an unusual implication of this seemingly straightforward effect—the case of the Manx cats.

Lethal Alleles and Manx Cats

Manx cats are peculiar animals, having rather large hind legs and practically no tails. No one has ever been able to develop a strain of true-breeding Manx cats for the simple reason that the tail-less animals are all heterozygotes. Normal cats, with tails, are **TT** homozygotes; Manx cats without tails, are **TM** heterozygotes. The problem is, the homozygous **MM** genotype is an embryonic lethal; that is, these cats die while still embryos. So already we see a strange thing. The **M** allele is dominant for one trait, and recessive for another. It is dominant for the absence of a tail, and it is recessive for the absence of a kitten. So when two Manx **TM** cats mate, 1/4 of the offspring will be normal cats, 1/2 will be Manx cats, and 1/4 will be dead cats. The dead ones are reabsorbed by the mother's body as embryos, so the only litter you would see from such a cross would be 2/3 **TM** Manx and 1/3 **TT** alleycat:

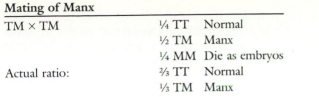

Mating of Manx			
TM × TM		¼ TT	Normal
		½ TM	Manx
		¼ MM	Die as embryos
Actual ratio:		⅔ TT	Normal
		⅓ TM	Manx

Now suppose that someone should populate a remote island with a shipload of Manx cats, turning them loose to run wild, yowling and scratching and mating randomly, in the fashion of cats. What would happen? We know that the frequency of the Manx allele, **M,** starts out at $q = 1/2$. But then we find that, in one generation, it is reduced to $q = 1/3$. What happens then? With random mating, the third generation of *zygotes* will be $p^2 = 4/9$ **TT**, $2pq = 4/9$ **TM** (Manx), and $q^2 = 1/9$ **MM** homozygous lethal.

But when the recessive homozygotes are removed by natural selection, 1/2 of the remaining cats are now Manx and 1/2 are alleycats. The frequency of the recessive lethal **M** allele has gone from 1/2 to 1/3 to 1/4 in three generations, and in succeeding generations it will fall further to 1/5, 1/6, and so on. Meanwhile, the proportion of homozygous lethal **MM** zygotes will also follow the Hardy-Weinberg distribution: 1/4, 1/9, 1/16, 1/25, 1/36, and so on. As you can imagine, Manx cats will become increasingly rare on our fair island. On the other hand, the severe selection against the **M** allele will diminish. Figure 18.5 plots the course of the genotypes over 70 generations. Note that the allele frequency of **M** has fallen to 1.37% by the end of the 70 generations, and that about 2.8% of the cats will then be Manx. It would take another 70 generations to bring the recessive allele frequency down to 0.7%.

Selection doesn't have to be so severe, of course. As a general rule, the rate of change in allele frequency in a population is proportional to the amount of selection against some genotype. For instance, in the case of Manx cats, suppose that the recessive genotype **MM** wasn't lethal, but merely reduced the individual cat's reproductive ability by 1/10. Then it would take 700 generations, rather than 70, to go from $q = 50\%$ to $q = 1.37\%$.

You might wonder why there are any Manx cats at all. It's because people tend to be impressed by anything bizarre in cats, and they are likely to keep Manx kittens while disposing of the alley-kittens. So artificial selection keeps the Manx gene going. Let's go to the real world now to consider a case of natural selection operating in nature, the classic case of the peppered moth.

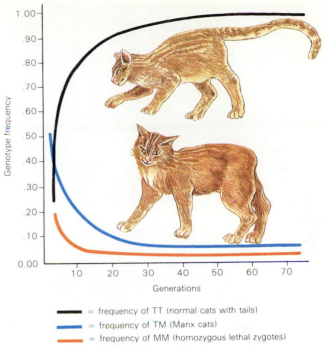

= frequency of TT (normal cats with tails)
= frequency of TM (Manx cats)
= frequency of MM (homozygous lethal zygotes)

FIGURE 18.5 Where lethal alleles are involved, selection is extremely strong at first, but as the frequency of the lethal allele decreases, it slows considerably. Why doesn't the Manx tailless allele simply disappear from a wild population?

Selection against harmful or **lethal** alleles is extremely strong at first, but rapidly decreases as the allele frequency falls.

Natural Selection in a Changing Environment: The Peppered Moth

The British peppered moth, *Biston betularia,* occurs in two forms, or **morphs** (Figure 18.6). One morph is light and mottled (or peppered), and the other is black. The British, who have a long tradition of collecting butterflies and moths, have kept excellent records on the peppered moth for two centuries. The black morph, whose color is controlled primarily by a single dominant gene, originally showed up in 18th-century collections as a rare, highly prized variant, or mutant.

In the early days of the industrial revolution (in the 1840s), the black morph began to appear more and more often, especially near cities. In fact, the black morph became so common in industrialized areas that it eventually outnumbered the light peppered morph. (In Manchester, England's industrial

FIGURE 18.6 In the absence of soot from industry, the light speckled variety of peppered moth is well concealed from predators, while its black counterpart is easily seen. But in the sooty environment the opposite is true.

center, the black morph came to comprise 98% of the population.) Meanwhile, the light peppered morph remained the predominant form in rural areas.

What had happened? It seemed clear that the species was adapting to some environmental change. That change was due to the burning of coal in the factories of heavy industry. Industrial England in the 19th century was quietly submitting to a dark cloak of carbon. As the countryside darkened and the mottled lichens began to disappear from the bark of trees, the frequency of the black morph increased in the population. It was hypothesized that this was because the black ones were harder for predatory birds to see against the soot, while the lighter, mottled individuals stood out in sharp contrast and were quickly taken.

From the historical data, J.B.S. Haldane calculated that the black morph survived and reproduced twice as well as the mottled in the industrial environment. A British naturalist, H.B.D. Kettlewell, performed the crucial experiment that validated the hypothesis. Kettlewell released known numbers of marked black and light peppered moths in unpolluted woodlands and two similar groups in polluted, soot-blackened woodlands. Later, he recaptured a portion of the released moths. The following are some of Kettlewell's mark-and-recapture data:

Dorset, England (unpolluted woodland)	Light morph	Black morph
Marked and released	496	473
Recaptured	62	30
Percentage recaptured	12.5%	6.3%
Relative survival	1.00	0.507

Birmingham, England (soot-blackened woodland)	Light morph	Black morph
Marked and released	137	447
Recaptured later	18	123
Percentage recaptured	13.1%	27.5%
Relative survival	0.477	1.00

In the first set of moths, released in the unpolluted woodland, twice as many light forms survived as black forms. In the second set, selection favored the black morph and acted against the light morph. About twice as great a percentage of the favored black type survived long enough to be recaptured.

Incidentally, England has been doing rather well lately in its battle against pollution. The woodlands near the cities are once again becoming covered with lichens and the soot is disappearing. And, as one might predict, the black morphs of *Biston betularia* are becoming scarce again.

Natural selection was observed in populations of peppered moths in which the frequency of those with coloration more closely mimicking their background increased.

Polygenic Inheritance and Natural Selection

The stories of the Manx cats on imaginary islands and peppered moths in polluted woodlands are instructive, but their simplicity can also be misleading. To be sure, evolution does proceed sometimes by the rapid sweep of a dramatically advantageous allele through a population. But most of the genetic differences between individuals in a population are not caused by a few genes with great effects, but by numerous genes with small, individual effects. A trait controlled by more than one gene is said to be under the influence of **polygenic inheritance** (see Chapter 12).

Many traits—such as height, weight, blood pressure, length of limbs, skin color, and swiftness of foot—are largely controlled by the cumulative action of many different gene loci, each gene with a vanishingly small effect. The cumulative effect of polygenic inheritance on the phenotypic variation in a population is enormous, and it is on this sort of variation that natural selection usually works.

Patterns of Natural Selection

The individual gene obediently follows Mendel's rules, but there are so many effects of gene interaction and other complications that the response of a population to natural selection is not simply one of allele increase and replacement. Let's take a look at how natural selection works with such continuous and graded traits. To approach this problem, we should first be aware that most individuals will be about average for most traits. Thus, for any given measurement, there will be relatively few individuals with extremely high or low values. If we group all of the individuals in a population according to a single trait, the resulting graph will almost always form a bell-shaped curve—the statistician's **normal distribution** (see Figure 12.5). In considering the effects of natural selection, the question is, how do the individuals in the middle of the distribution thrive compared with those on either extreme? Depending on how they fare, we can find three trends: **directional selection, stabilizing selection,** and **disruptive selection** (Figure 18.7).

FIGURE 18.7 **(a)** Stabilizing selection for a trait maintains a cluster about the mean. The shape of the bell-shaped curve resulting depends on the strength of selection for the mean. **(b)** In directional selection, the mean shifts to the right or left, and some alleles become scarce and others more common. **(c)** Disruptive selection can result in the two extremes in phenotypic expression being emphasized in a population.

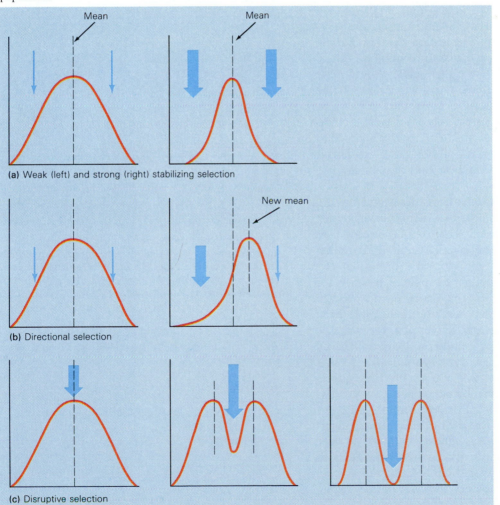

(a) Weak (left) and strong (right) stabilizing selection

(b) Directional selection

(c) Disruptive selection

Directional selection. Directional selection favors one extreme of the phenotypic range—one end of the curve. This is the kind of selection practiced by dairy breeders who want only the offspring of the cows that give the most milk. In nature, directional selection may be a response to a change in the environment that begins to favor individuals at one extreme. For example, a population may find itself in an unfamiliar territory, a new place offering new challenges. Or the species may suddenly lose a competitor and have new food sources open to it. In such cases, the formerly aberrant individuals at one end of a curve may be better adapted to the new conditions than are those at the center of the curve. Their previously unfavored traits may then become the new optimum. Subsequent evolution can be rapid, as the population quickly adapts to its new environmental demands. The peppered moth story, discussed earlier, is an excellent example of directional selection at work. Also, the early evolution of giraffes represents a classic case of directional selection, as shown in Figure 18.8.

Stabilizing selection. Stabilizing selection usually is associated with a population that has become well adapted to its particular surroundings. These surroundings usually are rather stable. Any genetic change in the population, therefore, is likely to be harmful. Although genetic variability still exists, selection tends to favor the mean, or average, individual. Because most populations are well adapted to their environments most of the time, stabilizing selection is the most common kind of natural selection.

Consider the giraffe. As far as necks and legs go, giraffes are now well adapted to their environment and are no longer subject to directional selection. In fact, they haven't changed much at all in 20 million years.

Perhaps the best-studied example of selection for an intermediate condition is that of birth weight in human babies. The data are readily available from hospital obstetric wards. If we plot survival rate against birth weight, we find that abnormally small babies have relatively low rates of survival, a fact that is not too surprising. But abnormally large babies also have lower survival rates (Figure 18.9). The highest survival rate is for babies around 3.4 kg (7.4 lb). In this case, the *optimal* birth weight (as determined by survival rate) is almost exactly the *average* birth weight. Selection works against genes for both high and low birth weight. In essence, the average tends to be the best, and "survival of the fittest" becomes "survival of the most mediocre."

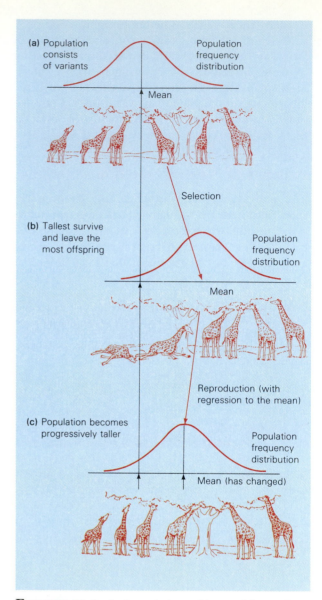

FIGURE 18.8 In the evolutionary history of the giraffe, an animal that browses on tall trees, height has been the critical factor. Among the antelope-like ancestors **(a)** height was variable, but as competition for the foliage increased **(b)**, natural selection began to favor taller individuals that could reach the still-untapped resources of the trees. (Natural selection was probably favoring taller trees as well.) As we see, the mean shifted. The taller individual survived, leaving the most offspring. **(c)** The offspring of the survivors tend to resemble their successful parents, although there is some regression to the mean. The average height increases over the course of one generation (exaggerated here). Over many generations, giraffes become taller and taller. (And so, incidentally, do the trees, as only the tallest trees escape defoliation by giraffes.)

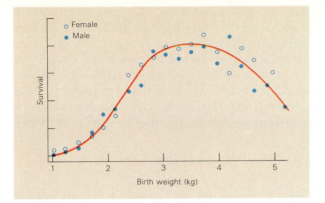

FIGURE 18.9 Plotting the survival rate of babies of different birth weight clearly indicates that there is an optimal weight of about 2.7 to 3.8 kg (6 to 8 lb).

FIGURE 18.10 Plotting the range of body weights for male and female elephant seals produces a decidedly bimodal curve.

Disruptive selection. In disruptive selection the intermediate types are selected against, and those at the extremes are favored. In this way, disruptive selection produces a *bimodal* (or two-humped) distribution curve. For example, it may be advantageous for males to be large and females to be small, as is the case in elephant seals (Figure 18.10). In such a situation, individuals of intermediate sizes would be weeded out of the population. That is, selection would not favor very small males and very large females. When bimodality results from differences in the sexes, the condition is called **sexual dimorphism.** If females tended to mate with the larger males, there would be a tendency for males to increase in size. The disparity of size, then, would be partly due to sexual selection, a form of natural selection operating through mate choice.

Directional selection favors individuals at one extreme of a continuous distribution of phenotypes, while **stabilizing selection** favors the average and status quo; **disruptive selection** favors the extreme phenotypes and selects against the average or intermediate phenotypes.

MUTATION: THE RAW MATERIAL OF EVOLUTION

If the environment is to select the "best" individuals from a population, the group must be variable. Variation implies inequality, and some individuals will simply have advantages over others. The question is,

how does this variation arise? Variation can arise in a number of ways such as through meiosis, crossing over, and the chance combination of gametes. This sort of variation, however, involves the shuffling of genes already present in the gene pool. So how do new *kinds* of genes arise? Even the best gamblers must draw new cards. In living things, gambling through evolution, new kinds of genes must arise from mutation, the random alteration of DNA. Earlier we saw how mutations arise through rare, unrepaired changes in base sequences and through chromosome breakage and rejoining. Let's find what happens to those mutations after they appear in the gene pool of populations.

Although meiosis and sexual reproduction introduce new combinations of existing genes, mutation is the source of new alleles and thus, new variation.

Mutation Rates: The Constant Input of New Information

Any given gene in a population is bound to mutate at one time or another. In fact, each gene undergoes mutation in a statistically regular and predictable manner, producing a constant and measurable input of new genetic information into the gene pool. The emphasis here is on the term *constant:* each specific gene mutation occurs at its own detectable rate. *Typically,* mutations arise at the rate of one per gene locus per 100,000 gametes. The range in humans, according to some authorities, is from 0.1 to 10 per 100,000 gametes. With this constant input of new genetic material, why do gene pools remain so stable? The reason is that each new mutation is tested by natural selection. A few are retained; most are discarded.

Balance Between Mutation and Selection

Any gene bearing a mutation that has an immediate beneficial effect can expect to rapidly increase in a population. However, as we have emphasized before, such changes are extremely rare. After all, our genes work remarkably well and most mutations can't be expected to make a gene work better than it did before. Most changes will have the opposite effect. It's as though you raised the hood on your new Mercedes and let your neighbor's kid randomly bang the internal workings with a hammer. He may make precisely the adjustment needed to make the car run better; all in all, though, you may not want to take the chance.

The point is, most mutations are harmful or at best neutral (neither harmful nor helpful). By definition, a mutation is harmful if it decreases the reproductive success of an individual. In some cases the effect is subtle, with the mutation causing a slight decrease in reproductive output; in other cases the effect may be more dramatic with total reproductive failure. Interestingly, the most harmful mutations may go undetected. It has been estimated that one third to one half of all human zygotes fail to develop because they bear such deleterious mutations. The potential parents are usually quite unaware that anything untoward has happened. The lethal gene carries the newly formed embryo into oblivion, its delicate tissues simply absorbed by the mother's body. Such lethal mutations are virtually impossible to detect in human populations, but they can be counted accurately in such experimental organisms as yeasts and fruit flies.

> **B**ecause most organisms are well adapted to their environment, very few mutations are actually helpful.

It is important to realize that, genetically, a mutation that proves lethal at the embryonic stage will have about the same effect on its bearer as a mutation that allows him to be born but kills him before he reproduces, or one that renders him sterile. That person's genes are not passed along; they die with him.

So although lethal alleles are constantly fed into the gene pool by mutation, they remain rare because they are not passed along. However, if the mutant allele is only *partially* limiting in its effect, and the afflicted individuals reproduce but at a reduced level, then the mutant form may become more common. From the known frequencies of recessive genetic diseases, it can be calculated that the average person carries about seven recessive alleles for serious genetic diseases.

Mutation and Natural Selection in Humans

The easiest mutations to study, of course, are those dominant mutations that cause *visible* changes. An invisible change might be an alteration in some enzyme that had little or no effect. One example of a visible change, a peculiar type of human dwarfism known as achondroplasia, occurs in one out of about 12,000 births to normal parents (Figure 18.11). In achondroplasia, the person's head and trunk are of normal dimensions, but the arms and legs are stunted or fail to grow at all. Since the condition is dominant, each new incident represents a newly mutated gene; the mutation for achondroplasia is one per 24,000 gametes. When achondroplastic dwarfs mate with normal individuals, about half of their children are afflicted by the condition.

Consider this: with an average mutation rate of about one mutation per gene locus per 100,000 gametes, and with an estimated 40,000 to 50,000 gene pairs per human zygote, *everyone* is likely to be carrying a newly arising mutation. The beneficial or neutral mutations, of course, will readily be passed on. If the mutation is harmful it is more likely to be transmitted if its effects are minor. Some of the more common of less-than-ideal genetic conditions are nuisances such as missing teeth, dental malocclusion, near-sightedness, and deviated nasal septum.

But, as we've just seen, some genetic conditions are severe. To achondroplasia we can add hemophilia, albinism, sickle cell anemia, and phenylketonuria, all discussed in earlier chapters. To these add schizophrenia, manic-depressive syndrome, early-onset diabetes, hereditary deafness, cystic fibrosis, Tay-Sachs disease, and thousands of other known genetic disorders. In spite of such devastating potential, however, you should remember that mutation is one of the reasons you are not an amoeba—or, for that matter, a random collection of carbon dioxide, hydrogen, and mud.

> **S**tatistics suggests that all humans are likely to carry a newly formed mutation.

FIGURE 18.11 Since achondroplasia (a form of dwarfism) is dominant in humans, its occurrence in a family with normal parents represents a new mutation in the father or mother. (*Milwaukee Journal* Photo.)

Human intervention and our genetic future. This brings us to a philosophical and moral question about genetic variation in future human populations. The question inevitably arises: If better medical and social care saves the lives of persons with adverse genetic conditions, thus allowing them to reproduce, what is to become of us?

It's not hard to find examples that illustrate the problem. One genetic condition, pyloric stenosis, an abnormal overgrowth of a stomach valve muscle, was once invariably fatal in infancy. Since the 1920s a simple surgical procedure has saved the lives of nearly all affected infants in developed countries. But about half of the offspring of the saved people are also affected, and they also need surgery. Since there are just as many new mutations as ever, the condition constantly appears anew; therefore, the genes that cause it have actually increased in frequency. Where will our species be in 10,000 years?

What has happened, in effect, is that a *severe* genetic condition—which 60 years ago meant certain death in infancy by intestinal obstruction—has been transformed to a relatively *mild* genetic condition that can be readily corrected surgically. Suppose that the remaining risk of the condition, including possible delayed diagnosis and surgical mishap, are such that now about one affected infant in 20 fails to survive. The mutant genes for the condition will continue to increase until, many millenia from now, there will be exactly 20 times as many affected individuals as there were before the operation was developed. In the meantime, many lives will have been saved, and many new people—with slightly aberrant genotypes—will have joined the human population. Is that good or bad?

This sort of thing has already happened repeatedly in a variety of cultures. For example, in primitive hunting and gathering tribes, myopia (nearsightedness) must be a nearly lethal condition. Presumably, nearsighted aborigines can't even find roots and berries efficiently, let alone a zebra. But long before the invention of corrective lenses, the stable social conditions that came with villages and agriculture allowed myopics to survive. In some cases they may have even benefited. For example, male myopics would have been of no value in hunting or in war, and might have stayed safely home to make tools, weave baskets, tell stories, and help the women around the hut. In any case, myopia is much more common among people with a long history of agriculture, writing, and urban civilization than among groups that have more recently given up nomadism or the hunting-gathering life. American Indians and American blacks are blessed with much better visual acuity, on the average, than are Americans of European or Oriental ancestry.

> **N**atural selection may operate differently in humans because of an ability to intervene and preserve alleles normally selected against.

GENETIC DRIFT

Genetic drift refers to *random* changes in gene frequency, when certain genes accumulate by chance—not because of the effects of selection. The phenomenon is seen most easily in small populations. For example, should some catastrophe, such as a flood or a plague, suddenly wipe out most of a population, the survivors would then begin to reproduce. Just by chance, however, the presence of certain alleles and the frequency of others in this small population might be different from that of the former, larger group. In the jargon of genetics, the population would have gone through a **bottleneck** (a brief period in which a population becomes drastically reduced, causing a random change in gene frequencies). The harmful alleles, which were once rare, may now be not so rare. Similarly, if a few individuals stray out of their normal habitat and establish a successful colony in a new place, any rare genes they happen to carry would become common among their descendants. This special kind of bottleneck is referred to as the **founder effect** (the genetic effect of the chance assortment of a few individuals from a larger population).

There are many examples of genetic bottlenecks and founder effects in human history. The Afrikaaners of South Africa are all descended from some thirty 17th-century families (Figure 18.12). (Remember, all humans carry their share of harmful, recessive genes, but they are seldom expressed in homozygotes.) The Afrikaaners' genes, having gone through a bottleneck of only 30 families, cause present-day Afrikaaners to suffer from a unique set of recurrent, recessive genetic diseases that are seldom seen in other populations. Among these is a version of porphyria, a metabolic disease that results in liver damage and bright red urine. Conversely, Afrikaaners are almost completely free of other recessive genetic diseases. The 30 families obviously did not carry those genes to Africa. Similarly, Jews of Eastern European ancestry harbor a different but equally distinctive array of recessive genetic diseases, one of which is the tragic Tay-Sachs disease—an enzyme deficiency that leads to blindness, mental deterioration, and death in infants. These high gene frequencies can be taken as circumstantial evidence for one or more population bottlenecks in the history of this group.

Genetic drift is evolutionary change brought about by chance events: random, unselected changes in allele frequencies.

Neutralism: A Different View of Evolution

We've built a strong case for natural selection as *the* molding force of evolution, and most biologists would agree with this position. We have seen, however, that evolutionary change can occur in the absence of selection, as in the Afrikaaners and in the Eastern European Jews. In these cases, genetic change exists that is clearly nonadaptive. Other genetic changes may be neither harmful nor beneficial, but completely neutral with regard to natural selection. The question of just how significant nonselective evolution is has led to raging arguments. In recent years, there has been some controversy over to what degree natural variation is due to **neutral mutations** and **random drift. Neutralists** say that much variation on the molecular level is simply incidental and nonadaptive. For example, there are frequently several slightly different forms of any enzyme in a population. These enormous molecules may differ from each other by only one or two amino acids. Neutralists hold that most of this kind of variation has no effect on the function of the enzyme. They believe that the responsible alleles are equivalent and appear by chance mutation, and that the allele frequencies "drift" meaninglessly. **Selectionists,** on the other hand, contend that virtually all variation is caused by natural selection and has some adaptive basis, even if we don't happen to know what it is.

FIGURE 18.12 Afrikaaners, the hardy decendants of 30 original European families that colonized South Africa, represent a population that has experienced a genetic bottleneck.

SUMMARY

THE POPULATION AND HOW IT EVOLVES

Evolution can be thought of as occurring at three levels: the gene, the population, and the species. A population is an interbreeding group whose alleles make up the total gene pool.

The Hardy-Weinberg Law and Populations in Equilibrium

The Hardy-Weinberg law, developed independently by Hardy, Weinberg, and Castle, proposes that if mating in a population is random and there is an absence of selective forces, the frequency of dominant and recessive alleles will remain constant. This explains why recessive traits do not simply disappear, swamped as it were, by dominants. It further relates to the fact that alleles are physical entities. Alleles in such instances are in genetic equilibrium.

An Algebraic Equivalent

In the example of brown and blue eyes in a population where the frequency of **B** and **b** are equal, all the matings taken collectively can be represented as $(\mathbf{B} + \mathbf{b})^2$ or $\mathbf{B}^2 + 2\mathbf{Bb} + \mathbf{b}^2$.

Since allele frequencies are rarely equal, the dominants and recessives can be represented as p and q. Thus all the alleles in the gene pool are represented by $p + q = 1$, and all possible matings by $(p + q)^2 = 1$. In the expanded form this becomes $p^2 + 2pq + q^2$, the Hardy-Weinberg formula.

By using an example in which recessive individuals make up 4% (0.04) of a population, the allele and genotype frequencies can be determined as follows:

1. The recessives or $q^2 = 0.04$. To find q, take the square root: $q = \sqrt{0.04} = 0.2$.
2. Next, find p. Since $p + q = 1$, and $q = 0.2$, p is found by subtracting q from 1, or $1 - q = p$; that is, $1 - 0.2 = 0.8$.
3. Substituting the values of p and q in the Hardy-Weinberg formula will provide the genotype frequencies, p^2 and $2pq$.

For alleles to be in genetic equilibrium the following restrictions apply:

1. Random mating
2. Alleles of the simple Mendelian alternatives
3. Interbreeding population with no individuals entering or leaving
4. An infinitely large population and sample size

In reality, most alleles are not in genetic equilibrium, and most gene pools are changing. Three forces affecting allele frequencies are natural selection, mutation, and genetic drift.

NATURAL SELECTION

Lethal Alleles and Manx Cats

In the Manx cat example, cats with normal tails, **TT**, and Manx, **TM**, survive, while the homozygous Manx, **MM**, dies as an embryo. Thus in an interbreeding popula-

tion of Manx cats, the M allele is subject to strong negative selection. Selection eventually eases off, simply because the chances of an MM combination become minute. In all but lethal alleles, selection is much less severe.

Natural Selection in a Changing Environment: The Peppered Moth

A classic study of natural selection involved the light and dark morphs of the peppered moth, *Biston betularia*. In the past years, soot from coal burning in England's industrial centers blackened tree trunks in nearby forests. The dark coloring hid the dark morph from bird predators, but it exposed the light morph, whose numbers dwindled. It was determined that natural selection was at work when comparative studies involving the release and recapture of the two morphs in both sooty and clean forests were made.

Polygenic Inheritance and Natural Selection

Since most traits are polygenic (the product of many genes), when the genotypes are plotted, they form a continuous distribution.

Patterns of Natural Selection

The distribution of phenotypes can be analyzed for trends in natural selection. Three such trends are directional, stabilizing, and disruptive selection.

In directional selection, individuals at one end of the spectrum are favored; thus a less common phenotype becomes the new average phenotype. In stabilizing selection the average phenotype is most favored, and selection is against the extremes. Disruptive selection occurs when the conditions affecting a population change from one extreme to another; thus different phenotypes may be favored, and the distribution becomes discontinuous. The favored phenotypes may even form a bimodal distribution, as happens in species where sexual dimorphism (male and female differences) are favored.

MUTATION: THE RAW MATERIAL OF EVOLUTION

New variation arises through mutation, genetic change brought about by random changes in base sequences in DNA, and through chromosome rearrangement.

Mutation Rates: The Constant Input of New Information

Typical mutation rates are one per gene locus per 100,000 gametes. Most are quickly selected out by natural selection.

Balance Between Mutation and Selection

Most mutations are harmful or neutral; few are helpful. While the frequency of helpful mutations tends to increase, that of harmful mutations decreases. The rate of decrease depends on how strongly they affect reproduction. Each human carries about seven recessive alleles for serious genetic diseases.

Mutations and Natural Selection in Humans

Dominant genetic abnormalities, such as achondroplasia (dwarfism), provide evidence of ongoing, constant mutation. Unlike a recessive abnormality, it cannot be hidden, so each appearance represents a new mutation. Less serious but continually arising mutations include those that cause missing teeth and nearsightedness. More serious examples include hemophilia, sickle cell anemia, diabetes, hereditary deafness, and Tay-Sachs disease.

In modern human societies the effects of natural selection are greatly moderated through medical intervention. Under primitive conditions the reproductive fitness of individuals with new harmful mutations would be decreased. Medical treatment not only assures the survival of such persons but also permits them to reproduce. Thus certain harmful alleles are likely to increase.

GENETIC DRIFT

Genetic drift refers to random changes in allele frequencies, changes not produced through natural selection. In the so-called bottleneck a population may suffer a drastic reduction wherein, just by chance, certain alleles may be reduced or lost and others increased. The same may happen through founder effect, where small groups establish colonies.

Neutralism: A Different View of Evolution

Neutralists attribute a significant amount of evolutionary change to mutations with neutral effects and to random drift. Although they do not discount natural selection as an important evolutionary force, they argue that most minor changes in alleles are simply meaningless drift.

KEY TERMS

natural selection	mutation	disruptive selection
artificial selection	genetic drift	sexual dimorphism
levels of evolution	lethal	bottleneck
population	morphs	founder effect
gene pool	polygenic inheritance	neutral mutation
population genetics	normal distribution	random drift
Hardy-Weinberg law	directional selection	neutralist
genetic equilibrium	stabilizing selection	selectionist

REVIEW QUESTIONS

1 Carefully define the terms *population, gene pool,* and *frequency.* (pp. 271–272)

2 Summarize the problem that vexed Punnett. What conclusion did Hardy reach when he applied his math skills to the problem? (p. 272)

3 From your knowledge of cells, explain why recessive alleles cannot simply disappear. (In reality, what are alleles?) (p. 274)

4 Basically, how does the approach of the population geneticist differ from that of the Mendelian geneticist? (pp. 273–274)

5 Briefly state a way to prove that in the absence of selection the frequency of recessive alleles remains constant. What term describes such stability? (pp. 273–274)

6 Briefly explain each of these three algebraic equations: $p + q = 1$, $(p + q)^2 = 1$, and $p^2 + 2pq + q^2$. What do the letters p and q represent? What does each expression actually represent in a population? What is another way of stating the number 1? (pp. 274–275)

7 How does one actually go about determining the value of q^2 in a real population? How would the number be expressed? (p. 275)

8 Consider a population in which 400 people have the recessive trait (a hypothetical one) hairless nostril (**hh**). The remainder, 9600 people, have normal, hairy nostrils (**HH** and **Hh**). What is the frequency of the hairless genotype? Find the frequency of each allele and the other two genotypes. (p. 275)

9 In a certain population, 36% cannot roll their tongues. People without this "talent" cannot produce tongue-rolling children, and children who can roll their tongues have at least one tongue-rolling parent. Is the trait dominant or recessive? How many heterozygotes might we expect in this population? (p. 275)

10 Find the genotype frequency of both kinds of dominant individuals (**RR** and **Rr**) in a population where the frequency of recessive Rh-negative individuals (**rr**) is 16%. (p. 275)

11 The term *random mating* has been used several times in this chapter. List as many of the attributes of random mating as you can. What effects might nonrandom mating have on alleles that are in equilibrium?

12 Since the Hardy-Weinberg concept has such stringent requirements, how can it be of any use to geneticists? (p. 276)

13 What do changes in allele frequencies indicate about a population? (p. 276)

14 Using the representative letters **T** and **M** carry out the cross between two Manx cats. State the expected phenotypic ratio. What ratio actually appears? How might this represent natural selection at work? (p. 276)

15 From a look at Figure 18.5, characterize the ongoing selection against the Manx allele, and in your own words explain what you see. (p. 277)

16 In the peppered moth story, what was the actual selective force? How did industrialization affect the fate of the dark morph? What happened after the curbs on air pollution became effective? (pp. 277–278)

17 In the absence of air pollution would the black morph be considered a lethal, sublethal, neutral, or helpful mutation? Explain. (pp. 277–278)

18 Using a simple graph, characterize directional selection. Relate this kind of selection to the peppered moth episode. (p. 280)

19 Giraffe neck-length is now believed to be under the influence of stabilizing selection. What does this mean? What condition might change this? (p. 280)

20 Under what geological conditions would one expect disruptive selection to occur? How might the loss of a major predator (say through bounty hunting) bring on disruptive selection? (p. 281)

21 Mutation aside for the moment, list several sources of genetic variation within a population. What limits this variation? Explain the statement, "Mutation is the raw material of natural selection." (p. 281)

22 What happens to most newly formed mutations? Why is this so? What obvious factor determines the strength of selection against an allele? (p. 282)

23 State the general mutation rate. Does this mean we all bear mutations? (p. 282)

24 How would you actually measure the effects of natural selection against a slightly harmful allele? What would you actually observe? In other words, what finally happens to the frequency of slightly harmful alleles? (p. 282)

25 Why would a recessive mutant allele persist more than a dominant mutant allele? Would such a dominant mutant allele disappear from a population? Explain your answer. (p. 282)

26 In what way does achondroplasia illustrate the regularity with which mutations occur? What is the chance that any human carries a harmful recessive mutant allele? (p. 282)

27 Briefly describe how humans overcome the usual effects of natural selection. How might this affect the human gene pool in generations to come? How might genetic engineering head off this effect? (p. 283)

28 Using bottleneck and founder effect as extreme examples, explain what genetic drift is about. (pp. 283–284)

29 What, according to the neutralist position, is the significance of genetic drift? At what level is drift most pronounced? (p. 284)

19

EVOLUTION AND THE ORIGIN OF SPECIES

One of the most interesting things about biology, and probably other sciences as well, is that although a great deal of attention is given to working out details, many of the larger, more basic questions remain unanswered. For example, some biologists may peer endlessly at the pattern of bristles on a fruit fly's back, while others stroke their chins and ask, *where do new species come from?* And if that question weren't basic enough, others point out that we still don't even know what a species *is*. No definition of the term is fully satisfactory to everyone. So let's look into some of these most fundamental questions. First, let's see how species arise and then let's look at some other questions, including the problem of defining species.

It is important to realize that speciation (the formation of new species) is not the same as evolution (descent with modification), but that it is an important *result* of evolution.

NAMING NAMES

First, we should explain how species are named and some of the problems of naming. The science of naming new species is called **taxonomy.** The first modern taxonomist of note was a Swede by the name of Karl von Linné (1707–1778), or Linnaeus, as he preferred to call himself. Linnaeus took upon himself the incredible task of naming all the plant and animal species known. He also was the first to fully apply the system of **binomial nomenclature**—the practice of giving species a **scientific name,** actually two Latin names: a **generic name** and a **specific name.** The generic name is the name of the **genus,** or group of closely related and ecologically similar species; the specific name identifies the **species** within the genus. Long-standing tradition and international regulations state that:

1. Both names must be in Latin or at least latinized
2. Both are to be written in italics
3. The first (generic) name is to be capitalized, while the second (specific) name is never capitalized.

Once assigned, this combination of names may never be used again. Also, the genus name is generally a noun, and the specific name should be an adjective. These rules are bent a little to allow the latinized adjectival version of the name of a friend, colleague, or authority figure (the rules prohibit anyone naming a species after himself or herself). Thus do taxonomists seek to impose order on a disorderly world.

As an example, we humans are called *Homo sapiens*. *Homo* is our generic name, and *sapiens* is our specific name. *Homo* means "man," while *sapiens* means "wise" or "discerning." (Make of this what you will.) Other species in the genus are *Homo habilis* (*habilis* means "able to do or make") and *Homo erectus* ("upright"), both extinct (Figure 19.1).

When necessary, the binomial nomenclature is extended to a third Latin term, the **subspecies,** or variety. Thus contemporary humans are sometimes referred to as *Homo sapiens sapiens,* to distinguish us from our recently departed cousins, *Homo sapiens neanderthalensis*. And one race of apes is called *Gorilla gorilla gorilla*. (Using the same name for genus and species is acceptable in zoology, but not in botany. A botanist friend was once heard to ask disparagingly, "Really, now, what kind of information is conveyed by a name like *Gorilla gorilla gorilla*?" To which a zoologist present muttered "all you need to know.") (For a look at higher taxonomic categories, see Essay 19.1.)

> **I**n the **binomial system, scientific names** consisting of **genus** and **species** are assigned to each species.

WHAT IS A SPECIES?

You can rattle a graduate student preparing for a doctoral examination in biology by asking, "Quick, what is a species?" This may be surprising because the question seems simple enough. But the simplicity is deceiving.

There usually isn't much difficulty in telling one species from another when you are out in the field—on safari, for instance. A giraffe is quite distinguishable from a lion. A tree fern clearly belongs to one species, and an African violet clearly belongs to a different species. For field work, then, a simple definition of species is adequate—*a species is a distinct and recognizable group of organisms* (Figure 19.2). This definition may not be very intellectually satisfying, but in truth it is usually adequate—except for evolutionary and biogeographic studies of sexually reproducing populations. For those, a more exacting definition will be needed.

Perhaps *interbreeding* is the critical criterion. Two groups clearly belong to the same species if they interbreed and produce viable, healthy offspring on a regular basis. But what about groups that are *capable* of interbreeding but are separated by geography? Now the issue becomes sticky (Figure 19.3). Ani-

FIGURE 19.1   Today's humans all fall within a single genus and species, *Homo sapiens*. We share our genus with two extinct species—*Homo habilis* and *Homo erectus*. We share many traits with these two, but the differences are sufficient to warrant individual species designations.

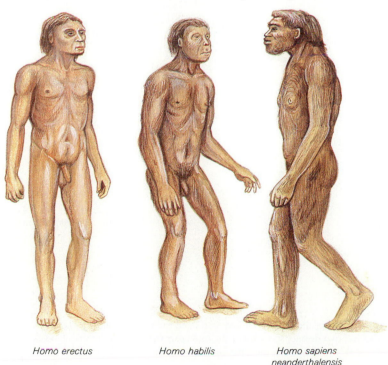

Homo erectus   Homo habilis   Homo sapiens
                                                                neanderthalensis

FIGURE 19.2 For most purposes, it is not difficult to distinguish a species. Here, for example, the zebras are obviously a single species, as are the wildebeest and the rushes and grasses along the bank. But perhaps not far away are zebras of another stripe. Are the two groups of the same species? How do we know?

Red-shafted flicker

Hybrid flicker

Yellow-shafted flicker

FIGURE 19.3 The red-shafted flicker, *Colaptes cafer,* of the western United States and the yellow-shafted flicker, *Colaptes auratus,* of the midwest and east, are considered two distinct species. For the most part they are geographically isolated, but their ranges come together in several states. Where they meet, they may mate. So are they of different species?

mals that interbreed successfully when confined together in zoos (Figure 19.4) may ignore one another in their own less stressful (and, perhaps, less boring) natural environments. Plants that set seed when pollinated by hand may depend on their own insect pollinators in the wild, and wouldn't necessarily cross-fertilize without our help. The interbreeding criterion is generally useful but far from absolute. It doesn't help at all, for instance, in the task of identifying species in asexual organisms. The criterion of interbreeding isn't much more help in defining species among plants, where hybridization between species is a common event.

Ranges, Clines, and Species

One of the problems with identifying species is that they may change across their **range** (the geographic areas over which they exist.) Larger ranges may encompass a variety of habitats and subject different parts of the population to different environmental pressures. If the environment varies gradually and the range is extensive, the population may also vary gradually, producing a **cline.** For example, field mice and frogs have extensive ranges from north to south in the United States, and because of the great ecological differences in their habitats, they may differ markedly at the extremes of their ranges.

In any such extensive range, there are also likely to be "pockets" of areas, quite different from their surroundings. If a subpopulation adapts to such a pocket, it may take on characteristics quite different from the rest of the population, while remaining a part of the same species because of some genetic mixing with the surrounding population. This genetic mixing is called **gene flow,** the exchange of genes between subpopulations of a species. The greater the gene flow between two groups, the fewer changes will arise between them. Conversely, if gene flow is stopped between two subpopulations, they may take off in different evolutionary directions and, in fact, become different, species.

> The problem of species description is compounded by **clines,** which are gradual changes produced across a species' **range** as the subpopulations of the species adapt to local conditions.

Another question to consider when defining *species* is, when (in evolutionary time) do two diverging groups start to qualify as separate species? It obviously can't happen suddenly, since the process is continuous. However, the human mind seems to love categories and hates having to make difficult decisions. Perhaps the best working definition, at least for the animal species, is one by the zoologist Ernst Mayr:

> A *Species* is a group of actually or potentially interbreeding natural populations that is reproductively isolated from other such groups.

Now that we have reached a reasonable definition of species, let's turn to our main subject, how species arise. We will begin with a brief overview of the processes and then turn to geography for a look at its influence.

FIGURE 19.4 Captive animals, subjected to conditions that do not exist in the wild, may behave differently from how they behave in nature. For example, African lions and Siberian tigers would not interbreed in the wild partly because they would never encounter each other. But such mating can occur in captive animals, as witnessed by this hybrid *tiglon* from a male tiger and a female lion. (©Jungle Larry's Safari Land, Inc.)

Kingdoms are the largest taxonomic category, each containing organisms that share basic features of cell structure. The number of kingdoms varies in different schemes according to what is considered to be important, but at the moment, most biologists would go along with five.

If we were describing political organization, kingdoms would be the equivalent of nations. They are generally subdivided into what taxonomists call **phyla** (singular, *phylum*)—equivalent, roughly, to our own states, if we continue the political analogy. Each phylum is itself subdivided into **classes** (counties), and so the subdivisions continue. It is easier at this point to look at the total organization as we make our way down to the species level. The increasingly finer divisions (and a useful way of remembering them) are as follows:

Kingdom	King
Phylum*	Philip
Class	Came
Order	Over
Family	From
Genus	Greece
Species	Singing
Subspecies	Songs
(race)	

We will find that there is no single "correct" way to place an organism into a scheme such as this. In fact, there is often a great deal of

*In botanical terms, the phylum is replaced by the *division*.

argument over such placement. Obviously, however, the smaller the group into which two kinds of organisms are placed, the more similar they must be. Those placed in the same species are likely to be so similar that they can interbreed. Those in the larger categories may be quite different. For example, even though both are animals, it is apparent that humans and sponges are not alike at all (your opinion of your next-door neighbor not withstanding).

The organization of life into the five kingdoms is as follows:

1. **Kingdom Monera.** The prokaryotes or bacteria are chiefly single celled or colonial, and nearly all lack membranous organelles. Included are chemo-

Kingdom:	Animalia	Animalia	Kingdom:	Plantae
Phylum:	Chordata	Chordata	Division:	Anthophyta
Subphylum:	Vertebrata	Vertebrata	Subdivision:	
Class:	Mammalia	Mammalia	Class:	Dicotyledonae
Order:	Cetacea	Insectivora	Order:	Sapindales
Family:	Mysticeti	Craseonycteridae	Family:	Aceraceae
Genus:	*Balenoptera*	*Craseonycteris*	Genus:	*Acer*
Species:	*B. musculus*	*C. phonglongyai*	Species:	*A. rubrum*

The two animals shown here represent the largest and smallest mammals. The great blue whale (*Balenoptera musculus*) grows to about 100 feet in length, can weigh over 150 tons, and devours 8 tons of food per day. Kitti's hog-nosed bat (*Craseonycteris phonglongyai*) weighs about 2 grams (0.07 oz), and has a wing span not exceeding 17mm—altogether about the size of a bumblebee.

The red maple (*Acer rubrum*) is a flowering plant of considerable size and is rather closely related to those other species that are called maples.

trophs, phototrophs, and heterotrophs. Heterotrophs include ecologically vital decomposers and numerous disease-causing parasites.

2. **Kingdom Protista.** The protists include the protozoa (single-celled, animal-like heterotrophs), and the **algae** (plantlike, photosynthetic autotrophs that may be single-celled, colonial, or multicellular).

3. **Kingdom Fungi.** The fungi are simple, multicellular, heterotrophs with lengthy, tubular cells, cell walls composed of chitin or cellulose, and elaborate sexual structures. Included are many ecologically important decomposers and a large number of parasites.

4. **Kingdom Plantae.** Plants are nonmotile (stationary), multicellular, photosynthetic autotrophs with cell walls of cellulose. Most have highly specialized tissues and organs.

5. **Kingdom Animalia.** Animals are motile, multicellular, heterotrophs that lack cell walls, and have highly specialized tissues and organs.

These descriptions summarize the more familiar characteristics of the five kingdoms, but there are obviously some problems. You may have noted that there is no mention of the viruses. They should probably have their own kingdom since they are unlike anything else (see Chapter 20). However, since kingdoms should be based on evolutionary relationships, we can't justify this step. We simply don't know their evolutionary origin.

Within the five-kingdom scheme there are further problems, specifically with regard to the protists. Kingdoms are supposed to be cohesive units with all of their members traceable to a common evolutionary ancestor. Such descent is called **monophyletic.** Yet there is no evidence that the various protozoa and algal protists are descended from a single line. In fact, they are definitely **polyphyletic,** having evolved from different ancestors. However, they will be lumped together provisionally until their evolutionary origins can be sorted out.

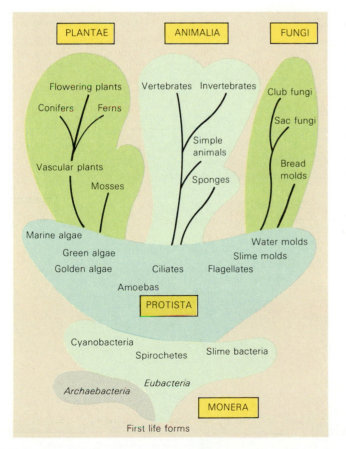

The five kingdoms are arranged in a manner that suggests their phylogenetic relationship to each other. The underlying kingdom, known as Monera, is now being reorganized into Archaebacteria and Eubacteria, two quite diverse groups of prokaryotes. Above this is the large assemblage provisionally called Protista or Protoctista. Some of its members are descended from the same lines that gave rise to kingdoms Plantae, Fungi, and Animalia.

MECHANISMS OF SPECIATION

Speciation, the formation of species, arises in two general ways (Figure 19.5). First, a species may simply change over time so that an existing animal might not even recognize its forebears. This kind of linear change over time is called **phyletic speciation.** Until recently many anthropologists believed that much of hominid (human line) evolution occurred in this "straight-line" fashion, at least from the advent of *Australopithecus* on to modern humans (see Chapter 30). Currently, though, anthropologists favor a branching tree of human evolution. In fact, evolutionists agree that *most* speciation occurs in a branch-ing fashion with one species giving rise to two in what has been called **divergent speciation.**

Divergent speciation theoretically occurs in two principal ways. The first is **allopatric speciation,** which involves geographically separated groups following their own paths of evolution. Allopatric speciation is believed to be the far more common means by which new species arise. Far less frequently **sympatric speciation** may occur. In this case new species spring from a single, interbreeding group.

Regardless of the way in which speciation occurs, once new species arise, certain barriers appear that generally prevent the new species from interbreeding again. Such barriers are called **reproductive isolating mechanisms.**

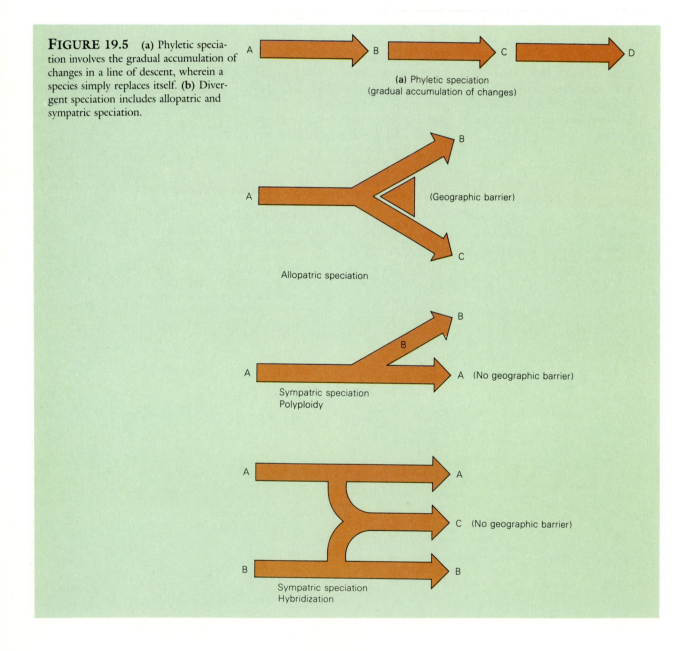

FIGURE 19.5 **(a)** Phyletic speciation involves the gradual accumulation of changes in a line of descent, wherein a species simply replaces itself. **(b)** Divergent speciation includes allopatric and sympatric speciation.

(a) Phyletic speciation (gradual accumulation of changes)

Allopatric speciation

(Geographic barrier)

Sympatric speciation Polyploidy

(No geographic barrier)

(No geographic barrier)

Sympatric speciation Hybridization

Reproductive Isolating Mechanisms

Typically, one species gives rise to two as a population is split geographically, each branch undergoing changes independently of the other as they adapt to different environmental conditions. Some of the changes the species undergo will eventually render them reproductively incompatible; that is, reproductive isolating mechanisms will appear.

Some reproductive isolating mechanisms are called **prezygotic** (before the zygote); they prevent successful fertilization. For example, the breeding seasons of the two branches may change enough so that they enter their reproductive cycles at different times. Also, the two groups might not attempt to interbreed if their courtship behavior changes so that they do not appropriately signal each other. Or perhaps even if copulation is successful, the sperm might encounter a less-than-ideal chemical environment. Prezygotic isolation includes behavioral, anatomical, and physiological changes that prevent fertilization.

Other reproductive isolating mechanisms are **postzygotic** (after the zygote) because they function after fertilization. For example, offspring may be physically weak or may die as embryos. Perhaps the offspring survive but grow into sterile adults (commonly because the chromosomes fail to synapse [pair up] properly during prophase I of meiosis). In any case, even closely related species (or, perhaps, *especially* closely related species) normally develop ways to foil interbreeding and thereby preserve their accumulated genetic adaptations for a particular environment.

> **P**rezygotic reproductive isolating **mechanisms** (operating through altered behavior, anatomy, and physiology) prevent fertilization; **postzygotic mechanisms** (loss of vigor or fertility) prevent success of hybrids.

Allopatry and Speciation

Since geographic separation is so important to the origin of species, let's review the principle of allopatric speciation and explore some of its causes and effects.

First, it is obvious that should a mountain range arise or a new river form, subgroups may become isolated, resulting in a halt in gene flow because of the new barrier. As we have seen, such isolated groups, subjected to different selective factors, are commonly the raw material of speciation. Eventually, such geographic isolation could lead to physical or

behavioral changes, as the isolated organisms became more and more different. Ultimately, should the opportunity to interbreed arise, it is no longer possible. Thus we have the formation of two species where before there was one (Figure 19.6).

Aside from the formation of such local barriers as rivers or mountains, large-scale geological changes can divide a previously continuous range. The most fundamental changes of the planet's surfaces occurred some 230 million years ago, when the most recent worldwide process of **continental drift** began; and again about 65 million years ago, when Africa and South America parted company. The uniqueness of species communities in the world's present-day continents, particularly those of Australia and South America, has been the result of millions of years of allopatric speciation made possible by continental drift (Essay 19.2).

FIGURE 19.6   After formation of the Grand Canyon and Colorado River, once continuous populations were geographically isolated and followed their own evolutionary paths. The Abert squirrel (as shown) and Kaibab squirrel, living on opposite sides of the canyon, are believed to have evolved from a single ancestral species present before the canyon formed.

In 1912, Alfred Wegener published a paper that was triggered by the common observation of the good fit between South America's east coast and Africa's west. Could these great continents ever have been joined? Wegener coordinated this jigsaw-puzzle analysis with other geological and climatological data, and proposed the theory of **continental drift.** He suggested that about 200 million years ago, all of the earth's continents were joined together into one enormous land mass, which he called Pangaea. In the ensuing millennia, according to Wegener's idea, **Pangaea** broke apart and the fragments began to drift northward (by today's compass orientation), to their present location.

Wegener's idea received rough treatment in his lifetime. His geologist contemporaries attacked his naïveté as well as his supporting data, and his theory was neglected until about 1960. At about that time, a new generation of geologists revived the idea and subjected it to new scrutiny based on recent findings. These findings buttressed Wegener's old notion and breathed new life into it.

The most useful data have been based on magnetism in ancient lava flows. When a lava flow cools, metallic elements in the lava are oriented in a way that provides a permanent fossil of the earth's magnetic field at the time, recording for future geologists both its north-south orientation and its latitude. From such maps it is possible to determine the ancient positions of today's continents. We now believe that not only has continental drift occurred, as Wegener hypothesized, but that it continues to occur today.

Geologists have long maintained that the earth's surface is a restless crust, constantly changing, sinking, and rising because of incredible, unrelenting forces beneath it. These constant changes are now known to involve large, distinct segments of the crust known as *plates.* At certain edges of these masses, immense ridges are being thrust up, while other edges sink lower. Where plates are heaved together, the buckling at the edges has produced vast mountain ranges. When such ridges appear in the ocean floor, water is displaced and the oceans expand. (Astoundingly precise satellite studies reveal that the Atlantic Ocean is 5 cm wider each year.)

In addition to its fascinating geological implications, an understanding of continental drift (or **plate tectonics**) is vital to the study of the distribution of life on the planet today. It helps to explain the presence of fossil tropical species in Antarctica, for example, and the unusual animal life in Australia and South America.

As the composite maps indicate, the disruption of Pangaea began some 230 million years ago, in the Paleozoic era. By the Mesozoic era, the Eurasian land mass, called **Laurasia,** had moved away to form the northernmost continent. **Gondwanaland,** the mass that included India and the southern continents, had just begun to divide. Finally, during the late Mesozoic era, after South America and Africa were well divided, what was to be the last continental separation began, with Australia and Antarctica drifting apart. Both the North and South Atlantic Oceans would continue to widen considerably up to the Cenozoic era, a trend that is continuing today. So we see that although the bumper sticker "Reunite Gondwanaland" has a third-world and trendy ring to it, it's an unlikely proposition.

There are other ways that populations of a species might become geographically isolated. One possibility is illustrated by a seed, an inseminated female, or a group of individuals finding itself—by some happy accident—in a new, yet hospitable, place. Ocean islands, for instance, are occasionally populated by the descendants of unwilling, drenched, and thoroughly disgusted passengers on driftwood logs. Birds and flying insects may be blown to some island by particularly violent storms, or perhaps through an error in navigation.

The Galapagos Islands and Darwin's finches. The finches of the Galápagos Islands (Figure 19.7a) provide the best known example of allopatric speciation (involving separated populations). Compared to the giant tortoises, strange flightless cormorants, and impish sea iguanas living there, the finches are not particularly interesting—that is, until the saga of their evolution is revealed.

All of the finches, also called Darwin's finches, are 10 to 20 cm long, and both sexes are drab brown and gray. Six are ground species, feeding on different,

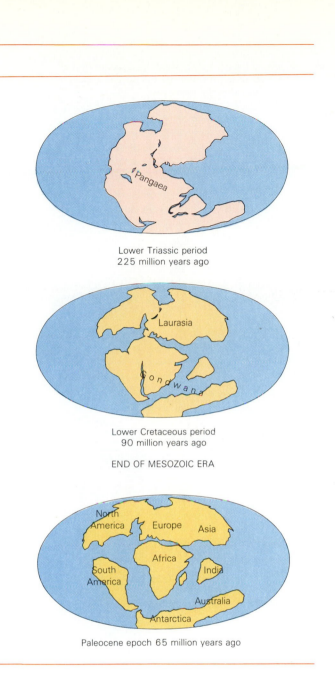

Lower Triassic period
225 million years ago

Lower Cretaceous period
90 million years ago

END OF MESOZOIC ERA

Paleocene epoch 65 million years ago

bird taxonomist examined the specimens and noted that the inhabitants of different islands—though they were very similar to one another—were clearly different species. Ordinarily, birds living in one locale tend to be very different from one another. These birds were all clearly finches, and, indeed, they were South American finches. But Darwin had seen many of them doing things that finches don't ordinarily do.

Darwin concluded (and his conclusions are supported by ensuing years of careful research by others) that the different species of birds were all descended from the same stock (Figure 19.7b). About 10,000 years ago the volcanic islands were colonized by South American finches that were probably blown out to sea by a storm. Apparently, conditions on the island were favorable and the "castaways" flourished. Their descendants eventually populated all the islands by their occasional island-hopping. However, the island hopping was rare enough to ensure the virtual isolation of each group. What followed is referred to as **adaptive radiation.**

The little birds had the islands to themselves, as far as they were concerned. They found food of all sorts everywhere. They were already well adapted for foraging for small seeds on the ground, but now there were other plentiful food resources—food not ordinarily eaten by finches.

Soon enough, the expanding populations were demolishing the supply of available small seeds. Thus, natural selection began to favor birds that could also cope with larger seeds as well as other types of food. In time, the birds' bill sizes began to change as each population began to adapt more closely to the food found on its island. Not only were bill sizes changing, but so were gene frequencies. Natural selection (undoubtedly influenced by genetic drift) was having its way. Eventually the isolated birds of the different islands differed genetically to the extent that any island hoppers would find themselves to be reproductively incompatible with the residents of other islands. In this way, new species were formed.

Even if some species invaded an island and found a genetically incompatible species already there, they might be able to coexist with the residents if the two groups tended to use different resources. This, of course, would mean the pressure for further change was on. With two species of finches trying to survive on one small island, natural selection would favor the individuals in *each* population that were as different as possible from those in the other population (and so would be less affected by competition from them). There would be a tendency toward further separation

appropriately sized seeds or cactus, and eight are tree finches. In such species, the bill has become modified for a specific diet. (In one case, the behavior, rather than the bill, has become modified. The woodpecker finch lacks the long, piercing tongue of the woodpecker, so it uses long cactus spines to pry insect grubs out of cracks and crevices in the trees.)

On the *Beagle's* historic visit to the Galápagos Islands, Darwin collected everything he could find or catch, including these ordinary little brown finches. He took no special interest in them. But a London

FIGURE 19.7 Galápagos (Darwin's) finches **(a)** include six species of ground foragers (9–14) and eight species of tree foragers (1–8). What does a comparison of the size and shape of beaks suggest about individual diets? Intensive studies of Galápagos finches have led to a scheme **(b)** suggesting a number of divergences in their evolutionary past.

Key to species names: The tree finches are 1, *Camarhynchus pallidus* (the woodpecker finch); 2, *C. heliobates*; 3, *C. psittacula*; 4, *C. pauper*; 5, *C. parvulus*; 6, *C. crassirostris*; 7, *Certhidea olivacea* (the warblerlike finch); and 8, *Pinaroloxias inornata* (the Cocos Island finch). The ground finches are: 9, *Geospiza magnirostris*; 10, *G. fortis*; 11, *G. fuliginosa*; 12, *G. difficilis*; 13, *G. conirostris*; and 14, *G. scandens*.

(a)

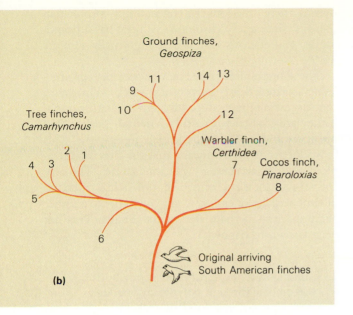

Ground finches,
Geospiza

Tree finches,
Camarhynchus

Warbler finch,
Certhidea

Cocos finch,
Pinaroloxias

(b)

Original arriving
South American finches

and divergence of the two groups as each became a specialist in utilizing the environment in a particular way. The tendency for differences in competing species to become exaggerated as each specializes is called **character displacement** (Figure 19.8).

After thousands of years of occupying these dismal islands and separating, changing, specializing, and rejoining, the different populations are now totally unable to interbreed. Today, several of the species exist side-by-side on every island. Each species utilizes the resources of the island in its own unique manner, in some cases filling niches that are occupied by other kinds of birds on the mainland.

Darwin's finches are not an isolated example. Exactly the same kind of adaptive radiation is seen in the birds of another archipelago—the honeycreepers of Hawaii.

Allopatric speciation is the formation of new species by the geographic separation of a population into groups that then take different evolutionary routes.

Sympatry and Speciation

Although allopatric speciation—that is, the formation of new species in geographically isolated groups—is by far the most common means, speciation within a single locale *without* geographic isolation indeed occurs. We have called it sympatric speciation. The best examples are found among plants where the fusion of two species, or hybridization, is common.

Sympatric speciation is the formation of new species within an interbreeding group.

Hybridization: meiosis and the sterile hybrid. Plants, unlike animals, regularly undergo hybridization. The best known examples of naturally forming hybrids come from species of woody flowering plants such as *Eucalyptus*, mountain lilacs (*Ceanothus*), and oaks (*Quercus*). Hybridization in these plants is usually associated with some form of environmental stress such as a disturbed habitat.

The success of plant hybrids may be surprising, since hybrids between animal species are usually infertile. The mule, for example, is a vigorous hybrid that is completely sterile. The reason is straightforward: a mule is a cross between a donkey and a horse; however, the number and organization of the chromosomes is so different in the donkey and horse that

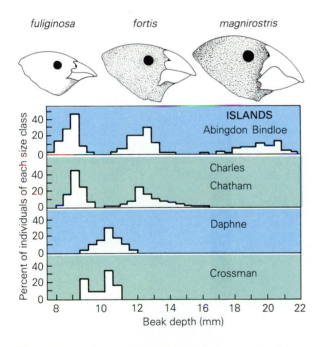

FIGURE 19.8 Character displacement is revealed in beak size changes in three species of Galápagos finches, *Geospiza fuliginosa, G. fortis,* and *G. magnirostris.* Where all three species are found together (*graph a*), the ranges in beak sizes are clearly separated with no overlap. Where *G. magnirostris* is absent (*graph b*), its beak size range is overlapped by *G. fortis.* However, notice that it and *G. fuliginosa* remain distinct. Where *G. fortis* and *G. fuliginosa* exist separately and alone (*graphs c* and *d*), their beak size ranges completely overlap.

they cannot pair in meiosis (see Chapter 10). This pairing up is essential for the proper metaphase alignment and anaphase separation of homologous chromosomes if normal gametes are to be produced. The question arises, then, why don't plants suffer from this problem?

Polyploidy. A rather dramatic way that plant species hybridize successfully involves **polyploidy,** where whole sets of chromosomes become doubled. This happens spontaneously from time to time in the mitotic divisions of a growing plant. The chromosomes double in preparation for cell division, but for some reason the cell fails to divide. Later, the cell will again double its chromosomes, as if nothing were unusual, and proceed with normal mitosis. Thus all of its progeny will have four complete sets of chromosomes. The abnormal cell is called a **tetraploid** cell, and its progeny may form tetraploid tissue and, even, tetraploid flowers.

Sexual reproduction in hybrids may fail early in meiosis because the hybrid cell has two different haploid chromosome sets. But when spontaneous tetraploidization occurs, there will suddenly be two different complete diploid chromosome sets. Such a tetraploid is called an **allotetraploid** ("other-tetraploid"). When flowers form in the allotetraploid

hybrid, there is no longer a compatibility problem in meiosis, since every chromosome now has a homologue, and meiosis can proceed normally (Figure 19.9).

The allotetraploid plants may at once be reproductively isolated from the parental stock. While they can successfully reproduce through self-fertilization, if they are crossed with either parental species, they produce only *triploid* seeds, which are infertile. This reproductive isolation means that the new allotetraploid plant constitutes an "instant" species. The new species will soon fail, of course, unless it happens to fill a new niche or unless it can outcompete another plant species—perhaps one of its parents. This has been known to happen.

Chromosome incompatibilities in hybrids can be overcome through **polyploidy,** through which chromosome doubling makes homologous pairing and separation possible in meiosis.

Plant breeders can repeatedly bring about polyploidy through the application of colchicine, a chemical agent that prevents chromatid separation during mitosis. Thus, it is possible to produce *hexaploids* (six

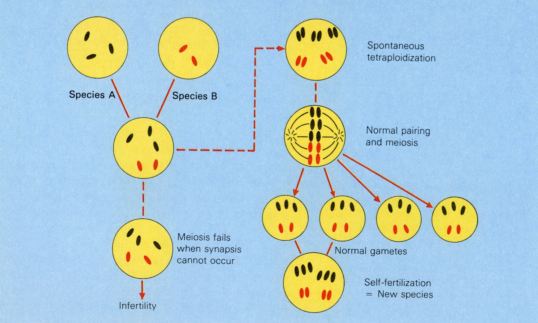

FIGURE 19.9 Species A is successfully pollinated by species B, producing a hybrid. Since there is no match in the chromosome complement, the hybrid cannot carry out meiosis and is therefore sterile. However, should a spontaneous doubling of chromosomes occur, as it sometimes does, normal pairing-up and meiosis occurs and normal gametes are produced. Following self-fertilization, a new viable species is produced.

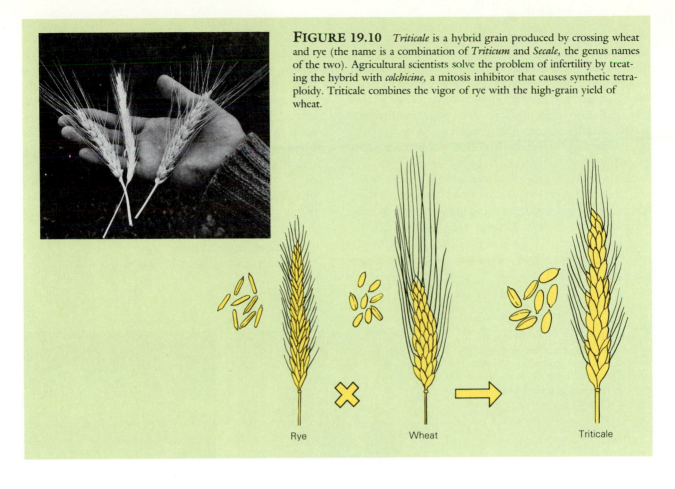

FIGURE 19.10 *Triticale* is a hybrid grain produced by crossing wheat and rye (the name is a combination of *Triticum* and *Secale,* the genus names of the two). Agricultural scientists solve the problem of infertility by treating the hybrid with *colchicine,* a mitosis inhibitor that causes synthetic tetraploidy. Triticale combines the vigor of rye with the high-grain yield of wheat.

Rye   Wheat   Triticale

genomes, or three doubled copies of three different parental genomes), *octaploids,* and so on. (The term *polyploid* covers any level of chromosome doubling higher than diploid.) Strange as it seems, polyploidy is common among many wild and domestic flowering plants. Wheat, for example, is actually an allohexaploid, a genetic combination of the chromosome complements of three entirely different Middle Eastern species of wild grasses. **Triticale** (Figure 19.10) is a human-engineered application of the tendency of wheat and rye grasses to form **allopolyploids.**

For reasons not fully understood, polyploid species often have a tolerance for harsh climatic conditions. In one study only 26% of the plants sampled in lush tropical regions were polyploids, while 86% of all the flowering plant species in the raw environs of northern Greenland were polyploids.

Hybridization followed by polyploidization creates instant, sympatric species of flowering plants, ready to be tested by the forces of natural selection. This versatility helps explain how flowering plants arose abruptly in evolution and how they quickly spread out over the landscape to create the incredible diversity of plant species that dominate our world.

Sympatric speciation in animals. Although there are polyploid species of animals, hybridization is not as likely in species that have sex chromosomes. This is because in polyploid meiotic cells, the Xs tend to pair with Xs and the Ys with Ys, instead of the normal XY pairing. The resulting gametes are therefore unbalanced for sex chromosomes. Polyploidy is frequently found among fish, reptiles, and amphibians; sex in these groups is influenced by factors such as temperature, rather than by chromosome ratios.

Evolutionary theorists argue over whether sympatric speciation could occur in animals in ways other than through polyploidy, but nowhere among the animals is the situation as clear-cut as in the polyploid plants.

MAJOR EVOLUTIONARY TRENDS

How can we put the concept of speciation into the larger context of evolutionary history? Let's begin by taking a look at some of the major trends in evolution as revealed by the fossil record, and by comparing living animals.

Divergent Evolution

We used the term *adaptive radiation* to describe the manner in which speciation occurred in the Galapagos finches. The finches developed new ecological niches, and in the process of adapting to their niches, they became less similar to one another. Thus adaptive radiation depends on **divergent evolution,** which simply means that newly emerging species tend to become increasingly different from each other over time.

Such changes proceed more slowly under some conditions than others. If ecological demands in different areas are severe and narrow, evolution will proceed rather rapidly. Change may also be accelerated by competition. This can happen, for example, when one species forces another into a more restricted, narrower niche.

The idea of such divergence has strong ecological overtones, since becoming different is often associated with finding some new way of utilizing the environmental resources—in Darwin's words, a new "place in the polity of nature." The opening of new niches is greatly encouraged by natural selection, since it relieves the unrelenting competition for resources. Such divergence is often represented in branching schemes called phylogenetic trees. The tree is a good analogy because of its constant branching and rebranching. We will look at several examples later in this chapter and in many chapters to come.

In **divergent evolution,** organisms with common origins become increasingly different.

FIGURE 19.11 The concept of convergent evolution is well supported by observations of Australian mammals. Although phylogenetically unrelated to their counterparts in other continents, they bear a striking resemblance to many.

A marsupial cuscus (*left*) and a placental sloth (*above*)

Marsupial rabbit bandicoots (*left*) and a placental arctic hare (*above*)

Convergent Evolution

We may be struck with the tendency toward divergence in long-term evolution, but it is not the only possible trend. In some cases, unrelated or remotely related species may grow more alike. This should not be unexpected in different species that are adapting to similar environments and establishing similar niches; that is, ways to exploit those environments. The process is called **convergent evolution.**

Darwin was impressed by the evidence of convergent evolution in his lengthy travels. He recorded in his journal that the South American mara or Patagonian hare, *Dolichotis patagonum,* was quite similar, in both appearance and ecological niche, to the European rabbit. Close examination of the mara revealed that it was not a rabbit at all, but a rodent. Thus, despite its resemblance to a rabbit, it is actually more closely related to the guinea pig (see Chapter 17).

Convergence is dramatically evident in comparisons between placental mammals and the distantly related marsupial (pouched) mammals of Australia. Marsupials and placental mammals have established very similar niches. Through a long period of isolation, selection, and adaptation, unrelated species have often taken on a striking resemblance to one another. In Australia we find the rabbit bandicoot, the marsupial mouse, the marsupial mole, the flying phalanger, and the banded anteater. All of these have a placental counterpart on other continents (Figure 19.11).

In **convergent evolution,** unrelated species adapting to similar environments come to resemble each other.

A marsupial sugar glider *(top)* and a placental flying squirrel *(above)*

The Tasmanian devil *(top)* and the placental wolverine *(above)*

The marsupial numbat *(top)* and the placental giant anteater *(above)*

Short- and long-nosed bandicoots *(above, right)* and the placental Norway rat *(far right)*

Coevolution

Quite often the direction of evolution in one species is strongly influenced by what is happening in the evolution of another species, particularly if either is dependent on the other. The most obvious examples of this sort of change are seen in predator-prey relationships. As natural selection improves the predator's skill, it also favors the development of behavior that will improve the prey's ability to escape. As the predator population gets better, so does the prey population. This two-way tracking by natural selection is called **coevolution.**

The great array of flowering plants on the earth has been so influenced by the coevolution of insect pollinators that today many flowering plant species are selectively pollinated by only one kind of insect. For example, yucca is entirely dependent on the yucca moth for pollination; the yucca moth, in turn, is entirely dependent on the yucca flower, where it lays its eggs and where its larvae grow on a diet of yucca seeds. The yucca moth goes to a considerable amount of trouble to ensure pollination, since only properly pollinated flowers will produce the seeds the moth larvae need.

As a remarkable example of herbivore-plant co-evolution, consider the relationship between passion flower vines and a butterfly *(Heliconius)* whose caterpillars specialize in eating them (Figure 19.12). This plant has succeeded in manufacturing poisons that prevent most other insects from devouring its leaves and young shoots, but these butterflies have evolved the ability to detoxify the poisons. The butterfly lays bright yellow eggs on the young leaves, which act as a warning to other female butterflies that it would be wiser for them to find their own leaves. The other butterflies avoid laying eggs where there are already eggs, an adaptive response since it cuts down the competition their own larvae will face. Through natural selection, the plant has taken advantage of this behavior and now has perfected rather good mimic eggs, little round lumps of bright yellow tissue scattered randomly on the leaves and shoots. These also tend to persuade the butterfly to hunt elsewhere. Furthermore, the same vines have mimicked the shriveling of leaves that usually accompany larval infestations.

Coevolution occurs when different species influence each other's direction of evolution of each other.

FIGURE 19.12 The passion flower vine *(Passiflora)* continually evolves new strategies to resist the parasitic activity of the *Heliconius* larvae. Displaced nectar glands (yellow spots) resembling the butterfly's eggs discourage "additional" egg laying. (In this case the mimicry has not worked. The brighter spot is the egg of *Helioconius* amid the less colorful spots produced by the plant.) Variation in leaf shape may also mislead egg-laying females searching for a specific shape and size.

The Evolutionary Pace and Punctuated Equilibrium

We noted in Chapter 17 a problem in the fossil record. There is a notable lack of transitional fossils that would, were they there, strongly support the notion of **gradualism**—a slow, continuous process of adaptive change. This common observation can be accounted for, however, by an evolutionary pattern called **punctuated equilibrium.** We touched briefly on the idea earlier.

Recall that Eldridge, Gould, and others who support the idea of a "punctuated" evolutionary history contend that species often persist virtually unchanged for millions of years (in "equilibrium") and then dramatically disappear, suddenly replaced by new species. They equate the bursts of extinction and speciation with the geological upheavals that periodically have shaken the earth and changed its face. Punctuated equilibrium has three main aspects:

1. Long periods occur with little evolutionary change.
2. New, seemingly unconnected lines arise rapidly replacing the old.
3. Evolutionary episodes are associated with geological upheaval.

Let's consider a scenario involving allopatric speciation suggested by this explanation.

In our scenario, the earth and its denizens have enjoyed a long period of geological calm. Then, however, the peace is disrupted by incredibly powerful movements of the earth. The result is that one large population of creatures is split apart. The main population remains intact, but a splinter group is isolated as the earth under it moves away from the main mass in the twinkling of a geological eye (perhaps in only a few thousand years). Since conditions are likely to be different in the two places, the groups would, of course, take different ecological directions.

The earth is a restless place, and let's suppose that before long (geologically) the two land masses were reunited, bringing together the two groups. Although differences would have occurred. The two groups would bear a common stamp and would, because of their common heritage, utilize their resources in similar ways. Thus, having gone their separate ways for a time, they would now be thrown into powerful competition. Suppose now that the smaller group should out-compete the larger one and bring about its extinction.

Some anthropologists suggest that this may be exactly what brought about the demise of Neanderthal man in human evolution. They theorize that smaller groups became glacially isolated from the main group, then advanced more rapidly than the larger group—physically or culturally or both—and later confronted and obliterated the main, more primitive line.

If things had proceeded according to our story, imagine what would happen to the fossil record. A paleontologist digging in a certain rock stratum might uncover two kinds of fossils that, although similar, were different enough to constitute separate species. One would have a long fossil history in older strata, ending abruptly in a certain stratum. The record of the second would suddenly begin there and extend into the newer strata above.

We can see that although compelling in its logic, the theory of punctuated equilibrium will need to hold up under closer scrutiny. In the meantime, some paleontologists will go on looking for those "links" missing in the saga of evolution.

> **G**radualism is slow, continuous adaptive change; **punctuated equilibrium** implies that species enjoy long periods of little change with periodic episodes of great change.

EVOLUTION AT THE MOLECULAR LEVEL

Molecular biology came of age in the early 1950s, with great fanfare and marching to the bugles of Watson and Crick. Since that time there has been an unimagined increase in the technical capability of the molecular biologist, culminating in the dazzling new technologies of genetic engineering. The powerful new investigative tools have now been focused, with considerable success, on questions of evolution. As a result, biologists now routinely describe evolutionary relationships based on deeply probing, computer-generated, protein–amino acid sequences and DNA nucleotide sequences. Their logic is based on the assumption that the proteins and nucleotide sequences of closely related organisms are more similar than are those of more distantly related organisms. Scientists still use the older methods of systematics and taxonomy to try to determine relatedness, of course. They ponder over the visible differences in various groups, they measure leg length, bill size, and carefully trace their embryological development. Their ancient search is powerfully supplemented, however, by the new molecular techniques.

In fact, it is often revealing to "test" the conclusions of the more traditional approaches with newer techniques. It is somehow comforting to see how

FIGURE 19.13 Minimum mutation trees include those developed by amino acid sequencing **(a)** and through DNA hybridization techniques **(b)**. The numbers along the branches of the cytochrome *c* tree represent the fewest numbers of mutations that could account for the differences in amino acid sequences. (Open circles represent extinct ancestors). The phylogeny of bird families was established by DNA hybridization studies. The most recent addition to bird families were the starlings; the crow is indeed ancient.

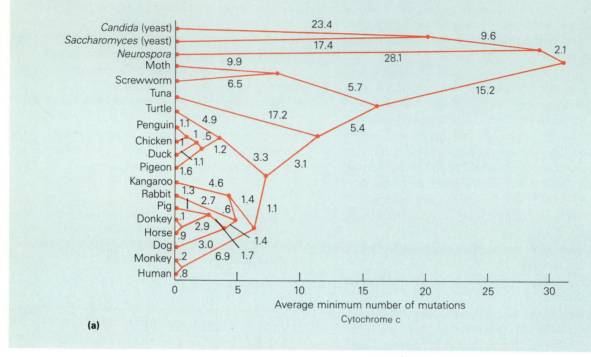

(a)

often the two agree. As the molecular data come in, crusty old biologists who know their bones have time and again been shown to have been on the right track all those years.

> The evolutionary relatedness of different species can be determined by comparing amino acid sequences in proteins and nucleotide sequences in the DNA of genes.

The Molecular Clock

Comparative analysis of the proteins and nucleotides of thousands of species has revealed fascinating evidence for the existence of a **molecular clock.** The molecular clock is based on the idea that point mutations (single nucleotide changes) and subsequent amino acid changes in proteins occur with clocklike regularity. If such regularity is present, not only can we use molecular differences to determine relatedness of species, but also we can tell *when* the divergences occurred. In other words, the data generated

from comparative molecular studies not only can be used to organize phylogenetic ("family") trees, they also give us an accurate *time* framework. This means that we can draw such trees with a once-unimagined accuracy. The length of each branch following a division reflects the actual time elapsed since the two species diverged.

Sometimes the findings from such studies are startling. For instance, in his comparisons of serum albumin, a primate blood plasma protein, Vincent M. Sarich came up with some surprising data on human divergence. Most researchers had concluded that humans diverged from other primates from 20 to 30 million years ago, but Sarich's data suggested that the divergence occurred only 5 million years ago. (This was later supported by nucleotide sequencing studies.)

> The regularity with which gene mutation occurs can be used to establish a **molecular clock,** a precise way of establishing an evolutionary time framework.

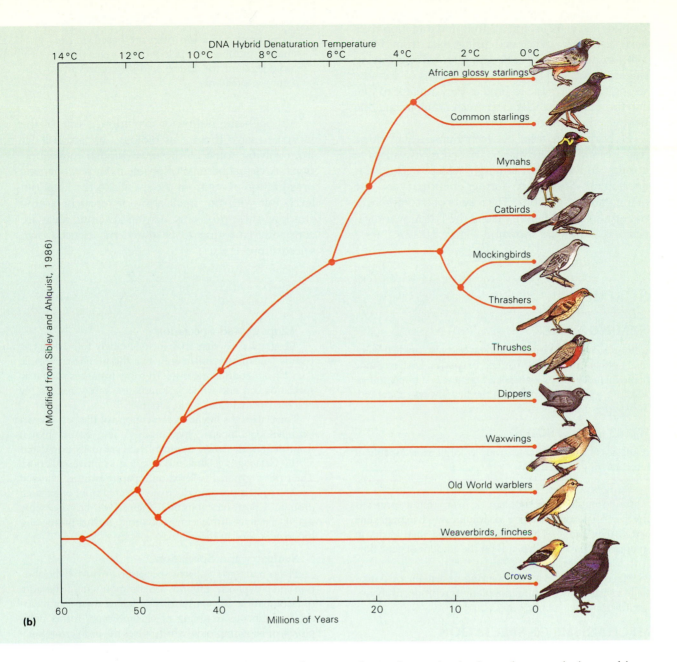

DNA Hybrid Denaturation Temperature

14°C   12°C   10°C   8°C   6°C   4°C   2°C   0°C

African glossy starlings

Common starlings

Mynahs

Catbirds

Mockingbirds

Thrashers

Thrushes

Dippers

Waxwings

Old World warblers

Weaverbirds, finches

Crows

(Modified from Sibley and Ahlquist, 1986)

60   50   40   20   10   0

Millions of Years

(b)

Minimum mutation trees. From comparative amino acid analyses, molecular biologists have developed what they call **minimum mutation trees,** phylogenetic schemes based on the smallest number of nucleotide changes that could have produced the observed amino acid differences. Such trees are designed to reveal the order in which various organisms appeared and how they are related to each other.

One of the earliest trees developed from amino acid analysis involved cytochrome *c,* a respiratory pigment (Figure 19.13a). Cytochrome *c,* which consists of 108 amino acids in most vertebrates and slightly more in other organisms, is believed to have

changed very slowly throughout evolutionary history. For example, humans and chimpanzees have identical sequences; humans and rhesus monkeys have only one amino acid difference, in spite of the 20 million years that have elapsed since the divergence of our ancestral lines. More impressively, the cytochrome *c* of humans and brewers yeast (a fungus) reveal only *38* amino acid differences in the protein chain! (It is perhaps somehow humbling to learn how closely we are related to yeast.)

Other amino acid sequences have also been analyzed in this manner, including those from the respiratory enzyme, carbonic anhydrase (see Chapter 38), which appears to have had a much faster rate of change than cytochrome *c*. Minimum mutation trees have also been developed using data from DNA hybridization studies. These studies involve mixing single strands of DNA from two strains to see how strongly they are able to bind as they attempt to join and form a double helix. The greater the binding, the stronger the relatedness.

Hybridization tests between humans and other primates still indicate that our closest relatives are the gorillas and chimps (although which is closest is debatable). Somewhat further removed are the orangutan and gibbons. The results of a comprehensive study of bird families using the DNA hybridization techniques are shown in Figure 19.13b.

> **Minimum mutation trees** are based on the smallest number of nucleotide changes that could account for amino acid differences in common proteins.

Although the notion of evolution is one of the most pervasive themes in biology, we are still far from solving some of the most fundamental questions. A virtual barrage of problems in phylogenetic organization exists from the species to the kingdom level. But with the small army of researchers now attacking these problems, new and exciting ideas are constantly emerging to be tested by science's own selective processes.

SUMMARY

NAMING NAMES

Linnaeus, an early naturalist and taxonomist, applied binomial nomenclature to the naming of species. Each scientific name includes genus and species, generally a noun and an adjective written in Latin with the first always capitalized. Subspecies designations may follow.

WHAT IS A SPECIES?

A species is a recognizable group of organisms capable of interbreeding.

Ranges, Clines, and Species

Compounding the problem of delimiting a species is the fact that some form a continuously changing cline across their range. The degree of change that occurs in semi-isolated pockets depends on the amount of gene flow with the main group.

Mayr defines species as "a group of actually or potentially interbreeding natural populations reproductively isolated from other such groups."

MECHANISMS OF SPECIATION

In phyletic speciation one species simply changes enough to become a new species. In divergent speciation, species branch off of main lines, or main lines diverge forming two new species. Included in the latter are allopatric speciation, where geographical isolation takes effect, and sympatric speciation, which occurs without geographic isolation. Reproductive isolation is a necessary prerequisite to both.

Reproductive Isolating Mechanisms

Where reproductive isolation occurs, two groups can no longer interbreed. Prezygotic isolation includes physical, physiological, or behavioral changes that preclude successful mating. Postzygotic isolation includes incompatibilities that interfere with the survival of offspring or that render them infertile.

Allopatry and Speciation

Geographic barriers may include newly formed rivers, islands, and mountain ranges, but the grandest example comes from continental drift. In some instances allopatric speciation occurs when colonists or castaways simply become isolated from main groups.

The Galápagos finches represent one of the best known examples of allopatric speciation. A few finches blown from the South American mainland eventually populated all the Galápagos Islands, undergoing adaptive radiation. The earliest groups, isolated on separate islands, changed enough to become reproductively isolated from other such groups. Upon reestablishing themselves on the same island, character displacement occurred, further promoting differences. Today there are 14 species.

Sympatry and Speciation

Plants undergo sympatric speciation through hybridization and polyploidy. Hybrids are commonly sterile because of incompatible chromosomes that fail to synapse at meiosis. Spontaneous doubling of chromosomes forms polyploids, or allotetraploids, which solves the problem of pairing. The progeny, immediately reproductively isolated, may form a new species if conditions are favorable. Producing successful hybrids through induced polyploidy is a common practice by plant breeders. Natural polyploids are commonplace in colder climates.

MAJOR EVOLUTIONARY TRENDS
Divergent Evolution

In divergent evolution, species become increasingly different from their ancestral type. Such changes are adaptive since they help relieve competition.

Convergent Evolution

In convergent evolution, unrelated or distantly related species adapt to similar niches and come to resemble each other. Many examples are seen in the marsupial and placental mammals.

Coevolution

In coevolution the adaptive changes of one species track those of another. This commonly occurs between predator and prey species. The defensive measures taken by the passionflower against insects have led to countermeasures by a butterfly whose larvae feed on the leaves.

The Evolutionary Pace and Punctuated Equilibrium

Because it does not support the idea of gradualism, many believe the fossil record to be incomplete. Others propose that species go through long periods of little change, interrupted suddenly by geological upheaval and accompanied by the sudden extinction of some species and the rise of others. In the punctuated equilibrium scenario small groups, separated from the parent group by geological change, were later reunited. Where reproductive isolation had occurred, the two groups remained separate, and strong competition ensued. In some instances the smaller group won out and the larger, older line became extinct. This would explain the sudden end of one line and the rise of another in the fossil record. The missing fossil link simply had no time to form.

EVOLUTION AT THE MOLECULAR LEVEL

The evolutionary origin and relationships of species is now being determined through DNA and amino acid sequencing methods. The logic used is that closely related species have the smallest numbers of differences. Thus far the results agree with earlier determinations based on traditional methods.

The Molecular Clock

The regularity with which mutations occur enables molecular biologists to equate nucleotide and amino acid differences among species to past evolutionary time. Thus evolutionary schemes represent both relatedness and time of divergence.

Minimum mutation trees are phylogenetic schemes based on the smallest number of nucleotide changes that could have produced the amino acid differences. Molecules such as cytochrome c, carbonic anhydrase, and DNA have been used to construct such trees. The new recombinant DNA technology offers many applications for molecular evolution studies.

KEY TERMS

taxonomy	phyletic speciation	tetraploid
binomial nomenclature	divergent speciation	allotetraploid
scientific name	allopatric speciation	triticale
generic name	sympatric speciation	allopolyploid
specific name	reproductive isolating mechanism	divergent evolution
genus	prezygotic	convergent evolution
species	postzygotic	coevolution
subspecies	continental drift	gradualism
range	adaptive radiation	punctuated equilibrium
cline	character displacement	molecular clock
gene flow	polyploidy	minimum mutation tree

REVIEW QUESTIONS

1 Explain the organization of binomial nomenclature and provide an example. (pp. 288–289)
2 Summarize the problems in delimiting species. In particular, explain why the criterion of interbreeding isn't always dependable. (pp. 289–291)
3 List some of the complications in identifying species along an extensive range. (p. 291)
4 State Ernst Mayr's definition of species. For what contingency does the term *potentially interbreeding* provide? (p. 291)
5 Using simple diagrams, compare phyletic and divergent speciation. Which is representative of gradualism as discussed in the previous two chapters? (p. 294)
6 Why is reproductive isolation so important to specia-

tion? What happens to populations that rejoin before it is complete? (pp. 294–295)
7 Make a technical distinction between prezygotic and postzygotic reproductive isolation. (p. 294)
8 List several ways in which geographic isolation of species populations might occur. What must happen before the formation of separate species would be assured? (p. 295)
9 List the hypothetical events that led to allopatric speciation in the Galápagos finches. What is character displacement and what role did it play in finch speciation? (pp. 296–297)
10 Essentially how does sympatric speciation differ from allopatric speciation? (p. 299)

11 What generally happens when meiosis occurs in a hybrid (such as the mule)? How do plants manage to overcome the problem? (pp. 299–300)

12 Prepare a diagram to show how the rise of polyploidy might create instant reproductive isolation in a hybrid? (p. 300)

13 Explain how the polyploid state can be artificially induced. Suggest a practical application for this practice. (pp. 300–301)

14 Is polyploidy simply an oddity in plants? In what regions is it most commonly seen? (p. 301)

15 Briefly explain the meaning of divergent evolution. How might the shape of a tree be a good analogy to divergence? (p. 302)

16 List three marsupials and three placental mammals that represent clear examples of convergent evolution. What European niche does the South American mara fill? (p. 303)

17 Define coevolution and provide three examples. (p. 304)

18 Compare the pace of evolution according to gradualism and punctuated equilibrium. (p. 304)

19 Scientists have long been troubled by so-called missing links in the fossil record. Explain how the theory of punctuated equilibrium addresses this problem. Why are transitional forms actually missing? (p. 305)

20 What is the logical basis for using nucleotide sequences in DNA and amino acid sequences in protein for establishing phylogenetic trees and schemes? (pp. 306–308)

21 What is the "molecular clock," and what does it add to phylogenetic schemes derived from nucleotide and amino acid sequencing? (pp. 306–308)

III

FROM PROKARYOTES TO PLANTS

20

BACTERIA, VIRUSES, AND THE ORIGIN OF LIFE

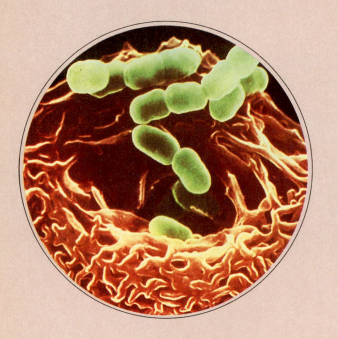

It's difficult to ponder the complexities of evolution for long without arriving at the ultimate question: how did life begin? The question is as old as humanity. The ancients throughout the world were absorbed by this mystery, and their conclusions have formed the bases for practically all religions.

Science is fettered with all manner of restraints, prejudices, hunches, and hopes. It may be said that in the sciences, faith is as strong as it is in religion or philosophy. Furthermore it must grow increasingly strong as solid evidence grows weaker. Thus in searching for an explanation of how life began, each researcher must have a measure of faith that he is on the right track. But faith in an idea is only a starting point. How does one legitimately investigate an improbable event that may have happened only once, several billion years ago? It's clear that we can never prove how life really first came to be on this planet. We can, however, examine a number of seemingly plausible notions of how life *might* have arisen. Most speculations about the possible origin of life involve suppositions and hypotheses that lead to predictions, and predictions, in turn, lead to testing. Many such suppositions have been trotted out, and many have been found wanting. But one proposed scheme offers enough promise to occupy the energies of a growing list of researchers.

THE ORIGIN OF LIFE

Although Darwin speculated that life might have arisen in a warm, phosphate-rich pond, the first serious proposals concerning the spontaneous origin of life (those that were based on sound biochemical and geological information) began to appear almost 50 years ago. Similar schemes were presented by J.B.S. Haldane, a Scottish biochemist, and by A.P. Oparin, his Soviet counterpart. They proposed that shortly after the earth's formation, under conditions quite different from those of today, a period of chemical synthesis occurred in the warm primeval seas. During this era, the precursors of life's molecules—amino acids, sugars, and nucleotide bases—formed spontaneously from the hydrogen-rich molecules of ammonia, methane, and water. Such synthesis was possible because there was no destructive oxygen in the atmosphere, and there was an abundance of energy in the form of electrical discharges, ultraviolet light, heat, and radiation (Figure 20.1). Since there were no organisms or oxygen to degrade the spontaneously formed organic molecules, they accumulated until the sea became a "hot, thin soup."

FIGURE 20.1 Scenario of early earth conditions. Torrential rains fed the young seas, while volcanoes released volatile gases into the forming atmosphere. Heat, ultraviolet light, and electrical discharge provided energy for chemical synthesis.

Haldane and Oparin suggested that continued synthesis and increasing concentrations led to the formation of polypeptides from amino acids, and, eventually, to a diversity of molecules, including the first enzymes. Proteins—especially enzymatic ones—catalyzed more synthesis, producing more interactive proteins. Collections of these new catalysts then became enclosed by simple, water-resistant protein or lipid shells that allowed certain molecules to pass through them.

These self-forming collections, termed **coacervates** by Oparin, supported and perpetuated themselves by making use of the energy-rich nutrients of the sea.

The **Haldane-Oparin hypothesis** suggests that simple molecules in the primitive seas and an abundance of energy led to the spontaneous formation of the precursor chemicals of life.

To continue with the Oparin-Haldane scenario, the coacervates initially were more or less random collections of molecules. They grew to a critical size and simply divided into smaller parts, only to increase again. But eventually the molecular structure of some became specific, and new, self-perpetuating forms arose. Included were molecules that encouraged energy-yielding reactions and others that used such energy to assemble replicas of the unique molecules. Such systems became more efficient at capturing and using the precursor molecules. Further, several unique lines began competing for the energy sources. The transition from coacervate to **protocell** (proto, "early") was under way.

After presenting his **coacervate hypothesis** in the 1930s, Oparin spent many years experimenting with versions of coacervate droplets. He and his co-workers tested great numbers of different combinations of molecules and succeeded in simulating simple versions of cell metabolism in their droplets. They added starch-synthesizing enzymes and glucose substrate, and starch appeared. They switched to starch-digesting enzymes and got their glucose back. Of course, these experiments must be kept in proper perspective. Coacervates are not "alive," and the impressive feats demonstrated by Oparin and his followers ultimately depended on the droplet being supplied with enzymes extracted from living cells. The experiments, however, do provide some information about a critical stage in the origin of life.

> Oparin maintained that **coacervates**— self-forming, growing, and dividing collections of molecules—represent an early stage in the evolution of cells.

With these developments in the scenario, the fundamental essentials of life are in place. Present are both energy-capturing and replicating mechanisms. Further, there is variation and competition for limited resources, key prerequisites for the operation of natural selection and evolution. From these beginnings the forces of evolution would produce the first protocells—true, if crude, living forms.

Haldane and Oparin's hypothetical scheme remained a neglected intellectual curiosity until 1952, when Nobel laureate Harold Urey and a younger colleague, Stanley Miller, began testing some of the assumptions in earnest.

The Miller-Urey Experiment

The crucial supposition of the Haldane-Oparin hypothesis was that *organic* (carbon-containing) molecules would form spontaneously under the primitive conditions. Urey and Miller created a laboratory apparatus at the University of Chicago that attempted to simulate what were then believed to be some of the primitive conditions of the earth (Figure 20.2). They introduced a small amount of water and a mixture of gases including methane, ammonia, water vapor, and hydrogen—but no free oxygen— into the apparatus. Energy was provided in the form of repeated electrical discharges (lightning?) through the atmosphere of the upper flask. After a week-long run, analyses of the sediments that collected in the lower flask revealed the presence of aldehydes, carboxylic acids, and, most interestingly, amino acids. All are common constituents of living cells.

> In the **Miller-Urey experiment** simple organic molecules were produced in an apparatus that simulated hypothetical early earth conditions.

Although these small molecules were a far cry from anything alive, their production under the simulated primitive conditions provoked a lively revival of interest in the Haldane-Oparin hypothesis. Until recently, the special atmosphere tested by Miller and Urey was believed to be representative of conditions on the early earth, conditions produced chiefly by volcanic activity.

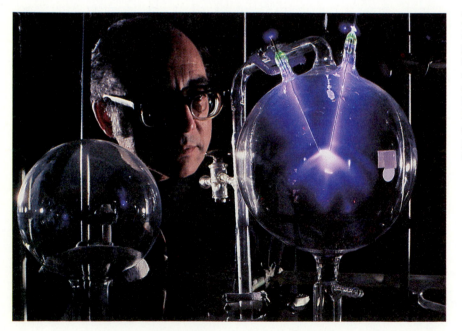

FIGURE 20.2 In the classic Miller-Urey experiment, the heated gases thought to comprise the primitive atmosphere were subjected to electrical discharges in a sealed, sterile environment. Residues were collected in the lower chamber and analyzed. Results indicated that some of the simple monomers of life could be produced spontaneously under test conditions.

Computer simulations now show that methane, ammonia, and hydrogen sulfide would be rapidly broken down by ultraviolet radiation, and that most of the hydrogen liberated would be lost to outer space. According to current theory, the principal constituents of the early atmosphere were water vapor, carbon dioxide, carbon monoxide, molecular nitrogen, and possibly some free hydrogen. Recent repeats of the Miller-Urey experiment, this time using the revised version of the probable primitive atmosphere, happily give even greater yields of appropriate small organic molecules. Included among these are the nucleotide bases of RNA and DNA.

We should keep in mind that there was no shortage of energy in the primitive atmosphere. Ultraviolet (UV) light was plentiful since the ozone layer (today's UV screen) had not yet formed. Other forms of readily available energy included lightning, heat, and radioactivity. Further, volcanic activity was intense. So the consensus of scientists today is that the major requirements of chemical evolution—reactive gases and concentrated energy—were abundant.

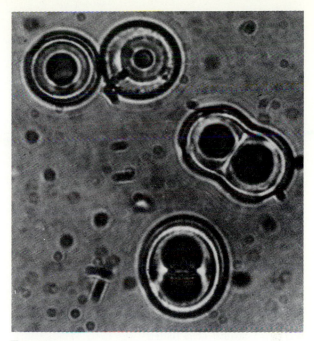

FIGURE 20.3 In water, thermal proteinoids spontaneously form proteinoid microspheres, each with a bilayer of molecules forming an isolating membrane.

Recent data suggest that the early atmosphere contained H_2O, CO_2, CO, N_2, and perhaps H_2. Energy sources included UV light, lightning, heat, radioactivity, and volcanic activity.

The Hypothesis Today

The spontaneous generation hypothesis is vigorously pursued today, but much of the effort is concentrated on its troublesome aspects. While the continued clarification of conditions on the primitive earth goes on—aided by NASA's planetary probes—and the spontaneous formation of monomers offers few problems, there are difficulties at the higher levels of the scenario, those involving **polymerization.**

Polymers. The polymerization of monomers into the familiar macromolecules of life—proteins, carbohydrates, lipids, and nucleic acids—without the assistance of enzymes presents many difficult problems. It is here that the original "hot, thin soup" hypothesis is weakest. Biological polymers in water slowly dissociate back into monomers, and heat accelerates the process. The reaction moves in the direction of spontaneous polymerization *only* when the concentration of monomers is very high and the concentration of water is very low.

How can this condition be achieved in nature? There have been many suggestions. Carl Woese of the University of Illinois, for example, has proposed that life began not in the sea, but in the hot, extremely dense atmosphere of the *very* early earth. His proposal has been supported by Sidney Fox of the University of Miami, who has demonstrated that amino acid polymerization occurs readily under hot, drying conditions, such as might be found in small pools alongside volcanoes and on the hot rocky beaches of ancient seas. Using drying heat and amino acids, Fox has succeeded in producing polypeptides of 200 or more amino acids. Fox calls these spontaneously generated polymers, **thermal proteinoids.** Importantly, when placed in water, the thermal proteinoids cluster into **proteinoid microspheres** (Figure 20.3). Such spheres automatically form two-layered membranes, isolating themselves from their watery surroundings much in the manner of coacervates.

Using Fox's methods, but in another approach, Israeli scientists have concentrated and polymerized amino acids on the surfaces of fine clay particles. They suggest that the first living, successfully reproducing organisms might have been made mostly of clay!

Fox polymerized amino acids under hot, drying conditions, forming **thermal proteinoids.** In water, proteinoids form **proteinoid microspheres** that are similar to coacervates.

The successful *spontaneous* polymerization of nucleotides is another matter. In the hope of proving something, investigators have boiled and dried concentrated solutions of energy-rich nucleoside triphosphates in the presence of single strands of DNA, loading all the dice toward the successful production of a second DNA strand. But without the appropriate enzymes, no recognizable polymers are formed. Spontaneous linkages can be forced, but they occur in the wrong places. Supporting evidence for the spontaneous formation of nucleic acids remains to be found.

The Earliest Cells

Having presumptuously taken the giant step between metabolically active aggregates to self-reproducing protocells—leaving huge gaps for future theorists to deal with—we can apply some informed speculation about early cellular life. What were the earliest cells like?

These first living beings probably relied heavily on the simple, anaerobic process of fermentation (see Chapter 8). Originally, their energy supply might have come from the monomers still being spontaneously formed. Such cells may have evolved ways to prey on each other, but with increasing competition in this limited energy supply system, natural selection would have strongly favored organisms that could exploit entirely new energy sources.

The early autotrophic cells. Autotrophs are of two main types: chemotrophs and phototrophs. Both require carbon dioxide as a source of carbon for their own cell structures, and simple, inorganic molecules, such as water or hydrogen sulfide, as a source of hydrogen to reduce the carbon dioxide. They also need a source of energy.

The most primitive living phototrophs obtain their hydrogen from dissolved hydrogen sulfide, and it's a good bet that the earliest successful phototrophs also utilized this source, using light energy in the simplest of photosystems to pry the hydrogen away (see Chapter 7). But the number of places in the world that provide both hydrogen sulfide and abundant sunlight are severely limited. At some point, a variant line of ancestral phototrophic bacteria began to obtain their hydrogen from a far more available source: water. This giant step was energetically difficult and probably required more complex photosystems, perhaps like those of cyanobacteria today (see Figure 20.13). The accomplishment was a smashing success but it was to change the earth forever.

> Hypothetical order of cell evolution: (1) Simple anaerobes used the energy of monomers; (2) phototrophs obtained hydrogen from hydrogen sulfide; (3) more complex phototrophs used H_2O as a hydrogen source.

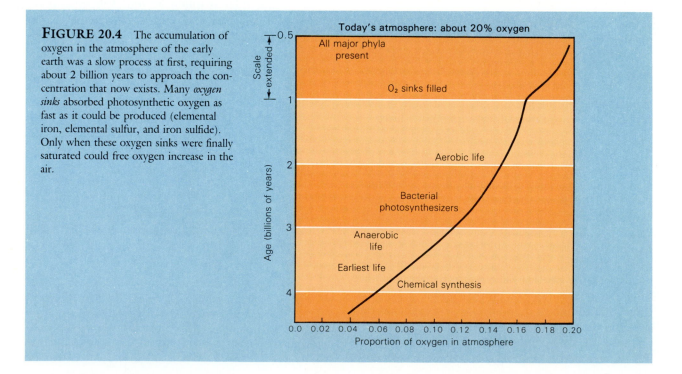

FIGURE 20.4 The accumulation of oxygen in the atmosphere of the early earth was a slow process at first, requiring about 2 billion years to approach the concentration that now exists. Many *oxygen sinks* absorbed photosynthetic oxygen as fast as it could be produced (elemental iron, elemental sulfur, and iron sulfide). Only when these oxygen sinks were finally saturated could free oxygen increase in the air.

Oxygen: a new atmosphere and the end of an era. A waste product of water-based photosynthesis is molecular oxygen. As the early phototrophs flourished, their ongoing release of oxygen became significant (Figure 20.4). The accumulation of spontaneously formed monomers ended since they were quickly degraded by the oxygen. Further, oxygen gradually poisoned the water for the anaerobic forerunners, eventually restricting them to anaerobic pockets in the sea bed and the earth's crust.

Newer kinds of heterotrophs. All life is capable of change, and although many oxygen-sensitive organisms undoubtedly became extinct—or were literally driven into the mud—new forms were to emerge through mutation and natural selection. The first step was to develop means of detoxifying oxygen. Later, ways were developed to harness the corrosive power of oxygen in order to extract the maximum amount of energy from organic foodstuffs, and oxidative respiration came into being in the biosphere.

New modes of nutrition arose, too. The burgeoning cyanobacteria themselves represented an abundant new source of food for any heterotroph that could engulf prey; thus the world saw the emergence of the first herbivores. The remaining anaerobes were soon relegated to a backwater in the progression of life, hidden away from poisonous oxygen in pockets of the earth's crust, in nutrient-rich muds, and in deep recesses of stagnant waters.

In this imaginative scenario, we have seen two metabolic forms of life emerging: the photosynthetic, oxygen-producing green phototroph and the aerobic, oxygen-using heterotroph. This is all we require to make the transition from the unknown to the known, for we have arrived at the time of the first fossil evidence of early life on our planet.

Much of the origin of life, therefore, remains unexplained, and what explanations we do have are based on conjecture and on our imperfect knowledge of what the primitive, inorganic earth was like. But this is the way of science, and whether current theory thrives and grows or dwindles into oblivion ultimately will depend on imaginative experiments and observations still to come.

Whereas increasing oxygen concentrations stopped monomer synthesis and drove many early cell lines into extinction, other lines evolved a means of using oxygen in cell respiration.

KINGDOM MONERA: THE PROKARYOTES

There is no longer any doubt that the prokaryotes preceded all of today's forms of life. In fact, there are clear indications of their presence in deposits 3.5 billion years old. What followed can be rightly called the Age of Prokaryotes, undoubtedly the longest period to be dominated by a single kingdom. The first eukaryotes probably arose only 1 to 1.2 billion years ago (Figure 20.5). The most widespread evidence of prokaryote antiquity is seen in strange columnlike deposits known as **stromatolites** (Figure 20.6). These highly laminated deposits of sedimentary rock feature layers produced by dense populations of bacteria—probably **cyanobacteria**—that were infiltrated over the eons by sand-bearing high tides. Modern cyanobacteria (formerly known as "cyanophytes" and "blue-green algae") are advanced photosynthetic prokaryotes.

Some paleontologists doubted that these strange geological formations were evidence of early life until the discovery of still-active stromatolite-forming cyanobacteria at work. They can be found in Yellowstone National Park in the United States and on the shores of Shark Bay on Australia's west coast.

The earliest fossils are prokaryotes, cyanobacteria that began forming **stromatolites** some 3.5 billion years ago.

Later in the chapter we will look into some startling ideas on prokaryote evolution and classification based on biochemistry. In the most recent taxonomy, the kingdom **Monera** has been discarded, its members divided into two apparently unrelated kingdoms, the **Archaebacteria** and the **Eubacteria** (giving *six* kingdoms). We will come back to this development after a general look at bacteria.

Bacterial Characteristics

Bacteria are single-celled prokaryotes. Whereas most forms exist singly, a few reveal signs of **colonial** organization, that is, clusters of cells living in some state of interdependence. Most bacteria are heterotrophs, relying on other organisms for their materials and energy. Of these, an immense number are **decomposers** (also called **reducers**)—soil and water bacteria whose decay activities are vital in recycling essential mineral ions. Others are **pathogens**—disease-

FIGURE 20.5 An earth calendar. The earth's history is shrunk into a period of 12 hours—midnight to noon. Note the long periods of time preceding life, and the age of prokaryotes.

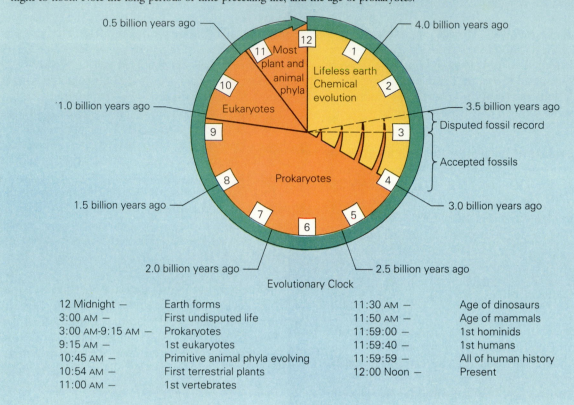

0.5 billion years ago

4.0 billion years ago

Most plant and animal phyla

Lifeless earth Chemical evolution

1.0 billion years ago

3.5 billion years ago
Disputed fossil record

Eukaryotes

Accepted fossils

1.5 billion years ago

Prokaryotes

3.0 billion years ago

2.0 billion years ago

2.5 billion years ago

Evolutionary Clock

Time	Event	Time	Event
12 Midnight —	Earth forms	11:30 AM —	Age of dinosaurs
3:00 AM —	First undisputed life	11:50 AM —	Age of mammals
3:00 AM-9:15 AM —	Prokaryotes	11:59:00 —	1st hominids
9:15 AM —	1st eukaryotes	11:59:40 —	1st humans
10:45 AM —	Primitive animal phyla evolving	11:59:59 —	All of human history
10:54 AM —	First terrestrial plants	12:00 Noon —	Present
11:00 AM —	1st vertebrates		

FIGURE 20.6 Fossilized stromatolites are believed to represent the most ancient evidence of life on the earth. They arose on rocky ledges in the tide pools of shallow preCambrian seas.

FIGURE 20.7 The prokaryotic bacterial cell.

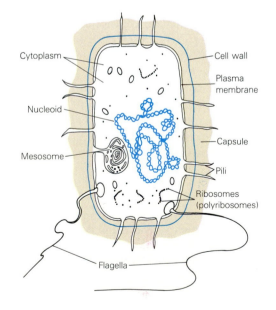

Cytoplasm

Cell wall

Plasma membrane

Nucleoid

Capsule

Mesosome

Pili

Ribosomes (polyribosomes)

Flagella

causing parasites—of plants and animals (including humans). Several groups are autotrophic, either **phototrophs** or **chemotrophs,** as we mentioned. The phototrophs utilize light-gathering pigments for photosynthesis, either **bacteriochlorophyll** or a uniquely prokaryote pigment called **bacteriorhodopsin.** Chemotrophs metabolize inorganic substances such as iron and sulfur compounds from the earth's crust.

Bacterial Cell

The bacterial cell is unique in a number of ways. Most are small, about one-tenth the size of typical eukaryotic cells, and their internal structure is much simpler (Figure 20.7). As we saw earlier (Chapter 4), membrane-surrounded organelles are rare. Exceptions include the well-formed thylakoid of cyanobacteria and the **mesosome.** The mesosome is an extension of the plasma membrane that may be involved in cell wall formation. There is no organized nucleus, and the single chromosome is essentially a naked, circular molecule of DNA, lacking the protein of eukaryotic chromosomes.

Bacterial cell walls differ from those of other eukaryotes. In most bacteria, the molecular building block is **peptidoglycan,** a complex polymer containing short amino acid chains interwoven with modified glucose units. Penicillin, the familiar antibiotic, interferes with peptidoglycan synthesis and is therefore lethal to many bacteria.

Many bacteria move about through the use of one or more flagella, as do some eukaryotes. However, unlike the microtubular, undulating eukaryotic flagellum, the bacterial version is an S-shaped, rotating, hollow tube—the only known rotating organelle (Figure 20.8).

> Most bacteria lack membrane-surrounded organelles. They have naked, circular DNA, cell walls of either **peptidoglycan** or protein, and a tubular, rotating flagellum.

FIGURE 20.8 Prokaryotic flagella are tubular structures, permanently bent into a gentle S-shape. The base inserts through the wall and into the plasma membrane, where it joins a ring of spherical proteins. The spheres rotate in place, spinning the flagellum.

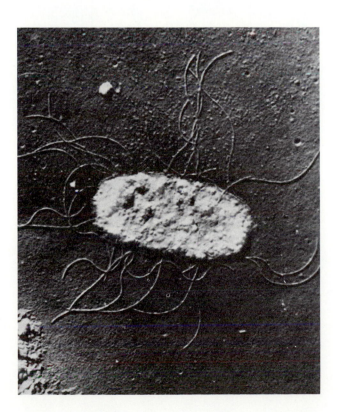

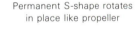

Permanent S-shape rotates in place like propeller

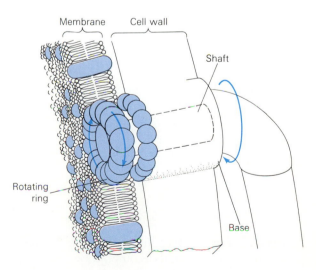

Bacterial reproduction. You may recall from Chapter 16 that some bacteria make use of a connecting sex pilus in a primitive and rare form of sexual reproduction called conjugation. Asexual reproduction is far more common. It occurs through **fission**, a primitive form of cell division without the use of a microtubular spindle apparatus (see Chapter 9). Following chromosome (DNA) replication, the two replicas attach to separate sites on the plasma membrane, and the cell wall is laid down between them (Figure 20.9).

The rate of fission can be phenomenal. For instance, under ideal growth conditions, the colon bacterium *Escherichia coli* can divide every 20 minutes. Potentially, 72 generations could form in just one day. (That's 2^{72} or 40 with 21 zeroes behind it.)

> Bacteria reproduce asexually by replication and simple **fission** and sexually through **conjugation**. Rapid growth rates are common.

Diversity in form and arrangement. The first criterion for classifying bacteria has been *shape*. The three primary shapes—rod, sphere, and spiral—are known, respectively, as **bacillus, coccus,** and **spirillum** (Figure 20.10).

The bacillus forms occur as single cells and in chains enclosed in sheaths. The spherical, or coccoid, forms occur singly (coccus), in pairs (diplococcus), in beadlike chains (streptococcus), or in grapelike clusters (staphylococcus) (see Figure 20.10). The spiral-shaped cells, or **spirochaetes,** occur singly. Many of these have lengthy flagella.

Many bacilli are also known for their ability to form highly resistant, thick-walled **endospores** (Figure 20.11) in response to unfavorable conditions. These dehydrated bodies contain the cellular components in a state of dormancy, ready to reabsorb water and resume their metabolic activities when conditions improve.

> Bacteria occur as rods **(bacillus),** spheres **(coccus),** and spirals **(spirillum).** They are arranged singly, in chains **(strepto-),** and clusters **(staphylo-).** Some form resistant, dormant **endospores.**

Heterotrophic Activities

Decomposers. Most heterotrophic bacteria gain their energy through decomposition, the break-

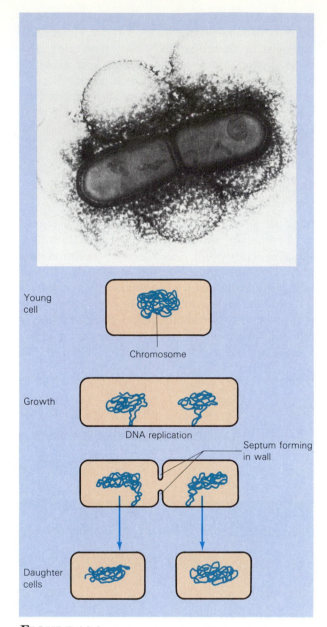

FIGURE 20.9 In bacterial fission, DNA replication occurs first, and each replica attaches to the cell membrane. The cell then divides and identical daughters emerge.

down of organic matter in dead organisms or their wastes. This activity is ecologically crucial since it releases such key ions as nitrates, phosphates, and sulfates for use by other organisms. This is particularly important to the growth and metabolism of phototrophs, organisms that bring energy into the living realm. (Of course, if the organic material being broken down is tonight's tenderloin, we may lose this objective view of decomposer activity.)

Bacterial species become quite specialized in their role as decomposers. Each has its own nutritional

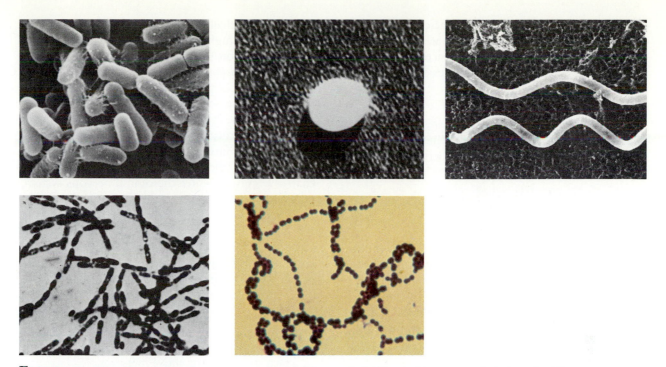

FIGURE 20.10 *(Top row)* The three common eubacterial forms—the bacillus (rods), coccus (spherical), and spirillum (spiral). *(Bottom row)* Two examples of bacterial aggregations: chains of bacilli and pairs of cocci. (Photo bottom right: Reprinted with permission of the present publishers, Jones and Bartlett Publishers, Inc., from Shih and Kessel: *Living Images,* Science Books International, 1982, page 3.)

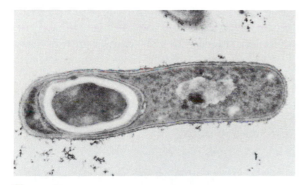

FIGURE 20.11 Endospore. Many bacteria, particularly those in the soil and water, survive unfavorable conditions by forming tough-shelled, resistant endospores.

requirements, and quite often the energy-rich products of one group are used by the next. Thus a succession of different bacterial decomposers arises in a food source. (Thus today's neglected tenderloin will take on a sequence of appearances and fragrances in succeeding days.). Nowhere is this better illustrated than in the **nitrogen cycle,** where the conversion of dead organisms to useful nitrates requires the activities of several specialists (see Chapter 46).

We often go to a lot of trouble to keep decomposers from getting at the tenderloin. The problem is not

an easy one, however, because in general, ideal growth conditions for such heterotrophs include only food, warmth, moisture, and (for many) oxygen. Thus our food is as attractive to decomposers as it is to us. Accordingly, there are many familiar ways of preventing or slowing their growth. We can interfere with their success by sterilization (canning and irradiation), cooling and freezing, and drying, salting, and sugaring. The last three effectively remove water from the food or set up unfavorable osmotic conditions. Heat can kill the decomposers as well. We are aware, for example, that pasteurization, the brief application of heat, kills disease-causing bacteria in milk. Chemical preservation, a favorite in the food industry (some food labels can be almost frightening), includes the use of small amounts of sorbic acid, sodium nitrate, calcium proprionate, and other chemicals to retard growth.

Although a lot of effort ordinarily goes into the prevention of bacterial growth in foods, there are some instances in which it is encouraged. Certain harmless bacteria provide many appetizing flavors in foods. For instance, we owe the tartness of pickles and sauerkraut to lactic acid bacteria. Add to the list yogurt, buttermilk, sour cream, and many of your favorite cheeses (Parmesan, Cheddar, Swiss, and

Camembert, to name a few), and bacteria may take on a whole new perspective. There are many other commercial and industrial uses for bacteria, but let's turn now to some bacterial activities we definitely want to discourage.

> Decomposer heterotrophs recycle vital mineral ions. Although many are food spoilers, some are used industrially in food processing.

Pathogenic Heterotrophs: The Villains

Pathogenic bacteria cause many serious, sometimes fatal, diseases. Diseases can be caused by all three bacterial forms. Pathogenic bacilli, for example, include the agents of such dread diseases as leprosy, typhus, black plague, diphtheria, and tuberculosis. These dangerous diseases have been the focus of intensive research over the years, and effective means of combatting them have been developed.

In spite of such notable progress with some pathogenic bacteria, we are still threatened by others. For instance, when the highly resistant spores of the soil anaerobe *Clostridium botulinum* are introduced into foods during the canning process, they can germinate and thrive in the nutrient-rich, airless environment. When contaminated food is eaten, the deadly bacterial secretions can cause a potentially fatal food-poisoning called **botulism.** With the decline of home canning, botulism is rare today, but the threat is always present.

Most coccoid pathogens are not as life threatening as *Clostridium* but they can also cause serious problems. Staphylococci, for example, are commonly involved in minor skin infections, boils, and pimples. One virulent strain of staphylococci, called "hospital staph," may sweep through hospital nurseries and cause numerous deaths before it can be contained.

The familiar strep throat is caused by streptococci. Because of the widespread use of antibiotics, strep throat isn't nearly as serious a health threat in the United States today as it was early in this century, or as it still is in less developed parts of the world. The body's own reaction to the streptococcus is the real threat: allergic reactions produce scarlet fever, rheumatic heart disease, and kidney inflammation. All can be fatal.

One highly persistent coccoid bacterium that is increasingly reported today is *Neisseria gonorrhoeae,* the diplococcus of **gonorrhea,** a sexually transmitted disease (Figure 20.12a). At one time, gonorrhea was readily cured with antibiotics, but bacteria evolve and adapt to the challenges of their environment, and now new and highly resistant strains exist.

The most notorious of the spirillum form of bacteria is *Treponema pallidum,* the corkscrew-shaped spirochaete of **syphilis,** another common sexually transmitted disease (Figure 20.12b). In its more progressive stages, syphilis has been called the "great pretender" because its effects on the body are widespread and it mimics the symptoms of a wide range of diseases. If the disease is untreated, the spirochaetes eventually enter the central nervous system, permanently damaging brain tissue and causing blindness, insanity, and death. Sadly, the spirochaete can cross the placenta, enter a growing fetus, and cause tragic birth defects. Before the development of antibiotics, syphilis was a serious threat, and many people died of the disease.

> Heterotrophic bacteria include **pathogens** that cause many important human diseases, some of which still resist preventive measures.

Autotrophic Activities

Photosynthetic bacteria. The best known of the photosynthetic bacteria are the cyanobacteria, which are mostly aquatic organisms that live singly or in colonies (Figure 20.13). Although the most ancient fossils, the 3.5 billion-year-old stromatolites,

FIGURE 20.12 Two common agents of sexually transmitted diseases are *Neisseria gonorrhoeae* and *Treponema pallidum,* the agents of gonorrhea and syphilis, respectively.

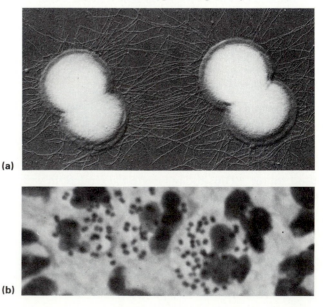

(a)

(b)

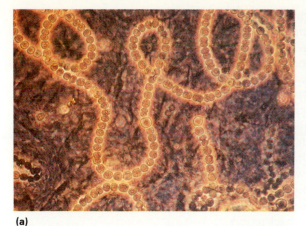
(a)

(b)

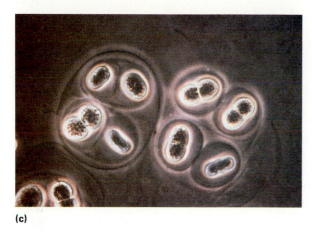
(c)

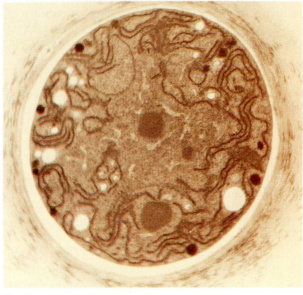
(d)

FIGURE 20.13   The diverse cyanobacteria include the beadlike *Nostoc* (**a**), the quietly undulating, filamentous *Oscillatoria* (**b**), and the spherical *Gleocapsa* (**c**), enclosed in its gelatinous wall. All are inhabitants of stagnant fresh water. The larger cells of *Nostoc* are known as *heterocysts*, which specialize in nitrogen fixation. Electron microscopic studies of cyanobacteria (**d**) reveal that their cellular organization can be quite complex. Note the membranous thylakoid (wavy structure).

may have been produced by cyanobacteria, the cyanobacteria are nevertheless considered to be *advanced* (highly evolved) organisms. This is because they capture light with bacteriochlorophyll *a* and carotenoids, plantlike pigments that are embedded in a complex thylakoid. Further, they use water as a source of hydrogen for fixing carbon during carbohydrate synthesis (see Chapter 7).

Another photosynthetic group, the **halobacteria** (halo, "salt"), get their name from the salty environment in which they thrive. In the simplest of photosystems, the halobacteria capture light energy with the purple pigment, bacteriorhodopsin, using the energy to pump protons out of the cell. This creates the usual steep chemiosmotic gradient that the bacterium uses to generate ATP. The ATP is then used in the synthesis of other molecules.

Photosynthesis in **cyanobacteria,** a **eubacterium,** employs chlorophyll *a* and an advanced thylakoid. In **halobacteria** the pigment **bacteriorhodopsin** is used in a very primitive photosystem.

Bacterial chemotrophs. Chemotrophic bacteria obtain their energy from the oxidation of inorganic compounds in the earth's crust. (Recall from Chapter 6 that oxidation is the removal of electrons or hydrogen from substrate.) One group breaks down sulfur compounds, producing sulfuric acid, which ionizes in soil water, releasing hydrogen ions and essential sulfate ions. Some chemotrophs get their energy by reducing hydrogen sulfide (H_2S) to sulfur, while others oxidize reduced forms of iron and manganese.

Cyanobacteria, along with some soil bacteria and certain bacteria that live in association with flowering plants, are **nitrogen fixers.** That is, they take in nitrogen gas (N_2) from the atmosphere and reduce it to ammonia (NH_3) and ammonium ions (NH_4^+) for their own use. This nitrogen, of course, is necessary for the synthesis of amino acids, nucleotides, and other essential molecules. But more significantly, the fixed nitrogen is also released into the environment where it becomes available to plants and algae. Thus **nitrogen fixation** is an important source of new usable nitrogen for other organisms. (The nitrogen cycle is discussed in greater detail in Chapter 46.)

Prokaryote Origins and Phylogeny

As recently as 1980, most biologists accepted the classification of prokaryotes into two major groups: the *bacteria* and the *cyanobacteria* (the cyanobacteria, in fact, were previously not considered to be bacteria at all, and were called *blue-green algae*). These two kinds of prokaryotes were grouped together into the kingdom Monera. As you are well aware, however, notions about how things should be grouped can change rapidly in biology. Intensive research, utilizing new molecular techniques for establishing phylogenetic relationships, has changed the way we classify microorganisms (see Chapter 19). Carl Woese, a leader in the new efforts, first suggested that the prokaryotes be divided into two kingdoms: the Eubacteria ("true bacteria") and Archaebacteria ("first, or ancient, bacteria"). Both qualify as prokaryotes, but they differ in enough ways to suggest, if not prove, that they evolved separately. Although the cells of the two bacterial groups look very much alike, they are as biochemically different from each other as they are from eukaryotes (Table 20.1). Let's look now at the archaebacteria.

In a phylogeny based on molecular differences in cell walls, membranes, pigments, and rRNA, prokaryotes are divided into two kingdoms, **Archaebacteria** and **Eubacteria.**

Archaebacteria

Although their name suggests a greater antiquity than the eubacteria, it is clear that these tough little creatures are about equally ancient. The two groups probably diverged over 3.5 billion years ago in an anaerobic world.

The best known archaebacteria are strict anaerobes but there are aerobes as well. One reason they have only recently been recognized is their peculiar living conditions. Archaebacteria live in improbable places such as acidic hot springs, ammonia-rich muck, salty ponds and mud flats, and dark, sediment-rich, anaerobic lake bottoms.

TABLE 20.1 Differences Between Archaebacteria and Eubacteria

	Archaebacteria	Eubacteria
Cell wall	Variety of substances, often proteinaceous	Peptidoglycans
Plasma membrane lipids	Modified branched fatty acids	Straight-chain fatty acids
DNA	Naked, circular	Naked, circular
Membrane-surrounded organelles	Absent	Absent (except for mesosome and thylakoid in some)
Ribosomes	30S, 50S subunits; structural similarity to eukaryotic	30S, 50S subunits, unlike archaebacteria and eukaryotic
Flagella	Unknown	Tubular, rotating (protein flagellin)
Photosynthetic pigments	Bacteriorhodopsin	Bacteriochlorophyll (chlorophyll *a*)
Cell division	Fission	Fission

Their habitat is not the only aspect of archaebacterial life that has the microbiologists' attention. Archaebacterial cell walls contain little-known proteins; unusual *branched* fatty acids occur in the cell membranes. Archaebacterial ribosomes look more like those of eukaryotes than those of eubacteria. As we've seen, phototrophic forms use a peculiar light-capturing pigment called bacteriorhodopsin instead of bacteriochlorophyll (Table 20.1). All in all, archaebacteria are definitely a strange lot.

The largest group of archaebacteria, the **methanogens** (methane-generators), are found in habitats where carbon dioxide and hydrogen are readily available, but where there is little or no oxygen. Among these habitats are anaerobic marshes, sewage treatment plants, mucky, anaerobic sea and lake bottoms (such as in the Black Sea), and the airless bowels of animals, including humans. There they ferment carbohydrates and reduce carbon dioxide, producing a mixture of methane gas (CH_4), or "marsh gas" as it was first called, and hydrogen gas (H_2). Well-designed sewage treatment plants can supply their own energy by utilizing the methane gas produced by methanogenic archaebacteria.

> **M**any archaebacteria are anaerobes that live in habitats that are hot, acidic, or salty. The best known are methane gas–producing, **methanogens.**

VIRUSES

Viruses don't really fit into any organizational scheme of living organisms, and, in fact, they may not be organisms at all. This odd speculation is based on the observation that dormant viruses can readily crystallize. Within their group, viruses are a mixed bag of unrelated entities. They share only a few features, such as their minute size and their inability to carry out the essential life processes outside a living host. Accordingly, all viruses are parasites. They must use the host's enzymes, raw materials, and energy supplies just to reproduce themselves.

Viruses are well-known agents of disease in virtually all forms of life. Human viral miseries include rabies, polio, smallpox, encephalitis, and yellow fever—each of which can be fatal. Less severe, but still dangerous, are the many forms of influenza, as well as the common cold, measles, chicken pox, and herpes. Viruses are also implicated in some animal cancers and are now known to be the agent of AIDS (acquired immune deficiency syndrome) (Table 20.2).

Outside their host, viruses consist of a core of nucleic acid, an enzyme or two, and a coat of protein. Many viruses are either cylindrical or polyhedral. Bacteriophages ("bacteria eaters") are more complex, with polyhedral heads and cylindrical tails (Figure 20.14). The infective form of a virus carries on no metabolism, has no cytoplasm, and can usually be crystallized. Viruses seem to fit somewhere between a very large molecule and a very small organism, but they are really neither.

> **V**iruses require the energy, enzymes, and protein-synthesizing machinery of a living host in order to reproduce.

Viral Genome

No one knows precisely how viruses originated, but it seems probable that they arose as aberrant genetic material of normal cells. Different kinds of viruses must have arisen independently of one another, since their basic mechanisms are so different. For example, in some viruses the genetic material is standard double-stranded DNA, just as it is in all metabolizing organisms. But in other viruses the genetic material varies, and we find (1) single-stranded DNA, (2) double-stranded RNA, (3) a single large molecule of single-stranded RNA, or (4) several small strands of RNA. The nucleic acid can be circular or linear, and the single-stranded nucleic acid can be either the transcribed strand or the nontranscribed strand. Furthermore, once the virus is inside its host cell, it may even change the kind of nucleic acid it uses: the RNA viruses often make DNA copies of their own genomes. Viruses are complicated entities indeed.

How Viruses Behave—or Misbehave

Most viruses contain one or more specialized enzymes that facilitate attachment to and penetration of a host cell. In some viruses, notably the bacteriophages, only the nucleic acid enters the host cytoplasm; but in other viruses, some enzymes are carried in as well. Once inside the host cytoplasm the virus can make a more or less permanent home. This is called the **lysogenic cycle.** Alternatively, it can take over the cell's metabolic apparatus, using it for its own ends. This more destructive process is called the **lytic cycle** (Figure 20.15a).

TABLE 20.2   Human Viruses and Associated Diseases

	Diseases
DNA Viruses	
Poxviruses (brick-shaped)	
Vaccinia type	Smallpox
Paravaccinia	Nodules on hands
Herpesviruses (icosahedral, enveloped)	
Group A	
Herpes simplex 1	Fever blisters, respiratory infections, encephalitis
Herpes simplex 2	Genital infections, cervical cancer (?)
B virus	Encephalitis
Group B	
Varicella-zoster	Chicken pox
Cytomegalovirus	Jaundice, liver/spleen damage, brain damage
Ungrouped	
Burkitt lymphoma	Burkitt lymphoma, Hodgkin's disease, infectious mononucleosis
Adenoviruses (icosahedral, naked)	
Human adenoviruses	Respiratory infections
Papovaviruses (icosahedral, naked)	
Human papilloma	Warts
RNA Viruses	
Picornaviruses (icosahedral, naked)	
Enteroviruses	
Poliovirus	Poliomyelitis
Coxsackie A	Muscle and nerve damage, common cold, meningitis
Coxsackie B	Meningitis, paralysis
ECHO	Paralysis, diarrhea, meningitis
Rhinoviruses	Common cold
Arboviruses (helical, enveloped)	
Dengue	Fever, rash
California encephalitis	Encephalitis
Myxoviruses (helical, enveloped)	
Influenza viruses	Influenza
Type A_0, A_1, A_2	
Type B_0, B_1, B_2	
Type C	
Paramyxoviruses	
Sendai virus	Common cold
Mumps virus	Mumps
Pseudomyxoviruses	
Measles	Measles, pneumonia, common cold
RNA tumor viruses	Breast cancer(?)
Retroviruses	
HTLV-I, HTLV-II	Leukemia, lymphoma (still in question)
HTLV-III	AIDS (acquired immune deficiency syndrome)
Miscellaneous Viruses	
Rubella virus	German measles
Hepatitis viruses	
Type A	Short incubation hepatitis (infectious)
Type B	Long incubation hepatitis (serum)
Type nonA-nonB or C	Hepatitis

FIGURE 20.14 A comparison of several representative viruses with the familiar bacterium *E. coli* shows how small viruses are as well as the range of sizes found. *E. coli* measures about 3000 nm in length (about half the diameter of a human red blood cell). The smallest virus, a bacteriophage, measures a minute 20 nm, while one of the largest, the tobacco mosaic virus, is just visible with the light microscope.

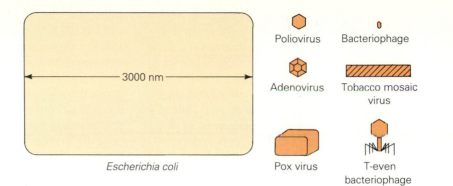

3000 nm

Escherichia coli

Poliovirus   Bacteriophage

Adenovirus   Tobacco mosaic virus

Pox virus   T-even bacteriophage

FIGURE 20.15 Some viruses are capable of both a lytic and a lysogenic cycle. **(a)** The virus invades, reproduces and lyses the cell. **(b)** The virus invades and inserts its nucleic acid into the host genome. It may later break out of the lysogenic cycle and enter the lytic cycle.

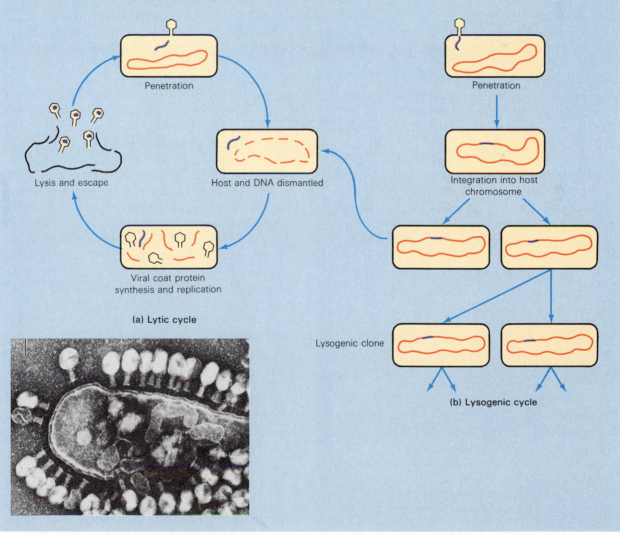

Penetration

Penetration

Lysis and escape

Host and DNA dismantled

Integration into host chromosome

Viral coat protein synthesis and replication

(a) Lytic cycle

Lysogenic clone

(b) Lysogenic cycle

The lytic cycle. In a typical host-killing lytic cycle a virus penetrates a cell and within minutes stops the host's protein synthesis by dismantling its DNA. Following this, the virus transcribes its own genes, forming viral messenger RNA. Using the host's protein assembling machinery, the virus makes its new penetrating enzymes and protein coats. Next, using either the host's replicating enzymes or its own, the viral invader assembles its new nucleic acid molecules.

Finally, the new infectious viral particles are assembled, and viral enzymes lyse or dissolve the remains of the host cell. The new viruses are then liberated, each fully capable of infecting and killing another cell. Some of the mammalian viruses provide a final insult to the host cell. Each partially assembled viral particle merges with a section of the host plasma membrane, which is then used to form a new viral envelope. (It's as if your favorite uncle, who, having eaten all of your groceries, borrows your overcoat on the way out.)

The lysogenic cycle. Events are even more bizarre in viruses that enter a lysogenic cycle (Figure 20.15b). Rather than killing the host they make a semipermanent home in the host cell. A virus does this by physically incorporating a copy of its genome (its total genetic material) into its host's DNA. This trick was first observed in bacteriophages (bacterial viruses) but human viruses do the same thing.

At some later time, the incorporated viral DNA cuts loose from the host chromosome and reverts to the lytic cycle, taking over the cell and making more infectious virus particles, thereby killing the cells. They will switch to this behavior whenever something goes wrong with normal host cell DNA replication. It is as if this is a sign that the host is in trouble and that it is time for the virus to jump ship.

> In the **lytic cycle,** the virus invades, reproduces, and lyses the cell. In the **lysogenic cycle,** the virus invades the cell and inserts its DNA into host DNA. Later the virus may enter a lytic phase.

Retroviruses. Certain RNA viruses called **retroviruses** infect humans in a remarkable way. The viral genome consists of single-stranded RNA, but they have an enzyme, **reverse transcriptase,** that can transcribe the single-stranded RNA into double-stranded DNA (see Chapters 15 and 16). The viral DNA is then inserted into one or more of our chromosomes. As the infected cell proliferates, the virus insert goes right along with it. It may even be passed down through generations in eggs and sperm. Some retroviruses ensure even more rapid proliferation by transforming the host cells into rapidly dividing cancer cells. In more recent developments, a retrovirus has been identified as the agent of the tragic disease AIDS (see Chapter 39).

Herpes simplex II. While AIDS is considered a fatal disease, herpes is often a somewhat painful nuisance. There are two types of the herpes virus. **Herpes simplex 1** causes troublesome fever blisters (cold sores). These are often activated by some trauma such as tension or direct sunlight on the lips. **Herpes simplex 2** is more serious. This is the notorious genital herpes. (There can be some transmission of type I to the genitals and vice versa, so sexual activity should be limited during either outbreak.)

So what is herpes all about? Surprisingly, the herpes virus resides in nerve cells, but it usually doesn't kill them. When the host's immune defenses are down, often because of stress, the virus buds off from its sanctuary, perhaps deep in the spinal cord, and travels along certain nerves to the skin. There it infects surface cells of mucous membranes, killing them and liberating numerous infectious virus particles. Time and again the host builds up antibodies, causing the virus to become quiescent and retreat into the nerve cells, where it is safe from the antibodies. Then the antibody level falls, and sooner or later herpes strikes again. There appears to be a direct relationship between early genital herpes infections and certain kinds of cervical cancer, which may develop years afterward. Herpes infections last a lifetime and are currently incurable, although intensive research is underway that may soon lead to at least a partial remedy. The drug acyclovir, a DNA replication suppressant, shows some promise in controlling active herpes, but it has no apparent effect on its dormant state.

We have begun our survey of life in the biosphere with an introduction to the simpler forms. It should be apparent, however, that the simpler forms are not so simple after all. Life at any level is complex, and our understanding of it is riddled with unknowns that, for some, translate into exciting challenge.

SUMMARY

THE ORIGIN OF LIFE

Ideas on the spontaneous generation of life were first formalized by J.B.S. Haldane and A.P. Oparin. They proposed that the conditions present on the primitive earth permitted the chemical precursors of life (such as sugars, amino acids, and nucleotide bases) to form spontaneously. From there, continued polymerization would form enzymes and other proteins, and collections of these surrounded by molecular shells might have formed coacervates. The growth of coacervates and inclusion of self-perpetuating systems might eventually have led to the first cells or protocells.

Since these ideas were first presented, many experiments with synthetic coacervates have been carried out, and many life processes observed. However, in each the enzymes at work were extracted from living organisms.

The Miller-Urey Experiment

S. Miller and H. Urey developed an apparatus in which they simulated the primitive conditions. Methane, ammonia, water vapor, and hydrogen were exposed to electrical discharge. Among the chemical products were amino acids. Since that time, many variations of reactants and energy sources have been tried, and similar results obtained.

Theorists today believe that the primitive atmosphere contained water, carbon dioxide, carbon monoxide, and nitrogen. Energy sources included ultraviolet light, lightning, heat, and radioactivity.

The Hypothesis Today

The weakest part of the spontaneous generation hypothesis involves polymerization—formation of the macromolecules. While some polymers form spontaneously, the reactions generally reverse with dilution in water. Some suggest that such chemical synthesis may have taken place in the atmosphere or on clay particles. S. Fox suggests that the proper concentrations of reactants could have occurred in small, hot, isolated pools. Accordingly, he has succeeded in producing polymers he calls thermal proteinoids, which in water form spherical collections called proteinoid microspheres.

The Earliest Cells

Theorists suggest that the first organisms were simple anaerobes, heterotrophs that utilized spontaneously forming monomers for energy and raw materials. Early phototrophs utilized sunlight energy and hydrogen from hydrogen sulfide in forming carbohydrates. Later the means for extracting hydrogen from the water molecule developed.

In the latter, oxygen was released as a by-product and began to accumulate, causing the spontaneous breakdown of monomers. The spontaneous generation of life was then impossible.

Heterotrophs adapted by evolving the means for detoxifying oxygen, eventually putting it to use in aerobic respiration. Their source of food became the autotrophs, along with other heterotrophs. The anaerobes persisted but were isolated in anaerobic habitats.

KINGDOM MONERA: THE PROKARYOTES

Prokaryotes were the first known forms of life. The oldest fossils, probably cyanobacteria, formed columnar **stromatolites.**

Bacterial Characteristics

Bacteria are single celled and colonial. The heterotrophs include decomposers and pathogens (disease producers). Autotrophs include phototrophs and chemotrophs. Phototrophs have the uniquely bacterial pigments, bacteriochlorophyll and bacteriorhodopsin.

Bacterial Cell

Bacterial cells are small, and with the exception of thylakoids and mesosomes membranous organelles are absent. The DNA is circular and lacks protein; the cell walls contain peptidoglycan; and the flagella are tubular and rotating.

Bacteria reproduce through simple fission, which follows replication. They have the fastest known cell cycles.

The three most common cell forms are the rodlike bacillus, spherical coccus, and spiral spirillum. Bacilli occur singly and in chains, whereas the arrangement of cocci may be single, paired, clustered, or in chains. Spirilla are single, usually with long flagella. Many bacteria become dormant by forming resistant endospores.

Heterotrophic Activities

Decomposers are ecologically vital since they recycle mineral nutrients. Different bacteria work in sequence throughout the decomposition process. Food spoilage can be prevented by sterilization—usually with heat—and inhibited by cooling, freezing, drying, salting, sugaring, and pasteurization. Chemical food additives are also effective. The food industry cultures certain bacteria in foods for the flavors they provide.

Pathogenic Heterotrophs: The Villains

The bacterial agents of most human disease can be controlled. Exceptions include the agents of food poisoning such as botulism. Staphylococcal and streptococcal infections persist, as do newer strains of the gonorrhea organism. Syphilis is still an important sexually transmitted disease that can impair the nervous system and infect the unborn fetus.

Autotrophic Activities

Many cyanobacteria are quite advanced; they produce plantlike, chlorophyll pigments and have an extensive, membranous thylakoid. Holobacteria utilize bacteriorhodopsin in a simple chemiosmotic system.

Chemotrophs oxidize inorganic materials in the earth's crust and take part in the nitrogen cycle. Some are nitrogen fixers, incorporating atmospheric nitrogen into useful compounds and ions. Nitrogen is needed for the synthesis of many molecules including amino acids and nucleotide bases.

Prokaryote Origins and Phylogeny

In newer schemes based on biochemical and molecular data, prokaryotes have been assigned to two kingdoms, archaebacteria and eubacteria. They differ in cell wall make-up, plasma membrane lipids, ribosomal RNA, and other factors.

Archaebacteria

Archaebacteria inhabit acidic hot springs, anaerobic lake-bottom mud, salty ponds, and the gut of many animals. The methanogens ferment carbohydrates, producing methane and hydrogen gases.

VIRUSES

The phylogenetic origin and relationships of viruses are unknown. Viruses consist of a protein coat, a nucleic acid core (the genes), and penetration enzymes. All are parasitic, unable to reproduce outside the host cell. Many are important disease agents of humans.

Viral Genome

The nucleic acid core of viruses may be single- or double-stranded DNA, double- or single-stranded RNA, or small strands of RNA.

How Viruses Behave—or Misbehave

Some viruses utilize enzymes to insert their nucleic acids into the host cell, whereas in others the entire viral particle is taken in through phagocytosis. Within the host, viruses may enter a lytic cycle in which they reproduce and lyse (destroy) the cell. The host's protein-synthesizing and replicating mechanisms are used by the virus. In the lysogenic cycle the viral genome is inserted into a host chromosome, and it may pass from generation to generation of cells and individuals in a dormant state. Later it may enter a lytic cycle.

Retroviruses are RNA viruses that use the enzyme reverse transcriptase to convert their single strand of RNA to a double strand of DNA. The DNA is then inserted into the host's chromosomes. This disrupts many gene functions. A retrovirus causes AIDS.

The herpes simplex 2 virus causes genital herpes. The virus infects genital and mouth lining cells, forming blisters as it reproduces and lyses the cells. Remissions occur periodically when the virus migrates back into the nervous system.

KEY TERMS

coacervate	Eubacteria	bacillus	nitrogen fixer
protocell	colonial	coccus	methanogen
coacervate hypothesis	decomposer (reducer)	spirillum	virus
polymerization	pathogen	spirochaete	lytic cycle
thermal proteinoids	phototroph	endospore	retrovirus
proteinoid microsphere	chemotroph	nitrogen cycle	reverse transcriptase
stromatolite	bacteriochlorophyll	botulism	Herpes simplex 1
Cyanobacteria	bacteriorhodopsin	gonorrhea	Herpes simplex 2
Monera	peptidoglycan	syphilis	
Archaebacteria	fission	halobacteria	

REVIEW QUESTIONS

1 Summarize Haldane's and Oparin's ideas on the spontaneous synthesis of molecular precursors. Why was an absence of oxygen essential? (pp. 312–313)

2 What steps did Haldane and Oparin suggest might have followed the formation of precursors? (pp. 312–314)

3 Describe the experiments carried out with coacervates. What is their main shortcoming? (p. 314)

4 Discuss the experiment of Miller and Urey. Include their apparatus, the substances energy-source tested, and the results. (p. 314)

5 Summarize what today's atmospheric scientists believe were the gases and energy sources in the primitive earth. (p. 315)

6 Discuss the problem of spontaneous polymer formation. What tends to happen when polymerization occurs in water? (p. 315)

7 Summarize the findings of Sidney Fox. Did he succeed in synthesizing cells? Explain. (p. 315)

8 What have been the results when attempts at the spontaneous synthesis of nucleic acids were made? What critical element of the replication process is apparently needed? Why not simply add it? (p. 316)

9 Briefly summarize the four hypothetical steps that lead from the protocell to more advanced autotrophs and heterotrophs. (pp. 316–317)

10 Why was the evolution of a photosystem that used

water for its hydrogen source so significant to life. Was this a sudden development? Explain. (p. 317)

11 What do prokaryotes and, in particular, cyanobacteria have to do with the origin of life? (p. 317)

12 What are stromatolites? How do we know they are authentic? (p. 317)

13 List four ways bacteria fulfill their material and energy requirements. (pp. 317, 319)

14 Prepare a simple illustration of a prokaryote cell. Label the flagellum, cell wall, cell membrane, and any internal structures. (p. 319)

15 How do the following differ between prokaryotes and eukaryotes: flagellum, cell wall, chromosomes, membrane-surrounded organelles? (p. 319)

16 Describe the fission process in bacteria. How does it differ from cell division in most eukaryotes? What is the apparent advantage of such a simple mechanism? (p. 320)

17 Prepare simple drawings of the three forms of bacterial cells. Label the three and then show the three arrangements seen in the spherical bacteria. (p. 320)

18 What is the single, most ecologically important activity of heterotrophic bacteria? Why is this role so essential? (pp. 320–321)

19 List five ways of preventing food spoilage by bacteria and explain how each works. (p. 321)

20 List five formerly important bacterial diseases and explain why they are no longer a threat. (p. 322)

21 Why is gonorrhea now an important disease when it was once almost completely controlled? (p. 322)

22 Name the light-absorbing pigments in the two kinds of phototrophic bacteria. Which bacterium would you consider more advanced? Why? (pp. 322–323)

23 List three activities of bacterial chemotrophs. (p. 324)

24 Why is nitrogen so essential to life? Explain why the work of nitrogen fixers is so important. (p. 324)

25 What changes are taxonomists making in the classification of prokaryotes? List four differences between members of the two new kingdoms. (pp. 324–325)

26 List four environments in which archaebacteria are likely to be found. (pp. 324–325)

27 Describe the structure of a virus. Why is it not considered to be a cell? (p. 325)

28 List five important human viral diseases. What is the latest important disease to be added to the list? (p. 325)

29 Into what taxonomic grouping do the viruses fall? Why? (p. 325)

30 Name four different ways the viral genome is organized. (p. 325)

31 Briefly summarize the events of the lytic cycle. (p. 328)

32 Explain how the lysogenic cycle operates. Which of the two cycles, the lytic and lysogenic, is most significant genetically, that is, to future generations? (p. 328)

33 Explain how retroviruses enter a lysogenic cycle. Why is there a greatly renewed interest in the retrovirus? (p. 328)

34 Distinguish between the infection caused by the Herpes simplex 1 and Herpes simplex 2 viruses. (p. 328)

35 Discuss the cyclic behavior of genital herpes. Is there a cure yet? (p. 328)

21

PROTISTS AND FUNGI
The Simpler Eukaryotes

The eukaryotes are a diverse lot. They range from fungal spores to Washington lobbyists. Protists and Fungi, the simplest eukaryotes, are among the most primitive living things on earth, and they vary greatly from one form to another. Some emit tiny bursts of light, setting aglow warm tropical seas. Others poison those waters and kill other marine creatures by the millions. Yet others are tiny filamentous predators that can entrap worms and send their fingerlike projections deep into the prey's nutrient-rich body.

Because protists are so primitive and relatively unorganized, some forms are believed to be similar to the distant ancestral species that gave rise to much of today's life. Some people believe that by understanding more about these simpler eukaryotes, we can gain a clearer picture of how life may have changed during the planet's distant past. For example, we may learn how the simplest eukaryotes arose from distant prokaryote ancestors. (A startling theory on the emergence of eukaryotes is presented in Essay 21.1.) Further, we may learn how *multicellularity* arose, since some of the simple, single-celled eukaryotes are related to others showing a hint of multicellularity and still others that are *clearly* multicellular. Through the rise of multicellularity, the evolutionary stage was set for the added specializations necessary for species to explore new resources and survive in an increasingly complex and competitive world.

WHAT IS A PROTIST?

The kingdom Protista contains the eukaryotic organisms that are not plants, animals, or fungi. Now we know what they aren't, but describing what they *are* takes a bit of doing. That's because there is no simple definition of a protist. In essence, protists are a grab-bag of disparate creatures. Whereas many are single celled, others occur in **aggregates** and **colonies** of cells, and a few are complex and truly multicellular. Although aggregates are more or less casual, temporary associations, colony members have developed a degree of interdependence. By contrast, the cells in multicellular species have reached a state of total interdependence and, for the most part, cannot function separately.

We have arranged the protists in three categories: heterotrophic, animal-like, **protozoans;** autotrophic (photosynthetic), plantlike **algae;** and heterotrophic, funguslike **water molds** and **slime molds.** The most diverse of these are the algae, since they range from the green, single-celled swimmer *Euglena* to the giant multicellular ocean kelp *Macrocystis,* which is over 50 meters in length. The large and complex kelps and seaweeds are sometimes included in the plant kingdom.

PROTOZOANS: ANIMAL-LIKE PROTISTS

"Proto" means first and "zoa" refers to animals, and indeed, many protozoans are clearly similar to animals. For example, they are heterotrophic, which means they derive their energy and carbon by feeding on other organisms or their products. Protozoans require amino acids, carbohydrates, lipids, and vitamins in their diet, much as we do. Further, like animals, they show a wide range of feeding specializations. Many are parasites; some are simple decomposers of dead organic material, and others actively capture and digest living prey.

The 65,000 known protozoans have been assigned into seven phyla, but we will focus on the three that contain the most numerous and best known species. Phylum **Sarcomastigophora** includes the **flagellates** and **amebas;** phylum **Apicomplexa** contains the nonmotile **sporozoans,** chiefly parasites; and **Ciliophora** contains the active, fast-moving **ciliates.**

Flagellates and Amebas (Phylum Sarcomastigophora)

Flagellates. **Flagellates** move their vase-shaped bodies by means of one or more whiplike, undulating flagella. Flagella occur singly, in pairs, or in greater numbers and they can either push or pull the cell about (Figure 21.1). Many flagellates are free-living, but others are parasites. As a rule, feeding is through either simple absorption or phagocytosis (see Chapter 5).

Like so many protists, flagellates reproduce asexually, employing mitosis and cell division through animal-like cleavage. Sexual reproduction occurs, but it is apparently infrequent. Curiously, sex in flagellates does not involve gametes; two flagellates simply fuse to form a zygote. Further, such fusions are not preceded by meiosis; there is no need for chromosome reduction beforehand, since flagellates, like so many protists, are haploid throughout most of their lives. As you would expect, the fusion of two haploid cells restores the diploid chromosome number—but not for long. The newly formed zygote soon undergoes meiosis, forming four haploid cells. This peculiar

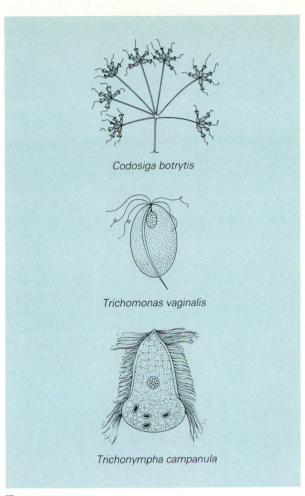

FIGURE 21.1 *Codosiga botrytis* forms a colony of stationary, stalked cells that use their flagella for feeding. *Trichonympha campanula* swims through the termite gut where it lives by digesting wood taken in by its host. *Trichomonas vaginalis* inhabits the human vagina where it sometimes causes serious discomfort.

zygotic life cycle contrasts sharply with our own **gametic** life cycle and that of all animals, in which, except for the haploid sperm and eggs, cells are diploid throughout life (see Essay 21.2).

Flagellates move through the action of a flagellum, have a **zygotic** life cycle, and are often serious parasites of animals.

Some parasitic flagellate protozoans cause severe diseases in humans. Among them are the **trypanosomes,** members of the genus *Trypanosoma.* A trypanosome can be identified by an undulating flap—actually a modified flagellum—that runs the length of its spindly body (Figure 21.2). *Trypanosoma gam-*

The evolutionary transition from the prokaryotic cell to the much more complex and elaborate eukaryotic cell has perplexed biologists for some time. One hypothesis proposes that eukaryotic organelles evolved when infoldings of the cell membrane pinched off and enclosed various cellular functions. Hypotheses such as this often seem reasonable enough, but they simply can't be tested readily.

In 1967, a totally different hypothesis was proposed by Lynn Margulis. Using information from a wide variety of fields, Margulis concluded that the primitive eukaryotic cell developed in at least three separate stages that involved the union of four different prokaryotic lines. Her conclusion has become known as the **symbiosis hypothesis.** Margulis proposed that mitochondria, which are found in all eukaryotic cells, are the descendants of once free-living bacteria that long ago formed such a mutualistic symbiosis with a host cell. She also proposed that chloroplasts and cilia are the descendants of other bacteria that also entered the eukaryotic cell in what began as mutualistic symbiosis, an association in which both parties benefited.

Margulis' symbiosis hypothesis was testable: specifically, it allowed her to predict that mitochondria, chloroplasts, and cilia should be biochemically and genetically more similar to certain free-living prokaryotes than they are to other parts of the eukaryotic cell. These predictions have held up remarkably well for mitochondria and for chloroplasts, but not for eukaryotic cilia. So far there has been no way to equate the solid, rotating, prokaryote flagellum with the undulating, microtubular eukaryote counterpart.

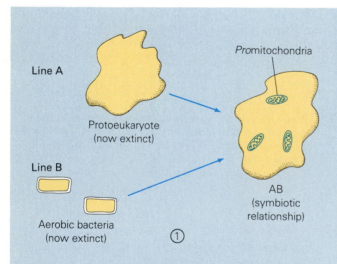

Line A

Protoeukaryote
(now extinct)

Line B

Aerobic bacteria
(now extinct)

Promitochondria

AB
(symbiotic
relationship)

①

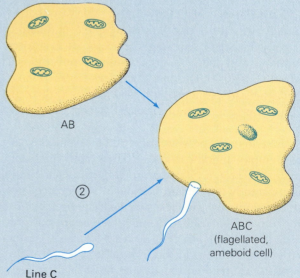

AB

②

Line C

ABC
(flagellated,
ameboid cell)

② The union of prokaryote lines AB and C. The new AB symbiont now took one step closer to a eukaryotic status by incorporating into its cytoplasm a cell from line C. These new cells brought with them microtubule proteins and the flagellate structure. In addition, it is hypothesized, the tubular centriolar structure arose from this new incorporation. The new development improved the ability of the symbiont to move about, becoming a more efficient heterotroph.

① The union of prokaryote lines A and B. Two hypothetical prokaryotes, now extinct, included a protoeukaryote (line A), which was a simple anaerobe with the ability to phagocytize its food. One organism it fed upon was an aerobic bacterium from line B. Eventually, line B cells became incorporated, and a symbiotic relationship developed. They became interdependent, with the mitochondrialike bacteria carrying on aerobic respiration within the line A cells. The line B cells lost their ability to live outside their hosts. As the host reproduced, the line B cells did likewise, just as mitochondria do in eukaryotic cells today.

Margulis' case seems strongest for the origin of chloroplasts. Their internal structure and biochemistry are very similar to that of cyanophytes. Like cyanophytes and chloroxybacteria, plastids store starch. Chloroplasts arise only by division of other chloroplasts. Both chloroplast and mitochondrial DNA are susceptible to certain antibiotics that do not affect the eukaryote nucleus—further evidence of similarity between the inclusions and prokaryotes. When the chloroplasts of *Euglena* have been destroyed by such antibiotics, the parent cell line can be kept growing indefinitely in a nutrient broth, but the chloroplasts never reappear.

The case for the bacterial origin of mitochondria is almost as good. True, mitochondria have internal membranes (cristae) unlike anything seen in bacteria, and they seem to have very few functional genes. But at least one mitochondrial protein, cytochrome c, is recognizably similar by shape and sequence—presumably by descent—to the cytochromes of certain bacteria, especially the photosynthetic nonsulfur purple bacteria. It now seems likely that the original mitochondrial symbiont was a photosynthetic symbiont, and that it later became restricted to respiratory tasks.

A lightweight ribosomal RNA is found in mitochondria, chloroplasts, eukaryote cytoplasm, bacteria, and cyanobacteria (but not in cilia): a computer analysis of such RNA sequences produces exactly the relationships that are uniquely predicted by Margulis' hypothesis. The symbiotic origins of mitochondria and chloroplasts are now as thoroughly established as any "fact" in biology today.

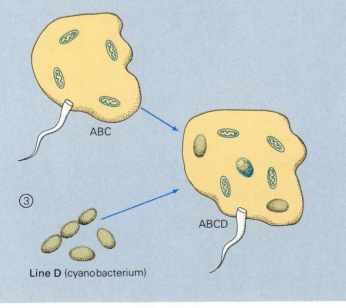

③ The union of prokaryote lines ABC and D. In the final step, the highly improved prokaryote incorporated a cyanobacterial cell with efficient photosynthesizing structures. By this step, the prokaryote had several of the organelles of today's eukaryotes, including mitochondria, contractile proteins, centrioles, cilia, and now chloroplasts. All that remained was for the membranous endoplasmic reticulum and the nuclear membrane to evolve and a modern eukaryote would emerge.

ABC

③

ABCD

Line D (cyanobacterium)

There are three basic themes in the life cycles of eukaryotes. Of course, we are most familiar with our own, so we will review it first. The other two may seem a bit bizarre by comparison.

1. The **gametic cycle.** The gametic cycle occurs in some protists and all animals, including humans. It is quite direct and uncomplicated. In the gametic cycle, the cells are diploid except for the gametes—the sperm and egg cells or their counterparts (isogametes)—which are haploid. In animals, gametes are produced as certain diploid cells undergo meiosis. The diploid state is restored as gametes unite in fertilization. While this is a conceptually comfortable cycle, many of the world's creatures have evolved quite different systems. The next theme, in fact, is pretty much the opposite of the animal life cycle.

2. The **zygotic cycle.** The zygotic life evolved much earlier than the gametic cycle. In fact, it is the most primitive of all the cycles. We find it to be the reproductive theme in some of the green algae, some protozoa, and the fungi. In these species nearly all of the individual's life is spent in the haploid state. At some point, certain haploid cells enter conjugation, their nuclei fusing through this primitive form of fertilization, thus forming diploid zygotes. The resulting zygote may enter an extended period of dormancy, but it is more likely that meiosis will immediately follow fertilization, restoring the usual haploid state.

3. The **sporic cycle.** The sporic life cycle can be quite varied in the algal protists, so we'll concentrate on its characteristics in plants. Meiosis in plants does not directly result in the formation of gametes. Instead haploid **spores** are formed (sometimes called **meiospores**). If conditions are suitable, the spores grow and divide, giving rise to a specialized multicellular phase in which gametes are produced. Because this phase is already haploid, the gametes are produced by simple mitosis. Because of its role, this phase of the life cycle is sensibly called the **gametophyte** ("gamete plant").

The fusion of gametes at fertilization produces a diploid zygote. Through growth and cell division, the zygote gives rise to a diploid, multicellular generation, which will again enter meiosis and give rise to more spores. The diploid, spore-producing phase is aptly called the **sporophyte** ("spore plant"). For most plants this is the prominent phase, the one most easily found. Thus, the sporophyte includes the plant body, the familiar roots, stems and leaves. The gametophyte is tucked away in the flower or cone. Biologists call this alternation between the sporophyte and gametophyte phases an **alternation of generations.**

In its more primitive state (some algae and plants such as ferns), the alternating gametophyte and sporophyte phases occur in physically separated individuals. At times, things get even stranger, and we find a highly dominating gametophyte and a highly reduced sporophyte.

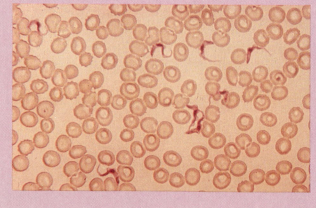

FIGURE 21.2 A complex flagella attached to an undulating membrane characterize the flagellate, *Trypanosoma gambiense,* the agent of African sleeping sickness. It is spread by the bite of a tiny tsetse fly, a second host.

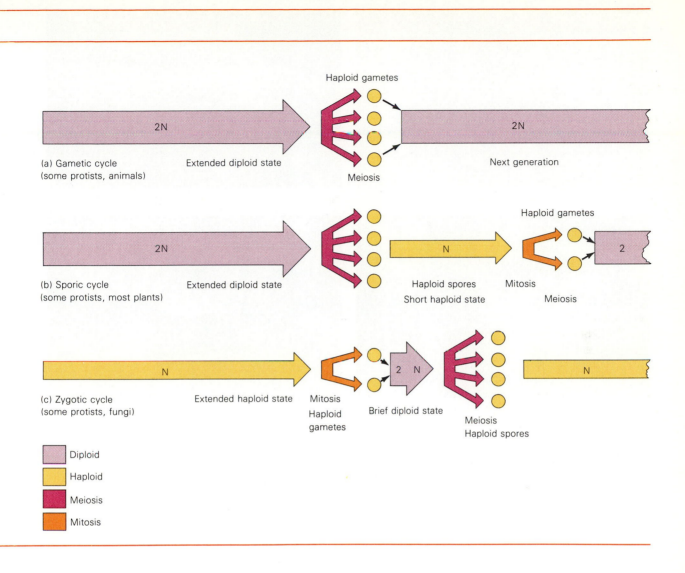

Haploid gametes

(a) Gametic cycle
(some protists, animals)

2N

Extended diploid state

Meiosis

2N

Next generation

(b) Sporic cycle
(some protists, most plants)

2N

Extended diploid state

Haploid spores

Short haploid state

N

Mitosis

Haploid gametes

Meiosis

2

(c) Zygotic cycle
(some protists, fungi)

N

Extended haploid state

Mitosis

Haploid gametes

2 N

Brief diploid state

Meiosis

Haploid spores

N

Diploid

Haploid

Meiosis

Mitosis

biense is the cause of African sleeping sickness. The bite of the infamous tsetse fly injects the parasite into the bloodstream of a mammalian host. Multiplying trypanosomes eventually enter the host's central nervous system, bringing on eventual coma and death.

Amebas (subphylum Sarcodina). Ameboid protozoans are fascinating creatures. Some of them are quite large as protists go. A few giants, such as *Pelomyxa,* may reach five millimeters ($^3/_{16}$ in.) in length, making them easily visible to the unaided eye (Figure 21.3a). (Their size may explain why they require numerous nuclei for protein synthesis.) Most amebas are free-living predators that feed by surrounding and engulfing prey through phagocytosis and digesting it in food vacuoles. Other amebas are

dangerous parasites. *Entamoeba histolytica,* for example, infects cells lining the human colon, causing amebic dysentery. Many an invading army has had to hastily retreat from areas harboring *E. histolytica.*

Typically, amebas move about and capture prey through the use of **pseudopods** ("false feet"). Pseudopods are temporary, lobelike extensions of the cytoplasm that involve the reorienting of microfilaments in the cytoskeleton, thus stiffening the walls of a false foot and softening the cytoplasm within. Once these changes occur, a pseudopod can extend in any direction and the rest of the cytoplasm then flows into it. Obviously, there isn't much point in describing the "shape" of an ameba.

The dramatically beautiful **heliozoans** or "sun animals" (Figure 21.3b) live in fresh water and are partially encased in glassy capsules of silicon dioxide.

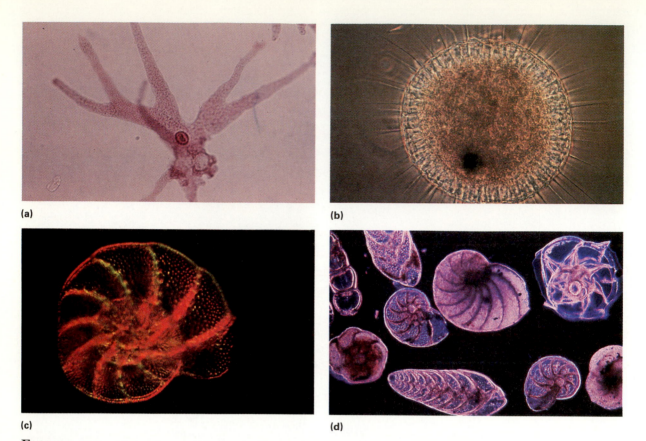

FIGURE 21.3   (a) *Amoeba* can reach several millimeters in diameter. (b) The heliozoan ameba, *Actinosphaerium,* has numerous spiny axopods, each with an overlayer of moving cytoplasm that actively engages in phagocytosis. (c) Radiolarians are often spherical with highly sculpted glassy skeletons. Radiolarians, along with the coiled foraminiferans (d), contribute significantly to ocean bottom sediments.

The radiating rays consist of lengthy **axopods,** pseudopods of motile cytoplasm, stiffened with long, straight bundles of microtubules. The microtubule bundles can quickly disassemble and reform later as they are needed. **Radiolarians** of the open sea (Figure 21.3c) have a similar body plan, and their glassy corpses litter the ageless ocean floor with deposits known as *radiolarian ooze.*

Foraminiferans belong to another group of planktonic ameboid protozoans. They produce chalky, not glassy, skeletons, sometimes in shapes remarkably reminiscent of the shells of garden snails (Figure 21.3d).

> Freshwater sarcodines include the formless ameba and the beautiful heliozoans. Marine amebas include spiny **radiolarians** and spiral-shelled **foraminiferans.**

Sporozoans (Phylum Apicomplexa)

Sporozoans have three major characteristics: (1) they form spores, (2) live as parasites, and (3) except for gametes, have no obvious means of moving about. Many sporozoans have complex life cycles, reproducing in both sexual and asexual phases, often completed in different hosts.

One group of sporozoans is of great importance to humans since it is the agent of malaria, a disease that has been called humanity's greatest curse. Malaria is spread from person to person by the female *Anopheles* mosquito, a tiny insect harboring the even tinier sporozoan parasite, *Plasmodium vivax.* (The female *Anopheles* is recognized by her habit of standing on her head as she draws blood.) Actually, there are some 50 species of *Plasmodium,* all carried by mosquitos and capable of infecting other vertebrates, primarily birds.

The life cycle of *P. vivax* and the course of malaria are summarized in Figure 21.4. Note particularly the organism's asexual stages in the malaria victim and the events that bring on cycles of fever and chills. Sexual reproduction, we see, takes place in the mosquito. (For a strange twist involving malaria and the sickle cell allele see Essay 15.1).

> **S**porozoans are chiefly parasitic with complex life cycles. Included is the human malarial agent *Plasmodium vivax,* whose asexual phase occurs in the human victim and sexual phase in the mosquito.

Ciliates (Phylum Ciliophora)

Among the most complex cells on earth are those of the **ciliates** (Figure 21.5). Ciliates range in size from about 10 μm to 3 mm, which is about the same relative difference that exists between a shrew and a blue whale. The ciliates' most obvious characteristic is that they are covered with cilia, in longitudinal or spiral rows. Like flagella, cilia can move, but they are so numerous that it wouldn't do for each cilium to beat wildly, independent of the rest. Their movement is highly coordinated by a network of connecting fibers that run beneath the surface of the cell. Other ciliates are sessile (fixed in place) and their cilia are used only for feeding.

Many ciliates feed by using cilia to sweep bacteria and organic debris into the **cytostome,** a mouthlike opening where phagocytosis occurs. The food then enters a **food vacuole,** receives enzymes, and, as the vacuole breaks away and moves through the cytoplasm, the digested food is distributed (Figure 21.6). Undigested residues are discharged from the cell through exocytosis, which occurs at another specific location, the **cytopyge.** (The specifics of phagocytosis and exocytosis are discussed in Chapter 5.)

Water regulation in freshwater ciliates and many other protozoans is carried out by **contractile vacuoles.** These specialized, permanently located organelles take in water from the cytoplasm and squeeze it out through the surrounding membrane. Contractile vacuoles fill and empty periodically, using ATP to power the contractions of surrounding microfilaments that do the squeezing.

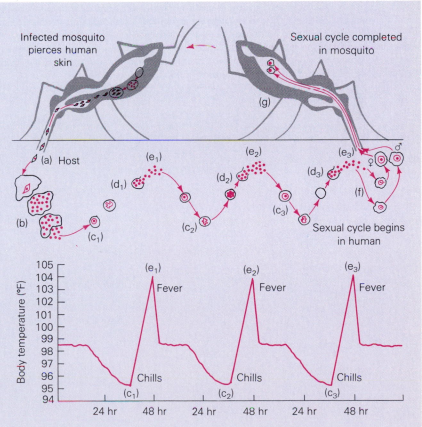

FIGURE 21.4 *Plasmodium* life cycle and malaria. The female *Anopheles* mosquito is a known carrier of the malarial parasite, *Plasmodium vivax.* The life cycle of *P. vivax* takes place partly in the mosquito and partly in the reservoir animal, in this case a human. **(a)** The cycle begins when the mosquito injects saliva containing **sporozoites** into the bloodstream. **(b)** From there, the sporozoites enter the liver and produce large numbers of **merozoites,** which **(c)** reenter the bloodstream and **(d)** invade red blood cells to reproduce once again. **(e)** The sudden, coordinated release of numerous parasites brings on a period of fever and chills. As the fever subsides, a new infection of red cells occurs, ultimately bringing about a new release of the parasites. Then fever and chills occur again. **(f)** Eventually, **gamonts** (sexual forms) are produced. When these are taken into the intestine of a mosquito, they begin a sexual cycle, forming sperm and eggs. After fertilization, the zygote develops in the intestinal wall of the mosquito. **(g)** Eventually, the maturing sporozoites venture into the salivary gland, from where they move into the saliva that may then be injected into another victim.

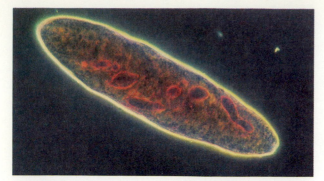

S. ambiguum

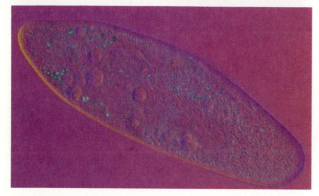

P. multimicronucleatum

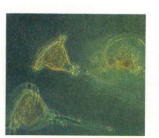

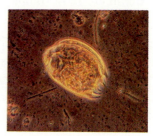

V. campanula, D. dentatum

FIGURE 21.5 Ciliates range greatly in size from that of *Diplodinium dentatum*, a commensal in the cow's stomach (20 to 40 μm), to *Spirostomum ambiguum*, a protozoan giant whose length is measured in millimeters (3 mm or 3000 μm). (This size difference is equivalent to the relative size of shrews and blue whales.) Of interest is the funnel-shaped *Vorticella campanula*, which pops up and down on its contractile stalk, using its cilia for sweeping in food particles. *Paramecium multimicronucleatum*, as its polysyllabic name implies, has numerous micronuclei.

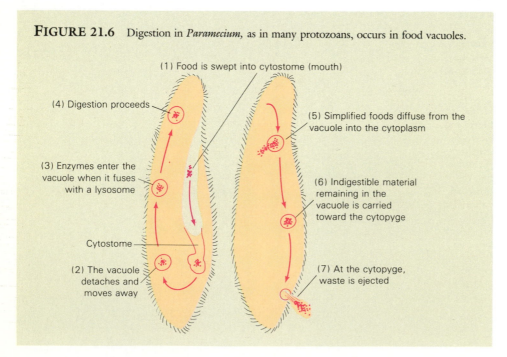

FIGURE 21.6 Digestion in *Paramecium*, as in many protozoans, occurs in food vacuoles.

(1) Food is swept into cytostome (mouth)

(4) Digestion proceeds

(5) Simplified foods diffuse from the vacuole into the cytoplasm

(3) Enzymes enter the vacuole when it fuses with a lysosome

(6) Indigestible material remaining in the vacuole is carried toward the cytopyge

Cytostome

(2) The vacuole detaches and moves away

(7) At the cytopyge, waste is ejected

Ciliates are unusual protists in that they maintain their DNA in two kinds of nuclei. A germ line DNA, set aside for replication, is kept in one or more tiny **micronuclei.** Micronuclei produce larger **macronuclei,** metabolically active bodies that specialize in RNA transcription and protein synthesis.

During asexual reproduction, the micronuclei undergo replication and mitosis, the macronucleus pinches in two, and cytokinesis occurs. Typically, sexual reproduction in ciliates occurs through **conjugation,** a fusion of two individuals of compatible **mating types** (there are no males and females, as such). Following cell fusion, the micronuclei undergo meiosis, and some of the haploid products are exchanged. As the haploid nuclei join, the diploid state in each partner is restored.

> **C**iliates—active, complex protozoans—use cilia in movement and feeding. Digestion occurs in **food vacuoles;** water regulation occurs through **contractile vacuoles.** Asexual reproduction is through mitosis and fission; sexual reproduction, through meiosis and conjugation.

ALGAE: PLANTLIKE PROTISTS

There are about 18,000 named species of **algae.** The oceans are laced with vast beds of seaweeds and kelps, and astronomical numbers of simpler algae congregate in drifting populations referred to as **phytoplankton.** Other algal protists live as symbionts* within the cells of corals, giant clams, sea slugs, and protozoans. Altogether, marine algae fix more carbon by photosynthesis than do all of the land plants and other algae combined. But not all algal protists are marine; many live in fresh water, and others occur on land, some of the latter in mutualistic* partnerships with terrestrial organisms.

Dinoflagellates (Phylum Pyrrophyta)

Visitors to tropical waters are often surprised and delighted as they are rowed in the evening between ship and shore. Each time the paddle slides into the water, the sea seems to explode with iridescent light. Even the wake of the canoe is aglow. The tiny, twin-

kling lights are the magic of minute living creatures, the microscopic **dinoflagellates,** or fire algae.

However, when conditions are favorable, their numbers can increase explosively, and these same little creatures can be responsible for another, equally dramatic and far more dangerous phenomenon: the **red tide.** Teeming trillions of dinoflagellates turn the sea a bloody color, and fish, subjected to deadly toxins, die by the thousands. Clams, oysters, and mussels survive, but accumulate the poisons as they filter-feed on the dinoflagellates. At these times—generally, from May through August—the poisoned mollusks can prove fatal to humans who eat them.

Dinoflagellates are flagellated, photosynthetic protists, covered with plates of cellulose and quite unlike anything else alive. Each typically has two flagella, one trailing and one confined to a groove that encircles its waist (Figure 21.7). Some dinoflagel-

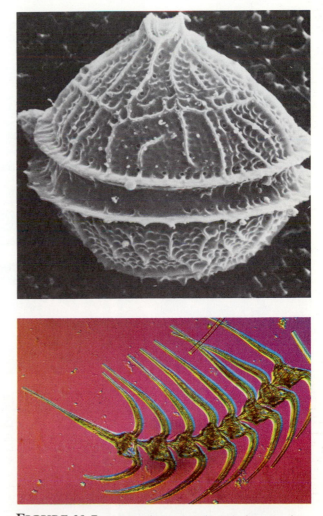

FIGURE 21.7 Among the marine phytoplankton are the dinoflagellates, which are primitive, single-celled photosynthesizers.

---

*In biological relationships, **symbiosis** simply refers to living in an intimate association, usually one organism within another. Symbiosis includes: **mutualism,** in which both symbionts benefit; **commensalism,** in which one partner benefits while the other is unaffected; and **parasitism,** in which one partner benefits while the other is harmed.

lates live most of their lives as photosynthetic symbionts in the cells of marine protozoa or animals, often imparting a peculiar green color to their larger symbiotic partners.

Diatoms and Golden-brown Algae (Phylum Chrysophyta)

The **golden-brown algae** are single-celled and colonial algae of both marine and fresh waters. Their colors derive chiefly from carotenoid pigments (accessory photosynthetic pigments; see Chapter 7). As photosynthesizers, the golden-brown algae join the diatoms in helping to provide the energy base of marine food chains.

The **diatoms** produce cell walls of glass (silicon dioxide). Over time, their numbers have been so immense that today we routinely mine rich diatomaceous earth deposits for use in filters and cleaning agents. The glassy walls of diatoms can be intricately sculpted in a variety of patterns, the result of numerous tiny perforations needed for permitting gases to enter and leave the cell (even glass houses need windows; Figure 21.8). The glassy walls are like tiny pillboxes, each with a lower lid and an overlapping

FIGURE 21.8 The most spectacular chrysophytes are the 5000 or so species of diatoms. Their glassy walls contain numerous types of finely etched patterns so regular and clear that mounted specimens are used to test the quality of microscope lenses.

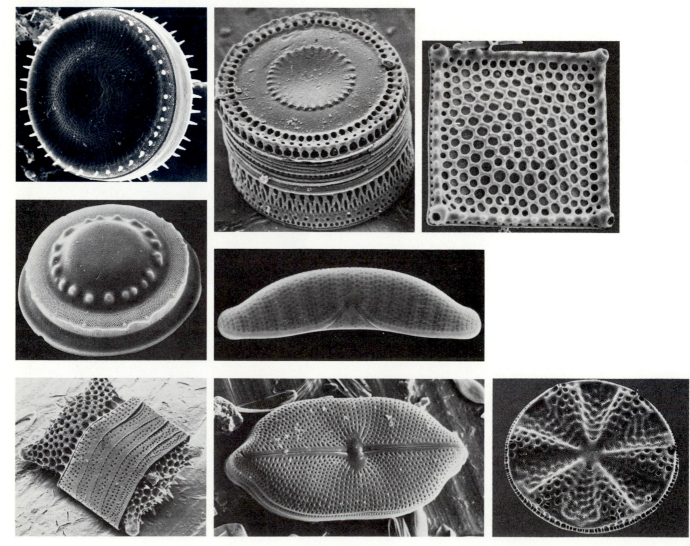

FIGURE 21.9 In their asexual reproduction, which occurs through mitosis and cell division, one diatom daughter cell gets the upper lid of the glassy box, while the other gets the lower, smaller lid. For some unknown reason, diatoms manufacture only lower lids after division, so some diatoms get smaller and smaller. The diatom's answer to this vexing problem is to stop mitosis and enter a sexual phase.

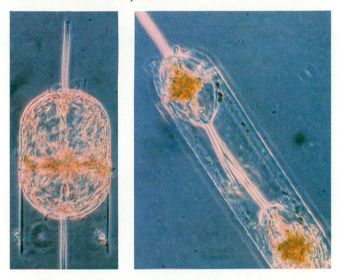

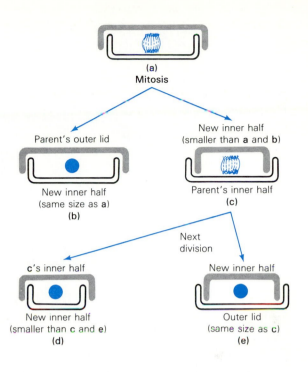

(a)
Mitosis

Parent's outer lid

New inner half
(smaller than **a** and **b**)

New inner half
(same size as **a**)
(b)

Parent's inner half
(c)

Next
division

c's inner half

New inner half

New inner half
(smaller than **c** and **e**)
(d)

Outer lid
(same size as **c**)
(e)

upper lid. This arrangement presents some interesting problems when the diatom grows and reproduces (Figure 21.9).

The glassy walls form excellent fossils, so we know that diatoms appeared in the late Mesozoic era but didn't really become numerous until the beginning of the Cenozoic era (65 million years ago).

> **D**iatoms are single celled, colonial photosynthesizers with glassy cell walls. Along with **golden-brown algae** they help form the energy base of marine food chains.

Euglenoids (Phylum Euglenophyta)

Euglena gracilis (Figure 21.10) is probably the best known euglenoid. Most of these single-celled, flagellated algae live in fresh water, often in nutrient-enriched or polluted waters where their numbers during algal "blooms" can turn the surface bright green. *Euglena* defies and confounds the taxonomist. With its flexible body, active flagella, and photoreceptor with a bright red lid (the "eye-spot"), it is surely a protozoan flagellate. However, also included in *Euglena's* repertoire of organelles is a well-formed chloroplast and numerous starch storage bodies—all

algal characteristics. Studying its life cycle isn't much help; although it reproduces asexually through mitosis and cell division, sexual reproduction hasn't been observed. Thus we find *Euglena* included in both the zoologist's and botanist's taxonomic schemes.

> **E**uglena is a complex species with both protozoan and algal traits. It moves about by flagellum, orients to light with a photoreceptor, has a chloroplast, and produces starch.

Red Algae (Phylum Rhodophyta)

The 4000 or so species of **red algae** are primarily seaweeds, although a few live on the land and in fresh water. Seaweeds attach to the rocky sea floor by fingerlike structures known as **holdfasts.** Some red algae are actually red; others are green, black, blue, or violet. Most are small and frilly, with lengths up to perhaps a meter (Figure 21.11). *Sushi* lovers are familiar with the thin, greenish-black edible red alga that is used to wrap the raw fish delicacy.

As in plants, the storage polysaccharide of many red algae is starch. Red algae are commercially important as a vegetable in the Asian diet and as a source of the polysaccharides **agar** and **carrageenan.** Agar is used in cosmetics, medicine capsules, and in

FIGURE 21.10 *Euglena gracilis,* a common pond protist, has both protozoan and algal characteristics.

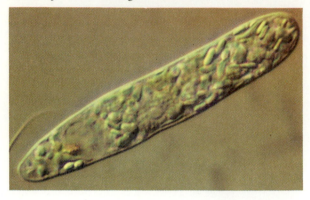

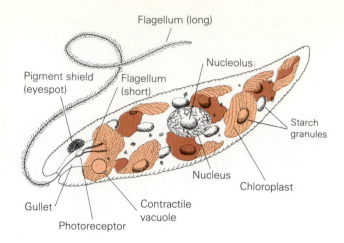

Flagellum (long)

Pigment shield (eyespot)

Flagellum (short)

Nucleolus

Starch granules

Gullet

Photoreceptor

Contractile vacuole

Nucleus

Chloroplast

FIGURE 21.11 Red algae are most common in warm marine waters, where they attach to rocks on the sea bed. The branched body of *Polysiphonia* is frilly and delicate.

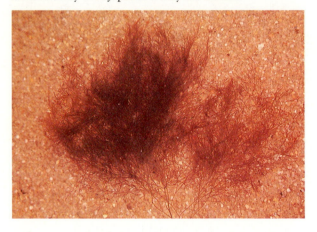

agar agar, the jellylike material upon which microbiologists grow bacteria and fungi. Carrageenan is used as a smoothing agent in paints and cosmetics, and it gives chocolate-flavored dairy drinks their fake creaminess.

When red algae reproduce, they form crawling, ameboid sperm rather than the usual flagellated form of other algae. The life cycle is plantlike, or **sporic.** That is, a diploid spore-producing or **sporophyte** phase alternates with a haploid, gamete-producing, or **gametophyte,** phase. The two-part life cycle is described as an **alternation of generations,** a term we will be saying more about shortly (see also Essay 21.2).

Red algae are primarily marine seaweeds, commercially important for their **agar agar** and **carrageenan.**

Brown Algae (Phylum Phaeophyta)

The **brown algae** include the large kelps, some of the seaweeds, and a few microscopic forms. They owe their color to the brown pigment, **fucoxanthin.**

Most of the 1000 or so named species of brown algae live in cold coastal waters, but one genus, *Sargassum,* grows in shallow tropical and subtropical waters. Storms regularly break *Sargassum* bodies from their holdfasts, and the broken plants are washed to sea, where they continue to photosynthesize and grow, although they can no longer successfully reproduce. In the middle Atlantic, vast tangled masses of *Sargassum* form the Sargasso Sea, which has spawned many salty legends about trapped ships and sea monsters.

The giant kelps can grow over 50 m (164 ft) in length (Figure 21.12). Their large flattened, leaflike **blades** can be close to the sunlit surface and their tangled, elaborate holdfasts can anchor them far below. Connecting the two ends of the plant are stemlike **stipes,** and the blades are kept near the surface by the buoyancy of hollow **floats.** Although they are listed among the protists, kelps actually have evolved food-conducting tissues very similar to those of higher plants. These conducting tissues allow photosynthetic products to be transported throughout the alga.

Like the red algae, the brown algae are commercially important. Kelps are harvested along the southern California coast on a regular basis for their rich sodium, potassium, and iodine content. Their structural polysaccharide, **algin,** is used as a thickening and stabilizing agent for foods and paints and as a paper-coating agent. In Asia some brown algae are eaten as a vegetable.

Also like the red algae, brown algae have a sporic life cycle, exhibiting a clear alternation of genera-

FIGURE 21.12 Giant kelps such as *Nereocystis* thrive in cold oceans where they form undersea "forests." After storms, their remains are a common sight along California beaches.

tions. In some species, the two alternating phases are amazingly plantlike. They have a highly dominating sporophyte that retains and protects its spores while they subsequently develop into tiny, protected gametophytes (see Essay 21.2). In addition, some species produce **heterogametes,** which means they have large stationary eggs and tiny, flagellated sperm, another advanced trait. The presence of dominant sporophytes, vascular tissue, and heterogametes in brown algae and plants is attributed to convergent evolution. That is, although the two groups are not closely related, they have made similar adaptive changes.

> Advanced characteristics of **brown algae** include a sporic life cycle, prominent sporophyte generation, heterogametes, and a protected gametophyte. They are commercially important for their **algin** and minerals.

Green Algae (Phylum Chlorophyta)

Most species of **green algae** live in fresh water, although a sizable number are marine and a few are terrestrial. Some are no longer independent and must live within the cells of certain ciliates and invertebrate animals. Other green algae live in a mutual associa-

tion with fungi, forming some of the many varieties of rock-encrusting lichens. The 7,000 or so species of this diverse group range from single-celled to colonial and multicellular.

Green algae are biochemically similar to plants. They make use of the light-gathering pigments chlorophyll *a* and *b* and carotenoids; they form typical plant starches, and build their cell walls of cellulose.

Single-celled green algae. Single-celled green algae may be nonflagellated, such as *Chlorella,* or flagellated. One of the best-known flagellated forms is *Chlamydomonas reinhardi,* which has been studied extensively by geneticists. Each tiny, oval cell has two anterior (pulling) flagella, a red, light-sensitive eyespot, and a single cup-shaped chloroplast that takes up much of the cell's volume. For most of its life cycle *Chlamydomonas* is haploid and reproduces asexually by mitosis and cell division.

Asexual and sexual reproduction in *C. reinhardi* are reviewed in Figure 21.13. Note the presence of haploid **isogametes** (so-called because they are identical in appearance), and the formation of a tough, resistant zygote called a **zygospore.** The long haploid phase and very limited diploid phase are typical of a **zygotic** life cycle (see Essay 21.2).

Colonial green algae. *Volvox,* a rather remarkable green alga, is comprised of an unusually organized spherical colony of flagellated cells (Figure 21.14). As a colony, *Volvox* is a community of cells behaving as a single organism. Although the cells are not wholly dependent on each other, their association appears to offer a degree of increased efficiency. Although *Volvox* is not directly related to any truly multicellular higher plant, nor even to truly multicellular green algae, its organization does suggest something about how multicellularity itself *might* have begun.

Multicellular green algae. Many green algae are multicellular. Some form thin filaments of cells, and others exist as leaflike blades. *Ulothrix,* a common freshwater **filamentous alga** (Figure 21.15a), is characterized by a zygotic life cycle. Following a long haploid phase, *Ulothrix* produces motile, flagellated isogametes that fuse to form a diploid zygospore. The zygospore enters meiosis to liberate haploid cells that will produce a new filamentous body.

Another multicellular green alga, *Ulva* ("sea lettuce") (Figure 21.15b), is quite different. It has a sporic life cycle with a clear alternation of generations (see Essay 21.2). The sporophytes and gametophytes

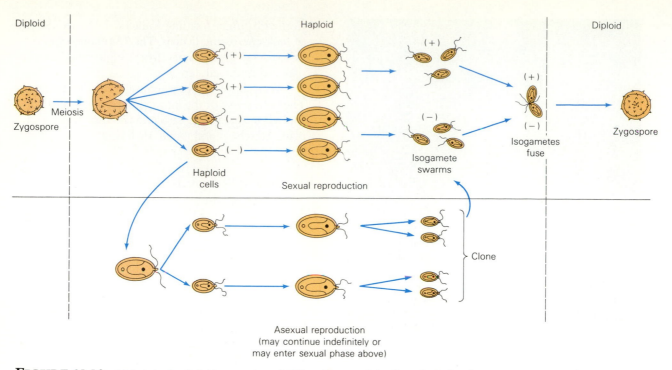

FIGURE 21.13 Meiosis in the diploid zygospores of *Chlamydomonas reinhardi* results in flagellated, haploid cells that can increase their number through asexual reproduction or enter a sexual cycle where they form isogametes. Different mating types fuse, forming new zygospores.

FIGURE 21.14 *Volvox* forms a spherical colony made up of an outer layer of interconnected swimming cells and smaller spheres representing new colonies within. The smaller spheres begin their development as zygotes after sexual reproduction has occurred. The spheres then grow through cell division and eventually emerge from the parent colony to begin life on their own.

take the form of large, leaflike blades that are two cells thick. Although their roles in the life cycle and their chromosome numbers differ, sporophytes and gametophytes are identical in size and shape.

Although they are interesting in their own ways, our main reason for lingering with the green algae is that they have relatives in "high places." At some time in the distant past, about 400 million years ago, during the Paleozoic era, one or more kinds of delicate but adventuresome multicellular green algae began what was to be the first successful transition to terrestrial life. It was from this humble beginning that today's great array of terrestrial plant life is believed to have emerged.

Green algae are single celled, colonial, and multicellular with various zygotic and sporic life cycles. Ancestral green algae are thought to have given rise to plants during the Paleozoic era.

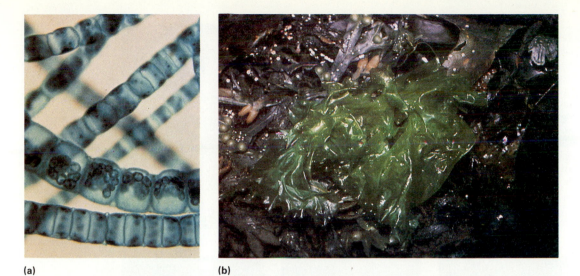

(a)   (b)

FIGURE 21.15 (a) The freshwater filamentous alga, *Ulothrix*. (b) The leafy marine alga, *Ulva*, known as "sea lettuce."

SLIME MOLDS AND WATER MOLDS: FUNGUS-LIKE PROTISTS

Now let's consider those protists that resemble fungi in certain ways, while retaining their protistan membership (some people, we should add, still consider them to be fungi).

Slime Molds

Although they are unrelated and dramatically different, the two groups of slime molds, **cellular slime molds** (phylum Acrasiomycota) and **acellular slime molds** (phylum Myxomycota), have something in common: they both lead double lives.

In one portion of their lives, cellular slime molds multiply and grow over their food supply (often a rotting log), each cell behaving like an ameba. But when their food source dries up, they change drastically. The individual cells crawl together and coalesce, forming a single body called a **slug.** The slug wanders blindly about like a mindless worm. Eventually, it stops and vertical stalks begin to arise from its mass. The stalks bear fruiting bodies that give rise to airborne spores, just like any respectable mold might do (Figure 21.16).

Acellular slime molds form huge multinucleate masses, forming what looks like a giant ameba—large enough to cover an entire log. The mass, however, may be only a millimeter thick. As it creeps along, it engulfs bits of organic matter and shows some sensitivity in that it avoids obstacles. When its habitat dries out, it produces slender stalks that will release haploid spores. These are released into the environment to later fuse and begin dividing, producing the diploid, amebalike mass again.

Water Molds (Phylum Oomycota)

Water molds include those unsightly, furry growths that plague the fish in our aquariums. Others are parasites of insects and plants, and one is blamed for the exodus of many Irish after the famous potato famine of the 1840s. (If you are an American of Irish descent, you may owe your citizenship to that very parasite.) The threadlike body of the water mold is reminiscent of some fungi, but there are important differences. For instance, water molds are essentially diploid, which means their life cycles are gametic, a characteristic of animals (see Essay 21.2).

FUNGI

Fungi are a strange lot, in many ways quite unlike other organisms. They are stationary, multicellular, and heterotrophic; most live as parasites, decomposers and mutualists. As decomposers, they join the bacteria in the ecologically essential task of *mineral recycling*. To some of us the most familiar fungi are

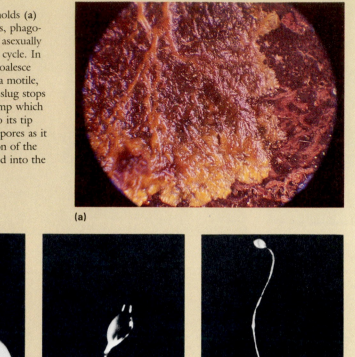

FIGURE 21.16 Cellular slime molds **(a)** live as independent, unicellular amebas, phagocytizing soil bacteria and reproducing asexually during the vegetative part of their life cycle. In the sexual phase **(b)**, individual cells coalesce into a heap, which differentiates into a motile, nonfeeding "slug." **(c)** Eventually the slug stops crawling; a stalk appears, first as a bump which then lengthens, lifting a ball of cells to its tip **(d).** The ball (sporangium) develops spores as it rises higher with the further elongation of the stalk. Eventually the spores are released into the wind.

(a)

(b)　　　　**(c)**　　　　**(d)**

the delicate mushrooms and enchanting toadstools, while others might think at once of furry growths on leftovers. Actually, most species live in association with other organisms as parasites. Thousands of species are mutualists; they help form lichens and **mycorrhizae,** the latter of which are fungus-plant associations in the roots of many plants. The fungi help absorb minerals and water, and the roots provide sugars (see Chapter 25).

Other Fungal Characteristics

Fungi spread over the world by forming tiny spores that can be carried by air currents. Under favorable conditions—when there is adequate moisture, food, and warmth—the spores germinate, and a **vegetative** (feeding) **stage** emerges. In most fungal species, the vegetative stage is marked by an extensive, spreading **mycelium,** which consists of numerous branching, threadlike growths called **hyphae** that secrete digestive enzymes into food and absorb the products. Some hyphae grow upward, later forming and releasing spores, as mentioned earlier. Individually, the hyphae are minute tubes of cytoplasm, surrounded by a cell wall that is usually composed of the complex carbohydrate **chitin** (the same tough, flexible materi-

al that is found in the skeletons of insects and their relatives). In some fungi, the cytoplasm is not organized into cells, but is continuous and contains many nuclei. Other fungi exhibit a typical cellular state, with one nucleus per cell.

Fungi are multicellular heterotrophs, feeding as parasites, decomposers, and symbionts. They have chitinous cell walls, a tubular vegetative mycelium, and often a large fleshy fruiting body.

In their life cycle, fungi spend most of the time in a haploid state typical of the zygotic life cycle (see Essay 21.2). As with many protists, sexual reproduction involves the union of different mating types, referred to here as "plus (+) strains" and "minus (−) strains." As usual, the union produces the diploid state, but in a most peculiar way in some species. Each mating partner contributes a haploid nucleus, but the two nuclei may not fuse for a long time. When fertilization is delayed, the zygote isn't really diploid. Such a cell is said to be in a **dikaryotic** state (two nuclei). We'll see shortly how such dikaryotic cells can develop into elaborate fruiting bodies, in which fusion and meiosis give rise to the next generation of spores. (Mushrooms, toadstools, and shelf fungi are familiar fruiting bodies.)

> Following conjugation, many fungi enter a lengthy **dikaryotic** (binucleate) state in which a fruiting body forms. With nuclear fusion, a brief diploid state is formed, followed immediately by meiosis and spore formation.

The fungal kingdom contains four phyla: **bread molds** (phylum **Zygomycota**), **sac fungi** (phylum **Ascomycota**), **club fungi** (phylum **Basidiomycota**), and the **fungi imperfecti** (phylum **Deuteromycota**). (The first three are also known more commonly as: **zygomycetes, ascomycetes,** and **basidiomycetes**.)

The origin of fungi from protist ancestors is obscure, but disputed funguslike fossils occur in Precambrian strata some 900 million years old. This places them among the oldest eukaryotes.

Bread Molds (Phylum Zygomycota)

One well-known bread mold, *Rhizopus stolonifer,* is a fuzzy, black invader that is bound to turn up in everyone's refrigerator at one time or another. *Rhizopus* grows vigorously on many foods but is partial to the starchy types (Figure 21.17a). The haploid mycelium develops long, horizontal hyphae that send branching rhizoids down into the food, where digestion and absorption occur. The hyphae of bread molds lack cell walls, so the continuous cytoplasm is multinucleate. The tiny black dots on moldy bread are the **sporangia,** asexual bodies that generate many tiny haploid spores through mitosis. Some of the spores may be dispersed over great distances by air currents.

Sexual reproduction in the bread molds occurs when a plus strain meets a minus strain. The hyphae of the two types connect, permitting the haploid nuclei from each strain to join. Their union brings about the development of a tough, black, diploid **zygospore.** The brief diploid state ends as soon as meiosis occurs in the zygospore. When the zygospore germinates, the hyphae that emerge are once again haploid (Figure 21.17b).

FIGURE 21.17 (a) *Rhizopus stolonifer* forms a vast spreading mycelium. Some hyphae (rhizoids) penetrate food, digesting and absorbing nutrients, while others grow erect, producing spores in black, spherical sporangia. (b) When plus and minus hyphae meet, opposing haploid nuclei join and a zygospore forms. After meiosis, a new hypha emerges, forms a sporangium, and liberates spores. (Photograph courtesy Carolina Biological Supply.)

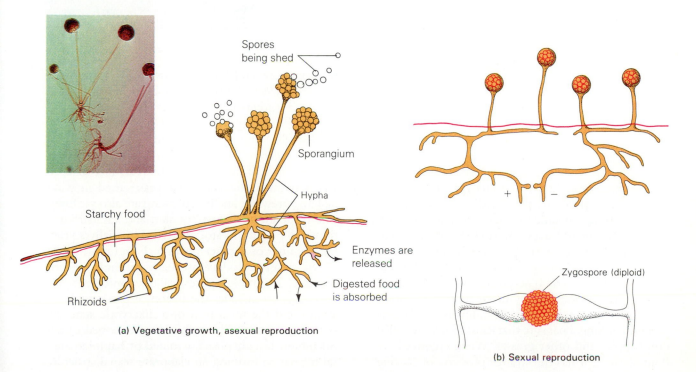

Spores being shed

Sporangium

Hypha

Starchy food

Enzymes are released

Digested food is absorbed

Rhizoids

(a) Vegetative growth, asexual reproduction

+ −

Zygospore (diploid)

(b) Sexual reproduction

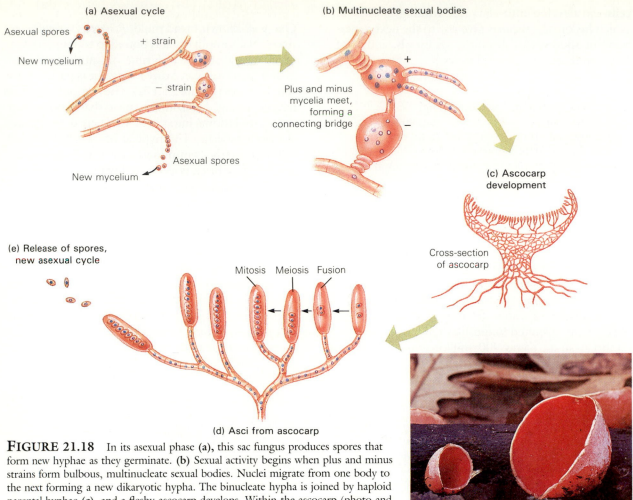

(a) Asexual cycle

Asexual spores

New mycelium

\+ strain

\- strain

Asexual spores

New mycelium

(b) Multinucleate sexual bodies

Plus and minus
mycelia meet,
forming a
connecting bridge

\+

\-

**(c) Ascocarp
development**

Cross-section
of ascocarp

**(e) Release of spores,
new asexual cycle**

Mitosis Meiosis Fusion

(d) Asci from ascocarp

FIGURE 21.18 In its asexual phase **(a)**, this sac fungus produces spores that form new hyphae as they germinate. **(b)** Sexual activity begins when plus and minus strains form bulbous, multinucleate sexual bodies. Nuclei migrate from one body to the next forming a new dikaryotic hypha. The binucleate hypha is joined by haploid parental hyphae **(c)**, and a fleshy ascocarp develops. Within the ascocarp (photo and **d**), the fusion of nuclei occurs in saclike asci. Fusion is followed by meiosis and mitosis, which leads to the emergence of many haploid ascospores.

Sac Fungi (Phylum Ascomycota)

The ascomycetes (and the basidiomycetes) have an essentially cellular structure, with **septa** (crosswalls) isolating each nucleus in the tubelike hyphae. The septa have large pores through which the nuclei are free to migrate. The names *ascomycetes* and *sac fungus* both refer to a characteristic, microscopic, saclike reproductive structure, the **ascus** (plural, **asci**), in which sexual spores are produced.

The sac fungi include the powdery mildews sometimes seen on plant leaves. Two of these, the chestnut blight and the agent of Dutch elm disease, have raised havoc in American forests. Edible morels and truffles and the red, blue-green, and brown food spoilers are also sac fungi. One sac fungus that holds rather ghastly implications for humans is *Claviceps purpurea,* a fungal parasite that causes a disease called **ergot** in rye and other grasses. When ergotized rye flour is eaten, it has the strange property of causing

hallucinations and burning sensations in the hands and feet, where blood vessels become constricted. (Some historians believe the Salem "witches" were suffering from ergot poisoning.)

Not all sac fungi are harmful however; the pink mold *Neurospora* helped geneticists discover the biochemical role of the gene in past years (see Chapter 14). Commercially important yeasts used in winemaking, brewing, and breadbaking are also sac fungi. The troublesome "yeast" of skin and vaginal infections can't spoil this story since it is actually a yeast-like member of another phylum, Fungi imperfecti.

Sac fungi reproduce asexually through the production of simple spores called **conidia.** Sexual reproduction includes the fusion of plus and minus strains and the formation of a dikaryotic state, the odd form of delayed fertilization mentioned earlier. Such binucleate hyphae are joined by haploid parental hyphae in forming an elaborate sexual structure, the **ascocarp** (Figure 21.18). (The edible truffle and morel are ascocarps.) Union of the plus and minus nuclei is followed immediately by meiosis and the formation of haploid **ascospores.**

> **S**ac fungi form cellular mycelia and asexual spores called **conidia.** Conjugation between plus and minus strains produces dikaryotic hyphae, which then form cuplike **ascocarps** where nuclear fusion, meiosis, and sexual spore formation occur.

Club Fungi (Phylum Basidiomycota)

The basidiomycetes, or club fungi, include the common forest mushroom, the shelf fungus, the puffball, and other fleshy species, in addition to the parasitic wheat rusts and corn smuts. The names *basidiomycetes* and *club fungi* both refer to a characteristic micro-

scopic reproductive structure from which the sexual spores are budded off: the **basidium** ("little pedestal"). To some, the same structure also resembles a club (Figure 21.19).

The familiar mushroom growing on the forest floor is only a part of the organism. Below the soil surface lies an extensive, unseen mycelium, silently secreting enzymes, digesting organic matter, and absorbing nutrients. The mycelium may also form the mycorrhizal relationship with plant roots, as was described earlier. The mushroom's above-ground portion—the part sold in supermarkets—is known, technically, as the **basidiocarp** (club-fruit). It is produced after hyphae of plus and minus strains have conjugated below ground (Figure 21.20a). Each cell produced after the union is dikaryotic, containing a haploid nucleus from each parental strain. The dikaryotic state persists in the mushroom, just as it did in the ascocarp of the sac fungus, its hyphae contributing to the growing basidiocarp. Nuclear fusion

FIGURE 21.19 Clubfungi (a) Bracket fungus. (b) The edible mushroom *Lepiota* looks too much like the poisonous *Amanita* (death angel) (c) even for experts to take chances. Corn smut (d) can be devastating to crops.

(a)

(b)

(c)

(d)

FIGURE 21.20 A constantly enlarging "fairy ring" *(photo)* is the product of continuous conjugations over an extended period of time. In the mushroom life cycle, conjugation occurs below ground and the dikaryote **(a)** give rise to a basidiocarp **(b)**. Within the cap **(c)**, nuclear fusion occurs in numerous basidia along the frilly gills. Fusion is followed by meiosis and haploid spore formation.

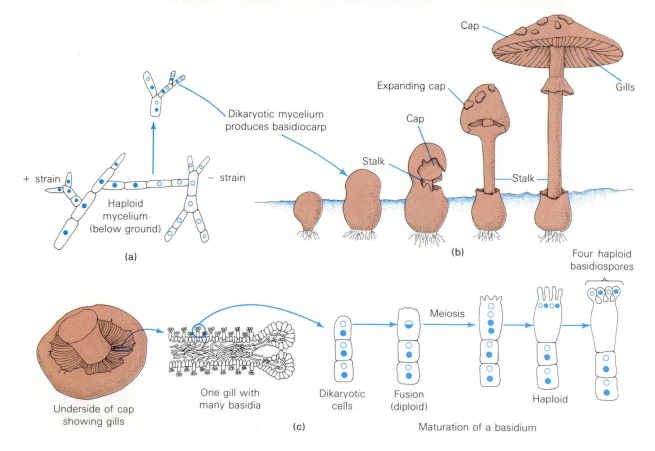

finally takes place in the numerous basidia lining the thin **gills** on the underside of the mushroom cap (Figure 21.20c).

As expected, the diploid state is brief, followed at once by meiosis and the formation of haploid spores. People who count such things tell us that a single mushroom can produce billions of spores in this manner—a sizable investment in its future.

Fungi Imperfecti (Phylum Deuteromycota)

Imperfect is a botanical term referring to the presumed absence of sexual reproduction. There are thousands of poorly understood species of Fungi imperfecti, which apparently will occupy the energies of taxonomists for decades to come. Undoubtedly, many of these species will eventually be placed among either the sac or club fungi. The Fungi imperfecti include a number of human parasites such as *Trichophyton mentagrophytes,* which causes athlete's foot. Another causes ringworm. A fascinating but

FIGURE 21.22 Lichens, a mutualistic association of fungi and algae or cyanobacteria, sometimes occur as a colorful though crusty growth on bare rock surfaces.

FIGURE 21.21 Among the Fungi Imperfecti is the bizarre, predatory species, *Dactylaria.* Its mycelium contains many looplike snares, each capable of swelling rapidly upon touch, to close the loop on anything passing through. Soil nematodes, moving through the soil water, are its usual victims. Once captured, they are penetrated by fast growing fungal filaments that secrete digestive enzymes.

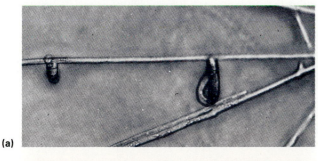

(a)

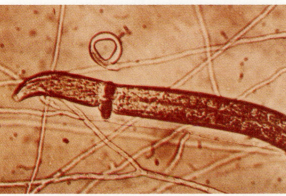

(b)

presumably unrelated species, *Dactylaria,* is a predator that catches certain roundworms that live in the soil (Figure 21.21).

> **Fungi imperfecti** include species with no known sexual stages. Included are parasites, predators, and decomposers.

LICHENS

We include **lichens** among the fungi, but they are actually composed of a symbiotic association of a fungus and a green alga or a cyanobacterium. A number of fungi may be involved in such associations, but the most common are the sac fungi. Whatever the species, however, the association is mutual; both partners benefit. The fungus provides moisture, mineral nutrients, and strong attachment to the substrate. The alga or cyanobacterium provides food produced through photosynthesis. This unique partnership permits the lichen to grow in unusual places where there is little competition from other organisms. We commonly find them on rocky outcrops, where, because of their erosive effects on the rocks, they may begin soil formation. Lichens also grow on trees and as luxurious ground cover in the frigid tundra (Figure 21.22). They rarely live in cities, since they are highly susceptible to the toxic effects of air pollution.

SUMMARY

WHAT IS A PROTIST?

The protist kingdom is wide ranging, including single-celled, colonial, and multicellular forms. The size range is enormous, and most protists are aquatic. Three major categories are the animal-like protozoans, the plantlike algae, and the funguslike water molds and slime molds.

PROTOZOANS: ANIMAL-LIKE PROTISTS

Protozoans are heterotrophic with animal-like nutritional requirements. Three major phyla contain the flagellates and amebas, the sporozoans, and the ciliates.

Flagellates and Amebas (Phylum Sarcomastigophora)

The flagellates bear flagella, are free living or parasitic, and feed through absorption or phagocytosis. Asexual reproduction is most common. Most of the zygotic life cycle is spent in the haploid state. Sexual reproduction is through cell fusion, followed by meiosis.

Parasites include *Trypanosoma gambiense,* the agent of African sleeping sickness, a disease spread by the tsetse fly.

Amebas include *Entamoeba histolytica,* the agent of ameboid dysentery. Free-living amebas are formless, moving and feeding through temporary cytoplasmic extensions called pseudopods. Food enters through phagocytosis and is digested in vacuoles. Heliozoans (freshwater) live in glassy capsules and feed via cytoplasmic streams covering spinelike axopods. Radiolarians (marine) are similar. Foraminiferans (marine) produce chalky, snail-like skeletons.

Sporozoans (Phylum Apicomplexa)

Sporozoans are nonmotile, parasitic, spore formers. The best known, *Plasmodium vivax,* is the mosquito-borne agent of malaria. Fever and chills follow regular cycles of the parasite's asexual activity, which is marked by red blood cell lysis. Sexual stages form in the host but must be completed in the mosquito.

Ciliates (Phylum Ciliophora)

Ciliates, the most complex protozoans, move and feed through the coordinated movement of cilia. In some, food is swept into a cytostome, whereupon it enters a food vacuole, where it is joined by digestive enzymes. The products diffuse into the cytoplasm, and the residues leave the cell through exocytosis at the cytopyge.

Water regulation is carried out by the contractile vacuole, which fills and empties through the action of microfilaments.

Micronuclei contain germ-line DNA reserved for reproduction, whereas macronuclei contain replicated DNA for use in transcription and protein synthesis.

In asexual reproduction the micronuclei undergo replication, followed by mitosis and cytokinesis. The cell cycle is gametic—the lengthy diploid state is interrupted by meiosis during sexual reproduction. Such reproduction occurs through conjugation between mating types. After two cells have fused, meiosis occurs in the micronuclei, and haploid products are exchanged. The cells, now diploid again and having undergone genetic recombination, separate, and asexual reproduction resumes.

ALGAE: PLANTLIKE PROTISTS

Included among the abundant marine algae are seaweeds, kelps, phytoplankton, and intercellular symbionts. Many algae live in freshwater, and a few are terrestrial.

Dinoflagellates (Phylum Pyrrophyta)

Dinoflagellates (fire algae) are mainly flagellated and photosynthetic. Many create an iridescent glow at night, and some, during their periodic blooms, cause the infamous red tide. The accumulation of their toxins in clams, oysters and other bivalves, renders them poisonous to humans.

Diatoms and Golden brown Algae (Phylum Chrysophyta)

The diatoms and golden brown algae make up an important part of the marine food chain. Diatoms have been so numerous in the past that their glassy walls have formed dense deposits called diatomaceous earth. Diatoms have upper and lower interlocking walls. During asexual reproduction they decrease in size and eventually enter a sexual phase, where gametes escape the walls and fuse. The large size is then restored.

Euglenoids (Phylum Euglenophyta)

Euglena is single celled, flagellated, and photosynthetic, with a flexible body, well-formed chloroplast, starch storage bodies, and a photoreceptor. Is it a protozoan or an alga? Taxonomists cannot agree.

Red Algae (Phylum Rhodophyta)

Red algae are frilly, multicellular, marine seaweeds. Holdfasts anchor them to the seabed. Agar and carrageenan are extracted for commercial use. They have an alternating, two-part, sporic life cycle made up of diploid, spore-forming sporophytes and haploid, gamete-forming gametophytes.

Brown Algae (Phylum Phaeophyta)

Brown algae, multicellular marine kelps and seaweeds, are often large and structurally complex. Some have elaborate holdfasts, large leaflike blades, stipes with conducting tissue, and bulbous floats. Algin and minerals are extracted for commercial use. Many have a plantlike, sporic life cycle that includes a dominating sporophyte and highly reduced gametophyte. The latter gives rise to heterogametes (minute sperm and large eggs).

Green Algae (Phylum Chlorophyta)

Most green algae live in freshwater and are biochemically similar to plants. Species are single celled, colonial, or multicellular.

Single-celled green algae include *Chlamydomonas reinhardi,* whose zygotic life cycle is principally haploid. A brief diploid state, called a zygospore, enters meiosis, restoring the haploid state.

Volvox, a spherical colony of interacting, flagellated cells, helps to illustrate one way in which multicellularity may have begun.

Multicellular green algae include the filamentous *Ulothrix,* with a primitive zygotic life cycle, and the more advanced marine seaweed *Ulva,* which has a sporic life cycle with identical, bladelike sporophytes and gametophytes. Plants are believed to have evolved from one of the multicellular green algal lines.

SLIME MOLDS AND WATER MOLDS: FUNGUSLIKE PROTISTS
Slime Molds
Acellular and cellular slime molds are protistlike in their ameboid vegetative or feeding stages and funguslike in their asexual reproductive stages. In the latter they give rise to stalks tipped by spore-forming fruiting bodies.

WATER MOLDS (PHYLUM OOMYCOTA)
Water molds are economically important because some (potato blight) damage crops, and they are biologically important because of their advanced sexual structures. They resemble fungi in growth and asexual reproduction, but unlike fungi, their life cycles are gametic.

FUNGI
Other Fungal Characteristics
Fungi are multicellular heterotrophs. Many are parasites, and some are free-living decomposers. The latter are essential in recycling minerals. Some associate with plant roots, forming mineral-absorbing mycorrhizae. Typically the vegetative or feeding fungal mycelium consists of threadlike, spreading and branching hyphae, whose walls are of chitin. Hyphae may be acellular (multinucleate), a primitive state, or cellular, an advanced state. The life cycle is zygotic with brief diploid states following the fusion of plus and minus mating types. Some retain separate plus and minus nuclei—a dikaryotic state—for a time, before actual fusion occurs. Large, elaborate, and fleshy fruiting sexual bodies are often formed. Fungi are among the oldest eukaryotes.

Bread Molds (Phylum Zygomycota)
The bread mold, *Rhizopus stolonifer,* has typical spreading hyphae with rootlike rhizoids that secrete enzymes and absorb nutrients. Vertical hyphae produce sporangia in which asexual spores are formed. Union of plus and minus hyphae form diploid zygospores that undergo meiosis and produce new, sexually recombined, haploid hyphae.

Sac Fungi (Phylum Ascomycota)
Hyphae in sac fungi have septa (cross walls). The group includes important parasites, edible forms, and common food spoilers. *Claviceps purpurea* produces a rye infection called ergot, which is highly poisonous to humans. Sexual reproduction includes fusion of plus and minus strains, a lengthy dikaryotic state, and the formation of a cuplike ascocarp. Following nuclear fusion, meiosis and ascospore formation occur in saclike asci.

Club Fungi (Phylum Basidiomycota)
Club fungi include mushrooms, toadstools, wheat rusts, corn smuts, and others. Fusion of plus and minus hyphae in the extensive underground mushroom mycelium results in a dikaryotic growth that emerges to form the basidiocarp, a fruiting body. Flattened gills within the cap contain numerous clublike **basidia,** in which nuclear fusion occurs. Meiosis ensues, and numerous **basidiospores** form.

Fungi Imperfecti (Phylum Deuteromycota)
The Fungi Imperfecti are species with no known sexual stages. Members include the parasite of athlete's foot and a nematode-trapping predator.

LICHENS
Lichens are a mutualistic fungus-alga or fungus-cyanobacterium association. They are ecologically important because of their soil-building activities.

KEY TERMS

aggregates	cytosome	alternation of generation	chitin
colonies	food vacuole	brown algae	dikaryotic
protozoan	cytopyge	fucoxanthin	bread mold
algae	contractile vacuole	blade	Zygomycota (zygomycete)
water mold	micronuclei	stipe	sac fungi
slime mold	macronuclei	float	Ascomycota (ascomycete)
Sarcomastigophora	conjugation	algin	club fungi
flagellate	mating type	green algae	Basidiomycota (basidiomycete)
ameba	phytoplankton	isogamete	Fungi Imperfecti
Apicomplexa	dinoflagellate	zygospore	Deuteromycota

sporozoans	red tide	filamentous alga	sporangia
Ciliophora	golden-brown algae	cellular slime mold	zygospore
ciliate	diatom	acellular slime mold	ascus
zygotic	red algae	slug	conidia
gametic	holdfast	mycorrhiza	ascocarp
trypanosome	agar	vegetative stage	basidium
pseudopod	carrageenan	mycelium	basidiocarp
heliozoan	sporic	hyphae	gill
axopod	sporophyte		imperfect
radiolarian	gametophyte		lichen
foraminiferan			

REVIEW QUESTIONS

1 Generally characterize the range of organisms in the kingdom Protista. What, if anything, do they have in common? (p. 332)

2 Clearly distinguish between the following: the single-celled state, the aggregate, the colony, and the multi-cellular state. (p. 332)

3 List two characteristics that protozoans have in common with animals. (p. 332)

4 List several characteristics of flagellates. What form of life cycle do they exhibit? Explain what this means. (pp. 333–336)

5 Name an important parasitic flagellate and describe the disease it causes. (pp. 333, 337)

6 Explain the manner in which free-moving amebas move about and capture food. What is the physical basis for this movement? (p. 337)

7 Compare the habitat, body form, and method of feeding in the heliozoans and foraminiferans. (p. 338)

8 List three important characteristics of sporozoans and name an important parasite. (pp. 338–339)

9 Relate the cyclic symptoms of malaria to the activities of the sporozoan agent. What must happen for the parasite to reproduce sexually? (p. 339)

10 Discuss movement, feeding, digestion, and water regulation in the representative ciliate *Paramecium*. (p. 339)

11 Describe the activity in the micronuclei during sexual reproduction in a ciliate. Would you expect the macronuclei to participate? Explain. (p. 341)

12 What are the phytoplankton? What is their major importance to marine life? (p. 341)

13 Describe the agent responsible for red tide. What must happen for this condition to arise and how is it important to us? (p. 341)

14 Describe the cell wall organization of a diatom. What problem does this present when asexual reproduction occurs and what is the solution? (pp. 343–344)

15 List the plantlike and animal-like characteristics of *Euglena gracilis*. (p. 343)

16 Describe the general body form, habitat, and economic importance of the red algae. (pp. 343–344)

17 *Polysiphonia* is characterized as having a sporic life cycle with equal sporophyte and gametophyte phases. With the aid of a simple diagram explain what this means. Be sure to use the terms *meiosis* and *fertilization* and *diploid* and *haploid*. (pp. 336, 344)

18 Describe the size and specialized body structures of a giant kelp. In what way is the provision for transport in the kelp similar to that in land plants? (p. 344)

19 Describe alternation of generations in the brown alga *Fucus* and compare its sporic life cycle to that of most land plants. Does this mean that *Fucus* and oaks are closely related? Explain. (pp. 344–345)

20 List the three types of green algae and provide an example of each. (p. 345)

21 List several ways in which the life cycle of *Chlamydomonas reinhardi* is similar to that of a protozoan flagellate. (Start by determining whether its cycle is gametic, zygotic, or sporic.) (p. 345)

22 Describe a typical *Volvox* colony. What important information might be yielded from studies of *Volvox*? (p. 345)

23 Describe the life cycle of *Ulva*. In what way or ways is *Ulva* advanced over the green algae mentioned above? (pp. 345–346)

24 Describe ways in which the slime molds are similar to both protists and fungi. (p. 347)

25 The water molds are commonly placed in the kingdom Fungi. Through a consideration of their cell structures and their life cycle argue against this assignment. (p. 347)

26 List three important activities of fungi. Include one that is vital to plant and animal life. (pp. 347–348)

27 What kind of life cycle do the fungi follow? Explain what a dikaryotic state is. (p. 348)

28 With the aid of a simple diagram, describe the vegetative stages and asexual reproduction in the bread mold *Rhizopus stolonifer*. (p. 349)

29 Explain how sexual reproduction occurs in the bread molds. (p. 349)
30 List three important parasites and two edible forms of sac fungi. (p. 350)
31 List the events that occur during sexual reproduction in a sac fungus, from the meeting of plus and minus hyphae through the formation of ascospores. (p. 350)
32 List three groups of club fungi that are on the list of dangerous parasites. (p. 351)

33 Describe the sexual cycle of a mushroom, starting with the union of plus and minus hyphae below ground. When does the fusion of plus and minus nuclei finally occur? (pp. 351–352)
34 What is the basis for assignment to the phylum Fungi Imperfecti? (p. 353)
35 Essentially, what is a lichen? What does each member contribute to the welfare of the whole? (p. 353)

22

EVOLUTION AND DIVERSITY IN PLANTS

We humans sometimes take delight in wondering aloud just who has inherited the earth: cockroaches, rats, houseflies, or us. Of course, it's a nonsensical question, but it is interesting that we never consider our silent partners, the plants. Everywhere we look we see green. Not only are plants the most prominent form of land life on our planet, but also they form the base of nearly every terrestrial food chain. In other words, they manufacture the organic molecules that are eventually passed along through both plant eaters and predators, the creatures that roam the earth in search of the food that is stored in the bodies of other individuals.

The plant kingdom includes two groups of terrestrial plants, one with vascular (conducting) tissue, one without: the nonvascular **bryophytes** (mosses, liverworts, and hornworts) and the vascular plants (also called **tracheophytes**). (The vascular plants not only have specialized conductive tissues but also true leaves, stems, and roots.)

WHAT IS A PLANT?

What distinguishes plants from the other life forms on earth? The question can be answered at a number of levels. For instance, plants make almost all of the food on the planet. Specifically, they are distinguishable as multicellular photosynthesizers with cells that are organized into specialized tissues, which, in turn, form organs such as roots, stems, and leaves. Perhaps, most obviously, plants are quite stationary: trees spend their entire lives just standing around (although the so-called lower plants have motile sperm).

Plants, as we know, are photosynthesizers. Their photosynthetic pigments include chlorophyll a and b and the carotenoids. Most of the food they store is in the form of starch, and the most common structural material is cellulose—the tough polysaccharide found in cell walls and plant fibers. Finally, plants are distinguished by the way they reproduce. Plant embryos develop within the confines of a gametophyte structure called the **archegonium,** where they are offered a measure of protection. The protected embryo is an important adaptation for living on land.

Plants are multicellular with specialized tissues and organs. Photosynthetic pigments include chlorophylls a and b and carotenes. Polysaccharides include starch and cellulose. The embryo is protected within the gametophyte.

Alternation of Generations in Plants

As we pointed out in Chapter 21, the plant life cycle is **sporic:** that is, it has alternating sporophyte and gametophyte phases. This is referred to as an **alternation of generations** (see Essay 21.2). Briefly, in the sporic life cycle the haploid products of meiosis are spores and not gametes (unlike in the **gametic** animal life cycle.) In plants, haploid spores form multicellular gametophytes, which in turn give rise to tissues in which gametes are formed. When gametes fuse in fertilization, the diploid sporophyte phase reappears and a new cycle begins. Certain cells in the multicellular sporophyte enter meiosis once more, and another cycle of spores and gametophytes begins.

> In the **alternation of generations** in plants, diploid multicellular sporophytes produce haploid spores, which then form multicellular gametophytes that give rise to gametes and house the embryo.

In its most primitive state, as seen in some filamentous green algae, the gametophyte phase is quite dominating and the sporophyte phase brief and simple. Further, the two phases tend to occur in separate individuals. But recall that the green alga *Ulva* and the red alga *Polysiphonia* are somewhat more advanced. Although they maintain separate sporophytes and gametophytes, the phases are about equal and are even similar in appearance. In the brown algae and in almost all plants the evolutionary trend is clearly in the opposite direction. The sporophyte dominates the life cycle, and the gametophyte is incorporated into the sporophyte body. The trend is most striking in the seed plants. In fact, in the most recently evolved plants—the flowering plants—the gametophyte is restricted to a relatively few haploid cells within the flower.

Another evolutionary trend in plants has been a departure from **homospory,** a primitive condition in which only one form of spore is produced. More advanced plants are **heterosporous** ("hetero," different), and, accordingly, they form **heterospores.** Thus in most plants we find **microspores** ("small spores") and **megaspores** ("large spores"). These descriptive terms are not really precise since microspores and megaspores are often similar in size. They are better distinguished by what they produce. Microspores give rise to male gametophytes (called **microgametophytes**), which in seed plants are minute pollen grains. Megaspores give rise to female gametophytes (**megagametophytes**), the large ovules of seed plants. Eventually, selected cells in the two will develop into sperm and egg.

With these two evolutionary trends in mind, let's look into an important exception, the *bryophytes,* nonvascular plants. They are evolutionary holdouts with highly dominating gametophytes and spores that all look alike.

> The life cycle of most plants follows an evolutionary trend away from primitive **gametophyte** dominance and **homospory,** and toward **sporophyte** dominance and the **heterosporous** (**microspore** and **megaspore**) state.

NONVASCULAR PLANTS: BRYOPHYTES

The bryophytes (division *Bryophyta*)—the mosses, liverworts and hornworts—are multicellular terrestrial plants with specialized tissues that efficiently divide the tasks of life. There are about 23,000 named species, most of which are mosses.

Bryophyte Characteristics

Bryophytes lack the specialized supporting and conducting tissues of vascular plants, although many mosses have primitive versions of such tissues. For the most part, water and nutrients move through the bryophyte body via the tedious process of cell-to-cell transport. For these and other reasons, bryophytes are generally small and ground-hugging (Figure 22.1).

The absence of vascular tissue in bryophytes also means that they lack *true* roots, stems, and leaves, each of which, by definition, requires such tissues. They do have leaflike scales that contain chloroplasts in which photosynthesis occurs.

Bryophytes anchor themselves in the soil by rootlike **rhizoids.** Unlike true roots, the rhizoids are not involved in water transport; the entire organism must absorb and retain moisture from rain and condensation. In spite of this many mosses can get by in fluctuating environments because they can survive a temporary drying out even becoming dry and brittle, but they revive and begin metabolizing again when

FIGURE 22.1 Bryophytes The gametophytes of *Polytrichum* (a) form the green leafy carpet we generally think of as moss. Emerging from gametophytes are the sporophytes, consisting of a brown stalk and capsulelike sporangia. The capsules will open to scatter the haploid spores. The liverwort gametophyte (b) is a flattened, ground-hugging growth. The erect bodies that look like miniature palms are egg-producing structures.

moist conditions return. In fact, some species do quite well in deserts and high mountains.

Despite their reasonably successful transition to terrestrial life, the mosses and their relatives have some of the same requirements for reproduction as did the ancient green algae from which they ultimately descended. Their sperm have flagella and must swim in order to reach the egg, which lies protected within the parent gametophyte in a vaselike structure called the **archegonium.** In some bryophytes swimming to the egg is not much of a trick, because the egg and sperm are produced on the same gametophyte. In other cases the sperm must travel from the **antheridium** (where it is produced) of one gametophyte to the archegonium of another gametophyte. It generally accomplishes this more frequently by

being splashed by falling raindrops than by its own flagellar activity, but it is a perilous trip all the same. The alternation of generations in a moss is seen in Figure 22.2.

> **B**ryophytes are small, ground-hugging plants that lack specialized vascular tissue and true roots, stems, and leaves. Bryophytes have a dominating **gametophyte** phase from which arises a dependent **sporophyte.**

Bryophyte Origins

While some botanists consider the bryophytes to be primitive—closely resembling the earliest plant life—many others disagree. They maintain that bryophytes branched from the vascular plant line some 350 million years ago, well after vascular plants arose (Table 22.1). Bryophytes, they assert, are not entirely primitive after all, but owe their unique traits to evolutionary simplification, the loss of certain complex ancestral characteristics. The fossil record supports the later divergence of bryophytes, since the oldest known plant fossils are clearly those of vascular plants.

VASCULAR PLANTS

The vascular plants (**tracheophytes**) comprise the vast majority of today's plant species. The tracheophytes have two types of specialized conducting tissues: **xylem,** which transports water and minerals, and **phloem,** which distributes organic food from one part of the plant to another. The xylem often has an important secondary function: it provides support for the plant body. Wood consists primarily of xylem. Xylem and phloem are discussed in detail in Chapters 24 and 25.

The earliest tracheophytes appear in the fossil record some time before the earliest bryophytes. These early vascular plants belong to an extinct group, called the Rhyniophytes, a division that flourished in the marshes of the early Paleozoic era (see Table 22.1). They were simple plants that lacked leaves and roots. A main **rhizome** (underground stem) produced vertical branches and simple, anchoring rhizoids (Figure 22.3). Within their stems lay a system of crude tubules, true xylem elements called

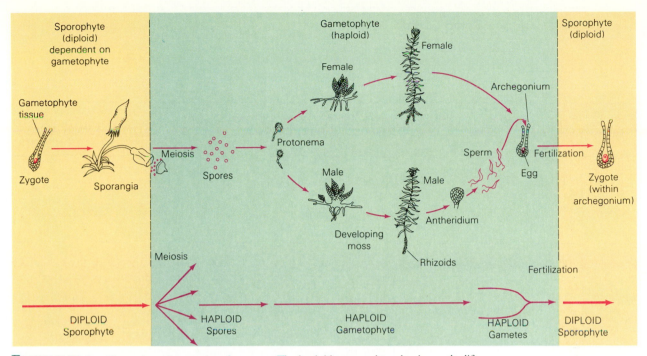

FIGURE 22.2 Alternation of generations in mosses. The haploid gametophyte dominates the life cycle. The diploid sporophyte, consisting of a stalk and spore-forming capsule, grows out of the gametophyte, releasing haploid spores that have formed through meiosis. Sperm and egg develop in antheridia and archegonia, which form in the leafy gametophyte. When water is available, flagellated sperm swim to the archegonium where fertilization occurs. The diploid zygote develops into another sporophyte.

tracheids, which are specialized for water conduction. With this innovation, the evolutionary future of the tracheophytes was assured.

> Specializations such as supporting tissue, water-conducting **xylem** and sugar-conducting **phloem,** help explain the great diversity and wide distribution of **vascular plants.**

Vascular Plant Divisions

According to most taxonomists, there are nine divisions of vascular plants, four of which release spores that develop into inconspicuous—but independent—gametophytes. The great 18th century taxonomist, Linnaeus, was so confounded by the apparent lack of reproductive structures in these plants that he named them **cryptogams,** which quaintly translates as "hidden marriage." The rest of the plants, with their highly visible cones and flowers, came to be known as **phanerogams,** or "apparent marriage." At

any rate, the nine vascular plant divisions are as follows:

I. **Seedless plants** (tiny independent gametophytes)
   Division Psilophyta ("naked plants"): whisk ferns
   Division Lycophyta ("spiderlike plants"): ground pine or club mosses
   Division Sphenophyta ("wedge plants"): horsetails
   Division Pterophyta ("winged plants"): ferns
II. **Seed plants** (tiny gametophyte incorporated into sporophyte)
   A. **Gymnosperms** (naked seeds)
      Division Cycadophyta: cycads
      Division Ginkgophyta (maidenhair tree): ginkgo
      Division Gnetophyta: gnetophytes
      Division Coniferophyta ("cone-bearers"): pines and other conifers
   B. **Angiosperms** (seeds with fruit)
      Division Anthophyta ("blossom or flower plant"): the flowering plants

The first three divisions of seedless plants, the whisk ferns, club mosses, and horsetails, were once

TABLE 22.1 Geological History of Plants

Era	Period(s) (Millions of years ago)	Conditions	Plant History	
Cenozoic	Quarternary Tertiary	Glaciation, mountain building, cooling	Extensive grasslands	**AGE OF ANGIOSPERMS**
	— 65 —			
Mesozoic	Cretaceous	Rocky mountains / Extensive lowlands	Flowering plants	**AGE OF GYMNOSPERMS**
	— 135 —		Conifers	
	Jurassic	Lowlands, inland seas	Cycads	
	— 197 —			
	Triassic	Mountains, drying		
	— 225 —		—— Most recent continental drift begins ——	
Paleozoic	Permian	Glaciers / Inland seas dry up	Gingkos	
			Earliest conifer fossils	
	— 280 —		Earliest fern fossils	**GREAT PALEOZOIC FORESTS**
	Carboniferous	Mountain building	Sphenophytes	
			Earliest bryophyte fossils	
	— 345 —			
	Devonian		Lycophytes	
	— 405 —			
	Silurian	Extensive shallow seas, mild climate	Earliest vascular plant fossils (Rhyniophytes)	Plants invade land
	— 425 —			
	Ordovician		First plant fossils	**PLANT LIFE BEGINS**
	— 500 —			
	Cambrian			
	— 570 —			
Precambrian			(Algae)	

an important part of the earth's flora. They were the giants of the Paleozoic forests. Vast coal deposits in the earth today are convincing evidence of the dominating size and vast numbers reached by these plants. But the heyday of such plants is over, and only a few stragglers remain (Figure 22.4). The fourth seedless plant division, the pterophytes, or ferns, is a different story. A close look at this holdout will help you to visualize the peculiar life cycle of the cryptogams.

Psilophytes, lycophytes, and **sphenophytes** were prominent in the Paleozoic era, but they have been replaced by seed plants (and ferns).

Ferns

The ancient Paleozoic forests were also graced with a much more familiar plant, the **fern.** Ferns have survived in great numbers and have adapted to both a vastly changing environment and competition from seed plants (Figure 22.5). They are widespread, thriving in both temperate and tropical climates. Some even live in the desert, and a few manage to survive in the dim recesses of smoky bars.

The fern sporophyte often consists of a number of lush, finely divided leaves that arise from a thick rhizome, or underground stem. The leaves function in both photosynthesis and spore production. As the plant grows, the leaves first appear as the familiar coiled **fiddleheads,** each of which then unrolls into a large, complex leaf. The stem also gives rise to a pro-

FIGURE 22.3 *Rhynia* is the oldest known fossil vascular plant. It flourished some 350 to 400 million years ago. It lacked leaves and true roots but had photosynthetic stems that grew up from an underground stem, or rhizome. Spore-producing sporangia developed on the tips of the erect stems. True conductive tissue is evident in the fossil traces. This is the sporophyte; the gametophyte is unknown.

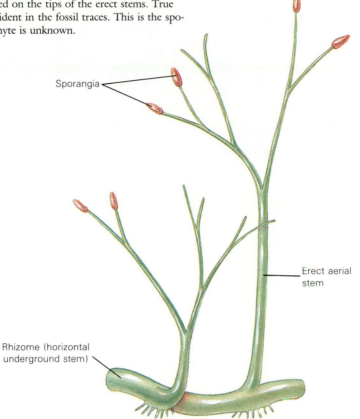

Sporangia

Erect aerial stem

Rhizome (horizontal underground stem)

FIGURE 22.4 **(a)** *Psilotum,* a psilophyte, produces an erect, highly branched stem with scattered sporangia. **(b)** Lycophytes, also called ground pines and club mosses, are neither pines nor mosses. Some produce complex, conelike sporangia at their tips. **(c)** *Equisetum,* a sphenophyte, also called a horsetail, has different photosynthetic and reproductive shoots rising from a single rhizome. Note the multiple sporangia clustered at the tip of the reproductive shoot.

(a)   (b)   (c)

FIGURE 22.5 Although many ferns are restricted in size and are confined to the forest floor, tree ferns may grow to a height of 15 m (about 50 ft).

FIGURE 22.6 (a) Anatomy of a fern. Below the soil, an extensive underground rhizome produces root growth and sends leaves above ground to form the cluster shown here. The leaves emerge from the rhizome as tightly curled fiddleheads, which gradually open. (b) Fern sporangia occur in a variety of forms and patterns, (see photo), but the sorus shown here is common. Spores are produced meiotically in the sporangia, and remain there until the sporangium splits and the spores are ejected.

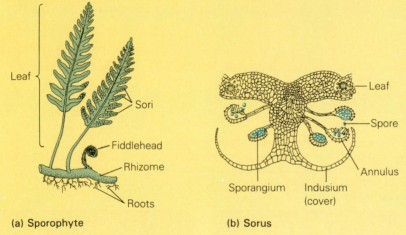

(a) Sporophyte

(b) Sorus

fusion of fine, hairy roots that absorb water and minerals (Figure 22.6a).

Most ferns are homosporous. The simple haploid spores are produced by meiosis in structures called **sori,** often seen on the undersides of leaves. The sori may be scattered, or they may occur in neat rows, appearing as brown or red dots (that have often sent alarmed gardeners to the store for pesticides). Each sorus is a group of **sporangia** (spore-forming organs) sometimes hidden under a scalelike cover, or **indusium** (Figure 22.6b). As the sporangia rupture, the spores are released, some becoming windborne and traveling great distances.

When a fern spore germinates, a tiny, heart-shaped, photosynthetic gametophyte, the **prothallus,** develops. Its purpose is to produce gametes. Sperm and egg form in antheridia and archegonia, structures that develop on the gametophyte's lower surface. After fertilization, the young, diploid sporophyte grows from the nurturing tissue of the gametophyte but soon becomes independent (Figure 22.7).

> **Ferns** are homosporous with a dominating, complex sporophyte with true roots, stems, and leaves, and a minute, separate gametophyte.

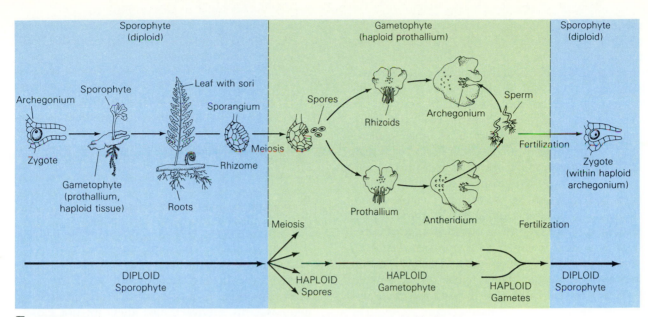

FIGURE 22.7 *Alternation of generations in a fern. In ferns, the sporophyte is highly dominant, and the generations are represented by separate plants. After fertilization, the young diploid sporophyte begins its growth from the archegonium, soon producing its own roots and photosynthetic tissue. The sporophyte produces spores. Those that succeed produce a heart-shaped gametophyte, which bears antheridia and archegonia.*

THE MESOZOIC ERA: TIME OF GYMNOSPERMS

The primitive vascular plants persisted through the Paleozoic era. At its close some 225 million years ago, much of the earth experienced vast geological upheaval, and plant life underwent dramatic change.

Throughout the first half of the Paleozoic era, the earth was a rather smooth globe, and the low-lying continents were largely covered with warm, shallow seas. Following this and into the next era—the Mesozoic—the surface of the earth itself began to shift as the soggy lowlands rose up and vast mountain ranges emerged. Great deserts formed in the shadows of newborn mountain ranges. The monotonously warm global climate changed, with gradual cooling at first and then fluctuation between extremes as ice ages came and went. Even the great land masses were restless and the most recent episode of continental drift began.

Toward the close of the Paleozoic era, an estimated 90% of the animal species rapidly died out. These extinctions, marking the end of the Paleozoic era and the beginning of the Mesozoic, were the greatest mass extinction of life known to the earth. Most of the great plants of the Paleozoic era perished, leaving behind only scattered remnants.

With the demise of the ancient forests, the competitive edge passed to the emerging Mesozoic seed plants: up to that time they had existed inconspicuously among the Paleozoic giants. The newly changed earth presented untried opportunities, for with the extinction of the older giants, countless new ecological niches were possible. (An ecological niche refers to the interaction of a species with its environment.) Soon the seed plants appeared everywhere over the Mesozoic landscape. These were primitive **gymnosperms,** the forerunners of today's conifers.

The rise of **seed plants** in the Mesozoic era followed vast changes in terrain and climate and the extinction of most Paleozoic plant life.

Gymnosperm Specializations

Why were the gymnosperms so successful? First, they had evolved extensive root systems that could draw water from the earth and transport it, through the increasingly well developed xylem tissue, upward to the leaves. Both the root and the stem were capable of extensive **secondary growth**—growth in diameter by the addition of rings of vascular tissue.

Second, the gametophyte became incorporated into the sporophyte. So this vital stage of the life cycle was protected from the rigors of a drying habitat, one which may have contributed to the demise of the Paleozoic giants. Further, the male gametophyte (gymnosperms are heterosporous, with male and female gametophytes) had evolved into the hardy, windblown **pollen grain,** which could travel for miles and withstand severe drying, thereby remaining viable for years (Figure 22.8a). Furthermore, fertilization did not require an outside source of water, since the windblown male gametophyte could form a deeply penetrating **pollen tube** that could deliver sperm directly to the hidden female gametophyte.

Third, and perhaps most importantly, there was the evolution of the **seed** itself (Figure 22.8b). The female gametophyte came to remain within the parental sporophyte tissue, where it could be supported, protected, and nourished. Then, after fertilization, the seed itself developed and could be released for dispersal and propagation. The gymnosperm seed consists of tough, nearly waterproof outer seed coats surrounding a mass of stored nutrients and a dormant, partly formed plant embryo—the

next sporophyte generation. Seeds, like pollen, can survive harsh conditions and may successfully germinate after years of dormancy.

> The success of seed plants can be attributed to more extensive vascular tissue (**secondary growth**), a protected male gametophyte (**pollen**), and a better-protected embryo (**seed**).

The Gymnosperms Today

The word *gymnosperm* means "naked seeds," a fitting term since the seed is not surrounded by fruit as is the case with the angiosperm. Further, while the reproductive structure of the angiosperm is the flower, in most gymnosperms it is the cone. Four divisions of gymnosperms survive today; they are not closely related to one another. These are the **ginkgos,** the **cycads,** the strange **gnetophytes,** and the familiar **conifers.**

The ginkgo, or maidenhair tree, qualifies as rare because there is only one surviving species, *Ginkgo biloba* (Figure 22.9a). Earlier, individuals of this single species were rare even in their native China. Now, however, the ginkgo has become a common decora-

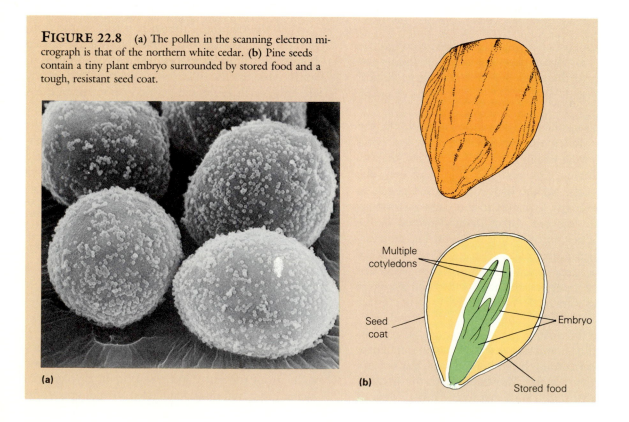

FIGURE 22.8 (a) The pollen in the scanning electron micrograph is that of the northern white cedar. (b) Pine seeds contain a tiny plant embryo surrounded by stored food and a tough, resistant seed coat.

Multiple cotyledons

Seed coat

Embryo

Stored food

(a)

(b)

(a)

(b)

(c)

FIGURE 22.9 The ginkgo *(Ginkgo biloba)*. Male sporophytes (sexes are separate) produce bright yellow pollen cones. **(b)** Palmlike cycads have separate sexes also. Note the bright yellow pollen cone of this male. **(c)** *Welwitschia mirabilis*, a gnetophyte, is seen in the remote Kalahari desert. It produces two ragged, splitting leaves with seed cones on the edges.

tive tree throughout the world—partly because it is quite pretty, partly because of its unusual appearance, and partly because it is relatively resistant to insects, disease, and even air pollution. The large, rather smelly seed is considered a great delicacy by some gourmets.

The cycads have done a little better than the ginkgos; about 100 species of cycads are alive in the world today. Most of these are native to the tropical and subtropical regions of the world. In hothouses and botanical gardens, cycads are often mistaken for palms, which they superficially resemble, just as ginkgos superficially resemble ashes or sycamores. But ashes, sycamores, and palms are all flowering plants, unrelated to either cycads or ginkgos. Palms produce flowers, and cycads produce massive cones (see Figure 22.9b).

The 70 or so named species of gnetophytes are a bizarre, diverse lot. Some botanists believe that the flowering plants evolved from this group, or at least that the two groups are related. The evidence is sparse but interesting. For example, plants of the genus *Gnetum* have leaves with netlike veins, rather resembling the leaves of a cherry tree. Another gnetophyte, the rare and rather weird *Welwitschia mirabilis* (see Figure 22.9c), has xylem **vessels.** Vessels are specialized xylem cells that are common in flowering plants (see Chapter 25), but do not exist in the xylem of any other gymnosperm. Finally, gnetophytes, like conifers and angiosperms, have nonmotile sperm.

The conifers. The conifers are made up of about 500 named species—not very many species, considering the vast coniferous forests of the world. Many conifers thrive in the cold climates of the earth (Figure 22.10), but some are also doing quite well in warm regions. Typically, they produce **needles:** narrow, tough leaves with thick, water-resistant cuticles. This is an adaptation to arid conditions, whether the habitat is simply dry or the water is periodically bound up as ice. Nearly all conifers are "evergreen";

FIGURE 22.10 Coniferous forests are found chiefly in the cold regions of the earth. They form a continuous belt across Northern Asia, North America, and Europe.

many species retain their leaves for two to four years, but continuously shed. (The long-lived, bristle-coned pine keeps its leaves for nearly 50 years.)

> Gymnosperms—**ginkgos, cycads, gnetophytes,** and **conifers**—are heterosporous (producing microspores and megaspores); they bear exposed, fruitless seeds, and form pollen tubes for sperm transfer.

The conifers include the pines, firs, spruces, red-woods, hemlocks, junipers, and larches. Of these, the most common and best-known group is the pine family, Pinaceae. Pines have separate male (pollen-bearing) and female (ovule-bearing) **cones,** and each tree is bisexual (that is, each sporophyte bears both male and female cones). The shapes and sizes of the cones are usually the most distinctive features of the different pine species. The seeds—pine nuts—remain in the female cones for about two years as they slowly mature (Figure 22.11). During this peri-od, the seeds of many pines develop a winglike struc-ture that will catch the wind, so that when the cone opens and they are released, they will float far from the parent tree. In some pines, the cones will not open to release their seeds until they first are scorched by fire and then cool off; each new genera-tion of such pines must await its own forest fire.

> Special adaptations of many conifers include perpetual, drought resistant needle-like or scaly leaves and wind-borne, resistant seeds.

In ancient Mesozoic times, the dominance of the gymnosperms and that of the dinosaurs were strangely intertwined, and both groups fell from prominence toward the end of the Mesozoic era. The giant reptiles—except for the lines that led to moni-tor lizards, alligators, and crocodiles—were to pass into oblivion, while the conifers, although managing to survive, decreased drastically in number. The Cenozoic era, which followed the Mesozoic era and began 65 million years ago, was the time of the **flow-ering plants.** The flowering plants came to dominate the landscape from the tropics to the temperate regions, leaving mainly the colder northern regions to most of the surviving gymnosperms. The conifers were well on their way to being rare, archaic relics, like the gnetophytes and the ginkgos, but in the Pleistocene period, which began only two million years ago, they began an amazing comeback. In these relatively recent times both their geographic range and the number of individuals, if not the number of species, have greatly increased.

THE CENOZOIC ERA: THE TIME OF THE FLOWERING PLANTS

When did the flowering plants evolve? Were they inconspicuously sprinkled among the dominant, if primitive, conifers, cycads, and ginkgos of the Meso-zoic era, or were they absent altogether in those days? What kinds of conditions promoted their rather sud-den explosion to dominance?

One theory is rather simple: the flowering plants had evolved two advantages, *animal pollination* and *seed dispersal*. Insects had been around for a very long time, but the gymnosperms had depended on wind pollination alone. It is generally agreed that the earliest flowering plants were animal pollinated, largely by insects. Most depend on insects for pollination today, although many flowering plants have reverted to wind pollination. Animal pollination, being efficient and rather specific, may have given the early flowering plants a decided advantage in the Darwinian struggle. As for seed dispersal, the key event was probably the emergence of birds. Birds were attracted to the fleshy, tasty, sugar-laden tissue encasing resistant seeds, and seeds passed through their digestive systems in viable condition, often after being carried to distant but suitable locations. This again was a major advantage to early flowering plants, as it is to many flowering plants today.

Other theories abound. Some investigators believe that the relatively rapid emergence of the flowering plants can be explained on the basis of geological and climatological changes; temperatures of the Cenozoic era were colder than those of the Mesozoic era, for instance. Any such change brings new adaptive opportunities, and flowering plants did well under these more rigorous conditions. At the end of the Mesozoic era, 65 million years ago, the drifting continents also had approximately reached their present positions, and life could begin adapting to the relatively constant conditions that prevailed, based on their stable positions on the globe. (See also Essay 29.1)

The rise and success of flowering plants are associated with efficient animal pollination and seed dispersal, along with opportunities arising from changes in weather, relatively stable geological conditions, and reduced competition.

The Angiosperms Today

Angiosperms, more technically, **anthophytes,** surround their seeds with **fruit,** often of the familiar soft and tasty kind, but also of the dry, hardened form such as those surrounding the seeds of grasses, hickory trees, and oaks. *Fruit* simply refers to the mature

FIGURE 22.11 Alternation of generations in a conifer. The conifers have no truly separate gametophyte generation. Cells in the male cones, known as microspore mother cells, enter meiosis and form haploid microspores. These microspores form a winged pollen grain and later the male gametes. Cells in the female cone, the megaspore mother cells, enter meiosis and produce haploid megaspores. These produce the female gametophyte. When pollen lands on the female cone, a pollen tube grows into the tissue surrounding the egg cell. Fertilization occurs when a sperm from a pollen tube reaches an egg cell.

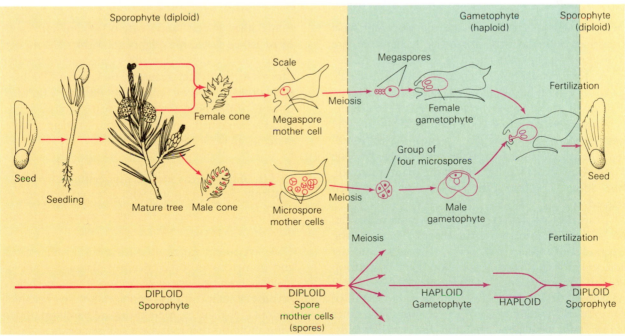

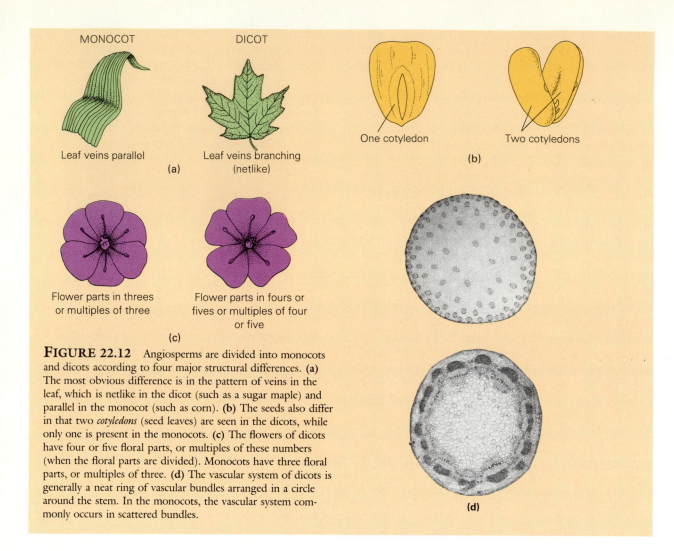

MONOCOT   DICOT

Leaf veins parallel   Leaf veins branching
(netlike)

(a)

One cotyledon   Two cotyledons

(b)

Flower parts in threes   Flower parts in fours or
or multiples of three   fives or multiples of four
or five

(c)

(d)

FIGURE 22.12 Angiosperms are divided into monocots and dicots according to four major structural differences. **(a)** The most obvious difference is in the pattern of veins in the leaf, which is netlike in the dicot (such as a sugar maple) and parallel in the monocot (such as corn). **(b)** The seeds also differ in that two *cotyledons* (seed leaves) are seen in the dicots, while only one is present in the monocots. **(c)** The flowers of dicots have four or five floral parts, or multiples of these numbers (when the floral parts are divided). Monocots have three floral parts, or multiples of three. **(d)** The vascular system of dicots is generally a neat ring of vascular bundles arranged in a circle around the stem. In the monocots, the vascular system commonly occurs in scattered bundles.

ovary in which fertilization and development have occurred. Angiosperms, like other seed plants, are heterosporous, producing megaspores and microspores, as we will see in the next chapter. The female gametophyte is highly reduced, generally just seven cells in all, tucked away in the ovules of the flower.

All you have to do is look around to see that the angiosperms—the flowering plants—have "inherited the earth," at least for the time being. No one knows how many kinds of flowering plants there are, but about 250,000 different species have been named.

In spite of such diversity, the flowering plants can all be divided into two great classes. These are the **Monocotyledonae** ("monocots," for short) and the **Dicotyledonae** ("dicots," for short). The first group is in the minority, since there are only about 50,000 named species of monocots. Among them are all of the grasses—including corn, wheat, and all the other cereal grains we depend on—and palm trees, orchids,

tulips, lilies, yuccas, and many other familiar plants. Most other flowering plants are dicots. Monocots and dicots are rather distantly related, and although they share many key features, they also differ from each other in several important aspects. The most obvious differences are in their leaf patterns, seeds, floral arrangement, and the pattern of their vascular systems, as we see in Figure 22.12.

The **angiosperms** include **monocots** and **dicots,** flowering plants with seeds enclosed in fruit.

As we might expect of such a successful, varied, and numerous group, flowering plants have developed a dazzling variety of life cycles. Nonetheless, because of their common heritage and their essentially similar challenges, their cycles are based on underlying unifying themes, as we will see next.

SUMMARY

WHAT IS A PLANT

Some plant characteristics are multicellularity, including specialized tissues and organs, the pigments chlorophyll a and b and carotenoids, the polysaccharides starch (food) and cellulose (structure), and embryonic development within the protective archegonium.

Alternation of Generations in Plants

Plants follow a sporic life cycle in which the evolutionary trend in the alternation of generations has been from separate sporophytes and gametophytes toward a highly dominating sporophyte that incorporates the gametophyte within reproductive structures. A second evolutionary trend has been away from homospory and toward heterospory. Thus most plants produce megaspores and microspores, which give rise to megagametophytes ("female") and microgametophytes ("male").

NONVASCULAR PLANTS: BRYOPHYTES

Bryophytes include mosses, liverworts, and hornworts.

Bryophyte Characteristics

Although bryophytes have some specialized tissues, most lack extensive conducting and supporting vascular tissue and, accordingly, have no true roots, stems and leaves and remain small. Rhizoids anchor the body, but water must be absorbed by other cells. Water is required for the transit of sperm from antheridium to archegonium, where fertilization occurs. In the moss alternation of generations the haploid gametophyte (the green leafy plant) is dominant.

Bryophyte Origins

Bryophytes are believed to have branched from vascular plants. Thus their lack of vascular tissue and dominant gametophyte are thought to represent evolutionary simplification rather than primitive traits.

VASCULAR PLANTS

Vascular plants—tracheophytes—have water-conducting xylem and food-conducting phloem. Vascular tissue also provides structural support. The more primitive tracheophytes have dominating sporophytes but retain minute, separate gametophytes. The earliest were the simple Rhyniophytes of the Paleozoic era. They had an underground rhizome from which simple, forking branches arose. Their xylem included tracheids but no vessels.

Vascular Plant Divisions

The primitive seedless plants or cryptogams contain four divisions (whisk ferns, ground pine, horsetails, and ferns). Most are homosporous, releasing simple, haploid, aerial spores that form separate, minute gametophytes. The seedless plants dominated the paleozoic forests but, except for ferns, are rare today.

The phanerogams, or seed plants, make up five divisions. They have minute gametophytes incorporated into the sporophyte and are heterosporous. The male gametophyte is released as pollen. Seed plants have dominated the forests since the Mesozoic era, although ferns are widespread.

Ferns

The fern sporophyte contains complex leaves that develop from fiddleheads. True roots absorb water. The ferns are homosporous, forming simple, haploid spores in leaf structures called sporangia. The spores grow into minute gametophytes, which form antheridia and archegonia.

THE MESOZOIC ERA: TIME OF GYMNOSPERMS

Mountain building, a drying landscape, and a cooling climate led to the demise of most seedless plant species. Their extinction cleared the way for the first seed plants, the gymnosperms.

Gymnosperm Specializations

Success in the drier Mesozoic environment was aided by an extensive vascular tissue, made possible by secondary growth. Other adaptations included incorporation of the gametophyte in the large sporophyte and the advent of highly resistant pollen grain and tough, resistant seeds containing the delicate embryo.

The Gymnosperms Today

Today's gymnosperms form pollen and seed cones, the latter of which bear naked seeds (without fruit). One species of the ginkgo (maidenhair tree) remains. Cycad species are more numerous but are restricted to warmer climates. The gnetophytes are mainly desert inhabitants.

Conifers are widespread in colder regions and have adapted to drier conditions. The needle (or scaly) leaves are always present, but shedding of older leaves is continuous. Pines produce separate male and female cones, in which pollen tube growth and seed maturation occur.

By the start of the Cenozoic era, conifers were replaced in many regions by newly expanding flowering plants, the angiosperms.

THE CENOZOIC ERA: THE TIME OF THE FLOWERING PLANTS

The success of flowering plants can be attributed in part to animal-assisted pollination by insects and seed dispersal. Rapid geological change may have also played a role.

The Angiosperms Today

Angiosperms or anthophytes, the flowering plants, surround their seeds with fruit (the mature ovary). They are heterosporous and maintain their gametophytes within the flower. Important to their success has been diversification; there are 250,000 species. They are grouped into two classes, Monocotyledonae (monocots) and Dicotyledonae (dicots).

KEY TERMS

bryophyte	rhizoids	sporangium	conifer
tracheophyte	xylem	indusium	vessel
archegonium	phloem	gymnosperm	needle
sporic	rhizome	secondary growth	cone
alternation of generation	tracheid	pollen grain	flowering plant
gametic	cryptogam	pollen tube	angiosperm
homospory	phanerogam	seed	anthophyte
heterospory	fern	ginkgo	fruit
microspore	fiddlehead	cycad	Monocotyledonae
megaspore	sori	gnetophyte	Dicotyledonae
megagametophyte			

REVIEW QUESTIONS

1 List five characteristics of plants. Which, if any, are exclusive? (p. 358)

2 Review the sporic life cycle. How does it differ from our own gametic life cycle? (p. 359)

3 What evolutionary trend do we see in sporophyte and gametophyte dominance during the evolution of plants? Where is the gametophyte in a flowering plant? (p. 359)

4 Carefully define the term *heterosporous*. Name the two kinds of spores and suggest where they are to be found in the flowering plant. (p. 359)

5 List three kinds of bryophytes. What is lacking in bryophytes that is present in most other plants? (p. 359)

6 Why should the absence of conducting tissues affect the size to which a plant can grow? (pp. 359–360)

7 In what way has the bryophyte failed to fully adapt to the dry, terrestrial environment? How does it make up for this? (p. 360)

8 Starting with the zygote, summarize the alternation of generations in a moss. Be sure to indicate where meiosis and fertilization occur, and specifically what parts of the life cycle are haploid and what parts are diploid (see Figure 22.2).

9 If bryophytes did not descend from the most primitive plants, how can we explain the scarcity of vascular tissue, their dominant gametophyte, and their simple organization? (p. 360)

10 When do vascular plants first appear in the fossil record? Describe the earliest known. (p. 360)

11 What are cryptogams? In what three primary ways do they differ from the phanerogams, the more advanced vascular plants? (p. 361)

12 In what part of the earth's history did cryptogams dominate the forests? What were conditions like at that time? Which group is still well represented? (p. 362)

13 Which portion of the fern's life cycle is definitely dominant? Describe this from your own experience. (p. 362)

14 Review the fern life cycle, beginning with the zygote. Be sure to explain where meiosis occurs, what the gametophyte is like, and when the diploid and haploid states are found. (p. 364)

15 List the physical changes that occurred at the end of the Paleozoic era. What effect did this have on animals? On the cryptogams? (p. 365)

16 What plant group became widespread during the Mesozoic era. List three or four important adaptations that helped these plants adapt to the new conditions. (p. 365)

17 List four groups of gymnosperms that made it into modern times. Which is obviously the most successful today? (p. 366)

18 Where do most conifers live today? Describe the leaf form and explain how it is adaptive to conditions in their habitat. (pp. 367–368)

19 Where do the microgametophyte and megagametophyte form in the pine? What other events go on in these structures? (Figure 22.11)

20 What common fate fell to both gymnosperms and reptiles at the end of the Mesozoic era? What geological event in more recent times led the way for the comeback of the conifers? (p. 368)

21 In what two ways were animals important to the early success of flowering plants? (p. 369)

22 Compare the number of species of angiosperms and their distribution on the earth with that of conifers. (p. 370)

23 To what reproductive characteristic do the names gymnosperm and angiosperm refer? Is this true of all angiosperms? (pp. 369–370)

24 Name the two angiosperm classes and list differences in flowers, vascular tissue, leaf venation, and seed structure. (p. 370)

The flowering plants, the angiosperms, began with a rich heritage. By the time their great invasion of the earth's varied habitats began, they were already well prepared for the rigors of terrestrial life. Their vascular systems were well developed, permitting great increases in size as they pushed their leaves toward the sun. Their massive but delicate roots were able to draw water from the soil. They produced pollen, and fertilization no longer required water. The embryo was protected by a hardened seed coat that could resist most environmental rigors. But the solution to one problem—how to get the sperm to the egg—represents one of the flowering plants' most fascinating adaptations.

Early in their evolutionary history, seed plants had to rely primarily on the winds to carry the male gametophyte to the female gametophyte. This works well where great numbers of the same species exist side by side (as in the great pine and spruce forests), but in mixed stands wind pollination begins to lose its efficiency. As we have seen, the key to angiosperm success has been diversity, and an important part of this development was greater control over pollen dispersion. Thus the emerging angiosperms began employing other forms of assistance, and the earth's animals, particularly its insects, were pressed into service. But insects were not in the business of raising plants. What was in it for them? How did plants enlist their little six-legged partners? The answer is one of our best examples of coevolution (see Chapter 19).

The earliest angiosperm insect lure was probably a device that oozed a sugary plant fluid, at least enough to interest some crawling Mesozoic beetle. Once the trend was established, the race was on as new insect-tempting devices arose to be tested by the forces of natural selection. As a result, plants developed ever more attractive and efficient ways of making use of the wandering insects. At the same time, the insects were also undergoing changes that would enable them to exploit more efficiently whatever it was the plant was offering them. In time, many insects had evolved remarkably specific and efficient sensory devices for detecting flowers and long tubular mouthparts for sucking up nectar. Plants, of course, competed among themselves for the attention of these creatures. Some even began a garish form of advertising that attracted insects—those remarkable displays we call *flowers,* which Darwin referred to as "contraptions" (see Table 23.1).

23

REPRODUCTION IN THE FLOWERING PLANTS

ANATOMY OF THE FLOWER

Although flowers take what seems like endless forms, most have structures in common (Figure 23.1). We can generalize by noting that flowers essentially have four parts: **sepals, petals, stamens,** and **pistils.** All of the parts are actually modified leaves, but the most leaflike are the sepals and petals. Sepals function in the bud stage, where they cover and protect the developing flower. In many flowers, the petals have the important task of attracting insects or other pollinators (Table 23.1). For instance, typical bee-pollinated flowers are brightly colored and fragrant and form sugary nectar in glandular **nectaries.** However, sepals and petals are accessory parts; the real business of reproduction goes on in the stamens and carpels.

Each stamen consists of a slender, stalklike **filament** ending in an enlarged **anther,** where, following meiosis, the male gametophyte is produced. So, we see that the stamen is a male floral structure.

The female parts taken together form the pistil, which is made up of one or more **carpels** (the exact number depends on the species). Each carpel con-

tains three principal parts: **stigma, style,** and **ovary.** The stigma and style play a role in bringing the sprem and egg together, as we'll learn, but it is within the ovary, in small rounded bodies called **ovules,** where the female gametophyte forms.

FIGURE 23.1 The generalized flower contains both accessory and reproductive parts. The ring of sepals is called a **calyx,** and the petals form the **corolla.** In this flower several carpels make up the **pistil,** or **gynoecium** as it is also known. The male counterpart, the **androecium,** is made up of stamens.

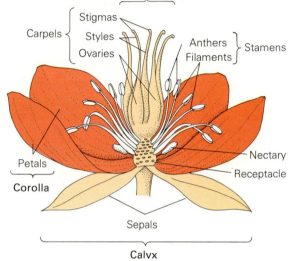

TABLE 23.1 Animal Pollinators and Floral Adaptions

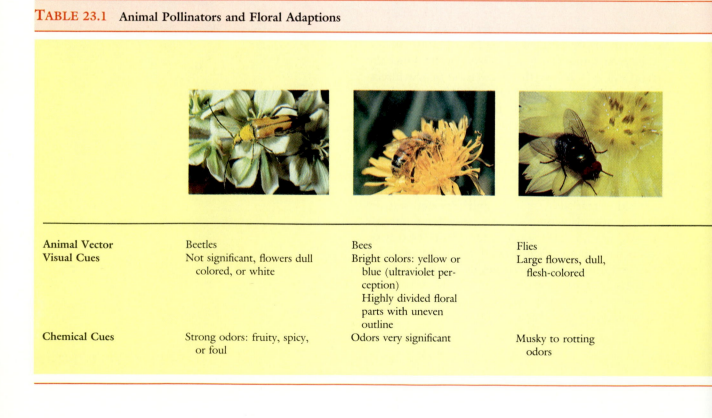

	Beetles	Bees	Flies
Animal Vector	Beetles	Bees	Flies
Visual Cues	Not significant, flowers dull colored, or white	Bright colors: yellow or blue (ultraviolet perception) Highly divided floral parts with uneven outline	Large flowers, dull, flesh-colored
Chemical Cues	Strong odors: fruity, spicy, or foul	Odors very significant	Musky to rotting odors

THE SEX LIFE OF THE FLOWERING PLANT

As a flowering plant prepares for sexual reproduction, changes begin in both the ovary and the anther. Certain of these diploid tissues contain special cells that will undergo meiosis in order to usher in the inconspicuous gametophyte generation. As you would expect, flowering plants are heterosporous: they produce two types of spores (see Chapter 22).

Inside the Ovary: Ovule and Embryo Sac

Within the soft tissues of the flower's young ovary, tiny ovules develop. Although the term *ovule* means "little egg," ovules are technically not eggs. In their early state, they contain sporophyte cells that have the ability to produce the female gametophyte. Each ovule consists of a **megaspore mother cell** surrounded by nutritive and protective tissues.

The megaspore mother cell is a large diploid cell that will produce the female gametophyte. This cell will undergo meiosis in the usual fashion (see Chapter 10) and produce four haploid spores. Three of

these will disintegrate, leaving one large cell, the **functional megaspore** that then begins three rounds of mitosis and produces eight haploid nuclei (one round produces two nuclei, which produce four, and the four produce eight).

In most species, cell walls form and isolate six of the eight nuclei. The other two remain together in a large central cell. At one end, one of the isolated cells becomes the **egg,** the female gamete. The final seven-celled, eight-nucleate structure is the mature female gametophyte, or **megagametophyte,** now called an **embryo sac** (Figure 23.2). As we will see, both the egg cell and the binuclate central cell will enter into fertilization.

Inside the Anthers: Pollen Formation

While the embryo sac has been developing in the ovary, changes have been occurring in the anthers that will produce the male gametophyte (Figure 23.3). The anthers typically contain four chambers known as **pollen sacs.** Within the pollen sacs are numerous diploid cells, the **microspore mother cells.** It is these cells that undergo meiosis. Each meiotic event forms four haploid cells called **microspores.** Each of these cells then doubles by mitosis—

Butterflies	Birds	Bats
Bright colors: red, orange, yellow, blue	Bright colors: red and yellows	Large, dull-colored flowers, color not significant (Bats are night flyers.)
Strong, sweet odor	Copious sugary nectar, little odor	Copious nectar, fruity and fermenting odors

FIGURE 23.2 The female gametophyte generation begins after meiosis in the megaspore mother cell (**a–e**). One of the haploid megaspores goes through three rounds of mitosis, eventually forming the seven-celled embryo sac (**g–j**). The embryo sac includes an egg cell and a central binucleate cell, both of which will participate in fertilization and embryo formation.

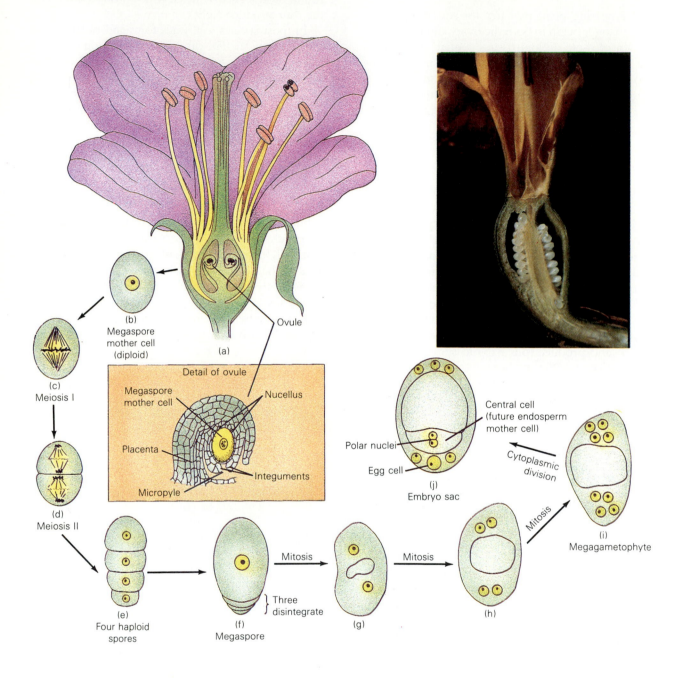

(a)

(b) Megaspore mother cell (diploid)

Ovule

(c) Meiosis I

(d) Meiosis II

Detail of ovule

Megaspore mother cell

Nucellus

Placenta

Integuments

Micropyle

(e) Four haploid spores

(f) Megaspore

} Three disintegrate

Mitosis

(g)

Mitosis

(h)

Mitosis

(i) Megagametophyte

Cytoplasmic division

Central cell (future endosperm mother cell)

Polar nuclei

Egg cell

(j) Embryo sac

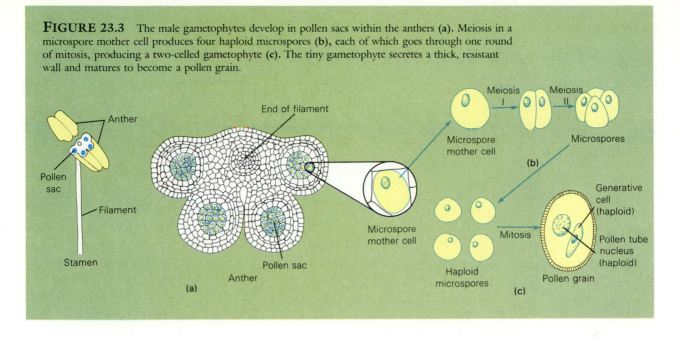

FIGURE 23.3 The male gametophytes develop in pollen sacs within the anthers (a). Meiosis in a microspore mother cell produces four haploid microspores (b), each of which goes through one round of mitosis, producing a two-celled gametophyte (c). The tiny gametophyte secretes a thick, resistant wall and matures to become a pollen grain.

just once—to produce the two-celled male gametophyte. Each of these two cells has its own role and name. One is called the **generative cell** and the other is called the **pollen tube cell.** The generative cell becomes completely enclosed within the cytoplasm of the pollen tube cell. Each gametophyte produces a tough, resistant coat and matures to become a small, light **pollen grain.** Most pollen is lost in this uncertain world, but some grains will land on the stigma of a receptive flower.

In the angiosperms, the gametophyte generation (which was so prominent in the more primitive plants) is represented only by the pollen grain and the embryo sac.

> The **egg** is one of seven cells within the **embryo sac,** the mature **female gametophyte.** The generative cell is one of two cells in a **pollen grain,** the **male gametophyte.** Both form through meiosis followed by mitosis.

Pollination and Fertilization

Technically, **pollination** occurs when pollen is deposited on a receptive stigma, but actual fertilization occurs somewhat later (Figure 23.4). The events leading to fertilization begin when pollen on the moist stigma germinates (emerges from dormancy). After the hard coat breaks open, a **pollen tube** emerges and grows through the stigma and down the style. The growing tube, under the direction of the pollen tube nucleus, produces enzymes that actually digest the soft tissues ahead of the tube. The tube nucleus remains near the tip as it grows downward. During this growth the single generative cell nucleus undergoes one round of mitosis, producing two genetically identical, haploid **sperm.**

Fertilization and fusion. Finally the pollen tube penetrates the ovule at a tiny opening, the **micropyle.** The two sperm then enter the embryo sac, and a double fertilization will occur. One sperm fertilizes the egg cell, that is, male and female haploid nuclei fuse to form the new diploid zygote. The zygote will develop into the plant embryo and eventually form the plant body of the sporophyte generation. The other sperm penetrates the large binucleate central cell and fuses with the two nuclei there to form a **triploid cell.** This unusual cell will undergo numerous mitoses to form a special nutritive tissue called the **endosperm.** The starchy triploid endosperm usually forms the food reserves of the seed.

The simple plant endosperm also plays a critical role in human affairs. This is because the starchy endosperm provides the flour and meal produced from wheat, corn, rice, rye, millet, and oats.

> **Pollination,** the transfer of pollen to the stigma, is followed by **pollen tube growth,** formation of two sperm, and fertilization of the egg and binucleate cell.

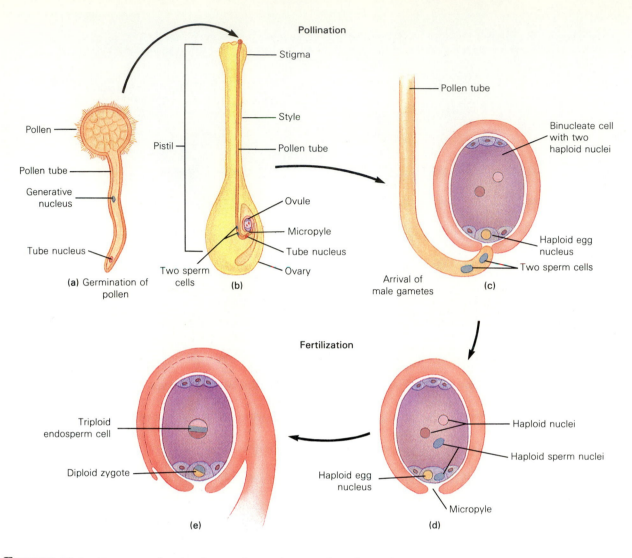

FIGURE 23.4 Upon contacting the stigma, pollen produces a pollen tube **(a)** that penetrates the style and ovary **(b)**. The generative nucleus divides forming two sperm cells **(c)**, which enter the ovule **(d)**, fertilizing the egg and binucleate cell **(e)**.

EMBRYO AND SEED DEVELOPMENT IN A DICOT

Soon after the triploid cell is formed, it repeatedly undergoes mitosis, thus forming the endosperm. While the endosperm grows, the embryo undergoes rapid cell division. Later, the embryonic cells will begin to differentiate (undergo changes leading to specialization) in preparation for different roles in the life of the plant. Among its first efforts, the young embryo will give rise to one or two wings of tissue called **cotyledons.** An embryo will thus reveal at an early stage whether it is a **monocot (monocotyledon)** or a **dicot (dicotyledon)** (see Chapter 22). Whereas monocots have one cotyledon, dicots have two. The cotyledon has a similar function in the two groups—feeding the growing and developing embryo—but there are differences. For instance, in corn and other grains, the single cotyledon lies alongside the endosperm, from which it absorbs food. While the cotyledon operates similarly in some dicots, in the bean, the endosperm is absorbed into the cotyledons during development; the cotyledons are essentially food storage organs.

The Mature Embryo

The embryonic development of the dicot *shepherd's purse* is shown in Figure 23.5. As the embryo completes its development, we can see two large cotyledons and the massive **hypocotyl,** which will have an important role in germination and early growth. (The hypocotyl is the region between the cotyledons and the root tip.)

We can also see several tissues known as **meristems.** Meristematic tissue remains somewhat unspecialized, ready to take any of a number of developmental paths. The meristems are the source of cells for new growth throughout the life of the plant. One of these, the **shoot apical meristem,** is located in the **shoot tip,** a small mound between the cotyledon bases. As you would expect, it provides cells for con-

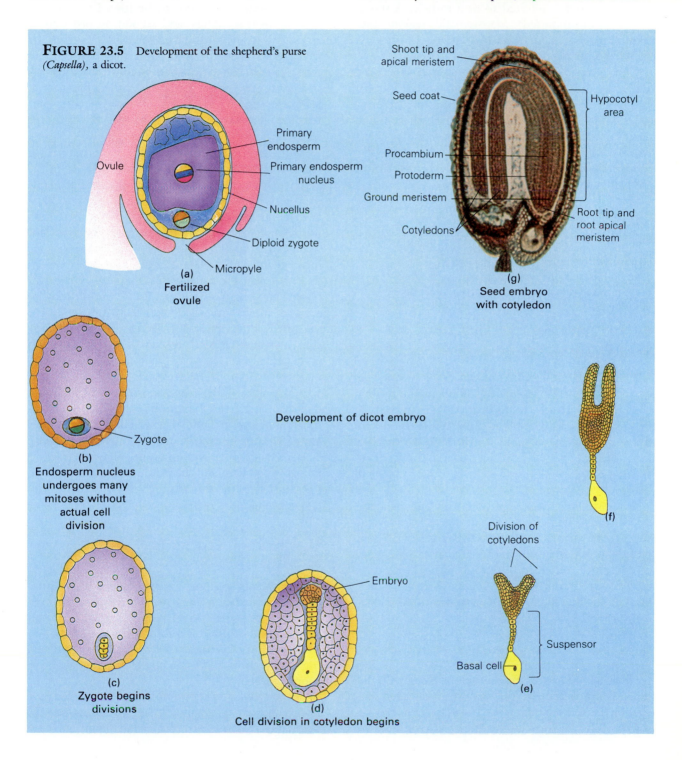

FIGURE 23.5 Development of the shepherd's purse *(Capsella),* a dicot.

(a) Fertilized ovule

Ovule
Primary endosperm
Primary endosperm nucleus
Nucellus
Diploid zygote
Micropyle

(b) Endosperm nucleus undergoes many mitoses without actual cell division

Zygote

(c) Zygote begins divisions

(d) Cell division in cotyledon begins

Embryo

Development of dicot embryo

(e)
Division of cotyledons
Suspensor
Basal cell

(f)

(g) Seed embryo with cotyledon

Shoot tip and apical meristem
Seed coat
Procambium
Protoderm
Ground meristem
Cotyledons
Hypocotyl area
Root tip and root apical meristem

tinued shoot (stem) growth. In some embryos (the peanut and bean, for example,), the shoot tip is quite developed, sporting a **plumule,** a tiny shoot complete with embryonic leaves. At the other end of the hypocotyl, a **root apical meristem** occurs in the developing **root tip.** Logically, this meristem provides for continuous root growth. In some embryos, root development begins early, and the well-defined embryonic root is referred to as a **radicle.** A more general (uncommitted) meristematic region, the **ground meristem,** gives rise to a variety of tissues, as we will see in the next chapter.

Other, more differentiated (committed) meristematic tissues (those undergoing specialization) include the **protoderm** and **procambium.** The protoderm ("first skin"), an outlying tissue, will form the plant's **epidermis** ("outer skin"). The centrally located procambium will provide the water- and food-conducting xylem and phloem, tissues that help form the plant's extensive **vascular system.**

Principal structures in the shepherd's purse embryo include two **cotyledons,** a **stem** and **root tip** containing **apical meristem,** uncommitted **ground meristem,** and committed **protoderm,** and **procambium.**

Seed Coats and Dormancy

After its initial differentiation and development, the embryo becomes dormant. It will undergo no further changes until germination, the metabolic awakening process in the seed. At that time, cell division and differentiation will resume. Until then, the embryo lies protected by a hardened seed coat. In its dormant state, the seed will lose water, becoming dry and hard.

Interestingly, seeds can lie dormant but viable for a long time. Most seeds can sustain at least several years of dormancy; certain lotus seeds, found in a peat deposit near Tokyo, germinated after 2000 years of dormancy. The record, though, is held by a delicate flower of the Yukon, *Lupinus arcticus,* which grew into a fine plant after having lain in the frozen soil for over 10,000 years!

Fruit

In all angiosperms, the fruit develops along with the seed. **Fruit** is actually the mature ovary that surrounds the seeds. You may be surprised to learn that some foods you know as vegetables are, technically,

fruits. Among these are squash, eggplant, cucumbers, and tomatoes, as well as corn, wheat, rye, and beans (if we include the pods). Essay 23.1 discusses the varieties of fruit.

Seed Dispersal

It is advantageous for any plant to be able to disperse its seeds—first, so as not to be forced to compete with its own seedlings, and second, in order to be able to invade new habitats. However, it is often the fruit, rather than the seed itself, that brings about seed dispersal. Such dry fruits as peas and beans pop open and expel seeds forcefully, projecting them at least a few meters away. Other, less dramatic fruits may use wind, water, or birds and foxes to scatter the seeds even more widely (see Figure 23.6).

Wind-dispersed fruit or seeds have plumes or wings that help in lofting them in breezes from the parent plant to some distant place. The winged maple fruit with its two seeds tends to drop straight down at first, but as its speed increases, it begins to spin horizontally away from the parent. The buoyant, water-borne coconut fruit (the husk) contains one huge, hollow seed. The coconut is tough and can float, so even the loneliest Pacific atoll is likely to boast a coconut tree. The cranesbill, foxtail, and clover burr are dry fruits adapted for clinging to the fur of animals. Burrs may be carried for miles before they split open and release their seeds. The cranesbill fruit is remarkable in that it lodges itself into the ground once it has been dropped. As the humidity rises and falls, the spiral fruit opens and closes, turning and ratcheting itself into the ground. Other seeds are distributed in a more familiar way. Their fleshy, sweet, and tasty fruit lures some animals into eating them. The seeds simply pass through the digestive tract, to be deposited here and there in the animal's feces. In some instances the animal's digestive enzymes stimulate germination.

Germination and Early Seedling Development

In most plants, germination is triggered by the presence of adequate water, proper temperature, and oxygen. But some species require some rather surprising conditions. For example, in some seeds, germination must be triggered by fire, others by freezing temperature, and some by the grinding action of running water.

Some seeds won't germinate at all unless they have been subjected to an animal's digestive processes. On the island of Mauritius in the Indian Ocean, there are

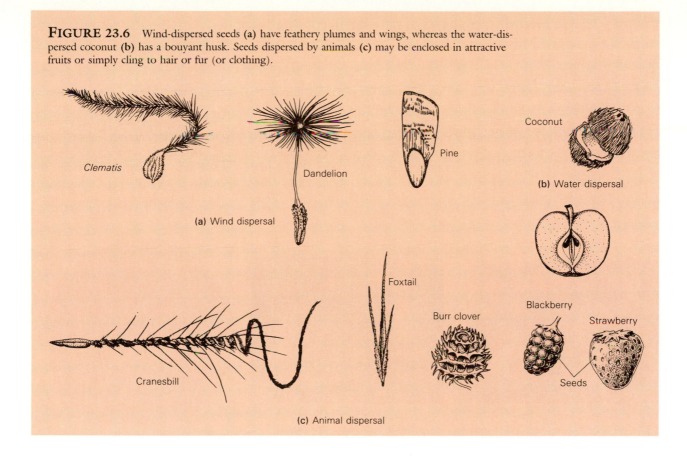

FIGURE 23.6 Wind-dispersed seeds **(a)** have feathery plumes and wings, whereas the water-dispersed coconut **(b)** has a bouyant husk. Seeds dispersed by animals **(c)** may be enclosed in attractive fruits or simply cling to hair or fur (or clothing).

Clematis

Dandelion

Pine

Coconut

(b) Water dispersal

(a) Wind dispersal

Foxtail

Blackberry

Strawberry

Burr clover

Cranesbill

Seeds

(c) Animal dispersal

only 11 huge Tombalacoque trees, a species found nowhere else. All of the trees are about 300 years old. Every year they produce a crop of fruit containing huge seeds with thick seed coats. But the seeds never germinate. In this species, germination cannot occur unless the seed is passed through the crop of a bird native to the island—*Raphus cucullatus,* better known as the dodo. The problem is, the trusting and helpless dodos were killed in great numbers by 17th-century Europeans, and the last one died about 300 years ago. So year after year the seeds just lie around "waiting for the bird that will never come." (This tragic tale may yet have a happy ending, as the naturalist who discovered this curious phenomenon recently managed to get several of the seeds to germinate by passing them through a turkey.)

The **fruit** surrounding seeds represents the enlarged, ripened ovary. It may be fleshy and sweet or hard and dry. Wind, water, and animals are common dispersal agents.

The Seedling

Let's now consider the early growth of two kinds of seedlings: the green bean, a dicot, and corn, a monocot. These were just arbitrarily chosen, and the two cannot be presumed to represent even most of the members of each group because there is such diversity in the early growth of plants.

Bean seed and seedling. The bean seed (Figure 23.7a) contains an embryo with two large cotyledons. When the bean absorbs enough water, the seed coats soften and split. The cotyledons open slightly as the embryo expands.

Growth in the bean embryo begins as the young root emerges from the seed and penetrates the soil, absorbing water and acting as an anchor. The rapidly expanding hypocotyl emerges next, and immediately forms a loop, the **hypocotyl hook.** The hook acts as a bumper as the lengthening hypocotyl "elbows" its way up through the soil, drawing the cotyledons after it (Figure 23.7b). As the hook emerges, it straightens, exposing the cotyledons and plumule to the sunlight. Just below the plumule, cells in the rap-

A fruit, for the most part, is a ripened ovary. There are three basic types of fruits: *simple, aggregate,* and *multiple,* depending on the number of ovaries in the flower or the number of flowers in the fruiting structure.

Simple fruits may be derived from a single ovary or, more commonly, from the compound ovary of a single flower. They can be divided into two groups according to their consistency at maturity: *simple fleshy fruits* and *simple dry fruits*.

Simple fleshy fruits include the *berry, pome,* and *drupe*. The **berry** has one or several united fleshy carpels, each with many seeds. Thus the tomato **(a)** is a berry, and each of the seed-filled cavities is derived from a carpel. Watermelons, cucumbers, and grapefruit are also berries (but, oddly enough, blackberries, raspberries, and strawberries technically are *not* berries). **Pome (b)** means "apple," and the group includes apples, pears, and quinces.

(a) Flower of tomato

Young, simple fleshy fruit (berry) of the tomato with only sepals remaining.

Mature fleshy berry of the tomato. A cut at right angles to its axis reveals five fused carpels, each containing the seed-bearing, fan-shaped parts of the ovary.

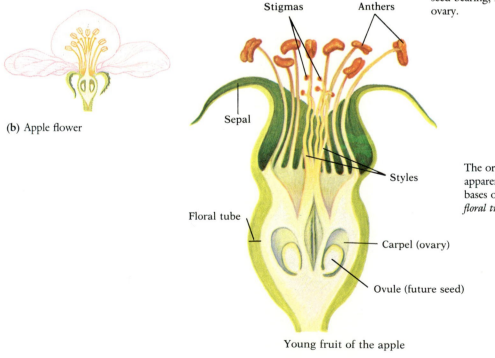

(b) Apple flower

Stigmas   Anthers

Sepal

Styles

Floral tube

Carpel (ovary)

Ovule (future seed)

Young fruit of the apple

The organization of a pome becomes apparent in the young fruit, as the bases of corolla and calyx form the *floral tube* surrounding the ovary.

In the pome, only the inner chambers (roughly, the "core") are derived from the ovary, and most of the flesh comes from the calyx and corolla. A **drupe**—what a wonderful word—is also derived from a compound ovary, but only a single seed develops to maturity. The ripened ovary consists of an outer fleshy part and a hard, inner *stone,* containing the single seed. Peaches and cherries are drupes.

There are many kinds of simple dry fruits, but they are neatly categorized as follows: (1) those with many seeds, which split open and release their seeds, and (2) those with few seeds, which do not split open or release seeds. The first group is called **dehiscent (c),** from the verb *dehisce,* to split or to open, and includes poppies, peas, beans, milkweed, snapdragons, and mustard. The second group is called **indehiscent (d)** (nonsplitting). Its members include sunflowers, dandelions, maples, ash and corn.

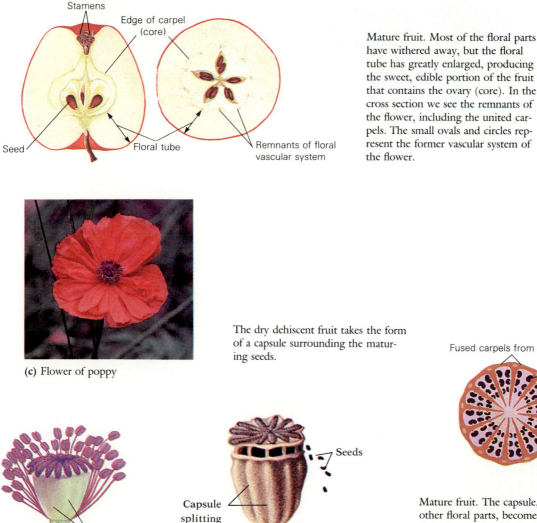

Mature fruit. Most of the floral parts have withered away, but the floral tube has greatly enlarged, producing the sweet, edible portion of the fruit that contains the ovary (core). In the cross section we see the remnants of the flower, including the united carpels. The small ovals and circles represent the former vascular system of the flower.

(c) Flower of poppy

The dry dehiscent fruit takes the form of a capsule surrounding the maturing seeds.

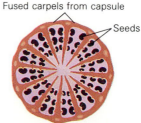

Mature fruit. The capsule, free of other floral parts, becomes a seed-dropping machine as it splits. In cross section, the united carpels are visible in this simple fruit. Each carpel contains numerous seeds in rows along its length.

Individual flower of sunflower. Note the yellow ray flowers.

(d) The sunflower, a composite form, consists of many individual disk flowers, making up the *head*. Each flower is simple, consisting of one carpel that will hold a single seed. As the dry indehiscent fruit matures, it will become surrounded by the familiar hardened "shell" or capsule.

Each of the small spheres, the carpels of this aggregate, is actually a simple fleshy fruit (drupes, in this case) containing a hard seed.

Individual sunflower fruits at two different stages

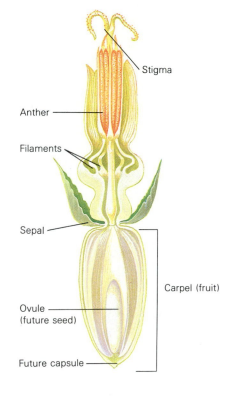

Stigma

Anther

Filaments

Sepal

Ovule (future seed)

Future capsule

Carpel (fruit)

Aggregate fruits (e) are derived from numerous separate carpels of a single flower. Blackberries, raspberries, and strawberries are aggregate fruits. Aggregate fruits consist of many simple fruits clumped together on a common base.

Multiple fruits (f) are formed from the single ovaries of many flowers joined together, as seen in the mulberry, fig, and pineapple. The pineapple starts out as a cluster of separate flowers on a single stalk, but as the ovaries enlarge, they coalesce to form the giant multiple fruit. (The commercial variety, the kind we most commonly see, is a seedless hybrid.)

(e) Flower of the blackberry

Maturing aggregate fruit of the blackberry

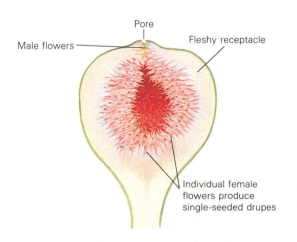

(f) In the common fig, functional male and female flowers both develop within vaselike receptacles, but on different trees. The male receptacle remains tiny (and inedible), producing staminate ("male") flowers within its porelike opening. However, it also contains nonfunctional female flowers that serve only to attract the female fig wasp who lays her eggs within. When the young hatch, the males fertilize the females and then usually die, but the females crawl out, becoming dusted with pollen as they leave. Later, as they prepare to lay their eggs, some will inadvertently enter female flowers. Since the pistillate ("female") flowers are not suitable for egg laying, the wasps soon leave, but not before pollinating all of the flowers within. Each flower then matures into a simple drupe, but forms a swollen, fleshy mass characteristic of the edible fig.

idly growing **epicotyl** elongate, raising the shoot tip further upward. (The epicotyl is the embryonic stem region, above the base of the cotyledons.)

As the food reserves in the coytledons begin to dwindle, the plumule enlarges, producing leaves that unfold to the sun. Soon the little plant becomes independent, producing its own foods through photosynthesis. The cotyledons wither and fall, as food reserves diminish.

> Upon germination in the bean, the **primary root** curves downward and the expanding hypocotyl draws the seed above ground where the **epicotyl** elevates the shoot tip and young foliage.

Corn grain and seedling. Corn germinates in a different way. Corn (a monocot) has only one cotyledon. It takes the form of a food-absorbing structure called the **scutellum.** Surrounding the scutellum is the starchy endosperm. During germination the corn kernel produces enzymes that digest starch, and the products are absorbed by the scutellum.

The corn embryo contains roughly the same tissue organization as the bean embryo but with some significant differences. For instance, both the embryonic leaves and roots are surrounded by protective sheaths: the **coleoptile** and **coleorhiza,** respectively (Figure 23.8a).

When germination and growth occur in corn, the kernel remains behind in the soil as the shoot emerges (Figure 23.8b). At first the young shoot remains surrounded by the protective, green coleoptile. Soon the young leaf within breaks through, enlarged by rapid cell division in the shoot apical meristem below. Thus the first of several leaves is exposed to sunlight.

> Upon germination, the corn shoot, surrounded at first by the **coleoptile,** emerges above ground. Below, the emerging root breaks through its protective **choleorphiza.**

In the next chapter, we will see just how drastically cells can change, how they can specialize, act in concert, and even die to meet the challenges faced by plants on earth.

FIGURE 23.7 Most of the bean seed consists of large cotyledons. The embryo, a miniature plant, contains an epicotyl and hypocotyl, both of which become very active upon germination and seedling growth. **(b)** Note the role of the hypocotyl hook in penetrating the soil and the rapid growth of the anchoring root. The epicotyl extends the shoot and raises the foliage leaves to sunlight.

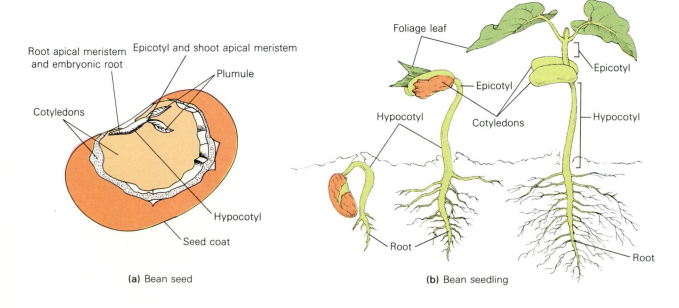

(a) Bean seed

(b) Bean seedling

FIGURE 23.8 In the corn kernel **(a)**, actually a fruit, the endosperm is a large starchy body. The embryo has a single cotyledon, the scutellum. Protective sheaths, the coleoptile and coleorhiza, surround the plumule and radicle. Upon germination **(b)**, only the shoot reaches the surface, where it breaks through the coleoptile to unfurl as a foliage leaf. The fast-growing root must also emerge from its sheath.

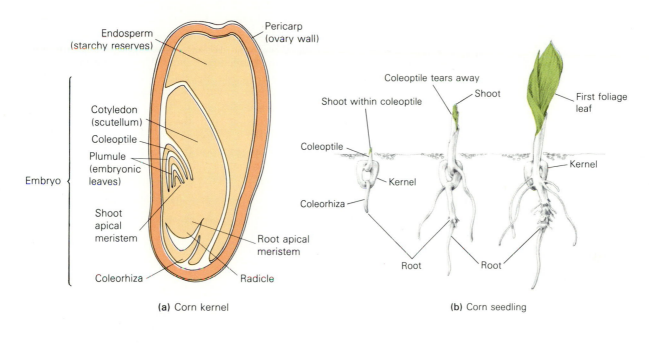

(a) Corn kernel

(b) Corn seedling

SUMMARY

The earlier seed plants were commonly wind pollinated, but as flowering plants emerged, part of their success was due to an increasing coevolution with animal pollinators. Included today are insects, birds, bats, and others.

ANATOMY OF THE FLOWER

Accessory floral parts include leaflike sepals and petals. The latter are often brightly colored and contain nectaries. Reproductive parts include stamens and pistils. The stamen holds the anther, in which the male gametophyte forms. The pistil is made up of one or more carpels, each of which contains a pollen-trapping stigma, a supporting style, and an ovary with one or more ovules. Female gametophytes form in the ovules.

THE SEX LIFE OF THE FLOWERING PLANT

Diploid sporophyte cells, committed to reproduction, enter meiosis and form heterospores.

Inside the Ovary: Ovule and Embryo Sac

Diploid megaspore mother cells within ovules enter meiosis. One of the four haploid megaspores continues into mitosis, giving rise to a seven-celled megagametophyte, the embryo sac.

Inside the Anthers: Pollen Formation

Within the anther's many pollen sacs, diploid microspore mother cells enter meiosis, yielding haploid microspores. Each enters mitosis, forming a two-celled microgametophyte—made up of a generative and a pollen tube cell. Each microgametophyte will become a pollen grain.

Pollination and Fertilization

Pollination is the transfer of pollen to the stigma. Following pollination, a pollen tube forms, penetrating the style and ovary, and entering the ovule through the micropyle. The generative cell divides forming two sperm. One fertilizes the egg cell, forming a zygote, while the other fertilizes the central cell forming a triploid cell that will give rise to the food-storing endosperm.

EMBRYO AND SEED DEVELOPMENT IN A DICOT

The monocot embryo forms one cotyledon, whereas the dicot forms two. Cotyledons provide nourishment to the germinating embryo.

The Mature Embryo

The shepherd's purse embryo forms two large cotyledons and a large hypocotyl. Early tissue differentiation produces a shoot apical meristem and a root apical meristem, a source of unspecialized cells that later provide for stem and root growth. Some embryos have developing shoots and leaves called **plumules** and well formed roots called radicles. Ground meristem, protoderm and procambium later give rise, respectively, to cortical tissue, epidermis and vascular system.

Seed Coats and Dormancy

Following dehydration of the embryo and hardening of seed coats a dormant period ensues. Some seeds may be preserved almost indefinitely.

Fruit
Seed Dispersal
Germination and Early Seedling Development

Fruit, the mature ovary surrounding the seeds, may take many forms, from fleshy to dry and hard. Seeds are adapted to a variety of dispersal agents, including wind, water, and animals. Seeds or fruits may simply cling to animal fur or they may be eaten and shed in the feces. Germination agents include water, fire, abrasion, freezing, the action of animal digestive enzymes, and others.

The Seedling

Germination in the common bean includes the uptake of water, splitting of the seed coats, and the rapid emergence of the hypocotyl. The latter curves, forming the bumperlike, hypocotyl hook, that breaks through the soil, drawing the cotyledons behind. Upon exposure to light, the hook straightens, the epicotyl lengthens and the first leaves form. The cotyledons wither and fall after their food supply diminishes.

In germinating corn, the scutellum absorbs digested food from the endosperm. The young shoot, emerges alone from the soil, soon breaking through the protective coleoptile. The rapidly growing root breaks through the coloerhiza, as it penetrates the soil.

KEY TERMS

sepal	functional megaspore	micropyle	radicle
petal	egg	triploid cell	ground meristem
stamen	megagametophyte	endosperm	protoderm
pistil	embryo sac	cotyledon	procambium
nectaries	pollen sac	monocot (monocotyledon)	epidermis
filament	microspore mother cell	dicot (dicotyledon)	vascular system
anther	microspore	hypocotyl	fruit
carpel	generative cell	meristem	hypocotyl hook
stigma	pollen tube cell	shoot apical meristem	epicotyl
style	pollen grain	shoot tip	scutellum
ovary	pollination	plumule	coleoptile
ovule	pollen tube	root apical meristem	coleorhiza
megaspore mother cell	sperm	root tip	

REVIEW QUESTIONS

1 Explain how the sudden spread and success of angiosperms during late Mesozoic and early Cenozoic was tied in with animal evolution. (p. 373)
2 Using Table 23.1 as a guide, list several of the adaptations of flowers to insect pollinators. (pp. 374–375)
3 Using an actual flower or a simple line drawing you prepare, identify or label the following parts: sepals, petals, pistil (stigma, style, and ovary), stamens (filaments and anthers). (p. 374)
4 State a general function for each of the floral parts identified above (question 3). (p. 374)
5 Beginning with the megaspore mother cell, summarize megasporogenesis—the events leading up to and including the formation of an embryo sac. (p. 375)
6 Beginning with the microspore mother cell, summarize microsporogenesis—the events leading up to and including the formation of a pollen grain. (pp. 375–377)
7 Carefully explain what constitutes the gametophyte in the flowering plant. (pp. 375–377)
8 List the steps involved in pollination and fertilization. What must happen to the generative cell before fertilization is possible? Why is the term, "double fertilization," appropriate? (p. 377)
9 What is the future significance of the triploid cell? Why is the triploid of such vast economic importance to us? (p. 377)
10 What events in early seed formation indicate whether the plant is a dicot or monocot? What is the function of the structure in question? (p. 378)

11 List the developmental events that occur in the shepherd's purse embryo from fertilization to seed formation. (pp. 379–380)

12 Locate the following tissues in the embryo and list their future roles: shoot and root apical meristems, ground meristem, protoderm, procambium. (pp. 379–380)

13 Technically, what is fruit? Is fruit always sweet and tasty when ripe? Explain. (p. 380)

14 List three agents of seed dispersal and five adaptations seeds have for dispersal. (p. 380)

15 What two factors do all seeds require for germination? List four germination conditions that probably represent special cases. (pp. 380–381)

16 What are the roles of the hypocotyl and epicotyl in bean germination? What function do the cotyledons serve during germination and what happens to them afterwards? (p. 381)

17 Contrast the germination and emergence of the corn seedling with that of the bean. What special tissues protect the young corn embryo? (pp. 381–386)

24

GROWTH AND ORGANIZATION IN FLOWERING PLANTS

Eons of plant evolution have molded seeds into tough, resilient, and effective genetic repositories. We have seen how seeds form and what they contain, and we have learned something about how they are adapted to their roles. We have also launched the tiny seedlings on their way to becoming mature plants. The story does not end there, though, because many plants continue to grow throughout their lives. So let's see just how they grow and how their tissues are organized.

OPEN OR INDETERMINATE GROWTH

Many of the familiar angiosperms (flowering plants) are **annuals,** short-lived species that germinate, mature rapidly, reproduce, and die, all within a single season. Probably most of the delicate flowers that grace our meadows are destined to live but a few months. Others, the **biennials,** complete their life cycle in two seasons, with the second reserved for flowering and seed production. However, the largest and most dramatic plants, the great trees, are among the plants called **perennials.** Perennials have **open** or **indeterminate growth;** barring an untimely death from injury, infection, or predation, these plants theoretically live and grow forever.

There are arguments over which tree holds the record for longest life. Among the oldest is a gymnosperm, a gnarled 4,900-year-old bristle-cone pine from the White Mountains in California. Of even greater antiquity are certain cottonwoods, some reportedly 8,000 years old. In any case, we can be sure that some tree, somewhere, is the oldest living thing on earth.

The plant's continued growth and development is assured by its meristem. Meristematic tissue, as we've seen, is composed of undifferentiated and immature tissues. Some of these tissues are always held in reserve—in a sense, they are the plant's investment in its own immortality. When new growth occurs, some of the meristematic cells simply divide mitotically. Some of the daughter cells remain as meristematic tissue, while others enlarge and differentiate, producing a variety of new tissue (see Essay 24.1).

> **Perennial** plants owe their ongoing, **open** or **indeterminate growth** to the continued presence of meristematic tissue.

PRIMARY AND SECONDARY GROWTH

Essentially, **primary growth** increases the length of a plant, while **secondary growth** increases its girth or thickness. More specifically, primary growth occurs when cells contributed through mitosis in the shoot and root apical meristems elongate and mature. Some of the specific products of primary growth are young roots, shoots (including new branches), leaves, and flowers. (Figure 24.1 shows the body of a "generalized" plant and illustrates the functions of these systems.) Primary growth is, of course, responsible for the emergence of the young plant from the seed. Some of the cells produced through primary growth remain simple and unspecialized, capable of resuming activity later. Such tissue, in some plants, will contribute to secondary growth.

Secondary growth generally originates in two sources, **vascular cambium** and **cork cambium,** both of which emerge from the unspecialized reserves of tissues mentioned earlier. They produce a variety of tissue types (these will be discussed later). Although all plants carry on primary growth, secondary growth is not universal. The most obvious examples of secondary growth are seen in the familiar trees, the woody dicots. Most monocots and many short-lived dicots show only primary growth.

FIGURE 24.1 The generalized plant and its organ systems.

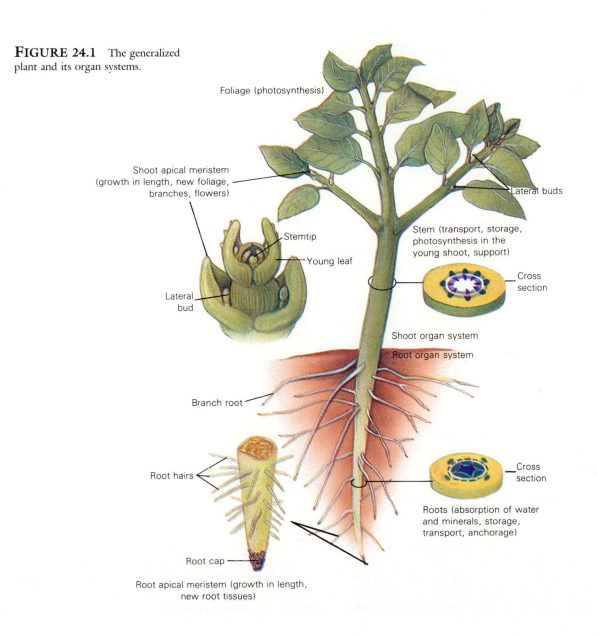

Foliage (photosynthesis)

Shoot apical meristem (growth in length, new foliage, branches, flowers)

Lateral buds

Stemtip

Young leaf

Stem (transport, storage, photosynthesis in the young shoot, support)

Cross section

Lateral bud

Shoot organ system

Root organ system

Branch root

Cross section

Root hairs

Roots (absorption of water and minerals, storage, transport, anchorage)

Root cap

Root apical meristem (growth in length, new root tissues)

In some ways, plants are ideal subjects for studying cell growth. Some plants have the ability to generate roots from stem cuttings, stems from bits of root, and even entire plants from leaves. These phenomena have been invaluable in agriculture through the ages, and for biologists they offer clues to the puzzle of differentiation.

From regeneration studies, we have learned that many, perhaps most, plant cells are **totipotent**—that is, they have the ability to produce the entire organism from which they come. Unlike most animal cells, their differentiation is often reversible. Let's look further into the idea of totipotency.

Some 50 years ago it was discovered that carrot tissue could be grown from individual cells of the carrot embryo. Once separated, they were cultured in a medium made from coconut milk (which contains critical nutrients and hormones). Then, in the 1950s, mature phloem (food-conducting) cells from carrots, cultured in a similar medium, grew into rootlike structures that, when planted, produced entire carrots. More recently, there has been progress in culturing redwood trees

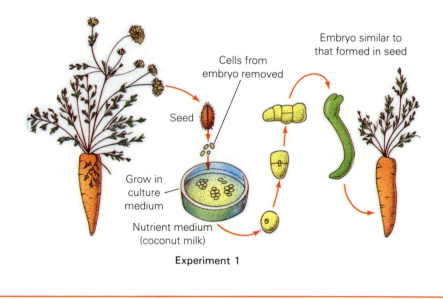

Cells from
embryo removed

Embryo similar to
that formed in seed

Seed

Grow in
culture
medium

Nutrient medium
(coconut milk)

Experiment 1

TISSUE ORGANIZATION

Plants, maintaining their passive vigils, may seem to be simple and inactive, but this appearance is deceptive. In fact, they are often highly organized, dynamic organisms that interact with their environments in very complex ways. Some of this complexity is revealed in their many kinds of tissues. In the last chapter, we described the early formation of three types, the protoderm, ground meristem, and procambium (see Figure 23.5g). It is from these three that the many types of plant tissue are derived. Table 24.1 summarizes tissue types and their derivations. The tissues are organized into organs that comprise two major systems: the **root** (usually underground) and the **shoot** (usually above ground). (Their func-

tions were shown in Figure 24.1.) For now, our discussions will concentrate on vascular tissue—the xylem and phloem.

The sources of specialized tissues in plants are **protoderm, ground meristem,** and **procambium.**

Since terrestrial plants are not bathed in life-sustaining waters as were their ancestors, they have had to develop the means to transport the necessities of life within their bodies, primarily in tissues called the **xylem** and **phloem.** Let's take a look at these fascinating, fluid-filled channels.

and orchids in a similar manner. In addition, botanist James Shepard of Kansas State University has dissolved the walls of mature potato cells, leaving behind the naked cells. He has grown individual cells in a nutrient medium and produced plants, proving again that mature plant cells have lost none of their genetic potency.

Although such work is in its early stages, the potential benefits are encouraging. An obvious outcome would be the use of **cloning** (the production of genetically identical individuals from a single cell) to produce selected crop plants. But even more in keeping with the new era of genetics would be the use of these techniques in gene splicing and recombinant DNA programs. Scientists have already succeeded in producing a potato-tomato hybrid by joining the nuclei from these plants. This capability is important because it lends itself to the ongoing search for ways to improve the resistance of crop plants to disease, drought, cold climates, and other agricultural problems. It is interesting and sobering to try to imagine just how far such techniques could conceivably take us in the future.

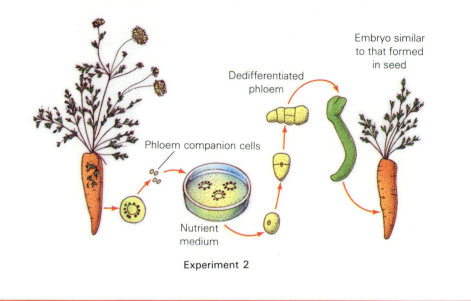

Embryo similar to that formed in seed

Dedifferentiated phloem

Phloem companion cells

Nutrient medium

Experiment 2

Vascular Tissues

Xylem. Xylem, the water- and mineral-transporting tissue, contains several types of fibers and cells, but the tissues most directly involved in transport are the **vessels** and **tracheids.** (You may recall that while tracheids are present in all vascular plants, vessels are found only in gnetophytes and angiosperms.) Vast numbers of these cells, laid end-to-end in the vascular system, form minute tubes through which water can pass from root to stem and leaf.

As young xylem cells mature, they die and their cytoplasm disappears, leaving them essentially hollow. From this time on they are referred to as **elements.** In their mature form, both vessels and tracheids are elongated elements with thick, pitted side walls. The **pits,** or **pit pairs** (their more technical name), are indentations containing only the thin, primary cell wall; water readily passes through. The end walls of tracheids also contain thin-walled pits, while the end walls of vessels are completely perforated or absent altogether (Figure 24.2).

Phloem. Whereas xylem carries water, phloem conducts **sap**—a solution containing foods made by photosynthesis. Although the principal food substances are sugars, amino acids and even hormones are carried in the phloem stream. Unlike the xylem, phloem must remain alive to be functional.

Phloem is also a complex tissue, comprising **sieve elements, companion cells,** and **phloem parenchyma** (Figure 24.3). The cells that actually carry out transport are the sieve elements. Sieve elements

TABLE 24.1   Meristem and Its Tissue Derivatives in Primary Growth

In primary growth, meristematic tissue produces:

Protoderm

Protoderm differentiates into covering tissues, including the epidermis of roots, stems, and leaves. More specialized examples include guard cells, leaf hairs, and root hairs.

Ground Meristem

Ground meristem differentiates into three basic tissue types:

Parenchyma is widely distributed in the stem and root and makes up the photosynthetic tissues of the leaf. The cells are large and thin-walled, often involved in storage.

Collenchyma is primarily involved in support. Its thick-walled cells form tough strands of tissue below the epidermis, within vascular tissue, and in the supporting portions of the leaf.

Sclerenchyma, in its *fiber* form, strengthens young shoots. In its *sclereid* form, it provides hardness for seed coverings and shells.

Procambium

Procambium differentiates into xylem and phloem, the conducting (vascular) tissue of roots, shoots, and leaves. Xylem specializes in water and mineral transport; phloem, in food transport.

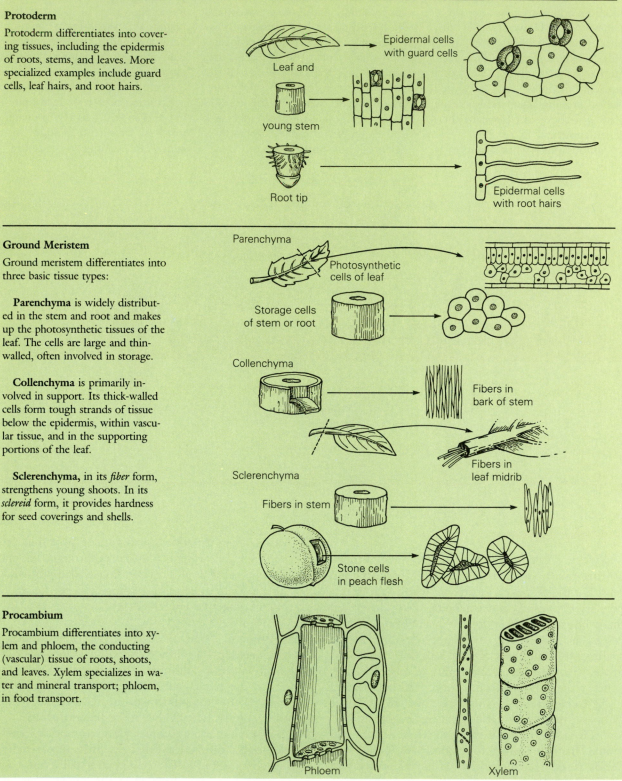

include primitive sieve cells, found in most vascular plants and the more advanced sieve tube members restricted to flowering plants. We will be referring primarily to the latter.

The term sieve comes from the prominent pores that pock the walls of sieve tubes. They occur in both the side walls and the end walls. Actually, they are enlarged *plasmodesmata* (see Chapter 5), through which the cytoplasm of one sieve tube member is continuous with that of the next. Anything in the cytoplasm, then, can move from one member to the next. The largest pores occur in the *sieve plates,* located in the end walls.

As we noted earlier, phloem is living. This may be stretching the definition a bit, however, since the cytoplasm of sieve tubes lacks a nucleus. How does a

FIGURE 24.2 The conducting elements of xylem include tracheids **(a)** and vessels **(b).**

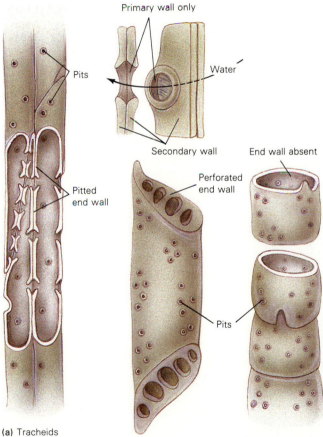

(a) Tracheids
(cutaway view)

(b) Vessels

FIGURE 24.3 The major components of phloem are sieve elements, companion cells, and phloem parenchyma.

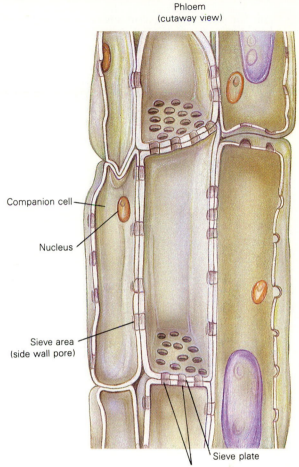

Phloem
(cutaway view)

Companion cell

Nucleus

Sieve area
(side wall pore)

Sieve plate

Plasmodesmata
(allow cytoplasmic stream)

cell—that is, a sieve tube member—survive without a nucleus? In the case of phloem, each sieve tube member lies against a nucleated **companion cell,** and the cytoplasm from one can move into the other. Since sieve tube members lack ribosomes as well as nuclei, it is believed that most metabolic activities are carried out in the companion cells. We do know that the death of a companion cell signals the immediate death of its sieve tube member.

Vascular tissues include water-conducting **vessels** and **tracheids** of **xylem,** and food-conducting **sieve elements** and associated **companion cells** and **parenchyma** of phloem.

THE ROOT SYSTEM

A walk through a forest convinces us of the great diversity of plant shoots, stems, leaves, and so on. But far from obvious is the forest beneath our feet, a hidden growth of vast root systems that are just as diverse as what we see above ground. Different kinds of roots boast their own special properties, and different parts of roots have their own important functions.

The principal tasks assigned to the root are providing anchorage and support to the stems and foliage, taking in water and minerals, and to a varied extent, storing substances for future use.

The Primary Root

The **primary root** includes two regions, the **root tip** and the maturing region above. While the root tip is the site of ongoing primary growth, events in the maturing region above set the stage for secondary growth.

Root tip. The root tip (Figure 24.4) is marked by intense activity in the **root apical meristem,** which is located just within the very end of the root. Root apical meristem includes numerous tiny, undifferentiated cells that continually divide and redivide, contributing cells to the protoderm, the ground meristem, and the procambium. Protoderm will produce

FIGURE 24.4 The root tip.

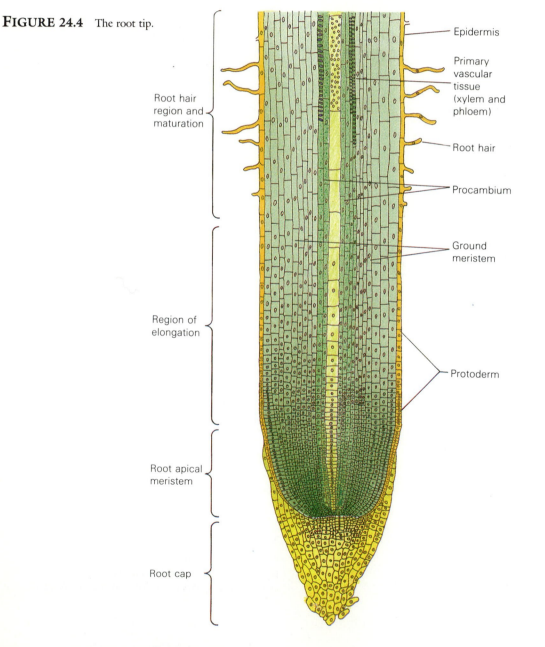

Root hair region and maturation

Region of elongation

Root apical meristem

Root cap

Epidermis

Primary vascular tissue (xylem and phloem)

Root hair

Procambium

Ground meristem

Protoderm

FIGURE 24.5 When germinated in a moist chamber, the seedling produces an enormous number of root hairs. Each is an extension of an epidermal cell. Their combined area provides the root with a great absorbing surface.

the epidermis, while procambium matures into vascular tissue. The ground meristem will later contribute to the cortex. Some of the cells from the root apical meristem replace those lost by the **root cap,** a cluster of cells at the very end of the root tip. Root caps are worn away as the root pushes through the abrasive soil.

Primary root growth occurs in the **root tip** where mitotic activity in the root apical meristem provides cells for the **root cap** and primary tissues above.

Push is the right word, since root tips are literally forced through the soil. As cell division in the root apical meristem continues, the new cells left behind grow rapidly in length. Their elongation is what pushes the root tip along. Elongation is brought about by the absorption of water into the cells, which stretches the young, elastic primary walls and lengthens the cells in the direction of the root axis. Soon, firmer secondary walls will be laid down, and elon-

gation will stop in those cells. In the meantime, a new generation of cells will elongate, and the pushing continues.

While the elongation process takes place, other changes occur in the root tip. Tiny **root hairs** form as extensions of the epidermal cells that surround the root tips. Root hairs grow in great profusion and provide an enormous surface area through which water and dissolved minerals can move into the plant (Figure 24.5). Since the mature root develops a waterproof covering of waxy **suberin,** the root tips provide most of the water uptake.

At the uppermost region of the root tip, procambium undergoes differentiation, forming vascular tissue. Primary xylem, primary phloem, and surrounding tissues begin to form. They will take the form of a cylinder called the **stele.**

The maturing root tip includes a region of elongation, **root hair** growth, and vascular tissue differentiation.

Stele. The stele is a remarkable example of plant differentiation and reorganization (Figure 24.6). In cross sections of some roots, the primary xylem forms a kind of star. The smaller, thinner-walled primary phloem lies between the arms of the star. Surrounding the primary xylem and phloem is a final cylinder of cells called the **pericycle,** which will be important to growth later on.

Just outside the pericycle lies the **endodermis**—a kind of "inner skin" that is actually a part of the **cortex.** The endodermis is important to water transport because its cell walls contain a waxy layer of suberin—the **Casparian strip** (see Chapter 25).

Outside the stele is an extensive cylinder of large, thin-walled parenchyma cells, often swollen with stored starches. Together with the endodermis they make up the cortex. Around the cortex lies the root's **epidermis,** or outer skin.

The **stele** is a cylinder of tissue inside the **endodermis** that includes **pericycle, primary xylem,** and **primary phloem.**

FIGURE 24.6 **(a)** The tissues of the primary root become established in regions just above the root tips. In their final arrangement, the tissues form concentric cylinders. The inner one, the stele, is surrounded by the endodermis. Outside the stele lies a region of storage parenchyma called the cortex. It is bordered by the epidermis. **(b)** The Casparian strip, the suberized cell walls between endodermal cells, directs water through the endodermal cytoplasm before it enters the stele.

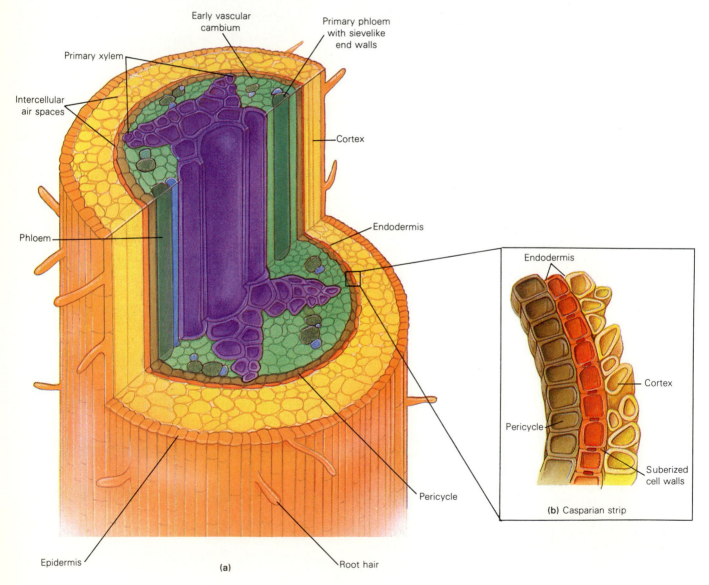

Early vascular cambium

Primary phloem with sievelike end walls

Primary xylem

Intercellular air spaces

Cortex

Phloem

Endodermis

Endodermis

Cortex

Pericycle

Suberized cell walls

(b) Casparian strip

Pericycle

Epidermis

(a)

Root hair

Lateral Roots and Root Systems

Most plants start out with a single primary root, which next gives rise to many **lateral roots.** Lateral roots originate in cells of the pericycle well above the root tip. As they grow they push across the cortex, eventually breaking through the epidermis (Figure 24.7). The vascular system of the young lateral root will join that of the primary root. As lateral roots mature, they produce side branches, which, in time, produce their own side branches, a process of subdivision that continues as long as the root grows. This branching from a central root is characteristic of the **tap root system.** Examples include the carrot, sugar beet, and dandelion (Figure 24.8a).

By contrast, in plants such as grasses, the original root is very temporary. It is quickly replaced by other roots that grow outward from the base of the stem. Roots that originate in this way are called **adventitious roots.** Adventitious roots form an extensive mat called a **diffuse** or **fibrous root system** (Figure 24.8b). In corn, adventitious roots are aerial, that is, they arise from the part of the stalk just above the ground, arching downward and forming **prop roots.** Prop roots help keep the heavy stalk erect.

It should be noted that adventitious roots have other functions. The aerial roots of Algerian ivy, for

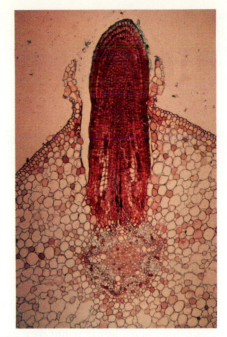

FIGURE 24.7 Lateral or branch roots are initially produced by the pericycle of tap roots. Cells in the pericycle undergo repeated divisions. The mass of cells produced breaks through the endodermis and begins to digest its way through the cortex.

FIGURE 24.8 (a) Taproot system of the dandelion. (b) Diffuse root system in grasses.

(a)

(b)

example, hold it to the sides of aging college dormitories (some claim the ivy is what holds the dorms up). And many plants can be propagated by cuttings that sprout adventitious roots when suspended in water.

> In **tap root systems,** lateral roots arise from the pericycle of primary roots; in **diffuse root systems, adventitious roots** arise from the stem.

THE SHOOT SYSTEM

Growth at the shoot tip continues throughout the life of a plant, just as it does in the root tip. New tissues arise from apical meristem and then elongate, resulting in stem growth. But aside from this, there are few similarities in the development of the root and the shoot. After all, the shoot must produce such structures as leaves, branches, and flowers.

The Primary Shoot

The shoot apical meristem (Figure 24.9) is somewhat dome shaped and is covered by a protective layer called the **tunica.** The shoot meristem does not simply lengthen, leaving behind differentiating tissue. Instead, as it grows, it leaves behind both differentiating tissues and patches of various kinds of meristem. One of these kinds of patches, the **leaf primordia,** gives rise to leaves; others, called **lateral bud primordia,** produce branches.

Behind the shoot meristem. Tissues behind the shoot meristem remain undifferentiated for a time, but strands of procambium mark the sites of future xylem and phloem, and certain large parenchyma cells form **pith.** The outer cells of the young shoot, still green with chloroplasts and carrying on photosynthesis, have begun differentiating into the young epidermis (see Table 24.1).

In dicots, as the young tissues left behind by the apical meristem mature, they reorganize into specific patterns quite unlike those of the monocots. Bundles of vascular tissue are often scattered in the monocots, but they tend to form ringlike patterns in the dicots (Figure 24.10). Also, in many dicots (but not in the

FIGURE 24.9 The shoot tip contains the second region of apical meristem *(center)*. It is located in a dome-shaped mass. The two small projections rising from the meristem are the newest leaf primordia. Older, much larger leaf primordia now rise up to cover the entire structure. In their axes, two patches of dark tissue mark the location of lateral bud primordia.

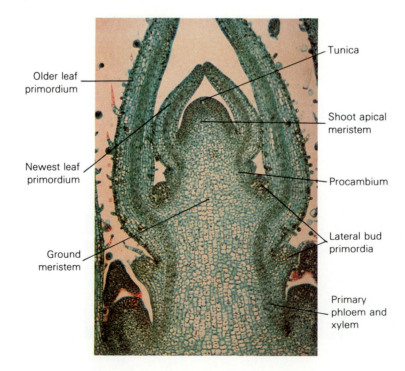

Older leaf primordium

Newest leaf primordium

Ground meristem

Tunica

Shoot apical meristem

Procambium

Lateral bud primordia

Primary phloem and xylem

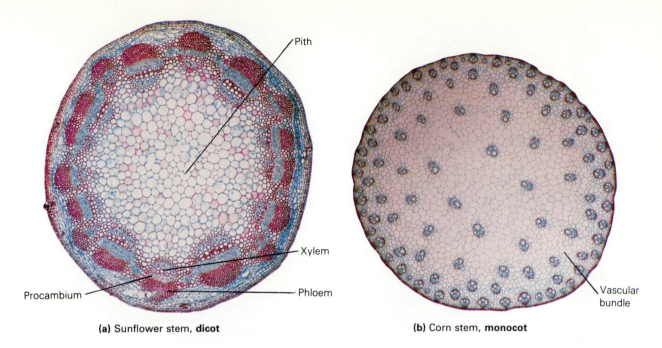

Pith

Xylem

Phloem

Procambium

Vascular bundle

(a) Sunflower stem, **dicot**

(b) Corn stem, **monocot**

FIGURE 24.10 After primary growth, the vascular system in the young shoot is organized into bundles or cylinders. In the dicot (a), The bundles are arranged in an orderly circle, just below the epidermis. Each bundle contains xylem and phloem, separated by a patch of procambium, along with supporting fibers. Most of the stem consists of soft pithy parenchyma. In the monocot corn (b), the vascular bundles are scattered in the stem. Each bundle contains xylem, phloem, and some tough supportive fibers.

monocots), a small region of procambium (a tissue that is critical to secondary growth) is retained between the xylem and phloem.

Secondary Growth in the Shoot

Since secondary growth in the root and shoot are quite similar, we will concentrate on the shoot. Secondary growth accounts for increases in thickness, but it does not occur in all plants. Instead, it is restricted to perennial dicots such as trees, in which it makes great size possible. (A few plants such as the coconut palm, a monocot, grow quite large even without secondary growth. Gymnosperms are also capable of secondary growth.)

The capability for secondary growth is quite ancient. Evidence is seen in fossils of the earliest vascular plants. Thus the restriction to primary growth is probably a more recent evolutionary development.

Transition from primary to secondary growth. Secondary growth in the stem begins just below the growing and differentiating shoot tip where primary growth ends. At this time the young primary vascular tissues have collected into a ring of

bundles containing xylem and phloem. Small patches of procambium remain between the two tissues, and it is this lingering procambium that plays a major role in secondary growth.

Procambium gives rise to **vascular cambium,** which produces **secondary xylem** and **secondary phloem.** In the mature stem, the vascular cambium forms a thin strip between the secondary xylem and phloem. Through continuing mitosis, the vascular cambium provides cells for xylem on its inner side and cells for phloem on its outer. Yet it perpetuates itself by holding some cells in reserve.

As the newly produced xylem grows, it pushes the vascular cambium and newly formed phloem outward. Likewise, the new phloem can only grow outward, crushing older tissue in its path. Secondary growth, the continuous outward expansion of the woody stem, is caused by an enlarging ring of dividing and growing cells within. The sequence of events in secondary growth is shown in Figure 24.11.

In secondary growth, procambium gives rise to **vascular cambium** from which secondary tissues, including **secondary xylem** and **secondary phloem** continually arise.

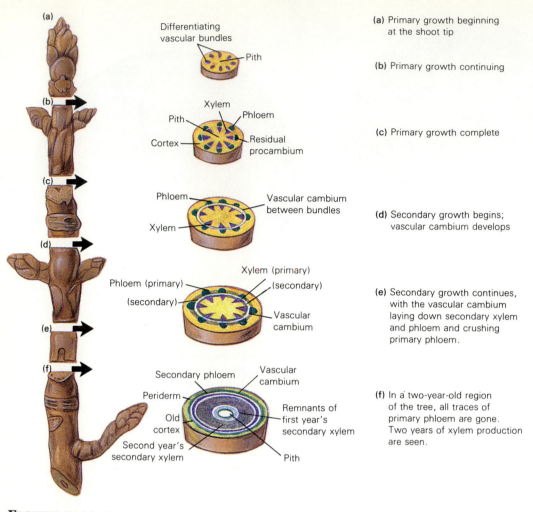

(a) Primary growth beginning at the shoot tip

(b) Primary growth continuing

(c) Primary growth complete

(d) Secondary growth begins; vascular cambium develops

(e) Secondary growth continues, with the vascular cambium laying down secondary xylem and phloem and crushing primary phloem.

(f) In a two-year-old region of the tree, all traces of primary phloem are gone. Two years of xylem production are seen.

FIGURE 24.11   In primary growth the vascular system of the dicot shoot matures (**a, b, c**) into distinct vascular bundles. (**d**) The vascular cambium produces secondary xylem on its inner side and secondary phloem on its outer side. This growth begins to push the primary xylem and phloem away (**e**), with the vascular tissue becoming a continuous ring. In an older region (**f**) the results of continued activity in the vascular cambium are seen. Secondary growth has also replaced the epidermis with a new tissue, the periderm.

Older woody stem.   Older regions of the stem, those that have gone through several seasons of secondary growth, are mostly composed of woody xylem tissue, referred to as "wood" (85% or more of the mature tree). The vascular cambium, the phloem, and the periderm all lie outside the wood, and together they form a rather thin ring of living material.

The growth rate of the xylem tissue is highly dependent on environmental conditions. For example, it may slow down drastically during winter seasons. A cross-section of an older stem or trunk reveals a definite pattern in trees that undergo seasonal growth. During periods of rapid growth, the xylem tends to consist of large, relatively soft cells. As growth slows, the differentiating xylem cells do not

expand as much and remain smaller and denser. The differences in seasonal rates of growth produce the **annual rings** of trees, most obvious in the trees of the earth's temperate zones where spurts of growth occur seasonally (Figure 24.12).

A second growth pattern seen in the older stem takes the form of radiating spokes that extend through the wood and secondary phloem. These are known as **vascular rays** or, simply, **rays**. They consist of sheets of thin-walled parenchyma cells and their thicker-walled descendants called **collenchyma** (a supportive tissue; see Table 24.1). Both are produced by the vascular cambium. Vascular rays provide a means of transporting nutrients laterally, a trait required in younger stems, in which much of the tissue is still alive. In older stems, the growth of rays is essential in relieving the forces created by the expanding cylinder of xylem inside the trunk.

Secondary growth at the perimeter. Secondary growth in the vascular tissues is accompanied by changes in the shoot epidermis. Cells in the cortex near the epidermis now take on a new role. They begin to divide rapidly, producing what is known as the **cork cambium** (see Figure 24.12). The cork cambium produces layer upon layer of cells that are continually pushed outward, rupturing and replacing the old epidermis. These new tissue layers constitute the shoot periderm. The outer layer of the periderm becomes impregnated with suberin, producing a waterproof covering. In this way, the plant has begun to produce **cork.** Cork is often mistakenly called bark, but technically, **bark** is everything outside the vascular cambium.

The corks in wine bottles are true cork. But such cork does not occur naturally. Cork growers remove the periderm of the cork oak, causing the tree to respond to the injury by obligingly forming a new, smoother cork cambium. The new tissue is removed and cut into cylinders. (These cork cylinders are then placed into wine bottles in such a way that they split or crumble at any attempt to remove them.)

Woody tissues include xylem (in annual rings), vascular cambium, phloem, **vascular rays, cork cambium,** and **cork.**

THE LEAF

Leaves are so much a part of our lives that we tend to take them for granted, except perhaps when they signal a change in season. When they are alive and functioning, they are primarily devoted to the conversion of sunlight energy into chemical bond energy in foods. As such, they are amazingly complex and efficient.

The development of even the simplest of leaves necessitates contributions from several basic tissues. Protoderm contributes to the highly specialized epidermis, which slows water loss and admits air. The layers of light-trapping, photosynthetic parenchyma cells within owe their presence to ground meristem, while the vascular tissues, so vital in bringing water and carrying sugars out of the leaf, arise from the versatile procambium.

Leaf Anatomy

The typical dicot leaf is a flattened **blade** attached to a stem by a stalklike **petiole.** The vascular system of the stem passes into the leaf through the petiole, and into the blade along a large central vein called the **midrib.** In typical dicots, the midrib supplies a network of smaller branches, or **veins,** that carry fluids through the blade. Within the blade, each smaller vein is surrounded by specialized cells that form the **bundle sheath.** Anything entering or leaving the veins must

FIGURE 24.12 A photomicrograph of a cross section through a three-year-old woody stem clearly reveals regions of different tissues. The outermost tissue is the protective cork, a suberized layer of cells produced by the cork cambium lying just inside. The conducting tissue consists of a circle of phloem divided by rays. Just inside the phloem is a thin cylinder of vascular cambium, which seasonally produces phloem and xylem. Inside the vascular cambium and making up most of the stem tissue is the xylem, or wood. At the very center, a small region of pithy parenchyma remains.

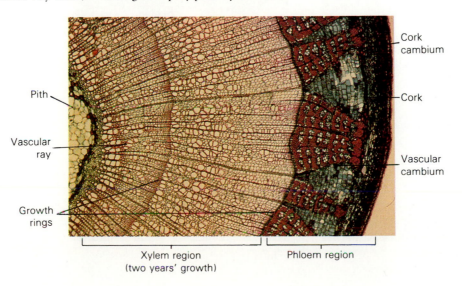

Pith

Vascular ray

Growth rings

Cork cambium

Cork

Vascular cambium

Xylem region (two years' growth)

Phloem region

pass through these cells. We found in Chapter 7 that bundle-sheath cells have special significance to C4 plants.

The organization of the monocot leaf is quite different. Such monocots as the grasses have no petioles. The leaves emerge from a tough sheath around the stem (which is why it is so frustrating to try to tear off a corn leaf). In most monocots the veins do not branch from a central midrib; they lie in parallel rows, interconnected by short, smaller veins (Figure 24.13).

Organization of the leaf. A cross-section of a dicot leaf (Figure 24.14) reveals outer layers of cells of the **upper epidermis** and **lower epidermis.** The upper epidermis, the part most often exposed to light, consists of fairly large, flattened cells whose outer walls are coated with a layer of a wax called **cutin.** Most epidermal cells lack chloroplasts and are transparent.

Within the leaf there are several layers of parenchymal cells that contain chloroplasts. Those cells nearest the upper epidermis are arranged in one or more tightly packed layers and, because of their elongated shape, are called **palisade parenchyma.** They are the first to receive incoming light. Below this lie less orderly layers of cells that are more rounded. They are scattered in such a way that spaces form between them into which air can move. This layer is the **spongy parenchyma,** aptly named for its appearance. The moist air spaces are important avenues of carbon dioxide diffusion, which is essential to photosynthesis. Air enters the leaf through minute openings called **stomata** (singular, **stoma**), which are found primarily in the lower epidermis—the underside of the leaf. Forming the stoma is a pair of kidney-shaped **guard cells** (see Chapter 25).

The undersides of leaves are often covered with fine **leaf hairs,** each of which arises from a single epidermal cell. Some leaf hairs are soft and downy, but some are sharp and hooked and can be lethal to insect larvae that attempt to eat the leaf. Leaf hairs also have another function: they impede the movement of air over the leaf's surface, slowing the evaporation of water.

FIGURE 24.13 **(a)** Dicot leaves are typically net-veined, with a central midrib giving rise to numerous smaller, branching veins. A leaf petiole forms the attachment to the stem. **(b)** Monocot leaves, on the other hand, contain parallel veins, and the leaves attach to the stem by a sheathlike arrangement.

(a)

(b)

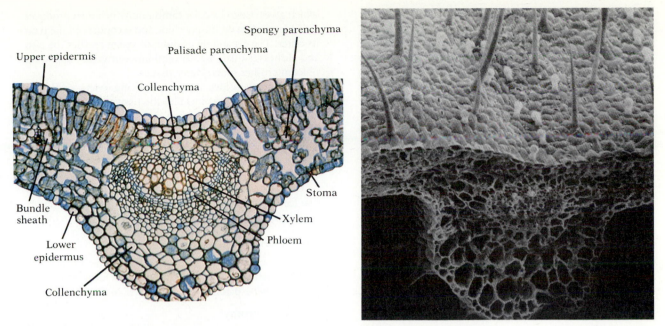

Upper epidermis

Collenchyma

Palisade parenchyma

Spongy parenchyma

Bundle sheath

Lower epidermus

Collenchyma

Stoma

Xylem

Phloem

FIGURE 24.14 The cross-sectional view of a leaf reveals its complex tissue organization. Many leaves have epidermal leaf hairs as well, as seen in the scanning electron micrograph. (*Left*, courtesy Carolina Biological Supply.)

Leaf tissues include **upper** and **lower epidermis, palisade** and **spongy parenchyma,** and **guard cells** that form the margins of **stomata.**

Plants are highly organized and complex organisms. This complexity is revealed in the many specialized tissues of a single plant, as well as in the diversity when species are compared. Still, there are common themes: the general similarity of tissue types, primary growth mechanisms, and systems of transport. In the next chapter we will take a closer look at these transport systems, and we will discover that the xylem and phloem are uniquely adapted to their vital tasks.

SUMMARY

OPEN OR INDETERMINATE GROWTH

In their life spans, plants are generally annuals, biennials, or perennials. The latter have open or indeterminate growth, and an indefinite life span. This is made possible by a reserve of undifferentiated meristematic tissue.

PRIMARY AND SECONDARY GROWTH

Primary and secondary growth are growth in length and girth respectively. Primary growth results in new shoots, leaves, flowers, and roots. Secondary growth originates from vascular cambium and cork cambium, occurring chiefly in woody dicots.

TISSUE ORGANIZATION

Mature plant tissues are derived from protoderm, ground meristem, and procambium. Tissues become organized into two systems: root and shoots. Procambium gives rise to xylem and phloem.

Vascular Tissues

The water and mineral conducting portion of xylem, vessels and tracheids, form continuous tubes throughout the vascular system. Mature xylem consists of non-living elements. Water moves between adjacent elements via thin-walled pits or pit pairs. Tracheids have end—wall pits, whereas vessels have open or perforated end walls.

Phloem, a living tissue, conducts sap (sugars and other substances). Included are sieve elements, companion cells, and phloem parenchyma. Sieve elements, arranged end to end, form the principal transport system. The presence of plasmodesmata in their sieve-like end—walls results in a continuous cytoplasm. The companion cells perform metabolic tasks and along with phloem parenchyma, actively transport materials in and out of sieve elements.

THE ROOT SYSTEM

Roots provide anchorage for stems, carry on water and mineral transport, and store foods.

The Primary Root

A primary root includes the root tip and maturing region. Continuous cell division in the root apical meristem provides cells for the root cap ahead and the maturing region behind. Cell lengthening in the latter pushes the root through the soil. Epidermal cells and their root hairs absorb water and minerals. Maturing procambium forms the vascular tissues of the stele.

The stele includes the pericycle, xylem, phloem, and residual procambium. The cortex surrounding the stele begins with the endodermis, a cylinder of cells that contains a waxy water-barrier called the Casparian strip. It directs incoming water through the endodermal cytoplasm. The root epidermis surrounds the cortex.

Lateral Roots and Root Systems

Tap root systems have a main root with many branches. Cells of the pericycle in the primary root give rise to lateral roots, whose pericycles, in turn, produce additional roots. In diffuse or fibrous root systems, adventitious roots arise from stem regions above. Included are the prop roots of corn.

THE SHOOT SYSTEM
The Primary Shoot

The shoot apical meristem provides cells for primary growth. Patches of meristem are left behind, forming leaf primordia and lateral bud primordia. Within the young shoot emerge future xylem, phloem and simple pith parenchyma. Vascular tissue forms scattered bundles in monocots and distinct rings in dicots. In some dicots, reserves of procambium provide for secondary growth.

Secondary Growth in the Shoot

Secondary growth is restricted to perennial (woody) dicots (and gymnosperms). It begins in procambium which gives rise to vascular cambium, which then produces secondary xylem on its inner side and secondary phloem on its outer. The expanding cylinder of xylem crushes the pith and pushes residual vascular cambium outward. Expanding phloem crushes older, outer tissues.

Most of the older stem is nonliving xylem or wood; living tissue, the bark, includes the tissues outside the vascular cambium. Differences in growth produces xylem of changing size which are viewed as annual rings. Spokelike vascular rays or rays, composed of parenchyma and collenchyma, provide lateral transport and relieve the stress of expansion.

Cork cambium divides continually, contributing cells that form the shoot periderm. Suberin impregnated outermost cells form waterproof cork.

THE LEAF

Leaves emerging from leaf primordia utilize protoderm, ground meristem, and procambium to form epidermis, photosynthetic parenchyma and vascular tissue.

Leaf Anatomy

The dicot leaves consist of a stalklike petiole, a flattened blade, and a midrib. The latter contains a central vein. Veins are surrounded by bundle sheath cells. Monocot leaves emerge from a broad sheath and have parallel veins.

A cross-section through a dicot leaf reveals an upper epidermis (cutin impregnated), photosynthetic tissues including a palisade parenchyma and spongy parenchyma, extensive air spaces, and a lower epidermis containing numerous stomata and leaf hairs. The stomata and leaf hairs inhibit water loss. The pore of each stoma is formed by paired guard cells.

KEY TERMS

annual	primary root	procambium
biennial	root tip	vascular cambium
perennial	root apical meristem	secondary xylem
open (indeterminate) growth	root cap	secondary phloem
primary growth	root hair	annual ring
secondary growth	stele	vascular ray
vascular cambium	pericycle	collenchyma
cork cambium	endodermis	cork
root	cortex	bark
shoot	Casparian strip	blade
xylem	epidermis	petiole
phloem	lateral root	midrib
vessel	tap root system	vein
tracheid	adventitious root	bundle sheath
element	diffuse (fibrous) root system	upper epidermis
pit pair	prop root	lower epidermis
sap	tunica	palisade parenchyma
sieve element	leaf primordia	spongy parenchyma
companion cell	lateral bud primorida	stomata
phloem parenchyma	pith	guard cell
		leaf hair

REVIEW QUESTIONS

1 List three plant categories according to life span. Which has indeterminate growth and what provides for such "immortality"? (p. 390)

2 Distinguish between primary and secondary growth in terms of their effects on plant size. Are all plants capable of primary growth? Of secondary growth? (p. 390)

3 List the three kinds of primary tissue and briefly state what they produce. (p. 392)

4 What is the general role of xylem? List the two principal types of xylem elements. (p. 393)

5 Name and describe the structures that permit water to move between adjacent xylem elements. How do the end walls of the two types of elements differ? Which of the two is absent in nearly all gymnosperms? (p. 393)

6 What is the general role of phloem? State a major difference between phloem sieve elements and vessels or tracheids. (pp. 393, 395)

7 List the two kinds of sieve elements. How do materials pass from one sieve element to the next? (p. 395)

8 What are the principal roles of the phloem parenchyma and companion cells? (p. 395)

9 List three primary functions of the plant root. (p. 396)

10 Prepare a simple longitudinal outline drawing of a primary root and label the following: root tip, root cap, root apical meristem, epidermal cells, root hairs, region of elongation, stele, and cortex. (pp. 396–397)

11 Explain how a primary root continually moves through the soil. Essentially, what provides the push? (p. 397)

12 List the tissues of a mature region of the primary root, starting outside and working to the center. (p. 398)

13 Describe the special feature of the endodermal cell walls. To what important function does this relate? (p. 398)

14 Describe the manner in which lateral branches form in the tap root system. How does repeated branching occur? (p. 399)

15 How do adventitious roots arise? What functions do they serve in corn and ivy? (pp. 399–400)

16 What are leaf primordia? Lateral bud primordia? From what tissue do they arise? (p. 400)

17 Compare the distribution of primary vascular tissues in dicots and monocots. In which does procambium persist? (pp. 400–401)

18 What role does residual procambium play during secondary growth in the stem? To what specific tissues does it give rise? (p. 401)

19 Explain what happens when secondary xylem and secondary phloem increase in size. What must the vascular cambium provide if secondary growth is to continue over the years? (p. 401)

20 What tissues make up the "wood" of a woody plant? What part of a tree is actually alive? (p. 402)

21 What can you determine by counting tree rings? Would this be true in a tropical rain forest where rainfall occurred year round? What actually produces the tree rings? (p. 402)

22 List the tissues of a woody stem from the vascular cambium outward. Distinguish the term *bark* from the term *cork*. (p. 403)

23 To what do the three primary tissues (protoderm, procambium, and ground meristem) contribute in leaves? (p. 403)

24 Distinguish between the organization of dicot and monocot leaves. To which do the terms *midrib* and *petiole* apply? (pp. 403–404)

25 Prepare a simple line drawing showing a cross-section through a dicot leaf and label the following: the upper and lower epidermis, the spongy parenchyma, palisade parenchyma, stomata, guard cell, and air spaces. (p. 404)

26 Explain how the arrangement of the spongy parenchyma provides for carbon dioxide uptake. (p. 404)

25

MECHANISMS OF TRANSPORT IN PLANTS

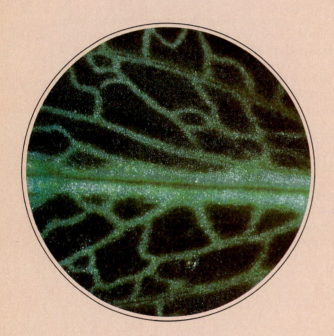

The leaves of a tall tree may discharge enormous amounts of water vapor into the air. And, in certain seasons, they do this day after day, dampening the forest air and lending authority to that glorious smell of the woodlands. Those leaves may be hundreds of feet from the ground, but the water they lose comes from the roots, deep in the earth (Figure 25.1). How does the water, pouring into millions of tiny root hairs, reach those lofty leaves? The question is a good one.

And what about the other fluids that move through such forest giants? In North America one often finds trees that have been girdled with a series of small holes, the work of a migratory little woodpecker called the sapsucker. The holes are shallow, but they penetrate the phloem and fill with sap that is intercepted on its way downward from the leaves. The sapsucker laps at the sugary fluid that seeps from the wounds. The question arises, what causes the sap to move along? The question is intriguing, and the search for the answer involves another good story from the saga of life.

THE MOVEMENT OF WATER AND MINERALS

Let's first ask how water moves as it travels through xylem from the root to the foliage. We should keep in mind that even within the tissues of living plants, water obeys certain physical principles (discussed earlier in Chapters 2 and 5). In fact, plants have evolved very precise means to take advantage of those principles. In a real sense, the vascular plant has evolved around the behavior of water.

Water Potential Revisited

Earlier, we used the term **water potential** in reference to the various forces that can cause water to move. These forces can account for such behavior as the swelling of cells due to osmotic pressure, and the downward flow of water due to gravity. Essentially, water potential describes the *free energy* of water (see Chapter 5).

To illustrate our definition, consider water potential in a cell, where it is dependent upon how dilute the cell's fluid is. Dissolved solutes within a cell *reduce* the cell's water potential. You may recall from our discussion of osmosis (see Chapter 5) that water tends to move through a semipermeable membrane from regions of lower solute concentration (higher water potential) to those of higher solute concentration (lower water potential). We can simplify this by remembering that the transport of water within the plant body always occurs from regions of higher water potential to lower water potential. Water thus moves from cell to cell along a **water potential gradient.** Since we know that water moves from the roots to the leaves, we can infer that the roots have a higher water potential than the leaves. And now we come to some basic questions regarding this phenomenon. Why should a leaf cell have the lower water potential? Not much is used in photosynthesis, so where does the water go? It simply evaporates from the leaf. Let's see why.

Under normal conditions a decreasing **water potential gradient** exists between soil water and foliage and between foliage and surrounding air.

The Transpiration-Adhesion-Cohesion-Tension Hypothesis

The problem of water loss. The problem is that leaves leak—they have to. As you know, plants use carbon dioxide from the air in photosynthesis. It diffuses through the stomata into the leaf's moist air spaces as a gas, but it must be dissolved before it can move into cells. This means that plants must continually bathe their leaf cells in water. However, plants have not evolved a way to let carbon dioxide in without also letting water escape. Water escapes because of evaporation, and it is constantly replaced by water moving upward from the roots. The loss of water from the leaf stomata is known as **transpiration.**

Energy for transpiration. The movement of water through a plant begins with transpiration in the leaf. The amount transpired daily is enormous (Figure 25.2 and Table 25.1), and all of it must be

FIGURE 25.1 This towering giant sequoia, *Sequoiadendron giganteum*, is one of the world's tallest trees 83 m (272 ft). It is truly awe-inspiring to stand in one of the remaining groves of such giants. If you are aware of the problems of water transport, the marvel of it all increases.

FIGURE 25.2 Plants transpire far more water than they use in photosynthesis. The amounts can be staggering. During the growing season, each wheat plant in this field transpires about 100 liters (26.4 gal.) of water.

TABLE 25.1	**Transpiration Rates**

	Liters per Day
Cactus	0.02
Tomato	1
Sunflower	5
Ragweed	6
Apple	19
Coconut palm	75
Date palm	450

replaced if the plant is to remain active and healthy. This movement requires the expenditure of large amounts of energy. Fortunately for plants, they do not have to provide this energy; the energy of evaporation is provided by the sun and the wind, and it is absolutely free. The sun's energy powers transpiration and subsequent water transport. But other mechanisms are also at work; let's look at these.

Transpiration pull. As water evaporates from the moist air spaces in the leaf parenchyma, it is replaced by water from surrounding cells (Figure 25.3). The mechanism of water replacement isn't entirely clear, but the loss of water in cells adjacent to the air spaces would presumably decrease water potential in those cells. This would begin a water potential gradient that, as water begins to move, would spread across the surrounding cells. The leaf parenchyma cells react to changes in water potential more or less as a unit. Their cell walls are very porous, and their cytoplasm is connected by numerous plasmodesmata; therefore, a rapid interaction occurs among the cells. That is, the cell walls and plasmodesmata permit water to move rapidly from cell to cell along a water potential gradient to the site of transpiration.

Some authorities maintain that **adhesion** is a principal force in the movement of water across the leaf and in setting up a pulling force against the xylem water. Adhesion in water is the tendency for water molecules to adhere or cling to certain other substances, in this case cellulose. These researchers suggest that water evaporating into the immense air spaces of a leaf is replaced as water molecules literally creep by adhesion along cellulose cell wall boundaries. Since the combined cell surface area is so large, adhesion becomes a major pulling force. The pulling force, whether osmotic or adhesive or both, is called **transpiration pull.**

Of course, for water movement to continue in the leaf, there must be a constant supply, and this supply comes from the xylem of the leaf vascular system. As we've mentioned, the xylem elements are lengthy, water-filled tubes. But in the xylem, the mechanisms of water movement change.

Transpiration pull includes the evaporation of water from leaf cells and the subsequent movement of water across the leaf from the source.

Cohesion and tension in the xylem. To understand what happens next, we must visualize the xylem as containing an unbroken *column* of water, extending from leaf to root. As water escapes through the stomata, its responding movement through the leaf cells exerts a pull, or **tension,** on the column. Any pull at the top of the column raises the entire column, permitting water to enter the leaf. The pull is substantial enough to raise a column of water to the foliage of the tallest trees. It is interesting that water in an ordinary hose or pipe cannot be lifted more than 10 m by any amount of suction, since suction is dependent on the force of atmospheric pressure *pushing* a heavy column of water upward. Yet transpiration can *pull* water 10 times higher than that. But let's look more closely at the notion of water being pulled through the vascular system, since it raises an important question: Why doesn't the column of water simply break up? There are at least two reasons.

Transpiration pull depends on both the extremely small diameter of the xylem elements and the cohesive quality of water. Water molecules, you may recall (see Chapter 2), cling together because of hydrogen bonding—the attraction between positively and negatively charged ends of adjacent molecules. This ten-

FIGURE 25.3 Water movement through the leaf tissues occurs as a result of a gradient between the xylem and the air surrounding the leaf. The gradient is established by water evaporating from the leaf, which lowers the water potential in the air spaces within. This decrease in water potential starts a chain of events resulting in a constant flow from the xylem to the outside.

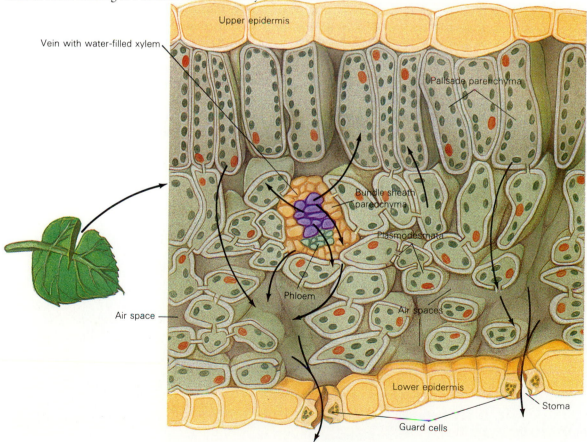

dency among molecules is called **cohesion.** The cohesive forces in water would be ineffective in a large tube, but xylem is microscopic, so the water molecules within cling together tenaciously. In fact, the tensile strength of water in such a thin column approaches that of surgical steel wire of the same diameter!

The tension exerted on water in the xylem through transpiration pull is not hypothetical. It can be demonstrated through the use of a sensitive instrument known as a **dendrograph** (Figure 25.4). Precise measurements of tree trunks over 24-hour periods have revealed that trunk diameters decrease significantly at midday, when transpiration is most intense. This clearly indicates that the tension within the trunk is both real and enormous.

> **T**ranspiration and molecular **adhesion** in the leaf exert a pull on water in minute xylem columns. Water there is held together by **cohesion** and the pull creates **tension** in the columns.

Water Movement in the Root

With water transpiring from the leaf and being pulled out of the xylem for replacement, the root must be able to meet the demands by bringing in new water from the soil. As long as the water potential in the surrounding soil water is greater than that in the root cells, there will be an inward gradient.

Water moves through the root along two pathways. Much of it occurs along the vast network of porous cell walls while some occurs through the cytoplasm of the root cells. Cytoplasmic passage is aided by numerous plasmodesmata. However, the easy passage ends at the endodermis. As we have

seen, *all* water entering the stele is directed by the Casparian strip through the endodermal cytoplasm (Figures 25.5 and 24.6). Plant physiologists believe that the endodermal cells can influence water uptake by varying their own concentration of mineral ions, thereby altering the osmotic pressure of their cell fluids. So the osmotic potential of the endodermal cells seems to help move water through roots. However, the osmotic mechanism can be overridden by even more powerful forces. During intense transpiration, the enormous pulling forces transferred to the root probably nullify the effects of osmosis. In fact, some plant physiologists believe that during intense transpiration most if not all water taken up by the root is through simple *bulk flow* along the steep water potential gradient.

One might expect that plants can literally run out of water at such times, and, of course, they sometimes do. When soil water supplies dwindle, the leaves and softer shoots simply wilt, actually shrinking. Unless the water shortage continues, though, they will recover. One way plants assure a continuous water supply is through rapid root growth allowing new sources to be tapped. Some roots, in fact, grow with remarkable speed. For instance, prairie grass roots grow at a rate of 12 to 14 mm per day; those of the corn plant tear along at 50 to 60 mm per day.

> Rapid, continuing root growth helps provide a constantly renewed source of water for plants.

In smaller plants, though, osmotic pressure is responsible for **guttation,** the exuding of water from openings in the leaves. For example, strawberries may be covered with water exuded in this way early in the morning before the sun dries them.

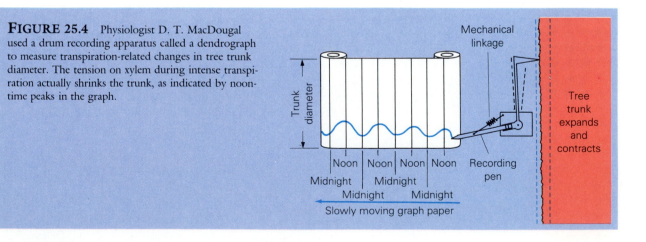

FIGURE 25.4 Physiologist D. T. MacDougal used a drum recording apparatus called a dendrograph to measure transpiration-related changes in tree trunk diameter. The tension on xylem during intense transpiration actually shrinks the trunk, as indicated by noontime peaks in the graph.

FIGURE 25.5 Most water moving through the root cortex follows the cell wall route *(dark arrows)* but some moves through the cytoplasm *(light arrows).* Upon reaching the endodermis, the Casparian strip directs all of the water into the endodermal cytoplasm before it reaches the stele.

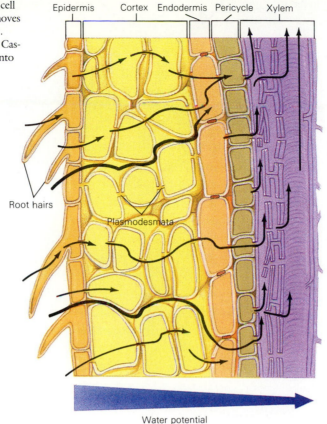

Epidermis   Cortex   Endodermis   Pericycle   Xylem

Root hairs

Plasmodesmata

Water potential

To sum up the transpiration-adhesion-cohesion-tension hypothesis, the energy needed to power water transport is provided by the sun and expressed in evaporation or transpiration. As transpiration occurs at the leaf, the loss is translated into a water potential gradient there. Water moving along the gradient exerts a substantial pull or tension on water in the xylem elements. The adhesive and cohesive qualities of water keep the moving column intact, but this water must be continually replaced by uptake in the root. The combined focus of transpiration, adhesion, cohesion, and tension can be thought of as the **TACT** forces (Figure 25.6).

Turgor and the Behavior of Stomata

We've seen that water loss is actually an essential factor in the pulling of water upward through the xylem. However, water loss must be correlated with the water supply and excessive losses avoided if soil water is limited. Water loss is regulated by numerous paired guard cells that alter the stomatal opening by swelling and shrinking.

Guard cells are somewhat sausage shaped. Their walls are thin along their outer margins but quite thick along the inner margins that line the stomatal opening (Figure 25.7). The difference in thickness is significant. When turgor pressure is high, the cell walls bend, opening the stoma. But when it is low, the springlike, thicker wall straightens, and the stomatal opening becomes a mere slit.

> Increases in turgor bend paired **guard cells,** opening the **stoma;** decreases in turgor permit the cells to relax, closing the stoma.

Stomata are light sensitive and tend to open during the day and to close at night. Thus carbon dioxide is allowed to pass into the plant mostly when the plant is actively involved in photosynthesis. Naturally, there are exceptions. The cells of a plant wilting for lack of water will lose turgor and the stomata will close, conserving precious fluids even at the expense of being unable to carry on photosynthesis.

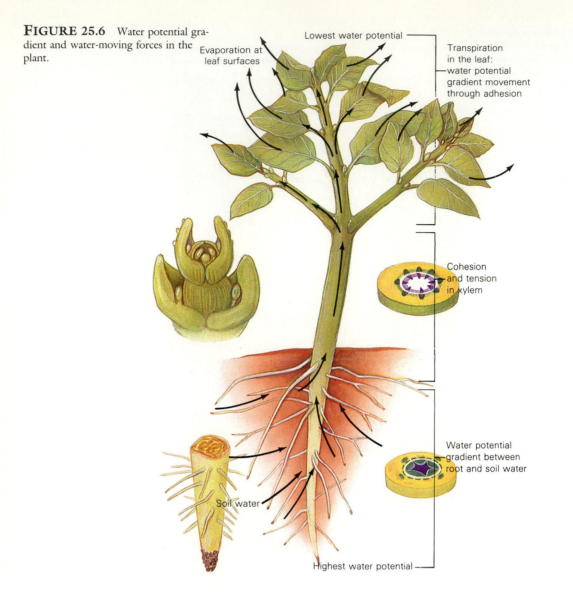

FIGURE 25.6 Water potential gradient and water-moving forces in the plant.

Lowest water potential

Evaporation at leaf surfaces

Transpiration in the leaf: water potential gradient movement through adhesion

Cohesion and tension in xylem

Water potential gradient between root and soil water

Soil water

Highest water potential

The precise mechanism of guard cell control remains unknown, but several hypotheses have been proposed. The most favored explanation at present involves a light receptor and the rapid active transport of selected ions. Under carefully controlled experimental conditions, the guard cells of some plants are shown to respond to light in the shorter, or blue, wavelength by pumping potassium ions into the cytoplasm. The ions are in solution, and their increased concentration brings about an inward movement of water by osmosis. Thus the guard cells swell and the stomata open.

Physiologists know that the potassium mechanism can be overridden under special circumstances, however. For instance, in times of severe water stress, as when soil water is depleted or evaporation from the leaf is too rapid, a plant hormone known as **abscisic acid** accumulates in the leaf. Since abscisic acid causes guard cells to lose their potassium ions, the solute concentration diminishes and water moves out. With the loss of turgor the stomata close.

Increases in guard cell turgor may involve a light receptor, and its activation triggers the inward pumping of potassium ions, followed by the passive entry of water.

In some plants the stomata close in the early afternoon to prevent excessive water loss in the heat of the day. In the desert, where excessive water loss must be

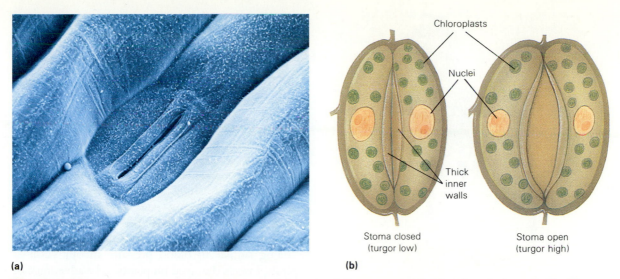

Chloroplasts

Nuclei

Thick inner walls

Stoma closed (turgor low)

Stoma open (turgor high)

(a)

(b)

FIGURE 25.7 **(a)** The scanning electron microscope shows the slitlike stoma (closed). Note the paired guard cells with thick inner cell walls, and the larger, surrounding epidermal cells. **(b)** When turgor is low in the guard cells, their thickened inner walls straighten, closing the stoma. Increased turgor, however, causes the guard cells to swell, which bends the thickened inner walls, opening the stoma.

avoided, some plants, notably the so-called CAM (crassulacean acid metabolism) plants, have evolved biochemical answers to the problem. Their stomata open only at night, admitting carbon dioxide that is incorporated into organic compounds until daylight. Then the stomata close, the biochemical reactions are reversed, and carbon dioxide is released for photosynthesis.

Mineral Uptake by Roots

For most plants, the only sources of mineral nutrients are the ions dissolved in soil water. Since the plant has to take a great deal of water from the soil to make up for transpiration losses, you might expect that it would simply passively extract its needed minerals from the water. However, plants must use active transport to obtain mineral nutrients, so ATP energy is expended. Once inside the root, minerals move from cell to cell by way of plasmodesmata (Figure 25.8). A second expenditure of ATP moves the ions across the endodermis where they readily enter the water flow in the xylem. The intake of minerals must be ongoing, but in many cases the plant gets a little help from certain friends.

Mutualism and Mineral Uptake

The roots of most vascular plants form peculiar fungal associations called **mycorrhizae** (Figure 25.9; see also Chapter 21). The fungal **mycelium** is vast,

FIGURE 25.8 The pathway of mineral ions through the root begins with active transport in the epidermis. Most ion movement is via the cytoplasmic route until the watery stele is reached.

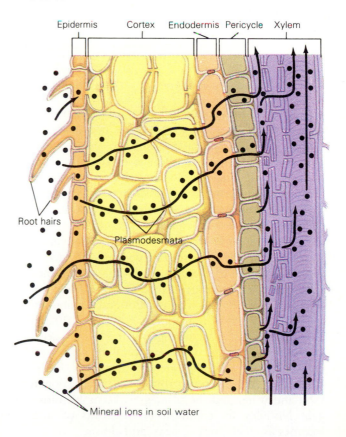

Epidermis   Cortex   Endodermis   Pericycle   Xylem

Root hairs

Plasmodesmata

Mineral ions in soil water

FIGURE 25.9 Three nine-month-old sweetgum seedlings grown in fumigated soil of moderate fertility. The fumigation killed the mycorrhizal fungi that live symbiotically with the plants. The fungi were restored in the two larger plants on the right. The stunted plant on the left developed without the fungi. The experiment illustrates the importance of such associations in the development of some plants.

extending far out into the soil. Some of these tubelike filaments penetrate the root itself. Once there, the fungus can take advantage of the plant's food resources. But the association is mutualistic: both parties benefit. The extensive mycelium concentrates mineral ions, particularly phosphates, in its mass. Thus the plant has ready access to some scarce minerals.

Bacteria provide another example of mutualism. In addition to the more routine decomposing activities that help in the recycling of mineral nutrients, some bacteria are nitrogen fixers. They convert atmospheric nitrogen (N_2) into nitrates and ammonium ions through nitrogen fixation (see Chapters 20 and 46). In some instances, nitrogen-fixing bacteria actually invade the root, which responds by forming a confining nodule (cystlike growth) around the bacterial colony. As in the mycorrhizae, the bacteria obtain food and water and the plant gets the usable nitrogen. Nodules are common in the roots of such legumes as alfalfa, beans, peas, and clover.

FOOD TRANSPORT IN THE PHLOEM

Now that we have considered the movement of water and minerals through the plant, let's see how sugars and other manufactured products move through the phloem.

We learned earlier that transpiration creates a substantial *pull* on water columns in the xylem. But things are different in the phloem. The **phloem sap** is subjected to a pushing force in the form of high **hydrostatic** (water) **pressure.** (Hydrostatic pressure is the pressure that is exerted in all directions by a fluid at rest. In this case, it might help to consider it as being similar to blood pressure in our vessels.) Aphids, insects that feed on plants, take advantage of the hydrostatic pressure of the phloem sap by using their long, hollow mouthparts to drill tiny holes in individual sieve tube members. They just let the nutrient-laden phloem sap flow into their bodies as if from an artesian well. In fact, researchers use aphids to obtain pure samples of phloem sap for analysis (Figure 25.10).

Sap is actually a rather thick fluid, especially when the plant is actively metabolizing and photosynthesizing. Nonetheless it moves rapidly through the phloem, up to a meter per hour. Sucrose makes up about 90% of the solutes in sap, but it also carries other sugars, mineral nutrients, hormones, and amino acids.

The onward movement of sap is brought about by high hydrostatic pressure in the phloem.

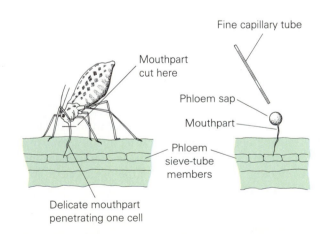

FIGURE 25.10 An ingenious means of obtaining pure sap involves the use of aphids. After the aphid has pierced the phloem, it is anesthetized and its mouthparts are severed so that they remain in place.

Flow from Source to Sink

Nutrients originally produced in the leaf are widely distributed in the plant, moving to the actively growing regions, into the root, into maturing fruit, and to storage regions. This transfer, or **translocation,** as it is known, is multidirectional; it can occur in different directions in the same tissue at different times. We will refer to areas where nutrients are to be used or stored as **sinks,** and to areas where they originate as **sources.**

The flow of sap is *from source to sink:* nutrients are actively transported into the sieve tubes at the source, and are actively transported out of the sieve tubes at the sink (Figure 25.11). The active transport at both sites requires an expenditure of ATP.

The Pressure Flow Hypothesis

Active transport loads nutrients into the sieve tubes at the source and unloads them at the sink, but what accounts for the flow between the two? There have been many hypotheses to account for this mecha-

nism, but the one currently favored, the **pressure flow hypothesis,** is an older one, first proposed in 1927. It is based on the differences in water potential and osmotic pressure between the xylem and the phloem.

The idea is this: the active transport of sugars from the source into the phloem greatly decreases its water potential in comparison to the high water potential in the nearby xylem elements. The result is that water leaves the xylem and moves into the phloem sieve tubes, raising the hydrostatic pressure there. The increased hydrostatic pressure then forces the sap to move as a stream through the phloem tubes.

Meanwhile, at the various sinks, solutes are being unloaded. This results in an increase in the water potential within the sieve tube compared to the surrounding cells. Because of this, water leaves the sieve tube, entering the sink tissues or moving back into the xylem. Within the phloem, the sap follows the gradient in water potential that is created by active transport at both ends of the pipeline—that is, at the sink and at the source (see Figure 25.11).

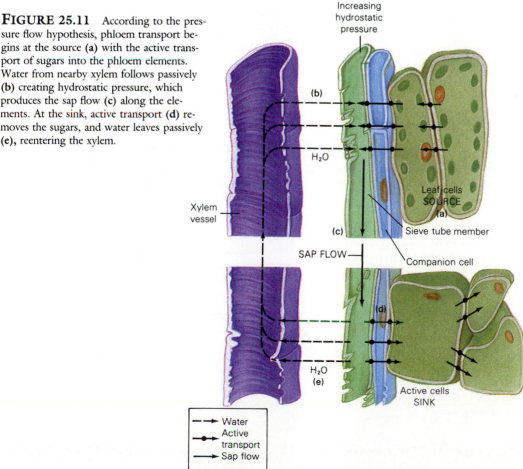

FIGURE 25.11 According to the pressure flow hypothesis, phloem transport begins at the source (a) with the active transport of sugars into the phloem elements. Water from nearby xylem follows passively (b) creating hydrostatic pressure, which produces the sap flow (c) along the elements. At the sink, active transport (d) removes the sugars, and water leaves passively (e), reentering the xylem.

The **pressure flow hypothesis**: sugar, actively transported into the phloem at the **source**, is joined by the passively moving water. The resulting hydrostatic pressure moves the sap along the phloem to the **sink.**

As you now see, the simple tree, standing among other simple trees, is not so simple after all. It is quietly and efficiently engaged in processes that dedicated scientists are only now beginning to understand.

SUMMARY

THE MOVEMENT OF WATER AND MINERALS

Plant evolution has been greatly influenced by the characteristics of water.

Water Potential Revisited

Water potential refers to the potential movement of water due to gravity and hydrostatic or osmotic conditions. Differing solute concentrations in cells create water potential gradients with water moving from regions of high water potential to regions of low. In plants this means from the soil to the root and from root to stem and leaf and then to the air outside.

Transpiration-Adhesion-Cohesion-Tension Hypothesis

In the process of transpiration, water evaporates through the stomata as carbon dioxide is admitted for photosynthesis. This loss starts the movement of water up through a plant. Thus the plant takes advantage of the energy of sunlight and wind to move water.

Evaporation from the stomata sets up a pulling force, transpiration pull. Some of the force may be due to the water potential gradient, but much of it may be a product of adhesion, the attraction of water to cellulose cell walls. The pull is reflected on the xylem columns.

Transpiration creates a tension in the xylem water columns as they are raised up by the pulling forces from above. The water columns resist breaking because water is greatly affected by its cohesion—the attraction between water molecules. In the minute xylem columns the cohesive force or tension is enormous. During intense transpiration, tension actually causes a tree trunk to decrease its diameter, an observation made through dendrograph measurements.

Water Movement in the Root

Water moves from the soil into the root because of a water potential gradient there. Most movement occurs along cell walls in the cortex, but some is through the cytoplasm. At the endodermis, water must pass through the cell cytoplasm, where its uptake may be influenced by osmotic conditions therein. During intense transpiration, bulk flow probably accounts for most movement. If the inward water potential gradient is lost, wilting occurs.

Turgor and the Behavior of Stomata

Stomata open when turgor pressure is great in the paired guard cells and close when it is low. This corresponds to photosynthetic activity. Theoretically the turgor-changing mechanism is a photoreceptor that reacts to light by causing potassium ions to be pumped into the cell. Water follows, and the guard cells swell, opening the stomata. In water stress, abscisic acid, a hormone, is believed to override the photoreceptor, turgor is lost, and stomata close. Desert CAM plants open their stomata at night and close them in daylight. At night they incorporate incoming carbon dioxide into organic compounds, releasing it during daylight for photosynthesis.

Mineral Uptake by Roots

Minerals in soil water must be taken into the root cells by active transport. The principal route of transport is the cytoplasm, facilitated by plasmodesmata.

Mutualism and Mineral Uptake

In mutualistic fungal-root associations called mycorrhizae the fungus provides minerals and uses some of the plant's food supply. Mutualistic nitrogen-fixing bacteria live in root nodules, exchanging nitrogen compounds for plant food.

FOOD TRANSPORT IN THE PHLOEM

Phloem sap (primarily sucrose and water) is moved by hydrostatic pressure. It builds as water enters the phloem after sugars and other solutes have been pumped there through active transport.

Flow from Source to Sink

In translocation, materials are moved from sources, tissues where foods are produced or stored, to sinks, tissues where new storage or usage goes on. Food moves into and out of both regions through active transport.

The Pressure Flow Hypothesis

In the pressure flow hypothesis, sugars actively transported into the phloem from the source cause the inward movement of water and a rise in hydrostatic pressure. The sap flow then occurs. When the sink is reached, active transport removes the sugars, and water subsequently follows, some of it returning to xylem.

KEY TERMS

water potential
water potential gradient
transpiration
adhesion
transpiration pull

tension
cohesion
dendrograph
guttation
TACT

abscisic acid
mycorrhizae
mycelium
phloem sap
hydrostatic pressure

translocation
sink
source
pressure flow hypothesis

REVIEW QUESTIONS

1 List three factors that can influence water potential. (p. 408)

2 Explain what a water potential gradient is and how cells can create such gradients. (p. 409)

3 Why is it necessary for plants to permit a water loss to occur? What is this process called? (p. 409)

4 If water is pulled through a plant, what is the source of the energy required to exert the pull? Could plants afford such an energy expenditure? (pp. 409–410)

5 Describe the stepwise changes in water potential in the leaf, as water is lost through the stomata. (p. 410)

6 What is adhesion? How might adhesive forces add to transpiration pull? In what part of the leaf are the pulling forces finally reflected? (p. 410)

7 Compare the pulling force of transpiration pull with sucking forces that might be created by a vacuum. Can the latter lift water to the tops of tall trees? (p. 411)

8 Account for the great tension possible in xylem water columns. What does cohesion and xylem diameter have to do with this? Is there any experimental evidence of tension? Explain. (pp. 411–412)

9 Describe the water potential gradient in the soil and root. Describe the two routes followed by water in the root cortex. Which is most important? (p. 412)

10 How does the Casparian strip affect water passage into the stele? How might this be important? At what times does bulk flow overwhelm osmosis? (p. 412)

11 Describe the arrangement of guard cells in the stoma. (p. 413)

12 What force brings about opening and closing of the stomatal pore? What is the significance of the thick inner walls of guard cells? (p. 413)

13 Explain the relationship between light and guard cell shape. In what way does this correspond to photosynthesis? (p. 414)

14 Explain the peculiar adaptation of the CAM plants. (p. 415)

15 Describe the principal differences between the uptake and movement of mineral ions across the root cortex and the uptake and movement of water. (p. 415)

16 Describe the mycorrhizal association. What makes it mutualistic? (pp. 415–416)

17 Explain the mutualistic exchange between nitrogen-fixing bacteria and leguminous plants. (p. 416)

18 Generally compare the forces involved in water and sap transport. Which, if any, requires ATP energy? (p. 416)

19 Distinguish between the source of materials and their sink. Name the process of nutrient movement. (p. 417)

20 Using a simple diagram explain how pressure flow accounts for the movement of materials from source to sink. Be sure to distinguish active from passive transport. (p. 417)

26

RESPONSE MECHANISMS IN PLANTS

You have probably noticed that plants tend to be a little short on personality, which is probably why many people have switched to hamsters. However, perhaps a few very patient people with time on their hands have learned that plants can and do respond to their surroundings in many ways. A plant, like any other organism, responds continuously to a variety of cues, signals both from within itself and from its environment. But a plant's responses are usually gradual and based on time-consuming chemical changes.

Regulation through chemical mechanisms frequently involves certain molecules known as **hormones.** Essentially, hormones are chemical messengers that are manufactured in one part of an organism and are transported to another part, where they can cause some sort of change. The cells in which the change takes place have specific receptor sites that recognize and respond to the hormones.

In addition to being very specific, hormones are effective in minute amounts, and they are almost always short-lived. They do not accumulate in cells and tissues but are rapidly broken down. This turns out to be important in the coordination of hormonal activity.

Plant hormones are important in a number of ways. They are involved in growth, cell division, seed germination, flowering, tissue differentiation, dormancy, and other vital activities. You may recall from our earlier discussions, for example, that primary growth itself occurs through cell division and cell elongation, both of which require the presence of certain hormones. Let's now consider a few specific plant hormones and see how they function to regulate and coordinate the activities of the plant.

PLANT HORMONES AND THEIR ACTIONS

Auxin

Auxin is a class of very small molecules with far-reaching effects. The principal naturally occurring auxin is indoleacetic acid (IAA). Auxin was chemically identified about 50 years after its presence was suspected (Figure 26.1).

Auxin is best known as a growth hormone. It affects nearly every aspect of growth, from root tip to foliage. It doesn't cause plants to grow by increasing the rate of mitosis, but by promoting cell enlargement in stems, particularly by elongation of cells behind the apical meristem (see Chapter 24). Although we still don't completely understand just how auxin works, it seems that, among other things, it promotes cell elongation by going to work on the soft primary cell walls of newly divided cells before they have reached their final, hardened state (that is, before they are impregnated with pectin and other wall hardeners). Auxin promotes the loosening of closely bound filaments of cellulose near the ends of the young cell walls, thus permitting turgor pressure to expand the cells in those areas. The increased turgor is due to enlarged central vacuoles, rather than to added cytoplasm.

Other roles of auxin. Working alone or in concert with other hormones, auxin influences cell differentiation, growth in the vascular cambium, fruit and leaf fall, and even the shape plants take as they grow. Two of these, leaf fall and tree shape, have been of great interest to naturalists.

In deciduous trees of the temperate zone, leaf fall is a seasonal event. It begins as auxin is withdrawn from cells in the **abscission zone** at the base of each leaf petiole (Figure 26.2). At this time, valuable materials within the leaf cells are withdrawn. Next, cellulose-splitting enzymes break down cell walls in the abcission zone. With the slightest autumn breeze the leaves break away, spinning and looping, to carpet the ground below.

Tree shape is often due to auxin's ability to both encourage and inhibit growth. It works through a principle called **apical dominance.** You may have observed that, generally, the uppermost growing tips of plants grow faster than those below. This is because auxin, produced in the growing tip, stimulates growth there, but as it moves downward, it suppresses growth in the stems below. The result is the familiar triangular shape of conifers such as the pine

FIGURE 26.1 The discovery of auxin was preceded by a number of key experiments. (**a**) Charles Darwin and his son, Francis, determined that a light-dependent agent in the tip of canary grass seedlings caused them to bend toward a light source. (**b**) P. Boysen-Jensen determined that the light-activated agent could diffuse through gelatin. This indicated that the agent was molecular. (**c**) A. Paal carried out his key experiment in the dark. He used severed coleoptile tips to direct the bending of oat seedlings, showing that the coleoptile was the source of the active agent. (**d**) Fritz Went removed coleoptiles and placed them on agar blocks for varying times. He then used the blocks to produce curvature. By experimenting with various concentrations of auxin, he related the amount of curvature to the amount of auxin present.

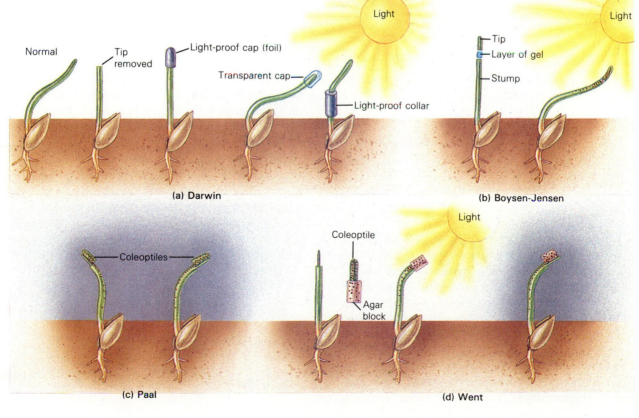

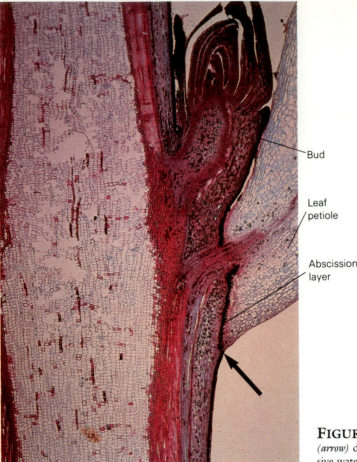

FIGURE 26.2 Before leaf fall, cells in the abscission layer *(arrow)* die and harden. The formation of a scar prevents excessive water and sap loss and prevents infection.

Bud

Leaf petiole

Abscission layer

and spruce. Should the growing tip be lost, one of the lateral branches will take over, soon restoring the graceful triangular form.

> **A**uxin influences cell differentiation, growth of vascular cambium, tree shape, and fruit and leaf fall.

Gibberellins

The **gibberellins,** a family of 57 known molecules, received their name from the fungus in which they were first found, *Gibberella fujikuroi.* This fungus, which once threatened rice harvests in Japan, causes the rice plant stem to elongate strangely and does not permit the plant to produce normal flowers. Gibberellins are now believed to be present in all plants and concentrated in the seeds.

The growth-promoting power of gibberellins has been dramatically illustrated in a number of experiments (Figure 26.3), particularly those involving genetic dwarfs. Dwarf corn, for instance, can be induced to grow to normal height after the application of gibberellins. Such experiments suggest that the dwarf corn is short only because of the lack of a hormone, the presence of which is genetically determined.

Gibberellins also have other roles. For example, they stimulate pollen germination and pollen tube growth. Later, during the germination of grain, the hormones stimulate the synthesis of the starch-digesting enzyme **alpha amylase.** Alpha amylase makes glucose available to the growing embryo. In other circumstances gibberellins have been used to inhibit seed formation and to produce seedless fruits.

> **G**ibberellins cause shoot lengthening, stimulate enzyme production in grains, and influence pollen germination and pollen tube growth.

FIGURE 26.3 Gibberellins have a dramatic effect on stem growth, as seen in these plants. The plants at the left were grown normally, while the ones at the right were treated with gibberellins.

Cytokinins

Cytokinesis refers to cell division (see Chapter 9), and **cytokinins** are a group of hormones that influence this process. Plant researchers first learned about cytokinins by using coconut milk in cell cultures (see Essay 24.1). They knew that some hormone in the coconut milk was encouraging cell division in their cultures. In 1964 the first of the cytokinins was isolated and named **zeatin.** Since then three others have been identified.

Botanists soon learned that cytokinins alone cannot stimulate cell division or other plant activities; they must function with other plant hormones. Figure 26.4 shows how varying mixtures of auxin and cytokinins can influence plant growth and differentiation.

Cytokinins can also prevent aging in plants. For example, if freshly picked leaves are treated with the hormones, they wither and die far more slowly. In treated leaves the chlorophyll remains active, protein synthesis continues, and carbohydrates remain intact. Synthetic cytokinins have been applied to harvested vegetables to extend their storage life. (Unfortunately, cytokinins have no such effect on humans.)

Ethylene

Ethylene is literally a lightweight among the plant hormones—light enough, in fact, to escape from the plant as a gas. Ethylene is a hormone whose development is promoted by auxin, and it often operates in concert with auxin. It is important in the ripening of fruit. Picked fruit will ripen much more rapidly if it is kept in an enclosed space, such as a paper bag, where the ethylene produced by the fruit itself can be concentrated. This finding has obvious commercial application. Fruits can be shipped in an unripe condition and, just before marketing time, exposed to synthetic ethylene gas, which hastens the ripening process. Ethylene is also known to promote fruit abscission (fruit fall), and growers who use mechanical harvesting devices sometimes apply the gas to loosen blackberries, cherries, and grapes.

Ethylene is also known to influence sex in species that produce separate male and female flowers. When young cucumber flower buds are treated with ethylene, most of the emerging flowers will be female (pistillate). In contrast, high levels of gibberellins encourage formation of male (staminate) flowers.

Ethylene may be important in maintaining the curved hypocotyl hook that acts as a bumper when some seedlings make their way out of the soil (Figure 26.5). It prevents the hypocotyl from straightening until it breaks through the soil surface. Once this happens, light apparently inhibits the production of ethylene, so that the stem straightens and the leaves unfold to the sun's rays.

> **E**thylene ripens fruit, influences sex in flowers, and affects hypocotyl curvature in seedlings.

Abscisic Acid

In the late 1940s, plant researchers, encouraged by the discovery of growth-promoting hormones, found new growth-inhibiting substances. In the mid 1960s one of the inhibitors was chemically identified and named **abscisic acid (ABA).** A chief source of ABA today is the cotton plant.

ABA is involved in the wilting response of stomata to excessive water loss (see Chapter 25). ABA is also believed to inhibit growth. It does this by suppressing protein synthesis. Thus its effects are opposite to those of auxin and the gibberellins. Also,

FIGURE 26.4 The effects of auxin and cytokinin on differentiation in the tobacco callus depend on the relative concentrations of the two hormones.

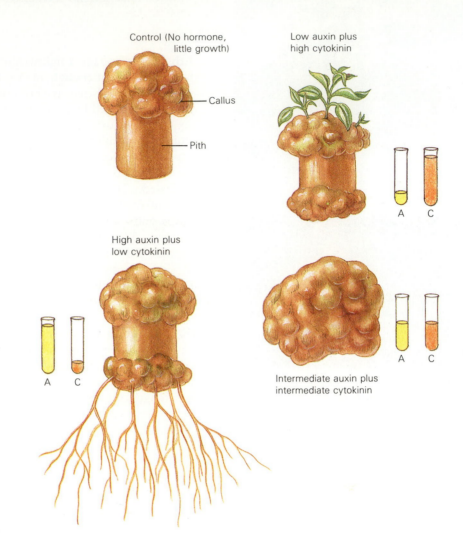

Control (No hormone, little growth)

Callus

Pith

Low auxin plus high cytokinin

A   C

High auxin plus low cytokinin

A   C

Intermediate auxin plus intermediate cytokinin

A   C

FIGURE 26.5 Ethylene is associated with shoot curvature in the seedling. **(a)** Note the typical curvature of seedlings as they emerge from the soil. The curved hypocotyl in the bean is thought to act as a protective "bumper." **(b)** The pea seedlings have been grown in increasing concentrations of ethylene gas. As the concentration is increased, the curvature also increases.

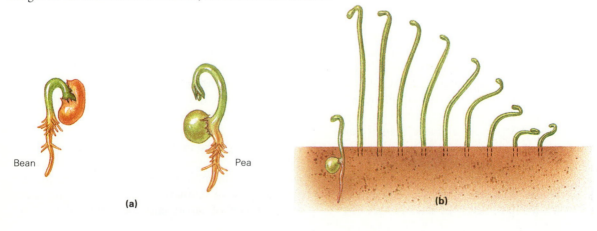

Bean

Pea

(a)

(b)

unlike the gibberellins, ABA is known to inhibit production of the starch-digesting enzyme alpha amylase in barley seeds, thus inhibiting germination. Although ABA shows some potential in agriculture, no practical applications have been discovered so far.

Abscisic acid inhibits growth and enzyme production in grain and promotes stomatal closure.

ARTIFICIAL AUXINS AND PLANT CONTROL

As we humans have learned more about plant hormones, we've increasingly utilized these chemicals to cause plants to behave in the ways we want—such as to grow, to die, and to bear fruit. We've also looked for cheaper and better ways to control plants. One way has been through the production of synthetic or artificial hormones. For example, industry can now produce a number of inexpensive artificial auxins or other growth-promoters. Some of these have even greater effects than the natural auxin because they are not rapidly broken down by the plant's enzymes. One growth promoter is the herbicide (plant killer) 2,4,5–T (2,4,5–trichlorophenoxyacetic acid). Whereas small amounts of 2,4,5–T promote growth, high concentrations kill plants. This compound is very commonly used in weed control because it is highly selective. It is usually highly toxic to the dicotyledonous plants (such as clover, dandelions and certain other "weeds") and spares the monocotyledonous plants (such as grasses, wheat, and oats). Fortunately, such herbicides are also **biodegradable,** which means they break down rapidly when exposed to the elements.

Use of 2,4,5–T is not exactly uncontroversial. There is some ominous evidence that it may interfere with the reproductive success of mammals, particularly by causing birth defects. Thus its value as a weed killer has to be measured carefully in terms of its risk.

Other artificially manufactured plant hormones used in agriculture (or to control the growth of unwanted flora) may have unexpected repercussions in organisms other than plants. Some of these effects may not appear until years after exposure. For example, contaminants in Agent Orange, a defoliant used during the Vietnam War, are now accused of being responsible for a horrible array of effects on the Vietnamese farmers and American veterans who were exposed to it.

Synthetic growth promoters, similar to hormones, are used as herbicides.

PLANT TROPISMS

Since plants must generally stay put, their responses to different environmental stimuli are largely restricted to specific growth patterns. Such growth responses, called **tropisms,** take many forms. For example, plants respond to light through **phototropism** and to gravity through **gravitropism** (formerly called geotropism). Tropisms can be either positive or negative—a plant bending toward the light shows *positive* phototropism. A shoot growing away from gravity (up into the air) illustrates *negative* gravitropism. As we will see, hormones are usually involved in tropisms. In addition to having hormonally induced growth responses, some plants are capable of short-term responses involving rapid movement. One of the most fascinating of these is the **touch response** (more technically, **thigmonastic movement**). It is seen in the sensitive plant *Mimosa pudica* and in certain carnivorous plants that trap insects.

Phototropism

Phototropism is a plant's growth response to light. We see this, for example, when a plant bends toward light (see Figure 26.1). Obviously, something in the shoot tip must respond to light. But what is it? So far, no one has positively identified the specific mechanism, but plant physiologists are on the trail of a yellow-colored pigment, possibly one of the flavoproteins, that specializes in the absorption of light in the blue range. The receptor is believed to have an effect on the distribution of auxin as it is produced in the shoot tip. In one series of experiments, investigators learned that the total auxin production in the tip is the same under lighted conditions as it is in darkened conditions. But in the light, the distribution can be quite different. In plants exposed to light on the right side, for example, much of the auxin diffused or was transported to the left side. The cells on the left responded by elongating more rapidly, producing a curvature toward light (Figure 26.6). (This is the reason you have to keep rotating your window plants unless you favor the "windblown" look.)

FIGURE 26.6 Cells in the apical meristem continually divide, producing cells which then elongate. **(a)** When light comes from all sides, elongation occurs equally around the entire stem. **(b)** But when light comes only from one side, only the cells on the unlighted side elongate. This is because auxin diffuses, or is transported to the unlighted side.

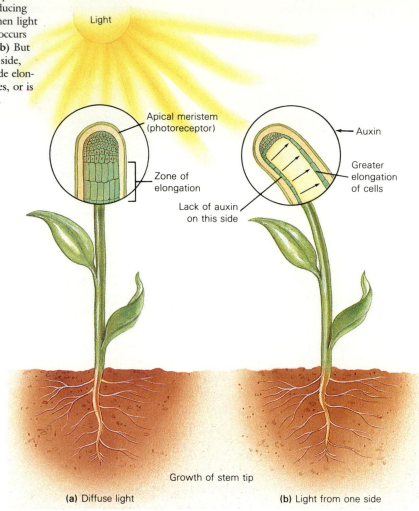

Light

Apical meristem (photoreceptor)

Zone of elongation

Auxin

Greater elongation of cells

Lack of auxin on this side

Growth of stem tip

(a) Diffuse light

(b) Light from one side

This migration of auxin away from the light has been fully substantiated through the use of auxin labelled with carbon-14, a radioactive tracer. Its use permits the experimenter to follow the telltale radiation wherever the molecule migrates. The migration of auxin suggests that the light receptor somehow produces selective changes in the permeability of cell membranes in the shoot, favoring the diffusion, or perhaps the active transport, of auxin away from the lighted side.

If light brings about the changes in the distribution of auxin, you might expect that plants kept in the dark would grow straight and tall, at least until their energy reserves were depleted. And you would be right. For example, bean seedlings grown in a dark-room go through a surge of growth, becoming tall and spindly (as well as ghostly white, since the production of chlorophyll requires light). However, the photoreceptor is quite sensitive, and a mere pinpoint of light from any direction will initiate the phototropic response.

In **phototropic responses** auxin migrates away from light, causing cell elongation and a bending toward the light.

Gravitropism

When a seedling is placed on its side in the dark, the shoot tip soon grows upward and the young root, downward. Again, this response is gravitropism. The shoot responds negatively to gravity while the root's response is positive. Certainly, it is adaptive for shoots to grow upward and roots down, but what is the mechanism for the response? The plain fact is that plant physiologists are stymied. Fortunately, they do have some promising clues. For example, they have detected increases in auxins, gibberellins, and abscisic acid on the lower side of the horizontal shoot, so perhaps these hormones influence the young shoot's negative response to gravity. However, such hormonal gradients have not been found in roots, so roots represent a different problem.

Researchers now believe that *calcium* is an important factor in gravitropism. Calcium is well known as an agent that stiffens cell walls, thus inhibiting cell elongation. When seedlings are arranged horizontally for a short time, calcium is detected in greatest amounts in cells on the upper side of the shoot and on the lower side of the root. These are the cells that *do not elongate*. However, the cells opposite, uninhibited by calcium, *do elongate,* bending the shoot and root in the directions observed (Figure 26.7). So, the distribution of calcium seems to explain the different growth responses of the two seedling parts. Researchers are stalled at this stage, however, and are looking for the mechanism that determines calcium distribution and the nature of calcium interaction with hormones.

The distribution of calcium in seedlings and its role as an inhibitor of cell elongation suggest a central role in **gravitropism** (response to gravity).

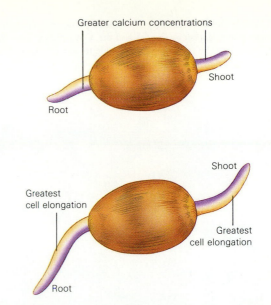

FIGURE 26.7 Gravitropism. Seedlings placed in the dark and in the position shown respond by negative gravitropism in the shoot and positive gravitropism in the root. The distribution of calcium, an elongation inhibitor, is believed to play a pivotal role in the two different responses.

Touch Response

Touching the leaflets of the "sensitive plant," *Mimosa pudica* (Figure 26.8a) causes the plant to "cringe." That is, the leaflets fold almost spasmodically and the petioles droop. Some theorists suggest this drooping, a thigmonastic movement, tends to discourage browsing animals. Others claim it helps the plant avoid excessive water loss when the leaves are stimulated by hot, dry winds, which are common in its usual habitat. The question remains, though, *how* do they do it?

Another example of the touch response is the Venus flytrap, *Dionaea muscipula* (Figure 26.8b). The trap, a highly modified leaf, lies open when at rest. Each half of the trap has three tiny, hairlike triggers that, when brushed by a wandering insect, spring the trap, quickly closing the leaf. The toothed leaf presses the insect against the digestive glands on its inner surface, and the plant gains nutrients, particularly nitrogen, from the insect's body. Like other insectivorous plants, the Venus flytrap is adapted to nitrogen-deficient bogs and marshes.

The ability of some plants to respond quickly to touch has presented an enduring problem to plant physiologists. The mechanism of sudden movement in plants is now thought to be based on the very rapid active transport of ions out of cells and a corresponding fast drop in their water content. (Such a change is easily detected as a minute current flow.) Since leaves are often held erect by turgor pressure, its sudden loss could explain the cringing and drooping effects.

Touch response in leaves may be based on fast ion transport and subsequent turgor changes.

PHOTOPERIODISM AND FLOWERING PLANTS

The response of an organism to changing relative lengths of the day and night is known as **photoperiodism.** A clear example of photoperiodism in plants is the production of flowers during their reproductive season, a season also measured by the length of day. There are essentially three responses flowering plants may have to changing day length. Depending

FIGURE 26.8 Examples of touch response are seen in the sensitive plant *Mimosa pudica* (**a**) and the Venus flytrap *Dionaea muscipula* (**b**). The responses may be due to active transport of ions that cause rapid changes in turgor.

(a)

(b)

on the species, the plants are called **short-day plants, long-day plants,** and **day-neutral plants.** The day-neutral plants can flower at any time of the year, so we won't bother with them.

Short-day plants begin to flower as the days grow shorter, that is, shorter than a certain critical length (depending on the species). For example, chrysanthemums and poinsettias (Figure 26.9 a,b) typically begin flowering in autumn. Long-day plants, on the other hand, begin to flower when the days begin to lengthen. The critical time period varies for different species, and none will react to any day length shorter than that specifically required. Thus long-day plants—like potatoes, spinach, and henbane (Figure 26.9c)—flower at different times in summer. Spinach, incidentally, will not flower in tropical regions, because days are never long enough to exceed its 14-hour critical photoperiod.

Photoperiodism and the Length of Night

The long- and short-day terminology is unfortunately misleading. (And so, perhaps, is the notion we left you with in the preceding section.) This is because the terms *long-day* and *short-day* were already fixed in the scientific vocabulary before it was discovered that plant photoperiodism isn't determined by changes in day length at all. Instead, it's determined by the length of *night*.

Photoperiodism is the response of plants to changes in the length of day and night periods.

How we know. By raising plants in darkness and controlling the time they are exposed to light, investigators have found that the length of darkness controls flowering. When the *light* periods are changed drastically, the plants show no response at all. If the *dark* periods are changed in the same way, however, the plants respond.

Another interesting experiment has provided us with fascinating information. A long-night (short-day) plant can be fooled into behaving as if any night were short enough for flowering by being subjected to a flash of light in the middle of the night. The flash of light resets what has come to be called the plant's "dark clock." The dark clock behaves like a countdown timer that tells you when the roast is done. The timer of each species is set to go off when the required length of darkness is reached. This triggers the flowering process. So it is the extended darkness that influences the plant's reproductive behavior.

The flash of light, or more precisely the red wavelengths in the light, sets the clock back to zero. The cool light of dawn soon comes and makes the night seem extremely short from the plant's viewpoint. Under natural conditions, of course, that same morning light will be sensed by the plant, and if the nights are too short to initiate flowering (in other words, if daylight comes before the clock runs out), the clock will be reset to zero and the timing process will begin again the next night.

Flowering in short-day and long-day plants occurs when a critical period of darkness is reached.

Phytochrome: The Light Receptor

Plant physiologists have never been able to pin down the biochemical mechanisms of photoperiodism, although research has been intense and many major hypotheses have been proposed and discarded. Scientists have, however, established the nature of the light receptor involved in this phenomenon, and have named it **phytochrome.** Phytochrome is a protein associated with a light-absorbing accessory pigment that, like chlorophyll, absorbs light in the 660 nm range. Through several ingenious experiments, it has been conclusively shown that phytochrome is located in the leaves (Figure 26.10). There it responds to the light stimulus by setting the flowering process in motion, probably through the release of a hormone. Although no such hormone has been isolated, botanists are confident enough that it exists to have tentatively named it **florigen.** In addition to its role in flowering, phytochrome has also been shown to be the receptor often involved in leaf

FIGURE 26.9 (a) The chrysanthemum is a short-day plant that produces flowers in the autumn. (b) Poinsettias are also short-day plants and will bloom when the night is longer than 13 hours. (c) The henbane requires long days (short nights) for flowering.

(a)

(b)

(c)

FIGURE 26.10 This experiment with the cocklebur, a short-day plant, establishes that the phytochrome photoreceptor is in the leaf. Only one leaf in this series of six grafted cocklebur plants is exposed to the proper photoperiod, yet all six plants produce flowers.

Wrong photoperiod

Correct photo-period

All six plants produce flowers

growth, seed germination, and the lengthening and branching of stems.

It is apparent that plants are not only structurally complex, with a variety of very specialized tissues, but also that they are highly regulated, coordinated, and responsive organisms. In this chapter we have explored some of the ways they are regulated and a few of the means by which they are able to respond to the environment. Of course, this has been only a brief glimpse at such responses, but it suggests the fascinating array of ways that plants have come to adapt to a complex environment.

Flowering photoperiodicity is based on activation of a leaf light receptor, **phytochrome,** that responds by instigating the release of flowering hormone.

SUMMARY

Plant regulation often involves hormones, chemical messengers that travel from their place of origin to target cells in which they initiate responses. Hormones have specific actions, are effective in minute amounts, and are short lived.

PLANT HORMONES AND THEIR ACTIONS

Auxin

Auxin (indoleacetic acid or IAA) affects growth by loosening cellulose wall fibers, thus permitting turgor pressure to bring about cell elongation.

Working with other hormones, auxin influences differentiation, fruit and leaf fall, and tree shape. In the first, specific combinations determine whether root or shoot tissue will form. In fruit and leaf fall, auxin withdrawal permits the breakdown of abscission zone cells and leaf separation. Apical dominance in conifers occurs as auxin promotes elongation in the uppermost shoot and partially inhibits those below.

Gibberellins

Gibberellins promote growth, pollen germination and pollen tube growth, and, in germinating grains, stimulate the release of a starch digesting enzyme.

Cytokinins

Cytokinins, along with other hormones, promote cell division and differentiation and prevent aging.

Ethylene

Ethylene, a gas, promotes fruit-ripening and fruit abscission, influences sex in flowers, and supports bending in the hypocotyl hook of emerging seedlings.

Abscisic Acid

Abscisic acid, also ABA, produces stomatal closure and slows growth by inhibiting protein synthesis.

ARTIFICIAL AUXINS AND PLANT CONTROL

Artificial growth promotors such as the herbicide 2,4,5-T are used to kill weeds, but their use is controversial since it may adversely affect mammal reproduction. Humans exposed to Agent Orange herbicide contaminants in Viet Nam reportedly developed serious health problems.

PLANT TROPISMS

Phototropism

Phototropism, the growth of shoots toward light,

occurs when a highly sensitive flavoprotein photoreceptor somehow causes auxin to concentrate on the unlighted side, thereby promoting cell elongation and curvature on that side. In total darkness the shoot grows straight.

Gravitropism

In gravitropism, growth toward gravity, roots respond positively, and shoots negatively. One hypothesis suggests that the different responses may be caused by opposing calcium distributions. Calcium is known to inhibit growth hormones.

Touch Response

Thigmonastic movement is the rapid response to touch, seen as a sudden drooping of leaflets and petioles in *Mimosa pudica* and in the closing of the Venus flytrap. The mechanism may be rapid, cell-to-cell, active transport of ions and subsequent losses of leaf-supporting water (turgor).

PHOTOPERIODISM AND FLOWERING PLANTS

Flowering in short-day and long-day plants is photoperiodic—dependent on seasonal changes in the length of day-night periods. For this reason, different species produce flowers in specific parts of the year.

Photoperiodism and the Length of Night

Studies support the idea that the length of darkness is the key factor in flowering photoperiodism. Interruptions in light periods have no effect on flowering, but even flashes of light during dark periods prevent flowering in long-night (short-day) plants, running the so-called dark countdown clock back to zero.

Phytochrome: The Light Receptor

The light receptor of flowering is phytochrome, a protein and accessory pigment located in the leaves. Its operating mechanism is unknown, but the presence of a flowering hormone is suspected.

KEY TERMS

hormones	zeatin	thigmonastic movement
auxin	ethylene	photoperiodism
abscission zone	abscisic acid (ABA)	short-day plant
apical dominance	biodegradable	long-day plant
gibberellins	tropism	day-neutral plant
alpha amylase	phototropism	phytochrome
cytokinesis	gravitropism	florigen
cytokinins	touch response	

REVIEW QUESTIONS

1 Define the term *hormone* and list several characteristics of hormones. (p. 420)
2 What specific effect does auxin have on cells? What is the result of this effect? (p. 421)
3 List the steps involved in leaf fall. Explain how auxin can have a "negative" role. (p. 421)
4 Explain auxin's role in forming the triangular shape of some trees. How might such shape be adaptive, say in snowy regions? (pp. 421–422)
5 How were the gibberellins first noticed? List three of their natural roles. (p. 422)
6 Describe the effects on plant differentiation of varying combinations of cytokinins and auxin. (p. 423)
7 List three of ethylene's effects on plants. (p. 423)
8 Compare the effects of gibberellins and abscisic acid on germinating seeds. (pp. 423–424)
9 List two instances in which the application of artificial herbicides has had undesirable effects. (p. 425)
10 Summarize the phototropic mechanism in the shoot, starting with light and the pigmented photoreceptor. (pp. 425–426)

11 In what ways do shoots and roots react to gravity? Why have the usual hormones been discounted as the agent responsible? (pp. 426–427)
12 Describe the hypothetical role of calcium in gravitropism. (p. 427)
13 Describe two examples of a thigmonastic movement. What is the importance of each to the plant involved? (p. 427)
14 Suggest a mechanism that explains the sudden dropping of leaf petioles and folding of leaflets in *Mimosa pudica*. (p. 427)
15 Define photoperiodism. To what do the terms short-day, long-day, and day-neutral refer? (pp. 427–428)
16 Discuss the experimental evidence supporting the notion that night length is the determining factor in flowering. (pp. 428–429)
17 Explain the mechanism believed to be involved in the flowering response. What evidence supports the idea that the response begins in the leaves? (p. 429)

IV

ANIMAL EVOLUTION AND DIVERSITY

27

ANIMAL ORIGINS AND THE LOWER INVERTEBRATES

What is an animal? This is one of those deceptively easy questions: almost anyone can come up with an answer, but probably no one can satisfy all the experts. Animals are so varied that exceptions can be made to almost any definition. For example, most animals move, have mouths, and eat things. If the trait of multicellularity were added, that would just about cover the animal kingdom. But, invariably, some creature would shout, "Not me!" One such exception is a peculiar giant red tube worm discovered near the Galápagos Islands. It lives near recently discovered vents in the ocean floor that spew mineral-laden water that is heated by the molten earth beneath (see Chapter 46). This creature has neither a mouth nor a gut, but derives its nourishment from bacterial symbionts living in its body. It doesn't move much; it just lies there, absorbing oxygen from sea water and hydrogen sulfide that spews from the vents. In almost every way, this creature is exempt from the animal kingdom. It's an animal, nevertheless.

Despite such exceptions, let's see if we can come up with a workable definition for the animal kingdom. We can cover *most* animals, at least for our purposes, with just seven criteria:

1. Animals are multicellular and eukaryotic.
2. Animals are heterotrophic; that is, they require food from other organisms.
3. Animals reproduce sexually, producing large, nonmotile eggs, and small, flagellated sperm.
4. Animals have a number of kinds of cells, tissues, and organs that carry out different functions.
5. Animals are essentially diploid throughout life with a gametic life cycle. When meiosis occurs, the products develop directly into gametes. (Only the diploid cells undergo mitosis.)
6. Animals can respond rapidly to stimuli through well-organized nervous and muscular systems.
7. Animals hold themselves together with an extracellular connective-tissue matrix of *collagen,* a protein.

Here's another deceptively easy question. Where did animals come from? Of course, there are few hard data to support any argument, but most scientists believe that animals as well as plants and fungi sprang from the ancient protists. It is generally believed that the animal kingdom evolved from two different protist lines. One, a flagellate protozoan, produced the **Parazoa,** a subkingdom with only one phylum— **Porifera,** the sponges. The rest of the earth's animals (comprising the 10 major phyla) are in the subkingdom **Metazoa,** all derived from a single ancestor which was, in turn, descended from a protozoan of some sort, probably a ciliate.

BODY ORGANIZATION

Animals have two basic types of bodies: those with *radial* symmetry, and those with *bilateral* symmetry. **Radial symmetry,** which is believed to have evolved earlier, is characterized by a cylindrical, spherical, or disk-shaped form. The body parts are arranged so that any radius extending from the center outward will pass through similar parts (Figure 27.1).

Only a few phyla today have radial symmetry. These include a few sponges, the **coelenterates** (the jellyfish, corals, hydroids, and sea anemones) and the **ctenophorans** (such as sea walnuts and comb jellies). **Echinoderms**—the starfish (sea stars), sea urchins, and sand dollars—as adults have a peculiar pentaradial (five-part) symmetry (see Chapter 28).

All other animal phyla consist of bilaterally symmetrical animals. **Bilateral symmetry,** as its name suggests, creates right and left sides. The overwhelming number of bilaterally organized animal species may suggest to you that there are disadvantages in radial symmetry, but beware of such conclusions. Radial animals are well adapted to their niches and perform quite efficiently within them.

Radial animals are disk shaped, spherical, or cylindrical. A line across any radius divides the animal into similar halves. **Bilateral animals** have one plane of symmetry, dividing right and left sides.

Within most animals there are four levels of organization: **cellular, tissue, organ,** and **organ system.** Most animals have achieved what is called the *organ system* level, a number of organs that carry out some major function or life process. Human digestion, for example, occurs in the digestive system, a collection of various organs, including the mouth, gut (intestinal tract), pancreas, and liver. Such organs are, in turn, made up of various specialized tissues—groups of cells—performing specific tasks within the organs. For instance, the tissues lining the gut specialize in secreting digestive enzymes and absorbing digested food.

PHYLOGENY OF THE ANIMAL KINGDOM

The history and relationships of animal phyla can be represented by phylogenetic trees that show the major milestones of animal evolution (Figure 27.2). As we saw in Chapter 19, such trees are constructed from several kinds of information, including the fossil record (paleontology) and the comparative anatomy, physiology, and embryology of living animals. More recently, data from protein and DNA sequencing has been employed as well.

The major branches of the tree represent the evolutionary events that produced the great variety of animals on earth today. The names shown in red reflect the two major divisions of animals: the **proto-**

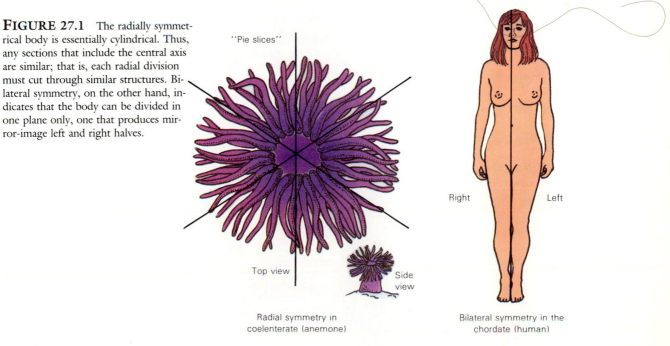

FIGURE 27.1 The radially symmetrical body is essentially cylindrical. Thus, any sections that include the central axis are similar; that is, each radial division must cut through similar structures. Bilateral symmetry, on the other hand, indicates that the body can be divided in one plane only, one that produces mirror-image left and right halves.

"Pie slices"

Top view

Side view

Radial symmetry in coelenterate (anemone)

Right   Left

Bilateral symmetry in the chordate (human)

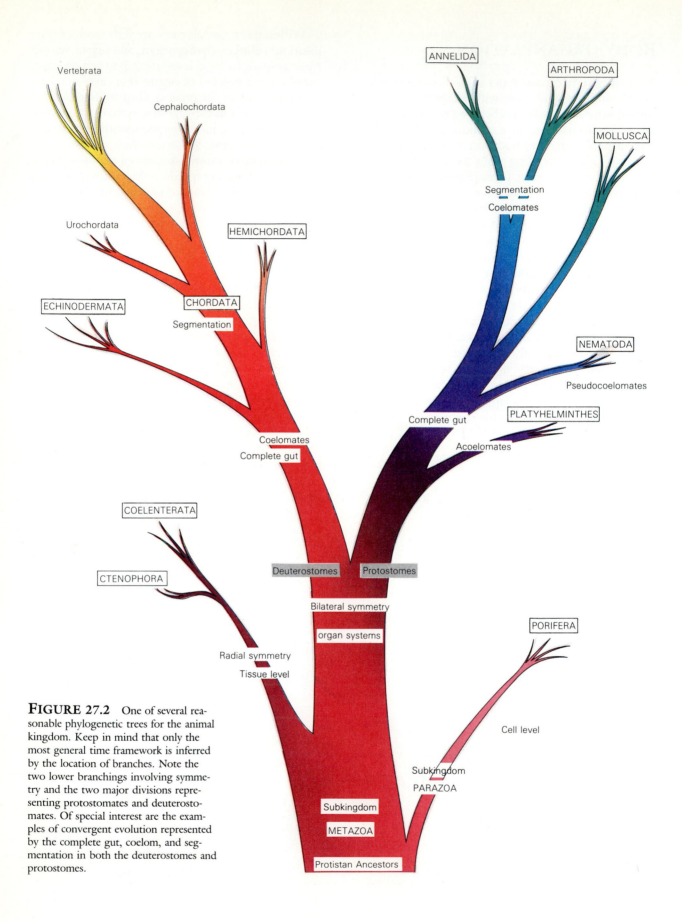

Vertebrata

Cephalochordata

ANNELIDA

ARTHROPODA

Urochordata

MOLLUSCA

HEMICHORDATA

Segmentation

Coelomates

CHORDATA

Segmentation

ECHINODERMATA

NEMATODA

Pseudocoelomates

PLATYHELMINTHES

Complete gut

Coelomates

Acoelomates

Complete gut

COELENTERATA

CTENOPHORA

Deuterostomes   Protostomes

Bilateral symmetry

organ systems

PORIFERA

Radial symmetry

Tissue level

Cell level

FIGURE 27.2 One of several reasonable phylogenetic trees for the animal kingdom. Keep in mind that only the most general time framework is inferred by the location of branches. Note the two lower branchings involving symmetry and the two major divisions representing protostomates and deuterostomates. Of special interest are the examples of convergent evolution represented by the complete gut, coelom, and segmentation in both the deuterostomes and protostomes.

Subkingdom

PARAZOA

Subkingdom

METAZOA

Protistan Ancestors

stomes ("first mouth") and the **deuterostomes** ("second mouth"). (These terms refer to the embryological origin of the mouth. We will cover these terms later in this chapter and in Chapter 28, but for now, just keep in mind that such seemingly trivial embryological events as the development of the mouth can tell us a great deal about evolutionary history.) Notice that this sort of tree implies nothing about evolutionary *time*.

The animal phylogenetic tree, based on the study of fossils and comparative anatomy, physiology, embryology, and biochemistry, includes a short trunk and two main branches, the **protostomes** and **deuterostomes**.

The Early Fossil Record

The earliest known fossil record, which appears to be fossil worm burrows, is estimated to be 700 million years old, but the burrows' authenticity is still being debated. However, the oldest indisputable animal fossils are found in rocks from 580 to 680 million years old. These rich beds, the **Ediacara fauna** of southern Australia, include abundant fossils of jellyfish, coelenterates, and worms (Figure 27.3). Interestingly, fossils in the extremely rich **Burgess Shale Formation** of western Canada represent all of the major living animal phyla and a number of extinct phyla as well (Figure 27.4). Yet the Burgess Shale Formation is almost as old (570 million years) as the Ediacara fauna. This means that either the Ediacara fauna is not representative of animals of that period, or most animal phyla appeared over an incredibly

FIGURE 27.3 The fossil record indicates that Ediacara fauna (animals) of the late Precambrian oceans probably was dominated by the thin-bodied coelenterates. Among these are (**a**) jellyfish—not unlike those seen today, and (**b**) stalked, featherlike corals, nearly identical to today's "sea pens." The bottom dwellers include several species of annelids (**c**), the segmented worms, identified by lines crossing the body. Representatives from the jointed-legged animals, the arthropods (**d**), are also present, as are a few shelled mollusks (**e**). In addition, there are fossil animals of phyla that are now entirely extinct (**f**). The egg-like mass at the left (**g**) is believed to be algae.

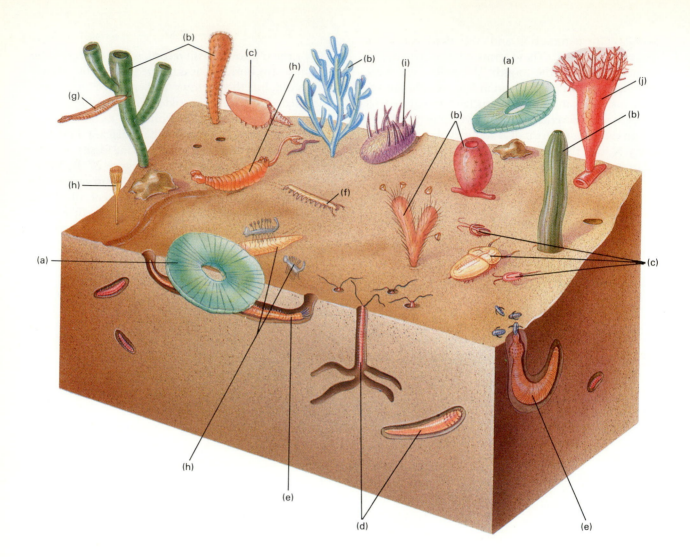

FIGURE 27.4 The Burgess Shale fauna of Canada include many familiar phyla and one that is unknown. The advanced state of many suggest a long evolutionary history.

(a) coelenterates   **(f)** onychophorans
(b) sponges   **(g)** chordates
(c) arthropods   **(h)** unknown
(d) tube annelids   **(i)** mollusk
(e) priapulids   **(j)** echinoderm

brief period of evolutionary time, perhaps 10 to 100 million years.

SPONGES: PORIFERA

We stated that most animals have four levels of organization. One of the exceptions is the **Porifera**—the sponges. Essentially, they consist of just a few types of cells, organized only at the cellular level, or at most, in loosely arranged tissues.

Sponges are primarily ocean dwellers, although about 150 species live in fresh water. They live unobtrusively, fastened securely to the ocean or lake bed, where they busily filter tiny food particles, organic detritus and microorganisms, from the surrounding water. Sponges lack organized muscles and nerves, so they are incapable of rapid, whole-body responses.

The simplest sponges are the vaselike **ascon sponges** (Figure 27.5). Their hollow bodies are just a few cell layers thick and consist of only four or five types of cells. Like all sponges, they feed by filtering particles from the surrounding water. The food is carried past them by a current of water produced by the beating flagella of the **collar cells (choanocytes)** that line the inner body. (The water enters through pore cells called **porocytes.)** The *collar,* which gives the cell its name, consists of a ring of stiff **microvilli** (fingerlike membrane extensions) circling the base of the long flagellum. Food particles are trapped in mucus secretions on the collar cells and are carried down to the base of the collar, where they are engulfed through phagocytosis and, later, digested in food vacuoles. The partly digested food is then transferred to wandering **ameboid cells (amebocytes)** that creep about the tissues, digesting the food further and distributing it throughout the body.

Sponges maintain their shape because of a kind of skeleton formed of **spicules,** or protein fibers. Spicules are secreted by ameboid, **mesenchyme** cells and, depending on the species, may consist of chalk (calcium carbonate), glass (silicon dioxide) (the glassy sponge, in fact, can be quite elaborate and beautiful), or **spongin.** Spongin, a fibrous protein consisting of collagen, forms the skeleton of the large "bath" sponges (rarely used today, having been replaced by synthetic sponges).

Now let's consider how an immovable animal reproduces. In some sponges, the sexes are separate. But other species are **hermaphroditic;** that is, the same animal produces both sperm and eggs. The eggs are stationary, lying just below the collar cells. They are fertilized by clouds of sperm from a neighboring sponge that are drawn into the body cavity. The sperm must penetrate the recipient's body wall to fertilize the eggs. The zygote will develop into a flagellated, swimming **larva** (an immature stage quite different from the adult form). Sponge larvae finally settle to the bottom, become attached, and mature into adults.

The **sponges (Porifera)** have a limited, cellular organization with only a few specialized cells. They are nonmotile, aquatic, filter feeders.

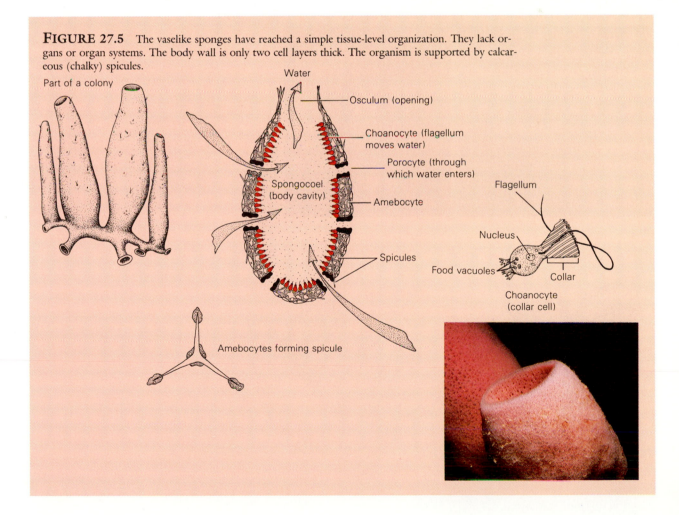

FIGURE 27.5 The vaselike sponges have reached a simple tissue-level organization. They lack organs or organ systems. The body wall is only two cell layers thick. The organism is supported by calcareous (chalky) spicules.

Part of a colony

Water

Osculum (opening)

Choanocyte (flagellum moves water)

Porocyte (through which water enters)

Spongocoel (body cavity)

Amebocyte

Spicules

Amebocytes forming spicule

Flagellum

Nucleus

Food vacuoles

Collar

Choanocyte (collar cell)

POLYPS AND MEDUSAS: COELENTERATA

As we've seen, the coelenterates (and the ctenophorans have radial symmetry. For that reason they are often called **radiates.** We have no firm ideas as to how the radial body form arose, but many zoologists theorize that the direct ancestor to all metazoans, including the radiates, was probably a bilateral inhabitant of the muddy ocean bottom (where bilateral symmetry works well). It may have resembled the **planula larva,** an early developmental stage of coelenterates that we will look at shortly. The theorists go on to suggest that a radial offshoot from these simple animals did well as a swimming form and that this line gave rise to the radiates.

Coelenterates (also called **cnidarians**—phylum **Cnidaria**) barely rise above the tissue level of organization, although some organ development is present. The coelenterate body is essentially a thin-walled sac, with an inner and outer tissue layer, each only one cell thick. Sandwiched between the two layers is a structureless, jellylike **mesoglea,** which holds the two cell layers together, acting as a kind of skeleton. The outer tissue layer is essentially protective, while the inner one forms the lining of the saclike **gastrovascular cavity.** This cavity extends everywhere, even into the tentacles. An example is *Hydra,* a freshwater coelenterate that stands a few millimeters high.

Hydra, like most coelenterates, has tentacles that are armed with stinging cells called **cnidocytes,** which are used in immobilizing prey and in defense. Cnidocytes are odd structures. Many contain stinging **nematocysts,** coiled, poisonous harpoons at the end of hollow threads (Figure 27.6). Other nematocysts release sticky, snaring threads that trap prey.

FIGURE 27.6 (a) Feeding in *Hydra,* a freshwater hydroid. The stinging nematocytes (b) release their harpoon-like nematocysts upon contact. Digestion occurs within the saclike gastrovascular cavity (c), carried out by its highly specialized lining (d).

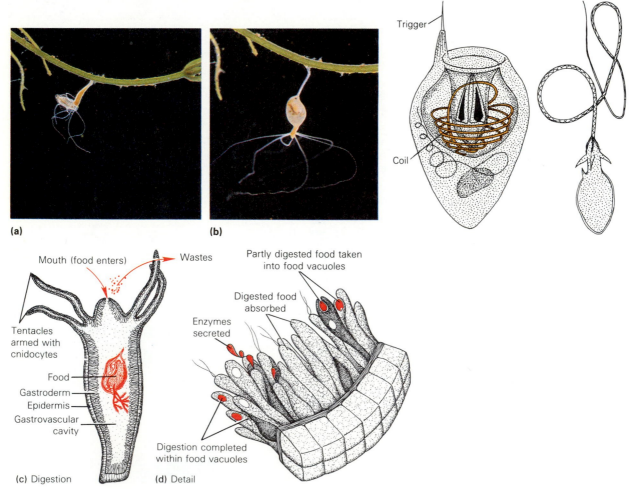

(a)

(b)

Trigger

Coil

Mouth (food enters)

Wastes

Tentacles armed with cnidocytes

Food

Gastroderm

Epidermis

Gastrovascular cavity

(c) Digestion

Partly digested food taken into food vacuoles

Digested food absorbed

Enzymes secreted

Digestion completed within food vacuoles

(d) Detail

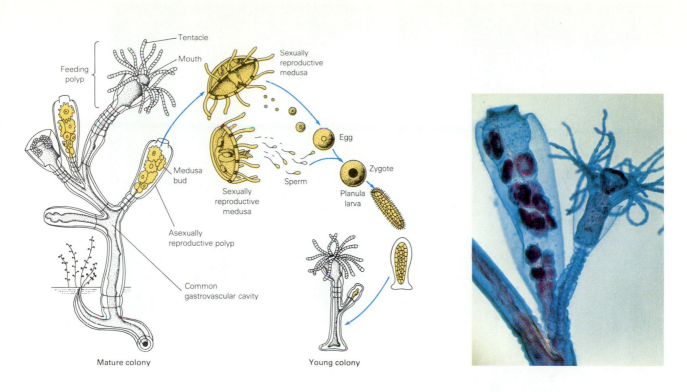

FIGURE 27.7 The highly branched body of *Obelia,* a marine hydroid, contains feeding and reproductive polyps. Reproductive polyps bud off swimming medusas that release sperm and eggs into the water, where fertilization occurs. The zygotes develop into swimming planula larvae that eventually fasten to the sea bed and develop into a polyp.

Hydra are the terrors of their tiny world. Any small creature moving by triggers the *Hydra's* stinging cells, and once it is immobilized, tentacles draw the stunned victim into the gastrovascular cavity. Once the victim is drawn inside the cavity, it will undoubtedly be impressed with the very specialized lining. Some gastrovascular cells produce digestive enzymes, others absorb digested food, some engulf whole food particles to be digested later in vacuoles, and still other cells have flagella with which they move particles around for greater ease of handling.

Polyp and Medusa Body Patterns

Two basic body patterns are found among the coelenterates, the **polyp,** or fixed and sedentary state (as in *Hydra*), and the **medusa,** a swimming jellyfish state. Interestingly, some groups alternate between the two body patterns, although one is usually the dominant or longer-lived state. In other groups, either the swimming medusa or the polyp state may be entirely absent. *Hydra,* for example, has the polyp state only. The organization of the coelenterates into their three classes is based principally on these factors.

Class **Hydrozoa** includes *Hydra,* along with many marine hydroids. The polyp is the dominant state. Typically, the tiny marine hydroids form highly branched colonies of polyps that feed on drifting plankton. Like *Hydra,* they produce new polyps on the sides of their bodies through an asexual process called **budding.** Unlike the buds of *Hydra,* which break away, the hydroid's buds remain attached, forming dense, branched, colonies. When hydroids reproduce sexually, they bud off tiny swimming medusas that form gametes and release them into the water. Following fertilization, the zygote develops into a ciliated planula larva. It soon settles to the ocean floor where it goes through a period of development, emerging as a polyp (Figure 27.7).

In the second class, **Scyphozoa,** the dominant stage is the swimming jellyfish (medusa). Like the hydroid medusa, it releases its gametes into the water and produces a swimming planula larva. But this larva grows into a small, inconspicuous polyp that fastens to the underside of a rocky ledge and buds off young jellyfish that grow into adults.

The third class, **Anthozoa,** includes the sea anemones and corals. In this class the medusa state is entirely absent; thus the life cycle is simple, essential-

FIGURE 27.8 (**a**) The jellyfish (class Scyphozoa) are free-swimming, trailing their stinging tentacles. A fish brushing against these will be stung until it is senseless and then digested. (**b**) Jellyfish larvae enter a brief polyp state, which buds off numerous young jellyfish. (**c**) Coral polyps (class Anthozoa) are also colonial, with the many individual polyps secreting hardened calcareous walls around themselves. (**d**) The anemone (also class Anthozoa) is a polyp frequently found in shallower waters.

ly going from polyp to polyp with only a brief larval stage between.

Many corals form massive colonies, constantly secreting limestone and forming awesome and beautiful coral reefs. (Representatives of classes Scyphozoa and Anthozoa are seen in Figure 27.8.)

Hydroids, jellyfish, anemones, and corals (Coelenterata) have a tissue level of organization, a thin, saclike body, and tentacles with stinging cells. They exist as swimming medusas or stationary polyps; some species alternate between the two body forms.

THE COMB JELLIES: CTENOPHORA

The **ctenophorans** ("comb carriers") should be mentioned because they appear to be closely related to the coelenterates. The two differ in that all comb jellies are free-swimming, and their tentacles lack stinging cells. Instead, their tentacles are coated with sticky secretions from what are known as **glue cells,** which are used to trap plankton. Some ctenophorans produce an intriguing—and sometimes eerie—luminescence that makes their watery home actually glow. Some are quite large. In fact, one species, *Cestum* ("Venus' girdle"), looks like a glowing ribbon, nearly a meter long.

CLEAVAGE PATTERNS AND THE VERSATILE MESODERM

The radial, hollow-bodied coelenterates with their two layers of cells may strike you as being quite different from what you expected of animals. However, in the groups to come we will encounter not only heads and tails and bilateral symmetry but also vast changes in internal structure. Bodies become dense, true muscle tissue appears, and soon we will come to those metazoans who can boast of skeletons that hold them erect, muscular hearts that pump blood, and centralized brains that integrate sensations and coordinate responses.

We can trace the appearance of these more characteristic animals to important changes in the embryo. In the development of coelenterate embryos, only two types of embryonic tissue ever form. These tissues, or **germ layers,** as they are known, are the **endoderm** and the **ectoderm.** During development the endoderm ("inner skin") forms many internal linings. Ectoderm ("outer skin") is primarily involved in forming outer linings. We will turn our attention to animals that develop an important middle germ layer, the **mesoderm** ("middle skin"). And it is from the mesoderm that muscle, blood, and skeleton are derived. We see some evidence of the importance of mesoderm in the next phylum of animals, the group that includes flatworms, but first let's look at another major evolutionary milestone.

> The three **germ layers** are the **ectoderm, endoderm,** and **mesoderm.** Each helps form specific parts of the developing embryo.

Protostomes and Deuterostomes

Notice that the great tree in Figure 27.3 is split into two major branches with **deuterostomes** at the left and **protostomes** at the right. Obviously, something important happened here, but you can't tell much about it from the names. So why is the distinction so important?

The answer is deceptively mundane. Early in its evolution, animal life diverged in the way the digestive tract formed in the embryo (Figure 27.9a). Briefly, in the protostomate animals with mouths and anuses the mouth forms early and the anus much later. (Some, such as the platyhelminthes, or flatworms, have only a saclike [or **incomplete**] gut. The

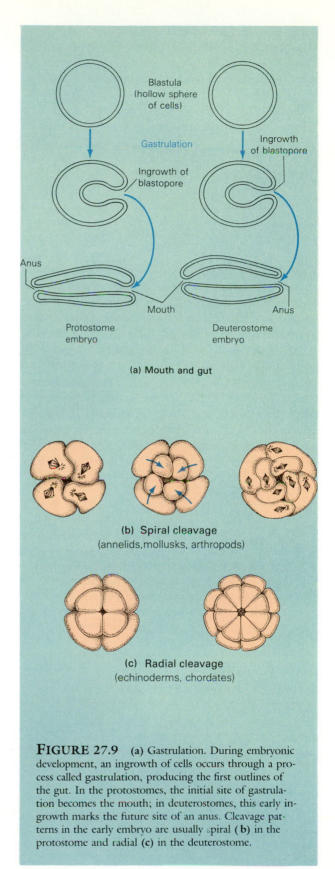

FIGURE 27.9 **(a)** Gastrulation. During embryonic development, an ingrowth of cells occurs through a process called gastrulation, producing the first outlines of the gut. In the protostomes, the initial site of gastrulation becomes the mouth; in deuterostomes, this early ingrowth marks the future site of an anus. Cleavage patterns in the early embryo are usually spiral **(b)** in the protostome and radial **(c)** in the deuterostome.

other protostomes have both a mouth and anus [a **complete** gut].) All deuterostomes have both openings, and in this group the anus forms early, and the mouth forms much later. This simple divergence led to two vastly different types of animals. Today, the protostomes include such major phyla as the flatworms and roundworms, as well as the mollusks, annelids, and arthropods. The major deuterostome phyla are the echinoderms and chordates, although there are a few minor phyla as well.

Protostomes and spiral cleavage. Any such fundamental organizational difference as we see in protostomes and deuterostomes is likely to signal other basic changes as well. And, indeed, we find marked differences in the early embryonic development of these two groups. For example, the protostomes reveal their particular developmental route long before the mouth forms. We see it first in their **spiral cleavage** (Figure 27.9b).

Deuterostomes, on the other hand, undergo **radial cleavage.** The cleavage planes are symmetrical, and each division produces daughters that lie one directly above the other (Figure 27.9c). Further, the embryo undergoes **indeterminate development.** That is, the fate of the daughter cells is not set in early cleavages. In fact, each cell remains quite versatile for a considerable time. If the first four cells to form are carefully separated, four miniature but normal embryos will emerge (Chapter 41).

The protostome mouth develops first; cleavage is **spiral;** and development is **determinate** (cells' fate is set early). The **deuterostome** mouth develops late; cleavage is **radial;** and development is **indeterminate** (cells remain flexible longer).

FLATWORMS: PLATYHELMINTHES

With the **Platyhelminthes,** or flatworms, we finally find animals with definite organ systems, and we can see how the mesoderm has increased their complexity (Figure 27.10). There are three major groups of flatworms, and we can't say that you will be thrilled to learn about all of them. You may feel okay about the free-living **Turbellaria,** but the other two groups are parasites, including some that attack humans. They are the tapeworms of class **Cestoda** and the flukes of class **Trematoda.**

But let's start on a cheerful note. Most streams and

ponds are inhabited by free-living **planarians,** fascinating little worms just a few millimeters long. (One terrestrial relative grows to 60 cm [23 in] and feeds on earthworms and leeches.) Planarians, like other flatworms, have flattened, bilateral bodies. The planarian moves slowly by means of cilia on its ventral (belly) side, and it steers with well-coordinated and well-defined muscles. The nervous system of this creature is rather simple and ladder-shaped, but here we see a major new evolutionary development. Most of the **neural ganglia** (masses of nerve cell bodies) are concentrated at the **anterior** (head) end. Two eyespots simply detect the presence and direction of light. While they do not form images, they enable the vulnerable creature to remain in the darker and safer regions of its domain.

The planarian's digestive system is a highly branched gastrovascular cavity. But it is still a saclike structure, with one opening. Nonetheless, it is rather specialized, with a protrusible pharynx (which means that the worm can extend its tubelike mouth out of its body). It uses its muscular pharynx like a vacuum cleaner hose, sucking up the juices and soft body parts of its prey.

Although some systems in the flatworm are very simple, the reproductive system is surprisingly complex. Planarians are hermaphroditic. They all have well-defined testes and ovaries, as well as long ducts through which gametes travel. The penis can extend from the chamber in which it rests, and a **genital chamber** acts as a vagina. Planarians usually don't self-fertilize; instead, they democratically exchange sperm.

Free-living flatworms (**Platyhelminthes**), have several complex organ systems and flattened, solid, muscular bodies. Parasitic flatworms include tapeworms and flukes.

Parasitic Flatworms

The parasitic flatworms—the tapeworms and flukes—are quite unlike the planarians. As is true of most successful internal parasites, their evolutionary specialization has led to a sometimes startling emphasis on some systems, while other systems have become reduced or have even disappeared. For example, the tapeworm, commonly found in its host's small intestine, has no gut whatsoever, but it has a complex and specialized head with suckers and grasping hooks that ensure a firm hold on the host's intestinal wall. It absorbs predigested food over its entire body surface, which is covered with tiny projections

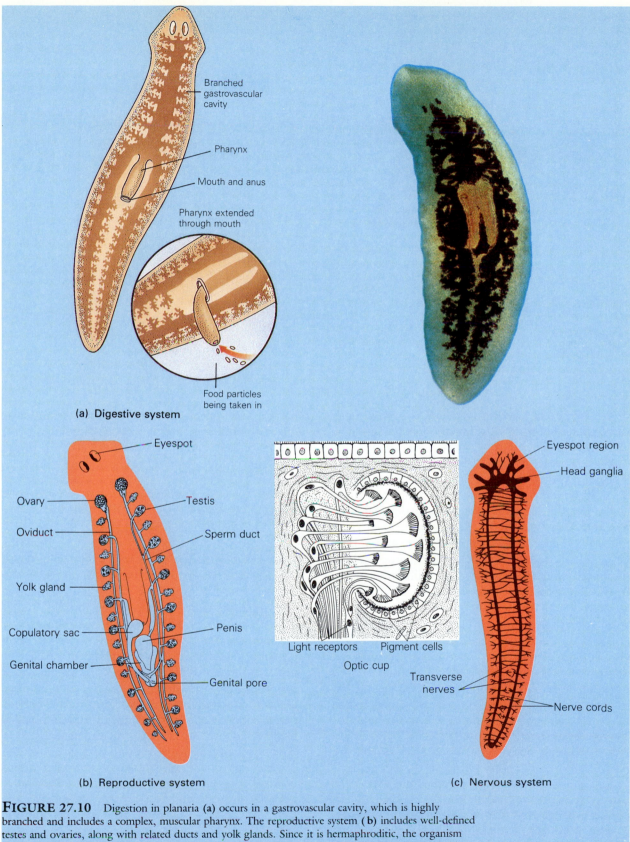

(a) Digestive system

- Branched gastrovascular cavity
- Pharynx
- Mouth and anus
- Pharynx extended through mouth
- Food particles being taken in

(b) Reproductive system

- Eyespot
- Ovary
- Testis
- Oviduct
- Sperm duct
- Yolk gland
- Copulatory sac
- Penis
- Genital chamber
- Genital pore

Light receptors — Pigment cells
Optic cup

(c) Nervous system

- Eyespot region
- Head ganglia
- Transverse nerves
- Nerve cords

FIGURE 27.10 Digestion in planaria (a) occurs in a gastrovascular cavity, which is highly branched and includes a complex, muscular pharynx. The reproductive system (b) includes well-defined testes and ovaries, along with related ducts and yolk glands. Since it is hermaphroditic, the organism has both penis and vagina. Light-sensitive eyespots detect the direction of a light source, and a ladder-like nerve network (c) coordinates its movement.

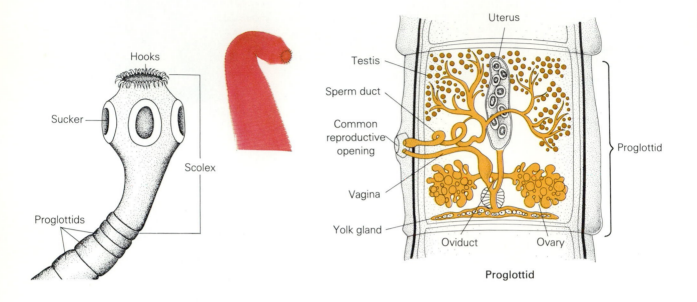

FIGURE 27.11 The tapeworm, a common intestinal parasite. The beef tapeworm of humans can grow to about 7 m (23 ft) in length, but the record is probably held by the broad (or fish) tapeworm of humans, which can exceed 18 m (60 ft).

that increase the absorptive area. In a sense, the worm is inside out, with what amounts to a gut lining the outside.

With so many of life's daily problems solved, the tapeworm can devote much of its energy to reproduction. Its body, which may be several meters long, is composed of segments called **proglottids** that contain both ovaries and testes. The proglottids are continually produced just behind the creature's tiny head, or **scolex.** Each mature proglottid may contain thousands of eggs, and following fertilization (tapeworms can self-fertilize) the proglottids break off and are passed out with the feces. When they rupture, the eggs are released, ready to renew the life cycle (Figure 27.11).

The eggs of beef and pork tapeworms must be swallowed by the cow or pig for the parasite to continue its life cycle. When an egg hatches, the minute offspring moves from the host's digestive tract to the bloodstream, thereby finding its way to the muscles. There it curls up and forms a protective, capsulelike cyst, remaining inactive until a human decides to have steak or pork chops a little on the rare side.

The life cycles of many parasites are extremely complicated. They may go through a number of physical changes and may inhabit a number of hosts. The timing and sequence of the changes must be precise, and a great deal is left to sheer luck. The odds against making it to that final host are so great that

natural selection has dictated that each worm maximize the number of eggs it produces, leaving the rest to chance. For example, consider the life cycle of the human liver fluke, as portrayed in Figure 27.12.

BODY CAVITIES, A ONE-WAY GUT, AND A NEW BODY PLAN

Now let's review a few of the important evolutionary events that have proved to be key developments—changes that made possible new trends and directions, and altered life on this planet forever.

With the development of bilateral symmetry, a significant and probably simultaneous trend in body organization arose. Animals developed a leading, or head, end and a trailing, or tail, end. At first, the head may well have been simply a concentration of muscles, an adaptation for burrowing in the soft sea beds of ancient oceans, which is where the oldest fossils of bilateral animals are found. But leading ends soon became equipped with sensory structures for the detection of food, light, vibrations, and other stimuli. Such structures require neural support and integration, so, as we might expect, clusters of nerve cells were located close by in what would become the brain.

With the bilateral plan well established, newer, far-reaching evolutionary developments were in

FIGURE 27.12   The human liver fluke *(Chlonorchis sinensis)*, common in many Asian regions, lives in the bile passages of the liver, where heavy infestations can bring on cirrhosis and death. Its life cycle is one of the most complex known, requiring three separate hosts: human, snail, and fish. Its primary, or sexual, stage occurs in humans, where the eggs are fertilized and the first of several intermediate stages, the *miracidium,* forms. The egg cases then pass into the intestine and out of the host with the feces. When the miracidia are eaten by a freshwater snail (in rice paddies or other poluted waters), they hatch from the egg case and bore into the snail's tissues, forming *sporocysts.* The sporocyst then enters an asexual phase, producing numerous *redia,* each of which, in turn, produces many swimming *cercaria.* The cercaria escape from the snail to seek out the next host, the fish, whereupon they bore into its muscles and secrete protective capsules (cysts) around themselves. The encysted cercaria (or *metacercaria*) remain there until some hapless human eats the fish—raw or partially cooked. The digestive enzymes of the human host weaken the capsules and the young flukes emerge and make their way up into the bile duct to the bile passages of the liver. The cycle then repeats.

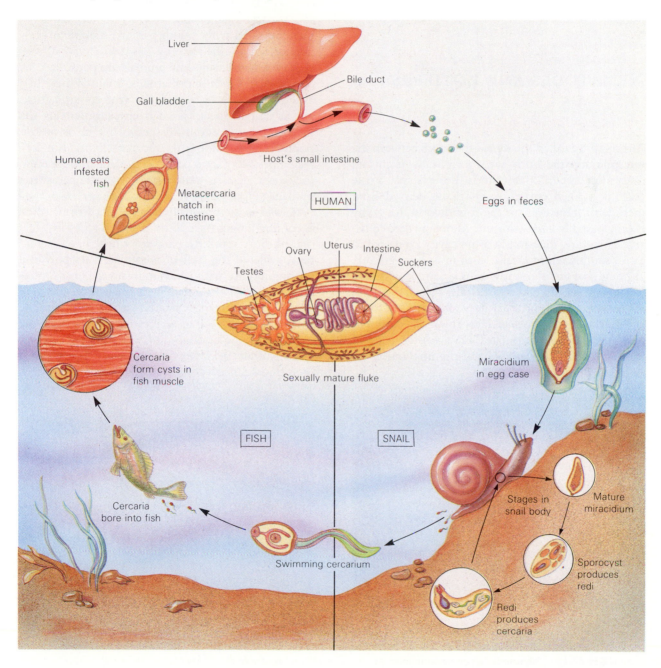

store. Two of these were to go hand-in-hand. One was the complete, tubelike, one-way digestive tract with a mouth, gut, and anus. So, with a gut inside a body wall, the body plan of these animals took on a tube-within-a-tube organization. Between the gut and the body wall—between the tubes—emerged a body cavity, known in its final form as the **coelom**. Apparently this organization was a huge success, paving the way for numerous modifications. Today, most animals have retained the tube-within-a-tube plan.

NEMATODES AND ROTIFERS

Pseudocoeloms and the Roundworms

Although we called the *coelom* the space between the intestine and the body wall, technically, a coelom must meet certain other criteria. For example, a true coelom is lined entirely with tissue derived from mesoderm. However, in the roundworm this cavity is only partially lined with mesodermally derived tissue. Therefore, the roundworm's cavity is referred to as a **pseudocoelom** ("false coelom"). Furthermore, although the gut in roundworms is complete (that is, it has both mouth and anus), it lies free in the fluid-filled pseudocoelom; also, its wall is not muscular and is usually only one cell layer thick, all conditions not typical of true coelomates. Let's consider a few of the pseudocoelomate phyla and the implications of this development.

Nematodes.   Some people might find it hard to believe that roundworms could be either important or interesting, but they are both, as we shall see. The word *nematode* means "threadlike," a description that applies to most of the species. There are many species of roundworms, and they are all monotonously cylinder shaped and tapered at both ends. Taxonomists have already described 10,000 of the estimated half-million species of nematodes, many of which are efficient predators, winnowing their way among moist soil particles, paralyzing prey with their saliva, or piercing them with mouth parts to suck their body juices (Figure 27.13).

Virtually all plants and animals are parasitized by one or more kinds of nematodes. Some of these parasites, in fact, have been devastating to agriculture, and at least 10 species are dangerous to humans. On the other hand, about 50 species live in or on our bodies without doing us apparent harm. But let's take a brief look at a particularly dangerous species, the giant *Ascaris lumbricoides,* which parasitizes humans (Figure 27.14).

Ascaris is an unusually large roundworm, often becoming longer than 20 to 35 cm (8 to 14 in). It is one of those repulsive parasites whose habits could be considered the stuff of nightmares. Its powerful sucking mouth, with which it grasps the host's intestinal wall, leads to a flattened, ribbonlike, but very simple gut, a tube that extends from the mouth to the anus. Thousands of these creatures can live in the intestine of one person.

Like other parasitic worms, *Ascaris* is a prodigious reproducer, an adaptation to a life cycle filled with

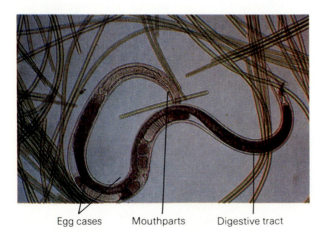

Egg cases   Mouthparts   Digestive tract

Cysts

FIGURE 27.13.   Nematodes are common in most soil, but abound in moist, fertile places. Many are scavengers or predators of soil organisms and are considered free-living, but a great number are agricultural parasites.

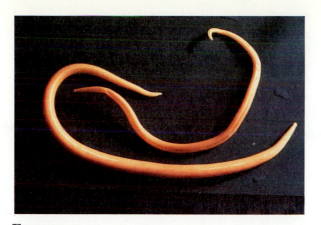

FIGURE 27.14 *Ascaris lumbricoides,* male and female. Female ascarid worms grow to 35 cm (14 in) in length, but the males are shorter and more slender. Males can immediately be distinguished from females by the presence of a curled tail with fine bristles emerging from the tip.

Rotifers. Rotifers are not parasites. They are microscopic and are often confused with the protists whose watery environment they share. They are interesting because in spite of their tiny size, they are distinctly more complex than other pseudocoelomates.

Rotifers feed in a most unusual way. The double rings of cilia that circle their heads in a wheel-like manner (*rotifer* means "wheel bearer") sweep food into a grinding gullet, or gizzard. The rotifer's digestive system is unusually complex for such a small animal. Who would suspect that it has a muscular, grinding pharynx, a stomach, two digestive glands, an intestine, and an anus?

We've learned something about the lives of a few of those often-neglected animals, the invertebrates. We may have also gained a new respect for their complexity, their life histories, and their place in the scheme of life. Such creatures sometimes are referred to as "primitive," but organisms cannot be classified in this way; only a particular trait can be described as **primitive** (retaining the ancestral condition of the group) or **advanced** (changed from the ancestral condition). We will soon see that there is no orderly progression toward "advanced" forms of life. Each type of animal is uniquely adapted to its role; it is likely to be very good at doing those things necessary to its own existence. It may survive quite well with traits we find trivial or unnecessary, and it may have no use whatsoever for ours.

perils. Some mature females produce up to 200,000 eggs per day. The eggs pass out of the body with the feces, and new infestations occur when the eggs are accidentally swallowed. If you can't imagine this, it's probably because you haven't lived in places without toilets and haven't eaten vegetables from a garden fertilized with untreated "night soil." However, many of the earth's billions live under such conditions and are parasitized by these creatures.

SUMMARY

Animals are multicellular, heterotrophic, sexual reproducers that produce heterogametes and follow a gametic life cycle. Most have organ systems and nervous and contractile tissue and produce collagen.

Most theorists think that the parazoan ancestors were protozoan flagellates, and the metazoan ancestors, protozoan ciliates. Protozoans have animal-like characteristics and dietary requirements.

BODY ORGANIZATION

A few phyla have radial symmetry—any cuts in the form of "melon" or "pie" segments made in their spherical or cylindrical bodies contain similar structures. Most phyla have bilateral symmetry—right and left, mirror image sides. Most animals have the organ-system level of organization.

PHYLOGENY OF THE ANIMAL KINGDOM

Phylogenetic trees, based on the fossil record, comparative anatomy, physiology, embryology, and biochemistry, portray major divergences that gave rise to the protostome and deuterostome lines.

The Early Fossil Record

Many animal phyla appear in the Ediacara fauna, from strata dated 580 to 680 million years old. All phyla appear in the Burgess Shale Formation, 570 years old. This suggests that the evolution of the major phyla was remarkably rapid.

SPONGES: PORIFERA

Sponges are roughly radial, containing a cellular level of organization (perhaps a rudimentary tissue level). They are filter-feeding aquatic animals with only a few cell types. Their names and functions are collar cells (feeding), porocytes (admitting water), amebocytes (ameboid feeding and reproduction), mesenchyme (producing spicules and other cells), and gametes (reproduction). Zygotes pass through a temporary ciliated larval stage.

POLYPS AND MEDUSAS: COELENTERATA

Radiates may be an offshoot of early bottom-dwelling bilateral animals. The earliest may have resembled the planula larva common to marine invertebrates.

Coelenterates may have reached the organ level of organization but definitely have tissues. The hollow, thin-walled body contains two cell layers and surrounds an extensive gastrovascular cavity lined with digestive cells. Tentacles armed with stinging cells (cnidocytes) discharge nematocysts that subdue prey. Digestion begins in the gastrovascular cavity and continues in food vacuoles. Movement is through contractile fibers, and the neural structures have a netlike arrangement.

Polyp and Medusa Body Patterns

Coelenterate body forms include stationary polyps and swimming medusas. In hydrozoans the polyp is prominent. It uses budding to produce swimming medusa that release sperm and eggs. The zygote forms a planula larva, which then develops into the polyp. In scyphozoans (jellyfish) the medusa dominates. Zygotes produce a brief polyp state that buds more jellyfish. Anthozoans (anemones and corals) have the polyp form only. Corals are ecologically important as reef builders.

THE COMB JELLIES: CTENOPHORA

Comb jellies are similar to coelenterates but use glue cells to trap prey. Included is the lengthy, ribbonlike "Venus girdle."

CLEAVAGE PATTERNS AND THE VERSATILE MESODERM

Although the embryos of coelenterates have only two germ layers, ectoderm and endoderm, other metazoans have a third, the mesoderm, which in vertebrates gives rise to blood, a skeleton, and organized muscle tissue.

Protostomes and Deuterostomes

The two major animal types differ in gut formation. In protostomes (e.g., most invertebrates) the mouth forms early, while in deuterostomes (e.g., echinoderms and chordates) it forms late. In the first group the earliest cleavages occur in a spiral pattern, and their developmental fate is set early (determinate development). In the latter, cleavages follow a radial pattern, and early development is indeterminate (cells remain uncommitted longer).

FLATWORMS: PLATYHELMINTHES

Flatworms have organ systems, with dense, mesodermally formed muscle layers. Planarian turbellarians are small and free-living aquatic worms. They have a ladderlike nervous system, eye spots, a well-developed pharynx for feeding, and a highly branched gastrovascular cavity. Ciliated flame cells eliminate excess water. They are hermaphroditic, each with well-developed male and female sexual structures.

Parasitic Flatworms

The adult tapeworm lives in the host's intestine. Most of its systems are highly reduced, and specializations include a gripping head or scolex that continuously forms proglottids. Each proglottid has testes and ovaries and is capable of producing great numbers of offspring. In many species the fertilized eggs must be taken in by a different animal, where the offspring upon hatching, bore into muscle tissue and encyst there. The second host must first be eaten if the sexually mature adult stage is to reoccur. The human liver fluke has three hosts, human, snail, and fish, each of which harbors a different stage of the parasite's life cycle.

BODY CAVITIES, A ONE-WAY GUT, AND A NEW BODY PLAN

Bilateral animals evolved a tubelike (tube-within-a-tube), complete gut with separate mouth and anus. A cavity, the coelom, formed between the gut and body wall.

NEMATODES AND ROTIFERS

Pseudocoeloms and the Roundworms

Nematodes (roundworms) and rotifers form a pseudocoelom, a body cavity incompletely lined by mesodermally formed tissue. The gut lacks muscular development.

All nematodes have threadlike cylindrical bodies with a pseudocoelom. Whereas most are minute, soil-dwelling, free-living predators, many are plant and animal parasites. The largest parasite, *Ascaris lumbricoides,* infects humans and hogs, where it can produce thousands of eggs daily. The cycle is direct, with no alternate hosts.

Rotifers are complex, free-living pseudocoelomates. They use a ciliated funnel in feeding and have a complex, complete gut.

Most animals have a mix of primitive and advanced traits, each adapting it to its niche in a unique manner.

KEY TERMS

Parazoa	Platyhelminthes	microvilli	planula larva
Porifera	coelenterates	ameboid cell (amebocyte)	Cnidaria
Metazoa	ctenophorans	spicule	mesoglea
radial symmetry	Ediacara fauna	mesenchyme	gastrovascular cavity
echinoderms	Burgess Shale Formation	spongin	cnidocyte
bilateral symmetry	ascon sponge	hermaphroditic	nematocyst
protostome	collar cell (choanocyte)	larva	polyp
deuterostome	porocyte	radiates	medusa

Hydrozoa	mesoderm	Trematoda	pseudocoelom
budding	incomplete gut	planaria	nematode
Scyphozoa	complete gut	neural ganglia	rotifer
Anthozoa	spiral cleavage	anterior	primitive
glue cell	radial cleavage	genital chamber	advanced
germ layer	indeterminate development	proglottid	
endoderm	Turbellaria	scolex	
ectoderm	Cestoda	coelom	

REVIEW QUESTIONS

1 List six or seven important animal characteristics. Indicate which, if any, are unique to the animal kingdom. (p. 434)

2 Briefly, what are parazoans and metazoans? What are their theoretical origins? (p. 434)

3 Compare radial and bilateral symmetry and cite an example of each. (p. 435)

4 List and define the four levels of organization in animals. (p. 435)

5 To what do the terms protostome and deuterostome refer? Looking at the phylogenetic tree of animals (Figure 27.2), list the phyla that appear under each category. (pp. 435–437)

6 To each of the phyla listed (question 5), state examples of representative animals.

7 What major phyla are represented in the Ediacara fauna? How old is this part of the fossil record? (p. 437)

8 What additional phyla do we find in the Burgess Shale Formation? How old is this deposit? (p. 437)

9 Describe feeding and digestion in the ascon sponge. (p. 438)

10 List the three kinds of spicules. What is the function of the spicule? (p. 439)

11 Describe reproduction in the sponge. Suggest how a swimming larval state might be adaptive to a sedentary animal. (p. 439)

12 Describe the general body form of the coelenterate and name several specialized cells. What if anything qualifies as an organ? (p. 440)

13 Describe typical feeding responses in *Hydra*. (p. 441)

14 Which of the two body forms predominates in the hydrozoan? The scyphozoan? The anthozoan? (p. 441)

15 Briefly contrast the life cycle of the hydrozoan with that of the scyphozoan. (pp. 441–442)

16 Name the three germ layers in the three-layered embryo. What new kinds of tissue were made possible by the new middle layer? (p. 443)

17 Compare gut development in protostomes and deuterostomes. (pp. 443–444)

18 Contrast cleavage in protostomes and deuterostomes. (p. 443)

19 Describe the general body appearance of the free-living flatworms (turbellarians). (p. 444)

20 Briefly describe the following systems in planarians: digestive, nervous, reproductive. What major systems are absent? (p. 444)

21 What systems are least apparent in the tapeworm? Most apparent? How does this make sense in terms of the worm's life-style (its adaptive significance)? (pp. 444, 446)

22 Why might successful reproduction in the beef or pork tapeworm be considered difficult? How does this affect its reproductive efforts? (p. 446)

23 Briefly summarize the stages and hosts in the life cycle of the human liver fluke (Figure 27.12). Where are the weak links in the cycle—vulnerable places where the chain of infestation might be broken? (p. 447)

24 Why was the evolution of a leading and following end in bilateral animals important? (p. 446)

25 Describe the complete gut and tube-within-a-tube body plan common in metazoan animals. Name the important body cavity resulting. (pp. 446, 448)

26 Clearly distinguish between a coelom and a pseudocoelom. Which appears in the nematodes? (p. 448)

27 How does the absence of mesodermally derived tissue in the roundworm gut affect its structure? (p. 448)

28 Roundworms are often thought of only as parasites. What's wrong with this viewpoint? Where do other roundworms live? (p. 448)

29 Describe the life cycle of the ascarid worm. What difficulties does its enormous reproductive effort help overcome? (p. 449)

30 Describe the feeding apparatus and gut of a rotifer. Which structures would you consider primitive? Advanced? (p. 449)

31 To what do the terms advanced and primitive refer? Why must they be used with caution in describing animals? (p. 449)

28

THE COELOMATE INVERTEBRATES

"Human beings are the most complex, the most advanced, and the most nearly perfect organisms on earth, just one cut above the majestic Indian elephant. Other animals are, by degrees, less advanced, less complex, and less perfect—which is to say, less and less human. Higher forms, such as birds and mammals, are more advanced—closer to perfection—than such lower forms as reptiles, fish, crabs, and worms."

We hope nothing so far has been touched by your yellow marking pen. These were the basic notions of an ancient idea called the *scala naturae,* or the natural scale. Of course, they haven't a grain of truth in them, but somehow the idea has been subtly preserved, as is evident in the almost inescapable notion of "higher" and "lower" species, the higher ones being those with more traits in common with humans. In actuality, each species of life on this earth is continually adapting to better utilize its own niche, and that niche may be quite different from our own.

Keep this in mind and consider a second group of invertebrates. These are the ones that traditionally have been referred to as the higher invertebrates, but you already know our opinion on this. At the same time, it can probably be assumed that these species have a greater number of advanced traits than those discussed in the preceding chapter. As we said, an "advanced" trait is one that is considered to be more unlike those of ancestral organisms than a "primitive" trait (so a primitive trait more closely resembles those of the animal's evolutionary forebear). Actually, every species is really a mix of primitive *and* advanced traits. We'll see how this is true of humans as well as other species.

THE COELOMATE BODY PLAN

The species we will consider in this chapter are **coelomates** (see Figure 27.2). These are the animals with a true, mesoderm-lined coelom. The coelomates have a complex, one-way gut lined with digestive and absorptive tissue surrounded by muscles and covered by a smooth epithelium that permits freer movement of the gut within the coelom. In most coelomates the gut has specialized regions along its length. For instance there are regions whose primary functions are grinding, swallowing, digesting, and absorbing food; there are others for the temporary storage of food, and yet others for the concentration and elimination of wastes. Such linear specialization permits food to be continuously processed, since, during a given time, food in different regions will be undergoing different stages of digestion (Figure 28.1). This arrangement is quite different from the saclike gastrovascular cavities of the flatworms and coelenterates.

We learned earlier that an embryonic distinction characterizes a great split in animal evolution, which led to the formation of two major animal groups: the protostomes and the deuterostomes (see Chapter 27).

In review, the protostomes primarily include the flatworms, roundworms, annelids, arthropods, and mollusks, which together make up the majority of today's named animal species. The deuterostomes include the echinoderms, the group that encompasses humans (the chordates), and a few minor phyla such as one containing the arrow worms (chaetognaths).

FIGURE 28.1 Acoelomates, pseudocoelomates, and coelomates. (a) Acoelomates lack a body cavity. Pseudocoelomates (b) have a body cavity, but it is only partially lined by mesodermally derived tissue. Coelomates (c) have a true coelom, a cavity completely lined by mesodermally derived tissue.

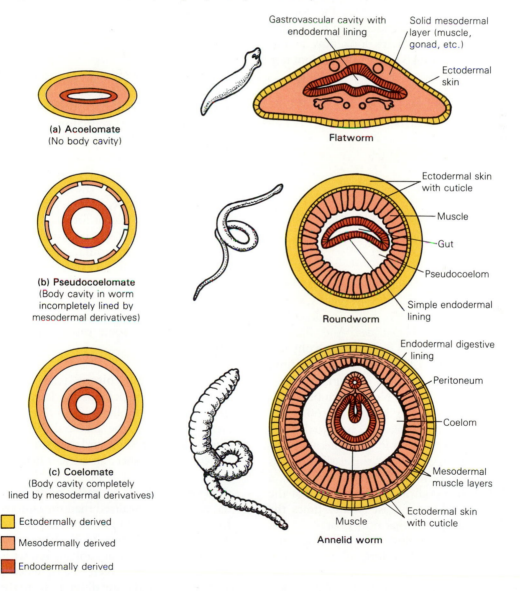

The Segmented Body

Along with the development of the coelom and the linearly specialized digestive system, some coelomates achieved a third evolutionary milestone: the **segmented body plan.** In its simplest form, this means that the body was organized into serially repeated units or segments, as seen in the centipede and earthworm. Each segment is divided from the next by transverse **septa,** or cross walls, and the structures within each are more or less repeated. In some cases, the basic segmentation has been modified to such a degree that it may no longer be apparent. For example, the segmentation in humans is relegated to repeated vertebrae, ribs, spinal nerves, and trunk muscles. Many zoologists believe that the coelom and segmentation arose independently in the protostomes and deuterostomes. Let's look now at the Mollusca, a phylum in which neither the coelom nor segmentation is obvious.

> The coelom and segmentation in both protostome and deuterostome lines are examples of convergent evolution.

SHELLS AND A MUSCULAR FOOT: THE MOLLUSKS (PHYLUM MOLLUSCA)

The earth is burgeoning with **mollusks.** In fact, biologists already know of about 100,000 species, which makes them third in numbers of species described after the arthropods and nematodes. And, like the arthropods, the mollusks are a highly diverse phylum (Figure 28.2). Some mollusks are minute—tiny, inconspicuous creatures huddled in fragile shells—but others are truly giant. The North Atlantic squid, for example, may reach a length of 18 m (60 ft).

The fossil history of mollusks goes back to the Precambrian period and is found in the Ediacara beds, (see Figure 27.2). Interestingly, the earliest fossils include an ancestral form very similar to *Nautilus,* a living shelled cephalopod. In fact, it seems that the Cambrian fossils include at least twenty times the number of mollusk species that now exist.

In many ways, the mollusks are a phylogenetic puzzle. For example, they show little, if any, evidence of segmentation, and the size of the coelom is so reduced that some scholars deny that mollusks have ever been coelomate animals. They hold that the mollusks share very little of their evolutionary history with the other protostomes.

Many biologists, however, believe that the mollusks are simply highly specialized relatives of the annelids and the arthropods. They note strong similarities in the earliest embryonic stages of mollusks and annelids, each with spiral, determinate cleavage and (when they occur), similar swimming larvae. Further, such theorists assert that mollusks and annelids diverged early in the history of coelomate protostomes.

> Because mollusks lack clear evidence of a coelom and segmentation, their relationship to other protostomes is uncertain.

Modern Mollusks

There are four major classes of mollusks and several minor ones. The major classes are the **chitons,** the **gastropods** (snails), the **bivalves** (clams and their relatives), and the **cephalopods** (octopuses and squids). As would be expected, no class of living animals conforms entirely to any simplified, generalized mollusk body plan. But all mollusk classes include at least some species with the basic molluscan characters: a muscular **foot,** a **shell,** a **mantle** and **mantle cavity,** and **gills.** Except for the bivalves, most mollusks have a highly specialized feeding device, the oscillating, rasplike **radula,** composed of hardened chitin. It is found in no other phylum.

All of these basic parts, however, have been subjected to intense evolutionary modification, and they may differ greatly from one group to the next (see Figure 28.2). In some cases, a part may even be entirely absent.

Chitons. The **chitons** (class Polyplacophora; Figure 28.2a) are perhaps the least modified of the major groups of mollusks. This class has changed relatively little from the ancestral condition. The chiton's eight-part shell and repetitious rows of gill structures may reflect an ancient heritage.

Gastropods. The **gastropods** (class Gastropoda) are more specialized than the chitons, and therefore have departed more from the ancestral line. For example, snails (Figure 28.2b) have retained the simple gliding foot but are able to retract it. They feed with a radula, but their shells, when present, are asymmetrical and quite different from the segmented shell of the chiton. Early in its development the snail embryo undergoes extreme *torsion,* or twisting (180 degrees), displacing the internal organs. Thus, the

FIGURE 28.2 Membership in any of the major molluscan classes depends on specializations in the shell, mantle and mantle cavity, foot, gut, and respiratory structures.

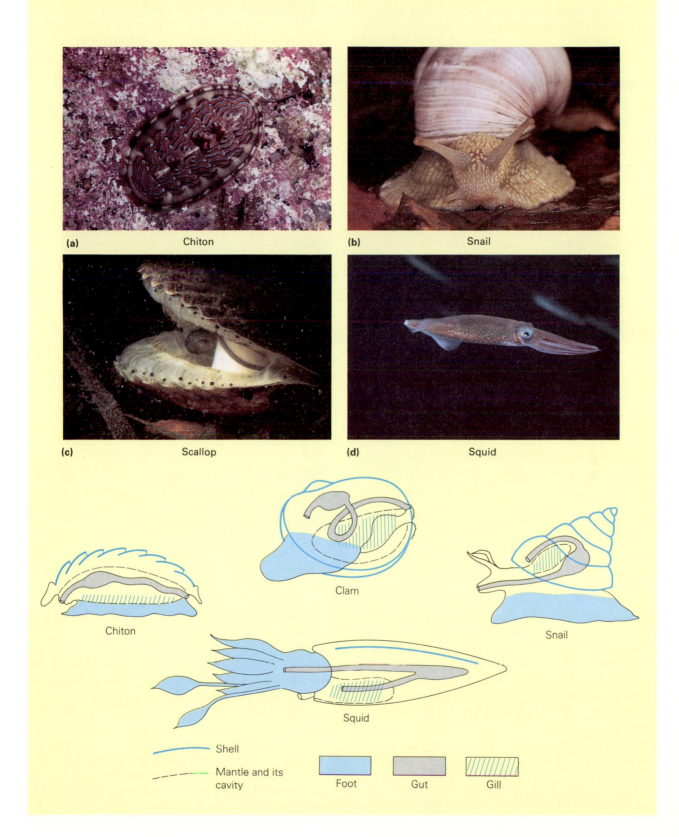

(a) Chiton

(b) Snail

(c) Scallop

(d) Squid

Chiton

Clam

Snail

Squid

Shell

Mantle and its cavity

Foot

Gut

Gill

anus ends up over the head, if you can imagine that. In addition, the genitals end up on one side of the head, in about the position of what would be the right cheek, if gastropods had cheeks. This torsion is then followed by an equally severe spiralling in the shell. Many gastropods are hermaphroditic and have large penises with which they fertilize each other. The sight of the organ extending from the side of the head is remarkable. Even more remarkable is the habit of garden snails of thrusting sharp "love darts" into the flesh of potential mates, seemingly just to get their attention.

Bivalves. The **bivalves** (class Bivalvia—"two shells") include clams, oysters, mussels, and scallops (Figure 28.2c). These species have followed yet another adaptive path: they have become **filter feeders,** filtering food from water, drawing the water through an **incurrent siphon** and directing it over and through their gills. The gills have been modified into sievelike feeding structures. Cilia covering the gill surfaces create the water currents that carry in food particles (minute algae), which become ensnared in a dense film of mucus that moves the food into the simple mouth. The water then passes on through the gills and exits through an **excurrent siphon.**

Cephalopods. The **cephalopods** (class Cephalopoda) have diverged the most from the basic molluscan body plan. This class includes the octopuses, squids (see Figure 28.2d), and the chambered nautilus. The first two are swift predators, in which the foot has been modified into a number of grasping tentacles. The mantle can rapidly contract, forcefully expelling water and jet-propelling the animal along its way.

The cephalopods are undoubtedly among the most fascinating of all the invertebrates. They all have excellent image-producing eyes, remarkably like those of vertebrates. Since cephalopods are not at all closely related to vertebrates, this is coincidence—an amazing example of convergent evolution. The nervous systems of these fascinating creatures reveal different evolutionary directions as well. For example, the cephalopod brain is quite large in comparison to the brains of other mollusks, and we know that cephalopods can learn certain things with surprising ease.

> **M**olluscan diversity involves dramatic specializations in the shell, foot, mantle, mantle cavity, and gills.

SEGMENTED WORMS: THE ANNELIDS (PHYLUM ANNELIDA)

Earthworms are commonly used to represent **annelids,** but most annelid species are **polychaete** ("many-bristled ones") worms that live in the sea (Figure 28.3). Typical polychaetes are the sedentary, filter-feeding *fan worm* and the active, predatory *clam worm.* Both marine and terrestrial annelids have highly segmented bodies.

The earthworms are land-dwelling **oligochaetes** ("few-bristled ones"). The "bristles," or **setae** are chitinous spines that aid the worm in burrowing. Another group of annelids, the **hirudinians**—the **leeches**—are blood-sucking, external parasites that inhabit moist or swampy environments (where they help liven up old Bogart movies).

Earthworm

Most of the earthworm's organ systems are well developed (Figure 28.4). The segmented body contains complex muscle layers. The coelom is fluid filled, and the fluid is under pressure, forming what is called a **hydrostatic skeleton.** This means of support is common to many soft-bodied animals and provides a firmness that helps with movement and the maintenance of body form. As in other coelomate protostomes, the nervous system includes a **ventral nerve cord** that extends along the entire body, below the intestine. Two large **ganglia** (nerve cell clusters) make up the brain—which, as in annelids, arthropods, and mollusks, is above and below the esophagus.

The earthworm's muscular, tubelike digestive system includes several unusual specializations. For example, the **typhlosole,** a large fold in the gut wall, aids digestion and absorption by greatly increasing the surface area. The excretory system, which is responsible for removing nitrogenous wastes and for water regulation, consists of paired, funnel-shaped **nephridia** that clear the wastes from the coelomic fluid in each segment and conserve body water by recycling it to the blood. Cell-by-cell diffusion of food and gases, which was quite sufficient in the smaller and simpler invertebrates, does not work in the comparatively dense body of the earthworm. Here we encounter, for the first time, an efficient circulatory system. Furthermore, it is a *closed* system, like our own. This means that blood remains within vessels rather than percolating through open cavities and sinuses, as it does in many other invertebrates.

FIGURE 28.3 The most diverse and numerous of the annelids are the polychaete worms. Many, such as the fan worms **(a)**, are tube dwellers that use feathery devices in feeding and respiration, popping them in and out of their tube houses. The oligochaetes—terrestrial annelids—lack complex outer structures that would complicate their burrowing activities. Segmentation, a prominent annelid characteristic, is readily evident in the earthworm **(b).** Hirudineans **(c)** specialize in ectoparasitism (external parasitism), using their sucker devices to attach to the host animal.

(a)

(b)

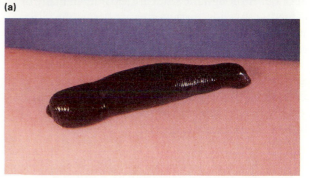

(c)

FIGURE 28.4 The most prominent characteristic of the earthworm is its pronounced segmentation. The smooth, unsegmented clitellum is a gland that secretes a slimy, protective cocoon over fertilized eggs. The body wall includes complex muscle layers and bristlelike setae. Within is the large, fluid-filled coelom and intestine. A large fold in the intestine, the typhlosole, increases surface area. The cutaway view (*below*) shows the closed circulatory system and specialized digestive and reproductive systems. One pair of water-conserving, excretory nephridia is also seen.

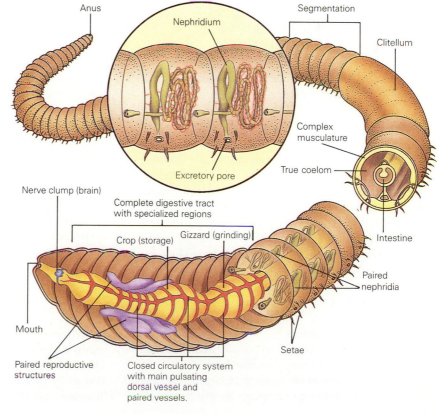

Anus

Nephridium

Segmentation

Clitellum

Complex musculature

True coelom

Excretory pore

Intestine

Nerve clump (brain)

Complete digestive tract with specialized regions

Crop (storage)   Gizzard (grinding)

Paired nephridia

Mouth

Setae

Paired reproductive structures

Closed circulatory system with main pulsating dorsal vessel and paired vessels.

Since the blood contains hemoglobin, it is red, like ours. The blood is pumped through five pairs of "hearts" or **aortic arches,** which send it coursing through large blood vessels that branch into dense beds of finer, thin-walled vessels called **capillaries.** The capillaries, passing through the thin, moist skin, permit oxygen to diffuse into the blood and carbon dioxide to diffuse out. The capillaries provide all tissues with food and oxygen.

The earthworm's reproductive system is quite elaborate. Although the sexes are separate in many of the marine annelids, earthworms are hermaphroditic, with each individual possessing both testes and ovaries. Earthworms mate by lying head to tail and exchanging sperm, which are then stored in **seminal receptacles.** Later, a sleevelike mucus cocoon is secreted. It passes over ducts that release eggs and then over ducts that release sperm. The earthworm embryos develop in the cocoon.

> **S**egmented worms (annelids) have a complex, muscular body wall, a fully formed coelom, specializations in the gut, a closed circulatory system, paired excretory structures, and a complex reproductive system.

A REMARKABLE SUCCESS STORY: THE ARTHROPODS (PHYLUM ARTHROPODA)

No one has any idea how many species of arthropods there are, but the most respected guesses range between 800,000 and 1,000,000. In any case, Arthropoda is the most successful phylum on earth.

What is an **arthropod?** *Arthropod* means "jointed foot," so arthropods have jointed feet. They are also segmented, but their segments are not the simple repeating units characterizing the earthworms. Instead, the segments may be specialized and modified for different tasks. Arthropods have exterior skeletons (**exoskeletons**) covering their bodies. The exoskeleton, or **cuticle,** is made up of **chitin,** a dense, flexible carbohydrate. In the aquatic crustaceans (order **Crustacea),** it is often hardened with calcium salts; in insects (order **Insecta**) it is hardened with various organic substances.

Chitin is also common to other protostomes, where it helps form many hardened structures. As they grow, all arthropods must periodically discard their hardened exoskeleton through **molting,** replac-

ing it with a larger one. Molting (also called **ecdysis**) is under hormonal control.

Arthropods Today

Arthropods have been incredibly successful in their expansion over the earth, sometimes establishing very narrow ecological niches. (Consider the mayfly, a delicate creature that emerges as an adult without mouthparts and must mate and leave offspring in the few precious hours of life allowed it; or strange green insects that live only on year-round alpine glaciers). In fact, arthropod niches are often so specialized that many species can live in very close association without seriously competing with each other.

Arthropods include omnivores, herbivores, filter feeders, carnivores, scavengers, ectoparasites, endoparasites, and even a few opportunistic cannibals. How did they become so successful? For one thing, the use of jointed limbs was an immediate evolutionary success. Limbs were subject to all sorts of modifications that could eventually permit crawling, burrowing, jumping, grasping, feeling, and even hearing. The mouthparts are derived from jointed appendages, and are also extremely specialized, modified for such actions as biting, chewing, sucking, stinging, or lapping.

Through such diversity the arthropods have been able to exploit just about every resource on earth. The development of wings in the insects greatly increased their ability to disperse and to exploit previously unavailable niches. And we must not forget the phenomenal reproductive capabilities of this group. In addition, a great many species produce larvae whose diet is entirely different from that of the adults. This results in subdivision of the niche and also helps to preclude parent-offspring competition.

> **A**rthropod characteristics include highly modified segmentation, a chitinous exoskeleton, jointed legs, paired limbs, and diverse and specialized mouthparts.

Arthropod Diversity

Since there is no concise way to deal with the enormous diversity of arthropods, we'll have to pick and choose a few examples. The living arthropods are traditionally divided into two huge subphyla, the **Chelicerata** and the **Mandibulata** (Figure 28.5). The

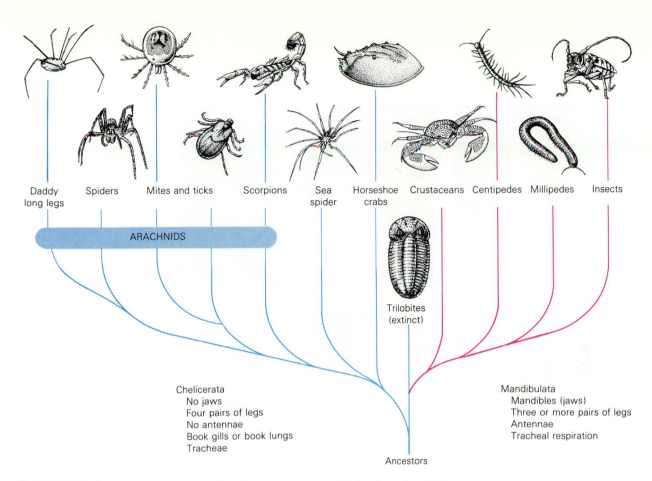

FIGURE 28.5 The immense arthropod phylum contains two subphyla: the jawless *Chelicerata,* and the jawed *Mandibulata.*

Chelicerata (arthropods that lack jaws) include the **arachnids** (spiders, scorpions, and others), the **sea spiders,** and the **horseshoe crabs.** The Mandibulata (the jawed arthropods) include the **crustaceans, centipedes, millipedes, insects** and a number of minor groups (Figure 28.6). Some scholars claim that the mandibulates are actually three unrelated phyla that are lumped together only because of convergent evolution. In any case, we'll concentrate on just three arthropod groups, the arachnids, the crustaceans, and the insects.

Arachnids: spiders and their relatives. Arachnids include spiders, scorpions, ticks, mites, and daddy longlegs. Typically, arachnids have a two-part body: a **prosoma,** which bears the appendages, and **opisthosoma** (or abdomen), which contains digestive, reproductive, and silk-producing organs. They also have six pairs of appendages, including the specialized **chelicerae** (or fangs). These are followed by sensory **pedipalps,** and then by four pairs of legs.

Spiders are carnivores, but they lack jaws and must suck their foods. Typically, a spider first injects venom into its prey's body to kill or paralyze it, then it pumps in digestive enzymes that liquefy the prey's tissues. Spiders breathe by **book lungs,** essentially sacs with slits that open to the outside. The sacs are lined with flattened folds that resemble the pages of a book. Blood passing through the thin sheets exchanges gases with air in the sac.

Nearly all spiders have silk-producing glands connected to external appendages called **spinnerets.** The system is used to form both the web and cocoon (Figure 28.7).

Spiders are **chelicerates** with a two-part body, six pairs of appendages, venomous **chelicerae, book lungs,** and complex silk-producing structures.

Grasshoppers

Centipede

Millipede

Ants and aphids

Aphid giving birth

Mayflies

FIGURE 28.6 Representative mandibulates. While insects make up the majority of mandibulates, crustaceans are also numerous. Minor groups include the millipedes and centipedes.

FIGURE 28.7 Most spiders have silk glands that are associated with external appendages called spinnerets. Many, like the orb spider, produce several kinds of silk, including a sticky thread used in trapping prey, and a dry type, upon which the spider can safely walk.

Crustaceans. Most species of crustaceans are aquatic and are common in both marine and fresh waters. This class includes crabs, shrimp, crayfish, and lobsters, as well as terrestrial wood lice (also called sow bugs). Crustaceans range in size from the microscopic freshwater ostracods to the gigantic king crabs of cold Pacific waters.

Typically, crustaceans breathe through gills that are covered by the tough exoskeleton. Blood continuously flows through delicate, feathery gills, releasing carbon dioxide and taking in oxygen. Crustaceans often have highly developed sensory structures. Interestingly, the general plan of the arthropod nervous system is similar to that of the earthworm and the mollusk: a "brain" surrounding the esophagus, and paired, solid, ventral nerve cords with paired ganglia at intervals.

Marine crustaceans and other saltwater inhabitants share the problem of life in a hypertonic environment—roughly a 3% salt solution. Some cope as **osmoconformers**—maintaining a salt content that roughly matches the surroundings. The **osmoregulators,** on the other hand, maintain a lower and relatively constant content in their bodies by secreting salt through special glands.

Among the most specialized of the crustacean sensory structures are the **compound eyes,** which are often borne on flexible stalks. The crustacean eye is similar to that of an insect, composed of a large number of visual units called **ommatidia.** Each ommatidium (singular) has a tough, transparent lens and pigmented, light-sensitive receptors (retinal cells) (Figure 28.8). With this arrangement the animal obtains

a nearly 360-degree view of its surroundings, though this "view" may be a shimmering mosaic of light and dark colors—quite different from the images we see.

Marine crustaceans such as crabs and lobsters have a hardened exoskeleton and compound eyes.

Insects. The crustaceans are the dominant, or most prevalent, arthropods in the sea, but insects dominate the land, both in number and in kind. Insects are of such ecological and economical importance that we literally could not have reached our own place in nature without understanding something about them. One reason is that we must continuously compete with them, and we don't always win. There are a great many humans who go hungry because their food is eaten or ruined by insects, and many live debilitated, shortened lives, victims of insect-borne diseases such as malaria, typhus, and African sleeping sickness. It is indeed a high price to pay to be able to share the planet with the butterflies.

The segmented body of insects as we know them today (Figure 28.9) has undoubtedly changed considerably from the ancestral form. For one thing, many of the segments have become fused. Segmentation in many adult insects is readily apparent only in the abdominal region. Typically, there are three body regions: the **head, thorax,** and **abdomen.** The

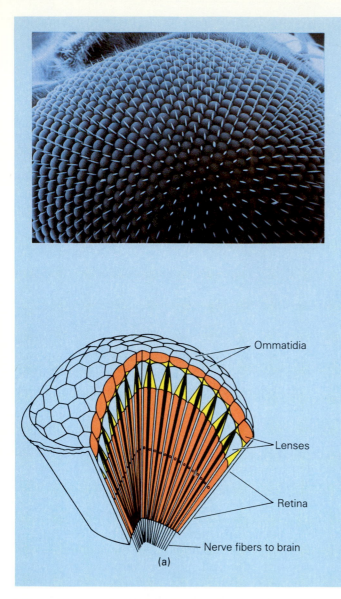

FIGURE 28.8 The compound eyes of crustaceans and insects consist of many individual light-receiving units called ommatidia.

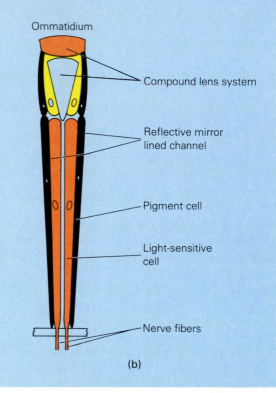

Ommatidium

Compound lens system

Reflective mirror lined channel

Pigment cell

Light-sensitive cell

Nerve fibers

Ommatidia

Lenses

Retina

Nerve fibers to brain

(a)

(b)

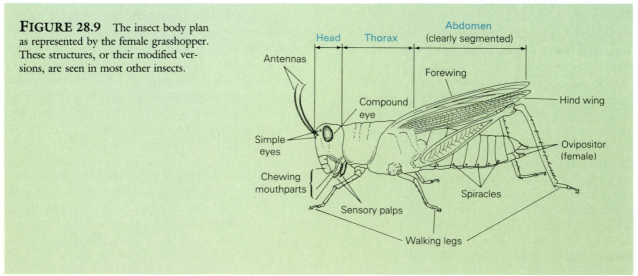

FIGURE 28.9 The insect body plan as represented by the female grasshopper. These structures, or their modified versions, are seen in most other insects.

Head   Thorax   Abdomen (clearly segmented)

Antennas

Forewing

Hind wing

Compound eye

Simple eyes

Ovipositor (female)

Chewing mouthparts

Sensory palps

Spiracles

Walking legs

sensory structures—the eyes, antennae, and sensory palps—are concentrated in the head region. The thorax gives rise to three pairs of legs, and commonly to two pairs of wings.

The wings of insects are thin, chitinous sheets, moved by powerful muscles in the thorax on elaborate, levered hinges. Wing movement in some insects is incredibly rapid. Fruit flies, for example, can maintain a continuous beat of 300 strokes per second for as long as two hours.

The rudimentary circulatory system of insects is not usually involved in respiration. Insects exchange gases with the environment by admitting air into a complex **tracheal system.** It consists of tubes (the **tracheae**) that pass throughout the body, branching to produce ever finer **tracheoles,** passages that finally end blindly. The air enters through valvelike body openings called **spiracles.**

There is enormous variety among the specialized insect mouthparts. For example, the mouthparts of grasshoppers are suited for tasting, shearing, and chewing. Moths have long sucking mouthparts that they coil neatly when not in use. Mosquitos have piercing and sucking mouthparts, as we are all aware. The crass housefly salivates on your chocolate cake, stirs it with its bristled tongue, and then sucks up the resulting mess.

The insect digestive system includes three parts: the **foregut, midgut,** and **hindgut** (Figure 28.10). Food is digested in the midgut and then moves to the hindgut, where water is removed and fecal wastes are concentrated. The area where the midgut and hindgut join receives metabolic wastes from the excretory system, which consists of numerous hairlike structures known as **Malpighian tubules.** The waste is eliminated as nearly dry crystals of uric acid.

Insects, like other arthropods, have an *open* circulatory system. The main dorsal blood vessel has several contractile areas called "hearts." Openings in the vessel allow blood to be drawn in from the surrounding spaces and then pumped along by the vessel's contractions. But the blood soon leaves the vessels and is pumped into sinuses and cavities. From there it sluggishly percolates through the tissue and back to the dorsal vessel.

The insects' reproductive adaptations contribute significantly to their success. The life span is typically short, but many species compensate by quickly producing incredibly large numbers of offspring. (A female housefly has the potential to leave over five trillion descendants in just seven generations, or one year's time!) In addition, each of the four parts in the life cycles of many insects has its own adaptive significance. The **eggs** are often well concealed and resistant. When the eggs hatch, the **larvae** go through **metamorphosis,** changing from larva to **pupa** before entering adulthood. The larva and adult often utilize entirely different food sources, so they are not in direct competition. The pupa lives on food stored in the larval stage. Egg and pupa often survive the

FIGURE 28.10 The insect digestive and excretory systems. The chewing mouth parts (**a**) are well adapted for feeding on vegetation. The three gut regions (**b**) have specialized functions. The Malpighian tubules absorb nitrogen wastes from surrounding body fluids.

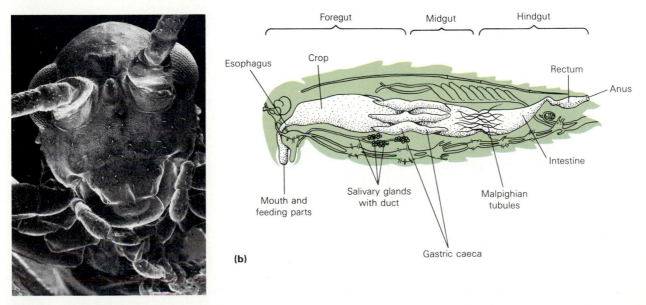

FIGURE 28.11 In a complete metamorphosis, as seen in this beetle, fertilization is followed by a three-part life cycle: larva, pupa, and adult. Because of their voracious appetite, many larvae are damaging agricultural pests, the target of relentless crop spraying and dusting. Pupae, while seemingly dormant, undergo great changes.

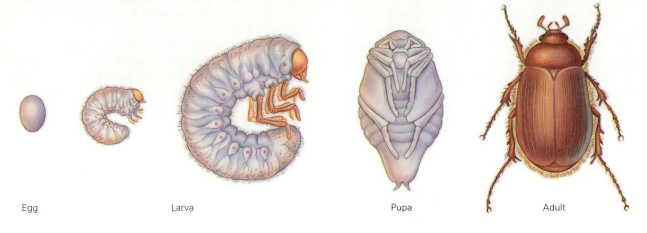

Egg   Larva   Pupa   Adult

winter in dormant states. Insect metamorphosis is delicately orchestrated by specific hormones (Figure 28.11).

> Insects have a three-part body, three pairs of legs, two pairs of wings (in many), a complex three-part digestive system, a water-conserving excretory system, an open circulatory system, a tracheal respiratory system, and highly specialized reproductive parts.

Insects, indeed, abound over the earth. They have exploited virtually every available nook and cranny on the planet. Their success, however, shouldn't be surprising considering their fundamental adaptations. In a real sense, their success can be attributed to varied diet, small size, rapid generation time, great reproductive output, and highly varied life cycles.

To sum up, we have pointed out that the protostome line produced three great coelomate phyla—Mollusca, Annelida, and Arthropoda—whose members make up the majority of animal species today. With relatively few (but notable) exceptions, this line emphasized great diversity, small bodies, rapid reproduction, and dense populations. It can be argued that such characteristics more than compensate for their limited intelligence and learning ability.

THE DEUTEROSTOMES: THE ECHINODERM-CHORDATE LINE

The earliest deuterostomes were small and simple, with extremely limited nervous systems. And yet there was an unsuspected potential in these animals. No one could be too surprised that the deuterostomes were to produce the witless starfish, but who would have imagined that they would also give rise to the chordates, and that from the chordates would come the vertebrates—the largest and brainiest animals on earth?

Spiny Skins and Radial Bodies: The Echinoderms

Echinoderms are exclusively marine animals, with many species living in the shallow waters of the continental shelf. Others, though, thrive in the deepest oceanic trenches.

There are five major classes of echinoderms (Figure 28.12), each with its own variation on the basic five-part body plan.

Echinoderms are unusual in many respects. Their radial symmetry, for instance, is not like that of the simple coelenterates, but is a modified form called **pentaradial symmetry** (*penta,* five). In other words, any "pie slices" could only be cut at certain places to produce nearly identical sections. However, the embryonic stages are not radially symmetrical at all. The larvae (and, indeed, the ancient fossilized adult echinoderms) are bilaterally symmetrical.

Even the spiny echinoderm skeleton is a true **endoskeleton.** That is, it is of mesodermal origin and actually it is located on the inside. Don't confuse the lengthy spines of many echinoderms with exoskeletons. They form inside the animal and emerge from bony (mesodermal) plates located below its skin.

One of the most unusual features of the echino-

FIGURE 28.12 Five-part radial symmetry is a basic feature of echinoderm anatomy, but many variations of this theme are seen in the phylum.

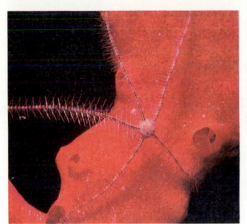

Brittle star

Sea urchin

FIGURE 28.13 In the sea star or starfish, the water vascular system consists of the madreporite (an inlet), a canal system, and numerous tube feet. The tube feet are used in moving about and feeding. To accomplish this, the animal contracts its ampullas, forcing water into the tube feet and extending them. When the tube feet contact a surface, their terminal suckers fasten on. Then, muscles in the tube feet contract, shortening them. As they shorten, water is allowed to escape back into the system, which has a number of check valves to regulate its flow. In this way, many tube feet, working in series, pull the animal along the ocean floor. The tube feet are powerful and can open the shells of bivalves. The sea star then everts its stomach and digests the bivalve within its own shell.

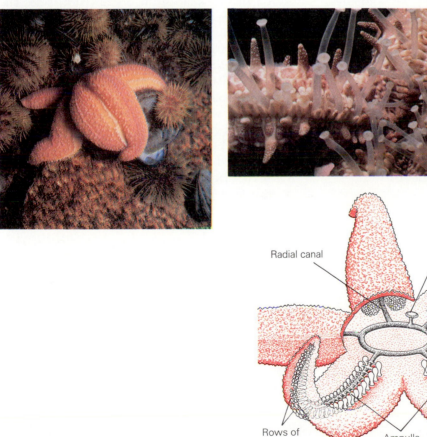

derms is the **water vascular system**. It is the principal mechanism of locomotion for some species (although some sea urchins also clamber about on their stiltlike, movable spines). The **madreporite** is the system's sievelike inlet. The major parts of the internal plumbing are the hardened **stone canal, ring canal,** and **radial canals.** The moveable parts are the **ampullas,** muscular "squeeze bulbs" that force water into the **tube feet,** thereby extending them. The mechanism and role of the water vascular system in the sea stars are described in Figure 28.13.

Other systems in the echinoderms are also strange, yet simple. Many are unique to this group. For example, respiration is carried out by **dermal branchiae,** simple ciliated extensions of the coelomic lining that stick out through the body wall and act in gas exchange. Dissolved gases can also readily cross the thin membranes of the tube feet. The sea star's nervous system is a simple ring, with extensions reaching into each of its five arms. There is no sign of centralization, no clumps of ganglia, and no concentration of nerve cells. This may explain why the animal can move in any of five directions with equal ease and full coordination. The digestive tract is *complete;* that is, it includes a mouth, a gut, and an anus. The reproductive system is simple, consisting of testes or ovaries (sexes are separate) that lead to ducts. In most echinoderms the gametes are simply released into the water, where fertilization occurs.

Among the **echinoderms** are sea stars, brittle stars, sea urchins, crinoids and sea cucumbers. Characteristics include a spiny **endoskeleton,** a unique **water vascular system,** and **pentaradial** (five-part) adult symmetry.

Hemichordates

The **hemichordates** (phylum **Hemichordata**) comprise a peculiar group, including a few rather uninspiring aquatic creatures such as the **acorn worms.** The acorn worms of this minor phylum have two primitive chordate characteristics, **gill slits** and a **dorsal hollow nerve cord** (which we will discuss in Chapter 29). Equally significant, the acorn worm's larvae are startlingly similar to those of some echinoderms (Figure 28.14).

Chordates

And now we come to the **chordates** (phylum **Chordata**), the group that includes humans. Some of the chordate traits may seem alien to you, but keep in mind that they may appear only briefly, at some embryonic stage (see Chapter 42).

Phylum Chordata includes three subphyla: **Urochordata, Cephalochordata,** and **Vertebrata.** In each chordate subphylum, the following characteristics are shared:

1. All chordates possess, at least at some time in their lives, a **notochord**—an internal, flexible, turgid rod that runs along the dorsal (back) side. The phylum derives its name from this structure.
2. All chordates possess, at some time in their lives, a number of **gill arches** (forming between them are the **gill slits**).
3. All chordates have, at some time in their lives, a **dorsal hollow nerve cord.**
4. At some time (in an early embryonic stage, at least), all chordates possess **myotomes**—serially repeated blocks of muscle along either side of the notochord.
5. All chordates have a **post-anal tail** at some time in their lives.

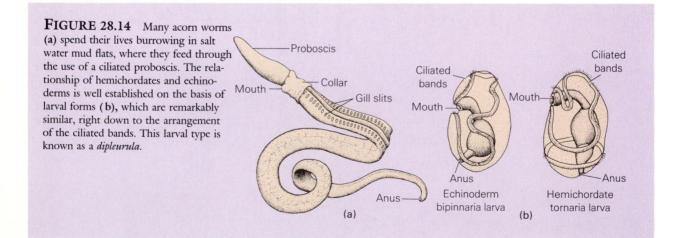

FIGURE 28.14 Many acorn worms **(a)** spend their lives burrowing in salt water mud flats, where they feed through the use of a ciliated proboscis. The relationship of hemichordates and echinoderms is well established on the basis of larval forms (**b**), which are remarkably similar, right down to the arrangement of the ciliated bands. This larval type is known as a *dipleurula.*

FIGURE 28.15 As an adult, the tunicate hardly represents what we expect in a chordate. The simple saclike body lacks nearly all of the typical chordate structures, except for the telltale chordate gill slits. The ciliated gill structure (called a *gill basket*) is used in gas exchange and for straining food particles from the sea water drawn into the incurrent opening of the tunic.

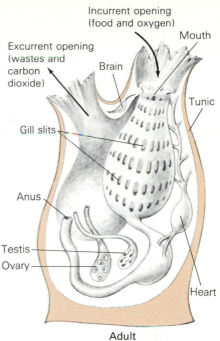

Adult

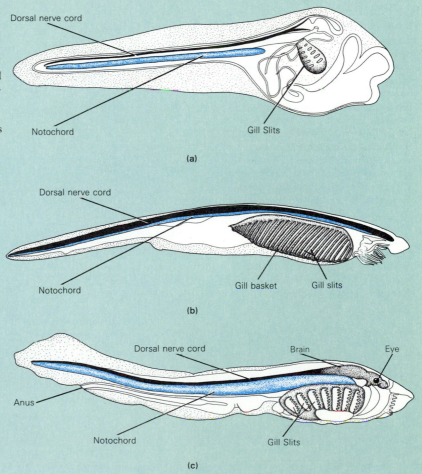

FIGURE 28.16 The chordate body plan is clearly seen in these three representatives. The tunicate larva **(a)**, unlike the adult, is truly bilateral with an elongated body. Similarly, the adult lancelet (*Branchiostoma*) **(b)** has a slender bilateral body with a well-defined tail. Also prominent are the gill slits, notochord, and dorsal hollow nerve cord. There are many similarities between these chordates and the so-called *ammocoete* larvae of the sea lamprey **(c)** a jawless vertebrate.

The **urochordates** include the stationary **tunicates** (sea squirts); the bizarre, transparent, free-swimming **salps;** and a minor, but highly significant group, the **larvacea,** planktonic forms with small, soft bodies.

Adult tunicates (Figure 28.15) have a hollow sac-like body composed of a tough **tunic.** A casual observer could confuse them with coelenterates—especially since, like sea anemones, they squirt sea water out of their bodies when they contract. But the larva of the tunicate unveils it as a chordate, with its bilateral form, a notochord, gill arches, myotomes, a dorsal hollow nerve cord, and a post-anal tail that permits vigorous swimming. (The adult larvacea retain this body form.) Larval tunicates are called **tadpoles,** and indeed they look and act a lot like the larvae of frogs and toads.

Cephalochordates have been found fossilized in the Burgess Shale deposits of the early Cambrian period. They are very similar to the living cephalochordates, the lancelets. They belong to the genus *Branchiostoma,* but are perhaps better known by their former scientific name, *Amphioxus.* They, at last, are clearly our relatives. In fact, the basic cephalochordate body plan seems almost like a simplified cartoon of the general vertebrate body plan. At the same time, it is similar in many ways to that of the urochordate larva (Figure 28.16). Like urochordates, cephalochordates are filter feeders. These similarities have strongly suggested how chordates may have evolved. (Such a scenario is seen in Figure 28.17.) Much later in the Cambrian period, ancestral cephalochordates gave rise to a new kind of animal in the oceans. At first it was an awkward, slow-swimming, jawless creature, sucking up its nutrients from the mucky bottom sediments. But it *was* the first vertebrate, a fishy ancestor to a group that would someday dominate and change the very face of the earth.

> The chordate body plan includes the **notochord, gill arches,** dorsal hollow **nerve cord,** trunk segmentation, and a **post-anal tail. Urochordates** and **cephalochordates** are subphyla with many primitive traits.

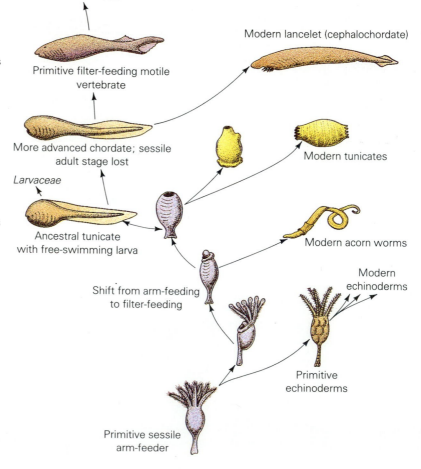

FIGURE 28.17 Theoretical chordate evolution. According to one theory, echinoderms, hemichordates, primitive chordates, and vertebrates arose from an ancestral arm-feeding deuterostome. From this ancestor arose the echinoderms and hemichordates, both of which still retain the free-swimming larva. Following these divergences, the deuterostomic line divided once more, but in a most unusual manner. One branch produced the urochordate line, today's tunicates and salps. The other arose from certain larvae that had somehow retained their juvenile body form while reaching sexual maturity. The best evidence of this strange capability is seen in *Larvaceae,* a group of living urochordates that remains permanently in a larval state. From this seemingly odd venture arose the cephalochordates and the vertebrates.

Modern vertebrates

Primitive filter-feeding motile vertebrate

Modern lancelet (cephalochordate)

More advanced chordate; sessile adult stage lost

Larvaceae

Modern tunicates

Ancestral tunicate with free-swimming larva

Modern acorn worms

Shift from arm-feeding to filter-feeding

Modern echinoderms

Primitive echinoderms

Primitive sessile arm-feeder

SUMMARY

THE COELOMATE BODY PLAN

Coelomates have a tube-like or complete gut, including regions specialized for swallowing, storing, grinding, digestion, and waste elimination. The body cavity is a mesodermally-lined true coelom. Its presence in protostomes and deuterostomes is attributed to convergent evolution.

The Segmented Body

Segmentation, the division of the body into repeated segments, is highly pronounced in annelids and arthropods and is common throughout the coelomate phyla. Its presence in protostomes and deuterostomes is also attributed to convergent evolution.

SHELLS AND A MUSCULAR FOOT: THE MOLLUSKS (PHYLUM MOLLUSCA)

Molluskan fossils are numerous in strata of the Cambrian period. Today's species reveal little evidence of segmentation or a coelom, but other characteristics reveal their relationship to other coelomate protostomes.

Modern Mollusks

The classes (chitons, gastropods, bivalves, and cephalopods) differ in specializations of the foot, shell, mantle, and mantle cavity. The presence of a radula for feeding is common.

Primitive characteristics in chitons include simple shell plates, a radula, and a simple mantle and foot. Advanced gastropod traits include body tortion, a twisted shell, and a retractable foot. Bivalves have two shells, powerful retracting muscles, and specializations for filter feeding. The fast-moving cephalopod predators have many advanced features, including tentacles (subdivided foot), jetlike use of the mantle, larger brain with learning capability, and image-producing eyes.

SEGMENTED WORMS: THE ANNELIDS (PHYLUM ANNELIDA)

Annelids include marine polychaete worms (clamworms, fanworms, tubeworms) and terrestrial types, the oligochaetes (earthworms) and hirudinians (leeches, which are ectoparasites).

Earthworms

Earthworms are highly segmented, have complex muscles, a hydrostatic skeleton (fluid-filled coelom), and well-developed systems. The nervous system includes large ganglia that form a brain and a ventral nerve cord. The digestive system has several specialized regions with an increase in the absorbing area provided by a typhlosole. Paired nephridia in most segments remove nitrogen wastes. Hemoglobin-rich blood in the closed circulatory system is pumped by five pairs of aortic arches, with all exchanges occurring through capillary walls. They are hermaphroditic with well-developed reproductive organs.

A REMARKABLE SUCCESS STORY: THE ARTHROPODS (PHYLUM ARTHROPODA)

Members of the largest phylum, arthropoda, have jointed apppendages, modified segmentation, and chitinous exoskeletons. Many molt as they grow.

Arthropods Today

Through enormous structural diversification (especially limbs and mouthparts), arthropods fill enormous numbers of niches. Most reproduce prodigiously, and many have complex life cycles.

Arthropod Diversity

Subphyla include chelicerata (spiders and others) and mandibulata (crustaceans, insects, millipedes and centipedes).

The spider body has two parts, a head and abdomen. Its six pairs of appendages include two chelicerae (fangs), two pedipalps and eight walking legs. Spiders kill their prey with venom, later sucking up its body fluids. Gas exchange occurs through book lungs. Silk is formed in glands, and spinnerettes spin webs and cocoons.

Crustaceans inhabit marine, freshwater, and terrestrial habitats. Gills are common in aquatic species. A brain and ventral nerve cord are present, as are compound eyes. The latter consist of ommatidia, visual units that detect movement. Species may be osmoregulators or osmoconformers.

Insects have had profound effects on human life, representing the most threatening animal competitors. The three-part body includes head, thorax, and abdomen. Many have two pairs of wings, and most have three pairs of walking legs. Insects have open circulatory systems and complex tracheal respiratory systems, with gas exchange occurring in thin-walled tubes called tracheae. Highy varied mouth parts permit great specialization. The digestive system includes a foregut, midgut, and hindgut. Malpighian tubules transfer nitrogenous wastes from body fluids to the digestive wastes.

Most insects have a short life span, but they produce great numbers of offspring. In species with complete metamorphosis, egg, larva, pupa, and adult stages form.

THE DEUTEROSTOMES: THE ECHINODERM-CHORDATE LINE

Deuterostomes arose from very simple animals with little neural development, yet this line produced the vertebrates, animals with the largest brains.

Spiny Skins and Radial Bodies: The Echinoderms

Echinoderms include sea stars, brittle stars, sea urchins, crinoids, and sea cucumbers. Adults have a pentaradial (5-part) symmetry, but larvae are bilateral. The spiny endoskeleton emerges from mesodermal plates. A unique water vascular system, including numerous canals, "squeeze-bulb" ampullas, and tube feet, provides for movement and feeding. Gas exchange occurs through dermal branchiae and tube feet, and digestion occurs in a complete tract. The nervous system is a simple ring of nerves with little centralization. Fertilization is external.

Hemichordates

Hemichordates include acorn worms whose relationship to chordates is revealed by gill slits and dorsal hollow nerve cords.

Chordates

Chordates include urochordates (sea squirts and salps), cephalochordates (simple fishlike *Branchiostoma*), and vertebrates. All form notochords, gill arches, and slits and have a dorsal hollow nerve cord, myotomes, and a postanal tail.

Sea squirts have hollow, thin-walled bodies and are stationary, but their larvae have typical chordate traits. Cephalochordates resemble vertebrates but in a highly simplified way, probably representative of the first vertebrates.

KEY TERMS

coelomate	ganglia	pedipalps	madreporite
segmented body plan	typhlosole	book lung	stone canal
mollusk	nephridia	spinneret	ring canal
chiton	aortic arch	osmoconformer	radial canal
gastropod	capillary	osmoregulator	ampulla
bivalve	seminal receptacle	compound eye	tube feet
cephalopod	arthropod	ommatidia	dermal branchiae
foot	exoskeleton	thorax	Hemichordata
shell	cuticle	abdomen	acorn worm
mantle	chitin	tracheal system	gill slit
mantle cavity	Crustacea	tracheae	dorsal hollow nerve cord
gill	Insecta	tracheole	Chordata
radula	molting	spiracle	Urochordata
filter feeder	ecdysis	foregut	Cephalochordata
incurrent siphon	Chelicerata	midgut	notochord
excurrent siphon	Mandibulata	hindgut	gill arch
annelid	arachnid	Malpighian tubule	myotome
polychaete	sea spider	larva	post-anal tail
oligochaete	horseshoe crab	metamorphosis	tunicate
setae	centipede	pupa	salp
hirudinian	millipede	endoskeleton	larvacea
leech	prosoma	pentaradial symmetry	tunic
hydrostatic skeleton	opisthosoma	water vascular system	tadpole
ventral nerve cord	chelicerae		

REVIEW QUESTIONS

1 List three important characteristics of coelomate animals and cite six phyla as examples. (pp. 452–453)

2 In what way do theorists explain the presence of segmentation and a true coelom in both protostomes and deuterostomes? (pp. 453–454)

3 What is segmentation? In what group of animals is it most obvious? List two or three examples of segmentation in our own bodies. (p. 454)

4 What factors suggest that mollusks are closely related to annelids and arthropods? Why do some authorities question this relationship? (p. 454)

5 List several examples of members in each of the four major mollusk classes. Describe the general appearance of the foot, shell, and mantle in each. (p. 454)

6 Why is the chiton's feeding apparatus, shell, mantle, and gills considered primitive? (p. 454)

7 What are the gastropods? Describe a peculiarity in the formation of body and shell. (pp. 454–456)

8 Describe the feeding apparatus in the clam. To which mollusk class does it belong? (p. 456)

9 In which of the mollusk classes have the foot and mantle become the most specialized or advanced? Explain. List two or three other advanced characteristics of this group. (p. 456)

10 Name the three annelid classes and cite a representative from each. Which class is largest and where do its members live? (p. 456)

11 What is a hydroskeleton? Suggest how it may function in the earthworm's movement. (p. 456)

12 List the regions of the earthworm digestive system. Why is specialization important to such an animal? Do humans share in this distinction? (p. 456)

13 Define "closed circulatory system" and describe its parts in the earthworm. (pp. 456–458)

14 The earthworm is described as "hermaphroditic." What does this mean? (p. 458)

15 List three "key" (unique) characteristics of the arthropods. (p. 458)

16 Characterize the habitats, feeding, and reproductive capacity of arthropods as a group. (p. 458)

17 Name the two subphyla of arthropods and list a principal difference. Also list three classes in each subphyla. (pp. 458–459)

18 List five traits that spiders have in common. (p. 459)

19 Characterize the aquatic crustaceans in the following areas: exoskeleton, size range, respiratory system, and nervous system (include eyes). (p. 461)

20 List four ways in which insects threaten and compete with humans? (p. 461)

21 Develop an outline that characterizes each of the following aspects of the insect body: major regions, appendages for movement, respiratory system, and feeding specializations. (pp. 461–463)

22 What is the function of each of the following in insects: midgut, Malpighian tubules, open circulatory system? (p. 463)

23 Name the stages insects pass through in which metamorphosis is complete. What is the specialization of each stage? (pp. 464–465)

24 Explain how a deuterostome skeleton differs from that of a protostome. (p. 464)

25 Name four or five examples of echinoderms. In which group does the body seem most different? Would this be a primitive or an advanced trait? (p. 465)

26 Describe the peculiar form of radial symmetry in echinoderms. Why are they considered actually to be bilateral? (p. 464)

27 Name the main parts of a water vascular system and explain how it is used for movement. (p. 466)

28 What features of the hemichordate indicate its relatedness to echinoderms? To chordates? (p. 466)

29 Summarize the five important chordate characteristics. Do humans express all of these? (p. 466)

30 What is there about the urochordate larvae and cephalochordates that evolutionary theorists find so interesting (Figure 28.17)?

29

THE VERTEBRATES

Now we come to the animals that we probably know the most about—the ones that cross our minds when we hear the word "animal." They have no ventral nerve cords; no open circulatory systems; no bodies growing from arms; no anuses above the eyes. These are the ones most people can relate to: the **vertebrates** (subphylum **Vertebrata**).

Most vertebrates share certain traits in addition to the standard chordate characteristics. Perhaps most striking is the **vertebral column** of bone or cartilage, the "backbone" that forms the body axis. In addition, vertebrates boast a centralized nervous sytem (brain), a closed circulatory system, a dorsal heart, gills or lungs, two pairs of appendages, two image-forming eyes, and a compact excretory system with paired kidneys. There are two distinct sexes in each species. These traits are characteristic of vertebrates, and although exceptions are inevitable, they are minor. Vertebrates, as a group, have distinct traits that leave little room for exceptions.

In this chapter we will focus on the evolutionary relationships of vertebrates. This group, of course, includes a staggering array of animals and life styles. We will see that in spite of the great diversity among backboned animals, there are a number of underlying similarities that virtually all of them share. So, we'll begin where vertebrate evolution began—with the jawless fishes.

> **V**ertebrates have a vertebral column of bone or cartilage, two pairs of appendages, closed circulation, dorsal heart, gills or lungs, paired kidneys, distinct sexes, and image-forming eyes.

HUMBLE BEGINNINGS AND THE JAWLESS FISHES: CLASS AGNATHA

The earliest vertebrate fossils ever found are of the **ostracoderms.** Their remains have been found in strata from throughout much of the Paleozoic era, for a period extending some 95 million years (Table 29.1). The earliest findings are about a half billion years old. The ostracoderms whose fossils have survived were slow, heavy, armor-plated fishes living on the ocean bottom. They lacked jaws and obtained their food by sucking up the bottom sediments and sorting out the nutrients. They were fearsome-looking creatures with large heads and huge gill chambers. Their bluff occasionally might have been called, however, because, their appearance notwithstanding, most species were quite small.

Jaws may seem trivial, but they are not. They are an important development and, probably because of this, the agnathans now are represented by only a few species. Most agnathan species had died out by about 345 million years ago, possibly because they were displaced by the rapidly evolving jawed fishes. The only survivors are the eel-like **lamprey** and the **hagfishes.**

In many ways the lamprey (Figure 29.1) has changed little since the Devonian period, and today it is wide ranging and quite successful. The success of the parasitic lamprey belies its ungainly features and unadmirable habits. After all, it clamps its round, jawless mouth onto the side of a larger fish, scrapes away the skin and flesh with a tough, rasping tongue, and sucks out the blood and juices of its living victim, dropping off only when gorged. The larval lamprey almost seems to pretend that it is unrelated to the adult. A shy and retiring filter feeder, the larva retains both the ecological niche and most of the physical characteristics of its cephalochordate ancestors (see Figure 28.16).

FIGURE 29.1 The lamprey is believed to be descended from the ostracoderms, jawless fishes of the early Paleozoic era. *Below*, the mouth of the lamprey.

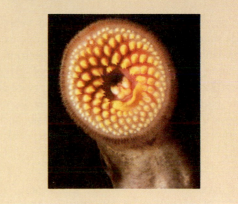

TABLE 29.1 Geologic Timetable

Eras (Years since Start)	Periods and Epochs	Extent in Millions of Years
Cenozoic	Quaternary	
	Holocene (present)	Last 10,000 years
	Pleistocene	0.01–2
	Tertiary	
	Pliocene	2–6
	Miocene	6–23
	Oligocene	23–35
	Eocene	35–54
65,000,000	Paleocene	54–65
	(Cretaceous-Paleocene discontinuity)	
Mesozoic	Cretaceous	65–135
	Jurassic	135–197
225,000,000	Triassic	197–225
Paleozoic	Permian	225–280
	Carboniferous	280–345
	Devonian	345–405
	Silurian	405–425
	Ordovician	425–500
570,000,000	Cambrian	500–570
Precambrian		570–4500

Origin of earth, 4.5 billion years

THE FIRST JAWS: CLASS PLACODERMI

There is little doubt that the evolution of jaws was one of the most significant events in vertebrate history. It almost immediately changed the behavior of many species, greatly increasing the feeding niche and encouraging new variations, some of which have succeeded to the present. All sorts of toothy creatures can bite the daylights out of you these days.

Figure 29.2 depicts one hypothesis regarding the evolutionary development of the vertebrate jaw. Note that it is derived from the gill arches (the bony structures that support the gills) in embryonic development. For gills to give rise to jaws would, of course, require a great many changes both in the position and in the strength of the arches, as well as in the surrounding muscles.

Placoderms apparently appeared in the Silurian period, about 405 million years ago. Once established, their numbers increased rapidly, and the

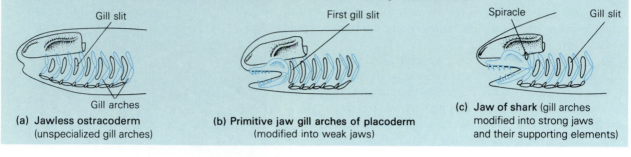

FIGURE 29.2 The forerunner of the jaw in the vertebrates was the primitive gill arch. In the jawless ostracoderms, the gill arches were all similar and unspecialized **(a).** As jaws evolved in the placoderms **(b),** the front gill arches became modified into very primitive upper and lower jaws. In the modern shark **(c)** the modifications involve more of the gill arches devoted to other specialized structures.

(a) Jawless ostracoderm (unspecialized gill arches)

(b) Primitive jaw gill arches of placoderm (modified into weak jaws)

(c) Jaw of shark (gill arches modified into strong jaws and their supporting elements)

group persisted for some 150 million years—an obvious success story. With the placoderms, we find the first evidence of paired pelvic and pectoral fins, which later gave rise to the four limbs of terrestrial vertebrates. One of the more fascinating placoderms was the gigantic *Dunkleosteus* (Figure 29.3), which was about the size of a modern gray whale, and one of the most fearsome predators that ever lived.

> The development of jaws from gill arches greatly broadened niche opportunities and was a pivotal event in vertebrate evolution.

CARTILAGINOUS FISHES: CLASS CHONDRICHTHYES

The cartilaginous fishes, those with skeletons of **cartilage,** include the sharks, rays, and chimeras—a large and successful group of predators and scavengers. The protective armor and heavy skeleton of the ancient species have been replaced in the modern species by a tough skin, slight frame, powerful muscles, and, in some cases, great speed. According to the fossil record, they first appeared in the early Devonian period, dwindled during the Jurassic period, and then began to increase again up to the present time.

The Shark

In addition to having cartilaginous skeletons, sharks are unusual in other ways. Their body and tail shapes are unlike those of most bony fishes (Figure 29.4),

FIGURE 29.3 Giant whale-sized placoderms such as *Dunkleosteus* retained some of the armor of their predecessors, but most of the creature's huge body lacked such protection.

Dunkleosteus

and their skin is rough, covered with minute, toothlike growths known as **placoid scales.** The shark's true teeth are not anchored into the jaw. They originate in soft tissues, forming many rows deep in the mouth, and gradually moving forward to become functional. They eventually fall out, to be replaced by new teeth from a seemingly inexhaustible supply. Some parts of the ocean floor are covered with discarded shark teeth.

The shark's short, cylindrical intestine has a curious structure called the **spiral valve** (also seen in agnathans and primitive bony fishes). It is essentially a twisted flap resembling a spiral staircase and consisting of absorbing tissue. The valve greatly increases the surface area of the intestine and causes food to move through it slowly. These are both adaptations to a diet that includes sizable chunks of unchewed flesh (sharks cannot chew) that require time for digestion. The shark's digestive system ends in a structure common to most vertebrates, the **cloaca.** This is a chamber that serves as a common passageway for solid and metabolic wastes. It also functions as the reproductive opening of the body, and is used by male and female sharks in copulation and by females in egg-laying.

The male shark lacks a true penis, but it has paired **claspers** on its pelvic fins that are grooved on the inner sides. When the claspers are brought together, they form a channel through which semen can flow into the female cloaca.

Sharks have keen senses and can locate prey by smell, by sight, and by vibration and water movement. Such patterns are detected in the **lateral line organ,** a sensory device found in bony fishes as well. The lateral line organ is composed of numerous sensory cells located in tiny canals that run along the head and body.

THE BONY FISHES: CLASS OSTEICHTHYES

The bony fishes are categorized into two subclasses represented by the **lobe-finned fishes** and the **ray-finned fishes.** The ray-finned fishes are the ones that probably come to mind when you hear the word "fish," since the lobe-fin subclass contains only a few living species. Ray-fins include such familiar fishes as perch, bass, tuna, swordfish, catfish, and seahorses, all with calcium-hardened bone. They are a very

FIGURE 29.4 Sharks are often described as eating machines because of their ravenous appetites. There is no doubt about their success as ocean predators, and they show a number of adaptations to this mode of life. The body shape **(a)** is, in fact, a perfect example of streamlining. Their sensory structures include an extensive lateral line organ running along the sides of the head and body, along with keen olfactory and visual senses. Within the intestine **(b),** a flaplike spiral valve increases the surface area and slows the movement of any chunks of food the shark swallows whole. The powerful jaws, with row after row of razor-sharp, replaceable teeth, tell their own story **(c).** The skin is tough and flexible, consisting of scales that resemble miniature teeth **(d).**

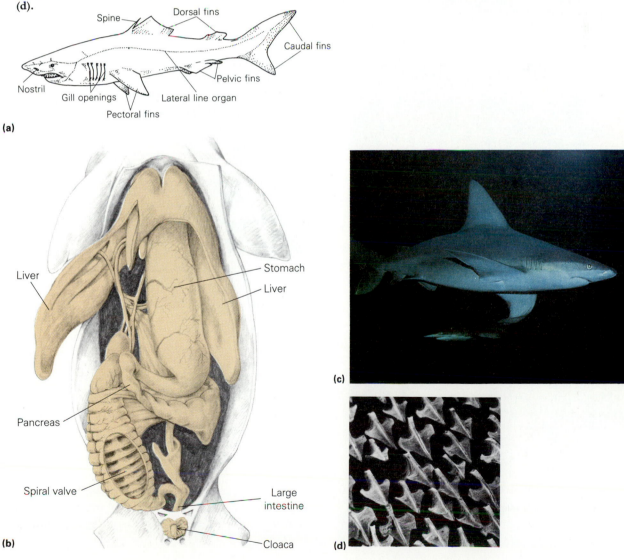

FIGURE 29.5 Most of the ray-finned fishes are similar in general body shape, with some variation in the fins. However, both the sea horse and angler fish of the deep differ quite markedly.

Flying fish

White-spot moray

Sturgeon

Lined seahorse

Ocellated frogfish

diverse group (Figure 29.5); presently, more than 20,000 species have been identified. We will consider the lobe-finned fishes and their enormous evolutionary impact after we compare bony fishes and sharks.

Bony Fishes

Some bony fishes may have a sharklike, "torpedo" appearance, but the two are not closely related (Figure 29.6). For example, the fins of bony fishes, especially the ray-finned fishes, are generally much more delicate and movable, with fan-shaped supporting elements. Such fins permit great maneuverability. The quick, darting movements of the bony fish are not possible in the shark.

Some bony fishes have a **swim bladder.** By controlling the gas volume in the bladder, the fish adjusts its buoyancy and is able to remain stationary at any depth. The swim bladder, surprisingly enough, is an evolutionary remnant of paired lungs, dating back to the time when the distant ancestors of modern bony fishes evolved in shallow, stagnant waters.

The skin of most bony fishes is covered with scales and numerous mucous glands. The slimy mucus covering the body is quite important to swimming. Studies reveal that its presence reduces water friction by up to 65%.

Sharks and bony fishes also differ in how they respond to their salty environment. Sharks are **osmoconformers.** They retain enough of the nitrogen waste, urea, in their blood to balance the 3% salt of the surrounding sea. Bony fishes, like most vertebrates, are **osmoregulators.** They expend energy to actively secrete sodium chloride from special glands in the gills, thereby maintaining a much lower salt content in their body fluids (about 1%).

Gas exchange in nearly all fishes occurs in the gills, where oxygen dissolved in the water crosses the thin gill membranes to enter the moving bloodstream, and waste carbon dioxide diffuses out into the water (see Chapter 38). In bony fishes there are usually five pairs of gills. These are located in **gill chambers,** each of which is covered by a protective bony flap called the **operculum.**

Reproduction in bony fishes occurs in a variety of ways, from simple, brief acts of spawning—where males and females come together just long enough to release their gametes—to intricate premating behavior, nest-building, internal fertilization (in some groups), and vigorous care of the eggs and young.

Development in bony fishes is also highly varied. In **oviparous** (egg-laying) fishes, such as the cod, the eggs are simply released to be fertilized, and the nutrients needed by the embryo are provided by the egg. In toothcarps (the family of the common aquarium guppy) and other **ovoviviparous** fishes, fertilization is internal—and the egg is retained within the female for development. The young emerge from the cloaca fully developed. However, in ovovivipary, nourishment is still provided by food stores in the egg itself. Other species of toothcarp provide rare examples of fish that are truly livebearing, or **viviparous,** a system usually associated with mammals. In vivipary, some or all nourishment is provided by tissues in the mother's uterus.

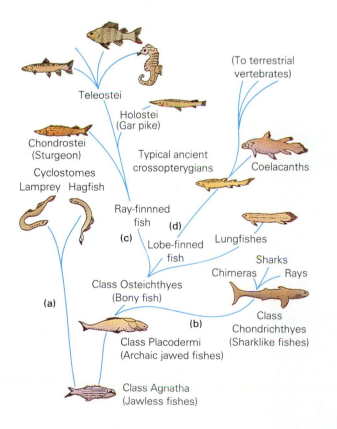

FIGURE 29.6 The phylogenetic tree of fishes. Four branches gave rise to (a) modern jawless fishes, (b) sharks and rays, (c) modern bony fishes, and (d) lobe-finned fishes. One line of lobe-fins is ancestral to the amphibians, from which reptiles, birds, and mammals arose.

Teleostei

Holostei (Gar pike)

(To terrestrial vertebrates)

Chondrostei (Sturgeon)

Cyclostomes Lamprey Hagfish

Typical ancient crossopterygians

Coelacanths

Ray-finned fish

(d)

(c)

Lobe-finned fish

Lungfishes

Sharks

Chimeras Rays

Class Osteichthyes (Bony fish)

(a)

(b)

Class Chondrichthyes (Sharklike fishes)

Class Placodermi (Archaic jawed fishes)

Class Agnatha (Jawless fishes)

Reproductive modes in vertebrates are **ovipary** (egg-laying), **ovovivipary** (egg retention with nourishment from egg reserves), and, in a few species, **vivipary** (placental support of embryo).

VERTEBRATES INVADE THE LAND

It was during the Devonian period that the bony fishes diverged into two separate groups: the ray-finned fishes and the lobe-finned fishes (see Figure 29.6). The ray-finned fishes quickly became the predominant group in waters around the world. The lobe-finned fishes didn't do as well and are rare today, but other descendants took some rather interesting evolutionary turns.

Lobe-Finned Fishes: A Dead End and a New Opportunity

The Devonian lobe-finned fishes were unusual in that they had a nasal opening that extended into the mouth (instead of dead-ending in a nasal sac, as in most fishes), and they had lungs as well as gills. (It seems peculiar that lungs first evolved in fishes.) The lobe-fins were also unusual in that their fins were heavy, fleshy appendages, probably best suited for resting on the muddy bottoms of shallow ponds or flapping along mud flats in search of deeper waters. In time the early lobe-fins diverged into two lines, one of which includes today's bizarre **lungfishes.** These sluggish, air-gulping oddities live in highly restricted shallow ponds in Australia, Africa, and South America. They are unusual in that they have retained the air-breathing lung, which in most fishes

has become the swim bladder. Thus these fish can hibernate in mud and remain active in water so stagnant that it lacks the oxygen most fishes require.

The second line of lobe-finned fishes, the **crossopterygians** ("fringed-wing ones"), and their close relatives, the **coelacanths,** died out in the Cretaceous period—at least that's what scientists thought until 1939, when a group of puzzled fishermen caught a live coelacanth—a species known as *Latimeria chalumnae*—in deep waters off of the east coast of South Africa. It was a startling find. These lobe-fins had survived for 80 million years. An intensive search began, and more of these "living fossils" have now been found (Figure 29.7).

With their heavy fins and their primitive lungs the early crossopterygians were in an ideal position to press on to new opportunities—those on the land. Great problems were associated with living in the drying air, so the first land invaders were **amphibians,** animals that spend part of the time on land and part in the water. We see evidence of the transition in fossils of the early lobe-finned fishes and the first amphibians (Figure 29.8).

> The ancestral terrestrial vertebrate line arose from a branch of lobe-finned fishes called **crossopterygians.** The same line produced the **lungfish** and **coelacanths.**

FIGURE 29.7 Coelacanths still exist off the coast of South Africa. *Latimeria,* a direct descendant of the crossopterygians, was long thought to be extinct.

FIGURE 29.8 By comparing ancient amphibian fossils and fossils of lobe-finned crossopterygians, we can see how the transition to land life might have occurred. For example, the first use of lobe fins as walking appendages may have simply involved getting from pond to pond, or even as a brief respite from relentless aquatic predators.

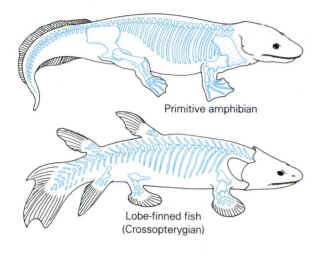

Primitive amphibian

Lobe-finned fish
(Crossopterygian)

THE TRANSITIONAL AMPHIBIANS

Those first fishy attempts to crawl out of the water were undoubtedly rather awkward, but the unfamiliar land must have offered some rewarding new opportunities, and some species were soon getting around with a certain ease (Figure 29.9). Some of the earliest efforts at developing locomotor structures are preserved in the modern salamander. Its frail upper limbs protrude nearly straight out to the side before angling down, and its body drags on the ground. (Try doing push-ups with your arms in this position.) It moves with an undulating, fishlike motion, its body first curving to the left and then to the right—an impressive show of vigor coupled with rather limited forward progress.

Amphibians reveal ancestral habits in other ways as well. For example, the thin, moist skin of amphibians contains dense capillary beds. This permits gases to be exchanged, augmenting the work of the limited, hollow lung. For this to work efficiently, the skin must be kept moist, so most amphibians must avoid dry places. (As we will see, there are exceptions.) In

FIGURE 29.9 The adaptation to terrestrial life involves the positioning of limbs in the tetrapods. Amphibians (a) such as the salamander and the newt have thin, lightly muscled legs splayed out to the side so that the body weight is borne on flexed joints. Reptiles (b) retain the legs alongside the body, and the limbs remain flexed as they carry the body weight. The bodies of mammals (c), the fastest moving land creatures, are raised above the ground, with the limbs essentially below them.

(a)

(b)

(c)

(a)

(b)

(c)

addition, many amphibians require water for reproduction. Such species fertilize the eggs externally, and the young develop in the water.

The amphibian heart has three chambers, one muscular **ventricle** (lower pumping chamber) and two smaller **atria** (upper receiving and pumping chambers). This organization differs from what is essentially a two-chambered heart in fishes. In the fish, blood is pumped from the single ventricle to capillary beds in the gills, where it is oxygenated. It then passes throughout the body, entering many capillary beds once more before returning to the single atrium for another trip. In amphibians, a second circuit is added for oxygenation (Figure 29.10).

Modern Amphibians

There are three existing orders of amphibians. The first two have been mentioned: the **Urodeles** ("with tails"—the salamanders); and the **Anurans** ("without tails"—the frogs and toads). The third order is the **Caecilians,** an obscure group of legless, worm-like tropical amphibians (Figure 29.11). Some species of urodeles and anurans have evolved toward an increasingly terrestrial life, while others have re-turned completely to the water, where they spend their entire lives.

There are some remarkable examples of specialization among the amphibians. For example, the desert spadefoot toad survives in its dry habitat by burrowing into the soil and waiting for one of the infrequent rains, whereupon it crawls out, quickly locates a temporary pond, and immediately mates. The offspring must develop quickly before the usual drought returns. As another example, while the young of most frogs and toads must develop in water, one species, *Pipa pipa,* the Surinam toad of South America, carries its fertilized eggs in moist pouches on its back, where the offspring completely develop.

Caecilians avoid the water problem altogether by actually copulating. The male has a copulatory organ and is able to deposit sperm directly into the female's cloaca. The eggs develop within the moist interior of the female, and the young caecilians are born fully formed.

Amphibians are transitional land-dwellers, most with moist skins used in gas exchange, simple saclike lungs, and external water-requiring fertilization.

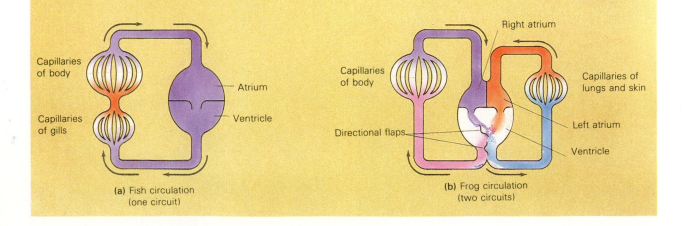

FIGURE 29.10 Schematic comparison of two- and three-chambered hearts. **(a)** The fish has a single circuit. Deoxygenated blood is received by the atrium, which delivers it to the ventricle. It is then pumped to the gill capillaries, where oxygenation occurs. From the gills the blood must pass through body capillaries before returning to the heart. **(b)** Two circuits are seen in the amphibian. Deoxygenated blood enters the right atrium of the three-chambered heart, from which it is pumped to the ventricle. Simultaneously, oxygenated blood enters the left atrium, and it too moves to the ventricle. The ventricle then pumps blood from the two sources to the lungs and body. Although it seems as though oxygenated and deoxygenated blood should totally mix in the single ventricle, a good separation is maintained by flaps and valves in the system.

Capillaries of body

Capillaries of gills

Atrium

Ventricle

(a) Fish circulation (one circuit)

Right atrium

Capillaries of body

Capillaries of lungs and skin

Directional flaps

Left atrium

Ventricle

(b) Frog circulation (two circuits)

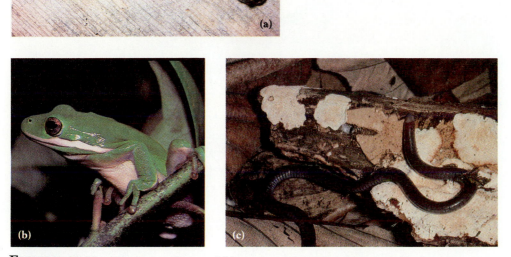

FIGURE 29.11 The three modern amphibian orders. Salamanders **(a)** are probably the most primitive representatives because of their body shape and limbs; but their method of reproduction is quite advanced. Frogs and toads **(b)** are reproductively primitive, but their limb structure is advanced. Caecilians **(c)** are in the minority, comprising only 160 species. They are nearly blind and lack limbs, using their wormlike bodies to burrow into the soil, but their reproductive mode is better adapted to land life.

REPTILES AND THE TRANSITION TO LAND

Amphibians and reptiles evolved from the same common ancestor, and the first reptiles probably appeared soon after the amphibians. The reptiles, however, took up an entirely different life-style. While the amphibians continued to exploit the planet's aquatic niches, the reptiles moved to the drier environment, eventually adapting to a completely terrestrial life.

One of the necessary adaptations was a tough, scaly, dry, water-repellent skin that controlled water loss and resisted wear. But this meant that the skin could no longer be used in gas exchange. Thus, a second adaptation included changes in the lung. Essentially, the lung's exchange surface was increased by the development of a spongy construction with many vascularized spaces, or **alveoli** (see Chapter 38).

On land, reptiles are swifter than salamanders because their legs do not act as simple pivots for the trunk muscles. Instead, reptile legs are very muscular. The muscles are necessary because reptile legs still tend to splay out to the side, bearing the animal's heavy weight at an awkward angle. But even large crocodilians can support their weight long enough for a remarkably quick dash to catch an unfortunate deer or dog—or human.

The greatest adaptive changes demanded of terrestrial reptiles were in their methods of reproduction and development. External fertilization was not possible on the dry and hostile land, so, like the caecilians, the reptiles developed the capacity for internal fertilization.

A new, drastically modified reproductive device—the **land egg**—first introduced by the early reptiles, was a vital adaptation to complete terrestrial life (Figure 29.12). The land egg was surrounded by a tough leathery shell (later replaced by a calcium shell in birds), which, while admitting air, protected the

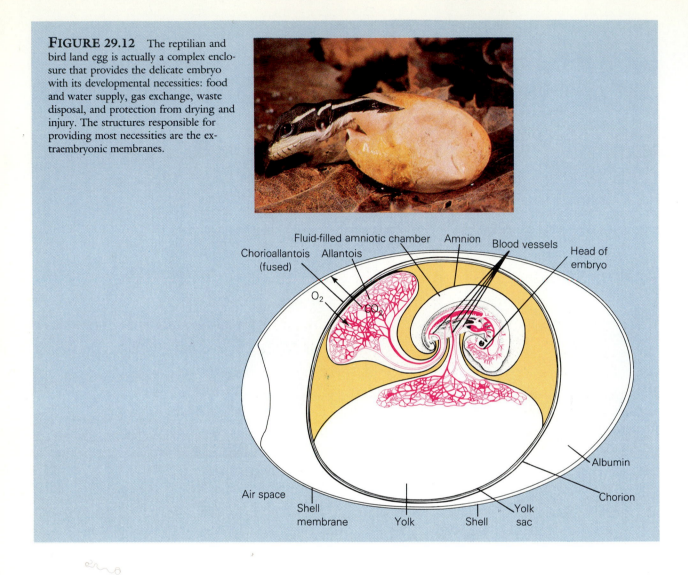

FIGURE 29.12 The reptilian and bird land egg is actually a complex enclosure that provides the delicate embryo with its developmental necessities: food and water supply, gas exchange, waste disposal, and protection from drying and injury. The structures responsible for providing most necessities are the extraembryonic membranes.

Fluid-filled amniotic chamber
Chorioallantois (fused)
Allantois
Amnion
Blood vessels
Head of embryo
O₂
CO₂
Albumin
Chorion
Air space
Shell membrane
Yolk
Shell
Yolk sac

embryo against desiccation and mechanical injury. Included within the egg was a supply of water and food, everything necessary for the embryo's development.

A second and equally important developmental adaptation involved the embryo itself. The developing reptile (and bird) produces a number of supporting **extraembryonic membranes,** with vast networks of blood vessels. The **yolk sac,** an extension of the embryo's gut, brings in food; the **chorion,** a thin but extensive membrane, exchanges respiratory gases; the **allantois,** an extension of the urinary bladder, receives and stores solid nitrogenous wastes (later in development, it fuses with the chorion and aids in gas exchange); and the **amnion** encloses the embryo, providing a protective, water-filled environment. All of these extraembryonic membranes are left behind when the animal hatches and leaves the egg.

The Age of Reptiles

Reptiles have faded somewhat from the stage, but they certainly had their day. In fact, the entire Mesozoic era, which lasted 160 million years (see Table 29.1), is referred to as the "Age of Reptiles." There were, indeed, many successful lines, each exploiting the planet in its own way.

By the start of the Mesozoic era (225 million years ago), the trend toward large size was well underway, and as time went on, natural selection favored even larger species. Even the flying reptiles—the **pterosaurs**—produced a giant called *Pteranodon*, which was about the size of a small airplane. Some of the great beasts were carnivores, and they were well equipped with huge claws and teeth like steak knives. The most fearsome of great reptiles was *Tyrannosaurus rex* ("tyrant lizard"), probably the largest terrestrial carnivore that ever lived. Although larger dinosaurs stalked the earth, these were herbivores. Even the foliage of very tall trees did not escape *Diplodocus,* which was 30 m long (98 ft) and weighed about 30 metric tons (33 tons) (Figure 29.13).

Exit the Great Reptiles

About 65 million years ago, at the end of the Mesozoic era, the great reptiles suddenly disappeared. The sudden passing of these reptiles has long presented a great puzzle. What could have caused such a massive extinction? Hundreds of hypotheses have been considered. For a time, the favored idea was that the dinosaurs were simply outcompeted by emerging numbers of smaller, more intelligent mammals of the time. Or perhaps, some thought, the furry little rascals ate so many eggs that the dinosaurs died out. Other ideas involved drastic climatic changes at the close of the Mesozoic era. The problem is that none of the explanations could account for the dramatic *suddenness* of the mass extinction or the fact that so many other species died out with them. (Essay 29.1 considers a rather startling answer to the riddle.)

> During the Mesozoic era, the age of reptiles, major evolutionary lines produced the great dinosaurs and the ancestors of today's reptiles, birds, and mammals.

Modern Reptiles

The four orders of modern reptiles (Figure 29.14) probably descended from four general lines of ancient reptiles. One line produced the turtles and the side-necked turtles. A second line produced the crocodiles and alligators. A third led to the lizards, monitor lizards, and snakes. A final reptilian evolutionary line is represented by only one living species, *Sphenodon punctatus,* the tuatara of New Zealand, whose third eye, a crude light receptor (the **pineal eye**), on the top of its head makes it one of the world's strangest creatures.

BIRDS TAKE TO THE AIR

The ancestors of modern birds can be traced back about 180 million years to the early Jurassic period (see Table 29.1). *Archaeopteryx,* the oldest known fossil bird, had feathers and presumably could fly (Figure 29.15).

It takes a great deal of evolutionary change for a reptile to fly, and birds have certainly changed from their reptilian stock. However, beneath their obvious flight modifications lie many ancient reptilian traits. Their legs, for example, are still covered with reptile-like scales. And feathers, complex as they are in today's birds, can be traced back to reptilian scales.

FIGURE 29.13   The ruling reptiles of the Mesozoic era included some of the largest animals ever to roam the land and take to the air.

No one knows what triggered the mass extinctions that heralded the end of the Mesozoic era. One explanation, though, springs from peculiar findings in the earth's crust. There are places in the crust where a stratum—a geological boundary—was formed 65 million years ago, marking the end of the Mesozoic and the beginning of the Cenozoic era. In the waters off Gubbio, Italy, the marine deposits are particularly well defined. Below this geological boundary, in the Mesozoic strata, are carbonate rocks containing many types of plankton skeletons, particularly very large foraminifera—early protists (Chapter 21).

But just above the boundary, in the rocks deposited in the early Cenozoic era, the life forms change drastically. Here, there are fewer and much smaller species. And there is something else in these rocks. At the boundary itself is a single layer of clay about a centimeter thick.

In 1980, paleontologist Walter Alvarez, along with his father, Luis Alvarez (a physicist and Nobel prize winner), noted that this thin layer of clay has peculiar concentrations of some unusual elements. In particular there is about 50 times more iridium and platinum in the clay than one would expect. Iridium is extremely rare on earth, but it is a common metal in meteors and asteroids. Why would iridium suddenly appear in the rocks being formed at the very time the dinosaurs were dying? The **Alvarez hypothesis,** as it has come to be known, suggests that an asteroid collided with the earth some 65 million years ago. The force was enough to vaporize the object, sending iridium into the atmosphere, later to fall, forming a sediment. Other research has supported the Alvarez hypothesis. In 1987, crystals from several places around the world were discovered that had been subjected to incredible stress. They contained fractures that could only have been produced by pressures of over 1.3 million pounds per square inch. Such pressures exist naturally on the earth only at the sites of meteor impacts. Apparently these small crystals were thrown out of the earth's atmosphere to reenter like ballistic missiles.

Judging from the amount of iridium found in that thin layer, the Alvarezes calculated that the Mesozoic asteroid was about 10 km (six miles) in diameter. A rock six miles across would certainly bring a quick end to any creature it happened to hit, but it may have also brought an end to the Mesozoic era.

The dust thrown up by such an impact would block out much of the sun's rays and darken the earth for months. With the darkness, photosynthesis could not occur, and the life that depends on it would begin to die. Some creatures would succumb to the freezing, wintry days on a darkened earth.

Only certain kinds of life would survive such events, and the clearing skies would have revealed a new kind of earth. Some species would have been untouched, such as marine plankton, which could form resistant spores, and the tough, protected seeds of plants. Many kinds of birds also somehow got through the event. Even some reptiles survived, although, for some reason, all species that weighed over 26 kg (about 60 lb) were eradicated.

The accident would have caused great shifts in the current of life as new niches opened over the entire planet. The remaining living things would have immediately spread out, taking advantage of new opportunities and adapting to their strange new world.

(a) Lizard   **(b)** Snake   **(c)** Turtles

(d) Crocodile   **(e)** Tuatara

FIGURE 29.14 There are four orders of reptiles today. (**a** and **b**) Lizards and snakes are members of the same order. (**c**) Turtles represent a second order. (**d**) The crocodile is a third, and (**e**) the tuatara represents the fourth order of living reptiles.

FIGURE 29.15 *Archaeopteryx,* the earliest known bird—or is it? Note the numerous teeth, long tail, and clawed fingers. Whatever it was, this pigeon-sized, rather weakly muscled animal was abundant in the Mesozoic era.

Today the feathers provide not only an aerodynamic flight surface but also insulation for a body that must carefully regulate its temperature. The upright, bipedal posture of birds, by the way, was already established in their thecodont ancestors.

More interesting, perhaps, are the specializations for flight developed by birds (Figure 29.16). The wrists and fingers have undergone extensive fusion and elongation, supporting the important primary flight feathers. The skeleton is light and strong. Many bones are hollow, containing extensive air cavities, and are crisscrossed with netlike, triangular bracings for strength. Further weight reduction occurs in the gonads. The weight of the testes is drastically reduced between breeding seasons (some 1500 times in starlings). The females have but one ovary. The largest flight muscles are found in active flyers such as the pigeon, where they make up about half of the body weight. In soaring birds, these muscles may be greatly reduced, but the tendons and ligaments that hold the wings in position are considerably strengthened.

The ancestral reptilian jaw has been drastically lightened, and teeth have been replaced with a light, horny bill. Bills vary enormously according to the feeding habits of the bird. The typical bird neck is long and flexible, and the bones of the trunk (pelvis, backbone, and rib cage) are fused into a semirigid unit. The breastbone is greatly enlarged and has a **keel** (a flattened, vertical bone) from which the large flight (breast) muscles originate. The tail is reduced, consisting of only four vertebrae. Finally, the feet are specialized in various ways for digging, swimming, grasping, running, or perching.

There are less obvious internal modifications for flight. Like mammals, birds are **homeothermic;** that is, they can maintain a relatively constant (and rather high) internal body temperature. Other vertebrates

FIGURE 29.16 Modifications for flight are seen in nearly every aspect of the bird's anatomy and physiology, from the streamlined form to the elevated metabolic rate. In spite of the demands placed upon it, the skeleton is extremely light. In general, the slender, hollow bones of birds have a deceivingly delicate appearance; in fact, however, they are strong and flexible, containing numerous triangular bracings within (see x-ray image). Part of the skeletal strength is due to fusion, as is seen in the hip girdle, tail vertebrae, and, most spectacularly, in the long finger bones. Flight feathers, which can weigh more than the skeleton, owe their extreme strength and flexibility to numerous vanes. These have an interlocking arrangement of hooklike barbules.

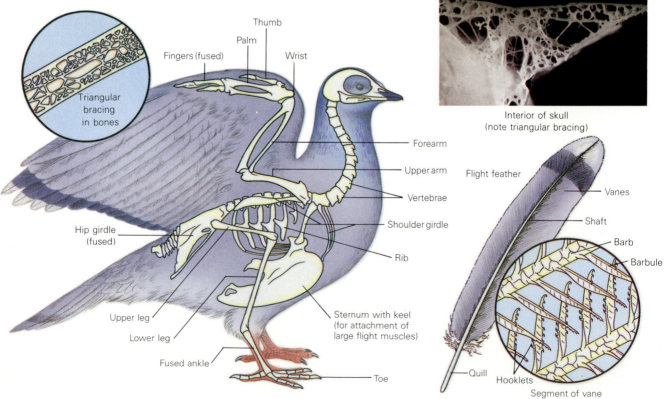

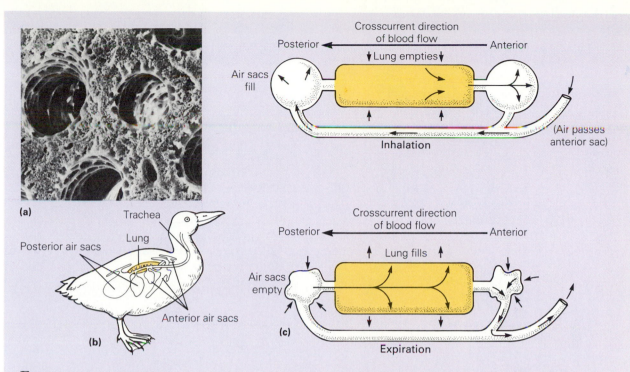

FIGURE 29.17 The extensive bird respiratory system includes posterior and anterior air sacs (a) that act as reservoirs and bellows for filling and emptying the lungs. Air flows *through* the lungs (b) rather than *in and out*, as in other air-breathing vertebrates. The one-way passage establishes a crosscurrent exchange of gases between the air and blood since they move in perpendicular directions. Oddly enough, the bird lung contracts on inhalation and expands on expiration (exaggerated here), but this is in response to expansion and contraction in the air sacs, rather than to air entering or leaving the body. (c) In the scanning EM of the lung tissue, cylinder-shaped parabronchi (branches of the bronchi) are surrounded by highly branched walls containing the capillaries.

are typically **poikilothermic;** the body temperature varies so that it is roughly the same as that of the surroundings. The constancy of temperature in birds and mammals is maintained at a metabolic cost, but it has permitted them to adapt to virtually all climates. Helping to meet birds' high metabolic requirements is an efficient four-chambered heart that ensures that oxygenated and deoxygenated blood follow fully separated pathways in the circulatory system. The birds' respiratory system is unique in that the air moves in a one-way flow through the lung (Figure 29.17), as opposed to the in-and-out movement of air in other vertebrates.

The flow of air in the bird lung opposes the flow of blood, and so a **crosscurrent exchange** is established. This results in a greater efficiency in the exchange of oxygen and carbon dioxide. Such efficiency is essential to flight at high altitudes where oxygen is less plentiful.

Birds continue the reptilian tradition of producing large, self-contained eggs. But as a rule, they produce fewer eggs than do reptiles, and tend to care for them more after laying them.

ANOTHER SUCCESS STORY: MAMMALS

The Age of Mammals

The reptiles owned the Mesozoic era, but mammals inherited the Cenozoic era, perhaps with a little help from an asteroid (see Essay 29.1). Whatever the cause, the survivors of that great extinction faced a new kind of world. With the extinction of the dinosaurs the mammals had countless new opportunities. They took advantage of what the new earth had to offer. Rapidly diverging and capitalizing on newly available resources, they established a variety of new niches for themselves.

Today, the surviving mammals are of three types (Figure 29.18): the **monotremes,** mammals that lay eggs; the **marsupials,** pouched mammals without true placentas; and the **placentals,** which constitute the great majority of mammals on all continents other than Australia. The placentals nourish their embry-

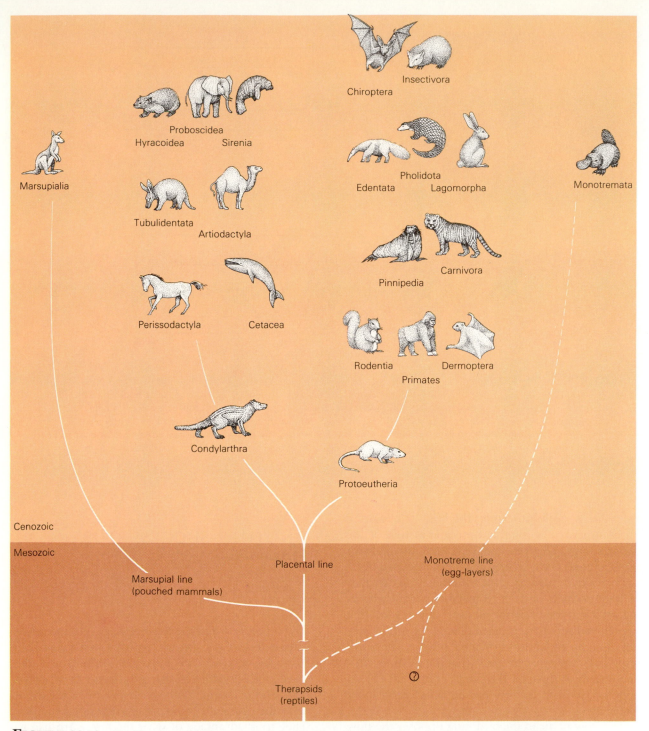

FIGURE 29.18 The 19 orders of modern mammals emerged from the Mesozoic era in three primary lines of descent: the egg-laying monotremes represented by the duckbilled platypus *(right)*, the pouched marsupials of Australia and New Zealand *(left)*, and the placental mammals *(center)*, which include 17 of the orders. The fossil record of monotremes is scanty, but they do have mammalian traits suggesting a similar origin *(dashed line)*. The marsupials entered the Cenozoic in their own line, and were once widespread in North America. Except for the opossum they were displaced by placental mammals. The marsupials were limited first to South America, then to Antarctica, and finally to Australia. They were isolated there, free from placental competition, by the final events of continental drift. The placental mammals entered the Cenozoic in two groups, represented in the early Cenozoic fossil record by *Condylarthra* and *Protoeutheria*.

os through a well-developed **placenta,** and give birth to relatively advanced young.

Modern Mammals

How did mammals become so well established in the Cenozoic era? Aside from a possible sigh of relief escaping from the mammals at the demise of the ruling reptiles, there is no explanation that doesn't arouse argument. But it does seem that mammals have evolved a particularly well matched group of critical traits that have enabled them to survive and flourish. If we concentrate on the placental mammals only, these traits include:

1. An efficient four-chambered heart supporting a constant, high body temperature and high metabolic rate.
2. Internal development, with the embryo nourished through a placenta.
3. Mammary glands (in the female) for milk production.
4. Specialized teeth and efficient jaws.
5. A muscular diaphragm separating the chest and abdominal cavities.
6. Hair.
7. A large and versatile brain.

The mammalian brain. Above all, the hallmark of a modern mammal is its brain. Modern mammals are "smarter" than other vertebrates; they rely less on genetically programmed instincts, basing much of their behavior on parental guidance, individual experience, and learning. Not only is the brain much larger in mammals than in reptiles, but the mammalian brain has parts not found in other vertebrates.

Keep in mind that increased learning capacity is only one evolutionary approach to survival; there are other adaptive routes. For example, the insects are our chief competitors for the earth's resources, and they have a comparatively limited ability to learn. But, obviously, the alternative path of evolution works well for them.

The story of the evolution of animals is indeed a fascinating one. Accounts such as this, though, must necessarily compress time so that we may be left with visions of some finny creature crawling ashore and growing fur before its tail left the water. Instead, we should remind ourselves that evolution is primarily a story of failure—slow failure. One "hopeful experiment" after another died at the water's edge.

The successes were not marked by suddenness or fanfare. They just continued on, changing all the while as sensitive cytoplasm responded to a wheedling environment. Such processes indeed led to successes, that is, to the continued existence of various lives, and one of those lives gave rise to the creature we will see next.

SUMMARY

Vertebrate characteristics include the vertebral column, highly centralized nervous system, closed circulatory system, two pairs of appendages, image-forming eyes, compact excretory system, and distinct sexes. The seven living classes include jawless fishes, cartilaginous fishes, bony fishes, amphibians, reptiles, birds, and mammals.

HUMBLE BEGINNINGS AND THE JAWLESS FISHES: CLASS AGNATHA

Ostracoderms, the first jawless fishes and first vertebrates, lived in Paleozoic. They were small, bottom dwelling, and armored. Survivors today include lamprey eels and hagfish. The lamprey larva resembles the more invertebrate chordates.

THE FIRST JAWS: CLASS PLACODERMI

The evolution of jaws in placoderms greatly expanded vertebrate niches. Jaws were derived from highly modified gill arches. Similar transitions can be seen in today's vertebrate embryos. Placoderms flourished for some 150 million years, some becoming whale size.

CARTILAGINOUS FISHES: CLASS CHONDRICHTHYES

Cartilaginous fishes lack bony skeletons, have tough, thin skins and powerful swimming muscles.

The Shark

Sharks have toothlike, placoid scales; replaceable, unsocketed teeth; simple, hingelike jaws; and a short digestive system with a spiral valve. The cloaca is a common urinary and reproductive opening. Fertilization is internal. In addition to smell and vision, sharks can detect electrical fields and water movement. Water movement is detected by the lateral line organ.

THE BONY FISHES: CLASS OSTEICHTHYES

Bony fishes include ray-finned and lobe-finned types. Although rare today, a branch of the latter produced the first terrestrial vertebrates.

Bony Fishes

Bony fishes have small ray-fins (greater agility), a swim bladder (buoyancy control), osmoregulation (through salt excretion), and a bony operculum (gill flap). Reproduction in bony fishes is through simple ovipary (egg laying), ovo-vivipary (retaining eggs until hatching), and (rarely) vivipary (retention and providing food and gas exchange for embryos).

VERTEBRATES INVADE THE LAND: THE TETRAPODS

Lobe-Finned Fishes: A Dead End and a New Opportunity

Lobe-finned fishes include lungfishes—freshwater species that gulp surface air into lungs and one marine species, the coelacanth. A related line produced the amphibians. The heavy, fleshy fins were forerunners of terrestrial limbs.

TRANSITIONAL VERTEBRATES: THE AMPHIBIANS

Some amphibians have primitive limb structure; most exchange gases across the skin and in simple, hollow lungs; many require water for development—the young going through a larval or tadpole state. Amphibians have a three-chambered heart, with a separate respiratory circuit.

Modern Amphibians

Amphibian orders include salamanders, frogs, toads, and caecilians (legless). Advanced terrestrial adaptations include desert survival by hibernation and rapid reproductive cycles, development in body pouches, and copulation rather than external fertilization.

REPTILES AND THE TRANSITION TO LAND

Reptilian terrestrial adaptations include a dry, waterproof skin and a spongy lung (great surface area). The outer skin is shed to permit growth. Reptilian legs are strong and better adapted to walking and running. All copulate and fertilize internally. Typically, embryos develop in special land eggs, supported by extraembryonic membranes (yolk sac, chorion, allantois, and amnion).

The Age of Reptiles

Reptile diversity peaked during the Mesozoic era, the Age of Reptiles. Some flew, and others were the largest known terrestrial vertebrates.

Exit the Great Reptiles

Changing conditions at the end of Mesozoic led to the demise of the dinosaurs and the rise of mammals. Many different hypotheses explain the sudden extinction of ruling reptiles. Among the most controversial is one proposing that a huge asteroid, having struck the earth, produced enough dust to drastically alter the climate for many months.

Modern Reptiles

Four orders of living reptiles include turtles, crocodiles, and alligators, lizards and snakes, and *Sphenodon,* the tuatara.

BIRDS TAKE TO THE AIR

The oldest bird fossils are dated early Mesozoic. They arose from a line that also produced crocodilians. Flight modifications include feathers (flight surfaces and insulation), forelimb elongation and fusion, hollowing and crossbracings in long bones, loss of teeth and lengthening of neck, fusion and reduction in trunk bones, sternum enlargement and keel formation (attachment of flight muscles), reduction in gonads, and specialization in bills and feet. Physiological changes include homeothermy (warm bloodedness) and a unique one-way, crosscurrent flow of air in the lungs. The bird embryo is supported by a reptilelike land egg and extraembryonic membranes.

ANOTHER SUCCESS STORY: MAMMALS

The Age of Mammals

Mammals began their greatest divergence in early Cenozoic, forming three lines: egg-laying monotremes, pouched marsupials, and placental mammals.

Modern Mammals

Mammalian traits include a four-chambered heart, constant (warm) body temperature, placental support of the embryo, mammary (milk) glands, specialized, socketed teeth, muscular diaphragm, hair. A large brain makes learning and complex behavior possible.

KEY TERMS

vertebral column	ray-finned fish	coelacanth	allantois
ostracoderm	swim bladder	ventricle	amnion
lamphrey	osmoconformer	atria	pterosaur
hagfish	osmoregulator	Urodele	pineal eye
cartilage	gill chamber	Anuran	keel
placoid scale	operculum	Caecilian	homeothermic
spiral valve	oviparous	alveoli	poikilothermic
cloaca	ovoviviparous	land egg	crosscurrent exchange
clasper	viviparous	extraembryonic membrane	monotreme
lateral line organ	lungfish	yolk sac	marsupial
lobe-finned fish	crossopterygian	chorion	placental

REVIEW QUESTIONS

1 List six important vertebrate characteristics. (p. 472)

2 List the eight vertebrate classes and representative species. Which class is extinct?

3 Describe the first vertebrates. Name the two surviving members. (pp. 472–473)

4 In general, what effect did the evolution of jaws have on vertebrate opportunities? Did this innovation persist? (p. 473)

5 Explain the theoretical derivation of jaws. What supporting evidence do we find in today's vertebrate embryos? (p. 473)

6 Briefly describe the following aspects of shark anatomy: skin, teeth, digestive tract, reproductive structures. (p. 474)

7 Name the two major lines of bony fishes. Which is apparently most common today? Name five or six examples. (pp. 475, 477)

8 The following in bony fishes: fin structure and movement, maintaining buoyancy, osmoregulation, gas exchange. (p. 477)

9 Explain the differences between the oviparous, ovoviviparous, and viviparous modes of reproduction. (p. 477)

10 To which major grouping of bony fishes do lungfish belong? In what ways are they different from other bony fishes? (p. 478)

11 How many known species of crossopterygians exist today? What was the most important thing about this evolutionary line? (p. 478)

12 Describe limb position in salamanders. Why is this considered to be primitive? (p. 479)

13 List several characteristics of amphibians that seem to link them to aquatic ancestors. (pp. 478–480)

14 What respiratory provision does the three-chambered heart make possible? Is a complete separation of oxygenated and deoxygenated blood possible? Explain. (p. 480)

15 List the modern amphibian orders and representatives. Which group appears most specialized for terrestrial life? (p. 480)

16 Briefly discuss two examples of terrestrial reproductive adaptations in amphibians. (p. 480)

17 Describe terrestrial adaptations in the reptilian skin and respiratory system. How are the two tied together? (p. 481)

18 Of what importance is copulation to terrestrial adaptation? (p. 481)

19 What provisions do the reptiles make for development of the embryo outside the mother? (p. 482)

20 Where do the extraembryonic membranes originate? List them and mention their functions. (p. 482)

21 In what era did the reptiles peak? What was the apparent physical trend at this time? Provide examples. (pp. 482–483)

22 List three possible reasons for the demise of the dinosaurs. (p. 483)

23 List five specific modifications for flight seen in the bird skeleton. (pp. 483, 486)

24 List two ways in which the bird reproductive system is modified for the lightness required by flight. (p. 486)

25 Describe the heart and respiratory system in the bird and explain how their advanced state relates to the bird's metabolic requirements. (pp. 486–487)

26 When did mammals undergo their most dramatic divergence? Name the three lines they formed. (p. 487)

27 List seven important characteristics of mammals. Which of these is unique to the class? (p. 489)

30

HUMAN EVOLUTION

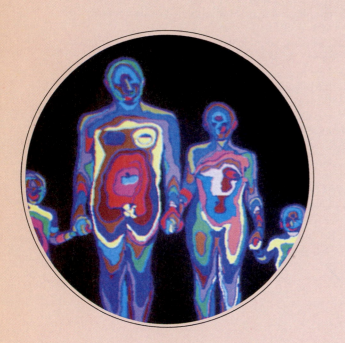

Much of the great debate about evolution occurs because of the sporadic surging of religionists against the bulwark of scientific evidence and opinion. Probably few people would be drawn to the fray, however, if scientists restricted themselves to worms and moles. Yet, when the principles of evolution are applied to other species, humans are bound to find themselves under this great explanatory umbrella as well. A lot of people resent being placed in the shade with the worms and moles and do not believe they share the expectations of other creatures. In their desire to be set apart the arguments begin. Those who are curious about scientific thinking, though, often begin with questions. Some questions currently being asked are:

When did the first human appear?
Did we really evolve from apes?
Are we still evolving?

The answers are, respectively, *it depends on what you mean by human; probably not in the way you're thinking;* and *yes, but things have gotten very complicated.* If these answers seem arbitrary and vague, it's because we are now dealing with a subject that has a remarkable ability to draw out deep emotions, one with a long history of conflicting ideas.

PRIMATE ORIGINS

Humans are, of course, primates, so we might best begin to trace our origins by reviewing what we know about our taxonomic order. **Primate** fossils, like those of most other placental mammals, first appear in the Paleocene deposits, formed about 60 to 65 million years ago, soon after the dinosaur extinction and the onset of the great mammalian expansion. The earliest primates, with their long snouts and claws, somewhat resembled modern tree shrews or even rodents. In fact, they may have occupied ecological niches similar to those of modern rodents, with some primate species living in trees and others scurrying about on the ground or living in burrows. People in technologically advanced societies may be a bit embarrassed to think of how many grubs our ancestors ate.

By the beginning of the Eocene epoch (about 60 million years ago), primates began to resemble those existing today. They had become primarily fruit eating and tree dwelling, and there was a general shortening of the snout, a more forward location of the eyes, and a more definite primate tooth structure. Toward the middle of the Miocene epoch, about 20 million years ago, lines that lead to all modern primate families (including **Hominoidea**—apes and humans) were well established (Figure 30.1).

Modern Primates

Primates differ from other mammals in a number of ways—for example, in their limbs. Most primates are well adapted for **arboreal** (tree-dwelling) life, as evidenced by their **prehensile** (grasping) hands and feet, long arms, and, in the case of the New World monkeys, prehensile tails.

But life in the trees had demanded other changes as well. Selection favored a more frontal location of the eyes, which improved both binocular and stereoscopic vision. With both eyes focused on an object, a fine, three-dimensional image could be produced that permitted more accurate estimates of distance.

Coupled with this visual precision was an acute eye-hand coordination, which undoubtedly continued to develop as visual information became more and more "informative." These traits are obviously important if one is to swing through the trees (Figure 30.2).

Such anatomical specializations would require a substantial degree of simultaneous brain development, with strong emphasis on brain centers dealing with coordination and vision. For example, we can propose that as the hand developed and became increasingly dexterous, its use would have gone beyond simply keeping the animal from falling out of trees. The hand could be used in other ways, but learning these would have demanded a correspondingly more complex (larger) brain. Such a brain might then discover new uses for the hand, but then an even more advanced brain would have been

FIGURE 30.1 This tentative phylogeny of the primates places *Plesiadapis* at the base. The earliest branches produced the tree shrew and prosimian lines, followed next by the New World monkeys. These two groups represent the greatest divergence in the living primates. Old World monkeys diverged some 10 million years later, subsequently followed by the great apes. The most recent divergence occurred between humans and chimpanzees.

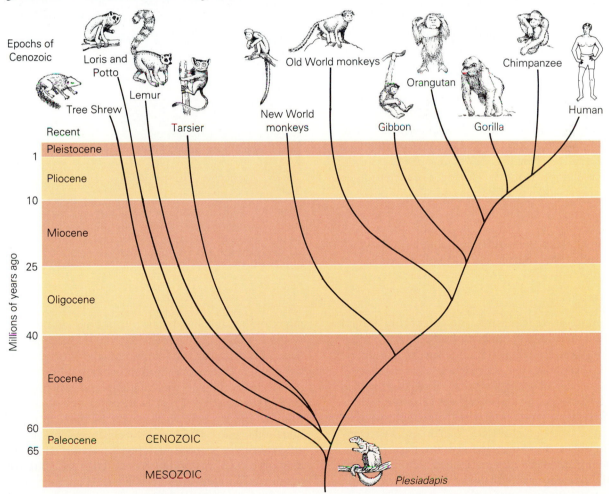

(a) Gibbon

(b) Hands and feet of orangutan

FIGURE 30.2   Brachiation (swinging from limb to limb) requires prehensile hands, long arms, stereoscopic vision, and hand-eye coordination.

required. Hand and brain development, then, might have occurred in a kind of positive feedback system in early primate evolution.

Primates tend to be omnivores, eating all sorts of food, and their mouths are relatively unspecialized. However, with the exception of humans, primates—particularly the males—have rather large canine teeth. These are used primarily in aggressive encounters with other male primates and in defense against predators (Figure 30.3). Human canines have become reduced in size, probably an adaptation to a changing diet. Their loss has since been more than compensated for by the development of such tools as rocks, spears, knives, and cruise missiles.

> **P**rimates have prehensile hands and feet, binocular, stereoscopic vision, good hand-eye coordination, and extensive learning capacity.

Human specializations.   It might be argued that human evolution has been markedly more mental than physical. This is because many of our physical traits are those of a generalist (a nonspecialist)—ones expected in a species with a high intelligence that tends to live an opportunistic existence. So, as our intelligence presents us with many opportunities, our generalized bodies are able to help us take advantage of them. Our principal evolutionary achievements outside of the nervous system are our **bipedal gait** and our **opposable thumb,** which can touch any

FIGURE 30.3   The large canines of many primates are important defensive weapons. They are often displayed to potential adversaries as a warning. In baboons, canines also are used in killing prey—often young mammals—to supplement their vegetable diet.

finger of the same hand. The upright human posture is quite unlike that of any other living primate. Savannah chimpanzees sometimes stand to see over tall grass, and they may walk bipedally a short way, but normally the apes are **quadrupedal,** walking on all fours (Figure 30.4). It is amusing to see an ape running on its rear legs, partly because it is so humanlike and yet so ungainly. Humans, however, are beautifully adapted to bipedal walking and running. We owe this ability to our enlarged **gluteus maximus** (buttock) and, in part, to our uniquely specialized foot with its springlike arched construction and broad first toe. Interestingly, a human sprinter can outrun a horse over 100 m (horses are slow getting started), and a marathon runner can outrun a horse in a 50 km race. Horses tire first. But on a 2 km (1.25 mi) run, bet on the horse.

As for the human thumb, it is merely a refinement of a specialization that is possessed, to some degree, by other primates. Originally, the opposable thumb evolved as an adaptation for grasping branches. But in most primates it is relatively short, poorly muscled, and much less capable of precise movement. The human thumb has evolved special musculature and can be rotated readily. Apes can be trained to use simple tools and to open beer cans, but they are comically clumsy all the same. With our much greater manual dexterity, we can make precise tools, even from rocks and sticks if we must, and many of us have been known to open beer cans with great dexterity. Other animals have been reported to use or even make tools, although the definition of "tool" must be stretched to include such things as the stone upon which a sea otter smashes a clam, or the twig that a chimpanzee uses to probe termite nests and to extract the excited insects. But no other species can build a watch that works or make tools that are used just to make other tools. To worry about how much of this has to do with thumbs and how much has to do with brains is to miss the point—which is that our intelligence and our manual dexterity evolved together.

Human anatomical specializations provide for upright posture, bipedal gait, thumb and hand dexterity, and keen hand-eye coordination.

Our intelligence has not evolved without costs. Like other mammals, we are born in a helpless state, but human infants seem to be particularly helpless, with fewer built-in adaptive responses than infants of

FIGURE 30.4 (a) Apes can assume a bipedal posture, but neither their hip nor leg structure supports this posture very well. In bipedal walking, the weight is borne on the outer edge of the archless foot. (b) The hands of humans and chimpanzees appear generally similar, but there are important differences. Chief among these are the length and musculature of the thumb. In the chimpanzee, the thumb doesn't quite reach the base of the forefinger, while in humans the thumb extends nearly to the middle joint.

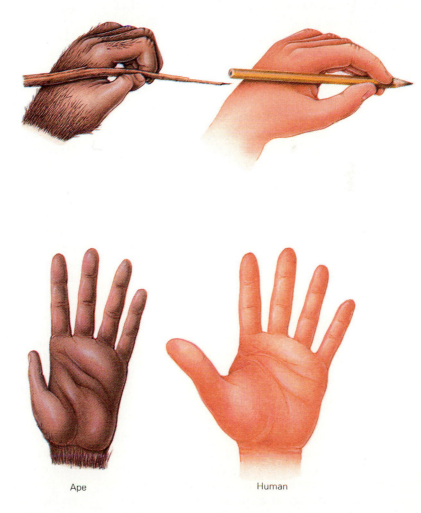

(a)

Ape   Human

(b)

many other species. A baby hare, for example, will lunge and hiss at an intruder. Newborn antelopes follow their mothers within minutes, and infant baboons quickly learn to ride on their mothers' backs. Virtually all baby primates will hold onto their mother's hair, so that she can move with ease. In comparison, our newborns seem witless and almost completely helpless. (And in what other species do 20-year-old offspring demand so much?)

Even the extensive development (some say *over*development) of the human brain merely extends a long-standing trend in mammalian and especially primate evolution. Over the millions of years, the consistent trend in most mammalian orders has been toward larger and larger brains. This is accompanied by a greater capacity for learning and for versatile behavior at the expense of stereotyped, genetically based, instinctive behavior.

The importance of intelligence to humans, coupled with our complex and highly interactive social system, has led to another unusual trait in our species: the development of language. Of course, wolves howl, birds sing, and bees "tell" each other the location of food by complex dances. And there are controversial reports that apes or dolphins can learn various nonverbal means of communicating with humans. However, humans so far can claim exclusive rights to the ability to communicate abstract ideas.

Humans also have an enormous capability for mathematics, some of us more than others. Why or how this ability evolved is not easy to fathom. Careful neurological measurements reveal that the human brain has a highly localized site for the process of multiplication—and an entirely different, equally localized site for long division. What these specialized parts of the brain were doing just a few thousand years ago, before mathematics had been invented, is anybody's guess.

> The large human brain provides for a large capacity for learning, verbal communication, the ability to deal in abstract thought.

THE HUMAN LINE

In the early 1960s, comparisons of proteins clearly indicated that humans are related more closely to African chimpanzees and gorillas than to Asian orangutans. Researchers were aware that such molecules as these change at a constant and predictable rate, and thus were able to provide us with kind of a molecular "clock" (see Chapter 19). This clock suggested that humans and African apes diverged from a common ancestor not more than five million years ago. The suggestion was startling at the time; anthropologists had always assumed that the separation had occurred much earlier. And so these findings were met with skepticism and in some cases, outright hostility. However, other data—both biochemical and paleontological—began to appear that supported the newer findings, and so we have adjusted our notions of human lineage.

The current theory is that about 3.5 to 4 million years ago, humanlike forms began to appear in the open grasslands of eastern and southern Africa. Fossils suggest that the line eventually consisted of four species, all of which have now been assigned to the genus *Australopithecus*. The name, which means "southern ape," is unfortunate in light of today's thinking, but let's see what they were like and what became of them.

The Australopithecines

The **australopithecines** (members of the genus *Australopithecus*) were rather small-boned, light-bodied creatures, about 1 to 1.5 m (3.5 to 5 ft) tall. They had humanlike teeth and jaws with small incisors and canines, and they walked upright (Figure 30.5). They apparently hunted baboons, gazelles, hares, birds, and giraffes. The australopithecine **cranial capacity** (a measure of brain size) ranged from 450 to 650 cc, as compared with 1200 to 1500 cc for modern adult humans.

To date, four species of australopithecines have been named. While their phylogeny is still tentative, a number of physical anthropologists go along with the scheme seen in Figure 30.6. There we see *Australopithecus afarensis* placed in a position of extreme importance, that of the common **hominid** (human) ancestor. According to this scheme the *A. afarensis* line produced two or three branches, one of which led to the genus *Homo*, which includes modern humans. The other line or lines produced *A. africanus*, *A. robustus*, and *A. boisei*.

A. boisei and *A. robustus*, as the latter's name implies, were larger boned—though not taller—than *A. africanus*, the oldest of the three. Most strikingly, the two newer arrivals had much larger jaws and teeth with greatly expanded cheek bones to accommodate the massive jaw muscles. These features reach their extreme in *A. boisei*. From a traditional view this progression may seem to be backward—toward an apelike condition—but other physical evidence and dating are to the contrary. The shape of the teeth and

FIGURE 30.5 The australopithecines were rather small, from 1 to 1.5 m (3.5 to 5 ft) tall. They were heavy boned, suggesting strong muscularity and a weight of up to 68 kg (150 lb). Their heads appeared more apelike than humanlike, with a low cranial profile and little or no chin. However, the jaws were large and forward-thrusting.

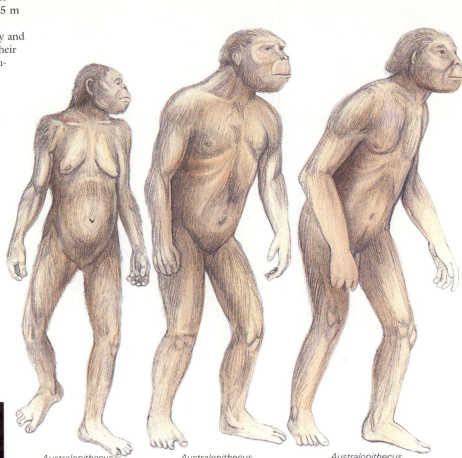

Australopithecus afarensis

Australopithecus robustus

Australopithecus africanus

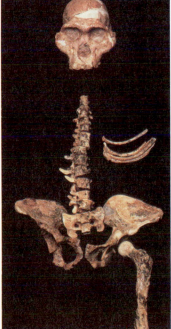

A. afarensis
(reconstructed from parts of several individuals)

A. robustus skull

A. africanus

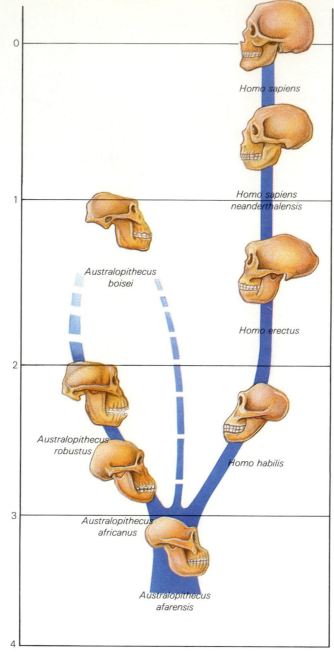

FIGURE 30.6 The known hominid history spans a period of nearly 4 million years. In a scheme based partly on the conclusions of Donald Johanson a line represented by *Australopithecus afarensis* produced a branch containing other australopithecines and one leading to *Homo*.

Homo sapiens

Homo sapiens neanderthalensis

Homo erectus

Australopithecus boisei

Homo habilis

Australopithecus robustus

Australopithecus africanus

Australopithecus afarensis

Millions of years ago

the curve in the jaws are decidedly human, not ape-like. The tooth wear, incidentally, suggests that much of the diet of these australopithecines consisted of plant food.

The first specimen of *A. afarensis,* the oldest known hominid (dubbed "Lucy" after a Beatles song from the '60s), was found in the northern Ethiopian desert region in 1974 by Donald Johanson. The fossil remains, estimated to be over 3 million years old, consisted of little more than half of the skeleton of an upright-walking female. The following year, Johanson's luck blossomed. He unearthed the remains of 13 more "Lucy" types, all in one area. After several years of puzzling over these slightly built creatures, Johanson reached a decidedly unorthodox yet insightful conclusion. He proposed that *A. afarensis* was indeed more primitive than other australopithecines, placing it at the base of the hominid tree. The idea, hotly contested at first, is now well accepted by many researchers.

Homo habilis

The earliest group to be placed squarely in the *Homo* line was **Homo habilis.** The group was represented by certain fossils found in Olduvai Gorge in Tanganyika, Africa, by the famed anthropologist Louis Leakey. The fossil remains show *H. habilis* to be clearly associated with tool making; crude tools were unearthed with their fossil skeletons. Critics have argued that the new find is simply a variant of the genus *Australopithecus* and that Leakey was unjustified in trying to include his fossils within the genus *Homo.* For the moment, though, *H. habilis* is placed in the early *Homo* line (see Figure 30.6).

Homo erectus

Even more recently, fossil beds of the eastern shore of Lake Turkana yielded fossils that are more similar to the modern human. The new species, called **Homo erectus,** is regarded as an extinct member of our own genus. The earliest African *H. erectus* skulls are known to be more than 1.5 million years old. What is most interesting about them is that they appear to be of the same species as some of the first hominid fossils ever found—those that were once called "Java Ape Man" and "Peking Man." The problem is that these fossils were only about half a million years old. Other *H. erectus* fossils have been found that may be

even less than 200,000 years old. In other words, *H. erectus* flourished, relatively unchanged, for well over a million years. Furthermore, during its first 300,000 years it coexisted with other more primitive hominid species, including the australopithecines and, possibly, *Homo habilis.* During at least the final 100,000 to 200,000 years of its existence, persistent members of *H. erectus* shared the planet with yet another species, **Homo sapiens.** Fossils of *H. erectus* have been found in China, Europe, and southern Africa, and, of course, East Africa. The evidence left by *H. erectus* provides fascinating grist for the mills of our imaginations.

H. erectus was obviously successful, but in time its tenure on the planet came to an end. Most passed from the earth just after the first glaciers of the Pleistocene epoch receded. At least one line of descendants is believed to have persisted, quietly changing and adapting and eventually leading to us. But there is still one more story to tell before we come to modern humans. The distribution of fossil hominids is seen in Figure 30.7.

A branch of the **hominid** line produced *H. habilis,* who was succeeded by *H. erectus. H. erectus* spread through the Old World and eventually gave rise to *H. sapiens.*

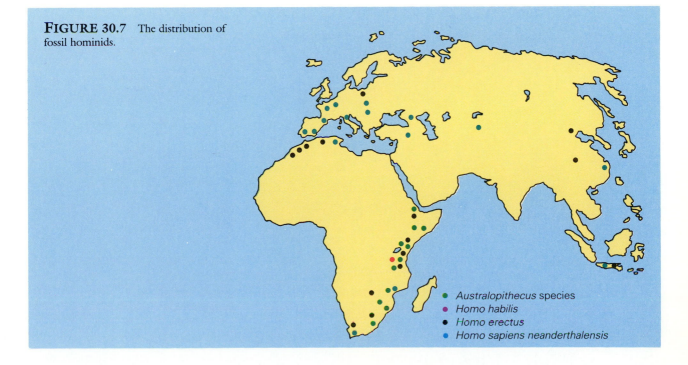

FIGURE 30.7 The distribution of fossil hominids.

- Australopithecus species
- Homo habilis
- Homo erectus
- Homo sapiens neanderthalensis

Neanderthals and Us

In 1856, while Darwin was puzzling over natural selection at his country estate, workmen in a steep gorge in the Valley of Neander (in German, *Neanderthal*) were pounding at a rock they didn't recognize. They finally saw that it was a skeleton, but by then it had been smashed to bits. Fortunately, they had left enough for researchers to study, and soon it was announced that there was clear evidence of a new and different kind of human. (Interestingly, a similar skull had been unearthed at Gibraltar a few years earlier but had not created much of a stir.)

Scientists are rarely at a loss for words, so an explanation of this peculiar find was immediately forthcoming. Professor E. Meyer of Bonn examined the heavy-browed skull, cleared his throat, and proclaimed that the skull and bone fragments belonged to a Mongolian cossack chasing Napoleon's retreating troops through Prussia in 1812. An advanced case of rickets had deformed his legs and had caused

him great pain. The pain had furrowed his brow and had produced the skull's great ridges. Because he was so distraught, he had crawled into a cave to rest, but, alas, he died.

This scenario now has been rejected in favor of the idea that the bones were those of an early form of human that became extinct—the so-called **Neanderthal man**—and that the skeleton's unusual features were actually common to the whole group. (Interestingly, the individual who originally owned that skeleton did indeed have rickets. Perhaps it was hard to get enough sunshine while living in a cave in Northern Europe during an Ice Age.)

At first, Neanderthal fossils seemed to show exactly what anyone of the 19th century would expect of an "ape-man." Neanderthals were depicted as being heavy boned and heavy browed, with low foreheads, wide faces, and little or no chin. "Reconstructions" drawn in the 19th and early 20th centuries always showed ugly, stooped, hairy, apelike bodies,

FIGURE 30.8 In a face-to-face confrontation **(a)**, a modern human and the Neanderthal reveal many general similarities and some striking differences. In the Neanderthal, note the sloping of the forehead, the large brow ridges, and the receding lower jaw. The facial reconstruction **(b)** produces an image quite different from the traditional view of Neanderthal, long considered an apelike creature. (Copyright © Jay H. Matternes—Courtesy Science '81.)

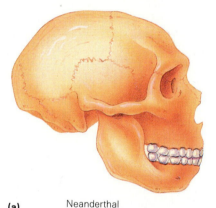

(a)   Neanderthal   Modern human

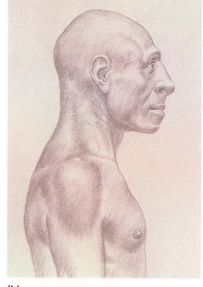
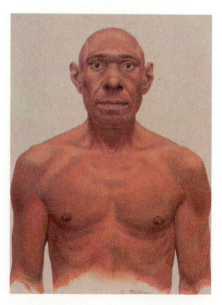

(b)

although we now know that the Neanderthal body was very similar to our own.

Later, it was found that, although the Neanderthals did indeed have large brow ridges, sloping foreheads, and small chins, their necks and bodies—when they didn't have rickets—were like ours (Figure 30.8). There is no way to know whether they had a spoken language, but we do know, from fossil pollens found with their remains, that Neanderthals sometimes covered their dead with flowers before burial. Whether or not that's sophisticated, it certainly is human—touchingly so.

Why did the Neanderthals disappear? One suggestion is that the classic (or more primitive) Neanderthal line and the line of modern humans diverged from each other as long as 250,000 years ago. For some reason, the Neanderthals flourished at the time the developing "sapiens" types were few in number. Then, about 40,000 years ago, the scarce *Homo sapiens sapiens* population suddenly burgeoned and expanded its range. This was when Neanderthal became extinct, possibly from attacks by *H. sapiens sapiens*.

A second theory suggests that the differences between the two groups were insignificant, because *H. sapiens* in the Neanderthal age was a highly variable species that included both the classic Neanderthal types as well as individuals much like ourselves. This theory implies that the Neanderthals were squarely in the mainstream of human evolution and not a dead-end side branch. The upshot is that modern humans evolved from Neanderthal ancestors. Therefore, the theory states, the Neanderthals didn't die out, but merely changed—into us.

Whatever the case, *Homo sapiens* became rather well established on earth, and, at the point record-keeping began, our account is called *history*. We will have more to say about our history, our present, and our future later. We deserve the attention, not only from an egotistical view, but because of the impact we had—and are continuing to have—on our limited planet.

SUMMARY

PRIMATE ORIGINS

Primate divergence from other mammals began in early Cenozoic, the earliest members resembling rodents. The divergence of modern families began just 20 million years ago.

Modern Primates

Primate characteristics include arboreal adaptations, prehensile hands, feet, and tails, improved frontal, stereoscopic vision, and good hand-eye coordination. Hand and brain evolution may have positively reinforced each other. Except for the canines, dentition is unspecialized.

Human specializations include a higher level of intelligence, an upright, bipedal posture and gait, and greater dexterity in the opposable thumb. The upright posture and gait is made possible by enlarged buttock muscles and the foot arch. Humans are not entirely unique as tool users but are the only animal that uses tools to fashion other tools.

Human development is slower than that of other primates, but the learning capacity is greater. Unique to humans is the use of complex language and abstracts such as writing and mathematics.

THE HUMAN LINE

Newer studies based on mutation rates and the molecular clock place the origin of the human line at only 5 million years. The australopithecines are known to have existed in the plains of Africa some 3.5 to 4 million years ago.

The Australopithecines

Australopithecines were smallish creatures, with cranial capacities generally about half that of modern humans. *A. afarensis,* the oldest, gave rise to two lines, one containing *A. africanus, A. robustus,* and *A. boisei.* The other began with *Homo habilis* and led to *H. erectus* and finally to *H. sapiens. A. afarensis* is the smallest. The other australopithecines were taller and had larger jaws.

Homo Habilis

One of Louis Leakey's discoveries, *H. habilis,* made crude tools and was a contemporary of the australopithecines.

Homo Erectus

The oldest fossils of *H. erectus* date at 1.5 million years, and they are known to have persisted until some 200 thousand years ago. In their last years they coexisted with *H. sapiens.* One line gave rise to *H. sapiens.*

Neanderthals and Us

Neanderthals closely resemble modern humans in stature and build, but the skull has larger brow ridges and a sloping forehead, and the chin is smaller. *H. sapiens neanderthalensis* ranged widely over Europe and Asia, persisting up until about forty thousand years ago. All newer fossils are of *H. sapiens sapiens.* Some anthropologists theorize that modern humans are one offshoot of *H. erectus* and that Neanderthal is another. Others state that modern humans are simply one of many variants of Neanderthal.

KEY TERMS

primate	bipedal gait	australopithecines	*Homo sapiens*
Hominoidea	opposable thumb	*Homo habilis*	Neanderthal man
arboreal	quadrupedal	*Homo erectus*	*Homo sapiens sapiens*
prehensile	gluteus maximus		

REVIEW QUESTIONS

1 From a close study of Figure 30.1 list the main divergences in the primate line and indicate when they occurred. What was the ancestor of all primates like?

2 List four important traits of most primates. (pp. 493–494)

3 Explain how evolutions of the eye and hand of primates reinforced each other over time. (pp. 494–495)

4 What is the theoretical significance of the large canines in most primates? (pp. 494)

5 Discuss human physical characteristics that go along with true upright posture and the bipedal gait. Do any other primates have these abilities? (pp. 494–495)

6 In what specific ways is the human thumb different from that of a chimpanzee? How might this have affected tool making and usage? (p. 495)

7 How does human tool use differ from that of other animals? (p. 495)

8 How has the human mental capacity affected the ability of newborn babies? Compare these abilities with those of other primate newborns. (pp. 495–496)

9 List three or four specific capabilities of humans that are not developed in other animals. (p. 496)

10 How long, according to recent molecular studies, have the hominids been around? What part of the world did hominids first inhabit? (p. 496)

11 Of the four species of australopithecines, which is probably the oldest? What happened to the australopithecine skull and jaw as evolution continued? (pp. 496–498)

12 With which hominid does the human line actually begin? How might this placement represent a departure from traditional thinking about the physical traits of the earliest humans? (pp. 496, 498)

13 Through what time period did *Homo erectus* extend? (p. 499)

14 From a look at Figure 30.7, comment on the success of *H. erectus*.

15 What is the traditional or historical notion of Neanderthal's appearance? Compare this to the modern view (Figure 30.8). (p. 500)

16 How long ago did Neanderthal cease to exist? Summarize the two theories about his demise. (p. 501)

V

ANIMAL REGULATION

31

VERTEBRATE SUPPORT AND MOVEMENT

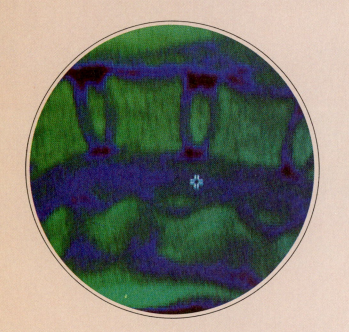

Now we focus our attention on the vertebrate body. But we must begin with the niggling awareness that there is no such thing as "the vertebrate body." Vertebrates are a highly varied group with a wide range of appearances. The most skilled physician might have difficulty performing an appendectomy on a turtle. Where would one begin to look?

On the other hand, all vertebrates have many traits in common. For example, they all obviously have backbones. The vertebrate head is always located at the anterior end of the body. The bodies of all vertebrates are composed of only a few types of tissues. The similarities continue even to the molecular level where we will find that the cell constituents of all vertebrates are remarkably similar, and even the chemical reactions that power the muscles reveal a common heritage.

VERTEBRATE TISSUES

There are four major types of vertebrate tissue: **epithelial tissue, connective tissue, muscle,** and **nerve.**

Epithelial Tissue

Epithelium, or **epithelial tissue,** forms the interior and exterior linings of most surfaces of the vertebrate organism. Wherever they are located, these tissues are commonly separated from other tissues below by a fibrous, noncellular **basement membrane.** Thus the **epidermis** ("outer skin") is epithelial, as are the linings of the mouth, the nasal cavities, the respiratory system, the coelom, the tubes of the reproductive system, the gut, and the interior of blood vessels. Some glands of the body are composed of thickened tissue called **glandular epithelium.** The cells there not only form the linings of the ducts but also produce the secretions that later will be released through the ducts to the exterior.

As you might expect, epithelial cells differ greatly from place to place, although there are only three main shapes: flattened, columnar, and cuboidal (Figure 31.1). In the epidermis, for example, we find an outer **stratified squamous epithelium,** containing many layers of flattened cells. The outermost cells are filled with the protein keratin and are hardened and dead. When these are shed as scales, they form dandruff and a startling proportion of household dust. The innermost cells of the epidermis, a living layer of relatively cuboidal cells, repeatedly divide to provide new cells to the flattened layers above.

FIGURE 31.1 Epithelial cells form linings that may be arranged in a simple, flattened layer (**a**) or one that is stratified (layered) (**b**), as seen in places of rapid wear. Cells lining the respiratory passages (**c** and **d**) often contain columnar cells, some of which may be ciliated or mucus secreting. The secretory linings (**e**) of glands are also formed by epithelial cells.

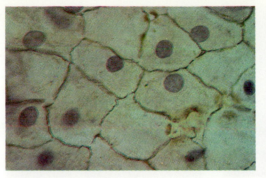
(a) Squamous cuboidal cells

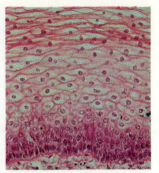
(b) Stratified cuboidal cells

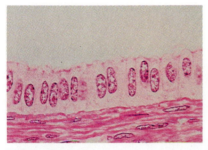
(c) Columnar cells

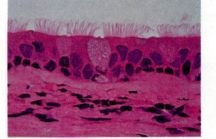
(d) Ciliated cells

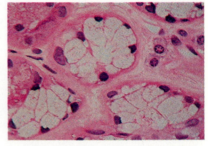
(e) Secretory cells

In the nasal lining and other respiratory linings, the epithelium is more complex, containing glandular, mucus-secreting cells and ciliated cells, both of which occur in columnlike rows and are known as **columnar epithelium.**

> Various **epithelial** tissues form the epidermis and internal linings of the gut, blood vessels, and air passages.

Connective Tissue

Connective tissue is found throughout the vertebrate body—which is probably a good thing, since it basically holds the body together. But some types of connective tissue have other roles, also. Essentially, connective tissue consists of cells plus their secretions, which together produce a noncellular **connective tissue matrix** (Figure 31.2). Familiar connective tissue includes bone, cartilage, ligaments, tendons, and, perhaps surprisingly, blood.

The principal substance in most connective tissue matrices such as tendons, ligaments, basement membranes, and muscle coverings is **collagen,** a fibrous protein that accounts for at least a third of the total body protein in larger vertebrates. Collagen serves as the "glue" of the animal body, as it is responsible for

binding various tissues together. It also forms such extremely tough structures as the cornea of the eye and the **intervertebral discs** (the cushions between the bones of the spine). Collagen is even a principal component of bone. It is found in all animals.

Collagen is secreted by special cells known as **fibroblasts,** forming tough, lengthy fibers (Figure 31.3). Fibroblasts are vitally important to wound healing (they produce scar tissue) and are essential in the mending of broken bones. They fill the fracture site with tough fibers of collagen. This specialized collagen remains in place only until new bone forms and hardens, permanently fusing the break.

Adipose tissue is a primary storage site of fats. These "fat cells" are found under the skin, between muscle fibers, in the breasts and buttocks, in intestinal membranes, and in other places in the body. Pinch tests provide one way to ascertain the amount and distribution of fat on your body. As a very simple test, if you can pinch more than one inch of fat in any area (usually the waist, the shoulder blade, and the back of the arm), you may be eating too much. Some parents consider a fat infant a healthy infant. According to some theories, however, overfeeding in infancy can build a surplus of adipose cells that may sentence the baby to a lifetime of obesity or constant dieting.

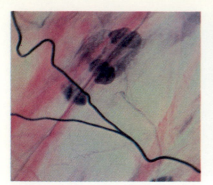
(a) Loose connective tissue

(b) Dense fibrous connective tissue

FIGURE 31.2 Loose connective tissue **(a)** contains a loosely arranged matrix of collagen fibers and fine elastic fibers. It forms beneath the skin, in the walls of blood vessels, and around nerves. Dense connective tissue **(b)** has many collagenous fibers and forms tough ligaments and tendons.

(a) Collagen fibers in tendons

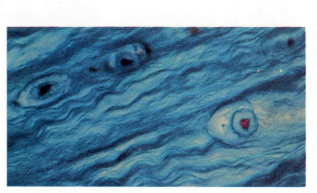
(b) Close-up of collagen fibers

FIGURE 31.3 **(a)** Collagenous fibers form a tough binding material that literally holds the vertebrate body together. Logically enough, collagen is the primary material of tendons—strong, cordlike structures that connect muscles to bones. **(b)** Individual collagen fibers in tendons form a wavy pattern, with distinct cross-banding of dense protein. (*a* from *Tissues and organs: a text atlas of scanning electron microscopy,* by Richard G. Kessel and Randy H. Kardon, W. H. Freeman and Company, copyright © 1979.)

Blood is also a connective tissue, according to the standard definition of the term. Its cells are suspended in a viscous fluid, the **plasma,** which is the connective tissue matrix. (The qualities of this peculiar fluid will be discussed in Chapter 39.)

Connective tissues such as cartilage, bone, and blood consist of cells surrounded by a noncellular matrix.

Muscle Tissue

Muscle tissue is unique in that it has the peculiar ability to contract. This contraction, of course, is responsible for movement in vertebrates. Aside from moving the skeleton, other muscular contractions, over which we have little control, are responsible for breathing, heartbeat, and digestion. We'll come back to muscle tissue shortly.

Nerve Tissue

Nerve tissue is excitable and irritable. These are not unpleasant traits, in this case. The statement simply means that nerve cells are responsive to external stimuli. Nervous tissue responds by conducting **neural impulses** along the nerve cells. The nerve cells, the functional units of nerve tissue, are called **neurons** (the basic parts of one kind of neuron are described in Figure 31.4). We will discuss the structure and function of nerve tissue in the next chapter.

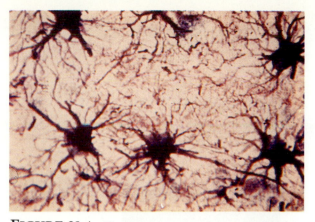

FIGURE 31.4 Neurons are very reactive to stimuli and impulses through the body. The *cell body* contains the usual cellular organelles, while other parts are adapted to either receiving or sending signals. Neurons range from a few micrometers to a meter in length.

THE VERTEBRATE SKELETON

The **skeleton** in nearly all classes of vertebrates, except for the cartilaginous fishes, is comprised of hardened bone, a connective tissue. The skeleton has four major functions: (1) it supports the body; (2) it provides a framework for muscle attachment and a resistant base for contraction; (3) it protects parts of the body; and (4) it is a site in which blood cells are formed.

Structure of Bone

Bones may form in different ways. The flattened, platelike bones of the skull, for example, are formed differently from the long bones of the appendages and most of the skeleton. We will concentrate here on the long bones.

In their general appearance, long bones (Figure 31.5a) have expanded **heads** and longer, narrower **shafts.** Except at the joints, the long bones are surrounded by a living layer of connective tissue called the **periosteum** ("around the bone"). Its cells are important in both bone formation and in the repair of broken bones. Most of the shaft is composed of **compact bone.** As the name suggests, it is thick and dense. Within the shaft is a tubular cavity containing a fatty material known as **yellow marrow.** The heads of long bones contain **spongy bone,** so-called because the hardened matrix is weblike rather than solid. The spaces within spongy bone are filled with soft tissue making up the **red marrow,** which in some bones is the site of red blood cell production.

Microscopic structure of bone. Despite its nonliving, stonelike appearance, compact bone contains vast numbers of metabolically active bone cells called **osteocytes** and numerous nerves and blood vessels. Most of the bony mass (about 65%), however, consists of hardened mineral salts, such as calcium phosphate, which are set in a matrix of collagen.

Microscopic sections of compact bone (Figure 31.5b) reveal intricate, repeated, structural units called **Haversian systems.** Each consists of a **central canal** that contains blood vessels, lymph vessels, and nerves surrounded by concentric **lamellae,** cylinders of calcified bone. The laminated lamellar arrangement, like layers of wood in plywood, imparts great strength and resilience to the bone.

Within the lamellae are the osteocytes (bone cells). Each resides in a tiny cavity—a **lacuna** (plural, **lacunae**). Tiny canals, the **canaliculi,** pass through the hardened bone from one lacuna to the next. The osteocytes touch each other with long extensions projecting through the canaliculi. Some of these projections reach the central canal, permitting the living bone cells to exchange materials with the circulatory system. Osteocytes help deposit or withdraw calcium deposits, according to the body's needs and the normal processes of change. The Haversian systems are in a constant state of flux—they are broken down and rebuilt continually through life.

> The unit of bone structure, the **Haversian system,** consists of concentric, hardened **lamellae** containing numerous interconnected **lacunae** that house the **osteocytes.**

Organization of the Human Skeleton

The human skeleton, a complex and fascinating system, can be divided into two parts: the **axial skeleton** and the **appendicular skeleton.** The axial skeleton includes the skull, the vertebral column, and the bones of the **thoracic region** (chest). The appendicular skeleton includes the **pectoral girdle** (shoulder) and **pelvic girdle** (hip), along with the **limbs** (the arms and legs) (Figure 31-6a). We'll begin with a look at places where various bones meet.

Joints. Where bones of the skeleton meet they form various kinds of **joints** (Figure 31.6). There are the free-ranging, rotating, **ball-and-socket joints** of the shoulder and hip and the less versatile **hinge**

FIGURE 31.5 **(a)** The sectioned long bone consists of a hard shaft and a central cavity of yellow marrow. Spongy bone is seen near the joints. **(b)** Numerous Haversian canals, responsible for carrying blood vessels and nerves, are surrounded by hardened concentric rings, or lamallae, containing bone cells (osteocytes). Such cells are entombed in lacunae, tiny cavities that communicate with each other via minute crevices called canaliculi. Such structures are grouped into Haversian systems.

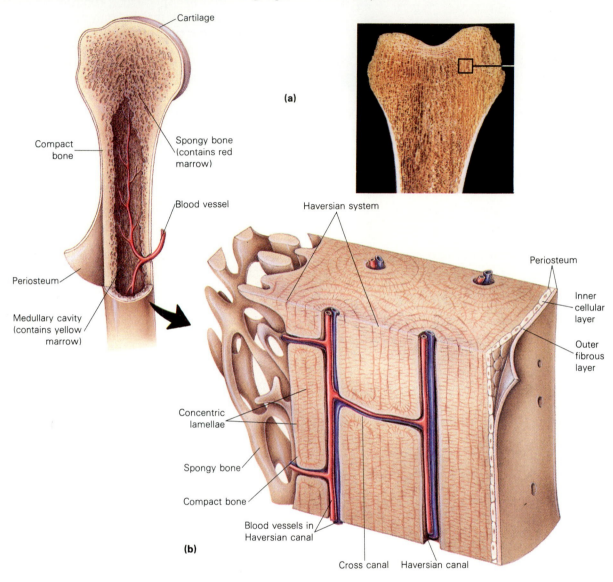

Haversian system of compact bone

FIGURE 31.6 The skull, vertebral column, sternum, and ribs make up the central axial skeleton (a) the pectoral and pelvic girdles and the limbs form the appendicular skeleton. Vertebrae from the three uppermost regions (b) have many features in common, but each has certain unique features (note the facets for rib attachments in the thoracic vertebra). Lumbar vertebrae support the most weight and are generally more massive than the others. Several kinds of joints (c) are formed by the hand, wrist, and arm bones. The knee, a hinge joint (d), is quite complex, bound with several ligaments that form a synovial capsule.

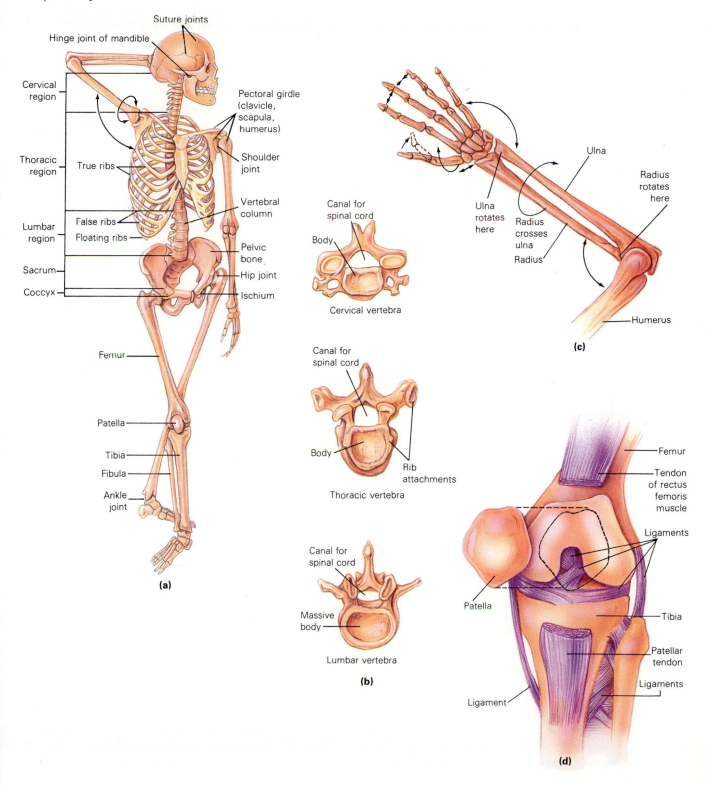

joints of the fingers, toes, and knee. Far less mobile **gliding joints** are found in the wrist and ankle; so-called **slightly movable joints** occur in the pelvic bones. Even the skull has joints, but these **sutures,** as they are known, are fused and immovable in the adult.

The articulating (contacting) surfaces of the bones of movable joints are covered with a thin layer of smooth, glistening cartilage. The joint itself is bound together by **ligaments** made up of tough, flexible connective tissue. In some instances the ligaments form a surrounding capsule. These are called **synovial joints,** and the lubricating fluid inside is called **synovial fluid.** Synovial fluid contributes to the silent efficiency of the active hip, elbow, shoulder, and knee joints. From an evolutionary point of view, it wouldn't have done for primitive human hunters to go creaking around in the underbrush.

Types of joints include rotating **ball-and-socket, hinge, gliding, slightly movable,** and **immovable. Synovial joints** are encapsulated by ligaments.

Axial skeleton. The axial skeleton, as its name implies, forms the central axis of the body. It is particularly interesting to anthropologists because it includes the skull and jaw, structures that fossilize well and have yielded a great deal of information about human evolution (see Chapter 30). The role of protection falls largely to the axial skeleton, since the skull offers protection to the brain, the rib cage surrounds the heart and lungs, and the vertebrae house the vulnerable spinal cord. The protective role of the skeleton is apparent in Figure 31.6a.

The human **skull** consists of 28 bones. Most of its volume makes up the **cranium** ("brain case"), which surrounds and protects the delicate and baffling organ within. Since the cranial bones of the skull do not fully meet until a child is about 18 months of age, there is a vulnerable soft spot on top of a baby's head for a time. The resulting flexibility of the skull helps in the birth process, wherein the large head is slightly compressed, permitting the baby to move more easily through the birth canal.

The **vertebral column,** or backbone, forms the flexible axis of the skeleton. It supports the weight of the upper body, delivering its load to the pelvic girdle below.

Since bones often serve as attachments for muscles, they usually have **processes** protruding from them, places where the muscles can attach. The vertebrae, in particular, have rather pronounced processes. Each vertebra also has a dense, rounded **body** that is joined to its neighbors above and below by cartilaginous disks. Most also have a prominent **foramen** (opening) in the vertebral column, through which the spinal cord passes (see Figure 31.6b). Exceptions are the **sacrum,** the wedgelike group of fused vertebrae, and the **coccyx,** the fingerlike remnant of the tail (a persistent reminder of our humbler origins).

The third region of the human axial skeleton includes the 12 pairs of **ribs** (one in 20 people have 13 pairs) and the shieldlike **sternum** (breastbone). The sternum and rib marrow are important sources of blood cells.

The **axial skeleton,** the skull, vertebral column, sternum, and ribs, acts as a body axis, protects vital organs, and produces blood cells.

Appendicular skeleton. The **pectoral girdle,** the **pelvic girdle,** and the **limbs** make up the appendicular skeleton. The appendicular skeletons of vertebrates, from amphibians to primates, have become enormously modified as species have become increasingly adapted to the terrestrial environment. Also, since humans are the only truly bipedal primates, our skeletons have required additional modifications (see Chapter 30).

The **pectoral girdle** consists of the paired **clavicles** (the collar bones) and **scapulae** (shoulder blades). The seemingly loose formation of the arm socket, for instance, is what makes the shoulder the most mobile of all our joints, providing a 360-degree rotation of the **humerus** (upper arm bone) (a movement employed by softball pitchers). The gently curved scapula glides smoothly over the rounded rib cage. This flexibility, coupled with the partially rotating, hinged elbow, the complex wrist, and the versatile hand, provides for a variety of motions characteristic of primates, but not typical of other vertebrates.

The **pelvic girdle** includes the end of the vertebral column and the three pairs of bones that make up the right and left halves of the pelvis. Each half includes a flattened **ilium** (hip bone), an **ischium** (sitting bone), and a **pubis** (pubic bone). Where the three meet on each side, they form the two prominent sockets that receive the rounded heads of the thigh bones. The ischium and pubis join in the front to form the **pubic joint,** or **pubic symphysis.** Flexibility of this joint allows the birth canal to expand during birth.

The limbs of humans are quite similar to those of other primates, yet the two differ in significant ways (see Chapter 30). We described the versatile shoulder joint previously, but we might add that much of the flexibility of the lower arm and hand is made possible by arrangement of the two lower arm bones. The **radius,** which articulates with the wrist on the thumb side, can cross over the **ulna** (see Figure 31.6c). The wrist itself cannot rotate but can merely do "wig-wag" and "goodbye" motions.

The articulation of the **femur** with the hip is another ball-and-socket arrangement. A far more peculiar and seemingly unlikely joint is the knee. While less versatile than the elbow hinge, the knee hinge does have some ability to rotate (in fact, over-rotation is the cause of many sports-related injuries). The knee, while essential to upright, bipedal posture and walking, is such a complex contraption that its evolution seems like the work of a committee. The femur perches on the upright **tibia** (the larger lower leg bone or shinbone), with some protection offered by the **patella** (kneecap). But, however flimsy it may seem, the knee has the toughest supporting capsule of any of the synovial joints.

VERTEBRATE MUSCLE AND ITS MOVEMENT

Any movement of cells, whether the waving of cilia, the contraction of the mitotic spindle fibers, or the flexing of an arm, relies on a universal principle. Certain long, filamentous proteins, by using ATP, are able to slide past each other. The result is an effective shortening of the filament pair. When a great number of such filaments are organized into a muscle, and that muscle is attached to a structure such as bone, it can move the structure.

Muscle Tissue Types

Vertebrate muscle can be classified into three types, **skeletal muscle** (also called "striated" or "voluntary" muscle), **cardiac muscle** (heart muscle), and **smooth muscle** (also called "visceral" or "involuntary" muscle). The three types of muscle tissue differ in appearance, location, function, and means of control.

Skeletal muscle. Skeletal muscle is often called "striated" (striped) because of the prominent cross-banding visible under the microscope (Figure 31.7a). Its multinucleate cells are referred to as **muscle fibers.** Groups of fibers with the same action are called **muscle bundles.** Most skeletal muscles, as you may have guessed, move the skeleton. Generally, movement is voluntary, which means that there is conscious control over the action. Contraction in skeletal muscle can be rapid, powerful, and often sustained.

Smooth muscle. Smooth muscle cells are long, spindly, and tapered. Each cell has one nucleus (Figure 31.7b). The cells commonly occur in flattened sheets and are found throughout the body, for example, in the walls of the gut, blood vessels, at the bases of hairs, in the iris of the eye, and in the uterus and other parts of the reproductive system. Smooth muscle is regarded as involuntary, meaning that there is little if any conscious control over its functioning, but there is evidence that some conscious control is possible. Smooth muscle tends to contract slowly and in a wavelike manner.

FIGURE 31.7 Skeletal muscle (a) is heavily striated and multinucleate. Smooth muscle (b) consists of long spindly cells, each containing a single nucleus. Cardiac muscle (c) tissue branches and rebranches and is interrupted by intercalated disks. Like skeletal muscle it is heavily striated (cross-banded).

(a)   (b)   (c)

Cardiac muscle. Cardiac muscle has traits in common with both smooth and skeletal muscle. For example, like smooth muscle, it is involuntary, and like skeletal muscle, it is highly striated. However, cardiac muscle differs from both in that its fibers are highly branched, forming a woven appearance. Furthermore, in cardiac muscle individual cells are separated by prominent **intercalated disks** (Figure 31.7c), which are not disks at all but interlocking, fingerlike foldings of adjacent plasma membranes. Because of the enormous interface created by this folding between adjacent cells, contractile impulses can pass rapidly from one cell to the other.

Compared to skeletal contraction, contraction of cardiac muscle is highly rhythmic and moderately slow. Further, its rhythmic contraction is intrinsic (from within); it needs no external stimulus. Even cells removed and grown in the laboratory lie pulsing in their dishes for as long as they remain alive.

Skeletal muscle (skeleton and body wall) is striated, specializing in voluntary movement. **Smooth muscle** (gut and blood vessels) is generally involuntary. **Cardiac muscle** (heart) is striated, branched, and involuntary.

Organization of Skeletal Muscle

Muscle fibers are held together by connective tissue composed largely of extracellular material. Skeletal muscles are richly supplied with blood vessels that run between and within the bundles of fibers, supplying oxygen and nutrients and carrying away wastes. An efficient circulatory system is critical to the efficient functioning of muscle. (What happens when a working muscle does not receive enough oxygen? See Chapter 8.) Nerves also penetrate the bundles, their branches dividing ever more finely until individual neurons finally innervate each muscle fiber at what are called **neuromuscular junctions.** These nerves carry the messages that cause the fibers to contract.

Muscle bundles are enclosed by **fascia,** a tough casing of connective tissue. At both ends of the muscle the fascia merges into increasingly denser collagenous tissue, forming cordlike **tendons** that attach to bone. One end of a muscle is usually attached to a more-or-less stationary base, the **origin,** while the other end is attached to a more movable part, the **insertion.** Examples of muscle origins and insertions are shown in Figure 31.8.

Not all skeletal muscles move bones. The muscles of your face, for instance, move your face. They enable you to produce all of your wonderfully attractive expressions. Tongue muscles also have complex origins and insertions, and you can move your tongue in an interesting variety of ways. Both smooth muscles and skeletal muscles may form rings around various passages or openings. These muscles, called **sphincters,** are found around the anus and in the gut, in the mouth, and even in many blood vessels. Other muscles form flattened sheets and have broad, thin tendons, such as the sheet of abdominal muscles that helps you pull in your stomach.

Opposing muscle groups. Muscles that move an appendage one way usually have opposing muscles that move it the other way. For example, the biceps flexes the arm and its opposing muscle, the triceps, straightens it. Such muscles with opposite actions are called **antagonists** (see Figure 31.8). The term suggests that they oppose or "fight" each other. In fact, however, they must cooperate in a highly coordinated fashion for most normal movements. Because of such interplay we are able to rise gracefully from our chair and to walk over to meet our fiancé's parents rather than leaping from the chair and sprawling at their feet.

Fibers are the units of skeletal muscle structure. They form **bundles,** each with a tendon of **origin** (stationary base) and one of **insertion** (movable part). **Antagonistic muscles** help with opposing movement and posture.

Ultrastructure of Skeletal Muscle

Now let's take a closer look at the finest level of muscle structure and see how such "ultrastructure" is important in muscle contraction. We found that the muscle bundle is made up of units called fibers. Thanks to the vast resolving power of the electron microscope we now know a great deal about the makeup of those fibers (Figure 31.9).

Skeletal muscle fibers range from a few millimeters in length to several centimeters—enormously long as cells go. Each muscle fiber is surrounded by a **sarcolemma,** the equivalent of a plasma membrane. **Motor neurons** (nerve cells carrying impulses to the muscle) join the muscle at neuromuscular junctions. The neuromuscular junctions are the nerve-muscle interfaces across which impulses pass, triggering contraction.

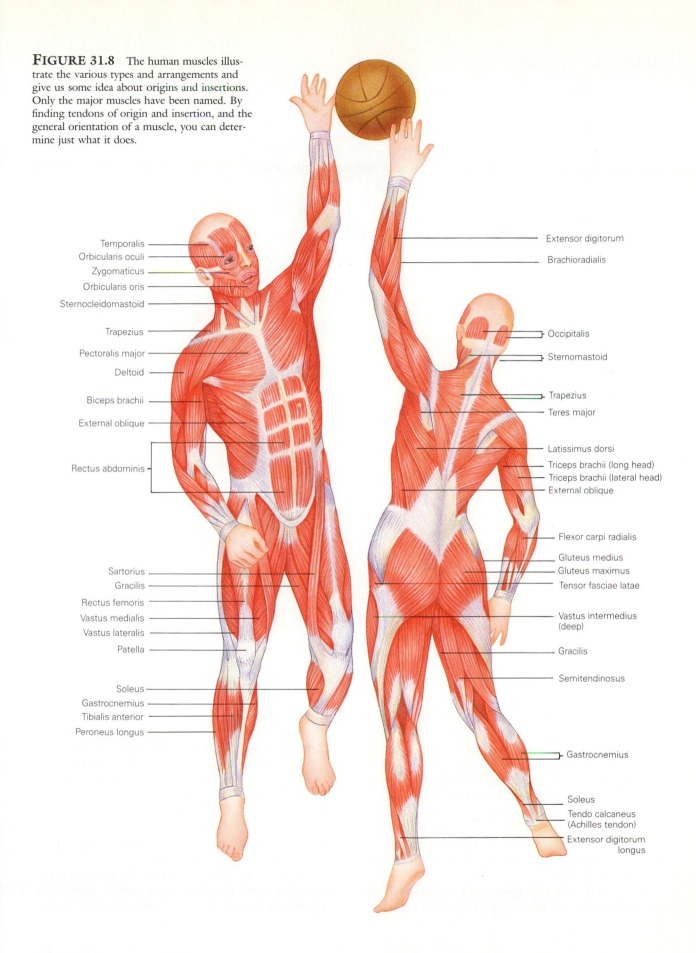

FIGURE 31.8 The human muscles illustrate the various types and arrangements and give us some idea about origins and insertions. Only the major muscles have been named. By finding tendons of origin and insertion, and the general orientation of a muscle, you can determine just what it does.

Temporalis
Orbicularis oculi
Zygomaticus
Orbicularis oris
Sternocleidomastoid
Trapezius
Pectoralis major
Deltoid
Biceps brachii
External oblique
Rectus abdominis
Sartorius
Gracilis
Rectus femoris
Vastus medialis
Vastus lateralis
Patella
Soleus
Gastrocnemius
Tibialis anterior
Peroneus longus

Extensor digitorum
Brachioradialis
Occipitalis
Sternomastoid
Trapezius
Teres major
Latissimus dorsi
Triceps brachii (long head)
Triceps brachii (lateral head)
External oblique
Flexor carpi radialis
Gluteus medius
Gluteus maximus
Tensor fasciae latae
Vastus intermedius (deep)
Gracilis
Semitendinosus
Gastrocnemius
Soleus
Tendo calcaneus (Achilles tendon)
Extensor digitorum longus

FIGURE 31.9 A trip through the levels of muscle organization begins with the whole muscle **(a),** which is subdivided into fasciculi (bundles of muscle fibers). Each muscle fiber **(b)** contains, at its core, several clusters of contractile proteins called myofibrils. A dense sarcoplasmic reticulum and intermittent T-tubules are prominent, as are a large number of mitochondria. A single myofibril is subdivided by T-tubules and Z lines into sarcomeres or contractile units, each of which contains a great many myofilaments. The arrangement of myofilaments forms the striated pattern so prominent in skeletal muscle.

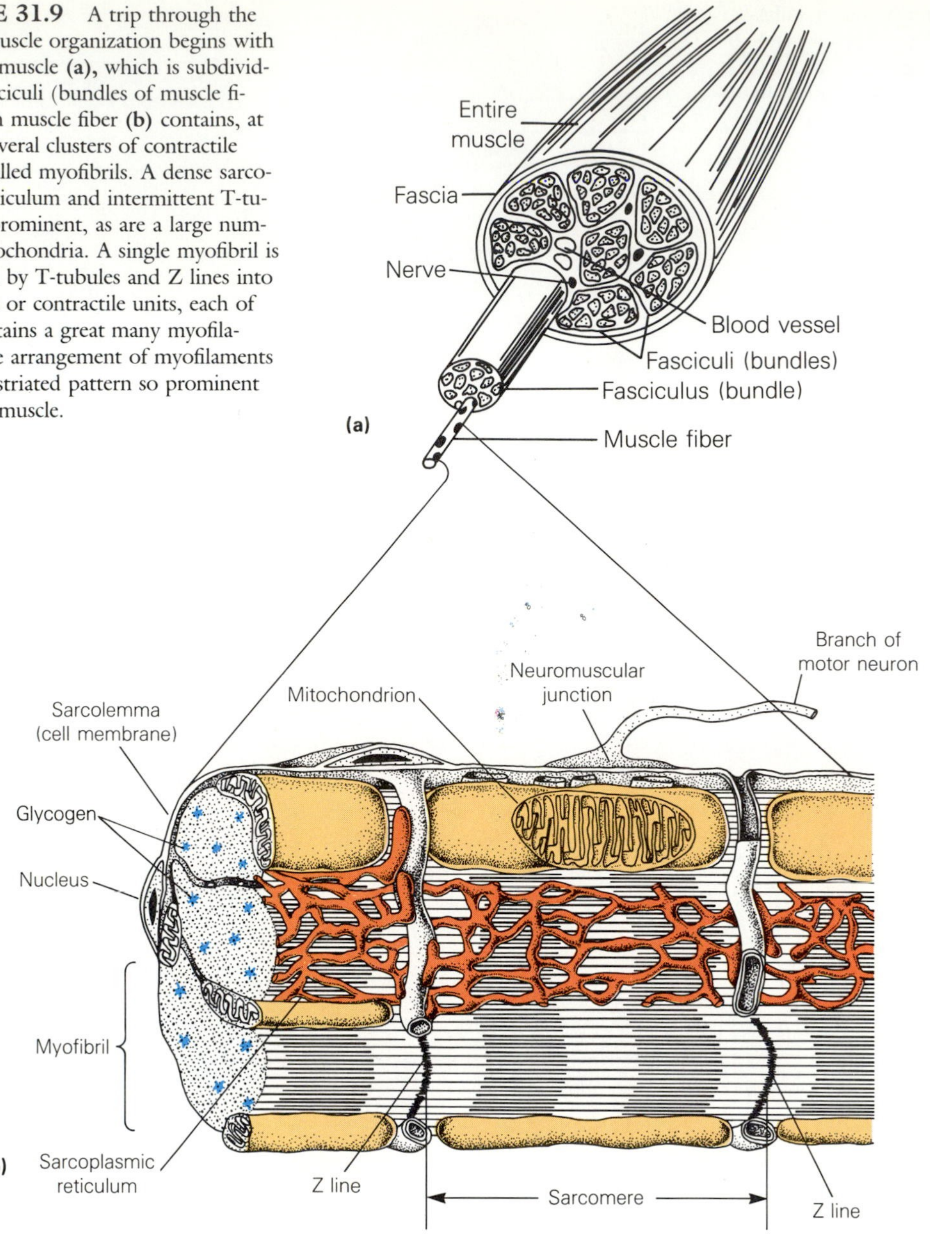

Within the muscle fiber, just below the sarcolemma, are found a number of nuclei and mitochondria and many glycogen granules—just what one would expect for such an active tissue. Lying just beneath the sarcolemma is the **sarcoplasmic reticulum,** which, like the endoplasmic reticulum of other cells, is a membranous, hollow structure. Somewhat larger than the sarcoplasmic reticulum are the **transverse tubules (T-tubules),** which mark the boundaries of functional, or contractile, units of the muscle fiber (see Figure 31.9b).

The actual contractile parts of the muscle fiber are the rod-shaped **myofibrils** (Figure 31.9b). Myofi-brils form the visible pattern of striations characteristic of skeletal muscle.

Each myofibril contains numerous rod-shaped filaments, or **myofilaments,** of the protein **myosin** and an even greater number of thinner filaments of **actin.** When a myofibril is viewed in cross-section, we usually find each thick myosin filament surrounded by six thinner actin filaments. The two kinds of filaments are arranged in a highly specific longitudinal manner, as shown in Figure 31.10.

Let's look at this arrangement from the surface, beginning with the very prominent **Z lines.** The region between the Z lines is the contractile unit, also

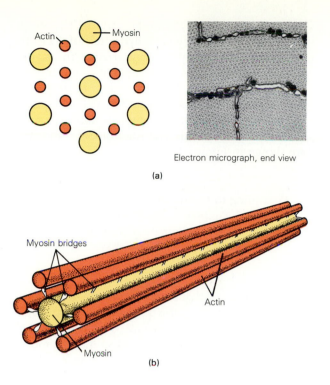

Electron micrograph, end view

(a)

(b)

FIGURE 31.10   **(a)** The electron micrograph of a cross-section through the myofibril; the accompanying illustration shows the arrangement of actin and myosin filaments in respect to each other. The three-dimensional drawing **(b)** shows the bridges between myosin and the surrounding actin.

known as the **sarcomere.** Moving inward from either Z line, we come to a very light zone called the **I band.** It consists of the protein actin only, with no overlapping of myosin. Further inward is a broad, dark **A band,** with a smaller and lighter central strip, the **H zone.** The two darker parts of the A band consist of overlapping actin and myosin myofilaments. The lighter central H zone represents myosin alone unless the muscle is contracted. When muscle contracts, the H zone tends to disappear, as we shall see.

Myofibrils include thick **myosin** and thin **actin myofilaments.** They form the distinct banded appearance of the contractile units.

Contraction of Skeletal Muscle

Painstaking studies of electron micrographs of relaxed and contracted sarcomeres reveal that, during contraction, the actin filaments move toward each

other, sliding through the stationary myosin filaments. This is now called the **sliding filament theory.** As seen through the electron microscope (Figure 31.11), the inward movement of actin from both sides brings the Z lines closer together and shortens the entire sarcomere. This movement continues until the actin filaments touch. At that time the H zone disappears and the A band is uniformly dense. This is not a local event in contracting muscle, but occurs simultaneously in each sarcomere, producing a rapid shortening of the entire muscle (which explains the deepening furrows in your brow as you read this). However, to understand how the actin moves we will need to examine the molecular structure of both myosin and actin.

The sliding action is made possible by the presence of numerous minute projections—the **myosin heads**—along the myosin filament (Figure 31.12). In relaxed muscle the myosin heads approach—but do not touch—the actin. In contraction the heads bend back and attach all along the actin filaments, forming **myosin cross bridges.** The bridges straighten and in so doing produce a "power stroke" that actually pulls the actin inward. As each myosin head completes its limited movement, it reattaches farther along and repeats its action. Therefore, the sliding of actin filaments is actually a ratcheting action.

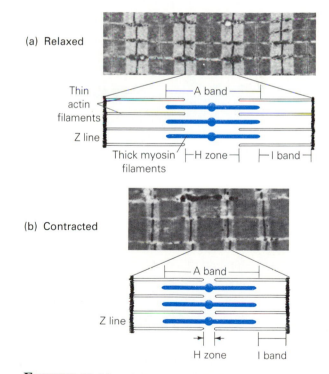

(a) Relaxed

(b) Contracted

FIGURE 31.11   The two electron micrographs clearly demonstrate what happens to the contractile unit when muscle contracts. Note the inward movement of the Z lines, the change in density of the A band, and changes in the H zone.

So, you may ask, why do the myosin bridges attach only in contracting muscle? The answer is in the actin filaments, which actually contain three proteins. In addition to actin there are **tropomyosin** and **troponin.** In the resting muscle, conditions around the troponin site inhibit myosin bridge formation. Bridge formation requires the presence of two substances: calcium ions (Ca^{2+})—the key to muscle contraction—and ATP, which, as you would expect, provides the energy. When Ca^{2+} is present, it alters

the troponin site and the bridges attach. The attachment triggers the enzymatic hydrolysis of ATP: the phosphate bond energy is transferred to the myosin head, which responds by straightening and tugging on the actin filament. For a myosin head to reattach farther along on the actin, another ATP is required, and the ratcheting action continues until maximum contraction is reached. The roles of Ca^{2+} and ATP are shown in Figure 31.12.

> According to the **sliding filament theory** an influx of Ca^{2+} permits myosin bridges to attach to actin, ATP energy is released, and the bridges straighten, pulling the actin inward.

FIGURE 31.12 (a) Without Ca^{2+} in the sarcomere, the myosin bridges cannot form. (b) When a neural impulse reaches a muscle, the calcium Ca^{2+} diffuses into the contractile units. In the presence of Ca^{2+}, the myosin bridges form, ATP transfers energy to the myosin bridges, and they contract and straighten, pulling the actin inward. ATP molecules continue to restore each bridge, permitting it to act again. (c) When Ca^{2+} is removed, bridge formation is inhibited, and the muscle rests.

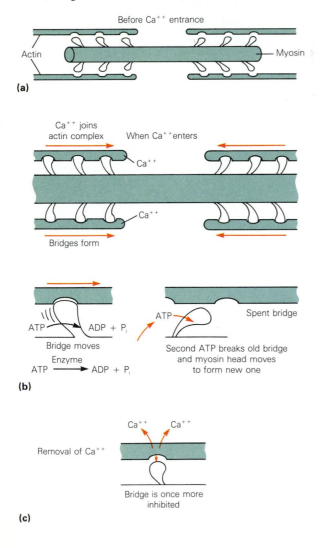

(a)

Before Ca^{++} entrance

Actin — Myosin

(b)

Ca^{++} joins actin complex — When Ca^{++} enters

Ca^{++}

Ca^{++}

Bridges form

ATP → ADP + P$_i$

Bridge moves

Enzyme

ATP → ADP + P$_i$

ATP — Spent bridge

Second ATP breaks old bridge and myosin head moves to form new one

(c)

Ca^{++} Ca^{++}

Removal of Ca^{++}

Bridge is once more inhibited

We have noted that calcium ions are a key factor in muscle contraction, so the questions now are, Where do the calcium ions come from? What controls their presence? How are they removed so that the muscle can relax? We find that in the relaxed muscle, calcium ions are sequestered within the membranous sarcoplasmic reticulum (see Figure 31.9b). Continuous active transport is required to move the ions there, which involves a pumping action by elements in the membrane itself. This is how muscles relax.

The events leading to contraction begin when a motor neuron relays a message across the neuromuscular junction. This creates a sweeping **polarity** change—a shift of plus and minus charges—in the muscle fiber, which passes along the T system to the sarcoplasmic reticulum. The polarity shift drastically alters the permeability of the sarcoplasmic reticulum, permitting the rapid escape of Ca^{2+}, which floods the sarcomeres (see Figure 31.12b). The presence of Ca^{2+} permits myosin bridges to form throughout the muscle, and contraction begins. More specifically, the calcium ions bind to a form of **troponin.** The calcium-activated troponin mobilizes enzymes that catalyze ATP, and its energy thereby becomes available to the myosin bridge.

When the motor impulse ends, it is the active pumping of Ca^{2+} back into the sarcoplasmic reticulum and the restoration of that membrane's ability to hold the ions that inhibit further bridge formation.

We have seen how individual skeletal muscle fibers react to an impulse from a motor neuron, but we should point out that individual muscle fibers rarely act alone. In fact, usually at least 10 or 12 fibers are activated at once. One motor neuron usually branches into at least that many muscle fibers. When an impulse arrives, all of the fibers served by that motor neuron will react simultaneously; thus the reacting group is aptly called a **motor unit.** Motor units of just a few muscle fibers are usually found where precision is important, as in the muscles of the hands or eyes. On the other hand, motor units in the calf muscle, which tends to react as a whole, may include hundreds of muscle fibers.

We now have some ideas on the basic tissue and skeletal organization in vertebrates, and we know some of the intricacies of muscle contraction. We have introduced the idea of nerve action, and in the next chapter we will take a closer look at this fascinating phenomenon as we consider some of the startling new finds of neurobiology, one of the fastest growing fields of biology.

SUMMARY

VERTEBRATE TISSUES

Epithelial Tissue

Epithelial tissue forms linings, separated from tissues below by a basement membrane. Examples include skin or epidermis and digestive, respiratory, and reproductive tracts. Glands have secretory or glandular epithelium. Specialized epithelial cells include flattened stratified squamous of the outermost epidermis and the continuously active cuboidal epithelium below. Columnar epithelium forms the secretory lining of the respiratory system.

Connective Tissue

Connective tissue forms bone, cartilage, tendons, ligaments, and blood. It includes cells and the surrounding matrix they secrete. The most common matrix is collagen, a fibrous protein secreted by fibroblasts. Adipose tissue stores body fats. Blood cells occur in a matrix of plasma.

Muscle Tissue

Muscle, a contractile tissue, has important functions in nearly all systems.

Nerve Tissue

Nerve tissue responds to stimuli by conducting neural impulses. The functional units are called neurons or nerve cells.

THE VERTEBRATE SKELETON

The skeleton's functions include support, movement, protection, and blood cell formation.

Structure of Bone

Long bones often have enlarged heads and long shafts, with regions of dense compact bone and spongy bone. The hollow shaft is filled with yellow marrow while red marrow occurs in spongy bone. The latter is often the site of red blood formation.

Microscopically, bone is organized into cylindrical Haversian systems, each with a central canal and concentric hardened layers or lamellae. Osteocytes (bone cells) reside within numerous lacunae and communicate via minute canaliculi. Osteocytes deposit or withdraw calcium salts as conditions warrant.

Organization of the Human Skeleton

The axial skeleton includes bones of the skull, vertebral column, and the thoracic or chest region. The limbs and the pectoral and pelvic girdles make up the appendicular skeleton.

Bones articulate at rotating ball and socket joints, hinge joints, gliding joints, slightly movable joints and immovable sutures. Bone surfaces at joints contain smooth cartilage, and the joints are bound by tough ligaments. Some ligaments occur as capsules forming synovial joints.

The skull protects the brain. Except during infancy, its 28 bones form immovable suture joints. The vertebral column forms a body axis, supporting upper body weight. Most vertebrae have rounded central bodies that connect to each other via intervertebral disks. Muscles fasten to bony processes and the spinal cord passes through the vertebral foramena (openings). Bones are fused in the triangular sacrum and tiny coccyx. The thoracic region includes the ribs and sternum.

The pectoral girdle includes the two clavicles and two scapulas, each pair forming ball and socket joints with a humerus (upper arm bone). The pelvic girdle has three pairs of bones (ilium, ischium, and pubis) joined at the rear by the sacrum. The three resulting joints are the pubic symphysis, sacroiliac, and hip joint.

Arm bones include the humerus, radius and ulna. The latter two form a rotating hinge at both ends. In the leg, the upper femur and hip form a ball and socket joint, and the lower femur, tibia, and patella form the hinged knee joint.

VERTEBRATE MUSCLE AND ITS MOVEMENT

All contractile tissue works through an ATP-dependent, sliding and shortening principle.

Muscle Tissue Types

Skeletal muscle (striated and voluntary) moves the skeleton, supports the trunk, and forms sphincters that control passageways. Muscle fibers are the structural units. Contractions are rapid, forceful and voluntary.

Smooth muscle (visceral and involuntary) occurs in the gut and blood vessels, iris, and uterus. Its contractions are slow, wavelike, and involuntary.

Cardiac (heart) muscle resembles skeletal muscle, but its fibers branch and are connected by intercalated disks. Its contractions are slow, rhythmic, involuntary, and intrinsic.

Organization of Skeletal Muscle

Skeletal muscle is bound by connective tissue and contains many blood vessels and nerves. Neurons form neuromuscular junctions on individual fibers. Fascia, enclosing muscle bundles, forms tough tendons that join muscle to bone. Such muscles have origins (stationary bases) and insertions (the part moved). Muscles also move the face and form sphincters and flattened sheets. Those with opposing functions, antagonists, work cooperatively in controlling movement and posture.

Ultrastructure of Skeletal Muscle

The muscle fiber is enclosed by a sarcolemma which receives motor neurons. Fibers contain mitochondria, glycogen granules, a web-like sarcoplasmic reticulum and a number of transverse tubules. Rod-shaped myofibrils are made up of thick myofilaments of myosin and thin surrounding myofilaments of actin.

In the surface patterns, Z lines form the boundaries of contractile units. Within are lighter I bands of actin, followed by darker A bands of both actin and myosin, and central H zones of myosin alone.

Contraction of Skeletal Muscle

The sliding filament theory maintains that during contraction actin slides past myosin, which remains stationary. Accordingly, the Z lines move together, the I band decreases, and the H zone disappears. The sliding movement occurs as myosin heads join actin, forming cross bridges and pulling the actin inward. In the resting state, bridge formation is inhibited. Contraction is triggered by calcium ions whose presence alters troponin, the bridge-inhibiting protein. Bridge attachment triggers ATP action and the myosin heads begin working on actin.

Membranal pumps concentrate calcium ions in the sarcoplasmic reticulum until a neural impulse reaches a fiber. This triggers their release and contraction ensues. When the impulse ends, the calcium ions are returned. Contraction generally involves entire motor units, many fibers served by a single motor neuron.

KEY TERMS

epithelial tissue	thoracic region	cardiac muscle
connective tissue	pectoral girdle	smooth muscle
muscle tissue	pelvic girdle	muscle fiber
nerve tissue	limb	muscle bundle
epithelium	ball-and-socket joint	intercalated disk
basement membrane	hinge joint	neuromuscular junction
epidermis	gliding joint	fascia
glandular epithelium	slightly movable joint	tendon
stratified squamous epithelium	suture	origin
columnar epithelium	ligament	insertion
connective tissue matrix	synovial joint	sphincter
collagen	synovial fluid	antagonist
intervertebral discs	skull	sarcolemma
fibroblast	cranium	motor neuron
adipose tissue	vertebral column	sarcoplasmic reticulum
blood	processes	transverse tubules (T-tubules)
plasma	foramen	myofibrils
neural impulse	sacrum	myofilament
neuron	coccyx	myosin
skeleton	sternum	actin
periosteum	clavicle	Z line
compact bone	scapula	sarcomere
yellow marrow	humerus	I band
spongy bone	ilium	A band
red marrow	ischium	H zone
osteocyte	pubis	sliding filament theory
Haversian system	pubic symphysis (joint)	myosin head
central canal	radius	myosin cross bridge
lamellae	ulna	tropomyosin
lacuna	femur	troponin
canaliculi	tibia	polarity
axial skeleton	patella	motor unit
appendicular skeleton	skeletal muscle	

REVIEW QUESTIONS

1 List four places where you would expect epithelial tissue to be located. (pp. 504–505)

2 Describe the kinds of cells and their arrangement in the human epidermis. What lies below epidermis? (p. 504)

3 Describe the kinds of cells that make up columnar epithelium. What special functions do such cells have in the respiratory passages? (p. 505)

4 What are the two elements of connective tissue? What is its general purpose? (p. 505)

5 Describe the appearance of collagen. List four places in the body where it is located. (p. 505)

6 Explain the role of fibroblasts in bone healing. (p. 505)

7 What is the role of adipose tissue? In what two ways is this tissue useful? (p. 505)

8 Name the functional unit of nerve tissue. What is its primary function? (p. 506)

9 Where are the two kinds of marrow located? What is the function of the red? (p. 507)

10 Using an outline drawing, illustrate the Haversian system. Label and give the role of the central canal, osteocytes, lacunae, lamellae, and canaliculi. (p. 507)

11 List the general parts that make up the axial and the appendicular skeleton. (p. 507)

12 List four types of movable joints and describe the range of movement in each. (p. 507)

13 Cite an example of a synovial joint and describe its makeup. (p. 510, Figure 31.6b)

14 What do the skull, vertebral column, and rib cage protect? (p. 510)

15 List the four regions of the vertebral column (Figure 31.6) and compare the general structure of vertebrae in each. (p. 510, Figure 31.6b)

16 Describe the pectoral girdle. In what way is this loose association with the humerus helpful? (p. 510)

17 List the three paired bones of the pelvic girdle and describe the importance of the pubic symphysis. (pp. 510–511)

18 Why is the knee joint sometimes described as "improbable?" Upon what does this joint rely for its strength? (p. 511)

19 List the three names for muscle that moves the skeleton. To what does each name refer? Characterize movement in this tissue. (p. 511)

20 List three structures in the body where smooth muscle is located. Characterize its movement. (p. 511)

21 List three unique characteristics of cardiac muscle. (p. 512)

22 What roles do blood vessels, connective tissues, and motor neurons perform in skeletal muscle? (p. 512)

23 Prepare a simple drawing of a skeletal muscle and its accompanying long bone. Label bundle, tendon of origin, and tendon of insertion. Now add in an antagonistic muscle. (p. 512)

24 List three places where sphincters are located. What is their function? (p. 512)

25 Briefly state what each of the following provides to a muscle fiber: sarcolemma, mitochondrion, neuromuscular junction, sarcoplasmic reticulum. (p. 514)

26 Describe the make up of a myofibril and provide a simple drawing of an end view. (p. 514)

27 Prepare an illustration showing the surface pattern of a contractile unit. Label the parts and explain what they represent. (pp. 514–515)

28 What happens to the pattern of bands and lines in the contractile unit when contraction occurs? (p. 515)

29 Explain contraction in terms of the formation and movement of myosin heads. (pp. 515–516)

30 Summarize the role of calcium ions in contraction. (p. 516)

31 Explain how calcium ions are released and what their specific role is in muscle contraction. (p. 516)

32 How does the muscle fiber restore its resting state? (p. 516)

33 What are the motor units and how do they increase the efficiency of movement? (pp. 516–517)

32

NEURONS AND HOW THEY WORK

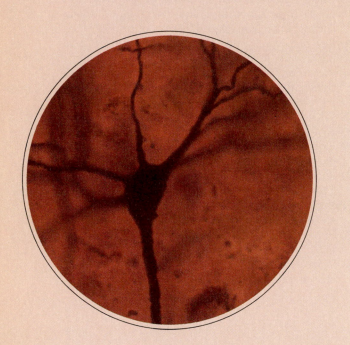

In the chill of morning, a browsing hare nips at tender buds on a hillside. Just inches away are other plants—fresh, dewy, and succulent. But the hare avoids these because its senses reveal that these plants contain toxins. The hare's movement attracts the attention of a bobcat that quickly crouches and begins a stealthy approach, ears forward, totally focused on the browsing hare. Each step brings the cat closer, and with each step it risks giving itself away. So although its attention is on the hare, it subconciously feels the ground before placing its weight on each tentatively advancing paw. Within seconds both animals will be rushing at full speed, their bodies a wonderful coordinated symphony of interactions. If the bobcat is successful, the hare's symphony will end in the dissonance of death (Figure 32.1).

Such sensitivity, coordination, and interaction are common in the animal world. After all, the earth is a variable and changing place, and from time to time and place to place it offers innumerable threats and gifts. It behooves animals, then, to be able to recognize the nature of their surroundings and to respond in an adaptive manner. This is possible because of specialized nerve cells that are sensitive to specific aspects of the environment and that can stimulate the body to respond appropriately.

Nerve cells, called **neurons,** respond to stimuli and effect changes in a similar fashion in all animals. As we will see, the mechanisms (electrical and chemical) operate on the same principles, whether in a starfish, a catfish, or a cat.

THE NEURON

Neurons, quite simply, are nerve cells. They exist in many sizes and shapes, but every neuron has a **cell body** from which extend a number of processes. Some processes are extremely long, reaching from one part of the body to another some distance away. For example, a single neuron can reach from your foot all the way to your spinal cord.

The cell body (Figure 32.2) contains the nucleus and most of the cell's cytoplasm. The cytoplasm includes such typical cell organelles as ribosomes, an endoplasmic reticulum, and numerous secretory bodies. In addition, the cell body produces **neurotransmitters,** which are chemicals that move to special sites in the neuron where they are secreted. When such chemicals reach adjacent neurons, these cells are stimulated to transmit an impulse. Neurotransmitters may also stimulate an **effector** (a structure capable of a response) such as a gland or a muscle.

FIGURE 32.1 Animals generally respond rapidly to incoming environmental cues. The ability is important in a number of ways, such as in finding food and recognizing danger.

FIGURE 32.2 (a) Neurons have cell bodies, dendrites, and axons; the latter are often myelinated. The direction of impulse movement is generally from dendrite to axon. (b) An important function of the cell body is the synthesis of neurotransmitter molecules, which are transported into the axon, destined for the synaptic knobs.

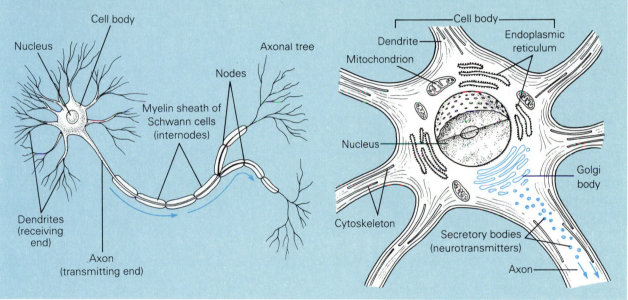

Two major types of processes extend from the cell body (see Figure 32.2): the **dendrites** and the **axons.** The dendrite ("little tree") is the receiving end of the neuron. Each dendrite can receive impulses from its surroundings or from other neurons, and it then generally converts this information into a nerve impulse that is transmitted *toward* the cell body.

The axon transmits the neural impulse *away from* the cell body. It may communicate with other neurons or directly with an effector. A neuron often has many dendrites, but it usually has only one axon. The single axon, however, may branch at any point along its length. An axon commonly divides and redivides at its tip, forming a terminal **axonal tree.** The axonal tree releases the neurotransmitters formed in the cell body, thus chemically relaying the message to the next neuron or to an effector. At the point where the tips of the axons **innervate** a muscle fiber (supply it with nerves), they branch and spread over the muscle fiber, each one ending in a footlike **neuromuscular junction** (see Chapter 31).

The axons of some neurons are surrounded by a

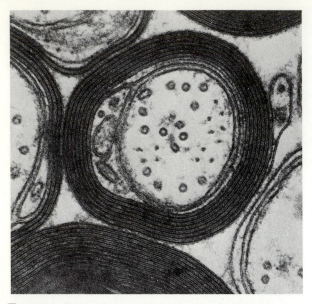

FIGURE 32.3 A cross-section through a myelinated axon shows the wrappings surrounding the axon itself. The wrappings are the membranes of an oligodendritic cell (similar to a Schwann cell), whose cytoplasm and nucleus produce the enlarged region.

fatty material called **myelin,** forming a **myelin sheath** (see Figure 32.2). Like any lipid, myelin has great electrical resistance, so it acts as an insulator. The myelin sheaths of neurons within the brain and spinal cord are formed by cells called **oligodendrocytes;** those of the neurons elsewhere in the body are formed by **Schwann cells** (Figure 32.3). In both cases the encompassing cells become wrapped around the neuron, but such wrappings are not complete. At frequent intervals called **nodes** the axon remains exposed to its ion-rich, watery surroundings, which is important to neural conduction.

> Neurons contain a **cell body** with typical organelles, **dendrites** that receive and conduct impulses toward the cell body, and **axons** that conduct impulses away. Some axons are myelinated.

Types of Neurons

Sensory neurons. There are three basic types of neurons: **sensory neurons, interneurons,** and **motor neurons** (Figure 32.4). Sensory neurons conduct impulses from **sensory receptors** to the central nervous system (the brain and spinal cord). We will say more about sensory receptors in Chapter 34, but let's note here that each type is specialized to detect specific environmental stimuli. Thus sensory neurons carry messages about conditions in the surroundings and in the body.

Interneurons. Interneurons communicate only with other neurons. They are largely responsible for integrating stimuli and initiating and coordinating responses. As you would expect, interneurons in the human nervous system make up much of the spinal cord and brain.

Motor neurons. Motor neurons are responsible for the body's final reactions to stimuli. They commonly receive impulses from the interneurons and transmit these impulses to effectors such as muscles and glands. Thus activated motor neurons enable us to yell, jump, blink, secrete, sweat, blush, squint, and perform any number of other such charming activities.

While the neurons carry impulses in the nervous system, the brain and spinal cord contain other types of cells. One type, the **glial cells** (or **neuroglia** as they are collectively known), outnumber neurons ten to one. Their functions are not well understood, but they serve some structural roles and provide metabolic support for the neurons. Neurobiologists have recently suggested possible information-processing roles for the glial cells as well.

> Sensory neurons carry impulses from sensory receptors to interneurons of the spinal cord and brain for integration and response. Motor neurons transmit impulses to responding organs.

Nerves

The axons and dendrites that extend throughout the body usually travel over the same routes, forming tracts called **nerves.** Thus, a spinal nerve, for example, might carry both sensory and motor impulses. A nerve is somewhat like a telephone cable carrying many individual lines, each insulated from the other. Nerves appear as white, glistening cords, and are surrounded by their own coverings of tough connective tissue (Figure 32.5).

THE NEURAL IMPULSE

While neurons can be said to conduct impulses from one part of the body to another, it's important not to confuse the term "conduct" with the usual electrical

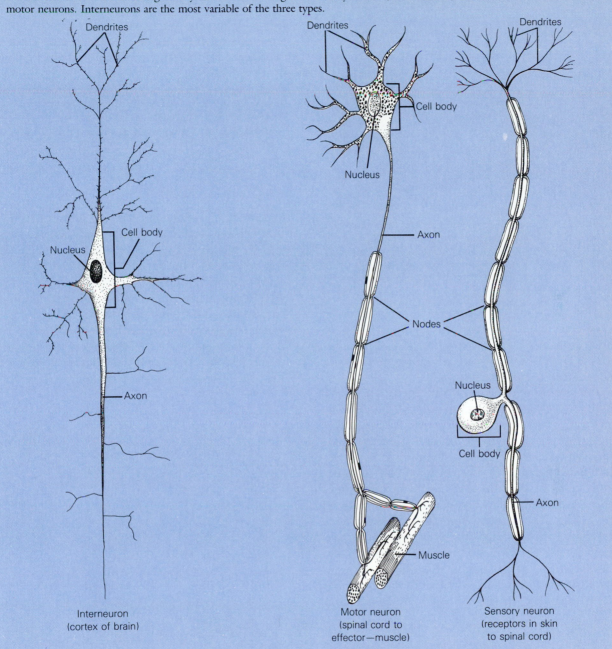

FIGURE 32.4 Nerve cells generally fall into three categories: sensory neurons, interneurons, and motor neurons. Interneurons are the most variable of the three types.

Dendrites

Cell body

Nucleus

Axon

Interneuron
(cortex of brain)

Dendrites

Cell body

Nucleus

Axon

Nodes

Nucleus

Cell body

Muscle

Motor neuron
(spinal cord to
effector—muscle)

Dendrites

Nucleus

Cell body

Axon

Sensory neuron
(receptors in skin
to spinal cord)

connotation. Neurons are far more than simple conductors, and a moving **neural impulse** is quite different from an electrical current passing through a wire conductor. Electrical current passing through a conductor diminishes over time and distance, but neural impulses, once started, do not diminish. As with a row of falling dominoes, the last falls with the same energy as the first.

We can divide the complex events of neural activity into three parts: (1) the resting state, (2) the action potential, and (3) repolarization.

The Resting State: A Matter of Ion Distribution

The resting state in a neuron refers to the period when no impulses are being generated. But more than that, it is a time when ions inside and outside

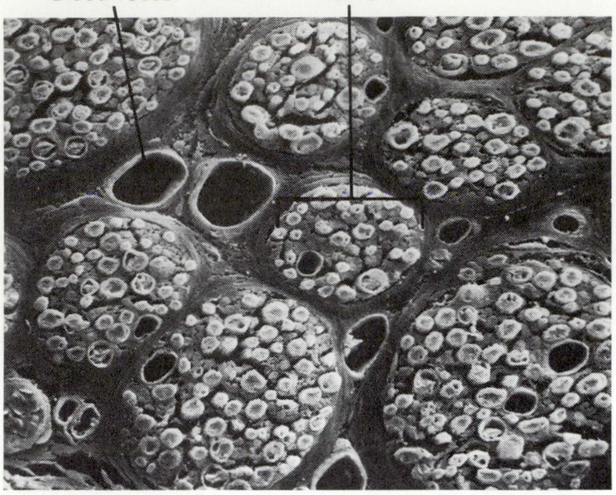

Blood vessel   Nerve

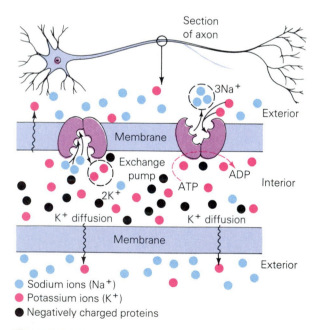

FIGURE 32.5 A nerve, as seen in cross-section through the scanning electron microscope, contains numerous neural processes, possibly both axons and dendrites. (From *Tissues and organs: a text-atlas of scanning electron microscopy,* by Richard G. Kessel and Randy H. Kardon. W.H. Freeman and Company, copyright © 1979.)

the neurons reach a precarious, unbalanced distribution—one that, if disturbed, will bring about a very sudden rush toward equilibrium.

The ions important to neural activity are chiefly sodium ions (Na^+), potassium ions (K^+), and larger immobile, negatively charged proteins. The negatively charged proteins remain within the neuron's interior. While at rest the membrane itself is impermeable to sodium, most of which remains outside. Potassium ions, freer to diffuse across the membrane, can be found on both sides.

The distribution of sodium and potassium does not result solely from passive movement and simple permeability. The ions end up where they are largely because of energy expenditure. Specifically, they are moved around by **sodium-potassium ion-exchange** pumps that are driven by ATP energy (Figure 32.6).

In the neuron's resting state, sodium-potassium ion exchange pumps maintain higher concentrations of Na+ outside and K+ inside the neuron. Immobile, negatively charged proteins remain inside.

Resting potential. During the resting state, with some positive ions excluded from the neuron and others leaving through diffusion, the interior of the cell becomes *negatively charged* relative to the outside. In other words, the neuron is **polarized.** If the

electrical charges inside and outside the resting axon's membrane are compared, we find that there is an electrical potential difference across the membrane, or **resting potential,** of −60 millivolts (mV: $1/1000$ of a volt) (Figure 32.7a). The resting potential represents a significant amount of potential energy.

Differences in charges inside and outside a resting neuron create a poised state of **polarization** with a voltage potential of −60 mV.

The Action Potential

When a neuron is stimulated, the point of stimulation becomes suddenly **depolarized,** and the depolarization sweeps rapidly along the length of the neuron, followed within about 1 millisecond ($1/1000$ second) by **repolarization.** The depolarization is created by a rapid change in membrane permeability and a corresponding shift in the precarious balance of ions, which was maintained during the resting state. This shift of ions and electrical charges produces the neural impulse or **action potential** (Figure 32.7b and c). Let's see what's behind these changes.

- Sodium ions (Na^+)
- Potassium ions (K^+)
- Negatively charged proteins

FIGURE 32.6 In its resting state a neuron maintains a negatively charged interior and positively charged exterior. In addition, through the action of numerous sodium-potassium exchange pumps, opposing diffusion gradients of sodium and potassium ions are maintained.

To begin, when a nerve impulse passes any point in an axon, the plasma membrane at that point suddenly becomes permeable to sodium ions, and the resting potential is rapidly lost as sodium ions rush down their steep gradient into the cytoplasm of the axon. The −60 mV differential is abruptly shifted to an electrical peak of +40 mV (Figure 32.7c).

Action potentials last briefly. The region just inside of the neuron becomes positively charged only for milliseconds. But as one area along the neuron experiences this shift in ions, it triggers the next area to do the same. Once started, the shift in ions continues in a cascading manner—in a *wave of depolarization*—down the length of the axon (Figure 32.7d). But in its wake an immediate recovery or repolarization begins, and the resting potential of the neuron is quickly reestablished.

An **action potential** is a moving, depolarizing wave caused by the sudden influx of sodium ions. It reaches a peak of +40 mV. The polarized state is immediately restored.

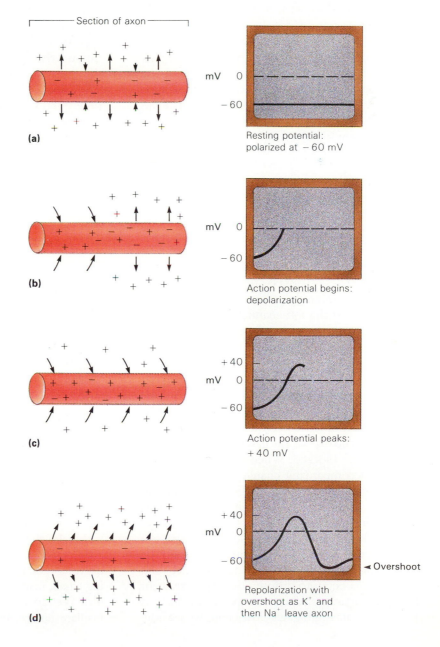

FIGURE 32.7 Action potentials occur when the polarized resting state (a) is suddenly lost. A rapid influx of positive sodium ions (b) creates a depolarizing shift, and the membrane voltage potential moves from −60 to +40 mV (c). The depolarized state is quite brief, as the inward movement of sodium ions soon stops. Its depolarizing effects are countered by the outward rush of positive potassium (c and d), which restores the resting state. Eventually the exchange pumps will eliminate the brief "overshoot" and restore the sodium and potassium distribution.

Section of axon

(a)
mV   0
     − 60
Resting potential: polarized at − 60 mV

(b)
mV   0
     − 60
Action potential begins: depolarization

(c)
     + 40
mV   0
     − 60
Action potential peaks: + 40 mV

(d)
     + 40
mV   0
     − 60   ◄ Overshoot
Repolarization with overshoot as K⁺ and then Na⁺ leave axon

Back to the resting state. As an action potential peaks, the membrane's permeability to sodium drops sharply, and this ion is again rejected. Then potassium becomes the essential ion of recovery. Potassium ions move out of the neuron until their number balances the sodium ions that moved in. This restores the resting potential. Interestingly, as soon as the resting potential of -60 mV is restored, the neuron may fire again, but not until. The time during which it cannot fire is called the **refractory period.**

It may have occurred to you that while the exodus of potassium ions restores the resting potential, the distribution of sodium and potassium ions is not as it was before. However, the sodium-potassium ion-exchange pumps eventually restore the earlier distribution of ions, and soon the neuron is back to its old balancing act.

This is about all we knew about the movement of ions until just a few years ago. Now biologists understand a great deal more, especially about the events underlying the sudden shifts in membrane permeability associated with the action potential and the act of recovery. For example, now we know about ion channels and gates.

Ion Channels and Ion Gates

What is it that makes the axonal membrane suddenly permeable to sodium ions when the nerve impulse begins? Studies reveal that, in addition to the sodium-potassium exchange pumps, the membrane contains a large number of very special voltage-sensitive **ion channels.** These channels are quite selective. For example, some admit only sodium, others only potassium. Controlling the ion channels are very specialized membrane proteins that form voltage-sensitive **sodium gates** and **potassium gates.** Let's see how the channels and gates help explain an action potential.

Briefly, the ion gates open and close through changes in shape, and these changes are triggered by voltage shifts around the neuron. In the resting neuron, as you would expect, the gates are closed and the ion channels are blocked. When an action potential arrives, the accompanying change in voltage causes the sodium gates to open, and sodium ions rush into the neuron (diffusing down their gradient). This continues for a brief period, about half a millisecond, and as the depolarizing wave peaks ($+40$ mV), the sodium gates suddenly close. During this period the slower-acting potassium gates will have opened, and potassium ions begin to diffuse down their gradient out of the neuron. When the polarized state is restored, the potassium gates close. Thus we see how

opening and closing of the gates account for the action potential. But we are left with questions. Why does the action potential proceed along a neuron? How do the sodium gates close at two vastly different voltages?

As we've seen, the shift from a polarized to a depolarized state represents a minute current flow that becomes self-sustaining as activity in one set of gates activates the next along the length of the neuron. The sodium gates, it turns out, are more versatile and complex than we have indicated. Since they respond to contrasting conditions—closing in the polarized state and closing again in the depolarized state—neurophysiologists suggest that each sodium gate is actually two gates in one. The first, a **sodium activation gate,** remains closed at the resting potential but is activated by electrical disturbances such as an approaching action potential. The second is a **sodium inactivation gate** that remains open except when the peak voltage of an action potential is reached. The second gate is vital to recovery since without its timely action the continued influx of sodium might put the neuron in a permanent refractory state—unable to recover and act again. Figure 32.8 illustrates the work of ion channels and gates.

> In an **action potential,** voltage-sensitive **sodium gates** open, admit sodium, and close at $+40$ mV. **Potassium gates** then open, release potassium, restore the resting voltage, and close.

Myelin and Impulse Velocity

Axons in vertebrates are commonly surrounded by **myelin sheaths** that both insulate the neuron and help to speed up impulses. Myelinated neurons in humans, for example, can conduct impulses at a speed of up to 100 m per second, many times faster than the nonmyelinated neurons found in many invertebrates.

Aside from myelination, the only other way to speed up impulses is by increasing the diameter of the axon. For example, the giant axons of the squid are several millimeters thick and can conduct impulses at 30 m per second—a rate that is fast for an invertebrate, but still far from vertebrate capabilities.

Myelin sheaths presumably evolved as a means of keeping the axons of vertebrates (with their extensive nervous systems) small. There are advantages to having small, insulated neurons that carry impulses rapidly. We can see how the fatty myelin sheaths would insulate nerves, but how do they increase impulse

FIGURE 32.8 (a) In the resting, or polarized, neuron the sodium inactivation gates are open while the activation gates and the potassium gates are closed. Opposite sodium and potassium ion gradients are maintained, and a large number of immobile negative ions remain inside. (b) An action potential begins as sodium activation gates open, and an inrush of sodium ions begins. (c) Recovery is almost immediate as the sodium inactivation gates close and the potassium gates open. Potassium ions rush from the interior, and the peak voltage of +40 mV drops rapidly toward −60 mV. (d) As the resting, or polarized, state returns, the sodium inactivation gates open while the sodium activation gates and the potassium gates close.

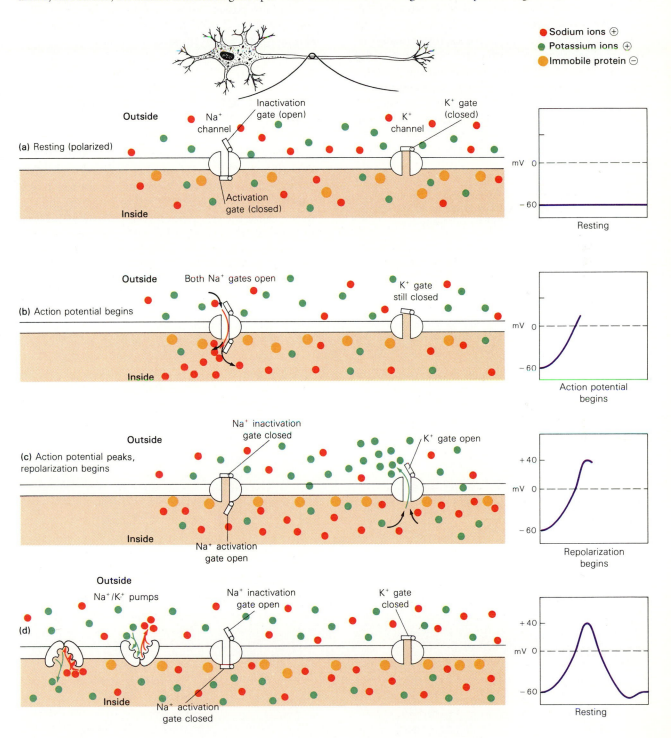

velocity? And, for that matter, how can an action potential be generated in an axon that is *insulated from* the surrounding sodium-rich fluid?

Actually there are many nodes in the myelinated neuron, places where the wrappings are absent (see Figure 32.4). It is in the nodes that action potentials occur. An action potential in a node creates a minute flow of electrical current that passes, instantaneously, to the next node, activating the voltage-sensitive sodium gates and creating a new action potential there. The neural impulse literally jumps from one node to the next, like a rock skipping along the surface of a pond. This is called **saltatory propagation** (salt-, "jump") (Figure 32.9).

> In **saltatory propagation**, current from an action potential in one node triggers an action potential in the next—and so on along the neuron.

Saltatory propagation not only increases the speed of the impulse but also conserves energy. This is because the ATP-driven sodium-potassium exchange pumps have far less work to do in maintaining the needed ion distribution. Experiments indicate that an impulse passing down a nonmyelinated neuron requires some 5,000 times as much energy as one skipping along a myelinated neuron.

COMMUNICATION AMONG NEURONS

The place where the axon of one neuron activates the dendrite or cell body of another is called a **synapse.** Most neurons come very close but do not touch one another; the tiny space between one neuron and the next is called the **synaptic cleft** (Figure 32.10). Thus, in a chain of neurons, one must stimulate the next across this cleft. It does this by releasing the chemi-

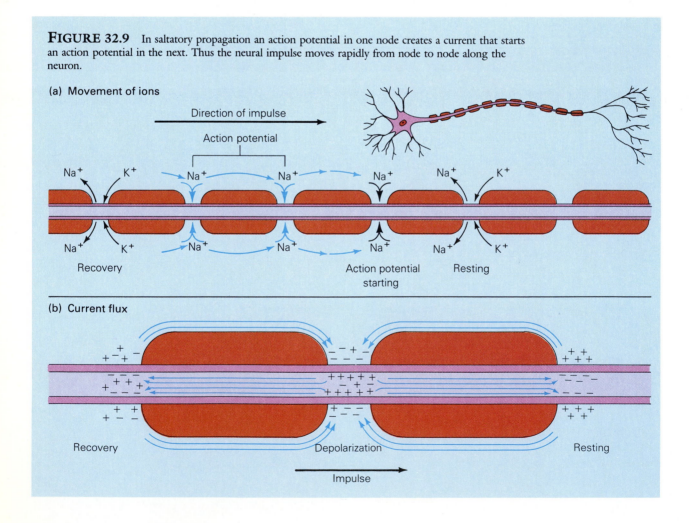

FIGURE 32.9 In saltatory propagation an action potential in one node creates a current that starts an action potential in the next. Thus the neural impulse moves rapidly from node to node along the neuron.

(a) Movement of ions

Direction of impulse

Action potential

Na⁺   K⁺   Na⁺   Na⁺   Na⁺   Na⁺   K⁺

Na⁺   K⁺   Na⁺   Na⁺   Na⁺   Na⁺   K⁺

Recovery   Action potential   Resting
                                  starting

(b) Current flux

Recovery   Depolarization   Resting

Impulse

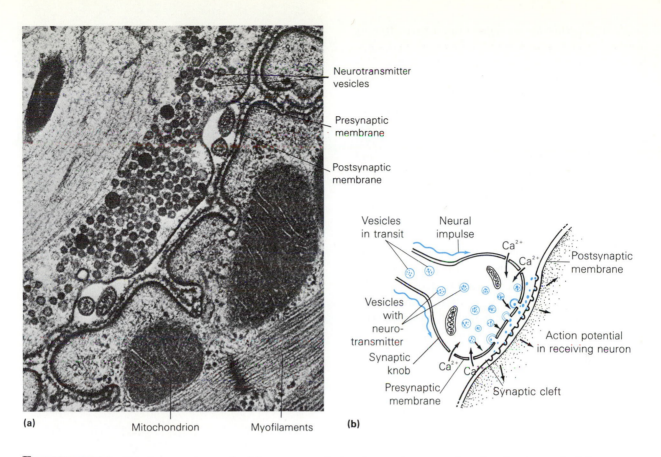

(a)

Neurotransmitter
vesicles

Presynaptic
membrane

Postsynaptic
membrane

Vesicles
in transit

Neural
impulse

Ca^{2+}

Ca^{2+}

Postsynaptic
membrane

Vesicles
with
neuro-
transmitter

Action potential
in receiving neuron

Synaptic
knob

Ca^{2+} Ca^{2+}

Presynaptic
membrane

Synaptic cleft

Mitochondrion   Myofilaments

(b)

FIGURE 32.10   The electron micrograph of the neuromuscular junction **(a)** shows a portion of a minute synaptic cleft between presynaptic *(left)* and postsynaptic *(right)* membrane. Note the many neurotransmitter-filled vesicles inside the presynaptic membrane. Also note the mitochondria just below the postsynaptic membrane and the strandlike myofilaments *(lower right)*. **(b)** Upon receiving a neural impulse, calcium gates in the presynaptic membrane open, and with the entry of calcium ions, the vesicles fuse with the membrane and rupture. Neurotransmitter diffuses to the postsynaptic membrane where it triggers an action potential.

cals called neurotransmitters. There are many different kinds of neurotransmitters, depending on the functions of the neurons involved. The most common outside the brain are **acetylcholine** and **norepinephrine** (others are discussed in Chapter 33).

Action at the Synapse

At the tips of the axonal tree are many tiny bulbs, the **synaptic knobs.** The knobs are filled with minute vesicles, or sacs, that contain the neurotransmitter. When an action potential reaches these synaptic knobs, voltage-sensitive calcium gates in the surrounding **presynaptic membrane** open and admit calcium ions (Ca^{2+}) from outside. Calcium ions are believed to activate a protein called **calmodulin,** which, as one of its many effects, brings about the attachment of microtubules to the vesicles. The vesicles are drawn to the membrane to which they fuse. They then rupture, and their cargo of neurotransmit-

ter molecules spills into the synaptic cleft. These molecules rapidly diffuse across the narrow cleft and attach to specialized receptors in the **postsynaptic membrane** (the membrane of the receiving dendrite or cell body; see Figure 32.10b).

Typically, when a critical number of receptor sites have filled, *chemically activated* sodium or potassium gates in the postsynaptic membrane open, and the positively charged ions rush into the receiving neuron. In this manner a new action potential is initiated. The depolarizing wave passes in the usual fashion along the dendrites, cell body, and axon.

A neural impulse ends at the **synaptic knob,** where it stimulates the release of a neurotransmitter that diffuses across the **synaptic cleft,** triggering an action potential in the next neuron.

What happens to the neurotransmitter after its work is finished? It is vital that it be inactivated. Otherwise the second neuron would simply keep on firing in an unorganized manner. So the neurotransmitters are quickly deactivated by enzymes. Acetylcholine, for instance, is broken down by **acetylcholinesterase.** (Interestingly, some military "nerve gases" and certain powerful insecticides called *organophosphates* do their work by inhibiting such enzymes and causing the loss of muscular control.)

Significantly, certain neurotransmitters from some neurons inhibit, rather than activate, the next neuron. Neurons that do this are called **inhibitory neurons,** and they are essential in bringing about a more controlled and coordinated action. Curiously, inhibitory neurons secrete neurotransmitters that activate **chloride ion** (Cl^-) **gates,** permitting the negative ion to enter the second neuron. This increases its polarized state beyond the resting voltage. For such a **hyperpolarized** neuron to react at all will require stimulation by several excitatory neurons.

An example of such inhibitory neurons at work might be those whose high threshold of activation permits sleep. Certain inhibitory neurons, by suppressing action potentials, might screen out incoming stimuli, such as noises or thought patterns or whatever else might interfere with sleep. But then a rustling sound under the bed might generate enough action potentials to overwhelm such inhibitory pathways.

THE REFLEX ARC

Now let's see how a system comprising countless neurons might assign just a few to produce a simple behavioral response. Consider the **reflex arc** (Figure 32.11).

The reflex arc is a complete reaction—one encompassing detection, integration, and response—that does not necessarily directly involve the brain. A familiar example of a reflex arc is the "jumping" of your leg when a doctor taps the tendon below the knee (thought by some to be for the physician's amusement, but actually used as a test to rule out certain neurological disorders).

Your leg jumps, or kicks, because the blow stretches the tendon, which also causes the muscle above to stretch (a stretch reflex). The change is detected by certain **stretch receptors,** specialized sensory neurons within muscles, that flash a message to the spinal cord. The impulse is immediately

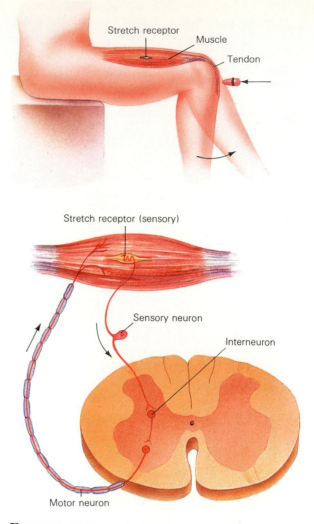

FIGURE 32.11   In the knee-jerk reflex, striking the tendon causes the muscle above to extend slightly. Stretch receptors, specialized sensory neurons in the muscles, are stimulated. They then transmit impulses to the spinal cord, where the appropriate motor neurons are activated, causing muscle contraction.

relayed through interneurons to nearby motor neurons, whose axons pass back down to the same muscle, which contracts, producing the kick. The reflexive response is sudden and involuntary, since the brain is not involved except as a passive and possibly surprised observer.

The response may be adaptive in certain situations, say when you twist your ankle and your leg buckles. The reflexive straightening of the leg can keep you from falling onto the cat.

Complete reflexive responses may be brought about by the simple action of a sensory neuron, an interneuron, and a motor neuron—a **reflex arc.**

Stretch receptors are also responsible for your head snapping up as you doze off during lectures, announcing to everyone your opinion of the class. Such reflex systems are essential to the delicate processes that enable you to maintain posture and limb position. Highly coordinated contractions in opposing muscles must be adjusted constantly by neural behavior, but this involves little conscious intervention. (When's the last time you thought to yourself, "I really must contract my left sternocleidomastoid; my head seems to be leaning to the right"?)

Reflexes are a particular and relatively simple type of neural response. In general, they are identified by a few special traits. Reflexes usually: (1) are involuntary; (2) are stereotyped (always performed the same way); (3) are adaptive; (4) involve relatively few neurons; and (5) are rapid.

Our neural structures, then, are important to our adjusting to a complex and variable world. Neurons, the individual nerve cells, are highly sensitive, reactive, and complex structures that, when properly coordinated, allow us to assess our situation and to make the proper responses to the challenges and opportunities of our environment.

SUMMARY

THE NEURON

Neurons or nerve cells have three primary parts: a cell body (with most of the cytoplasm and organelles), dendrites (receiving processes) and axons (transmitting processes). The cell body synthesizes neurotransmitters that are released by the axonal tree, permitting impulses to move from neuron to neuron and from neuron to effector.

Myelinated neurons have myelin sheaths formed by oligodendrocytes and Schwann cells. Nodes are regular interruptions in the sheath.

Types of Neurons

Sensory neurons conduct impulses from specialized sensory receptors to the central nervous system. There, impulses are relayed to interneurons in the spinal cord and brain whose task is to coordinate information and initiate responses. Responses are made through motor neurons that activate muscles, glands and other parts of the body. Glial cells have structural and chemical supporting roles in the central nervous system.

Nerves

Nerves are cable-like collections of neural axons and dendrites surrounded by insulating sheaths.

THE NEURAL IMPULSE

Neural impulses are regenerated along the length of a neuron.

The Resting State: A Matter of Ion Distribution

In the resting state, the region immediately outside a neuron is positive to the region inside, thus the resting neuron is polarized. Sodium ions predominate outside and potassium ions are found on both sides. Negative ions outnumber the positive ions inside. Ion distribution is maintained by sodium-potassium ion-exchange pumps. At rest, the measured voltage potential or resting potential across the neural membrane is -60 mV.

The Action Potential

A neural impulse begins when a stimulus depolarizes part of a neuron. The depolarization sweeps along the neuron in what is called an action potential. Repolarization follows immediately. Depolarization is brought about by a sudden change of membrane permeability resulting in a massive influx of sodium ions. The voltage shifts from -60 mV to $+40$ mV. Repolarization begins as sodium movement stops and potassium diffuses outward, its positive charges restoring the resting potential. Later the pumps will restore the sodium-potassium balance.

Ion Channels and Ion Gates

The rapid passage of sodium and potassium in and out of the neuron is facilitated by specific ion channels that are controlled by sodium and potassium gates. At the start of an action potential, voltage dependent sodium gates open admitting sodium ions. Near the peak of depolarization, the sodium gates close and potassium gates open, permitting the escape of potassium ions and a return to the resting state. An action potential moves along a neuron because the current it produces activates sodium gates further along the neuron. Actually, sodium channels have two different gates. One is opened by the initial stimulus or current and closes when the resting potential is restored. The other remains open except during a peaking action potential.

Myelin and Impulse Velocity

Myelinated neurons conduct impulses much faster than non-myelinated neurons because action potentials occur only at nodes. The current flow created by an action potential in one node, instantaneously activates sodium gates in the next node, thus the impulse jumps from node to node (called saltatory propagation). This speeds up transmission and greatly reduces the amount of ATP used by sodium-potassium ion-exchange pumps.

COMMUNICATION AMONG NEURONS

One neuron activates another at a synapse.

Action at the Synapse

An action potential reaching a synaptic knob activates calcium ion gates and calcium aids in neurotransmitter release at the presynaptic membrane. Such molecules cross the synaptic cleft, joining receptor sites in the postsynaptic membrane of the next neuron. Chemically activated sodium or potassium gates are opened, the ions enter and an action potential begins. Neurotransmitters are quickly deactivated by enzymes.

A measure of control is provided by inhibiting neurons whose neurotransmitters activate chloride gates in the postsynaptic membrane. The negative ions hyperpolarize the neuron, and a number of excitory neurons must then act to depolarize it and start an action potential.

THE REFLEX ARC

The simplest complete reaction, the reflex arc, involves as little as one sensory neuron, a spinal cord interneuron, and a motor neuron. A motor unit may then contract without the intervention of the brain. Reflex arcs make it possible for sudden involuntary but protective movements to occur. Upright body posture involves many reflex arcs.

KEY TERMS

neurotransmitter
effector
dendrite
axon
axonal tree
innervate
neuromuscular junction
myelin sheath
oligodendrocyte
Schwann cell
node
sensory neuron
interneuron
motor neuron

sensory receptor
glial cell (neuroglia)
neural impulse
sodium-potassium ion-exchange
polarized
resting potential
depolarized
repolarization
action potential
refractory period
ion channel
sodium gate
potassium gate
saltatory propagation

synapse
synaptic cleft
acetylcholine
norepinephrine
synaptic knob
presynaptic membrane
calmodulin
postsynaptic membrane
acetylcholinesterase
inhibitory neuron
chloride ion
hyperpolarized
reflex arc
stretch receptor

REVIEW QUESTIONS

1 Prepare an outline drawing of a motor neuron, labelling cell body, nucleus, dendrites, axon, axonal tree, and axonal knobs. (pp. 520–521)

2 Add to your drawing, a myelin sheath, labelling nodes and internodes. How do such sheaths form? (p. 521)

3 Summarize the general roles of sensory neurons, interneurons, and motor neurons. In what two structures are interneurons located? (pp. 522–523)

4 Describe the structure of a nerve. How are its neurons protected from stimulating each other? (p. 522)

5 In what major way do neural impulses differ from electrical current? How are they similar? (pp. 522–523)

6 Describe the concentration of positive and negative ions in the resting neuron. (pp. 523–524)

7 Explain the distribution of charges in and around the resting neuron in terms of sodium and potassium ions and protein. How does the exchange pump help with this? (p. 524)

8 The resting potential is said to be -60 mV. What does this have to do with polarization and how is such a measurement made? (p. 524)

9 What happens to the following when an action potential begins: the polarized state, the positive charges, the negative charges? (pp. 524–525)

10 Explain in terms of membrane permeability and sodium ions how an action potential starts. (pp. 524–525)

11 Repolarization immediately follows depolarization. Explain this in terms of behavior of specific ions. At what voltage potential does repolarization begin? (p. 526)

12 Recent discoveries about the neural membrane help explain how the rapid movement of ions can occur. What makes this rapid movement possible? (p. 526)

13 Explain, in terms of sodium gates, how an action potential can move along a neuron? (p. 526)

14 At what voltage does the potassium gate open? Close? (p. 526)

15 Which events are clarified by considering the presence of two differently activated sodium gates. (p. 526)

16 How does the presence of a myelin sheath affect the speed of an action potential? What other way is there to speed up an action potential? (pp. 526–527)

17 Where do action potentials actually take place in myelinated neurons? How does the depolarizing wave move along a myelinated region? (p. 528)

18 Saltatory propagation saves a great deal of ATP. Explain why. (p. 528)
19 What is the role of the following at the synapse: calcium ions, neurotransmitter molecules, postsynaptic receptor sites, enzymes, neurotransmitter vesicles? (p. 529)
20 Specifically, how does the postsynaptic membrane first react when neurotransmitters fill the critical number of receptor sites? What does this cause? (p. 529)
21 Why is it so essential that the neurotransmitter be broken down by enzymes soon after it acts? (p. 530)

22 What is the effect of organophosphates at the synapse? How might this affect an insect? (p. 530)
23 What effect does neurotransmitter from an inhibiting neuron have on the postsynaptic membrane and receiving neuron? How is this overcome? (p. 530)
24 How might inhibiting neurons offer a measure of control in the nervous system? (p. 530)
25 List the events associated with the knee jerk reflex. How might such acts be important in avoiding injury? (p. 530)

33

THE CENTRAL NERVOUS SYSTEM

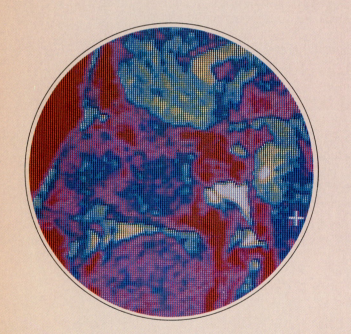

We now come to the part of biology where the brain discusses itself. We can only begin to guess at what lies ahead in this area of research, but we will get some very tantalizing glimpses as we concern ourselves with some of the work that has already been done. So now that we've learned something about the anatomy of neurons and the chemistry of neural behavior, let's learn something about our highly regarded brain (are these the words of a brain complimenting itself?) and the great thick cord that communicates with it. The brain and the spinal cord together comprise the **central nervous system (CNS).** Here we will take a closer look at this great system and the neural apparatus that lies outside the CNS connecting its functions to the rest of the body. First let's consider how the CNS may have evolved.

EVOLUTION OF THE CENTRAL NERVOUS SYSTEM

Clues to the evolutionary development of nervous systems can be gleaned from a cross-species survey from simple to complex (Figure 33.1). One of the simplest neural arrangements (hardly a system) is that of the freshwater *Hydra*. It consists simply of a two-dimensional net of interconnecting neurons, or nerve cells, spread throughout the outer body layer. The entire surface of the animal is about equally covered. There is no part that controls the rest; no nerve center that functions in the regulation or coordination of the nerve net. Thus if one part of the animal is stimulated, the entire body responds and shows awareness of the stimulus.

The flatworm has a somewhat more centralized nervous system (Fig. 33.1b). The neurons are arranged in two longitudinal nerves connected by **transverse nerves,** producing a "ladder" as opposed to the *Hydra's* "net." Your keen eye will undoubtedly also have noted the consolidation of nerves in the head region. These are the **cephalic** (head) **ganglia,** which are composed of clumps of neural cell bodies.

A somewhat more complex nervous system is found in the earthworm (Figure 33.1c). The earthworm has a single longitudinal nerve, but it shows vestiges of a paired arrangement in that it is two lobed, much like two cords pressed together. The nerve is ventral, with the heart and digestive tract lying dorsal to it. The distinct cerebral ganglia together form a primitive brain. Note the segmental nodes along the nerve cord, each with paired nerves reaching into a segment of the body.

The frog nervous system (Figure 33.1d) is relatively primitive for that of a vertebrate, but it can be used to illustrate the basic neural plan in vertebrates. In this group, we find a distinct brain and spinal cord that together form a true central nervous system. In frogs, as in all vertebrates, the longitudinal nerve (the spinal cord) is dorsal, hollow, filled with fluid, and protected by bone. The anterior end is marked by a brain, an elaboration of the primitive ganglionic mass of ancient forebears. The vertebrate brain shows marked specialization; that is, different parts of it are associated with very specific functions. The central nervous system of vertebrates shows traces of the paired and segmented neural arrangements of their distant ancestors. For example, the brain is two-lobed and paired nerves extend from it and from the spinal cord. However, the pair branching is no longer so regular and apparent because of specialization along the spinal cord as the vertebrate body plan became more complex. Figure 33.2 illustrates relative differences in parts of the brain from fish to reptile to mammal.

Vertebrates have strongly centralized nervous systems with a relatively large, specialized brain and a lengthy dorsal, hollow, segmentally organized spinal cord.

Nerve centralization, absent in the coelenterate's netlike nervous system, occurs as a ladderlike arrangement in flatworms and in the annelids as a more complex brain, ventral nerve cord, and segmental ganglia in the annelids.

The **central nervous system** is only one of two parts of the vertebrate neural structure. The other is the **peripheral nervous system.** The central nervous system, we know, comprises the brain and spinal cord. The peripheral nervous system includes the vast network of neurons and nerves outside the central nervous system. Neurons enter and leave the central

FIGURE 33.1 Invertebrate nervous systems include (a) the simple nerve net of the coelenterate *(Hydra)*, a radial animal. The ladderlike system in the planarian **(b)**, a bilateral animal, reveals some anterior consolidation and marked segmentation. The earthworm, an annelid **(c)**, has a sizable brain and a highly segmented arrangement of ganglia in its ventral nerve cord. The frog, a vertebrate **(d)**, has a highly consolidated brain with segmentation along the cord somewhat masked by specialization.

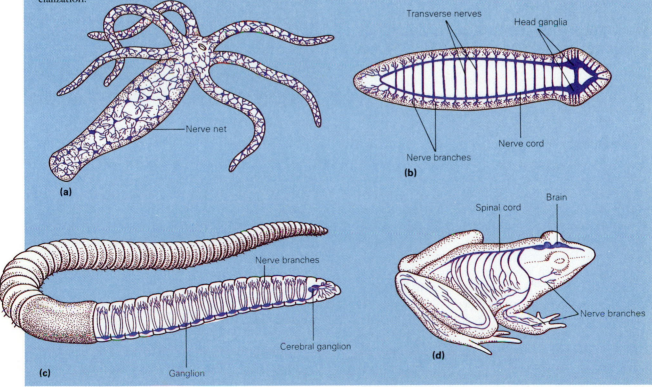

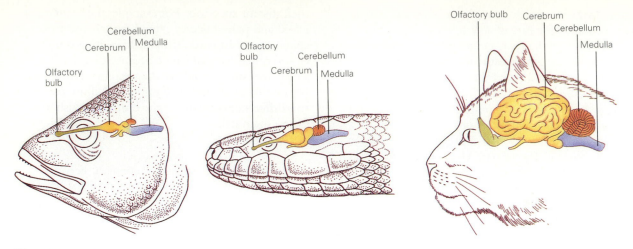

FIGURE 33.2 A comparison of the brains of a fish, reptile, and a mammal. Notice the diminutive size of the cerebrum relative to the olfactory bulb in the fish. Also note the relative mass of the lower brain (here, the cerebellum and medulla) compared to that of the cerebrum. Reptiles have a somewhat larger, but still smooth, cerebrum and a reduced olfactory area. The brain of the cat is dominated by the convoluted cerebrum. The cerebellum, involved in coordination, is well-developed in the cat, as is the olfactory bulb.

nervous system through **cranial** and **spinal nerves.** The peripheral nervous system is divided functionally into two systems. They are the **somatic nervous system** and the **autonomic nervous system** (about which we will say more shortly).

THE HUMAN BRAIN

The human brain (Figure 33.3) is a fascinating structure. To this day, we know very little about the brain, but even the things that we do know are often hard to believe. For example, there is some evidence that every word you have ever said or heard is filed away in your brain, even though you will go to your grave having retrieved hardly any of that information.

The human brain weighs about 1.4 kg (3 lb), has a volume of 1200 to 1500 cc, contains over 100 billion neurons, and has about 10 times that number of supporting glial cells. Since each neuron may synapse with several other neurons, there are a number of alternative pathways for impulses, and the coordination necessary to produce even a simple response must be due to a veritable neural symphony.

The brain, which has a consistency somewhat like gelatin, is obviously fragile, but it is well protected. In addition to the surrounding skull, the brain—like the spinal cord—is directly enclosed by the tough, elastic coverings called the **meninges.** The spaces within these membranes, and the cavities within the brain itself, are filled with the pressurized, shock-absorbing **cerebrospinal fluid.** The billions of deli-

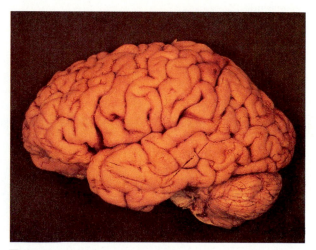

FIGURE 33.3 Under the wrinkled exterior of the human brain resides an incredibly complex array of neurons.

cate neurons themselves are embedded in the vast numbers of glial cells that make up much of the brain's mass.

The vertebrate brain consists of three regions: **hindbrain, midbrain,** and **forebrain.** In humans, the midbrain is not easily seen, since most of it is enclosed by the prominent forebrain (Figure 33.4).

THE HINDBRAIN

The **hindbrain,** which consists of the **medulla oblongata,** the **pons,** and the **cerebellum,** is continuous with the spinal cord. As a rough generality, the

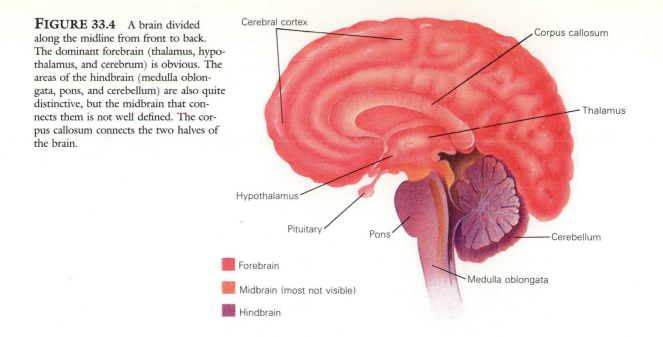

FIGURE 33.4 A brain divided along the midline from front to back. The dominant forebrain (thalamus, hypothalamus, and cerebrum) is obvious. The areas of the hindbrain (medulla oblongata, pons, and cerebellum) are also quite distinctive, but the midbrain that connects them is not well defined. The corpus callosum connects the two halves of the brain.

Cerebral cortex

Corpus callosum

Thalamus

Hypothalamus

Pituitary

Pons

Cerebellum

Medulla oblongata

■ Forebrain
■ Midbrain (most not visible)
■ Hindbrain

more unconscious, involuntary, and mechanical processes are directed by these more posterior parts of the brain. For example, the medulla oblongata (or, more simply, the medulla), which can be considered an enlargement of the spinal cord, controls such functions as breathing rate, blood pressure, and heart rate. All communication between the brain and spinal column must pass through the medulla. The medulla also contains **nuclei** that help regulate respiratory, digestive, cardiovascular, and urogenital functions. (Nuclei, in this sense, are clumps of neural cell bodies that develop in the same way and that innervate the same region.)

The pons, which lies just above (anterior to) the medulla, contains the ascending and descending tracts that run between the brain and spinal cord. It also receives tracts to and from large nerves that extend from the brain itself (primarily to regions of the head and face). These are called the **cranial nerves.** The pons also links the functions of the forebrain with those of the cerebellum.

The **cerebellum** is a paired, bulbous structure, about the size and general appearance of the two halves of a large walnut. It lies above the medulla and somewhat toward the back of the head. The cerebellum is concerned with balance, equilibrium, and muscle coordination. It receives input from muscle proprioceptors and from areas of the cerebral cortex concerned with vision, hearing, and equilibrium. (Because of its role, do you suppose that the cerebellum of a ballet dancer or tumbler might differ from that of others? It now appears that it does, but the differences are subtle.)

Hindbrain functions include: regulation of body processes **(medulla)**, linking of forebrain and midbrain **(pons)**, balance and muscle coordination **(cerebellum).**

THE MIDBRAIN

Essentially, the **midbrain** connects the hindbrain and forebrain. All of the tracts between the two must pass through this area. Certain parts of the midbrain receive sensory input from the eyes and ears. All auditory (sound) input of vertebrates is processed here before being sent to the forebrain. In most vertebrates, visual input is first processed here also. But in mammals, the visual information is possibly sent directly to the forebrain. Although the midbrain is involved in complex behavior in fishes and amphibians, many of these functions are assumed by the forebrain in reptiles, birds, and mammals.

THE FOREBRAIN

The **forebrain,** the largest and most dominant part of the human brain, is responsible for conscious thought, reasoning, memory, language, sensory decoding, and certain kinds of movement. The embryonic forebrain gives rise to such important structures as the **thalamus,** the **reticular system,** the **hypothalamus,** and the **cerebrum.**

The Thalamus

The **thalamus** is located at the base of the forebrain. It has been rather unpoetically called the "great relay station of the brain" (see Figure 33.4). It consists of densely packed clusters of neurons, which provide connections between the various parts of the brain—between the forebrain and the hindbrain, between different parts of the forebrain, and between parts of the sensory system and the cerebrum.

The Reticular System

The thalamus also contains most of an extensive area called the **reticular system,** comprised of interconnected neurons that are almost feltlike in appearance. These neurons run throughout the thalamus and into the midbrain. The reticular system is still somewhat of a mystery, but several interesting facts are known about it. For example, we know that it monitors the brain. Every pathway to and from the various portions of the brain sends side branches to the reticular system as it passes through the thalamus, so it virtually taps all incoming and outgoing communications. Also, reticular neurons appear to be rather unspecific. The same reticular neuron may be stimulated by impulses from the hand, foot, ear, or eye. As for its function, the leading hypothesis is that the reticular apparatus is something of an alarm system that serves to activate the appropriate parts of the brain upon receiving a stimulus. The portion of the reticular system involved in such arousal is logically called the **reticular activating system (RAS).** The more messages it intercepts, the more the brain is aroused.

The reticular system also seems to function importantly in sleep. You may have noticed that it is much easier to fall asleep when you are lying on a comfortable bed in a quiet room with the lights off than on a noisy bus. With fewer stimuli, the reticular system receives fewer messages, and the brain is allowed to relax. Some people can sleep under almost any condition, perhaps because their reticular systems more effectively screen out sensory signals on their way to the cortex.

T**he reticular system** monitors incoming information, relaying it to other parts of the brain; it screens out stimuli during sleep.

The Hypothalamus

As the name implies, the **hypothalamus** lies below the thalamus (see Figure 33.4). It is densely packed with cells that help regulate the body's internal environment as well as certain aspects of behavior. The hypothalamus helps control heart rate, blood pressure, and body temperature. It is also involved in such basic drives as hunger, thirst, sex, and rage. Electrical stimulation of various centers in the hypothalamus can cause a cat to act hungry, sexy, cold, hot, benignly, or angry. In humans it is known that a tumor pressing against the hypothalamus can cause a person to behave violently, even murderously.

A major function of the hypothalamus is its coordination of the nervous system with the **endocrine (hormonal) system.** In fact, the hypothalamus has a certain monitoring control over the so-called "master gland," the pituitary (see Chapter 35). The hypothalamus actually may be called an endocrine gland itself, since it produces some of the pituitary gland hormones.

H**ypothalamic** regulatory functions include heart rate, blood pressure, body temperature, basic drives, and coordination of many hormones.

The limbic system. The hypothalamus and the thalamus, along with certain pathways in the cortex, are functionally part of what is called the **limbic system** (Figure 33.5). The limbic system links the forebrain and midbrain and is composed of a number of nuclei that are also centers of emotion. For example, the **amygdala** lying within the limbic system can produce rage if stimulated and docility if removed. The **hippocampus,** another limbic structure, may figure importantly in the memory of recent events. Without the hippocampus, a person may be unable to complete a sentence because he or she forgot how it began.

The Cerebrum

The word *brain* usually conjures up an image of two large, convoluted (wrinkled) gray lobes. Those lobes make up much of the **cerebrum,** the largest and most prominent part of the human brain. If we had to ascribe one prominent responsibility to the cerebrum, we would probably say it is *intelligence*.

The left and right halves of the cerebrum are the **cerebral hemispheres,** and the outer layer of gray, unmyelinated cells is the **cerebral cortex.** (*Cortex* means "rind," and is a general biological term for the outer layer of any organ.) The cerebral cortex consists of a thin but extremely dense layer of about 15 billion nerve cell bodies and their dendrites. It overlies the whitish, more solid region of myelinated nerve fibers below (Figure 33.6).

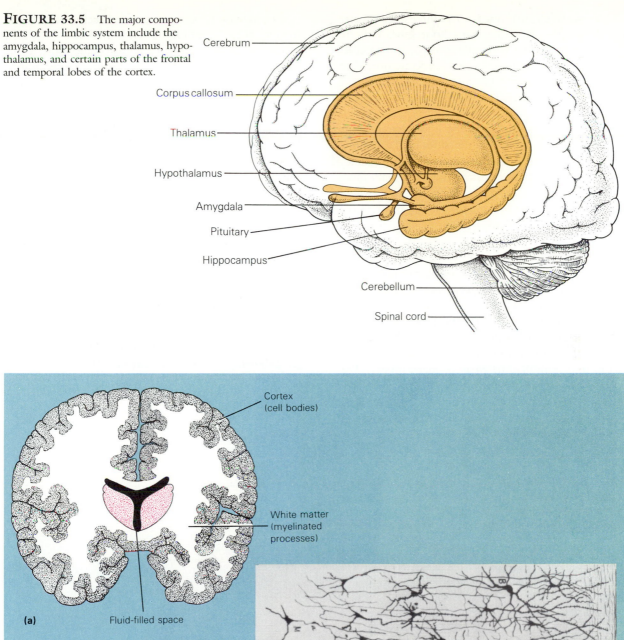

FIGURE 33.5 The major components of the limbic system include the amygdala, hippocampus, thalamus, hypothalamus, and certain parts of the frontal and temporal lobes of the cortex.

Cerebrum

Corpus callosum

Thalamus

Hypothalamus

Amygdala

Pituitary

Hippocampus

Cerebellum

Spinal cord

Cortex (cell bodies)

White matter (myelinated processes)

(a)

Fluid-filled space

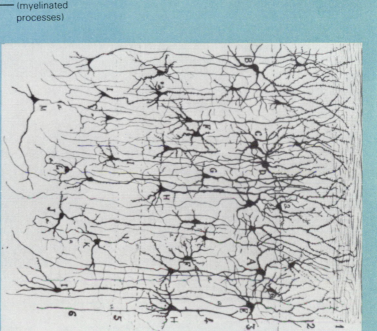

(b)

FIGURE 33.6 **(a)** A cross-section of the cerebrum reveals an outer layer of gray matter, the cortex, that contains several very dense layers of neurons. **(b)** Cells of the cortex from a micrograph made in 1888.

Hemispheres and lobes. In humans, each cerebral hemisphere is divided into four lobes (Figure 33.7). At the back on each side is the **occipital lobe,** which receives and analyzes visual information. The *visual field* of the cerebral cortex is stimulated by the images formed on the retinas of the eyes. If the occipital lobe is injured, black "holes" appear in the part of the visual field that occurs in the injured area.

The **temporal lobes**—at the sides of the brain—roughly resemble the thumbs on boxing gloves. They help process visual information, but their main function is in hearing. The **frontal lobes** are right where you would expect to find them—at the front of the cerebrum. (This is the part of your head that you hit with the palm of your hand when you suddenly remember what you have forgotten.) Part of the frontal lobe regulates precise voluntary movement. Another part controls movements that produce speech.

The very front of each frontal lobe is called the **prefrontal area.** Its principal function is to sort out sensory information. In other words, it places information and stimuli into their proper context. The gentle touch of a mate and the sight of a hand protruding from the bathtub drain will both serve as stimuli, but each stimulus will be processed differently by the prefrontal area.

The **parietal lobes**—located directly behind the frontal lobes—contain the sensory areas for the skin receptors, as well as the areas that detect body position. Damage to the parietal lobe may cause numbness and can also cause grossly distorted visual perceptions.

By probing the brain with electrodes, investigators have determined exactly which areas of the cerebrum are involved in the body's various sensory and motor activities and have mapped these functions on the cortex. Figure 33.8 shows the results of such mapping. The figures are distorted to demonstrate the relative area of the cerebrum devoted to each body part. The sensory areas of the cortex are largely devoted to integrating sensations from the face, tongue, hands, and genitals, while the motor areas are devoted primarily to the muscles of the tongue, face, and thumbs.

Functions in cerebral regions include: vision **(occipital lobes)**, hearing **(temporal lobes)**, voluntary movement and speech **(frontal lobes)**, sorting sensory input **(prefrontal areas)**, visual and sensory perception **(parietal lobes)**.

FIGURE 33.7 The human cerebrum is divided into four prominent lobes: occipital, temporal, frontal, and parietal.

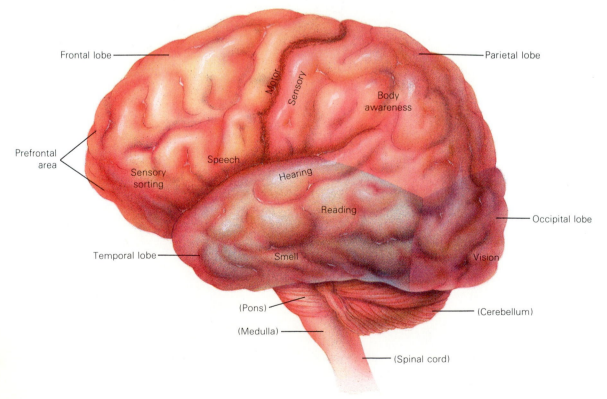

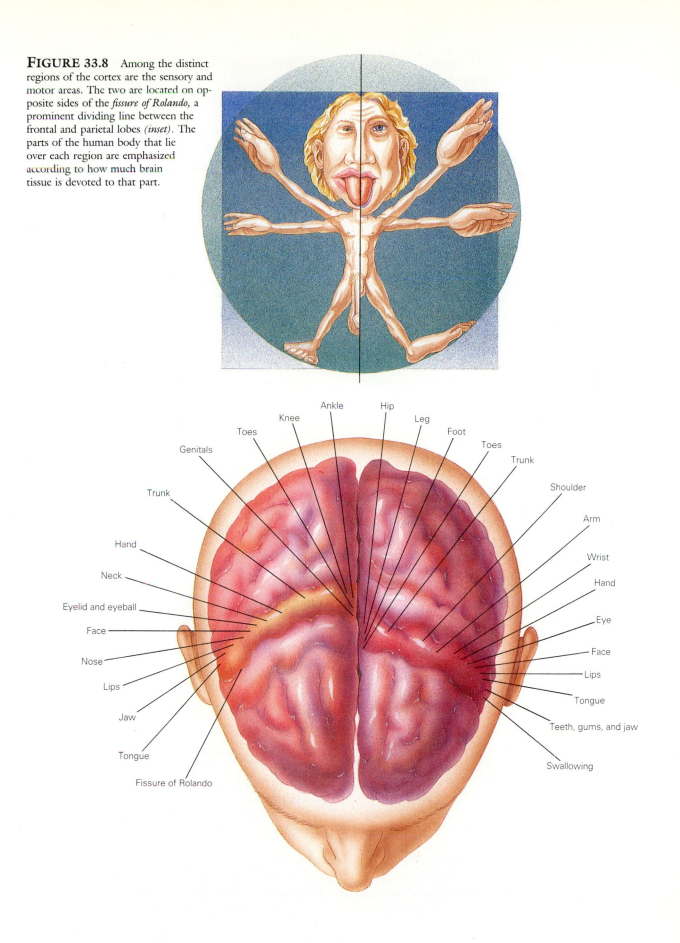

FIGURE 33.8 Among the distinct regions of the cortex are the sensory and motor areas. The two are located on opposite sides of the *fissure of Rolando,* a prominent dividing line between the frontal and parietal lobes *(inset).* The parts of the human body that lie over each region are emphasized according to how much brain tissue is devoted to that part.

Right and left halves of the brain. Although the two cerebral hemispheres are roughly equal in size and in potential, they are quite different in function. Moreover, their differences apparently are accentuated by learning, because certain learned patterns are associated primarily with one hemisphere.

Because neural tracts cross from one side of the brain to the other, the right side of the body is controlled by the left side of the brain, and vice versa; thus in right-handed people, the left half of the brain is dominant.

Functions such as speech, perception, and different aspects of IQ test performance are also more likely to be controlled by one hemisphere than the other. The primary speech center of all right-handed people (and most left-handed people as well) is located in the left hemisphere. The left hemisphere also seems to be the seat of analytical thinking, while spatial perception is a right-hemisphere function. Left-hemisphere brain damage can result in *aphasia*—the inability to speak or understand language—while damage to the right hemisphere of the brain may result in the inability to draw the simplest picture or diagram (but does not affect the ability to write letters and numbers, which is a left-hemisphere function).

In spite of these specializations, the right and left hemispheres operate as an integrated functional unit, connected primarily by the **corpus callosum** (Figure 33.9). If one side of the brain learns something—for instance, by feeling an object with just one hand—the information will be transferred to the other hemisphere. However, if the corpus callosum has been severed, the left side of the brain literally doesn't know what the left hand is doing.

> Although anatomically similar, the **cerebral hemispheres** are functionally distinct, specializing in learning, speech, analytical thought, and handedness. Information is shared via the **corpus callosum.**

THE SPINAL CORD

The **spinal cord** (Figure 33.10) serves as the primary link between the brain and other parts of the nervous system. Essentially, its outer areas consist of incredible numbers of myelinated axons running parallel to each other and forming **spinal tracts.** Myelin gives these tracts a white, glistening appearance. Inside this area is a butterfly-shaped gray region (the **gray mat-**

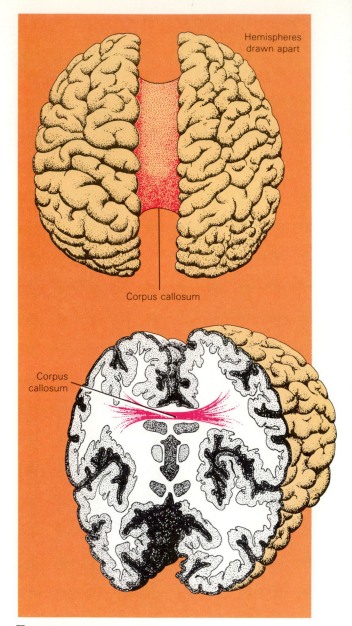

Hemispheres drawn apart

Corpus callosum

Corpus callosum

FIGURE 33.9 The corpus callosum is a neural bridge between the cerebral hemispheres, relaying information from one half to the other.

ter), which is composed not only of nonmyelinated nerve tracts but also of the nonmyelinated cell bodies of all the spinal neurons.

The spinal cord begins as a narrow continuation of the brain, passing through the **foramen magnum** ("big opening") at the base of the skull. It lies sheltered within the **vertebral canal,** a continuous channel lying within the vertebral column (see Chapter 31). Paired **spinal nerves,** which are part of the peripheral nervous system, emerge from the cord through the spaces between adjacent arches.

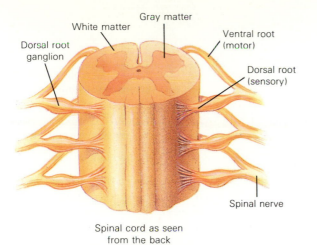

FIGURE 33.10 A three-dimensional view of the spinal cord reveals gray matter (cell bodies), surrounded by white matter (myelinated fibers). Incoming neural impulses from sensory neurons synapse in the dorsal root ganglia, passing then into the cord for transfer to the brain. Motor neural impulses emerge from the cord via the ventral roots, on their way to muscles, glands, blood vessels, and other effector organs.

CHEMICALS IN THE BRAIN

We know that the brain contains billions of neurons and that these neurons interact in a delicate and coordinated manner, integrating and shunting information from one place to another. This interaction includes both the excitation and inhibition of adjacent neurons through very specific actions in the trillions of synapses. The brain has at least 50 neurotransmitters, with more being discovered all the time. This number probably shouldn't be too surprising, considering the specificity necessary in orchestrating the brain's vast network of cells.

The brain's neurotransmitters—synthesized in the cell bodies of neurons—may be simple **monoamines,** such as norepinephrine, dopamine, histamine, and serotonin. Other neurotransmitters may be modified or unmodified amino acids. One more recently discovered class of transmitters, the **neuropeptides,** are short chains of amino acids varying in number from two to about 40.

Among the more interesting brain neuropeptides are the **enkephalins** and **endorphins.** These modify our perception of pain and also have an elevating effect on mood. Anything acutely painful, such as running a marathon race or being shot in the foot, will stimulate the release of enkephalins. The "runner's high," the slight euphoria that may result after about a 10-mile run, is also attributed to the release of enkephalins (although some runners may simply be ecstatic at having covered that distance without

dying in the process). These peptides are called **opioid neurotransmitters** because morphine and other opiates will also bind to the enkephalin neuron receptors and mimic their action. Our rapidly expanding knowledge of the neurotransmitters is shedding some light on the action of certain drugs that affect the central nervous system. It is also being found that neurotransmitters are implicated in certain disease conditions (Essay 33.1).

Endorphins and enkephalins, brain neurotransmitters, are known to reduce pain and produce euphoria. Their effects are imitated by opiates.

ELECTRICAL ACTIVITY IN THE BRAIN

Each firing neuron in the brain creates impulses that generate a form of electrical activity. If, perhaps, a million neurons fire simultaneously, this electrical energy can be detected experimentally from outside the body. The instrument used in such detection is called an **electroencephalograph,** and the record obtained is called an **electroencephalogram (EEG).** Electrodes leading to the instrument are fastened at various places on the cranium, and the very faint electrical currents they pick up (primarily from the cortex) are amplified and recorded.

The EEG is not very useful in determining specifically what is going on the brain, but it is useful in detecting certain abnormalities or changes in brain activity—certain kinds of brain damage, for example, or the differences between wakefulness and sleep. Figure 33.11 compares the EEG of a normal person with that of a person with epilepsy. As the recording shows, the brains of epileptics are subject to sudden, random bursts of electrical activity. In a few instances, this abnormality can be traced to physical defects, such as scars or lesions in the brain tissue, but most forms of epilepsy are simply not understood.

Sleep

Electrical activity in the brain does not cease with sleep—quite the contrary is true. EEGs reveal that sleep is accompanied by a considerable amount of brain activity. Sleep has four distinct phases (Figure 33.12). By far the most intriguing of these is called **rapid eye movement (REM) sleep.** During this period, the skeletal muscles are very relaxed—except for the eyes, which dart about beneath the eyelids. The EEG recording at this time is similar to that pro-

We are all unhappily aware that some people may become forgetful, foolish, and incompetent as they age. They may regress to reliving the distant past, no longer functioning in the present. Such people suffer from **senile dementia,** the most prevalent form of which is called **Alzheimer's disease,** a relentlessly progressive condition that afflicts 5 to 10% of all people over 65. (It can also be found in younger people.) Many patients in nursing homes have been placed there because their cognitive abilities, and especially their memories, have deteriorated too far for family members to be able to care for them at home.

Alzheimer's disease first manifests itself as an inability to recall recent events. At this stage, afflicted people cannot remember what happened an hour or a week ago, but they can often remember childhood experiences in vivid detail. As short-term memory lapse continues, other cognitive functions begin to fail. In the second stage of the illness, victims gradually forget how to read or write or perform simple calculations, and their speech may become garbled and irrational. The impair-

ment of these abilities is often accompanied by irritability, paranoia, and hallucinations. Yet afflicted people remain alert (and aware of their degeneration) until the final stages of the disease.

Whereas any form of senile dementia was once considered to be simply a natural part of aging—the mind deteriorating as the body does—researchers now recognize certain variables associated with Alzheimer's disease. For example, the disease seems to be strongly influenced by genetic factors. However this is difficult to fully substantiate, since the disease appears so late in life that there is a strong possibility that the individual may die before the traits ever have the opportunity to be expressed. One genetic indicator is due to a nondisjunction at meiosis resulting in a condition similar to Downs' syndrome. The connection between the two conditions is being extensively investigated. Another indicator of Alzheimer's disease is a reduction in the level of **choline acetyltransferase,** an enzyme that helps synthesize the neurotransmitter **acetylcholine,** in the brain cells of victims. In 1986,

researchers reported a blood indicator of Alzheimer's. Some healthy people were reluctant to be tested for the indicator, however, since there is no cure. They would simply live out their "normal" years knowing what lay ahead.

People suffering from Alzheimer's show a marked decrease in the number of neurons in the cortex of the brain (the gray matter) and especially in the **nucleus basalis,** a structure in the base of the forebrain that has many neural extensions to the cerebral cortex. (If you point your finger directly at your temple, you will be pointing at this somewhat mysterious structure.) Alzheimer's is also marked by dense tangles ("plaques") of neurons and their remnants in other parts of the brain.

Scientists continue to investigate the physiological causes of what was once thought to be a mental condition. Their discoveries regarding Alzheimer's disease's effects on the brain raise possibilities of counteracting these effects with medication or surgery, and offer new hope for treating this affliction of the elderly.

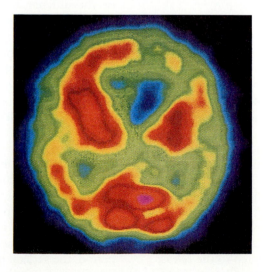

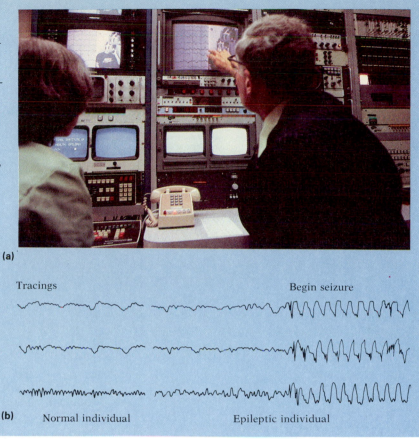

FIGURE 33.11 **(a)** An electroencephalogram (EEG) is produced by fastening a number of electrodes on the patient's scalp and then recording differences in the electrical potential between or among the leads. **(b)** The normal electrical activity of the brain is seen at the left, showing several EEG tracings from different locations on the cranium. In an epileptic person, the brain may show normal electrical activity between seizures, but when these episodes do occur, the electrical disturbances are obvious.

(a)

Tracings   Begin seizure

(b)   Normal individual   Epileptic individual

duced by wakefulness. A person awakened at this time will report vivid dreams (that will otherwise be forgotten if the person is allowed to waken naturally).

Psychologists and biologists generally agree that, for whatever reason, sleep appears to be essential, especially to mental concentration and balance, and is somehow restoring. Theorists suspect that sleep (and REM sleep in particular) is a period of information sorting and storage, and may be essential to long-term memory storage.

MEMORY

Mammals have two distinct kinds of memory. **Short-term memory** lasts for just a few hours, whereas **long-term memory** is relatively permanent. The two apparently function together because the neural events that form memories must be encoded in the short-term memory first. These short-term memories may or may not be consolidated into long-term memory. No one knows just what physical form

either kind of memory takes. Experimental manipulation of rats suggests that whereas short-term memory does not require protein synthesis, the consolidation into long-term memory does require it.

We do know that the **hippocampus** part of the limbic system (see Figure 33.5) is necessary for long-term memory consolidation. Rats with experimental lesions in the hippocampus must be taught the same maze every day, because they will have forgotten it by the next day. Humans with hippocampal lesions are in the same kind of a fix. They may be perfectly rational, intelligent people, with the ability to learn and with an unimpaired memory of events that occurred before their brain damage. But they will have no recollection whatever of anything that has happened to them since, unless it has happened within the previous few hours.

Memory may be **short-term** and transient or, when consolidated by the hippocampus, **long-term** and permanent.

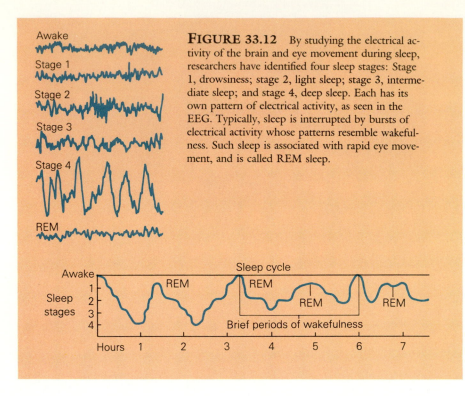

Awake

Stage 1

Stage 2

Stage 3

Stage 4

REM

FIGURE 33.12 By studying the electrical activity of the brain and eye movement during sleep, researchers have identified four sleep stages: Stage 1, drowsiness; stage 2, light sleep; stage 3, intermediate sleep; and stage 4, deep sleep. Each has its own pattern of electrical activity, as seen in the EEG. Typically, sleep is interrupted by bursts of electrical activity whose patterns resemble wakefulness. Such sleep is associated with rapid eye movement, and is called REM sleep.

Sleep cycle

Awake
Sleep stages 1 2 3 4
REM REM REM REM
Brief periods of wakefulness
Hours 1 2 3 4 5 6 7

THE PERIPHERAL NERVOUS SYSTEM

As was mentioned, the vertebrate nervous system is divided into two major parts: the central nervous system and the peripheral nervous system. The peripheral nervous system includes all the neural structures that lie outside the central nervous system. The peripheral nervous system can be further divided into two functionally different systems. One is the **somatic system,** which includes sensory pathways (from sensory structures, to be discussed in the next chapter) and motor pathways (to effectors such as muscles). The other system is the **autonomic nervous system.**

The Autonomic Nervous System

The **autonomic nervous system (ANS)** is essentially a *motor system*. This means that it carries impulses from the brain and spinal cord to the organs it serves. In doing this, it works in concert with the central nervous system in regulating and sensing the activity of the **viscera,** the internal organs. In addition to the prominent contents of the chest and abdominal cavities (the heart, lungs, digestive tract, kidneys, and bladder), the ANS also coordinates activities in such body parts as the arteries, the veins, the irises of the

eyes, the nasal lining, the sweat glands, the salivary glands, and the tiny muscles that cause our hair to stand on end when we learn who's been elected (Figure 33.13).

The general function of the autonomic nervous system is to promote **homeostasis.** Essentially, homeostasis is the maintenance of stability or constancy in the face of changing conditions. The ANS, under the direction of the central nervous system, constantly adjusts and coordinates the internal organs to meet changing demands. For such a system to function efficiently requires a considerable amount of sensory feedback from the organs served. This is carried out by sensory nerves of the somatic nervous system, which, by keeping the brain informed, also play an important role in homeostasis.

> The **autonomic nervous system (ANS)** is basically **homeostatic.** It responds to sensory feedback from the internal organs by continuously making the fine adjustments needed by the body in meeting changing conditions.

The autonomic nervous system is divided into two parts: the **sympathetic division** and **parasympathetic division.** These divisions usually have opposite effects, but they operate in a highly coordinated manner to produce an overall adaptive effect. One example of this is control of heart rate. The human heart, without outside influence, contracts about 70 to 90 times per minute. It speeds up when stimulated by the sympathetic **cardioaccelerator** nerve, and slows down on a signal from a parasympathetic **vagus** nerve (see Figure 33.13). How can neural impulses from two different nerves have opposing effects on heart rate? The answer has to do with the specific neurotransmitters released by those neurons. Most (but not all) of the sympathetic neurons secrete the chemical **norepinephrine** at their target organs, while neurons of the parasympathetic system secrete **acetylcholine** (as do motor neurons that move skeletal muscle.) Norepinephrine accelerates heart rate, while acetylcholine slows it down.

> The two ANS divisions, the **sympathetic** and **parasympathetic,** work cooperatively but oppositely in regulating many internal body functions.

FIGURE 33.13   The autonomic nervous system, showing the sympathetic and parasympathetic components. The central nervous system is shown in the center.

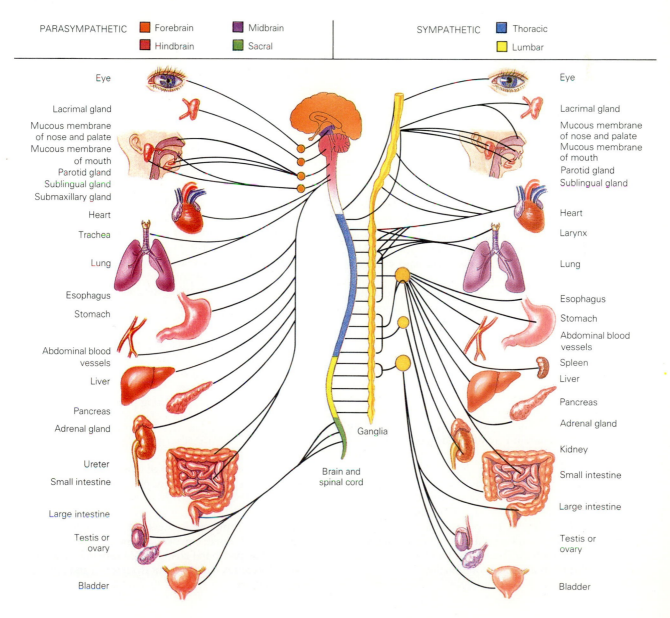

An interesting example of how the two ANS divisions effect such changes in the viscera is seen in emergencies—the so-called "flight-or-fight" response. In an emergency, the heart and breathing rates increase, accompanied by an increase in blood pressure, the shunting of blood from the digestive tract to the brain and skeletal muscles, and a general slowing of all functions not essential to immediate survival. After the emergency has passed, the parasympathetic nervous system takes over, and the internal situation reverses.

As you might expect, the divisions of the autonomic nervous system differ anatomically as well as physiologically. As shown in Figure 33.13, most of the parasympathetic nerves originate in the brain, with a few coming from the lower region of the spinal cord. Some go directly to their target organs; others end in external ganglia, where they relay their messages to nerves continuing toward the target organ. The sympathetic system originates only in the gray matter of the spinal cord. Furthermore, all of the sympathetic nerves leaving the cord pass through or synapse within rows of **sympathetic ganglia** just outside the cord. Some sympathetic nerves synapse once again in ganglia at various locations in the body.

We can see that the vertebrate body is never at rest. It is virtually abuzz with neural signals flashing in all directions but in a highly coordinated fashion. In many cases those signals are responses to stimuli, both from within and without. Next we will see just how environmental stimuli are perceived by the special receptors we call the senses.

SUMMARY

The central nervous system consists of the brain and the spinal cord.

EVOLUTION OF THE CENTRAL NERVOUS SYSTEM

The neurons in coelenterates lack consolidation and form a simple net. Planarian flatworms have a ladder-like system with transverse nerves and an anterior consolidation called the cephalic ganglia. Annelids (and arthropods) have a distinct brain, where ganglia mass, and a paired but fused ventral nerve cord with segmental branches. The frog has a definite central nervous system; the brain has specialized regions. It still reveals a general paired construction. Also present is a complex, dorsal hollow nerve cord with segmented branching.

Nerves outside the CNS make up the peripheral nervous system, which includes the somatic and autonomic nervous systems.

THE HUMAN BRAIN

The many billions of neurons and glial cells making up the brain occupy a volume of 1200 to 1500 cc. The fragile tissue is cushioned by cerebrospinal fluid and protected by the meninges, three tough membranes. In humans the usual vertebrate's hindbrain, midbrain, and forebrain are present but the midbrain is reduced and obscured.

THE HINDBRAIN

The hindbrain includes the medulla oblongata, pons and cerebrum. The first controls many involuntary acts such as breathing and heart rate. Some of its functions are assigned to cell masses called nuclei. The pons contains neural tracts from the brain, cord, and cranial nerves and also links the forebrain and cerebellum. The cerebellum functions in balance, equilibrium and muscle coordination.

THE MIDBRAIN

The midbrain in humans is greatly reduced, acting primarily in processing audio input and forming connecting tracts between brain regions.

THE FOREBRAIN

The forebrain, the largest brain region in humans, is involved in both voluntary and involuntary activities.

The Thalamus/Reticular System

The thalamus forms numerous relay connections between brain regions. It contains most of the reticular system, which monitors incoming and outgoing impulses. It contains the reticular activating system that sorts incoming stimuli, at times filtering them out and permitting sleep and at other times arousing the conscious centers.

The Hypothalamus

The hypothalamus regulates internal functions such as heart rate, blood pressure, temperature and basic drives such as sex, anger, and thirst. It also interacts with the endocrine system regulating the pituitary gland and producing its own hormones.

The limbic system, consisting primarily of nuclei, links the forebrain and midbrain and is involved in emotions and recent memory.

The Cerebrum

The cerebrum is made up of two cerebral hemispheres. Its outermost gray layer, the cerebral cortex, contains dense layers of cell bodies. The cerebral lobes and their functions are as follows. (1) Occipital: processes visual input from the eyes. (2) Temporal: processes auditory and some visual input. (3) Frontal: invokes voluntary movement and speech. The prefrontal area sorts sensory information. (4) Parietal: receives sensory input from touch and body position receptors.

Right and left hemispheres have somewhat different functions. One side controls speech, perception, and IQ. Physical control of each side of the body is centered in the opposite hemisphere. Learned information is transferred between hemispheres through the corpus callosum.

THE SPINAL CORD

The spinal cord exits the skull through the foramen magnum and passes through the vertebral canal carrying spinal neural tracts to and from the brain. White matter (outside) represents myelinated fibers, while gray matter (inside), the cell bodies.

CHEMICALS IN THE BRAIN

Relays of neural impulses in the brain are controlled by at least 50 neurotransmitters. Included are monoamines, modified and unmodified amino acids, and neuropeptides. The latter include enkephalins and endorphins associated with the relief of pain and emotional well-being. They work similarly to opioids.

ELECTRICAL ACTIVITY IN THE BRAIN

Gross electrical activity in the brain is detected through electroencephalography. General patterns can be studied for evidence of abnormalities such as epilepsy.

Sleep

EEG studies of sleep reveal several phases, one of which is REM (rapid eye movement) sleep, a time of vivid dreams.

MEMORY

Memory storage begins with short-term memory, where information is encoded. Most of this is temporary, but some events enter permanent long-term memory. The hippocampus is essential to long-term memory.

THE PERIPHERAL NERVOUS SYSTEM

The peripheral nervous system includes all neurons outside the brain and cord. Its somatic branch includes primarily sensory pathways to the brain.

The Autonomic Nervous System

The autonomic branch is principally motor, its neurons affecting the functioning of many internal functions such as circulation, respiration and digestion. The autonomic nervous system promotes homeostasis, a state of stability and constancy.

The sympathetic division of the ANS generally speeds up activity in its target structures, while the parasympathetic division slows things down. They do this through the secretion of different neurotransmitters. The two divisions cooperatively produce the flight-or-fight emergency response—one slowing irrelevant functions, the other speeding the essential ones.

Parasympathetic nerves emerge from the brain and lowermost spinal cord. Some go directly to target organs, while others relay their impulses at synapses. Sympathetic nerves emerge from the spinal cord only. They also follow direct and relay routes.

KEY TERMS

central nervous system (CNS)
transverse nerve
cephalic ganglia
peripheral nervous system
cranial nerve
spinal nerve
somatic nervous system
autonomic nervous system (ANS)
meninges
cerebrospinal fluid
hindbrain
midbrain
forebrain
medulla oblongata
pons
cerebellum
thalamus
reticular system
hypothalamus

cerebrum
reticular activating system (RAS)
endocrine (hormone) system
limbic system
amygdala
hippocampus
cerebral hemisphere
cerebral cortex
occipital lobe
temporal lobe
frontal lobe
prefrontal lobe
parietal lobe
corpus callosum
spinal cord
spinal tract
gray matter
foramen magnum
vertebral canal

monoamine
neuropeptide
enkephalin
endorphin
opioid neurotransmitter
electroencephalograph
electroencephalogram (EEG)
rapid eye movement (REM) sleep
short-term memory
long-term memory
homeostasis
sympathetic division
parasympathetic division
cardioaccelerator nerve
vagus nerve
norepinephrine
acetylcholine
sympathetic ganglia

REVIEW QUESTIONS

1 Compare the nervous systems of *Hydra,* a planarian, and an earthworm. Why would you expect to find similarities between planarian and earthworm? (p. 534)

2 Describe the frog's central nervous system. In what ways is it similar to that of the earthworm? What are some striking differences? (p. 535)

3 What is included in the following: central nervous system, peripheral nervous system, somatic nervous system, and autonomic nervous system? (pp. 535–536)

4 In what ways are the meninges and the cerebrospinal fluid important to the brain? What group of cells also plays a supporting role? (p. 536)

5 List the principal parts of the hindbrain. In general what kinds of acts does this region regulate? (p. 537)

6 What part of the hindbrain would be most affected by the ongoing training of a gymnast? Why? (p. 537)

7 What were some prior functions of the vertebrate midbrain? What has happened to these functions in humans? (p. 537)

8 What general function is ascribed to the thalamus? (p. 538)

9 Where is the reticular system located? List its two important functions. (p. 538)

10 List five specific functions or behaviors that are influenced by the hypothalamus. (p. 538)

11 What are two endocrine (hormonal) functions of the hypothalamus? (p. 538)

12 What specific parts of the limbic system are involved in emotions and memory? (p. 538)

13 Where is the cerebral cortex? Describe its makeup. (p. 538)

14 Name a function that would most likely be impaired if severe damage occurred in the following: occipital lobe, temporal lobe, parietal lobe, prefrontal region. (p. 540)

15 Locate the cerebral regions responsible for voluntary movement and sensory input from touch receptors. What factor reveals the importance of movement and touch in a specific part? (p. 540)

16 In general how does the control of body movements relate to specific cerebral hemispheres? What familiar information about stroke victims supports this? (p. 541)

17 Which side of the brain is in control in right-handed persons? (p. 542)

18 Specifically, how does one hemisphere learn what the other has learned? How do we know this? (p. 542)

19 What is the general function of the spinal cord? What are its white and gray regions made of? (p. 542)

20 Why is it not surprising to find a great number of neurotransmitters in the brain? List three main types. (p. 543)

21 When are enkephalins and endophins released? What is their general effect? (p. 543)

22 What do electroencephalographs actually detect? How is such information used? (p. 543)

23 What is REM sleep? (p. 543)

24 Describe the recent theory of memory storage. What evidence supports the idea that memory is a biochemical phenomenon? (p. 545)

25 Summarize the general functions of the autonomic nervous system. Why is it called a motor system? (p. 546)

26 In general, what effect does activity in the sympathetic division have on the body? (p. 547)

27 If both the sympathetic and parasympathetic divisions have identical action potentials, how can this produce different effects on target organs? (pp. 547–548)

28 Summarize the flight-or-fight response. Which division is most involved? (p. 548)

29 Compare the sources and arrangement of the parasympathetic and sympathetic nerves. (p. 548)

If we were asked by some space traveler about the nature of our planet, what the earth is like, we would have a ready answer. We would talk about colors and feelings and textures and distances. We would describe sounds and music and pain. In essence, we would be trying to convey to the visitor what our senses had conveyed to us. If the visitor were able to communicate with another species and ask the same question, he might become confused, however, because other species are likely to know a different kind of world. They have different impressions of the world because they have different kinds of receptors. Furthermore, they tend to perceive the things that are important to them. Since scent is more important to dogs than color is, for example, a dog might describe a gray world of stunning odors. A fly, on the other hand, might tell about a world of shimmering mosaics with swirling eddies and delicious surfaces. A tapeworm might know nothing of colors or sounds (perhaps occasional rumbling vibrations), but might describe a watery world filled with food. Each species is able to detect those things that are important to its survival.

We must keep in mind, then, that we are aware of only a small part of our environment, that the world is far richer than we imagine. Simply put, we, too, know what we need to know: Life is often a conservative, waste-abhorring process; the irrelevant is soon discarded, with precious energy and materials invested only in paying propositions. Let's see, then, how organisms become aware of certain aspects of their surroundings through a look at sensory reception.

First, we should be aware that there is a great deal of variation in the complexity of sensory receptors. They can be quite simple—little more than specialized dendrites, as in the free neural endings in the skin—or they can be incredibly complex, as in the light-activated retina of the vertebrate eye and the acute sound receptors of the mammalian ear.

No matter what their level of complexity, though, sensory receptors have several characteristics in common. For example, they all convert the varied stimuli they receive into action potentials in the associated sensory neurons. Receptors themselves undergo depolarization, but through **generator potentials.** Unlike the "all or none" ("go or don't go") action potentials, generator potentials can increase in intensity. If you think about it, such "grading" of stimuli can be quite useful, since it is through such input that we make very fine distinctions between bright and dim light, soft and loud sounds, and faint odors and damaging toxic fumes. In addition, receptors are highly specialized for certain stimuli, so that a taste

34

THE
SPECIAL SENSES

receptor cannot respond to light wavelengths and vice versa.

Sensory receptors convert incoming stimuli into **generator potentials** which then stimulate action potentials in sensory neurons.

MECHANORECEPTORS: TOUCH AND PRESSURE

In almost all species, **mechanoreceptors,** also called **tactile** (touch) **receptors,** involve extremely sensitive, fast-firing neurons that respond when anything alters the shape of the neural membrane. In some animals the body surface overlying the touch receptor has bristles or hairs, and objects in the environment are detected before the rest of the body makes contact (Figure 34.1). The minute sensory hairs on the cockroach abdomen are a good example, since they can actually detect the slight movement of air that might signal a descending foot.

Vertebrates have two kinds of mechanoreceptors. Distance receptors, such as the **lateral line organ** of fish, detect stimuli in the form of water disturbances from distant sources. Sharks, as we saw in Chapter 29, have highly developed lateral line organs and are attracted to any unusual disturbances, such as the distress or panic movements of an injured fish. The second kind of mechanoreceptor detects two types of stimuli, direct touch and pressure.

Mechanoreceptors are located in the skin (Figure 34.2). Touch receptors include **Meissner's corpuscles** and **free nerve endings,** both of which are located near the skin surface. Free nerve endings also register pain. Pressure is detected by bulbous **Pacinian corpuscles** that are located deeper in the skin. Human touch receptors are more concentrated in the fingertips, lips, nipples, face, and genitals. Body hairs can also transmit signals since at their base they are generally wrapped by free nerve endings. (Try moving one hair without feeling it.)

Until very recently it was generally believed that human hairs, in their sensory function, were simply dead, mechanical levers that when touched would jostle the sensory nerves surrounding their roots. Then another theory was developed based on information that the hair protein keratin is so highly structured as to be essentially crystalline. In fact, it was found that each hair comprises a single **piezoelectric crystal.** A piezoelectric crystal discharges electricity when it is deformed. (Cheaper phonograph pickups use piezoelectric crystals to translate needle movements into electric currents.) Researchers found that like other transducers, a perfectly dead hair generates a small electrical discharge when it is bent, and that nerve endings respond to this electricity.

Incidentally, the outer layer of skin is also made primarily of keratin, and it too has a piezoelectric effect. Bending or depressing the epidermis generates detectable electric discharges that are picked up by the touch-sensitive free nerve endings.

Mechanoreceptors include **distance receptors** such as the **lateral line organ** of the fish and **touch receptors** located in the skin of animals, including humans. The latter receptors respond to deformations of **piezoelectric crystals.**

THERMORECEPTORS

Thermoreceptors are sensitive to temperature. While thermoreception may be important to many invertebrates, little is known about its mechanisms. Heat detection is somewhat important to the ectoparasites of birds and mammals: leeches, fleas, mosquitoes, ticks, and lice—parasites that must find a warm-blooded host. Their thermoreceptors are generally located on the antennae, legs, or mouthparts.

Most human thermoreceptors are located in the skin. These receptors respond not only to temperature, but particularly, to *changes* in temperature (so that a change from cold to cool might be registered as

FIGURE 34.1 Invertebrates commonly sense objects they contact through sensory hairs whose movement sends action potentials to the brain. Among the most acute are those of cockroaches.

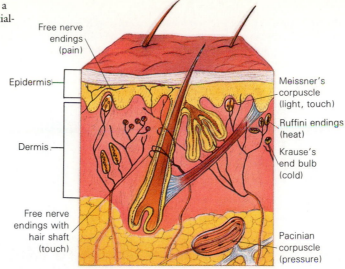

FIGURE 34.2 The skin contains a variety of sensory structures, each specialized for detecting certain stimuli.

Free nerve endings (pain)

Epidermis

Dermis

Free nerve endings with hair shaft (touch)

Meissner's corpuscle (light, touch)

Ruffini endings (heat)

Krause's end bulb (cold)

Pacinian corpuscle (pressure)

warmth). Their precise mechanism of detection remains a mystery, although some physiologists ascribe thermoreception to the free nerve endings and to specialized skin receptors called **Ruffini corpuscles** and **Krause end bulbs** (see Figure 34.2). The latter are far more numerous and are stimulated by a greater temperature range than are the former.

CHEMORECEPTORS: TASTE AND SMELL

Chemoreceptors detect various chemicals and are stimulated by many kinds of molecules. For the most part the molecules must be in solution to activate the chemoreceptor. Chemoreception is common in invertebrates, particularly arthropods, where it is important to feeding, defense, and reproduction. The most powerful chemical sensitivity known is found in the male silk moth. It can detect a single molecule of the sex attractant *bombykol*. (Human chemoreceptors normally begin to respond only after stimulation by several million molecules.) Among vertebrates, the most sensitive chemoreceptors are found in the mammals, especially carnivores and rodents, where scents are important in feeding and in social and reproductive activities.

In humans, **gustation** (the sense of taste) is closely related to our sense of smell, and both forms of chemoreception are often active at the same time. In fact, much of what we taste is actually being smelled. (You've probably noticed that food is not so tasty when you have a cold.)

"True" taste receptors are located in the **taste buds** of the tongue. There are four categories of taste: sweet, sour, salty, and bitter. Taste buds that specialize in each are distributed strategically on the tongue (Can you suggest a reason for the location of the bitter receptors?) (Figure 34.3).

Olfaction, the sense of smell, is not nearly as well developed in humans as it is in some other mammals. Furthermore, there seem to be great differences among humans in the ability to taste and smell. But whatever the ability, human olfactory neurons (like those of other mammals) are located in the **olfactory epithelium,** where stimulating molecules of the air are dissolved in the moist surface (Figure 34.4). The olfactory neurons send their signals to the **olfactory bulb** of the brain, where the information provided by the stimulating molecules is processed and interpreted.

In humans, **chemoreception** involves the detection of molecules by taste buds or by the **olfactory epithelium.**

AUDITORY RECEPTORS

Audition, or hearing, is similar in some respects to lateral line reception in fishes since in both a distant stimulus is transmitted to the receptors via a medium (air or water). In fact, evolutionary theory holds that the structure of balance and hearing in the vertebrates evolved from increasingly complex lateral line organs.

Most invertebrates don't have specialized sound receptors, but many are sensitive to vibrations in the

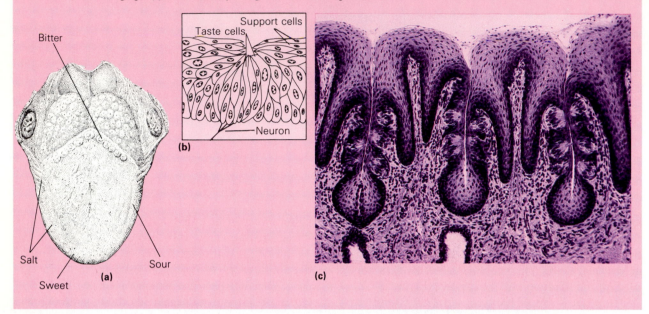

FIGURE 34.3 The arrangement of taste buds on the tongue **(a)** is such that certain regions specialize in detecting each of the four primary tastes: bitter, sour, sweet, and salty. Within the taste buds **(b)**, clusters of specialized neurons converge at tiny pits in which solutions form. Individual taste buds, as seen in the micrograph **(c)**, are constantly being worn out and replaced.

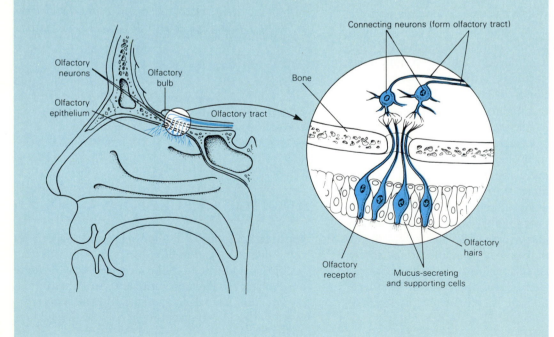

FIGURE 34.4 Olfactory neurons are scattered among the cells of the moist nasal epithelium. Odors are detected by olfactory hairs that emerge from the receptors. The olfactory neurons synapse with other neurons in the olfactory bulb located at the base of the brain. From there, impulses travel to the frontal region of the brain, which is responsible for their interpretation.

air, water, or soil in which they live. One notable exception among the invertebrates is the insects, a group that boasts several kinds of sound receptors. For example, most species have sensory hairs that respond to low-frequency vibrations of air, but others have a specialized organ, located in a leg, that is sensitive to movements of whatever the insect is standing on. Yet others, including grasshoppers, moths and crickets, have **tympanal organs** that respond to high-frequency vibrations, much like the human eardrum. For a special case of insect hearing and its adaptiveness, see Essay 44.3.

Auditory Receptors in Humans

The human ear, like that of other mammals, consists of three basic regions: the **external, middle,** and **internal ear** (Figure 34.5). The **external ear** includes the **pinna,** the **auditory canal,** and the **tympanic membrane** (eardrum). The **pinna** directs sound waves inward, through the auditory canal to the tympanic membrane, which vibrates in response.

The **middle ear,** an air-filled cavity, contains three tiny and unusual bones: the **malleus, incus,** and **stapes.** Acting as a jointed lever, they transfer vibrations of the eardrum to the **cochlea** of the internal ear

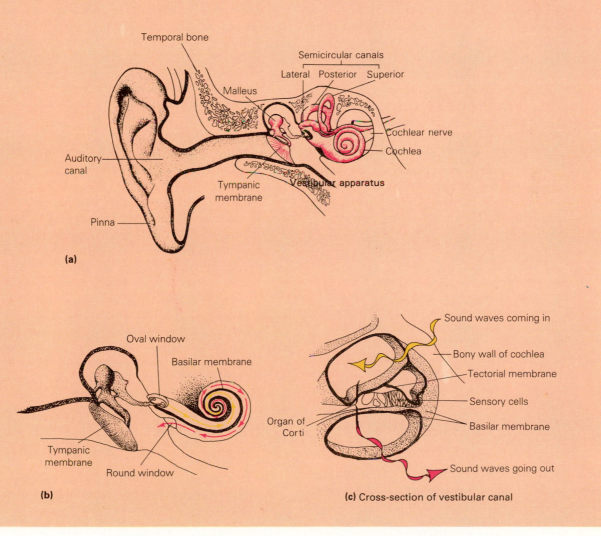

FIGURE 34.5 **(a)** When sound waves vibrate the human eardrum (tympanic membrane), they set in motion three tiny leverlike bones: the malleus, incus, and stapes. The stapes, attached to the oval window, sets fluids in motion within the snail-shaped cochlea. **(b)** The cochlea is actually a U-shaped tube, divided by the basilar membrane. **(c)** Sensory hair cells of the membrane are embedded in the gelatinous tectorial membrane. The two membranes and the sensory hair cells are called the organ of Corti. Sound impulses are transmitted by the middle ear bones from the tympanic membrane to the oval window of the fluid-filled cochlea and from there over the cochlear nerve to the brain.

(malleus, incus, stapes, and cochlea translate, respectively, as "hammer", "anvil," "stirrup," and "snail shell"). The middle ear, therefore, transfers the energy of sound through an intricate lever system (via the bones of the middle ear) to the internal ear.

The **internal,** or inner, **ear** consists of the cochlea and the vestibular apparatus (discussed below). The cochlea is a lengthy, fluid-filled tube that doubles back on itself and then coils like a snail in its shell. The coiling makes it hard to imagine how it works, but if we were to assume that it is straight (as it is, in fact, in birds), we would see a tube, divided into two chambers along its length by a complex membrane, containing the sensory neurons that are stimulated by the energy of sound (see Figure 34.5). One end of the U-shaped tube contains the **oval window,** to which the stapes is attached. The other end holds the flexible **round window.**

As sound waves strike the eardrum, it vibrates and moves the three middle ear bones that transfer the energy of sound to the oval window, causing it to vibrate rapidly. This vibration moves the fluid of the outer tube, and at its far end, it causes the round window to move back and forth. (The round window serves to dissipate the sound energy.) As the fluid pulsates within the tube, it activates what is called the **organ of Corti.** As shown in Figure 34.5c, the organ of Corti consists of a **basilar membrane,** from which arise sensory **hair cells** (actually modified cilia). The tips of these hair cells are embedded in the gelatinous **tectorial membrane.** As the basilar membrane moves, the sensory hairs are bent, creating impulses in the neurons. The impulses travel along the **cochlear nerve,** eventually reaching hearing centers in the cortex.

In humans and other mammals, sound waves vibrate the **tympanum** and **middle ear bones,** which sets **inner ear** fluids in motion. Moving fluid excites sensory **hair cells,** generating action potentials that reach the brain via the **cochlear nerve.**

GRAVITY AND MOVEMENT RECEPTORS

In humans and other mammals, body movement, position, and balance are detected by the vestibular apparatus of the inner ear (Figure 34.6). It is composed of the **semicircular canals,** the **saccule,** and the **utricle.** These three structures are closely associated with those of hearing. Each semicircular canal lies in a different plane, at right angles to each of the other two. This arrangement permits the sensing of movement—acceleration or deceleration—in any direction. Each canal is filled with fluid, and its movement jostles sensory hairs that extend into the canals. As the fluids move, they bend the hairs, creating generator potentials, which in turn activate sensory neurons that send impulses to the brain.

The saccules and utricles contain sensory hairs coated with fine granules of calcium carbonate. Shifts in these granules pressing on the sensory hairs change the rate of neural impulses, providing information about the position of the head with respect to gravity. Some impulses travel to the spinal cord, where body position can be adjusted by reflex action; others are sent to the cerebellum, where other reflexive muscular coordination is orchestrated; and yet others move on to higher centers involved with the control of eye movement. Input from the eyes is important in maintaining balance. (Try to close your eyes and stand on one leg.)

The movement of granules against sensory hairs in the human vestibular apparatus creates action potentials that detect movement.

VISUAL RECEPTORS

Visual receptors are sensitive to a particular part of the spectrum of electromagnetic energy—primarily the part we call visual light, although some animals can detect ultraviolet light. Visible light wavelengths range from about 430 to 750 nm.

Among the best-developed invertebrate eyes are those of the cephalopod mollusks, such as the octopus and squid. They are unique among invertebrates in that they have image-forming eyes, quite like those of vertebrates. Arthropods, such as spiders, crayfish, and insects, also have exceptionally good vision, although their eyes are adapted to detecting movement rather than producing sharp images. As we saw in Chapter 28, insects and crustaceans have compound eyes (see Figure 28.8).

Among invertebrates, cephalopods have image-forming eyes; the simple and compound eyes of arthropods detect movement.

Humans are very visual creatures. We rely on vision in nearly every aspect of life, and we have quite a remarkable visual apparatus. The **eyeball** (Figure 34.6), a spherical, fluid-filled structure, contains three tissue layers: the outermost, tough, white **sclera,** to which muscles of eye movement attach; the middle **choroid coat,** rich in blood vessels; and the inner, light-sensitive **retina.** Light entering the eye first passes through the **cornea,** a transparent portion of the sclera that forms a slight bulge at the front of the eyeball. It then passes through the **iris,** an adjustable circle of pigmented tissue that controls the amount of light entering the **pupil.** Next, light enters the **lens** and is focused on the retina, but to reach this dense region of neurons it must cross the large, fluid-filled interior of the eye. We'll return to the retina, but first, let's see how the lens does its work.

A camera lens, as you may know, adjusts to distance by moving back and forth. Interestingly, sharks focus on objects in the same way. However, human eye lenses do not move back and forth; they adjust to varying distances by changing their shape.

The Retina

The **retina** consists of four layers of cells (Figure 34.7). The deepest layer, attached to the inner surface of the choroid coat, is pigmented. It absorbs light that might otherwise be reflected inside the eyeball, creating visual problems. Overlying the pigmented layer are the **rods** and **cones,** the actual light receptors. You might expect them to be in the direct path of light, but they are covered by two more layers of rather transparent neurons. When the rods and cones are stimulated by light, they send their impulses to the overlying **bipolar cells;** these, in turn, synapse with the **optic neurons** just above. Optic neurons gather from all parts of the retina to form the **optic nerve,** which carries visual impulses to the brain.

In many vertebrates, including cats and dogs, the absorptive pigment layer can be altered at night by movement of the pigment granules within the cells. This reveals another layer of reflecting crystals. The reflective layer bounces the excess light back through the layer of rods and cones, which doubles the sensitivity of the eye. This reflective layer in animals' eyes can be quite startling at night to human travelers on lonely highways.

In the human eye the iris adjusts the amount of entering light; the lens focuses images on the retina; and the retina generates action potentials that reach visual centers in the brain via the optic nerve.

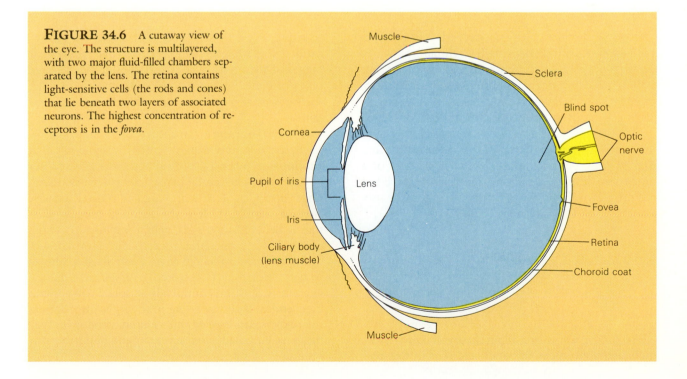

FIGURE 34.6 A cutaway view of the eye. The structure is multilayered, with two major fluid-filled chambers separated by the lens. The retina contains light-sensitive cells (the rods and cones) that lie beneath two layers of associated neurons. The highest concentration of receptors is in the *fovea*.

Muscle

Sclera

Blind spot

Optic nerve

Cornea

Fovea

Pupil of iris

Lens

Retina

Iris

Choroid coat

Ciliary body (lens muscle)

Muscle

FIGURE 34.7 A scanning electron micrograph view of the retina (a) reveals thickened cones and slender rods. A diagrammatic view (b) reveals a layer of light-sensitive rods and cones. Overlying the rods and cones are transparent layers of bipolar cells. These are sensory neurons that, when excited by the rods and cones, stimulate the ganglion cells. The latter respond by producing their own impulses that travel out over the optic nerve.

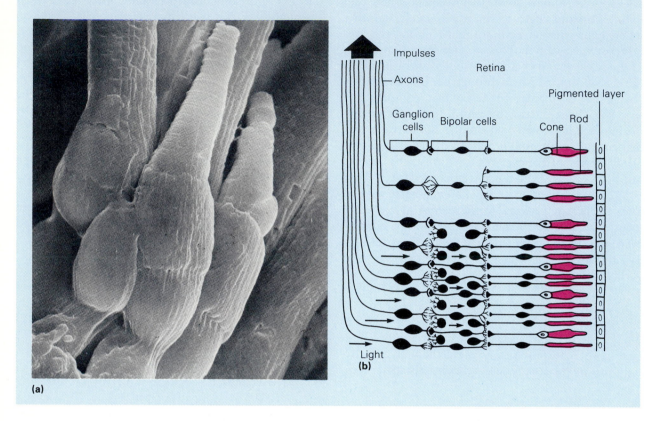

Rods and cones. The slender rods cells are especially light-sensitive, particularly to the shorter wavelengths (purple). They cannot distinguish colors, but rather they detect degrees of brightness that are interpreted by the brain as various shades of gray. Nearly all of our night vision depends upon the rods.

Cones, which are actually cone-shaped, specialize in detecting various parts of the visible spectrum, that is, they detect colors. Cones are capable of a much finer level of discrimination than rods are but require relatively bright light and are practically useless at night.

> Whereas **rods** distinguish levels of brightness and work well in dim light, **cones** distinguish colors and require bright light.

According to the prevailing theory of color vision, there are three types of cones: red-sensitive, green-sensitive, and blue-sensitive. With these, we can see many colors because these receptors overlap in their ranges of sensitivity. The sensitivities of the different types of cones to a given color depend upon what sorts of visual pigments (light absorbers) they contain.

The rods operate on an entirely different principle. Each rod contains a light-sensitive pigment called **rhodopsin.** When rhodopsin absorbs light, it loses its color and chemically breaks down into two subunits: **opsin,** a colorless protein, and **retinal,** a derivative of vitamin A. It is the chemical process itself that is believed to trigger neural impulses to visual centers in the brain. After their chemical breakdown, opsin and retinal enter into a chemical pathway where rhodopsin is restored. Apparently, dietary vitamin A must be continually supplied to keep the biochemical pathway going in the right direction. If the body is deprived of this vitamin, rhodopsin synthesis is curtailed, and severe night blindness can result.

The earth is a complex place, with an incredible interplay of energetic forces dancing across its surface. The various species of the planet have developed ways to detect some of those forces, particularly those that might be important to their survival, while remaining completely oblivious to others. Our world, then, is simplified by our ability to detect only limited aspects of it. Nonetheless, it remains a complex, fascinating, and often puzzling place, based on what we *do* know.

SUMMARY

Sensory receptors vary from simple to complex, but most have the same characteristics. They convert stimuli into generator potentials, a special type of impulse that can vary in a graded manner.

MECHANORECEPTORS: TOUCH AND PRESSURE

Mechanoreceptors fire impulses when their surface is altered by touch. In invertebrates they generally occur as sensory hairs. Such receptors in vertebrates include distance receptors, such as lateral line organs of fishes, and touch and pressure mechanoreceptors of the skin.

Human touch receptors include Meissner's corpuscles and free nerve endings. Pressure is registered by deeper-lying Pacinian corpuscles. Body hairs have free nerve endings around their roots. Hairs and skin react to touch as piezoelectric crystals, discharging current when deformed.

THERMORECEPTORS

Invertebrate heat detection is important to ectoparasites of warm-blooded hosts but the receptors are not well understood. Human thermoreceptors include free nerve endings, Ruffini corpuscles, and Krause end bulbs. They work in a comparative rather than an absolute manner.

CHEMORECEPTORS: TASTE AND SMELL

Chemoreception in arthropods is important to feeding, defense and reproduction. Silk moth antennae are activated by trace amounts of sex attractants.

Vertebrate carnivores and rodents have keen chemoreception. Gustation (taste) in humans occurs in taste buds that specialize in sweet, sour, salty, and bitter. Olfaction in humans is the role of the olfactory epithelium in the nasal passages. Its receptors synapse with the olfactory neurons.

AUDITORY RECEPTORS

Insects perceive low frequency sound through sensory hairs in the legs and higher frequencies through tympanal organs.

Auditory Receptors in Humans

The human external ear includes the pinna, auditory canal, and tympanic membrane, the latter of which is vibrated by sound. In the middle ear, three minute bones transfer tympanic vibrations to the oval window of the cochlea. The cochlea, part of the inner ear, is a coiled tube divided by a membrane that bears the sensory cells. The vibrating oval window moves fluids within the cochlea that activate hair cells in the basilar membrane of the organ of Corti. The bending hair cells generate impulses that travel the cochlear nerve.

GRAVITY AND MOVEMENT RECEPTORS

Body movement, position, and balance are sensed by the semicircular canals, and saccule and utricle of the inner ear. Moving fluid in the canals activates sensory hairs whose impulses are perceived by the brain as acceleration or deceleration. Sensory hairs in the saccules and utricles are activated by head movement. Impulses inform the brain of head position.

VISUAL RECEPTORS

Visual receptors in most animals respond to the visible light spectrum. In invertebrates, receptors range from simple eye spots in planaria to complex image-forming eyes in cephalopod mollusks.

The human eye contains several tissue layers, including the light-sensitive retina. The iris adjusts light entering the eye, while the lens focuses images upon the retina. Focusing is done by ciliary muscles that change the lens shape.

The Retina

The retina's light activated cells are the rods and cones. They synapse with a layer of bipolar cells above, which activate overlying optic neurons that form the optic nerve. A reflective layer below the rods and cones occurs in many nocturnal animals.

Rods detect all wavelengths and are sensitive to dim light. Cones specialize in reds, greens, and blues, and work best in bright light. Overlaps in reception provide the intermediate colors. Rods contain rhodopsin that breaks down in light initiating action potentials and forming opsin and retinal. Rhodopsin is restored in a chemical pathway requiring vitamin A.

KEY TERMS

REVIEW QUESTIONS

1 How does the activation of a sensory receptor differ from that of the sensory neuron? How is this adaptive? (p. 551)

2 Transducers are electronic devices that convert mechanical movement into electrical current. Would the term transducer apply to sensory receptors? Explain. (p. 551)

3 What insect structures act as touch receptors? How do such receptors actually work? (p. 552)

4 How would a shark detect a swimmer that was beyond visual and olfactory range? (p. 552)

5 List three kinds of touch receptors in the human skin. How would the simplest of these be activated? (p. 552)

6 Explain how any touch on the skin surface of an animal might start an action potential in nearby free nerve endings. (p. 552)

7 To what specific group of invertebrate might thermoreception be highly essential? (pp. 552–553)

8 Do human skin thermoreceptors actually detect specific temperatures? Explain. (pp. 552–553)

9 Describe the sensitivity of the male silk moth to its sex attractant. What other animals are aroused by such scents? (p. 553)

10 Using a simple illustration, indicate the location of specific taste receptors on the human tongue. (p. 553)

11 Describe the arrangement of sensory cells in the human olfactory epithelium. Where are their generator potentials sent? (p. 553)

12 List two kinds of auditory receptors in insects. (p. 554)

13 Trace the pathway of air disturbances from the surroundings of humans to the oval window of the cochlea. (pp. 555–556)

14 Suggest reasons why the use of the three inner ear bones to transfer vibrations might be adaptive. Why not a direct stimulation of the oval window by air? (pp. 555–556)

15 Describe the organization of the human cochlea. What is the purpose of the fluid within? (p. 556)

16 Describe the organization of the organ of Corti. In what structures do generator potentials originate? (p. 556)

17 What is the significance of the length of the tube forming the cochlea? Why not a short tube? (p. 556)

18 What function do the semicircular canals serve? What is the significance of the arrangement of the three vessels? (p. 556)

19 Explain how changing the position of the head affects the structures within the saccule and utricle. (p. 556)

20 List three visual specializations in the invertebrates. Which represents an example of convergent evolution? (p. 556)

21 Trace the pathway followed by light in the human eyeball. Name each structure along the way and state its function. (p. 557)

22 Name the four layers of the retina and state their functions. (pp. 557–558)

23 Under what conditions are the cone cells most effective? How are colors other than red, green and blue produced? (p. 558)

24 When do we rely most on the rod cells? What might be the effect of continuous bright light on these receptors? How does this explain the temporary night blindness that occurs when we go from a brightly lighted room into darkness? (p. 558)

25 Describe the chemical pathway generated by light striking the rod cells. What does the chemical change do to the cone cells? (p. 558)

In a real sense, life is an unlikely condition. A smart celestial gambler would bet against its appearance. Of course, life didn't appear all at once, full blown and operational. Instead, small, mindless molecules finally became associated in precise ways so that the simplest forms of life took their place on the planet, and from these more complex types arose. The process was a slow one, and as it unfolded, life became ever more complex and organized.

In more complex forms of life, maintaining the appropriate conditions for its continuance presents problems that stagger the imagination. Yet life continues, its processes delicately balanced and coordinated in ways we are only beginning to understand. We do know, though, that each small action must be a part of some larger process. Each time a cell goes about its business, handling this ion or that, allowing this molecule through and barring that one, its actions must ultimately benefit the body of which it is a part. Its behavior must be coordinated with the activities of other kinds of cells in some distant part of the body. Some sort of means of signalling becomes necessary, and one kind of signal involves chemical messengers called **hormones.** Hormones are chemicals formed in one part of the body that travel (usually through the bloodstream) to another part of the body, where they cause changes.

Hormones are chemical messengers. They are produced in one region of the body and carry out their action in another.

Hormonal regulation is common throughout the animal world, in invertebrates as well as vertebrates. In fact, a great deal of hormone research has been carried out on arthropods, such as insects and crayfish. For example, hormones have been found to regulate the change in the body organization of insects as they pass through their larval and pupal stages. The importance of hormones in insect development is illustrated in Figure 35.1

NATURE OF HORMONES

Hormones have a number of very special characteristics. First, they are quite effective in minute quantities—sometimes trace amounts. Many hormones have highly specific **target cells** (cells they arouse) and equally specific actions. Target cells often have unique plasma membrane **receptor sites,** molecular configurations that match one hormone only. Fur-

35

CHEMICAL MESSENGERS IN ANIMALS

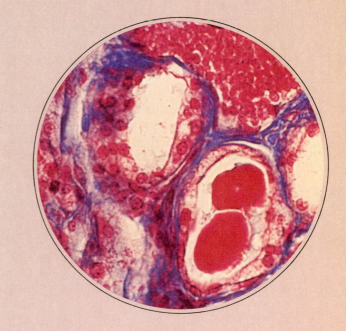

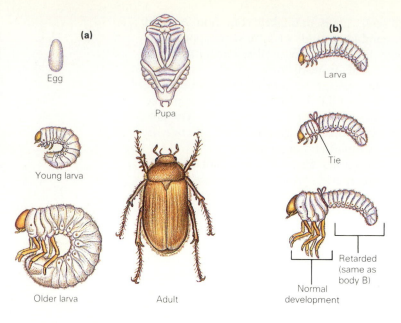

FIGURE 35.1 **(a)** Development in a beetle. Not all insect species go through the sequence of egg, larva, pupa, adult, but whatever their pattern, each stage is brought on at a specific time by a different hormone. **(b)** An experiment showing the importance of hormones in insect development. When growth hormones produced in the head are kept from reaching other parts of the body by tying off those parts, the hormone-deprived areas do not mature.

(a)

Egg

Pupa

Young larva

Adult

Older larva

(b)

Larva

Tie

Normal development

Retarded (same as body B)

ther, hormones are transient; once a hormone has found and aroused its target, it is quickly inactivated by enzymes. The elimination of a lingering effect is a vital component of control.

The best-known vertebrate hormones fall into several classes according to their structures. Included are **steroids, proteins, polypeptides,** and modified **amino acids.** A fifth group of chemical messengers we will consider, the **prostaglandins,** not generally recognized as hormones, are modified fatty acids (Figure 35.2).

The cell-specific, temporary action of hormones is made possible by the presence of matched receptor sites and enzymes that quickly degrade the hormones after they act on the specific **target cells.**

Hormones and Feedback Mechanisms

The tiny hormonal molecules that ebb and flow through our bodies, lightly touching our life processes and causing them to shift this way or that, may seem to be a rather delicate and fragile way to control such critical processes. However, those tiny molecules have a sledgehammer impact. Some of the changes they bring are swift, dramatic, and irreversible. Obviously, they must be subject to controls.

One of the basic ways they are controlled is through **negative feedback mechanisms.** Essential-

ly, negative feedback is an automated process in which the result of an activity, decreases that activity (Figure 35.3). When the body needs a substance such as a hormone, it begins to manufacture it. But then the accumulation of the product begins to inhibit the system that produced it thus forming a **feedback loop.** However, as the hormone level drops, the producing mechanism is freed to begin making the product again. As you can see, negative feedback mechanisms can rigidly and automatically control a hormone's release.

In **negative feedback** the product of an action has a negative, or reducing, effect on the mechanism that produced it.

In **positive feedback mechanisms** (Figure 35.3b), the result of an activity causes that activity to increase, thereby further increasing the action in what can become a "vicious circle." Positive feedback is relatively uncommon in nature and is often associated with abnormalities. For example, high blood pressure can damage arteries, and the damaged vessel walls can become infused with fatty materials, scar tissue, and cellular growth. This restricts the size of the vessel opening, further increasing blood pressure.

Not all positive feedback is bad. Adaptive positive feedback loops are found in a few physiological processes that require rapid amplification. Examples

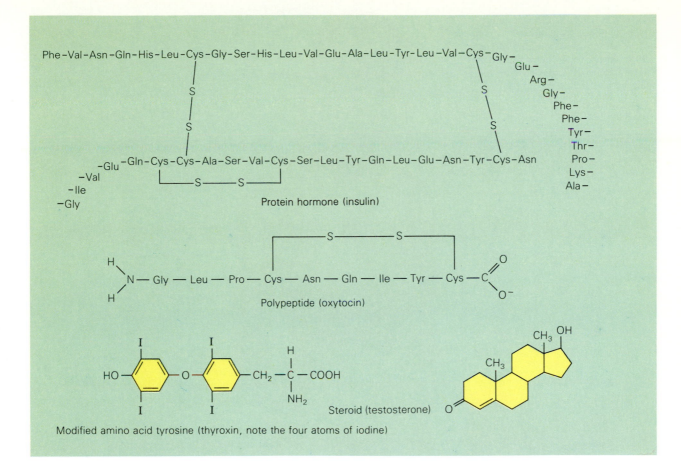

Phe–Val–Asn–Gln–His–Leu–Cys–Gly–Ser–His–Leu–Val–Glu–Ala–Leu–Tyr–Leu–Val–Cys–Gly–

Protein hormone (insulin)

Polypeptide (oxytocin)

Modified amino acid tyrosine (thyroxin, note the four atoms of iodine)

Steroid (testosterone)

FIGURE 35.3 Two types of feedback systems. In negative feedback (**a**) a rather constant water level is maintained as long as there is enough rain. As the amount of water increases, more is allowed to run out; as it decreases, the drain is plugged. This is a typical negative feedback system. In positive feedback (**b**) as the water level rises, less is allowed to escape so the water rises out of control. As it falls, even more is released until the barrel is empty. This is a positive feedback system. Which do you suppose more closely approximates biological feedback systems?

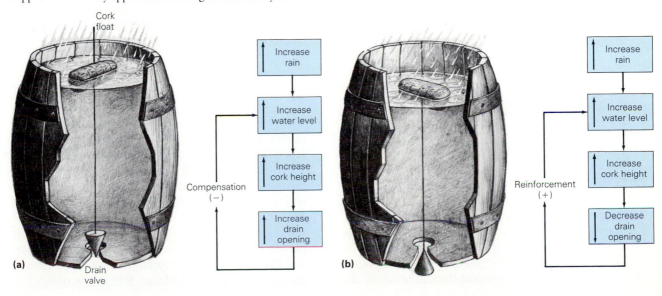

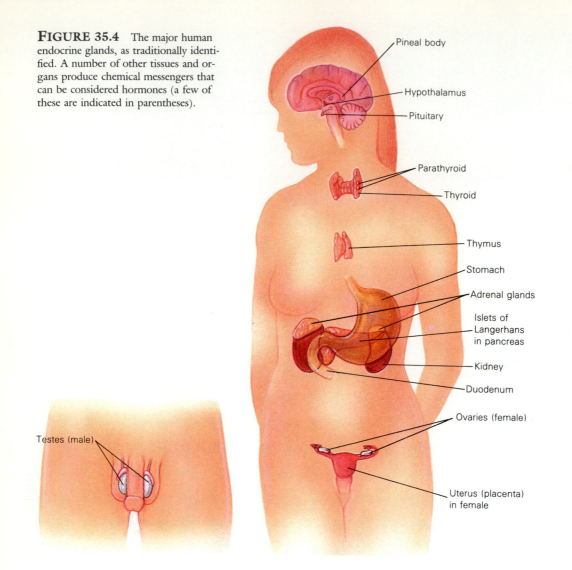

FIGURE 35.4 The major human endocrine glands, as traditionally identified. A number of other tissues and organs produce chemical messengers that can be considered hormones (a few of these are indicated in parentheses).

Pineal body
Hypothalamus
Pituitary
Parathyroid
Thyroid
Thymus
Stomach
Adrenal glands
Islets of Langerhans in pancreas
Kidney
Duodenum
Ovaries (female)
Uterus (placenta) in female
Testes (male)

include the blood-clotting mechanism and the disease-combating reactions within the immune system (Chapter 40).

Positive feedback is an amplifying process wherein the product of an action increases that action.

HUMAN ENDOCRINE SYSTEM

In humans, most hormones are produced in distinct glands and a number of scattered tissues that make up the **endocrine system** (Figure 35.4). The term "endocrine" means ductless; the products are not secreted into ducts but enter the blood for distribution. By contrast there are many **exocrine glands,** such the salivary glands, sweat glands, and mucous glands whose products enter ducts to be carried away.

The Pituitary

The **pituitary** is a tiny, bilobed structure about the size of a kidney bean, but its size belies its importance. The pituitary releases at least eight hormones important to the body's metabolism, growth, reproduction, and other activities. The pituitary lies at the end of a stalk that emerges from the hypothalamus of the brain (Figure 35.5). The stalk, as we'll see, represents one of the main functional connections that permit the nervous and endocrine systems to interact. The relationship between the hypothalamus and the pituitary clearly illustrates this interaction.

Pituitary and hypothalamus. Both lobes of the pituitary, under the influence of the brain's hypothalamus, release important but very different hormones (since the lobes are actually different glands). The **posterior pituitary** *(neurohypophysis)* is actually part of the nervous system; embryologically, it arises from the central nervous system. The posterior lobe doesn't manufacture its own hormones; it simply stores and releases two hormones that are synthesized in nerve cell bodies in the hypothalamus and are transmitted to the posterior lobe by the nerve cell axons.

The **anterior pituitary** differs greatly from the posterior lobe in structure, function, and origin. Embryologically, it originates in a pocket of ectodermal epithelium on the roof of the mouth. It is a true hormone-synthesizing gland, producing and releasing six hormones. It is also intimately influenced by the hypothalamus. The hypothalamus is drained by a network of capillaries that merge into a short blood vessel, which then travels down the pituitary stalk. There the blood vessel divides again into a second capillary bed that spreads through the anterior pituitary. It is through this circulatory connection that minute quantities, actually fleeting traces, of **releasing hormones** and **inhibiting hormones** travel from the hypothalamus to the anterior pituitary. When these hypothalamic messengers reach the anterior pituitary, they stimulate or inhibit the release of major pituitary hormones. Describing the quantity of these messengers as "fleeting traces" is no overstatement. In the early search for them, 4 tons of hypothalamic tissue was needed to yield 1 *milligram* of the first releasing hormone to be identified.

More importantly, it is clear that the pituitary, called the "master gland" by earlier endocrinologists, functions at the bidding of the hypothalamus, which is not itself an endocrine gland. The hypothalamus is largely under the control of other parts of the brain, and as we will see, it is subservient to a number of negative feedback loops. (So who's running things?)

> The **posterior pituitary** stores and releases two hormones secreted there by neurons from the hypothalamus. The **anterior pituitary** produces six hormones which it releases in response to **releasing hormones** from the hypothalamus and then ceases in response to **inhibiting hormones.** The hypothalamus, in turn, is controlled through **negative feedback.**

FIGURE 35.5 The hypothalamus, anterior pituitary, and posterior pituitary (see Figure 35.4 for their general locations in the brain). Note that the hypothalamus communicates with the anterior pituitary by sending releasing factors through blood vessels. However, hormones of the posterior pituitary are actually produced in neurons of the hypothalamus and carried there via the axons of those neurons.

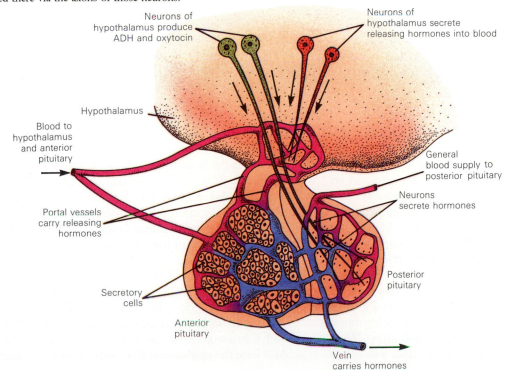

Hormones of the anterior pituitary. Five of the anterior pituitary's hormones influence other endocrine glands. The sixth stimulates body growth in a general way.

Let's begin with the exception, **growth hormone,** or **GH.** Proper levels of growth hormone in the body are essential to normal growth, but sometimes something goes wrong. Too much GH during the early years of development can produce **pituitary giants** (gigantism). People severely affected by this condition may grow to be 7 to 9 feet tall. Conversely, lower-than-normal GH levels in children results in **pituitary dwarfs** (dwarfism). Pituitary dwarfism is now treatable with GH produced through recombinant DNA techniques (see Chapter 16).

As shown in Figure 35.6 the production of **adrenocorticotropic hormone (ACTH)** is first stimulated by a hypothalamic releasing factor and is then regulated by a negative feedback control system. The target of ACTH is the cortex (outer layer) of the adrenal gland, which is located on top of the kidney. When stimulated by ACTH, the adrenal cortex secretes an entire battery of hormones. As the levels of these hormones rise in the blood, they inhibit the hypothalamus, which then slows ACTH production in the pituitary. Besides activating the adrenal cortex, ACTH regulates the metabolism of fats. Under its influence, the body releases fatty acids into the bloodstream for redistribution through the body.

ACTH prompts the adrenals to release their hormones, which then form a negative feedback loop to the hypothalamus. The latter responds by slowing its prompting of the anterior pituitary, and ACTH secretion diminishes.

Thyroid-stimulating hormone (TSH, also known as **thyrotropin)** is another anterior pituitary hormone. It is responsible for stimulating the thyroid to release two thyroid hormones, **thyroxin** and **triiodothyronine.** These thyroid hormones regulate the metabolic rate of the body and influence the growth of the nervous system.

Prolactin promotes milk production in mammals. Toward the end of pregnancy, the blood level of prolactin increases dramatically.

Follicle-stimulating hormone (FSH) and **luteinizing hormone (LH)** are both involved in stimulating the production of gametes and sex hormones in the gonads, and are called **gonadotropins.** These hormones will be considered in Chapter 41.

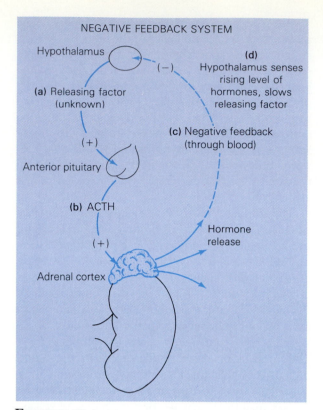

FIGURE 35.6 The release of ACTH by the anterior pituitary is controlled by a negative feedback loop. Feedback in this instance involves the rising level of a specific hormone of the adrenal cortex.

Hormones of the posterior pituitary. Two hormones released by hypothalamic neurons and stored in the posterior lobe are **oxytocin** and **antidiuretic hormone (ADH).** Oxytocin is important to reproduction—it stimulates the contraction of uterine muscle during labor, and after delivery it helps slow bleeding as the uterus continues to contract. Suckling the baby also stimulates the mother's posterior lobe to release oxytocin (apparently the sensory nerves of the nipples communicate with the brain and, finally, with the hypothalamus). Oxytocin then stimulates the smooth muscle around the milk ducts, and milk flow begins. Interestingly, oxytocin in women is also released during sexual stimulation and orgasm. Again, the uterus responds by contracting. Researchers studying human sexual behavior suggest that the contractions may cause the uterus to draw in the semen, assisting in fertilization.

A **diuretic** is an agent that increases the water content, and thus the volume, of urine (see Chapter 36). An **antidiuretic** does the opposite. ADH decreases urine volume by withholding water, a part of the body's homeostatic maintenance. The target cells of ADH are the epithelial cells of urine-collecting ducts in the kidneys. ADH is released when the hypothalamus detects a decrease in the blood's water content, and the target cells respond by shunting water back into the blood, bringing osmotic conditions to a more optimal level.

The posterior pituitary produces oxytoxin (important in female reproductive behavior) and ADH (decreases water concentration in urine).

The Thyroid Gland

The **thyroid gland** is shaped somewhat like a bow tie and is located in an appropriate place—in front of and slightly below the larynx (Figure 35.7). Two of its three hormones, **thyroxin** and **triiodothyronine,** are very similar in structure; they are synthesized from the amino acid tyrosine. Thyroxin has four iodine atoms added, and triiodothyronine has three (you can see why iodine is an essential mineral in the diet). Actually, most physiologists now believe that triiodothyronine is merely an inactive form of thyroxine.

The secretion of thyroxin is controlled by negative feedback. The hypothalamus sends specific releasing factors to the anterior pituitary, which responds by releasing TSH. TSH causes the thyroid to secrete thyroxin. Thyroxin levels in the blood are monitored by the hypothalamus, which moderates its TSH production accordingly.

Thyroxin influences the rate at which carbohydrates are oxidized by cells and, accordingly, the amount of body heat produced. The rate of oxidation, called the **basal metabolic rate (BMR),** is determined by measuring a resting subject's rate of oxygen consumption. Thyroxin is believed to work by activating genes that direct the synthesis of certain respiratory enzymes.

Thyroid abnormalities include **hyperthyroidism** (overactive thyroid), and **hypothyroidism** (underactive thyroid). A form of hyperthyroidism called Grave's disease is characterized by rapid metabolism, weight loss, nervousness, and insomnia. In some instances, the eyes may bulge out noticeably, a condition known as **exophthalmic goiter.**

Hypothyroidism—thyroxin insufficiency—produces a general slowing of the metabolic rate. Hypothyroid adults are usually sluggish and overweight, have low blood pressure, and may have an enlargement of the thyroid called **simple goiter.** This is an adaptive response to insufficient iodine in the diet, but since the availability of iodized salt, few cases have been reported.

Calcitonin, the third thyroid hormone, works in concert with a hormone from the **parathyroid glands** to regulate calcium ions in the body.

Under the influence of the pituitary the **thyroid gland** secretes hormones that regulate metabolic rate and calcium distribution.

The Parathyroid Glands and Calcium Regulation

The **parathyroid glands** are pea-sized bodies embedded in the tissue of the thyroid (Figure 35.8). The parathyroids secrete **parathyroid hormone (PTH),** a polypeptide that helps raise the calcium levels of the

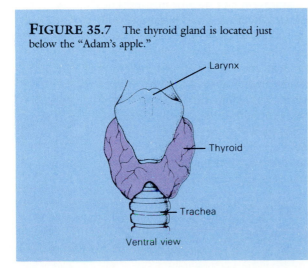

FIGURE 35.7 The thyroid gland is located just below the "Adam's apple."

Larynx

Thyroid

Trachea

Ventral view

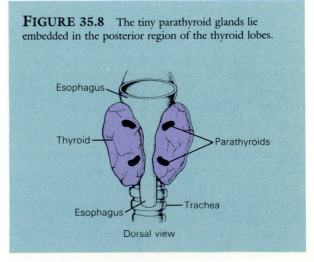

FIGURE 35.8 The tiny parathyroid glands lie embedded in the posterior region of the thyroid lobes.

Esophagus

Thyroid

Parathyroids

Esophagus

Trachea

Dorsal view

blood, acting as an antagonist of calcitonin. In their regulation of calcium, parathyroid hormone and calcitonin affect such things as bone deposition, release and reabsorption in the kidneys, and absorption by the intestine. Overall, the net effect of parathyroid hormone is to increase the calcium ion (Ca^{2+}) concentration in the blood; the net effect of calcitonin is to decrease it.

Abnormally low levels of parathyroid hormone cause muscle convulsions and, eventually, death. This can occur when the parathyroid glands are destroyed, as sometimes happens in an **autoimmune reaction,** when the body's own immune system mistakenly begins to treat the parathyroid tissue as "foreign" and attacks it. The opposite condition, abnormally high levels of parathyroid hormone, results in a severe decalcification of bone *(osteoporosis),* with the subsequent formation of fibrous cysts in the skeleton. If the condition is severe, death follows.

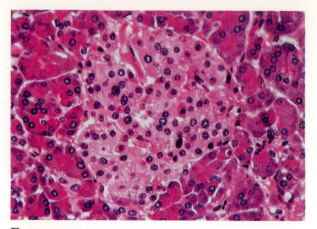

FIGURE 35.9 The islets of Langerhans are clearly distinguishable from the surrounding exocrine tissue. Within the clusters of endocrine tissue are patches of three types of secretory cells that produce the hormones.

> Parathyroid and thyroid hormones cooperatively adjust calcium intake and excretion and influence its storage and removal from bone.

The Pancreas and the Islets of Langerhans

The **pancreas** is, for the most part, a ducted exocrine gland, since its major secretions are digestive enzymes and sodium bicarbonate, which are released into the small intestines. Scattered through the pancreas, however, are groups of true endocrine cells that secrete their products directly into the bloodstream. These clumps of cells are the **islets of Langerhans,** or, simply, the **pancreatic islets** (Figure 35.9). Each cluster consists of at least three types of secretory cells, named **alpha, beta,** and **delta.** Alpha cells produce the hormone **glucagon,** while the beta cells secrete the more publicized hormone **insulin.** Each of these polypeptide hormones has a role in the regulation of carbohydrate metabolism (Figure 35.10). Delta cells produce **somatostatin,** a puzzling hormone whose specific action remains unknown. However, physiologists now suspect that pancreatic somatostatin inhibits the release of digestive hormones at times when they are not required.

Glucagon is a polypeptide consisting of a single chain of 29 amino acids. Its principal role is to stimulate the liver to break down glycogen into glucose. Glucagon is released into the bloodstream when blood glucose levels fall below a certain level; the glu-cose that is released from the liver restores the proper level of blood sugar, which in turn slows down the production of glucagon in the pancreatic islets—a classic negative feedback loop.

Insulin, in its active form, consists of 51 amino acids, arranged in two polypeptide chains joined by disulfide linkages (covalent bonding between sulfur side groups). The hormone is large and complex enough to be called a protein. The specific role of insulin is to help glucose move across cell membranes, but it also has other actions: it is involved in fatty acid metabolism and glycogen synthesis, it seems to be directly necessary for capillary function, and it stimulates cells, in tissue cultures, to divide.

> Pancreatic islet cells release the hormones **glucagon** and **insulin** that influence glucose uptake, storage, and release by cells.

Deficiency in the insulin system produces **diabetes mellitus.** In *juvenile-onset diabetes,* its most severe form, the deficiency is caused by the destruction of beta cells, either by a viral infection or by an autoimmune response. In the more common *adult-onset diabetes,* affected persons have normal levels of insulin, but they may lack enough receptor sites on the membranes of the target cells.

> Diabetes mellitus results from a destruction of beta islet cells or from a lack of insulin receptor sites on plasma membranes.

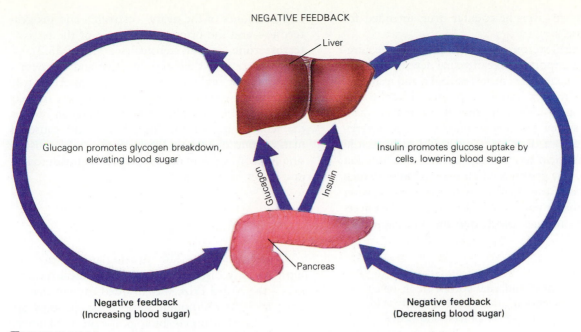

Glucagon promotes glycogen breakdown, elevating blood sugar

Insulin promotes glucose uptake by cells, lowering blood sugar

Liver

Glucagon

Insulin

Pancreas

Negative feedback (Increasing blood sugar)

Negative feedback (Decreasing blood sugar)

FIGURE 35.10 Low blood sugar **(a)** and high blood sugar **(b)** bring on the release of glucagon and insulin, respectively. While they have opposing actions, the controlling factors are the same. In both instances it is the actual correction of the condition that initiates a negative feedback loop that then inhibits the hormonal release.

FIGURE 35.11 The adrenal glands. The adrenal cortex synthesizes a variety of steroid hormones, while the adrenal medulla produces only epinephrine and norepinephrine.

The Adrenal Glands

"Ad" means upon, and "renal" refers to the kidney. So, in humans, the **adrenal glands** are perched atop the kidneys just as one might suspect. Each adrenal gland is essentially two glands. The outer layer, or **cortex,** produces a number of steroid hormones and has a different origin, structure, and function than the inner layer, the **medulla** (Figure 35.11).

Adrenal cortex. The hormones of the adrenal cortex fall into three categories according to their functions: **mineralocorticoids, glucocorticoids,** and **steroid sex hormones.** The mineralocorticoids regulate minerals. The best known, **aldosterone,** promotes the retention of sodium ions and the release of potassium ions by the kidney. The mineralocorticoids also promote inflammation as part of the body's immune defense reactions. In this role, they oppose—in a cooperative manner—the action of glucocorticoids.

One of the most common glucocorticoids, **cortisol,** is involved in the metabolism of foods, facilitating the conversion of amino acids and fatty acids into glucose. In addition, some glucocorticoids act as anti-inflammatory agents, suppressing inflammation. (A pharmaceutical preparation, hydrocortisone, is

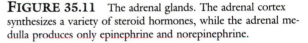
Adrenals

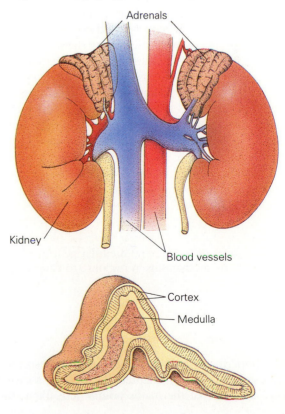

Kidney

Blood vessels

Cortex

Medulla

available as an over-the-counter drug intended for this purpose.)

The cortical steroids (sex hormones) of the adrenals play an important role in sexual development. In fact, the adrenal cortex makes estrogen and testosterone—the same sex hormones produced by the ovaries and testes—although generally in smaller quantities. Thus they promote secondary sex characteristics, such as beards in men and enlarged breasts in women, and help to maintain reproductive function and libido. The principal adrenal steroid in both men and women is testosterone, with estrogens making up only a minor part of the total output. The effects of sex hormones are described further in Chapters 41 and 42.

> Hormones of the **adrenal cortex** are involved in sodium retention, amino acid and fatty acid metabolism, sexual development, and sexual functions.

Adrenal medulla. The adrenal medulla produces two fascinating *amine* hormones: **epinephrine** and **norepinephrine** (commonly known as adrenaline and noradrenaline; *epinephros* in Greek and *adrenal* in Latin both mean "on top of the kidney"). Epinephrine and norepinephrine can cause very specific changes in the body, usually in response to sudden fright or anger. They reduce blood flow in the capillaries near the body surfaces, causing the skin to pale. The blood is diverted to the muscles, which may need to perform some strenuous activity, like getting you out of a car after an accident. At such times, digestive functions cease, blood pressure increases, the pupils of the eyes dilate (to see better), and glucose is released from the liver into the bloodstream. Other changes also occur to prepare the body for emergencies, called the "flight-or-fight" responses—a capability of the autonomic nervous system as well (see Chapter 33).

> Hormones of the **adrenal medulla** generally speed body mechanisms in response to danger or fright.

Ovaries and Testes

The endocrine functions of the ovary and testes are discussed in detail in Chapters 41 and 42, so we'll note just some of the major points here. First, the two hormones of the ovary—**estrogen** and **progesterone**—and the principal hormone of the testis—**testosterone**—are all steroids (see Figure 35.2).

In addition to their reproductive and behavioral functions, the sex hormones have an important role in skeletal development. The sudden increase of their levels in the blood at the onset of puberty stimulates the lengthening of the long bones and causes a marked spurt of growth. Interestingly, it also causes a simultaneous spurt in mental growth, as measured by raw scores on IQ tests.

Other Chemical Messengers

Prostaglandins. The **prostaglandins** are the most recently discovered class of chemical messengers—the Nobel Prize was awarded to their discoverers in 1981. Although some prostaglandins are among the most potent biological materials known, perhaps one reason for their late discovery is that they are not produced by specialized organs. Various prostaglandins are produced by most kinds of tissues. For this reason they are not universally regarded as hormones.

Prostaglandins may be released by the activity of other hormones or by almost any irritation of the tissues. Some prostaglandins are involved in inflammatory responses and in the sensation of pain. Aspirin inhibits the synthesis of prostaglandins, which is why aspirin is effective against pain, inflammation, and fever.

Prostaglandins also have other actions. For instance, one type causes uterine contractions. Blood platelets, which are involved in blood clotting, produce a prostaglandin called **thromboxane** that causes platelets to stick together in clots and can also cause the walls of arteries to contract. Another prostaglandin, **prostacyclin,** has exactly the opposite effects—it prevents clots, keeps blood thin, and prevents arteries from closing. Since prostacyclin is produced by cells that line the blood vessels, prostaglandins may be important in complex ways in maintaining normal circulation.

We mentioned that aspirin inhibits prostaglandin synthesis. It turns out that thromboxane synthesis is inhibited by very low levels of aspirin, while such levels have little effect on prostacyclin. So is aspirin good or bad for us? It can be both. First, there is evidence that some heart attacks, arterial disease, and stroke are caused by an imbalance in thromboxane, where spontaneous clotting (embolus formation), and arterial constriction bring on the familiar symptoms. Seemingly, one answer is lowering thromboxane levels, and here is where aspirin can help. On the basis of circumstantial evidence, it seems that aspirin in low doses (one tablet a day or every other day) is *beneficial*. Habitual aspirin users have *far lower* rates of arterial disease and heart attacks than do nonusers. However, heavy users, such as arthritics, also run the risk of serious stomach hemorrhages.

HOW HORMONES WORK

Cellular Biology of Hormone Action

In 1971 a Nobel Prize was awarded for the discovery of **cyclic adenosine monophosphate (cAMP)** as a participant in hormone activity. Cyclic AMP is so important that it is often referred to as the **second messenger**—the molecular messenger that acts inside the cell. But, as we will see, this is only one way hormones work.

Second messengers. In light of the second messenger theory, we could refer to the hormones we've been talking about as "first messengers," since it appears that many of them bring their message only as far as the target cell membrane. Within the cell, the actual response is often triggered by cAMP, which apparently then works through what might be called third and fourth messengers. For example, epinephrine, released from the adrenal medulla, is carried by the blood to a target, such as the liver (Figure 35.12). It turns out that the liver cells have very specific receptor sites along their cell membranes. Once fixed to the membrane, epinephrine activates an enzyme known as **adenylate cyclase,** which immediately converts ATP in the cytoplasm to cAMP. The cAMP then triggers the activity of some enzymes and decreases the activity of others; in the case of epinephrine, the result is a decrease in the synthesis of glycogen (stored chains of glucose molecules) and an increase in its rate of breakdown, with a net release of glucose into the blood.

An important aspect of cAMP control represents yet another role of the widespread calcium-activated protein calmodulin. Activated calmodulin mobilizes an enzyme called **phosphodiesterase,** which subsequently converts cAMP to simple adenosine monophosphate (AMP). The AMP is simply recycled to form more ATP.

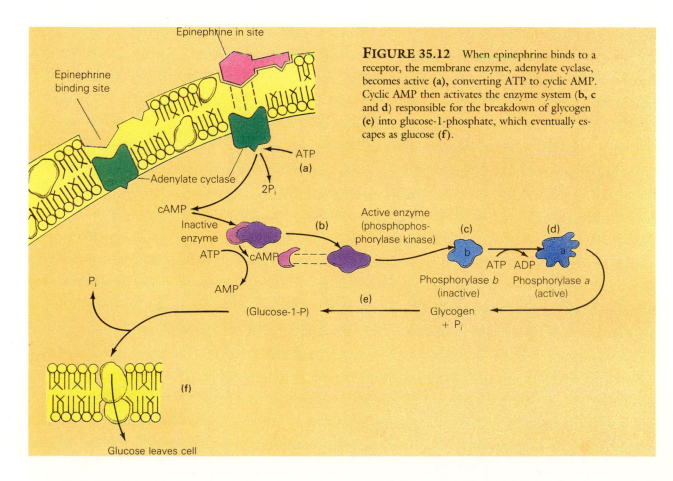

FIGURE 35.12 When epinephrine binds to a receptor, the membrane enzyme, adenylate cyclase, becomes active **(a)**, converting ATP to cyclic AMP. Cyclic AMP then activates the enzyme system **(b, c** and **d)** responsible for the breakdown of glycogen **(e)** into glucose-1-phosphate, which eventually escapes as glucose **(f)**.

At least 12 other hormones are known to stimulate the production of cAMP, utilizing it as a second messenger. But the question arises: How is the activity of so many hormones regulated if they all activate the same second messenger? The answer incorporates two important points. First, hormones have target cells, and a target cell has a specific binding site for a specific hormone. Thus, no other hormone can bind to that particular site (although a cell may have binding sites for more than one hormone). Second, while cAMP has a similar role in all cells—the activation of enzyme systems—different kinds of cells have different enzyme systems waiting for activation. All of this must, of course, be determined ahead of time when cells become specialized.

Hormones as Gene Activators

Not all hormones remain outside of their target cells. Steroid hormones may or may not join with cell-surface receptors—the point is still being argued—but it is certain that many do enter the cell. Once inside, such steroid hormones are tightly bound by a **cytoplasmic binding protein.** Then the steroid-binding protein complex moves into the nucleus, where it joins with other proteins that are permanently bound to the chromosomes. In this way, they can act directly on the chromosomes; the whole complex of hormone, cytoplasmic receptor, and chromosomal protein initiates gene activity, with the production of appropriate mRNA and protein (Figure 35.13).

Some steroid hormones enter the cell, where they activate cytoplasmic agents that enter the nucleus and trigger transcription in certain genes.

A better understanding of those chemical messengers called hormones can provide us with continuing insight into the precise coordination of life's processes. Because of such coordinated interaction, organisms are not solely dependent on the whims of the environment; they can, through automated and precise chemical responses, adjust and fine tune their internal environment as the need arises.

FIGURE 35.13 Steroid hormones are known to enter the cell cytoplasm, where they join cytoplasmic receptors, enter the nucleus, and activate specific genes. Once active, the genes transcribe mRNA, and protein synthesis begins.

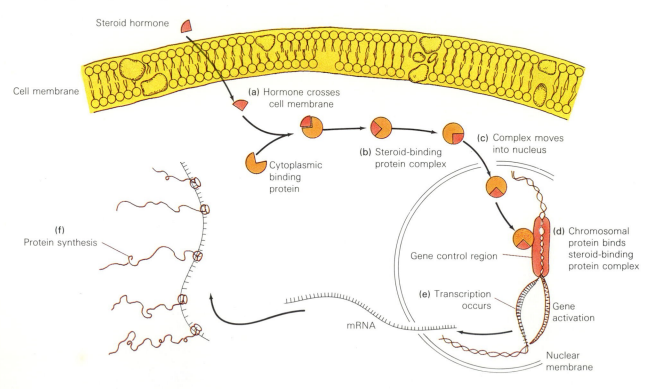

SUMMARY

Communication in the body occurs through neural impulses and through chemical messengers called hormones. Hormones occur throughout the animal kingdom. Studies of hormones and insect metamorphosis are numerous.

NATURE OF HORMONES

Hormones work in minute amounts, have specific actions and target cells with specific receptor sites, and are short-lived. Chemically, they include steroids, proteins, polypeptides, and modified amino acids.

Hormones and Feedback Mechanisms

Hormone release is automated because of negative feedback. Their accumulation or the accumulation of some product they promote, "feeds back" to their place of origin, inhibiting their release. In positive feedback, the presence or product of a substance increases its output, thereby forming an increasing spiral or vicious circle.

HUMAN ENDOCRINE SYSTEM

The human endocrine system includes distinct glandular organs and tissues. Their products enter the blood for transport.

The Pituitary

The pituitary is two glands in one, both of which are under the immediate influence of the hypothalamus. The posterior pituitary secretes two hormones that it receives from neurons originating in the hypothalamus.

The anterior pituitary is a true gland, producing and secreting six hormones. Their release is controlled by specific releasing and inhibiting hormones secreted by the hypothalamus. The hypothalamus is, in turn, controlled by the brain and by its own negative feedback loops.

The anterior pituitary hormones and their functions are as follows. Growth hormone (GH) promotes body growth. Oversecretion can produce pituitary giantism while undersecretion produces pituitary dwarfism. Adrenocorticotropic hormone (ACTH) stimulates the adrenal cortex to secrete steroid hormones. ACTH also regulates fat metabolism. Thyroid-stimulating (TS) hormone prompts the thyroid to release its hormone. Prolactin promotes milk production. Follicle-stimulating hormone (FSH) and luteinizing hormone (LH) prompt gamete and hormone production and release in the ovary.

The posterior pituitary receives oxytocin and antidiuretic hormone (ADH) from the hypothalamus. Oxytocin stimulates uterine contraction during delivery and sexual excitement and causes milk release. ADH increases the recovery of water during urine formation.

The Thyroid Gland

Thyroxin release, prompted by TSH, increases the basal metabolic rate, thereby increasing ATP energy and body heat. Oversecretion produces the hyperactivity of Grave's disease and undersecretion produces hypoactivity and often goiter, thyroid gland enlargement.

The Parathyroid Glands and Calcium Regulation

Parathyroid hormone (PTH), along with calcitonin from the thyroid, regulates calcium uptake, excretion, and deposition in bone. Undersecretion of PTH causes convulsions and death. Oversecretion causes skeletal deterioration.

The Pancreas and the Islets of Langerhans

Pancreatic delta islet cells secrete somatostatin, which may regulate certain digestive hormones. When the blood glucose is low, alpha islet cells secrete glucagon which prompts the breakdown of glycogen and release of glucose. When the blood glucose level is high, beta islet cells secrete insulin which prompts glucose uptake by cells throughout the body. Diabetes mellitus occurs when beta cells fail to produce enough insulin, when receptor sites are too few.

The Adrenal Glands

The adrenal cortex secretes mineralocorticoids, which regulate mineral ions and promote inflammation, and glucocorticoids, which prompt the conversion of fatty and amino acids to glucose and are antiinflammatory. Steroid sex hormones prompt secondary sexual development and influence sex drive.

The adrenal medulla secretes epinephrine and norepinephrine, both of which causes responses that prepare the body for an emergency.

Ovaries and Testes

Ovaries and testes produce the steroid sex hormones estrogen, progesterone and testosterone, all of which influence reproduction and sexual behavior. They also promote bone growth and mental development during puberty.

Other Chemical Messengers

Prostaglandins act as antiinflammatory agents, cause uterine contraction, promote blood clotting in wounds (a function inhibited by aspirin), and prevent spontaneous clotting in vessels (a function promoted by aspirin).

HOW HORMONES WORK

Cellular Biology of Hormone Action

Many hormones prompt the formation of cyclic AMP which initiates the response. When epinephrine attaches to liver cell receptor sites, it activates the membranal enzyme adenylate cyclase, which converts ATP to cAMP. The latter activates an enzyme system that breaks glycogen down into glucose. Many hormones can utilize the cAMP mechanism because different target cells have different enzyme systems poised to act.

Hormones as Gene Activators

Steroid hormones may penetrate the cell, join cytoplasmic binding proteins, enter the nucleus, and activate certain genes. Thus the response is genetic.

KEY TERMS

hormone
target cell
receptor site
steroid
polypeptide
prostaglandin
negative feedback
  mechanism
feedback loop
positive feedback
  mechanism
endocrine system
exocrine gland
pituitary
posterior pituitary
anterior pituitary
releasing hormone
inhibitory hormone
growth hormone
  (GH)

pituitary giant
pituitary dwarf
adrenocorticotrophic
  hormone (ACTH)
thyroid-stimulating
  hormone (TSH)
thyrotropin
thyroxin
triiodothyronine
prolactin
follicle stimulating
  hormone (FSH)
luteinizing hormone
  (LH)
gonadotropin
oxytocin
antidiuretic hormone
  (ADH)
diuretic
thyroid gland

basal metabolic rate (BMR)
hyperthyroidism
hypothyroidism
exophthalmic goiter
simple goiter
calcitonin
parathyroid gland
parathyroid
  hormone (PTH)
autoimmune reaction
pancreas
islets of Langerhans
alpha cell
beta cell
delta cell
glucagon
insulin
somatostatin
diabetes mellitus
adrenal glands

adrenal cortex
mineralocorticoid
glucocorticoid
steroid sex hormone
aldosterone
cortisol
adrenal medulla
epinephrine
norepinephrine
estrogen
progesterone
testosterone
thromboxane
prostacyclin
cyclic adenosine
  monophosphate (cAMP)
adenylate cyclase
phosphodiesterase
cytoplasmic binding protein

REVIEW QUESTIONS

1 Carefully define the term hormone. Are all chemical messengers hormones? (pp. 561–562)

2 Review an experiment involving insect metamorphosis and hormones. What do such hormones prove about insect growth? (Figure 35.1)

3 List three factors that account for the highly specific action of hormones, and one factor that prevents an unending, uncontrolled action. (pp. 561–562)

4 Contrast negative and positive feedback. Why is the latter often considered abnormal? (pp. 562–563)

5 Draw a general scheme showing the work of a negative feedback loop. (p. 562)

6 Name and locate the major endocrine glands. (p. 564)

7 Explain how the anterior and posterior pituitary differ in origin and secretory activity. (pp. 564–565)

8 Explain how the hypothalamus exercises chemical control over the anterior pituitary. (p. 565)

9 List the six hormones of the anterior pituitary and give an example of the action of each. (p. 566)

10 Using growth hormone as an example, discuss the dramatic effects of both the oversecretion or undersecretion of hormones. (p. 566)

11 Name the two hormones of the posterior pituitary and summarize their actions. (pp. 566–567)

12 Prepare a diagram illustrating negative feedback control of thyroxin secretion. How might this hormone relate to the body temperature regulation in humans? (p. 567)

13 Name and explain two opposing kinds of thyroid abnormalities. (p. 567)

14 Summarize the dual control mechanism for calcium regulation in the body. (p. 568)

15 List the hormones secreted by the islet cells and state the action of each. (p. 568)

16 Describe the glucose-regulating interplay between glucagon and insulin, including negative feedback aspects. (Figure 35.10)

17 What is diabetes mellitus? List two abnormal situations that can bring on the condition. (p. 568)

18 List three families of hormones secreted by the adrenal cortex and state one action for each. (pp. 569–570)

19 Explain, specifically, how the hormones of the adrenal medulla complement the work of the sympathetic part of the autonomic nervous system. (p. 570)

20 Describe an important growth effect of steroid hormones. When is this most pronounced? (p. 570)

21 Distinguish between action of thromboxane and prostacyclin. Which effect is reinforced by aspirin? Why? What group of people might this help? (pp. 570–571)

22 What is the second messenger? How is it produced? (p. 571)

23 List the events surrounding the activity of epinephrine in liver cells. (p. 571)

24 How can cyclic AMP create so many different effects? (p. 572)

25 Explain how some steroids take their action directly to the gene. (p. 572)

Morning comes and your eyes slowly open. As you rustle about, life seems simple and routine. You hardly notice what you are doing. But this is because evolution has not burdened you with the constant awareness of the many processes that enable you to do simple things. While you slept, poisonous nitrogenous substances were washed from the bloodstream. After awakening, you felt certain urges and while one part of your brain was deciding how to satisfy them, another part was coordinating your muscular movements so that you didn't fall flat on your face. And you probably paid no attention to the remarkable fact that you were alive at all; while you slept, various mechanisms were operating that kept your bodily processes within very precise limits. For example, your body temperature fell ever so slightly during the night, but at some point it stabilized and you did not die of hypothermia. When things are going well, your body's activities are, indeed, kept within certain critical limits. The maintenance of a stable internal environment is called **homeostasis.**

THE NATURE OF
HOMEOSTATIC MECHANISMS

The body has basically two types of homeostatic responses to changing conditions: physiological and behavioral. *Physiological* responses generally are made without conscious intervention, and, as we have seen so far, they involve the autonomic nervous system and endocrine system. An animal that has these capabilities does not really have to think much about increasing its metabolic rate to produce more body heat, or about shunting blood into its extremities to cool its body. However, the animal may curl up in a ball to retain more heat, or move into the shade to cool itself. These conscious changes are examples of *behavioral* responses.

To illustrate the adaptiveness and complexity of homeostatic mechanisms, let's consider two processes that involve multiple, interacting controls. One is *thermoregulation,* the animal's control over its internal temperature. The other is *osmoregulation,* through which the animal controls its body-fluid and mineral-ion balances. The latter is often closely associated with the *excretory system,* which rids the body of nitrogenous wastes.

36

HOMEOSTASIS AND LIFE'S DELICATE BALANCE

THERMOREGULATION

Thermoregulation is the ability of an organism to maintain its body temperature either at a constant level or within an acceptable range. Some animals have very little ability to regulate their temperature; some have a moderate ability; and yet others are highly specialized for it.

Why Thermoregulate?

The most apparent reason for thermoregulation is that life can only exist within certain temperature limits. Under the most extreme conditions, low temperatures can freeze the water in living cells resulting in ice crystals disrupting delicate membranes and the inclusions in the remaining fluids becoming dangerously concentrated. High temperatures, on the other hand, can accelerate rates of biochemical reactions to unacceptable levels and can denature enzymes, rendering them biochemically inactive.

Animals in an environment cooler than their bodies cannot completely avoid heat loss, and since the primary source of heat for animals is their cellular respiratory process (see Chapter 8), we have a paradoxical situation. As the body cools, greater metabolic heat is required. Yet the loss of body heat ordinarily slows all chemical activity, including the respiratory activity required to produce heat. The result, under frigid conditions, is an accelerated (positive feedback) cooling of the animal, unless it can take measures to counteract the phenomenon.

Animals have just a few adaptive options when environmental temperatures fall below optimal levels. Most can attempt to avoid heat loss through behavioral strategies (Figure 36.1), or, as is often the case, the metabolic machinery will simply slow down, sending the animals into a metabolic stupor, their biochemical processes becoming so slow that

FIGURE 36.1   Vertebrate adaptions to cooling external temperatures include a variety of behavioral responses. Humans may pile on clothing and voluntarily increase their muscular activity, a primary source of metabolic heat. Birds tend to crouch into a ball shape, drawing the extremities in. At this time their inner down feathers may be fluffed up, trapping air and improving their insulating quality. Reptiles of temperate regions are baskers. Lacking a physiological means of maintaining warmth, they often use the morning sun to raise their body temperatures.

they become sluggish or immobile. Another option for some animals is to take physiological measures to replace lost metabolic heat and to restrict what heat remains to those parts of the body that are most critical. Keep in mind that behavioral and physiological strategies usually work in concert. In the winter, for example, humans tend to take in more calories *and* put on warmer clothing.

Thermoregulation, of course, also involves the loss of unwanted heat under high environmental temperatures. In fact, overheating often causes more problems than does overcooling. The associated problems may also be more severe, because physiological damage created by excessive heat is often irreversible, whereas damage done by low temperatures, within certain limits, is more likely to be temporary.

> Thermoregulation involves physiologically or behaviorally keeping the body temperature at a certain level or within a certain range.

Homeotherms and Poikilotherms

Some species maintain rather constant internal temperatures. These are called **homeotherms** (sometimes called "warm-blooded" animals). The major homeothermic groups are the birds and mammals. In other species the internal temperatures may fluctuate wildly With the environmental temperatures. These are the **poikilotherms** (sometimes called "cold-blooded" animals). Examples include many invertebrates, most fishes, amphibians, and reptiles.

The advantage of homeothermy is that the body is kept within a certain (usually relatively warm) temperature range; therefore, heat-dependent chemical processes can go on with a certain constancy (not requiring, for example, warm-up periods). The disadvantage is that the maintenance of constant internal temperatures requires a great deal of energy, and internal temperature changes that exceed certain limits can be dangerous. Poikilothermy, on the other hand, requires little expenditure of energy in producing body heat. Most poikilotherms can tolerate a great deal of internal temperature variation.

Animals gain heat in two basic ways. The **endotherms** generate a great deal of their heat through internal, metabolic means, primarily cell respiration. The source of this energy is food, of course, which means that endotherms must feed frequently. In contrast, the **ectotherms** require external sources of heat—heat from their surroundings. Some regulate their temperatures by exposing themselves to the sun

in specific ways. To cool themselves the ectotherms simply avoid heat, such as by seeking shade or burrowing. Simply put, endotherms heat themselves from the inside out, and ectotherms heat themselves from the outside in. When cooling is needed, sun exposure is kept to a minimum, and some burrow to escape the sun's rays altogether. These strategies and others like them are commonly seen in invertebrates and reptiles.

> **Homeotherms** maintain a rather constant body temperature. **Endotherms** generate heat internally. **Ectotherms** derive heat from the environment. **Poikilotherms** are able to allow their body temperature to vary with that of the environment.

The lines between endothermy and ectothermy are not clearly drawn, as anyone can tell you who has ever seen a dog lying in the sun on a cold day. Then there are fast-moving fishes that remain highly active in very cold ocean water (Essay 36.1). Insects are another puzzle. Some beetles, moths, butterflies, and bees thermoregulate metabolically at times like typical endothermic homeotherms. In fact, some flying insects generate so much heat that they must shunt warm blood to the abdomen, which acts as a heat radiator. Yet at other times these same insects are poikilothermic. They expend no energy on body heat at all, letting their bodies cool down to environmental temperatures. Physiologists often characterize such animals as **heterotherms.** The point is, except for birds and mammals, which are clearly endothermic homeotherms, there are few reliable taxonomic dividing lines limiting thermoregulation.

> The ability to thermoregulate is not confined to certain taxonomic groupings but varies from species to species.

Thermoregulation in Humans

Humans, like other mammals, maintain internal body temperatures within rather narrow limits. Any consistent variation of more than a few degrees from the optimum usually means trouble. We adjust our body temperature physiologically by varying the rate of metabolic heat production and controlling heat loss or gain from our body surfaces. The two mechanisms work in close harmony through the efforts of the hypothalamus, the body's internal thermostat (Figure 36.2).

The bluefin tuna was once believed to be coldblooded, like many other fishes. Yet it is among the fastest of all bony fishes and often lives in extremely cold water. This does not seem possible; speed and cold bodies just don't go together. How could a poikilotherm generate the metabolic energy needed to swim so fast in its chilling habitat? For one thing, the bluefin tuna is not the "cold fish" we once thought it was. In fact, even in the coldest water its internal temperatures can be quite high, up to nearly 32°C (almost 90°F). This is far better physiological regulation than we (as efficient endotherms) are capable of. How does this fish keep its body warm in frigid surroundings?

Much of the answer seems to be in the bluefin's circulatory system, which is quite different in some ways from that of truly cold-bodied bony fishes. In the bluefin tuna, the major arteries leaving the head and warm internal regions, and the veins returning blood from cool external regions, run paired with and parallel to each other; those of other fishes tend to branch individually. This is the basis for the bluefin's unusual ability. The parallel vessels set up the mechanism for a *countercurrent heat exchange*. It works this way: warmer blood leaving the deeper tissues passes cooler blood coming back from the surface. As the two opposing streams pass each other, heat moves to the cooler returning blood, and so much of the heat never reaches the extremities.

We find two differently colored regions of muscle in the bluefin, light and dark. The dark muscle occurs in a region of higher temperature (as much as 10°C higher than the skin). Its dark color is due to an immense network of blood vessels consisting of parallel arteries and veins. This vascularized region, known as the *rete mirabile* (wonderful net, see illustration), is a very dense countercurrent heat exchanger and conserver. Because of its arrangement, the *rete mirabile* produces a comparatively warm, lively group of swimming muscles. And that's why the bluefin tuna (and a number of other fast-swimming predatory fish) can swim rapidly in very cold water.

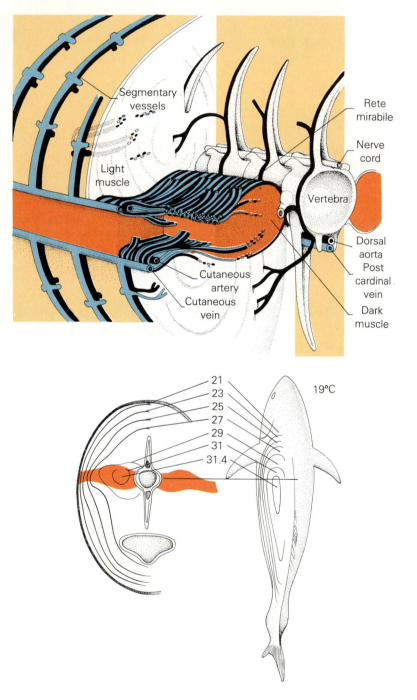

FIGURE 36.2 The hypothalamus receives thermal information both from thermoreceptors in the skin and by direct sensing of the temperature of blood arriving from the core of the body. Its response to changing temperatures is carried out in two ways: through activation of the autonomic nervous system and the endocrine system. Negative feedback occurs through the continued sensing of blood temperature.

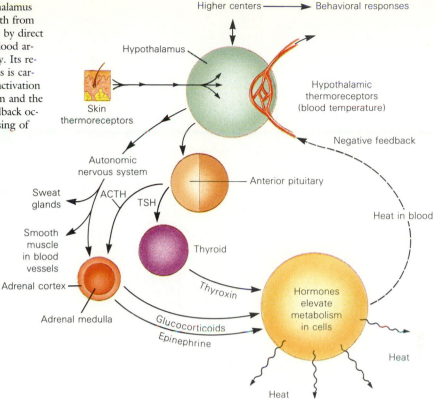

The hypothalamus: a thermostat. The temperature-regulating portion of the hypothalamus works a bit like an ordinary home thermostat. The hypothalamus, however, is far more sensitive and precise. In fact, physiologists have detected responses in the hypothalamus when blood temperature changed as little as 0.01°C. The hypothalamus receives information from thermoreceptors in the skin and from its own thermoreceptors, which monitor blood coming from various parts of the body (see Figure 36.2).

When the hypothalamus detects a drop in body temperature, it can respond in a number of ways. It can influence the autonomic nervous system to decrease blood flow to the skin, conserving heat. Working through the autonomic nervous system, it can increase heat production by stimulating the adrenal medulla. In response, the gland releases epinephrine into the bloodstream, which increases the conversion of glycogen to glucose in the liver and muscles. This provides the fuel required for increased metabolic activity and heat release. The effects of epinephrine are short-lived, but the hypothalamus can produce a longer lasting increase in metabolism by causing the pituitary to release TSH and ACTH, which stimulate the thyroid to release its metabolism-elevating hormones and the adrenal cortex to release glucocorticoids that mobilize fats and proteins in preparation for cell respiration (see Chapter

35). The result in all instances is an increase in body heat. As body heat increases, the hypothalamus senses it (negative feedback) and eases off on its heat-generating activity.

At temperatures below optimum the hypothalamus prompts the autonomic nervous system to decrease surface blood flow, and heat is retained internally. It also prompts the release of hormones that elevate metabolism.

Skin and lungs as thermoregulators. Two important structures for managing heat loss and gain in humans are the skin and respiratory passages. The skin is beautifully adapted to this function (Figure 36.3). The arrangement of the blood vessels ensures that blood flow to surface capillaries can be increased or decreased to dissipate or conserve heat, respectively. Blood flow in these areas is directly controlled by smooth muscle sphincters (circular muscles) in the tiny arteries leading to the capillary bed. Contraction of the sphincters is brought about by the hypothalamus, operating through the autonomic nervous system. When these sphincters close due to cold, blood is kept deep in the warmer parts of the body, an adaptive mechanism that sacrifices the less critical parts of the body first.

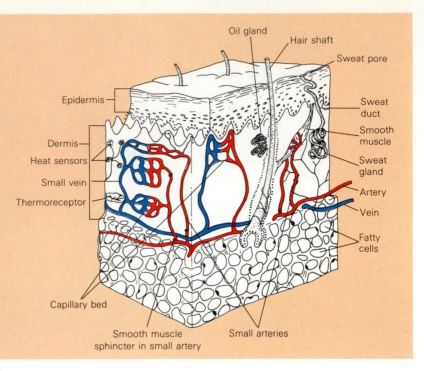

FIGURE 36.3   The human skin is an important thermoregulatory organ. Sweat glands secrete water through ducts. The evaporation of the sweat cools the skin. Sebaceous glands secrete oils that keep the hair and skin pliable and waterproof. Capillary beds below the surface can be opened, bringing blood near the skin for cooling, or alternately can be closed, keeping blood in deeper regions and thereby conserving heat. The direction of blood flow is controlled by sphincters (circular valves in the small arteries). Heat and cold receptors are abundant in the skin. Layers of fatty tissue provide heat-retaining insulation.

Heat loss through breathing is unavoidable and is an important factor in frigid climates. Air entering the nasal passageways is warmed by blood in the highly vascularized nasal lining, thus protecting the lungs from drastic local heat loss. The nasal passages themselves are then rewarmed by exhaled air. (Physiologists tell us that by the time cold winter air reaches the lungs, it is warmed almost to body temperature.)

When excess heat is a problem, the vessels near the skin dilate (enlarge), bringing more blood to the skin, thereby permitting the heat to radiate into the cooler air. Heat escape is even faster if aided by the evaporation of perspiration. Humans are unusual in their ability to sweat over virtually their entire bodies. Sweat glands are present in only a few mammals. Horses have them over most of the body, whereas in dogs the glands are found only on the footpads. They are entirely lacking in reptiles and birds.

At temperatures above optimum the hypothalamus slows heat generation and prompts the autonomic nervous system to increase surface blood flow and sweating, permitting heat loss.

Humans, like some other animals, are able to regulate body temperature by countercurrent heat exchangers as we see in Figure 36.4. Note the great temperature effect of simply rerouting the blood.

Countercurrent heat exchangers make use of heated and cooled fluids passing in opposite directions in closely parallel vessels. Heat transfer occurs along the entire route.

OSMOREGULATION AND EXCRETION

Osmoregulation, or the way that water and ion concentrations are regulated in the animal body, presents another fascinating problem for physiologists. It is sometimes said that most cells are about two-thirds water, but to the animal, "about" won't do. In fact, for all living things the amount of intracellular water is critical, as is the relative abundance of various ions in the cell fluids since the two problems are inseparable.

The problem is to understand how the balance of water and ions is maintained. In particular, the question centers on the way excess water or ions are removed from the body by **excretion.** Excretion refers to the removal of metabolic wastes from the body, particularly the removal of the nitrogenous wastes produced by the metabolism of amino acids.

To a great degree, the animal's environment dictates the methods by which nitrogenous wastes are removed.

The maintenance of specific ion and water content in the body is called **osmoregulation. Excretion,** removing nitrogen wastes, often involves the same system.

The Human Excretory System

Because humans are terrestrial creatures, we must conserve water, just like our fellow landlubbers. At the same time, we must wash potentially poisonous nitrogenous wastes from our bodies and regulate such ions as sodium, potassium, chloride, and hydrogen. Most human nitrogenous waste occurs in the form of **urea,** a relatively harmless by-product of ami-

no acid metabolism. The specific process, which occurs in the liver, is called **deamination.** Both the osmoregulatory and the excretory functions are handled by the kidneys and their associated ducts (with assistance from the lungs and sweat glands).

Excretory structures. The human excretory system comprises the **kidneys, ureters, bladder,** and **urethra** (Figure 36.5). Each kidney receives a small blood vessel, the **renal artery** ("renal" means "pertaining to the kidney"), which branches directly from the **descending aorta,** a major artery from the heart. (All arteries carry blood from the heart through the rest of the body.) The renal artery is small, but blood passing through it is under extremely high pressure. Blood leaves each kidney through the **renal vein.** (Veins carry blood back to the heart.)

The excretory system removes excess water, excess salts, and urea from the blood. And while the kidneys filter about 180 liters (190 qt) of fluid per day, more

FIGURE 36.4 Countercurrent heat exchangers are common in human extremities. In the arm, for instance, the larger arteries and veins travel close together deep in the muscle. When the arm is cold, blood returns through the deeper veins, where the countercurrent exchange of heat between the arteries and veins conserves internal body heat. An alternate route for returning blood is through the veins that lie near the surface, just below the skin. When the arm is warm, returning blood follows the surface route, increasing the radiation of heat from the skin.

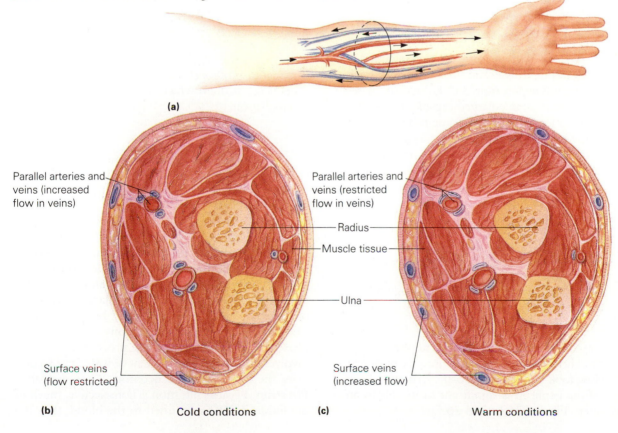

(a)

Parallel arteries and veins (increased flow in veins)

Parallel arteries and veins (restricted flow in veins)

Radius

Muscle tissue

Ulna

Surface veins (flow restricted)

Surface veins (increased flow)

(b)   Cold conditions   (c)   Warm conditions

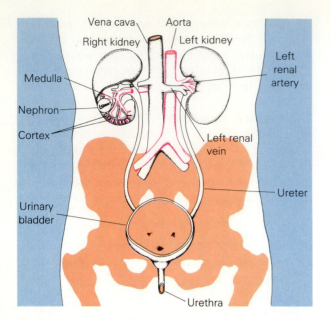

Vena cava   Aorta
Right kidney   Left kidney
Medulla   Left renal artery
Nephron
Cortex   Left renal vein
Urinary bladder   Ureter
Urethra

FIGURE 36.5   The human excretory system consists of the paired kidneys, their associated blood vessels, the renal arteries and veins, the ureters, bladder, and urethra.

A nephron begins as a hollow bulb or cup known as **Bowman's capsule.** From the Bowman's capsule, the nephron forms a slender tubule that is organized into three distinct parts. The first, the **proximal (near) convoluted tubule,** gets its name from the twisting route it follows before it is directed downward into the second part, a long, hairpin loop known as the **loop of Henle.** The loop of Henle is made up of a **descending limb** that dips down toward (or into) the renal medulla and an **ascending limb** that returns upward. (Such hairpin loops are found in all water-conserving vertebrate kidneys and are extremely prominent in the kidneys of desert-dwelling mammals.) The ascending limb of Henle's loop then gives rise to the last part of the nephron, the **distal (far) convoluted tubule.** Like its proximal counterpart, the distal convoluted tubule follows a twisting path. It finally joins a **collecting duct,** which also receives the distal tubules of neighboring nephrons.

Since it is the blood that is filtered, the blood vessels associated with the nephron are of equal importance to its function. The Bowman's capsule contains a dense ball of capillaries known as the **glomerulus,** which arises from the **afferent vessel,** a tiny branch of the renal artery (see Figure 36.6d). The capillaries of the glomerulus, having followed their tortuous route within the Bowman's capsule, rejoin to form a small emerging **efferent vessel.** This vessel immediately divides again, this time into the **peritubular capillaries,** a network that surrounds the tubule and the collecting duct. Eventually these capillaries will merge into venules (little veins) that join to form the renal vein, through which filtered blood is returned to circulation.

than 99% of that fluid is recycled back to the blood before the urine (about 1.2 liters [1.3 qt] per day) is formed. At any time, the actual volume and content of the urine depends on water intake and diet.

The **kidney** (Figure 36.6a) has three major regions: the outer **renal cortex,** the **renal medulla,** and the **renal pelvis.** Much of tissue of the first two regions is made up of **nephrons,** the filtering units of the kidney, and their associated blood vessels. Each of the one million nephrons in each kidney originates in the renal cortex as an enlarged capsule that is continuous with a lengthy **tubule.** Some tubules extend into the medulla, while others are confined to the cortex; all of the tubules eventually join with the tubules of neighboring nephrons to form larger ducts that carry urine into the renal pelvis. Of equal importance are the blood vessels that are closely associated with the nephrons.

The human excretory and osmoregulatory system includes the renal vessels, kidneys, ureters, bladder, and urethra. The filtering units are numerous microscopic nephrons.

Microscopic structure of the nephron. To understand how the nephrons function, we must first take a close look at their microscopic structure. Each aspect of the nephron is significant to its role as an active filter (Figures 36.6c and 36.7).

The **nephron** and related structures are Bowman's capsule, proximal tubule, loop of Henle, distal tubule, collecting duct, and associated blood vessels.

Filtering activity of the nephron. The role of the kidneys and their nephrons, as mentioned, is to rid the body of nitrogenous wastes and to maintain the body's delicate water and salt balance. As it turns out, there is no simple way for the body to do this. The filtering work of the nephrons occurs in three phases, each involving several processes. The first involves nonselective movement of water and solutes from the blood into the nephron, a process called **filtration.** Because filtration is nonselective, much of the filtrate must be returned to the blood, thus the second process, **reabsorption,** is aptly named. The third process, **tubular secretion,** is highly selective, involving the transport of several substances from the blood to the tubule.

The role of the nephron is to receive a crude filtrate from the blood at one end, selectively return essential materials to the blood along the tubule, and produce finished urine at the end.

Filtration takes place at the glomerulus, the ball of capillaries within Bowman's capsule. Blood entering the glomerulus is under considerable pressure, and the force literally presses most of the water and solutes it carries right through the capillary walls and into Bowman's capsule. The fluid entering the nephron, which is not urine, is referred to as the **crude filtrate.**

The filtration of fluid from the glomerulus into Bowman's capsule removes urea from the blood, but it also removes many valuable constituents. Thus the

FIGURE 36.6 **(a)** The kidney contains an outer cortex, an inner medulla, and a final collecting region known as the renal pelvis. **(b)** Note the relationship between the cortex and medulla of the kidney and the loop of Henle. **(c)** The functional units of the kidney are the nephrons. Each nephron consists of four anatomical regions: Bowman's capsule, proximal convoluted tubule, loop of Henle, and distal convoluted tubule. Each nephron is joined to a nearby collecting duct. Note the blood supply to the nephron. Blood enters the nephron at the Bowman's capsule, where an afferent arteriole has branched into a mass of smaller vessels that comprise the glomerulus. Emerging from the glomerulus is an efferent arteriole that immediately branches to form the extensive peritubular capillary network over the entire nephron. **(d)** The juxtaglomerular region of the nephron is essential to the reabsorption of sodium.

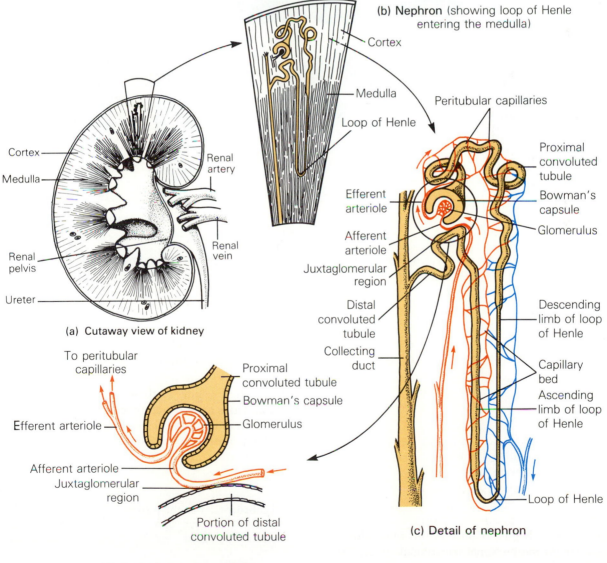

(a) Cutaway view of kidney

(b) Nephron (showing loop of Henle entering the medulla)

(c) Detail of nephron

(d) Juxtaglomerular complex

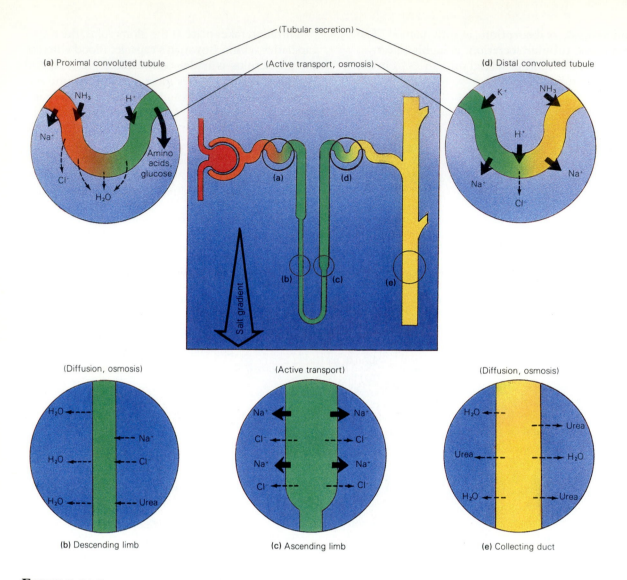

FIGURE 36.7 A diagrammatic view of the nephron includes the various active and passive processes involved in filtration and reabsorption. Note the steep salt and urea gradient around the loop and collecting duct, important to the recovery of water (increasing color).

blood leaving the glomerulus to enter the peritubular (peri, "around") capillary bed (around the nephron), is in a very dense, hypertonic state. It is loaded with large particles such as cells and proteins but little water.

> **Filtration** in the glomerulus forces water and many blood solutes into Bowman's capsule, forming **crude filtrate.** The blood leaving Bowman's capsule is hypertonic.

Reabsorption begins at once as the crude filtrate passes through the proximal convoluted tubule. As

you see in Figure 36.7a, water, sodium ions, chloride ions, glucose, and amino acids leave the crude filtrate to reenter the peritubular capillaries. Both active and passive transport are responsible for reabsorption in this region. In spite of these efforts, more of the water and ions must be reclaimed if a balance is to be maintained in the body. This brings us to one of the most fascinating parts of kidney function.

> **Reabsorption** in the proximal tubule returns some of the water, salts, glucose, and amino acids to the blood.

The loop of Henle. The principal role of the loop of Henle is to create a dense salt concentration in its surroundings, the kidney medulla. With a million nephrons participating, the salt concentration in the medulla becomes considerable. A high salt concentration means a low water concentration—much lower than the water concentration inside the nephron, so that a natural osmotic gradient forms. Simply stated, where salt goes, water will follow. But how does the loop accomplish this? The answer lies in its peculiar hairpin shape and some very capable cells in the ascending limb.

As the crude filtrate makes its way through the loop, cells in the ascending limb actively transport salt out of the filtrate. Much of the salt leaving the ascending limb moves across to the decending limb, where, as you see in Figure 36.7b and c, it simply diffuses back into the loop. (The transfer between two oppositely moving streams is another example of a countercurrent exchange at work.)

We see then, that the continuous cycling of salt in and out of the loop produces the necessary osmotic gradient. Further, active transport also moves some of the salt into the nearby capillary bed, thus extending the gradient. As a result, water continually leaves the descending loop, moves through the salty medulla, and enters the peritubular capillaries.

Interestingly, the osmotic gradient we've been describing gets a boost in a seemingly odd way. Urea, which is concentrating in the collecting duct, moves out, thereby adding another solute to the salty medulla. It reenters the nephron at Henle's loop, returning to the collecting duct and thereby forming its own cycle (Figure 36.7e). So urea, the primary nitrogenous waste, also plays a role in water retention.

A countercurrent exchange in the loop of Henle produces a dense salt concentration that results in additional water leaving the crude filtrate and reentering the capillaries.

The final steps. The fluid leaving the loop of Henle is close to its final form, but as it enters the distal tubule, more adjustments are made. Salt, apparently still in excess, is once more actively transported out of the filtrate, and some water passively follows.

The final phase of the nephron's action, tubular secretion, occurs in the proximal and distal tubules and in the collecting ducts. Tubular secretion is the active transport of substances from the blood into the nephron, so the movement is opposite that of reabsorption. Included are nitrogenous wastes in the form of ammonium ions, creatine, potassium ions, and hydrogen ions. Tubular secretion is quite important, for in addition to ridding the body of the two nitrogenous wastes, it helps maintain the body's critical ion and pH balances.

In **tubular secretion,** hydrogen and potassium ions are transported from the blood into the nephron, eliminating waste and adjusting potassium ion and pH balances.

The filtrate leaving the distal tubule is now urine. It will enter the collecting duct, where, as we will see, yet one more adjustment of the urine will occur. From the collecting ducts urine passes into the renal pelvis and, eventually, into the ureters to the bladder. From the bladder it leaves the body through the urethra.

Just how much water is removed by the kidneys depends, of course, on the person's physiological state. If water intake has been excessive, the urine volume will be considerable and may be quite diluted. If a person is dehydrated, the urine volume may be small but highly concentrated. The amount of salt present in the urine depends on the intake of sodium chloride in the diet. Of course, the nephron does not control water and salt retention all by itself. Controlling the reabsorption of water and salt, as we saw in the last chapter, involves the intervention of hormones.

Hormonal Control in the Nephron

Antidiuretic hormone. One role of the hypothalamus is to monitor the osmotic state of the blood passing through its capillaries (the relative water and solute content). If the blood is becoming hypertonic with the water content below optimum, the hypothalamus secretes the hormone ADH into the posterior pituitary, which then releases it into the bloodstream. Its targets are the epithelial cells of the distal convoluted tubule and the collecting ducts of the nephron (Figure 36.8). The hormone renders those passageways permeable to water, which flows freely from the nephron to reenter the bloodstream via the capillaries associated with the system. As the proper osmotic pressure becomes reestablished, less ADH is released, the tubules become less permeable, and the urine is more dilute.

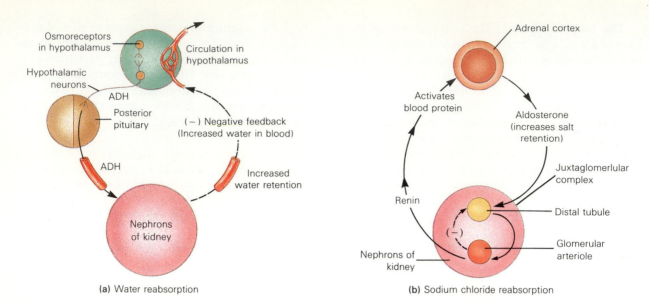

Osmoreceptors
in hypothalamus

Circulation in
hypothalamus

Hypothalamic
neurons

ADH

Posterior
pituitary

(—) Negative feedback
(Increased water in blood)

ADH

Increased
water retention

Nephrons
of kidney

(a) Water reabsorption

Adrenal cortex

Activates
blood protein

Aldosterone
(increases salt
retention)

Juxtaglomerlular
complex

Renin

Distal tubule

(—)

Glomerular
arteriole

Nephrons of
kidney

(b) Sodium chloride reabsorption

FIGURE 36.8 **(a)** Water reabsorption is controlled in part by the hypothalamus, which secretes ADH via the posterior pituitary. Negative feedback is direct, since the osmoreceptors in the hypothalamus respond to the increased water content of the blood. **(b)** Salt reabsorption is influenced by the adrenal cortex hormone, aldosterone, which is released when renin is present. Aldosterone increases the active transport of sodium in the distal tubule, which forms a negative feedback loop that slows renin secretion.

The hormone ADH increases the reabsorption of water by altering the permeability of the distal tubules and collecting ducts.

Aldosterone. Another hormonal mechanism operates to control the retention of sodium chloride (Figure 36.8b). In this case the hormone is **aldosterone,** a mineralocorticoid (see Chapter 35) that is released by the cortex of the adrenal gland. The link between sodium chloride retention and aldosterone release is indirect and not entirely understood.

Cells of the juxtaglomerular complex of the nephron's distal tubule (see Figure 36.6d) monitor minute changes in blood pressure in the nearby afferent vessel (the one carrying blood into the glomerulus). If blood pressure is below optimum, the complex stimulates the release of the hormone **renin** into blood passing through the afferent vessel. Renin has no effect on the nephron, but it does activate a blood protein that, on reaching the adrenal cortex, stimulates aldosterone secretion. Aldosterone's target cells are in the nephron's distal tubule and the collecting ducts. The target cells respond by speeding up their transport of sodium ions out of the tubule and back to the blood. As expected, water follows, and the additional water increases blood pressure enough to form an inhibiting feedback loop back to the juxtaglomerular complex.

This mechanism has two important aspects. First, it assures that the blood pressure in the kidney itself is great enough to maintain an efficient filtration phase. Second, the aldosterone-related increase in sodium transport also means an increase in the tubular secretion of potassium ions, mentioned earlier. The active transport mechanism involved is identical to the familiar sodium-potassium ion-exchange pump of blood and nerve cells.

Decreasing blood pressure, sensed by juxtaglomerular cells, leads to aldosterone secretion. The distal tubule and collecting ducts respond by increasing their sodium reabsorption.

In this chapter we have seen only a few of the many delicate, interacting, and highly coordinated mechanisms that keep the body's internal environment within the extremely precise limits critical to life. Remember, we live in what is essentially a disruptive environment. To remain organized in the face of such potential disruption requires an uphill battle against a variety of forces. That battle is best fought under optimal conditions, which is what homeostasis is all about.

SUMMARY

THE NATURE OF HOMEOSTATIC MECHANISMS

Homeostasis involves maintaining stability through ongoing adjustments to change. Such responses are physiological and behavioral.

THERMOREGULATION

Animals that thermoregulate maintain a certain body temperature despite surrounding changes.

Why Thermoregulate

Excessively low or high temperatures can have damaging effects on cells. As heat is lost, chemical activity slows, setting up a positive feedback situation. Some animals simply cool down as surrounding temperatures fall, eventually becoming immobile. Others have a physiological response to maintain heat and some have behavioral responses.

Homeotherms and Poikilotherms

Homeotherms maintain relatively constant, generally warm, temperatures. Poikilotherms permit their temperatures to change with surroundings. Homeotherms remain in a constant state of activeness, but at a cost of energy. Poikilotherms have no such energy expenditure, but are often inactive.

Endotherms utilize metabolism to maintain body heat, whereas ectotherms find ways of utilizing heat from the surroundings. Many animals utilize both means. Heterotherms may be homeothermic for a time and then switch to poikilothermy.

Thermoregulation in Humans

Humans utilize physiological mechanisms to generate and retain heat, to slow heat production, and to speed its escape. Body heat is monitored by the hypothalamus.

Avoiding heat loss. As body temperature falls, the hypothalamus stimulates activity in the autonomic nervous system and the endocrine system. Circulatory changes shunt blood away from the skin and extremities. Metabolic heat output is increased through glucose release and cell respiration speeds up. Highly vascularized air passages help avoid cooling by warming incoming air before it gets to the lungs.

Speeding heat loss. Cooling is done by shunting more blood to the skin, generating sweat, and slowing the metabolic processes. Alternative surface arrangements and deeper countercurrent arrangements in blood vessels help in regulating body heat.

OSMOREGULATION AND EXCRETION

In humans osmoregulation, the precise regulation of body water and ion content, is closely associated with excretion, the removal of nitrogen wastes.

The Human Excretory System

Humans must conserve water and ions as they excrete wastes. Urea, the primary nitrogenous waste, is produced following the deamination of amino acids.

The excretory system includes the kidneys and associated blood vessels, ureters, bladder, urethra. The kidneys remove excess water and salts and also urea. Nephrons, the filtering units, are concentrated in the renal cortex, but the tubules of many dip down into the medulla. They join ducts that lead to the renal pelvis.

The parts of nephrons and their functions are as follows.

Bowman's capsule and the glomerulus: force filtration from the glomerulus to the capsule, creates the crude filtrate.

Peritubular capillaries: surround nephron and receive reabsorption products.

Proximal convoluted tubule: reabsorption begins. Active transport and diffusion return water and other critical substances to capillaries. Tubular secretion actively transports ammonium ions, creatinine, K^+, and H^+ into the urine.

Loop of Henle: countercurrent mechanism creates a dense salt (solute) concentration in the kidney medulla, prompting the exodus of more water from the filtrate. (Urea increases the solute concentration.)

Distal convoluted tubule: further active and passive transport returns more critical substances to capillaries. Tubular secretion actively transports ammonium ions, creatine, K^+, and H^+ into the urine.

A final adjustment of water and ions in the filtrate is made in the collecting duct as the urine forms.

Hormonal Control of the Nephron

ADH is released through the posterior pituitary when the blood's water content is low. It alters permeability in the distal tubule and collecting duct, permitting water to leave.

Aldosterone is released by the adrenal cortex when cells of the juxtaglomerular complex sense solute-related blood pressure changes. Aldosterone increases salt retention which leads to increased water reabsorption and a favorable change in blood pressure.

Both hormones are regulated by negative feedback loops that influence the hypothalamus.

KEY TERMS

thermoregulation
homeotherm
poikilotherm
endotherm
ectotherm
heterotherm
countercurrent heat exchanger
osmoregulation
excretion
urea
deamination
kidney
ureter

bladder
urethra
renal artery
descending aorta
renal vein
renal cortex
renal medulla
renal pelvis
nephron
tubule
Bowman's capsule
proximal convoluted tubule
loop of Henle

descending limb
ascending limb
distal convoluted tubule
collecting duct
glomerulus
afferent vessel
efferent vessel
peritubular capillaries
filtration
reabsorption
tubular secretion
crude filtrate
homeostasis

REVIEW QUESTIONS

1 Review the concept of homeostasis, referring to Chapter 35 as necessary. (p. 579)

2 Briefly discuss two kinds of homeostatic responses available to animals. (p. 579)

3 In comparing the risks of cooling and heating, why is the latter considered more dangerous? (p. 580)

4 Explain the "paradoxical situation" arising when the animal body cools. (p. 580)

5 Make a general distinction between homeothermy and poikilothermy. In general, what animal groups would you expect to find in each category? List an apparent drawback to each. (p. 581)

6 Distinguish between maintaining body heat through endothermy and ectothermy. (p. 581)

7 Describe heterothermy in flying insects. (p. 581)

8 Which of the four descriptive terms (homeothermy, poikilothermy, endothermy, ectothermy) is suitable when describing thermoregulation in humans? Support your answer. (p. 581)

9 What structure in humans acts as a central thermostat? What does it measure? (pp. 581–583)

10 List several responses the human body makes to a lower than optimal body temperature. (pp. 583–584)

11 Discuss how the skin provides for heat retention and heat loss. (pp. 583–584)

12 Explain how certain arrangements of arteries and veins result in a countercurrent exchange. How does this affect body temperature? (p. 584)

13 What is osmoregulation and why is it important to the individual? (pp. 584–585)

14 What is the source of nitrogen waste in humans? (p. 584)

15 List the organs of the human excretory system and explain the arrangement of the associated blood vessels. (pp. 585–586)

16 Describe the peculiar shape of the nephrons and their arrangement in the kidney. (p. 586)

17 Prepare a large outline drawing of the nephron, labelling Bowman's capsule, proximal convoluted tubule, loop of Henle, and distal convoluted tubule. Be sure you get the thick and thin parts of the loop right. Finally, add in a collecting duct. (pp. 586–587)

18 Referring to the diagram you just drew, add in the following blood vessels: branch of the renal artery, afferent vessel, glomerulus, efferent vessel, peritubular capillaries. Turning to the tubule, indicate with a "CF," where the crude filtrate is formed, with a "Re," where reabsorption occurs, and with a "TS," where tubular secretion occurs. (pp. 586–588)

19 Make a list of the nephron's parts, and after each, indicate what forces are at work, what substances (if any) move into the nephron and what substances (if any) move out. (pp. 586–588)

20 What is the general purpose of the long hairpin shaped loop of Henle? What familiar mechanism is suggested by the ongoing movement of substances from one part of the loop to the other? (p. 589)

21 What are the substances affected by tubular secretion? Which way do they move? What important aspect of homeostasis does this process serve? (p. 589)

22 Is osmoregulation complete when the urine moves into the collecting duct? Explain. (p. 589)

23 Under what conditions does the hypothalamus cause ADH to be secreted? Where are its target cells? What is their response to ADH? (pp. 589–590)

24 Describe the negative feedback aspect of ADH secretion. (pp. 589–590)

25 Describe the events leading up to aldosterone secretion. What does the juxtaglomerular complex actually measure? (p. 590)

26 If aldosterone causes salt retention to increase, how might this bring the blood pressure up to the optimum? What effect does this have on aldosterone secretion? (p. 590)

VI

ANIMAL MAINTENANCE AND REPRODUCTION

37

DIGESTION AND NUTRITION

Within the thin veil of precious gases and water in which life exists on this planet, a constant and often deadly pageant unfolds as a means of rearranging energy to permit that life. Wherever life exists, there is a relentless search for food and the energy it contains. Some species make their food; others prowl in search of living things whose bodies hold nutrients. We humans are not exempt from the search, although we often distance ourselves from the death and carnage as much as is seemly. We may sell real estate and shop for our veal and the makings for the salad that goes with it. And in so doing we deliberately distance ourselves from recognizing that we, as our forebears before us, must respond to the call of our heterotrophy. Nevertheless we can only continue with the strength we glean from other living things. When the calf and the lettuce lived, they too needed energy-laden molecules to be able to continue their existence. The calf and lettuce are now gone, and our time will come, but life goes on. As part of the living world we share a common heritage and common problems. We not only must acquire food but also must have the means to handle its energy. The problem for animals is twofold: first, they must find the proper kind of food. This addresses the problem of nutrition. Then they must break it down efficiently so its components can be used by their bodies. Essentially, this is what digestion is all about.

DIGESTION IN INVERTEBRATES

Few foods can be absorbed and used in the form in which they are acquired. They must first be broken down into their chemical components, taken into the animal's cells, and used according to that animal's requirements. In all cases the chemical breakdown of bulk foods during digestion requires specific hydrolytic digestive enzymes. As we have seen, such enzymes use water in breaking the chemical bonds linking the molecular building blocks of carbohydrates, fats, and proteins. There are many ways in which this happens in animals, but there are several basic digestive plans (Figure 37.1).

When the sponge, a simple filter feeder, captures a morsel of food, the food is phagocytized, entering the cell cytoplasm in a food vacuole. There it is joined by powerful digestive enzymes, and the food is broken down into simpler molecules that can be used by the cells. Wandering ameboid cells then distribute the digested food to other cells throughout the sponge's simple body. The digestion within food vacuoles, a primitive process generally associated

FIGURE 37.1 Invertebrates reveal several kinds of digestive arrangements.

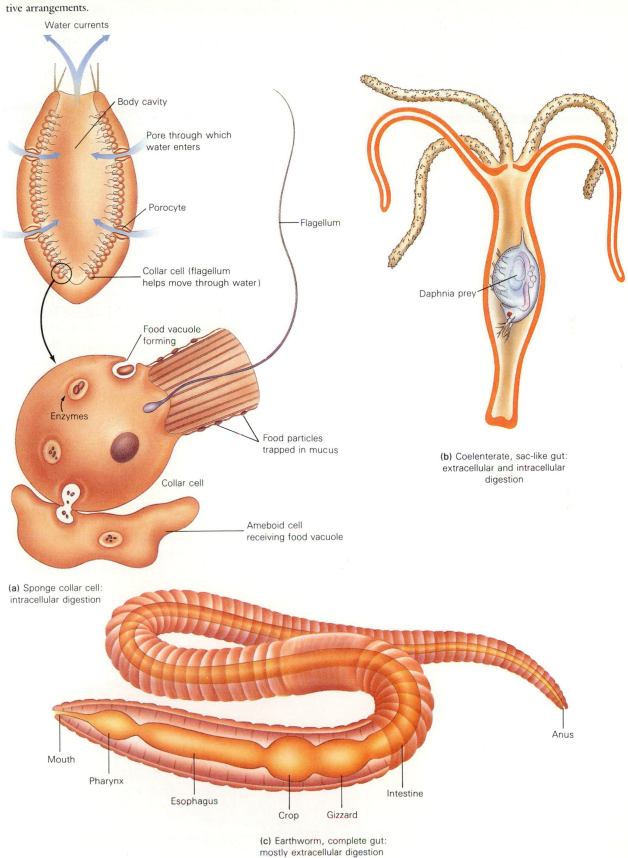

Water currents

Body cavity

Pore through which water enters

Porocyte

Flagellum

Collar cell (flagellum helps move through water)

Food vacuole forming

Enzymes

Food particles trapped in mucus

Collar cell

Ameboid cell receiving food vacuole

(a) Sponge collar cell: intracellular digestion

Daphnia prey

(b) Coelenterate, sac-like gut: extracellular and intracellular digestion

Mouth

Pharynx

Esophagus

Crop

Gizzard

Intestine

Anus

(c) Earthworm, complete gut: mostly extracellular digestion

with protists, is called **intracellular digestion** ("inside cells").

More advanced animals evolved a primitive digestive surface, as we see in today's coelenterates and flatworms. Here food is taken into a saclike gastrovascular cavity (which is highly branched in the flatworm). While some food is captured by phagocytic cells and digested intracellularly, the rest is digested through **extracellular digestion** ("outside cells") by enzymes released into the digestive cavity. We should add that there is a certain inefficiency in the saclike digestive cavity. Ingested food must be digested and the residue expelled before more food can be taken in. Further, there is little specialization within the sac.

In **intracellular digestion** undigested food is taken into the cell by phagocytosis, and enzymes carry out digestion in food vacuoles. In **extracellular digestion** enzymes carry out digestion in digestive cavities before the food enters the cell.

The development of the longitudinal body plan made a tubular gut possible. With an entrance (mouth) at one end and an exit (anus) at the other, digestion becomes not only more civilized but more efficient. Food can be handled serially. While some food is being digested, other food can enter the process and begin its sequence. Enzymes are secreted into the digestive tract, and the food is broken down through extracellular digestion.

We find a highly specialized tubelike gut in many invertebrates, including the nematodes, mollusks, annelids, and arthropods. In earthworms, for example, various regions of the gut have different roles: food enters through the mouth, passes through the esophagus, is stored in the crop, and ground in the gizzard before most digestion begins. The grinding is an important advancement since food is mechanically broken down thereby increasing the surface area available to digestive enzymes.

In most invertebrates, digestion is extracellular, with ingested food exposed to a gut surface that secretes powerful and specific enzymes. Things are more or less the same in vertebrates, as we will see.

Invertebrate digestive arrangements include primitive saclike cavities, simple tubular tracts, and more specialized tubular tracts.

VERTEBRATE SPECIALIZATIONS

The vertebrate digestive system follows the usual metazoan tube-within-a-tube plan. It begins at the mouth cavity, in which teeth may be present to tear or grind food as it is manipulated by the tongue. The chewed or "gulped" food passes into a pharynx at the rear of the mouth and then through a muscular esophagus that squeezes it into a temporary storage and digestive organ—the stomach. The stomach empties into the small intestine, which is the major organ of digestion. Here, products of digestion pass through the gut and into the bloodstream. Next, in the large intestine, excess water is absorbed into the blood. The residue of waste is stored in the rectum until it is emptied through the anus.

Any variation from the usual vertebrate gut (see

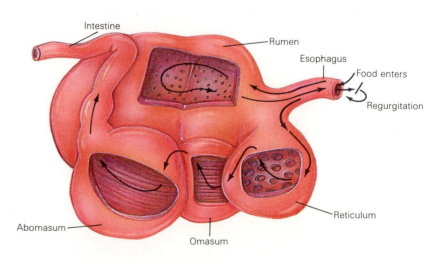

FIGURE 37.2 The four-part stomach of ruminants is specialized for the digestion of cellulose, a mainstay of the animals' diets. Food first enters the *rumen*, where microorganisms digest the cellulose. The food is regurgitated, thoroughly chewed (as a "cud"), and then reswallowed, this time passing into the *reticulum*, then the *omasum*, and finally the *abomasum* (true stomach). During its second transit, the food and microorganisms are digested through chemical processes similar to those of other mammals.

Chapter 29), as you might expect, would be an evolutionary specialization for some particular diet. In no other group has the stomach become so extensive and specialized as in the **ruminants,** such as cattle, deer, giraffes, antelope, and buffalo. They eat cellulose-containing plants, but they cannot digest cellulose. In fact, few animals have this capability (the linkages of the beta glucose found in cellulose, you recall, are difficult to break enzymatically). These animals solve the problem by harboring in the gut immense numbers of protozoa and bacteria that *can* digest cellulose and, when they die, are themselves quite nutritious to the host (Figure 37.2).

Many vertebrate guts have a blind sac where the small intestine joins the large intestine. This is the **cecum,** a pouch that serves as a food-storage organ and as a fermenting vat in a diverse group of mammals, including primates, horses, rabbits, ground squirrels, elephants, coneys, and marsupials. The cecum allows nonruminants to digest plant materials by retaining them in the bacteria-ridden sac. The human gut has a rather small cecum, from which extends a small, fingerlike pouch, the **vermiform appendix,** which is extremely prone to infection (see Figure 37.3).

Vertebrate specializations for cellulose digestion include a long intestine, a four-part ruminant stomach and a pouchlike cecum.

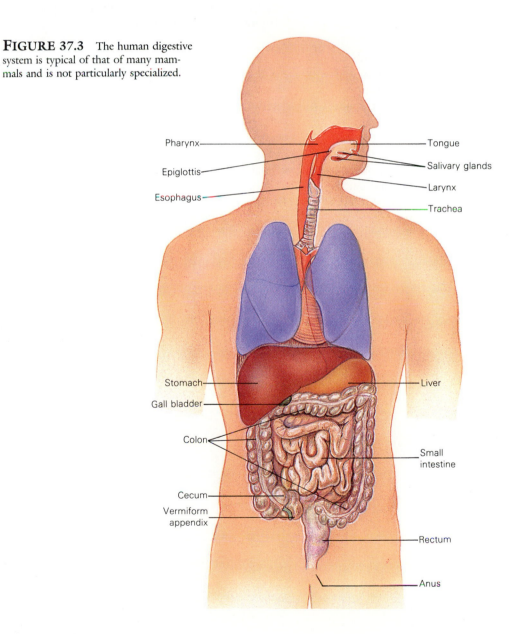

FIGURE 37.3 The human digestive system is typical of that of many mammals and is not particularly specialized.

Pharynx

Epiglottis

Esophagus

Tongue

Salivary glands

Larynx

Trachea

Stomach

Gall bladder

Colon

Cecum

Vermiform appendix

Liver

Small intestine

Rectum

Anus

THE HUMAN DIGESTIVE SYSTEM

As mammalian digestive systems go, ours is rather ordinary and generalized. But this allows us to serve as a good representative of our class. As shown in Figure 37.3, the human digestive system includes the mouth, esophagus, stomach, small intestine, and large intestine. The organs are held loosely in place by folds of the **peritoneum,** called **mesenteries.** The peritoneum is an extensive connective tissue that also lines the inner wall of the abdominal cavity. The folds carry blood vessels, nerves, and lymphatic vessels—all important to digestion.

The Mouth and Esophagus

The digestive structures of the mouth include the lips, teeth, tongue, pharynx, and salivary glands. In case you're wondering what the lips have to do with eating, they help seal the mouth. (Try eating and swallowing with your lips open—but do it somewhere else.)

The tongue is also surprisingly important in eating. In addition to its role in moving food into position for chewing, swallowing, and sorting out fish bones, it constantly monitors the texture and chemistry of foods. This is a valuable chore, since it tells us about food in time to prevent us from swallowing something we shouldn't. In addition, the tongue can distinguish certain chemicals by specialized chemoreceptors called taste buds. These receptors can distin-

guish four basic tastes: salty, sour, sweet, and bitter (see Chapter 34).

Saliva is produced by three pairs of **salivary glands:** the **parotid, sublingual,** and **submandibular glands** (Figure 37.4). These glands secrete saliva through ducts that empty into the mouth. Saliva is about 95% water; the remaining 5% includes various ions, an enzyme (**salivary amylase)** that begins starch digestion, and a slippery substance called **mucin,** which is a lubricating glycoprotein. Salivary amylase is probably less important in digestion than in oral hygiene, since it helps break down starchy food particles remaining in the mouth.

> **S**aliva is important in moistening and lubricating food; its enzyme **salivary amylase** begins the digestion of starch.

The **pharynx,** located in the rear of the oral cavity, joins with the nasal cavity to form a common passageway. The pressure-equalizing **eustachian tubes** of the middle ear, an otherwise sealed chamber, also open into the pharynx. Just below the root of the tongue the pharynx divides, forming the **larynx** and esophagus. The larynx is a complex, muscular structure containing the **voice box** and several ringlike cartilages along with the flaplike **epiglottis.** During swallowing the larynx rises and the epiglottis presses against it, directing food into the esophagus (Figure 37.5). If this fails, food will enter the larynx, producing violent choking or coughing spasms.

FIGURE 37.4 Three pairs of salivary glands—the parotids, sublinguals, and submandibulars—secrete mucus and salivary amylase.

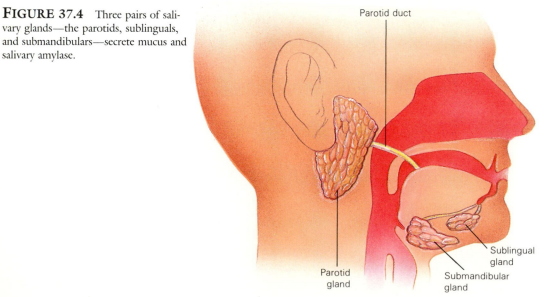

Parotid duct

Parotid gland

Sublingual gland

Submandibular gland

FIGURE 37.5 The important structures of swallowing are the tongue, pharynx, soft palate, epiglottis, larynx, and laryngopharynx. The act is initially voluntary and then becomes involuntary or reflexive.

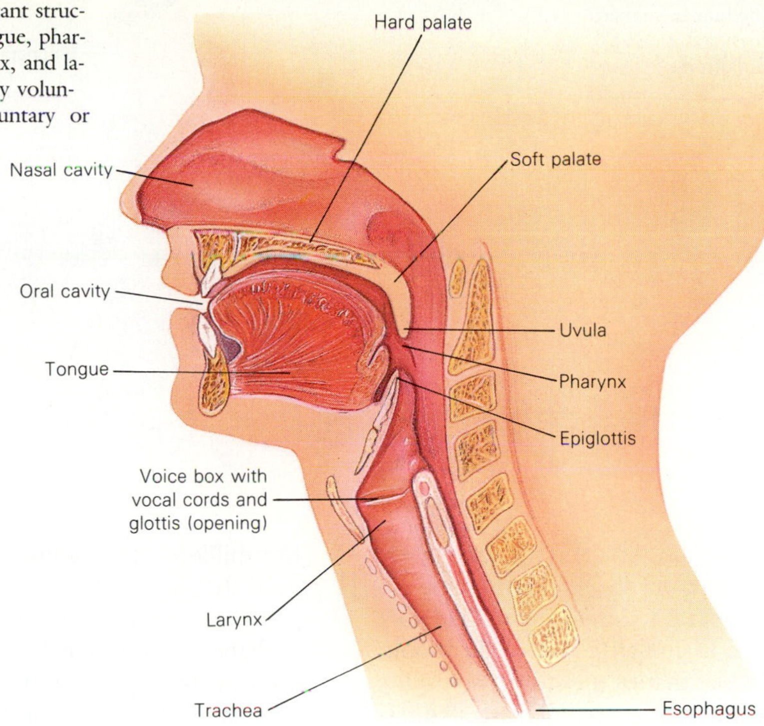

The **esophagus** lubricates food and directs it to the stomach. Its upper region contains skeletal (voluntary) muscle; the rest is involuntary, containing circular and longitudinal layers of muscle. Swallowing begins as a voluntary act but continues as an involuntary one. Food is moved through the esophagus and the remainder of the digestive tract by **peristalsis**—coordinated contractions of smooth muscle.

> Swallowing involves the pharynx and larynx and is a voluntary act: **peristalsis,** the movement of food through the esophagus, is involuntary.

The Stomach

The human **stomach,** a muscular, J-shaped sac, has a complex glandular inner lining and is surrounded by three criss-crossed layers of smooth muscle (Figure 37.6). Its functions include temporarily storing ingested food, intensive churning and mixing with **gastric juices,** the initial digestion of some foods, and (not insignificantly) making use of its acidic environment (pH 1.6 to 2.4) to destroy ingested bacteria and other potential parasites.

Churning and mixing of food occur in the stomach through a wringing, squeezing action made pos-

sible by the arrangement of its smooth muscle layers in three directions. Ringlike **cardiac** and **pyloric sphincters** seal the stomach during churning, preventing the escape of food until it is ready to be released into the small intestine. (Failure of the cardiac sphincter to completely close the esophagus can produce the familiar condition called "heartburn.")

Gastric juices are secreted by specialized glands and cells of the stomach lining. **Chief cells** secrete the protein **pepsinogen,** and **parietal cells** secrete **hydrochloric acid** (HCl). The acid is required to activate the pepsinogen, which then forms the digestive enzyme **pepsin.** Other glands secrete **rennin,** an enzyme that helps young mammals to digest milk, and **gastric lipase,** a fat-splitting enzyme.

The acid is strong enough to threaten the stomach lining. We usually don't digest our stomachs because a layer of insoluble mucin, also found in saliva, coats the stomach lining.

> The principal functions of the stomach are food storage, churning, and protein digestion. Its acidic fluids control bacterial growth.

The Small Intestine

Food, well churned and liquefied by stomach action, is then squirted into the upper part of the small intes-

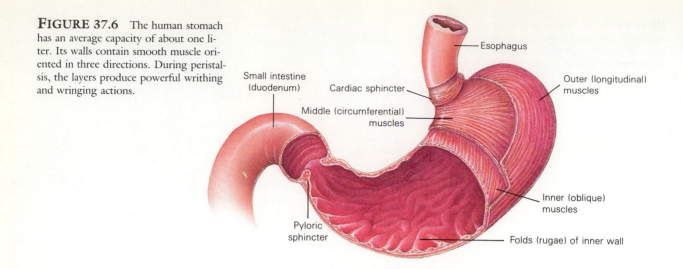

FIGURE 37.6 The human stomach has an average capacity of about one liter. Its walls contain smooth muscle oriented in three directions. During peristalsis, the layers produce powerful writhing and wringing actions.

Esophagus

Small intestine (duodenum)

Cardiac sphincter

Middle (circumferential) muscles

Outer (longitudinal) muscles

Inner (oblique) muscles

Pyloric sphincter

Folds (rugae) of inner wall

tine, the **duodenum.** The duodenum itself is only about 25 to 30 cm long, but the **small intestine** is a highly coiled tube about 6 m long. The musculature of the small intestine is similar to that of the esophagus, but its lining, like that of the stomach, is quite intricate and well suited for its tasks. The small intestine completes the process of digestion and absorbs nutrients before it passes the undigested residue to the large intestine.

The lining of the small intestine (Figure 37.7) has an enormous surface area—estimated at 700 m² (about the floor area of four or five three-bedroom houses). The great surface area is produced by four specializations. First, *coiling* makes great length possible. Second, within the tube's lining are numerous folds, or **rugae.** Third, the surface of the folds contains tiny fingerlike projections called **villi** (singular, **villus**), giving a velvety appearance to the gut lining. Finally, villi themselves are bristling with **microvilli,** fine foldings in the cell membranes that form what is called a **brush border** (Figure 37.8).

The absorbing surface of the small intestine is enhanced by its overall length, made possible by coiling, a highly folded inner surface, and numerous villi and microvilli.

Villi specialize in food absorption and contain dense capillary beds and saclike vessels called **lacteals.** While most digested foods enter capillaries, digested fats enter lacteals, extensions of the **lymphatic system.** This system has several functions. One is to drain digested fats away from the intestine, as we will discuss later (see Figure 37.8). Villi contain smooth muscle fibers that enable them to move vigorously,

like millions of wiggling fingers, further mixing the food that passes through the small intestine.

It has only been recently discovered that most—perhaps all—nutrients enter the lining of the small intestine through active transport processes; further, each kind of nutrient probably has its own specific ATP-powered transport mechanism. Recent studies also reveal that many small intestinal enzymes are actually bound to the lining cells and are not free, as was once believed.

Absorption by intestinal villi occurs along its elaborate **brush border.** While certain fats enter the **lacteals,** other foods enter capillaries.

The Liver

The upper region of the small intestine, the duodenum, receives secretions from two organs: the liver and the pancreas (Figure 37.9). The **liver** secretes **bile,** which helps break down fats.

The bile is stored in the **gall bladder** and is released by rather weak muscular contractions brought about by hormones whose release is triggered by fats in the small intestine. Bile reaches the duodenum through the **common bile duct,** which is joined by the **pancreatic duct** just before it reaches the intestine (see Figure 37.9). The bile carries off metabolic wastes and breaks down fats into tiny droplets. The smaller the droplets, the relatively greater the surface area on which enzymes can act. An obstructed bile duct results in an inability to properly digest fats. Surgeons sometimes move the bile duct of a dangerously obese patient to the lower end of the

FIGURE 37.7 The surface area of the small intestine is accounted for by coiling **(a)**, folding of the lining **(b)**, the presence of numerous villi **(c)**, and microvilli (not shown).

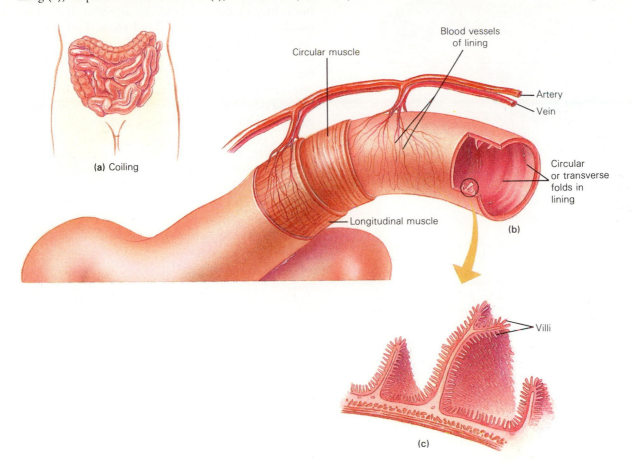

(a) Coiling

Circular muscle

Blood vessels of lining

Artery

Vein

Circular or transverse folds in lining

Longitudinal muscle

(b)

Villi

(c)

FIGURE 37.8 Villi *(left)* may be from 0.05 to 1.5 mm long and are densely packed over the intestinal surface, with 100 to 400 per cm³. The microvilli *(right)*, as seen in the scanning electron micrograph. These form a brush border that greatly increases the surface area of the small intestine. (Photo from *Tissues and organs: a text-atlas of scanning electron microscopy*, by Richard G. Kessel and Randy N. Kardon. W. H. Freeman and Company, copyright © 1979.)

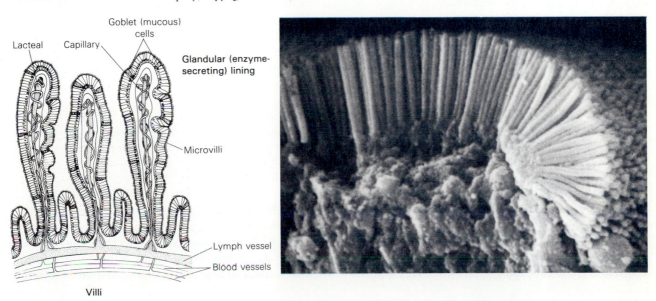

Lacteal

Capillary

Goblet (mucous) cells

Glandular (enzyme-secreting) lining

Microvilli

Lymph vessel

Blood vessels

Villi

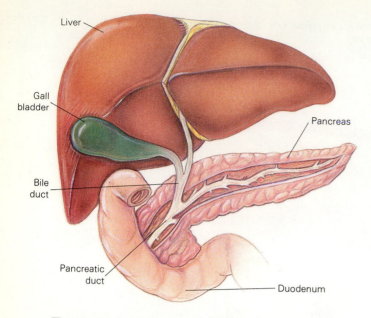

Liver

Gall
bladder

Bile
duct

Pancreatic
duct

Pancreas

Duodenum

FIGURE 37.9   The liver and pancreas are accessory digestive organs. The ducts from both the gall bladder and the pancreas meet to form a common duct that empties into the duodenum of the small intestine.

small intestine. The patient, unable to absorb dietary fat, loses weight dramatically.

The Pancreas

The human **pancreas** is a long, glandular organ nestled between the stomach and the duodenum (see Figure 37.9). It secretes sodium bicarbonate, which neutralizes the acid that enters from the stomach. In addition, the pancreas secretes a battery of digestive enzymes that act in the digestion and metabolism of fats, carbohydrates, proteins, and, incidentally, nucleic acids, which are also digested.

The liver secretes bile, a fat emulsifier; the pancreas secretes several important digestive enzymes and sodium bicarbonate, a stomach acid neutralizer.

The Colon

The **colon** consists of the large intestine and rectum. The large intestine absorbs water and minerals, transferring them to the blood, and forms and stores feces before they leave the digestive tract. Nutritionists argue over the role of the large intestine in digestion. The lining of the colon is glandular, but it secretes only mucus—no enzymes. The mucus protects the colon lining and lubricates it for the passage of feces.

Recent evidence indicates that some digestion and absorption of food does occur in the large intestine, but it may be due solely to the activities of the vast numbers of bacteria that dwell there. You may be surprised to learn that virtually all the material entering the gut is used by these numerous and varied bacteria in the large intestine. The result is that about one third of the fecal material actually consists of living and dead bacteria. The remainder includes undigested residues, some nutrients, and inorganic material.

Actually, intestinal bacteria are quite useful. In fact, an overdose of antibiotics can kill the bacteria, which often results in diarrhea. More importantly, the bacteria provide humans with certain essential vitamins, including vitamin K, biotin, and folic acid. Our relationship with our fecal bacteria is clearly mutualistic.

The **colon** absorbs water and houses vast bacterial populations that break down digestive residues and provide certain essential vitamins.

Chemical Digestion and Absorption

We considered the molecular structure of proteins, fats, and carbohydrates in Chapter 3. Digestion can be viewed as the process of breaking these molecules down into smaller particles that can cross membranes and move into the bloodstream.

The bonds of the large molecules are broken through a process called **hydrolytic cleavage,** or **hydrolysis** (see Figure 6.7). Essentially, this means that enzymes add water to the linkages, disrupting them and yielding molecular subunits. Thus, in digestion, carbohydrates are dismantled into simple sugars; fats, into fatty acids and glycerol; proteins, into their various amino acids; and nucleic acids, into nucleotides.

All digestion occurs through **hydrolytic cleavage,** a process in which enzymes make use of water in breaking foods down into their molecular subunits.

Carbohydrate digestion.   Simple sugars, such as glucose, can be absorbed "as is" by the intestinal lining. But more complex carbohydrates must first be broken down into simple sugars. Even disaccharides, such as sucrose and lactose, must first be enzymati-

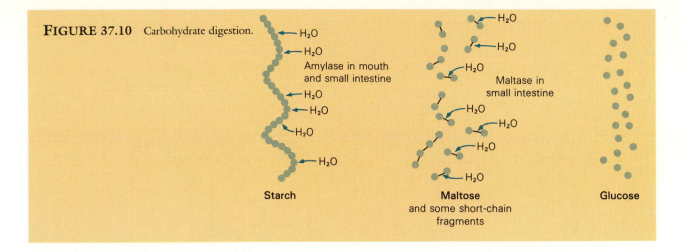

FIGURE 37.10   Carbohydrate digestion.

Starch
Amylase in mouth and small intestine
H₂O
H₂O
H₂O
H₂O
H₂O
H₂O

Maltose and some short-chain fragments
Maltase in small intestine
H₂O
H₂O
H₂O
H₂O
H₂O
H₂O
H₂O

Glucose

cally split into their component parts. In fact, if sucrose is injected into the blood it will be secreted by the kidneys unchanged, because **sucrase** exists only as a membrane-bound enzyme of the gut epithelium.

Starch digestion begins in the mouth, where salivary amylase breaks some linkages, producing maltose and some larger fragments (Figure 37.10). In the small intestine, pancreatic amylase converts all starch into maltose, which is finally cleaved into two molecules of glucose by the enzyme **maltase.**

Fat digestion.   Fats are first dispersed into tiny droplets by bile salts, and most are then hydrolyzed into fatty acids and glycerol by pancreatic lipase (Figure 37.11). The products along with cholesterol, another lipid, then enter cells lining the villi. Once inside, triglycerides are reformed and, along with cholesterol, are gathered into minute protein-surrounded bodies called **chylomicrons.** Then through pinocytosis the chylomicrons pass into a nearby lacteal. The lacteals from each villus empty into lymph vessels that carry the lipids directly into the circulatory system for distribution throughout the body.

Protein digestion.   Proteins are the largest and most complex of the food molecules, so it is not surprising that their digestion also is complex. Essentially, protein digestion occurs in three steps, beginning in the stomach. Here, pepsin attacks the molecule, splitting it more or less randomly into peptide fragments of various lengths. The fragments are then subjected to a more specific disruption in the small intestine, where the pancreatic enzymes **trypsin** and **chymotrypsin** break only specific amino acid linkages. This leaves the protein in the form of peptide fragments only two to ten amino acids long. These

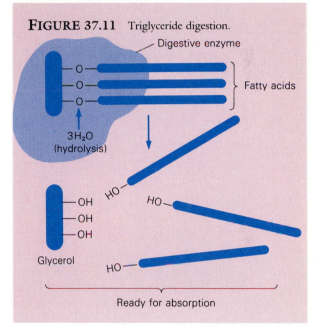

FIGURE 37.11   Triglyceride digestion.

Digestive enzyme
O
O
O
Fatty acids
3H₂O (hydrolysis)
Glycerol
OH
OH
OH
HO
HO
HO
Ready for absorption

are finally cleaved by enzymes of the small intestine into single amino acids. Following protein digestion, the amino acids enter capillaries in the villi and are carried directly to the liver, where they are used according to the body's metabolic needs. Figure 37.12 reviews protein digestion in greater detail.

Because of the number of different amino acids, protein digestion involves several classes of enzymes and proceeds in several stages: protein to polypeptide; polypeptide to dipeptide; and dipeptide to amino acid.

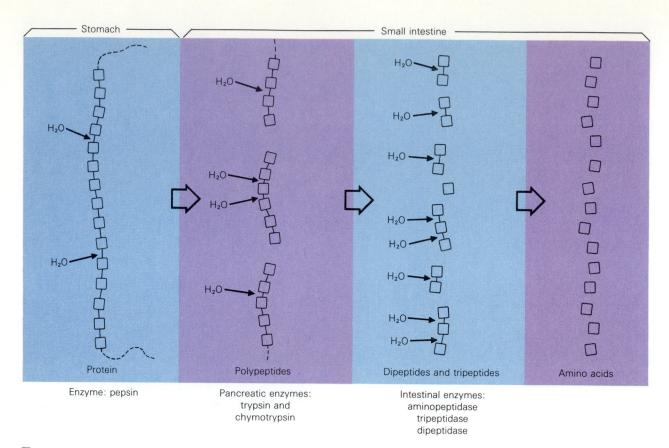

Stomach — Small intestine

| Protein | Polypeptides | Dipeptides and tripeptides | Amino acids |

Enzyme: pepsin

Pancreatic enzymes:
trypsin and
chymotrypsin

Intestinal enzymes:
aminopeptidase
tripeptidase
dipeptidase

FIGURE 37.12   Proteins contain hundreds—often thousands—of amino acids. The complete digestion of protein to free amino acids requires at least three chemical steps.

Integration and Control of the Digestive Process

The timing of the release of digestive juices is under at least three types of control: mechanical, neural, and hormonal. For instance, just thinking about something good to eat or smelling food cooking can trigger the secretion of saliva and start the gastric juices flowing. Enzyme release can also occur through more subtle means. Cells lining the stomach and small intestine apparently detect the presence of specific foods and trigger the release of digestive hormones. One of these, **gastrin,** is released when protein enters the stomach. Its targets are other stomach lining cells, which respond by secreting the gastric juices.

SOME ESSENTIALS OF NUTRITION

Nutrition has become not only an interesting and trendy topic, but a critical one as well, as we are made aware of increasing numbers of contradictory options. Unfortunately, interest in food doesn't necessarily equal knowledge of nutrition. Many food faddists are virtually ignorant of the *science* of nutrition. Some food "experts" do not understand that organically grown food is no better for you than that grown with chemical fertilizers; that rose hip vitamin C is no different from synthetic vitamin C produced by bacteria; that large doses of vitamins may be harmful; that dietary protein that exceeds body needs is simply stored as glucose in the liver or is converted to fat on the hips; or that high-protein diets have not been shown to be beneficial, and, in fact, can be both fattening and harmful. We can best make sense of such findings by reviewing certain large molecules in the context of their roles as food.

Carbohydrates

Carbohydrates are common sources of energy, as we saw in our discussion of their use in cell respiration (see Chapter 8). Their usefulness, however, is quite varied and complex.

Once glucose makes its way from the gut into the circulatory system, it is immediately removed and stored as glycogen, primarily in the liver. From there it is meted out as glucose according to the body's needs. This keeps the blood glucose level rather constant, with a temporary 10% to 20% increase immediately after a high-carbohydrate meal.

The skeletal muscles store a considerable amount of glucose as glycogen. During anaerobic activity, glycogen is again broken down into glucose, which is then used as an energy source. Long-distance runners build up muscle glycogen by continually depleting those reserves in long training runs and then building them back to even higher levels. Excess glucose is simply converted into body fat.

> Carbohydrates are stored as glycogen, oxidized for energy, and, when present in excess, converted to fats.

Fats

People generally assume that it is good to avoid fats in the diet. But fats are not all bad. In fact, some amount of polyunsaturated fat is essential in the diets of many animals, including humans. Fats have a number of uses. They have twice the energy value of carbohydrates. In addition, they contain the essential fat-soluble vitamins A, D, E, and K. Unsaturated fats are also part of all cell membranes. Some fats can be synthesized in the body; others must be provided in the diet. These are known as **essential fatty acids.**

You are probably aware of the persistent controversy over the connection between saturated fats and cholesterol. You may have even switched to foods with high levels of unsaturated fats—the ones so heavily touted in advertisements for margarine and cooking oils. Incidentally, if you are trying to cut down on fat intake, keep in mind that some fats can be synthesized not only from excess carbohydrates, but from excess protein as well. For this reason, high-carbohydrate or high-protein diets may defeat their own purpose if intake is not carefully measured.

> Fats are oxidized for energy, incorporated into membranes, and, when present in excess, stored in adipose (fatty) tissue.

Protein

Protein, an essential nutrient, must be constantly present in the diet since we don't store it well. Although some protein is stored in the liver and muscles, there is a steady turnover of *total* body protein,

and we need even more when we are growing. (Low supplies of protein in the first two years of life can produce permanent brain damage.)

When protein is digested, its amino acids are utilized in several ways. For example, they are the building blocks of our own protein; they are used to form nitrogen bases such as those of DNA; they can be oxidized for energy; and they can be stripped of their amino groups and converted to fats and carbohydrates.

Animals generally are able to convert certain amino acids to others. In fact, we can convert 12 of the 20 amino acids we require into others, if necessary. However, the other eight must be supplied in the diet. These are referred to as the **essential amino acids**—a phrase that delights advertising agencies. Actually, all 20 are essential at some level.

The quality of some proteins is lower than that of others, meaning that some kinds are deficient in one or more of the essential amino acids. The synthesis of any protein depends on the presence of all of the required constituent amino acids. This means that the usefulness of any protein in food, for anything other than calories, depends on the relative concentration of its most scarce essential amino acid. In general, animal proteins are of much higher quality than plant proteins.

Vegetarians, therefore, must select their foods with great care. Legumes, including beans, peanuts, and especially soya products, have fairly high-quality protein. But the best rule is to eat combinations of protein-rich vegetable products, and *know your plants*. An intelligently planned vegetarian diet is unquestionably more healthful than the typical American diet, which includes an excess of animal fats. A well-balanced vegetarian diet that is stretched to include fish as an honorary vegetable may lead to healthy old age.

> Amino acids are reassembled into protein for cell structures, enzymes, and other uses. Some are oxidized for energy, and excesses, which cannot be stored, are converted to fat.

Vitamins

Vitamins are essential in the diets of animals. Biochemists have identified most of them, so we know not only their molecular structures but also their precise functions. There are still a few vitamins, however, that are understood to only a limited extent. All we can say about those is that if you don't have them, you will probably develop some unpleasant condition or another.

Most vitamins function as *coenzymes.* For example, respiratory enzymes cannot function without the coenzymes NAD and FAD, which are derived from vitamin B_6 and riboflavin, respectively. Shortages of these vitamins can lead to serious illness. Vitamins C and E have a somewhat more general function: both are *antioxidants,* which means that they remove spontaneously forming free radicals that would otherwise damage our tissues.

Mineral Requirements

Animals also require a number of inorganic ions that are generally referred to as **minerals.** Those required in the largest amounts include calcium (a major constituent of bone and of many cellular processes), magnesium (necessary as a cofactor [see Chapter 6] for many enzymatic activities), and iron (a component of hemoglobin as well as the cytochromes of the electron transport chain). Sodium, potassium, and chloride are also needed in fairly substantial quantities in order to replace daily losses; sodium and potassium are involved in nerve cell conduction and osmotic regulation.

Trace elements.   In addition to the various elements that are necessary in large amounts for life and good health, others are necessary only in very small amounts. Included are iodine (thyroid hormones), copper (hemoglobin formation and enzyme action), fluorine (protection of teeth), zinc (enzyme action and insulin synthesis), selenium and manganese (enzyme action), and cobalt (red blood cell formation). Recently added to the list of trace elements is silicon, a mineral constituent of rock and one of the commonest elements on the earth. But to be useful to the body silicon must be in a soluble form, as it is in plant fibers. So, getting your "roughage" may be important for more than enhancing bowel regularity. Silicon is now believed to be an important constituent in the elastic walls of arteries, and its absence in diets of highly processed foods may be a significant cause of arterial disease—another strong argument for eating fresh fruits and vegetables.

Moderation Is Its Own Reward

We've seen that low- and high-cholesterol diets are both potentially harmful; that the balance between saturated and unsaturated fats mustn't be tipped too far in either direction; and that too much protein is harmful, but too little is worse. Careless vegetarianism can be dangerous, and so can a diet laden with red meat. One can get sick from having too much vitamin A or from not having enough. Most people consume too much sodium, but everyone needs a certain amount. Ocean fish can be extremely good for you, unless it is contaminated with high levels of mercury. How can one make intelligent nutritional decisions in the face of such complex scientific evidence?

There is no simple answer. It is clear that most people in developed nations, whatever their diet, eat too much. We must resort to generalities and cliches, such as "moderation in all things," or "variety is the spice of life," or "no one ever suffered from eating sensible amounts of fresh fruits and vegetables." We might stroke our chins in our wisest fashion and say, "get enough roughage." At any rate, it is probably best to avoid diet fads; and to avoid saturated fats—but not fanatically.

SUMMARY

As heterotrophs, animals have a two-fold problem: obtaining food and assuring that it fulfills their nutritional requirements.

DIGESTION IN INVERTEBRATES

Digestion is the breakdown of foods by hydrolytic enzymes into their molecular components.

Sponges carry on intracellular digestion, taking food in by phagocytosis and breaking it down within food vacuoles. Coelenterates continue the use of some intracellular digestion, but extracellular digestion occurs in the gastrovascular cavity. A complete tubular gut occurs in most invertebrates, with specialized regions processing food in different ways.

VERTEBRATE SPECIALIZATIONS

The tube-within-a-tube system of vertebrates often includes special adaptations. Plant eaters may have an exceptionally long intestine. Ruminants have four-part stomachs housing microorganisms that digest cellulose. Others have a large pouchlike cecum in which microorganisms also breakdown plant material.

THE HUMAN DIGESTIVE SYSTEM

Humans have a generalized digestive system with typical vertebrate digestive organs.

The Mouth and Esophagus

The tongue is important to moving and mixing food, detecting foreign objects, and tasting. The salivary glands secrete saliva which moistens and lubricates food and begins starch digestion.

Swallowing begins with voluntary movement in the pharynx—the larynx elevates, thereby closing off the air passage and helping direct food into the esophagus. Then, peristalsis, an involuntary action, propels food toward the stomach.

The Stomach

The stomach stores and actively churns food and secretes gastric juices. Hydrochloric acid activates pepsinogen, forming pepsin, which begins protein digestion.

The Small Intestine

The small intestine completes digestion of all foods. Its great coiling length, rugae or folds, villi, and microvilli produce a large surface area for absorption. Fingerlike villi contain capillaries and lacteals that receive digested foods carried in by active transport.

The Liver

The liver produces bile, a fat emulsifier, which it stores in the gall bladder. It is released when fats are present. The liver takes in much of the digested food for further processing and storing.

The Pancreas

The pancreas secretes sodium bicarbonate and digestive enzymes into the small intestine.

The Colon

The colon (also large intestine and bowel) absorbs water and minerals and processes digestive wastes. Immense bacterial populations break down digestive residues and make useful vitamins available.

Chemical Digestion and Absorption

All foods are broken down into molecular subunits through hydrolytic cleavage. The products are glucose, fatty acids, glycerol, amino acids, and nucleotides.

Carbohydrate-digesting enzymes include salivary and pancreatic amylase which yield maltose and maltase which yields glucose. Lactase and sucrase break down lactose and sucrose, respectively.

Pancreatic lipase breaks down fats into fatty acids and glycerol. Along with cholesterol, they enter the villus where they are gathered into chylomicrons that are then carried into the lacteal for lymphatic transport.

Protein requires several enzymatic steps, proceeding from proteins to polypeptides, then to peptide fragments and dipeptides, and finally amino acids.

Integration and Control of the Digestive Process

Hormones, whose release is stimulated by the presence of foods, prompt the release of enzymes whose action breaks down the food. The absence of food acts as a negative feedback loop.

SOME ESSENTIALS OF NUTRITION

Care must be taken in accepting nutritional information since much of it is misleading or wrong.

Carbohydrates

Carbohydrates are important as energy sources. Glucose is stored as glycogen and meted out by the liver. Skeletal muscles rely on glycogen, breaking down into glucose for glycolysis. Excesses are stored as fat.

Fats

A certain level of fat intake is essential. Lipids are used for energy, incorporated into structure, converted to glucose, and stored in adipose tissue. A balance of saturated and unsaturated fats seems desirable.

Protein

Protein must be part of the daily diet, it cannot be stored. Amino acids are used for protein and nucleotide synthesis, oxidized for energy, and the excesses converted to fats and carbohydrates. Eight of the twenty (essential amino acids) must be in the diet. They are most readily available from animal protein. Except for certain seed combinations, plant foods are usually deficient in certain amino acids.

Vitamins

Vitamins are generally important as coenzymes and antioxidants.

Mineral Requirements

Many mineral ions are needed as bone elements, enzyme cofactors, for heme groups in hemoglobin and cytochromes, in nerve action, and for osmotic regulation. Trace elements have varied uses. For instance, roughage is important to bowel regularity, and it is now known that the silicon it contains is important to arterial elasticity.

Moderation Is Its Own Reward

The key to proper nutrition appears to be eating a variety of foods, avoiding too much animal fat, and restricting the intake of highly processed foods.

KEY TERMS

intracellular digestion
extracellular digestion
ruminant
cecum
peritoneum
mesenteries
saliva
salivary gland
parotid
sublingual
submandibular
salivary amylase
mucin
pharynx
eustachian tube

larynx
voice box
epiglottis
esophagus
peristalsis
stomach
gastric juice
cardiac sphincter
pyloric sphincter
chief cell
pepsinogen
parietal cell
hydrochloric acid
pepsin
rennin

gastric lipase
duodenum
small intestine
rugae
villus
microvilli
brush border
lacteal
lymphatic system
liver
bile
gall bladder
bile duct
pancreatic duct
pancreas

colon
hydrolytic cleavage
sucrase
maltase
chylomicron
trypsin
chymotrypsin
gastrin
essential fatty acid
essential amino acid
vitamin
mineral

REVIEW QUESTIONS

1 Write an accurate definition of digestion, contrasting it with dehydration linkage (Chapter 3). (p. 594)

2 Using examples, distinguish between intracellular and extracellular digestion. (pp. 594–595)

3 Briefly summarize functioning of the tube-within-a-tube plan. What digestive innovations did it permit? (p. 596)

4 Briefly describe three vertebrate innovations for cellulose digestion. Why is such cellulose digestion a problem to most organisms? (pp. 596–597)

5 What are the digestive functions of the following: salivary glands, tongue, pharynx? (p. 598)

6 Explain the voluntary and involuntary aspects of swallowing. What kind of muscle tissue acts in each? (p. 598)

7 Describe the masculature of the stomach and its specific action. What keeps the contents inside? (p. 599)

8 List the components of gastric juice. What are two ways in which a very low pH is important? (p. 599)

9 What prevents the stomach lining from being eroded by harsh gastric juices? (p. 599)

10 What are the specific functions of the small intestine? (p. 600)

11 List four factors that provide great surface area to the small intestine. Why is a large surface important? (p. 600)

12 Prepare an outline drawing of one villus, labelling the smooth muscle, capillary bed, lacteal, and microvilli. (p. 600)

13 What digestive agent does the liver secrete? Explain how it is released and what it does. (p. 600)

14 How is the pancreas important to digestion? (p. 602)

15 List three important functions of the colon. Why are its bacterial populations classified as mutualistic? (p. 602)

16 Describe the chemical process of hydrolytic cleavage. Is water a reactant or a biproduct? (p. 603)

17 List the four enzymes responsible for carbohydrate digestion and name the substrates and products of each. (p. 603)

18 What are the products of pancreatic lipase? What happens to these products inside the villus? How are digested fats carried out of the villus? (p. 603)

19 List the general events in protein digestion and state where they occur. Why are so many steps needed? (p. 603)

20 Using gastrin as an example, explain how hormones function in digestion. What is the value of such a system? (p. 604)

21 Why is it more urgent than ever that accurate nutritional information be made available? (pp. 604–605)

22 Where is most glycogen stored? To what use is most glycogen put? (p. 605)

23 What happens to excess glucose, fatty acids, and amino acids taken in? Why does a high protein weight-reducing diet defeat its own purpose? (p. 605)

24 To what does the phrase "essential amino acid" refer? What are the best sources of essential amino acids? Why do they have to be taken in each day? (p. 605)

25 List two common uses the body makes of vitamins. (p. 606)

26 List five specific ways the body makes use of minerals. (p. 606)

27 List four or five general rules of eating that might help assure proper nutrition. (p. 606)

The story of how life evolved is largely about the behavior of gases. For example, the masses that coalesced to form the planet and the waters from which life arose were gaseous. Some theorists suggest that, as life continued its struggle to establish itself, it did so in a gaseous sea that was the earth's first atmosphere. That atmosphere was far different from what it is now. To begin with, at first there was little oxygen over the earth's surface. In time, however, oxygen began to accumulate, manufactured by early phototrophs and also as a by-product of molecular interactions in the upper reaches of the atmosphere. As it accumulated, it placed severe demands on the life that it touched. Many life forms fell before this strange, corrosive force. But others found ways to utilize it and, in so doing, to create greater stores of energy than had ever been possible.

Here, then, we will consider just how various forms of life have come to deal with oxygen and how they handle another gas, carbon dioxide (CO_2). We will first consider some general ideas about the exchange of gases in living things and then review exchange mechanisms in various kinds of animals, focusing finally on our own species.

GAS EXCHANGE: AN EVOLUTIONARY PERSPECTIVE

As various forms of life began to find ways to use oxygen, a general problem arose: How does one get oxygen? Further, how does one get rid of carbon dioxide, which, as we know, builds up as a metabolic waste? Simple-bodied, oxygen-using life forms, like their counterparts today, probably relied on simple diffusion alone. Diffusion worked well because in their metabolic activities such organisms would have created the concentration gradients needed to encourage the inward diffusion of oxygen and the outward diffusion of carbon dioxide. As we will see, many simple animals today rely on unassisted diffusion to meet all their respiratory needs. Even simple multicellular forms have no special mechanisms of gas exchange—they rely on direct cell-to-cell diffusion.

Unassisted diffusion was satisfactory for early life because organisms were simple, and favorable diffusion gradients were created naturally through metabolism.

38

GAS EXCHANGE

While the diffusion of oxygen and carbon dioxide is a primary means of gas exchange in all animals today, larger, more complex animals cannot rely on a simple cell-to-cell transfer. Thus, various ways have evolved to more effectively bring these gases to special exchange surfaces, or interfaces, across which oxygen and carbon dioxide may diffuse (Figure 38.1).

We will have a look at some of these interfaces next, but first, since we will be using the term respiration quite often, we should make a distinction: **cell respiration** is the metabolic process by which cells utilize oxygen in obtaining energy from fuels. Here, though, we will consider what is called **organismic respiration**—the physical processes by which oxygen passes into and out of the body.

THE RESPIRATORY INTERFACE

If gas is to move into and out of a body, it must cross some boundary. That boundary can be called the **respiratory interface.** This interface—generally a living membrane—must be thin, moist, and of sufficient area to accommodate the animal's physiological needs. A thin membrane, of course, is easier for gases to cross than a thick one, and moistness is essential because gases normally must be dissolved in liquid in order to cross solid barriers easily.

How do animals meet these requirements? As you might expect, the answer varies for different kinds of animals. But three factors appear to be involved in determining the nature of the organism's interface:

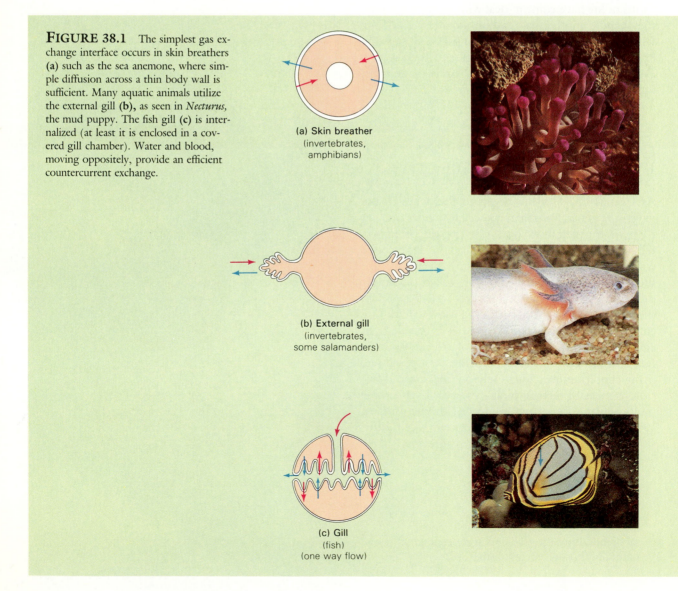

FIGURE 38.1 The simplest gas exchange interface occurs in skin breathers **(a)** such as the sea anemone, where simple diffusion across a thin body wall is sufficient. Many aquatic animals utilize the external gill **(b),** as seen in *Necturus,* the mud puppy. The fish gill **(c)** is internalized (at least it is enclosed in a covered gill chamber). Water and blood, moving oppositely, provide an efficient countercurrent exchange.

(a) Skin breather
(invertebrates, amphibians)

(b) External gill
(invertebrates, some salamanders)

(c) Gill
(fish)
(one way flow)

the size and complexity of the organism, its metabolic needs, and the nature of the surrounding environment. The problem of gas exchange cuts across phylogenetic lines, so we are led to review some points made in Chapters 27 to 29.

A fundamental problem of all life is to provide a suitable **interface**—a thin, moist, membrane—with the environment for an adequate respiratory exchange.

Variations in the Interface

Skin exchange. Skin exchange, or "skin-breathing" as some call it, involves gas exchange across the skin or body surface. Simple, unassisted skin exchange, even in invertebrates, is not very common, being restricted primarily to sponges, coelenterates, and flatworms. More complex invertebrates generally require the aid of a circulatory system or its equivalent to provide adequate gas exchange. With a circulatory system, gases can be brought to the respiratory interface from other parts of the body.

Gill exchangers. Most complex aquatic animals require a greater exchange of gas than can be accommodated by the skin, and so various means of increasing the respiratory interface have evolved. The most common is the **gill.** Gills are feathery, thin-walled extensions of the body wall that are rich in tiny capillaries (thin-walled blood vessels). Since the vessels passing through the gills have walls only one cell

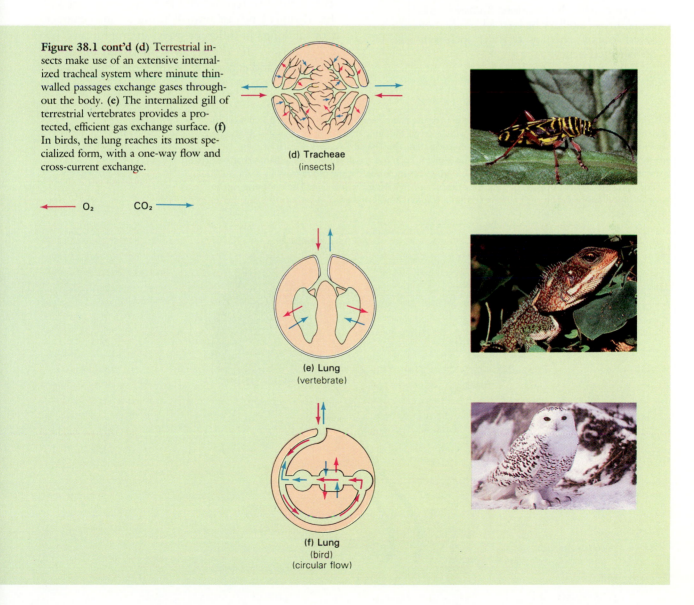

Figure 38.1 cont'd (d) Terrestrial insects make use of an extensive internalized tracheal system where minute thin-walled passages exchange gases throughout the body. **(e)** The internalized gill of terrestrial vertebrates provides a protected, efficient gas exchange surface. **(f)** In birds, the lung reaches its most specialized form, with a one-way flow and cross-current exchange.

O_2 ⟵ CO_2 ⟶

(d) Tracheae
(insects)

(e) Lung
(vertebrate)

(f) Lung
(bird)
(circular flow)

thick, the blood in these areas is very near the surrounding water. Thus gases are easily exchanged. Gills of one kind or another are found in such animals as marine annelids, mollusks, arthropods, nearly all developing amphibians, and, of course, fishes.

Gills reach their greatest complexity in the fishes, where an efficient exchange is provided by a countercurrent flow of water and blood (Figure 38.2; also see Chapter 29). The gills of bony fishes are protected within the gill chambers by a tough flap, the **operculum.** Muscular movement of the gill chamber, together with the action of flaps and valves and the rhythmic opening and closing of the mouth area, ensures a one-way flow of water across the gill surfaces.

> **Gills** are thin walled, feathery, external or internal body-wall extensions. In fishes, gills contain rich capillary beds in which the flow of blood counters the flow of water, increasing gas exchange efficiency.

Lung exchangers. Most terrestrial vertebrates have solved the problem of keeping their respiratory membranes moist by bringing the respiratory interface inside the body, where it is sheltered from the drying air. In terrestrial vertebrates, the **lungs** provide the moist internal interface for the exchange of gases. The lungs of most land vertebrates are paired structures consisting of inflatable, highly vascularized, and somewhat spongy tissue. (In amphibians the lungs are simply hollow sacs.) A vast capillary network spreads throughout the lung tissue, across which the oxygen must pass. The oxygen is transported from the capillaries of the lung throughout the body by joining temporarily with molecules of hemoglobin, which, in all vertebrates, is contained in red blood cells.

Gas enters and exits the lung through a single, ventral, tubelike **trachea** and its branches, the **bronchi.** Various kinds of animals bring air into contact with the lungs in different ways: in amphibians, by movements in the throat; in reptiles and birds, by contraction and expansion of the surrounding body

FIGURE 38.2 (a) The supporting structures of the fish gills are the cartilaginous gill arches. Inside the curve of the arch are the gill rakers, which screen foreign particles out of the gills. At the outer curve, two rows of gill filaments protrude from each arch. (b) The surface area of each filament is greatly increased by the presence of lamellae, as shown. Each has a rich supply of capillaries that branch from afferent vessels, carrying deoxygenated blood. Crossing a lamella, the blood loses its carbon dioxide and picks up oxygen before entering the efferent vessel leaving the filament. The opposing movement of blood and water in each lamella sets up a countercurrent exchange, greatly enhancing the exchange of gases.

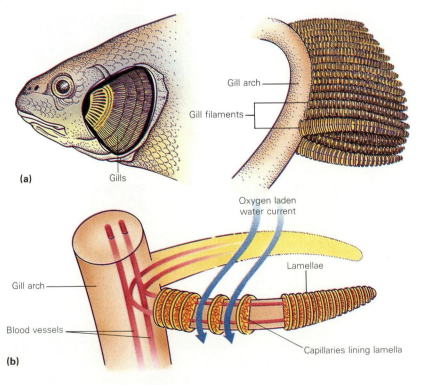

FIGURE 38.3 The human respiratory system is made up of extensive passages forming the bronchial tree and spongy lungs that provide an extensive gas exchange surface. The shelflike, muscular diaphragm is strictly a mammalian characteristic.

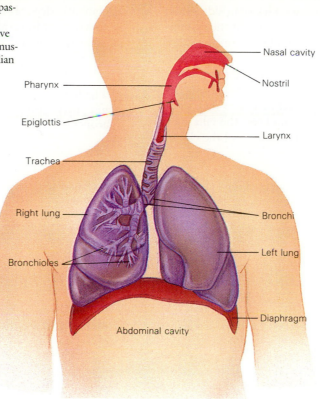

Nasal cavity

Nostril

Pharynx

Epiglottis

Larynx

Trachea

Right lung

Bronchi

Left lung

Bronchioles

Diaphragm

Abdominal cavity

---

wall; and in mammals, by body-wall movement and contractions of a muscular **diaphragm**.

> The vertebrate **lung**, an adaptation to terrestrial life, is a thin-walled, moist, highly vascularized infolding, within which gas exchange is supported by blood with oxygen-carrying hemoglobin.

THE HUMAN RESPIRATORY SYSTEM

The human respiratory system (Figure 38.3) is typical of that of most mammals. Its major parts include the nasal passages, the buccal (mouth) cavity, the larynx, trachea, bronchi, and lungs. Gases are exchanged primarily in the lungs.

Air first enters the system through the nasal passages or the mouth. Within the nasal cavity, it passes over a special nasal epithelium that filters, warms, and moistens it before it enters the lungs. The nasal epithelium has mucus-secreting **goblet cells** scattered among numerous ciliated cells. The mucus traps dust and other fine particles, and the ciliated cells sweep the dust-laden mucus toward the throat, where it is swallowed. Bacteria in this mucus are usually killed by harsh stomach acids.

The Larynx

Inhaled air passes through the nasal passages into the pharynx, and from there through the larynx into the trachea. The **larynx,** or **voice box,** contains the opening of the trachea. The vocal cords are stretched over this opening to form a triangle that narrows to a slit as the cords are tightened (Figure 38.4). During swallowing the larynx is elevated, closing it against the epiglottis. At the same time the vocal cords come together, usually preventing anything from entering the respiratory system below (Figure 38.4b and c).

The Trachea and Bronchial Tree

The **trachea** is essentially a ribbed tube that is reinforced by C-shaped rings of cartilage. At the point where the trachea enters the **thoracic cavity** (chest cavity), it divides into right and left **primary bronchi.** The bronchi enter the lungs, where they branch and rebranch until they form the smallest branches, the **bronchioles.** These make up what is called the **bronchial tree** (because it resembles an upside-down tree). The trachea and larger passages of the respiratory tree are lined with an epithelium similar to that of the nasal passages, complete with mucus-secreting and ciliated cells. The moving cilia sweep the mucous film upward, carrying trapped dust particles or other such substances out of the trachea where they, too, are swallowed. In persistent smokers, the cilia may have become paralyzed by the smoke and the chem-

ical toxins it contains, and the epithelium may have permanently degenerated, leaving the lungs vulnerable to a host of intruders. These intruders, of course, include **carcinogens,** cancer-causing chemicals (Figure 38.5).

> The human respiratory system includes nasal and pharyngeal passages, **larynx, trachea, bronchi, bronchioles,** and **alveoli.**

FIGURE 38.4   A principal function of the larynx is to guard the entrance of the trachea, preventing foods from entering as they are swallowed **(a).** In swallowing, the larynx is elevated (you can check this with your fingers), and the epiglottis is folded over the respiratory openings, directing food into the esophagus **(b).** The larynx consists of cartilage and muscle. Toward the front is a bulging mass of cartilage, the so-called Adam's apple **(c).** In addition, the larynx houses the vocal cords.

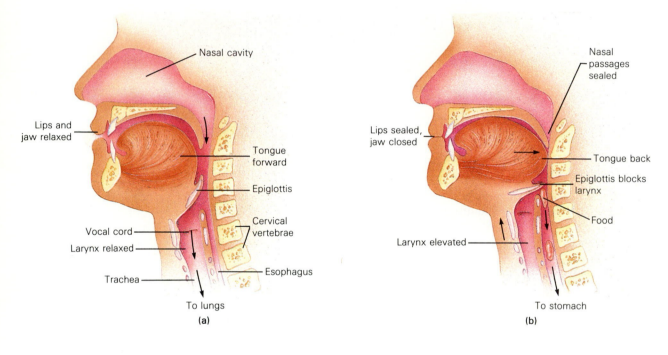

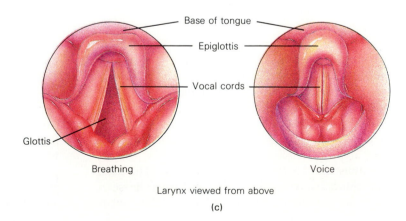

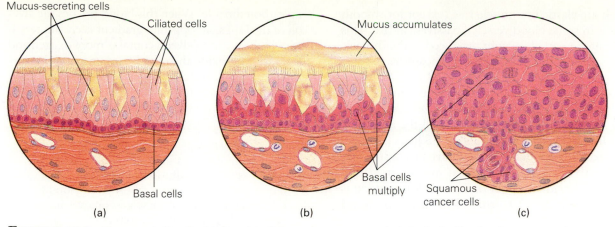

FIGURE 38.5 The normal ciliated epithelium **(a)** of the respiratory passages includes both ciliated and mucus-secreting columnar cells. The cilia sweep the dust-trapping mucus out of the passages and toward the throat. In the smoker's respiratory lining **(b),** the cilia become partially paralyzed, and mucus accumulates on the irritated lining. Where an early cancerous state exists, basal cells divide more rapidly and begin to displace normal columnar cells. As the cancer progresses **(c),** most of the normal columnar cells are replaced by crowded, squamous cancer cells that form a spreading tumor. In advanced cases, clusters of cancer cells may be carried away in the lymphatic system, spreading to other parts of the body.

The Alveolar Interface

The tiniest branches of the respiratory tree end in grapelike clusters of air sacs called **alveoli** (Figure 38.6). Alveoli are extremely thin walled and are surrounded by tiny capillaries; here, the atmospheric air is separated from the bloodstream by exceedingly thin layers of tissue. The numerous alveolar clusters provide an enormous total surface area. In fact, our lungs hold some 300 million alveoli, with a combined surface area of nearly 100 m² (over 1,000 sq ft)—about the area of a tennis court.

The Lungs and Breathing

Human lungs are roughly triangular with a broad base. Each lung is enclosed by two layers of saclike membranes, the **pleurae.** The inner pleura is tightly attached to the spongy lung surface; the outer pleura lines and encloses the thoracic cavity. Inflammation of these membranes produces a condition known as *pleurisy.*

At the base of the lungs is a muscular shelf, the **diaphragm,** which divides the abdominal and thoracic cavities. In its relaxed condition—during expiration—the diaphragm is dome shaped. During inspiration the diaphragm is contracted, resulting in lowering and flattening of its dome shape. In addition, the muscles between the ribs contract, causing the rib cage to rise and enlarge. These changes increase the volume of the thoracic cavity. The lungs,

FIGURE 38.6 The bronchioles terminate in grapelike clusters of alveoli—blind, thin-walled sacs whose surfaces contain extensive capillary beds.

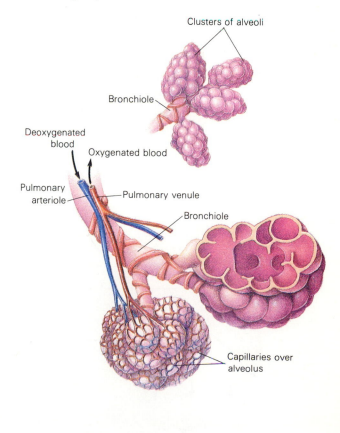

which are elastic but muscle free (except for smooth muscle in some blood vessels), passively inflate. This is because a partial vacuum produced in the thoracic cavity permits the weight of the atmosphere to force air down into the lungs (Figure 38.7). The elastic lungs compress and deflate when the muscles relax and pressures are once again equalized. No matter how hard you try, you can't force all the air out of your lungs. There is always about 1.5 liters left. This is called the **residual volume.** This air ensures that some carbon dioxide is retained in our circulation with each breath, a matter of life and death since it is the presence of CO_2 that stimulates continued breathing.

The Exchange of Gases

As we've seen, the underlying mechanism of gas exchange in the body is diffusion. In diffusion, molecules move from regions of greater concentration to those of lesser concentration. There are two general areas in the body where major gradients of oxygen and carbon dioxide exist. One is in the body's active tissues, where oxygen concentrations are low because it is used in cell respiration, and carbon dioxide concentrations are high because it is produced as a waste product. This activity establishes a gradient between the active tissue and the blood passing through that tissue. Thus the blood readily loses oxygen and picks up carbon dioxide. When this blood reaches the alveoli of the lungs, an opposite gradient is encountered. Air within the lung alveoli contains more oxygen and less carbon dioxide than the blood entering the surrounding capillary beds, so a reverse exchange occurs in the lungs. Carbon dioxide is lost into the lungs as oxygen passes into the bloodstream (Figure 38.8).

Diffusion gradients in metabolically active tissues assure the diffusion of CO_2 from cells to blood and the movement of O_2 from blood to cells. The diffusion of these gases moves in opposite directions in the alveoli.

Hemoglobin and oxygen transport. The key to the efficiency of oxygen transport in vertebrates (and some invertebrates) is a complex protein called **hemoglobin,** which makes up most of the content of red blood cells. The total hemoglobin content is so great that, if it were not compressed in red cells, our blood would be too thick to circulate. Actually, oxygen could be carried in the fluid part of blood plasma without hemoglobin, but the maximum would be only about 0.3 ml of oxygen for each 100 ml of blood. Because of hemoglobin, the blood can carry about 20 ml of oxygen per 100 ml of blood—about 67 times as much!

FIGURE 38.7 At inspiration **(a)** the flattening action of the diaphragm and the rib-elevating action of the rib muscles increase the volume of the thoracic (chest) cavity, and the lungs fill. The opposite movements bring on expiration **(b),** which is generally a passive process in both the muscles and the lungs.

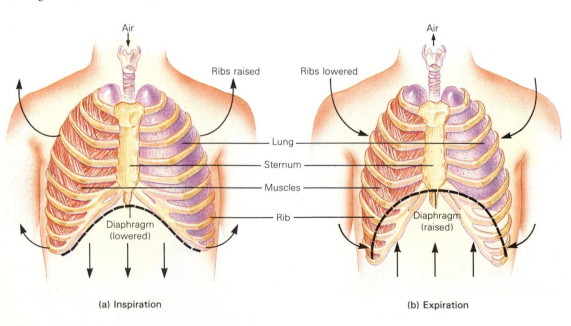

(a) Inspiration

(b) Expiration

FIGURE 38.8 Diffusion gradients for oxygen and carbon dioxide in the alveoli and surrounding capillaries **(a)** permit the required exchanges of gases. In a closer view **(b)**, oxygen enters a capillary to be taken up by hemoglobin-containing red blood cells. The moving stream of red cells ensures the continuous uptake of oxygen until saturation occurs. Carbon dioxide, in solution in the plasma, escapes across the capillary wall into the alveolar space.

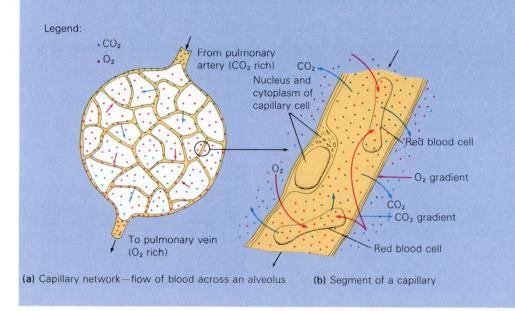

Legend:
• CO_2
• O_2

From pulmonary artery (CO_2 rich)

Nucleus and cytoplasm of capillary cell

CO_2

Red blood cell

O_2

O_2 gradient

CO_2
CO_2 gradient

To pulmonary vein (O_2 rich)

Red blood cell

(a) Capillary network—flow of blood across an alveolus

(b) Segment of a capillary

What precisely is this magical molecule, and how does it work? Hemoglobin is a rather large protein, made of four polypeptide chains and four **heme** groups, each containing an iron atom to which an oxygen molecule can attach (see Figure 3.12d). But the bonds are reversible. The four oxygen molecules are quickly released under the right conditions. The association and dissociation of O_2 and hemoglobin (Hb) can be written:

$$Hb \; + \; 4O_2 \longleftrightarrow Hb \cdot (4O_2)$$

Hemoglobin Oxygen Oxyhemoglobin

This simply means that one hemoglobin molecule plus four oxygen molecules yields one oxyhemoglobin molecule, and the two-headed arrow shows that the association is readily reversible. The hemoglobin molecule is able to pick up an entire load of four oxygen molecules in the lung and to release all four in the tissues, where they are needed, before it returns to the lungs for another load.

Oxygen joins the heme groups of hemoglobin forming oxyhemoglobin in a loose, reversible association.

Carbon dioxide transport. Carbon dioxide transport is quite complex. To begin, carbon dioxide is readily soluble in water—in fact, it is 30 times more soluble than oxygen. Therefore, some of the carbon dioxide picked up by the blood (about 8%) goes into solution in the blood plasma. The rest of the carbon dioxide (92%) enters red blood cells, where it is transported in two ways. Some forms a loose, reversible association with hemoglobin the way oxygen does. However, carbon dioxide does not join the heme groups like oxygen, but reacts with amino acids of the huge protein, forming what is called **carbaminohemoglobin.**

The remaining carbon dioxide entering the red cells reacts with water, forming carbonic acid (H_2CO_3). Carbonic acid, in turn, dissociates into hydrogen ions (H^+) and bicarbonate ions (HCO_3^-). This reaction can occur in plasma, but there it is very slow. Red cells, however, contain the enzyme **carbonic anhydrase,** which not only speeds up the formation of carbonic acid but operates reversibly, and can rapidly convert carbonic acid back into carbon dioxide and water. This is quite important, since carbon dioxide must be reformed quickly if it is to leave the body when the blood reaches the lungs.

When carbonic acid dissociates into hydrogen

ions and bicarbonate ions in the red cells, the hydrogen ions are buffered (resisting pH changes) by the protein hemoglobin itself. The bicarbonate ions diffuse out into the plasma, where they are joined by sodium ions, forming sodium bicarbonate ($NaHCO_3$). In addition to providing a means of transporting carbon dioxide, **sodium bicarbonate** in the blood forms an important part of the body's **acid-base buffering system**—that is, it helps neutralize any acids or bases that might form, keeping the blood pH near neutral. (The sodium bicarbonate of the blood is identical to both commercial baking soda and the main buffering ingredient in many familiar stomach acid neutralizers.) The reactions, so far, are:

1) $CO_2 + Hb \longleftrightarrow$ Carbaminohemoglobin

$$\text{Carbonic} \atop \text{anhydrase}$$

2) $CO_2 + H_2O \longleftrightarrow H_2CO_3 \longleftrightarrow H^+ + HCO_3^-$

3) $Na^+ + HCO_3^- \longleftrightarrow NaHCO_3$

As we have seen, the reactions are all reversible, and in each it is the quantity of carbon dioxide present that dictates the direction. This is typical of the way some enzymes work. So in the active tissues, where carbon dioxide levels are high, the direction of the reactions is toward carbaminohemoglobin and toward the formation of hydrogen and bicarbonate ions and sodium bicarbonate. But in the capillaries of the alveoli, any free carbon dioxide escapes from the blood, so its concentration decreases. Then in a speedy cascade of reversing chemical events: (1) The carbaminohemoglobin releases its carbon dioxide; (2) the bicarbonate of sodium bicarbonate in the plasma reenters the red cells; (3) it joins hydrogen ions to form carbonic acid; and (4) with a boost from carbonic anhydrase it is converted back to carbon dioxide and water.

Some carbon dioxide is carried in solution in plasma, but most is carried in the red cells as **carbaminohemoglobin, carbonic acid** and its ions, and **sodium bicarbonate.** All reactions reverse in the lung.

The Bohr effect. The **Bohr effect** is named for its discoverer, Christian Bohr, who found that the binding of oxygen to hemoglobin is strongly influenced by carbon dioxide levels. When CO_2 levels are high, hemoglobin releases oxygen more readily (Figure 38.9). The release of oxygen from oxyhemoglobin involves more than just diffusion gradients. This is an interesting biochemical adaptation. It means that oxygenated blood passing metabolically *inactive cells* does not tend to give up much oxygen. But in active cells, where CO_2 levels are high, oxygen is more readily released by hemoglobin. This, of course, corresponds to the oxygen demand in such tissues. The Bohr effect, incidentally, may be due more to the increase in acidity that accompanies rising CO_2 levels than to the CO_2 molecule itself.

The more rapid release of oxygen from oxyhemoglobin in the presence of carbon dioxide is called the **Bohr effect.**

Respiratory Control

We can vary the rate and depth of our breathing, but only up to a point. If your little brother holds his breath to get his way, don't worry. He may begin to lose his rosy complexion, but the ruse won't work. No matter how hard he tries, as the CO_2 level in his blood rises, his autonomic nervous system will take over and he will be forced to breathe.

As you see, breathing is under both voluntary and involuntary neural control. In addition, a number of chemical sensors in the body monitor the blood's carbon dioxide and oxygen levels and its hydrogen ion content (pH), sending their information to the brain. Thus respiratory control has a chemical as well as a neural component. Both are only partially understood, but let's look at some of what we know.

Breathing movements are coordinated by voluntary centers in the cortex (those that permit your little brother to make the threats about holding his breath) and by involuntary centers in the pons and medulla (those that defeat his strategy). While the anatomy of the involuntary centers is far from clear, it is apparent that it includes **inspiratory centers** and **expiratory centers.** Activity by the expiratory center, as we'll see, is restricted to periods of strenuous breathing.

During quiet breathing, the inspiratory center is self-excited creating impulses on its own. Its impulses pass through the spinal cord to the diaphragm and rib muscles, which contract and bring on inspiration. After about two seconds of activity, the inspiratory center spontaneously rests for three seconds when expiration (a passive process) occurs.

During periods of more strenuous activity, the breathing rate increases sharply. Whereas the inspiratory center still brings on inspiration, now at a faster rate, other factors come into play. For instance, stretch receptors in the lungs—activated by prolonged inspiration—fire inhibiting signals back to the inspiratory center thus permitting expiration and

FIGURE 38.9 In the Bohr effect, hemoglobin surrenders its oxygen load more readily in the presence of increasing amounts of carbon dioxide. In the organism **(a)**, this chemical behavior means that metabolically inactive cells will receive less oxygen than metabolically active ones, regardless of the oxygen gradient. The Bohr effect is readily revealed when the rate of oxygen dissociation from hemoglobin versus carbon dioxide partial pressure is plotted on a graph **(b)**.

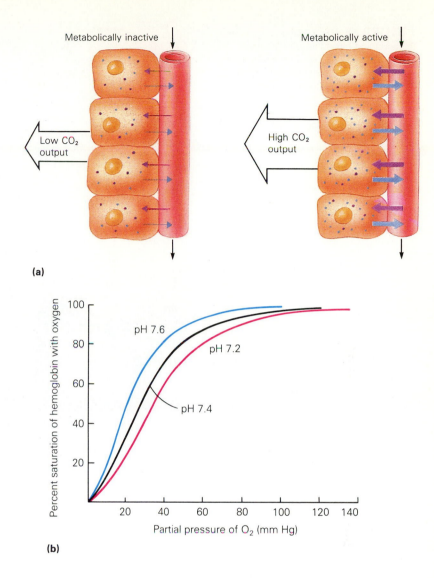

preventing overinflation. In addition, the expiratory center now comes into play. It sends its messages to different muscles, some in the chest and some in the abdomen, whose contraction adds force to passive expiration thus increasing the expulsion of air from the lungs.

> Breathing is initiated and regulated by automated respiratory control centers in the pons and medulla. Lung **stretch receptors** prevent overinflation.

Chemical control is based on input from several chemoreceptors, two in major arteries and one in the brain (Figure 38.10). The arterial **carotid bodies** and **aortic bodies** are aroused when blood CO_2 levels rise and when the hydrogen ion level (acidity)

increases. They also sense decreases in oxygen, but, surprisingly, to a much lesser extent. Chemoreceptors in the fluid-filled spaces of the medulla oblongata in the brain monitor hydrogen ion levels in the cerebrospinal fluids. When neurons in any of these regions become active, their impulses are relayed to the respiratory centers in the pons and medulla, and the rate and depth of breathing increases. Such breathing, of course, decreases the level of CO_2 and hydrogen ions in the blood and increases the level of oxygen. The chemoreceptors, sensing these changes, slow their output of neural impulses (another example of negative feedback at work). Interestingly, during vigorous exercise this straightforward chemical regulatory mechanism is overridden by new input from the cerebrum and input from other kinds of sensors, possibly proprioceptors, located in the joints and muscles.

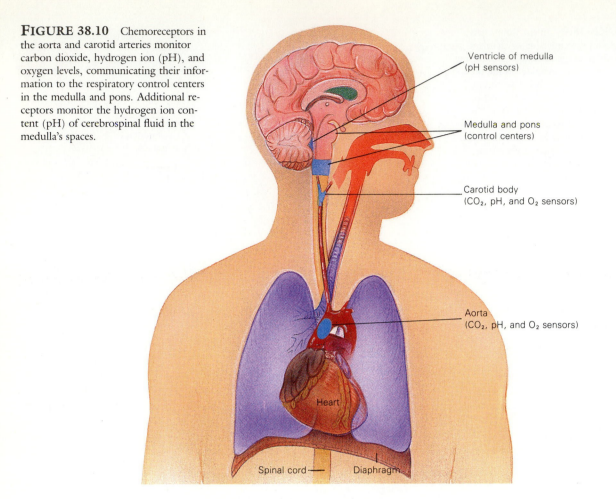

FIGURE 38.10 Chemoreceptors in the aorta and carotid arteries monitor carbon dioxide, hydrogen ion (pH), and oxygen levels, communicating their information to the respiratory control centers in the medulla and pons. Additional receptors monitor the hydrogen ion content (pH) of cerebrospinal fluid in the medulla's spaces.

Ventricle of medulla (pH sensors)

Medulla and pons (control centers)

Carotid body (CO_2, pH, and O_2 sensors)

Aorta (CO_2, pH, and O_2 sensors)

Heart

Spinal cord — Diaphragm

Here we set out to discuss the exchange of certain gases in the body. Few topics relating to life, though, can be discussed singly, apart from the rest. Life's processes are far too coordinated and interactive to focus on any narrowly without losing sight of the overall picture. So we've found ourselves considering anatomy and physiology, gases and liquids, chemistry and neurology. The interplay, though, stands as one more testimony to the wonderous properties and harmonious balance of this thing called life.

SUMMARY

GAS EXCHANGE: AN EVOLUTIONARY PERSPECTIVE

The earliest aerobic life forms, like today's simpler animals, relied on simple cell-to-cell diffusion for exchanging oxygen and carbon dioxide with the environment. Diffusion remains a primary agent of gas exchange, but complex animals have evolved more efficient transport mechanisms and exchange interfaces.

THE RESPIRATORY INTERFACE

The respiratory interface is generally an extensive, thin, moist membrane. Its complexity varies with the animal's size, metabolic activity, and the environment.

Variations in the Interface

Many simpler invertebrates utilize simple, cell-to-cell skin exchange. More complex species receive an assist from circulatory systems.

Most complex aquatic animals have gills, thin-walled, capillary-rich extensions of the body surface. The bony fish gill consists of rows of filaments whose blood flow opposes water flow, thus forming a countercurrent exchange. Water is pumped by the mouth chamber.

Vertebrate lungs are saclike or spongy, internalized structures with vast capillary beds that help form enormous, thin-walled exchange surfaces. Oxygen transport is greatly improved by the presence of hemoglobin. Air is moved in and out by movements of the body wall with the added assistance of the diaphragm in mammals.

THE HUMAN RESPIRATORY SYSTEM

The nasal epithelium includes goblet cells that secrete dust-trapping mucus, and ciliated cells that sweep the mucus toward the pharynx.

The Larynx/Trachea and Bronchial Tree/Alveolar Interface

The respiratory tree begins with the larynx or voice box (vocal cords). Its elevation during swallowing blocks and protects the air passage. The trachea, a reinforced tube, branches into the two bronchi, which rebranch into bronchioles forming the respiratory tree. The epithelial lining includes cleansing goblet and ciliated cells. The lung interface is composed of grapelike clusters of thin-walled alveoli surrounded by capillaries.

The Lungs and Breathing

Pleural membranes line and seal the chest cavity and form the surfaces of the paired lungs. The diaphragm closes the cavity below. At inspiration, the flattening diaphragm and elevating rib cage expands the chest cavity, decreasing its pressure. Air rushes into the bronchial tree, expanding the lungs from inside. Relaxation at expiration produces the opposite effect, forcing air back out. Air that cannot be exhaled, the residual volume, is about 1.5 liters.

The Exchange of Gases

The necessary diffusion gradients for oxygen and carbon dioxide exchange in the active tissues are produced naturally by metabolic activity with oxygen leaving the blood and carbon dioxide entering. The gradient reverses in the alveoli with oxygen entering the blood and carbon dioxide leaving.

Because of hemoglobin the blood can carry 67 times the oxygen otherwise possible. Each hemoglobin molecule carries four oxygen molecules (one per heme) in a reversible association that breaks down in the tissues.

While some carbon dioxide enters solution in the plasma, most enters red blood cells. Some join hemoglobin forming carbaminohemoglobin, and some, with the aid of carbonic anhydrase, enter solution forming carbonic acid. The acid ionizes whereupon the hydrogen ions are buffered by hemoglobin and the carbonate ions join sodium which becomes a pH buffer. The reactions simply reverse in the lungs, reforming water and carbon dioxide. The latter diffuses out.

In the Bohr effect, the rate at which oxygen disassociates from oxyhemoglobin is directly proportional to the amount of carbon dioxide present. This means that metabolically active tissues receive the most oxygen.

Respiratory Control

Breathing involves neural and chemical factors. In quiet breathing the neural inspiratory center in the medulla instigates rhythmic inhaling. Exhaling is passive. With strenuous activity, this action speeds up. Stretch receptors in the lung also act, preventing overinflation by inhibiting the inspiratory center. The neural expiratory center also begins to act, producing more forceful expiration. Breathing rate is influenced chemically by input from several chemical sensors that become active when carbon dioxide levels rise and pH falls (acidity increases).

KEY TERMS

cell respiration	goblet cell	carbaminohemoglobin
organismic respiration	thoracic cavity	carbonic anhydrase
respiratory interface	bronchiole	sodium bicarbonate
skin exchange	bronchial tree	acid-base buffering system
gill	carcinogen	Bohr effect
operculum	alveoli	inspiratory center
lung	pleurae	expiratory center
trachea	residual volume	carotid bodies
bronchi	hemoglobin	aortic bodies
diaphragm	heme	

REVIEW QUESTIONS

1 Describe the manner in which gas exchange occurs in the simplest animals. How are favorable diffusion gradients produced? (p. 609)

2 Summarize the basic gas exchange problem faced by animals as their complexity increased. (p. 610)

3 List three characteristics of an efficient gas exchange interface. (p. 610)

4 List three groups of multicellular animals that rely on simple cell-to-cell diffusion for gas exchange. (p. 611)

5 Mention three or four vertebrates that make significant use of the skin for gas exchange. (p. 610)

6 What structural features do most gills have in common? (pp. 611–612)

7 Describe the structure of the bony fish gill and explain how it provides for a countercurrent exchange with the water. (A simple diagram will help.) (p. 612)

8 Larger aquatic animals must devote a considerable amount of energy to gas exchange. What are the underlying reasons for this? How do bony fishes assure that their gills will be sufficiently ventilated? How about sharks (Chapter 29)? (p. 612)

9 Relate your answer to the question above (number 8) to gas exchange mechanisms in all aquatic reptiles, birds and mammals. (p. 612)

10 What is the general make up of the vertebrate lung? How does the breathing mechanism in the amphibians, reptiles and birds differ from that of the mammal? (pp. 612–613)

11 List the structures (6 or 7) through which air flows as it enters the human respiratory system. (p. 613)

12 Describe the epithelium of the respiratory passages and explain how it functions. (p. 614)

13 How is the respiratory tree protected from the accidental introduction of food or fluids during swallowing? (p. 614)

14 Describe a typical cluster of alveoli including the circulatory structures. (p. 615)

15 Describe the role of the diaphragm and rib muscles in inspiration. What actually causes the lungs to fill? In general, how does expiration occur? (pp. 615–616)

16 Why is a residual volume essential? (p. 616)

17 Describe the diffusion gradients of the two respiratory gases in the metabolically active tissues and in the lungs. (p. 616)

18 Describe the hemoglobin molecule. In what part of the molecule is oxygen bound? How much can each molecule carry? (pp. 616–617)

19 List the changes carbon dioxide goes through when it enters a red blood cell. Name the enzyme that facilitates both the formation and the breakdown of carbonic acid. (pp. 617–618)

20 What factors determine the direction followed in the carbon dioxide reactions? List the events that occur as deoxygenated blood reaches the alveoli. (p. 618)

21 Describe the Bohr effect and explain how it is adaptive. (p. 618)

22 Describe the neural aspect of breathing under restful conditions. List two additional factors that enter in when rapid forceful breathing is required. (p. 618)

23 Locate the three groups of chemoreceptors that monitor blood conditions. What activates these sensors? Explain how negative feedback might work here. (pp. 618–619)

Even the crustiest and most jaded biologists may be fascinated by—and perhaps in awe of—something they have undoubtedly seen many times before: the formation of new life. The sight of a living chick embryo cannot help but touch something basic in each of us.

Already one can distinguish familiar landmarks in this fragile form. One can see the great, dark orbs that will form the eyes and the bulbous lobes that will be the brain. One can also see vague channels through which fluid flows jerkily in halts and starts. That fluid is being moved along by the regular contractions of a simple and still tubular heart.

The heart has an important role in the development of this kind of life and so it begins functioning early. In fact, the first timorous heart beats can be seen only two days after fertilization. In response, blood cells move through rough-hewn channels. Here, then, is the developing **circulatory system**—that vascular arrangement that moves blood and other fluid throughout the body.

Why does the circulatory system develop so early, and why is its presence so critical? The answers are found in its transport functions, which prove to be central to all other systems. The circulatory system does just what its name suggests. It moves substances via the blood from one part of the body to another; substances such as oxygen, carbon dioxide, nutrients, water, ions, hormones, antibodies, and metabolic wastes. Further, in homeothermic animals, the circulatory system also transports heat, shunting it to surface parts for release or sending it to core regions for retention (see Chapter 36). This system also plays a vital role in supporting the immune system, helping to combat bacteria, viruses, and other invaders. From this impressive list, the circulatory system's pivotal role becomes obvious. But before we get further into the details of our own circulatory system, let's look into the ways this system is organized in other animals.

ANIMAL CIRCULATORY SYSTEMS

Invertebrates

In the simpler-bodied invertebrate phyla, the sponges, coelenterates, flatworms, and a few others, there is little problem in moving substances from one part of the body to another. A relatively thin body with a large surface area and large internal spaces, such as gastrovascular cavities, preempt the need for complex systems in delivering food, disposing of metabolic wastes, and exchanging respiratory gases, all primary functions of circulatory systems. Cell-by-

39

CIRCULATION

cell transport through diffusion and active transport are generally sufficient in these animals.

However in other, more complex invertebrates things become more difficult. The bodies are larger, the distances greater, and the tissues and organs can be quite dense. Just as in the simpler invertebrates, cell-by-cell transport is important, but it is simply too slow to do the job unassisted. For these reasons, the body works to shift molecules around, carrying them in an extensive fluid stream to places where they will be needed, sometimes through great channels, sometimes along minute openings, sometimes across membranes. Among the more advanced invertebrate systems are those of the annelids and arthropods.

Annelids—earthworms and their aquatic relatives—have a well-formed circulatory system (Figure 39.1a). The blood never leaves the vessels, so it is called a **closed circulatory system.** Interestingly, annelid blood contains hemoglobin, although it is chemically different from our own and free, rather than bound to red blood cells. Other respiratory pigments occur in invertebrates, including a blue, copper-containing one called hemocyanin.

The circulatory system of earthworms includes two great longitudinal vessels, one dorsal, one ventral. They are connected anteriorly by five pairs of primitive hearts called **aortic arches,** whose tireless contractions move the blood along. Smaller vessels branch from the larger vessels, entering dense tissues where they rebranch, eventually forming extensive capillary beds. It is through the thin-walled **capillaries** that substances enter and leave the blood.

> In **closed circulatory systems,** the blood remains within the vessels, while transport materials enter and leave through thin-walled capillaries.

Earthworms and many other coelomate invertebrates (see Chapter 28) have essentially two circulatory systems since the coelomic fluid (in the space between the gut and the body wall) carries many of the same substances as does the blood and helps distribute them throughout the body.

Arthropods have **open circulatory systems,** that is, the blood is not always enclosed in vessels. While a fairly extensive system of vessels is seen in crustaceans (Figure 39.1b), primarily to assure a steady flow of blood through the gills, insects usually have only one large dorsal vessel. (Figure 39.1c). As the dorsal vessel contracts, it forces blood into the few vessels that arise from it. From there the blood simply flows free-

ly into tissue spaces, bathing the cells and exchanging materials as it percolates through the body. Eventually (largely due to the insect's movements) it ends up back at the dorsal region, where it enters the heart through tiny openings called **ostia.** One reason a sluggish circulatory system is sufficient in insects is that the blood is not important to gas exchange.

> In **open circulatory systems,** blood is pumped into vessels, but it soon enters open sinuses and body cavities, where exchanges with cells occur.

Vertebrates

The vertebrate circulatory system is essentially closed. In fishes the heart (Figure 39.1d) is two chambered, with a receiving chamber, or **atrium,** and a sending chamber, or **ventricle.** Note also the widened vessel, the **sinus venosus** leading into the atrium, and the heavy-walled **conus arteriosus** leaving the ventricle. The sinus venosus and conus arteriosus (which some consider to be bona fide chambers) are finally lost in the four-chambered heart. Curiously, the two structures show up early in the development of all vertebrate embryos (seemingly the vertebrate embryo reviews its evolutionary history as it develops). You may recall from Chapter 29 that the vertebrate heart has varied through evolution from essentially a two-chambered arrangement in fishes, to three chambers in the amphibians and reptiles, to four in the birds and mammals. We can consider the human circulatory system as representative of mammals.

THE HUMAN CIRCULATORY SYSTEM

The Heart

The four-chambered human heart is a remarkably efficient organ. Although anatomically it is only one structure, it can be said to function as two separate pumps (Figure 39.2). The right side, comprising the **right atrium** and the **right ventricle,** receives *deoxygenated* blood by way of **veins** from the body and pumps it to the lungs, where it picks up oxygen and releases carbon dioxide. The *oxygenated* blood returns to the **left atrium,** from which it is pumped to the **left ventricle,** and then, via **arteries,** throughout the body. Because the two sides are completely separate, oxygenated and deoxygenated blood do not

FIGURE 39.1 A closed circulatory system, as in the earthworm **(a)**, retains blood inside vessels, with exchanges occurring in capillary beds only. In the crustacean's and insect's open circulatory systems **(b** and **c)**, blood is pumped through vessels to open sinuses through which it gradually makes a return to the heart. Before its return trip in the crustacean, it is shunted through the gills for oxygenation. The fish **(d)**, like all vertebrates, has a closed circulatory system. The lone ventricle of its two-chambered heart must provide the thrust to pump blood through two or more sets of fine capillary beds prior to its return to the heart.

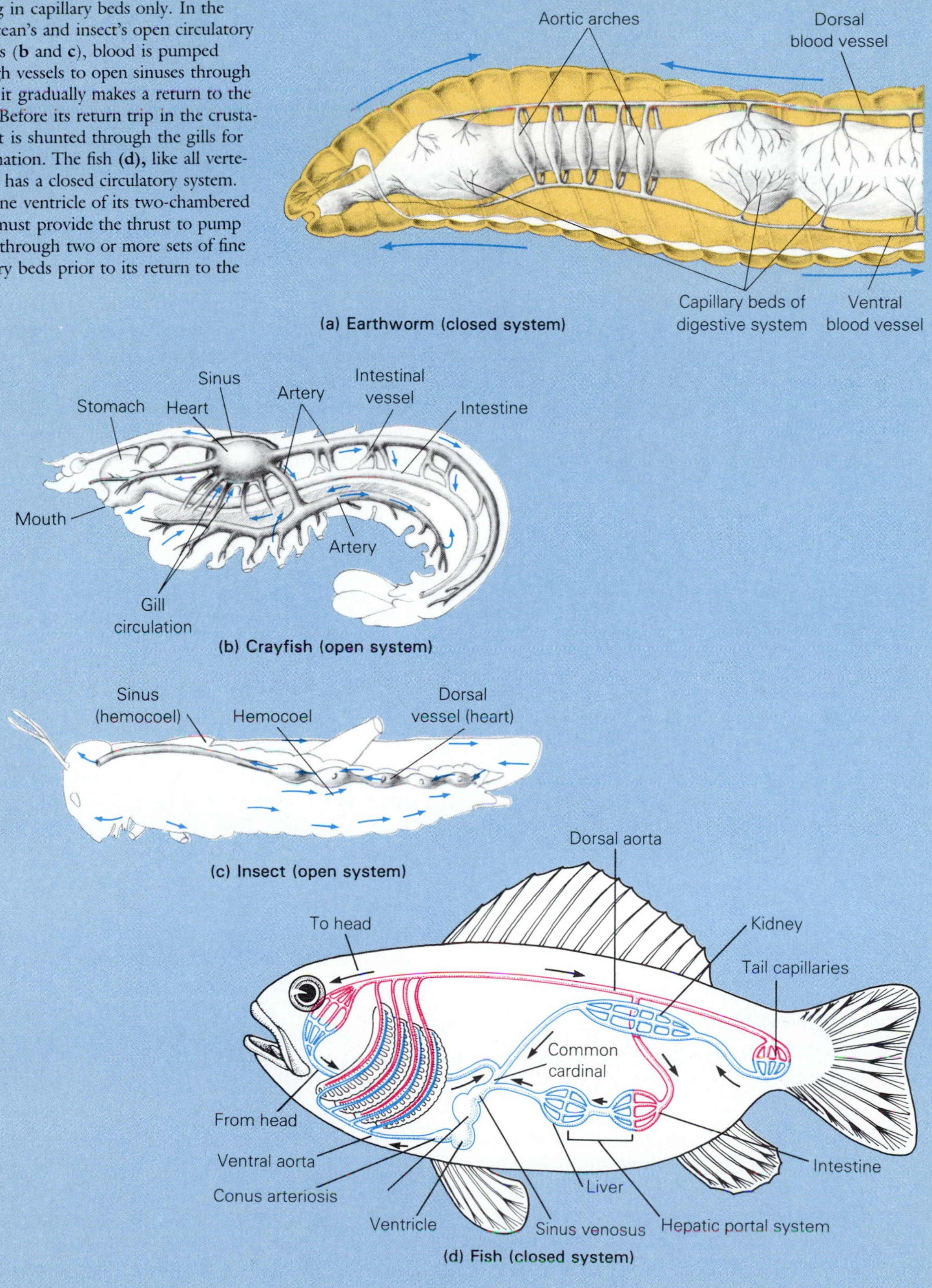

Aortic arches

Dorsal blood vessel

Capillary beds of digestive system

Ventral blood vessel

(a) Earthworm (closed system)

Stomach   Heart   Sinus   Artery   Intestinal vessel   Intestine

Mouth

Gill circulation   Artery

(b) Crayfish (open system)

Sinus (hemocoel)   Hemocoel   Dorsal vessel (heart)

(c) Insect (open system)

Dorsal aorta

To head

Kidney

Tail capillaries

Common cardinal

From head

Ventral aorta

Conus arteriosis

Ventricle

Sinus venosus

Liver

Hepatic portal system

Intestine

(d) Fish (closed system)

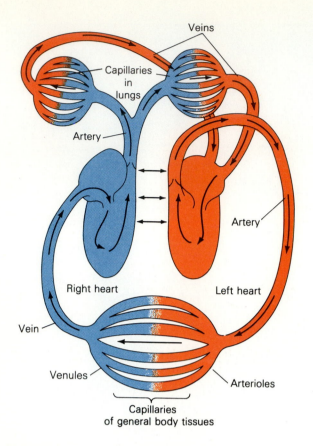

Veins

Capillaries in lungs

Artery

Right heart

Left heart

Artery

Vein

Venules

Arterioles

Capillaries of general body tissues

FIGURE 39.2 If we emphasize the separation of right and left chambers, the four-chambered heart becomes two pumps in one. One side serves the lungs; and the other side, the rest of the body. The "right heart" receives deoxygenated blood from the body and pumps it through the lungs, where carbon dioxide is replaced by oxygen. The "left heart" receives the oxygenated blood from the lungs and pumps it to all parts of the body.

mix. You may recall that this is not the case with the three-chambered hearts of amphibians and reptiles (see Chapter 29).

> The four-chambered heart can be thought of as two hearts in one. The right side pumps deoxygenated blood to the lungs; the left pumps oxygenated blood to the body.

Structures of the Heart

In keeping with its endless task, the heart is an enormously powerful and virtually tireless muscle. Since the left ventricle must pump blood throughout the body, it is particularly large and powerful. This coupled with the fact that the heart is slightly tilted, causes many people to assume the heart is located on the left side. Thus people swear to all sorts of things

with the right hand held over the left lung. Tracing the flow of blood through this magnificent muscle (Figure 39.3), we begin with the deoxygenated blood returning to the heart from the body. This blood is delivered through two great veins, the **superior vena cava** (from the upper part of the body) and the **inferior vena cava** (from the lower part of the body). They empty into the right atrium, a thin-walled receiving chamber. When the right atrium contracts, it forces blood into the right ventricle, the thicker-walled chamber below. Contraction of the right ventricle forces blood into the **pulmonary artery**, which branches, carrying blood to both lungs. Freshly oxygenated blood is returned to the heart through the **pulmonary veins**, first entering the left atrium. (Note that although arteries usually carry oxygenated blood and veins usually carry deoxygenated blood, in this case the situation is reversed.)

Incoming oxygenated blood passes from the left atrium to the left ventricle, the extremely thick-walled chamber that must force blood through most of the body. When the left ventricle contracts, blood is forced into the **aorta**, the largest artery in the body.

> The path of blood through the heart is:
> body → right atrium → right ventricle →
> lungs → left atrium → left ventricle → body.

Heart valves. As the atria and ventricles contract, blood is prevented from flowing backward by four one-way valves (Figure 39.4). The **tricuspid valve** lies between the right atrium and right ventricle, while its counterpart, the **bicuspid valve,** is between the left atrium and left ventricle. The "cusps" are extremely strong, thin-walled membranes that balloon out (like parachutes) and come together as blood in the ventricle starts to back up. Under pressure, the membranes are held in position by tough tendonous cords, the **chordae tendineae,** that are attached to the cusps at one end and to cone-shaped **papillary muscles** arising from the chamber walls at the other.

The two other valves, the **pulmonary semilunar valve** and the **aortic semilunar valve,** lie at the base of the pulmonary artery and the aorta, respectively. These valves each consist of three small pockets attached to the inside artery wall. They prevent the backflow of blood from the arteries into the ventricles.

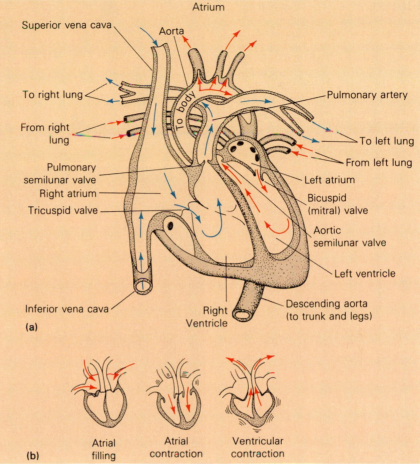

FIGURE 39.3 In its circulation through the heart, blood is directed by the two **vena cavae** to the **right atrium.** (The blue coloring signifies that this is deoxygenated blood.) It then moves into the **right ventricle,** which pumps it into the **pulmonary artery** for a trip through the **lungs.** Blood returns from the lungs via the **pulmonary veins** and enters the **left atrium.** (Bright red coloring signifies oxygenated blood.) It passes to the **left ventricle,** which pumps it into the **aorta** for its trip through the body.

Atrium

Superior vena cava

Aorta

To right lung

To body

Pulmonary artery

From right lung

To left lung

From left lung

Pulmonary semilunar valve

Left atrium

Right atrium

Bicuspid (mitral) valve

Tricuspid valve

Aortic semilunar valve

Left ventricle

Inferior vena cava

Right Ventricle

Descending aorta (to trunk and legs)

(a)

Atrial filling

Atrial contraction

Ventricular contraction

(b)

The valves have a great deal to do with the familiar "lub-dup" heart sounds. The first—the "lub"—is produced primarily by the snapping shut of the tricuspid and bicuspid valves as they respond to the two contracting ventricles. The second sound—the "dup"—is the closing of the semilunar valves, which tells us when blood has filled the pulmonary artery and the aorta. (The sound is actually created by the turbulence in the heart chambers as the valves close.)

The heart valves assure a one-way flow of blood by directing it from atria to ventricles and from ventricles to arteries.

Control of the Heart

Any such highly coordinated organ as the heart must operate under remarkable forms of control. In fact, the human heart is controlled in two ways: *intrinsically,* from within, and *extrinsically,* from without.

Intrinsic control. We saw earlier (see Chapter 31) that cardiac muscle is *intrinsically contractile;* that is, it contracts without external influences. It is also extremely conductive, with many of the characteristics of nerve tissue. Recall the presence of intercalated disks—those extensive, interlocking regions between fibers that enhance cell-to-cell conduction. Because of its intrinsic contractility, severing of controlling nerves from the autonomic nervous system will not cause contraction to stop; the heart will go on beating quite rhythmically at 70 to 80 beats per minute.

The rhythm or frequency of contractions is also partly controlled by factors within the heart itself. It stems from a specialized group of cells in the right atrium. This control center is technically known as the **sinoatrial (SA) node,** but it is usually called the **pacemaker** (Figure 39.5). The pacemaker generates repeated action potentials similar to those of neural impulses. These are transmitted to both atria, which respond by contracting simultaneously. Then the action potential reaches a second node, the **atrioventricular (AV) node,** which relays the impulse to the

FIGURE 39.4 The valves of the heart. **(a)** The aortic and pulmonary semilunar valves have simple three-part flaps. **(b)** The larger valves are between the atria and ventricles. The bicuspid (mitral) valve has two flaps of tissue; the tricuspid has three. The valves are supported by the chordae tendineae, stringlike cords that attach to papillary muscles projecting from the base of the ventricles.

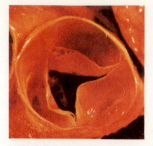 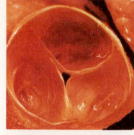

(a) Semilunar valve open   Valve nearly closed

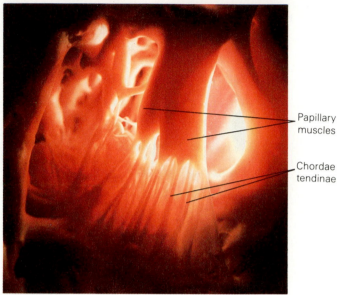

Papillary muscles

Chordae tendinae

(b) Papillary muscles and tendons below tricuspid

ventricles. They, too, contract simultaneously. Should the pacemaker fail, the heart rhythm will go awry. In such cases, it may be necessary to install an artificial pacemaker, an electronic device about the size of a pocket watch. Such surgery is now fairly routine.

> The heart's **intrinsic impulses** originate in the **sinoatrial** (SA) **node,** trigger atrial contraction, move to the **atrioventricular** (AV) **node,** and down the septum, triggering ventricular contraction.

Extrinsic control. While the heart can pump blood without outside influence, it must respond to varying oxygen needs and changing blood pressure in the organs it serves. Input from the nervous system, specifically from the autonomic division, permits the necessary adjustments to be made (see Chapter 33).

You may recall that the heart is innervated by two groups of nerves from the autonomic system—one sympathetic, the other parasympathetic. The parasympathetic nerves slow the heart rate by releasing the neurotransmitter **acetylcholine** into the pacemaker and the cardiac muscle. The sympathetic nerves accelerate the heart rate by releasing the neurotransmitter **norepinephine.** The release of extrinsic neurotransmitters must be coordinated very precisely to control the heart's response to the body's changing demands. **Epinephrine** (or adrenalin) and norepinephrine released by the adrenal medulla and carried by the bloodstream can also elevate the heart rate (see Chapter 35).

> **Extrinsic control** of the heart is over autonomic nerves. Acceleration is primarily by **norepinephrine** from sympathetic nerves; slowing is by **acetylcholine** from parasympathetic nerves.

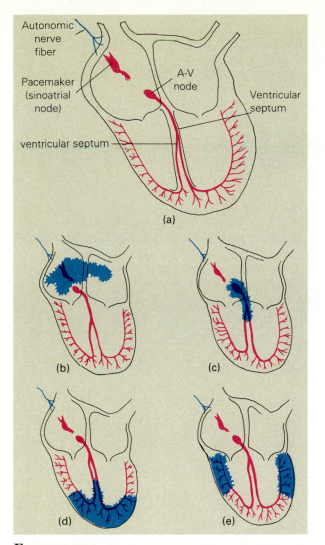

Autonomic
nerve
fiber

Pacemaker
(sinoatrial
node)

A-V
node

Ventricular
septum

ventricular septum

(a)

(b)

(c)

(d)

(e)

FIGURE 39.5   The heart's contractile impulses originate in the sinoatrial node, or pacemaker (**a**), and spread over the atria (**b**) (which contract), quickly reaching the atrioventricular (AV) node. From the AV node (**c**) impulses pass down the bundle of His in the ventricular septum to the first Purkinje fibers (**d**), whereupon ventricular contraction begins. Contraction proceeds upward in both ventricles (**e**) producing a squeezing effect that directs the blood into the large arteries leaving the heart.

Blood Vessels and Circulatory Routes

With contraction of the ventricles, the blood begins its journey through the body. Now we will see where the blood goes and what happens when it gets there.

Arteries and blood pressure.   Arteries carry blood away from the heart. They are not simple conduits, however; one of their major functions is to maintain blood pressure. The great vessel that receives blood from the left ventricle, the aorta,

receives the full impact of the heart's powerful surges. The sudden swell of blood during **systole** (ventricular contraction) expands the elastic walls of the aorta. As the blood moves from the last contraction of the ventricle onward, the elastic walls of the expanded aorta contract automatically. Therefore, during **diastole** (between contractions, when the ventricle is filling), blood pressure remains high because of the force of the contracting aorta on the remaining blood in the vessel. However, there is some drop in pressure as the ventricles fill. This is called the **diastolic pressure**. A typical **systolic pressure** is 120 mm Hg; a typical diastolic value, 80 mm Hg. The blood pressure in this case would be "120 over 80" (Figure 39.6). (Millimeters of mercury—mm Hg—is a standard way of expressing blood pressure.)

> **S**ystolic blood pressure is the maximum force exerted against the arterial walls by ventricular contraction. **Diastolic blood pressure** is the minimum residual force between contractions.

Arterial circulation.   As the aorta leaves the heart, it gives rise at once to its first branches, the **coronary arteries,** which go directly to the heart muscle, providing it with nutrients and oxygen. The aorta then curves to the left and forms the **aortic arch,** from which additional arteries arise, their branches extending into the head and arms. From the arch, the aorta proceeds downward, sending branches into viscera, trunk muscles, and the vertebral column. It then divides, in the lower abdomen, to form the major arteries of the legs.

The arteries eventually form **arterioles** (small arteries), which branch once again to form capillaries. Many arterioles contain **precapillary sphincters,** rings of smooth muscle that regulate the flow of blood into the capillary beds (Figure 39.7). The sphincters respond to the autonomic nervous system and to certain hormones. (The role of the arteriolar sphincters of the skin in thermoregulation was discussed in Chapter 36.)

Capillaries.   The capillaries are fascinating structures. Some are so small that blood cells must squeeze through them in single file. While the blood is in those vessels, it carries out some remarkable and essential tasks. There are so many vessels in a capillary bed that virtually no cell is far from these tiny rivers of life. This is critical, since the cells must draw sustenance from the vessels and deposit metabolic wastes into them.

FIGURE 39.6   The sphygmomanometer consists of an inflatable pressure cuff and a pressure gauge or mercury column. The cuff is wrapped around the upper arm and inflated until its pressure exceeds the pressure in the brachial artery. As the air in the cuff is gradually released, the first pulse sounds can be detected through a stethoscope. The gauge at this point will give the systolic pressure. With the continued release of air, the sounds become louder, but then disappear. At this instant the gauge will reveal the diastolic pressure.

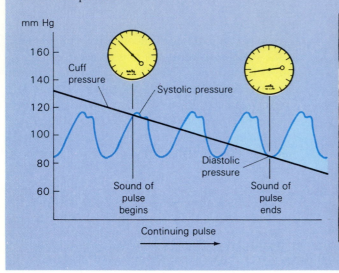

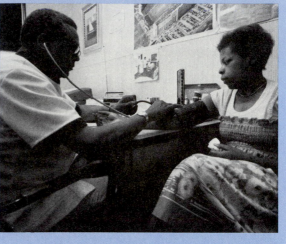

FIGURE 39.7   Capillaries (a) are thin walled, consisting of a single layer of cells. Some substances move readily through the capillary walls, while others must be actively transported. Capillaries usually occur in highly branched beds (b) and arise from arterioles. They pass through tissue layers and among individual cells. Blood may be shunted from one bed to another by smooth-muscle sphincters.

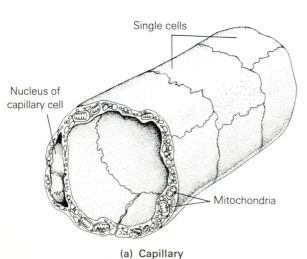

(a) Capillary

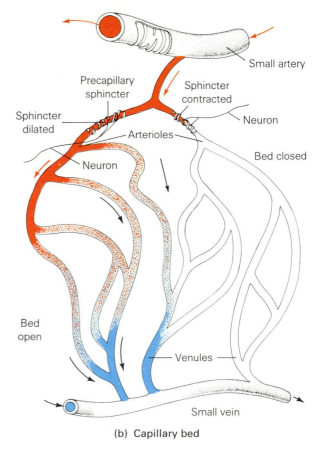

(b) Capillary bed

At the time the Declaration of Independence was signed, the most common cause of death in this new country was, ostensibly, indigestion. Either the quality of our food has improved since then or, more likely, the problem was misdiagnosis. What the founding fathers and mothers were really suffering from were heart attacks (or heart failure).

What *is* a heart attack? In most instances, the problem is caused by an insufficient blood supply to the heart muscle. The heart attack was once referred to as **coronary thrombosis** ("blood clot in a coronary vessel"). A coronary artery may indeed be blocked by a moving blood clot, but the blockage is more likely to be due to **coronary arteriosclerosis,** a hardening and narrowing of the vessel. A specific form of this condition, **artherosclerosis,** occurs when **plaque** coats the inside of arteries, reducing the inside diameter and restricting blood flow. Plaque is a flaky, crumbly substance that frequently breaks away from artery walls to be carried through the bloodstream, increasing the risk of a blockage. It may break away only partially, forming a flap that blocks blood flow. A blockage near the aorta is particularly dangerous, and most deaths from heart attacks result from such incidents. Blockages farther along in the coronary arteries affect less tissue.

However a vessel is blocked, the muscle deprived of blood soon dies. The death of heart tissue is called **myocardial infarction.** Tissue death is significant because it disrupts the heart rhythm. Impulse conduction and contraction of the heart muscle are precisely coordinated, so a loss of conduction in one area affects the coordinated contraction of the entire heart.

Today, blocked coronary vessels can be routinely treated, either medically or surgically. For example, blocked vessels can be surgically repaired in what is known as **coronary bypass surgery.** In this procedure, the damaged arteries are removed and replaced by corresponding lengths of vein, usually taken from the leg. Double, triple, and quadruple bypass procedures are becoming common, and the prognosis for many heart attack victims is now a long and healthy life.

Scanning electron micrograph of red blood cells caught in fibrous network of blood clot

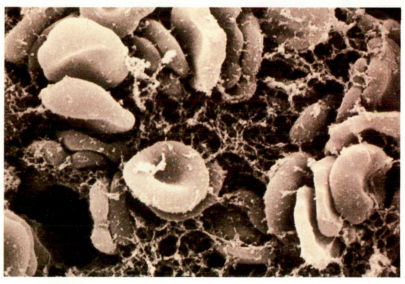

The capillary wall is formed by a single layer of interlocking cells (Figure 39.7a). It is so thin that some substances can cross by simple diffusion. The movement of other substances may be encouraged by the high hydrostatic pressure that forces smaller molecules across the thin walls. Such movement is facilitated by tiny pores at cell junctions. In addition, some movement is due to active transport in the form of pinocytosis (see Chapter 5). In this process, fluids and suspended materials are drawn into a pocket formed by the membrane of a capillary cell. The pocket then breaks off, forming a vesicle that is transported across the cytoplasm, and the materials are squeezed out on the opposite side (Figure 39.8).

Arterioles direct blood into **capillary beds** where substances leave and enter through hydrostatic pressure, active transport, diffusion, and osmosis.

Veins and the return to the heart. Once the blood has nourished the various tissues of the body and carried away their wastes, it begins its return to the heart. Immediately upon leaving the capillary bed, the blood enters the tiny **venules,** which merge to form the veins. Veins have thinner walls than arteries, but they contain the same types of tissues.

Blood has reached the capillary beds under great pressure, forced along by the heart and squeezed by arterial muscles. But in its passage through the capillary beds, its pressure has been dissipated, and it enters the venules sluggishly. Venous blood must rely on a number of mechanisms to return to the heart. For example, many veins have one-way flap valves that allow the blood to move in only one direction—toward the heart. Also, veins in or near skeletal muscles are squeezed when the muscles contract, pushing the blood along. During breathing, changing pressure in the thoracic cavity helps blood move through the veins there. (Veins and arteries are compared in Figure 39.9.)

Venus blood, under very low pressure, receives an assist in returning to the heart by muscle movement, breathing, and one-way valves.

FIGURE 39.8 Many substances are taken into capillary cells through pinocytosis. Pinocytic vesicles capture materials on one side of the cell, pass to the other side in the form of vacuoles, and deposit the materials outside the cell through exocytosis.

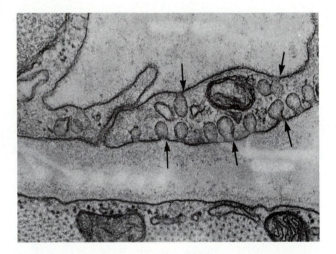

FIGURE 39.9 Both arteries and veins are composed of three layers of tissue, including a smooth inner endothelium, a middle layer of circular smooth muscle and elastic connective tissue, and an outer layer of fibrous connective tissue.

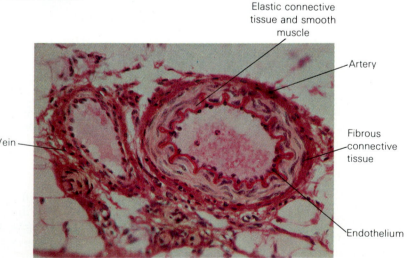

Elastic connective tissue and smooth muscle

Artery

Fibrous connective tissue

Vein

Endothelium

BLOOD

As we've seen, the blood performs many vital and varied functions. Its volume is substantial, 5 to 6 liters in adult men and 4 to 5 liters in adult women; on the average, blood makes up about 7.7 percent of a person's total body weight. The blood volume includes a generous safety factor, since any healthy adult can lose—or donate—about 1/10 of the total volume (roughly a pint) without ill effects. Blood is indeed a critical and fascinating fluid, but what exactly is it?

Components of Blood

Structurally, the blood can be divided into two parts, the straw-colored **plasma** (about 55% by volume) and the **formed elements** (about 45%). Formed elements include the **erythrocytes** (red cells), **leukocytes** (white cells), and **platelets** (noncellular bodies important in blood clotting).

Plasma. Blood plasma is about 90% water; most of the remainder is made up of three proteins: **albumin, globulin,** and **fibrinogen.** Albumins are important in maintaining osmotic conditions in the blood; globulins function as part of the immune defenses; and fibrinogen operates in blood clotting. Less than 2% of the plasma includes transient ions, hormones, vitamins, urea, and various nutrients, particularly sugars.

> Plasma is mainly water and plasma proteins. Other constituents include ions, hormones, vitamins, nutrients, and wastes.

Red cells. Erythrocytes (erythro, "red"; cyte, "cell") are among the smallest and most specialized of our cells. They are only about 8 μm in diameter, and in most mammals take the form of a biconcave disk (Figure 39.10). Mature erythrocytes lack nuclei, mitochondria, and ribosomes. They function essentially as little bags of hemoglobin (see Chapter 38).

Normally, there are about 5 million red cells per cubic microliter (μl) of human blood. Each cell lives about four months, after which it is destroyed in the liver or spleen. So the erythrocytes must be constantly replaced. In adults, new red cells are produced by **stem cells** in the red bone marrow. Their rate of pro-

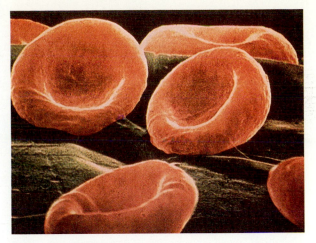

FIGURE 39.10 Red blood cells (erythrocytes) are biconcave disks only 8 μm in diameter.

duction is controlled by a kidney hormone known as **erythropoietin,** which is released into the blood when cells in the kidney detect a drop in blood oxygen levels—a function of the number of red cells. As red cells increase, the stimulus is removed and erythropoietin secretion diminishes (a typical negative feedback mechanism).

White blood cells. Unlike red cells, white cells **(leukocytes)** do not discard their nuclei as they mature. As was indicated, the white blood cells are active in the immune system, which will be discussed in more detail in Chapter 40. For now it is important to know that the **neutrophils,** whose numbers make up the majority of leukocytes, are important phagocytic cells. They aggregate at infection sites, engulfing invading microorganisms. **Basophils** are involved in the inflammatory response, releasing histamines and serotonin at infection sites. **Eosinophils** are also involved in inflammatory responses, but in addition, they help destroy larger parasites. **Lymphocytes** are the backbone of the immune system. In lymphatic tissue they carry out many tasks that aid in fighting off infectious organisms, destroying foreign molecules and providing longer-lasting immunity from disease. The **monocytes,** once activated at infection sites, develop into **macrophages** which, like neutrophils, specialize in phagocytizing foreign cells and any cellular debris they encounter. They also play a special role in activating the immune system, as we will see in the next chapter.

White blood cells vary in diameter from 9μm—only slightly larger than an erythrocyte—to 15 μm or more, about the size of most other cells of the

FIGURE 39.11 The white blood cells (leukocytes).

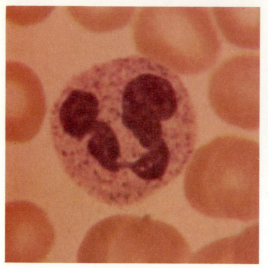

Neutrophil

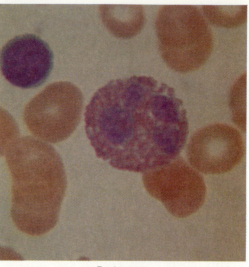

Eosinophil

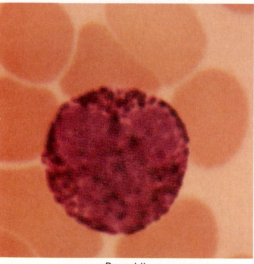

Basophil

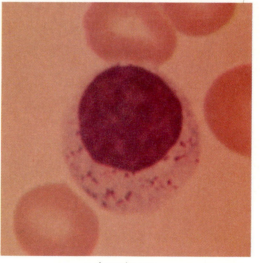

Lymphocyte

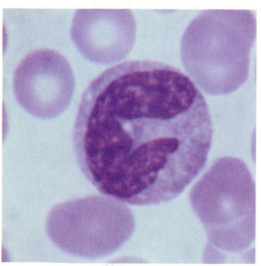

Monocyte

body (Figure 39.11). Under normal conditions there is about one white blood cell for every 700 red blood cells (an average of about 7000 leukocytes per μl of blood). Low white cell counts (below 5000 per μl) indicate damage to elements in the bone marrow that form the white cells. High counts (above 10,000 per μl) are a sign of infection or of a more serious condition such as leukemia (in which the count may increase to well over 100,000).

Erythrocytes transport O_2 and CO_2, and outnumber leukocytes 700 to 1. The latter carry out immune responses and phagocytize cell debris. Both groups originate from stem cells in red bone marrow.

Platelets and blood clotting. Platelets are actually fragments of cells that contain enzymes and other agents that act in blood clotting. The clotting process is quite complex and not completely understood, but there are about 15 participants, some of which act as fail-safe mechanisms to prevent accidental clotting.

When an injury occurs, platelets gather at the wound site, form lengthy extensions, and adhere to collagen fibers, essentially forming a plug. In addition, platelets release **vasoconstrictors,** chemicals that stimulate smooth muscle in nearby blood vessels to contract, slowing the leakage of blood into the wound area. Most significantly, platelets at wound sites release **thromboplastin,** an enzyme that starts a cascading series of reactions that result in the actual clotting events. The final clot contains lengthy fibers of the protein **fibrin** (derived from fibrinogen), which forms a woven net across the wound.

> **P**latelets form plugging fibers over wounds, release **vasoconstrictors** (which help close off injured vessels), and **thromboplastin** (which begins blood clotting).

THE LYMPHATIC SYSTEM

The **lymphatic system** is the "secondary circulatory system," and, anatomically, a rather simple one at that. Basically, it is the system of channels through which **lymph** flows. Lymph is composed of fluid that has leaked, or been pressed, out of the capillaries by high hydrostatic pressure. The lymph moves between cells, percolating slowly through the body, occasionally collecting into distinct channels. It returns to the bloodstream through ducts entering large veins near the heart. Because fluids can enter and leave blood vessels, the lymphatic system is important in maintaining water balance in the blood. We've already mentioned its role in the absorption and transport of digested fats (see Chapter 37), and we will discuss a third function shortly.

Figure 39.12 illustrates the anatomy of the lymphatic system. As you can see, it consists of a large number of **lymph ducts, lymph nodes,** and **lymph vessels.** The lymphatic system lacks a pumping heart, so the fluid is pushed along primarily by the squeezing action of muscles and the normal movement of

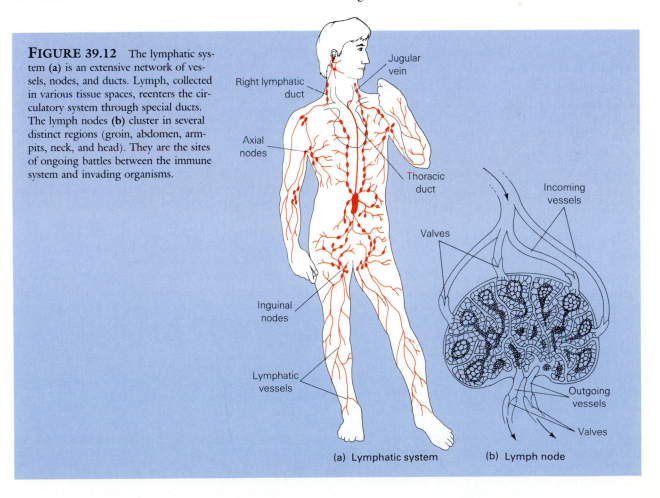

FIGURE 39.12 The lymphatic system **(a)** is an extensive network of vessels, nodes, and ducts. Lymph, collected in various tissue spaces, reenters the circulatory system through special ducts. The lymph nodes **(b)** cluster in several distinct regions (groin, abdomen, armpits, neck, and head). They are the sites of ongoing battles between the immune system and invading organisms.

Right lymphatic duct

Jugular vein

Axial nodes

Thoracic duct

Valves

Incoming vessels

Inguinal nodes

Lymphatic vessels

Outgoing vessels

Valves

(a) Lymphatic system

(b) Lymph node

various organs, as well as the pulsing of adjacent arteries. A system of check valves prevents the lymph from backing up, so it flows continuously toward the heart.

The **lymph nodes** are scattered throughout the body, but they are concentrated in the neck, armpits, and groin. Each node is a clump of tissue harboring multitudes of fixed macrophages and roving lymphocytes. The nodes act as filters of a sort, since foreign materials, bacteria, viral particles, and cancerous cells that have managed to enter the body eventually accumulate in a node, where they are immediately attacked by resident white blood cells. This, then, is the third function of the lymphatic system—the removal of foreign materials and invading microorganisms from the body's fluids. (The spleen and tonsils aid in this task.) Swollen nodes may be a sign of infection.

The lymphatic system, which is made up of a number of nodes, ducts, and vessels, cycles fluids from tissue spaces to the bloodstream, transports fats, and houses invader-destroying white blood cells.

SUMMARY

The circulatory system transports many substances, aids in thermoregulation, and supports the immune system.

ANIMAL CIRCULATORY SYSTEMS

Invertebrates

Although simpler invertebrates rely on cell-to-cell transport, more complex types require circulatory systems. Annelids have a closed system with hemoglobin-rich blood. Exchanges occur through capillary walls. Arthropods have open systems in which blood leaves vessels to percolate through body spaces.

Vertebrates

Vertebrates have closed systems. The vertebrate heart consists of two chambers in fish, three in amphibians and reptiles, and four in birds and mammals.

THE HUMAN CIRCULATORY SYSTEM

The Heart

The four-chambered heart provides for separate pulmonary and systemic circuits. Deoxygenated blood is received and sent to the lungs by the right side, and oxygenated blood from the lungs is received and sent to the body by the left.

Structures of the Heart

The superior and inferior vena cava return deoxygenated blood to the right atrium It then passes through the tricuspid valve to the right ventricle, which pumps it past the pulmonary semilunar valve into the pulmonary arteries. They direct it into the lung circulation for gas exchange. Following this, pulmonary veins carry oxygenated blood to the left atrium, which sends it past the bicuspid valve into the thick-walled left ventricle. (Both tricuspid and bicuspid valves have thin flaps held in place by tough chordae tendineae.) From there blood is pumped past the aortic-semilunar valve into the aorta for distribution. The two heart sounds are produced by the two sets of valves.

Control of the Heart

Intrinsic control originates in the sinoatrial node (pacemaker), which directs impulses across the atria, which contract. The impulses are then relayed to the atrioventricular node, which directs them to the ventricles bringing on their contraction.

Extrinsic control occurs via the autonomic nervous system. Decreases in heart rate are brought about by acetylcholine secreted by parasympathetic nerves. Increases occur when norepinephrine is secreted by sympathetic nerves.

Blood Vessels and Circulatory Routes

Maintenance of blood pressure is aided by the elasticity of arteries. Arterial pressure peaks during systole (ventricular contraction) and falls during diastole (between contractions.)

The aorta's first branches go to the heart itself, after which the curving arch sends branches to the rest of the body. Arteries branch into arterioles, vessels with smooth muscle precapillary sphincters that control flow into capillary beds.

All exchanges occur through the one cell-thick capillary walls. Exchange occurs through hydrostatic pressure, diffusion, osmosis and pinocytosis.

Capillaries form venules which join to form veins. Venus blood pressure is low and blood return to the heart is assisted by one-way valves, muscle movement, and pressure changes in the chest cavity.

BLOOD

Components of blood

Plasma (55% of blood volume) consists of water, resident blood proteins, and various substances being transported.

Formed elements (about 45% of blood volume) include erythrocytes, leukocytes and platelets. Erythrocytes (red blood cells) are biconcave, hemoglobin-filled cells that lack organelles. Their formation from stem cells is regulated by an automated hormonal system involving erythropoietin.

The leukocytes (white blood cells) are larger cells that retain their organelles, and occur in far fewer numbers. They perform immune functions and, accordingly, their numbers increase during infections.

Platelets are essential to blood-clotting, releasing the enzyme thromboplastin that acts in fibrin (clot) formation.

THE LYMPHATIC SYSTEM

The lymphatic system includes simple ducts, vessels, and nodes. Its roles include maintaining fluid balances and transporting digested fats. The lymph nodes contain certain leukocytes involved in immune responses.

KEY TERMS

closed circulatory system	aorta	diastolic pressure	neutrophil
aortic arch	tricuspid valve	systolic pressure	basophil
capillary	bicuspid valve	coronary artery	eosinophil
open circulatory system	chordae tendineae	arteriole	lymphocyte
ostia	papillary muscle	precapillary sphincter	monocyte
atrium	pulmonary semilunar valve	plasma	macrophage
ventricle	aortic semilunar valve	formed element	vasoconstrictor
sinus venosus	sinoatrial (SA) node	erythrocyte	thromboplastin
conus arteriosus	pacemaker	leukocyte	fibrin
vein	atrioventricular (AV) node	platelet	lymphatic system
artery	acetylcholine	albumin	lymph
superior vena cava	norepinephrine	globulin	lymph duct
inferior vena cava	epinephrine	fibrinogen	lymph node
pulmonary artery	systole	stem cell	lymph vessel
pulmonary vein	diastole	erythropoietin	

REVIEW QUESTIONS

1 List six substances transported in the circulatory system. List five systems served by the human circulatory system. (p. 623)

2 List several examples of invertebrates that have no need for a circulatory system and explain how they carry on transport. (pp. 623–624)

3 What is a closed circulatory system? How can a closed system exchange materials with tissues? (p. 624)

4 Describe the anatomy of the closed circulatory system of the earthworm. (p. 624)

5 Describe the flow of blood through the insect open circulatory system. (p. 624)

6 List the four structures of the fish heart and describe a complete circuit of blood in its circulatory system. (p. 624)

7 Explain how the four-chambered heart represents two pumps in one. What does it provide that is not possible with a three-chambered heart? (p. 624)

8 Starting at the vena cavae, trace the flow of blood through the human heart, finishing at the aorta. Name all chambers, valves, and vessels. (pp. 624–626)

9 Compare the appearance and operation of the tricuspid and bicuspid valves with that of the semilunar valves. (p. 626)

10 Relate the heart sounds to activity in the heart valves. (p. 627)

11 Describe the intrinsic events accompanying a complete cycle of contractions in the atria and ventricles. (pp. 627–628)

12 Explain how sympathetic and parasympathetic nerves can have different effects on the heart rate. (p. 628)

13 Discuss how the structure and work of arteries affects blood pressure in the circulatory system. (p. 629)

14 A typical blood pressure is 120 over 80. What does each measurement actually reflect and how are such measurements made? (p. 629)

15 What is the role of the precapillary sphincter? Cite an example from your reading about thermoregulation (Chapter 36). What two systems control this function? (p. 629)

16 List forces involved in substances leaving the blood at the start of a capillary bed and those involved in returning materials on the other side. (p. 631)

17 Relate the structure of a capillary to its principal functions. (pp. 625–627)

18 Characterize blood pressure in the veins and cite three factors that aid in returning blood to the heart. (p. 628)

19 Make a list of the blood plasma components, indicating whether each is generally permanent or transient. (p. 629)

20 Erythrocytes are often cited as examples of highly specialized cells. List several characteristics that support this point. (p. 629)

21 How long do erythrocytes live? Explain the mechanism that assures an ongoing supply. (p. 629)

22 Compare the size, structure, and relative numbers of leukocytes with that of erythrocytes. (pp. 629–630)

23 What would a white cell count of 10,000 or higher indicate? A count of over 100,000? (p. 630)

24 Discuss the general role of platelets. What triggers their activity? (p. 631)

25 List the three main structures of the lymphatic system. What propels the lymph along? (p. 631)

26 What are the three principal functions of the lymphatic system? (pp. 631–632)

27 Describe the structure of a lymph node and explain what goes on in these bodies. (p. 632)

If an alien from another world landed on our planet, his biggest worry might not be a trigger-happy farmer or even our corrosive, oxygen-laden atmosphere. A greater problem might be the vast army of tiny life forms that relentlessly attack other kinds of life. We, of course, evolved in a sea of these bacteria, viruses, and other parasitic invaders, and we have mechanisms that usually contain or repel their advances. The visitor would probably have no such protection and might quickly fall to their wheedling intrusions.

Even among our own species, we may find that one group has good protection against a certain microbe while another group that has no experience with it is defenseless. In the Ecuadorian Amazon, for example, tiny, remote branches of the Waorani tribe have been occasionally devastated by outsiders who carried in common cold viruses.

How, then, have we managed to survive while literally surrounded by tiny, opportunistic exploiters? Certainly, as natural selection worked its way, many of our forebearers didn't survive. Those who did survive and their descendants were left with mechanisms that conferred some degree of immunity from such infective agents. Let's now take a brief look at the immune mechanisms that we depend on to defend us.

CHEMICAL DEFENSES: THE FRONT LINE

The first responses to invaded or injured cells stem from the cells themselves. The injured tissue releases specific chemicals that call the body's defenses into action. One such group of chemicals is called **histamines.** Histamines bring on the redness and swelling associated with inflammation and infection by dilating the tiny arterioles at the site, thereby increasing the flow of blood into the area. They also increase the permeability of blood vessels in the area, allowing fluids (such as plasma) to seep out, further increasing the swelling. (**Antihistamines,** then, reduce this reaction, especially in the nasal passages of hayfever sufferers and those with that charming condition known as the common cold.)

Other released substances include polypeptides from a group called **kinins,** molecules that further increase the permeability of vessels and local swelling. The subsequent pressure placed on nerve endings may cause pain or tenderness and discourages further injury by encouraging us to treat the area with care while the healing process is underway.

40

IMMUNITY

Infections also trigger activity in the dormant **complement system,** a defense mechanism comprising about eleven plasma proteins. Activation begins as the first protein binds to an invading bacterium or infected cell, setting off an avalanche of reactions from one protein to the next. Once activated, the complement system reinforces the other chemical responses and attracts phagocytic **neutrophils.** More dramatically, it destroys invaders directly, altering cell permeability so that the inrush of water and ions literally bursts the cell.

Another chemical defense involves the antiviral protein **interferon,** whose action can effectively slow the increase of viruses that have successfully invaded the body. As we explained in earlier chapters, viruses routinely dismantle the host DNA and produce many new viral particles by transcribing their own genes using host replicating and protein-synthesizing machinery. Interferon is known to block this action in some viruses. Further, interferon produced in one cell can protect other cells from viral invasion. Interferon is also believed to offer protection against virally induced cancer and also cancers brought about by radiation and chemicals. Interferon, incidentally, is one of the proteins that has been produced through genetic engineering.

CELLULAR RESPONSES: ROVING DEFENDERS

Five kinds of white blood cells (or **leukocytes**) and a cell of unknown origin, **the natural killer cell,** are involved in immune responses. Of the white blood cells, three are phagocytes; that is, they engulf and dispose of invaders. The phagocytes include **natural killer cells, eosinophils, neutrophils,** and **monocytes** (Figure 40.1). A fourth type, the **basophil,** is important in inflammation, and a fifth, the **lymphocyte,** is critical to a wide range of immune responses, including identifying and killing invaders and producing antibodies against them. We will briefly consider the roles of the natural killer cells, neutrophils, and monocytes, while focusing mainly on the lymphocytes.

In early cellular responses, **natural killer cells** destroy cancerous and virus-infected cells; **neutrophils** and **monocytes** phagocytize invaders.

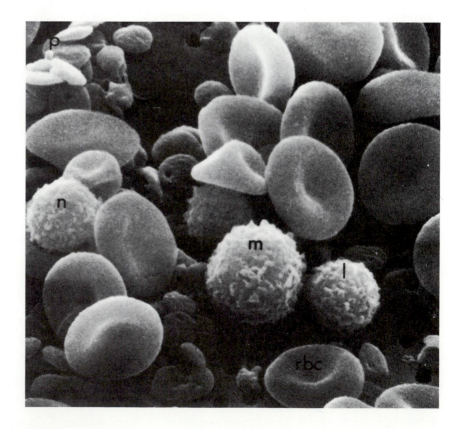

FIGURE 40.1 Frontline defenders caught by the scanning electron microscope include a large monocyte **(m)** (which undergoes a transition into a macrophage), one of the countless neutrophils **(n),** and an immature lymphocyte **(l).** Compare their sizes to that of the much more common red blood cell **(rbc). P** indicates platelets.

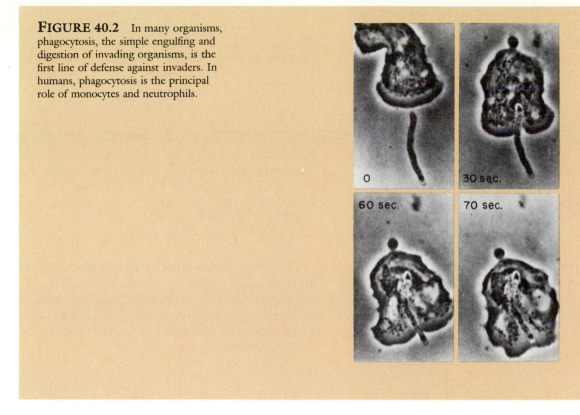

FIGURE 40.2 In many organisms, phagocytosis, the simple engulfing and digestion of invading organisms, is the first line of defense against invaders. In humans, phagocytosis is the principal role of monocytes and neutrophils.

0   30 sec.   60 sec.   70 sec.

The natural killer cells, or **NK cells,** routinely rove the body, touching and searching body cell surface features as they go. In ways we have yet to fully understand, the NK cells uncover abnormal cells—those infected by viruses or those in the early stages of cancer—and promptly kill them. As more becomes known about the NK cells we may find that it is the failure of these first-line defenders that permits the early spread of cancerous cells.

The neutrophils are the expendable, frontline foot soldiers. Perhaps 100 billion neutrophils are produced each day. They survive only a few days and suffer great casualties with every invasion. They are the first to arrive at any invasion site, drawn toward chemicals emitted from bacteria, injured tissue, and clotting blood. They quickly swarm at an infection site, engulfing any intruder they can manage (Figure 40.2). (Sometimes, though, the invaders win the fight.) The monocytes arrive next, and once at the site they undergo remarkable changes, growing and swelling until they are transformed into huge **macrophages,** whose numbers further increase in the later stages of infection.

The macrophage is a huge, relentless, "eating-machine" that may live for years. *Macrophage* means "big eater"; they eat not only microorganisms but old, worn-out blood cells and dead tissue. Further, they do it with astonishing speed. They can engulf a foreign particle in 1/100 second. In some cases, even if they can't digest the offending particle, they engulf it anyway and hold it within their bodies where it can do no harm. As the phagocytes continue to engulf bacteria, they accumulate the bacterial poisons and eventually begin to die in great numbers, their tiny corpses forming pus.

The Macrophage as an Antigen-Presenting Cell

In addition to engulfing invaders and hydrolyzing them with their potent enzymes, the macrophages have another rather amazing role. While most of what they consume is simply digested, some of the ingested molecules are saved and later brought to the cell surface where they are incorporated into the macrophage's plasma membrane. Following this, the macrophages roam through the body wearing bits and pieces of what they ate. Like natural killer cells, they touch surfaces with the various cells they encounter. But, unlike the NK cells that search for diseased cells, **antigen-presenting macrophages** are interested only in friendly cells. Specifically, their role is to find and activate **helper T-cell lymphocytes** whose cell surfaces carry molecules that match the antigen worn by the macrophage.

When an antigen-presenting macrophage finds the right helper T-cell, the immune system, is quickly aroused and responds by forming a veritable army of highly specific cells, a massive clone with just one task. Like angry bears aroused from hibernation, they track down and deal with the agent that brought about their arousal. The method by which the immune system prepares its leukocytes for the key step of antigen recognition is an interesting story that we will return to shortly, but for now let's look more closely at this amazing, single-minded army.

> **A**ntigen-presenting macrophages, those displaying invader molecules on their membrane, activate helper T-cells with matching surface receptors.

Introducing the B-cell and T-cell Lymphocytes

There are two broad categories of lymphocytes, **B-cell lymphocytes** and **T-cell lymphocytes,** or simply, B-cells and T-cells. When activated, the B-cells produce large amounts of proteins called **antibodies,** or more technically, **immunoglobins.** Immunoglobins carry out what is called the **humoral immune response,** which basically amounts to finding and immobilizing any matching antigens in the body. The term "humoral" refers to the fluid (blood) in which antibodies are distributed.

T-cells carry out the **cell-mediated response,** a very different task, in which specific antigen-bearing invaders and infected body cells are sought out and killed before (one would hope) the parasite can reproduce. This response depends not on released protein immunoglobins but on similar proteins embedded in the cell surface of the T-cells. Both B- and T-cells originate from stem cells in the red marrow, but they mature in different places (Figure 40.3).

With these points in mind, let's return to where the antigen-presenting macrophage met its match and see how B- and T-cells are aroused. The details were first suggested some 30 years ago by Australian immunologist Sir Macfarlane-Burnett, when he proposed his **clonal selection theory.**

> **M**ature activated **B-cell lymphocytes** form and release immunoglobins; **T-cell lymphocytes** attack infected and invading cells.

FIGURE 40.3 **(a)** Virgin B-cells and T-cells are identical in appearance. Following activation, however, the B-cell lymphocyte **(b)** produces a vast, rough endoplasmic reticulum, a sign of intense protein synthesis, which presumably would include its specific immunoglobin. The T-cell lymphocyte **(c)** produces very little rough endoplasmic reticulum.

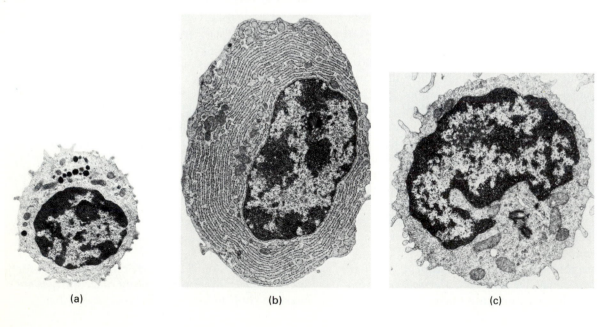

(a) (b) (c)

AROUSING THE LYMPHOCYTES: THE PRIMARY IMMUNE RESPONSE

When an antigen-presenting macrophage encounters a matching helper T-cell lymphocyte, the macrophage secretes a powerful activating substance called **interleukin-1,** a chemical from a group known as **lymphokines** ("lymphocyte activators"). The helper T-cell responds to the chemical agent by at once seeking out and contacting any inactive lymphocytes with similar surface recognition molecules. Upon contact, the excited helper T-cells secrete their own lymphokine, logically called **interleukin-2.** Interleukin-2 activates other sleeping brothers, which, once aroused, quickly mature and enter into a frenzy of mitotic activity.

Activated helper T-cells amplify the lymphocyte response by seeking out and activating other inactive lymphocytes with matching surface receptors.

According to Macfarlane-Burnett's clonal selection theory, there are enough kinds of inactive, or "virgin," B- and T-cells to react against any potential antigen imaginable. The theory maintains that any time helper T-cells are activated and the alarm sounded, only a few virgin B- and T-cells are aroused, those with matching cell-surface recognition molecules. Upon arousal, they give rise to two lines of cells, the B-cells that make antibodies and three kinds of T-cells. (Figure 40.4).

Aroused B-cell Lymphocytes

B-cell descendants include **plasma cells** and **memory cells.** The plasma cells are short lived, lasting only a few days, but during that period they begin the humoral response. Each plasma cell synthesizes and secretes copious amounts of immunoglobin, constructed according to specifications in the original captured antigen. Immunoglobins circulate freely in the blood. When they encounter matching antigens, whether on an invader's cell surface or as molecules, they become firmly attached. As the reaction goes on, massive antigen-antibody complexes are formed. Such complexes, as we will see, occur as immobile clumps that are readily cleaned up by phagocytes. The interaction of immunoglobulin and antigen also activates the complement system as discussed earlier. Memory cells live much longer, forming a small but effective residual force that, if aroused, can quickly mount new attacks.

Immunoglobins released by plasma B-cells attach to matching antigens, forming antibody-antigen complexes that can be phagocytized by other cells. Memory B-cells are much longer-lived.

Aroused T-cell Lymphocytes

Activated T-cell lymphocytes give rise to several specialized subpopulations. These include **cytotoxic T-cells** (sometimes called "killer" or "effector" T-cells), **helper T-cells, suppressor T-cells,** and **memory T-cells.** Their tasks, respectively, are: destroying infected cells, arousing virgin lymphocytes, and (through delicate negative feedback processes) slowing down and stopping the immune response.

Cytotoxic T-cells.   The role of identifying and killing invading cells and friendly but infected body cells goes to the cytotoxic T-cell. Upon identifying such cells, cytotoxic T-cells cluster about, releasing substances that lyse, or rupture, the cell. Recognition occurs when the antibody-like protein carried by the T-cell forms a match with the antigen site on the invader. If the infection is viral, the aroused cytotoxic T-cells will be carrying a surface antibody that matches an antigen that has formed on the cell surface. Recall that when viruses invade cells, they make specific molecular changes in the host membrane, rendering it impenetrable by other viruses (a viral adaptation that eliminates competition). Upon contact, the two sites bind together, and the cytotoxic T-cells then destroy the infected cell and its invader.

In addition, all T-cells have surface receptors that recognize "self." The term "self," of course, refers to one's own tissues. This is also important since it safeguards against inadvertent attacks on normal cells and tissues. In the case of infected or invading cells, this permits a dual recognition to go on (see Essay 40.1).

Cytotoxic T-cells attack infected cells with matching antigenic sites. Their dual recognition sites prevent attack on "self."

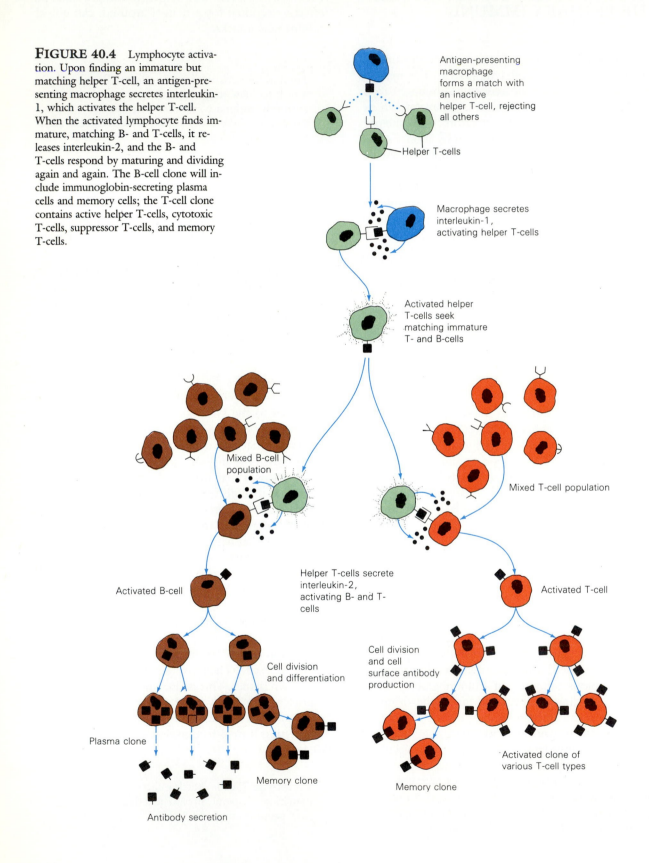

FIGURE 40.4 Lymphocyte activation. Upon finding an immature but matching helper T-cell, an antigen-presenting macrophage secretes interleukin-1, which activates the helper T-cell. When the activated lymphocyte finds immature, matching B- and T-cells, it releases interleukin-2, and the B- and T-cells respond by maturing and dividing again and again. The B-cell clone will include immunoglobin-secreting plasma cells and memory cells; the T-cell clone contains active helper T-cells, cytotoxic T-cells, suppressor T-cells, and memory T-cells.

Antigen-presenting macrophage forms a match with an inactive helper T-cell, rejecting all others

Helper T-cells

Macrophage secretes interleukin-1, activating helper T-cells

Activated helper T-cells seek matching immature T- and B-cells

Mixed B-cell population

Mixed T-cell population

Activated B-cell

Helper T-cells secrete interleukin-2, activating B- and T-cells

Activated T-cell

Cell division and differentiation

Cell division and cell surface antibody production

Plasma clone

Memory clone

Memory clone

Activated clone of various T-cell types

Antibody secretion

Helper T-cells. As we have seen, mature helper T-cells assist other lymphocytes in responding to antigen. Activated helper T-cells amplify the original activating process by continuing to secrete interleukin-2, prompting even more virgin B- and T-cells to divide and mature. While the name "helper" doesn't sound very impressive, immunologists are now convinced that the helper T-cells tasks are quite pivotal, indeed critical, to the overall operation of the immune system. The helper T-cells, for example, stimulate not only the formation of cytotoxic T-cells, but **memory T-cells** as well. Memory T-cells (like memory B-cells) are long-lived survivors that are readily activated if stimulated by a second invasion of the same antigen. They quickly produce more cytotoxic T-cells.

Chilling verification of the importance of helper T-cells comes to us from a relatively new saga in the story of infectious disease. Immunologists now believe that the deadly agent of AIDS (acquired immune deficiency syndrome) prefers to attack helper T-cells, thus devastating the immune system. Specifically, the AIDS virus is believed to genetically alter those genes in the helper T-cell that specify the vital surface recognition complex. This may be invasion in its most insidious form; although the defending army is still intact, the invader has quietly but inexorably removed the victim's ability to sound the alarm.

Suppressor T-cells. Once an invader has been successfully subdued, the task of shutting down the immune response goes to **suppressor T-cells.** The role is vital because, as we've seen, the immune response is self-amplifying (an example of positive feedback) and could easily soar out of control. Once the arousal subsides, the immense clones answering the call die off and eventually the only B- and T-cells remaining will be the "quieter," long-lived memory cells. The events described so far are often referred to as the **primary immune response.** While the primary response is being organized by the body, we may become quite ill as the invaders have their way. But given a little time and if all goes well, the offenders will be dealt with and we will recover. We are left weaker but "wiser," that is, our immune system is wiser. Such new wisdom is to be found in the memory B- and T-cells, which are responsible for what is called the **secondary immune response.**

Suppressor T-cells inhibit the immune response, leaving only memory T- and B-cell lymphocytes.

Memory Cells and the Secondary Immune Response

Memory cells have the ability to recognize the specific antigen that earlier aroused their sister cells. While the other activated B- and T-cell clones live short, busy lives, memory cells live on and on, perhaps for decades. This is important, for should the same invader show up a second time, it is immediately recognized, and the body's response is much quicker than before. A massive new army of B- and T-cells will soon arise and repel the second invasion. We may not even be aware of the renewed struggle, for symptoms of illness are often absent or quite mild. So, thanks to our memory cells, we suffer many diseases just once.

When the long-lived memory T- and B-cells recognize former invaders, they rapidly arouse the immune system bringing on a secondary immune response.

Active and passive immunization. When you got your first vaccinations your body was provided with shortcuts to the secondary immune response. You skipped most of the primary immune response because you developed **artificial active immunity.** The vaccine you received contained weakened or killed disease agents that promoted the primary immune response with little of the misery and risk of the actual disease. During this shortened response, banks of memory cells were produced as usual, but the aroused lymphocyte army, having found itself with little real work to do (no positive feedback going on), quickly retired. But had you later been confronted with the real disease agent, your immune system would have gone right into the streamlined secondary immune response, and the invader would never have known what hit it.

Where vaccines aren't available or where the disease has already begun, alternatives are possible. One is the injection of an **antiserum** containing the specific immunoglobins against the agent. Such immunoglobins are routinely obtained from animals exposed to the disease agent under carefully controlled laboratory conditions. When injected, the immunoglobins go about the task of immobilizing the invader's antigens. Since the immune system is not activated, this treatment is known as **passive immunization.** This, incidentally, is the only treatment available against the fatal rabies virus. Antibodies are short lived, so the protective effects are temporary.

We've still left a few questions unanswered, as you

ESSAY 40.1 RECOGNIZING "SELF"

The very capability that makes the immune system so versatile has within it the potential for disaster. Thus arises yet another of those endless questions: What keeps the immune system from reacting against proteins and other molecules in the very body in which it resides? There are two answers. First, the immune system must learn *not* to react against "self," a process called **immunological tolerance.** Second, sometimes the immune system does react against self, a response we will consider shortly. Let's first see how the immune system "learns."

At some determined time during the embryo's development, the many kinds of virgin lymphocytes begin to rove the body, essentially becoming familiar with their parent organism. But when a wandering cell finds a chemical match with its specific antigen recognition protein, it is not activated as happens in the primary immune response. Instead, it becomes permanently suppressed. The workings of the suppression process are unknown, but some evidence suggests that suppressor T-cells are involved. Once they have learned to identify self, they interact with B- and T-cells, preventing them from attacking the body. The accompanying figure illustrates an experiment that generally supports the notion of immunological learning.

Considering the enormous complexity of the immune system, it should be no surprise that it sometimes goes awry and reacts against self. Such a condition is called an **autoimmune disease.** Among the many known or suspected autoimmune diseases are arthritis, nephritis, rheumatic fever, systemic lupus erythematosis, various hormone disorders, certain forms of diabetes, and possibly even schizophrenia.

The source of at least some autoimmune diseases is the body's own response to infection. When antigens closely resemble the body's own chemistry, the immunoglobins produced may affect the body's tissues, bringing on a severe autoimmune reaction. The *Streptococcus* bacteria that cause "strep throat" are notorious for this. An infection in the throat creates antibodies that can attack tissue elsewhere, notably in the kidneys or heart valves, with serious and sometimes fatal results.

Experiments with larval tree frogs have verified that a developmental period of "self-identification" occurs that suppresses autoimmune responses. In this experiment, the pituitary gland of one tadpole has been transplanted to another early in development. Later, the pituitary is returned but is rejected as foreign tissue. Hypothetically, during the pituitary's absence, the young lymphocyte population completed its identification of self. In the control, only half the pituitary was removed, and when returned to its original owner, fails to provoke an immune response and is accepted as "self." This shows that the rejection was not based on changes that may have occurred while the pituitary was growing in the temporary host.

may have noticed. For instance, what is an immunoglobin and how does it actually do its work? How can so many different types arise? Further, how does the body provide for the incredible diversity needed in virgin lymphocytes? After all, there is a seemingly endless number of different antigens around. Certainly, recognition is the key to many of the answers, and recognition involves the immunoglobins and related cell surface recognition molecules.

Vaccines confer **artificial active immunity** by harmlessly stimulating the primary immune response. The administration of a specific **antiserum** (immunoglobulin) confers **passive immunity.**

IMMUNOGLOBIN STRUCTURE

Immunoglobins (or antibodies) are globular proteins, each containing at least four polypeptide chains. Because of the many ways the amino acids can be arranged in the chains, there is a great range of specificity. The basic four-part structure includes two identical **heavy** (long) **chains** of amino acids and two identical **light** (shorter) **chains,** arranged in a Y shape (Figure 40.5). The two double chains making up the Y contain a **constant region** (the stalk of the Y) and a **variable region** (the separate forks). Whereas the constant regions may be the same in thousands of different immunoglobins, the variable regions are different in each kind of immunoglobin. Variable

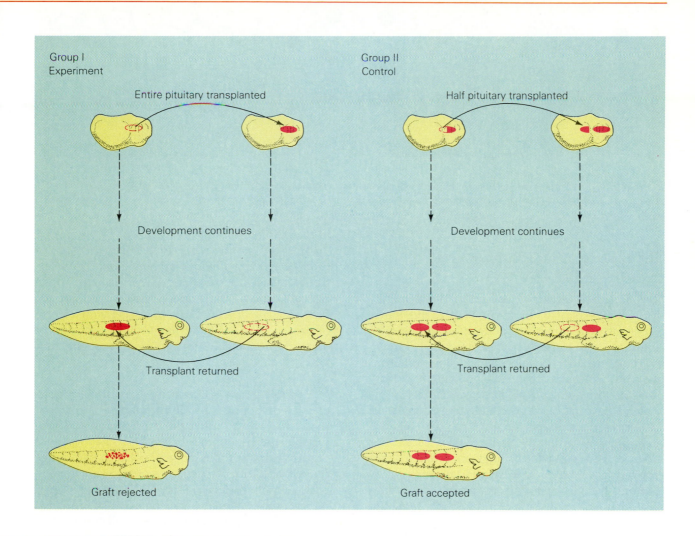

Group I
Experiment

Entire pituitary transplanted

Development continues

Transplant returned

Graft rejected

Group II
Control

Half pituitary transplanted

Development continues

Transplant returned

Graft accepted

regions, like the active sites of enzymes, have a highly specific shape, the **antigen recognition region,** which is capable of binding to its matching antigen only. Actually, because of their Y shape and two variable regions, immunoglobins can attach to two antigens at once. When many immunoglobins attach to many antigens, the foreign molecules agglutinate into great clumps (Figure 40.6). (The clumping process often gets a boost by the presence of complement, as mentioned earlier.)

Immunoglobins are Y-shaped globular proteins containing two short and two long chains. Two highly specific antigen recognition regions form matches with specific antigens.

FIGURE 40.5   In the Y-shaped immunoglobin, short and long amino acid chains are joined through disulfide bridges. Each has two specific antigen recognition regions at the tip of the Y.

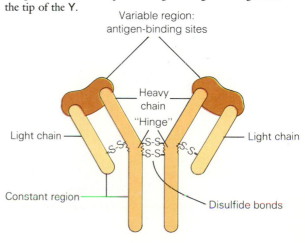

Variable region:
antigen-binding sites

Heavy
chain

"Hinge"

Light chain

Light chain

Constant region

Disulfide bonds

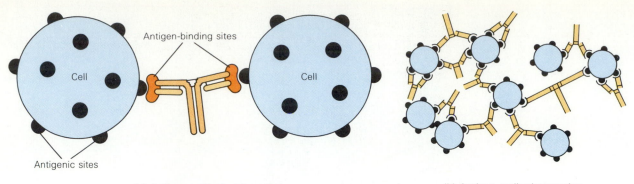

(a) Antigen-antibody interaction

(b) Antigen-antibody complex

FIGURE 40.6 Each immunoglobin can bind to two antigenic sites, in this instance on the surface of two cells. The resulting clumps of invading cells makes the work of phagocytic cells much more efficient.

The Source of Cell Surface and Immunoglobin Diversity

Now let's look into the question of the seemingly unlimited diversity of virgin lymphocytes and immunoglobins. Remember that antigen-presenting macrophages can be carrying virtually any kind of foreign molecule and, after touching many, many virgin lymphocytes, will almost invariably find one that recognizes the foreign molecule. How can this be?

As we have indicated, specific immunoglobins and cell surface recognition sites can be prepared that will react against virtually any large foreign molecule. For instance, when crocodile hemoglobin is injected into rabbits, the rabbit's B-cell lymphocytes respond by forming specific opposing antibodies. Does this mean that, somehow, some of the rabbit's lymphocytes are *preprogrammed to combat crocodile hemoglobin*? Why should this be? And if it's so (and it is), how does the immune system do it?

If we are to understand the genetic basis for immunoglobin diversity, we must shake off what we have come to accept as the "central dogma" (see Chapters 14 and 15). The central dogma holds that proteins are formed according to directions encoded in triplets of nucleotides established in DNA and this coding is passed intact, through faithful replication, from generation to generation. Although a mountain of data support this idea, in this instance the genetic coding for producing the endless variety of immunoglobins *is not inherited*.

According to current theory, the DNA responsible for the variable regions of immunoglobins and for cell surface proteins are generated from a small number of inherited genes, but these genes can be rearranged in nearly countless ways. Thus, during the development of lymphocytes, *gene rearrangement* provides the enormous genetic diversity necessary to produce so many kinds of immunoglobins and surface recognition molecules. (A few years ago, when our confidence in the central dogma was firming up, such a statement would have been met with a storm of protest. But today we know that genes are not quite the stable entities we once thought they were.)

Variable genes. Geneticists have actually located a few hundred "variable region gene segments," those that direct both light-chain and heavy-chain variable regions, but they believe there are thousands of such genes. A thousand genes of each type, when clipped out and rearranged, would give a million possible combinations (Figure 40.7). And so we harbor an army of lymphocytes (some 2×10^{12}), and the virgins of each clone bear on their cell surfaces one out of a million different recognition molecules. When a virgin cell is activated, it arouses its unique genome and begins producing its own special immunoglobin.

> The vast amount of diversity (immunoglobin and cell surface) in the immune system is not inherited but is provided for by specific rearrangements of variable genes.

Monoclonal Antibodies

Since 1976 it has been possible to grow clones of any plasma B-cell desired and, as a result, to obtain pure samples of the specific immunoglobins produced by that B-cell. Such immunoglobins are called **monoclonal antibodies,** proteins that have been very much in the news in recent years.

The first step in the manufacturing process is to use recombinant techniques to fuse a desired line of B-lymphocytes with B-lymphocyte myeloma cells—tumor cells that have lost the ability to produce antibody. Tumor cells do especially well in tissue culture; so well that their cell lines are sometimes referred to as "immortal." The fused cells, called **hybridomas,** then go on through their cell cycles, producing clones. And as is the case with plasma cells, each produces only one specific antibody, a "monoclonal" antibody.

The medical potential for monoclonal antibodies is staggering. Theoretically, one could order a supply of antibodies against any protein, whether in a viral coat, bacterial cell wall, or plasma membrane of a cancerous cell. The available antibody would be highly specific for whatever was causing any problem. Monoclonal antibodies also show great potential in getting specific cytotoxic (cell-killing) drugs to their specific target cells. Getting drugs into the desired cells and tissues is often a problem for the clinician, and using specific monoclonal antibodies as piggy-back carriers has great promise.

Through recombinant DNA technology and cell culturing, specific B-cell lymphocytes can be grown and useful quantities of pure, monoclonal antibodies extracted.

AIDS AND THE CRIPPLED IMMUNE SYSTEM

Over the past few years the new and terrible disease called **acquired immune deficiency syndrome (AIDS)** has gained worldwide attention. The problem results from suppression of the immune system. The symptoms may begin as a simple but persistent cold, but as the disease progresses AIDS victims grow increasingly susceptible to all sorts of diseases, even very rare ones. In fact, the appearance of some rare diseases, such as Kaposi's sarcoma and pneumocystic pneumonia, assists in identifying the condition in its later stages. By this time, unfortunately, such information is often more useful to the pathologist than to the patient.

The Growing AIDS Epidemic

The first cases of AIDS were recognized late in 1979. By mid-1986 the disease had appeared throughout most of the United States and in 100 other nations. Worldwide, it is estimated that 10 million persons have been infected by the virus, and it is feared that probably most will develop AIDS. (People can carry the virus for 10 years without expressing symptoms other than the presence of specific viral antibodies.)

By mid-1987, nearly 36,000 active cases of AIDS have been diagnosed in the U.S. and nearly 21,000

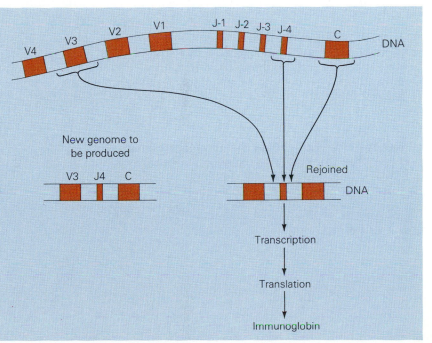

FIGURE 40.7 During their development, lymphocytes undergo seemingly unlimited kinds of gene rearrangement, resulting in their great diversity. A variable region gene (here, V3) is excised and joined to one of several joining genes. The two are then fused to the end of a larger gene, designated "C," the one responsible for the constant region of the immunoglobin. The new unique gene is then transcribed into mRNA, its introns removed, and translated into the polypeptides of an immunoglobin.

have died. Public Health Service authorities now believe that the virus is present in one out of 30 men between 20 and 50 years of age. While most AIDS victims are men, by mid-1987 some 2,000 women and several hundred children had the disease. (In Africa fully half the AIDS victims are women.) The highest risk group (about 66%) continues to be male homosexuals and bisexuals, followed by intravenous drug users (17%), hemophiliacs (8%), transfusion recipients (4%), and heterosexuals (4%). While the disease is just now making inroads into the heterosexual population, the next significant increase is expected to be in this group.

Fewer than 14% of AIDS victims survive for three years after onset of the condition. No treatment has been successful. Intensive research into AIDS is continuing, however, and some clues show promise as avenues of attack.

The Agent of AIDS

The agent of AIDS is almost exclusively transmitted through semen and unsanitary intravenous drug injection (generally, street drugs), but as mentioned, it has also been transmitted through routine medical blood transfusions and from mother to newborn. It can also enter the body if infected blood contacts even a slight open wound on the skin. Public health officials tell us that recently improved safeguards make the risk from transfusions extremely low. However, blood screening tests are still not 100% reliable.

> In AIDS, the immune system fails, and rare, fatal diseases appear. Although most frequently seen in homosexual and intravenous street drug users, AIDS is on the increase among heterosexuals.

Scientists now know that the agent is a human retrovirus (of the HTLV, or human T-lymphotrophic virus, group) that specifically attacks lymphocytes, preferring the T-cells. Apparently, the B-cells continue to function, actively producing antibody against the viral agent. In fact, the presence of the antibody is how AIDS carriers and those exposed to AIDS are identified. (In case you are wondering, the antibody is not enough to destroy the virus. Once the virus invades a cell, the intervention of T-cells is needed.) Let's see why the T-cells fail to act.

Retroviruses, you may recall (see Chapters 15 and 20), use reverse transcription to convert their RNA genes to DNA genes, which are then integrated into the DNA of the host chromosome. The new genes then play havoc with the host's genetic mechanisms. As we mentioned earlier, for T-cells to carry out the cell-mediated response, they must use a dual recognition process, one involving a match between antibody and antigen and the other a self-recognition match. Although some details are yet to be clarified, researchers now think that the AIDS retrovirus may produce an aberrant self-recognition site on helper T-cells, whereupon they fail in their primary task of identifying and activating other lymphocytes.

The virus may also interfere with the dual recognition processes essential to cytotoxic T-cells. Ordinarily, cytotoxic T-cells would simply seek out and destroy any virus infected cells, including afflicted helper T-cells. But the AIDS virus is truly insidious. Among the genes it alters are those specifying some of the helper T-cell's surface proteins, effectively disguising its infected state. Unhappily, the cytotoxic T-cell's dual recognition process fails, and the AIDS virus deftly escapes from the immune system safeguards.

> The agent of AIDS is a retrovirus: An RNA virus transcribes its genome into DNA, which then becomes integrated in the host genome. It is known to disrupt recognition sites on helper T-cells and cytotoxic T-cells.

SUMMARY

CHEMICAL DEFENSES: THE FRONT LINE

Histamine release from injured tissues produces an increase in blood flow resulting in inflammation. Kinins increase swelling, usually bringing on pain. Complement injures bacterial cells, causing lysis, prompts inflammation, and attracts neutrophils. Interferon blocks protein synthesis in virus-infected cells.

CELLULAR RESPONSES: ROVING DEFENDERS

Leukocytes carry out cellular responses. Natural killer cells identify and destroy abnormal (cancer) cells. Neutrophils, the most numerous white cells, act early in infections, engulfing invading cells. Monocytes undergo transformation into phagocytic macrophages which activate lymphocytes.

The Macrophage as an Antigen-Presenting Cell

Macrophages incorporate invader molecules in their plasma membranes, thereby becoming antigen-presenting cells. They activate T-cell lymphocytes with matching surface molecules.

Introducing the B-cell and T-cell Lymphocytes

B-cells specialize in the humoral response, producing and releasing specific immunoglobins. T-cells specialize in the cell-mediated response, identifying and killing invading and diseased cells.

AROUSING THE LYMPHOCYTES: THE PRIMARY IMMUNE RESPONSE

In the primary immune response, antigen-presenting cells making contact with helper T-cells secrete interleukin-1. The activated helper T-cells then seek out matching virgin lymphocytes, whereupon they secrete interleukin-2. In response, the virgin cells grow and differentiate into B-cells and T-cells, which then produce immense clones.

Aroused B-Cell Lymphocytes

B-cells synthesize and secrete specific immunoglobins that recognize and attach to invading cell surface antigens and free antigens, forming masses that are easily engulfed by phagocytes. Memory cells are held in reserve, activated only if reinfection occurs.

Aroused T-Cell Lymphocytes

Cytotoxic T-cells kill any invading and diseased cells whose surface antigens match their surface antibodies. Because of dual recognition complexes, friendly cells ("self") are avoided.

The immune response is amplified as helper T-cells arouse virgin lymphocytes, which give rise to additional helper T-cells. As invaders are subdued, suppressor T-cells inhibit the primary response.

Memory Cells and the Secondary Immune Response

When a second invasion occurs, memory B- and T-cells quickly form immense clones whose members immediately subdue the invader.

Artificial active immunity is brought about by the use of vaccines. They contain killed or weakened disease organisms that initiate the primary immune response without most of the disease symptoms. Passive immunity is conferred by the injection of antiserum, which contains active immunoglobins.

IMMUNOGLOBIN STRUCTURE

Immunoglobins contain paired heavy and light chains of amino acids that have constant and variable regions. The latter is the highly specific antigen recognition region that binds to matching antigen.

The Source of Cell Surface and Immunoglobin Diversity

The vast number of different cell surface recognition proteins and potential immunoglobins is attributed to the behavior of lymphocyte genes during development. Certain genes undergo rearrangement, during which each kind of lymphocyte has its variable gene segments rearranged in its own specific way. Because of the great numbers of rearrangements carried out, virtually any antigen can be matched by a lymphocyte.

Monoclonal Antibodies

Using recombinant DNA techniques researchers have been able to produce clones of B-lymphocytes that produce any desired immunoglobin.

AIDS AND THE CRIPPLED IMMUNE SYSTEM

AIDS is a condition in which the immune system fails to fight off disease. Victims often die of rare diseases.

The Growing AIDS Epidemic

AIDS, a worldwide problem, is concentrated primarily among homosexuals and users of intravenous street drugs, but is now increasing in the heterosexual population.

The Agent of AIDS

Common agents of transfer are semen and blood. The retroviral agent favors T-cells, particularly helpers. Following reverse transcription, the viral genes are inserted into the lymphocyte genome, effectively wrecking the vital dual recognition complex.

KEY TERMS

histamine
antihistamine
kinin
complement system
neutrophil
interferon
leukocyte
natural killer (NK) cell
eosinophil
neutrophil
monocyte
basophil
lymphocyte
macrophage
antigen-presenting macrophage

helper T-cell lymphocyte
B-cell lymphocyte
T-cell lymphocyte
antibody
immunoglobulin
humoral immune response
cell-mediated response
clonal selection theory
interleukin-1
lymphokine
interleukin-2
plasma cell
memory cell
cytotoxic T-cell
helper T-cell

suppressor T-cell
memory T-cell
primary immune response
secondary immune response
artificial active immunization
antiserum
passive immunization
heavy chain
light chain
constant region
variable region
antigen recognition region
monoclonal antibody
hybridomas
acquired immune deficiency
   syndrome (AIDS)

REVIEW QUESTIONS

1 List four chemical agents that help combat infection and briefly summarize their role. (pp. 635–636)

2 List the six types of leukocytes indicating which are the phagocytes. (p. 636)

3 Contrast the defensive roles of NK cells and neutrophils. (pp. 636–637)

4 Describe the change that occurs when a monocyte is activated at an infection site. What are two roles of these transformed cells? (p. 637)

5 Explain how a macrophage becomes an antigen-presenting cell. What does such a cell seek? (p. 637)

6 In what two general ways do activated lymphocytes respond? (p. 638)

7 What happens to an antigen-presenting cell when it identifies a matching helper T-cell? What is the helper T-cell's response? (p. 638)

8 Describe the effects of interleukin-2 on virgin lymphocytes. (p. 639)

9 What kinds of cells make up an activated B-cell clone? What is the specialized role of each of its kind? (p. 639)

10 In what way do immunoglobins participate in the immune response? (p. 639)

11 Discuss the work of the cytotoxic T-cell. (p. 639)

12 Describe the dual recognition mechanism of T-cells. Why is such a system vital? (p. 639)

13 Explain how helper T-cells amplify the primary immune response. Specifically, how might the agent of AIDS affect this function? (p. 641)

14 In what two different situations do suppressor T-cell carry out their functions? (p. 641)

15 Why is the secondary immune response so much faster than that of the primary response? (p. 641)

16 Briefly contrast artificial active and passive immunization. (p. 641)

17 Using a simple diagram, describe the typical immunoglobin, include light and heavy chains, disulfide bonding, constant regions and variable regions. Label the antigen recognition regions. (pp. 642–643)

18 What, if any, appear to be the limits in cell surface recognition and immunoglobin capabilities in lymphocytes? (p. 644)

19 Explain how gene rearrangement provides for the vast molecular diversity of lymphocytes. In what way does this seem to violate the central dogma? (p. 644)

20 What are potential ways in which monoclonal antibodies may be used? (pp. 644–645)

21 Is AIDS itself a disease? What actually kills the AIDS victim? (p. 645)

22 List, in descending order of risk, the four groups in which AIDS is most prevalent. (p. 646)

23 In what two specific ways is AIDS known to be transmitted? (p. 646)

24 Specifically, what is the AIDS agent? What specific cells does the agent favor? (p. 646)

25 How does this agent become part of the host genome? What is its effect on the host cell's functions? (p. 646)

The reproductive imperative of all living things is: "Reproduce or your genes will disappear from the population." This expresses nothing more than the unprejudiced arithmetic of evolution, and its meaning is deceptively simple: each generation is made up of the descendants of the reproducers of previous generations. Furthermore, most of the individuals of any generation are derived from the best reproducers of previous generations. Stated another way, natural selection favors traits that result in greater reproductive success. We will now look into some of the ways animals reproduce. As you might expect, they do so in a great number of ways and with a variety of techniques and strategies. Nonetheless, as usual among such diversity, there are underlying common themes.

REPRODUCTION IN REPRESENTATIVE ANIMALS

Asexual vs Sexual Reproduction

We are aware by now that animals may reproduce asexually (without sex) or sexually. **Asexual reproduction** involves just one individual and occurs through such processes as budding and binary fission (as we saw in *Hydra* and planaria) (Figure 41.1a; see also Chapter 27). Animals that reproduce asexually have the great advantage of each of their offspring carrying 100% of the parent's genes. (From an evolutionary perspective, reproduction involves simply getting one's genes into the next generation, and a parent that can produce offspring bearing all that parent's genes would seem to have an advantage.)

In many species, though, the parents "dilute" the genes in their offspring through **sexual reproduction,** in which copies of their own genes are combined with those of another individual. The main advantage of such dilution seems to be in increasing the variation in one's offspring so that, as a group, they are likely to succeed under a wide range of environmental conditions. Thus, as animals have dispersed over the earth, invading every nook and cranny and reproductively isolating themselves from other species, they have developed a great variety of techniques for getting their gametes together.

Asexual reproduction involves one individual and does not increase genetic variability. **Sexual reproduction** involves two individuals and promotes genetic variability.

41

REPRODUCTION

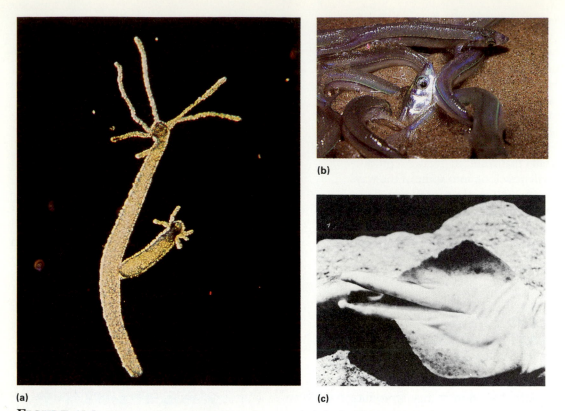

(a)

(b)

(c)

FIGURE 41.1 (a) Asexual reproduction in coelenterates includes budding, wherein miniature individuals arise from the bodies of others. Sexual reproduction may involve external fertilization as seen in the Pacific grunion **(b)**, a fish that comes ashore to reproduce. Internal fertilization occurs in all environments. The claspers of the male shark **(c)** serve as a penis. The male inserts them into the female's cloaca and ejects his sperm along the groove they form.

Modes of Sexual Reproduction

External fertilization. Perhaps the least intimate means of joining eggs and sperm is found among aquatic animals that simply discharge their gametes into the water, leaving the rest to chance. When all goes well, the gametes join in **external fertilization** (fertilization that takes place outside the body). Because the chances of fertilization are small, such species release very large numbers of gametes. There are ways to increase the likelihood of success, however, for example, by some coordination in space and time, that is, by the sexes coming together for mating. Such timing is everything to the grunion, a small fish that squirms ashore on California beaches on certain nights each year, generally at a peak tide (Figure 41.1b). The females frantically dig depressions in which they lay their eggs as males curl around them, releasing their sperm. The adult fish are then washed back out to sea with the next waves, but the eggs remain buried in the sand where they develop. At the next high tide the hatched young are carried out by receding waves.

Internal fertilization. With **internal fertilization,** sperm and egg join within the female body. Accordingly, animals need not produce prodigious numbers of eggs and sperm (thereby conserving some energy), although they may need to develop elaborate mating behaviors to bring the partners together. Internal fertilization, of course, requires some form of copulation. In copulation, the male penis (or some counterpart), is inserted into the female vagina or cloaca (or some variation of these receptacles), and the sperm are released. Copulatory organs vary enormously with seemingly no relationship to advances in other systems. The penis is well-formed in flatworms, but sharks rely on specialized parts of the pelvic fins, the claspers, for sperm transfer. And although birds are even more recent evolutionary arrivals, males lack copulatory organs (with a few exceptions). However, sperm are transferred quite successfully through the simple but precarious act of briefly pressing cloacas together (some do it while flying).

Some of the mating practices of animals can only be regarded bizarre by human standards. For example, in the bedbug (which, as ladies and gentlemen, you have certainly never seen) the male thrusts his sharp penis directly through the back of the female. The female can survive only a few matings. Some snails stimulate each other by thrusting sharp darts into each other's bodies before mutually exchanging sperm through enormous penises that emerge from over the eye. Other snails start off as wandering males that gradually slow their pace to become sessile females, waiting to be found by a younger male before he, too, changes. In some fish, males do not exist. A female entices a male of another species to mate with her, but his sperm only stimulate her eggs to develop; they do not actually fertilize them. In certain mites the females are born pregnant, having been ravaged by their brothers while still in the uterus. Others are impregnated seconds after being born, probably wondering as they crawl away, what kind of place is this, anyway?

Although there are various means of mating and reproduction, the principle remains the same: perpetuating one's genes by passing them to a new generation. Now we will focus on the reproductive patterns of the usual representative species and see, up close and personal, how it goes about perpetuating itself.

In **external fertilization,** eggs and sperm are released outside the body, generally in water. Large numbers of gametes are often involved. **Internal fertilization** is generally accomplished through **copulation,** wherein the male deposits sperm directly into the female's reproductive tract.

HUMAN REPRODUCTION

Compared to some mammalian species, the reproductive system of *Homo sapiens* seems rather ordinary. It is, in fact, almost identical to those of the other primates. However, humans do have some unique traits, such as an extremely high level of sexuality (see Essay 41.1), nonseasonal sexual behavior, and, in the male, an inordinately large penis for a primate.

Males

In men, the external genitalia include the **penis** and the paired **testes** (singular, **testis**), or testicles, suspended in the saclike **scrotum** (Figure 41.2a). The penis consists of a cylindrical shaft ending in the enlarged **glans,** with the urethral opening at its tip. It is an extremely sensitive organ with an abundance of touch receptors, especially around the glans.

During sexual excitement the penis becomes erect, lengthening and thickening (Figure 41.2b) and curving upward as its spongy **erectile tissues** fill with blood. These changes occur because the flow of arterial blood entering the penis increases, while venous outflow is retarded. Erection is brought about chiefly through a spinal reflex action, especially in response to touch, but higher brain centers intercede significantly through erotic thought, odors, sounds, and visual images. When erection occurs, the glans emerges from the **foreskin,** unless the foreskin has been removed by circumcision. Physical stimulation then brings on **ejaculation,** the release of sperm-bearing **semen.**

Blood trapped in spongy **erectile tissue** of the **penis** produces the erect state needed for copulation.

The testes and sperm production. Sperm and male sex hormones are produced in the testes. In many mammals, these dense oval bodies descend during the mating season and are withdrawn into the safer region of the body cavity when the season ends. But in humans the testes normally descend permanently shortly before birth. Their descent into the scrotum is essential, since developing sperm are quite heat sensitive and the scrotum is cooler than the higher internal body temperatures. The scrotum can also help regulate the temperature of the testes. In response to heat, its slender muscles relax, permitting the testes to descend away from the body, where it is cooler. Cold causes the scrotum to tighten and contract, drawing the testes closer to the warm body.

Much of the tissue of the testes consists of highly coiled **seminiferous tubules** (Figure 41.3a). It is from very active tissue lining the seminiferous tubules—the **germinal epithelium**—that sperm are formed. Following meiosis, each haploid daughter cell becomes a **spermatid,** an immature form of sperm cell. Spermatids lie embedded in supporting and nourishing **Sertoli cells,** while they complete their development (Figure 41.3b). Even then, sperm cannot enter into fertilization until they undergo a final period of maturation in the **epididymis,** a sperm storage structure perched above and along one side of the testes. The epididymis is formed by the union

Because of the pioneering research efforts of William H. Masters and Virginia E. Johnson of the Reproductive Biology Research Foundation in St. Louis, our knowledge of human sexual behavior is far more precise then it was before. Using volunteers, Masters and Johnson carefully monitored and recorded the physiological changes that occur during intercourse and orgasm.

Masters and Johnson described four phases of sexual response during intercourse. They labeled them **arousal, plateau, orgasm,** and **resolution.** Arousal is characterized in both sexes by increased heart rate, blood pressure, and breathing rate. In women, the response is quite pronounced: the clitoris enlarges and becomes more sensitive, the labia majora elevate and part, and the labia minora redden and increase in size. Meanwhile, secretions lubricate the vagina. In men, excitement causes the penis to become erect. Secretions of the bulbourethral glands moisten the glans. The scrotum may elevate and become firmer. Now the penis may readily be inserted into the vagina.

During the excitement stage, the plateau phase may be reached. This may last for some minutes and is marked by an increased intensity in the level of pleasure. Either partner may begin involuntary thrusts of the pelvis as various muscles contract. The uterus may elevate and tilt backward at this time. Interestingly, the clitoris may become smaller and recede into its hood, having become exquisitely sensitive to touch.

Orgasm is an intensely pleasurable sensation that accompanies complex contractions of several voluntary and involuntary muscles. In women, the contractions begin in the pelvic floor and surge through the vagina and uterus. In both men and women, involuntary orgasmic contractions occur at about 0.8-second intervals. In women, the upper part of the vagina may expand as the cervix moves downward (called "tenting"), a response that may help draw semen into the uterus.

In men, orgasm accompanies ejaculation, which involves rhythmic, involuntary contractions of the vas deferens, seminal vesicles, and prostate gland. The semen, containing its hordes of sperm, is forced into the urethra. The semen may be ejected from the penis in spurts, often propelled with considerable force by powerful muscles at the base of the penis.

Orgasm in men and women is compared in the accompanying figure. The most obvious difference between female (**a**) and male (**b**) orgasm is in the orgasmic peaks. Some women normally experience a single orgasm (3), but multiple orgasms are quite commonplace. These may occur as several minor episodes (2), or as fewer but more intense ones (1). In men, a single orgasm is the rule, followed by at least a partial state of resolution.

Resolution is apparently more pronounced in men than in women. At this time, erection may be lost rapidly, and most men cannot be aroused again for a time. The length of the resolution period is highly variable and usually depends on a number of factors. Resolution is more gradual in women, and immediate rearousal is often possible. This is often a quiet, relaxed, tender time that can provide pleasure of its own.

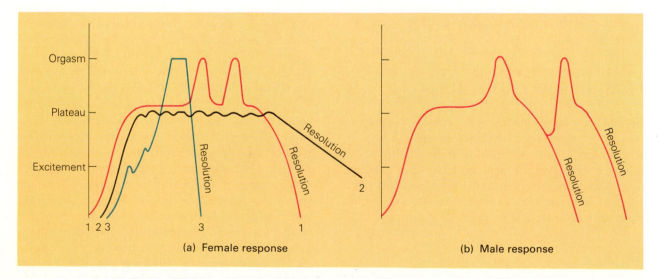

(a) Female response   (b) Male response

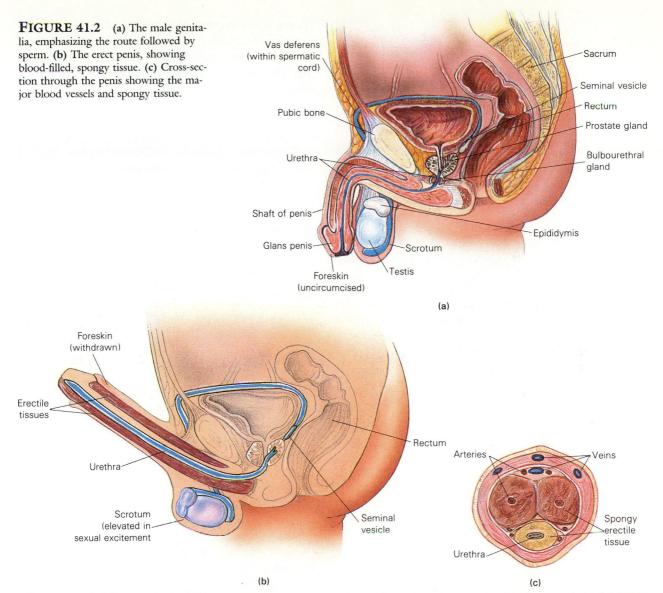

FIGURE 41.2 (a) The male genitalia, emphasizing the route followed by sperm. (b) The erect penis, showing blood-filled, spongy tissue. (c) Cross-section through the penis showing the major blood vessels and spongy tissue.

Vas deferens (within spermatic cord)

Pubic bone

Urethra

Shaft of penis

Glans penis

Foreskin (uncircumcised)

Sacrum

Seminal vesicle

Rectum

Prostate gland

Bulbourethral gland

Epididymis

Scrotum

Testis

(a)

Foreskin (withdrawn)

Erectile tissues

Urethra

Scrotum (elevated in sexual excitement

Rectum

Seminal vesicle

(b)

Arteries

Veins

Spongy erectile tissue

Urethra

(c)

of many seminiferous tubules. Supporting tissue surrounding the seminiferous tubules contains **interstitial cells,** whose specialization is manufacturing the male sex hormone **testosterone.**

Sperm pathway. Prior to ejaculation, the sperm are propelled to the urethra by the wavelike action of smooth muscles and cilia lining the epididymis and **vas deferens.** The latter is a slender duct that extends from the epididymis to the urethra (joined, of course, by its counterpart from the other testis). The vas deferens, along with nerves and blood vessels, and an outer sheath make up the **spermatic cord.**

Near the urethra, the sperm receive fluids from two glands, the **seminal vesicles** and the **prostate gland.** The seminal vesicles add fluid containing fructose (fruit sugar), which provides the sperm with an energy source. The prostate produces an alkaline

secretion that gives semen its characteristic thickness and odor. (The increased alkalinity later helps neutralize the vagina's acidic fluids.) The male urethra carries both urine and semen, but during sexual excitement the urine-releasing muscle sphincter below the bladder is involuntarily contracted. During sexual excitement and prior to ejaculation, the **bulbourethral glands** secrete clear slippery mucus into the urethra, lubricating the glans and adding lubricant to the semen. During ejaculation, powerful rhythmic contractions propel semen through the urethra.

Sperm passing through the **vas deferens** receive secretions from the **seminal vesicles** and **prostate** as **semen** forms. Upon ejaculation the semen is propelled through the **urethra.**

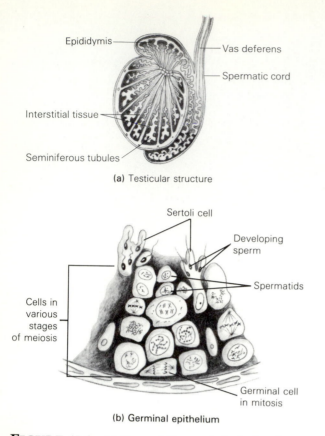

(a) Testicular structure

(b) Germinal epithelium

FIGURE 41.3 **(a)** The seminiferous tubules lead to the epididymis, whose duct continues as the vas deferens. Spermatogenesis occurs in the germinal epithelium **(b)** where cells in all stages of meiosis can be seen. Spermatids come to reside within Sertoli cells as they complete their development. The scanning electron micrograph of a seminiferous tubule nicely illustrates the germinal cells and sperm (tails).

Females

In women, the external genitalia are collectively known as the **vulva** (Figure 41.4). The most prominent part is the hair-covered **mons veneris,** a fatty mound overlying the bony pubic arch. Below the mons veneris lie the outer folds of the vulva, the **labia majora** (major lips), which cover a number of sensitive structures. Just within the labia majora are the less prominent, thinner folds of the **labia minora** (minor lips). These join at their upper margins, forming a kind of hood over a small, sensitive prominence, the **clitoris.** The clitoris is derived from essentially the same embryonic tissue as is the glans of the penis. The two are both erectile and have a rich supply of sensory receptors. In an excited state, the clitoris becomes erect, firm, and highly sensitive.

Enclosed by the labia minora, and near their lower border, lies the vaginal opening, the **introitus.** The introitus may be partially blocked by a membrane

known as the **hymen.** The strength of this membrane varies considerably, and its rupture, perhaps by the first intercourse, may produce discomfort and bleeding. The urethral opening in females lies just above the vaginal opening.

The **vulva** includes protective outer and inner lips, or **labia,** the sensitive, erectile **clitoris,** and the vaginal opening, or **introitus.**

Internal anatomy. The internal anatomy of the human female reproductive system includes the **vagina,** the **uterus,** the **ovaries,** and the **oviducts** (or Fallopian tubes) (Figure 41.5a). The vagina, a distendable tube about 8 cm (3 in) long when relaxed, receives the penis during intercourse and is the passageway through which birth occurs. It is well adapted for both functions, with its highly folded, muscular walls and a lining that secretes a lubricating mucus.

The vagina leads to a soft, muscular, pear-shaped organ, the **uterus,** which is capable of great expansion. The lower tip of the uterus, called the **cervix,** extends slightly into the vagina. The uterus is lined by a soft, vascular **endometrium,** which will receive the embryo should fertilization occur.

The **oviducts** emerge from each side of the upper end of the uterus, extend outward and downward toward the **ovaries,** and terminate in movable, fingerlike **fimbriae.** Although the ovaries produce the eggs, they do not directly connect with the oviducts. Instead, currents produced by the beating fimbriae draw eggs into the oviduct, where they are then swept along toward the uterus by cilia and by muscular contractions.

Internal female reproductive anatomy includes the **vagina, cervix, uterus, oviducts,** and **ovaries.**

The ovary and egg production. Like the testes, the ovaries produce both gametes and hormones. Each oval-shaped ovary is about 2.5 cm (1 in) long (Figure 41.6). The egg cells, actually **oocytes,** are produced in the germinal epithelium. At puberty the ovaries contain a total of about 400,000 oocytes, a surprisingly large number considering how few can ever be fertilized. You may recall from our discussion

FIGURE 41.4 The vulva—external female genitalia.

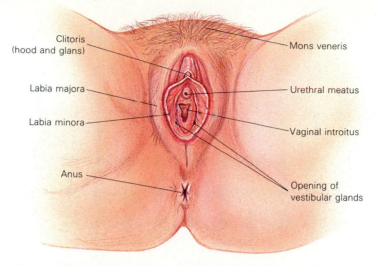

Clitoris (hood and glans)

Mons veneris

Labia majora

Urethral meatus

Labia minora

Vaginal introitus

Anus

Opening of vestibular glands

FIGURE 41.5 **(a)** The internal reproductive structures in the human female. **(b)** The scanning electron microscope reveals the numerous cilia that line the oviduct and help move sperm along to the egg. (Photo from *Tissues and organs: a text-atlas of scanning electron microscopy,* by Richard G. Kessel and Randy N. Kardon. W. H. Freeman and Company, copyright © 1979.)

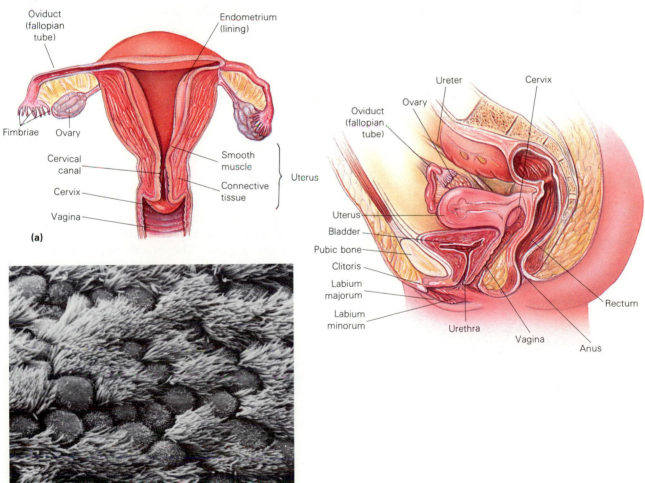

Oviduct (fallopian tube)

Endometrium (lining)

Fimbriae   Ovary

Cervical canal

Cervix

Vagina

Smooth muscle

Connective tissue

Uterus

(a)

Ureter   Cervix

Oviduct (fallopian tube)   Ovary

Uterus

Bladder

Pubic bone

Clitoris

Labium majorum

Labium minorum

Urethra

Vagina

Rectum

Anus

(b)

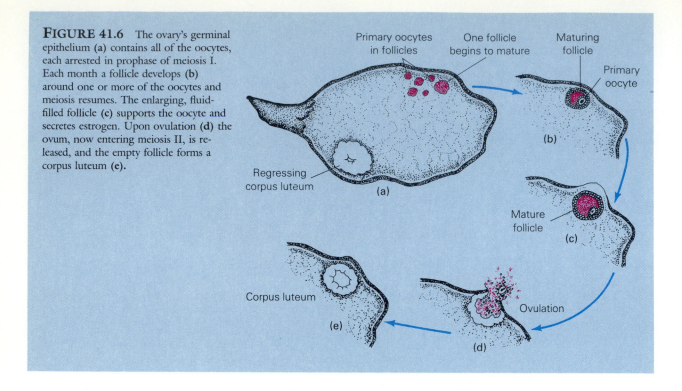

FIGURE 41.6 The ovary's germinal epithelium (**a**) contains all of the oocytes, each arrested in prophase of meiosis I. Each month a follicle develops (**b**) around one or more of the oocytes and meiosis resumes. The enlarging, fluid-filled follicle (**c**) supports the oocyte and secretes estrogen. Upon ovulation (**d**) the ovum, now entering meiosis II, is released, and the empty follicle forms a corpus luteum (**e**).

of meiosis (see Chapter 10) that the oocytes are produced during embryonic development; they remain inactive, suspended in prophase I of meiosis. A few are activated each month by pituitary hormones. The activated oocytes tend to suppress each other hormonally so that one usually gains a developmental advantage, and it alone matures. The release of mature eggs from the ovary is referred to as **ovulation.** We will look into fertilization in the next chapter.

> Unlike sperm, which are produced continuously, all eggs form during fetal development. A monthly cycle provides a steady supply of mature eggs as meiosis resumes and **ovulation** occurs.

HORMONES AND HUMAN REPRODUCTION

Sex hormones undoubtedly play an extremely important role in our lives. They determine not only our sex but our sexual behavior, our sexual development, and our sexual physiology as well. An increasing body of evidence implies that they also play a role in aggressiveness. Their effects are particularly obvious during puberty, when sexual differences between girls and boys are emphasized. At full sexual maturity, these hormones cause the continued production of sex cells as well as an increased sex drive. They begin to wane at about the time we enter our "golden years." The timing appears to be adaptive since a couple who conceived at too late an age might not live long enough to raise their child.

The sex-regulating hormones in both males and females are primarily produced in the pituitary gland and the gonads. The brain's hypothalamus (see Chapter 35) helps to regulate them by sensing the level of gonadal hormones in the blood and increasing or decreasing their secretion by the pituitary through a negative feedback system.

Prompted by the hypothalamus, the anterior lobe of the pituitary releases two hormones into the blood of both males and females: **FSH (follicle-stimulating hormone),** and **LH (luteinizing hormone,** in males called **interstitial cell–stimulating hormone,** or **ICSH**). Both are important to human reproduction.

> Sex-regulating hormones from the pituitary and gonads are important to physical and sexual development and to sex drive.

Hormonal Control in Males

FSH in men causes the seminiferous tubules to increase their meiotic activity and sperm to differentiate. LH stimulates the interstitial tissues that lie in the outer region of the tubules to produce testosterone, which also stimulates sperm production. In the adolescent male, testosterone initiates a number of changes. For instance, the voice deepens (or "cracks" in an embarrassingly intermittent manner), body hair appears, and bones and muscles enlarge, as do the penis and testicles, all heralding the difficult and puzzling years of puberty. While it is known that increasing levels of testosterone inhibit continued LH secretion through negative feedback, the factors controlling FSH are not clear.

Hormonal Control in Females

FSH and LH alter the **ovarian follicles,** the groups of cells surrounding the oocytes. Briefly, under the influence of these hormones, the follicles begin to grow, the oocytes resume meiosis, and the ovaries begin to secrete the hormones **estrogen** and **progesterone.** Estrogen and progesterone primarily affect the uterus, where the life-supporting lining, the endometrium, is prepared to receive an embryo if fertilization occurs. As we will see, the cycles of FSH and LH are closely correlated with changes in the uterus at the time of ovulation.

Estrogen is also responsible for the changes that girls undergo at puberty. Worldwide, puberty begins anywhere from nine to 13 years of age (the average age in the United States is now 12.8 years). Estrogen causes the breasts and nipples to enlarge, the hips to broaden, and a layer of fatty tissue to collect under the skin. Less noticeably, estrogen prompts the growth of the uterus, thickens the vaginal lining, and causes enlargement of the vulva. Estrogen cannot be credited for all pubertal changes, however. For example, body hair in women, usually restricted to the armpits and pubic region, is under control of the "male hormone," testosterone, which is produced by the adrenal cortex.

Ovarian and Menstrual Cycles

Puberty in girls is marked by the onset of the **ovarian** and **menstrual cycles,** during which the pituitary and ovarian hormones rise and fall—haltingly at first, but soon reaching a cyclic regularity. Cooperatively, they initiate conditions leading to the menstrual cycle. The sex drive also may increase sharply at puberty but (fortunately for concerned parents) it will not peak for several more years. Actual fertility, the physical ability to conceive, ordinarily follows the first menstrual flow, or "period," by about two years.

The ovarian cycle (Figures 41.7 and 41.8) is one of the more fascinating and important aspects of human sexuality. It is closely keyed to two related events: (1) the maturation and release of an egg cell; and (2) the thickening of the **endometrium** (uterine lining) in preparation for implantation of an embryo. Since these events involve different hormones acting in a highly coordinated and complex way, things can become a bit complicated. For convenience, let's break this 28-day cycle into two parts, bearing in mind that while the events are clear enough, the causal relationships remain hypothetical.

> During the **ovarian** and **menstrual cycles,** hormones correlate the timing of ovulation and fertilization with preparations in the uterus for receiving the embryo.

Days 1 through 14. The first day ("day 1") of the cycle is marked by the onset of **menstruation.** In the absence of pregnancy the endometrium begins to slough away, causing several days' bleeding as delicate capillaries rupture. Now the pituitary begins to secrete FSH (and some LH), stimulating the growth of an ovarian follicle and its oocyte. After a few days, the cells of the follicle begin to release estrogen, causing the uterine lining to undergo **growth** and **repair,** beginning the events that prepare the endometrium for an embryo. At about day 14, the estrogen in the blood reaches a critical level that, probably by negative feedback, slows the activity of the hypothalamus (see Figure 41.8a).

As the hypothalamus reduces its stimulation of the pituitary, FSH secretion diminishes and the pituitary dramatically increases the release of LH (see Figure 41.8b). As LH begins to stimulate the ovary, the follicle releases its egg (ovulation). Ovulation occurs at midcycle, and the event is marked by a slight, temporary rise in body temperature of about 0.3°C (0.6°F). (Awareness of this temperature change is important for women using the rhythm method of birth control.) Normally, ovulation occurs on day 14, and by then the endometrium has been growing for about 10 days.

> The cycle begins as increasing FSH stimulates follicle development and estrogen secretion. Estrogen later stimulates growth of the endometrium. The release of LH brings on ovulation.

FIGURE 41.7 Graphic representation of the menstrual cycle. The endometrium undergoes growth and repair during the first 14 days and reaches its fullest development a short time later. At midcycle (day 14) body temperature is slightly elevated, a fairly reliable indicator of ovulation.

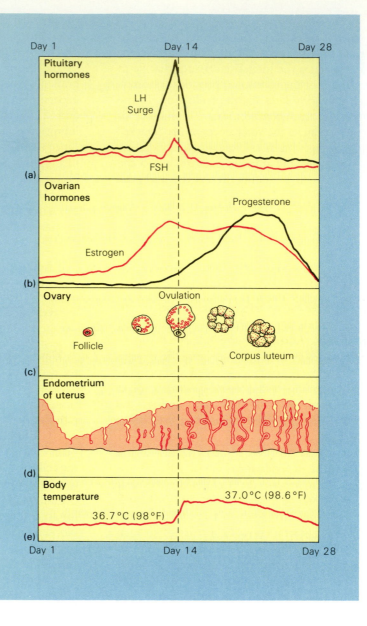

Days 15 through 28. After ovulation, cells of the vacated follicle undergo change, forming what is called the **corpus luteum** ("yellow body"). Under the influence of LH, the corpus luteum continues to secrete estrogen and increases its secretion of **progesterone** (see Figure 41.8c). Progesterone and estrogen together help bring the endometrium to a thick, fluid-filled, glandular state, fully prepared to receive an embryo. Should an embryo actually implant (attach) in the uterine wall (see Chapter 42), its membranes will begin to release a hormone, **human chorionic gonadotropin,** that enters the mother's bloodstream and imitates LH—prompting the continued release of progesterone from the corpus luteum. (The presence of HCG is the basis for most pregnancy tests.) After about two months, the source of progesterone will be the placenta. Progesterone is present throughout pregnancy.

In the cycle's second half, LH stimulates the **corpus luteum** to secrete progesterone and estrogen, further supporting endometrial growth.

FIGURE 41.8 **(a)** Hormonal control of the ovarian cycle. From day 1 to 14, FSH and estrogen dominate the cycle, bringing on follicle development and endometrial growth and repair. At midcycle **(b)**, negative feedback brings on a pituitary shift to LH secretion. LH stimulates ovulation and the development of a corpus luteum. From days 15 to 28 **(c)**, LH, estrogen, and progesterone dominate the cycle, bringing the endometrium to a fully receptive, glandular state. Without the implantation of an embryo the hormones diminish and the cycle ends.

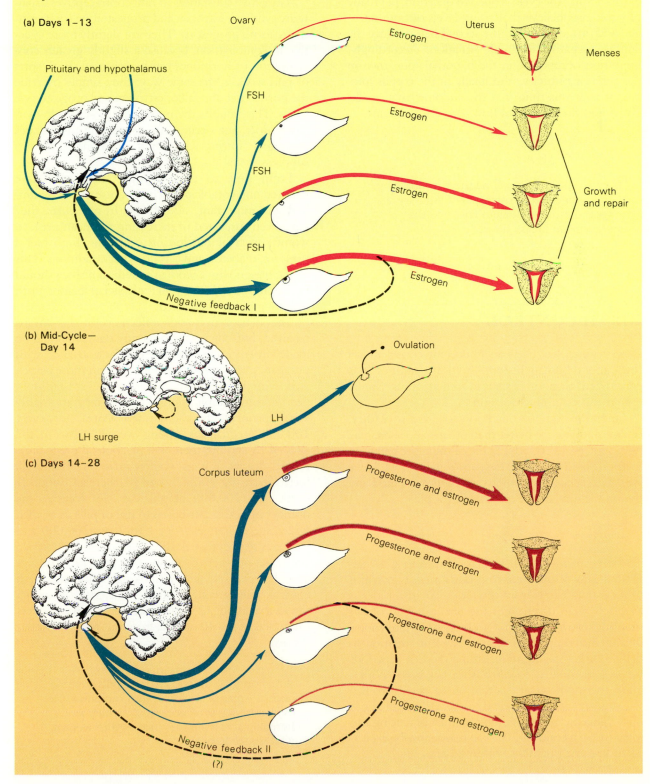

(a) Days 1–13

Ovary

Uterus

Estrogen

Pituitary and hypothalamus

Menses

FSH

Estrogen

FSH

Estrogen

Growth and repair

FSH

Negative feedback I

Estrogen

(b) Mid-Cycle— Day 14

Ovulation

LH

LH surge

(c) Days 14–28

Corpus luteum

Progesterone and estrogen

Progesterone and estrogen

Progesterone and estrogen

Negative feedback II (?)

Progesterone and estrogen

In the absence of pregnancy, the corpus luteum will begin to wither by day 26 or so, and progesterone levels will begin to fall. Without progesterone, the endometrium will start to deteriorate, bringing on menstruation. The precise sequence of hormonal events ending the cycle is open to question, but many physiologists believe that rising levels of both estrogen and progesterone in the second half produce the familiar negative feedback situation. Accordingly, inhibition occurs first in the hypothalamus, then in the anterior pituitary, and finally in the corpus luteum. It is at this time that the endometrium breaks down and the menstrual flow, or period, begins.

> Toward the cycle's end, negative feedback by progesterone and estrogen slows pituitary output, the corpus luteum fails, and the endometrium breaks down.

BIRTH CONTROL

Birth control has been an important consideration throughout human history. In some cultures it is considered a moral issue; in others, it is almost entirely an economic decision.

Since methods of birth control vary so widely, obviously some are better than others, and some may have serious side effects. Some of the more common methods used today are described in Table 41.1; we will give special attention to the rhythm method and the oral contraceptive (birth control pills).

The Rhythm Method

The **rhythm method** has been referred to as a "natural" means of birth control, but some say that this distorts the definition of the term. The main idea is that a woman determines the fertile period of her monthly ovarian cycle and abstains from intercourse during that time. This requires careful attention to daily routine (including recording menstrual periods for several months to establish a baseline). With a good thermometer and attention to detail, women with *very regular* cycles reach a success rate of about 80%. This means that among women practicing this form of birth control, 20% can reasonably be expected to become pregnant within a year.

Birth Control Pills

The **birth control pill** is among the most widely used and most effective of all contraceptives available today (success rate of up to 99%). It is now being used by about 100 million women worldwide.

The active substances in oral contraceptives usually are synthetic estrogen and progesterone (or its synthetic form, progestin). They are slightly more effective in combination, because a slightly greater concentration of hormones can be achieved. Both sorts of pills work in the same way: they simply override the normal rise and fall of estrogen and progesterone levels. This inhibits the midcycle LH surge, so ovulation does not occur. In a sense, the pill mimics pregnancy, during which high hormone levels also suppress ovulation.

From time to time, birth control pills have received unfavorable publicity because of certain limited, but important, side effects. In particular, they have been suspected of increasing the health risk to women with blood-clotting problems, high blood pressure, diabetes, and certain other conditions. This is one reason why a woman's medical history should be carefully studied by her physician before birth control pills are prescribed.

The debate over side effects is by no means resolved, but one point about any danger should be made: in *every* age group, the risks associated with pregnancy are significantly greater than those associated with taking birth control pills. In addition, deaths from complications of pregnancy are highly age dependent. In the United States, for every 100,000 pregnancies among women between the ages of 15 and 30, there will be about 7 pregnancy-related deaths. But as women grow older the risk increases steadily, until by age 40, there are about 21 deaths per 100,000 pregnancies. By contrast the number of deaths attributed to use of pills in women under age 35 ranges from 1 to 2 per 100,000 and increases to about 4 per 100,000 as women approach age 40. A number of factors may influence such figures. For example, heavy smoking by users of birth control pills greatly increases the risk. Research shows that about 12 of every 100,000 heavy smokers using pills at age 40 will die from pill-related complications.

> The hormones in birth control pills override normal negative feedback, thus inhibiting ovulation. Risks of side effects, which are normally acceptable, are increased in women who smoke heavily.

TABLE 41.1 Methods of Birth Control

Method	Application	Effectiveness	Drawbacks
Surgical Intervention (by qualified medical persons)			
Abortion (vacuum aspiration, up to 20 wks)	Cervix dilated, embryo and placenta removed by scraping or suction	Virtually 100%, hospital stay not required	Psychological effect common; strongly controversial
Abortion (saline injection, after 16 wks)	Saline (NaCl) solution injected into uterine cavity; labor and expulsion of fetus and placenta ensues	Usually 100%	Psychological effect; some risk from saline poisoning
Sterilization			
Vasectomy	Incisions through scrotum, section of ductus deferens removed and remainder tied	Virtually 100%, sometimes reversible	Some psychological effects
Tubal ligation	Incision through abdominal wall, oviducts cut and tied; sperm cannot reach egg	Nearly 100%	Not reversible; newer microtechniques produce less surgical risk
Chemical and/or Mechanical Intervention (with advice of qualified physician when needed)			
Oral contraceptives (the Pill)	Estrogen and progestins or progestin alone (minipill); taken daily, prevents ovulation	95%–99%	Costly; must be prescribed and monitored by physician; temporary side effects; greater risk to heavy smokers
Diaphragm with spermicide	Rubber dome; fits over cervix; blocks sperm; spermicide kills sperm	98% with spermicide and completely regimented use	Must be fitted by physician; strong motivation required; somewhat messy
Condom	Rubber sheath worn over penis	70%–93%, depending on quality and strict usage	Requires strong motivation since it is interruptive
Spermicide alone (foams, jellies, creams, or suppositories)	Placed in vagina with applicator before each intercourse; kills sperm	About 90% when properly used; otherwise, about 75%	Generally messy and short-lived (newer foams somewhat better); interruptive
Rhythm (natural method)	Intercourse avoided during carefully determined fertile period	Under ideal conditions, about 80%	Requires great motivation; fails when cycles are irregular
Douche	Vagina flushed with water or chemical solution (vinegar common) after intercourse	Below 60%	Slightly better than no precautions—in other words, worthless
Sponge	Polyurethane sponge saturated with spermicide placed in vagina before intercourse	Believed to be same as diaphragm (98%), but data not yet available	Interruptive; reliability not proven; implicated in toxic shock syndrome
Coitus Interruptus			
(Withdrawal)	Penis withdrawn just before ejaculation	About 70%	Mental stress for both partners; sperm can leak prior to ejaculation

SUMMARY

REPRODUCTION IN REPRESENTATIVE ANIMALS

Asexual vs Sexual Reproduction

Asexual reproduction occurs through budding, binary fission, and regeneration. One individual is involved so there is no genetic recombination. Sexual reproduction involves two individuals and genetic recombination occurs.

Modes of Sexual Reproduction

In external fertilization, gametes (often large numbers) are shed into the surroundings where fertilization and development occur.

Internal fertilization (fewer gametes) requires some form of copulation. Typical copulatory organs are the penis and vagina, although numerous variations exist. Mating behavior also varies greatly.

HUMAN REPRODUCTION

Males

Male external genitalia includes the penis, testes, and scrotum. Spongy erectile tissue in the penile shaft and glans make erection possible.

Sperm originate in germinal epithelium that lines the seminiferous tubules of the testes and develop within Sertoli cells. Storage and further maturation occur in the epididymis. Testosterone is produced in interstitial tissue surrounding the tubules.

Sperm pass through the vas deferens, joined by semen that forms from secretions of the seminal vesicles and prostate. In ejaculation, muscular contraction propels semen through the urethra.

Females

The female external genitalia (vulva) includes the mons veneris, labia majora, labia minora, clitoris, and vaginal introitus (opening). The highly sensitive clitoris contains erectile tissue.

Internal anatomy includes the distendable, tube-like vagina that extends to the cervix, the thickened opening of the uterus. The uterine endometrium is a temporary lining in which an embryo can implant. Oocytes, formed in the embryo, mature in the germinal epithelium of the ovary prior to ovulation. They are carried to the oviducts by waving fimbrae and cilia, where fertilization takes place.

HORMONES AND HUMAN REPRODUCTION

Sex hormones determine sex, influence sexual behavior, and bring on developmental changes during puperty. Their release by the gonads is regulated by the pituitary hormones, FSH and LH (ICSH in males).

Hormonal Control in Males

FSH stimulates sperm development and ICSH stimulates testosterone secretion. Testosterone determines sex in the embryo, initiates changes at puberty, and influences sex drive.

Hormonal Control in Females

FSH and LH in females influence oocyte and follicle development, stimulating sex hormone production in the latter. Estrogen prompts sexual differentiation in the embryo and development during puberty. Estrogen and progesterone support endometrial growth.

Ovarian and Menstrual Cycles

Ovarian and menstrual cycles begin at puberty; fertility requires two more years. The ovarian cycle includes oocyte maturation, ovulation and endometrial development.

The 28 day cycle begins with menstruation. Pituitary FSH stimulates follicle development and estrogen secretion in the ovary. Estrogen supports endometrial regrowth, but at about day 14 rising estrogen produces a negative feedback loop. The hypothalamus responds by prompting the pituitary to secrete LH. This initiates ovulation. Following ovulation, FSH and LH secretion support estrogen and progesterone secretion by the corpus luteum, and the endometrium matures. In the absence of pregnancy, negative feedback near the cycle's end once again inhibits the hypothalamus, which ceases prompting FSH and LH release in the pituitary. Accordingly, the corpus luteum fails, estrogen and progesterone secretion dwindles, and the endometrium begins to break down. In pregnancy, the corpus luteum receives support from hormones originated in the embryo.

BIRTH CONTROL

The Rhythm Method

In the rhythm method sexual intercourse is avoided during the fertile period. This period is determined through certain observations and careful recordkeeping.

Birth Control Pills

The most commonly used birth control measure is the oral contraceptive. Ongoing doses of estrogen and progesterone override the normal cycle, inhibiting ovulation. Whereas their use involves substantial risk in women with certain medical conditions, in the general population the risk accompanying pregnancy is significantly higher. Heavy smoking significantly increases this risk.

KEY TERMS

asexual reproduction
sexual reproduction
external fertilization
internal fertilization
penis
testes
scrotum
glans
erectile tissue
foreskin
ejaculation
semen
seminiferous tubule
germinal epithelium
spermatid

Sertoli cell
epididymis
interstitial cell
testosterone
vas deferens
spermatic cord
seminal vesicle
prostate gland
bulbourethral
  gland
vulva
mons veneris
labia majora
labia minora
clitoris

introitus
hymen
vagina
uterus
ovary
oviduct
cervix
endometrium
fimbrae
oocyte
ovulation
follicle stimulating
  hormone (FSH)
luteinizing
  hormone (LH)

interstitial cell-
  stimulating hormone
  (ICSH)
ovarian follicle
estrogen
progesterone
ovarian cycle
menstrual cycle
menstruation
corpus luteum
human chorionic
  gonadotropin (HCG)
rhythm method
birth control pill

REVIEW QUESTION

1 Describe how asexual reproduction occurs in *Hydra* and planaria. Compare the genetic make-up of the adult form with that of its offspring. (p. 647)

2 What, if any, are the advantages of asexual reproduction? (p. 649)

3 Under what conditions would the genetic advantage go to sexual reproducers? (p. 649)

4 Compare the number of gametes—particularly eggs—in external fertilization and internal fertilization. (p. 650)

5 Why do mating behaviors in internally fertilizing animals tend to be more complex than in those that fertilize externally? (p. 650)

6 What are the most common copulatory organs? List examples of animals that achieve internal fertilization without such structures. (pp. 650–651)

7 List the three modes of development available to internal fertilizers and cite an example of animals that use each. (p. 477)

8 Describe the anatomical basis for the male erection. What is the neural basis? (p. 651)

9 State the functions of the seminiferous tubules, the interstitial cells, and the epididymis. (p. 651)

10 List the structures through which sperm pass from their point of origin and indicate which contribute to semen production. What is the significance of the semen's alkaline condition? (p. 653)

11 List the structures that make up the female vulva. Which is in some ways similar to the penis? (p. 654)

12 What characteristics of the vagina suit it for its two tasks? (p. 654)

13 Describe the manner in which an egg moves from the ovary into the oviduct and from the oviduct to the uterus. (p. 654)

14 In what specialized tissues do oocytes reside? When do they initially form? (p. 654)

15 Where does fertilization occur? (p. 654)

16 List the sources of the sex hormones and name the structures that regulate their manufacture and secretion. (p. 656)

17 List two pituitary hormones in males and describe their effects. What controls their secretion? (p. 657)

18 List several important roles of testosterone. (p. 657)

19 Describe several important pubertal effects of estrogen. (p. 657)

20 What are two important outcomes of the ovarian cycle? (p. 657)

21 Name the pituitary and ovarian hormones that are prominent during the first 14 days of the ovarian cycle? What are their effects? (p. 657)

22 Describe the hormonal changes leading up to and accompanying ovulation. (pp. 657–658)

23 Name the pituitary hormone dominating the second half of the ovarian cycle. What becomes of the follicle following ovulation? (p. 658)

24 Approximately when in the ovarian cycle must fertilization occur if implantation is to be successful? (p. 658)

25 Describe the hormonal conditions that lead up to the end of an ovarian cycle. (pp. 659–660)

26 Explain the operation of the rhythm method of birth control. What must one know in a precise way? (p. 660)

27 Specifically, how do oral contraceptives prevent pregnancy? (p. 660)

28 Summarize the risk problem associated with oral contraceptives. In which groups is the risk greatest? Compare the risk among younger women with the risk of pregnancy. (p. 660)

29 Outside of surgical intervention, what are the four most effective birth control methods? State their success rates. (p. 660)

42

DEVELOPMENT

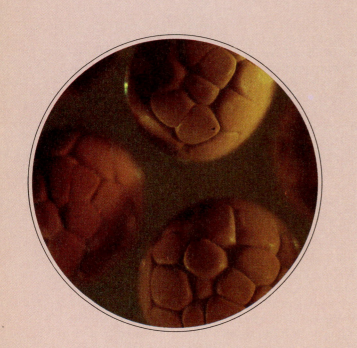

One of the most fascinating biological moments is that brief instant when sperm and egg join in fertilization. Clearly, that instant triggers a remarkable series of events that makes us pause in wonder and realize how little we really understand about life.

Yet it is here, at the very beginning, that many believe we will come closest to understanding just how life occurs at all. This, then, is our chance to begin at the beginning, to see what happens at the union of delicate "half-cells" and during the momentous changes afterward. It is a precisely timed and rigorously choreographed ritual that is remarkably similar across the range of life.

It shouldn't surprise you to learn that the study of the developmental period is called **embryology** (the study of the embryo), although embryologists have more recently begun to call their field developmental biology. Embryologists have described three phases in the development of an animal: **growth, cellular differentiation,** and **morphogenesis.** Growth is simply an increase in size brought about through repeated cycles of cell enlargement, mitosis, and cell division. Cellular differentiation is the process whereby cells become different; that is, the process by which various cells of an organism become increasingly specialized in shape, chemical makeup, and function. Morphogenesis is the emergence of an organism's overall recognizable form as individual structures become increasingly developed. Morphogenesis involves not only the movement, division, and change in shape of specialized cells, but also, in some cases, their programmed death.

GAMETES AND FERTILIZATION

Sperm

Except for a few differences in size and shape, the sperm cells of most animals are essentially similar. Perhaps this similarity stems from their common mission: to move about and penetrate the egg. The principal structures of a sperm are the **head, midpiece,** and **tail** (Figure 42.1). The head contains highly condensed *chromatin* (chromosomal DNA and its related proteins). At the tip of the head is an enzyme-laden **acrosome,** which helps the sperm penetrate the egg. The midpiece contains curiously shaped, spiralling mitochondria, along with a centriole and the roots of the microtubules that make up the **flagellum,** or tail. The midpiece provides the sperm's propulsive power. It contains the mitochondria that generate the ATP needed to sustain the action of the flagellum.

The three sperm regions include the **head** (with condensed chromatin and acrosome), the **midpiece** (with mitochondria and centriole), and **tail** (flagellum).

Eggs

Sperm are generally much smaller than eggs, although eggs of different species vary greatly in size. Even among vertebrates the range in size of eggs is enormous with the largest being those of birds and reptiles (see Figure 29.12). The size of the vertebrate egg relates closely to the quantity of yolk, the embryo's food supply. This, in turn, relates to the mode of development. Mammals require only a small quantity of yolk, because the young embryo soon implants itself in its mother's nutrient-rich endometrium, and its needs are provided by the placenta.

Humans, like other mammals, produce eggs that, while far larger than the sperm, are still tiny—barely visible to the unaided eye. (At ovulation the human egg is only about 0.15 mm in diameter, smaller than the period following this sentence.) The human egg (Figure 42.2) emerges from the ovary surrounded by a dense covering of follicle cells known collectively as the **corona radiata** ("radiating crown"). Below the corona radiata lies a thick, glassy area, the **zona pellucida** ("clear zone"), which is secreted by corona cells. Finally, below the zona pellucida is the plasma membrane, which in the egg is called the **plasmalemma.**

Human egg structures include a **plasmalemma** surrounded by a clear **zona pellucida** and a cluster of follicle cells, the **corona radiata.**

Fertilization

Fertilization is the process in which the sperm penetrates the egg and their haploid nuclei join. Fortunately, the process is somewhat similar in all animals, so we can apply what we know from studies of species that happen to lend themselves to experimentation. Echinoderms, such as sea urchins, sand dollars, and sea stars, are good subjects because they can be readily induced to shed eggs and sperm, which survive and function well in the laboratory.

FIGURE 42.1 (a) The human sperm, with its inclusion bodies, is similar to the sperm of other mammals. (b) Scanning electron microscopic view.

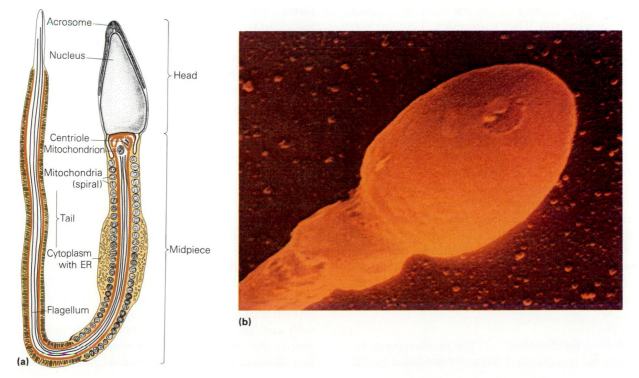

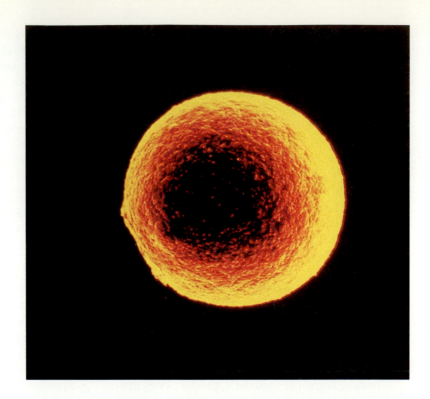

FIGURE 42.2 The human oocyte contains a haploid nucleus and cytoplasm, complete with the usual cellular organelles. The cytoplasm is surrounded by the plasmalemma, and outside of that is the zona pellucida. The sphere of cells surrounding it is the corona radiata.

Echinoderm fertilization. At fertilization the echinoderm sperm get a lot of help from the egg, which is anything but passive in this process. For example, the egg has specialized membranal receptor sites to which a sperm may attach. The sperm attaches through the **acrosomal process,** an extension of the acrosome (Figure 42.3a and e). Once this happens, the egg's plasma membrane suddenly extends its many microvilli. They surround and ensnare the sperm head, forming what is called a **fertilization cone.** Next the sperm head is drawn into the egg cytoplasm (Figure 42.3b and c).

At this time a number of **cortical granules,** storage bodies lying just below the echinoderm egg membrane, rupture, releasing substances that bring on the formation of a **fertilization membrane.** As it forms, the membrane's role becomes apparent. The clear, halo-like structure rises up all along the egg surface (Figure 42.3d) and, in so doing, carries with it many unsuccessful sperm that had also attached, effectively preventing their penetration and the penetration of any others in the vicinity. Penetration by more than one sperm can cause the zygote to fail. Later, the single, successful sperm will release its nucleus, or **pronucleus,** as it is known, which will fuse with the egg pronucleus, completing fertilization.

Human fertilization. The human sperm, by moving along a chemical attractant produced by the egg, reaches the egg somewhere in the upper oviduct. Even though only one sperm normally fuses with an egg, thousands are required to supply the quantity of acrosomal enzymes needed to dissolve the corona radiata. Once penetration has occurred, changes in the zona pellucida (altered sperm-binding sites) prevent the entry of other sperm. It then completes its second meiotic division (in fact, medical researchers use the appearance of another polar body as a signal that fertilization has occurred). The fusion of male and female pronuclei is followed by a round of DNA replication as the diploid zygote prepares for what will be the first of seemingly countless cycles of mitoses and cell division.

EARLY DEVELOPMENTAL EVENTS

Cleavage

The zygote now enters its first mitotic division, or **cleavage,** as it is known in the early stages of development. This division produces two cells, which then form four, which form eight, and so on. Mitosis occurs before each division. Because there is no cell growth during this period, the cells become smaller with each cleavage. The process is slower in some species than in others. For example, although the first cleavage in sand dollars may begin within an hour of fertilization, cleavage in fertilized frog eggs does not begin until after about 90 minutes; and cleavage in human zygotes does not begin until about 36 hours after fertilization.

Patterns of cleavage vary greatly among different animal groups. As we saw earlier (Chapter 27 and Figure 27.9), many protostomes undergo a **spiral, determinate cleavage.** Here, in the earliest stages of development, each new generation of cells arises at an angle from the parent cell. Furthermore, as each new cell arises in the protostome, its future is already determined.

Most deuterostomes undergo cleavage that is **radial** and **indeterminate.** Each new cell lies in the same plane as its parent cell, and each will continue to have a great deal of developmental flexibility for some time. Patterns of cleavage also vary according to the amount of yolk present in the fertilized egg. Yolk, an inert material, is inactive in the cleavage process. As you see in Figure 42.4, cleavage is complete in the frog embryo, but soon the quantity of yolk has a telling effect. Cleavage occurs equally at first, but by the third event this changes. A more rapid cleavage rate at one side produces smaller, active cells that

FIGURE 42.3 (a) After passing through the jelly coat, the echinoderm sperm attaches to a receptor site on the egg membrane. Following attachment, the membrane forms numerous microvilli (b) that ensnare the sperm head, drawing it into the cytoplasm. During this time, cortical granules below the membrane rupture, releasing a chemical into the membrane (c). As a result, a fertilization membrane forms (d) rising up from the egg surface, carrying unsuccessful sperm along with it. The electron micrograph (e) shows a sperm head embedded in the egg cytoplasm.

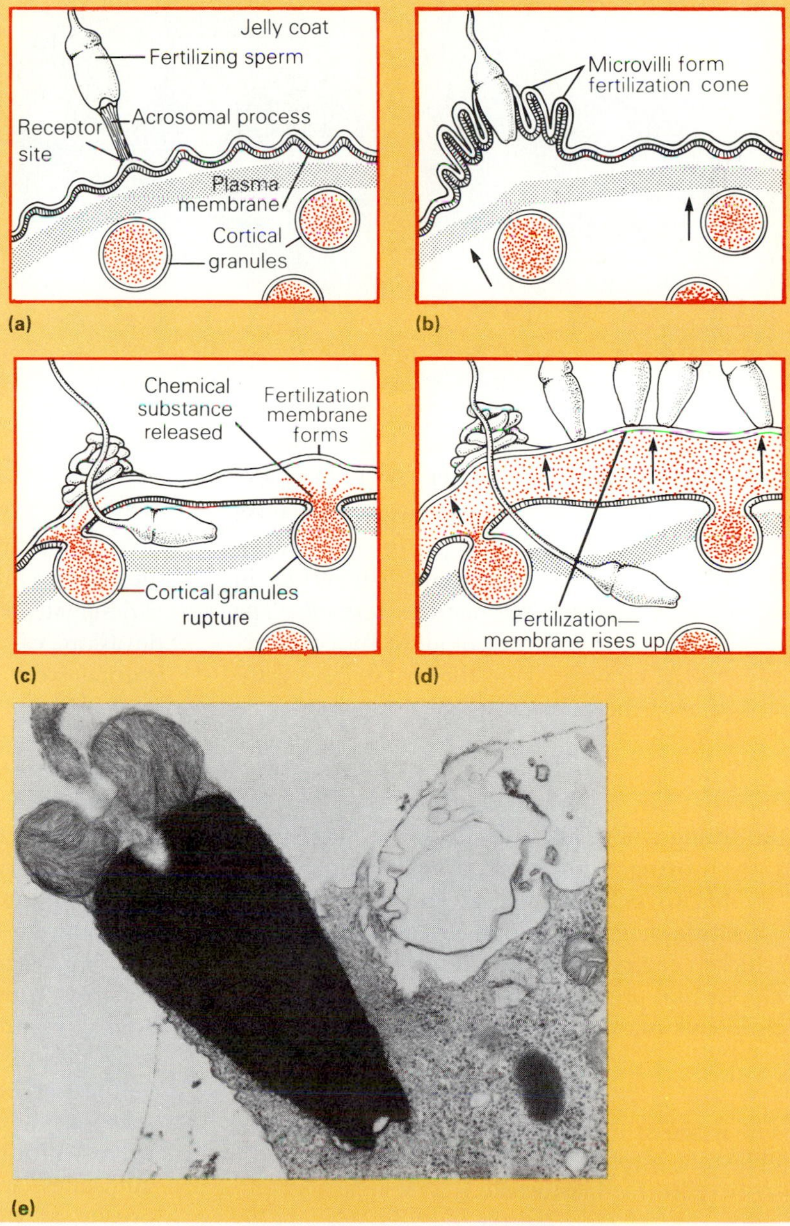

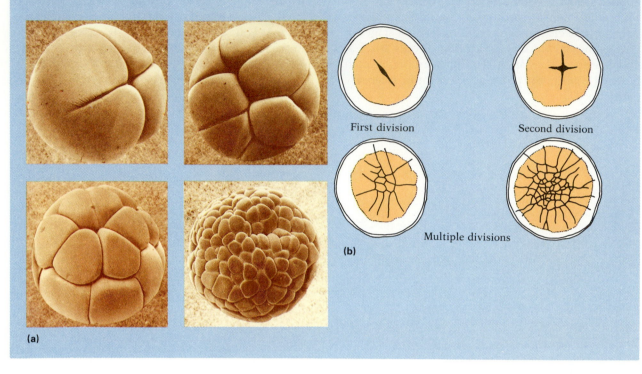

FIGURE 42.4 (a) Cleavages in the amphibian embryo begin simply enough, with the first two producing cells of equal size and content. The cleavages following, however, are highly unequal. This trend will continue, with the upper cells, or animal pole, dividing much more rapidly than the lower, vegetal pole cells. (b) The immense yolk of the bird makes complete cell division impossible, so at first, a small group of cells lying at the surface actively divides. This disk of cells will form the embryo proper.

First division

Second division

Multiple divisions

(b)

(a)

form the **animal pole.** Meanwhile, at the opposite side the rate is much slower, and larger, yolk-filled cells form the **vegetal pole.** This pattern will continue and will affect events in the immediate future. In birds, unequal cleavage reaches the extreme. The immense bulk of the yolk present in the bird egg prevents complete cleavage. Thus the bird embryo actually forms atop the yolk mass.

Morula and Blastula

As the young embryonic cells divide, a solid mass of cells (the **morula**) is produced, which develops a cavity, the **blastocoele,** as the embryo reaches the hollow **blastula** stage. Development in human, frog, and chicken embryos is similar in many ways, but the developmental process is still adapted to accommodate the yolk mass.

The **morula,** a solid ball of cells, later becomes a **blastula,** a sphere of cells surrounding a cavity called the **blastocoele.**

Gastrula

In all three types of embryos, rapidly dividing cells next form a migrating surface wave that rolls under at a designated region, invading the cavity within. This invasion, called **gastrulation,** is a critical developmental event that ushers in the **gastrula** stage. The gastrula stage is important because it marks the point at which the three embryonic **germ layers** first appear. You may recall from our discussions of animal evolution (see Chapter 28) that animals with three germ layers in their embryos are capable of developing complex organs and systems. The important point here is that gastrulation produces the first pronounced embryonic tissue organization. This new organization marks the beginning of the differentiation between internal and external parts of the animal. Figure 42.5 illustrates the differences in gastrulation in frog and bird embryos.

We learned earlier that the **ectoderm** will form such parts as the nervous system and skin; the **endoderm** will form such structures as the lining of the gut, lungs, and most glands; and the other internal organs, as well as bones and muscles, are derived

FIGURE 42.5 In the amphibian **(a)**, gastrulation begins as rapidly moving cells of the animal pole form an ingrowth into the blastula. The continued ingrowth displaces the original cavity of the blastula, and subsequently forms a new cavity, the archenteron, or primitive gut. With the continuation of gastrulation, a three-layered embryo forms with outer ectodermal, middle mesodermal, and inner endodermal cell layers. The bird embryo **(b)** will follow a different pattern of gastrulation. The epiblast will provide cells that form the three germ layers: ectoderm, mesoderm, and endoderm. During gastrulation, cells along the primitive groove roll under, entering the cavity below.

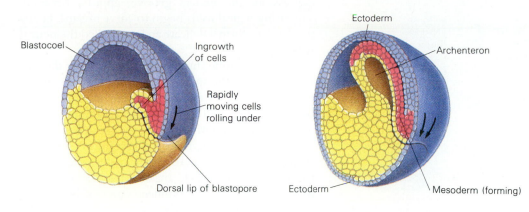

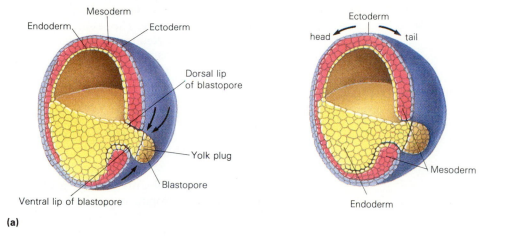

(a)

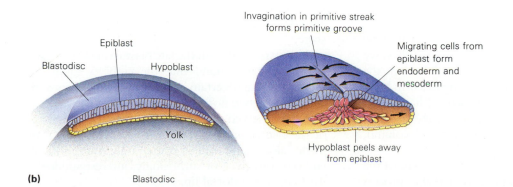

(b)

TABLE 42.1 Derivatives of the Three Germ Layers

Ectoderm	Mesoderm	Endoderm
Epidermis	Skeleton	Linings of:
Hair	Muscle	Gut
Milk glands	Skeletal	Pancreas
Oil glands	Smooth	Respiratory system
Sweat glands	Cardiac	Pharynx
Mouth lining	Dermis	Liver
Lens of eye	Blood	Urinary bladder
Inner ear	Gonads	
Nervous system	Kidney	
Brain		
Spinal cord		
Spinal nerves		
Adrenal medulla		

NOTE: The germ layers do not generally produce entire structures, but are responsible for their basic format during development. All organs eventually contain tissues derived from all three germ layers.

from **mesoderm.** (Table 42.1 indicates the structures primarily derived from each germ layer.)

> **G**astrulation, an inward migration of surface cells in the **blastula**, gives rise to a **gastrula.** It will produce three germ layers, **ectoderm, mesoderm,** and **endoderm,** each of which is involved in the formation of specific body tissues.

Neurulation and the Body Axis

Soon after gastrulation, newly formed mesodermal cells coalesce to form a dense, rodlike cylinder along the length of the developing embryo. This is the **notochord,** the structure that gives the chordate phylum its name. In the cephalochordates (lancelets) and in the sea lamprey and hagfish (jawless fishes; see Chapter 29), the rodlike notochord will become the principal supporting structure, serving as a firm body axis. In most vertebrates the notochord has a brief embryonic existence, as its supporting and organizing roles are taken over by the vertebral column, which also lies along the body's axis.

Following the organization of the notochord the chordate embryo enters into a remarkable process called **neurulation,** in which ectodermal cells along the embryo's dorsal area crudely form the beginnings of the brain and central nervous system (Figure

42.6). The events at this stage are so striking that the embryo is referred to specifically as a **neurula.**

In the first indication of neurulation, ectodermal cells overlying the lengthy notochord begin to thicken, forming what is called the **neural plate.** Next, the outer edges of the plate rise up as **neural folds,** and a depression, the **neural groove,** appears between. The rising neural folds begin to curve inward, finally touching to form a delicate archway called the **neural tube.**

The neural tube thickens and sinks below the surface to become the spinal cord. At the anterior (head) end of the neural tube, the tube expands into a bulbous form that will later become the brain.

Mesoderm on either side of the notochord forms two lengthy masses, then breaks up into blocks of tissue called **somites.** In all chordates, the somites form segmental muscle masses, but in vertebrates they also produce a prominent series of bones that make up the vertebral column.

> **I**n **neurulation,** dorsal ectodermal cells form a neural plate whose edges rise up as **neural folds** bordering a **neural groove.** The closing folds form the **neural tube.** Neurulation produces the rudiments of the central nervous system.

TISSUE INTERACTION AND EMBRYONIC INDUCTION

While developmental biologists know a great deal about the events of development, precise knowledge of developmental processes is hard to come by. Much of what we know has grown out of work done in the 1920s by Nobelist Hans Spemann and his protege, Hilde Mangold. Their experimental subject was the amphibian embryo, in particular its late blastula stage.

In experiments with the late blastula and early gastrula, Spemann found that the embryo could be divided through certain planes into two halves and still produce two normal embryos. The plane of division, he observed, had to pass through the dorsal lip of the blastopore (see Figure 42.5). If the cut was made along any other plane, only one normal embryo formed. Not surprisingly, interest suddenly focused on the dorsal lip.

In the next series of experiments, tissue from the dorsal lip of one blastula was transplanted to another embryo, specifically, to the recipient's ventral (belly)

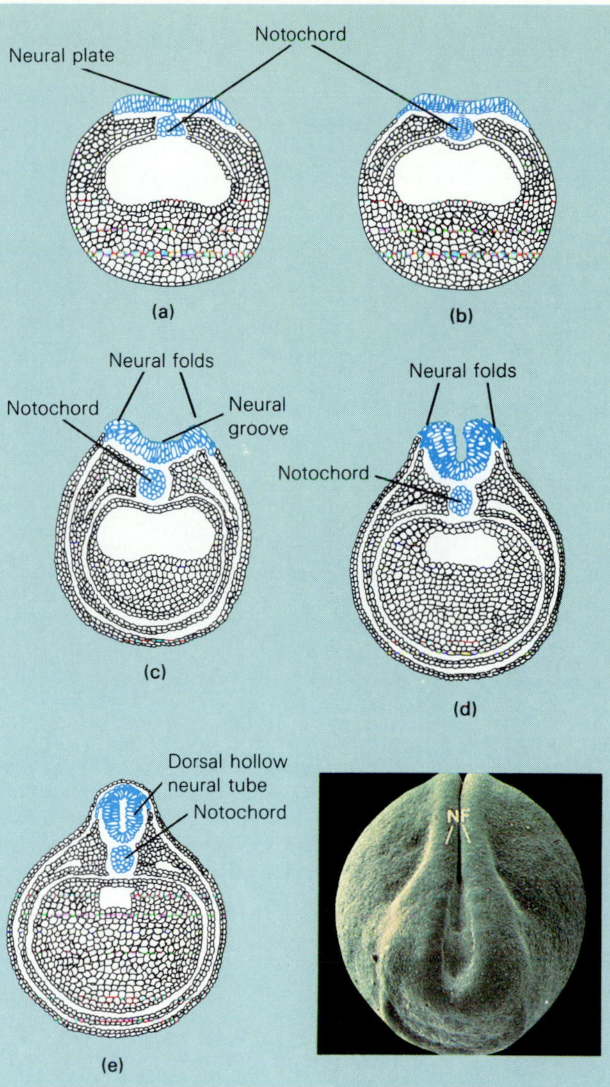

FIGURE 42.6 At the start of neurulation in the frog **(a)** ectodermal cells form a thickened plate along the embryo. **(b, c)** The edges then grow, rising up into folds. **(d, e)** These will join above, grow together, and form the dorsal hollow nerve cord. This then sinks below the surface and becomes covered by new ectoderm. With our surface view, we see that the closure of the neural folds first begins at the center, proceeding in both directions, but lagging behind at the anterior end. The folds there become greatly enlarged as they form the crude outlines of the rudimentary brain. (Photograph courtesy Carolina Biological Supply.)

side (Figure 42.7). The transplanted tissue went on to form a perfectly good notochord, which in itself wasn't too surprising, since that is what it would have formed in the donor. But what was surprising was that a second neural plate formed over the notochord, and then, following the usual events of neurulation, a second rudimentary nervous system formed. The startling reorganization continued until the area of the transplant formed sort of a Siamese twin to the first (Figure 42.7b and c). The question was, where did the material that formed the second embryo come from? Did it all come from grafted tissue?

Using dorsal lip transplant tissue from an amphibian that was highly pigmented, the researchers found the answer. The Siamese twin that developed was without the pigment of the donor. That meant it was

formed from host tissues. The experiments were repeated again and again, but the results were always the same. Somehow the dorsal lip tissue was prompting the surrounding tissues to enter neurulation and go on to form the second embryo.

The researchers deduced that the dorsal lip tissue had an organizing role in normal development. Spemann therefore called the dorsal lip region the **primary organizer.** The ability of one tissue to *induce,* or determine, the developmental future of another became known as **embryonic induction.** Spemann and Mangold's work led to a veritable barrage of experiments, and it soon became clear that development involved many primary organizers and many episodes of embryonic induction. One of the most complex involves the vertebrate eye, as we see in Figure 42.8.

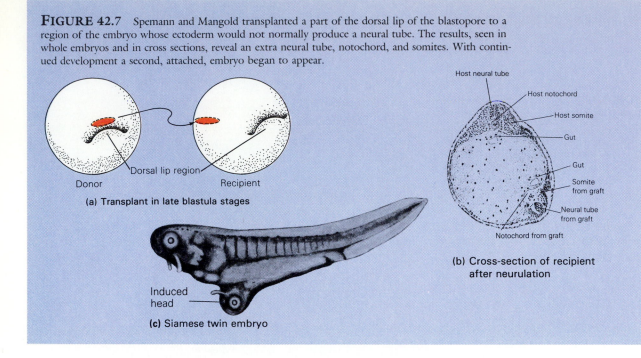

FIGURE 42.7 Spemann and Mangold transplanted a part of the dorsal lip of the blastopore to a region of the embryo whose ectoderm would not normally produce a neural tube. The results, seen in whole embryos and in cross sections, reveal an extra neural tube, notochord, and somites. With continued development a second, attached, embryo began to appear.

Donor
Recipient
Dorsal lip region

(a) Transplant in late blastula stages

Induced head

(c) Siamese twin embryo

Host neural tube
Host notochord
Host somite
Gut
Gut
Somite from graft
Neural tube from graft
Notochord from graft

(b) Cross-section of recipient after neurulation

FIGURE 42.8 Experiments on the development of the eye in frogs showed that there is a complex two-way interplay among the embryonic tissues. **(a)** As the brain begins its development, two bulges of tissue, the *optic vesicles,* begin their growth outward toward the surrounding ectoderm. **(b)** When contact is made, the ectoderm responds by forming the thickened *lens placode*. **(c)** The lens placode then becomes an inducer to the optic vesicle which responds by forming the curved *optic cup*. **(d)** In a final episode, the optic cup then induces the lens placode to invaginate, and it forms the sphere that will later become the lens **(e)**.

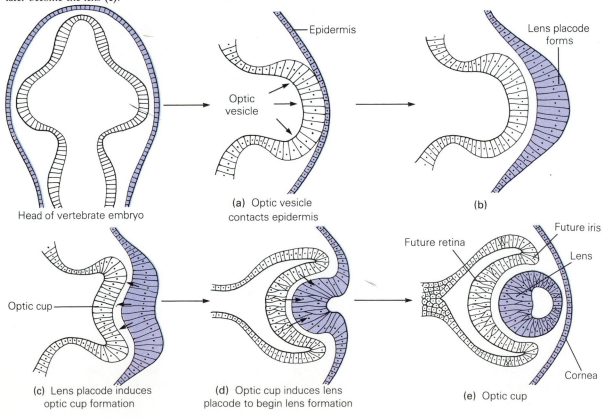

Head of vertebrate embryo

Epidermis
Optic vesicle

(a) Optic vesicle contacts epidermis

Lens placode forms

(b)

Optic cup

(c) Lens placode induces optic cup formation

(d) Optic cup induces lens placode to begin lens formation

Future retina
Future iris
Lens
Cornea

(e) Optic cup

Interestingly, the process of embryonic induction has resisted the concerted efforts of molecular biologists to uncover its chemical nature. What, precisely, are the messages passing from one tissue to the next? The suspects include inorganic ions, messenger RNA, and hormones. But the question is still open. To this day no single substance has been conclusively identified as a major inducing agent.

HUMAN DEVELOPMENT

Early Events

After the human sperm and egg join in fertilization in the upper reaches of the oviduct, the zygote begins to develop even as it continues its journey along the tube (Figure 42.9). Development is slow at first, with the first cleavage occurring about a day and a half after fertilization. The next four cleavages, though, occur more rapidly, forming a rough ball of 32 cells. (Recall that a zygote, when composed of a solid ball of cells, is called a morula.)

As the embryo moves on toward the uterus, a journey totaling some 3 days, its cells continue to divide. Eventually certain cell rearrangements of the morula usher in the next stage, the hollow sphere of cells called a **blastocyst** (roughly equivalent to a blastula) (Figure 42.9, inset). The sphere has a denser group of cells clustered on one side, the **inner cell mass,** destined to become the embryo proper. The thinner, single-celled layer forming most of the sphere, the **trophoblast,** is specialized for invading the uterine lining (the endometrium) and making the first maternal nourishment available to the young embryo. It is the blastocyst, the six-day-old embryo, that implants in the mother's endometrium.

The human zygote undergoes transition to a morula and then a **blastocyst.** The **inner cell mass** in the latter forms the embryo, while the **trophoblast** is important to implantation and early nutrition.

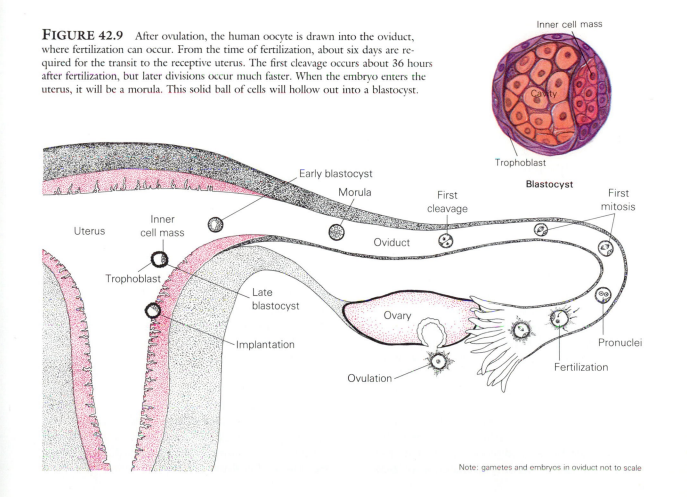

FIGURE 42.9   After ovulation, the human oocyte is drawn into the oviduct, where fertilization can occur. From the time of fertilization, about six days are required for the transit to the receptive uterus. The first cleavage occurs about 36 hours after fertilization, but later divisions occur much faster. When the embryo enters the uterus, it will be a morula. This solid ball of cells will hollow out into a blastocyst.

Inner cell mass

Cavity

Trophoblast

Blastocyst

Early blastocyst

Morula

First cleavage

First mitosis

Uterus

Inner cell mass

Oviduct

Trophoblast

Late blastocyst

Implantation

Ovary

Pronuclei

Ovulation

Fertilization

Note: gametes and embryos in oviduct not to scale

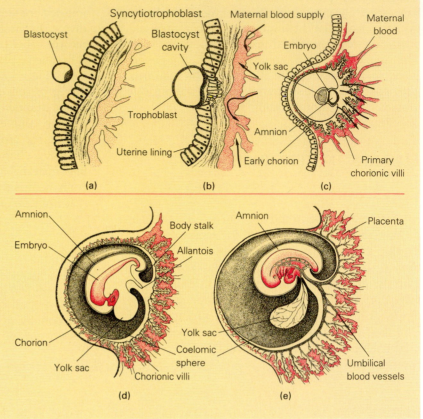

FIGURE 42.10 (a) The human blastocyst implants in the uterine lining about six days after fertilization. As implantation begins (**b** and **c**), fingerlike growths penetrate the endometrium, secreting enzymes that will clear a small blood-filled cavity into which the blastocyst will sink. During this brief period, the embryo continues to change. The amnion, first of the extraembryonic structures, then begins to balloon out. Later, cells on the opposite side will form a second cavity, the yolk sac, which resides within the trophoblast cavity. At this time, the embryo itself is represented by an elongated plate, only two cell layers in thickness. (**d** and **e**) Following gastrulation the embryo takes on an elongated shape with a definite head and tail organization. The allantois contributes to the body stalk, where blood vessels will form. The primary chorionic villi also expand, increasing exchange surfaces.

Implantation and Early Life Support

Implantation begins as the blastocyst touches the soft lining of the uterus (Figure 42.10a and b). Upon contact, the blastocyst releases the hormone **human chorionic gonadotropin** (HCG), which finds its way back to the corpus luteum, signaling it to continue its secretion of progesterone (see Chapter 41). Without this vital step, the usual negative feedback from the ovary to the hypothalamus would begin, the corpus luteum would fail, and the soft, receptive endometrium would be lost.

Next, secretions from cells of the trophoblast break down the endometrial surface and the blastocyst sinks into the soft tissues below. While its first food is provided by nutrient-rich blood from its surroundings, rapid cell division in the trophoblast sends slender fingerlike projections, the **primary chorionic villi,** deeper into the endometrium (Figure 42.10c). For a time this will be the connection between the embryo and the mother's tissues. But soon a more complex feeding structure, the **placenta,** will form. The placenta is a matlike, spongy structure formed from membranes and blood vessels that arise from the trophoblast to become intimately associated with the soft, highly vascular endometrium of the mother's uterus.

Upon implantation, trophoblast cells form lengthy **primary chorionic villi** that absorb nutrients from maternal blood.

Early Development and Formation of the Placenta

Meanwhile, there have been many changes in the inner cell mass. A cavity arises in the inner cell mass, forming what will become the **amnion.** The remaining cells of the inner cell mass form the **embryonic disk,** which is about two cells thick. At this point, the embryonic disk resembles a shelf and divides the blastocyst into two fluid-filled chambers: the smaller **amniotic cavity** above the disk, and a larger cavity (the **blastocyst cavity**) below (see Figure 41.10b). The fluid-filled amniotic cavity will surround the embryo throughout its development, constantly enlarging to accommodate fetal growth. The **amniotic fluid** will cushion the delicate embryo and help lubricate developing limbs and digits, preventing them from fusing during growth. (The amnion and its fluid are later referred to as the "bag of water"— the one that breaks, announcing the impending birth).

The lower layer of the two-layered embryonic disk, the endoderm, soon behaves in a remarkable way: It spreads outward at the edges and then folds under to form a **yolk sac** (see Figure 41.10c). In the bird egg these same cell movements enclose the yolk mass, but in the human embryo, they enclose clear fluid, forming a third fluid-filled chamber. Blood cells and blood vessels form in the yolk sac, which remains small and becomes increasingly insignificant as the embryo itself grows.

Following implantation, embryonic tissue forms the **amnion** and **amniotic cavity** above the embryo and, later, the **yolk sac** below.

It is at this time, some three weeks into development, that the unstructured, two-layered embryonic disk begins to change rapidly. The disk takes on an elongated slipper shape; the **primitive streak** appears down its center; and the mammalian version of gastrulation occurs. By the third week of development, neurulation begins. In the usual vertebrate manner, neural folds rise up on either side of the dorsal surface, their tips growing toward each other and finally closing to form the tubelike spinal cord. As this happens, the blocklike somites begin to appear along its length. Progress is rapid, and at 26 days, the brain is outlined, the crude S-shaped heart has formed, and the embryo has elongated, its postanal tail announcing its vertebrate status. At this time the embryo is about 3.6 mm (⅛ in) long.

In the third week the simple **embryonic disk** undergoes gastrulation, forming the three germ layers. Neurulation follows, and the embryo takes on a more definite vertebrate form.

As these fast-moving events progress, the **allantois,** the fourth and final extraembryonic membrane, develops. This is important, since it will contribute blood vessels during the formation of the placenta. This is its only function in primates, although in other mammals and in birds and reptiles, it collects wastes and fuses with the chorion to form the chorioallantois. The connections between the embryo proper and the extraembryonic membranes narrow somewhat to become the **body stalk.** Later, the body stalk will become the **umbilical cord.** Its point of attachment to the embryo is the **umbilicus** ("belly button"). The blood vessels of the allantois become the arteries and veins of the umbilical cord (see Figure 42.10d and e).

With the development of the chorion, allantois, and the embryo's circulatory system, the placenta emerges. The chorionic villi enlarge, forming numerous microvilli, and blood vessels form extensive capillary beds (Figure 42.11). The maternal and embry-

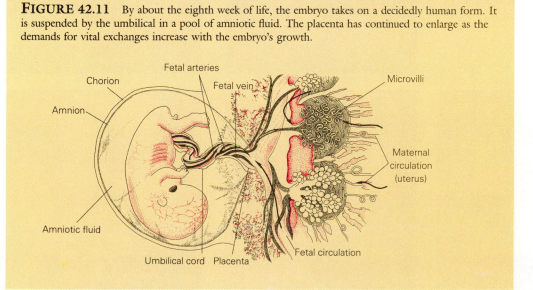

FIGURE 42.11   By about the eighth week of life, the embryo takes on a decidedly human form. It is suspended by the umbilical in a pool of amniotic fluid. The placenta has continued to enlarge as the demands for vital exchanges increase with the embryo's growth.

onic blood are separated by only a thin layer of cells, which permits oxygen and growth-supporting substances to be readily exchanged for metabolic wastes.

The **allantois** and **chorionic villi** contribute to formation of the **placenta.** Exchanges are facilitated by vessels in the chorionic villi and **microvilli,** which are in close association to endometrial vessels.

Despite the great changes that have occurred so far, the embryo will not be clearly recognizable as human until after eight weeks of development (see Figure 42.11). At that time, it will be about 25 mm (1 in) in length and growing rapidly. The embryo is commonly referred to as a **fetus** from this time until birth. The eight-week-old fetus, decidedly human, floats in a sea of amniotic fluid. As growth progresses, the placenta comes to contain so many blood vessels that it takes on a fibrous appearance. Its exchange surface by now consists of numerous mounds of tissue, each containing many microvilli that drastically increase its surface area; each microvillus contains its own capillaries from the placental vessels.

By the third month of pregnancy, the placenta assures its own survival by secreting estrogen and progesterone, replacing the corpus luteum as the primary source.

Further Human Development

Clinically, the 280-day gestation period of human development is divided into three parts called **trimesters.** Most of the significant morphological events occur during the first trimester. (Various stages of development are seen in Figure 42.12.)

Several of the morphological events of the first trimester are quite fascinating. For example, the early heart—one of the first functional organs—begins as a simple tube, which must grow into an S-shape before the atria and ventricles can emerge. At one stage the early human embryo even has pharyngeal gill arches. In fish they will largely form the gills, but in humans, the arches will contribute to the lower jaw, tongue, larynx, middle ear, pharynx, and other structures. The limbs make their appearance as tiny, rounded buds. The ends of these buds will form flattened paddles before finger and toe separations occur.

The reproductive organs form in an unusual way. At about seven weeks, they reach what is called an

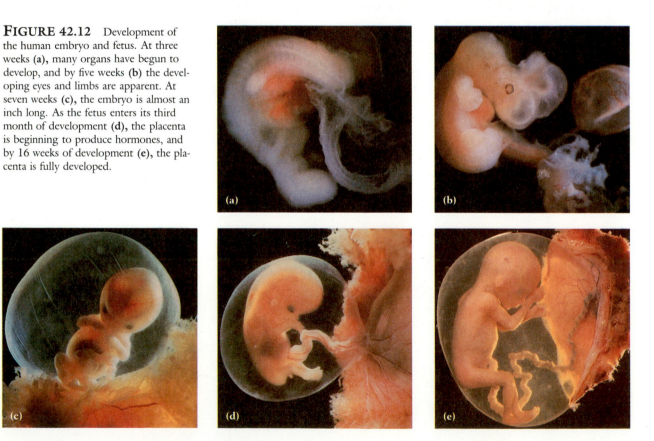

FIGURE 42.12 Development of the human embryo and fetus. At three weeks (a), many organs have begun to develop, and by five weeks (b) the developing eyes and limbs are apparent. At seven weeks (c), the embryo is almost an inch long. As the fetus enters its third month of development (d), the placenta is beginning to produce hormones, and by 16 weeks of development (e), the placenta is fully developed.

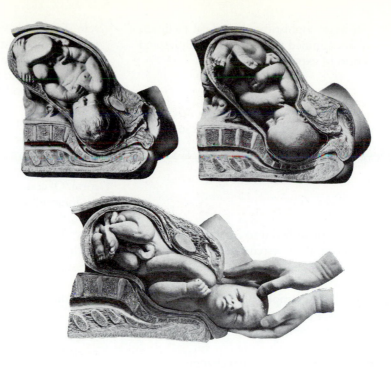

FIGURE 42.13 The birth process. In the first stage of labor, dilation of the cervix occurs and the baby's head eventually crowns *(top)*. The second stage of labor involves the actual expulsion of the fetus *(bottom)*. Expulsion of the placenta—the third stage—follows the birth of the baby.

"indifferent state"; that is, they are indentical in both sexes. The stage is marked by a protrusion called the **genital tubercle.** Then, depending on genetic instructions and hormonal output, it will enlarge as the glans penis or withdraw as the glans clitoris. Folds at either side will emerge as scrotal growth or as labia majora. In males, two ridges along the developing penis will grow together, forming the urethra. In females, similar ridges will form the labia minora. Sexual differentiation is completed by the eighth week, about the time when the embryo begins to be called a fetus.

> First **trimester** events include formation of the heart, the rise and differentiation of **pharyngeal gill arches,** and sexual differentiation.

By the end of the first trimester, all of the physiological systems will have reached a fairly advanced state of development. The second and third trimester are devoted primarily to continued growth and refinement. The central nervous system requires all of this time to grow and differentiate, and the bones, which began as beds of cartilage, will continuously take in minerals and harden. These activities place a high demand on the mother's reserves of mineral and protein. Antibodies from the mother cross the placenta during the last month of pregnancy. They will provide the newborn baby with immunity against

viral and bacterial infections for a month or two. As the third trimester ends, the fetus, now crowding the mother's abdomen, will weigh about 3200 g (7 lbs) and measure close to 50 cm (20 in) in length.

BIRTH

It might be argued that the birth process is far too emotional and momentous an event to be analyzed clinically. Nonetheless we're dealing with science here, so we will begin by dividing the process into three stages (Figure 42.13). The first stage involves **dilation** of the cervix, accompanied by a softening of the cervical tissue. The period of dilation is highly variable, lasting from a few to many hours. It is accompanied by periodic contractions of the uterus called "labor pains." These contractions increase in frequency through the first stage. When they begin to occur every three to four minutes, the head of the fetus **crowns** as it begins to push through the vaginal opening. This begins stage two, the **expulsion** of the fetus.

The expulsion process may last from a few minutes to hours. An anesthetic may be required at this time. The pain is highly variable, depending on the mother's emotional state, pain threshold, cultural conditioning, and preparedness.

The final stage of birth is the separation of the placenta and its expulsion from the uterus as the

afterbirth. In most sophisticated medical facilities, the afterbirth is examined for any abnormalities and for completeness of expulsion.

Birth phases include (1) **dilation** of the cervix and **crowning** (appearance of the fetal head), (2) **expulsion** (actual birth), and (3) the delivery of the placenta.

Physiological Changes in the Newborn

Because babies are propelled into a harsh new world with startling speed, their systems must be prepared for a new and threatening existence. They have left the most secure world they will ever know. The vital exchange of gases, for example, formerly provided by the placenta, now must occur independently. The infant's respiratory system must function on its own for the first time.

The circulatory system must also change in order to accommodate the newly functioning lungs. After all, as we see in Figure 42.14, the fetus receives oxygenated blood from the placenta via the umbilical vein. From this vein it enters the inferior vena cava and then the right atrium. Since the mother provides oxygen across the placenta, there is no reason for the blood to travel to the collapsed, nonfunctional lungs. So instead blood bypasses the lungs over two different routes.

First, an opening between the atria called the **foramen ovale** lets blood cross into the left atrium, and second, a vessel called the **ductus arteriosus** permits blood to pass from the pulmonary artery to the aorta. Of course, both must close at birth in order for the lungs to take over. The newly inflating lungs help solve the problem by suddenly permitting the free flow of blood into the pulmonary circuit. The return of this blood to the left atrium produces enough pressure to close the foramen ovale so that it can grow shut, and constriction of the ductus arteriosus soon disposes with this short circuit.

Circulatory changes in the newborn include closing of the **foramen ovale** and **ductus arteriosus,** thereby permitting blood to pass through the lungs. The **ductus venosus** closes and permits circulation to the liver.

FIGURE 42.14 Circulation in the fetus. Note the ductus venosus, which directs incoming oxygenated blood directly into the vena cava. Structures short-circuiting the pulmonary circuit include the foramen ovale and the ductus arteriosus.

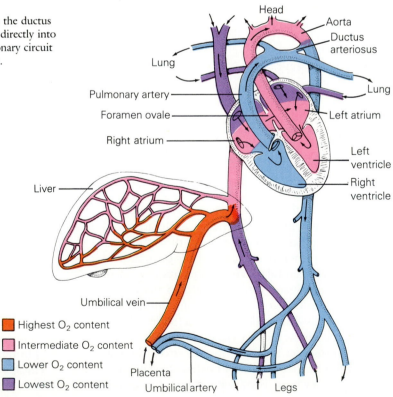

Head

Aorta

Ductus arteriosus

Lung

Lung

Pulmonary artery

Foramen ovale

Left atrium

Right atrium

Left ventricle

Right ventricle

Liver

Umbilical vein

■ Highest O₂ content

■ Intermediate O₂ content

■ Lower O₂ content

■ Lowest O₂ content

Placenta

Umbilical artery

Legs

The processes of fertilization, growth, and development are, indeed, remarkable. Each of us goes through these stages, which may partially explain our fascination with the newcomers to our small planet. We generally want them to get off to a good start, so a great deal of attention has been focused on ensuring normality through the developmental stages, but this area remains one of the most mysterious and compelling in biology.

SUMMARY

Development includes growth (increase in cells and body size), differentiation (cell and tissue specialization), and morphogenesis (emergence of form).

GAMETES AND FERTILIZATION

Sperm

Sperm structures include the head (chromatin and acrosome), midpiece (organelles including the centriole and mitochondria), and tail (flagellum).

Eggs

Egg size depends on yolk quantity, which relates to mode of development. At ovulation, the human egg is surrounded by cells that form the corona radiata, which merges with the zona pelucida.

Fertilization

Following attachment by the acrosomal process, sperm are actively drawn into the egg by microvilli. Cortical granules rupture and the fertilization membrane rises up, lifting extra sperm with it. Male and female pronuclei fuse.

Human fertilization requires thousands of sperm, but only one penetrates the egg. Upon completion of meiosis, a second polar body appears.

EARLY DEVELOPMENTAL EVENTS

Cleavage

Mitosis and cell division follow fusion of pronuclei. Cleavage in protostome is spiral and determinate, while in deuterostomes it is radial and indeterminate. Because of the large yolk reserves in the bird egg, cleavages occur in one small region only. In frogs, more rapid cleavage at one end produces an active animal pole, whereas slower cleavage at the yolky opposite end results in a sluggish vegetal pole.

Morula and Blastula

Continued cleavages produce a solid morula. A blastocoel cavity forms next and the hollow blastula emerges.

Gastrula

Gastrulation, an inward migration of cells, follows, and a three layered gastrula emerges. The three germ layers include ectoderm, endoderm, and mesoderm. Each has its own developmental role in producing body tissues.

Neurulation and the Body Axis

The notochord, a mesodermally derived structure, becomes the embryonic axis. Neurulation adds to the axis by giving rise to the rudimentary central nervous system.

Ectoderm thickens, forming the neural plate. Its edges rise up as folds and close, forming a neural tube which sinks below the surface. The wider end forms the brain. Somites, forerunners of the vertebral column and segmented muscles, form on each side of the notochord.

TISSUE INTERACTION AND EMBRYONIC INDUCTION

Spemann and Mangold transplanted tissue from the dorsal lip region of the late blastula to the opposite side of a recipient blastula and a second rudimentary nervous system arose. Further study established that the transplanted tissue induced the host tissue nearby to undergo neurulation. The dorsal lip tissue became known as the primary organizer and its effect on the host, embryonic induction. A triple induction system occurs in the vertebrate eye.

HUMAN DEVELOPMENT

The Early Events

From fertilization to implantation requires about 6 days during which the human embryo progresses to the blastocyst stage. The inner cell mass forms the embryo while trophoblast cells provide for implantation.

Implantation and Early Life Support

Upon implantation, the blastocyst releases a hormone that stimulates continued progesterone release, thus assuring endometrial maintenance. Nutrient uptake is increased as fingerlike primary chorionic villi emerge from the trophoblast.

Early Development and Formation of the Placenta

Cells of the inner cell mass form the amnion and fluid-filled amniotic cavity. Cells below form a fluid-filled yolk sac in which blood cells and vessels form.

Gastrulation and neurulation in the embryo follow, and by the fourth week the embryo takes on definite form. The emerging allantois contributes blood vessels to the placenta. Chorionic villi enlarge and are invaded by blood vessels soon forming the matlike placenta.

At eight weeks human form is recognizable and the embryo is called a fetus. The placenta rapidly increases in size and soon secretes its own progesterone.

Further Human Development

All systems form during the first trimester. The heart, a simple tube at first, forms an S-shape and the chambers emerge. Pharyngeal gill arches appear and contribute to neck and jaw structures. Male or female genitalia develop from a simple genital tubercle. The primary activities in the second and third trimesters include growth and refinement.

BIRTH

Stage one includes softening and dilation of the cervix, increasing labor pains, and crowning. In stage two, the fetus passes through the birth canal, and in stage three the placenta (afterbirth) is expelled.

Physiological Changes in the Newborn

The first breaths are accompanied by rapid changes in circulatory structures that earlier shunted blood away from the fetal lungs. The foramen ovale, a flap-covered opening between atria, closes and later fuses. The ductus arteriosus, a vessel connecting the pulmonary artery and aorta, constricts.

KEY TERMS

embryology	pronucleus	neurula	blastocyst cavity
growth	cleavage	neural plate	amniotic fluid
cellular differentiation	spiral determinant cleavage	neural fold	yolk sac
morphogenesis	radial indeterminant cleavage	neural groove	primitive streak
head	animal pole	neural tube	allantois
midpiece	vegetal pole	primary organizer	body stalk
tail	morula	embryonic induction	umbilical cord
acrosome	blastocoele	blastocyst	umbilicus
flagellum	blastula	inner cell mass	fetus
corona radiata	gastrulation	trophoblast	trimester
zona pellucida	gastrula	implantation	genital tubercle
plasmalemma	germ layer	HCG	dilation
fertilization	ectoderm	primary chorionic villi	crowns
acrosomal process	mesoderm	placenta	expulsion
fertilization cone	endoderm	amnion	afterbirth
cortical granule	notochord	embryonic disk	foramen ovale
fertilization membrane	neurulation	amniotic cavity	ductus arteriosus

REVIEW QUESTIONS

1 Carefully distinguish between growth, differentiation and morphogenesis. (p. 664)

2 List the three main parts of the animal sperm cell and name their components. (pp. 664–665)

3 To what aspect of vertebrate reproduction and development does the amount of egg yolk relate? (p. 665)

4 Prepare a simple line drawing of the human egg at ovulation and label: nucleus, cytoplasm, corona radiata, zona pellucida and plasmalemma. (p. 665)

5 How does each of following pertain to echinoderm fertilization: sperm attachment, fertilization cone, cortical reaction, fertilization membrane, and pronuclear fusion? (pp. 665–666)

6 What is the importance of a fertilization membrane? Do they form during human fertilization? (p. 666)

7 Why are so many sperm required for human fertilization? What evidence is there that meiosis has been completed? (pp. 666–667)

8 Compare early cleavages in protostomes and deuterostomes. (p. 667)

9 Describe how the yolk affects the early cleavages in frog and bird embryos. (p. 668)

10 Summarize the events accompanying the formation of an amphibian morula, blastula, and gastrula. (p. 668)

11 Name the germ tissues that form during gastrulation. What is the significance of the germ tissues? (pp. 668, 670)

12 Describe the formation of the notochord. In what chordates does this become permanent? (p. 670)

13 Starting with the neural plate, explain how the neural tube forms. To what two structures does it give rise? (p. 670)

14 Describe Spemanns critical transplant experiment. Why was the dorsal lip of interest? Where was the transplant placed and what was the result? (pp. 670–671)

15 How did Spemann determine whether the newly formed nervous system originated from host or donor? (p. 671)

16 In what ways are the terms primary organizer and embryonic induction fitting? (p. 671)

17 Describe changes in the human embryo from time of conception to implantation. How many days does this involve? (p. 673)

18 Draw a simple diagram of the human blastocyst, labeling the inner cell mass, cavity, trophoblast. What roles do the two cellular regions play? (p. 673)

19 How are the primary chorionic villi formed? What is their function? (p. 674)

20 List the three extraembryonic membranes and describe their formation. (pp. 674–675)

21 When do the following occur: gastrulation, neurulation, heart formation? (p. 675)

22 Describe the structures of the fully formed placenta. (p. 675)

23 What is the significance of the eighth week of human development? (p. 675)

24 Describe the fate of the pharyngeal gill arches in humans. (p. 676)

25 Summarize the events in sexual differentiation. When do these events take place? (p. 676)

26 List the three stages of birth and briefly explain what happens in each. (pp. 676–678)

27 What functions do the foramen ovale and ductus arteriosus have in the fetus? What must happen to them directly after birth? (p. 678)

VII

BEHAVIOR AND ECOLOGY
Interrelationships in a Complex Biosphere

43

THE MECHANISMS AND DEVELOPMENT OF BEHAVIOR

A cheetah crouches in the grass on some African plain. The wary gazelles are on the lookout, but step by step it stealthily draws near. When the cat finally moves, the effect is like the explosion of a granite statue. The gazelles immediately dart off in all directions. The cheetah is the fastest land animal on earth, but in most cases its chase is futile. The gazelles escape.

We have seen such chases before. They are almost standard fare on televised nature programs, although on film we rarely see the cheetah fail. And think of the countless other animals we have watched on film, many of them species we have never seen in real life (and probably never will). Why do we watch these films? Is it mere curiosity? Why would people in St. Louis watch a film about penguins? Anything they learn from the program is more than they will ever need to know about penguins. Could it be that people are naturally curious about other species because our evolutionary history is inextricably linked to theirs?

For whatever reason, people are interested in animals and how they behave. So here we will take a close look at some of the ways they behave, paying particular attention to the mechanisms and development of the patterns.

INSTINCT

It was long believed that humans *learn* their behavior whereas other animals respond only to unalterable **instincts** stamped into their nervous systems at birth. Since mounting evidence over the years did not support this sweeping generalization, the instinct concept fell into some disrepute. The major questions, however, were largely answered by the work of two Europeans, Konrad Lorenz of Germany and the Dutchman Niko Tinbergen, who did most of his work in England. The two (along with Karl von Frisch) received the 1973 Nobel Prize for their work.

Tinbergen and Lorenz called themselves ethologists. **Ethology** is the study of animals under natural conditions or in laboratory experiments that are designed to discover the role of a behavioral pattern in the wild. The greatest resistance to the ethological approach to the study of behavior came primarily from Americans who called their own approach **comparative psychology** and who concentrated primarily on learning, especially in laboratory rats, under extremely artificial conditions.

There has been a lot of controversy over the precise definition of an instinct. However, it is generally assumed that it is based on innate, genetically influenced behavioral patterns. However, as we will see, instinctive behavior can undergo alteration through experience, especially in higher vertebrates, where learning is important.

There are two theoretical components to an instinctive behavior, the **appetitive** and **consummatory stages.** The appetitive part is marked by more or less variable acts that are, to some degree, responsive to environmental cues. As the appetitive stage continues, however, each part is increasingly more stereotyped. Finally, the inflexible, unalterable consummatory act is performed, and this leads to a measure of temporary satisfaction. The instinct theory presumes that an animal is born with a predisposition to perform basic behavioral patterns, and that the performance of these patterns usually benefits the animal.

> **I**nstinct is genetically determined, or innate, behavior, modifiable by learning and with variable **appetitive** and fixed **consummatory stages.**

The environmental stimulus that brings about an instinctive action is called a **releaser** (or sign stimulus). Theory has it that an increasing tendency to perform an act builds up in an animal, and that the proper stimulus then "releases" that behavior. For example, there seems to be an innate urge in cats to perform hunting behavior. Thus we see them hide from, peer at, and stalk balls of yarn. Of course, the pattern is more likely to be performed when the cat is actually hungry (and has no expectations of receiving a bowl of Friskies). Such a cat will grow restless and begin to hunt. At first the search may be quite variable; the cat may literally hunt high and low. But when it spots a mouse, the behavior becomes less random, more focused. The sight of a mouse may cause the cat to crouch and freeze. Its behavior grows increasingly less flexible; each action in the sequence becomes more stereotyped. The stalk, the spring, the slap and the kill are each performed with less variation than the preceding action. Finally the cat performs the final consummatory behavior that leads to relief, or satiation. In this case the consummatory behavior consists of swallowing actions. Swallowing is done with very stereotyped actions indeed, varying little from one time to another or from one cat to the next.

In an experiment designed to assess the source of relief in performing one specific consummatory behavior, Russian scientists connected a tube to the esophagus of a dog in such a way that, as it swallowed, the food it ate emptied into a collecting bowl, rather than entering its stomach. After the dog had swallowed a certain number of times, it stopped eating and left the remaining food, not one morsel having entered its stomach. The only difference between the behavior of the experimental animal and that of a control animal was that the experimental dog returned to its food sooner. The implication is that animals may be motivated not by the presence of some commodity, but by the need to perform a fixed-action pattern. Of course, natural selection favors the performance of particular patterns—ones that usually result in the acquisition of something that is rewarding and beneficial to the animal.

The theory thus assumes that the motivation or drive to perform an act usually leads to biological benefit. The releaser triggers a particular set of behavioral patterns by stimulating something in the nervous system that causes the animals to behave in such a way that the consummatory pattern is finally performed. No one knows what is activated by the perception of a releaser, but the hypothesized neural response center has been called the **innate releasing mechanism (IRM).** Each releaser activates an IRM that then controls behavior by activating muscles that produce the instinctive action. The first phases are variable, and depend on what's going on in the environment. The final phase, the consummatory act, brings relief (and the sequence of behavior patterns may not appear again for some time). This, then, is the basic idea. Now let's consider each of these processes in more detail.

> **T**heoretically, releasers (sign stimuli) activate **innate releasing mechanisms** that trigger instinctive behaviors.

Fixed-Action Patterns

Many kinds of animals are born with a tendency to perform certain complex behavioral patterns. For example, a young blue-footed booby, unable yet to leave the nest, will toss and catch twigs, handling them in the unmistakable manner of an adult preparing to gulp down a fish. Furthermore, we know that the first time a tern chick is given a small fish, it jerks its head around in such a way that the fish is swallowed head first, the spines on its back safely flattened. We have all seen tiny kittens teetering around on uncertain legs; even before they have mastered the art of walking, they try to pounce on whatever their bleary eyes can find. What compels them to attempt such a complex act so soon? We will examine *why* such behavioral patterns are performed in the next chapter, but for now let's just note that many very young animals are capable of quite complex behavioral patterns, and they apparently are born with the tendency and the ability (more or less) to perform them. Some of these behaviors are **fixed-action patterns.**

A fixed-action pattern is a precise and identifiable behavior pattern that is innate and characteristic of a given species. Certain fixed-action patterns do not arise until later in an animal's development. They seem to develop and mature, just as physical structures do, and generally appear at about the time they might be useful. For example, vigorous wing flapping and other fixed-action patterns associated with flight normally appear at about the time a young bird is physically ready to begin flying. (Of course, the physical structures associated with flight, such as feathers and flight muscles, also must have matured.) Because some innate patterns have a delayed onset, researchers once assumed that the animal had learned the behavior. In experiments, however, young birds restrained from wing flapping were still able to fly when the time came and the restraints were removed. We must keep in mind, however, that even innate patterns can be improved by practice (Figure 43.1).

These acts may require specific movements that are performed in the same way by every member of the species. As an example, a bird may build its first nest by using peculiar sideways swipes of the head to jam twigs into the nest mass. If you watch other birds of the same species building their nests, you may notice that they all use the same motion. And have you noticed that all dogs scratch their ears the same way, by moving the rear leg outside the foreleg? There are numerous other examples of fixed-action patterns, but they all have certain traits in common. They are innate (present at birth); and they are characteristic for each species.

FIGURE 43.1 A young eagle crashes head first into the ground near an adult. Its fixed-action patterns associated with learning will later be modified by learning (one would hope) and its landing will be more graceful.

Orienting the Fixed-Action Patterns

Orienting movements, by which the fixed-action pattern is appropriately positioned and directed, are also components of instinctive behavior. A cat may pounce, but its chances for success are best if it pounces in the direction of the mouse. The scratching motion of a dog is most successful if it is applied directly to the itch. A young bird could get in a lot of trouble by jamming a twig meant for the nest into the wrong place.

Let's consider some examples of how a fixed-action pattern is oriented. The insect-capturing tongue flick of the frog (Figure 43.2) is a fixed-action pattern that does not occur until the frog moves around so that the fly is in the center of the frog's field of vision. This centrally oriented image, then, is what triggers the tongue flick. Once this flicking

> **F**ixed-action patterns commonly involve precise voluntary movements. While they are innate, they may arise at various but characteristic times in life and improve with practice.

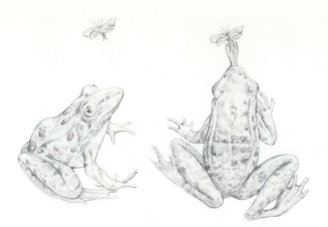

FIGURE 43.2 A leopard frog orienting to catch a fly. The tongue flick, a fixed-action pattern, is not released until the central nervous system is stimulated by the sight of an insect in the proper position (close and in the midline).

Thresholds and Releasers

Changing thresholds over time. There is some evidence that the desire to perform a fixed-action pattern can increase in a stimulus-deprived animal so that the cues that can trigger the performance of the act become increasingly less appropriate or less realistic. Some researchers believe that an instinctive act might even be performed in the absence of an environmental stimulus—just because of an overwhelming urge to do it.

Daniel Lehrman of Rutgers University found that a caged male blond ring dove, when in a courting mood and during a period of isolation from female doves, in time would accept something other than the ideal. When his hormones were running rampant, his urge to bow and coo before a female became overwhelming. When no female appeared, he began to bow and coo to a stuffed model of a female—a model he had previously ignored. When the model was removed and replaced by a rolled cloth, he began to court the cloth; and when this surrogate was removed, the bird directed his attention to a corner of the cage, where he could at least focus his gaze. With the continued absence of a live female dove, the threshold for eliciting the fixed-action courtship pattern became increasingly lower as time went by. It is almost as though there were some sort of building urge (an increasing "energy" that could be released only in a specific way). As this energy increased, the **response threshold,** that is, the minimum stimulus that could elicit a response, decreased to the point at which almost anything would stimulate the dove to perform the behavior. This urge, or "energy," is called **action-specific energy,** although neurologic evidence of its existence remains to be found.

behavior begins, it cannot be changed; if the fly moves now, the frog misses. The point is that the orienting component is performed according to certain specific environmental cues; it is adjustable. The fixed-action pattern (the tongue flick) is *not* adjustable; once it starts, it cannot be altered.

In some kinds of behaviors, the orienting and fixed components may be done simultaneously or they may even alternate in very complex ways, making them difficult—if not impossible—to distinguish. In the case of a frog zapping an insect, the two components of the instinctive act are easily distinguishable. But in other cases, the two components are hard to separate. A simple but remarkable experiment by Lorenz and Tinbergen showed the two components operating together in a way that initially was not apparent. They saw that if an egg of a nesting goose rolls out of the nest, she will roll it back, drawing it along under her chin (Figure 43.3). She keeps the egg rolling in the right direction simply by moving her head from side to side. If the egg rolls to the right, she moves her head to the right as she continues to draw the egg toward her. In the experiment, the egg was removed while the goose was retrieving it. Surprisingly, she continued to draw her head back (the fixed component)—but in a straight line, without the orienting side-to-side movements. This indicated that the fixed-action pattern, once initiated, is independent of additional environmental cues; and that once it starts, it continues.

FIGURE 43.3 In a classic experiment, Lorenz and Tinbergen showed that the behavior of a greylag goose rolling an egg back to her nest had two components: fixed and orienting.

> Unlike the fixed-action pattern, which is highly stereotyped, **orienting movements** vary with the conditions under which an act is performed.

FIGURE 43.4 A male European robin in breeding condition will attack a tuft of red feathers placed at a certain height in his territory.

You will recall that environmental factors that evoke, or release, instinctive patterns are called releasers. The releaser itself may be only one aspect of a general situation, but that aspect alone can be the cue that signals the existence of an appropriate situation for the release of the instinctive act. For example, a territorial male European robin will attack even a tuft of red feathers at a certain height within his territory (Figure 43.4). Of course, such a response usually is adaptive because tufts of red feathers at that height normally are on the breast of a competitor. So we see that the instinctive act may be triggered by only parts of the total environmental situation.

The effect of a releaser can be increased by exaggerating certain of its aspects. For example, an oystercatcher will abandon its own spotted egg to try to sit on an even larger egg with even more spots. Such exaggerated and artificial stimuli are called **supernormal releasers** (Figure 43.5). (Tinbergen found what may be the classic example of supernormal releasers—incubating geese that tried to roll volleyballs into their nests.)

Theoretically, as **action-specific energy** builds, the urge to carry out a behavior increases and the **response threshold** decreases as does the specificity of the cues that act as releasers.

Perspectives on Instinct

Obviously, the term *instinct* has very specific connotations and is often misapplied. For a behavioral pattern to qualify as instinctive, it should meet a number of conditions. For example, does the pattern show an appetitive phase? Is it characteristic of the species? Is it found throughout the species? Will it appear, even in rough form, without practice? Is it stimulated by releasers? Is it useful? Does it ever appear without a stimulus and out of context? Is there a period of satiation immediately following its performance when the threshold for its release is raised?

You have undoubtedly noted that there are certain problems with the classic instinct model. For example, how can an animal perform a complex chain of

FIGURE 43.5 Egg size as a supernormal releaser. An oystercatcher shows a preference for a giant egg rather than a normal egg *(foreground)* or a herring gull's egg *(left)*.

fixed-action patterns without intervening appetitive patterns? And why haven't the critical parts of the neural apparatus been identified? Actually, the instinct concept we've described is probably most useful when accounting for the behavior of rather stereotyped creatures such as insects and the lower vertebrates. It also may help to explain the behavior of other animals when it is not applied too rigidly. In any case, it's the best explanatory model we have.

LEARNING

We have seen that natural selection can produce inherent patterns and preferences, and that they can be especially critical in species that have little time or ability to develop critical adaptive behavior patterns. However, animals can behave adaptively by individually acquiring information from experience, a process referred to as **learning.** We will see how the ethological and comparative psychological theories have matured, expanded, and merged, so that behavioral scientists generally now agree that adaptive behavior has both innate and learned components.

Reward

Before considering some of the ways animals learn, we should be aware that there has been some argument regarding the concept of **reward.** Relevant questions might be: What does an animal seek by expending effort to acquire information? What does it want? How is it rewarded?

In the evolution of *populations,* changes are preserved through their survival value. If the net effect of any genetic change helps an organism to survive, that change is "good," and is retained in the behavioral repertoire. But how does an *individual* ascertain which behavioral patterns to keep in its repertoire? Generally, if an act fulfills or relieves a need, then it is considered good. The fulfillment or satiation is the reward for having performed that action. The quality of "good" has also been construed as something that lowers motivation. This will surely draw howls from those who subscribe to the "work ethic," but it really only means that a cheetah that has just eaten (received "good") is less motivated to go hunting for a while. A reward, then, is something "good," something that fulfills a need and lowers the motivation to perform the act that led to the fulfillment. If the reward for an action results in a greater probability of the animal's performing that action again, **reinforcement** is said to have occurred.

Reward is the result of relief or satiation upon completing an action. **Reinforcement** increases the probability of that action being performed again.

Instinct and learning: acting together as a reward. Konrad Lorenz proposed that the performance of a fixed-action pattern is pleasurable (rewarding) and reinforcing, and that this is one way instinct and learning operate together to strengthen the tendency to behave adaptively. He also suggested that the completion of certain acts (such as eating) has a reinforcing effect through **reafference,** or sensory feedback. Consider nest building in crows.

A crow standing at the site of an incomplete nest with a twig in its beak will try to shove the twig into the unfinished nest. It sweeps its head downward and sideways, forcing the twig against the wall of the nest. When it feels the twig meet some resistance, it shoves harder; if the resistance is not strong enough, it shoves again and again. When the twig is wedged more firmly, its resistance increases; this, in turn, increases the bird's efforts until, when the twig sticks fast, the bird consummates its activities in what Lorenz describes as an "orgiastic maximum of effort." After the act is finished, the bird loses interest in that twig.

Some species of birds have no innate preference for suitable nest material. At first, young birds of these species will attempt to build a nest with just about anything they can carry, and some of the things they show up with simply won't do. For example, they may bring such unlikely materials as light bulbs or icicles. In such cases, the young bird tries time and again, but a light bulb will not allow it to reach the consummatory stimulus situation, that final push that leads to both relief and biological success. After a failure or two with light bulbs, it chooses other material until, in time, it becomes a true connoisseur of twigs. Reinforcement, then, occurs through reafferent feedback produced by the performance of a fixed-action pattern.

Kinds of Learning

When experience alters the behavior of an animal, we can say that **learning** has occurred. However, the importance of learning in the lives of different kinds of animals varies widely. For example, tapeworms probably are not able to learn much. But then, why should we expect differently? Adult tapeworms, after all, live in an environment that is soft, warm, moist,

ESSAY 43.1 PLAY

Play is difficult to define, not least because it may appear in forms that are not recognizable to the human observer. Playlike behavior has been described in fish, but some imagination is required. For instance, "shooters" (*Jaculator*) may squirt water at their aquarium keeper, but this could be because they associate him with food and they tend to shoot at food. It was believed for a time that birds do not play, but in recent years, eider ducks have been seen "shooting the rapids" in Iceland, and a hummingbird was once repeatedly observed to float down a small stream of water that was flowing from a hose.

Ethologists categorize play as a type of learning, and while its importance as such in fish and birds remains to be proved, it does seem to have a role in the behavioral development of many other vertebrates. It can only be expected, to any great degree, in those species for which learning or socialization is important and in those that are behaviorally flexible. Also, play should only be expected in species in which appetitive behavior is not always strongly bound to a consummatory act. In many mammals, for instance, appetitive behavior is actually flexible enough to be broken off without leading to a consummatory

act. In fact, play can appear without environmental cues and without being preceded by normal appetitive behavior.

We have all noticed that dogs remain playful throughout their entire lives. Consider the fact that, in ordinary appetitive behavior, the animal learns how to overcome obstacles, so that the consummatory act becomes more easily reached as time goes by. But if the consummatory "goal" (such as food) is already provided for an animal—by an "owner" or by a parent—the appetitive search may become an end in itself. When this happens, the learning that takes place may not be primarily adaptive in helping to reach the consummatory situation, but instead may be more useful in encouraging the exploration of the environment. So, the adaptiveness of play may not be in helping the animal to learn to reach a goal, but in helping to expand its horizons, in giving it a better overall understanding of its world. This understanding is important to a behavioral process called *insight*. In the simplest terms, insight is learning that occurs through a kind of mental trial and error.

Play also provides practice; when young foxes play at biting each others' necks and knocking each other

down, they may be "practicing" being predators. But what about patterns of behavior that appear *only* in play? (Why would a duck shoot the rapids?) There are many accounts of otters racing uphill just to be able to slide down again. To include such behavior, the practice theory would obviously have to be modified to include patterns that improve coordination or some other general faculty.

Play has a socializing function in some species. In primate play groups, youthful experiments may be tried, and mistakes go largely unpunished. While playing, young primates can also learn about each others' temperaments and physical abilities, thus setting the stage for later formation of dominance hierarchies.

In many primates and other mammals the incidence of play decreases with age, but the trend is especially evident among males. Reduction in play may reduce the risk of misinterpreted signals among increasingly dangerous peers. Also, young mammals are explorative, curious, and innovative, and are more apt to "test" the environment than adults; adults tend to be more conservative, less explorative, and less playful

and filled with food. The matter of leaving offspring also requires the simplest of responses (since self-fertilization is common); tapeworms merely lay thousands and thousands of eggs and leave the rest to chance. By contrast, chimpanzees live in variable and often dangerous environments, and they must be able to cope with a number of complex conditions. They are long lived, highly social, and have very few offspring. This is because each infant must be tended as it gains experience, learning all the while (see Essay 43.1). Learning is important in the world of the

chimpanzee, but when a tapeworm dies, it probably carries very little information to its grave.

The value of learning in animals becomes even more difficult to generalize about when we see "unintelligent" species do some rather remarkable things. We must remind ourselves that natural selection will ensure that animals are able to learn what they need to know and usually not much more. In some cases, however, animals that are not known for their intelligence are able to perform some surprising mental feats in those few areas in which natural selec-

Juvenile polar bears

Female cheetah and young

Young red foxes

Female moose with young

tion has blessed them. For example, a bird may be able to locate a nut that it buried with hundreds of others some months ago. That may be on the very day that you can't recall where you left your car.

Let's now take a look at a few of the ways in which animals learn, and then see how various behavioral patterns help them adjust more finely to their environment. We will consider three types of learning: *habituation, classical conditioning,* and *operant conditioning*. We should keep in mind, however, that there are other ways that learning can occur and that learn-

ing and instinct can operate in quite complex ways, as we see in Essay 43.2.

Habituation

Habituation is a peculiar kind of learning, and yet probably one of the most important for animals. Essentially, habituation involves learning *not* to respond to certain stimuli, particularly those that are irrelevant to an animal's well-being. The first time an animal encounters a stimulus, its response may be

ESSAY 43.2 ON IMPRINTING BY PETER KLOPFER

Who has not seen a photo of Konrad Lorenz, large and white-bearded, leading his flock of goslings across a pasture? The goslings, like many birds that hatch in a precocial (developmentally advanced) state (ducks, geese, chickens, for instance), will follow almost any object that slowly moves away from them during a short period after hatching. Once it has been followed, that object becomes favored over others. In the case of Lorenz's goslings, they preferred him to their natural parents, and, on reaching sexual maturity, also courted him rather than their own kind. Lorenz in his long studies of the phenomenon was reminded of sealing wax, which can receive an impression only for the short time it is soft, and having once received the impression, retains it. So he called the process "imprinting."

The features which, according to Lorenz, set imprinting apart from other forms of learning include its rapidity—often only a few minutes of exposure to the imprinting model suffice; its limitation to a specific critical period—in Lorenz's Greyling geese, from 18 to 28 hours after hatching;

its permanence and irreversibility; and the absence of reinforcements or rewards. In fact, ducklings continue to follow their imprinted model even when they receive electric shocks for doing so.

The discovery of imprinting (though not the term) goes back to Aristotle (which is probably true of most psychological concepts). It was later rediscovered by the German ornithologist O. Heinroth, who was one of Lorenz's mentors. Since then it has been widely studied, and although a range of interpretations is possible, a comprehensive summary has been written by one of the early pioneers, Ekhard Hess.

Since Lorenz's early work, imprinting has been found in a great many species and to involve many different senses: Insect larvae may develop feeding preferences on the basis of the first food they eat. Songbirds may, as adults, sing the songs they heard for a short time many months earlier. Mother goats form attachments to their kids by smelling and tasting them as they are born. If prevented from licking them for the first hour after birth, they may fail to accept them. These are all situations in

which rapid learning is essential. Ducklings could easily lose their mothers if they didn't follow them from the nest and thereafter prefer them to passing moorhens or cormorants. Some species, however, may show no immediate imprinting behavior. Young robins, for example, apparently have no need of it; they are physically helpless for the first several days of their lives, and in the confines of their nest they have ample time to learn the appearance of their parents.

Unfortunately for those who like neat, discrete categories, the work of the last decade reveals imprinting to grade into other ing; none of its identifying characteristics are unique. Many kinds of learning take place without obvious rewards. Imprinting is no more permanent than many other experiences, nor is the "critical period" either sharply bounded or unique. Nonetheless, the notion as popularized by Lorenz did focus attention on a fascinating aspect of ethological research, and it stimulated an enormous amount of study that may someday help us form a comprehensive picture of learning and how and why it occurs.

immediate and vigorous. But if it encounters the same stimulus again and again without harm, the response gradually diminishes until finally the stimulus may be ignored. Habituation is not necessarily permanent, however. If an animal becomes habituated to some sight or sound that then is no longer encountered for a time, the response may reappear when the stimulus is encountered later.

There are several ways in which habituation is important in the lives of animals. For example, a bird learns not to waste energy by taking flight at the sight of every skittering leaf. A reef fish, holding a territo-

ry, habituates to its neighbors, whereas a strange fish wandering through the area elicits an immediate attack. Habituation also may help animals flee from furtive, and therefore unfamiliar, predators, while they ignore other, more commonly encountered species that have no reason to hide and intend them no harm.

Habituation, learning to ignore irrelevant stimuli in the surroundings, is adaptive in that it conserves energy and increases efficiency.

form of meat powder, was mechanically blown into the dog's mouth through a tube. After every few trials, the light was presented *without* being followed by food. (Food followed the light more frequently in some sets of trials than in others.) After each experiment was repeated several times, Pavlov measured the amount of saliva that was secreted when the dog only saw the light. He found that the amount of saliva elicited by the light alone was in direct proportion to the number of previous trials in which the light had been followed by food; the more frequent the rewards, the more the response was reinforced. The food was the unconditioned stimulus; the light was the conditioned stimulus. Salivation in response to food was termed the **unconditioned response,** and salivation brought on by the light alone was called the **conditioned response.**

Pavlov then found that this sort of conditioning, or learning process, also worked in reverse. When a conditioned animal (a dog that associated the light with food) was shown a light that was never followed by food, the conditioned response gradually underwent **extinction;** the dog began to salivate less each time until the response was extinguished (see Figure 43.6).

Other of Pavlov's experiments demonstrated more than the ability to substitute one stimulus for another in eliciting the same response. They also demonstrated two aspects of conditioning now called **generalization** and **discrimination.** Generalization, the ability to recognize similar qualities in different stimuli, was demonstrated when a dog that was conditioned to salivate in response to a green light also responded to a blue or red light. In other words, the dog was able to "generalize" regarding the qualities of lighted bulbs.

Discrimination, the ability to detect differences among similar stimuli, was demonstrated when, with careful conditioning, it was found that a dog could be taught to respond only to a light with certain properties. Dogs do not see color well, so they are more likely to be responding to differences in light intensity than to variations in color. In any case, if food was consistently presented only with a green light and never with a red or blue light, eventually the dog would respond only to green lights, demonstrating its ability to discriminate.

> **C**lassical conditioning is learning to respond to a normally irrelevant stimulus (e.g., light) that, through continued association, has come to represent a more meaningful stimulus (e.g., food).

Classical Conditioning

Classical conditioning was first described in the 1920s by the well-known Russian biologist Ivan Pavlov (Figure 43.6). In classical conditioning, a response to a common and relevant stimulus (an **unconditioned stimulus**) can come to be elicited by a normally irrelevant stimulus (a **conditioned stimulus**). Pavlov found that a dog normally salivates at the sight of food, and he built a device to measure the number of drops of saliva generated. He then began a set of experiments in which he presented a dog with a signal light precisely five seconds before food, in the

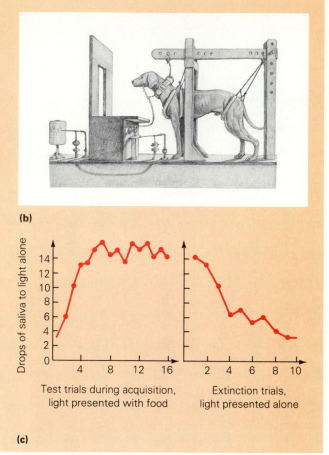

FIGURE 43.6 Ivan Pavlov (a) devised this apparatus (b) to demonstrate classical conditioning. (c) Note in the graph on the left that the dog salivated at maximal levels after only seven trials. When the experiment was reversed and food no longer followed the light, the dog stopped salivating after only nine more trials, as shown by the graph on the right.

(a)

(b)

Drops of saliva to light alone

14
12
10
8
6
4
2
0

4   8   12   16

Test trials during acquisition,
light presented with food

2   4   6   8   10

Extinction trials,
light presented alone

(c)

Operant Conditioning

Operant conditioning differs from classical conditioning in several important ways. In classical conditioning, the reinforcer (or reward, such as food) follows the *stimulus*. In operant conditioning, the reinforcer follows the *response* (Figure 43.7). Also, in classical conditioning the animal has no control over the situation. For example, in Pavlov's experiment all the dog could do was wait for the lights to go on and food to appear. The dog could not make anything happen. In operant conditioning, the animal can determine whether the reward or, in some cases, the stimulus, will appear.

In the 1930s, B. F. Skinner demonstrated operant conditioning with a device known as a **Skinner box.** Once a hungry animal is placed inside a Skinner box, it must perform some action (such as pressing a bar) in order to receive a reward (such as a food pellet from a dispenser). The bar pressing obviously must be learned (Figure 43.8).

When the animal (often a rat or a hamster) is first placed in the box, it usually begins to randomly wander around and investigate its surroundings. As it does so, sooner or later it accidentally presses the bar and a food pellet appears. It doesn't immediately associate the two events, but in time its movements become less random, and it begins to move closer and closer to the bar. Finally, it learns to associate getting food with pressing the bar. After this, it spends most of its time just sitting around, pressing the bar. Operant conditioning, then, is based on the premise that if an action is rewarded, there is an increasing probability that the action will be performed again.

A modified Skinner box can show other aspects of behavior. For example, after a pigeon in a Skinner box learns to peck at a bar to receive food, the experiment can be altered so the pecking is rewarded only if the action is performed within a certain interval after a sign that says "Peck" lights up. Soon the pigeon will peck the bar mostly at that time, largely ignoring it until the "Peck" sign is lit. A pigeon will continue to peck for a time after a new sign is presented that clearly says "Don't Peck." The "Peck" sign is always followed by food; the "Don't Peck"

FIGURE 43.7 In classical conditioning an unconditioned stimulus elicits a response. (Food causes salivation). As another, often irrelevant, stimulus becomes associated with the unconditioned stimulus, finally it alone will elicit the response. Here light (the conditioned stimulus) elicits salivation (now a conditioned response). In operant conditioning, when an unconditioned stimulus, such as light, becomes associated with a certain response and is rewarded, that response will tend to be performed when the unconditioned stimulus is perceived.

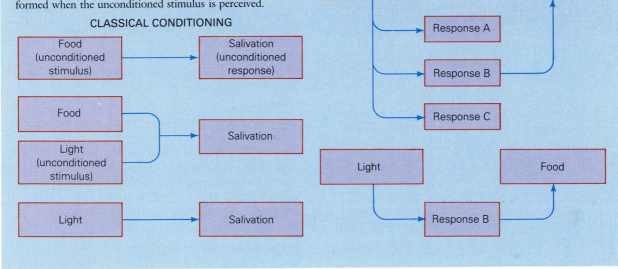

OPERANT CONDITIONING

CLASSICAL CONDITIONING

FIGURE 43.8 A rat in a Skinner box, a device designed to demonstrate operant conditioning.

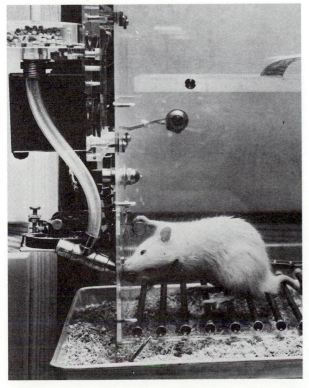

sign never is. The result is that the pigeon will begin to ignore the bar when the "Don't Peck" sign is lit. This is another case of discrimination. (Pigeons can also be trained to peck in response to the "Don't Peck" sign—pigeons can't really read.)

Habituation, classical conditioning, and operant conditioning are three examples of kinds of learning in animals. There is no way to know their relative importance in the wild, but it is generally assumed that most acquired behavior patterns in nature are the result of several types of learning.

In **operant conditioning** a specific but randomly arising response to a situation is rewarded. Where such rewards are consistent, the performance of that act becomes more frequent.

So, most behaviors have rather complex origins. Some are primarily based on inborn mechanisms, others are largely the result of experience. But it is increasingly apparent that adaptive behavior is often the result of the interaction of both genetic and environmental influences.

SUMMARY

INSTINCT

Instinct refers to inborn and stereotyped behavior patterns that often include both genetic and learned elements. Fixed-action patterns are specific movements that are innate and are characteristic for each species.

Releasers or sign stimuli are environmental factors that trigger instinctive patterns of behavior. Exaggerating certain aspects of a releaser can increase its effects. Releasers may be perceived by neural centers called innate releasing mechanisms (IRMs); many IRMs may need to be stimulated to release a complex behavior pattern.

Fixed Action Patterns

Certain fixed-action patterns may arise later in an animal's development when such actions are likely to be most useful. They are precise and identifiable acts that may be improved with practice and are characteristic of each species.

Orienting the Fixed Action Pattern

The orienting component of instinctive behavior is performed according to certain cues and, unlike fixed-action patterns, is adjustable.

Thresholds and Releasers

Releasers vary, triggered by parts of the total environmental situation. If certain aspects are exaggerated, they become supernormal releasers (geese trying to return volleyballs to their nests).

Perspectives on Instinct

Instinct has an appetitive phase, is species-specific, occurs spontaneously, and is followed by satiation. In this context it applies best to simpler animals that have little learning capability.

LEARNING

Learning occurs when experience alters behavior, and is usually a response to a reward.

Reward

A reward is something that brings a measure of relief or fulfills a need, while reinforcement increases the likelihood that the behavior will be repeated. If the performance of a fixed-action pattern is both pleasurable and reinforcing, instinct and learning may be operating together to enhance adaptiveness. The completion of certain acts may have a reinforcing effect through sensory feedback or reafference.

Kinds of Learning

The importance of learning in different animals varies widely; the need for adaptability and flexibility tends to encourage a higher level of learning that enables individuals and species to survive in complex and unpredictable environments.

Habituation

Habituation, classical conditioning, and operant conditioning are three types of learning. Habituation involves learning not to respond to stimuli that may be irrelevant to well-being. The response to such a stimulus diminishes until the stimulus is ignored. Habituation, though not necessarily permanent, can help animals conserve energy by responding only to meaningful environmental stimuli.

Classical Conditioning

In classical conditioning, first described by Pavlov, a response to a common (unconditioned) stimulus can come to be elicited by a normally irrelevant (conditioned) stimulus. Conditioned responses can undergo extinction if the reward or reinforcement is withheld. It was found that animals could generalize about or learn to discriminate among stimuli.

Operant Conditioning

In operant conditioning, the reinforcer or reward follows the response rather than the stimulus. The animal can often determine whether the reward (or even the stimulus) will appear, rather than simply acting as a passive receiver. In a Skinner box, a device used to demonstrate operant conditioning, an animal must learn to perform certain behaviors to earn a reward. Such conditioning can be used to teach an animal to detect subtle differences among stimuli and respond only to very specific conditions. Operant conditioning is based on the premise that an action rewarded is likely to be repeated.

KEY TERMS

instincts	action-specific energy	conditioned stimulus
ethology	supernormal releaser	unconditioned response
appetitive	learning	conditioned response
consummatory stage	reward	extinction
releaser	reinforcement	generalization
innate releasing hormone (IRM)	reafference	discrimination
fixed-action pattern	habituation	operant conditioning
orienting movement	classical conditioning	Skinner box
response threshold	unconditioned stimulus	

REVIEW QUESTIONS

1 What is the basic difference between the ethological and comparative psychological interpretations of behavior? How does this relate to instinct? (p. 684)

2 Using the hunting behavior of a cheetah, describe appetitive and consummatory behaviors, and provide examples of both orienting and fixed components of a fixed-action pattern. (p. 685)

3 What factor in the greylag goose's egg-retrieving behavior suggests that once fixed-action patterns are initiated, they are independent of additional environmental cues? (pp. 686–687)

4 Using the behavior of the male blond ring dove as an example, explain action-specific energy and its relationship to response threshold. (p. 687)

5 In general, what are releasers, and how do ethologists explain their neural effect? (p. 688)

6 Using nest-building in crows as an example, suggest how the innate aspects of behavior might be modified by experience. (p. 689)

7 Briefly describe the roles of reward and reinforcement in learning. (p. 689)

8 In what way is learning through habituation adaptive and essential to young animals? (pp. 691–692)

9 What are the significant differences between classical conditioning and operant conditioning? (pp. 693–694)

44

THE ADAPTIVENESS OF BEHAVIOR

An owl sits quietly on the beam of a barn, upright, eyes closed, almost unnoticeable until two mares pass by and one thumps the gate as it looms in the stall door. The owl suddenly lunges forward, feathers abristle and eyes staring widely. The mares walk into the pasture and stand together head to tail, the tail of each swishing across the face of the other. Overhead a crow methodically beats its way toward the nearby woods, a group of small songbirds swooping and diving around it. As evening draws on, the songbirds fall silent as first one kind of insect, then another and another, fills the night with sound. The mares, by now, have eaten, each immediately surrendering her mound of hay as the stallion resolutely approaches, his own hay unfinished.

The animals around us behave as animals will, each according to its tendencies, abilities, and perceptions. We observe them and we often have an explanation for their behavior. It is easy to believe that the owl lunged as a threat, that the horses stood so as to have insects brushed from their faces, and that the songbirds chased the egg-eating crow to protect their young. We can also imagine that the more aggressive stallion was making sure the mares were aware of his dominance as the chorusing insects sang to attract mates in their own way. But there are two problems with such explanations. First, such reasoning suggests that each animal knew its behavior would achieve a desired result. The same effect could be realized if the animal was only responding to a stimulus, according to an inherent set of movements that the stimulus triggered. The second problem is that we cannot know the adaptive response—the benefit—of any behavior without developing a hypothesis and testing it through careful experimentation. Here, then, we'll see how some animals behave and how their specific behavioral patterns are important to their survival. Some of our information will be derived from rigid experimentation while other conclusions will be more tentative, based largely on observation and still open to analysis. Some of the most rigorous experimentation has involved the ways animals arrange themselves in space.

ARRANGING ONESELF IN SPACE

The earth is a variable place. An animal's environment may abruptly change as it travels from one place to another, or any single place may change over time. Thus, many animals arrange themselves so as to take maximum advantage of the more desirable areas, and others move from one place to another more appropriate to their needs.

Kinesis and Taxis

The simplest type of spatial adjustment is called **kinesis,** in which the vigor of the animal's movement is proportional to the *strength* of the environmental stimulus, which is usually some form of negative (unpleasant) signal. This means that an animal is strongly stimulated to move about under undesirable conditions but less so under more favorable conditions. For example, if wood lice are placed in a box with both damp and dry areas, the dryness sends them scrambling, but they slow down or even stop in the damp areas, and so they tend to aggregate there.

A **taxis** is a movement that is influenced by the *direction* of the stimulus. There are a number of tactic responses: positive **geotaxis,** for instance, results in movement toward the pull of gravity; negative **phototaxis** involves movement away from light. The list of known taxic responses is long, and it is not always easy to label them. For example, tubeworms bend their bodies toward light (Figure 44.1). Newly hatched blowfly larvae are positively phototactic (a response that causes them to leave their dark but crowded hatching area), while older larvae become negatively phototactic (which enables them to end up in new hiding places). The adults also retreat from light (and thus avoid predators). So a tactic response may vary according to a number of environmental and developmental barriers.

FIGURE 44.1   Positive phototaxis. These tubeworms were planted in an aquarium after being stripped of their tubes. As the worms slowly built new tubes, they bent toward the experimenter's light, regardless of the direction from which it came.

> **K**inesis involves responsive movement with the vigor of the movement being related to the strength of the stimulus. **Taxis** involves movement determined by the direction of the stimulus.

Orientation and Navigation

Some of the most fascinating studies in animal behavior have stemmed from investigations of the remarkable abilities of some animals to know directions and to find far-off places—in some cases, places they have never seen.

Orientation.   **Orientation** simply involves being able to face the right direction. It seems a rather unimpressive talent—some worms can innately do it—but you can't. Humans seem to have little aptitude for orientation if denied our usual clues, such as landmarks. Some of the most fascinating instances of animal orientation are found among birds. They largely began with the pioneering studies initiated in

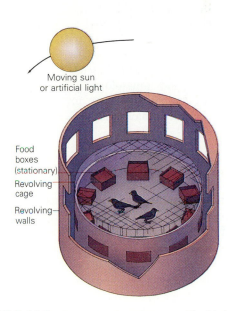

FIGURE 44.2   Kramer's orientation cage. The birds can see only the sky through the glass roof. The apparent direction of the sun can be shifted with mirrors.

the 1950s by a young German scientist, Gustav Kramer (Figure 44.2).

Kramer found that caged migratory birds became very restless at about the time they would normally begin their migration in the wild (see Essay 44.1). Furthermore, he noticed that as they fluttered around in the cage, they tended to launch themselves in the direction they would have migrated. Kramer then devised experiments with caged starlings and

It's the night before a big test. You are trying to study, but your pet hamster, active this night as usual, has a squeaky running wheel. The sound is so distracting that you decide to put your furry friend in the closet. A few nights later, the squeak coming from the closet reminds you that the hamster hasn't seen the sun, or anything else, for three days. Although it has no environmental time cues, such as a light-dark or temperature cycle, the hamster was still active at night, the customary time.

How did the hamster do it? How did it know when it was night? Most researchers assume many living things can measure the passage of time by an internal or biological clock.

Hamsters are not the only organisms with a biological clock. Indeed, the behavior and physiology of most organisms from protists to humans are rhythmic. In fact, rhythms are so common that rhythmicity should be considered a fundamental property of life.

The prevalence of biological rhythms is not surprising when we remember that life evolved in a cyclic environment. Behavior fluctuates in a repeating pattern so that any pattern ideally occurs at the appropriate time of day, in keeping, say, with the state of the tides, phase of the moon, or the season of the year. The rhythmicity on earth reflects the rhythmic movements of certain heavenly bodies, such as the earth, the moon, and the sun. The relative movements of the earth, moon, and sun cause regular changes in such things as light, temperature, geomagnetism, barometric pressure, humidity, and cosmic radiation. Because these environmental changes have been so regular and so predictable, evolution has been able to adjust behavior and physiology to match these cycles.

It has been argued that living things do not possess an internal clock, but they are merely responding to environmental stimuli. But the evidence does not support this. If you recorded the activity of your hamster while it was in the perpetual darkness of your closet, you would notice that, although bouts of activity regularly alternate with rest, the length of this activity cycle varies slightly from 24 hours. In other words, in constant conditions, daily rhythms are "about a day" in length, or circadian (*circa,* about; *diem,* day). If the hamster were responding to environmental cues, it would stay on a 24-hour cycle. Instead, environmental cues seem to keep its clock precisely "set."

Although biological rhythms continued without environmental cues, they are not completely independent of such cues. For example, light-dark cycles will set, or entrain, the rhythm so that its period length

found that their movement was, in fact, in the proper migratory direction—except when the sky was overcast. When the starlings couldn't see the sun, there was no clear direction to their restless movements, so Kramer surmised that they were orienting by the sun. To test his hypothesis, he blocked their view of the sun and used mirrors to reflect the sunlight, shifting the apparent position of the sun. The birds did indeed orient according to the position of the new "sun." Subsequent experiments have shown that many birds, particularly daytime migrators, possess the ability to orient by a sun compass.

A sense of timing is crucial to such an ability. Birds with **sun-compass orientation** (the ability to use the sun to orient) must know not only the normal course of the sun, but also the precise time of day (Figure 44.3). In other words, incredible as it seems, they apparently know where the sun should be at any time of day. Such an ability is obviously largely innate, but in many cases it is at least partly learned. In one experiment, a starling was reared entirely under artificial light, and then allowed to see the sun. It was able to orient itself fairly well, although not as well as birds that had seen the sun before. (This would appear to be another example of the interaction of innate behavior and learning.) Sun-compass orientation has also been found in a variety of other animals, including insects, fish, reptiles, and even some mammals.

The sun-compass studies raised other questions. What about birds that migrate at night? To test for their ability to orient without the sun, caged night-migrating birds were placed on the floor of a planetarium during their migratory period. A planetarium, of course, is essentially a theater with a domelike ceiling onto which a night sky can be projected for any night of the year. When the planetarium sky matched the sky outside, the birds fluttered in the direction of their normal migration. But when the dome was rotated, the birds changed their direction to match the artificial sky.

Nighttime migrators, too, must be able to precise-

matches that of the environment. Internal clocks have another advantage over clocks set by external cues. For example, some animals must be able to *anticipate* critical changes in their surroundings so that they have adequate time to prepare. A fiddler crab scurrying along the beach must return to its burrow before the tide returns or the waves will wash it away. Other animals use clocks to synchronize their behavior to an event that they cannot sense directly. This is the case for honeybees that travel to distant patches of flowers to gather nectar. Different types of flowers open their petals at different times of the day. The bees' clocks allow them to time their nectar-gathering forays so that they arrive when the flowers are open. They might visit morning glories early in the day but wait to visit four o'clocks in the afternoon.

Clocks can be used not only to determine the time of day, but how long it has been since some event. For animals such as the birds and the bees, the second function of a clock, measuring the passage of time, is particularly important because it is essential for sun compass orientation (see text). A homing pigeon flying south would be required to keep its path of flight at a 45-degree angle to the right of the sun at 9 A.M., but would have to change that angle by about 15-degrees an hour as the sun moved across the sky.

What makes the biological clock tick? We don't know. However, because rhythms exist in single cells and protists, we conclude that the clock must be intracellular. Cellular processes that may play a role in the timing process are protein synthesis on the cytoplasmic ribosomes, transport of ions across the plasma membrane or perhaps proton transport in the mitochondrion.

If a single cell can tell time, does every cell in a multicellular organism have its own "wristwatch"? Apparently so. Also, isolated tissues often remain rhythmic. For example, it has been found that if the heart of a hamster is removed and kept alive in a tissue culture, it will continue to beat more rapidly at night than during the day. Even a single heart cell will display a daily rhythm.

If there are many clocks in an animal, then they must be set to the same time or there would be internal chaos. Indeed, animals may have master clocks that synchronize the timepieces in individual cells. In mammals such as the rat, the master clock seems to be in a region of the brain called the suprachiasmatic nucleus. When neurosurgeons destroy this tiny group of cells, the rat's running activity, its drinking patterns, and several of its normal hormone rhythms disappear.

ly measure time, but they may have an even more complex task than daytime migrators. The apparent movement of the stars is much more complex than that of the sun. It seems that birds use a constellation of several stars, whose positions shift at different rates, to "fix" their positions. Birds can also use the stars to correct their migratory course. In one experiment, birds that normally migrate north and south between Western Europe and Africa were shown a planetarium sky with the stars as they would appear at that time over Siberia. The birds, behaving as if they were thousands of miles off course, correctly oriented toward the "east."

Orientation is the ability to face the right direction. **Sun compass orientation** is the ability to use the sun to orient.

Navigation. The ability to orient is indeed remarkable, but **navigation** is a far more complex phenomenon, primarily because it involves not just finding a certain direction but a particular destination. Navigation involves the ability to start at place A and find place B. The difference between orientation and navigation would become clear if you were blindfolded, driven out into the Mojave desert, and released with only a compass. Finding north would be easy; finding Bakersfield wouldn't be, not even if you had also been given a map—you would need to know your *position* on the map. And, as you sat on a rock, distraught and staring hopelessly at your map, birds might be passing nonchalantly overhead on their way to Argentina.

Adaptiveness of migration. Birds are probably among the greatest natural navigators on earth. The arctic tern actually makes two trips between the North and South Poles annually, a distance each way of 18,000 km (11,185 miles). Other species may not travel that far but still show remarkable endurance—such as the geese that fly from James Bay in Canada

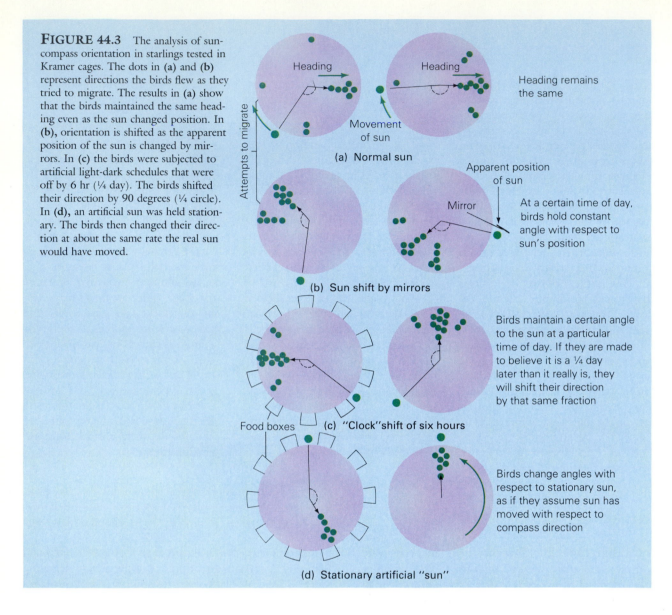

FIGURE 44.3 The analysis of sun-compass orientation in starlings tested in Kramer cages. The dots in **(a)** and **(b)** represent directions the birds flew as they tried to migrate. The results in **(a)** show that the birds maintained the same heading even as the sun changed position. In **(b)**, orientation is shifted as the apparent position of the sun is changed by mirrors. In **(c)** the birds were subjected to artificial light-dark schedules that were off by 6 hr (¼ day). The birds shifted their direction by 90 degrees (¼ circle). In **(d)**, an artificial sun was held stationary. The birds then changed their direction at about the same rate the real sun would have moved.

Attempts to migrate

Heading — Heading — Heading remains the same

Movement of sun

(a) Normal sun

Apparent position of sun

Mirror

At a certain time of day, birds hold constant angle with respect to sun's position

(b) Sun shift by mirrors

Birds maintain a certain angle to the sun at a particular time of day. If they are made to believe it is a ¼ day later than it really is, they will shift their direction by that same fraction

Food boxes   (c) "Clock" shift of six hours

Birds change angles with respect to stationary sun, as if they assume sun has moved with respect to compass direction

(d) Stationary artificial "sun"

to Louisiana, apparently without stopping, covering 2700 km (1677 miles) in only 60 hours. And tiny hummingbirds, with their minute food reserves, regularly cross the Gulf of Mexico. Such seasonal or periodic movement as part of the species' normal cycle is referred to as **migration.** Migrations are not the exclusive province of birds. Studies of monarch butterflies reveal that some travel as many as 3200 km (about 2000 miles) seasonally. Migrating fish also make legendary journeys. The European eel begins life in the Sargasso Sea, southeast of Bermuda, and then follows the Gulf Stream in a three-year odyssey that carries it to the coastal waters of Europe. The females swim into various rivers and streams, spend eight to fifteen years growing, and move back to sea, where they join the males for the return to the

Sargasso breeding grounds. The California gray whale makes an annual autumn trek from the frigid waters of the Arctic Ocean and Bering Sea to the warmer coastal waters of Baja California. After calves, conceived some 13 months earlier, are born, the group begins its return trip.

Migration is such a common phenomenon in the animal world that it obviously must have powerful adaptive advantages. Focusing on the well-documented data from bird studies, let's briefly consider some of these advantages.

The advantages of going south to warmer climates for the winter, or even of moving from mountains to lower, more protected altitudes, are clear; it's about like coming in out of the rain. But there are also more specific and less blatant benefits to such movements.

For example, harsh winter conditions can kill populations of any size and can throw remaining populations into stronger competition for scarce resources. Migrators returning in the spring may therefore find fewer predators, which may have been killed either by the winter or the sudden disappearance of some of their prey.

One might ask, if the areas to the south are so inviting, why don't the migrators just stay there? Possibly, they leave the tropics because of the great numbers of species there. Tropical residents are well adapted to their environments, and as competition begins to increase in the spring with the appearance of new broods, the visitors would probably not fare well. Also, migrators might return because the annual flush of life in the temperate zone provides predictable and temporarily underexploited resources. Finally, as the breeding season draws on, the days become longer in the north, giving animals more time to find food and rear young.

> **M**igration is a regular, often seasonal, movement. Animals routinely migrate great distances, usually as part of their reproductive cycles. Migration may help assure food supplies and avoid competitors and predators.

COMMUNICATION

If you come upon a large dog eating a bone, walk right up to him and reach out as if to take the bone away. If you do, you might notice several changes in his appearance. The hair on his back might rise, his lips might curl and expose sharp teeth, and he might utter peculiar guttural noises. He is communicating to you. (To see what the message is, grab the bone.)

Communication is any signal that passes from one individual to another. To make a monumental understatement, **communication** is important in the animal world. We are all aware that animals communicate in many ways and with innumerable adaptive effects. Ultimately, however, the adaptiveness of any behavior depends on how it affects reproductive success. Communication may be directly involved with reproductive success (as when it attracts a mate) or it may be indirectly involved, as when it reduces offspring mortality (for example, by warning the young of danger). It may also simply help the reproducing animal to live longer, enabling it to mate again. Remember, the evolutionary charge to all living things is "reproduce or your genes will be lost." Communication helps animals to carry out that reproductive imperative.

Deception

It was once thought that communication was essentially a method by which one organism informed another of its situation or intention. But it seems that animals have brought the art of communication a step further—they lie. An animal may lead another animal to believe it is about to do one thing, and then do another instead (Essay 44.2). For example, a fish with an eyespot on its tail easily escapes a predator that attempts to head it off; it darts in the opposite direction. This deception is in the form of a permanent marking. Other deceptions are behavioral. The dog with the bone, you recall, raised its hackles, which increased its apparent size. As two dogs approach each other in a belligerent manner, they walk stiffly erect, hackles raised, each looking as large as possible. Threatening bears stand sideways, showing you what you're up against. Other animals also deceive: Baby hares may hiss and lunge at an intruder in their burrow as if they were a dangerous species. An intruder may be startled at the prospect of being attacked by an enraged baby hare. When some moths are approached by a predator, they quickly open their wings and expose eyespots, suddenly taking on the appearance of a staring predator. Plants may even deceive animals. Flowers that look and smell like female wasps are pollinated by male wasps that land on them after visiting other flowers.

Now let's consider some of the ways animals communicate with one another.

Visual Communication

Visual communication is particularly important among some fish, lizards, birds, and insects, as well as some primates. Such messages may be transmitted in several ways, such as by color, posture, shape, movement, and timing. As an example, we saw in Chapter 43 that the color red can elicit territorial behavior in European robins. Certain lizards use a head-bobbing version of Morse code in identifying members of their own species. Some male butterflies are attracted to females by their specific flight movements. Communication by timing is found in fireflies that are attracted to each other through specific flash intervals. (One species flashes at another species' frequency and then eats whatever comes to call, an example of deceptive communication through mimicry.)

Because of the potentially high information con-

It was once thought that animal communication is essentially a way for one animal to let another know what it is about to do. Now, however, we are aware that this notion is a bit naive. Communication is more realistically thought of as a kind of "enabling device"; it enables the communicator to increase its likelihood of being successful at survival and reproduction. In other words, communication can enable an animal to more effectively manipulate its environment. In some cases, this manipulation involves deception.

For example, a fish may develop an "eyespot" near its tail while concealing its own eye with a stripe; an animal seeking to head it off moves in one direction while the fish moves off in another. A variety of dangerous species take on common coloration such as yellow and black patterns, as we see in the wasps of the genera *Vespula, Bembex,* and *Odynerus.* (This kind of convergent evolution is called *Müllerian mimicry.*) The harmless banded king snake mimics the red, yellow, and black stripes of the dangerous coral snake (an example of *Batesian mimicry*), and is also avoided by predators.

The orchid *Cryptostylis* emits a scent like that of the female Ichneumon wasp. The male wasps thus pollinate the orchids by *pseudocopu-* *lation* (shown here). In another example, the *Ophrys* orchids resemble the female black wasp, and they are pollinated as male wasps try to copulate with first one, then another.

The message of some animals such as the ghost crab is "I am not here." Others essentially say "I am something else." The walking stick is an edible insect that resembles an inedible twig. The angler fish seems to be a rock as it lies on the bottom, waving what appears to be a distressed worm near its gaping mouth, ready to snap up whatever curious fish draw near.

In some cases, animals deceive

Ghost crab

Walking stick

Frilled lizard

Killdeer

others about their conditions. Belligerent Australian frilled lizards unfurl flaps of skin on their necks, appearing to be larger than they really are. Then they may rear up and charge an intruder on their hind legs, collar abristle, turning tail and ignominiously scurrying away if the ruse doesn't work. Some birds, such as the common killdeer, feign injury and flutter along the ground in the "broken wing display," drawing predators away from their nesting areas. A great deal of communication involves living things deceiving each other in a variety of fascinating, unexpected, and bizarre ways.

Coral snake

King snake

Ichneumon (male)

Odynerus

Vespula

Angler fish

Bembex

tent of visual signals, they can be **graded;** that is, they can be of different intensities rather than "on-off, either-or," like many signals (Figure 44.4). Another advantage of visual signals is that the same message may be conveyed by more than one means, say, through both color and posture.

A visual signal can be a permanent part of the animal, as in the coloration of the male pheasant or the striking facial markings of the male mandrill (Figure 44.5). These two advertise their maleness at all times, and are continually responded to as males by members of their own species. Visual signals also may be more temporary. For example, the pheasant may strut and the mandrill may glare. Temporary signs may be of different durations, such as the reddened rump of an estrous female chimpanzee or the more short-term signal of a male baboon exposing his long canine teeth as a threat (see Figure 44.5).

Visual signals also have certain disadvantages. For example, a sender that can't be seen can't communicate, and all sorts of things can block vision (such as mountains) or reduce the signal's impact (such as fog). Visual signals are generally useless at night or in dark places (except in light-producing species). Also, distance reduces a signal's impact. As distance increases, the signal must become bolder and simpler, carrying less information.

> **V**isual communication, occurring as posture, marking, movement, luminescence, and coloration, can have high information content but is easily blocked by objects and mostly restricted to daylight.

Sound Communication

Communication by sound is so important in our own species that you may be surprised to learn that, for the most part, it is employed mostly by other vertebrates and arthropods. (They may even influence each other's evolution through sound—see Essay 44.3.) The familiar sounds of evening may include the songs of the cricket and the cicada. Insect sounds such as these are usually produced by some sort of friction, such as rubbing the wings together or the legs against the wings. Their message is carried in the cadence (or rhythm) rather than in pitch or tone, as is the case with most birds and mammals.

Vertebrates communicate by sound in a number of ways. Some fish may produce sound by frictional devices in the head or by manipulating the swim bladder. Land vertebrates, on the other hand, usually produce sound by forcing air through vibrating membranes across the respiratory tract. Vertebrates also communicate by sound in other ways: Rabbits thump the ground, and woodpeckers hammer on hollow trees and on drainpipes early on Sunday mornings.

Most of the amphibians and reptiles do not communicate by sound, but some exceptions are certain species of salamanders that squeak and whistle. (One even forces air out its cloaca in a most indelicate manner.) The croaks of male frogs and toads advertise their territories and their size, and females respond to certain qualities of the sounds. Territorial bull alligators can be heard roaring in the remote swamps of the South. In the last century, Darwin described the roaring and bellowing of mating tortoises when he visited the Galápagos Islands.

FIGURE 44.4 An example of graded display. At left, the bird *Fringilla coelebs* is showing a high-intensity threat. The posture at center is a medium-intensity threat, and that below is a low-intensity threat.

FIGURE 44.5 A male mandrill has permanent markings that advertise his sex, but his signals of anger are temporary and depend on his mood. It is probably often to his advantage to be perceived as a male, but less frequently advantageous to be perceived as an angry male.

Sounds may vary in cadence (as we saw with insects), pitch (low or high), volume, and tonal quality. The last is demonstrated when two people hum the same note, yet their voices remain distinguishable. Such differences in sounds can be shown visually by use of a sound spectrogram. In effect, this recording translates sound into visual markings. Sound spectrograms enable very precise description and analysis of this type of animal communication.

The function of a sound signal may dictate its traits. A bird calling others to help mob a predator may give low *chuk* sounds that are easy to locate. But when a hawk is spotted overhead, a high-pitched *twee* sound that is hard to locate can warn others without drawing undue attention to the caller. The warning calls of some animals, such as the pica (a rodent), prairie dog, and various primates, vary depending on the type of predator that threatens the group.

Sound signals can carry a high information load through variations in frequency, volume, timing, and tonal quality. In addition, sounds are transitory; they don't linger in the environment after they have been emitted. Thus, an animal can stop sending a sound signal should its situation suddenly change—for example, if a predator appears. Further advantages are that an animal doesn't ordinarily have to stop what it is doing to produce a sound, and unlike visual messages, sound can go around or through many environmental obstacles.

The disadvantages of sound communication include its diminished usefulness in noisy environments. Some sea birds that live on pounding, wave-beaten shorelines must rely primarily on visual signaling, while their close relatives in quieter areas signal vocally. Also, sounds grow weaker with distance, and the source of a sound is sometimes difficult to locate.

Sound information is provided by cadence, pitch, volume, and tone. Its information load is high but it can be drowned out by other sounds and it diminishes with distance.

Chemical Communication

You have probably seen ants rushing along, single file, as they sack your cupboard. You may also have taken perturbingly slow walks with a dog that stops to urinate on every bush. In both cases the animals are communicating by means of chemicals. The ants are following chemical trails laid down by their fellows, and the dog is advertising his presence to those who care to know.

Insects make extensive use of chemical signals, and many of the responses elicited by such chemicals follow quite rigid, stereotyped patterns. For example, ants produce an alarm chemical if they encounter some sort of threat. When an alarmed ant releases such a chemical, it permeates the area, causing every ant in the vicinity to rush about in a very agitated manner and attack anything foreign.

A chemical produced by one animal that alters behavior in another is referred to as a **pheromone** (*pherein*, "to carry", *horman*, "to excite"). The most powerful pheromone known is a sex attractant called bombykol produced by female silkworm moths. Even diluted to one part in a trillion, it can arouse male moths (Figure 44.6).

It was first believed that only insects possessed pheromones and that they triggered only stereotyped, genetically programmed behavior. This notion fell apart when pheromones were found in mammals. For example, it was discovered that if pregnant rats of some species smelled the urine of a strange male, they would abort their fetuses and become sexually receptive. (It was suggested that this trait enabled them to bear the offspring of a "better" male more quickly, one that apparently had displaced the former dominant male.) Another pheromone causes females of most mammalian species to signal their sexual receptivity by scent.

Recent research on human pheromones suggests

Noctuid (night-flying) moths are a favorite prey of certain bats. These bats fly swiftly and can turn on a dime to capture their prey on the wing. They avoid obstacles and locate prey by *echolocation*—emitting pulsing, high-frequency sounds that bounce back ("echo") from objects in the environment. These echoes provide the bat with information that allows it to intercept hapless moths. But just as bats have evolved ways of catching moths, noctuid moths have developed ways of avoiding bats. When they are about to encounter a bat, they take evasive measures. As you might suspect when dealing with bats, this is easier said than done, but the moth accomplishes it with a very simple hearing apparatus.

Noctuid moths have two tympana (drumlike hearing organs), one on either side of the thorax (the insect midsection), and each tympanum has only two kinds of sound receptors. One, called the A1 cell, is sensitive to low-intensity sounds. The other, the A2 cell, responds only to loud sounds. As any sound becomes louder, the A1 cell fires more frequently, responding best to pulses of sound—and it just so happens that bats emit pulses of sound.

In a sense, the moth has beaten the bat at its own game. Its very sensitive A1 neuron is able to detect bat sounds long before the bat is aware of the moth. Not only can the moth detect the distance of the bat, but it can tell whether the bat is coming nearer, since the sound of an approaching bat grows louder. It can also detect the direction the bat is taking. The directional mechanism is simple. If the bat is on the left or right, one or the other tympanum will be shielded by the body, and only one A1 cell will fire. If it is directly behind the moth, both A1 cells will fire simultaneously. If the bat is above, the upward beat of the moth's wings will deflect the sound intermittently; bat sounds from below will not be deflected.

What does the moth do with this information? If the bat is quite far away, the moth will simply turn and fly in the opposite direction. The moth probably turns until the A1 cell firing from each tympanum is equalized. When the bat changes direction, so does the moth. Should the faster-flying bat draw within a few meters of the moth, the moth's number is probably up. However, it has one more strategy. As the two approach each other on a collision course, the sounds of the onrushing bat will become very loud, and at this point the A2 cells fire.

As the A2 cells fire, the highly coordinated directional mechanism is inhibited and a new tactic begins. The moth's wings beat in peculiar, irregular patterns or not at all. The insect itself has no way of knowing where it is going as it begins a series of unpredictable loops, rolls, and dives, ideally bringing it near the ground where the echoes of the earth will mask the echoes the bat is receiving.

The noctuid moth's evolutionary response to the bat's hunting behavior serves as a beautiful example of the adaptive response of one organism to another. Also, it shows clearly that the sensory apparatus of any animal is not likely to respond to elements that are irrelevant to its well being. It is not important for moths to be able to distinguish frequencies of sound, but it is important that they be sensitive to differences in sound volume.

FIGURE 44.6   The antennae of the male silkworm moth are remarkably large, complex, and sensitive. These devices are able to detect minute quantities of sex attractant released by a receptive female. Each large bristle of the antenna has numerous hairs extending outward. Within each is a fluid-filled cavity containing sensory neurons. Chemical substances in the air enter these cavities through pores in the hairs, stimulating the neuron. Impulses thus created are transmitted to the brain.

that women produce a sexual attractant when they are most fertile, and that certain scents produced by men may have a stimulating effect on some women.

Chemical signals are advantageous not only because they can elicit responses in very small amounts, but also because they persist in the environment. This means that the sender and receiver do not have to be precisely situated in either time or space in order to communicate. Also, chemicals can drift around environmental obstacles.

The disadvantages of chemical communication may be due to the same qualities that make them useful. By lingering in the environment, they may alert predators to the communicator's presence. The specificity of chemicals limits their information load, and gradations can be produced only by varying the concentration of the molecules.

Chemical signals include **pheromones,** such as sex attractants and alarm chemicals. They are effective in minute amounts, but their information load is small, they linger in the environment, and they can attract predators.

Why Communicate?

Now that we have some idea of *how* animals communicate, we might wonder *why* they communicate at all. Clearly, there are many reasons, but let's try to organize our ideas a bit. We can begin by considering why it is important to inform other animals of what species you are in.

Species recognition. Animals tend to inform others of their species affiliation. This may not seem too important—unless one is interested in reproduction. Animals have a number of ways to advertise their species. In places where very similar species share the same area, the ritual of advertising one's affiliation may be rather elaborate and extended, and mating may be a slow process. After all, mating between individuals that are very similar but of different species will not produce healthy, viable offspring. Where species are so similar that interbreeding could occur, they often develop quite distinct signals and displays that, along with other isolating mechanisms, readily establish species identification (see Chapter 19).

Individual recognition. It is often important for animals to be able to recognize not only members of their own species, but also individuals within the species. You may have noticed that the gulls at the beach all look alike—at least the adults do. In gulleries, where gulls nest by the thousands, the birds are quite able to recognize their own mates by both sight and sound amid the raucous crowd wheeling above. Mate recognition ensures that a pair will attend to the nest that harbors their own offspring, thus increasing the chances of reproductive success. This is particularly important in species where males and females cooperate in rearing the young.

Communication makes species and individual recognition possible, thereby providing for mating, rearing offspring, and maintaining social organization.

Individual recognition is also important in social species that maintain **dominance hierarchies.** In such species, each individual generally assumes a rank that determines how it will behave toward others. Once animals in a group assume their rank among the others, there will be less fighting over various resources; the subordinate will almost always yield. In any hierarchical group where rank is unknown or not yet established, there is often more fighting, confrontation, and disruption. Rank can be maintained, however, only when each animal can recognize each of the others and therefore respond according to status.

AGGRESSION

The old image of "Nature, red in tooth and claw" apparently has been replaced by the notion that most animals normally get along with their own kind and that humans are the only species that kills its own members. Let's take a closer look at what's happening in the real world. We can first note that **aggression** is the belligerent behavior of one animal toward another, usually in response to competition of some sort.

Fighting

First we'll consider the most obvious form of aggression—fighting. We can discount those old films of leopards and pythons battling to the death; it's not likely to happen. After all, what does a python have that a leopard needs badly enough to risk dying for, or vice versa? Since fighting is much more likely between animals that compete, it is most likely to occur between members of the same species. Moreover, if there is competition for mates, fighting is even more likely to occur between members of the same sex within that species.

Fighting may take many forms, but in most species it is stylized—the combatants do not injure each other (Figure 44.7). Such restraint is highly adaptive because, first, no one is likely to get hurt. This may mean the combatants may continue to compete, but such competition may be far less risky than serious fighting. Also, since animals tend to breed with those individuals around them, the opponent could well be a relative, and current theory suggests that it is disadvantageous to harm those bearing copies of one's own genes. (We will consider other aspects of this "inclusive fitness" theory later in this chapter.) In any case, the restraint is not purposeful. If there is a reproductive advantage to such behavior, most individuals will behave this way because they are the descendants of generations that behaved in such a way. But notice that the "motive" (adaptiveness) is essentially selfish, not altruistic.

Fighting between members of the same dangerous species is usually harmless and stylized. Horned antelope may gore an attacking lion, but when they fight each other, they are apparently inhibited from attack-

FIGURE 44.7 In many species, individuals are genetically constrained to fight in relatively harmless ways among themselves. Most, if not all, of the gestures used in fights between members of the same species are stylized—that is, same-sex combatants will use the same gestures to fight each other throughout the species.

ing the vulnerable flank of an opponent (see Figure 44.7). Stylized fighting enables the combatants to establish which is stronger, and the weaker is usually permitted to retreat.

On the other hand, all-out fighting may occur between animals that are not able or likely to injure each other seriously, such as hornless female antelope. It may also occur between animals that are so fast that the loser probably can get away without serious injury—house cats, for example.

Fighting, of course, is always dangerous because, even when the fight is stylized, accidents can happen, and an injury can lead to retaliation and escalation. Furthermore, some animals commonly engage in dangerous fighting that often results in death. If a strange rat is placed in a cage with a group of established rats, the group may sniff at the newcomer carefully for a time, but finally they will attack and kill it. Male guinea pigs and mice may fight to the death. Male sea elephants occasionally kill each other in fights for mating rights. Male lions may kill a stranger from another pride (social group), and hyenas often will try to kill any member of another pack. Even gangs of male chimpanzees will occasionally ambush and kill isolated males from other troops.

> Fighting, an outward expression of aggression, is most often a product of competition between members of the same species and sex. It is usually stylized, but in some species it is dangerous or deadly.

Territories

Territoriality, the act of animals claiming real estate and defending it against competitors, has intrigued us since it was first described by the ancient Greek philosophers (and perhaps because it so often mirrors our own behavior). However, the notion was largely ignored by the modern scientific community until 1920, when Eliot Howard wrote *Territory in Bird Life,* a book describing his observations of birds expelling each other from certain plots of land. He noticed that one bird might always win fights on one plot of land, but lose to the same opponent on another plot. It seemed as if each bird claimed ownership of a piece of land and would fight particularly well in defense of it. Each bird would immediately attack any intruder of the same species and sex. Of the same species and sex? Clearly, the bird was driving out competitors. Members of the same species compete for commodities such as food and nest sites, and members of the same sex compete for mates. So here was a working hypothesis: **Territories** are areas that are held against competitors and, once established, reduce competition within their boundaries. Territoriality is also an important factor in population control (as we will see in Chapter 47). It has been suggested that territories might have the following additional functions: (1) protection against predators, disease, and parasitism; (2) selection of the most vigorous to breed; (3) division of resources among dominant and subordinate individuals; (4) stimulation of breeding behavior; (5) assurance of food supply; and (6) increased efficiency of habitat utilization of a familiar area.

> The establishment of **territories** reduces continuing competition and tends to control population density.

COOPERATION

Cooperation, or working together toward an adaptive result, seems to be a much "nicer" concept than aggression, and many of the animal stories of our youth involved animals helping each other in some way. Certainly, cooperation is highly developed in some species, and its complexity and coordination occasionally surpass imagination. But again we must sift fact from fiction.

Cooperative behavior occurs both within and between species. The relationship between the warthog and the tickbird is an example of **interspecific**

FIGURE 44.8 Interspecific cooperation, exemplified by the wart hog and the tick bird, is also referred to as mutualism, a form of symbiosis in which both partners benefit.

FIGURE 44.9 Intraspecific cooperation includes behavior intended for common defense. When predators approach herds of muskoxen, they form defensive circles around the more vulnerable females and young.

(between species) **cooperation** (Figure 44.8). The relationship is mutually beneficial; the little bird eats ticks infesting the warthog, while the warthog harbors a wary little lookout. In general, however, cooperation is most highly developed among members of the same species.

Let's consider a few examples of **intraspecific** (within species) **cooperation** (Figure 44.9). Groups of porpoises, for instance, will swim around a female in the throes of birth, driving away any predatory sharks attracted by the blood. They may also carry a wounded comrade to the surface, enabling it to breathe. Their behavior in such cases is highly flexible, constantly adjusted to fit the circumstances. Such

flexibility indicates that some aspects of their behavior are not a blind response to innate genetic influences.

Mammals often cooperate in both defense and hunting behavior. Adult male Himalayan yaks form a circle around the females and young at the approach of danger. They stand shoulder-to-shoulder, their massive horns directed outward—an effective defense against all predators except humans, since the yaks maintain their stance, the only defense they know, even as they are shot one by one. Wolves, African cape dogs, jackals, and hyenas often hunt in packs and may cooperate in bringing down their prey. In addition, members of these species may bring food to others of their group that are unable to participate in the hunt.

Because intelligence is often associated with cooperation, we might expect the highest levels of cooperative behavior among mammals, but in fact social behavior and cooperation are most highly developed in the insects. Their rigid, complex, and highly coordinated behavior patterns are generally considered to be genetically programmed, highly stereotyped, and usually not greatly influenced by learning. One of the more intricate, highly regulated, and cooperative of insect societies is that of honeybees (Figure 44.10).

Cooperative behavior, or working together toward an adaptive result, is particularly common in social insects such as bees and termites and in social mammals.

ALTRUISM

A current theme in modern biology is that animal behavior is essentially selfish and that animals behave as if they were seeking to perpetuate their kinds of genes. (Evolutionarily, it doesn't matter whether an animal is actually *trying* to perpetuate its genes, as long as it behaves *as if* it does.)

But we often find seemingly contradictory instances of animals behaving **altruistically.** That is, their behavior results in another being benefited at their own expense. On the surface it would seem that any animal that behaved in such a way would leave fewer descendants by not spending its energies looking after its own reproductive welfare. In time, the genes of altruists might be expected to disappear from the population, replaced by the genes of more selfish individuals.

FIGURE 44.10 Honeybees tending a queen. These social insects show extremely high levels of cooperation and self-sacrifice. Members of the hive live regimented lives, each with well-defined roles. While the *queen's* role is to lay eggs, the *workers,* all sterile females, begin life as "house bees," preparing cells in the hive to receive food. After a day or so, special *brood glands* develop and they begin to feed larvae. Next they build combs, or become hive *guards;* eventually each becomes a field worker or *forager,* gathering nectar, pollen, or water. The watchword of the hive is efficiency, and this applies to the treatment of males—the *drones*—whose only role in many species is to fertilize a queen. Upon completion of this task, they are quickly killed and shoved out of the hive.

However, perhaps apparently altruistic behavior persists through generations because it is not so altruistic after all. We know that **reproductive fitness** (or reproductive success) is a measure of one's success at leaving one's genes in the next generation. Reproductive fitness has traditionally been measured by the number of offspring an individual produces. However, biologists are now aware of the importance of a broader concept known as **inclusive fitness.**

Inclusive fitness is a measure not only of the genes one is able to leave in the next generation, but also a measure of one's *kinds* of genes. Thus, it includes the genes shared with one's relatives. We must remember that just as our own offspring bear our kinds of genes, so do our brothers, sisters, cousins, and other relatives, as we know by the rules of simple Mendelian inheritance. Animals can increase reproductive success by assisting relatives who bear the same kinds of genes. Thus, we can expect the greatest altruism in groups in which the individuals are more strongly related. The greatest self-sacrificing, to carry the idea further, could be expected toward those who are most strongly related (who carry more of the altruistic genes). As relatedness decreases, so would the tendency toward altruism.

From this we can deduce that in a highly related troop of baboons, a male might fight a leopard to the death in defense of the troop. By the same token, a bird can be expected to give a warning cry when the chance of attracting a predator to itself is not too great, and when the average neighbor is not too distantly related.

Altruism can be carried to extremes in social insects such as honeybees. Since workers are sterile, they can propagate their own genes only by maximizing the egg-laying output of the queen. In some species, the queen is inseminated only once (by a haploid male), resulting in all the workers in a hive being sisters with three-fourths of their genes in common. In such a system, then, almost any sacrifice is worthwhile for its net gain to the hive and to the queen.

We have seen how evolution has molded social behavior in other species, and we have noted the apparent influence of genetics and natural selection on a trait that we humans are often proud to exhibit: altruism. The question arises, is the ultimate foundation of our altruism different from that of other species? It has been suggested that we are altruistic mainly because in human societies there is a high probability of having the favor returned: **reciprocal altruism.** The idea implies that even our altruism is motivated by selfishness. Reciprocal altruism requires individual recognition, a stable social system (where one is likely to encounter an altruist again), a good memory, and a good chance that cheating will become known. Thus, so far, it is expected to appear only in humans.

> **R**eproductive fitness is a measure of reproductive success. **Inclusive fitness** involves increasing the frequency of one's genes in the next generation through reproduction by relatives. **Altruism** can be expected between individuals that are related. **Reciprocal altruism** occurs when there is some expectation of the favor being returned.

SOCIOBIOLOGY

In the mid-1970s an evolutionary concept that had been around for decades in one form or another was revived, reviewed, analyzed, refined, supported, and presented to the public. Since it was a generally familiar concept and was stated very carefully in a professional format, the scientific community was surprised by the turmoil that followed. It has not yet subsided.

The fundamental idea behind **sociobiology** is that social behavior is partly the result of evolutionary processes. This idea is certainly innocuous enough. The problem arose because of the suggestion that even human behavior is influenced to some degree by natural selection. That idea might have gone unnoticed except for a small group of people who believed that the idea was socially dangerous. They attacked it vigorously, drawing a great deal of attention to an idea they wanted people to ignore.

In essence, it was feared that a sociobiological explanation of human behavior would lead to a revival of the notion of **biological determinism,** which is the idea that any genetic influence on human behavior cannot be changed. It was argued that the acceptance of such an idea promotes resignation to the status quo and supports such undesirable social patterns as racism and sexism. The opponents of sociobiology generally prefer to believe that culture is the primary molder of our behavior and that we can change any undesirable behavior by education, social programs, or other environmental influences.

Sociobiologists, on the other hand, believe that the discipline holds real promise for building a better society. Perhaps to some it may seem irreverent to suggest that human behavior, to any degree, is preprogrammed through evolution, and that natural selection plays a role in how we treat each other. But sociobiologists argue that if our behavior *is* genetically controlled or influenced to *any* degree, we should know it. They note that we can't hope to find solutions if we don't understand the problem, and that one reason for our notable lack of success in improving society's condition is that we have ignored our biological heritage.

Sociobiology, in its refurbished form, is quickly maturing as data now appear from long-term studies and as new researchers approach the problem from many angles. The next few years should be interesting, as sociobiologists tighten their premises, more precisely define their terms, and present us with new approaches to an old idea.

The view of **sociobiologists** is that social behavior is partly the product of evolution. Some opponents believe that, for humans, it suggests **biological determinism.**

SUMMARY

ARRANGING ONESELF IN SPACE

Animals tend to take maximum advantage of desirable areas, and some travel or migrate to areas appropriate to their needs.

Kinesis and Taxis

Kinesis is movement related to the strength of the stimulus, while taxis is movement influenced by the direction of the stimulus.

Orientation and Navigation

Animals also have the ability to orient themselves and navigate from one area to another with the aid of such environmental cues as the position of the sun or stars. Their behavior is largely innate, but also reflects learning and experience.

Migration is adaptive in a number of ways. Movements to more seasonally benign environments enable migrators to leave areas of reduced commodities. They also leave behind certain predators and parasites and reduce the ease with which they could adapt to a constantly available food supply.

COMMUNICATION

Communication in animals has many adaptive effects, but each adds up to reproductive success.

Deception

Communication may sometimes involve deception, either in the form of permanent markings or in terms of behavioral traits. In some cases, the communication techniques of one animal will produce adaptive changes in another, such as the coevolution of hearing in bats and noctuid moths. Signals simply send messages, while displays typically function in attracting or repelling others.

Visual Communication

Visual communication is particularly important among some fish, lizards, birds, insects, and primates. Visual messages can be conveyed through color, posture, shape, movement, and timing. Signals can be graded according to their intensity, communicated through more than one means, and may be either permanent or temporary characteristics of organisms. Visual signals are limited, however, to direct observation.

Sound Communication

Communication through sound is used mostly by arthropods and nonhuman vertebrates. Arthropods produce sounds through some type of friction, and messages are carried by cadence. Vertebrates make sounds with frictional devices, by forcing air through vibrating membranes, or by using various nonvocal means. Sound messages can vary in cadence, frequency, pitch, volume, timing, and tonal quality and can carry a high information load, but sound communication is not as effective in noisy environments or over long distances.

Chemical Communication

Chemical communication involves substances produced by one animal that alter behavior in another. Both insects and mammals use pheromones, which can be employed to mark territory, signal sexual receptivity, warn other animals, or intimidate rivals or predators. Chemical signals are effective in small amounts and persist in the environment, permitting senders and receivers to find one another. However, the signals may also lead predators to their prey.

Why Communicate?

Communication allows for species recognition and individual recognition, which ensure that mating produces viable, healthy offspring and that, in some cases, mates can join in caring for young. Individual recognition is also important in maintaining dominance hierarchies, in which each member of the group must be able to distinguish the rank and status of the others.

AGGRESSION

Aggression is outwardly belligerent behavior of one animal toward another.

Fighting

Aggression is actually quite a complex behavior. It has been found that fighting is more likely to occur between members of the same species over commodities, or between individuals of the same sex within a species for mates. Fighting is most likely to occur between competitors. It is likely to be a harmless, stylized ritual in dangerous species or sexes. Harmless or evasive animals are more likely to engage in vigorous combat.

Territories

Territories can reduce competition within an area; limit populations; protect individuals against predators, disease, and parasitism; aid in the selection of the most vigorous individuals to reproduce; divide resources among dominant and subordinate individuals; stimulate breeding behavior; assure ample food supplies; and increase the efficiency of habitat use.

COOPERATION

Cooperative behavior occurs both within a species (intraspecific) and between species (interspecific). Animals often cooperate in defensive and hunting behaviors. Social behavior and cooperation are most highly developed among social vertebrate carnivores and the social insects such as honeybees.

ALTRUISM

Animals that benefit others at their own expense behave altruistically. Altruistic behavior may be related to a concept known as inclusive fitness. The results of any altruistic behavior must be a net gain to the group, though individuals may be sacrificed.

SOCIOBIOLOGY

Sociobiology involves studying the effects of natural selection on social behavior. Opponents fear that such study will revive the concept of biological determinism. Sociobiologists, on the other hand, feel that determining which behaviors are genetically preprogrammed will give us a better understanding of human nature and may help us create more humane societies.

KEY TERMS

kinesis	navigation	aggression	reproductive fitness
taxis	migration	territory	inclusive fitness
geotaxis	communication	cooperation	sociobiology
phototaxis	graded	interspecific cooperation	biological determinism
orientation	pheromone	intraspecific cooperation	
sun-compass orientation	dominance hierarchy	altruism	

REVIEW QUESTIONS

1 How did Gustav Kramer support his hypothesis regarding the cue used in orientation by caged starlings? What observation suggests that this ability is innate? (p. 699)

2 List four navigational cues known to be used by birds. (p. 700)

3 Give examples of visual communication in insects, fish, lizards, birds, and primates. (pp. 703, 706)

4 Describe a general advantage and disadvantage to an individual using each of the following: visual communication, sound communication, and chemical communication. (pp. 706–707)

5 Discuss two ways in which pheromones are used by insects. (p. 707)

6 Using two examples, describe the way in which fighting is typically carried out between individuals of the same species. How is this adaptive? Cite an exception. (p. 710)

7 List four specific adaptive advantages of establishing and holding territories. (p. 711)

8 Give two examples of interspecific cooperation and explain how such behavior is adaptive to both species. (pp. 711–712)

9 In which invertebrate group has intraspecific cooperation reached the highest level of organization? Discuss one example. (p. 712)

10 In which instances does altruism become most adaptive? Explain the theoretical basis for this conclusion. (pp. 712–713)

11 Summarize the major proposal of sociobiology. Why has this idea met with such vigorous opposition? (p. 714)

The earth is a very large place. The concept of a small planet may be true in the sense that we can alter vast parts of it, even changing its air or waters. However, any tendency to trivialize the earth's size after a glance at some NASA photo or a coast-to-coast flight can be quickly dispelled by a hike along Alaska's North Slope, an afternoon in a Louisiana woods, or even a walk to the next town. The earth is indeed huge, formidable, fascinating, and very different from one place to the next. Considerations of such differences and their effect on the distribution of life on this planet lead us to the broadest of all biological disciplines, ecology.

Ecology (eco, *oikos,* "the house") is the study of the interaction between organisms and their environment. Interaction implies reciprocity, and the two are indeed reciprocal—they shape each other. The ecologist's task is formidable, since such relationships are immensely complex, and understanding them requires expertise in a number of biological and physical areas. In a real sense, then, ecology is where the sciences come together. We will begin with a brief look at some rather grand concepts that encompass the biosphere and its physical conditions.

THE BIOSPHERE

The **biosphere** is the thin veil over the earth in which the wondrous properties of air, light, water, and minerals interact to permit life. The biosphere includes not only land areas and their subterranean realms, but the waters as well. In essence, on a worldwide basis, we will consider a great deal of surface area but not much depth. This is because organisms cannot live very far above or below the earth's surface. To be precise, the habitable regions of the earth lie within an amazingly thin layer of approximately 14 miles, from the highest mountains to the deepest ocean trenches. If the earth were the size of a basketball, the biosphere would be about the thickness of one coat of paint. Within these thin limits, the biosphere is a place with very special conditions.

The Atmosphere

The earth's atmosphere may indeed be wispy and ethereal, but virtually all life depends on this fragile veil. Chemically, it is a protective envelope of gases— 78% nitrogen, 21% oxygen, 0.04% carbon dioxide, and a number of other, quite rare gases. Water vapor is, of course, present, but in greatly varying amounts from place to place.

45

THE BIOSPHERE AND ITS ORGANIZATION

Most of the earth's atmosphere clings close to the planet, not extending more than 5 to 7 miles high. The atmosphere helps to screen out much of the dangerous ultraviolet radiation that would otherwise make the earth's surface inhospitable to life. In the upper atmosphere, ozone (O_3) protects us from many of the sun's harmful rays. (Unfortunately, the ozone is becoming seriously depleted in certain areas, and there may be serious problems ahead; see Chapter 47.)

The atmosphere also acts as a gigantic "heat sink," temporarily holding heat close to the earth's surface. (see Essay 45.1). A major factor in this fortunate, life-sustaining characteristic is water. One of the earth's unusual traits is the presence of water in all three states—solid, liquid, and gaseous. We have discussed the role of water in life before, but a major point to reveiw is that water is resistant to temperature change; it absorbs heat slowly and releases it slowly. Its ability to change from liquid to gas permits it to move rather freely through the biosphere and greatly facilitates the wide distribution of heat. Its presence in the atmosphere slows the dissipation of radiant heat from the earth's surface, helping the biosphere to remain at a relatively constant temperature.

The **biosphere** is that part of the earth's surface that can support life. Water and atmosphere moderate climate by retaining and distributing energy.

Solar Energy

Solar energy provides the vital energy for photosynthesis, but it has other roles in the pageant of life. Only about half of the incoming solar radiation ever reaches the earth's surface; about 30% is reflected back into space, while 20% is absorbed by the atmosphere. The 50% that does reach earth is absorbed by the land and waters, from which it radiates back into the atmosphere as heat (Figure 45.1). Although the energy reaching the earth's surface eventually escapes back into space, a great deal of work is accomplished during the time it interacts with the biosphere.

Less than 1% of incoming solar energy is used in photosynthesis. Most of that energy is used in shuffling water around in the **hydrologic cycle,** the ongoing evaporation and condensation of the earth's waters. This cycle, of course, is responsible for the earth's rainfall pattern. In addition to distributing water more equitably over the earth's surface, the cycle redistributes an immense amount of heat.

Solar energy penetrating the atmosphere warms the earth's surface and powers the **hydrologic cycle,** widely distributing water and heat. A small percentage powers photosynthesis.

Climate and the Tilted Earth

Although solar energy strikes the equatorial regions of the earth fairly evenly, in the northern and south-

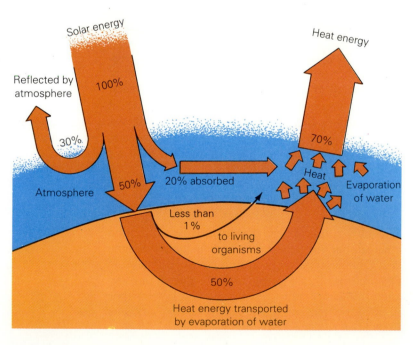

FIGURE 45.1 The earth's energy budget. The relative constancy of conditions in the biosphere depends ultimately on an equilibrium between energy entering and energy leaving. Most of the absorbed energy reenters the atmosphere through evaporation from the earth's waters. The thin arrow represents energy released by organisms.

ern latitudes this energy varies markedly from one season to the next because of the earth's tilted rotational axis (about 23.5 degrees from vertical). As the earth makes its appointed rounds, circling the sun, first the Northern Hemisphere, then the Southern, is struck broadside by the sun's rays. This is the basis for the changing seasons. Without these fluctuations, the temperate zones, where much of the earth's human population now lives, would be perpetually frozen.

ESSAY 45.1 CARBON DIOXIDE AND THE GREENHOUSE EFFECT: A DESTABILIZED EQUILIBRIUM

In recent years, atmospheric scientists have become greatly concerned about the increasing levels of carbon dioxide in the air. The CO_2 comes from a variety of sources. As we know, it is produced by the metabolism of most living things. In addition, the enormous amount of carbon dioxide released by the burning of fossil fuels has been a concern for many years (see graphs **a** and **b**), but today we face a new source of CO_2 production—the carbon dioxide that was once part of the living mass of the tropical rain forests. Such forests have always been a great CO_2 *sink* (region of concentration), but they are being cleared at the alarming rate of 1% each year. As they are cleared, the logs are burned and a great concentration of CO_2 is released into the atmosphere. This has all happened quite suddenly, and the earth's waters, which absorb CO_2, have not kept up.

Why the alarm? It has to do with the storage of heat in the atmosphere. One of the physical characteristics of CO_2 gas is that it absorbs the infrared (heat) energy that emanates from the surface of the sunlit earth. So light from the sun passes unhindered through CO_2, radiates from the earth, and warms the CO_2 in the earth's atmosphere. As atmospheric CO_2 increases, the air becomes capable of holding more heat, and so it begins to get warmer.

Since greenhouses maintain their warm temperature in a similar manner—by letting in short-wave light and retaining longer-wave radiation (heat)—the CO_2 phenomenon has been called the **greenhouse effect.** So far, the actual effect seems to have been minor, hypothetically because of geophysical changes that would normally have resulted in a cooling of the earth.

Still, according to the experts, the temperature cycle will eventually reverse, and when it does, the greenhouse effect will be accelerated. Adding to the problem is a steady increase in ocean temperatures. As the oceans warm even a little, their ability to hold CO_2 in solution will decrease. The oceans contain much greater reserves of CO_2 than the atmosphere, and a rise of one or two degrees would unload more of the gas into the air. It has been suggested that a warming earth will result in the melting of the polar ice caps (which has already begun). Not only would this cause ocean levels to rise drastically, but the ice caps play a role in maintaining the energy equilibrium by reflecting solar energy back into space. The greenhouse effect, then, is expected to increase in the coming years, with results that will be varied and far reaching and that are probably not completely anticipated.

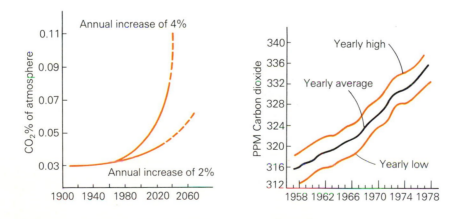

BIOMES AND WATERS OF THE EARTH

Because of the earth's varying climate and topography, the distribution of life—both in amount and kind—varies. Ecologists and geographers alike recognize a number of major plant associations in the terrestrial environment, which they refer to as **biomes.** Specifically, a biome is a particular array of plants within a geographic area. Each has distinctive climatic conditions. As you would expect, each biome also has specific, recognizable animal associations. The primary factors that influence the forma-

tion of biomes are chiefly climatic (precipitation, temperature, seasonal extremes, winds), although topography and light may also be important.

Different people have different ideas about how many biomes there are, but we will discuss eight (Figure 45.2)—in addition to the aquatic realm (including fresh and marine waters). We should first note that biomes tend to be arranged along particular latitudes, especially in the Northern Hemisphere. Starting at the equator and moving northward, the order of major biomes is equatorial forests, grasslands and deserts, temperate forests, northern coniferous forests, and tundra. Interestingly, we find a similar distribution arranged vertically in high moun-

FIGURE 45.2 The biomes. Each biome can be identified primarily by its plant life. The plant life has adapted to the specific biome's climatic conditions, including precipitation, availability of light, and, of course, temperature. Both latitude and altitude affect all these variables.

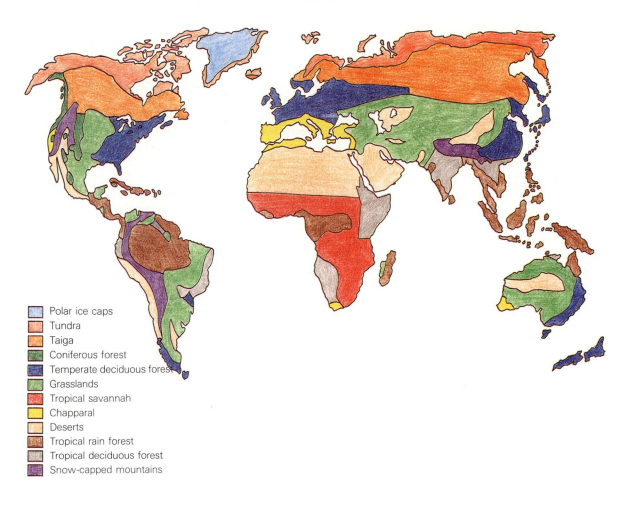

Polar ice caps
Tundra
Taiga
Coniferous forest
Temperate deciduous forest
Grasslands
Tropical savannah
Chapparal
Deserts
Tropical rain forest
Tropical deciduous forest
Snow-capped mountains

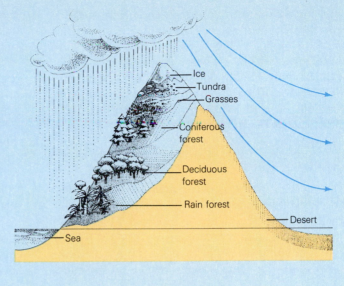

FIGURE 45.3 The altitudinal variation provided by mountains often mimics latitudinal biome distributions. On the leeward side of the mountain, air masses holding little moisture rush down the slopes and across the barren terrain, leaving typical desert conditions.

tain ranges. There, we see that the effects of altitude can mimic those of latitude (Figure 45.3).

Each biome consists of a number of **communities.** Communities are populations of plants, animals, and other organisms that interact more or less independently of other such groups. Communities are usually described as they are in their **climax state,** a "steady state" where there is little change and the organisms have established an equilibrium with the physical environment. As we will see in the next chapter, a great deal of ecology is focused on the community level of organization. We'll now consider the major biomes of the earth, beginning at the equator and moving through the temperate regions toward the poles.

THE TROPICAL RAIN FOREST BIOME

The first biome we encounter is the **tropical rain forest.** Typically, this lush and varied biome receives from 250 to 450 cm (100 to 180 in) of annual rainfall. There are a great number of plant species packed into such areas. Rain is usually rather evenly distributed throughout the year. In tropical rain forests there is little seasonal variation in temperature, often less than the change between day and night temperatures. The largest tropical rain forest is in the Amazon River Basin in South America; the second largest is in the wilds of the Indonesian Archipelago (see Figure 45.2).

The great amount of rainfall of the tropical rain

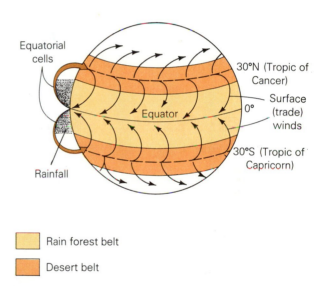

☐ Rain forest belt

☐ Desert belt

FIGURE 45.4 Air nearest the equator rises, forming equatorial air cells that carry abundant moisture. As an air cell rises, cooler, drier air rushes in underneath and the cell rotates. The rising air masses cool and dump most of their water in belts north and south of the equator. Rainfall is far more limited just above and below these belts and here are found some of the earth's great deserts.

forests can be traced to equatorial heat, an enormous source of energy. Heated air masses rise rapidly at the equator and are replaced by cooler air from the north or south. This activity results in the formation of enormous rotating **air cells,** which are thrown into a diagonal direction by the earth's rotation (Figure 45.4). The rising equatorial air cells lift great amounts of moisture, but as they gain altitude, they cool, and the moisture condenses and begins to fall as rain. By the time the air cells reach their northern and southern limits (roughly 30 degrees north and south), most of the moisture has been released. In addition to explaining the immense tropical rainfall, the behavior of equatorial air cells also explains why many of the earth's great deserts have formed just above and below the equatorial forests.

Plant and Animal Associations

A tropical rain forest is a verdant and beautiful place. The floor is dark and wet, the damp air ripe with smells. Unlike the situation in most other biomes, no single kind of plant is predominant. Any tree is likely to be a different species from its neighbors; the nearest tree of the same species may even be miles away.

The forest floor is usually shadowed by the nearly continuous leafy canopy of trees some 30 to 45 m tall. Below, smaller trees form rather distinct layers of subcanopies (Figure 45.5), interwoven by large numbers of vines. Both trees and vines may be festooned with **epiphytes,** plant species that have evolved an interesting way of competing for sunlight. Epiphytes live on the stems and branches of tall trees in the canopy and do not touch the soil below. They absorb water directly from the surrounding humid air.

The forest floor is often nearly devoid of foliage, but it is teeming with fungal and bacterial decomposers and insect scavengers. The darkness, warmth, and incredible humidity are ideal for rapid decomposition. However, the products of decomposition do not accumulate as humus (partially decayed organic material) and enrich the soil as they do in other forests. Instead, they rapidly cycle back into the living

FIGURE 45.5   The tropical rain forest as seen from a cleared area reveals its lush growth and hints at its stratification. Most of the animals live in the canopy or subcanopies, rarely descending to the dark forest floor.

FIGURE 45.6 Animals of the tropical rain forest are generally arboreal, each species specialized for life in specific parts of the canopy and subcanopy.

Scarlett macaw

Three-toed sloth

plants, leaving the soil notoriously poor. This is a major reason that clearing the tropical rain forests for any major agricultural undertaking is foolhardy—the benefits are short lived and marginal. Burning the trees cleared from such areas places an added CO_2 burden on the atmosphere (see Essay 45.1).

The tropical rain forest harbors an incredible number of animal species, more than any other terrestrial region. Insects and birds are particularly abundant, as are reptiles, small mammals, and amphibians. Many of the animal species are stratified according to the layers established by the plants, becoming specialists at occupying certain levels of the canopy and subcanopy. In one study of the Costa Rican rain forest, ecologists found 14 ground-foraging species, 59 species occupying the subcanopy, and 69 in the upper canopy. They further found that about two-thirds of the mammals were arboreal (tree dwellers), as were a number of frogs, lizards, and snakes (Figure 45.6).

Tropical rain forests are characterized by little temperature variation, heavy, rather evenly distributed annual rainfall, high species density, great species diversity, and marked stratification of the canopy.

Jungles, by the way, are the result of a disturbance of tropical rain forests. Where the sunlight strikes the ground, new growth abounds. Such growth is found in areas where the great canopy of trees has been

cleared and the area reclaimed by nature, and also along river banks. The myth of the dense, impenetrable jungle arose from river travelers who had little interest in going into it and traipsing around with the snakes.

THE TROPICAL SAVANNA BIOME

The **tropical savanna** biome is a special kind of grassland that often borders tropical rain forests. Unlike other grasslands, the savanna contains scattered trees or clumps of trees (Figure 45.7). And unlike tropical rain forests, savannas have a prolonged dry season and an annual rainfall of only 100 to 150 cm (40 to 60 in). The dry season is often marked by frequent and extensive fires, a phenomenon to which plants have had to adapt.

Plant and Animal Associations

The largest tropical savannas occur in Africa, but they are also found in South America and Australia. In Africa, while grasses are the dominant form of plant life, the strange, misshapen baobab trees, along with palms and colorful acacias, bring relief to the drab landscape. The number and variety of hooved animal species exceeds that of any other biome in Africa, and includes zebras, wildebeests, giraffes, and antelopes. This is also the domain of such infamous predators as lions and cheetahs.

FIGURE 45.7 Large hooved mammals are prominent among the savanna's herbivore population.

THE DESERT BIOME

The **desert** is both a dreaded place and a setting for uncounted fables, but the image most people have of deserts probably reflects only a few parts of the actual desert biomes. Deserts are actually quite varied places. The world's largest desert is the Sahara, followed by the vast Australian desert. A primary characteristic of the desert is severely limited, seasonal precipitation, usually less than 25 cm (10 in) per year. But while all deserts are dry and most are hot, there are cool northern deserts where winter snows are common. And all deserts have dramatic day-night extremes in temperature. Without the buffering effect of atmospheric moisture, the desert floor heats rapidly during the day and cools just as rapidly at night.

Plant and Animal Associations

Plants adapted to the extremely dry climates of deserts are known as **xerophytes** (*xeric,* "dry"). In the American desert, perennials such as the cactus, ocotillo, Joshua tree, creosote bush, sagebrush, and palo verde (Figure 45.8) are adapted to living for long periods with little water. The various cacti have greatly reduced water loss by replacing leaves with spines and producing a thick, waxy cuticle over their photosynthetic stems. Other perennials shed their small leathery leaves and remain dormant throughout the drier seasons.

Compared to other plants, leafy desert perennials tend to have fewer and more widely scattered guard cells, and even these are located mostly on the protected underside of their small leaves. Smaller leaves and fewer stomata help in conserving water, but the price is a considerably slower growth rate, since CO_2 uptake and photosynthesis are retarded. Some desert perennials close their stomata during the day and open them at night, storing CO_2 temporarily in intermediate compounds (see the CAM plants in Chapter 25).

The tiny but colorful desert annuals reveal another strategy. Their life cycle is short, an adaptation to the desert's infrequent rainfall. In many species, the tough, resistant seeds require a critical amount of water before germinating. If there is not enough water to trigger germination, the seed coats fail to split, and they just sit it out, perhaps for several seasons.

The animals of the desert are primarily arthropods, reptiles, birds, and mammals. Just as plants have had to adapt to the rigors of the desert, so have animals. Animals have the advantage of being able to adapt not only anatomically and physiologically, but behaviorally as well (see thermoregulation in Chapter 36).

Many desert animals avoid the heat by simply staying out of the daytime sun and becoming nocturnal (active at night). Mammals are largely represented by rodents, for which nocturnality has very clear advantages. (Rodents tend to lose water quickly, because of rapid breathing and because small animals have a large surface area relative to their volume.) The desert kangaroo rat (*Dipodomys deserti*) of the southern California deserts is particularly interesting because it *never* drinks. It survives on the water contained in its food and the metabolic water it produces through cell respiration. Its remarkably efficient kidney produces small quantities of highly concentrated urine, but most of the rat's water loss occurs through simple breathing.

Of course, predators such as owls and rattlesnakes must follow their prey, so they hunt mostly at night or in the cool of the evening. The relatively few species that are out and about in the daytime—such as the long-legged and swift lizards—are preyed on by hawks and roadrunners, which are also adapted to daylight conditions. Even the daytime animals, however, restrict most of their activity to the morning and evening hours (Figure 45.9).

THE CHAPARRAL BIOME

The **chaparral** biome (also, Mediterranean scrub forest) is rather insignificant among the forests of the world. It does, however, have unique characteristics and its own peculiar plant associations. For example, it is exclusively coastal, found mainly along the Pacific coast of North America and the coastal hills of Chile, the Mediterranean, southern Africa, and southern Australia. This biome is unique in that it consists of broad-leaved evergreens in regions marked by a very limited winter rainfall—an average of 25 cm (10 in)—followed by drought that extends through the rest of the year. The climate is moderated, however, by moist, cool air from the oceans (Figure 45.10).

During the dry season, the chaparral places the same demands on its inhabitants as does the desert; both plants and animals must adapt to long dry spells. In fact, some species in the two biomes are quite similar. But many of the chaparral plants are adapted to another factor—fire. Fire is a natural phenomenon encouraged by drought, resinous plants, and a deep layer of dry, slowly decomposing litter on the forest floor. Brush fires periodically sweep across the terrain, leaving behind the charred remains of plants and animals. Since the chaparral is made up chiefly of fire-adapted plant species, in most instances recovery is rapid, with shoots sprouting quickly from burned stumps and fire-resistant seeds. Ecologists describe the chaparral as a **fire-disclimax** community, which means that because of fire it never reaches a state of maturity. Virtually every stand of trees is in some state of recovery.

> The **chaparral** has a marine air flow but desert conditions. Its drought-resistant plants are often fire adapted. Animals are often nocturnal.

FIGURE 45.8 Both of the North American desert plants shown here (the saguaro, *left*, and the Joshua tree, *right*) have adapted to limited water; such plants are called *xerophytes*. Their thorny epidermis discourages browsing and helps shield the green surfaces from the harsh direct sunlight.

Saguaro

Prickly pear (foreground) and Joshua tree

(a) Roadrunner

(b) Desert iguana

(c) Desert kangaroo rat

(d) Great horned owl

FIGURE 45.9   Animals of the desert tend to forage in two shifts, day and night. Much of the activity occurs during early evening and early morning hours.

FIGURE 45.10   The chaparral in southern California may lack the glamour and luster of many other forests, but its plants are tenacious and hardy. These scrubby plants resist an annual drought that would discourage most other plants.

THE GRASSLAND BIOME

In the Northern Hemisphere, **grasslands** can form huge inland plains, such as the North American prairie and the vast Asian steppes. Extensive grasslands also occur in South America (pampas) and in Australia, where their area equals that of the desert (Figure 45.11). There are several similarities between grassland and desert; in fact, grassland often gradually fades into desert. The chief climatic difference between the two is precipitation—grasslands get more rain (between 25 and 100 cm per year). The rain, however, is of a seasonal nature, often not sustained or abundant enough to support forests. Another factor that prevents forest penetration is fire, a natural and recurring phenomenon in grasslands.

FIGURE 45.11 Grasslands, like savannas, support many herbivores. This South American grassland is made up mostly of bunchgrasses, the primary food of llamas, alpacas, and many smaller animals.

Plant and Animal Associations

As you might expect, the dominant plants of grasslands are grasses. But since there are many kinds of grasses, grasslands are very different from one place to the next. For example, on the American prairie (at least the part that is still identifiable), the grasses east of the Mississippi may grow nearly 3 m tall, while those in the West rarely exceed 0.5 m. Again, the difference is principally due to variation in rainfall.

Since rains are commonly seasonal in most grasslands, the plants have developed strategies for drought survival. In lowland regions, roots may penetrate as far as 2 m below the surface to the permanent water table. Some grasses, however, rely on a vast, spreading diffuse root system. In addition, grasses readily become dormant, reviving when water is once again available. Some grasses produce underground stems (rhizomes) that remain alive after all the foliage has died. Historically this matlike growth, or sod, prevented agricultural intrusion into the prairie until plowing implements were improved—hence the term "sodbuster." (As you are probably aware, there is little virgin grassland in the world today, because most of the natural grasses have been replaced by grains and other crops.)

Grasses are highly efficient at rapidly converting solar energy into the chemical-bond energy of their living matter, so it is not surprising that the grasslands can support large animal populations. Chief among the mammals are the hooved and burrowing types. In North America the hooved animals include bison and antelope, animals whose teeth and digestive systems are well adapted to a diet of tough grassland plants. Both groups were drastically reduced in number by hunting and agriculture, and are now seen only in protected areas.

Grasslands persist because of fire and limited, seasonal rainfall. Perennial grasses support immense populations of grazing insects and mammals.

THE TEMPERATE DECIDUOUS FOREST BIOME

If you live east of the Mississippi River, you may be well acquainted with the **temperate deciduous forest** biome. (A deciduous forest is one in which trees tend to lose their leaves seasonally.) The temperate deciduous biome extends over much of the eastern United States and northward into southeast Canada. It is also found in Europe and parts of China. Rainfall in the deciduous forest is rather evenly distributed throughout the year, often averaging more than 100 cm (39 in)—enough to support a variety of plant life.

Temperate deciduous forests are usually characterized by marked seasonal changes, but unlike more northerly biomes, they have a quite long growing season. With the onset of winter, much of the water

FIGURE 45.12 The deciduous forest changes its appearance with the seasons. The gently blushing spring turns to the lovely green hillside of summer that explodes in a riot of colors when autumn arrives. All in sharp contrast to the starkness of winter.

becomes frozen and unavailable to plants, so most perennial deciduous species become dormant (Figure 45.12).

Plant and Animal Associations

The American deciduous forest is generally subdivided into a number of forest types in which certain species dominate. For example, beech and maple forests dominate in the north, while oak-hickory and oak-chestnut complexes are prevalent farther south (mostly oak today, since most chestnuts have been killed by fungi).

The deciduous forests were once the home of the gray wolf, the mountain lion, and black bear. Now these once important predators are restricted to protected areas or, as in the case of the wolf, have been virtually eliminated from all but the more inaccessible areas of the north. Carnivores of the North American deciduous forest today include the bobcat, racoon, opossum, skunk, and an occasional red fox.

Animals of the deciduous forest adapt to the drastic seasonal changes in a number of ways. Some, primarily birds, migrate to southerly winter habitats. Others lapse into the long chilled stupor called *hibernation*, their metabolism drastically lowered. Yet others—bears, for example—fall into a deep sleep, occasionally rousing themselves for brief foraging expeditions. Some species like the bobcat and fox must simply brave the cold and its food shortages.

> **Temperate deciduous forests** have moderate amounts of precipitation and seasonal temperature extremes. Winter adaptations include leaf shedding and dormancy in plants, and migration, dormancy, and hibernation in animals.

THE TAIGA BIOME

The **taiga**, a **northern coniferous** or **boreal forest**, is almost exclusively confined to the Northern Hemisphere. There is nothing comparable in the Southern Hemisphere. It is made up of great forests of pine,

FIGURE 45.13 The taiga is an extensive biome, found almost exclusively in the Northern Hemisphere. Since the conditions of the taiga are duplicated in high mountains, similar communities are found here.

(a) Elk

(b) Grizzly bear

(c) Lynx

(d) Taiga biome

spruce, hemlock, and fir that extend across the North American and Asian continents. Smaller forests are found at higher elevations in many mountain ranges (Figure 45.13). The taiga is unmistakable; there is nothing else like it. It is subject to long, frigid winters and short summer growing seasons.

Plant and Animal Associations

Although the taiga is characterized by conifers, communities of poplar, alder, willow, and birch may be found in disturbed places. Furthermore, the taiga is interrupted in places by extensive bogs, or muskegs, the remnants of very large ponds. The most common

trees are spruce; low-lying shrubs, mosses, and grasses form the spongy ground cover.

Conifers have adapted to their cold dry environment through reduced needle-like or scale-like leaves that are covered by a waxy secretion. This specialization retards water loss, an important factor since arid conditions are common and ground water is frozen and unavailable throughout most of the year. (One is reminded of the spines and waxy cuticles of desert plants.)

The taiga harbors such large herbivores as moose, elk, and deer. It is also practically the last refuge of both grizzly and black bears. Wolves still roam here, as do lynx and wolverines. Rabbits, porcupines, hares, and rodents abound, but insect populations aren't as large as they are in deciduous forests. However, there is a disconcerting abundance of mosquitos and flies in some regions during the summer.

> The **taiga,** a northern coniferous forest, has low precipitation and vast seasonal extremes. Plant drought adaptations include needle-like and scalelike leaves. Some animals remain active; others migrate, become dormant, or hibernate.

Coniferous forests are also found in high mountains such as the Sierra Nevadas, where conditions mimic those of the taiga, and in regions of more moderate climate. Examples include the famous coastal redwood stands of Oregon and California, the sequoia forests of central California, and vast pine forests in our southeastern coastal plain.

The taiga is a continuing target of the lumber industry, as are more southerly coniferous forests. The forests have been partially protected so far by their very size, but the lumber companies seem to be taking whatever they can reach, including ancient stands of redwoods. Their much-publicized replanting programs usually replace mixed forests of genetically diverse and disease-resistant plants with artificially developed and genetically homogeneous trees that are fast-growing and can quickly be reharvested. Biologists are still trying to assess the dangers of such genetic uniformity in a large system.

THE TUNDRA BIOME

Tundra, the northernmost biome, has no equivalent in the Southern Hemisphere (except for a few alpine meadows where similar conditions are found). The annual precipitation is meager, often less than 15 cm (6 in), and much of this falls as snow. During the greater part of the year, much of the water is ice and is unavailable to most forms of life.

The tundra's growing season lasts about two months. During this time, the frozen surface waters thaw and ponds begin to form everywhere. Since the soil remains permanently frozen as **permafrost** a few feet below, the surface water cannot percolate down. Although the growing season is short, the summer days are long, permitting an extended *daily* growing period.

Plant and Animal Associations

Tall trees and shrubs are entirely absent from the tundra, except around streams. While the tundra at higher elevations may be composed of only scattered and rather drab plants, in the lower areas growth may be luxurious, dense, and colorful. Pioneering lichens and mosses are common, as are dwarfed versions of some familiar trees, among them willows and birches. Grasses, rushes, sedges, and other low-lying plants complete the summer ground cover (Figure 45.14).

Surprisingly, animal life isn't rare in this peculiar and rugged northern biome. In fact, the tundra supports some rather large herbivores. In North America we find the caribou and musk oxen, and in Europe and Asia, the reindeer. Other animals of the tundra include the ptarmigan, the snowshoe hare, the arctic ground squirrel, and the ever-present, legendary lemmings (see Figure 45.14).

Winter comes early in the tundra, and with the rapidly shortening days the migratory animals begin their southerly trek. The caribou, for example, leave for the forested taiga, where winter food is more plentiful. Those species that remain prepare for survival in a number of ways. Lemmings retreat to food-laden burrows; ptarmigans tunnel into snow banks, to emerge only periodically on foraging expeditions. Since the larger resident herbivores don't hibernate, they must rove the barren, windswept landscape to feed on subsistence foods such as mosses and lichens.

> The **tundra** is characterized by **permafrost,** limited precipitation, long winters, and flooding in summer. In winter, many animals migrate, a few remain active, while others become dormant or hibernate.

THE MARINE ENVIRONMENT

Even a casual glance at a globe reveals that most (about 71%) of the earth's surface is oceanic and the greatest depths of these oceans are deeper than the peaks of the highest mountains are high. The **marine environment** is indeed extensive and complex, containing a vast array of communities. These are divided among two major *provinces:* the deeper, open sea or **oceanic province,** and the shallower seas along the coastlines, the **neritic province.** The marine envi-

FIGURE 45.14 In summer, the treeless low tundra becomes a marsh as the snow melts. With little runoff, the landscape becomes dotted with small ponds. Plants include a number of dwarfed trees, grasses, and abundant lichens called reindeer moss.

(a) Tundra biome

(b) Snowy owl

(c) Lemming

(d) Caribou

ronment can also be subdivided vertically into the light-penetrating **euphotic zone** and the perpetually dark **aphotic zone** (Figure 45.15).

The Oceanic Province

The seas are not uniformly filled with life; in fact, life may be quite sparse in the oceanic province. Nevertheless, because of the vastness of the open seas, the *total* amount of life there is enormous. Much of this life is found in the sunlit euphotic zone, which contains populations of minute **plankton,** floating and drifting organisms, and **nekton,** the swimmers that feed on the plankton.

Perhaps the greatest mysteries on earth lie in the dark waters of the oceanic province, the depths of the **abyssal region.** The deepest part of the ocean is the Marianas Trench, which is 10,680 m (over 6 mi)

deep. These mysterious depths are places of tremendous pressure and chilling cold. Nevertheless, the abyss supports a surprising number of peculiar scavengers and predators. Generally lacking a producer population (although we will encounter a startling exception in the next chapter), these **benthic** (bottom-dwelling) creatures rely on the continuous rain of the remains of creatures from the euphotic zone above.

The **euphotic zone** of the **oceanic province** (open sea), contains plankton and a limited food chain. **Benthic** decomposers and scavengers of the **abyss,** rely on detritus from above.

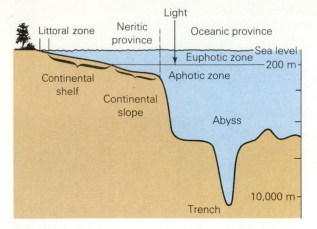

FIGURE 45.15 Organization of the marine environment.

The Neritic Province

In the neritic province, the land masses extend outward below the sea, forming the highly variable **continental shelf.** The neritic province ends at the **continental slope,** where the shelf drops off, often abruptly. In the shallower areas of the shelf, light penetrates to the ocean bottom. Such regions are constantly stirred by waves, winds, and tides, which keep nutrients suspended and support many forms of swimming and bottom-dwelling life. Just off shore, giant kelps and other seaweeds form extensive beds, offering hiding places for many fish.

One of the more productive* regions in the marine environment is found farther offshore, particularly in the province's colder waters. Here we find regions of **upwellings,** where deep, nutrient-laden colder waters move to the surface. Little is known about such vertical movement of water in the open sea, but we have a better idea of what causes coastal upwellings. They are generally seasonal and occur when coastal winds blow either seaward or parallel to the coast, moving the surface layers, which are then replaced by deeper layers. This stirring brings up nutrients that would otherwise be forever locked in the bottom sediments. The nutrients can then help support photosynthetic organisms, which provide the base for marine **food chains**—the passage of energy and essential molecules from one group of organisms to the next. (The vast anchovy fisheries off the coast of Peru are dependent upon such upwellings.) Let's look more closely at how the marine food chain is organized.

*Productivity is the rate at which biomass is produced per unit area by autotrophs.

Marine producers. As light passes through the waters of the euphotic zone, its energy is utilized by a variety of microscopic photosynthesizing organisms—chiefly diatoms and dinoflagellates—that are collectively called **phytoplankton.**

Phytoplankton, along with the seaweeds, are the **primary producers** of the sea. This means that energy enters the marine ecosystem via these minute creatures. It has been estimated that 80% to 90% of the earth's photosynthetic activity is carried on by marine organisms. Thus, the sea's food chain begins with tiny floating phototrophic marine protists capturing the sun's energy within their fragile bodies. The phototrophs are fed upon by heterotrophs only a little larger than themselves, the **zooplankton.** A variety of animals, from the fishes to the great baleen whales, also feed on both sorts of plankton. In ecological terms, heterotrophs are known, quite logically, as **consumers** (Figure 45.16).

The **upwelling** of nutrients supports abundant life in the neritic province. Complex food chains begin with **phytoplankton producers.** They support **zooplankton,** which in turn supports larger **consumers.**

Coastal Communities

The varying physical makeup of the coast—sandy beaches, rocky shores, bays, estuaries, tidal flats, and reefs—provide for a number of coastal communities. Such communities fall within the **littoral zone** (the shallow coastal water including the intertidal area, which is exposed at low tide only). Life is quite diverse here because of the presence of shelter and hiding places, abundant sunlight, and nutrients swept in by water runoff from the land. In fact, coastal communities are among the most biologically productive of the marine environments. However, the very nature of the shallow, littoral zone imposes critical survival problems on its inhabitants. Included are violently surging waves and surf, cyclic flooding and drying as the tides come and go, and often significant variations in salinity because of evaporation at low tide and the presence of freshwater runoff from the land.

Estuaries, where rivers run into oceans, can produce the problem of changing salinity, while low tides in mud flats require that their inhabitants be burrowers. Along rocky coasts (Figure 45.17), a number of plants and animals have adapted to the surging waves by developing means of holding fast

FIGURE 45.16 The oceanic food chain. Tiny phytoplankton capture the energy of the sun. They are eaten by animals larger than themselves, which are, in turn, eaten by larger animals. At the top are the largest carnivores of the sea.

FIGURE 45.17 Rocky tide pools. The rocky coast is home for numerous marine animals. Each is adapted in some way to withstand both the surging and pounding of waves and intermittent periods of exposure to the air at low tide.

to the rocks. In other cases, animals may seek refuge in burrows, or they may lodge themselves in crevices and on the undersides of rocks.

Among the most fascinating of the shore communities are coral reefs. **Coral reefs** are common in tropical and subtropical waters where the temperatures average between 23°C and 25°C (Figure 45.18). Corals are vast colonies of coelenterates that secrete heavy walls of calcium carbonate around themselves (Chapter 27). Their irregular growth provides natural refuges for marine animals, including sponges, bryozoans, mollusks (such as the octopus), and many kinds of fishes. Sharks commonly patrol the deep waters alongside the reefs. Where these formations appear along coastlines, they are called **barrier reefs.** The largest is the Great Barrier Reef, which extends for 1200 mi along the east coast of Queensland, Australia.

THE FRESHWATER ENVIRONMENT

The freshwater communities of rivers and streams, lakes and ponds are among the most heavily studied places on earth. Most of the lakes that grace the

earth's surface have been formed rather recently in our geological history. In fact, most northerly lakes were born at the time of the last glacial retreats (10,000 to 12,000 years ago). Lakes are also produced through volcanic activity, as was Crater Lake in Oregon, and through uplifting of the land, which created the typically shallow lakes of Florida. Lake Baikal in Russia, the world's deepest at 1750 m (5742 ft), is especially ancient, having been formed in the Mesozoic era.

Limnologists (*limne;* "pool or lake"), ecologists who study freshwater communities, have divided lakes into zones, each with its own physical features and each harboring a characteristic array of life. The zones are called **littoral, limnetic,** and **profundal** (Figure 45.19). Although the terminology is different, the organization is similar to that of the marine environment.

Life in the Lake Zones

The littoral zone is the area where light penetrates to the bottom of the lake. Producers in the littoral zone include a variety of free-floating and rooted plants

FIGURE 45.18 The coral reef and its inhabitants.

that form a progression of types as the water deepens. Some rooted plants break the lake's surface; others are completely submerged. As in marine waters, freshwater producers include numerous species of photosynthetic bacteria, protists, and algae. Together, these form the phytoplankton (Figure 45.20). Consumers in the littoral zone include protists, snails, mussels, aquatic insects, and insect larvae. Salamanders and frogs also prefer the littoral zone, as do

both herbivorous and carnivorous fish and turtles. And here we find a number of wading birds and birds that step gingerly along the mats of broad-leaved plants.

The limnetic zone is in open water, but includes only the depths penetrated by light. Almost all the producers here are microscopic. They include the phytoplankton that extend from the littoral zone, along with flagellated algal forms such as *Euglena*

FIGURE 45.19   Lake zonation. Each zone differs in its physical conditions and inhabitants.

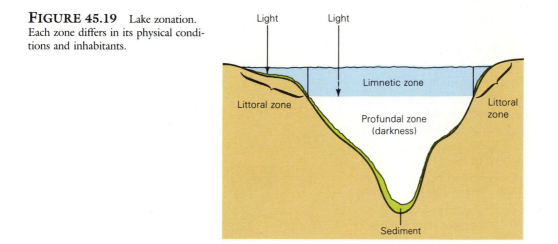

FIGURE 45.20   Producers of the littoral zone include (a) bottom-rooted, aquatic plants such as cattails, bulrushes, and arrowheads, floating water lilies, and pond weeds. (b) Microscopic producers (phytoplankton) include many filamentous and single-celled green algae, along with diatoms and cyanobacteria. (c) Primary consumers include the familiar freshwater snails, bottom-dwelling water mites, crustaceans, insect larvae, and nymphs. (d) Smaller aquatic predators of the littoral zone include the diving beetles, water scorpions, and nymphs of the damsel and dragon flies. There are also larger carnivorous species such as fish, frogs, and wading birds.

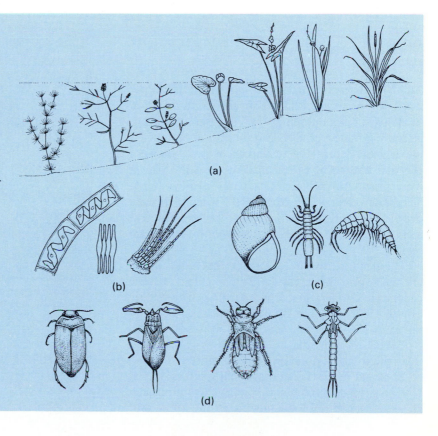

and *Volvox*. In northern lakes, phytoplankton populations undergo seasonal **blooms** during which their productivity exceeds that of the plants of the littoral zone. These blooms are a response to available nutrients, sufficient light, and favorable temperatures, and often follow a bloom of nitrogen-fixing **cyanobacteria.** The primary consumers are the zooplankton, composed largely of tiny crustaceans. Their great numbers are made up of only a few species, whose populations rise and fall in response to the numbers of producers. At the higher consumer levels we find principally the lake fishes, which consist mainly of plankton-feeding species and the carnivorous species that feed upon them. The food web of the limnetic zone is often simple and direct.

The profundal zone begins where light ceases to penetrate the lake waters and extends to the muddy, sediment-rich lake floor. There are, of course, no producers here. Life is represented mainly by decomposers such as bacteria and fungi, and by a few detritus-feeding clams and wormlike insect larvae. All of the profundal species are adapted to periods of very low oxygen concentrations. The sparse life here is critical to the organisms above, because decomposers convert deposits formed of corpses raining from above into mineral nutrients. As in marine environments, the distribution of these nutrients throughout the lake depends on the vertical movement of the waters.

Thermal Overturn and Lake Productivity

There is no aerobic (oxygen-using) life in the deeper waters of the tropical Lake Tanganyika, (at 1450 m, or almost a mile) but temperate Lake Baikal, which is about 300 m deeper, does much better at supporting life at great depths. The difference is the amount of **thermal overturn,** the vertical movement of water masses brought on by seasonal temperature changes. Thermal overturns carry dissolved oxygen to the lake depths and bring nutrients to the surface. The seasons, of course, are more marked in temperate regions.

Thermal overturn in temperate lakes occurs in the fall and spring, when surface waters undergo drastic changes in temperature. It is a peculiar characteristic of water that, as its temperature decreases, its density increases—it gets heavier—until it reaches 4°C. Below 4°C water's density *decreases* sharply, and at 0°C (the freezing point) it is at its lightest.

These properties mean that cooling surface waters tend to sink, displacing and stirring the warmer layers below, which subsequently rise to the surface. But

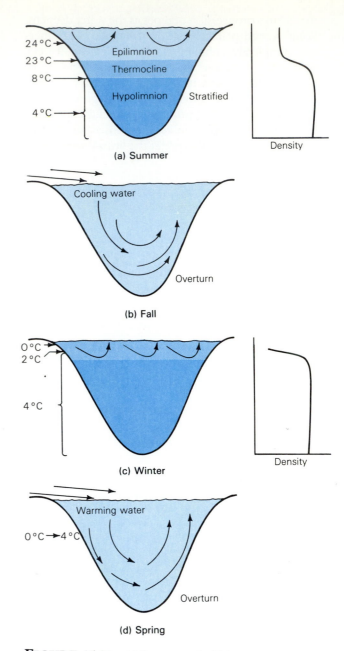

FIGURE 45.21 **(a)** In summer the highest water temperature is in the epilimnion and the lowest is in the hypolimnion. Between the two, a steep temperature gradient, or thermocline, occurs. Movement in the less dense epilimnion cannot disturb the denser cooler layers below, so overturn cannot occur. **(b)** In the fall, cooling surface waters approach 4°C (maximum density), sink to the bottom, and permit a wind-driven overturn to occur. **(c)** In winter, the summer temperature gradient is reversed, with the coldest temperatures at the surface (no thermocline forms), yet the density gradient is roughly similar to that of summer, preventing overturn. **(d)** In early spring, warming surface waters reach 4°C (maximum density) and sink, starting another wind-driven overturn.

later in the season, the sinking and stirring stop as surface waters cool below 4°C (reaching their lightest state at freezing). In case you've ever wondered, that's why lakes start freezing at the surface. The effects of changes in temperatures and density are seen in Figure 45.21.

The conditions that prevent overturn in Lake Tanganyika are similar to those that occur in temperate-zone lakes during the summer. A temperature gradient exists between top and bottom waters. The lighter, warmer, upper waters may be well mixed by wind action, but they cannot move into the dense, colder waters below. The result is that many temperate-zone lakes have three distinct summer temperature regions. There is an upper warm-water region, the **epilimnion** (upper lake), and a lower cold-water region, the **hypolimnion** (lower lake), each with relatively constant temperatures throughout. Between the two is a region called the **thermocline,** where temperatures drop as depth increases. Typically, oxygen depletion begins just below the thermocline.

In this chapter we have seen that the vastness of our "small" planet permits a wide range of environments and a huge array of habitats. Keeping in mind the constant exceptions we encounter in biology, it is possible to categorize the earth's environment according to the arrangement of the life it supports. Such generalization may help us to understand the present status of life on the planet and may also yield clues regarding the historical progression that led to what we see today.

SUMMARY

THE BIOSPHERE

Ecology is the study of the interaction between organisms and their environment. The biosphere includes land areas, water habitats, and life-supporting air.

The Atmosphere

The atmospheric gases are primarily water vapor, nitrogen, oxygen, and carbon dioxide. It is relatively thin, but effectively screens out UV radiation. The presence of water confers a heat-retaining characteristic that provides a moderate climate.

Solar Energy

Of the incoming solar energy, 30% is reflected back, 20% is retained in the atmosphere, and 50% reaches the surface. The resulting heat energy powers the hydrologic cycle, redistributing water and heat over the earth.

Climate and the Tilted Earth

The earth, spinning on a tilted earth's axis as it orbits the sun, experiences continuously changing seasons, making most of the earth readily habitable.

THE BIOMES AND WATERS OF THE EARTH

The uneven heating of the earth and the variable climate it produces result in the varied distribution of life across the planet. A biome is an array of plants and animals distributed over a geographic area that has distinctive climatic conditions. Life on earth is distributed into 10 major terrestrial biomes, plus the marine and freshwater realms. Each biome consists of communities, which are usually described in their climax states (in which organisms have established a sort of equilibrium with the environment).

THE TROPICAL RAIN FOREST BIOME

Plant and Animal Associations

Tropical rain forests receive about 250–450 cm (or 100–180 in) of rainfall per year. Equatorial heat produces rising air cells that rotate in northerly and southerly directions dumping most of their water in the tropics. The great variety of plant species precludes the predominance of any single species. Trees form canopies and subcanopies, while the forest floor supports primarily fungal and bacterial decomposers and insects. The soil is poor because the products of decomposition are washed away or rapidly recycled into living plants. The tropical forest harbors an incredible number of animal species, many of which have become adapted to life in specific layers of the canopies and subcanopies.

THE TROPICAL SAVANNA BIOME

Plant and Animal Associations

The tropical savanna is a special kind of grassland that often borders on tropical rain forests. It contains scattered trees or clumps of trees and has a prolonged dry season, with an annual rainfall of 100–150 cm (40–60 in). The largest tropical savannas occur in Africa, where grasses are the dominant form of plant life. There are many hooved animals, as well as predators such as lions and cheetahs.

THE DESERT BIOME

Plant and Animal Associations

Deserts receive less than 25 cm (10 in) of seasonal precipitation per year. They also have dramatic day-night extremes in temperature. Xerophytes have adapted to the dry climate and temperature extremes with waxy cuticles, fewer stomata and leaves, and seeds that can remain dormant for many seasons. Animals adapt by staying out of the sun and being active at night.

THE CHAPARRAL BIOME

The chaparral is exclusively coastal and consists of broad-leaved evergreens in regions marked by winter rainfall and summer droughts. Plants and animals have adapted in much the same way as those in desert biomes, with additional plant adaptations for fire.

THE GRASSLAND BIOME

Plant and Animal Associations

Grasslands receive more moisture than deserts but resemble them in other respects. Plants must adapt to periods of drought and be resistant to fire; many have vast diffuse root systems or produce rhizomes and stolons that remain alive after foliage has died. Abundant plant life supports a variety of insects, birds, and hooved and burrowing mammals.

THE TEMPERATE DECIDUOUS FOREST BIOME

Plant and Animal Associations

Temperate deciduous forests cover large sections of the world's landmasses. Precipitation is evenly distributed throughout the year and supports a variety of plant life. The forests have a long growing season, but many deciduous species become dormant in winter. Beech and maple trees dominate northerly American forests, while oak, hickory, and chestnut trees are prevalent farther south. Animals in deciduous forests, a mixture of herbivores and carnivores, adapt to seasonal changes by migrating, by hibernating, or by altering hunting patterns to adjust to food shortages.

THE TAIGA BIOME

Plant and Animal Associations

The taiga, made up of coniferous forests, is almost exclusively confined to the Northern Hemisphere. It is subject to long, severe winters and short growing seasons. Taiga is marked in places by muskegs, the remnants of large ponds. Conifers have adapted to the climate with needle-like leaves that retain water. The taiga supports large herbivores and a variety of other mammals.

THE TUNDRA BIOME

Plant and Animal Associations

Tundra is the northernmost land biome. During most of the year much of its water is tied up as ice; a few feet below the surface, the soil is permanently frozen. The growing season is short but days are long. Only a few species of plants grow in upper regions, but lichens, mosses, grasses, and some trees grow in lower areas. The tundra can support large herbivores and predators as well as smaller animals. Animals must migrate or otherwise adapt to the long, frigid winters.

THE MARINE ENVIRONMENT

The extensive marine environment can be divided into neritic provinces along coastlines and oceanic provinces in the deeper open sea. (It can also be divided into euphotic and aphotic zones.)

The Oceanic Province

The oceanic province's deep abyssal regions are characterized by tremendous pressure and cold waters, yet support a surprising array of scavengers and predators.

The Neritic Province

The neritic province covers the continental shelf, ending at the continental slope. In shallower areas, suspended nutrients support many forms of swimming and bottom-dwelling life. The most productive areas are farther offshore, in regions of upwellings, where deep, nutrient-laden waters move to the surface. The nutrients help support photosynthesizing organisms (primarily phytoplankton) that are the base of the marine food chain. These primary producers are eaten by zooplankton, which are in turn eaten by many fish and marine mammals.

Coastal Communities

Coastal communities include sandy beaches, rocky shores, bays, estuaries (where rivers meet the ocean), tidal flats, and reefs. These areas can change dramatically with tides and weather, so the inhabitants have adapted in a number of ways to such forces as pounding waves, changing salinity, and periodic dry conditions.

THE FRESHWATER ENVIRONMENT

Most lakes are recent in origin, products of glaciation. Limnologists divide lakes into littoral, limnetic, and profundal zones.

Life in the Lake Zones

Lakes, like terrestrial communities, have producers, consumers, and reducers, with nutrients and gases cycling through the trophic layers. Lake ecosystems can be divided into littoral, limnetic, and profundal zones. Littoral zones, where light penetrates to the bottom, include shorelines and shallow waters where sunlight and nutrients are abundant. Plants form a progression from the shore outward. Limnetic zones, in which there is still light, can support many types of producers and consumers. The profundal zone is the deepest level, where light ceases to penetrate the water. Although few producers are found there, it is rich in nutrients filtering down from above and supports a large population of bacteria and fungi.

Thermal Overturn and Lake Productivity

Thermal overturn, the vertical movement of water masses brought on by seasonal climatic changes, carries dissolved oxygen to lake depths and brings nutrients to the surface. Many temperate-zone lakes have a warm epilimnion, a cold hypolimnion, and a thermocline between the two (in summer).

KEY TERMS

ecology	desert	euphotic zone	littoral zone
biosphere	xerophyte	aphotic zone	estuary
solar energy	chaparral	abyssal region	coral reef
hydologic cycle	grassland	benthic	barrier reef
biome	temperate deciduous forest	continental shelf	limnologist
community	taiga	continental slope	limnetic zone
climax state	northern coniferous (boreal) forest	upwellings	profundal zone
tropical rain forest	tundra	food chain	bloom
air cell	permafrost	phytoplankton	thermal overturn
epiphyte	marine environment	primary producer	epilimnion
jungle	oceanic province	zooplankton	hypolimnion
tropical savanna	neritic province	consumer	thermocline

REVIEW QUESTIONS

1 Define the term biosphere and characterize its actual extent. (p. 717)

2 List the contents of the atmosphere. Which is largely responsible for the earth's moderate climate? (p. 717)

3 Discuss two vital aspects of the earth's atmosphere that are being disrupted by human activities. (p. 718)

4 Describe what happens to solar energy reaching the earth's atmosphere. What does the presence of water vapor have to do with this? (p. 718)

5 What would the earth's climate be like had the axis not been tilted? Explain. (pp. 718, 719)

6 Define the term biome and suggest three or four factors that determine a biome's characteristics. (p. 720)

7 List three physical factors that make the presence of a tropical rain forest biome possible. (pp. 721–722)

8 Discuss the special organization of plant life in the tropical rain forest. How does this affect the distribution of animals? (pp. 722–723)

9 Suggest reasons why modern agriculture fails in the tropical rain forest biome. In what ways are such activities affecting the biosphere? (pp. 722–723)

10 Specifically, how does the tropical savanna differ from the grassland biome? List several familiar animal inhabitants. (p. 723)

11 List several physical characteristics of deserts. (p. 724)

12 Where do deserts occur? Summarize the two major situations responsible for desert formation. (p. 724)

13 Discuss 3 ways plants adapt to desert conditions. (p. 724)

14 Describe the kangaroo rat's physiological and behavioral adaptations to desert life. (p. 725)

15 List four specific locations of the chaparral forest biome. What physical characteristics do all have in common? (p. 725)

16 Explain what the term "fire-disclimax" means. To what biomes does this apply? (p. 725)

17 List four regions where major grasslands occur and summarize the contributing climatic factors. (p. 726)

18 What is there about grasses that enables grasslands to support vast numbers of large herbivores? (p. 727)

19 To what special climatic conditions must life in the temperate deciduous forest adapt? (p. 727)

20 List the alternatives open to animals facing winter in the temperate deciduous forest biome. (p. 728)

21 Characterize the dominating plants and describe their special adaptations. (pp. 729–730)

22 Name several more southerly regions supporting large coniferous forests. In which do conditions mimic those of the taiga? (p. 730)

23 Where is the tundra located? List several unique characteristics. How do these affect plant life? (p. 730)

24 Prepare a simple scheme showing the organization of the marine biome into provinces and zones. (p. 730)

25 List several animals that inhabit the abyss. Is there a producer population? What is the basic source of energy? (p. 731)

26 Where is most ocean life concentrated? Describe the phenomenon that assures the producers of a continuing supply of nutrients. (p. 732)

27 Starting with primary producers, diagram a typical marine food chain. (p. 732)

28 To what special conditions must marine animals adapt in the estuaries? Along the rocky coast? (p. 732)

29 What geological force produced most of the world's northern lakes? In which regions do lakes experience the least amount of thermal overturn? (p. 734)

30 Prepare a diagram showing the zonation of a lake. In which of the zones are producers most numerous? In which are they absent? Why? (p. 734)

31 In which lake zone is the food chain most complex? Describe this. (pp. 734–735)

32 What chain of events determines the extent of life in the limnetic zones? (p. 736)

33 Characterize temperature conditions of tropical lakes or temperate zone lakes in summer. How do these conditions affect the distribution of oxygen? (p. 736)

34 In what parts of the year does thermal overturn occur? Explain what brings this on and how it affects life in the lake. (pp. 736–737)

46

ECOSYSTEMS AND COMMUNITIES

Over the long eons during which life has evolved on the planet, it has invaded, groped, held, thrived, yielded, and died. Its watchword, in a very real sense, has been exploitation, as it reached into every available nook and cranny of the earth, gleaning whatever essentials were available and interacting with other life forms all the while. The result has been myriad life forms that have adapted not only to the habitats offered by the earth but also to each other. Thus we find "constellations" of organisms that have specific roles in the larger picture. To best understand living things and their places in nature, we must not consider them singly but rather as part of a system, a grand interacting group.

We will first consider a particular kind of interacting system called an **ecosystem.** In ecology, each unit of interacting organisms and the physical environment of which they are a part is known as an **ecosystem,** a handy operational term that can be applied at just about any level, from the earth itself to a tiny pool of microorganisms. Of course, few researchers would want to consider any such unwieldy system as the earth itself, so most choose to describe ecosystems in terms of energy flow through **trophic levels** (positions in the food chain) within a specific interacting group. Our plan here is to first discuss the common characteristics of ecosystems and then to learn how they influence organisms. We can begin with the concept of energy flow.

> **Ecosystems** are units of interacting organisms and their physical environment.

ENERGETICS IN ECOSYSTEMS

In the last chapter we saw that about 50% of the solar energy reaching the atmosphere finds its way to the earth's surface. This enormous amount of energy is vitally important in warming the earth and shifting its waters about. But a comparatively small amount (about one-tenth of one percent, as a worldwide average) is captured by photosynthesizers of the earth's ecosystems. Meager as it seems, this energy is enough to produce 150 to 200 billion metric tons of dry organic matter each year.

Trophic Levels

Let's review a few basic terms regarding the flow of energy through ecosystems. It is first captured by **producers** (autotrophs: phototrophs and chemotrophs). From there, energy passes to various **consumers,** organisms that must rely on others for the organic compounds they require. In the last chapter we described food chains in the marine ecosystem. There we saw that phytoplankton, the producers, were fed upon by zooplankton, which were fed upon by several levels of larger and larger marine creatures. The bodies of both the producers and the consumers must finally yield to the decomposers. Figure 46.1, a rather generalized view, traces the flow of energy through several trophic levels. As you would expect, the passage of energy is, in effect, the passage of food molecules.

Producers. The phototrophic producers account for the preponderance of food molecules. They include plants, algal protists, and phototrophic bacteria. The photosynthesizers use light energy captured by various pigments to produce organic materials from carbon dioxide, water, and a few minerals (see Chapter 7). The chemotrophic producers are bacteria that obtain energy from inorganic substances in the earth's crust (see Essay 46.1). The combined mass of the earth's producers is about 99% of the total present in the biosphere.

Consumers. Consumers include animals, fungi, predatory protists, and bacteria. In other words,

these are the earth's heterotrophs. (The fungi and bacteria make up a special category, which we will come to next.) Since some consumers eat producers, others eat other consumers, and some eat both, the flow of energy through the consumers involves several trophic levels. Thus we have **primary consumers,** the herbivores that feed directly on producers; **secondary consumers,** carnivores that feed on primary consumers; and so on through **tertiary, quaternary,** and even higher consumer levels (with increasingly rare representatives).

Organizing the trophic levels in this manner is obviously reminiscent of the simple food chains we considered earlier. But in reality, nothing is ever that simple. Most consumers cross trophic levels. For example, there are few true carnivores (sharks and some flies are examples). Consider humans. At how many trophic levels do we feed? Do we have salad with our steak? The steak comes from a herbivore, of course—but what if we eat a tuna sandwich? Tuna eat other carnivores. Because of such complexities, feeding patterns in a community are better represented by **food webs,** such as we see in Figure 46.2.

Decomposers. Decomposers are great in number but small in size. This becomes apparent when we realize that they primarily comprise fungi and bacte-

FIGURE 46.1 Sunlight energy is captured by producers during photosynthesis. It then passes, as chemical bond energy in foods, from one trophic level to another. Eventually the energy passes to decomposers. Each transfer is about 10% efficient. The remaining energy escapes as heat.

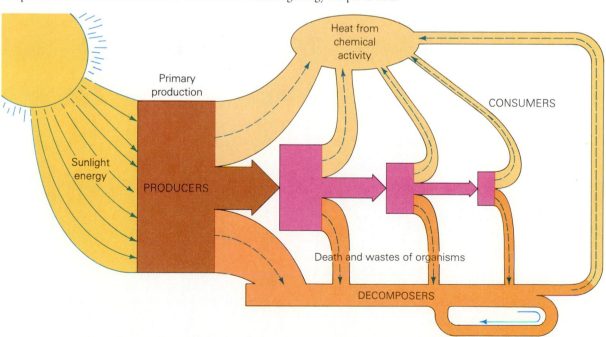

Deep down on the ocean floor, well over a mile beneath the surface, a number of benthic (bottom) communities thrive in the cold blackness. There are no producers here, but there is life. The source of nutrients and energy is the constant deluge of organic debris, raining down from the food webs above. Such sources of nutrients rarely go unexploited in nature.

Until 1977, this might well have summarized our knowledge of life on the ocean floor. Scientists believed that scavengers and decomposers were the only inhabitants of benthic communities. But in that year the research submarine *Alvin,* cruising at a depth of 2500 m near the Galápagos Islands, came upon a startling sight.

The scientists aboard *Alvin* saw some sort of turbulence on the ocean floor. On closer examination it was found to be a vent in the seabed spewing forth hot matter that, upon analysis, turned out to be hydrogen sulfide and carbon diox-

ide. This in itself was not entirely unexpected, but what they saw nearby was surprising indeed. The waters around the vent were cloudy (a condition later attributed to dense aggregations of bacteria). Enormous, strange tubeworms—blood-red, nearly 3 m long, and as thick as a man's wrist—bristled from the ocean floor. They were later classified as **pogonophorans,** mouthless and gutless animals, cleverly named *Riftia pachyptila. Riftia's* mode of feeding represents one of the most recently discovered and truly fascinating examples of mutualism. An extensive organ in the worm, the **trophosome,** houses vast numbers of chemoautotrophic vent bacteria, a type capable of extracting energy from simple chemicals and using that energy to reduce carbon dioxide, forming carbohydrates much in the manner of plants and other phototrophs (they have their own version of the Calvin cycle). The raw materials, hydrogen sulfide, oxygen, and carbon dioxide, are absorbed by

the worm's feathery plume and transported to the trophosome bacteria. In return, the bacteria provide a steady source of nutrients for distribution and use by the worm. Not surprisingly, a number of other rift animals have developed similar symbiotic relationships with the vent bacteria.

Smaller unknown wormlike animals, arranged in spaghetti-like masses, were found with more familiar filter-feeding crabs, mussels, barnacles, and a variety of other animals common to benthic communities. The seabed around the vents also gave rise to large clusters of huge, smooth-shelled clams with blood-red flesh caused by high levels of hemoglobin.

The discovery of the vent communities intrigued the scientific world, and an immediate effort was made to collect and study specimens and to sort out the organization of this bizarre assemblage. Finally, the pieces of the puzzle began to fit together. It was then that scientists

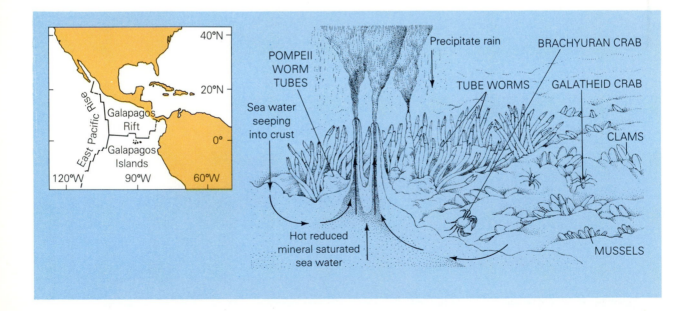

learned primary consumers in this community do not feed upon detritus falling from above, but are totally independent of life in the upper realms. The source of energy around the vents was found to be the enormous population of chemosynthetic bacteria that crowds the vent opening. These bacteria thrive on the matter boiling forth, using the hydrogen of hydrogen sulfide to reduce carbon dioxide to carbohydrates. The same bacteria live symbiotically in the skin of the giant tubeworms.

The rift has a seemingly endless supply of food. Oxygen is abundant in the cold abyssal water, so metabolic activity is rapid. The large Galápagos Rift clams, for instance, grow at a rate of 4 cm per year, about 500 times faster than their relatives in other waters. The extraordinary amount of hemoglobin is believed to be an adaptation for times when the oxygen level in the water is low.

At first, scientists aboard *Alvin* believed that the rift community they had discovered was unique to the Galápagos area, but other rift communities were discovered, and now it appears that they are quite extensive, cropping up here and there among the innumerable faults in the ocean floor. In fact, in time they may prove to be among the most widespread and richest of marine communities. Rich and active though they are, the rift communities can pass quickly. Like volcanoes, the hot springs eventually die down, leaving behind ghostly monuments of empty shells. But as some vents close, others appear in cracks torn in the sea bottom by the earth's restless, shifting crust.

Here, then, was a system that did not rely on energy emanating from the sun, but from some primordial heat that was captured by our small planet when the sun was young.

Tube worms

Clam field

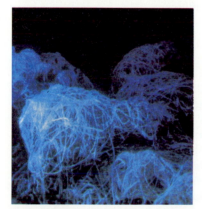

Spaghetti worms

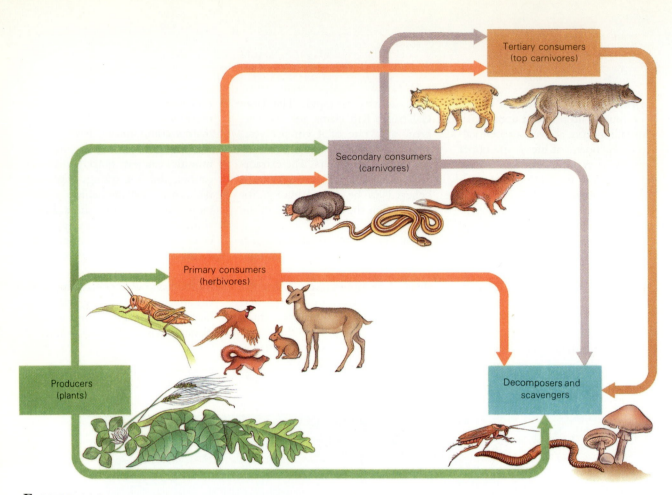

FIGURE 46.2 A simplified food web. Food webs reflect the complex feeding patterns in an ecosystem. The arrows indicate the direction of the flow of energy and matter. In nature, some animals feed from more than one trophic level, particularly during shortages when usual food sources become reduced.

ria. Decomposers generally feed by secreting digestive enzymes into their food and then absorbing the breakdown products (Figure 46.3). They are somewhat unique: unlike animals, they readily digest the cellulose-laden corpses of plants and the nitrogenous wastes of animals. In so doing they produce carbon dioxide and water, as do all consumers, but in addition they release sulfates, nitrites, and nitrates and other mineral ions. Without decomposers the world would be a far different place—a corpse-strewn, mineral-deficient wasteland.

The decomposer level is somewhat arbitrary; some ecologists refer to any species that feeds on the dead as **detritivores.** The list would include the usual bacteria and fungi, but added to it would be all of the scavengers or carrion eaters such as crows, jackals, crabs, vultures, and veritable armies of beetles and ants.

Decomposers are consumers that specialize in feeding on dead plants and animals and on animal wastes. They are essential to the recycling of mineral ions.

Ecological Pyramids

The pioneering ecologist Charles Elton first conceived of the **ecological** (or **Eltonian**) **pyramid** as a way of graphically handling some complex data. Essentially, ecological pyramids are an easy way to show the relationships between the different elements in an ecosystem. Their simplicity is deceiving, however, because the data are often hard won. The most common ecological pyramids are **pyramids of numbers, pyramids of biomass** (weight of the total living matter), and **pyramids of energy.**

FIGURE 46.3 Decomposers break down the wastes and remains of plants and animals, making simple mineral nutrients available again to the ecosystem. Although many are microscopic, the bracket fungi often seen on fallen trees are quite large.

Pyramids of numbers. In pyramids of numbers, counts of individuals at each trophic level provide the data. Consider, for example, a grassland community. The graph of the numbers of individuals at each level produces a typical "stepped" pyramidal shape (as seen in Figure 46.4).

Pyramids of biomass. Typically, the biomass of the producers is far greater than that of the consumers (Figure 46.4c), and the biomass of any level of consumer is less than that of the level below. As was mentioned earlier, 99% of the earth's biomass is tied up in the primary producer level. But, surprisingly little of the producer biomass and energy are transferred to the primary consumer level. Of the plant biomass that is eaten by herbivores, some is not actually absorbed but is disposed of in the feces. Of the part that is absorbed and utilized, a considerable amount is broken down during cell respiration. The result is that very little of the plant biomass becomes consumer biomass.

Pyramids of energy. Any consideration of energy transfers must, of necessity, return us to the second law of thermodynamics. We should be

FIGURE 46.4 Ecological pyramids. **(a)** A *pyramid of numbers* in a grassland community produces a typical broad-based, stepped form. **(b)** An inverted pyramid of numbers in the forest, although curiously shaped, simply reflects the fact that the forest producers are trees, thus a few individuals support many consumers. **(c)** A *pyramid of biomass* in a tropical forest reveals a great difference between producer mass and consumer mass. The seemingly large decomposer mass *(D)* tells us that nutrients are rapidly recycled in the tropical forest. **(d)** An energy pyramid from a freshwater aquatic community, one of the first developed, takes on a rather classic form. How might the stepped shape illustrate the second law of thermodynamics?

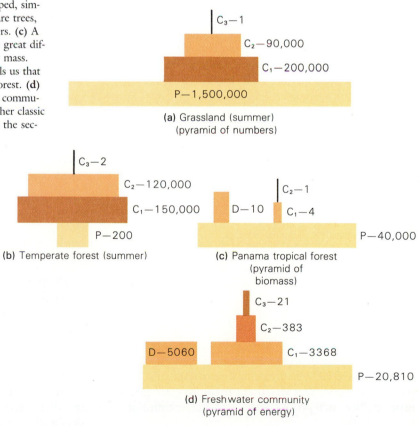

C_3-1
$C_2-90,000$
$C_1-200,000$
$P-1,500,000$
(a) Grassland (summer)
(pyramid of numbers)

C_3-2
$C_2-120,000$
$C_1-150,000$
$P-200$
(b) Temperate forest (summer)

C_2-1
$D-10$ C_1-4
$P-40,000$
(c) Panama tropical forest
(pyramid of biomass)

C_3-21
C_2-383
$D-5060$ C_1-3368
$P-20,810$
(d) Freshwater community
(pyramid of energy)

reminded that in the living as well as the nonliving realm, energy transfers are inefficient—there is no perfect exchange. While energy pyramids may not be as radical in appearance as biomass pyramids, they do show the usual stepped configuration (Figure 46.4d). The energy transfers from one trophic level to the next show only about 10% efficiency, because about 90% of the energy in the food eaten by consumers is not stored (some of the energy-laden molecules are not assimilated at all).

Ecological pyramids generally reveal that each trophic level tends to have fewer numbers, less energy, and less mass than the one below.

Humans and Trophic Levels

Energy pyramids may seem abstract, but they can suggest fundamental lessons in economics when they are applied to human populations. We know that humans are basically **omnivores,** capable of feeding at several trophic levels, and obviously the availability of food determines which trophic level is most heavily utilized. As economic conditions worsen, people tend to increasingly shift to lower trophic levels. The poorest people tend to act largely as primary consumers; they eat more plant foods and less meat. The reason is clear—the primary level holds more energy, or calories. To feed people at the secondary level or higher requires costly energy transfers. Since raising cattle, sheep, hogs, and other animal stocks is a wasteful process with little conservation of calories or biomass, meat becomes too expensive for them (Figure 46.5). Exceptions are seen where food is available from the sea and where livestock includes scavengers such as chickens and hogs that tend to fend for themselves.

Although humans are omnivorous, their primary trophic level depends heavily on their economic status. Less affluent people avoid costly energy transfers by feeding as primary consumers.

Productivity in Ecosystems

The rate at which producers in an ecosystem store energy is referred to as the system's **primary productivity,** a concept that has three main aspects: gross productivity, net productivity, and net community productivity.

FIGURE 46.5 Humans feeding on beef are secondary consumers. The energy differences between trophic levels are rather typical. Note that for every 1000 calories gained by humans, 2 million would have been processed at the producer level.

Gross productivity is the total rate at which energy is assimilated by producers over a certain period of time. Gross productivity doesn't really tell us how much energy the photosynthesizers are storing or how fast they are growing. After all, plants must expend a considerable amount of the assimilated energy for their own growth and maintenance.

Net productivity, a more useful measurement, takes energy utilization into account. It is determined by subtracting the rate of respiration by photosynthesizers (energy utilization) from gross productivity. In other words, the rate of energy stored minus the rate of energy released equals net productivity. Net productivity is reflected in new growth, seed production, and simple storage of such energy-rich compounds as lipids and carbohydrates.

Net community productivity takes the whole community into consideration, so respiration in both producers and consumers is subtracted from gross productivity. Productivity is expressed in calories or grams (or kilocalories or kilograms) per unit of area over some period of time. Using **GP, NP,** and **NCP** to represent gross, net, and net community productivity, respectively, and R_a to represent respiration in producers (autotrophs) and R_h, consumers (heterotrophs), the three aspects of productivity can be summarized as:

$$GP = \text{Energy assimilated by producers}$$
$$NP = GP - R_a$$
$$NCP = NP - R_h$$

By measuring the net productivity of a community, ecologists can compare energy efficiency within systems and can answer such questions as: Is it growing? Has it reached a climax state (full maturity)? Is it declining? Net community productivity, as you might expect, occurs only in communities that are growing. As they approach the climax state, the rates of energy assimilation and energy use begin to equalize. A net decrease in productivity signals a dying or declining community (or perhaps just the approach

TABLE 46.1

TABLE 46.1 Estimated Gross Primary Production (Annual Basis) of the Biosphere and Its Distribution Among Major Ecosystems

Ecosystem	Area, Millions of km²	Gross Primary Productivity, kcal/m²/yr	Total Gross Production, 10^{16} kcal/yr
Marine			
Open ocean	326.0	1,000	32.6
Coastal zones	34.0	2,000	6.8
Upwelling zones	0.4	6,000	0.2
Estuaries and reefs	2.0	20,000	4.0
Subtotal	362.4	—	43.6
Terrestrial			
Deserts and tundras	40.0	200	0.8
Grasslands and pastures	42.0	2,500	10.5
Dry forests	9.4	2,500	2.4
Northern coniferous forests	10.0	3,000	3.0
Cultivated lands with little or no energy subsidy	10.0	3,000	3.0
Moist temperate forests	4.9	8,000	3.9
Fuel-subsidized (mechanized) agriculture	4.0	12,000	4.8
Wet tropical and subtropical (broad-leaved evergreen) forests	14.7	20,000	29.0
Subtotal	135.0	—	57.0
Total for biosphere (round figures; not including ice caps)	500.0	2,000	100.0

SOURCE: From Fundamentals of Ecology, 3rd Edition by Eugene P. Odum. Copyright © 1971 by W.B. Saunders Company. Reprinted by permission of Holt, Rinehart and Winston, CBS College Publishing.

of winter). The results of productivity studies in several major regions of the earth are summarized in Table 46.1.

In determining the rate at which a community stores energy, **net community productivity** (the total respiratory energy release) is deducted from the energy that producers store.

Productivity in a forest community. In 1969, ecologist George Woodwell and his associates completed a 10-year study of productivity in a scrub oak-pine forest community near the Brookhaven National Laboratory on Long Island. Oak-pine forests are common in this area, a product of the disturbance of the great deciduous forests that once graced the rural landscape. Woodwell's study was enormous in scope; it is through such efforts that we are beginning to understand the basic principles of community ecology.

Woodwell and his group concluded that the annual gross productivity of the forest community was 2650 g/m² (about 5.8 lbs), while the annual net productivity was 1200 g/m². Further tests revealed that the rate at which new organic material was appearing—the net community productivity (net productivity minus heterotroph respiration)—was 550 g/m²/year (about 1.2 lbs). The forest study is summarized in Figure 46.6.

Similar studies have since been done in other forests, and we now know that, compared to some communities, the net productivity of this forest is modest. Annual net productivity in each square meter of some tropical rain forest communities, for example, can reach several thousand grams. Net productivity is also high where intensive agriculture is carried out. For instance, in tropically grown sugarcane, an efficient C4 plant (see Chapter 7), the annual net productivity can exceed 9000 g/m², while the productivity of grain fields ranges between 6000 and 10,000 g/m². (Of course, when we consider the energy of fossil fuels used to operate farm machinery and the

FIGURE 46.6 The rate of biomass formed in an oak-pine forest is expressed as 2650 g of organic matter per square meter per year. The pathways point out where the matter ended up. Only 21% occurs as new biomass. While a small amount was leached away, the rest was used in respiration.

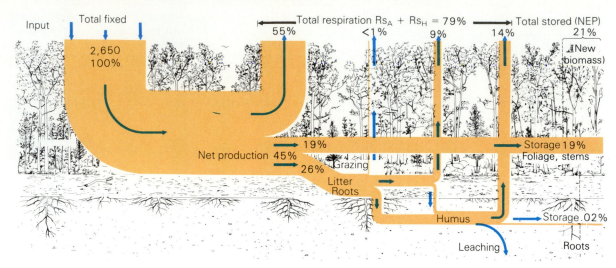

energy used to manufacture and apply pesticides and fertilizers, net yields fall drastically.)

One more observation—perhaps an obvious one—was made by Woodwell. The oak-pine community was growing; it had not reached its climax state. As we mentioned earlier, communities that have reached their climax state have no net community productivity. Their respiratory output equals their photosynthetic input.

> The Woodwell group estimated a forest's NCP in terms of grams per square meter per year by first determining the rate of biomass increase and then deducting the carbon given off as CO_2 in respiration.

NUTRIENT CYCLING IN ECOSYSTEMS

While energy flows through an ecosystem, emerging eventually as heat, the chemical elements essential to life *cycle* within ecosystems. Some of these elements are incorporated into the molecular makeup of the organism, while others are shuffled through complex metabolic pathways and drained of their bond energy. Ultimately, all the molecules will become available for recycling either as the organism's waste or as its corpse. At that time, the molecules are sub-

jected to the decomposers that release the products of decomposition into the environment where they once again become available to the producers. Most of the elements cycle in the form of mineral nutrients (mineral ions). Since the cycling of such nutrients involves both geological and biological activity in the ecosystem, the pathways are often called **biogeochemical cycles.**

Some biogeochemical cycles can be rather simple, involving only a few steps. For example, some of the water a plant takes in is simply transpired, passed to the leaves, where it is released through the stomata, back to the atmosphere (see Chapter 25). However, water may be used in photosynthesis. In this case, the water molecules are split, hydrogen is used to reduce carbon (forming foods), and oxygen is released into the atmosphere. Animals and other consumers may then breathe in the oxygen, using it in cell respiration where it is reunited with the hydrogen, forming water, which is then returned to the environment. Two other cycles, the **phosphorus cycle** and the **carbon cycle,** are described in Figure 46.7.

> In **biogeochemical cycles,** simple molecules are incorporated by producers, moving next to consumers, and finally to decomposers. The latter release the mineral ions, which recycle to producers.

FIGURE 46.7 (a) The phosphorus cycle. Usable phosphorus in the form of soluble phosphates is found in soil water and in aquatic systems. Some phosphates pass to consumers through the trophic levels, while some are taken in through drinking water. During decomposition, reducers make some phosphates available again, but some locked in animal remains (bones, teeth, shells, etc.) is unavailable for long periods. The loss of phosphates through leaching (from soil water) and through runoff (to the sea) is considerable. Some end up as insoluble phosphorus in deep sediments. A gain in available phosphates occurs through erosion and from pollutants introduced by humans. (b) The carbon cycle. Carbon dioxide must enter the trophic levels through producers that fix carbon into organic molecules during photosynthesis. CO_2 is released during respiration by producers, consumers, and decomposers and some is released from the earth's crust through volcanic action.

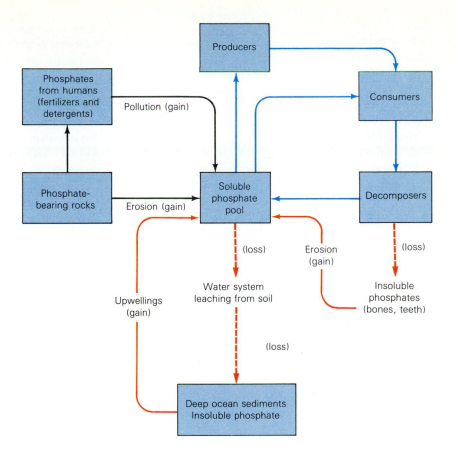

(a) Phosphorus cycle

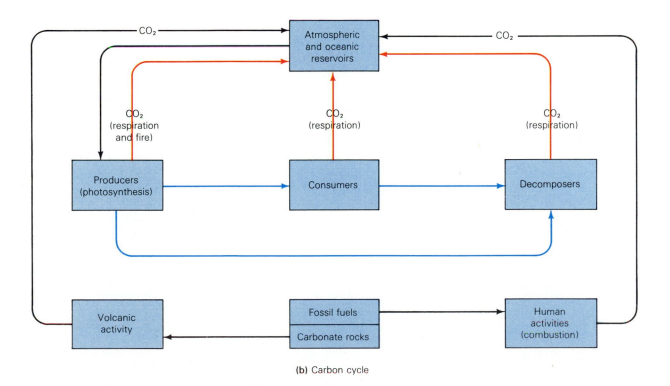

(b) Carbon cycle

The Nitrogen Cycle

One of the best-known biogeochemical cycles is the **nitrogen cycle.** We have referred to the cycle in another context, but here let's consider it in more detail. Nitrogen is essential to life, since it is a principal constituent of proteins, nucleic acids, chlorophyll, coenzymes, and several other important kinds of molecules.

Essential nutrients such as nitrogen are generally held in one of two places: **exchange pools,** where they are readily available, and **reservoirs,** where they are less available to living systems. The largest nitrogen reservoir is the atmosphere, about 79% of which is nitrogen gas (N_2). But atmospheric, or molecular, nitrogen as such is not available to the earth's organisms, except to certain nitrogen-fixing bacteria. Plants and most other producers must incorporate nitrogen primarily in the form of nitrate and ammonium ions (NO_3^- and NH_4^+), which are produced by soil and water bacteria over two complex pathways: *decomposition* and *nitrogen fixation*. These ions in the soil and water constitute the major exchange pool of nitrogen.

Role of decomposers. The details of the nitrogen cycle are summarized in Figure 46.8, using a

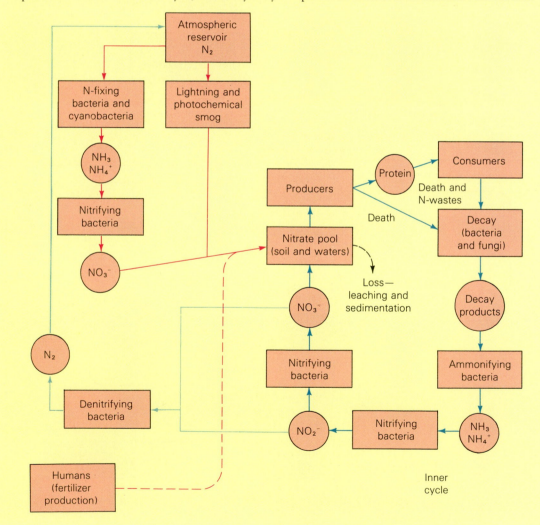

FIGURE 46.8 The nitrogen cycle becomes simpler when viewed as two cycles in one. The inner, main cycle is represented by producers, consumers, and decomposers, with the useful nitrogen compounds and ions present in an exchange pool. The outer cycle contains the nitrogen fixers, whose activities represent a gain in useful nitrogen from the nitrogen reservoir. Also present are the denitrifiers, whose activities represent a loss in useful nitrogen. Human activities, *(lower left)* represent an addition to the inner cycle, believed by many to represent an overload to an otherwise balanced state.

simple system involving plants, animals, and decomposers. As we see, plants take in nitrate ions and incorporate them into their own amino acids, where they are used to make plant protein. The molecules then pass through the consumer levels from herbivore to carnivore, where some of the amino acids are used in the production of the animal's proteins while many of the rest are metabolized. The nitrogen byproduct is excreted in urine. Eventually, all organisms and their nitrogen wastes enter the realm of the decomposers, where they are broken down into their component parts.

During decomposition, several populations of microorganisms, each with a specific role in the process, carry out **ammonification** (production of ammonia) and **nitrification** (production of nitrites and then nitrates). The nitrates (the end product) can then join the exchange pool, from which they can return to the plant. This may all seem quite efficient, but in fact there are complications that lead to losses. For example, certain anaerobic soil bacteria—the **denitrifiers**—metabolize nitrates, converting them to nitrogen gas that diffuses from the soil, reentering the atmospheric reservoir.

In the nitrogen cycle, a succession of bacterial species **ammonify** and **nitrify** plant and animal remains. The products enter **exchange pools,** becoming available to producers.

Role of nitrogen fixers. The denitrifiers remove nitrogen from the ecosystem, but the element is never depleted because of the action of **nitrogen fixers.** Nitrogen-fixing soil bacteria and cyanobacteria are able to "fix" atmospheric nitrogen, by combining it with hydrogen, producing ammonium ions (NH_4^+). Nitrogen fixation is energetically costly because the nitrogen molecule (N_2) is inordinately stable, resisting any chemical change. Reducing nitrogen (by adding hydrogen) requires powerful enzymes and a considerable expenditure of ATP.

Cyanobacteria and other free-living nitrogen-fixers release surplus ammonia into their watery surroundings where much of it is converted to nitrite and nitrate by soil bacteria. Bacteria living mutualistically in the roots of plants make ammonium ions available directly to their host's cells, where it is used in generating amino acids and other essentials.

While cyanobacteria generate their own ATP through photosynthesis, mutualistic bacteria use the host's supply. In fact, fully one fifth of the ATP generated by the pea plant is used for nitrogen fixation by its guest bacteria.

Nitrogen gas from the atmospheric reservoir is converted to useful nitrogen compounds by free-living and mutualistic **nitrogen fixers.**

Farmers have used the nitrogen fixers for many years. Crop rotation (planting different crops in a rotating sequence) commonly includes such legumes as alfalfa. Nitrogen-fixing bacteria of the genus *Rhizobium* invade the alfalfa roots, which respond by forming cystlike nodules around the bacterial colony (Figure 46.9).

FIGURE 46.9 (a) Root nodules in a leguminous plant. (b) Such nodules contain large colonies of irregularly shaped nitrogen-fixing bacteria from the genus *Rhizobium*.

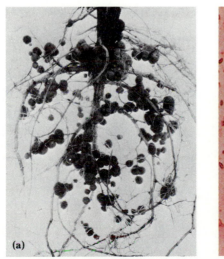

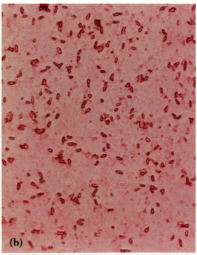

COMMUNITIES OVER TIME: ECOLOGICAL SUCCESSION

As time passes, communities change. In some cases they grow and their biomass increases. In other cases more energy is released in respiration than is stored, indicating a state of decline. Even when biomass and energy are stabilized, the community may be changing. Sometimes the change produces a sequence of organisms within the community itself, resulting in a process known as **ecological succession.** Eventually, a steady state or **climax** state may be reached, whereupon no further change will occur as long as the environment remains stable.

As populations within a community alter the environment, they set the stage for invasions by different species. The result is that the community takes on new traits, and with new species altering the environment in their own manner, the change goes on. The entire sequence from start to climax is called a **sere,** while its parts are **seral stages.** Ecological succession is somewhat predictable and sequential, although ecologists are finding it less so than they once believed. Not only do invasions by unexpected, opportunistic species break up the orderly progression, but unanticipated physical changes—perhaps a drought—can alter the usual events of succession.

Ecological succession occurs in two fundamental ways. **Primary succession** occurs where no community previously existed, such as on rocky outcroppings, newly formed deltas, sand dunes, emerging volcanic islands, and lava flows. (The volcanic slopes of Mount St. Helens are presently a good place for studying primary succession.) **Secondary succession** occurs where a community has been disrupted. We find it, for example, where a neglected farm is reverting to the wild, or in a forest community that has been subjected to clear cutting, the controversial lumbering practice in which all trees are removed.

Primary Succession

In primary succession (Figure 46.10), the first organisms to invade are usually hardy, drought-resistant species, often called **pioneer organisms.** For example when a sere begins, lichens are often the first to invade rocky outcroppings, held fast by their tenacious, water-seeking fungal component while the algal component provides food as its chloroplasts are exposed to the sun. Lichens gradually erode the rock surface as they probe into tiny crevices and help pry them open. Sand then accumulates in tiny fissures, and the bodies of dead lichens add to the humus. Soil is being born, and with it come opportunities for such plants as grasses and mosses to establish themselves.

In subsequent seral stages the plant roots penetrate the rocky crevices, exerting a remarkable pres-

FIGURE 46.10 Succession begins here with a bare rock outcropping and ends with a fir-birch-spruce community. Pioneering lichens and mosses begin the soil-building process, followed by the invasion of increasingly larger plants until a more stable long-lived, climax forest community emerges.

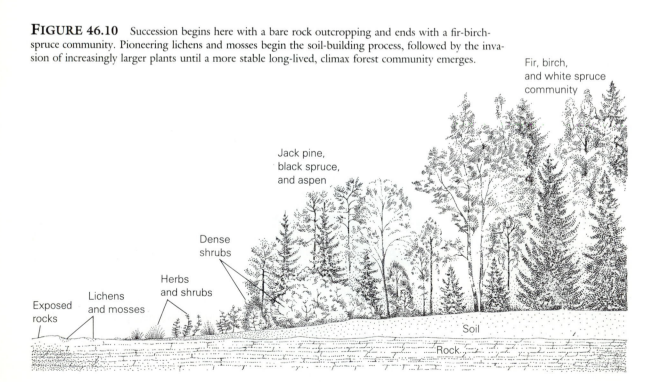

Fir, birch, and white spruce community

Jack pine, black spruce, and aspen

Dense shrubs

Herbs and shrubs

Lichens and mosses

Exposed rocks

Soil

Rock

1909

1925

1937

1979

FIGURE 46.11 Four stages of secondary succession are revealed in a series of photos taken in the same section of the Bitterroot National Forest in Montana.

sure, prying at the rocks and gradually widening the fissures. By now certain insect and decomposer populations will also have established themselves. As these early plants gain a toehold, the lichens that made their penetration possible give way; they cannot compete with the emerging plants for light, water, and minerals. Similarly, when the grasses and mosses have contributed significantly to the soil-building efforts, they will be replaced by fast-growing shrubs, and new kinds of animals will continue to invade.

Primary succession in bare rock outcroppings is an extremely slow process, often requiring hundreds of years. But once the soil has formed, the process can accelerate. Studies of succession from sand dune to climax forest community on the shores of Lake Michigan indicate that this transition took about 1000 years.

Secondary Succession

In secondary succession, the same principles apply, but events occur at a more rapid pace. Soil is often already in place, eliminating the long soilbuilding stages of primary succession. In deserted farms, grasses, shrubs, and saplings are often the first to appear, along with a variety of "weeds." The species we call weeds are usually imported—carried accidentally into a region. In balanced, well-adapted communities that are undisturbed, weeds are held in check, but since they tend to be fast-growing, opportunistic plants, they quickly invade disturbed communities.

As secondary succession progresses, the initial invaders are eventually replaced by plants from the surrounding community. Larger, faster-growing trees block the sunlight, and a new generation of shade-tolerant shrubs emerges below the canopy. Eventually the lines between the area in succession and the surrounding community begin to fade (Figure 46.11).

The time involved in secondary succession varies widely. In grassland communities, for example, succession to a climax community may take only 20 to 40 years. At the other extreme, fragile tundra may require hundreds of years to recover from a disturbance—if it ever recovers at all. Wagon tracks made more than 100 years ago are still clearly visible in this delicate biome.

In **secondary succession**—recovery from a disturbed state—a region takes on the characteristics of the surrounding community.

Succession in the Freshwater Aquatic Community

Like terrestrial communities, freshwater communities undergo ecological succession. A major determining factor in the rate at which succession occurs is the availability of nutrients. Lakes and ponds that are rich in nutrients and high in productivity are called **eutrophic** ("true foods"), while those that have a very limited nutrient supply and little productivity are called **oligotrophic** ("few foods"). The general trend in freshwater bodies is toward increased nutri-ent enrichment, a process of change called **eutrophication,** but if any essential nutrient becomes unavailable the trend can be quickly reversed.

As lake succession progresses, new organic materials are produced at an increasing rate, sediments increase, and the lake depth decreases. Littoral zone plants crowd the shallows along the lakeshore, gradually extending across the water. They are followed by increasing numbers of weather-tolerant shore plants (Figure 46.12). Unless the trend is interrupted, the lake will eventually convert to a wetland, such as a marsh, and with the invasion of terrestrial plants from the surrounding community, the last traces of the lake will disappear.

Succession is slow in nutrient-poor **oligotrophic** waters, but where **eutrophication** (nutrient enrichment) occurs, aquatic life increases, and the transition to a terrestrial state accelerates.

FIGURE 46.12 Aquatic succession: **(a)** Early in succession, aquatic plants begin to spread from the edges of the pond. **(b)** Eventually these plants extend across the open water. **(c)** As the pond's waters disappear, invading marsh grasses, cattails, and sedges replace the floating plants, converting the pond into a marsh.

Eutrophication: Human Impact

Interestingly, the ancient oligotrophic Lake Baikal has shown alarming indications of eutrophication, but not through natural means. Wastes from the human community along its shores are artificially fertilizing the water and enabling the rapid production of organic material.

Eutrophication is ordinarily an extremely slow process in lakes. Its progress is typically checked by a scarcity of two nutrients, phosphates and nitrates. In recent years, however, these nutrients have become readily available as humans dump sewage into water systems or permit the runoff of surface water from heavily fertilized farms or cattle feedlots. The addition of phosphates to laundry detergents has also added a heavy burden to natural water systems. The sudden increase of nitrates and phosphates in fresh waters produces unprecedented algal blooms, a first step in eutrophication through pollution.

The impact of humans on natural communities is profound, and our ability to alter such systems grows as our technological abilities increase. Even as we learn about the effects of our previous alterations, we continue to manipulate the intricate and myriad factors that contribute to the equilibrium of ecosystems. Of course, we are aware of our impact to some degree, and we often make well-intentioned, if unsuccessful, efforts to set things right. Our efforts often falter simply for lack of basic information. The bottom line seems to be that we just don't know how to live in harmony with the ecosystems of which we are a part; our technology has far outstripped our basic understanding of our environment. As we turn to the scientific community for answers, ecologists will play an increasingly important role in changing the ways in which we interact with the biosphere. In fact, ecologists may one day be recognized as the most important scientists on earth.

SUMMARY

Ecosystems are interacting units including organisms and their environment. Each contains characteristic trophic levels through which energy flows.

ENERGETICS IN ECOSYSTEMS

Energy reaching the biosphere accounts for 150 to 200 billion metric tons of organic matter per year.

Trophic Levels

Energy flows from producer through consumer levels. Producers, the autotrophs (phototrophs and chemotrophs) account for 99% of the earth's biomass.

Consumers, the heterotrophs, include primary consumers (herbivores), secondary and higher levels (carnivores). Food webs realistically portray feeding interactions.

Decomposers include bacteria and fungi, heterotrophs that secrete enzymes into food and release mineral ions.

Ecological Pyramids

Ecological pyramids include pyramids of numbers, biomass, and energy. Most are broadbased and stepped, indicating a loss at each level. The losses are represented by matter and energy not actually assimilated in the level above, or matter and energy expended in the ongoing metabolic processes. Energy transfer through the trophic levels is about 10% efficient (predictable by the second law of thermodynamics).

Affluent humans feed partly at secondary or higher consumer levels, while the more impoverished feed mainly at the primary or herbivore level. At that level, protein deficiencies may occur.

Productivity in Ecosystems

Productivity, the rate of energy storage in ecosystems, is measured as gross productivity (total rate of energy uptake by producers), net productivity (gross minus respiratory consumption by producers), and net community productivity (gross minus respiratory output by all organisms). Productivity measurements are useful in determining growth status and making community comparisons. The highest productivity occurs in estuaries and reefs, tropical forests and in intensive agriculture. Gross and net community productivity determinations were made in a scrub oak-pine forest. The end result indicated that the forest had not reached its climax state and that its net community productivity was modest. Greater yields are seen in tropical forests and agricultural regions.

NUTRIENT CYCLING IN ECOSYSTEMS

Mineral nutrients in ecosystems cycle between organisms and the environment in biogeochemical cycles. Examples include water, phosphorous, carbon, and nitrogen.

The Nitrogen Cycle

Nitrogen, an element required in most molecules of life, occurs as nitrogen gas in reservoirs and as nitrate and nitrite ions in exchange pools. Nitrogen gas is fixed into useful compounds by nitrogen-fixing bacteria and nitrogen compounds are cycled through decomposition.

A series of decomposers break down nitrogen compounds through ammonification and nitrification. Some loss occurs through bacterial denitrification which yields nitrogen gas.

Nitrogen-fixing soil bacteria, living mutualistically in leguminous plant root nodules, and cyanobacteria living in water, convert nitrogen gas to ammonium ions. Excesses are made available to exchange pools. Genetic engineers are trying to use gene-splicing techniques to give other crop plants the nitrogen-fixing capability.

COMMUNITIES OVER TIME: ECOLOGICAL SUCCESSION

Community change occurs through ecological succession. Basically, as transitional communities develop, they produce changes that lead to their being succeeded by other communities until a climax state is reached. The sequence is a sere, and its parts, seral stages.

Primary Succession

Primary succession begins with soil-building, often by lichens and other pioneer organisms. Grasses and mosses may follow eventually replaced by a succession of more complex communities until a climax state is reached.

Secondary Succession

A disturbed community may first go through a weed stage, but eventually the seral stages that produced the sur-

rounding community occur and the disturbed region blends in.

Succession in the Freshwater Aquatic Community

Change in eutrophic lakes is limited by the availability of mineral nutrients. Their increasing availability (eutrophication) speeds succession. As succession goes on, plant and other life rapidly increases, and the lake diminishes until it blends in with the surrounding terrestrial community.

Eutrophication: Human Impact

Limited phosphates and nitrates generally restrict succession in lakes, but both are common in pollutants introduced by humans.

KEY TERMS

ecosystem	ecological (Eltonian) pyramid	R_h	nitrogen fixer
trophic level	pyramid of numbers	biogeochemical cycle	climax
producer	pyramid of biomass	phosphorus cycle	ecological succession
consumer	pyramid of energy	carbon cycle	sere
primary consumer	omnivore	nitrogen cycle	seral stage
secondary consumer	primary productivity	exchange pool	primary succession
tertiary	gross productivity (GP)	reservoir	secondary succession
quarternary	net productivity (NP)	ammonification	pioneer organism
food web	net community productivity (NCP)	nitrification	eutrophic
decomposer	R_a	denitrifer	oligotrophic
detritivore			

REVIEW QUESTIONS

1 List the components that make up any ecosystem. (p. 740)
2 Why is energy in ecosystems described as a flow instead of a cycle? (pp. 740–741)
3 Review the general distribution of solar energy in the biosphere. How much do living organisms capture? (pp. 740–741)
4 List the two fundamental trophic levels and describe the general makeup of each. (p. 741)
5 List four levels in which consumers occur and provide an example of each. (p. 741)
6 How do food webs differ from food chains? (p. 741)
7 List two important groups of decomposers. In what ways do their activities differ from those of other consumers? (pp. 741, 744)
8 What is the general shape taken by number pyramids? Cite an exception. (p. 745)
9 Explain the great difference between biomass in producers and biomass in consumers. (p. 745)
10 Explain how the second law actually predicts the shape of an energy pyramid. What do energy losses actually represent? (pp. 745–746)

11 Relate the economic status of humans to their trophic levels. (p. 746)
12 Define gross, net and net community productivity. Don't forget to include the term "rate." (p. 746)
13 What did Woodwell conclude about the growth state of the scrub oak-pine community? How did he know this? (p. 747)
14 In general, which communities reveal the greatest productivity? Why are the high productivity measurements in agricultural communities misleading? (p. 747)
15 What is a biogeochemical cycle? Describe one involving carbon. (p. 749)
16 Distinguish between exchange pools and reservoirs in biogeochemical cycles. (p. 750)
17 In general, what goes on in the inner cycle of the nitrogen cycle? List the main steps. (pp. 750–751)
18 Briefly explain how losses and gains occur in the nitrogen cycle. (pp. 750–751)

19 List two types of nitrogen fixing organisms and describe their habitats. (p. 751)

20 In general, why does ecological succession occur? When, if ever, does it stop? (p. 752)

21 List three or four stages that one might expect in primary succession. Which apparently takes the longest? (p. 752)

22 Where would one expect to look for signs of secondary succession? When does secondary succession end? (p. 753)

23 Essentially, what determines the rate of succession in freshwater bodies? Name the process that greatly speeds succession. (p. 754)

24 Lake Baikal has long been considered as oligotrophic. What does this mean and why is this categorization changing? (p. 755)

25 List several human activities that increase eutrophication. (p. 755)

47

POPULATIONS AND HOW THEY CHANGE

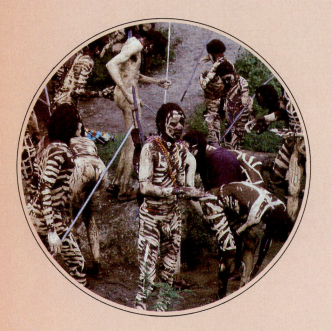

Informed people all over the world are becoming increasingly concerned about human population growth. Their concern is understandable; as a species, we have never been in this situation before. The earth has never supported so many humans, and our numbers are growing by the second. We can't begin to predict our future or even guess intelligently at our fate. Our best-educated guesses have been foiled time and again because our population seems to have a disconcerting lack of respect for the rules.

Or perhaps there are few "rules" when it comes to humans. Perhaps other species are more predictable, which is why we study them to learn how populations behave—about what causes them to change, grow out of control, or dwindle away. In this chapter, then, we will look into some fundamental principles of population behavior. In the next we will consider whether they apply to us.

POPULATION GROWTH PATTERNS

Populations, as we have seen, are interbreeding assemblages of a single species. And as we know, populations change. How they change is what interests us here. Essentially, the story of population changes can be told by two simple curves, the **J-shaped (exponential) curve** and the **S-shaped (sigmoid) curve**. First, consider the J-shaped curve (Figure 47.1a); this is the one environmentalists are so concerned about.

Let's suppose a few reproductive organisms are placed in an ideal environment with unlimited resources. Under such conditions they can be expected to reproduce at their maximum rate. Since there are only a few to start with, their numbers may rise slowly at first (say, from two to four, to eight, and so on). However, as new reproducers are added to the population, not only will the *numbers* increase, but the **population growth rate** will increase as well. (Growth rate is the change in percentage of growth over time.) This pattern, known as **exponential growth,** is marked by doublings, as 1, 2, 4, 8, 16, 32 . . . and so on.

The maximum physiological rate at which any individual can reproduce is called its **biotic potential.** Over time, such increases would produce a J-shaped curve of the most radical sort. Most species never reach their biotic potential, or reach it only briefly, because environmental conditions are rarely ideal. The expanding population encounters environmental situations that impede growth. These factors collectively are called **environmental resistance.**

A clear example of exponential growth occurs when a small number of bacteria are introduced into a rich laboratory culture medium. Under ideal conditions the familiar *E. coli*, a champion reproducer, will divide every 20 minutes. At this rate, after 24 hours one bacterium would have given rise to 40 sextillion descendants. But even as simple as *E. coli*'s growth requirements are, such a rapidly expanding rate of increase could not be sustained. Probably sometime midway through the 24-hour period, the waste produced by the bacteria would reach dangerous levels and the resources supporting such phenomenal growth would be reduced to a point where the biotic potential could no longer be reached. Thus, there are limits to the numbers of individuals any environment can support. This limit is known as the environment's **carrying capacity.**

Populations, then, are likely to encounter environmental resistance that depresses their growth rate so that their biotic potential is never achieved.

Populations approaching their **biotic potential** begin to encounter **environmental resistance,** whereupon growth slows as the **carrying capacity** is approached.

As the rate of increase slows, a gentler slope is produced that finally tends to level off around the environment's carrying capacity. The result produces the less dramatic S-shaped, or **logistic, growth curve** (Figure 47.1b). As we see, then, the S-shaped curve is identical to the J-shaped curve in its early

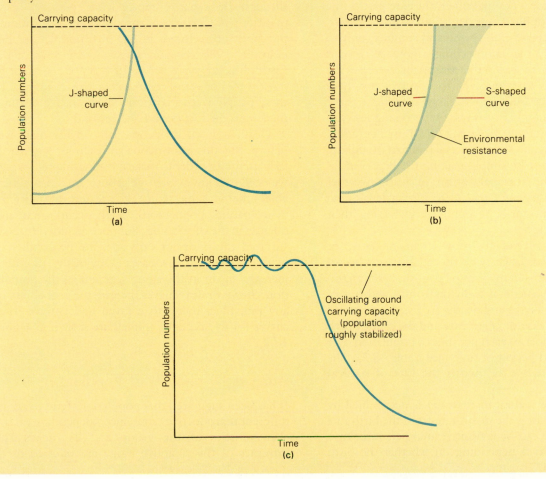

FIGURE 47.1 (a) Exponential growth produces the J-shaped growth curve. It is produced when species reproduce at or near their biotic potential. (b) When population growth is responsive to environmental resistance, it forms the S-shape or logistic growth curve. (c) Such populations hover at or below the carrying capacity.

phases, but as the population reaches the environment's carrying capacity, the curve levels off, its growth rate decreasing. The population finally fluctuates around the population size that the environment can support, sometimes rising slightly above it and sometimes dropping beneath it (Figure 47.1c).

Rapidly growing populations sometimes **overshoot** (quickly rise above) the environment's carrying capacity so drastically that they bring harsh pressures on their own numbers. The population may suddenly decrease, falling well below the original carrying capacity. Such a rapid decline is known as a **population crash.** A crash can be due to a number of factors, such as a rapid depletion of resources or damage to the environment. Populations that overshoot the carrying capacity can drastically abuse the environment—to such a degree that they permanently decrease the carrying capacity of the environment so that it could no longer support the numbers that it once sustained. For example, the elephants crowded into reserves in East Africa have destroyed acres of the slow-growing trees (such as acacias and baobabs) on which they feed, and some ecologists believe that the area will never recover.

In some cases, population crashes are part of the normal cycle of life. Consider populations of insects, those that increase each spring and summer, only to dwindle with the approaching rigors of winter. Winter is a harsh season that seasonally decreases the environment's carrying capacity. Species that have evolved under such fluctuating conditions have adapted in a number of ways: by becoming less vulnerable, for example, by laying on fat, by migrating, by hibernating, by altering social patterns (huddling, for instance), or by simply making the best of it (as deer do). The seasonal return of warm weather restores the carrying capacity to higher levels, and populations normally respond by increasing their numbers quickly.

Populations tend to grow, remain static, or decline in accordance with the relative number of births and deaths in the group (if we discount migration, the movement of individuals into and out of populations). Births and deaths are usually expressed in terms of the **crude birth rate** and the **crude death rate:** the number of each per unit of population over some specified period of time (see Table 48.2). The difference between the two is the **rate of natural increase.**

The rate of natural increase (*r*) is determined by simply subtracting the death rate from the birth rate (*b* − *d*). So *r* can be a positive number, zero, or a negative number, depending on whether the birth rate is greater than, equal to, or less than the death rate. In 1981 the estimated crude birth rate of humans was 28 per 1000 and the crude death rate was 11 per 1000; thus the rate of natural increase was 17. This translates into an annual growth rate of 1.7%, a number that alarms many people, since it means a doubling time for the human population of just 41 years. We'll come back to this point in the next chapter.

The **rate of natural increase** is determined by subtracting **crude death rate** from **crude birth rate.**

Life Span and the Population

Information about life span and age structure is important in characterizing a population and predicting its course. How many individuals in a population are below, within, or beyond the reproductive age? What is their life span? Do most individuals survive through their entire reproductive period? These questions are extremely important in determining probable future trends in our own population. For example, 1986 censuses revealed that 35% of the earth's humans were below 15 years of age. That is, most were not yet of reproductive age. And most of these people were statistically likely to live through their reproductive period and beyond.

Death now claims people later in life than ever before. But this information in itself is not particularly useful. In order to make meaningful predictions, we need to know which age groups are most vulnerable—that is, subjected to the greatest mortality. In many natural populations, death occurs quite frequently in the very young. But once an individual has survived the rigors of early life, the probability of living to old age increases. Obviously, mortality increases again in the aging segment of the population. **Survivorship curves** indicate the probability of any individual living to a given age. Survivorship curves for five types of animals are shown in Figure 47.2.

Adaptive Strategies of Populations

It has been suggested that populations tend to adopt different reproductive "strategies," depending on the characteristics of the group and its niche. The extremes of this adaptive range are referred to as

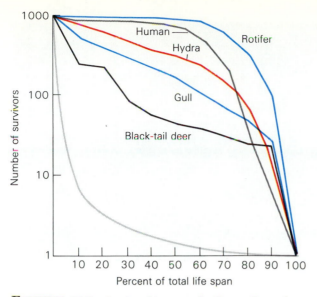

FIGURE 47.2 Survivorship curves for five species, each beginning with a population of 1000 *(vertical axis)*. Points along each line represent the percentage of the life span reached as the populations age *(horizontal axis)*. In blacktail deer, a species that experiences a high death rate among its young, the numbers drop off rapidly, with the average individual achieving only 6% of its potential life span.

r-selection and **K-selection.** (The letters r and K are borrowed from population formulas.) The reproductive strategy of any group of animals theoretically falls somewhere along the r-K spectrum.

K-selected species are those whose population growth curves closely resemble the idealized S-shape. Their numbers hover about the carrying capacity, to which they are highly responsive. Thus, they are less subject to dramatic change. K-selected species tend to be large animals, such as mammals and birds, with long life spans, continuous reproduction—year after year—and lengthy growth periods. At the other extreme are the r-selected species, sometimes referred to as "boom and bust" types. In their adaptation to large population size, they tend to have short life spans, to be small, to mature early, and to produce prodigious numbers of offspring—which they generally take no part in raising. Thus their populations suddenly boom, shooting up beyond the carrying capacity, following the familiar J-shaped growth curve before crashing. While population crashes can be quite dramatic in r-selected species, they are really a routine part of life, and recovery is just as routine and predictable. You might want to keep in mind, also, that K and r adaptations do not necessarily follow general taxonomic lines—thus while one might expect insects to be r-selected, and the locusts certainly are, bees are excellent examples of K-selected species. Perhaps we can make the distinction between r- and K-selected species clearer with a couple of examples.

Tapeworms are extremely r-selected animals. They maximize their reproductive output by simply producing as many offspring as possible (with very little investment in any single one). Their strategy is to lay thousands of eggs, leaving the rest to chance. A good deal of their energy, then, goes into simply manufacturing their offspring, and no energy or time is spent in caring for them.

At the other extreme are the K-selected chimpanzees. They produce few offspring, but each one receives a great deal of attention. Even the most prolific individuals have only a few offspring, but the mothers tend them carefully until they can survive independently, often a matter of several years. The father may make his investment in other ways, such as defending the group that includes his offspring. The longer developmental periods of K-selected species give them time to prepare for the rigors of a competitive world.

Another way of viewing r- and K-selection is to keep in mind that maximizing the *quantity* of offspring (r- selection) rather than the *quality* (K-selection) is particularly adaptive where conditions are unpredictable. The advantage of producing numerous offspring if conditions are unstable or unpredictable is the increased probability that more of them will encounter conditions that enable them to mature. Most of the offspring will be lost, but the parental investment in their care and rearing is low or absent, so the loss is minimized. K-selected species can be expected under more stable or predictable conditions in which the likelihood is high that a properly prepared offspring will survive.

INFLUENCES ON POPULATION DENSITY

Thus far, we have lumped the various factors that tend to control populations under the catchall terms of *biotic potential* and *environmental resistance*. Now let's take a closer look at some of these factors and how they operate. First, we should note that populations are controlled in two major ways.

Density-Independent and Density-Dependent Controls

In some cases, populations are controlled by factors that have nothing to do with their size or density.

FIGURE 47.3 The effects of natural disasters, such as fire, flood, landslide, and volcanic eruption, are usually density-independent.

Such factors are said to exert **density-independent control.** As an example, the parching sun does not respond to the density of drought-stricken corn plants in a field; it kills them all. Such controls are almost always **abiotic** (nonliving)—physical forces such as weather patterns or geological events (Figure 47.3). On the other hand, if that field of corn is densely planted, the plants may crowd each other. They may compete for sunlight, or nutrients, or water. In the competition, then, some fail as others thrive. Those that die, we can say, have succumbed to the effects of **density-dependent controls.** In such cases the level of environmental control on a population is related to the density of the population. Such controlling influences are usually **biotic,** or living ones.

More about Biotic Controls

Let's have a closer look at some ways in which populations can be controlled by *biotic* influences.

Specifically, let's consider four such influences:
1. Competition
2. Toxic wastes
3. Disease and parasitism
4. Predation

> Population controls may be nonliving **(abiotic)** or living **(biotic).** Density-independent controls are usually abiotic; **density-dependent controls** are usually biotic.

Competition and the ecological niche. Competition exists where two individuals attempt to use some resources that may be in short supply. Such competition can be **interspecific** (between species) or **intraspecific** (within a species). We will look at interspecific competition first, but we must preface our discussion by briefly reviewing the concept of the ecological niche. This is necessary since we can only judge the degree of competition between species by considering how much of an overlap exists between one niche and another. It is in the overlap that competition really exists.

The term *niche* is notoriously difficult to define; in fact, cynics say there is no record of any two biologists ever completely agreeing on a definition. Earlier we described the niche as the interaction between an organism and its environment. Here we will focus more narrowly on the niche as the role a species plays in a community of interacting species—how it affects them and how they affect it.

Often two species will attempt to occupy the same niche. This, of course, leads to intense competition. If the level of competition were overly intense—say, if both species attempted to interact with the environment in identical ways (that is, to occupy the same niche)—one species would simply replace the other in the area of overlap (due to the operation of the **principle** of **competitive exclusion,** seen where one species is replaced by a superior competitor). In the wild the situation is often not so desperate. In fact, very similar species often coexist as neighbors without apparent undue conflict. This is because, over long periods of adjustment, they have adapted to each other by subdividing the niche. The result is that similar species that would appear to be strongly competitive have instead become specialists, each species exploiting only a narrow part of the environment and generally ignoring the other species.

Probably the classic study of such specialization was performed by the American ecologist R. H. MacArthur (Figure 47.4). He found that five species of North American warblers coexisted in the same spruce tree groves, and he wondered if they were simply *sharing* the same food resources. It turns out that the sharing is minimized. Careful observation revealed that each species tends to feed in a different part of the tree. Thus, the different species MacArthur studied reduced competition among themselves by becoming specialists. But at the same time, by restricting themselves to certain feeding areas the warblers effectively reduced their food supply. This reduction could be expected to have an influence on their numbers.

Organisms may subdivide available resources by specializing in exploiting certain parts, thereby forming different niches.

Intraspecific competition is most clearly apparent in two forms of social organization common among animals. (It is interesting that these very behaviors not only illustrate such competition but also reduce it, as we will see.) The two forms of social organization with such importance in controlling population density are **territoriality** and **dominance hierarchies.**

Territoriality in birds was first discussed in the writings of the ancient Greek philosophers. Territorial birds occupy an area—a territory—and defend it, particularly against intruders of the same species and sex. As we have seen, territoriality has a number of advantages. A territory may reserve a food supply and a nest site; it enables the territorial animal to become very familiar with a specific area; and it advertises that the territory holder is a healthy and able animal. In some species of birds, the males must have a good territory in order to attract females; even a splendid male cannot attract a mate if he holds an inferior territory. If good territories are in short supply, those birds unable to acquire one will not be able to reproduce. In such species, the availability of attractive territories affects population size (see Chapter 44).

Dominance hierarchies, or pecking orders (Figure 47.5), can also be important in regulating populations. In hierarchical groups, the dominant individuals have freer access to resources than subordinate individuals do. The rankings may be established by combat, play, or by formal threats and confrontation

FIGURE 47.4 Five species of the North American warbler often use the same spruce trees for feeding and nesting, but each species tends to use a specific zone. The darkened areas indicate where each species spends at least half of its feeding time.

without contact. While dominance hierarchies encourage stability by decreasing the likelihood of confrontation, this social structure is also important in the way such populations change. For instance, when food is scarce, the low-ranking individuals are the first to starve, since higher-ranking individuals have priority for commodities. However, it is assumed that the subordinate's chances are better if he seeks other resources rather than challenges a superior.

Population density in territorial species is limited by the availability of suitable territories, while in those with dominance hierarchies it is limited by the assignment of necessities to those of higher rank.

Toxic wastes. Almost all species produce toxic (poisonous) material of some kind. In fact, toxic wastes can have a drastic influence in reducing population growth. Those that cannot escape their own wastes may well be poisoned by them. (Bacteria growing in a petri dish will finally die of their own waste.)

Toxic waste may also be used to influence the population of other species. For example, some ecologists have suggested that bacteria may render food rotten and therefore unpalatable to most other organisms. They then live for a time steeped in their own wastes, but with their decomposing food reserved for themselves.

Some plants manufacture poisons that they secrete from their roots. The poisons do somewhat retard the growth of the plant that produced them, but they have a stronger effect on other plants, including their own species. In this way they reduce the level of competition for water and minerals (Figure 47.6).

Humans have, in recent years, managed to escape many of the biological checks on our population growth. Now we, like the yeast and bacteria, are faced with the possibility of polluting ourselves into extinction (also see Essay 47.1). Never mind that the poisons are made by mines, factories, and automobiles, and not directly by our simple primate bodies; the principle is the same. It's difficult to say whether the effects on humans will be (or are) density dependent or density independent. If, in the future, finding an appropriate shelter with filtered air or bottled oxygen spells the difference between life and death during "smog alerts," then the control could well be density dependent. If we are caught in a wave of some

FIGURE 47.5 Complex social interaction characterizes baboons, providing a measure of both safety and order. Individuals and subgroups are organized in a hierarchy, with dominant members receiving first priority in feeding and reproduction.

manufactured poison, then its effects will likely be density independent. In 1985, thousands of people were killed and maimed by the accidental release of poisonous gases from a Union Carbide plant in Bhopal, India. The population density of the adjacent slum had no influence on the gas's effect. We are also now beginning to see the more subtle and widespread effects of a different kind of problem as we change the rain (Essay 47.2).

Population density is often limited by the effects of the population's own toxic wastes. The most dangerous by far are biproducts of human activities.

ESSAY 47.1 HOLES IN THE SKY

The 1970s were a time of consciousness raising. People with all sorts of drums to beat and causes to advance saw to it that the rest of us became fully aware of whatever it was they had in mind. Some of the causes were indeed important, and we, in fact, needed to be reminded of them. So we learned (again) about discrimination and redwoods and whales. We learned about new ways of fighting mysterious little wars, and we had it firmly impressed upon us that the Amazon is disappearing and the oceans are used as dumps. Some of the concerns thrust upon us were admittedly bizarre or even amusing (the Cabbage Rights Society?), but others that seemed just as odd on the surface had quite serious, even ominous, undertones. What were we to think when we were warned that our hair spray caused holes in the sky?

Indeed, in the mid-1970s we were warned that propellants in spray cans were contributing to the depletion of the earth's shield against ultraviolet radiation. That shield was the upper atmosphere's layer of ozone (O_3). Without the ozone the earth is bombarded by devastating levels of ultraviolet light of the sort that causes skin cancer. (The National Academy of Sciences estimates that each 1% decrease in ozone can be translated into 12,000 to 30,000 new skin cancers in the United States alone.)

The propellants in question were chlorofluorocarbons (commonly called Freons), which were subsequently banned for spray can use by the United States government. Problem solved? Not quite. Worldwide production of the propellants has not slowed at all; in fact, it has been increasing at a rate of about 5% per year. The pollutant now makes up about 3500 parts per trillion (ppt), whereas in 1970 the figure was 1500 ppt and in 1965, 1000 ppt. In 1987, rather than impose restrictions on industrial use of chlorofluorocarbons, thereby reducing profits, Ronald Reagan's Secretary of the Interior is said to have suggested that humans begin wearing hats and sunscreen.

At first the concern was that the ozone levels of the upper atmosphere were being reduced around the globe. Then in 1986 a problem of a different sort was discovered. An international group of some 150 scientists, including California chemist F. S. Rowland, startled us with the news that a gigantic "ozone hole," a region of dramatically decreased ozone concentration, had developed above Antarctica. The ozone hole was roughly twice the size of the United States.

The scientific world was greatly concerned about the potential worldwide effects of any atmospheric change of this proportion. We just don't know what events any such large-scale change can bring about. Furthermore, the worst may not be over. There is great concern that the hole will grow or that new ones will appear, perhaps over a more heavily populated continent.

The scientists suspect that the chlorofluorocarbons are responsible, but they admit they know little about such atmospheric chemistry. In fact, the development over Antarctica was a complete surprise. Many are concerned that yet other surprises are in store.

FIGURE 47.6 The sandy, grass-free zone bordering the cluster of purple sage is a product of volatile growth-inhibiting poisons released by the sage.

In the 1970s it became clear that the rain was changing. In fact, in some areas the gentle raindrops were downright dangerous. The rain was becoming a dilute mixture of acids. It was first noticed in Scandinavia, then in the northeast United States and southeast Canada, then in Northern Europe and Japan.

Rainwater, of course, had always been slightly acidic because the water dissolved atmospheric carbon dioxide, forming carbonic acids. But now the rain was showing alarming concentrations of the more dangerous sulfuric acid and nitric acid. Where were they coming from? They were the result of accumulations of nitrous oxides and sulfuric oxides in the atmosphere. The nitrous oxides, it turned out, were from power plant and automobile emissions; the sulfuric oxides, mainly from power plants and smelters. Dissolved in the water of cloud formations, they formed nitric acid and sulfuric acid, then fell to earth to bathe our forests and cities and to fill our lakes with the corrosive mix.

The relative proportions of the two acids in rain depends on where one lives. In the northeastern United States the acidity is primarily due to sulfuric acid, in California, to nitric acid. So we do have a choice.

The rain has caused the reduction and even the elimination of fish in many of our lakes. The rain apparently doesn't kill the fish, it just keeps them from reproducing. So no young fish are found as the old ones gradually go the way of all flesh. In fact, about 700 lakes in southern Norway are now *entirely devoid* of fish, and our own northeastern lakes are following one by one. As our Adirondack lakes reach pH levels of 5 (not uncommon), 90 percent have no fish whatever. They are also curiously devoid of frogs and salamanders.

Entire patches of forests worldwide are sickening and dying as ecologists busily try to find out just what effects the rain is having. In fact, such studies have masked action by the polluting countries. The Reagan administration (undoubtedly under heavy attack by industrial lobbyists) refused steadfastly for years to take action. Instead, it initiated one "study" after another, finally admitting in 1985 that there was a problem and that it had to do with industrial pollution.

Interestingly, the solution is clear to everyone. We simply need to reduce the levels of our effluent from power plants, smelters, and automobiles. Most of the technology exists, but its implementation would be too expensive for the polluters to willingly bear. Are we willing to pay higher prices for manufactured goods to save our lakes and rivers? The question is a fundamental one and is asked over and over in one form or another in today's technological world.

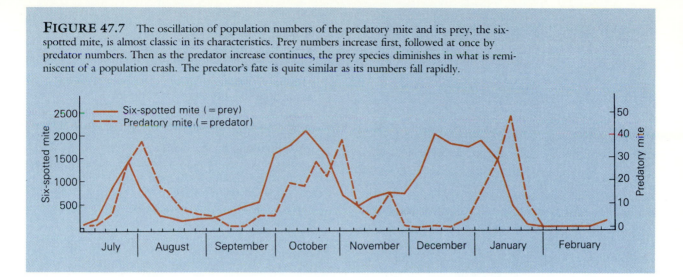

FIGURE 47.7 The oscillation of population numbers of the predatory mite and its prey, the six-spotted mite, is almost classic in its characteristics. Prey numbers increase first, followed at once by predator numbers. Then as the predator increase continues, the prey species diminishes in what is reminiscent of a population crash. The predator's fate is quite similar as its numbers fall rapidly.

Disease and parasitism. Among the most important density-dependent regulators of many populations are **disease** and **parasitism.** One reason is that increased density means greater proximity, which in turn facilitates the transmission of diseases and parasites. Also, disease and parasitism work hand in hand in times of hunger and starvation, helping to eliminate any weakened individuals. In some instances, disease helps to reduce a population by increasing the incidence of predations. For example, a two-week-old caribou can already outsprint a full-grown wolf, and healthy adult caribou seldom fall prey to wolves. But caribou are susceptible to a laming hoof disease, and it is these lamed animals that a wolf is likely to cull out of a herd. So both factors can influence population size, and it has been suggested that their effects might benefit their prey by removing the weak and sick.

> **D**isease and **parasitism** depress population growth because their spread increases with density.

Predation. There is little doubt that predators can influence the numbers of their prey. If a lion eats a zebra, that's one less zebra. But in the long run, the effect of a predator on its prey (and vice versa) may be quite complex. Predators normally do not—and probably cannot—eliminate their prey species altogether (barring human intervention, of course). This is because of their *reciprocal* effects—the influence of each species on the other.

The conventional explanation for the reciprocal influence is that under natural conditions, a feedback principle governs the interaction of predator and prey. As a prey species multiplies, it provides more food for predators. As a result, the well-fed predators increase in number. Their numbers do not rise immediately, however, because it takes time for the energy derived from food to be converted into successful reproductive efforts. When the number of predators finally does rise, they begin to exert increasing pressure on the prey. But as they begin to kill off the prey, they find themselves with less food, and so their own numbers fall, due perhaps to less successful reproductive efforts or perhaps to outright starvation. Again, the response lags a bit. Because of such lags, the prey population may be well on the road to recovery before the predator population begins to rise again (Figure 47.7).

We see, then, that the size and density of populations are influenced by a wide range of factors, from simple abiotic influences to the complex and interacting biotic factors. We are aware of some of the forces operating on populations, but we are still woefully short of understanding the underlying, fundamental principles of population change. The sooner we learn about such things the better, though, because our own numbers are rising at a rate unprecedented in human history.

> **I**n nature, predators reduce the numbers of their prey, but they rarely eliminate them because the predator numbers often track those of the prey.

SUMMARY

POPULATION GROWTH PATTERNS

Population growth follows J-shaped or S-shaped curves. The addition of reproducing members changes the population growth rate. In exponential growth, increases occur as doublings. J-shaped growth is limited because of environmental resistance. Bacterial growth is clearly exponential. Growth is limited by the environmental carrying capacity.

In S-shaped, or logistic, growth, increases are rapid at first, but they begin tapering off as the carrying capacity is reached. Overshoots may produce a crash in which most or all members die. Some crashes occur as a part of normal cycles, particularly in short-lived seasonal insect species.

Life Span and the Population

Survivorships curves are plots of rates against age groupings. They reveal that portion of the life span in which most individuals die.

Adaptive Strategies of Populations

K-selected species are those whose population growth curves are S-shaped. Members are long-lived, produce few offspring and assure survival by providing extensive parental care. At the other extreme, r-selected species follow J-shaped growth curves, have a brief life span, produce great numbers of offspring most of which perish, and offer little if any parental care. Both strategies work, but in different ways.

INFLUENCES ON POPULATION DENSITY

Density-Independent and Density-Dependent Controls

Most density-independent population controls are abiotic, and most density-dependent controls are biotic.

More About Biotic Controls

Competition, which may be interspecific (between species) or intraspecific (within species), occurs when the same resources (parts of the niche) are required by two individuals. When two species try to occupy a single niche, replacement or subdivision occur.

Intraspecific competition is reduced by social organization, as occurs in territories and dominance hierarchies. In hard times, individuals without territories and farther down in hierarchies will die off, but superior individuals will survive and reproduce.

Population density is reduced by self poisoning—the production of toxic metabolic wastes. In the long run, humans are undoubtedly subject to the effects of their toxic wastes, but the long-run effects of such pollution are still to be discovered.

Disease and parasitism, and their effects on reproduction, increase and decrease according to population density illustrating a negative feedback aspect.

Predator and prey numbers closely influence each other with predator population size closely tracking prey.

KEY TERMS

J-shaped (exponential) curve
S-shaped (sigmoid) curve
population growth rate
exponential growth
biotic potential
environmental resistance
carrying capacity
logistic growth curve
overshoot

population crash
crude birth rate
crude death rate
rate of natural increase
survivorship curve
r-selection
K-selection
density-independent control
abiotic

density-dependent control
interspecific
intraspecific
principle of competitive exclusion
territoriality
dominance hierarchy
disease
parasitism

REVIEW QUESTIONS

1 Construct graphs that illustrate J-shaped and S-shaped growth patterns. Does the "J" ever take on a vertical form? Explain. (pp. 758–759)

2 Describe the manner in which exponential growth occurs. What factors limit continued exponential growth? (p. 759)

3 What does the term carrying capacity include? How is the carrying capacity affected by populations that surpass it? (p. 759)

4 What is an overshoot? What commonly happens to populations that experience this? Is this result always considered abnormal? Explain. (p. 760)

5 Explain how the rate of natural increase is obtained. What would be a rapid rate of natural increase in the human population? (p. 760)

6 List two species in which the mortality rate is highest in the young. Characterize the human survivorship curve. (p. 761)

7 Name two K-adapted species and characterize the following: growth curve, number of offspring, life span, parental care. (pp. 761–762)

8 Name four r-adapted species. What can you surmise about the life span and the number of offspring? (pp. 761–762)

9 Name three examples of abiotic population controls, one of which might affect humans. Determine whether each is density dependent or independent. (p. 762)

10 Carefully define the term niche. Use the glossary if needed. (pp. 762–763)

11 Can two different species occupy the same niche? What are two common results of such an interaction? (p. 763)

12 Why would competition be greatest between members of the same species? The same species and sex? (p. 763)

13 Name two species that are definitely territorial. How might territoriality reduce the undesirable effects of competition? (pp. 763–764)

14 How might the establishment of dominance hierarchies assure survival? (p. 764)

15 Provide an example of toxic waste reducing population density. (p. 764)

16 Cite three or four examples of toxic waste production by humans. (pp. 764–766)

17 How might disease affect population density in a manner similar to negative feedback? (p. 767)

18 Prepare a graph illustrating the effects of predation on population size. Does this have a negative feedback aspect? Explain. (p. 767)

48

THE HUMAN POPULATION

Now we turn our attention to a set of numbers that has stimulated a great deal of concern and controversy in recent years: 4.94, 27, 11, 1.7, 41, and 35. You may not at first glance be particularly impressed. However, a look at Table 48.1 shows that the numbers represent, respectively, the human population (in billions) our crude birth rate, crude death rate, percentage annual growth, population doubling time (in years), and percentage of people below the age of 15.

It still may not be clear why we are bringing up such figures, but the reasons will soon be obvious. For example, we will see that the population of the world will have doubled between the time most of today's college students were born and about the year 2010.

The gloom and doom statistics are abundant, and anyone who is at all interested has probably heard enough of them by now. But just in case, here is one more: There are 27 more humans living now than there were 10 seconds ago when you began reading this paragraph. By tomorrow at this time, 230,000 will have been added, and by next year, 84 million. That is slightly more than the population of Mexico—and most of them will live in a style similar to that of the average citizen of that struggling nation (Figure 48.1).

We can generate such statements all day, but once we understand the problem, do we wallow in depression? Do we simply look away? Or do we join the ranks of hopeful and determined people who intend to learn as much as they can about the problem and then try to find ways to help? Obviously, we will assume you are in this last group, and so we'll begin by delving into the history of our numbers. The first thing we should know is that throughout most of our 3 to 4 million year history, populations remained fairly stable, but in the past million years that stability has been interrupted by three significant growth surges (Figure 48.2).

HUMAN POPULATION HISTORY

Let's begin our overview with a look at the early population of *Homo erectus,* an ancestor that lived about one million years ago. In those days we might have seen small bands roaming distant, grassy plains, a hunched figure stopping occasionally to dig at a root or pick at the soft parts of an insect. The hominid population, estimated to have been about 125,000 at that time, was not having much impact on the environment.

TABLE 48.1 World Population Data: 1970 and 1986

Region	Year	Total (millions)	Crude Birth Rate	Crude Death Rate	Natural Increase (annual %)	Doubling Time (years)	% Below 15 Years of Age
World	1970	3632	34	14	2.0	35	37
	1986	4942	27	11	1.7	41	35
Africa	1970	344	47	20	2.6	27	44
	1986	583	45	16	2.8	24	45
Asia	1970	2045	38	15	2.3	31	40
	1986	2876	28	10	1.8	39	37
North America	1970	228	18	9	1.1	63	20
	1986	267	16	9	0.7	98	22
Latin America	1970	283	38	9	2.9	24	42
	1986	419	31	8	2.3	30	38
Europe	1970	462	18	10	0.8	88	25
	1986	493	13	10	0.3	248	22
Nations of Special Interest							
United States	1970	205	17.5	9.6	1.0	70	30
	1986	241	16.0	9.0	0.7	99	22
Soviet Union	1970	243	17.9	7.7	1.0	70	28
	1986	280	20.0	11.0	0.9	79	25
People's Rep. of China (estimate)	1970	760	34.0	15.0	1.8	39	?
	1986	1050	18.0	8.0	1.0	72	34
India	1970	554	42.0	17.0	2.6	27	41
	1986	785	35.0	13.0	2.3	31	39

SOURCE OF DATA: Population Reference Bureau.

The lives of these uninspiring creatures must have been rigorous indeed. Yet they survived. They adapted and they changed. In time, they gave rise to creatures of a different sort, the earliest humans of the species, *Homo sapiens*.

These ancient peoples were probably not much to look at either. They, too, roamed the earth as hunters and gatherers. And life for them was undoubtedly rigorous. Infants and children probably suffered high mortality rates, but such losses were quickly replaced in a species where fertility was not a seasonal event. The average life span is estimated to have been 30 years; but there were undoubtedly a number of old folks in the group, their numbers balanced by the high infant mortality rate.

The low average life span of early humans was largely due to a high infant mortality rate.

The First Population Surge

The first growth surge in the human population was probably due to the development of increasingly efficient tools. With them, early people could more effectively modify and exploit their environment. In addition, humans—inveterate wanderers—had by then penetrated and established themselves on all of the continents. By 10,000 years ago, the earth probably supported about 5 million people. (Estimates of these early human populations are based on limited data, partly from anthropological studies of surviving primitive cultures.)

The Second Population Surge

About 10,000 years ago (some say 8000), the human population began its second growth surge, this time with more authority. With the development of agriculture and the domestication of animals came increasing densities of local populations. There was

FIGURE 48.1 What does population growth mean to a nation? The two largest urban centers in the world are located in Japan and Mexico, nations that have far different social and economic prospects. What would happen to each of these vast urban areas if population doubling were to occur in 27 years? Japan has its population growth under control, so the question is academic. In the case of Mexico, a 27-year doubling time is precisely what demographers predict, so the question is frightening.

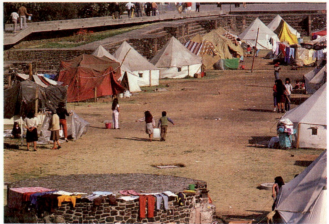

FIGURE 48.2 (a) A simple numerical plot of human population history clearly reveals the near vertical rise of the J-shaped curve, a danger signal for most species. (b) A logarithmic plot, where time is compressed, shows three distinct growth surges.

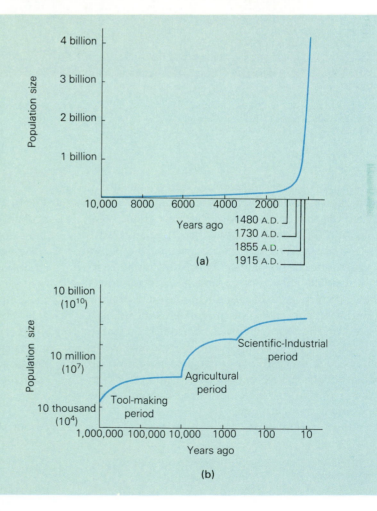

TABLE 48.2   Basic Population Arithmetic

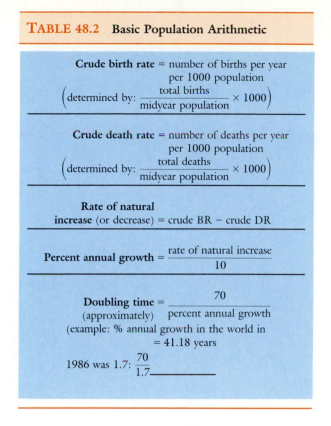

Crude birth rate = number of births per year per 1000 population

$$\left(\text{determined by: } \frac{\text{total births}}{\text{midyear population}} \times 1000\right)$$

Crude death rate = number of deaths per year per 1000 population

$$\left(\text{determined by: } \frac{\text{total deaths}}{\text{midyear population}} \times 1000\right)$$

Rate of natural increase (or decrease) = crude BR − crude DR

$$\text{Percent annual growth} = \frac{\text{rate of natural increase}}{10}$$

$$\text{Doubling time} = \frac{70}{\text{percent annual growth}}$$

(approximately)
(example: % annual growth in the world in 1986 was 1.7: $\frac{70}{1.7}$ = 41.18 years)

less need to roam the countryside in search of food; in fact, there was a great need to stay put and tend the fields and livestock. With the storage of surplus food, winter and drought no longer exacted such a great toll on human life.

With the increased quantity and dependability of the food supply, humans probably experienced a lower death rate, particularly among the young. Furthermore, there was quite possibly an increase in the birth rate because of better nutrition. Large families may have been encouraged because they meant more hands to till the fields. But life was by no means simple, since the crops were subjected to the inconsistencies of weather and to infestation by insects and other herbivores whose own numbers responded to the novel food supply.

The unprecedented population growth of the early days of agriculture did not continue at its initial soaring rate, but settled into a steadier, more gradual climb. Yet between the advent of agriculture and the time of Christ, the human population rose from 5 million to about 133 million. By 1650 A.D., it had reached an estimated 500 million.

History reveals that on a regional level this growth was interrupted many, many times by the decimating effects of disease, famine, and war. These are largely density dependent and closely interrelated factors. A severe example of the effects of disease occurred in the 14th century, when one-fourth of Europe's population was killed by the "Black Death"—the bubonic plague. Such other diseases as typhus, influenza, and syphilis also took their toll on the crowded and incredibly filthy towns of the medieval period.

Interestingly, the loss of such numbers is insignificant in view of population growth today. At today's population growth rate, for example, the number of deaths from the 14th-century bubonic plague could be recouped in one year, while the number of people killed in all the wars of the last 500 years could be replaced in about six months.

The Third Population Surge

The third population growth surge began in Europe in the mid-17th century, after the unexplained decline of the plague (perhaps only those who were naturally immune were left alive). A number of explanations have been advanced to account for this third surge. For one thing, the crowded populations of Europe expanded into the New World, with its array of opportunities and unexploited resources. More significantly, Pasteur and others postulated the "germ theory" and people were becoming aware of some of the causes of disease. By the 19th century public sanitation programs had begun, vaccines were developed, and rapid advances in food storage and transportation technologies led to a marked increase in food supplies. Between 1750 and 1850 the population of Europe doubled; that of the New World increased fivefold.

> In the most recent growth surge, the death rate fell after the discovery of bacteria as an agent of disease led to vast improvements in health and medical practices. Other factors were improved agriculture and industry as well as the colonization of the New World.

Populations were surging in other parts of the world as well, for reasons that are not completely understood. In China, the most heavily populated nation at that time, agriculture had made great gains, and a long period of comparative political stability followed the overthrow of the Ming dynasty in 1644. India, however, had known little rest from turmoil and periodic famines. In 1770, the worst famine of all reportedly killed three million people in India. African populations are believed to have remained stable until about 1850, when the impact of imported European medical advances began to depress the death rate. However, recent experiences in Africa, namely the Ethiopian drought and famine, remind us of our often fragile relationship with the environment and that we are not yet free of ancient hazards (Figure 48.3).

The third surge has continued into modern times, and the rate of the rise has constantly accelerated. This is due largely to a host of innovations in industry, agriculture, and public health. Many of these innovations arose in industrialized, developed countries and were exported to heavily populated developing regions.* In the developed nations, famine was all but eradicated with the advent of pesticides, chemical fertilizers, and high-yield crops. Potential disease epidemics were routinely controlled by vaccines, antibiotics, and insecticides.

In conclusion, we can note that the human population grew from about 5 million at the dawn of agriculture to 500 million by 1650. In the next 200 years the world population doubled, reaching 1 billion. (**Doubling time** is the number of years required for a population to double in numbers. See Table 48.2.) In the 80 years between 1850 and 1930 the numbers doubled again, to 2 billion. The next doubling took only 45 years, and in 1975 our world population stood at 4 billion. By 1970, thoroughly alarmed population experts were predicting another doubling, to 8 billion, by the year 2000—a span of only 35 years.

THE HUMAN POPULATION TODAY

To the surprise of nearly everyone, the rate of natural increase in the world population slowed toward the end of the 1970s, and that deceleration continues today (see Table 48.1). (Note the implications of the word *rate*. The occupants of a car approaching a cliff at 30 miles per hour might take little comfort in knowing that its rate is slowing and it will be traveling at only 15 miles per hour by the time it goes over the edge.)

At the end of 1986, demographers estimated the world's population to be near 5 billion. The annual

---

Developed nations are those that have a slow rate of population growth; a stable, industrialized economy; a low percentage of workers employed in the agricultural sector; a high per capita income; and a high degree of literacy. *Developing* nations have the opposite traits. Of course, many countries have intermediate conditions, and some have a combination—a privileged upper class and a poor lower class.

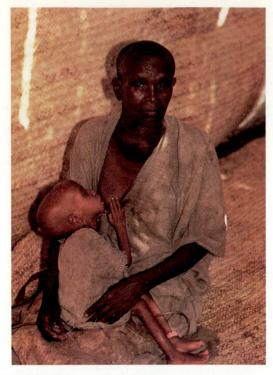

FIGURE 48.3   In spite of modern achievements, undeveloped and developing nations are still subject to disruptive episodes of famine.

growth rate had fallen slightly and the doubling time had increased to 41 years. These data suggest some headway in our attempts to control our population, which can be at least partially attributed to changing attitudes of women toward their role in society, changes in preferences in family size, advances in methods of birth control, and the liberalization of abortion laws in developed nations.

Growth in the Developing Regions

The new data generated a measure of relief and even a growing optimism. But it turns out that the depressed growth rates occurred primarily in the most developed nations, those that could best support increased populations, such as the United States, Japan, Western Europe, and the Soviet Union. Most poorer, developing nations of the world show few signs of controlling their populations. The annual rate of growth in those regions (excluding China) is an ominous 2.2% and the doubling time is 31 years. While the crude birth and death rates in the U.S. in 1986 were 16 and 9 per thousand, respectively, those rates in Africa were 45 and 16. Further, the doubling time in Africa is an alarmingly brief 24 years. How do you suppose these shifting population trends will affect political, social, and economic stability in the near future? What effects are they having now?

At first glance, the news from Latin America seemed hopeful: In the past few years there has been a decrease in the crude birth rate. But again, the numbers are misleading. In this region, the birth rate is already four times the death rate. Furthermore, many Latin American nations already troubled by political unrest and dismal economic conditions face a doubling time about the same as Africa's.

Asia has traditionally troubled demographers because so little is known about it and yet it has enormous reproductive potential. (It is instructive to keep in mind that well over half of the people walking the earth today are Asians, and one in every five humans alive today is Chinese.) However within the last decade the birth rate in China (reportedly) declined 53%, with an equivalent fall in the death rate. Partly because of this shift in China, the doubling time for Asian populations has increased from 31 to 39 years. Massive birth control programs in China and several other Asian nations have been instrumental in the declining birth rates. Similar efforts in India have been somewhat successful, but India's annual increase is still over 2% and its doubling time is only 31 years.

The fastest population growth today occurs in the developing regions: Africa, Asia, and Latin America, those places that can least support increased numbers of people.

The successes Asia is currently enjoying, however, may be swamped by another problem, one of momentum. Specifically, 37% of these people are under the age of 15 and have yet to enter the breeding population. Asia could well be in for another population explosion.

It is difficult if not impossible to predict what the future holds, but there are ways of making educated guesses. Let's gaze into the crystal ball of demography and see how populations are forecast.

Demographic Transition

There is an interesting relationship between a country's developmental progress and its population structure: As nations undergo economic and technological development, their population growth tends to decrease. According to the theory of **demographic transition,** nations go through several developmental phases, the earliest of which is characterized by high birth and death rates and slow growth. As they begin to develop, the birth rate remains high but the death rate falls. The result is that the population begins to grow rapidly. Then as industrialization peaks, the birth rate falls and begins to approximate the death rate. The population enters a fluctuating equilibrium state (Figure 48.4).

One major prediction based on the theory of demographic transition is that population growth in developing parts of Asia, Africa, and Latin America will slow as they become further industrialized. But can the answer to the enigma of world population growth be that simple? Not quite. First, it is the developed nations that must pay the enormous costs

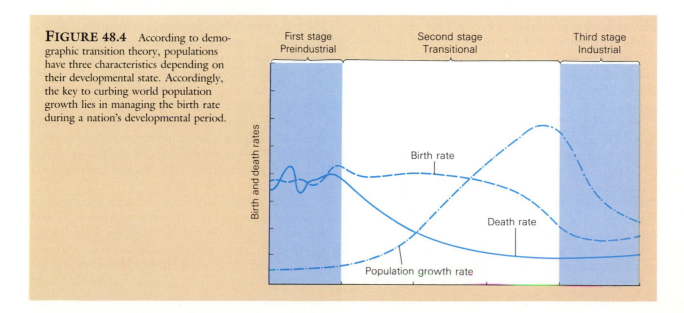

FIGURE 48.4 According to demographic transition theory, populations have three characteristics depending on their developmental state. Accordingly, the key to curbing world population growth lies in managing the birth rate during a nation's developmental period.

First stage
Preindustrial

Second stage
Transitional

Third stage
Industrial

Birth and death rates

Birth rate

Death rate

Population growth rate

of such a massive industrialization program, and this could place a great burden on their own economies. (Also, who needs more competition in the marketplace?) Second, there are severe risks in encouraging developing countries to go through such transitions. For example, if massive development programs stall in the second and most difficult phase, soaring populations will preclude the third stage and send the hopeful developing nation into a deadly population spiral. Thus, any such developmental program must be approached with extreme caution.

> **Demographic transition** theory maintains that populations that were stable in the undeveloped state increase rapidly during development because of depressed death rates. Upon development, birth rates decrease and stability resumes.

THE FUTURE OF THE HUMAN POPULATION

Changing Attitudes

Our track record in predicting population growth is not very impressive; demographers in the U.S. were taken by surprise by the baby boom of the 1950s, and they are still trying to explain the latest downward trend. However, increasingly sophisticated and precise calculations show some promise of improving the accuracy of our projections.

The infamous "baby boom" in the post–World War II years—1945 through 1960—witnessed an incredible rise in fertility rates, a time when the "good life" meant a home in the suburbs and three or four kids playing in the yard. Then came the "awakening," as ecologists and population biologists began to spread the alarm about unprecedented population growth.

The attitude of American women in their reproductive period toward domestic life and family size changed radically in the 1960s and 1970s (as did that of women in many other developed nations). Women began to assume new roles in industrialized societies. They entered new areas of the work force, challenged male enclaves, demanded rights and privileges previously reserved for men, and placed less emphasis on children. Their new attitudes were duly noted by the demographers, who then predicted a reduced rate of population growth. But such trends can change quickly, and if attitude is an important

variable in forecasting population sizes, demographers must remain current. In any case, measuring attitudes is a very risky business.

Population Structure

Knowing the age structure of any population is critical to understanding growth patterns and making predictions. One way to portray such data is by **age structure histograms.** In Figure 48.5, you can see how such diagrams are formed. Note the marked differences in the shapes of such histograms between developed and developing nations. In developed areas, recent population increases have been comparatively slow, so the base is not very wide. Also, people tend to live longer and thus to occupy the upper levels in greater proportions. In developing nations, on the other hand, the rate of increase is still expanding, swelling the lower levels. Obviously, these lower levels are important to population forecasting since they represent future reproducers. Finally, such shapes illustrate that people in developing regions have fewer health advantages and are more likely to die sooner, resulting in a significant decrease in the upper third of these regions' age brackets.

Growth Predictions and the Earth's Carrying Capacity

The fundamental question of how large the human population can become is irrevocably tied to what the earth can support—its human carrying capacity. If we have learned anything from population studies of other species, it is that this capacity cannot be exceeded for long without severe risk—especially, the risk to the environment. Any such damage would lower the environment's carrying capacity and set the stage for a devastating population crash.

The range of estimates of the earth's human carrying capacity is enormous. In other words, the experts cannot agree. Some population biologists believe that we have already exceeded our limits and that our present population represents a drastic overshoot. At the other end of the spectrum are the optimists who believe the human population can increase to 50 billion and still survive easily. (Biologists don't take this latter estimate very seriously.)

Recent estimates by more moderate population experts suggest that the human population could be sustained *temporarily* at 8 to 15 billion. From there, they suggest, our numbers could gradually decrease to new, more stable levels, If we fail to restrain ourselves when we reach the higher numbers, we can expect not a gradual decrease in numbers but a mas-

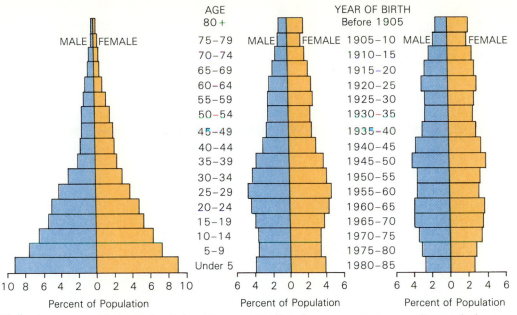

FIGURE 48.5 Age structure histograms break down the population into five-year age groups, revealing much about past history and permitting predictions of future trends to be made. *Left*, expanding nation, e.g., Mexico. *Middle*, moderately stable nation, e.g., United States. *Right*, long-term stable nation, e.g., Sweden. Source: Population Reference Bureau.

sive increase in our death rate—a dieback or crash. It has been calculated that such a crash might kill 50% to 80% of the human population. Population biologist Paul Ehrlich, writing in 1977, emphasized that this is probably the way our population will stabilize. The dieback, says Ehrlich, will likely be due to a combination of famine, war, disease, and ecological disruption. With the exception of war (which is rare among other species) these are common density-dependent controls.

> **M**any biologists maintain that the earth's carrying capacity for humans has been substantially exceeded. They predict that the usual biological controls, along with war, will produce a crash.

To leave the subject on a note of cautious optimism, we reiterate that world population growth is slowing down somewhat and that some of the more heavily populated nations have recently joined this trend. Further, it is within the power of the world's family of nations to see that the decreasing trend is continued and accentuated. Our goal, if we are to avoid chaos, is to reach a **replacement level.** Essentially, it means that each couple simply replaces itself,

by having only two children. (The popular belief that the United States has achieved this goal is inaccurate.) Because of the burgeoning numbers of young people, the future size of the world's population depends largely upon when that replacement level is reached.

Scenarios portraying a stable world population are admittedly utopian, but then attainment is not impossible. Some population experts maintain that many slow-growing developed nations are now reaching the desired level and that others can do so within a few decades. The trend toward family planning and use of birth control is increasing, and one hopes that efforts to stimulate such interest in developing nations will continue. Under the best of circumstances, the developing nations could reach some state of population stability in about 50 years.

The bottom line is that we must assume our species is not special; it is not exempt from the natural laws that govern population control in other species. Our only special feature is our mental capacity. We have the ability to analyze, predict, imagine, and finally to *choose.* Of course, we can choose by deciding not to choose, not to take a stand, not to be involved. But the time for that luxury is past. We must now learn as much as possible about the nature of overpopulation, apply ourselves to solving the problem, and stand ready to be accountable for our actions when we are judged by future generations.

SUMMARY

HUMAN POPULATION HISTORY

The First Population Surge

In the past 50,000 to 100,000 years, the human population has experienced three significant growth surges. The first growth surge probably occurred with the development of increasingly efficient tools with which people could more effectively modify and exploit the environment.

The Second Population Surge

Around 10,000 years ago, the second growth surge coincided with the development of agriculture and the domestication of animals; humans probably began to experience a lower death rate, and possibly a higher birth rate. This growth was interrupted numerous times by a variety of factors such as disease, famine, and war.

The Third Population Surge

In the mid-17th century, the third population surge began, possibly because of expansion into the New World, the introduction of sanitation programs and sophistication of medical practices, advances in the preservation of food, and political stability in some areas. Between 1650 and 1850, the world population doubled (from 500 million to 1 billion). There were 2 billion people by 1930, and 4 billion by 1975; in 1970, some predicted that there would be 8 billion people on earth by the year 2000.

THE HUMAN POPULATION TODAY

The rate of natural increase of the world's population slowed in the late 1970s, and is continuing to decelerate.

Growth in Developing Regions

The doubling time of the human population has increased, primarily in developed nations that could theoretically support increased populations. Developing nations, however, show few signs of controlling their populations. Some developing nations, such as China, have instituted major birth-control propaganda programs to stem their high rates of natural population increase.

Demographic Transition

A country's developmental progress and its population structure are related in an interesting way; as development increases, population growth tends to decrease. Several developmental phases occur, according to the theory of demographic transition, with the earliest characterized by high birth and death rates, the next by high birth rates and lower death rates, and the next by low birth and death rates, which reflect a fluctuating equilibrium state. This theory is the basis for the prediction that population growth in developing parts of Asia, Africa, and Latin America will slow as those areas become further industrialized. Programs based on the theory must be approached cautiously, however.

THE FUTURE OF THE HUMAN POPULATION

Changing Attitudes

Whereas American couples of the 1950's favored a large family size, attitudes changed abruptly in the 1960's and 1970's, contributing to a sharp decline in population growth.

Population Structure

Age structure histograms are useful devices for portraying the age structure of a population. Such information is important in understanding growth patterns and in making predictions.

Growth Predictions and the Earth's Carrying Capacity

The basic issue in human population studies is the carrying capacity of the earth. Estimates vary greatly, and some population biologists believe that humans have already exceeded the carrying capacity and are in a phase of overshoot. A population crash could result in stabilization—or the population could gradually decrease, possibly through zero population growth programs, through which we could reach our replacement level.

KEY TERMS

doubling time
demographic transition
age structure histogram
replacement level

REVIEW QUESTIONS

1 Describe the innovations that brought about the first two great population surges in human history. (p. 771)

2 List the three major causes of death during the Middle Ages. Were these density dependent or density independent? Explain. (p. 773)

3 List three innovations that may explain the most recent human population growth surge, and explain how each may have affected the birth rate and the death rate. (p. 773)

4 What is the status of human population growth today? Specifically, where is growth most rapid? What are some of the possible political and social ramifications of this? (p. 774)

5 Briefly predict the future of human population growth according to the theory of demographic transition. Upon what specific observations is this theory based? What are some of the theory's pitfalls? (p. 775)

6 With simple drawings, depict the population age structure for Mexico, the United States, and Sweden. What future conditions can we predict according to the base of the diagram? According to the top? (p. 777)

7 What are experts telling us about the earth's carrying capacity? Should human numbers be maintained at our current level? Explain. (p. 776)

APPENDIX A
GEOLOGIC TIMETABLE

Eras (Years Since Start)	Periods and Epochs	Extent in Millions of Years	Geological Events
Cenozoic	Quaternary		
	Holocene (present)	Last 10,000 years	
	Pleistocene	.01–2	Four ice ages, glaciation in N. Hemisphere; uplift of Sierras
	Tertiary		
	Pliocene	2–6	Continued uplift; drastic cooling
	Miocene	6–23	More uplift in Rockies; isthmus of Panama formed; climate drying
	Oligocene	23–36	Mountain uplift in Europe, Asia; volcanic action in Rockies
	Eocene	35–54	Inland seas diminished
65,000,000	Paleocene	54–65	Continents formed, separations continuing

(Cretaceous-Paleocene discontinuity. Asteroid collides with earth; dust obscures sun [recent hypothesis])

Eras (Years Since Start)	Periods and Epochs	Extent in Millions of Years	Geological Events
Mesozoic	Cretaceous	65–135	Two major land forms (Laurasia and Gondwana); continental separation occurs through era; Rockies forming, other continents low; seas over Europe
	Jurassic	135–197	Continued mountain building, most continents low, inland seas
225,000,000	Triassic	197–225	Mountain building in Pangaea (North America); most recent continental drift begins
Paleozoic	Permian	225–280	Very cool; mountain building, glaciation in south, seas diminish, Appalachians formed; vast extinction
	Carboniferous	280–345	Lowlands, shallow seas, coal swamps, mountain building in Pangaea (North America)
	Devonian	345–405	Landscape varies, Appalachians forming
	Silurian	405–425	Flattened landscape, some mountains; shallow seas, lowlands
	Ordovician	425–500	
570,000,000	Cambrian	500–570	Temperature increases
Precambrian		1000	Cooling; atmosphere has become oxidizing rather than reducing
		2000	Low-lying, vast, inland seas; tropical climate with little latitudinal variation
Origin of earth, 4.5–5.7 billion years		3000	Oxygen production
		4000	Oldest rock formation, crust hardening
		4500	Chemical evolution; solar system forms

APPENDIX B
CLASSIFICATION OF ORGANISMS

THE PROKARYOTES

KINGDOM MONERA Single-celled organisms, tough cell wall, no membrane-bounded organelles or organized nucleus. Circular DNA, not joined with protein. Reproduction mostly by fission; some by conjugation. Flagella tubular and rotating.

ARCHEBACTERIA ("beginning" bacteria): Unique, proteinaceous cell walls. Cell membrane with branched fatty acids. Mostly anaerobic; includes methanogens, halophiles, and thermophiles (Chapter 20).

EUBACTERIA ("true" bacteria): Cell walls of peptidoglycan, membranes with straight-chain fatty acids; includes many pathogens, free-living decomposers, phototrophs, and chemotrophs. Found in coccus, bacillus, and spirochaete forms, occurring singly, in clusters, or in chains. The cyanobacteria are colonial, with membranous photosynthetic thylakoid, and can fix nitrogen (Chapter 20).

THE EUKARYOTES

All other organisms. Membrane-bounded cellular organelles, linear chromosomes join protein. Cell division by mitosis and meiosis, sexual reproduction common. Flagella or cilia are microtubular. Single-celled, colonial, and multicellular.

KINGDOM PROTISTA Includes photosynthetic, plant-like (algal), heterotrophic, funguslike, and animal-like (protozoan) forms. Single-celled, colonial, and multicellular (Chapter 21).

PHYLUM SARCOMASTIGOPHORA (13,000 species; flagellated and ameboid protozoans): Single-celled, heterotrophic, some phagocytic, fresh and marine waters.

PHYLUM APICOMPLEXA (6000 species; nonmotile protozoans): Single-celled parasitic sporeformers.

PHYLUM CILIOPHORA (7200 species; ciliated protozoans): Single-celled, extremely complex and diverse heterotrophs.

PHYLUM PYRROPHYTA (1100 species; "fire algae," the dinoflagellates): Single-celled, flagellated, chitinous cell walls, phototrophic.

PHYLUM EUGLENOPHYTA (800 species; euglenoids): Single-celled, flagellated, flexible body wall, phototrophs or heterotrophs reproduce mitotically.

PHYLUM CHRYSOPHYTA (11,500 species; diatoms, yellow-green and golden-brown algae): Single-celled or colonial, glass walls, phototrophic.

PHYLUM RHODOPHYTA (4000 species; red algae): Coastal seaweeds, floridean or carageenan as storage carbohydrates. Phototrophic.

PHYLUM PHAEOPHYTA (1000 species; brown algae): Coastal seaweeds and kelps; fucoxanthin pigments; laminarin and mannitol storage carbohydrates. Often large; some with vascular tissue. Phototrophic.

PHYLUM CHLOROPHYTA (7000 species; green algae): Single-celled, colonial, and multicellular; pigments mostly chlorophylls and carotenoids; usually aquatic. Phototrophic.

PHYLUM CHAROPHYTA (250 species; stoneworts): Freshwater algae with apical growth; calcium in cell walls. Phototrophic.

PHYLUM OOMYCOTA (475 species; water molds): Flagellated fungi; many parasitic. Heterotrophic.

PHYLUM ACRASIOMYCOTA (26 species; cellular slime molds): Heterotrophic, individual amebas that live alone or join to form multicellular plasmodia.

PHYLUM MYXOMYCOTA (450 species; acellular slime molds): Heterotrophic; form multinucleate feeding plasmodia.

KINGDOM FUNGI Multicellular heterotrophs, including decomposers and parasites. Mycelial organization with chitinous cell walls. Sexual and asexual spores; primarily haploid with brief diploid stage (Chapter 21).

PHYLUM ZYGOMYCOTA (600 species; bread molds): Mycelium without cell end walls; simple sexual zygospore.

PHYLUM ASCOMYCOTA (30,000 species; sac fungi): Extensive mycelium with cell end walls. Complex sexual dikaryotic asci; ascospores produced through meiosis. Many species symbiotic with cyanobacteria or algae, forming *lichens*.

PHYLUM BASIDIOMYCOTA (25,000 species; club fungi): Extensive mycelium with cell end walls. Large complex dikaryotic basidiocarp produces basidiospores.

PHYLUM DEUTEROMYCOTA (also, Fungi Imperfecti) (25,000 species): Various fungi with no known sexual stage.

KINGDOM PLANTAE Nonmotile, multicellular organisms with dense cell walls of cellulose. Specialized tissues and organs. Phototrophic. Alternating generations. Embryo protected in archegonium (Chapter 22).

Nonvascular Plants

DIVISION BRYOPHYTA (16,000 species; mosses, liverworts, hornworts): Multicellular, nonvascular, terrestrial. Simple aerial spore, motile sperm, predominant gametophyte. Generally small with little supportive tissue.

Seedless Vascular Plants (Cryptogams)

Vascular tissue in roots, stems, and leaves. Predominant sporophyte; separate gametophyte. Aerial spore; motile sperm.

DIVISION PSILOPHYTA (4 species; whisk ferns): Simple, with few surviving species. Vascular stem, scalelike leaves.

DIVISION LYCOPHYTA (1000 species; club mosses): Vascular roots, stems, and leaves.

DIVISION SPHENOPHYTA (12 species; horsetails): One surviving genus, upright vascular stems, prominent nodes and tiny, scalelike nonphotosynthetic leaves.

DIVISION PTEROPHYTA (11,000 species; ferns): Widespread distribution. Complex leaves emerge as fiddleheads from rhizome.

Vascular Plants With Seeds (Phanerogams)

Gametophytes develop within sporophyte tissue; male and female spores produced; and microspores released within pollen grains. Embryo develops within seed that includes stored foods and protective seed coats.

Gymnosperm Divisions

DIVISION CYCADOPHYTA (100 species; the cycads): Palmlike leaves, exposed seeds, wind-dispersed pollen, motile sperm within pollen tube.

DIVISION GINKGOPHYTA (1 species; ginkgo): Trees with fan-shaped leaves, exposed seeds, wind-dispersed pollen, motile sperm within pollen tube.

DIVISION CONIFEROPHYTA (500 species): Usually large trees with needlelike or scalelike leaves. Evergreens; exposed seeds borne upon cones; nonmotile sperm.

DIVISION GNETOPHYTA (71 species): Some angiosperm features: xylem vessels, flowerlike cones, nonmotile sperm.

Angiosperm Divisions

DIVISION ANTHOPHYTA Flowers present; seeds enclosed by fruit; xylem vessels present. Nonmotile sperm.

   CLASS DICOTYLEDONEAE (200,000 species; the dicots): Diverse, net-veined leaves; secondary growth common; floral parts in fours, fives, or multiples of these; two cotyledons.

   CLASS MONOCOTYLEDONEAE (50,000 species; the monocots): Diverse, parallel-veined leaves; secondary growth rare; floral parts in threes or multiples of threes; one cotyledon.

KINGDOM ANIMALIA Multicellular, heterotrophic eukaryotes. Specialized tissues, most with organ systems. Most highly responsive. Diploid except for gametes. Fertilization without intervening haploid life cycle. Small, flagellated sperm and large stationary egg (Chapters 27 to 30).

Subkingdom Parazoa

Animals of flagellate origins, simple developmental progression.

PHYLUM PORIFERA (5000 species; the sponges): cellular organization. Nonmotile adults; filter feeding; skeletal elements of calcium carbonate, silicon dioxide, or spongin. Asexual reproduction by budding; sexual reproduction by fertilization of internalized egg (Chapter 27).

Subkingdom Metazoa

Animals of ciliate origin. Organ level of organization or higher.

Radiates

Acoelomates (no coelom)

PHYLUM COELENTERATA (9000 species): Radial body of two cell layers; saclike gastrovascular cavity; tentacles and stinging cells. May alternate between medusa and polyp stages; or only one stage may be present. Three classes: Hydrozoa (hydroids), Scyphozoa (jellyfish), Anthozoa (corals and anemones) (Chapter 27).

PHYLUM CTENOPHORA (90 species; comb jellies): Radial body of two cell layers. Tentacles with glue cells (Chapter 27).

Bilateral Protostomes

PHYLUM PLATYHELMINTHES (13,000 species; flatworms): Flattened body; branching gastrovascular cavity; dense bodies with many cell layers. Three classes: Turbellaria (free-living planarians), Trematoda, and Cestoda (parasitic flukes and tapeworms) (Chapter 27).

Pseudocoelomates (coelom not completely mesodermally lined)

PHYLUM NEMATODA (10,000 species named—estimated half million unnamed; the roundworms and rotifers): Class Nematoda (roundworms) includes free-living and parasitic species; slender body, pseudocoelom (not completely mesodermally lined), tube-within-tube body plan (complete gut) (Chapter 27).

PHYLUM ROTIFERA (2000 species; rotifers): free-living, minute, with complex organ systems (Chapter 27).

PHYLUM NEMATOMORPHA (230 species; horsehair worms)

PHYLUM RYNCHOCOELA (650 species; proboscis or ribbon worms)

Coelomates (coelom completely lined by mesoderm; all remaining phyla)

PHYLUM MOLLUSCA (47,000 species): Controversial classification—segmentation and coelom may not exist. Diversification through modifications of head, foot, mantle, and radula. Includes seven classes: Aplacaphora (solenogasters—wormlike, radula only clear characteristic), Monoplacophora (*Neopalina*, deep-sea form, believed to be extinct), Scaphopoda (tooth shells), Polyplacophora (chitons), Bivalvia (bivalves: two shells—clams, etc.), Gastropoda (snails, slugs), and Cephalopoda (octopus, squid—rather intelligent, fast, predators, foot subdivided into tentacles. Covering mantle, large brain, keen eyesight) (Chapter 28.)

PHYLUM ANNELIDA (9,000 species; segmented worms): Body subdivided into repeating segments; well-developed digestive system; closed circulatory system. Three classes: Oligochaeta (earthworms), Hirudinea (leeches), and Polychaeta (marine worms) (Chapter 28).

PHYLUM PRIAPULIDA (9 species; proboscis worms)

PHYLUM POGONOPHORA (100 species; beard worms)

PHYLUM SIPUNCULA (300 species; peanut worms)

PHYLUM TARTIGRADA (350 species; water bears)

PHYLUM ARTHROPODA (800,000 to 1,000,000 species; "jointed-footed" animals): Paired, jointed appendages with chitinous exoskeleton, varied segmentation, wide distribution (Chapter 28).

   SUBPHYLUM CHELICERATA Six pairs of appendages, four pairs being legs, with paired chelicerae (fangs). Three classes: Meristomata (horseshoe crabs), Arachnida (spiders, ticks, scorpions, mites, daddy-longlegs), and Pycnogonida (sea spiders).

SUBPHYLUM MANDIBULATA   Most with three pairs of walking legs, mandibles, compound eyes, antennas; some with wings. Four classes: Crustacea (aquatic with crusty exoskeleton, gills), Chilopoda (centipedes), Diplopoda (millipedes), and Insecta (insects—commonly three pairs of legs, wings at some time, three-part body, diverse mouth parts).

PHYLUM ONYCOPHORA   (70 species; *Peripatus):* Possessing both annelid and arthropod characteristics.

PHYLUM BRACHIOPODA   (250 species; lampshells): Appear similar to bivalves, but shell mounted differently, lopophore (ring of ciliated tentacles) present (Chapter 28).

PHYLUM PHORONIDA   (18 species):   Lopophore present.

PHYLUM ECTOPROCTA   (4000 species; moss animals or bryozoans): Lopophore present.

Deuterostomes

PHYLUM ECHINODERMATA   (6000 species): Spiny, skinned animals, five-part radial symmetry as adults, bilateral larvae, endoskeleton, water vascular system. Five classes: Crinoidia (sea lilies), Holothuroidia (sea cucumbers), Echinoidea (sea urchins, sand dollars), Asteroidea (sea stars, basket stars), and Ophiuroidea (serpent stars, brittle stars) (Chapter 28).

PHYLUM HEMICHORDATA   (80 species; acorn worms): Gill slits show relatedness to chordates (Chapter 28).

PHYLUM CHORDATA   (43,000 species): Gill slits, notochord, postanal tail, dorsal hollow nerve cord all present at some time (Chapters 28–30).

SUBPHYLUM UROCHORDATA   (1300 species; sea squirts): chordate characteristics seen mainly in bilateral larva.

SUBPHYLUM CEPHALOCHORDATA   (28 species; lancelet): fishlike body, permanent notochord and gill slits, filter feeder.

SUBPHYLUM VERTEBRATA   (41,700 species; the vertebrates): Vertebral column of bone or cartilage, heads well developed, ventral heart, dorsal aorta, two pairs of limbs. Seven classes: the fishes: Agnatha (jawless fishes), Chondrichthyes (cartilagenous fishes: sharks, rays, chimera), and Osteichthyes (bony fishes). Also, Amphibia (frogs, toads, salamanders), Reptilia (reptiles), Aves (birds), and Mammalia (mammals).

SUGGESTED READINGS

The readings listed here are of two types. For each Part of the book, relevant texts and other primary sources are listed first, then a selection of recent *Scientific American* articles is given. Further articles are listed and annotated in each chapter of the Instructor's Manual.

PART I

Alberts, B., et al. 1983. *Molecular Biology of the Cell*. New York: Garland Publishing Co.

Calvin, M., ed. 1973. *Organic Chemistry of Life; Readings from Scientific American*. San Francisco: W.H. Freeman Co.

The Chemical Basis of Life: An Introduction to Molecular and Cell Biology: Readings from Scientific American. Intro. by P.C. Hanawalt and R.H. Haynes. 1973. San Francisco: W.H. Freeman Co.

Darwin, C. 1859. *On the Origin of Species through Natural Selection*. A facsimile of the first edition. Cambridge, Mass: Harvard University Press.

de Beer, G. 1965. *Charles Darwin: A Scientific Biography*. New York: Doubleday.

Lehninger, A.L. 1982. *Principles of Biochemistry*. New York: Worth.

Life: Origin and Evolution: Readings from Scientific American. Intro. by C.E. Folsome. 1979. San Francisco: W.H. Freeman Co.

Moorehead, A. 1969. *Darwin and the Beagle*. New York: Harper & Row.

Porter, E. 1971. *Galapagos*. New York: Ballantine.

Ricklefs, R.E. 1978. *Ecology*, 2d ed. Newton, Mass.: Chiron Press.

Scientific American Editors. 1970. *Biosphere: A Scientific American Book*. San Francisco: W.H. Freeman Co.

Skinner, B.F. 1938. *The Behavior of Organisms: An Experimental Analysis*. New York: Appleton-Century-Crofts.

Stryer, L. 1981. *Biochemistry*. 2d ed. San Francisco: W.H. Freeman Co.

Weissmann, G., and Clairborne, R., eds. 1975. *Cell Membranes: Biochemistry, Cell Biology and Pathology*. New York: HP Publishing Co.

Scientific American articles. San Francisco: W.H. Freeman Co.

Allen, R.D. 1987. "The Microtubule as an Intracellular Engine." *Scientific American*, February.

Dautry-Varsat, A., and Lodish, H. 1984. "How Receptors Bring Proteins and Particles into Cells." *Scientific American*, May.

de Duve, C. 1983. "Microbodies in the Living Cell." *Scientific American*, May.

Dustin, P. 1980. "Microtubules." *Scientific American*, August.

Gingerich, O. 1982. "The Galileo Affair." *Scientific American*, July.

Lederman, L. 1984. "The Value of Fundamental Science." *Scientific American*, November.

Lerner, L.S., and Gosselin, E.A. 1986. "Galileo and the Specter of Bruno." *Scientific American*, November.

Scientific American, 1985. "The Molecules of Life," Entire October Issue. San Francisco: W.H. Freeman Co.

Youvan, D.C. and Marrs, B.L. 1987. "Molecular Mechanisms of Photosynthesis." *Scientific American*, June.

PART II

Avery, O.T. et al. 1944. "Studies on the Chemical Nature of the Substance Inducing Transformation of Pneumococcal Types." *Journal of Experimental Medicine* 79:137. (Classic early experiment on identifying DNA)

Dawkins, R. 1976. *The Selfish Gene*. New York: Oxford University Press.

Gilbert, L.E., and Ravin, P.H. 1975. *Coevolution of Plants and Animals*. Austin, Tex.: University of Texas Press.

Joravsky, D. 1970. *The Lysenko Affair*. Cambridge, Mass.: Harvard University Press. (A penetrating look at science under the influence of Soviet politics)

Klug, W.S., and Cummings, M.R. 1986. *Concepts of Genetics*, 2d ed. Westerville, Ohio: Charles E. Merrill Publishing Co.

Lack, D. 1947. *Darwin's Finches*. New York: Cambridge University Press.

Lewin, R. 1983. "A Naturalist of the Genome." *Science* 222:402.

Mendel, G. 1965. "Experiments in Plant Hybridization (1865)." Translated by Eva Sherwood. In *The Origin of Genetics*. Edited by C. Stern and E. Sherwood. San Francisco: W.H. Freeman Co.

Menosky, J.A. 1981. "The Gene Machine." *Science 81*, July/August.

Meselson, M., and Stahl, F.W. 1958. "The Replication of DNA in *E. coli*" *Proceedings of the National Academy of Sciences* (U.S.). 44:671.

Scientific American Editors. 1978. *Evolution: A Scientific American Book*. San Francisco: W.H. Freeman Co.

Shine, I., and Wrobel, S. 1976. *Thomas Hunt Morgan: Pioneer of Genetics*. Lexington: University of Kentucky Press.

Volpe, P. 1981. *Understanding Evolution*. 4th ed. Dubuque, Iowa: Wm. C. Brown.

Watson, J.D. 1968. *The Double Helix*. New York: Atheneum.

Watson J.D., and Crick, F.H.C. 1953. "Molecular Structure of Nucleic Acids: A structure of deoxyribose nucleic acid." *Nature* 171:737. (This is the one that started it all: the most influential single paper in scientific history.)

Scientific American articles. San Francisco: W.H. Freeman Co.

Aharonowitz, Y., and Cohen, G. 1981. "The Microbiological Production of Pharmaceuticals." *Scientific American*, September.

Anderson, W.F., and Diacumakos, E.G. 1981. "Genetic Engineering in Mammalian Cells." *Scientific American*, July.

Bishop, J.M. 1982. "Oncogenes." *Scientific American*, March.

Brill, W.J. 1981. "Agricultural Microbiology." *Scientific American*, September.

Chambon, P. 1981. "Split Genes." *Scientific American*, May.

Chilton, M. 1983. "A Vector for Introducing New Genes into Plants." *Scientific American*, June.

Cohen, S.N., and Shapiro, J.A. 1980. "Transposable Genetic Elements." *Scientific American*, February.

Feder, J. and Tolbert, W. 1983. "The Large-Scale Cultivation of Mammalian Cells." *Scientific American*, January.

Gilbert, L.E. 1982. "The Coevolution of a Butterfly and a Vine." *Scientific American*, August.

Grivell, L.A. 1983. Mitochondrial DNA." *Scientific American*, March.

Hopwood, A. 1981. "The Genetic Programming of Industrial Microorganisms." *Scientific American,* September.

Howard-Flanders, P. 1981. "Inducible Repair of DNA." *Scientific American,* November.

Kornberg, R.D., and Klug, A. 1981. "The Nucleosome." *Scientific American,* February.

Lake, J.A. 1981. "The Ribosome." *Scientific American,* August.

Novick, R.P. 1980. "Plasmids." *Scientific American,* December.

Pestka, S. 1983. "The Purification and Manufacture of Human Interferons." *Scientific American,* August.

Stahl, F.W. 1987. "Genetic Recombination." *Scientific American,* February.

Wilson, A. 1985. "The Molecular Basis of Evolution." *Scientific American,* October.

PART III

Alexopoulos, C.J. 1962. *Introduction to Mycology.* New York: Wiley.

Baker, H.G. 1963. "Evolutionary Mechanisms in Pollination Biology." *Science* 139:877.

Fox, G.E. et al. 1980. "The Phylogeny of Prokaryotes." *Science* 209:457.

Galston, W.W., and Davies, P.J. 1970. *Control Mechanisms in Plant Development.* Englewood Cliffs, N.J.: Prentice-Hall.

Lehner, E., and Lehner, J. 1973 *Folklore and Odysseys of Food and Medicinal Plants.* New York: Tudor.

Raven, P.H. et al. 1981. *Biology of Plants,* 3d ed. New York: Worth.

Salle, A.J. 1979. *Fundamental Principles of Bacteriology.* 7th ed. New York: McGraw-Hill.

Sporne, K.R. 1971. *The Mysterious Origin of Flowering Plants.* Burlington, N.C.: Carolina Biological Supply Co.

Went, F.W. 1963. *The Plants.* Life Nature Library. New York: Time, Inc.

Scientific American articles. San Francisco: W.H. Freeman Co.

Blakemore R.P., and Frankel, R.B. 1981. "Magnetic Navigation in Bacteria." *Scientific American,* December.

Cairns-Smith, A.G. 1985. "The First Organisms." *Scientific American,* June.

Eigen, M. et al. 1981. "The Origin of Genetic Information." *Scientific American,* April.

Evans, M.L. et. al. 1986. "How Roots Respond to Gravity." *Scientific American,* December.

Gallo, R.C. 1986. "The First Human Retrovirus." *Scientific American,* December.

Gallo, R.C. 1987. "The AIDS Virus." *Scientific American,* January.

Groves, D.I.; Dunlop, J.S.R.; and Buick, R. 1981. "An Early Habitat of Life" *Scientific American,* October. (Stromatolites).

Kaplan, D.R. 1983. "The Development of Palm Leaves," *Scientific American,* July.

Ptashne, M.; Johnson, A.D.; and Pabo, C.O. 1982. "A Genetic Switch in a Bacterial Virus." *Scientific American,* November.

Shepart, J.F. 1982. "The Regeneration of Potato Plants from Leaf-Cell Protoplasts. *Scientific American,* May.

Simons, K.; Garoff, H.; and Helenius, A. 1982. "How an Animal Virus Gets into and out of Its Host Cell." *Scientific American,* February.

Woese, C.R. 1981. "Archebacteria." *Scientific American,* June.

PART IV

Animal Engineering. Intro. by D.R. Griffin. 1974. San Francisco: W.H. Freeman Co.

Cornejo, D. 1982. "Night of the Spadefoot Toad." *Science 82,* September.

Johanson, D.C., and Edey, M.A. 1981. "Lucy: The Inside Story." *Science 81,* March.

Johanson, D.C., and White, T.D. 1979. "A Systematic Assessment of Early African Hominids." *Science,* 203:321.

McMenamin, M.A.S̈. 1982. "A Case for Two Late Proterozoic—Earliest Cambrian Faunal Province Loci." *Geology,* June.

Rensberger, B. 1981. "Facing the Past." *Science 81,* October. (Neanderthal man)

Storer, T.I. et al. 1979. *General Zoology,* 6th ed. New York: McGraw-Hill.

Scientific American articles. San Francisco: W.H. Freeman Co.

Gehring, W. 1985. "The Molecular Basis of Development." *Scientific American,* October.

Langston, Jr., W. 1981. "Pterosaurs." *Scientific American,* February.

McMenamin, M.A.S. 1987. "The Emergence of Animals." *Scientific American,* April.

Mossman, D.J., and Sarjeant, W.A.S. 1983. "The Footprints of Extinct Animals." *Scientific American,* January.

Roper, C.F.E., and Boss, K.J. 1982. "The Giant Squid." *Scientific American,* April.

Rukang, W., and Shenglong, L. 1983. "Peking Man." *Scientific American,* June.

Russell, D.A. 1982. "The Mass Extinctions of the Late Mesozoic." *Scientific American,* January.

PART V

Jaret, P. 1986. "Our Immune System, The Wars Within." *National Geographic,* June:169(6), 702–734.

Kolata, G. 1982. "New Theory of Hormones Proposed." *Science* 215:1383.

Landau, B.R. 1980. *Essential Human Anatomy and Physiology.* 2d ed. Glenview, Ill.; Scott, Foresman and Co.

Oppenheimer, J.H. 1979. "Thyroid Hormone Action at the Cellular Level." *Science* 203:971.

Sperry, R. 1982. "Some Effects of Disconnecting the Cerebral Hemispheres." *Science* 217:1223.

Scientific American articles. San Francisco: W.H. Freeman Co.

Bloom, F.E. 1981. "Neuropeptides." *Scientific American,* October.

Caravoli, E. and Penniston, J. 1985. "The Calcium Signal." *Scientific American,* November.

Dunant, Y. and Israel, M. 1985. "The Release of Acetylcholine." *Scientific American,* April.

Eastman, J.T. and DeVries, A.L. 1987. "Antarctic Fishes." *Scientific American,* November.

Heinrich, B. 1987. "Thermoregulation in Winter Moths," *Scientific American,* March.

Hudspeth, A.J. 1983. "The Hair Cells of the Inner Ear." *Scientific American,* January.

Laurence, J. 1985. "The Immune System and AIDS." *Scientific American,* December.

Llinas, R.R. 1982. "Calcium in Synaptic Transmission." *Scientific American,* October.

Marrack, P., and Kappler, J. 1986. "The T cell and its Receptor." *Scientific American,* October.

Morell, P., and Norton, W.T. 1980. "Myelin." *Scientific American,* May.

Morrison, A. 1984. "A Window on the Sleeping Brain." *Scientific American,* April.

Newman, E.A., and Hartline, P.H. 1982. "The Infrared 'Vision' of Snakes." *Scientific American,* March.

Schnapf, J.L., and Baylor, D.A. 1987. "How Photoreceptor Cells Respond to Light." *Scientific American,* April.

Snyder, S. 1985. "The Molecular Basis of Communication Between Cells." *Scientific American,* October.

Tonewaga, S., 1985. "The Molecules of the Immune System." *Scientific American,* October.

PART VI

Katchadourian, H. 1974. *Human Sexuality: Sense and Nonsense.* San Francisco: W.H. Freeman Co.

Money, J., and Ehrhardt, A.A. 1972. *Man and Woman, Boy and Girl: The Differentiation and Dimorphism of Gender Identity from Conception to Maturity.* Baltimore: Johns Hopkins University Press.

Shell, E.R. 1982. "The Guinea Pig Town" *Science 82,* December. (Framingham, Mass.)

Shodell, M. 1983. "The Prostaglandin Connection." *Science 83,* March.

Weisman, I.L. et al. 1978. *Essential Concepts in Immunology.* Menlo Park, Calif.: Benjamin Cummings.

West, S. 1983. "One Step Behind a Killer" *Science 83,* March. (AIDS)

Scientific American articles. San Francisco: W.H. Freeman Co.

Beaconsfield, P. et al. 1980. "The Placenta." *Scientific American,* August.

Buisseret, P.D. 1982. "Allergy." *Scientific American,* August.

Degabriele, R. 1980. "The Physiology of the Koala." *Scientific American,* July.

Gehring, W.J. 1985. "The Molecular Basis of Development." *Scientific American,* October.

Jarvik, R.K. 1981. "The Total Artificial Heart." *Scientific American,* January.

Leder, P. 1982. "The Genetics of Antibody Diversity." *Scientific American,* May.

Lerner, R.A. 1983. "Synthetic Vaccines." *Scientific American,* February.

Mishkin, M and Appenzeller, T. 1987. "The Anatomy of Memory." *Scientific American,* June.

Moog, F. 1981. "The Lining of the Small Intestine." *Scientific American,* November.

Rose, N.R. 1981. "Auoimmune Disease." *Scientific American,* February.

Winfree, A.T. 1983. "Sudden Cardiac Death: A Problem of Topology." *Scientific American,* May.

Zapol, W.M. 1987. "Diving Adaptations of the Weddell Seal." *Scientific American,* June.

Zucker, M.B. 1980. "The Functioning of Blood Platelets." *Scientific American,* June.

PART VII

Brown, J.L. *The Evolution of Behavior.* New York: W.W. Norton.

Gould, J.L. 1982. *Ethology: The Mechanisms and Evolution of Behavior.* New York: W.W. Norton.

Hess, E.H. 1973. *Imprinting.* New York: Van Nostrand Reinhold.

Mech, L.D. 1970. *The Wolf: The Ecology and Behavior of an Endangered Species.* Garden City, New York: Natural History Press.

Odum, E.P. 1983. *Basic Ecology.* Philadelphia, Penn.: Saunders.

Ricklefs, R.E. 1978. *Ecology,* 2d ed. Newton, Mass.: Chiron Press.

Scientific American Editors. 1970. *Biosphere: A Scientific American Book.* San Francisco: W.H. Freeman Co.

Skinner, B.F. 1938. *The Behavior of Organisms: An Experimental Analysis.* New York: Appleton-Century-Crofts.

Trivers, R.L. 1971. "The Evolution of Reciprocal Altruism." *Quarterly Review of Biology* 46:35.

Wallace, R.A. 1979. *Animal Behavior: Its Development, Ecology, and Evolution.* Glenview, Ill.: Scott, Foresman and Co.

———. 1979. *The Genesis Factor.* New York: William Morrow.

Wilson, E.O. 1975. *Sociobiology, The New Synthesis.* Cambridge, Mass.: Harvard University Press.

———. 1978. *On Human Nature.* Cambridge, Mass.: Harvard University Press.

Scientific American articles. San Francisco: W.H. Freeman Co.

Alkon, D.L. 1983. "Learning in a Marine Snail." *Scientific American,* July.

Beddington, J.R., and May, R.M. 1982. "The Harvesting of Interacting Species in a Natural Ecosystem." *Scientific American,* November.

Childress, J.J. et al. 1987. "Symbiosis in the Deep Sea." *Scientific American,* June.

Cloud, P. 1983. "The Biosphere." *Scientific American,* September.

Edmond, J., and Von Damm, K. 1984. "Hot Springs on the Ocean Floor." *Scientific American,* April.

Hauser, P.M. 1981. "The Census of 1980." *Scientific American,* November.

Heinrich, B. 1981. "The Regulation of Temperature in the Honeybee Swarm." *Scientific American,* June.

Ingersoll, A.P. 1983. "The Atmosphere." *Scientific American,* September.

Likens, G. et al. 1979. "Acid Rain." *Scientific American,* October.

Lloyd, J.E. 1981. "Mimicry in the Sexual Signals of Fireflies." *Scientific American,* July.

Partridge, B.L. 1982. "The Structure and Function of Fish Schools." *Scientific American,* July.

Perry, D. 1984. "The Canopy of the Tropical Rain Forest." *Scientific American,* November.

Revelle, R. 1982. "Carbon Dioxide and World Climate." *Scientific American,* July.

Tschirley, F. 1986. "Dioxin." *Scientific American,* February.

GLOSSARY

PRONUNCIATION KEY

a	act, bat	o	ox, box
ā	cape, way	ō	over, no
â	dare, Mary	o͝o	book, look
ä	alms, calm	o͞o	ooze, fool
e	set, merry	ô	ought
ē	equal, bee	s	see
ə	like *a* in alone	u	up, love
	or *e* in system	û	urge, burn
g	give	y	yes, lawyer
i	if, big	z	zeal, lazy
ī	ice, bite		
j	just, Jerry		

A band a band in striated muscle corresponding to the region of myosin filaments.

abdomen (ab′də mən) 1. in mammals, the body cavity between the diaphragm and the pelvis. 2. in other vertebrates, the body cavity containing the stomach, intestines, liver, and reproductive organs. 3. in arthropods, the posterior section of the body.

abiotic (ā′bī ot′ik) *adj.,* characterized by the absence of life.

abscisic acid (ab sis′ik) in plants, the hormone that causes leaves to separate from a plant. Also *ABA.*

abscission zone (ab′si′shən) in plants, a layer of specialized,cutinized parenchyma cells at the base of a leaf petiole, fruit stalk, or branch in which normal separation occurs.

absorption spectrum a graph indicating the wave lengths of light absorbed by a molecule.

abyssal region (ə bis′əl) the lowest depths of the ocean, especially the bottom water; also called *abysmal region.*

acellular (ā′sel′yu lər) not composed of cells; also called *noncellular.*

acetylcholine (ə sē′təl kō′lēn) a chemical agent that when released by one neuron crosses the synapse to activate a second neuron as effector.

acetylcholinesterase (ə sē′təl kō′lēn es′tə rās) a membrane-bound enzyme that hydrolyzes acetylcholine in the course of synaptic nerve impulse transmission.

acetyl-coA (ə sē′təl kō′ā′) an intermediate compound in cell respiration, to which most fuels are converted before entering the citric acid cycle.

acid a proton donor that yields hydrogen ions in water; a compound capable of neutralizing bases and of lowering the pH of solutions.

acrosome (ak′rə sōm) an organelle in the tip of a sperm which ruptures in fertilization with the release of enzymes and (in echinoderms) of an acrosomal filament.

actin (ak′tən) a cytoplasmic contractile protein and a constituent of muscle.

action potential in a neuron, a travelling depolarizing wave; a short-lived change in membrane potential that produces a neural impulse or, in a muscle, a contraction. Compare *resting potential.*

action-specific energy (ASE) in behavior, a hypothetical endogenous tension that increases in the nervous system until it is discharged, either on its own or due to the perception of an appropriate stimulus.

activation energy the energy input needed before an exergonic chemical reaction can proceed.

active site the part of an enzyme that interacts directly with the substrate molecule.

active transport energy-requiring transport of a substance across the cell membrane, usually against the concentration gradient.

adaptive radiation evolutionary divergence of two or more species from an ancestral form with the establishment of new, more specialized niches.

ADH. See *antidiuretic hormone.*

adipose tissue (ad′ə pōz) fatty tissue.

adenine (A) (ad′n ēn) a purine, one of the nitrogenous bases found in both DNA and RNA, as well as in ATP and several coenzymes.

adenylate cyclase (ə den′ə lāt sī′clās) an enzyme, usually incorporated into the cell membrane, that is capable of transforming ATP into cyclic ATP and pyrophosphate.

adhesion the attraction between two dissimilar substances, such as a solid and a liquid.

ADP (adenosine diphosphate) (ə den′ə sēn dī′fos′fāt) a compound of adenine, ribose, and two phosphate groups; a degraded form of ATP.

adrenal gland (ə drē′nəl) a vertebrate endocrine gland; the outer area (*adrenal cortex*) produces steroid hormones, the

inner area (*adrenal medulla*) produces *epinephrine.*

adrenaline (ə dren′ə len). See *epinephrine.*

adrenal cortex (ə drēn′əl kôr′teks) the outer portion of the adrenal gland, produces steroid hormones.

adrenal medulla (ə drēn′əl mə dul′ə) the inner portion of the adrenal gland, produces *epinephrhine* and *norepinephrine* (*adrenaline* and *noradrenaline*) as its principle hormonal products.

adrenocorticotropic hormone (ACTH) (ə drēn′ kôrt′ə kō trō′pik) a pituitary hormone that stimulates the production of hormones of the adrenal cortex.

adventitious root (ad′vən tish′əs) a secondary root growing from stem tissue.

aerobic (er ō′bik) *adj.,* requiring oxygen.

afferent vessel (af′er ənt) any blood vessel carrying blood toward a specific structure such as a gill filament or kidney nephron.

age structure histogram also *age profile, population pyramid;* a graph of a population divided into age groups. Each age group is represented by a horizontal bar with that of the youngest group forming the base.

aggression in behavior, hostility (attack or threat), especially unprovoked, usually against a competitor or potential competitor.

aggregate a number of independent organisms grouped together either in a casual, temporary way or for more permanent mutual reasons.

aggregate fruit a fruit developing from multiple carpels of the same flower.

AIDS (acquired immune deficiency syndrome) a viral disease that results in severely reduced immunity. No cure is known.

albumin (al byo͞o′men) 1. any of a class of clear, water-soluble plant or animal proteins. 2. *serum albumin,* a clear, water-soluble constituent of blood plasma, thought to serve detoxifying and osmotic functions. 3. *albumen,* egg white.

aldehyde (al′də hīd) any of a class of organic compounds containing the group −CHO, which yields acids when oxidized and alcohols when reduced.

aldosterone (al′dos′tər ōn′) a steroid hormone produced by the adrenal cortex, involved in potassium reabsorption by the kidney.

algae (al′jē) (*sing.*, alga[al′gə]) plantlike, photosynthetic autotrophs that may be single-celled, colonial, or multicellular; protists.

algin (al′jən) a structural polysaccharide of the brown algae.

alkali (al′kə lī′) any of various bases which neutralize acids to form salts and turn red litmus paper blue.

allantois (ə lan′tō is) one of the extraembryonic membranes; in birds and reptiles, serves as a repository for the embryo's nitrogenous wastes.

allele (əlēl′) a particular form of a gene at a gene locus.

allopatric speciation (al′əpat′rik spē′shē′ā′shən) formation of new species from populations that become geographically separated. Compare *sympatric speciation*.

allopolyploid (al′ə pol′ē ploid) *adj.*, having more than two haploid sets of chromosomes that are dissimilar and derived from different species. See also *allotetraploid, polyploid, tetraploid*.

allosteric site (al′ə ster′ik) in certain enzymes, a secondary binding site for small metabolites involved in the regulation of enzymatic activity.

allotetraploid (al′ə tet′rə ploid) *adj.*, derived from the hybridization of two distinct species, carrying the full diploid chromosome complements of both. See also *polyploid, tetraploid*, chromosome complements of both. See also *polyploid, tetraploid, allopolyploid*.

alpha amylase (al′fə am′ə lās) a starch-digesting enzyme.

alpha cell an endocrine cell within the pancreas, which secretes insulin.

alpha helix (al′fə hē′liks) the right-handed helical configuration spontaneously formed by certain polymers. See *secondary level*.

alternation of generations the existence in the life cycle of an individual of a haploid (1N) gametophyte stage that alternates with a diploid (2N) sporophyte stage.

altruism (al′trū iz′əm) behavior that is directly beneficial to others at some cost or risk to the altruistic individual.

Alvarez hypothesis (al′və rez hī poth′ə sis) a hypothesis which proposes that much of the massive extinction of life that accompanied the end of the Mesozoic era was produced by the aftereffects of a gigantic asteroid's collision with the earth.

alveolus (al′vē′ə ləs) (*pl.*, alveoli) one of the air sacs that occur in grapelike clusters at the ends of bronchioles in the vertebrate lung. Alveolar walls contain dense capillaries where gas exchange occurs.

Alzheimer's disease (Älts′hī merz) presenile dementia usually occurring in a middle-aged person and associated with sclerosis and nerve degeneration.

amebocyte (ə mē′bəcīt) in many individuals, an ameboid cell that functions in reproduction, digestion, and so on.

amino acid (ə mē′nō) 1. any organic molecule of the general formula R—CH(NH₂)COOH, having both acidic and basic properties. 2. any of the twenty molecular subunits that make up protein.

ammonification (ə mōn′ə fə kā′shən) the formation of ammonia or its compounds, as in soil by soil organisms.

amnion (am′nē ən) the innermost extraembryonic membrane of reptiles, birds, and animals.

amniotic cavity (am′nē ôt′ik) the smaller, upper division of the blastocyst, formed by the embryonic disk.

amniotic fluid (am′nē ôt′ik) the watery fluid in the amniotic sac, in which the embryo is suspended.

AMP (adenosine monophosphate) (ə den′ə sēn′ mon′ə fos′fāt) a molecule consisting of adenine, ribose and one phosphate group.

amphibian (am fib′ē ən) any member of the class of cold-blooded vertebrates (frogs, salamanders, etc.), the larva of which are typically aquatic, breathing by gills, and the adult of which are terrestrial, breathing by lungs and through moist, glandular skin.

anabolic (an′ə bol′ik) *adj.*, referring to metabolic activity that results in the chemical building up of molecules. See also *catabolic*.

anaerobic (an′ə rō′bik) *adj.*, in the absence of oxygen.

analogous (ə nal′ə gəs) in comparative morphology, similar in form or function but derived from different evolutionary or embryonic precursors (e.g., the wings of insects and birds).

anaphase (an′ə fāz) the stage of mitosis or meiosis II in which the centromeres divide and separate and the two daughter chromosomes travel to opposite poles of the cell.

androecium (an′drē′shē əm) a whorl of stamens; the stamens of a flower taken together.

angiosperm (an′jē ə spûrm) a plant in which the seeds are enclosed in an ovary; a flowering plant.

annelid (an′ə lid) any member of phylum Annelida, comprising segmented worms and leeches.

annual plant a plant that completes its life cycle—germination, growth, reproduction, and death—in a year. Compare *perennial*.

annual rings the concentric rings seen in the cross-section of a woody stem, each of which corresponds to one season's growth.

antagonistic muscles (an tag′ə nis′tik) a pair of skeletal muscles (or groups of muscles) whose actions cooperatively oppose one another.

anterior pituitary (pi tōō′i ter′ē) part of an endocrine gland communicating with the hypothalamus only by way of a small vascular portal system; secretes several hormones.

anther (an′thər) in a flower, the pollen-producing organ of the stamen.

antheridium (an′thə rid′ē əm) (*pl.*, antheridia) in plants, a male reproductive organ that produces motile sperm.

anthophyte (an′thə fīt′) a plant of the division Anthophyta; a flowering plant.

antibody (an′ti bod′ē) a protein molecule of the immune system that can recognize and bind to a foreign substance or invader, such as a bacterium or virus. See *immunoglobulin*.

anticodon (an′ti kō′don) a region of a tRNA molecule consisting of three sequential nucleotides that will have a matching codon in mRNA.

anticodon loop (an′ti kō′don) the region of a tRNA molecule containing the anticodon; one of the three or four loops of a tRNA molecule.

antidiuretic (an′ti dī′yōo ret′ik) any substance that helps the body conserve water by increasing water reabsorption in the nephrons.

antidiuretic hormone (ADH) (an′ti dī′yōo ret′ik) also called *vasopressin;* a polypeptide hormone secreted by the posterior pituitary that increases the resorption of fluid from the kidney filtrate.

antigen (an′tə jen) 1. any large molecule, such as a cell-surface protein or carbohydrate, that stimulates the production of specific antibodies or that binds specifically with such antibodies. 2. any antibody-specific site on such a molecule.

antigen recognition region (an′tə jən) the separate part of a Y-shaped antibody that matches specific antigens.

antiserum (an′ti ser′əm) blood serum containing antibodies specific to some particular antigen.

aorta (ā ôr′tə) in vertebrates, the principal or largest artery; carries oxygenated blood from the heart to the body.

aortic semilunar valve (ā ôr′tik sem′i lōō′nər) in the heart, a one-way valve at the base of the aorta that prevents backflow into the left ventricle during systole.

aphotic zone (ā′fō tik) "without light"; in a body of water, the depth to which light never penetrates.

apical dominance (ā′pə kəl) in the uppermost growing tip of a plant stem, the hormonal inhibition of the upward growth or formation of other branches.

apical meristem (ā′pə kəl mer′ə stem). See *meristem*.

appendicular skeleton (a pen dik′yə lər) in vertebrates, bones of the pectoral and pelvic girdles and of the appendages. Compare *axial skeleton*.

appetitive stage (ap'i tī'tiv) a variable, nonsterotyped part of instinctive behavior that involves searching (for food, water, a mate) for the opportunity to perform. Compare *consummatory stage.*

arachnid (ə rak'nid) any member of the class of arthropods which contains the spiders, scorpions, ticks, mites, etc.

arboreal (är bôr'ē əl) *adj.,* pertaining to dwelling in trees.

Archaebacteria (är'kə bak tir'ēə) one of the two suggested prokaryote kingdoms (or phyla in some schemes); contains bacteria such as methanogens (methane producers), thermaphiles (heat lovers), and acidophiles (acid lovers). See also *Eubacteria.*

archegonium (är'kə gō'nē əm) (*pl.,* archegonia) the female (egg-producing) reproductive structure in the gametophytes of ferns and bryophytes.

arteriole (är tir'ē ōl) a small artery, usually giving rise directly to capillaries.

artery (är'tər ē) a vessel carrying blood away from the heart toward arterioles and capillary beds.

arthropod (är'thrō pôd) any member of the phylum containing segmented invertebrates with joined legs, primarily insects, arachnids, and crustaceans.

artificial active immunity immunity developed within the body as the result of innoculation with a vaccine.

artificial selection the intentional selection (by humans) of domesticated animals or plants for breeding according to desired characteristics. See also *natural selection.*

ascocarp (as'kə karp) a cuplike or saclike body in the Ascomycota in which ascospores are produced.

ascomycete (as'kə mī sēt') a fungus of the division Ascomycota, which includes the yeasts, mildews, truffles, and so on; characterized by bearing the sexual spores in a sac, the *ascus.*

ascus (as'kəs) (*pl.,* asci) in ascomycetes, the sac in which meiosis occurs and in which four or eight ascospores are subsequently formed.

asexual reproduction reproduction by one individual that does not involve the union of genetic material from two sources.

asters (as'tərz) "stars"; paired, radiating mitotic structures, each consisting of microtubules and microfilaments.

atom the smallest indivisible unit of an element still retaining the element's characteristics.

atomic mass the average weight of the atoms of an element; also called *atomic weight.*

atomic number the number of protons in an atomic nucleus, specific to each element.

ATP (adenosine triphosphate) (ə den'ə sēn trī fos'fāt) a common molecule involved in many biological energy-exchange reactions; consists of the nitrogenous base adenine, the sugar ribose, and three phosphate groups joined by two energy-rich bonds.

atrioventricular (AV) node (ā'trē'ō ven trik'yə lər) a small mass of specialized muscle fibers at the base of the wall between the atria of the heart; conducts impulses to the bundle of His.

atrium (ā'trē əm) (*pl.,* atria) a thinner-walled compartment of the heart that receives venus blood.

audition (ô di'shən) the act, sense, or power of hearing.

auditory canal (ô'di tor'ē) the open, bony canal from the outer ear to the eardrum.

australopithecine (ô strā'lo pith'ə sēn) *adj.,* pertaining to members of the extinct hominid genus *Australopithecus.*

autoimmune disease (ô'tō i myōōn') an abnormal condition in which the organism's immune system attacks and destroys one or more of the organism's own tissues.

autonomic nervous system (ANS) (ô'tə nom'ik) the system of motor nerves and their ganglia arising from the brain and spinal cord; controls involuntary functions, chiefly in the internal organs. Compare *somatic nervous system.*

autosome (ô'tə sōm) any chromosome other than a sex (**X** or **Y**) chromosome.

autotroph (ô'tə trōf) "self-feeder"; an organism capable of using simple compounds (such as carbon dioxide) as its only source of carbon and sunlight (phototrophs) or simple inorganic compounds (chemotrophs) as its only source of energy. Compare *heterotroph.*

auxin (ôk'sin) a class of natural or artificial substances that act as the principle growth hormone in plants.

axial skeleton in vertebrates, the skull, vertebral column, and bones of the chest. Compare *appendicular skeleton.*

axon (ak'son) the extension of a neuron that conducts nerve impulses away from the cell body.

axonal tree (ak'son əl) the branching, terminal region of an axon. See *neuron.*

axopod (ak'sō pod) in sarcodines, slender, microtubular spines upon which feeding pseudopods move. See also *pseudopod.*

bacillus (bə sil'əs) a rod-shaped bacterium.

bacteriochlorophyll (bak tir'ē ə klôr'ə fil) a light-sensitive pigment used by certain eubacteria for capturing light energy to be used in photosynthesis.

bacteriophage (bak tir'ē ə fāj) also called *phage;* a virus that infects and destroys bacteria.

bacteriorhodopsin (bak tir'ē ə rō dop'sən) a purple photosynthetic pigment used by photosynthetic archaebacteria.

ball-and-socket joint a joint allowing maximum rotation and flexion; consists of a ball-like termination on one part, held within a concave, spherical socket on the other (e.g., the hip joint).

bark the portion of a stem outside of the vascular cambium; consists of phloem, cortex, epidermis, cork cambium, and cork.

Barr body a dark-staining feature in the nuclei of the cells of female animals; represents the condensed **X** chromosome.

barrier reef a reef of coral running roughly parallel to the shore and separated from it by deep water.

basal body a structure found beneath each eukaryotic flagellum or cilium; consists of a circle of nine short triplets of microtubules.

basal metabolic rate (BMR) a measure of oxygen consumption of an individual at rest.

base 1. a compound that reacts with an acid to form a salt. **2.** a substance that releases hydroxide ions when dissolved in water. **3.** a nitrogenous base (purine or pyrimidine) of nucleic acids.

basement membrane in animals, a sheet of collagen that underlies and supports the cells of a tissue. Also called *basal membrane, basilar membrane.*

base pairing the specific manner in which the nitrogenous bases of nucleic acids pair up and form hydrogen bonds; adenine always opposes thymine or uracil (A-T or T-A, A-U or U-A) and cytosine always opposes guanine (C-G or G-C).

base substitution a mutation in DNA in which one nucleotide is replaced by another, or modified into another.

basidiocarp (bə sid'ē ō kärp') "club fruit"; the spore-producing organ in mushrooms and other Basidiomycota.

basidiomycete (bə sid'ē ō mī sēt') a fungus of the division Basidiomycota, which includes the smuts, rust, mushrooms, puffballs, etc.; characterized by bearing the spores on a basidium.

basidium (bə sid'ē əm) "little pedestal"; the clublike structure of basidiomycetes such as mushrooms; produces basidiospores by meiosis.

basilar membrane (bās'ə lər) in the vertebrate ear, a membrane whose movement stimulates the sensitive hair cells that transmit neural impulses to the brain.

B-cell lymphocyte (limf'ə sīt) a lymphocyte that circulates in the blood and is involved in the immune response, especially in the production of free antibodies.

benthic (ben'thik) *adj.,* referring to the benthos, or bottom-dwelling, community of organisms.

berry a simple fruit, including a fleshy ovary and one or more carpels and seeds.

beta cell (bā'tə) an endocrine cell in the pancreas; secretes glucogon.

bicuspid valve (bī'kûs'pid) also *mitral valve;* the two-flapped valve between the left atrium and the left ventricle of the heart.

bilateral symmetry having left and right sides that are approximate mirror images; having a single plane of symmetry.

bile (bīl) a pigmented, alkaline liquid

secreted by the liver; contains bile salts and bile pigments and functions in fat digestion.

binomial nomenclature (bī nō′mē əl nō′mən clā′chər) the tradition (introduced by Linnaeus) whereby each species is given two Latin taxonomic names, a generic term and a specific term (genus and species).

biodegradable capable of being rendered harmless upon exposure to the elements and organisms of the soil or water.

biogenetic law (bī′ō jə net′ik) the fact that, under the current planetary conditions, life can arise only from preexisting life.

biogeochemical cycle the pathway of elements (e.g., carbon, nitrogen) or compounds (water) as they are taken up and released by organisms into the physical environment.

biogeography the study of the geographical distribution of living things.

biological determinism the influence of genetics, particularly on the social behavior of an organism.

biomass the total weight (dry) of all the organisms in a prescribed area.

biome (bī′ōm) a major plant association, e.g., a tundra.

biosphere the entire part of the earth's land, soil, water, and atmosphere in which the living organisms are found.

biotic (bī ōt′ik) *adj.*, pertaining to life.

bipedal gait (bī ped′əl gāt) walking on two feet.

birth control pill an oral steroid contraceptive that inhibits ovulation, fertilization, or implantation causing temporary infertility in women.

bivalve (bī′valv) a mollusk having two shells hinged together, such as the oyster, clam, or mussel.

bladder any membranous sac serving as a receptacle for fluid or gas, such as urinary bladder, gall bladder.

blade any broad, thin part of the thallus (body) of a red, green, or brown alga or of a leaf.

blastocoel (blas′tō sēl′) in embryonic development, the cavity of a blastula, arising in the course of cleavage.

blastocyst (blast′ ə sist) the early preimplantation stage in the mammalian embryo.

blastula (blas′chə lə) an early embryonic stage in many animals, consisting of a single layer of cells that forms a hollow ball enclosing a central cavity, the blastocoel.

blending inheritance a theory of inheritance which states that parental characteristics blend to produce an intermediate character in the offspring.

blue-green alga. See *cyanobacteria*.

body stalk in embryology, the connection between the early embryo and the extraembryonic tissues.

Bohr effect (bôr) the accelerated release of oxygen by hemoglobin when carbon dioxide is present.

book lungs the respiratory organ of a spider, scorpion, or other terrestrial arachnid; consists of thin, membranous structures arranged like the leaves of a book.

boreal forest (bôr′ē əl) a northern forest; see *taiga*.

bottleneck in population genetics, a period of time when the size of a population becomes small, resulting in a random change in allele frequencies. See also *genetic drift, founder effect*.

botulism (bôch′ə liz′əm) a bacterial disease caused by the presence in foods (usually canned foods) of *Clostridium botulinum*, whose nerve toxins are among the most powerful poisons known.

Bowman's capsule a curved sac at the beginning of a nephron that surrounds the glomerulus.

bread mold a member of the fungal phylum Zygomycota.

bronchial tree. See *respiratory tree*.

bronchiole (brong′kē ōl) a minute airway in the lung that is a small branch of a bronchus and part of the respiratory tree.

bronchus (brän′kəs) (*pl.*, bronchi) either of the two main branches of the trachea.

brown algae any algae of the division Phaeophyta, usually brown due to fucoxanthin pigment, e.g., kelp.

brush border. See *microvillus*.

bryophyte (brī′ə fit) a moss, liverwort, or hornwort of the division Bryophyta; nonvascular terrestrial plants.

budding asexual reproduction seen in yeasts and other organisms where smaller cells or entire offspring bud or grow from a parent cell.

buffer a solution of chemical compounds capable of neutralizing both acids and bases, thus resisting changes in pH.

bulbourethral glands (bul′bō yōō rēth′ rəl) a pair of small glands that secrete a mucous substance into the urethra in males, especially on sexual arousal. Also called *Cowper's glands*.

bulk flow the one-way movement of water or another liquid brought about by pressure, gravity, or solutes, generally from areas of greater water potential to areas of lesser water potential.

bundle sheath cell a specialized parenchyma cell, one of many forming compact layers to enclose the small veins in a leaf.

calcitonin (kal′sē tō′nin) one of the two major hormones of the thyroid gland whose major action is to inhibit the release of calcium from the bone.

calmodulin (kal′moj′ ə lin) a protein responsible for activating many kinds of enzymes, itself activated by its union with calcium ions.

calorie 1. *small calorie* (calorie proper), the amount of heat (or equivalent chemical energy) needed to raise the temperature of one gram (roughly one milliliter) of water by 1° C. 2. *large calorie, kilocalorie* (1000 small calories), the heat needed to raise the temperature of a kilogram of water by 1° C.

Calvin cycle the biochemical cycle in photosynthesis in which carbon dioxide, with the aid of NADPH and ATP, is fixed into carbohydrate. Also called *CO_2 fixation*. See also *light-independent reaction*.

calyx (kā′liks) (*pl.*, calyces) the outermost whorl of floral parts (the sepals), usually green and leaflike.

canaliculus (kan′ə lik′yə ləs) (*pl.*, canaliculi) a small canal or tubular passage, as in bone.

capillary a small blood vessel (with walls one cell thick) in which exchanges between the blood and tissues occur.

carbaminohemoglobin (carb′ə mēn′ō hē′mə glō′bən) hemoglobin complexed with carbon dioxide.

carbohydrate a class of organic compounds with the empirical formula $(CH_2O)_n$, characterized by many –OH and –H side groups and an aldehyde or ketone group; sugars, starches, cellulose, and chitin.

carbon cycle the pathway of carbon as it is taken up and released by organisms into the physical environment.

carbon dioxide fixation. See *Calvin cycle*.

carbonic anhydrase (kär bon′ik an hī′ drās) an enzyme that catalyzes the reversible conversion of carbonic acid to carbon dioxide gas and water.

carboxyl group (kär bok′sil) the proton-releasing acid group, –COOH, present in organic acids.

carcinogen (kär cin′ə jən) any substance that tends to cause cancer.

cardiac circuit the blood vessels of the heart, including the coronary arteries and veins and the capillaries.

cardiac muscle specialized involuntary muscle of the heart whose fibers are striated and branching.

cardiac sphincter (sfingk′tər) also *gastroesophageal sphincter;* the ring of muscle that closes the passageway between the lower esophagus and the stomach.

carotenoid (kə rōt′ə noid) any of a group of red, yellow, and orange plant pigments chemically and functionally similar to carotene; light-gathering accessory pigments associated with chlorophyll.

carotid body a mass of cells and nerve endings on the carotid arteries that senses blood carbon dioxide and pH levels and responds by affecting the rate of breathing and the heart beat.

carpel in flowers, a simple pistil, or a single member of a compound pistil; one sector or chamber of a compound fruit.

carrageenan (kar′ə gēn′ən) a polysaccharide produced by Irish moss, a red alga; used as a thickening and smoothing agent.

carrying capacity in ecology, a property of the environment defined as the size of a population that can be maintained indefinitely.

cartilage a firm, elastic, flexible, translucent type of connective tissue; in development, a precursor of bone formation.

Casparian strip (kas per'ē ən) in plants, a waxy, waterproof strip on cell walls of root tip endodermis that permits some active control of water uptake by directing incoming water through the cytoplasm of the endodermal cells.

catabolic (kat'ə bol'ik) *adj.*, referring to metabolic activity that results in the chemical breakdown of molecules and the release of their energy. See also *anabolism*.

catalyst an agent that greatly accelerates a chemical reaction while not being permanently altered itself.

cecum (sē'kəm) in vertebrates, a blind pouch of the intestine at the juncture of the small and large intestine.

cell the structural unit of life; consists of metabolically active cytoplasm and genetic macromolecules (DNA and RNA) enclosed in a semipermeable membrane. See also *prokaryote, eukaryote*.

cell body the region of a neuron containing the cell nucleus and most of the cytoplasm and organelles.

cell cycle the typical cycling events in the life of a cell, including the G1, S, G2, and M phases.

cell division in a general sense, both nuclear (mitosis or meiosis) and cytoplasmic division; more specifically, the division of cytoplasm. See *cytokinesis*.

cell plate the plant cell division, the forming plasma membrane between newly forming daughter cells.

cell theory the universally accepted proposal that cells are the functional units of organization in living organisms and that all cells today come from preexisting cells.

cellular differentiation during development, the commitment of immature cells or tissues to a specific morphological and functional type.

cellular slime mold a mold of the phylum Acrasiomycota.

cellulose an inert, insoluble carbohydrate; a principal constituent of plant cell walls; consists of unbranched chains of beta glucose.

cell-mediated response the immune response carried out by cells that arouses other cells to seek out and kill specific antigen-bearing invading organisms and infected body cells.

cell respiration the energy-yielding metabolism of foods in which oxygen is used. See also *respiration*.

cell wall the semi-rigid enclosure of a plant, fungal, algal, or bacterial cell that gives it support and a definite shape.

central dogma the proposition that all biological information is encoded in DNA, transmitted by DNA replication, transcribed into RNA, and translated into protein; includes several exceptions for certain viruses.

central nervous system in vertebrates, the brain and spinal cord to which sensory impulses are transmitted and from which motor impulses are sent.

centriole (sen'trē ōl) a paired, microtubular organelle in animals, protists, fungi, and lower plant cells; absent in the cells of seed plants.

centromere (sen'trə mir) the specialized region of a chromosome to which spindle fibers are attached; also called *kinetochore*.

centromeric spindle fiber any of a group of microtubules attached to each centromere and proceeding to a spindle pole in mitosis or meiosis.

cephalic ganglia (sə fal'ik gang'glē ə) neural aggregations at the anterior ends of some invertebrates.

cephalochordate (sef'ə lə kôr'dāt) "head cord animal"; a lancelet of the chordate subphylum Cephalochordata.

cerebellum (ser'ə bel'əm) the double, walnut-shaped portion of the hindbrain that coordinates voluntary movement, posture, and balance.

cerebral cortex (ser'ə brəl kôr'teks) the outermost region of the cerebrum, the "gray matter", consisting of several dense layers of neural cell bodies and including numerous conscious centers as well as regions specializing in voluntary movement and sensory reception.

cerebral hemisphere either the right or left half of the cerebrum.

cerebrospinal fluid (sə rē'brō spī'nl) a cushioning fluid that surrounds the central nervous system.

cerebrum (sə rē'brəm) the anterior portion of the vertebrate brain; the largest portion in humans, consisting of two *cerebral hemispheres* and controlling many localized functions (among others voluntary movement, perception, speech, memory and thought).

cervix (sir'viks) the opening to the uterus and the surrounding ring of firm, muscular tissue.

CF1 particle an enzyme-containing body on the outer surface of the thylakoid in which chemiosmotic phosphorylation occurs.

C4 plant a plant in which carbon dioxide is fixed into four-carbon compounds in leaf mesophyll cells, transported to the bundle sheath cells, and released and concentrated for the Calvin cycle in chloroplasts there. Compare *C3 plant*.

chain-terminating mutation a base substitution mutation in which the new codon created is a chain termination codon.

chaparral (shap'ə ral) a vegetation type common in coastal California, characterized by a dense growth of low, evergreen shrubs and trees.

character displacement where similar species share a niche, the tendency for natural selection to favor and accentuate physical differences.

Chargaff's rule in DNA, the amount of adenine present always equals the amount of thymine and the amount of cytosine always equals the amount of guanine.

chelicerae (kə lis'ər ī) the first pair of usually pincerlike appendages of spiders and other arachnids.

chelicerate (kə lis'ə rāt') any member of the subphylum Chelicerata.

chemical bond any of several forms of attraction between atoms in a molecule.

chemical communication the transmission of information between individuals by the use of pheromones.

chemical reaction the reciprocal action of chemical agents on one another; chemical change.

chemiosmosis (kem'ē ôz mō'sis) the process in mitochondria, chloroplasts, and aerobic bacteria in which an electron transport system uses the energy of photosynthesis or oxidation to pump hydrogen ions across a membrane, resulting in an electrochemical proton concentration gradient, or chemiosmotic differential, that can be used to produce ATP.

chemiosmotic gradient in ATP-generating systems, a steep proton gradient whose free energy is utilized in driving chemiosmotic phosphorylation.

chemiosmotic phosphorylation (kem'ē oz mot'ik fos'fər ə lā'shən) the phosphorylation of ADP to ATP using the free energy of the chemiosmotic differential in the CF1 and F1 particles.

chemoreceptor a neural receptor sensitive to a specific chemical or class of chemicals.

chemotroph (kēm'ə trōf) an organism that obtains energy from inorganic chemical reactions. Compare *autotroph, heterotroph*.

chiasmata (kī'az'ma'tə) (*sing.*, chiasma) after repulsion during prophase I of meiosis, X-shaped points of residual connection between homologous chromatids; they are believed to represent prior crossover events.

chitin (kīt'in) a structural carbohydrate that is the principle organic component of arthropod exoskeletons and fungal cell walls.

chlorophyll (klôr'ə fil) a green photosynthetic pigment found in chloroplasts and in some photosynthetic prokaryotes; occurs in several forms, *chlorophyll a, b,* and *c*.

chloroplast photosynthetic organelle (plastid) common in plants and algal protists; numerous internal membranous thylakoids containing photosystems with chlorophyll, electron/proton transport systems, and CF1 particles.

choanocyte (kō an'ə sīt'). See *collar cell*.

cholesterol (kəles tə rōl') a common steroid occurring in all animal fats; a vital component of cell membranes; an important constituent for bile for fat absorption; a precursor of vitamin D and a controversial dietary constituent.

chordae tendineae (kôr'di'tin din'ē ī) in the heart, tough, cordlike tendons that prevent backflow by holding the tricuspid and bicuspid valves in place where the ventricles contract.

chordate (kôr′dāt) belonging to the phylum Chordata, which contains the true vertebrates and those animals having a notochord, like the lancelet.

chorion (kôr′ē on) the outermost extraembryonic membrane of birds, reptiles, and mammals; contributes to the formation of the placenta in placental mammals.

human chorionic gonadotropin (HCG) (kôr′ē on′ik gə nad′ə trōp′ən) the hormone released by an implanted embryo that prompts the continued release of progesterone from the corpus luteum.

chromatid in the G2 chromosome, one of the two identical chromosome replicas held together by the centromere prior to mitosis or meiosis.

chromatin the substance of chromosomes; consists of DNA and chromosomal proteins.

chromatin net the netlike appearance of chromatin in the interphase nucleus.

chromosomal mutation a massive spontaneous change in DNA; generally, breakage involving a whole chromosome that is not repaired or has been repaired improperly. Also *chromosomal rearrangement*.

chromosome 1. in eukaryotes, a linear DNA molecule (or two DNA molecules when replication has occurred), one centromere, and associated proteins. 2. in prokaryotes, a naked, circular DNA molecule (lacking in protein). 3. the DNA or genetic RNA molecule of a virus.

chromosome puff in polytene chromosomes, an enlargement of one band associated with transcriptional activity (mRNA production).

chylomicron (kī′lə mī′kron) in digestion, a minute, protein-coated fat droplet formed during lipid transport in the intestinal villi.

cilia fine, hairlike, motile organelles found in groups on the surface of some cells.

ciliary muscles ring of muscles around the lens which bring about changes in lens shape.

ciliate any protozoan of the phylum Ciliophora, having cilia on part or all of the body.

circulatory system the system consisting of blood-forming organs or tissue, vessels, the heart, and blood; also called *vascular system*.

cisterna slender, membranous channels making up much of the Golgi apparatus.

citric acid cycle in cell respiration, the biochemical pathway in the mitochondrion or bacterial cell where pyruvate, newly converted to acetyl CoA, is combined with oxaloacetate and sequentially oxidized and decarboxylated, thereby producing CO_2, reducing NAD^+ and FAD^+ to NADH and FADH, and producing a small amount of ATP. Also called *Krebs cycle*.

claspers a pair of specialized grooved pel-

vic fins used by male sharks and rays as a penis.

class a major taxonomic grouping intermediate between phylum and order.

classical conditioning in behavior, the process by which a conditioned response is learned and elicited. Compare *operant conditioning*. See also *conditioned response*.

cleavage 1. the breaking down of a molecule or compound into simpler substances. 2. the cytoplasmic division of a zygote and young embryo.

climax state in ecological succession, the stage of a plant or animal community that is stable and self-perpetuating.

cline (klīn) 1. a simple geographic gradient, or regular change, in given character. 2. a regular change in allele frequency over geographic space.

clitoris (klit′ər əs) a touch sensitive, erogenous organ of the female genitalia considered to be homologous to the penis in the male.

cloaca (klō′ā kə) the common cavity into which the intestinal, urinary, and reproductive canals open in many vertebrates.

clonal selection theory in immunology, the proposition that all potential antibody specificity is present in differentiated cells early in development and that the specific immune response consists of inducing appropriately differentiated cells to proliferate clonally.

cloning the production of genetically identical individuals from a single cell.

closed circulatory system a circulatory system in which the blood elements remain in blood vessels. Compare *open circulatory system*.

club fungi fungi of the phylum Basidiomycota.

cnidocyte (nī′də sīt) in coelenterates, a stinging cell.

coacervates (kō as′ər vāts) droplets of protein or other substances that form spontaneously in colloidal suspensions, surrounding themselves with a lipid shell; important in some theories of the origin of life.

coccus (kok′əs) (*pl.,.* cocci) any spherical bacterium.

coccyx (kok′sikz) the tailbone or lowest portion of the vertebral column.

codon 1. a series of three nucleotides in mRNA that specify a particular amino acid (or chain termination) in protein synthesis. 2. the colinear, complementary series of three nucleotides or nucleotide pairs in the DNA from which the mRNA is transcribed.

codominance the individual expression of both alleles in a heterozygote.

coelenterate (si lent′ə rāt′) an animal of phylum coelenterata, characterized by a thin, sack-like body wall and only one digestive opening, such as the jelly fish.

coelom (sē′lōm) a principal body cavity, or one of several such cavities, between the

body wall and gut entirely lined with mesodermal epithelium. Compare *pseudocoelom*.

coelomate *adj.,* having a true coelom.

coenzyme a small organic molecule required for an enzymatic reaction in which it is often reduced (i.e., NAD, NADP).

coevolution evolutionary change in one species that is influenced by the activities of another (i.e., the behavior of a predator and its prey).

cofactor any organic or inorganic substance, especially an ion, that is required for the function of an enzyme.

cohesion the attraction between molecules of a single substance.

coitus (koy′təs) the act of sexual intercourse, especially between humans.

coleoptile (kō′lē op′təl) in the embryos and young shoots of grasses, a temporary tubular leaf structure that completely encloses and protects the plumule during emergence.

coleorhiza (kō′lē ə rī′zə) a temporary protective sheath over the radicle in the embryo of grasses and grains.

colinearity (kō lin′ē ar′ə tē) the principle that the linear arrangement of nucleotides in DNA corresponds to the linear arrangement of nucleotides in RNA, which in turn corresponds to the linear arrangement of amino acids in a polypeptide.

collagen a common, tough, fibrous animal protein occurring principally in connective tissue.

collar cell also called *choanocyte;* one of certain flagellated cells in sponges that create a current and ingest food particles from the water.

collecting duct the part of a nephron that collects fluids from the nephron and discharges it into the renal pelvis.

collenchyma in plants, a strengthening tissue; a modified parenchyma consisting of elongated cells with greatly thickened cells walls.

colon the large intestine.

colony 1. a group of animals or plants of the same kind living in a close semidependent association. 2. an aggregation of bacteria growing together as the descendents of a single individual, usually on a culture plate.

columnar epithelium (kol′əm nər ep′ə thē lē əm) epithelium consisting of one (simple columnar) or more (stratified columnar) layers of elongated, cylindrical cells.

commensalism (kə men′sə liz′əm) a symbiotic relationship in which one partner benefits while the other is neither helped nor hurt. Compare *mutualism, parasitism*.

community in ecology, an assemblage of interacting populations forming an identifiable group within a biome (i.e., a sage desert community or a beech-maple deciduous forest community).

compact bone dense, hard bone with spaces of microscopic size.

companion cell in plants, a nucleated cell adjacent to a sieve tube member and believed to assist in its functions.

competition in ecology, the utilization of the same limiting resource by two or more individuals or species.

complement a group of blood proteins that interact with antibody-antigen complexes to destroy foreign cells.

complete dominance the expression of a gene with the complete lack of expression of its allele.

complete gut a digestive tract which has both a mouth and an anus.

compound in chemistry, a pure substance of a single molecular type consisting of two or more elements in a fixed ratio.

compound eye an arthropod eye consisting of many simple eyes closely crowded together, each with an individual lens and a restricted field of vision, so that a mosaic image is formed.

concentration gradient a slow, consistent decrease in the concentration of a substance along a line in space. Also called *diffusion gradient.*

conditioned response an involuntary response (mouth-watering) that becomes associated with an arbitrary, previously unrelated stimulus (bell-ringing) through repeated presentation of the arbitrary stimulus (bell-ringing) simultaneously with a stimulus normally yielding the response (pizza).

conditioned stimulus in animal behavior, an environmental situation or condition that is normally irrelevant to a desired behavior but can come to stimulate the behavior. Compare *unconditioned stimulus.*

cone 1. a reproductive structure of conifers consisting of a cluster of scalelike modified leaves and either pollen or ovules, or the seed. 2. one of a class of conical photoreceptors in the retina that detect color.

conidium an asexual spore borne on the tip of a fungal hypha.

conifer an evergreen gymnospore of the division Coniferophyta, bearing ovules and pollen in cones; included are spruce, fir, pine, cedar, and juniper.

conjugated protein (kon′jə gā′tid prō′tēn) protein containing one or more nonprotein substances; e.g., hemoglobin, which contains four heme groups.

conjugation (kon′jə gā′shēən) sexual reproduction in which organisms (usually single-celled) fuse to exchange genetic materials.

connective tissue a primary animal tissue of mesodermal origin, with scattered cells and abstract extracellular substance or interlacing fibers, usually including collagen.

constant region the C-terminal portion of an immunoglobulin (antibody) light or heavy chain, not involved in antigen-specific binding.

consumer in ecology, an animal that feeds on plants (primary consumer) or other animals (secondary consumer).

consummatory stage a part of instinctive behavior that involves highly stereotyped (invariable) behavior and the performance of a fixed-action pattern, e.g. swallowing food. Compare *appetitive stage.*

continental drift the slow movement of the continents relative to one another on the earth's surface. See also *plate tectonics.*

continental shelf the part of a continent that is submerged in relatively shallow water.

continuous spindle fiber one of two partially overlapping spindle fibers (not actually continuous), each originating near a pole and extending across the chromosomes without attaching. Also called *polar spindle fiber.*

continous variation continuous gradation in the expression of a trait where two or more pairs of alleles contribute to such expression, i.e., height and skin color in humans.

contractile vacuole (kən trak′təl vak′yüōl) an organelle of many freshwater protists that maintain the cell's osmotic equilibrium by expelling excess water through an active, ATP-powered process.

control 1. a standard of comparison in scientific experiment; a replicate of the experiment in which a possibly crucial factor being studied is omitted. 2. a function of the nucleus of a cell—the direction of virtually all cellular activity.

controlled experiment a scientific study in which a number of subjects are randomly divided into two or more groups, and each group is treated exactly the same in all respects except one, which becomes the variable.

conus arteriosus (kōn′əs är tir′ē ō′səs) in a two-chambered vertebrate heart, the heavy-walled blood vessel that leaves the ventricle.

convergent evolution the independent evolution of similar structures in distantly related organisms; often found in organisms that occur in similar ecological niches, such as marsupial moles and placental moles.

cooperation working or acting together for a common purpose or benefit; joint action by several individuals.

copulation sexual union or sexual intercourse.

cork in plants, secondary tissue produced by the *cork cambium,* consisting of cells that become heavily suberized and die at maturity, resistant to the passage of moisture and gases; the outermost layer of bark.

cork cambium (kam′bē əm) in plants, the outermost meristematic layer of the stem of woody plants, from which the outermost layer of bark is produced.

corona radiata (kôr ōn′ə rā′dē′at′ə) "radiating crown"; an aggregation of follicle cells surrounding the mammalian egg at ovulation.

coronary arteriosclerosis (kôr′ə ner′ē är tir′ē ō skle rō′sis) an inelasticity and thickening of the arterial walls of the heart, resulting in a decreased blood flow.

corpus callosum (kôr′pəs kəlo′səm) a broad, white neural tract that connects the cerebral hemispheres and correlates their activities.

corpus luteum (kôr′pəs loo′tē əm) "yellow body"; a temporary endocrine body that develops in the ovarian follicle after ovulation; secretes estrogen and progesterone.

cortex (kôr′teks) 1. in animals, the outer layer or rind of an organ, such as the adrenal cortex. 2. in plants, the portion of stem between the epidermis and the stele.

cortical granule (kôrt′ə kəl gran′yool) a membranous vesicle beneath the surface of unfertilized echinoderm eggs; at fertilization these rupture to form the fertilization membrane during the cortical reaction.

countercurrent exchange a heat or molecule concentrating mechanism in endothermic animals, e.g., the presence of parallel arteries and veins permit an efficient heat exchange as the outward flow of warmer blood opposes the inward flow of cooler blood from the extremities.

covalent bond (kō vā′lənt) a relatively strong chemical bond in which an electron pair is shared by two atoms.

cranial nerve in humans, one of 12 pairs of major nerves that emerge directly from the brain.

cranium (krā′nē əm) 1. the skull. 2. the part of the skull enclosing the brain.

creatine phosphate (krē̄ətēn fos′fāt) Also called *phosphocreatine.* In vertebrate muscles, a source of high-energy phosphate for restoring ATP expended during muscle contraction.

crista (kris′tə) (*pl.,* cristae) a shelflike fold of the inner mitochondrial membrane, containing numerous electron transport systems, proton pumps, and F1 particles.

cross current exchange in the bird lung, the flow of blood at right angles to the passage of air.

crossing over 1. the exchange of chromatid (DNA) segments by enzymatic breakage and reunion during meiotic prophase. 2. a specific instance of such an exchange; a cross over.

cross-opterygian (kro sop′tə rij′ē an) any fish of the group Crossopterygii, extinct except for the coelacanth, regarded as being ancestral to amphibians and other land vertebrates.

crowning in the human birth process, the appearance of the head of the fetus.

crude filtrate in the kidney, the fluid entering the nephron.

crustacean (kru stā shēən) any member of the class Crustacea.

cryptogam (krip'tə gam') any of the Cryptogamia, an old primary division of plants without true flowers and seeds, such as ferns and horsetails.

C₃ plant a plant in which carbon dioxide is fixed into carbohydrates directly in the Calvin cycle. Compare *C₄ plant*.

cuticle (kŭ tə kəl) a tough, often waterproof, nonliving covering, usually secreted by epidermal cells.

cyanobacteria (sīanō bak tir'ēə) in older terminology, *cyanophytes* and *blue-green algae*, a photosynthetic eubacterium that uses water as a source of protons and whose cells exhibit membranous chlorophyll-containing lamellae; many are capable of nitrogen fixation.

cycad (sī'kad) a plant of the division Cycadophyta.

cyclic adenosine monophosphate (cAMP) (sik'lik ə den'əsin mon'ō fos'fat) "second messenger"; synthesized in response to certain hormones arriving at the cell membrane; stimulates further activity in the target cell.

cyclic photophosphorylation (sik'lik fō'tō fōs far ə lā'shən) light reactions employing only photosystem I, during which electrons from the P700 reaction center pass through the associated electron transport system and cycle back to P700, thus serving chemiosmosis only.

cytochrome (sī'tə krōm) iron-containing compounds including carrier proteins, found in electron/hydrogen transport chains in the thylakoid, mitochondrion, and bacterial membranes.

cytokinesis (sī tō ki ne'səs) division of the cell cytoplasm following mitosis or meiosis.

cytokinin (sī'tō kin'in) a plant cell hormone, mitogen, and plant tissue culture growth factor that interacts with other plant hormones in the control of cell differentiation.

cytological map (sī'tə loj'əkəl) a map locating genes on the physical chromosome by means other than recombination or genetic mapping.

cytoplasm (sī'tə plaz'əm) in eukaryotes, that region of the cell between the cell membrane and nuclear membrane, including the cytoplasmic organelles and matrix.

cytophyge (sī to'pij) the fixed position on the surface of a protist from which wastes are discharged by exocytosis.

cytosine (C) (sī'tə sēn') a pyrimidine, one of the four nucleotide bases of DNA and RNA.

cytostome (sī'to stōm) the mouth of a ciliate.

cytotoxic T-cell (sī'tō toks'ik tē'sel). See *T-cell lymphocyte*.

daughter cell either of the two cells formed when one cell divides.

day-neutral plants plants that can flower at any time of the year regardless of the relative amounts of light and darkness.

deamination (dē am'ə nā'shən) the removal of an amino group.

deciduous rain forest (di sij'oo əs) a lush forest biome, typically receiving 250 to 450 cm (100 to 180 in) of annual rainfull, with seasonal variations, in which trees drop their leaves in the "dry" season.

decomposer (dē'kəm pō'zər) an organism that breaks down organic wastes and the remains of dead organisms into simpler compounds, such as carbon dioxide, ammonia, and water. Also called *reducer*.

decomposition (dē'kom pə zish'ən) the act or process of breaking down large molecules into simpler ones.

deductive reasoning (di duk'tiv rē'zən ing) the logical process in which specific conclusions are drawn from generalities. Compare *inductive reasoning*.

dehydration chemically, an enzymatic reaction during which water is lost and a covalent bond forms between the reactants.

dehydration synthesis the process by which a covalent bond is formed between two compounds by the removal of one oxygen atom and two hydrogens, which form water.

deletion 1. the removal of any segment of a chromosome or gene. 2. the site of such a removal after chromosome healing—a mutation. 3. the deleted chromosome.

delta cell an endocrine cell in the pancreas, which secretes somatostatin.

demographic transition also *theory of demographic transition;* the proposal that in the development of nations, population growth has distinct stages: (1) high birth and death rates and slow growth; (2) high birth rate, low death rate, and very rapid growth; (3) low birth and death rates, and very slow growth.

denatured (dē nā'chərd) *adj.,* of a protein, altered so as to destroy its properties, through heating or chemical treatment.

dendrite (den'drīt) an extension of a neuron that receives impulses and conducts them toward the cell body.

dendrograph (den'drə graf) a device for recording fluctuations in the diameter of a tree trunk.

denitrifier (dē ni'trəfī'er) any one of several common soil and manure bacteria that break down nitrates and nitrites into nitrogen gas.

density-dependent control a factor affecting population size, the severity of which depends on the density of the population in question, i.e., competition.

density-independent control a factor affecting population size that is independent of population density, i.e., temperature, salincty, fire, meteorites, etc.

deoxynucleotide (dē ok'si nü klē ə 'tīd) any nucleotide of DNA.

deoxyribose (dē ok'si rī bōs) a five-carbon sugar identical to ribose except that one hydroxyl group is replaced by a hydrogen atom.

deoxyribose nucleic acid. See DNA.

depolarized (dē pō lə rīz'd) loss of a net-charged state.

dermal brachiae (der'məl brang'kē ī) "skin gills" of echinoderms, consisting of outpocketings of the coelom and body wall.

dermis (der'məs) in animals, the inner mesodermally derived layer of skin beneath the ectodermally derived epidermis.

descending limb in the kidney nephron the part of the loop of Henle that goes down into the renal medulla.

desert a region characterized by scanty rainfall, especially less than 25 cm (10 in) annually.

desmotubule (des'mə tü'byül) within the plasmodesmata of plant cells a continuation of the endoplasmic reticulum of one cell with that of the adjacent cell.

determinate cleavage in animal embryos the very early designation of cells to specific developmental pathways resulting in a loss of flexibility in individual cells and tissues. Also *determinate development*. See *indeterminate cleavage*.

deuterostome (dū'tər ə stōm') a bilateral animal (i.e., an echinoderm or chordate) whose anus arises early and whose mouth arises later as a second embryonic opening. Compare *protostome*.

diabetes mellitus (dī ə bē tēs'mel'ət əs) a genetic disease of carbohydrate metabolism characterized by abnormally high levels of glucose in the blood and urine and the inadequate secretion of utilization or insulin.

diaphragm (dī'ə fram) 1. in mammals, a dome-shaped, muscularized body partition that separates the chest and abdominal cavities and is involved in breathing movements. 2. a birth control device; a thin rubber cup with a springlike rim that, when inserted to cover the cervix, acts as a physical barrier to sperm.

diastole (dī'ə stōl) the period of expansion and dilation of the heart during which it fills with blood; the period between forceful contractions (systole) of the heart. See *systole*.

diastolic pressure (di'ə stol'ik pressure) the blood pressure between the heart's contractions; see also *blood pressure* and *systolic pressure*.

diatom (dī'ə tōm) an acellular or colonial yellow-green photosynthetic protist, having a silicon-impregnated cell wall in two parts.

dicot (dī'kot'). See *dicotyledon*.

dicotyledon (dī kot'l ē dən) a flowering plant of the angiosperm class Dicotyledonae, characterized by producing seeds with two cotyledons. Compare *monocot*.

differentially permeable. See *selectively permeable*.

diffuse root system also *fibrous root system*. A root system of a plant in which there are many roots all about the same size.

diffusion (di fyü'zhən) the random movement of a gas or solute under thermal agitation, resulting in a net movement from regions of higher concentration to regions of lower concentration.

diffusion gradient. See *concentration gradient*.

dihybrid cross (dī hī′brid krôs) in Mendelian genetics, a cross involving two unlinked pairs of factors or alleles.

dikaryotic (dī′kar′ē ot′ik) *adj.* pertaining to a condition in many fungi arising after conjugation, wherein parental plus and minus haploid nuclei remain separated for a time before fusion occurs.

dinoflagellate (din′ə flaj′ə lat) a flagellated, photosynthetic, marine protist of the group Dinoflagellata.

dipeptide (dī pep′tid) two amino acids united by a peptide linkage; a common intermediate product of digestion.

diploid (2n) *adj.*, doubled; having a double set of genes and chromosomes, one set originating from each parent. Compare *haploid, polyploid*.

disaccharide (dī sak′ə rīd) "two sugars"; a carbohydrate consisting of two monosaccharide simple sugar subunits, e.g. sucrose and lactose.

disruptive selection in population genetics, selection that through changing or cycling conditions shifts back and forth, favoring first one end of a phenotypic range and then another.

dissociating coming apart into discrete units; ionizing.

disulfide linkage (dī sul′fīd ling′kij) in protein, a covalent link formed between sulfur groups in one polypeptide or adjacent polypeptides.

directional selection in population genetics, selection favoring one extreme of a continuous phenotypic distribution (e.g., the darkest of several colors present).

disease a condition of an organ, part, structure, or system of the body in which there is incorrect function resulting from the effect of heredity, infection, diet, or environment; illness, sickness.

distal convoluted tubule (dis′təl kon′və lū′tid tū′byool) a portion of the nephron between the loop of Henle and the collecting duct.

diuretic (dī′ yoo ret′ ik) a substance that increases the volume of urine excreted.

divergent evolution (də vėr′jənt ev′ə lū′ shən) branching evolutionary change away from the ancestral type, with selection favoring differences in newly arising species.

divergent speciation. See *divergent evolution*.

division a major primary category or taxon of the plant kingdom, sometimes fungal moneran and protist kingdoms, equivalent to *phylum*.

DNA (deoxyribonucleic acid) (de ok′sə rī′bō nü kle′ik as′īd) a double-stranded nucleic acid polymer; the genetic material of all organisms (except RNA viruses).

DNA polymerase (pol′ə mə rās′) an enzyme that catalyzes the replication of DNA.

DNA probe a short, specific segment of single-stranded DNA nucleotides, some of which are radioactive, used in identifying and retrieving desired gene segments from DNA libraries.

DNA repair system a complex of enzymes that identifies and repairs spontaneous changes in the nucleotide bases of DNA.

DNA replication the semiconservative synthesis of DNA in which the double helix opens, the two strands separate, and each is used as a template for producing a new opposing strand.

dominance the phenotypic expression of only one of the two alleles in a heterozygote.

dominance hierarchy behavioral interactions established in a troop, flock, or other species group in which every individual is dominant to those lower on the order and submissive to those above. Also called *pecking order*.

dorsal hollow nerve cord (dôr′səl hol′ō nėrv kôrd) a characteristic neural structure of chordates, which in vertebrates forms the *brain* and *spinal cord*. "Hollow" refers to the presence of fluid-filled foldings and cavities.

double helix the configuration of the native DNA molecule which consists of two strands of nucleotides wound spirally around each other.

doubling time the number of years required for a population to double in size.

Down syndrome. See *trisomy 21*.

drumstick a small projection (not unlike a chicken leg) of the nucleus of the polymorphonuclear leukocytes of human females, attributed to the condensed second X chromosome.

drupt (drūp) in plants, a simple fleshy fruit, usually with a single seed, derived from one carpel; i.e., olive, peach, cherry.

ductus arteriosus (duk′təs är tir′ē ō səs) in the mammalian fetus, a short, broad vessel conducting blood from the pulmonary artery to the aorta, thus bypassing the fetal lungs.

duodenum (doo′ə de nəm) the first segment of the small intestine posterior to the stomach.

eardrum. See *tympanic membrane*.

ecdysis (ek′dī sis) also *molting*; 1. in arthropods, the shedding of the outer, noncellular cuticle. 2. this shedding together with associated changes in size, shape, or function.

ecdysone (ec′də sōn) the molting hormone of insects.

echinoderm (ikī′nə dūrm) any organism of the marine, coelomate, deuterostome phylum Echinodermata, i.e., starfishes, sea urchins, sea cucumbers, etc.

ecological niche (ē′kə log′ə kəl nich) the position or function of an organism in a community of plants and animals; the totality of adaptations, specializations, tolerance limits, functions, biological interactions, and behaviors of a species.

ecological pyramid (ē′kə loj′ə kəl pir′ ə mid). See *pyramid of numbers, energy* and *biomass*.

ecological succession the gradual progression or change in the species composition of a community; the progression of one community into another.

ecology the branch of biology dealing with the relations between organisms and their environment.

ecosystem in ecology, a unit of interaction among organisms and between organisms and their physical environment.

ectoderm in animal development, the outermost of the three primary germ layers of the embryo; the source of all nerve tissue, sense organs and outer skin.

ectotherm an animal that lacks the ability to thermoregulate physiologically. Compare *endotherm*.

ectothermic *adj.* pertaining to a condition in which the body temperature cannot be metabolically regulated.

effector any structure that elicits a response to neural stimulation, e.g., a muscle gland.

efferent vessel any blood vessel carrying blood away from a structure under consideration, specifically in a gill filament or kidney nephron.

egg the ovum or female reproductive cell. See *egg cell*.

eidetiker (i′det′i kər) a person with a "photographic" memory.

ejaculation (ē jak′yoo lā′ shən) the forceful expulsion of semen from the penis.

elastin (i las′tən) an extracellular structural protein that forms long, elastic fibers in connective tissue.

electroencephalogram (EEG) (i lek′trō en sef′ə lə gram) a clinical record of electrical activity within the brain.

electroencephalograph a clinical device for detecting and recording electroencephalograms (EEGs) of electrical activity within the brain.

electromagnetic spectrum the range of electromagnetic radiation from low-energy, low-frequency radio waves to high-energy, high-frequency gamma rays.

electron one of the three common components of an atom; its mass is 1/1837 of a proton's, and its electrostatic charge is −1.

electron acceptor a molecule that accepts one or more electrons in an oxidation-reduction reaction (and thus becomes reduced), i.e., a cytochrome or coenzyme.

electron carrier a molecule that behaves cyclically as an electron acceptor and an electron donor; a common constituent of electron transport systems.

electron donor a molecule that loses one or more electrons to an electron acceptor in an oxidation-reduction reaction (and thereby becomes oxidized).

electron orbital 1. a path traveled by an electron. 2. the space in which an electron is found 90% of the time.

electron transport system (ETS) a series of cytochromes and other proteins, bound within a membrane of a thylakoid, mitochrondrion, or prokaryotic cell, that passes electrons or hydrogen atoms or both in a series of oxidation-reduction reactions that result in a net movement of hydrogen ions across the membrane.

element 1. a substance that cannot be separated into simpler substances by purely chemical means. 2. in plants, any one of the hollow xylem cells with thick, pitted walls.

elongation growth by lengthening; in plant development, the expansion in one direction of stem or root cells under turgor and the subsequent growth in length of the plant.

eltonian pyramid (el tōn′ē ən pir′ə mid). See *pyramid of numbers*.

embryology (em′brē ol′ə jē) the scientific study of early development in plants and animals.

embryonic disk the part of the inner cell mass from which a mammalian embryo develops.

embryonic induction an influencing action, employing chemical or physical agents, during which one embryonic tissue influences the developmental fate of another.

embryo sac in flowering plants, the mature megagametophyte after division into six haploid cells and one binucleate cell, enclosed in a common cell wall.

endergonic *adj*. relating to a chemical reaction that requires an input of energy from some outside source and in which the products contain greater energy than the reactants (e.g., the synthesis of ATP and ADP and P_1). Compare *exergonic*.

endocytosis (en′dō sī tō′sis) the process of taking food, solutes, or invading cells into the cell (into vacuoles) by engulfment (a form of active transport). See also *phagocytosis*.

endoderm in animal development, the innermost of the three primary germ layers of a metazoan embryo and the source of the gut epithelium and its embryonic outpocketings (in vertebrates, the liver, pancreas, and lung); also called *entoderm*.

endodermis (en′dō dèr′ mis) a single layer of cells around the stele of vascular plant roots that forms a moisture barrier—its lateral cell walls are pressed tightly together and waterproofed, forming the *Casparian strip*.

endometrium (en′dō mē trē əm) in mammals, the tissue lining the cavity of the uterus; it responds cyclically to ovarian hormones by thickening in preparation for the implantation of an embryo, and is shed as the menstrual flow.

endoplasmic reticulum (ER) (en′dō plaz′mik ri tik′yə ləm) extensive and dynamic membranes of the cell cytoplasm, usually a site of synthesis, packaging and transport. **Rough ER** with bound ribosomes, the site of protein synthesis. **Smooth ER** without bound

ribosomes, the site of synthesis of nonprotein materials.

endorphin (en dôrfən) a brain neurotransmitter that reduces pain and produces euphoria.

endoskeleton (en′dō skel′ə tən) a mesodermally derived supporting skeleton, inside the organism and surrounded by living tissue, as in vertebrates.

endosperm a nutritive tissue of angiosperm seeds, formed around the embryo.

endospore a resistant, thick-walled spore formed from a bacterial cell.

endotherm an organism with the ability to metabolically thermoregulate; also called "warm-blooded."

endothermic *adj*., pertaining to the condition in which animals regulate their body temperature through the metabolism of cellular fuels, usually maintaining it at some constant optimal level.

energy the capacity or potential to accomplish work (with work defined as the movement of matter); it exists in several forms, including heat, chemical, electrical, magnetic, and radiant (electromagnetic).

energy pyramid the ecological pyramid comparing the energy content of producers, consumers, and decomposers.

energy shell one of several distinct energy levels at which the electrons of any element may be found; also called *electron shell*.

enkephalin (en kef′ə lən) a brain neurotransmitter that reduces pain and produces euphoria.

entrophy (en′trə pē) in thermodynamics, the energy in a closed system that is not available for doing work; also a measure of the randomness or disorder of such a system. See also *energy, potential energy,* and *second law of thermodynamics*.

environmental resistance the sum of environmental factors (e.g., limited resources, drought, disease) that restrict the growth of a population below its biotic potential (maximum possible population size).

enzyme a protein that catalyzes chemical reactions.

enzyme-substrate complex (ES) the unit formed by an enzyme bound by noncovalent bonds to its substrate.

epicotyl (ep′ə kot′l) in the embryo of a seed plant, the part of the shoot above the attachment of the cotyledon.

epidermis (ep′ə der′mis) 1. in plants, the outer protective cell layer in leaves and in the primary root and stem. 2. in animals, the outer epithelial layer of the skin.

epididymis (ep′ə did′ə mis) in mammals, an elongated soft mass lying along side each testis, consisting of convoluted tubules; the site of sperm maturation.

epiglottis (ep′ə glot′əs) in the lower pharynx, a flexible cartilaginous flap that folds over the glottis during swallowing.

epilimnion (ep′ə lim′nē on′) in lakes, the layer of water above the thermocline.

epinephrine (ep′ə nef′rən) a hormone with numerous effects produced by the adrenal medulla and by nerve synapses of the autonomic nervous system; also called *adrenaline*.

epiphyte (ep′ə fit′) a plant that grows nonparasitically on another plant, or sometimes, on an object, e.g., orchids.

epistasis (i pīs′tə sis) the masking of a trait ordinarily determined by one gene locus by the action of a gene or genes at another locus.

epithelial tissue (ep′ə thē lē əl tish′ū). See *epithelium*.

epithelium (ep′ ə thē′ lē əm) a basic animal tissue type, which covers a surface or lines a canal or cavity; it serves to enclose and protect.

erectile tissue spongy tissue of the penis, which fills with blood during sexual arousal, causing the penis to become erect, lengthen, and thicken.

erythroblastosis fetalis (i rith′rō bla stō′ sis fi tal′is) during Rh incompatibility, the destruction of red blood cells in the Rh^+ fetus or newborn through the action of maternal Rh^- antibodies that have crossed the placenta.

erythrocyte (i rith′rō sīt) a red blood cell, oxygen carrier.

erythropoietin (i rith′rō poi ē′tən) a hormone that stimulates the production and differentiation of erythrocytes during erythropoiesis.

esophagus the muscular tube connecting the pharynx to the stomach.

estrogen a female hormone; one of the hormones involved in the production of secondary sex characteristics and the menstrual cycle.

ethology (ə thol′ə jē) the scientific study of animal behavior, usually under natural conditions.

ethylene (eth′ə lēn) a colorless, sweet-smelling, unsaturated hydrocarbon gas emitted by ripening fruit and inducing further ripening.

ETS. See *electron transport system*.

eubacteria (yü bak tir ē ə) "true bacteria"; the better-known prokaryote group containing many familiar human pathogens and important soil and water bacteria. See also *Archaebacteria*.

eukaryote (y ü kar′ē ōt) a cell or organism with cells containing a membrane-bound nucleus, chromosomes complexed with histones, and other proteins and membrane-bounded cytoplasmic organelles. Compare *prokaryote*.

euphotic zone (yōō fō′tik zōn) the area of a body of water that receives sufficient light for photosynthesis to occur.

eustachian tubes (yōō stā′shən) a canal extending from the middle ear to the pharynx.

eutrophic (yōō trō′fik) *adj*. pertaining to fresh waters, rich in nutrients essential to plant algal growth, thus rich in life and usually in rapid ecological succession. Compare *oligotrophic*.

eutrophication (yōō trof′fə kā′shən) the aging process whereby a body of water supports increasing numbers of organisms, often causing lakes to become marshes and terrestial communities.

evolution 1. any gradual process of formation, growth, or change. 2. descent with modification. 3. long-term change and speciation (division into discrete species) of biological entities. 4. the continuous genetic adaptation to populations through mutation, hybridization, random drift and natural selection.

exchange pool in biogeochemical cycles, the readily available reserves of a mineral nutrient, such as a soluble phosphate or nitrate pool in the soil water; compare *reservoir*.

excretion the removal of cellular metabolic wastes from the body.

exergonic (ek′ sər gon′ ik) *adj.*, describing a chemical reaction that releases energy, with the products containing less free energy that the reactants; compare *endergonic*.

exocrine gland also called *ductless gland;* a gland that releases its secretions externally, into the gut or anywhere other than the blood stream.

exocytosis (ek′sō sī tō′sis) the process of expelling material from vacuoles through the cell membrane; compare *endocytosis*.

exon (ek′son). See *expressed sequence*.

exoskeleton an external skeleton and supportive covering (as in arthropods, where it consists of chitin).

experiment a procedure conducted for the purpose of discovering something unknown or for testing a hypothesis, supposition, etc.

experimental group in a controlled experiment, the group subjected to the variable being tested or studied.

expiratory center part of the respiratory control center in the medulla oblongata, increases the expiratory rate and volume during strenuous activity.

exponential curve (eks′pō nen′chəl). See *J-shaped curve*.

exponential growth also *geometric growth;* population growth in which the population size increases by a fixed proportion in each time period, successive values forming an exponential series.

expressed sequence also called *exon;* the nucleotide sequences that remain in a messenger RNA molecule after tailoring and thus are expressed in a polypeptide. See also *intron*.

expulsion in the human birth process, the phase of labor lasting from minutes to hours, during which the fetus is pushed out of the uterus.

external ear all parts of the ear external to the eardrum, comprising the external ear canal, the external auditory meatus, and the pinna.

external fertilization fertilization outside the body, as in echinoderms and most bony fish.

extinction behaviorally, the loss of a conditioned response as a result of the absence of reinforcement.

extracellular digestion digestion outside of cells (usually in the gut).

extraembryonic membrane (ek′strə em′ brē on ik) any of several external life-supporting structures produced by the vertebrate embryo (i.e., amnion, chorion, allantois, and yolk sac).

facilitated diffusion diffusion of molecules across a cell membrane assisted by carrier molecules.

FAD (flavin adenine dinucleotide) a coenzyme that is a hydrogen carrier in mitochondrial metabolism.

fascia (fāsh′ē ə) a heavy sheet of connective tissue covering or binding together muscles or other internal structures of the body, often connecting with ligaments or tendons.

fatty acid an organic acid consisting of a linear hydrocarbon "tail" and one terminal carboxyl group.

feedback the return of part of the output of a system to be reintroduced as input that regulates or affects the system's functioning.
  negative feedback the output damps the activity of the system, reducing the flow of output.
  positive feedback the output stimulates the activity of the system, further increasing the flow of output.

female gametophyte. See *megagametophyte*.

fern any of the pteridophytes, having few leaves large in proportion to the stems and bearing sporangia on the undersurface or margin.

fertility rate. See *general fertility rate*.

fertilization the sexual process by which gametes or gamete nuclei are united.

fertilization cone a cone-shaped mound of egg cytoplasm that, upon activation of the egg by a fertilizing sperm, rises to engulf the sperm.

fertilization membrane in echinoderms, a membrane formed upon egg activation by the rupture of cortical granules, preventing further sperm penetration.

fetus in vertebrates, an unborn ovum-hatched individual past the embryo stage; in humans, a developing unborn individual past the first eight weeks of pregnancy.

fibrin an insoluble fibrous protein forming blood clots and also contributing to the viscosity of blood. See *fibrinogen*.

fibrinogen (fī brī′ə gin) a globular blood protein (globulin) that is converted into fibrin by the action of thrombin as part of the normal blood clotting process.

fibroblast a cell in the connective tissue group that produces fibers and matrix substances such as collagen.

fibroin (fī′brō in) the insoluble fibrous protein of silk and spider webs.

fibrous root system. See *diffuse root system*.

fiddlehead the coiled new leaves of a fern, having a form similar to the curved head of a fiddle or violin.

filament in flowers, the slender stalk of the stamen, on which the anther is situated. See also *myofilament*.

filamentous alga a group of green algae that tend to form lengthy filaments of cells.

filter feeder an animal that obtains its food by filtering minute organisms from a current of water.

fimbriae (fim′brē ē) (*sing.*, fimbria) a fringe of ciliated tissue surrounding the opening of the oviduct into the peritoneal cavity.

first law of thermodynamics the physical law that states that energy cannot be created or destroyed and that the total amount of energy in a "closed" system remains constant.

fission the division of an organism into two (binary fission) or more organisms, as a process of asexual reproduction.

fixed-action pattern in behavior, a precise and identifiable set of movements, innate and characteristic of a given species. See also *instinct*.

flagellate (flaj′ə lāt′) any protozoan of the phylum Sarcomastigophora, having one or more flagella.

flagellum (flə jel′əm) (*pl.* flagella) 1. long, whiplike, motile eukaryote cell organelles projecting from the cell that propel the cell by undulations. 2. in prokaryotes, consisting of a solid, helical protein fiber that passes through the cell wall and propels the cell by rotating.

flame cells. Also called *protonephridia;* in flatworms, rotifers, and lancelets, a cup-shaped cell with a tuff of cilia in its depression, the flamelike beating of which creates suction that draws waste materials into an excretory duct.

fluid mosaic model a description of the cell membrane as a phospholipid bilayer that has a fluidlike core and contains an assortment of specifically oriented proteins and other surface molecules.

follicle-stimulating hormone (FSH) a hormone produced by the anterior pituitary that stimulates the growth and maturation of eggs and sperm.

F_1 generation in genetics, the first generation of offspring in cross-breeding. Subsequent generations are designated F_2, F_3, etc.

F_1 particle an enzyme-containing body or the mitochondrial membrane in which chemiosmotic phosphorylation takes place.

F plasmid a smaller bacterial chromosome, responsible for producing the sex pilus whose formation precedes conjugation.

food chain a sequence of organisms in an ecological community, each of which is a food for the next higher organism, from the primary producer to the top producer.

food vacuole (vak′yü ōl) in animals and protists, an intracellular vacuole that arises by the phagocytosis of solid food materials and in which digestive processes occur.

foodweb a group of interacting food chains; all of the feeding relations of a community taken together.

foramen (fō rā′mən) (*pl.*, foramina) openings or perforations.

foramen magnum the large opening at the base of the skull through which the spinal cord passes.

foramen ovale in the fetal mammalian heart, an opening in the septum between the atria; it normally closes at the time of birth.

foraminiferan (fō ram′ə nif′ər ən) a shelled marine sarcodine protist with one or more nuclei in a single plasma membrane, the carbonate shell having numerous minute openings (foramina) through which slender, branching pseudopods are extended.

forebrain the anterior of the three primary divisions of the vertebrate embryonic brain.

foregut the upper part of the embryonic alimentary canal from which the pharynx, esophagus, stomach, and part of the duodenum develop. A similar region in the gut of insects.

foreskin the fold of skin that covers the head of the uncircumcised penis.

founder effect in population genetics, the chance assortment of genes carried out of the original population by colonizers (or founders) who subsequently give rise to a large population.

frame-shift mutation an insertion or deletion of a nucleotide which results in a frame's change and the misreading during translation of all mRNA codons "downstream."

frontal lobe an anterior portion of the cerebrum believed to be a site of higher cognition.

fruit the mature, seed-bearing ovary of a flowering plant; it may be swollen and sweet or starchy.

fucoxanthin (fū kō zan′thin) a brown carotenoid pigment characteristic of brown algae.

fungi imperfecti yeast-like fungi of the phylum Deuteronmycota which cause skin and vaginal infections.

fungi (fun′je) (*sing.*, fungus) organism of the kingdom Fungi; included are yeasts, mushrooms, molds, mildew, puffballs, etc.

gall bladder a muscular saclike organ that is the temporary receptacle of bile.

gametes (gam′ētz) haploid cells that unite in sexual reproduction, producing a diploid zygote; typically the haploid sperm or egg cell.

gametic cycle in all animals (and some protists) a life cycle dominated by the diploid chromosome state, with the haploid state present only in the gametes.

gametophyte (gə mē′tō fīt) in plants with alternation of generations, the haploid form, in which gametes are produced; compare *sporophyte*.

ganglia (gang′glē ə) (*sing.* ganglion) a mass of nerve tissue containing the cell bodies of neurons.

gap junction dense structure that physically connects membranes of adjacent cells along with channels for cell-to-cell transport.

gastric juice the digestive fluid, containing pepsin and other enzymes, secreted by the glands of the stomach.

gastropod any mollusk of the class Gastropode, comprising the snails.

gastrovascular cavity the cavity of coelenterates, ctenophores, and flatworms which opens to the outside only via the mouth and functions as a digestive cavity and crude circulatory system.

gastrula (gas′trū la) a young metazoan embryo consisting of three germ tissue layers, with an inner cavity (archenteron).

gastrulation (gas′trə lā′shən) the process of cellular migration by ectoderm whereby a blastula becomes a gastrula.

gel electrophoresis (jel i lek trō for ē sis) an analytical procedure in biochemistry, whereby a mixture of molecules enters a gel and separates by the differential migration of its constituents in an imposed electrical field.

gene (variously defined) 1. the unit of heredity that controls the development of a hereditary character. 2. a continuous length of DNA with a single genetic function.

gene cloning technique whereby pieces of DNA from any source are spliced into plasmid DNA, cultured in growing bacteria, purified and recovered in quantity. See also *recombinant DNA technology*.

gene flow the exchange of genes between populations through migration, pollen dispersal, chance encounters, and the like.

gene interaction occurring when the genes at one locus affect the phenotypic expression of genes at another locus.

gene locus specific place on a chromosome where a gene is located.

gene pool all the genetic information of a population considered collectively.

generalization in behavior, the act or process of responding to a stimulus similar to but distinct from the conditioned stimulus.

general fertility rate the average number of live births per 1,000 females in their reproductive years (in the U.S., women 15 to 44).

generative cell a cell in the microgametophyte of a seed plant, capable of dividing to form two sperm cells.

generator potential in sensory receptors, depolarizations that differ from action potentials in that they may be graded in intensity.

generic name 1. the first part of a scientific name as in the binomial system. 2. a group of closely related and ecologically similar species, always italicized and capitalized.

gene amplification the presence in the genome of many copies of a specific gene, particularly where that gene's product is needed in large quantities.

gene sequencing determining the specific sequence of nucleotides in a gene.

gene splicing using recombinant DNA techniques to insert selected DNA fragments or genes into foreign strands of DNA or bacterial plasmids.

genetic code the specific groupings of nucleotides in DNA and RNA that specify the order of amino acids in a polypeptide or protein.

genetic continuity in generation after generation of cells and individuals of a species the preservation of the specific genetic code through preciseness in the processes of replication, mitosis, and meiosis.

genetic drift in population genetics, changes in gene frequencies through chance rather than through natural selection. See also *founder effect* and *bottleneck*.

genetic engineering modern techniques of gene management; including gene cloning, gene splicing, amino acid, DNA and RNA sequencing, and gene synthesis.

genetic equilibrium the genetic state of a population wherein the frequency of certain alleles remains constant generation after generation.

genetic recombination the exchange and subsequent recombination of genes as in crossing over in meiosis I.

genetics 1. the science of heredity, dealing with the resemblances and differences of related organisms resulting from the interaction of their genes and the environment. 2. the study of the structure, function, and transmission of genes.

genital tubercle (jen′ə təl tyōōb′er kəl) in the sexually undifferentiated mammalian embryo, a structure that, in the male, will form the head and shaft of the penis, and in the female, the *glans clitoris* and the *labia majora*.

genome (jə nōm′) the full haploid complement of genetic information of a diploid organism, usually viewed as a property of a species.

genotype 1. the genetic constitution of an organism (specific genes present). 2. *total genotype*, the sum total of genetic information of an organism.

genus in taxonomy, a major subdivision of a family, consisting of one or more species.

geotaxis (jē′ō tak sis) oriented movement of a motile organism toward or away from a gravitational force.

geotropism (jē′ot′rə priz′əm). See *gravitropism*.

germinal epithelium (jėr′mə nəl ep′ə thē lē əm) the epithelium of the gonads, which through mitosis gives rise to gametocytes, i.e., sperm and eggs.

germ layer any of the three layers of cells formed at gastrulation: *ectoderm, endoderm*, and *mesoderm*.

germ theory the proposal by Pasteur and others that bacteria were the primary cause of disease.

gibberellin (jib′ə rel′ən) any of a family of plant growth hormones that control cell elongation, bud development, differentiation and other growth effects.

gills 1. in fungi, the thin, flattened structures on the underside of a mushroom (basidiocarp) that bear the spore-forming basida. 2. in animals, a thin-walled organ of great surface area, for obtaining oxygen from water.

gill arches also called *pharyngeal arches*. 1. in fish, a row of bony curved bars extending vertically between the gill slits on either side of the pharynx, supporting the gills. 2. in land vertebrate embryos, a row of similar rudimentary ridges that give rise to jaw, tongue, and ear bones.

gill chamber in fishes, one of the two chambers housing the gills, covered by a bony flap, the *operculum*.

gill slit a chordate characteristic, permanent openings into the pharyngeal cavity of primitive chordates; associated with gills in fishes and represented only as transitory structures in the embryos of terrestrial vertebrates; also called *pharyngeal gill slits*.

ginkgo (gingki′gō) a plant of the division Ginkgophyta.

glans the enlarged vascular, sensitive body forming the end of the penis.

glandular epithelium simple columnar epithelial tissue that lines glands and the intestine, specializing in synthesis and secretion.

glial cells (glē′əl) numerous nonconducting supporting cells of the central nervous system that may play some role in information storage; also called *neuroglia*.

gliding joint a skeletal joint in which the articulating surfaces glide over one another without twisting.

globulin (glob′yə lin) any of a class of globular proteins occurring in plant and animal tissues and in blood.

glomerulus (glə mer′ə ləs) (*pl.* glomeruli) the tuft or mass of capillaries within Bowman's capsule.

glucagon (glü′kə gon) a polypeptide hormone secreted by the pancreatic islets of Langerhans, whose action increases the blood glucose level by stimulating the breakdown of glycogen in the liver.

gluconeogenesis (gloo′kō nē′o′jen′i sis) in the liver, a biochemical pathway in which, at the expense of ATP lactate from active muscle is converted back to glucose or glycogen.

glucose a six-carbon sugar, occurring in an open chain form or either of two ring forms; the subunit of many carbohydrate polymers; also called *dextrose, blood sugar, corn sugar,* and *grape sugar*.

glue cell a glandular, thread-bearing cell, found only in ctenophores, used to capture prey by adhesion.

glycerol (glis′ə rōl′) the three-carbon backbone with a hydroxyl group on each carbon; a component of neutral fats and of phospholipids.

glycogen (glī′kə jən) animal starch, a highly branched polysaccharide consisting of alpha glucose subunits; a storage carbohydrate in the liver and muscles of animals.

glycolysis (glī kol′ə sis) the enzymatic anaerobic breakdown of glucose in cells yielding ATP (from ADP), pyruvate, and NADH.

glycolytic pathway the sequence of enzymes and reactions responsible for the conversion of glucose to pyruvate and for the accompanying substrate level phosphorylation.

glycoprotein any of a group of complex proteins containing a carbohydrate combined with a simple protein.

gnetophyte (net′ə fīt) a plant of the division Gnetophyta.

goblet cells a mucus-secreting epithelial cell; common in the lining of the respiratory system.

golden brown alga any of the single-celled and colonial algae of the phylum Chrysophyta, found in both marine and fresh waters, deriving its color from carotenoid pigments.

Golgi body (gōl′jē) a membraneous organelle found especially in the cytoplasm of secretory cells, involved in the packaging of cell products from the endoplasmic reticulum into secretion granules; also called *Golgi complex* or *Golgi apparatus*.

gonadotropin (gō nad′ə trō′pin) a hormone that stimulates growth or activity in the gonads; in vertebrates, a specific peptide hormone of the anterior pituitary.

G₁ (gap one) in the cell cycle, the first part of interphase, during which the cell doubles in size.

gonorrhea a sexually transmitted bacterial disease caused by the diplococcus *Neisseria gonorrhoeae*.

gradualism the Darwinian proposal that the pace of evolution is slow but steady with an ongoing accumulation of minor changes leading eventually to the formation of new species; compare *punctuated equilibrium*.

granum (grā′nəm) (*pl.,* grana) a stack of thylakoid disks in chloroplast.

grassland one of the natural biomes of the earth, characterized by perennial grasses, limited seasonal rainfall, and great numbers of herbivorous mammals, birds, and insects.

gravitropism (grav′i trō piz əm) in plants, a growth response to gravity.

gray matter a butterfly-shaped region within the spinal cord, composed of cell bodies of interneurons and motor neurons; the cerebral cortex.

green algae any algae of the phylum Chlorophyta, biochemically similar to plants.

greenhouse effect the warming principle of greenhouses, in which high-energy solar rays enter easily, while less energetic heat waves are not radiated outward; now especially applied to the analogous effect of increasing atmospheric concentrations of carbon dioxide through the burning of fossil fuels and forests.

gross productivity (GP) the amount of biochemical energy captured by photosynthesis in a particular area per unit of time.

ground meristem the primary plant tissue from which the ground tissues, collenchyma, parenchyma, and sclerenchyma, are developed.

growth increase in size through cell division and/or enlargement.

growth hormone (GH) 1. a polypeptide hormone of the anterior pituitary that regulates growth invertebrates. 2. any hormone that regulates growth, e.g., auxin or gibberellin in plants.

G₂ (gap two) in the cell cycle, a period of renewed protein synthesis during which tubulin is made.

guanine (G) (gwä′nēn) one of the nitrogenous bases of DNA and RNA.

guard cell in a plant leaf or stem, one of a pair of crescent-shaped cells of a stoma whose changes in turgor regulate the size of stomatal opening.

gustation (gəs tā′shən) the sense of taste; the act of tasting.

gutation (gə tā′shən) the normal exuding of moisture from the tip of a leaf or stem in certain plants, presumably due to root pressure.

gymnosperm (jim′nə spėrm′) a nonflowering seed plant of the group Gymnospermae, producing seeds that lack friut; included are conifers, cycads, gnetophytes, and ginkgos.

gynoecium (ji nē′sē əm) the pistil, or the pistils collectively of a flower.

hair cell. See *organ of Corti*.

half-life in a radioisotope, the time it takes for half of the atoms in a sample to undergo spontaneous decay.

halobacteria a photosynthetic bacteria that thrives in a salty environment, capturing light energy with bacteriorhodopsin.

haploid (n) (hap′loid) *adj.* halved; having a single set of genes and chromosomes; compare *diploid, polyploid*.

Hardy-Weinberg Law in population genetics, a statement of the genotype frequencies expected given allele frequencies in a population of randomly mating diploid individuals.; also called *binomial law*.

Haversian system (hə vėr′shən) a Haversion canal together with its surrounding concentrically arranged layers of bone, canaliculi, lacunae, and osteocytes.

HCE. See *human chorionic gonadotropin*.

heavy chain the longer pair of polypeptides in an immunoglobulin.

helicase (hel′ə kās′) also called *unwinding enzyme;* one of the enzymes required to break the hydrogen bonds of the double helix of DNA during replication.

heliozoan (hē′lē ə zo′ən) a protist of a group in the class Sarcodina, consisting of free-living, freshwater forms looking rather like tiny suns, with multiple thin, stiff, radiating pseudopods.

helper T-cell a cell that activates elements of the immune system.

heme group an iron-containing, oxygen-binding, porphyrin ring present in all hemoglobin chains and in myoglobin.

hemichordate (hem′i kôr′dāt) any member of the phylum Hemichordata.

hemizygous (hem′ə zī′gəs) *adj.*, the condition of x-linked genes in males, which are neither homozygous nor heterozygous.

hemocyanin (hem′ə sī′ə nin) a copper-containing respiratory pigment occurring in solution in the blood plasma of certain invertebrates.

hemoglobin a protein, a respiratory pigment consisting of four polypeptide chains, each associated wtih a heme (iron-containing) group.

hemophilia also called *bleeder's disease;* uncontrolled bleeding in humans due to the lack of a necessary blood-clotting constituent; a genetic disease caused by recessive alleles at either of the two sex-linked loci.

hepatic portal circuit in the circulatory system, the assemblage of vessels that direct blood from the intestine to the liver.

hermaphroditic (hər maf′rə di′tik) *adj.,* pertaining to an individual animal or plant with both male and female reproductive organs.

herpes simplex II a highly contagious, sexually transmitted virus, causing intermittent outbreaks of painful, infective blisters on the mouth and genitals, followed by a period of remission.

heterogamete (het′ər ə gam′ēt) male and female gametes differing in form, size, or structure. See *isogametes.*

heteromorphic (het′ər ə môr′fik) *adj.,* dissimilar in shape, structure, or magnitude.

heterosporous (het′ər ə spôr′əs) in plants, producing morphologically distinct spores, microspores, and megaspores.

heterotherm animals that periodically switch from homeothermy to poikilothermy (insects).

heterotroph (het′ər ə trof) an organism that requires organic compounds as an energy and/or carbon source (i.e., all animals and fungi).

heterozygous (het′ər ə zī gəs) *adj.,* having two different alleles, commonly a dominant and a recessive, for a specific trait.

Hfr strain (high frequency of recombination) strain of bacteria with a strong tendency to conjugate and transfer the main chromosome.

high-energy bond a molecular bond in ATP and ADP that releases a comparatively large amount of energy when it is cleaved.

hindbrain 1. the posterior of the three primary divisions of the embryonic vertebrate brain. 2. the parts of the adult brain derived from the embryonic hindbrain, including the *cerebellum, pons,* and *medulla oblongata.*

hindgut the lower part of the embryonic alimentary canal from which the colon and rectum develop.

hinge joint a joint that moves in one plane like a door hinge, e.g., the knee.

hippocampus (hip′ə kam′pəs) a long, curved ridge of gray and white matter on the inner surface of each lateral ventricle of the brain, involved in memory consolidation, visual memory, and other functions.

histamine (his′tə mēn) an amino compound released in allergic reactions that dilates blood vessels and reduces blood pressure.

histocompatibility protein a protein which is highly specific for each individual organism, which is the basis for organ or tissue transplant rejection.

histone any of a class of protein substances, as globin, having marked basic properties.

holdfast a rhizoidal base of a seaweed, serving to anchor it to the ocean floor.

homeostatic mechanism (hō′mē ə stat′ik mek′ə nīz əmz) any mechanism involved in maintaining a stable internal equilibrium, especially one involving self-correcting negative feedback.

homeostasis (hō′me ə stā′sis) the maintenance of a stable internal environment in the body of a higher animal through interacting physiological processes involving negative feedback control.

homeotherm an organism capable of maintaining a stable high internal body temperature; also called *warm-blooded.*

homologue either of the two members of each pair of chromosomes in a diploid cell.

homologous (ho mol′ə gəs) *adj.,* 1. similar because of a common evolutionary origin. 2. derived from a common embryological source, i.e., the *glans clitoris* and the *glans penis.*

homospory (hom′ə spôr′e) in plants, a primitive condition in which only one form of spore is produced.

homozygous (hō′mə zī gəs) *adj.,* having identical pairs of alleles for any given pair of hereditary characteristics.

hormone a chemical messenger transmitted from one part of the organism to another, producing a specific effect on target cells.

humoral immune response the immune response carried out by immunoglobulins, which find and immobilize matching antigens in the body.

Huntington's disease a lethal hereditary disease of the nervous system developing in adult life and attributed to a dominant allele. Formerly, *Huntington's chorea.*

hybridization sexual reproduction between different species.

hydrogen bond a weak electrostatic attraction between the positively polar hydrogen of a side group and a negatively polar oxygen of another side group.

hydrologic cycle the cyclic evaporation and condensation of the earth's waters, driven by heat in the atmosphere including the biogeochemical cycling of water through photosynthesis and perspiration; also called *water cycle.*

hydrolytic cleavage the breaking of a covalent bond with hydrozide and hydrogen of water joining the subunits; also called *hydrolysis.*

hydrolysis. See *hydrolytic cleavage.*

hydrophilic *adj.,* "water-loving"; pertaining to the tendency of polar molecules or their polar side groups to mix readily with water.

hydrophobic *adj.,* "water-fearing"; pertaining to the tendency of nonpolar molecules or their nonpolar side groups to dissolve readily in organic solvents but not in water; resisting wetting.

hydrostatic pressure the pressure exerted in all directions within a liquid at rest.

hydrostatic skeleton a supporting and locomotory mechanism involving a fluid confined in a space within layers of muscle and connective tissue; movement occurring when muscle contractions increase or decrease the hydrostatic pressure of the fluid.

hydroxyl (hī drok′sil) *adj.,* containing the univalent group, –OH.

hymen also *maidenhead;* a fold of thick mucous membrane partially closing the orifice of the vagina, especially in virgins.

hyperthyroidism an abnormal condition caused by an excess of circulating thyroid hormone.

hypertonic *adj.,* having a higher osmotic potential (e.g., higher solute concentration and lower water potential) than the cytoplasm of a living cell (or other reference solution).

hypha (hī′fə) (*pl.,* hyphae) one of the individual filaments that make up a fungal mycelium.

hypocotyl (hīp ə kot′ l) the part of a plant embryo below the point of attachment of the cotyledon.

hypocotyl hook (hī pə kot′l hůk) in some seedlings, the curved region of the hypocotyl that acts as a bumper as the seedling emerges from the soil.

hypolimnion (hī′pō lim′nē on′) in lakes, the layer of water below the thermocline.

hypothalamus (hī′pə thal′ə məs) the region that lies in front of the thalamus in the forebrain; it regulates the internal environment, pituitary secretions, and some of the basic drives.

hypothesis a conjecture set forth as a possible explanation for some observation or phenomenon and that serves as a basis for experimentation or argument; compare *theory.*

hypothyroidism a condition caused by abnormally low levels of circulating thyroid hormones.

hypotonic *adj.,* having a lower osmotic potential (e.g., lower solute concentration and greater water potential) than the cytoplasm of a living cell (or other reference solution).

H zone clearer, centermost zone of the relaxed contractile unit consisting of myosin alone.

I band one of the striations of striated

muscle, of variable width, corresponding to the distance between the ends of the myosin filaments of adjacent units.

immune system in vertebrates, widely dispersed tissues that respond to the presence of the antigens of invading microorganisms or foreign chemical substances.

immunoglobulin (i myōo'nō glob'yə lən) a protein antibody produced by B-cells in response to specific foreign substances; it consists of four subunits that are joined through disulfide linkages and have specific antigen-binding sites.

immunological tolerance the process by which the immune system becomes inhibited from reacting against "self."

implantation in mammalian reproduction, the invasion of the uterine endometrium and attachment therein of the mammalian embryo (blastocyst).

imprinting in behavior, learning occurring rapidly and very early in life, characterized chiefly by resistance to extinction or forgetfulness.

inclusive fitness increasing the frequency of one's genes in the next generation through reproduction by relatives.

incomplete gut a digestive system consisting of a blind sac, as in flatworms.

incomplete penetrance (pen'ə trəns) a variability in the expression of a dominant allele where it may not be expressed or may be only partially expressed (i.e., polydactyly).

independent assortment the rule which indicates that the segregation of one pair of unlinked factors, or alleles, has no influence over the way any pair segregates.

indeterminate cleavage in newly forming cells in early animal embryos, the retention of developmental flexibility. Also *determinate development*. See *determinate cleavage*.

indeterminate life span the potentially endless life span in organisms such as perennial plants, where new growth is ongoing.

induced fit the proposition that enzymatic actions proceed because their active site forms an inexact fit with their substrate, producing physical stress.

inductive reasoning the logical process that moves from the specific to the general, reaching a conclusion based on a number of observations; compare *deductive reasoning*.

indusium (in dōo'zē əm) in ferns, a covering over the sorus (spore forming organ).

inhibiting hormone a chemical messenger produced by the hypothalamus that inhibits the release of the major pituitary hormones.

inhibitory neuron a nerve cell that functions by increasing the polarity of the next nerve cell, thus inhibiting it from firing.

initiation the first steps in the translation of the genetic code; the beginning of polypeptide synthesis.

initiation complex the physical association of a messenger RNA, two ribosomal subunits and methionine-charged transfer RNA required to begin synthesis of a polypeptide.

innate releasing mechanism (IRM) an ethological term referring to a neural mechanism that produces a specific behavioral event when triggered by a particular stimulus from the environment.

inner cell mass in a mammalian *blastocyst*, the portion that is destined to become the embryo proper.

insect any animal of the class Insecta.

insertion 1. in genetics, the addition of extra genetic material into a chromosome, gene, or other DNA sequence. 2. in anatomy, the distal attachment of a tendon or muscle, i.e., the attachment on the part to be moved; compare *origin*.

inspiratory center part of the respiratory control center in the medulla oblongata, rhythmically stimulates inspiration by causing contraction in the diaphragm and rib muscles.

instinct any inherent, unlearned behavioral pattern that is functional the first time it happens that can occur in animals reared in total isolation.

insulin a polypeptide hormone secreted by the islet of Langerhans of the pancreas, whose principal action is to facilitate the transport of glucose into cells; it has many other functions as well.

intercalated disk in heart muscle, the highly convoluted double plasma membrane between two adjacent cells in heart muscle.

interferon a cellular substance that interferes with viral replication.

interleukin-1 (in'tər lōo'kən) a powerful activating substance secreted by an antigen-presenting macrophage, which causes a helper T-cell to seek out any inactive lymphocytes and arouse them with interleukin-2.

interleukin-2 a lymphokine secreted by helper T-cells to arouse inactive lymphocytes.

internal ear the portion of the ear enclosed within the temporal bone; included are the three *semicircular canals*, the *cochlea*, and the *round* and *oval windows*; compare *external ear, middle ear*.

internal fertilization in animals, fertilization involving copulation, in which sperm release and fertilization occur within female.

interneuron a neuron of the central nervous system that makes connection between sensory and motor neurons.

interphase all of the cell cycle between successive mitoses; included are G_1, S, and G_2 *phases*.

interspecific *adj.*, pertaining to interaction between species.

interspecific cooperation cooperation between members of different species.

interstitial cells (in'tər stit'chəl) cells of the testis that have an endocrine function.

interstitial cell-stimulating hormone (ICSH) in males, an anterior pituitary hormone (identical to LH) that stimulates testosterone production in the interstitial cells of the testis.

intervening sequence also called *intron*; nonexpressed portions of messenger RNA, removed from the message prior to translation; compare *expressed sequence (exon)*.

intervertebral disc one of the tough, elastic, fibrous disks situated between adjacent vertebrae.

intrauterine device (IUD) a plastic device, sometimes containing copper, that is inserted into the uterus as a means of preventing conception.

intrinsic heart rhythm rhythmic contraction of the heart originating through the inherent capacity of cardiac muscle to contract without outside influence.

introitus (in troy'təs) the external opening of the vagina.

intron. See *intervening sequence*.

inversion the transposition of a portion of a chromosome following breakage and repair, altering the relative order of gene loci.

invertebrate any animal lacking a vertebral column.

involuntary muscle. See *smooth muscle*.

ion any electrostatically charged atom or molecule.

ion channels in the neural membrane, sodium and potassium (and chloride) channels that, through opening and closing of gates, selectively admit or reject ions.

ionic bond a chemical attraction between ions of opposite charge.

ionizing the dissociating of a molecule into oppositely charged ions in solution.

ionizing radiation radiation, including x-ray and gamma rays, energetic enough to create free radicals within the cell; may cause genetic damage.

islets of Langerhans clumps of alph, beta, and delta endocrine cells in the *pancreas*, which secrete *insulin, glucagon*, and *somatostatin* respectively.

isogametes (ī'sə gam'ēts) gametes that are identical in size and appearance, such as the (+) and (−) isogametes of *Chlamydomonas*.

isotonic *adj.*, having the same osmotic potential (e.g., same solute concentration and water potential) as the cytoplasm of a living cell or other reference solution.

isotope a particular form of an element in terms of the number of neurons in the nucleus; see also *radioisotopes*.

J-shaped curve a plot of population growth where growth approaches the biotic potential of the species and generally exceeds the environment's carrying capacity; compare *S-shaped curve*.

karyotype (kar'ē ō tīp) a mounted display of enlarged light photomicrographs of the chromosomes of an individual, arranged in order of decreasing size.

keel (kēl) the enlarged breastbone to which the flight muscles of birds are attached.

kidney in vertebrates, paired excretory organs serving to excrete nitrogenous wastes and regulate water and ion balances.

kinesis (ki nē′sis) in behavior, responsive movement with the vigor of the movement being related to the strength of the stimulus.

kinetic energy energy associated with motion (accomplishing work).

kingdom the largest taxonomic category.

Krause corpuscle a sensory receptor in the skin that responds to temperature changes; also called *Krause end bulb*.

K-selection reproductive strategy of a species adapted to a fairly constant environment, with a small number of offspring and considerable parental care; compare *r-selection*.

labia majora in human females, the outer, fatty, often hairy pair of folds bounding the vulva.

labia minora the smaller inner folds of skin that border the vagina.

lac operon (an inducible operon) in the chromosome of *E. coli*, composed of genes that code for three lactose-metabolizing enzymes and the region that controls their transcription. See also *operon*.

lactose a digestive enzyme that hydrolyzes lactose to glucose and galactose.

lactation the secretion of milk.

lacteal lymphatic vessels of the intestinal villi.

lactose a disaccharide consisting of glucose and galactose subunits; also called *milk sugar*.

lacuna (lə kyōō′nə) (*pl.,* lacunae) a minute cavity in bone or cartilage that holds an osteocyte or chondrocyte.

lagging strand also called *discontinuous strand* and *following region;* in DNA replication, the S′ end of a DNA strand, where nucleotides are first assembled into Okazaki fragments and then added in using the enzyme ligase.

lamella (lə mel′ə) (*pl.,* lamellae) 1. within chloroplasts, membranes that extend between grana (stacked thylakoids). 2. one of the bony concentric layers (ringlike in cross-section) that surround a Haversian canal in bone.

lamprey any eellike, marine or freshwater jawless fish, having a circular, suctioning mouth with horny teeth for boring into the flesh of other fish.

larva in animals, an early, active, feeding stage of development during which the offspring may be quite unlike the adult.

larvaceae (lar′vā′see āy) a class of urochordates in which a larval-like state is retained although sexual maturity occurs. The process, called neotony, suggests how the chordate line may be evolved.

larynx in terrestrial vertebrates, the expanded part of the respiratory passage at the top of the trachea.

lateral bud primordia one of the patches of shoot meristem which give rise to branches.

lateral line organ in nearly all fish, a canal-like sensory organ containing a line of pitted openings and believed to be responsive to water currents and vibrations; distantly homologous to the mammalian inner ear.

lateral root in plants, a root which originates in the cells of the pericycle well above the root tip, growing perpendicular to the primary root.

law a statement of a relationship or a sequence of phenomena invariable under the same conditions.

leading strand also called *continuous strand* and *leading region;* in DNA replication, the 3′ end of a DNA strand, where nucleotides are added one at a time to the growing strand.

leaf hairs hairlike projections from leaf epidermal cells, generally those on the underside of the leaf.

leaf mesophyll cell (mes′ə′ fil) photosynthetic parenchymal cells within the leaf.

learning in animal behavior, the process of acquiring a persistent change in a behavioral response as a result of experience.

left atrium the chamber of the heart which receives oxygenated blood from the lungs and pumps it to the left ventricle.

left ventricle the chamber of the heart which receives oxygenated blood from the left atrium and pumps it to the body via the arteries.

lesion random spontaneous changes in DNA, subject to repair.

leukocyte a vertebrate white blood cell, it aids in resisting infection.

leukoplast a colorless body in plant cells that stores proteins, lipids, and starch.

lichen (lī′kən) a combination of a fungus and an alga growing in a symbiotic relationship.

ligament a tough, flexible, but inelastic band of connective tissue that connects bones or supports an organ in place; compare *tendon*.

ligase (lig′ās) an enzyme that joins broken DNA strands or Okazaki fragments; used in gene-splicing technology.

light chain the shorter two of the four polypeptides making up an immunoglobin.

light harvesting antenna part of a photosystem; clustered chlorophyll *a*, chlorophyll *b*, carotene molecules, and an associated reaction center; functions in absorbing light energy.

light-independent reaction the part of photosynthesis not immediately requiring light; specifically the fixation of CO_2 into carbohydrate using the NADPH and ATP produced by the light reactions; also called *Calvin cycle* and *dark reaction*.

light reaction the part of photosynthesis directly dependent on the capture of photons, specifically the photolysis of water, electron and proton transport, and the chemiosmotic synthesis of ATP and NADPH; also called *light dependent reaction*.

lignin (lig′nin) an amorphous substance that helps give wood its rigidity.

limbic system a region of the brain concerned primarily with emotions.

limnetic zone (lim′net′ik) the open waters of a lake beyond the littoral zone, but including only the depths through which light penetrates and in which photosynthesis can occur.

limnologist (lim nol′ə jəst) an ecologist who specializes in the study of interaction in the fresh waters.

linkage group also called *linked genes;* a group of gene loci located on the same chromosome; ultimately an entire chromosome.

linked *adj.,* of two gene loci, not segregating independently.

lipase (lī′pas) a fat-digesting enzyme of the stomach or pancreas.

lipid an organic molecule that tends to be more soluble in nonpolar solvents (such as petroleum products) than in polar solvents (such as water.)

lipoprotein any of the class of proteins that contain a lipid combined with a simple protein.

littoral zone 1. a coastal region including both the land along the coast, the water along the shore, and the intertidal area. 2. a similar area in lakes.

liver an accessory digestive organ that serves many metabolic functions including glycogen storage, detoxification, production of blood proteins, food storage, and production of bile.

lobe-finned fishes any fish with fleshy pectoral and pelvic fins, including lung fishes and crossopterygians.

logistic growth curve. See S-*shaped growth curve*.

long-day plants plants that begin flowering at some specific time before the summer solstice when day length exceeds night; flowering is triggered by a critical established period of darkness; compare *short-day plants*.

long-term memory 1. learning that persists more than a few hours, the memory trace of which is physically located in a different part of the brain than short term memory. 2. the part of the brain and the general neural function with which such persistent memory traces are associated.

loop of Henle the prominent u-shaped loop in the nephron of the mammalian kidney.

lower epidermis in plants, an outer layer of leaf cells, commonly containing numerous stomata and projecting leaf hairs.

lumen the cavity or channel of a hollow tubular organ or organelle.

lung in land vertebrates, one of a pair of compound, saclike organs that function in the exchange of gases between the atmosphere and the bloodstream.

lung fish any fish of the group having a functional, lunglike air bladder as well as gills.

luteinizing hormone (LH) a pituitary hormone that causes ovulation and stimulates hormone production in the corpus luteum.

lymph watery intercellular fluid in the lymphatic system.

lymphatic system the system of lymphatic vessels and ducts and lymph nodes that serves to redistribute excess tissue fluids and to combat infections.

lymph node a cluster of cells and blind channels in the lymphatic system in which foreign cells and material are attacked by the immune system. Commonly called *lymph glands*.

lymphocytes any of the several varieties of similar-looking leukocytes involved in the production of antibodies and in other aspects of the immune responses; see also *B-cell, T-cell*.

lymphokine a lymphocyte activator channel.

Lyon effect the mosaiclike gene expression of X-linked genes in human females resulting from the random inactivation of one X chromosome in each cell of the human female embryo.

lysis (lī'səs) the destruction or lysing of a cell by rupture of the plasma membrane.

lysogenic cycle the cycle during which a bacteriophage chromosome is incorporated into the bacterial host chromosome, together with mechanisms preventing further infection and lysis; in later cell generations, the incorporated DNA may excise, replicate, and eventually cause cell lysis. See also *lytic cycle*.

lysosome (lī'sə som) a small, membrane-bounded cytoplasmic organelle, generally containing strong digestive enzymes or other cytotoxic materials.

lytic cycle the short cycle following bacteriophage invasion during which viral replication, capsid synthesis, viral assembly and cell lysis occur, the latter releasing new infective phage particles. See also *lysogenic cycle*.

macromolecule any large biological polymer, such as a protein, nucleic acid, or complex polysaccharide (for example, cellulose, or glycogen).

macronucleus the larger of the two nuclei of *Paramecium* and certain other ciliate protozoans, carrying somatic line DNA; compare *micronucleus*.

macronutrient a plant nutrient required in relatively substantial quantities, e.g., nitrogen, phosphorus, potassium, sulfur, magnesium, and calcium. Compare *micronutrient*.

macrophage (mak'rō fāj) a large phagocyte, i.e., leukocyte, previously a monocyte.

madreporite (mad'rə pōr'īt). See *water vascular system*.

male gametophyte in seed plant reproduction, the pollen grain.

Malpighian tubules (mal pig'ē ən) numerous blind, hollow tubular structures that empty into the insect midget and function as a nitrogenous excretory system.

maltose a disaccharide consisting of two glucose subunits in an apha linkage; a digestion product of starch.

mammal any member of the vertebrate class Mammalia, most of which are characterized by the presence of hair, a muscular diaphragm, milk secretion, and placental development.

mandibulate (man di'byū lāt) any member of the subphylum Mandibulata containing jawed arthropods, including crustaceans, insects, centipedes, and millipedes.

mantle in mollusks, a fleshy covering that secretes material to form the external shell.

marsupial (mär sü'pe əl) a mammal of the subclass Metatheria; the female has a pouch (marsupium); included are the kangaroo, wombat, koala, Tasmanian devil, opossum, and wallaby.

mating types genetically different clones or strains of fungi, protists, and certain plant algae, where sexual reproduction can occur between clones (mating types) but not within a clone; males and females do not exist.

mechanist one who believes biological phenomena, and everything else in the universe, can be explained by physical laws; compare *vitalism*.

mechanoreceptor a sensory neuron specialized in detecting touch or pressure against the skin or hair.

medulla the inner portion of a gland or organ; compare *cortex*.

medulla oblongata a part of the brainstem developed from the posterior portion of the hindbrain and tapering into the spinal cord.

medusa the motile, free-swimming jelly fish form of coelenterate; compare *polyp*.

megagametophyte the female gametophyte produced from a megaspore in flowering plants. See also *embryo sac*.

megaspore in flowering plants, the "female" spore, a product of meiosis that gives rise to the megagametophyte.

megaspore mother cell in flowering plants, a large diploid cell in the ovule that will give rise to the megaspore by meiosis.

meiosis in all sexually reproducing eukaryotes, the process of chromosome reduction, in which a diploid cell or diploid cell nucleus is transformed into four haploid cells or four haploid nuclei (the usu-

al manner of sperm and egg production); also called *reduction division*.

meiospore any haploid spore produced by meiosis.

Meissner's corpuscle (mīz nərz) in mammals, a small touch-responsive neural end organ.

memory cell a mature, long-lived, B- or T-cell lymphocyte, specialized in retaining specific antigen information.

Mendel's first law the law of paired factors and segregation; includes the concepts of paired factors, segregation, chance recombination, and dominance.

Mendel's second law the inheritance of one pair of factors (alleles) in an individual will occur independently of the simultaneous inheritance of a second pair of factors (alleles) (except where gene linkage groups occur).

meninges (mi nin'jēz) the tough, protective, connective tissues covering the brain and spinal cord.

menstrual cycle the cycle of hormonal and physiological events and changes involving growth of the uterine endometrium, ovulation, and the subsequent breakdown and discharge of the endometrium in menstruation (menses); the cycle averages 28 days; also *ovarian cycle*.

meristem also called *apical meristem*; the undifferentiated tissue at the stem and root tip that contributes cells for primary growth.

mensenteries (mes'ən ter'ēz) folds of the membrane which hold the organs of the human digestive system in place, carrying blood vessels, nerves, and lymphatic vessels.

mesoderm in animal development, the middle layer of the three primary germ layers of the gastrula, giving rise in development to the skeletal, muscular, vascular, renal and connective tissues and to the inner layer of skin and the epithelium of the coelom (peritoneum).

mesoglea (mes'ə glē'ə) the loose, gelatinous middle layer of the bodies of coelenterates between the outer ectoderm and the inner endoderm.

mesosome in many bacteria, an inward extension of the plasma membrane that forms a spherical membranous network.

messenger RNA (mRNA) in eukaryotes, RNA directly transcribed from a gene modified and transported to the cytoplasm; specifying a polypeptide sequence.

metabolic pathways a sequence of enzymatic reactions through which a metabolite passes before the formation of the final product or products.

metamorphosis a change or successive changes of form during the postembryonic or embryonic growth of an animal; in insects, the transition from egg to larva, to pupa, and adult.

metaphase the stage of mitosis or meiosis in which the chromosomes are brought to a well-defined plane in the middle of the mitotic spindle prior to separation in anaphase.

metaphase plate the equatorial plane of the mitotic spindle on which the centromeres are oriented in mitosis.

metastasis (mə tas′tə sis) the spread of malignant cells to other parts of the body by way of the blood vessels, lymphatics, or membranous surfaces.

metazoa all animals other than sponges; that is, all animals whose bodies are composed of cells differentiated into tissues and organs and who usually have a digestive cavity lined with specialized cells.

methanogen (me than′ə jən) a methane-generating archaebacterium.

microfilament a submicroscopic filament in the cytoskeleton, involved in cell movement and shape.

micronucleus in ciliate protists, the smaller of the two nuclei and the one carrying germ-like DNA; compare *macronucleus*.

micronutrient an element necessary for plant growth but needed only in extremely small quantities; compare *macronutrient*.

micropyle in seed plants, a minute opening in the integument of an ovule through which sperm enter.

microspore in seed plants, one of the four haploid cells formed from meiosis of the microspore mother cell; it undergoes mitosis and differentiation to form a pollen grain.

microspore mother cell in the anther of a flowering plant, the diploid cells that will undergo meiosis to form the haploid microspores.

microtrabecular lattice in the cell cytoplasm, a weblike system of microtubules and microfilaments that form a cytoskeletal framework upon which many organelles are suspended.

microtubular organizing center (MOC) in certain mitotic cells an amorphous region surrounding the centrioles, believed to be responsible for assembly and disassembly of microtubular proteins into spindle fibers or microtubules.

microtubule a cytoplasmic hollow tubule composed of spherical molecules of tubulin, found in the cytoskeleton, the spindle, centrioles, basal bodies, cilia, and flagella.

microvilla 1. tiny, fingerlike outpocketings of the cell membrane of various epithelial secretory or absorbing cells, such as those of the kidney tubule epithelium and the intestinal epithelium. 2. cellular projections form in the placenta and containing capillaries.

midbrain 1. the middle of the three primary divisions of the vertebrate embryonic brain. 2. the parts of the adult brain derived from the embryonic midbrain.

middle ear the middle portion of the ear consisting of the tympanic membrane and an air filled chamber lined with mucus, which contains the malleus, incus, and stapes.

middle ear bones the *malleus, incus,* and *stapes.*

middle lamella a layer of cementing material between adjacent plant cell walls.

midgut 1. the middle part of the embryonic alimentary canal from which the intestines develop. 2. the central portion of the three-part insect gut.

midpiece the central region of a spermatozoan, containing the mitochondria and centriole.

midrib in plants, the large central vein of a dicot leaf, containing vascular and supporting fibrous tissue.

migration the act or process of moving periodically from one region to another, as in certain animals.

millipede a nonpoisonous, herbivorous, terrestrial anthropod of the class Diplopoda, with a long cylindrical, segmented body, and two pairs of legs per segment.

mineral nutrient an inorganic compound, element or ion needed for normal growth of all organisms.

mineralocorticoid (min′ə ral′ə kôr′ti koid) any mineral-regulating steroid hormone of the adrenal cortex.

minimal medium the least complex medium capable of sustaining the growth of a specific microorganism.

minimum mutation tree in systematics, a hypothetical phylogenic tree selected because it represents the smallest number of evolutionary changes needed to account for known relationships.

mitochondrian (*pl.,* mitochondria) self-replicating, membrane-bounded eukaryotic organelle, functions in oxidative respiration and chemiosmotic phosphorylation.

mitosis nuclear division in eukaryotes, involving chromosome condensation, spindle formation, precise alignment of centromeres, and the regular segregation of daughter chromosomes to produce identical daughter nuclei; followed by cytoplasmic division.

model a contrived biological mechanism that, when applied, is expected to yield data consistent with past observations; a biological hypothesis with mathematical predictions.

mole in chemistry, the quantity of a substance whose weight in grams is equal to the substance's molecular weight, or Avogadro's number: 6.023×10^{23} molecules of a substance; the combined atomic weights of all the atoms of a substance, expressed in grams.

molecular orbital the shell formed by the shared pair of electrons in a covalent bond.

molecule a unit of chemical substance consisting of atoms bound by covalent bonding.

molecular clock an analogy based on the proposition that the rates at which specific mutations occur is regular and clocklike and can thus be used to establish an evolutionary time framework.

mollusk any invertebrate of the phylum Mollusca, typically having a hard shell that wholly or partly encloses the soft, unsegmented body, such as the chitons, snails, bivalves, squids, etc.

molting. See *ecdysis*.

monosaccharide "single sugar"; the molecular carbohydrate subunit; a simple sugar (e.g., glucose, fructose).

monotreme (mon′ə trēm) a platypus, echidna, or extinct egg-laying mammal of the order Monotremata.

mons veneris (monz′ven′ər is) in women, a rounded usually hairy bulge of fatty tissue over the pubic symphysis and above the vulva.

morph one of the particular forms of an organism that exists in two or more distinct forms in a single population.

morphogenesis the emergence of final form and structure in the embryo.

morula an early embryonic state consisting of a ball of cells.

motor neuron a neuron that innervates muscle fibers; its impulses stimulating muscle contraction.

Monera (mə nir′ə) the kingdom of prokaryotes, comprised of the bacteria.

monoamine a brain neurotransmitter, composed of a single amino acid group, such as norepinephrine, dopamine, histamine, and serotonin.

monoclonal antibody a specific immunoglobin produced by hybrid cells artificially cloned in the laboratory.

monocot a flowering plant of the angiosperm class Monocotyledonae, characterized by producing seeds with one cotyledon; included are palms, grasses, orchids, lilies, irises, and others.

monocotyledon (mon′ə kot′l ē′dən). See *monocot*.

monocyte a large, phagocytic leukocyte, formed in bone marrow and in the spleen.

monophyletic *adj.,* of a taxonomic group, deriving entirely from a single ancestral species.

motor unit a motor neuron together with the muscle fibers it innervates, which contract as a unit.

M phase See *cell cycle*.

mucin (myoō′sin) any of a class of mucoproteins that bind water and form thick, slimy, viscid fluids in various secretions.

multiple alleles the alleles of a single gene locus when there are more than two alternatives in a population.

multiplicative law of probability in mathematical probability theory, the statement that the probability of two independent outcomes both occurring is equal to the product of their individual probabilities.

muscle a contractile tissue, in vertebrates including skeletal, smooth, and cardiac muscle.

muscle fiber in skeletal muscle, one of the multinucleate cells, which takes the form of a long contractile cylinder.

mutagen a chemical or physical agent that causes mutations.

mutation any abnormal, heritable change in genetic material.

mutualism a mutually beneficial association between different kinds of organisms; a form of symbiosis beneficial to both partners; compare *commensalism*, *parasitism*.

mutualistic symbiosis. See *mutualism*.

mycelium (*pl.*, mycelia) the mass of interwoven hyphae that forms the vegetative body of a fungus.

mycoplasma a tiny, nonmotile, wall-less bacterium of irregular shape, occurring as an intracellular parasite of animals and plants; smallest cellular organism.

mycorrhiza (mī′kō rī′zə) a mutualistic fungus-root association with the fungal mycelium either surrounding or penetrating the roots of a plant; also *mycorrhizal association*.

myelin a soft, white, somewhat fatty, material derived from plasma membrane, that forms a myelin sheath around certain nerve axons.

myelin sheath a fatty sheath surrounding the axons of some vertebrate neurons.

myocardial infarction the necrosis of the muscular substance of the heart caused by blood deprivation.

myofibril a tubular subunit of muscle fiber structure, consisting of many myofilaments organized into sacromeres, the contractile units.

myofilaments the highly organized fibrous proteins of striated muscle, including the thin, movable *actin myofilaments* and the thicker, stationary *myosin myofilaments*.

myosin a protein involved in cell movement and structure, especially in muscle cells; see also *myofilament*.

myosin cross bridge an ATP-activated, movable connection between myosin and actin which is responsible for muscle contractions.

myosin head a globular projection of the protein myosin, which forms the myosin cross bridge.

myotome 1. the portion of a vertebrate embryonic somite from which skeletal musculature is developed. 2. one of the muscular segments of the body wall of a fish or lancelet.

NAD (nicotinamide adenine dinucleotide) "nad"; a coenzyme that is an electron and hydrogen carrier in glycolysis and cell respiration.

NADP (nicotinamide adenine dinucleotide phosphate) "nad-phosphate"; a coenzyme which is an electron and hydrogen carrier in photosynthesis.

nasal epithelium. See *olfactory epithelium*.

natural killer cell (NK cell) a non-specific phagocyte that destroys cancerous and otherwise diseased cells.

natural selection the differential survival and reproduction in nature of organisms having different heritable characteristics, resulting in the perpetuation of those characteristics and/or organisms that are best adapted to a specific environment. Also called *survival of the fittest*.

navigation the act or process of finding one's way.

Neanderthal an extinct, highly variable type or race of *Homo sapiens* of the middle Paleolithic.

nectary a flower gland whose nectar secretions attract animal pollinators.

negative feedback. See *feedback*.

nematocyst one of the minute stinging cells of the coelenterates, consisting of a hollow thread coiled within a capsule and an external hair trigger.

nematode an unsegmented worm of the phylum or class Nematoda, having an elongated, cylindrical body; roundworm.

nephridium (*pl.*, nephridia) an annelid excretory organ, occurring paired in each body segment and typically consisting of a ciliated funnel and a duct to the exterior.

nephron a single excretory unit of a kidney, consisting of a glomerulus, Bowman's capsule, proximal convoluted tubule, loop of Henle, and distal convoluted tubule.

neritic province (ni rit′ik) the coastal sea from the low-tide line to a depth of 100 fathoms; generally, waters of the continental shelf.

nerve a number of neurons following a common pathway, covered by a protective sheath and supporting tissue.

nerve cell. See *neuron*.

nervous system the brain, spinal cord, nerves, ganglia, and the neural parts of receptor organs, considered as an integrated whole.

net community productive (NCP) in ecology, the rate at which a biotic community gains in biomass or stored energy; determined by subtracting the total energy released in respiration from the total energy incorporated.

net productivity (NP) in ecology, the rate at which producers store energy or biomass; determined by subtracting the rate of energy release or biomass during respiration from the rate of energy or biomass incorporation.

neural folds in early vertebrate embryology, a pair of longitudinal ridges that arise from the neural plate on either side of the neural groove and that fold over and give rise to the neural tube, which eventually becomes the spinal cord.

neural groove an ingrowth of the neural plate of a vertebrate embryo; eventually forms the spinal cord in mammals.

neural impulse a transient membrane depolarization, followed by immediate repolarization, traveling in a wavelike manner along a neuron.

neural plate in embryology, a thick plate formed by rapid cell division over the notochord on the dorsal side of the embryo; eventually forms the nervous system in mammals.

neural tree 1. in early vertebrate embryology, the hollow dorsal tube formed by the infusion of the neural folds over the neural groove. 2. the spinal cord.

neuroglia (núr′rog′lēə). See *glial cell*.

neuromuscular junction the synapse between a neural motor end plate and a muscle fiber.

neuron a cell specialized for the transmission of nerve impulses.

neuropeptide a brain neurotransmitter composed of short chains of amino acids varying in number from 2 to 40.

neurotransmitter a short-lived, hormone-like chemical such as acetylcholine that stimulates a second neuron to transmit a nerve impulse. See also *synapse*, *synaptic cleft*.

neurulation the development of a neurula from a gastrula including formation of the neural plate, neural folds, and neural tube.

neutralist one who argues that a substantial proportion of the protein and DNA changes in evolution have been due to selectively neutral mutations fixed by random drift.

neutral mutation mutational change in DNA that has no measurable effect on the fitness of an organism, and which may sometimes be incorporated into the genome of a species. Also called *selectively neutral mutation*.

neutron one of the two common components of an atomic nucleus; has no charge and no effect on chemical reactions.

neutrophil the most common mammalian phagocytic leukocyte.

niche. See *ecological niche*.

nitrification the chemical conversion of ammonia to nitrites and nitrates by the action of soil bacteria.

nitrogenase an enzyme that catalyzes nitrogen fixation.

nitrogen base a purine or pyrimidine used in the synthesis of nucleic acids and other molecules; specifically adenine, cytosine, guanine, thymine or uracil.

nitrogen cycle the cyclic transfer of nitrogen compounds in a biogeochemical cycle, including the gain of nitrogen compounds through nitrogen fixation and lightning and their loss through denitrification.

nitrogen fixation the conversion of atmospheric nitrogen (N_2) to more readily utilized forms; usually by the action of cyanobacteria and other nitrogen-fixing bacteria, but sometimes by lightning, automobile engines, or the industrial preparation of synthetic fertilizers.

nitrogen fixer any of the bacteria or cyanobacteria which are able to use atmospheric nitrogen, combining it with hydrogen to produce ammonium ions.

node 1. in plants, region of leaf attachment in the stem; see *internode*. 2. in neurons, a constriction in myelin sheath, corresponding to a gap between successive Schwann cells; see *saltatory propagation*.

noncyclic photophosphorylation light reactions employing both photosystem II and photosystem I during which electrons from water pass through both photosystems reducing NADP to NADPH and H+, thus serving both chemiosmosis and carbohydrate synthesis. Also *noncyclic events*.

nondisjunction the failure of homologous chromosomes to segregate properly in meiosis, resulting in daughter cells with extra or missing chromosomes.

norepinephrine (nôr ep'ənef'rən) a compound that serves as a synaptic neurotransmitter and as an adrenal hormone. Also called *noradrenaline*.

normal distribution the idealized, symmetrical distribution taken by a population of values centering on a mean, when departures from the mean are due to the chance occurrences of a large number of individually small independent effects; often approached in real populations. Also called *bell-shaped curve*.

notochord a turgid, flexible rod running along the back beneath the nerve cord and serving as a body axis; exists in all chordates at some point in development, but is replaced in most vertebrates by the vertebral column.

nuclear envelope the double cellular membrane surrounding the eukaryote nucleus, the outermost of which is continuous with the endoplasmic reticulum. Also called *nuclear membrane*.

nucleic acid either DNA or RNA; DNA is a double polymer of deoxynucleotides and RNA is a single polymer of nucleotides.

nucleic acid hybridization through base-pairing the union of single strands of DNA from different sources, as occurs when DNA probes are used. See *DNA probe*.

nucleolar organizing region within the nucleus, multiple copies of a DNA loop that transcribes ribosomal RNA.

nucleolus (*pl.*, nucleoli) a conspicuous, dark-staining region of DNA, RNA, and protein within the cell nucleus.

nucleotide a compound consisting of a nitrogenous base and a phosphate group linked to the l′ and s′ carbons of ribose or deoxyribose, respectively the repeating subunit of DNA or RNA.

nucleus 1. in all eukaryote cells, a prominent, usually spherical or elipsoidal double membrane-bounded organelle containing the chromosomes and providing physical separation of the DNA and the cytoplasm. 2. a clump of neural cell bodies that develop in the same way and that innervates the same region.

occipital lobe one of the four major lobes of the brain; involved in the reception and processing of visual information.

oceanic province the open sea, as distinguished from the neritic province.

Okazaki fragment (ō'kə za'kē) during DNA replication in the lagging strand, an assembly of some 200-300 bases, incorporated through use of the enzyme ligase.

olfaction 1. the sense of smell. 2. the process of smelling.

olfactory bulb an extension of the brain that receives neurons from the olfactory receptors in the nasal passage.

olfactory epithelium the chemically sensitive neural tissue lining of the nasal cavity.

oligochaeta (ol'ə gō kēt) a member of the class of annelids that have locomotory setae sunk directly into the body wall, such as earthworms.

oligodendrocytes (ō'lə gō den'drə sītz) a neuroglial cell that forms the myelin sheath over axons of the central nervous system.

oligotrophic *adj.* a lake rich in dissolved oxygen and poor in plant and algal requirements; producer growth is thus held in check, and the lake ages very slowly. Compare *eutrophic*.

ommatidium (om'ə tid'ē em) (*pl.*, ommatidia) one of the elements of compound eye, consisting of a corneal lens, crystalline cone; rhabdome, light-sensitive retinula, and sheathing pigment cells.

omnivore "eating everything"; an organism that feeds on both animal and plant material.

oocyte (ō'ə sīt) an egg cell before maturation: *primary oocyte*, a diploid cell precursor of an egg before meiosis; *secondary oocyte*, an egg cell after formation of the first polar body.

oogenesis the meiotic process that results in the production of an egg cell or ovum.

oogonium (*pl.*, oogonia) a cell that gives rise to oocytes, the large, spherical, unicellular female sex organ of some protists in which egg cells are produced.

open circulatory system a circulatory system in which blood passes from vessels into intercellular spaces before returning to the heart. Compare *closed circulatory system*.

open life span. See *indeterminate life span*.

operant conditioning in behavior, learning through conditioning in which the reward or reinforcement follows a particular response that is desired over other possible responses.

operator. See *operon*.

operculum (ō pûr kyə ləm) a lid or cover, e.g., the skin-covered bony plates that cover the gill chambers of a bony fish.

operon in prokaryotes, a gene-controlling mechanism that includes structural genes and the genes controlling them; transcription may be *inducible*, remaining shut down until activated by an inducer substance, or *repressible*, remaining active until shut down by a repressor substance. See *lac operon*.

opsin one of the two chemicals that rhodopsin breaks down into when exposed to light.

optic nerve the nerve carrying impulses from the retina to visual centers in the brain.

orbital the approximate and hypothetical path on which an electron moves around the nucleus of an atom.

organ a distinct structure that consists of a number of tissues and carries out a specific function.

organelle a specialized part of a cell.

organismic respiration the physical processes by which oxygen and carbon dioxide are exchanged by the body.

organ of Corti on the basilar membrane in the cochlea, an organ containing the neural receptors for hearing.

organ system a number of organs participating jointly in carrying out a basic function of life (e.g., respiration, excretion, reproduction, digestion).

orgasm in humans, the climax of sexual excitement and pleasure, usually accompanied in men by ejaculation and in women by rhythmic contractions of the cervix.

orienting movement in behavior, the directing of bodily position according to the location of a particular stimulus; may be part of an instinctive action.

origin 1. evolutionary ancestry. 2. the nonmoving, skeletal base to which a muscle or tendon attaches. Compare *insertion*.

osculum (os'kyə ləm) an opening in a sponge through which water exits.

osmoconformer (oz'mō kən for'mər) an aquatic organism that does not regulate the solute content of its body tissues, but allows it to fluctuate with that of the environment.

osmoregulation (oz'mō reg'yə lā shən) in aquatic organisms, the retention of a specific solute content in the body in spite of fluctuations in the salinity of the environment.

osmoregulator an aquatic organism that osmoregulates. See *osmoregulation*.

osmosis the movement of water across a membrane from an area of high water potential to an area of lower water potential when the difference was brought about by the presence of solutes.

osmotic pressure the actual hydrostatic pressure that builds up in a confined fluid because of osmosis; the amount of force necessary to equal the water potential.

osteocyte a bone cell isolated in a lacuna of bone tissue.

ostia in an arthropod's open circulatory system, the tiny openings through which blood reenters the heart.

ostracoderm (os trak'ə derm) any of a group of extinct jawless fish.

oval window in the cochlea, a membrane articulating with the stapes that moves in response to its vibrations.

ovarian cycle. See *menstrual cycle*.

ovarian follicle the cluster of cells in which a mammalian oocyte matures, and which later gives rise to a corpus luteum.

ovary 1. in animals, the (usually paired) organ in which oogenesis occurs and eggs mature. 2. in flowering plants, the enlarged, rounded base of a pistil, consisting of a carpel or several united carpels, in which ovules mature and megasporogenesis occurs.

overshoot the condition in which a rapidly growing population rises above the environment's carrying capacity so drastically that it places harsh pressure on its own numbers, frequently leading to a population crash.

oviduct a tube, usually paired for the passage of eggs from the ovary toward the exterior or to a uterus often modified for the secretion of a shell or a protective membrane; in humans it is also known as a *fallopian tube*.

oviparity *n.*, the condition of producing eggs that mature and hatch outside the body, common to many vertebrates other than mammals.

oviparous. See *oviparity*.

ovipositor in invertebrates, an organ specialized for the depositing of eggs and often for boring holes in which eggs may be deposited.

ovoviviparity *n.*, the condition of producing eggs which are hatched within the body so that the young are born alive but without placental attachment, as in certain reptiles, fishes, etc.

ovoviviparous. See *ovoviviparity*.

ovulation the release of one or more eggs from an ovary.

ovule in seed plants, an oval body in the ovary that contains the megagametophyte mother cell and later the female gametophyte.

ovum the female reproductive cell or gamete of animals which is capable of developing, usually only after fertilization, into a new individual.

oxidation 1. the loss of electrons from an element or compound. 2. the addition of oxygen to an element or compound. 3. a multistep process in which oxygen is added or hydrogen or electrons are removed (e.g., the oxidation of glucose).

oxidative *adj.*, requiring oxygen.

oxygen debt a state of oxygen depletion after extreme physical exertion; measured by the amount of oxygen required to restore the system to its original state.

oxytocin (ok′sə tō′ sin) a polypeptide hormone of the posterior pituitary that stimulates the contraction of the uterus and the release of milk.

pacemaker. See *sinoatrial (SA) node*.

pacinian corpuscle (pa sin′ē ən) in oral pressure receptor of the skin, containing the ends of sensory neurons, especially in the hands and feet.

palisade parenchyma (pə reng′kə ma) in plants, a tissue of a lengthy, vertically arranged photosynthetic cell in the leaf, forming a closely packed layer (or layers) just below the upper epidermis.

pancreas a large digestive and endocrine gland of vertebrates, which secretes various digestive enzymes and hormones.

pancreatic islet cells. See *islets of Langerhans*.

papillary muscle one of the small bundles of muscles attached to the ventricle walls and to the chordae tendineae that tighten those tendons during ventricular contractions.

paradigm a broad, major concept in science, usually representing a new way of viewing natural phenomena (e.g., the theory of relativity in physics, continental drift in geology, the central dogma in biology).

parasitism a symbiotic relationship in which an organism of one kind (the parasite) lives in or on an organism of another kind (the host), generally to the host's detriment. Compare *commensalism, mutualism*.

parasympathetic division that part of the autonomic nervous system whose nerves emerge from the brain and lower spinal cord and whose action generally slows activity in the viscera. Compare *sympathetic division*.

parathyroid glands four small endocrine glands embedded in or adjacent to the thyroid gland and involved in the regulation of body calcium.

parathyroid hormone (PTH) the internal secretion of the parathyroid glands, involved in maintaining calcium balance.

Parazoa phylum Porifera, the sponges. See also *Metazoa*.

parenchyma the fundamental tissue of plants, composed of thin-walled cells and commonly specializing in photosynthesis and storage.

parietal cells large cells of the stomach lining that secrete hydrochloric acid.

parietal lobe one of the four major lobes of the cortex; the detection of body division and sensory input are the major functions.

partial dominance where the combined expression of two alleles in the heterozygote produces an intermediate trait (i.e., in the blossoms of four o'clocks, red + white = pink).

passive immunization short-lived immunity resulting from the injection of an antiserum containing specific immunoglobins against the invading agent.

passive transport in organisms, the movement of fluids, solutes, or other materials without the expenditure of ATP energy (e.g., by diffusion), especially across a membrane.

pathogen any disease-producing organism.

pathogenic *adj.*, disease-producing.

pectoral girdle the bones and cartilage supporting and articulating with the vertebrate forelimb; in humans, consisting of the clavicle and scapula.

pedipalps in arachnids, the pair of usually longer appendages immediately behind the chelicerae.

pelvic girdle the bones and cartilage supporting and articulating with the vertebrate hindlimbs; in humans, consisting of the fused bones of the pelvis.

penis the male intromittent sex organ in species where internal fertilization is carried out through copulation.

pentaradial symmetry a modified radial symmetry in which there are five repeated radial parts; seen in echinoderm adults.

pentose a five-carbon monosaccharide (i.e., ribose, deoxyribose).

pepsin an enzyme secreted as *pepsinogen* by glands of the stomach lining that is active only at low pH and that acts primarily to reduce complex proteins to simple polypeptides.

pepsinogen the initial, inactive form of pepsin as occurring in and secreted by gastric glands that readily converts to pepsin in an acid medium.

peptide bond the dehydration linkage formed between the carboxyl group of one amino acid and the amino group of another; also *peptide linkage*, a covalent bond.

peptidoglycan chemical material of the cell wall in Eubacteria; consists of sugars and short peptide strands cross-linked by strands of the amino acid glycine.

peptidyl transferase (pep′tī del) during translation, the enzyme involved in the formation of peptide bond between adjacent amino acids in the growing polypeptide.

perennial in plants, a species that lives for an indefinite number of years. Compare *annual, biennial*.

pericycle a layer of tissue that sheaths the stele of the root and is associated with the formation of lateral roots.

periosteum tough connective covering of bone.

peripheral nervous system in vertebrates, all neurons outside the central nervous system.

peristalsis successive waves of involuntary contractions passing along the walls of the esophagus, intestine, or other hollow muscularized tubes, forcing the contents onward.

peritoneum the smooth, transparent membrane lining the abdominal cavity of a mammal.

peritubular capillaries in the kidney, a capillary bed surrounding the nephron and involved in tubular reabsorption and secretion, related to osmoregulation and excretion.

permafrost in arctic and high-altitude tundra, the permanently frozen layer of soil or subsoil or both.

permeability the degree to which materials are able to pass through a substance, membrane, or barrier.

permease a membranal carrier that functions in facilitated transport of a specific substance across a plasma membrane.

peroxisome a cytoplasmic organelle involved in the detoxification of peroxides.

petal one of the usually white or brightly colored leaflike elements of the corolla of a flower.

petiole in dicot plants, the small stalk that emerges from the stem and supports the leaf.

phagocytosis engulfment of solid materials into the cell and the subsequent pinching off of the cell membrane to form a digestive vacuole.

phanerogam (fan′ər ə gam′) any of the Phanerogamia, a former primary division of plants comprising those having readily visible reproductive organs such as cones or flowers; a seed plant.

pharyngeal gill arches. See *gill arches.*

pharynx 1. in most vertebrates, the cavity between the mouth and the esophagus (contains the gills in fishes); 2. an analogous region in the alimentary canals of various invertebrates, including some in which it is reversible and toothed.

phenotype the final effect of the total interaction of genes with each other and with the environment, expressed in the individual.

pheromone a substance that is released into the environment by one individual and affects the behavior of another (i.e., the sex attraction in moths).

phloem a complex vascular tissue of higher plants that consists of sieve tubes, companion cells, and phloem fibers, and functions in transport of sugars and other solutes, e.g., phloem sap.

phloem parenchyma (flo′əm pəreng′kə mə) part of the phloem tissue complex; parenchymal cells that lie adjacent to phloem sieve tubes.

phosphate ion an ion of phosphoric acid.

phospholipid any of a class of phosphate-esterified lipids, including *lecithin, cephalin,* and *sphingomyelin;* a major component of cell membranes.

phosphorus cycle the pathway of phosphorus as it is taken up and released by organisms into the physical environment.

phosphorylation reaction the enzymatic addition of a phosphate group to a compound, e.g., the addition of phosphate to ADP yielding ATP and water.

photon (fō′ton) a "pocket" (quantum) of electromagnetic radiant energy; a unit of light energy.

photoperiodism the response of an organism to the length of daylight or dark periods (photoperiods), involving sensitivity to the onset of light or darkness and a capacity to measure time.

photophosphorylation phosphorylation that utilizes light as an initial source of energy.

photorespiration in C3 plants, the addition of oxygen rather than carbon dioxide to ribulose diphosphate and the subsequent loss of Calvin cycle components.

photosynthesis in phototrophic organisms, the organized capture of light energy in photosystems and its transformation into chemical bond energy in carbohydrates (glucose and other compounds).

photosystem in the thylakoid, light-harvesting antennas and electron/hydrogen transport systems, both of which function in the light reactions of photosyn-

thesis; also *photosystem I (P700)* and *photosystem II (P680).*

photosystem I (P700) the second in the two photosystems in the electron pathway of photosynthesis in cyanobacteria and chloroplasts, and in the cyclic reactions, the one involving the reduction of NADP to NADPH2.

photosystem II (P680) the first of two photosystems in the electron pathway of photosynthesis in cyanobacteria and all photosynthetic eukaryotes, and the one involving the photolysis of water.

phototaxis a tendency to move toward light.

phototroph an autotrophic organism that derives its energy initially from light; a photosynthetic organism.

phototropic response See *phototropism.*

phototropism the growth response of a plant to light.

pH scale a common measure of the acidity or alkalinity of a liquid, based on hydrogen ion concentration.

phyletic speciation the linear change over time of one species into another.

phylum 1. a major taxonomic unit of related, similar classes of animals, e.g., phylum Annelida; 2. a division of the plant kingdom.

phytochrome a red-light and far-red-light-sensitive protein complex of certain plant cell membranes; involved in many light-induced phenomena, including flowering, leaf formation, and seed germination.

phytoplankton in the aquatic environment (marine and fresh waters), minute photosynthesizing organisms, such as diatoms; the base of the marine food chain.

piezoelectric crystal crystalline structures, including the keratin of skin and hair, that when touched or otherwise deformed generate weak electrical currents.

piloerection the lifting up of hair by tiny involuntary muscles in response to cold or fright; bristling.

pineal gland also called *pineal organ, pineal body;* a small body in the brain directly sensitive to light in reptiles and birds.

pinna in common terms, the "ear."

pinocytic vesicle inpocketing of the plasma membrane of a cell formed as pinocytosis (cell "drinking") occurs.

pinocytosis a form of endocytosis in which dissolved molecular food materials are taken into the cell by an inpocketing of the plasma membrane. See also *pinocytic vesicle.*

pioneer organism during ecological succession, a type of organism specialized for the initial invasion of an uninhabited or seriously disturbed area (e.g., a rocky outcropping, landslide, or burned-out region).

pistil in flowering plants, the female reproductive structure, composed of one or more carpels and ovaries, and a style and a stigma. See also *carpel* and *gynoecium.*

pith thin-walled parenchymous tissue in

the central strand of a stem's primary growth; the dead remains of such tissue at the center of a woody stem.

pit pairs also called *pits;* the thin, porelike regions in adjacent plant cell walls where only the primary cell wall remains.

pituitary also called *hypophysis;* a small, double endocrine gland lying just below the brain and intimately associated with the hypothalamus in all vertebrates, consisting of an anterior and a posterior lobe. See also *anterior pituitary* and *posterior pituitary.*

pituitary dwarf an abnormally small individual resulting from the failure of the anterior pituitary to secrete growth hormone.

pituitary giant an abnormally large individual whose excessive growth is due to excessive secretions of growth hormone.

placenta in mammals other than monotremas and marsupials, the organ formed by the union of the endometrium and the extraembryonic membranes of the fetus; it provides for nourishment of the fetus, elimination of waste products, and the exchange of dissolved gases.

placental mammal mammals that provide support to the embryo via the placenta.

Plantae the plant kingdom. Plants are non-motile (stationary), multicellular, photosynthetic autotrophs with cell walls of cellulose, having highly specialized tissues and organs.

planula larva the early, ciliated, free-swimming form of a coelenterate.

plaque 1. pathological deposit of lipid, fibrous material and often calcium salts in the inner wall of a blood vessel; 2. a film of bacterial polysaccharide, mucus, and detritus harboring dental bacteria.

plasma the fluid matrix of blood tissues; it is 90% water and 10% various other substances, including plasma proteins, ions, and foods.

plasma cell a mature, short-lived B-cell lymphocyte specialized in secreting antibodies.

plasma membrane the external, semipermeable, limiting layer of the cytoplasm.

plasmid in bacteria, a small ring of DNA that occurs in addition to the main bacterial chromosome and is transferred from host to host; also used in recombinant DNA techniques.

plasmodesma (*pl.,* plasmodesmata) in plants, minute cytoplasmic junctions between cells, occurring at pores in the cell wall through which the plasma membrane of one cell becomes continuous with that at the next; highly significant to transport.

platelets minute, fragile noncellular discs present in the vertebrate blood; upon injury they are ruptured, releasing factors that initiate blood clotting and wound healing.

plastid any of several forms of self-replicating, semiautonomous plant cell organelles, including *chloroplast* (specialized for photosynthesis), *chromoplast* (specialized for pigmentation), and *leukoplast* (specialized for starch storage).

plate tectonics the movement of great land and ocean floor masses (plates) on the surface of the earth relative to one another. See also *continental drift*.

pleura *pl.*, pleurae in mammals, the tough, clear, serous connective tissue membrane covering a lung and lining the cavity in which the lung lies.

plumule the apex of certain plant embryos, consisting of immature leaves and an epicotyl.

pogonophoran (pə gō nə fŏr′ən) one of the large, red tubeworms found near gas vents on the ocean bottom.

poikilotherms (poi′kə lō thûrm) organisms with body temperatures that fluctuate with the temperature of the environment.

point mutation a mutation involving a minor change in a DNA sequence, such as a base substitution, addition, or deletion.

polar referring to the charged portion of a chemical or part of a molecule capable of forming hydrogen bonds with water and other polar molecules.

polar body a small, functionless daughter cell produced by the highly unequal cleavage during meiosis I and II in oogenesis.

polarity in chemistry, the presence or manifestation of two opposite or contrasting charges.

polarization the process in which the outside of a resting neuron becomes positively charged relative to the inside.

polarized in a neuron, the period when the region outside a neuron is positive and the region inside is negative, producing a membrane voltage potential of -60 mV. See also *resting state*.

pollen the male gametophyte of a seed plant; contains a generative nucleus and a tube nucleus and is enclosed in a hardened, resistant case.

pollen grain. See *pollen*.

pollen sac one of two or four chambers in an anther in which pollen develops and is held.

pollen tube a tube that extends from a germinating pollen grain and grows down through the style to the embryo sac, into which it releases sperm nuclei.

pollen tube cell in plant reproduction, the cell directly behind the pollen tube as it grows through the style of a flower before actual fertilization by one of the nuclei that follow it.

polychaete (pol′ē kēt) a member of the class of annelids having unsegmented appendages with many chaetae or bristles.

polydactyly (pol′ē dak′tə lē) the genetically derived state of having extra fingers or toes.

polygenic inheritance inheritance involving many interacting variable genes, each having a small effect on a specific trait.

polymer (pol′ə mər) a molecule made up of a string of more or less identical subunits (e.g., starch, nucleic acid, polypeptide).

polymerization the combination of many like or unlike molecules to form a more complex product of higher molecular weight.

polyp (pol ĭp) the typical attached, nonswimming form of coelenterate. Compare *medusa*.

polypeptide a strand of amino acids linked by peptide bonds, longer than a peptide but not usually a complete, functional protein. See also *protein*.

polyphyletic of a taxonomic group, having two or more ancestral lines of origin.

polyploidy (pol′ē ploid′ē) the condition of having a chromosome number that is more than double the basic or haploid number.

polyribosome several ribosomes simultaneously transcribing the same messenger RNA strand; also called *polysome*.

polysaccharide "many sugar"; a polymer of sugar subunits.

polysome See *polyribosome*.

polytene chromosome in certain insects, enlarged chromosomes created by chromatin replication without chromosome division.

pome (pōm) a simple fleshy fruit, formed in its outer portions by the floral parts themselves, i.e., apple, pear.

P₁ generation in genetics, the first generation of parents in cross-breeding; subsequent generations are designated P_2, P_3, etc.

pons (ponz) a broad mass of nerve fibers running across the ventral surface of the mammalian brain.

population 1. the total number of persons inhabiting a given geographical or political area (demography); 2. an aggregate of individuals of one species, interbreeding or closely related through interbreeding and recent common descent, and evolving as a unit (genetics); 3. the assemblage of plants or animals or both living in a given area; or all of the individuals of one species in a given area (ecology).

population crash the usually rapid depletion of a population that has exceeded the carrying capacity of its environment.

population genetics the scientific study of genetic variation within populations, of the genetic correlation between related individuals in a population, and of the genetic basis of evolutionary change.

population growth rate in population dynamics, the change in the percentage of growth over time. See *exponential growth*.

porocyte (por′ə sīt) a pore-bearing cell in the body wall of a sponge, specialized for admitting water.

positive feedback mechanism occurring when the result of an activity causes that activity increase, thereby further increasing the action; relatively uncommon in nature.

postanal tail a tail that extends from the anus posteriorly.

posterior pituitary also called *neurohypophysis;* not actually a gland but the enlarged, glandlike termini of axons of cell bodies in the hypothalamus, the hormones being synthesized in the cell bodies and translocated to the posterior pituitary within the axons, to be stored pending release; among these are *oxytocin* and *antidiuretic hormone*.

postsynaptic membrane the receptive surface of a dendrite or receiving cell body adjacent to a synapse. See also *synapse*.

posttranscriptional processing following RNA transcription, modification of raw transcripts through the removal of introns and other changes.

postzygotic reproductive isolating mechanisms biological mechanisms that function after fertilization to create reproductive incompatibility between species; i.e., embryo death, sterile adults.

potassium gates. See *ion channel*.

potential energy energy stored in chemical bonds, nonrandom organization, elastic bodies, elevated weight, or any other static form in which it can theoretically be transformed into another form or into work. Also called *free energy*.

precapillary sphincter (spingk′tər) in arterioles, rings of smooth muscle capable of regulating blood flow into capillaries; controlled by the autonomic nervous system.

prefrontal area in the brain, the anterior portion of the frontal lobe which functions in sorting sensory input.

prehensile adapted for seizing, grasping, or wrapping around, as the tail of a New World monkey or the upper lip of a rhinoceros.

pressure flow hypothesis an explanation of sap movement in the phloem based on the active transport of sugars into the phloem stream from the source, followed by an inward movement of water and the formation of hydrostatic pressure which pushes the stream to the sink.

presynaptic membrane the membrane of an axon or of the synaptic knob of an axon in the region of a synaptic cleft, into which it secretes neurotransmitters in the course of the transmission of a nerve impulse. See *synapse, synaptic cleft*.

prezygotic reproductive isolating mechanisms biological mechanisms that operate through altered behavior, anatomy, and physiology to prevent fertilization, thereby producing reproductive incompatibility between species.

primary bronchus the left or right division of the trachea. See also *respiratory tree*.

primary chorionic villi (kôr′ē on′ĭk) slender, fingerlike projections sent into the endometrium by the trophoblast, providing connection between the embryo and the mother's tissues prior to placental formation.

primary consumer in ecology, a herbivore; an organism that feeds directly on producers.

primary growth the initial growth or elongation of a plant stem or root, resulting mainly in an increase in length and the addition of leaves, buds, and branches. Compare *secondary growth*.

primary immune response the relatively slow response of the immune system upon its first contact with an invading organism or foreign protein. Compare *secondary immune response*.

primary lesion (lē zhən) a damaged or mismatched segment of DNA, subject to repair. See *DNA repair system*.

primary level in proteins, the first level of structure, the arrangement of amino acids into a simple, linear polypeptide.

primary oocyte (ō'ə sīt) a diploid cell of egg-producing potential prior to its first meiotic division. See also *oocyte*.

primary organizer in development, any tissue that induces or influences the future development of other subservient tissues.

primary phloem (flō'em) phloem developed from procambium, the phloem of primary growth.

primary producers in ecology, a plant, alga, or other photosynthetic (or chemosynthetic) organism that forms the base of a food chain.

primary productivity. See *gross productivity*.

primary root the root of a plant that grows through the production of primary tissues.

primary succession the succession of vegetational states that occurs as an area changes from bare earth to a climax community.

primary xylem (zī'lem) in primary growth, xylem produced by procambium rather than vascular cambium.

primate any member of the order Primates including humans, apes, monkeys, lemurs, tarsiers, and marmosets.

primitive streak in bird, reptile, and mammalian embryos, a thickening in the blastoderm formed by convergence of cells in preparation for gastrulation.

procambium (pro kam'bē əm) in plants, the primary tissue that gives rise to primary xylem and primary phloem.

producer. See *primary producer*.

profundal zone the depths of a lake below the penetration of light.

progeny testing (proj'ə nē) determination of an organism's genotype by crossing it with one of a known genotype and observing the resulting offspring.

progesterone (prō jes'tə rōn) an ovarian hormone, produced by the corpus luteum; assists in the preparation of the uterus for implantation of a fertilized egg and maintains the placenta during gestation.

proglottid one of many segments of a mature tapeworm, containing male and female organs and being shed when full of mature fertilized eggs.

prokaryote any organism of the kingdom Monera, including *Archaebacteria* or *Eubacteria*; its cells lack a membrane-bounded nucleus and membrane-bounded organelles. Compare *eukaryote*.

prolactin a hormone of the anterior pituitary that in mammals induces milk production.

promoter a DNA sequence to which RNA polymerase must bind in order for transcription to begin. See *operon*.

pronucleus the haploid nucleus of either gamete after the entry of a sperm into an egg and before nuclear fusion.

prophase the first stage of mitosis or meiosis, characterized by the condensation of chromosomes.

prop root in plants, an aerial adventitious root which functions to help keep the main stem erect.

prostacyclin a prostaglandin.

prostaglandin any of a group of hormone-like substances derived from long-chain fatty acids and produced in most animal tissues.

prostate gland a pale, firm, partly muscular and partly glandular organ that surrounds and connects with the base of the urethra in male animals; its viscid, opalescent secretion is a major component of semen.

protein one of the molecules of life, a functional macromolecule consisting of one or more polypeptides, often joined by disulfide linkages and frequently including one or more prosthetic groups.

proteinoid microspheres minute globes of protein that form spontaneously when proteins are concentrated in solution; possible precursors to the first cellular life.

Protista the polyphylitic kingdom of protozoa, algae, slime molds, and water molds.

protocell in the origin of life, a hypothetical cell containing the simplest organization and chemical substances needed to carry on life.

protoderm in plants, primary meristematic tissue; it gives rise to the epidermis of roots, leaves, and stems.

proton 1. one of the two particles composing the atomic nucleus in ordinary matter; it has an electrostatic charge of $+1$ and a mass 1837 times that of an electron; 2. a hydrogen ion.

proton pump an active transport system that uses energy to move hydrogen ions (protons) from one side of a membrane to the other against a concentration gradient, as in chemiosmosis.

protostome an animal in which the mouth derives from the region of the first embryonic opening (the blastopore). Compare *deuterostome*.

Protozoa the phylum containing single-celled, animal-like heterotrophs of the kingdom Protista.

proximal convoluted tubule See *nephron*.

pseudocoelom (sü də sē'ləm) in nematodes and rotifers, the body cavity between the body wall and the intestine that is not entirely lined with mesodermal epithelium.

pseudocoelomate animals that form pseudocoeloms.

pseudopod "false foot" any temporary protrusion of the protoplasm of a cell serving as a structure of locomotion or engulfment.

P700. See *photosystem I*.

psilophyte (sī'lə fītə) any whisk fern; among the earliest known vascular plants, lacking roots, cambium, leaves, and leaf traces.

P680. See *photosystem II*.

pterophyta (ter'ō fīt'a) "winged plants"; ferns.

pubic joint. See *pubic symphysis*.

pubic symphysis (sīm'fə sis) in mammals, the usually semirigid fibrous articulation of the two pubic bones.

pubis also called *pubic bone;* one of the constituent bones of the coxa or innominate bone.

pulmonary circuit blood vessels carrying blood to and from the lungs.

pulmonary semilunar valve a one-way valve at the base of the pulmonary artery that prevents back flow of blood into the right ventricle during systole.

punctuated equilibrium a theory stating that evolution does not proceed in a gradual manner but rather in sudden bursts of activity, followed by very long time-intervals during which little evolutionary activity is seen.

Punnett square in genetics, a grid used to predict the outcome of cross-breeding.

pupa (pyü'pə) in insects, the period of development between the larval and adult stages, during which time extensive body transformations occur prior to the emergence of the adult; the pupa generally is enclosed in a hardened pupal case or cocoon.

pupil the contractile aperture in the iris of the eye.

purine a nitrogenous, double-ringed base of DNA or RNA consisting of five-membered and six-membered rings (e.g., adenine, guanine).

pyloric sphincters also *pyloric valve;* a ring of muscle capable of closing off the opening between the stomach and the small intestine.

pyramid of biomass ecological pyramid based on the dry weight of the total living matter.

pyramid of energy. See *energy pyramid*.

pyramid of numbers an ecological pyramid based on relative numbers of producers and consumers.

pyrimidine a nitrogenous, single-ringed base of DNA or RNA consisting of a six-membered ring (e.g., cytosine, uracil, thymine).

pyruvate the ionized form of pyruvic acid, the final organic product of glycolysis in animal cells and the initial substrate of the citric acid cycle; also *pyruvic acid* (nonionized).

pyruvic acid. See *pyruvate.*

quadrupedal (kwä drü′pi dəl) *adj.,* four-footed.

quaternary structure (kwä′tər neŕ ē) in protein, the interaction of two or more polypeptides through disulfide linkages; the fourth level of structure.

radial cleavage in deuterostome embryos, a radial pattern in the early cleavages in which the cleavage planes come to lie one atop the other. See also *spiral cleavage.*

radial symmetry circular or spherical body symmetry where a radius cut through any part will intersect the same body parts (e.g., jelly fish, comb jelly).

radiates those organisms which are disk-shaped, spherical, or cylindrical; a line across any radius divides the animal into similar halves.

radicle (rad′ə k′l) the lower portion of the axis of a plant embryo, including the part that will become the root.

radioactive relating to the phenomenon exhibited by certain elements of spontaneously emitting radiations resulting from changes in the nuclei of atoms of the elements.

radioisotope an unstable isotope that spontaneously breaks down with the release of ionizing radiation; also called *radioactive isotope.*

radiolarian any minute marine protozoan of the phylum Sarcomastigophora, having an amebalike body with radiating pseudopods and an elaborate skeleton

radius one of the two bones of the forearm of land vertebrates, rotating about the ulna and articulating with the wrist.

radula (raj′ü lə) in all mollusks except bivalves, a toothed, chitinous band that slides backward and forward, scraping and tearing food and bringing it into the mouth

random drift. See *genetic drift.*

range the geographical area occupied by a species.

rapid eye movement (REM) sleep that part of sleep characterized by a high degree of relaxation in the voluntary muscles, but rapid movement of the closed eyes and considerable alpha activity registering on an electroencephalogram.

rate of natural increase in population dynamics, the difference between the crude birth rate and the crude death rate.

reabsorption in the kidney, the return of water, ions, amino acids, sugars, and other valuable substances from the crude kidney filtrate back into the blood following force filtration.

reaction the reciprocal action of chemical agents on one another; chemical change.

reaction center the part of a light-harvesting antenna in which light-activated chlorophylla transfers an electron to the electron transport system. See also *photosystem.*

reafference (rē af′ə renz′) in behavior, the presumed reward associated with the performance of a particular movement when an animal is performing an adaptive or instinctive pattern; behavior as its own reward.

receptor site a specific site on a cell membrane, usually a protein, that is capable of recognizing and binding with a specific hormone or other informational molecule.

recessive *adj.,* of an allele, not expressed in a heterozygote.

recessivity the lack of expression by one allele of a gene when a different, dominant allele for that gene is present.

reciprocal altruism in behavior, an action by one individual at some cost that benefits another individual in the expectation and probability that the favor will be returned.

recombinant DNA technology general term for laboratory manipulation of DNA; includes gene splicing, sequencing, and gene cloning.

recombinant virus technique in genetic engineering, the splicing of donor genes into a viral genome and using the virus to transfer such genes into a host cell.

red alga any alga of the division Rhodophyta.

red marrow regions within the ribs, sternum, vertebrae, and hip bones where red blood cells are produced.

red tide sea water discolored by a dinoflagellate bloom in a density fatal to many forms of life.

reducer. See *decomposer.*

reduction the addition of electrons or hydrogen atoms to a substance.

reductionism in science, the theory which attempts to divide phenomena and mechanisms to their most elemental parts, isolating as far as possible the effects of individual factors and testing these effects in separate controlled experiments.

reflex arc the simplest form of a complete neural reaction, involving a *sensory neuron, interneuron,* and *motor neuron,* where the integration of information involves only the spinal cord.

refractory period a brief period of depolarization when a neuron cannot generate a second impulse.

regulator. See *operon.*

releaser. Also *sign stimulus;* a stimulus that acts as a cue, releasing a certain behavior in an animal.

releasing hormone. Also *releasing factor;* a chemical messenger produced by the hypothalamus that stimulates hormonal release by the pituitary gland.

REM sleep. See *rapid eye movement (REM) sleep.*

renal circuit in mammals, the renal arteries, the glomerulus, the capillary beds of the nephron, and the renal veins.

renal cortex the outer region of the kidney, containing the upper portions of the nephrons.

renal medulla the region of the kidney below the cortex, consisting mainly of loops of Henle, capillaries, and collecting ducts.

renal pelvis the cavity of the kidney into which the collecting ducts empty.

rennin (ren′in) an enzyme produced by the stomach linings of young mammals, the action of which is to coagulate milk.

replication DNA synthesis; the process whereby a DNA helix is unwound, the hydrogen bonds between adjacent nitrogen bases broken, and a new strand assembled through base pairing along each old strand.

replication complex during replication, a grouping of the essential enzymes of that process including the unwinding enzymes, helicase, and DNA polymerase.

replication fork the point at which unwinding proteins separate the two DNA strands in the course of DNA replication.

repolarization in the neuron, reestablishment of the resting potential or polarized state following an action potential.

repressible operon the point at which unwinding proteins separate the two DNA strands in the course of DNA replication.

repressor protein in bacterial operons, a protein that binds the operator and prevents transcription.

reproduction the natural process among organisms by which new individuals are generated and the species perpetuated. See *asexual reproduction* and *sexual reproduction.*

reproductive fitness a measure of one's success at leaving one's genes in the next generation.

reproductive isolating mechanisms biological factors which prevent interbreeding between species.

reproductive potential the maximum physiological rate at which any population can increase.

reptile any member of the class Reptilia, composed of cold-blooded vertebrates such as turtles, lizards, snakes, crocodilians, and the tuatara.

repulsion during prophase I, the process during which homologous chromosomes move apart after crossing over.

reservoir in biogeochemical cycles, the less readily available reserves of mineral nutrients, such as atmospheric nitrogen, which is only useful to nitrogen-fixing organisms. Compare *exchange pool.*

residual volume. Also *residual air;* the volume of air remaining in the lungs following maximum, forceful exhalation.

resolution the final phase of sexual intercourse, marked by the loss of erection in males.

resolving power the ability of the eye to distinguish objects near each other as distinct and separate; also the chief factor limiting useful magnification in light microscopes.

respiration. See *cell respiration* and *organismic respiration.*

respiratory tree in air breathing vertebrates, the passageways of the respiratory system, including the trachea, paired bronchi, highly branched tracheoles, and alveoli.

response threshold in behavior, the minimum stimulus required to elicit a response.

resting potential the charge difference across the membrane of a polarized neuron (while it is not transmitting an impulse). Compare *action potential.*

restriction enzyme in bacteria, a defensive enzyme that recognizes and cuts out specific, short, viral DNA sequences, thus protecting the cell against most viruses; useful in genetic engineering.

reticular activating system (RAS) the portion of the reticular system involved in activating the appropriate parts of the brain upon receiving a stimulus.

reticular system. Also called *reticular formation;* a major neural tract in the brainstem containing neural pathways to other parts of the brain and to the *reticular activating system (RAS),* and arousal center.

retina the layer of light sensitive cells in the vertebrate eye.

retinol one of the two chemicals formed from *rhodopsin* when it is broken down by light.

retrovirus an infectious single-stranded RNA that copies itself into double-stranded DNA which is then inserted into a host chromosome; represents a rare instance of RNA producing DNA.

reverse transcriptase an enzyme of retroviruses that copies RNA sequences into single-stranded and double-stranded DNA sequences in a minor reversal of the central dogma. Also called *RNA-dependent DNA polymermase.* See *retrovirus.*

reward in behavior, reinforcement; something positive given to strengthen the probability of a specific response to a given stimulus.

R-group a chemistry shorthand where R stands for the variable part of an amino acid.

rhizoid (rī′zoid) 1. a rootlike structure that serves to anchor the gametophyte of a fern or bryophyte to the soil. 2. a portion of a fungal mycelium that penetrates its food medium.

rhizome (rī zōm) an underground, horizontal plant stem that produces shoots above and roots below, and is distinguished from a true root in possessing buds and nodes.

rhodopsin (rō dop′sən) the light-sensitive protein pigment of retinal rods that bleaches in the presence of light, somehow starting an action potential, and is restored in darkness. Also called *visual purple.*

rhythm method a method of contraception whereby copulation is avoided during periods when conception is likely. Also called *natural birth control.*

riboflavin (rī′bō flā′vin) a derivative of vitamin B₂ and an active group in the coenzyme FAD (flavin adenine dinucleotide).

ribonucleic acid See *RNA.*

ribose (rī bōs) a five-carbon aldose sugar, a constituent of many nucleosides and nucleotides.

ribosome a two-part cytoplasmic organelle upon which translation occurs, consisting of ribosomal RNA and proteins.

ribosomal RNA (rRNA) the RNA that forms the matrix of ribosome structure.

right atrium the chamber of the heart which receives the deoxygenated blood from the body via the veins, and then pumps it to the right ventricle.

right ventricle the chamber of the heart which receives deoxygenated blood from the right atrium and then pumps it to the lungs.

ring chromosomes a genetic mutation in which a broken chromosome is repaired improperly with its two ends fused, forming a circle; may be associated with hereditary mental retardation.

RNA (ribonucleic acid) a single-stranded nucleic acid macromolecule consisting of adenine, guanine, cytosine, and uracil; divided functionally into rRNA (ribosomal RNA), mRNA (messenger RNA) and tRNA (transfer RNA).

RNA-dependent DNA polymerase. See *reverse transcriptase.*

RNA polymerase the enzyme or enzyme complex catalyzing transcription.

rod one of the numerous, long, rod-shaped sensory bodies in the vertebrate retina; responsive to faint light but not to variations in color. Compare *cone.*

root the portion of a vascular plant that functions as an organ of absorption, anchorage, and sometimes food storage, and differs from the stem in lacking nodes, buds, and leaves.

root apical meristem in plants, region of undifferentiated tissue just above the root cap; gives rise to primary growth in the root.

root cap a protective mass of parenchymal cells that covers the root apical meristem.

root hair one of the many tiny tubular outgrowths of root epidermal cells, especially just behind the root apex, that function in absorption.

root pressure modest pressure in the root prompted by osmosis, causing water to rise in the stem.

root tip in plants, the actively growing end of a primary or secondary root, where root apical meristem is found.

rotifer (rō-tə fər) any microscopic animal of the phylum Rotifera, found in fresh and salt waters, having a ciliary apparatus on the anterior end.

round window at the termination of the cochlea, a membranous window that moves in response to perilymph movement started by the oval window. See also *oval window.*

roundworm any nematode that infests the intestine of humans and other animals.

r-selection the reproductive strategy seen in disruptive environments, where the organism produces large numbers of offspring but offers little if any parental care. Compare *K-selection.*

Ruffini corpuscle sensory receptors of the skin that respond to temperature changes.

rugae (roo g′ē) (*sing.,* ruga) wrinkles, folds, or ridges, especially of the lining of the small intestine.

ruminants hooved grazing mammals that digest cellulose through the action of microorganisms in a four-part stomach.

saccule (sak′yoo/) 1. a small sac. 2. the smaller of two chambers of the membranous labyrinth of the ear. Compare *utricle.*

sac fungi fungi of the phylum Ascomycota.

sacrum the part of the vertebral column that connects with the pelvis; in humans, consists of five fused vertebrae with transverse processes fused into a solid bony mass on either side.

saliva a viscous, colorless, mucoid fluid secreted into the mouth by ducted salivary glands.

salivary amylase an enzyme in the mouth that begins starch digestion.

salivary glands in land vertebrates, any of several glands secreting saliva into the mouth.

salp any free-swimming, oceanic tunicate of the genus *Salpa,* having a transparent, more or less fusiform body.

saltatory propagation in myelinated neurons, the skipping movement of an impulse from one node to another.

sap the watery fluid transported by the phloem that transports dissolved sugars, other organic compounds, and mineral nutrients from one part of the plant to another.

sarcolemma the membranous sheath enclosing a muscle fiber.

satellite DNA unexplained, frequently occurring short segments of chromosomal DNA containing mainly the base pairs adenine and thymine.

sarcomers the contractile unit of striated muscle.

sarcoplasmic reticulum a membranous, hollow tubule in the cytoplasm of a muscle fiber; similar to the *endoplasmic reticulum* of other cells; calcium ions are sequestered here when the muscle is at rest.

saturated *adj.,* in lipid chemistry, having accepted as many hydrogens as possible.

Schwann cells (shwän) one of the many cells that constitute the myelin sheath, wrapped around the axon of a myelinated neuron.

scientific method a research system in which a problem is identified, relevant data are gathered, hypotheses are formulated, and predictions are made and tested through experimentation or additional observation.

scientific name in biological taxonomy, the two Latin names (generic and specific) used to identify a species.

sclera (sklēr'ə) the heavy, white connective tissue enclosing most of the eyeball; the white of the eye.

sclerenchyma in plants, a protective or supporting tissue composed of cells with greatly thickened, lignified, and often mineralized cell walls.

scolex the hook-bearing head of a larval or adult tapeworm, from which the proglottids are produced by strobilation.

scrotum the external pouch of skin that contains the testis in most adult male mammals.

scutellum in monocots, the cotyledon in its specialized form as a digestive and absorptive organ.

secondary consumer a carnivorous animal that feeds upon herbivores (primary consumers).

secondary growth growth in dicot plants that results from the activity of secondary meristem, producing chiefly an increase in the diameter of stem or root. Compare *primary growth*.

secondary immune response the more rapid arousal of lymphocytes and conquest of an invader during a second or subsequent infection, due to memory cells. Compare *primary immune response*.

secondary level the second level of organization of a protein; the formation of helices or sheets by polypeptides.

secondary oocyte. See also *oocyte*; a developing egg cell after the first polar body has been produced and before the second polar body appears after meiosis I.

secondary phloem phloem produced by the vascular cambium during secondary growth.

secondary succession ecological succession occurring in a disturbed community.

secondary xylem xylem produced by the vascular cambium during secondary growth.

second law of thermodynamics the statement that all systems proceed toward entropy and that all chemical transformations are imperfect, that is, energy is lost as it goes from one form to another; the free energy in any closed system constantly decreases.

second messenger an intracellular chemical compound activated by a hormone that becomes active in the cytoplasm or nucleus.

secretion vesicle a small, bladderlike cavity which periodically breaks away from the maturing face of the Golgi body and moves to the plasma membrane where the substances it contains are released outside the cell.

seed the fertilized and ripened ovule of a seed plant, comprising an embryo, including one or two cotyledons, and usually a supply of food in a protective seed coat.

seedless plants any species that does not produce seeds in its reproduction. See *cryptogam*.

seedling any recently germinated seed plant.

seed plants any plant capable of seed production; includes gymnosperms and angiosperms.

segmented body plan a plan in which the body is divided into segments, originally repetitions of nearly identical parts (as still seen in some annelids, chilopods, diplopods, and *Peripatus*); frequently followed in evolution by the specialization of different segments as seen in most arthropods, some annelids, and vertebrates.

segregation the random separation of alleles in different gametes during meiosis.

selectionists biologists who attribute most, if not all, evolutionary change to natural selection.

selectively permeable in cellular membranes, the characteristic of permitting selected substances to pass through while rejecting others. Also called *differentially permeable*.

SEM (scanning electron microscope) a device for visualizing microscopic objects in three dimensions by scanning them with a moving beam of electrons, recording impulses from scattered electrons, and displaying the image by means of the synchronized scan of an electron beam in a cathode ray (television) tube.

semen in mammals, a viscous white sperm-bearing fluid produced in the male reproductive tract and released by ejaculation.

semicircular canals any of the three curved, tubular, fluid-filled canals in the labyrinth of the ear, associated with the sense of equilibrium.

semiconservative replication replication of DNA molecule in which the original molecule divides into two complimentary parts, both halves being preserved while each half promotes the synthesis of a new complement to itself.

seminal receptacle a storage organ for sperm in certain invertebrate females.

seminal vesicle 1. in various invertebrates, a pouch in the male reproductive tract serving as the temporary storage of sperm. 2. in male mammals, paired outpocketings of the vas deferens producing much of the fluid substance of semen.

seminiferous tubule any of the coiled, thread-like tubules that make up the bulk of a testis and are lined with germinal epithelium from which sperm are produced.

sensory neuron also *afferent neuron*; a neuron that conducts impulses carrying sensory information from a receptor to the brain or spinal cord.

sensory receptor a cell or tissue, specialized in responding to specific kinds of stimuli.

sepal the green, leaflike floral parts that surround the flower bud before it opens and later forms a whorl (the calyx) beneath and outside the petals.

seral stage one stage in a *sere*.

sere a recognizable sequence of changes, sometimes predictable, occurring during community development or succession.

Sertoli cells also *nurse cell*; elongated cells of the tubules of the testis that support spermatid development.

seta (*pl.*, setae) the bristlelike, chitinous structure in the body wall of annelids, arthropods, and certain other invertebrates.

sex-influenced trait a genetic trait that can occur in either sex but is more common in one (i.e., breast cancer in women, baldness in men).

sex-limited trait a variable trait that affects members of one sex only.

sex linkage inheritance of traits based on genes present exclusively in either the **X** or the **Y** chromosome.

sex pilus in some prokaryotes, an enlarged pilus (tube) through which a DNA replica can presumably pass from one cell to another.

sexual dimorphism differences in size, color, anatomy, etc. between the sexes.

sexual reproduction reproduction involving the union of genetic material from two individuals.

shaft of bone the long, comparatively straight part of a bone.

shell 1. the space occupied by the orbits of a group of electrons of approximately equal energy. 2. a hard, rigid, usually calcareous covering of an animal. 3. the covering of an egg. 4. the hard, rigid outer covering of a fruit or seed; e.g., walnut shell.

shoot the plant stem and foliage.

shoot apical meristem in plants, undifferentiated tissue at the stem tip that produces primary growth in the stem.

shoot tip in plants, the actively growing end of a primary or secondary stem, where shoot apical meristem is found.

short-day plant a plant that begins flowering after the summer solstice and in which flowering is triggered by periods of dark longer than some innately determined minimum. Compare *long-day plant*.

short-term memory transient, newly acquired memory that has not been consolidated through long-term memory processing.

sickle cell anemia a severe recessive condition attributable to homozygosity for an allele producing an abnormal, crescent-shaped erythrocyte.

sieve element a thin-walled phloem cell having no nucleus at maturity and forming a continuous cytoplasm with other such cells to form *sieve cells* and *sieve tubes*, functioning in the transport of organic solutes, hormones, and mineral elements.

sigmoid curve. See *S-shaped curve*.

sign stimulus. See *releaser*.

silent mutation a change in a DNA codon in which a synonymous codon forms (third letter change), having no effect on the amino acid sequence of the polypeptide.

simple goiter a visible enlargement of the

thyroid gland resulting from iodine deficiency.

sinoatrial (SA) node conducting tissue embedded in the musculature of the right atrium, serving as an intrinsic source of regular contractile impulses to the heart.

sinus arteriosus in the heart of some vertebrates, the widened blood vessel that leads into the atrium.

skeletal muscle muscle under direct and conscious control; striated with multinucleate unbranched fibers. Also called *voluntary muscle, striated muscle.* Compare *cardiac muscle, smooth muscle.*

skin breather any organism in which a significant proportion of the exchange of respiratory gases occurs through a vascularized moist skin (for example, earthworms, most amphibians).

skin exchange. See *skin breather.*

Skinner box in behavior, a device for investigating operant conditioning, named after B.F. Skinner, who invented it.

sliding filament theory the widely accepted explanation of skeletal muscle contraction in which actin myofilaments in the sarcomere are actively drawn past myosin myofilaments, thus shortening the contractile unit.

slime mold a funguslike protist with an ameboid feeding stage and a funguslike spore-forming stage.

small intestine the region of the digestive tract between the stomach and the cecum; the region in which most food digestion and absorption occurs.

smooth muscle the muscle tissue of the glands, viscera, iris, pilo-erectors, and other involuntary structures; consists of masses of uninucleate, unstriated, spindle-shaped cells, usually occurring in thin sheets. Also called *involuntary muscle.*

sociobiology the area of biological science concerned with the genetic basis of human individual and group behavior.

sodium activation gate. See *sodium gate.*

sodium gate either of the two gates controlling sodium ion passage through an ion channel, including a *sodium activation gate* and *sodium inactivation gate.* See *ion channel.*

sodium inactivation gate. See *sodium gate.*

sodium potassium ion exchange pump a membrane active transport mechanism that utilizes ATP energy to move sodium ions out of the cell and potassium into it.

solar energy energy obtained from the sun.

somatic system the voluntary or conscious part of the peripheral nervous system. Compare *autonomic nervous system.*

somatostatin a hormonal secretion of the *hypothalamus* and of *delta cells* in the *islets of Langerhans.*

somite in the early vertebrate embryo, one of a longitudinal series of paired blocks of tissue that are forerunners of body muscles and the axial skeleton.

sorus (*pl.,* sori) one of the clusters of sporangia on the underside of a fern frond.

specialization the process of narrowing abilities so that fewer roles are performed with greater efficiency; the process of becoming increasingly differentiated.

speciation an evolutionary process by which new species are formed, often by the division of one species into two.

species 1. the major subdivision of a genus, regarded as the basic category of biological classification; 2. related individuals that resemble one another through recent common ancestry and that share a single ecological niche; 3. in sexual organisms, a group whose members are potentially able to breed with one another but are unable to breed with members of any other group.

specific heat the heat, expressed in calories, required to raise the temperature of 1 gram of some substance 1°C; a way of considering the quantity of heat that various substances are capable of holding (for example, water has great specific heat).

specific name the second part of a formal scientific name, indicating a species with a genus, always italicized, but usually not capitalized.

sperm 1. a male gamete. 2. a spermatozoan. 3. a spermatozoid. 4. *adj.,* pertaining to the male gamete or male gamete function.

spermatic cord in the male reproductive system, a cordlike structure consisting of a tough, fibrous coat containing the vas deferens, the nerves and blood vessels supplying the testis, and a retractory muscle, the last being vestigial in humans.

spermatid one of the cells that result from the meiotic division of a spermatocyte and mature into spermatozoa.

spermatogenesis the meiotic process resulting in the production of haploid sperm.

S phase in the cell cycle, the stage during which DNA replication occurs.

sphincter a ring of muscle surrounding a body opening or channel that is able to close off the opening; e.g., oral sphincter, anal sphincter.

spicule a tiny calcareous or siliceous pointed body embedded in and serving to stiffen and support the tissues of sponges, sea cucumbers, and other invertebrates.

spinal cord the complex band of neurons that runs through the spinal column of vertebrates to the brain.

spinal nerves any of the many nerves that enter and leave the spinal cord, including both somatic and autonomic. Compare *cranial nerve.*

spindle a system of microtubules present in the cell during mitosis and meiosis, resembling the spindle of a primitive loom; it serves in the separation of chromosomes during the division process. Also called *spindle apparatus.*

spindle fiber one of the microtubule filaments constituting the mitotic spindle.

spindle pole one of the two points of origin of the mitotic apparatus; represents the microtubular organizing center and contains the centriole in cells where these bodies appear.

spinneret an arthropod organ for producing threads of silk from the secretion of a silk gland.

spiracles the external openings to the respiratory system of terrestrial arthropods.

spiral cleavage in protostome embryos, a spiral pattern in the early cleavages in which the cleavage planes become offset from those below. See also *radial cleavage.*

spiral valve a helical fold of the intestinal wall in the short intestine of sharks and certain bony fishes; slows the passage of food and provides additional absorptive surfaces.

spirillum spiral-shaped bacteria, primarily of the genus *Spirillum.*

spirochaete any of an order of slender, corkscrew-shaped bacteria.

sponge any animal of the phylum Porifera.

spongin a tough, insoluble protein that makes up the skeleton of a class of sponges including the once commercially important bath sponge.

spongy bone bone with a network of thin, hard walls and numerous spaces; spongelike in appearance.

spongy parenchyma (pə reng′kə mə) in a leaf, the loosely arranged photosynthetic tissue, containing many air spaces, below the palisade parenchyma.

spontaneous generation the production of living organisms from inanimate matter.

sporangium (*pl.,* sporangia) a structure in which spores are produced; found in algae, fungi, bryophytes, and ferns.

spore a minute unicellular reproductive or resistant body, specialized for dispersal, for surviving unfavorable environmental conditions, and for germinating to produce a new vegetative individual when conditions improve. See also *endospore.*

sporic cycle in some algae and all plants, a life cycle in which meiosis leads to a haploid generation of cells that later produces gametes through simple mitosis. The cycle is often described as an alternation of generations, wherein a diploid sporophyte generation alternates with a haploid gametophyte generation.

sporophyte in plants having an alternation of generations, a diploid individual capable of producing haploid spores by meiosis; the prominent form of ferns and seed plants. Compare *gametophyte.*

sporozoan any parasitic protozoan of the phylum Sporozoa, certain species of which cause malaria.

S-shaped curve a plot of population growth where growth is rapid at first but then slows when *environmental resistance* is met, and levels off at some point near or below the *carrying capacity*. Compare *J-shaped curve*. Also *logistic growth curve*.

stabilizing selection in population genetics, selection against both extremes of a continuous phenotype, favoring the intermediate.

stamen the male reproductive structure of a flower, consisting of a pollen-bearing anther and the filament on which it is borne.

staphylococcus (staf′ə lə kok′əs) spherical bacteria arranged in grape-like clusters.

stele in roots and stems of vascular plants, a central cylinder containing vascular tissue.

stem 1. the ascending axis of a plant, whether above or below ground; 2. the stalk which supports a leaf, flower, or fruit; 3. the main body of that portion of a plant which is above ground. Also *shoot*.

stem cell also *hemocytoblast;* generalized cell of red bone marrow from which all blood cells form.

steroid any of a class of lipid-soluble compounds, some of which are hormones, consisting of four interlocking saturated hydrocarbon rings and their side groups; included are *cholesterol, estrogen, testosterone, cortisol,* and others.

steroid sex hormone part of a class of hormones consisting of the steroid molecule with various side group substitutions; e.g., estrogen and testosterone.

stigma in the floral pistil, the top, slightly enlarged and often hairy or sticky end of the style, on which pollen grains adhere and germinate.

stipe the stemlike structure in red or brown algae that supports the blades or blade.

stoma (*pl.,* stomata) minute pores in the *epidermis* of leaves, stems and other plant organs, including *guard cells;* allows the diffusion of gases into and out of intercellular spaces.

stomach a saclike enlargement of the digestive tract functioning in storage, churning, and digestion.

storage vesicle. See *lysosome.*

stratified squamous epithelium multilayered, flattened epithelial cells as seen in the epidermis of the skin, esophagus, and vagina.

streptococcus (strep′tə kok′əs) spherical bacteria arranged in a chain.

stretch receptor a sensory receptor that is stimulated by stretching, as in a tendon, muscle, or bladder wall.

striated muscle. See *skeletal muscle.*

stroma the enzyme-containing fluid region that surrounds the thylakoids of a chloroplast.

stromatolite a macroscopic living or fossil geological structure of layered domes of deposited material, attributed to the presence of shallow-water photosynthetic prokaryotes.

style the stalk of a pistil in a flower, connecting the stigma with the ovary.

suberin a complex fatty substance of cork cell walls and other waterproofed cell walls.

subspecies a more or less clearly defined, morphologically distinct, named, geographic variety of a species; a third part of the scientific name (*genus, species, subspecies*).

substrate a substance acted upon by an enzyme.

substrate level phosphorylation (fos fər ə lā′shən) the production in one or more steps of ATP from ADP, P$_1$, and an appropriate organic substrate; the capture of high-energy phosphate bonds directly from metabolic transformations. Compare *chemiosmotic phosphorylation.*

subunit disassembly a hypothetical explanation of spindle shortening, an anaphase process during which spindle fiber microtubules are broken down into tubulin molecules.

sucrase an enzyme that digests sucrose, forming fructose and glucose.

sucrose a sweet, twelve-carbon disaccharide consisting of glucose and fructose subunits. Also called *table sugar.*

sun-compass orientation a behavioral mechanism utilizing the angle of the sun and the time of day to compute direction for navigation.

super-normal releaser in behavior, an environmental stimulus with exaggerated features that produces an instinctive response; not normally encountered in nature.

suppressor T-cell a type of white blood cell that shuts down the immune response after the risk of infection has passed.

surface volume hypothesis the proposal that cells are restricted to a size that assures a surface-volume ratio that provides a sufficient membrane area to support the transport needed to maintain metabolic activity.

survival of the fittest. See *natural selection;* the principle of the survival of the forms of animal and vegetable life best fitted for existing conditions, while related but less fit forms become extinct.

survivorship curve a graph with numbers of individuals plotted on the X axis and percentage of total life span completed plotted on the Y axis; useful in comparing periods of greatest mortality in several different species.

suture in anatomy, immovable joints formed by the articulation of skull bones.

swim bladder also called *air bladder;* a gas-filled sac giving controlled bouyancy to most bony fish; homologous with the lungs of land vertebrates and lungfish.

syllogism in logic, an argument the conclusion of which is supported by two premises, of which one contains the term that is the predicate of the conclusion, and the other contains the term that is the subject of the conclusion; common to both premises is a term that is excluded from the conclusion; e.g., all A is B; all B is C; therefore all A is C.

symbiont (sim′bē ənt) a symbiotic organism, one of two intimately associated species.

symbiosis the living together in intimate association of two species; includes three categories: *mutualism* (both organisms gain), *commensalism* (one gains at little or no expense to the other), and *parasitism* (one gains at the expense of the other).

symbiosis hypothesis the hypothesis that the eukaryotic cell evolved from the mutualistic union of various prokaryotic organisms, one of which gave rise basically to the cytoplasm, nucleus, and motile membranes; a second to mitochondria; a third to chloroplasts and other plastids; and a fourth to cilia, eukaryotic flagella, basal bodies, centrioles, and spindle, and all other microtubule structures.

sympathetic division that portion of the autonomic nervous system whose nerves emerge only from the spinal cord and function to speed up the usual pace of the visceral organs served. Compare *parasympathetic division.*

sympatric speciation speciation in populations without geographic separation. Compare *allopatric speciation.*

synapse (sin′aps) the junction between the axon of one neuron and the dendrite or cell body of another; crossed by neural impulses.

synapsis the pairing up and fusing of homologous chromosomes during the first meiotic prophase, whereby preparations are made for crossing over.

synaptic cleft the minute space between communicating neurons or between motor neurons and effector organs; the space crossed by neurotransmitters.

synaptic knobs one of the multiple bulbous swellings at the axonal endings, containing neurotransmitters in secretion granules and forming one side of the synaptic cleft.

synaptonemal complex (sə nap′tə nē′mal) in crossing over, a complex, zipperlike structure composed of protein and RNA formed between homologous chromatids in meiotic prophase.

synonymous codons in the genetic code, codons that represent the same amino acid.

synovial fluid a transparent, viscid lubricating fluid secreted by the synovial membranes of joints, bursae, and tendon sheaths.

synovial joint a freely movable joint surrounded by a fibrous capsule lined by a synovial membrane that secretes lubricating synovial fluid.

synthesist in science, one who attempts to draw broad general principles from widely disparate observations, or one who reinterprets established relationships in support of a new general idea or synthesis.

syphilis (sif'ə lis) a sexually transmitted disease caused by the spirochete *Treponema pallidum*.

system an assemblage of organs cooperatively performing a body process (i.e., the *nervous system* or *digestive system*).

systole the period of heart contraction, particularly of the ventricles. Compare *diastole*.

systolic pressure the highest arterial blood pressure of the cardiac cycle, a product of ventricular contraction.

tactile receptors. See *mechanoreceptor*.

taiga (tī'gə) a subarctic forest biome dominated by spruce and fir trees; found in Europe and North America and at high altitudes elsewhere.

tap root system a root system consisting of a large primary root and its secondary and lateral branches.

target cell a cell acted upon by a specific chemical messenger, generally containing or bearing specific receptor proteins not found in other cells.

taste bud a sensory receptor sensitive to taste, found chiefly in the epithelium of the tongue.

taxis the movement of an organism toward or away from a stimulus.

taxonomy the science of identifying, naming, and classifying organisms.

T-cell lymphocyte a lymphocyte specializing in cell-mediated responses; interacts in complex ways with other types of cells in the immune system; eliminates foreign or infected cells it encounters.

TDF gene the "testis determining factor" which stimulates the development of the testes in male embryos.

tectorial membrane a membrane of the cochlea, overlying and contacting the hair cells of the organ of Corti.

telophase the stage of mitosis or meiosis in which new nuclear membranes around each group of daughter chromosomes, the nucleoli appear, and the chromosomes decondense; at this time the cell membrane and cytoplasm usually divide to form two daughter cells.

TEM (transmission electron microscope) a device that uses an electron beam, rather than light, to form magnified images.

temperate deciduous forest a forest biome of the temperate zone, in which the dominant tree species and most other trees are deciduous (shedding) and are bare in winter months.

temporal lobe a large lobe on the lateral portion of each cerebral hemisphere.

tendon a dense tough cord of fibrous connective tissue that is attached at one end to a muscle and at the other to that part of the skeleton that moves when the muscle contracts.

termination the end of polypeptide synthesis, when "stop" codons on the messenger RNA are encountered by the ribosome, which releases the polypeptide and comes apart at its subunits.

territory the space defended by a territorial animal.

territoriality the behavior of an animal defending its territory.

tertiary consumer (tẽr'shē er'ē) a carnivorous animal that feeds on secondary consumers, which in turn feed on herbivores.

tertiary level (tẽr'shē er'ē) the third level of organization of a protein, the pattern of folding of a polypeptide upon itself, which is generally quite specific for each protein type.

test cross the cross of a dominant individual with a homozygous recessive individual to determine whether recessive alleles exist.

testes (*sing.,* testis) the male gonads, in which spermatozoa are produced by meiosis.

testicles. See *testes*.

testosterone a male hormone, produced in the testes, important in the sex drive and producing secondary sex characteristics.

tetrahedron in geometry, a solid contained by four plane faces; a triangular pyramid; the shape taken by methane (CH_4).

tetraploid *adj.,* having four complete sets of chromosomes in each cell. Compare *allotetraploid, allopolyploid, polyploid*.

tetrapod. Also *land vertebrate;* any vertebrate of the classes Amphidia, Reptilia, Mammalia, and Aves, including some that don't have four feet (e.g., birds, people).

thalamus (thal'ə məs) a subdivision of the forebrain, just above the brainstem, concerned with relaying information.

theory 1. a coherent group of general propositions used as principles of explanation for a class of phenomena (i.e., Darwin's theory of the origin of species). 2. a more or less verified explanation accounting for a body of known facts or phenomena. Compare *hypothesis*.

thermal overturn the seasonal overturn of lake waters brought about by decreasing surface temperatures that increase the density of surface waters, allowing them to sink, thereby disrupting the thermocline and permitting windblown revolving of water.

thermal proteinoids polymers spontaneously generated using dry heat and amino acids, which when placed in water cluster to form proteinoid microspheres.

thermocline in a body of water, a temperature gradient where the temperature changes rapidly as a function of depth; thermoclines act as barriers to the vertical movement of water.

thermodynamics 1. the branch of physics that deals with the interconversions of energy as heat, potential energy, kinetic energy, radiant energy, entropy, and work. 2. the processes and phenomena of energy interconversions. See *first and second law of thermodynamics*.

thermonastic movement in plants, a sudden reaction to touch, associated with rapid ion transport and sudden changes in turgor.

thermoreceptor a sensory receptor that responds to changes in temperature.

thermoregulation an animal's control over its internal temperature: the behavioral or physiological mechanisms that maintain a body at a particular temperature.

thoracic region the portion of the vertebral column that articulates with ribs, between the cervical and lumbar regions.

thorax 1. in animals, the part of the body anterior to the diaphragm and posterior to the neck, containing the lungs and the heart; 2. the middle of the three parts of an insect body, bearing the legs and wings.

thromboplastin (throm'bō plas'tin) in the blood-clotting reactions, a protein released from damaged platelets that catalyzes the conversion of the prothrombin into the active enzyme thrombin.

thromboxane (throm bôx'ān) a prostaglandin.

thylakoid (thī'lə koid) the membranous structure of chloroplasts consisting of a *thylakoid membrane,* containing light-harvesting antennas and the photosynthetic electron transport chain; an inner lumen that collects protons during active photosynthesis; and CF_1 particles, the sites of chemiosmotic phosphorylation.

thymine a pyrimidine, one of four nitrogenous bases of DNA.

thymus a glandular body above the lungs, believed to stimulate T-cell lymphocyte development through the secretion of thymosin.

thyroid gland a large endocrine gland in the lower neck region of all vertebrates, the thyroxin secretions of which regulate the rate of metabolism.

thyroid-stimulating hormone (TSH). Also *thyrotropin;* a peptide hormone of the anterior pituitary, the action of which is to stimulate the release of thyroxin from the thyroid.

thyrotropin. See *thyroid-stimulating hormone* (TSH).

thyroxin a thyroid hormone that functions in regulating metabolism.

tissue a grouping of cells of similar origin, structure, and function. Compare *organ*.

totipotent *adj.,* a cell or tissue retaining developmental flexibility; undifferentiated; having the ability to produce the entire original organism.

trace element. See *micronutrient*.

tracer a radioactive element or compound that is put into a biological system to be later located by detection of the radioactivity.

trachea (trā'kē ə) (*pl.,* tracheae) 1. in land

vertebrates, air passages between the lungs and the larynx; 2. one of the air conveying tubules in the respiratory system of an insect, millipede, or centipede.

tracheal system the respiratory system of insects, composed of thin-walled air-conducting tubules opening to *spiracles* and extending to finer, branched *tracheoles*, some terminating in *air sacs*.

tracheid a long, tubular xylem element that functions in support and water conduction; distinguished from *xylem vessels* by having tapered, pitted end walls.

tracheoles. See *tracheal system*.

tracheophyte a vascular terrestrial plant.

transcription RNA sequence in which the RNA nucleotide sequence is determined by specific base pairing with the nucleotide sequence of DNA.

transcription complex enzymes essential to the process through which DNA is transcribed into RNA, including helicase and RNA polymerase.

transducer a device that receives energy in one form and retransmits it in a different form, e.g., the conversion of touch (pressure) to action potentials.

transfer RNA (tRNA) in the synthesis of polypeptides, a class of RNA molecules with the task of identifying and bonding with specific amino acids and then, on the ribosome, identifying and bonding with corresponding sites on the messenger RNA.

transformation in a bacterium, the direct incorporation of a DNA fragment from its medium into its own chromosome.

translation polypeptide synthesis as it is directed by mRNA and assisted by ribosomes and tRNA; the transfer of linear information from a nucleotide sequence to an amino acid sequence according to the genetic code.

translocation 1. during protein synthesis in which a transfer RNA molecule is moved (translocated) from one ribosomal tRNA attachment site (pocket) to the other; 2. in chromosomes, the breakage and improper (nonhomologous) rejoining of chromosome segments; 3. the movement of solutes through the phloem from one part of a plant to another.

translocation Down syndrome. See *trisomy 21*.

transpiration 1. in plants, the evaporation of water vapor from leaves, especially through the stomata; 2. the physical effects of such evaporation taken together.

transpiration pull the pulling of water up through the xylem of a plant using the energy of evaporation, the water potential gradient in the leaf, and the tensile strength of water.

transposon a segment of DNA capable of being moved from one chromosomal location to another, containing insertion sequences and forming a complete transposable unit. Also *transposable gene*.

transposable gene. See *transposon*.

transverse tubule also called *T-tubule;* one of a specialized system of tubules in a muscle fiber, transmitting the contractile impulse from the sarcolemma to the sarcomeres.

tricuspid valve the valve between the right atrium and the right ventricle consisting of three triangular membranous flaps.

triglyceride a nonpolar, hydrophobic lipid consisting of three fatty acids, covalently bonded to one molecule of glycerol.

trimester one of the three-month periods of the nine months of human gestation.

trinucleate cell in plant reproduction, the triploid cell formed when a sperm penetrates the binucleate central cell in the embryo sac.

triphosphate nucleoside one of the components occurring in a nuclear pool, having two high-energy bonds available for use in DNA replication.

trisomy 21 a severe human congenital pathology attributable to the presence of three rather than two homologues of chromosome 21. Also *Down syndrome* and *translocation Down syndrome*.

trophic level relating to nutrition; a level in a food pyramid.

trophoblast in mammals, the thin-wall side of a blastocyst that forms the chorion when implantation occurs. See also *blastocyst*.

trophosome an extensive organ in a tubeworm which houses vast numbers of chemotrophic vent bacteria capable of extracting energy from simple chemicals and forming carbohydrates.

tropical rain forest a tropical woodland biome that has an annual rainfall of at least 250 cm (100 in.) and often much more; typically restricted to lowland areas and characterized by a mix of many species of tall, broad-leaved evergreen trees that form a continuous canopy, with vines and woody epiphytes, and by a dark, nearly bare forest floor.

tropical savanna a biome that is primarily grassy but frequently interrupted by groves of drought-resistant trees; commonly occurs between tropical rain forest and desert.

tropism growth toward or away from an external stimulus, in plants usually accomplished by differential cell elongation in the stem or root. See also *gravitotropism* and *phototropism*.

tropomyosin (trō pō mī'ə sən) a low-molecular weight filamentous protein that accompanies the globular protein actin in making up actin microfilaments.

troponin a protein of low molecular weight that binds calcium in muscle contraction, a specific variant of the ubiquitous calcium-binding molecule *calmodulin*.

true-breeding homozygous; containing one form of an allele only so the offspring always resemble the parents and each other for a particular trait.

trypanosome a parasitic, flagellated proto-

zoan of the genus *Trypanosoma*, infecting mammals and transmitted by insect vectors, responsible for *chagas disease* and *sleeping sickness*.

trypsin a powerful proteolytic enzyme secreted by the pancreas in the inactive form *trypsinogen* and activated in the intestine.

tryptophan operon (trip'tə fan' op'ə ron) (a repressible operon) a region of DNA in *E. coli* that includes structural genes coding for enzymes that synthesize tryptophan, and a region that controls their transcription. See also *operon*.

tubular secretion in the nephron, the active transport of certain substances from the crude filtrate back into the blood.

tubulin a protein consisting of two dissimilar spherical polypeptides making up the subunits of microtubules.

tundra a biome characterized by level or gently undulating treeless plains of the arctic and subarctic that support dense growth of mosses and lichens as well as dwarf herbs and shrubs; underlain by permafrost and seasonally covered by snow.

tunica in plants, the protective layer covering the short apical meristem.

tunicate any marine chordate having a sac-like body enclosed in a thick membrane (or tunic) from which protrude two openings or siphons for the entry and exit of water.

turgor the normal state of turgidity and tension in living plant cells by the uptake of water through osmosis.

turgor pressure the actual hydrostatic pressure developed by the fluid of a swollen plant cell.

tympanal organs. See *tympanum*.

tympanic membrane also *tympanum, eardrum;* a thin, clear, tense double membrane dividing the middle ear from the external auditory canal; on the surface in frogs and toads, and intermediate in birds and reptiles.

tympanum (tim'pən əm). See *tympanic membrane*.

typhlosole (tif'lə sōl) in the earthworm, an infolding in the roof of the intestine that greatly increases the digestive and absorptive surface.

ultrastructure the submicroscopic structure of organelles of the cell.

umbilical cord in placental mammals, a vascular cord connecting the fetus with the placenta.

umbilicus the navel; point on the abdomen at which the umbilical cord was attached to the embryo. Also "belly-button."

unconditioned response in behavior, an involuntary reaction to a common stimulus.

unconditioned stimulus the normal or usual stimulus that produces a certain predictable behavior. Compare *conditioned stimulus*.

unlinked *adj.*, gene loci of different chromosomes, independently assorted.

unsaturated *adj.*, in lipid chemistry, capable of accepting hydrogens.

upper epidermis in plants, the upper (light-exposed) layer of cutinized epidermal cells in a leaf.

upwelling in oceans, the wind-driven rise of deep water layers to the surface; associated with the circulation of mineral nutrients and a consequent increase in productivity and biomass.

uracil one of the nitrogenous bases of RNA.

urea a highly soluble compound that is the principle nitrogenous waste of the urine of animals.

ureter the tube that conducts urine from the kidney to the bladder.

urethra the tube that conducts urine from the urinary bladder to the outside of the body.

urochordate any member of the subphylum *Urochordata*: tunicates, salps, larvaceae.

uterus 1. in female mammals, a muscular, vascularized, mucous membrane-lined organ for containing and nourishing the developing young; 2. an enlarged section of the oviduct of various vertebrates and invertebrates.

utricle the chamber of the membranous labyrinth of the middle ear into which the semicircular canals open.

vaccine killed or weakened disease agents, injected to stimulate the primary immune reaction.

vacuole (vak′yü ōl) a general term for any fluid-filled, membrane-bounded body within the cytoplasm of a cell.

vagina the female copulatory organ and birth canal in mammals and other animals.

variability the general qualitative term for the presence of genetic differences between individuals in a population.

variable experimental variable; the focus of an experiment, tube tested and compared with a control.

variable region the portion of an immunoglobulin polypeptide concerned with the binding of an antigen, which varies with the specific immunoglobin.

vascular cambium the cylinder of meristematic tissue that in secondary growth produces xylem on its inner side and phloem on its outer side, thus contributing to growth in circumference.

vascular plant a plant with xylem and phloem; a tracheophyte.

vascular rays in woody stems, radiating, spokelike lines of parenchyma and collenchyma tissue that conduct materials laterally and help relieve pressure caused by expansion during circumferential growth.

vascular system 1. the xylem and phloem of a vascular plant; 2. the circulatory system of an animal.

vascular tissue any tissue that contains vessels through which fluids are passed.

vas deferens the duct of the testis which transports the sperm from the epididymis to the penis.

vasoconstrictor a nerve or drug that causes the constriction of the blood vessels.

vasopressin. See *antidiuretic hormone.*

vegetative stage. Also *vegetative state;* in fungi, a spreading mycelium specialized in feeding and growth.

vein 1. a vessel returning blood toward the heart. 2. a vascular bundle in a leaf or petiole.

ventral nerve cord a common feature of many invertebrate phyla, the main longitudinal nerve cord of the body; solid and paired, with a series of ganglionic masses.

ventricle one of the large muscular chambers of the four-chambered heart.

venule a small vein.

vermiform appendix a hollow, fingerlike, blind extension of the cecum, having no known function in humans.

vertebral canal the pathway of the spinal cord through the vertebral column.

vertebral column the articulated series of vertebrae connected by ligaments and separated by intervertebral discs that in vertebrates form the supporting axis of the body and of the tail in most forms.

vertebrate an animal in the subphylum Vertebrata, phylum Chordata; an animal with a vertebral column of bone or cartilage.

vessel a conducting tube in a dicot formed in the xylem by the end-to-end fusion of a series of cells (vessel elements) followed by the loss of adjacent end walls and of cell protoplasm. Compare *tracheid.*

vestigial (ve stij′ē əl) *adj.*, pertaining to a degenerate or imperfectly developed organ or structure no longer functional.

villi (*sing.*, villus) minute cellular processes that cover the inner surface of the small intestine, containing blood vessels and lacteals and serving in the absorption of nutrients.

virus a noncellular, parasitic organism transmitted as DNA or RNA enclosed in a membrane or protein coat, often together with one or several enzymes; replicates only within a host cell, using host ribosomes and enzymes of synthesis.

viscera the internal organs within the body cavity, e.g., heart, lungs, intestines, liver.

visible light electromagnetic wave lengths longer than about 400 nm and shorter than about 750 nm, which can serve as visual stimuli to most photoreceptive organisms.

vital capacity the maximum amount of air that can be exhaled after a fully forced inhalation.

vital force a discredited notion of mysterious life-giving force that animates and perpetuates living beings.

vitalism an untestable doctrine that attributes the functions of a living organism to a *vital principle* or *vital force* distinct

from chemical and physical forces; no longer taken seriously.

vitamin an organic substance taken in with food that is essential to the metabolic activity of an organism, usually because it supplies part of a coenzyme not made by the organism.

vitelline membrane the membrane surrounding the egg yolk in some animals.

viviparity *n.*, the condition of bringing forth living young rather than eggs, as most mammals and some reptiles and fishes.

viviparous *adj.*, producing young from within the uterus; during development, nourishment is supplied by the mother's tissues, usually via a placenta. Compare *oviparous, ovoviviparous.*

voluntary muscle. See *skeletal muscle.*

vulva the external female genitalia.

water potential the potential energy of water to move, as a result of concentration, gravity, pressure, or solute content.

water potential gradient the difference in potential energy of water between a region of greater water potential and a region of lesser water potential. Because of gravity, pressure, or an osmotic pressure, water moves down its water potential gradient.

water vacuole. See *contractile vacuole.*

water vascular system in echinoderms, a system of vessels that contains sea water and is used as a hydraulic system in the movement of tube feet.

white matter the portion of the spinal cord consisting of myelinated axons and dendrites. See *gray matter.*

wilting the loss of turgor, especially because of an inadequate supply of water to a plant or plant cell.

X chromosome one of the two heteromorphic sex chromosomes of mammals, flies, and certain other insects. In most cases **XX** = female and **XY** = male.

xerophyte a plant adapted to dry areas.

x-ray crystallography a procedure of directing x-rays at a crystal of a protein or other large molecule, recording the pattern produced as the rays are bent by the regular, repeating molecular structures within the crystal, and using this pattern to reconstruct the three-dimensional structure of the molecule.

xylem one of the two complex tissues in the vascular system of plants; consists of the dead cell walls of vessels, tracheids, or both, often together with sclerenchyma and parenchyma cells; functions chiefly in water conduction and strengthening the plant. See also *tracheid.* Compare *phloem.*

Y chromosome one of the two heteromorphic sex chromosomes of mammals, flies, and certain other insects. In most cases, **XY** = male and **XX** = female; in general, nearly devoid of genes not concerned with maleness.

yellow marrow yellow, fatty material within the central cavity of long bones.

yolk one of the extraembryonic membranes of a bird, reptile or mammal.

zeatin a plant cytokinin hormone and growth factor extracted from corn.

Z-line in striated muscle, the partition between adjacent contractile units to which actin filaments are anchored.

zona pellucida (zō′nə pel lū′sədə) "clear zone"; a thick, transparent, elastic membrane or envelope secreted around an ovum by follicle cells in some vertebrates.

zooplankton the nonphotosynthetic, minute, animal life drifting at or near the surface of the open sea.

Z-scheme a graphic presentation of the energy levels in the oxidation-reduction reactions occurring in the light reaction of photosynthesis.

zygospore a diploid fungal or algal spore formed by the union of two similar sexual cells; has a thickened wall and serves as a resistant resting spore.

zygote (zī′gōt) a cell formed by the union of two gametes; a fertilized egg.

zygotic *adj.*, pertaining to the cell formed by the union of two gametes or the fertilized egg.

zygotic cycle in some protists and all fungi, a life cycle in which the haploid state dominates. The diploid state, which follows fertilization, is usually a very brief interlude followed by meiosis and resumption of the haploid state.

ILLUSTRATION ACKNOWLEDGMENTS

Unless otherwise acknowledged, all photos are the property of Scott, Foresman and Company.

FRONT COVER egret © David Smart/DRK Photo; background © Fred Bavendam/Peter Arnold, Inc.
BACK COVER cheetah © Peter Pickford/DRK Photo; background © Fred Bavendam/Peter Arnold, Inc.

FRONT MATTER Page i/© Photo Researchers, Inc. Page iv/© Peter Arnold, Inc. Page vii/© Bruce Coleman, Inc. Page x/© Peter Arnold, Inc. Page xi/© Photo Researchers, Inc. Page xiii/© Peter Arnold, Inc. Page xiv/© Black Star Page xv/© Peter Arnold, Inc. Page xvi/© Tom Stack & Associates Page xvii/© Donald Perry Page xviii/© Tom Stack & Associates Page xix/© Jeff Rotman Page xx/© Tom Stack & Associates Page xxi/© Peter Arnold, Inc. Page xxii/© Peter Arnold, Inc. Page xxiii/© Peter Arnold, Inc. Page xxiv/© Tom Stack & Associates Page xxv/© Peter Arnold, Inc.

CONTENTS IN BRIEF Part I/© G. Ziesler/Peter Arnold, Inc. Part II/© Michael Nichols/Black Star Part III/© Donald Perry Part IV/© Jeff Rotman Part V/© Rod Planck/Tom Stack and Associates Part VI/© John Shaw/Tom Stack and Associates Part VII/© G. Ziesler/Peter Arnold, Inc.

CHAPTER 1 Page 2/© Steven Allen/Peter Arnold, Inc. 1.1/"Galileo Before the Holy Office" by Robert Fleury. Louvre, Paris 1.2/NASA 1.5a/Manfred Kage/Peter Arnold, Inc. 1.5b/E.R. Degginger 1.5c/Dwight R. Kuhn 1.5d/Dwight R. Kuhn 1.5e/Rajesh Bedi/*Life Magazine* © 1979 Time, Inc. (aphid); Dwight R. Kuhn (gharial) 1.5f/Baron Hugo Van Lawick, © National Geographic Society (chimpanzee); Stephen J. Krasemann/DRK Photo (bald eagles) 1.5g/Dr. Frank Carpenter

CHAPTER 2 Page 17/© Phil Harrington/Peter Arnold, Inc. 2.2/Courtesy of Eric M. Reiman, M.D. 2.13(tl)/© Department of Citrus 2.13(tc)/© Sam Griffith, Click/Chicago 2.13(tr)/© Al Gardner, Click/Chicago 2.13(bl)/© Ray Reiss, 1984, Click/Chicago 2.13(br)/© Coca-Cola USA

CHAPTER 3 Page 31/Courtesy Tripos Associates, Inc. 3.4/Brown, R. M. and J. H. M. Willison, 1977. In *International Cell Biology 1976-1977*, ed., B.R. Brinkley and K.R. Porter, pp. 267–283. © 1977 by The Rockefeller Univ. Press. 3.9/National Institutes of Health

CHAPTER 4 Page 45/© Manfred Kage/Peter Arnold, Inc. 4.3(bl)/© Fred Hossler/Visuals Unlimited 4.3(bc)/Macmillan Science Co., Inc. 4.3(br)/L.N.A. Lott, McMaster Univ./BPS 4.5/Dr. Daniel Branton 4.6/© J.J. Wolosewick, Univ. of Illinois at the Medical Center/BPS. 4.7a/Courtesy of Dr. Emma Shelton 4.7b/Dr. Daniel Branton Page 57(r)/Dr. Morton/American Society for Microbiology Page 57(1)/Dr. Daniel Branton 4.10/© D.W. Fawcett/Photo Researchers, Inc. 4.12a/Hugh Spencer 4.12b/W.P. Wergin and E.H. Newcomb, Univ. of Wisconsin—Madison/BPS 4.13a/Courtesy Abbott Laboratories 4.14b/P.R. Burton, Univ. of Kansas/BPS 4.16a/Bouck, G.B. 1971. *J. Cell Biology* 50:362-384. Reproduced by copyright permission of The Rockefeller University Press 4.16b/Dr. G.B. Bouck 4.17(l)/Dr. William E. Barstow 4.17(r)/Turner, F.R. 1968. *J. Cell Biology* 37:370. Reproduced by copyright permission of The Rockefeller Univ. Press 4.18(l)/Dr. Tony Brain SPL/Science Source, P.R. 4.18(r)/Courtesy of D.L. Findley, P.L. Walne, and R.W. Holton, U. of Tennessee, Knoxville. From *J. Phycology* 6:182-188, 1970.

CHAPTER 5 Page 68/Courtesy Lennart Nilsson © Boehringer Ingelheim International, GmbH 5.5b/H.E. Buhse, Jr., and R.C. Holsen, U. of Illinois at Chicago 5.5c/D.W. Fawcett/Photo Researchers 5.6/James D. Hirsch, Rockefeller Univ.

CHAPTER 6 Page 78/© Stephen Dalton/Photo Researchers, Inc. 6.1/© Rod Allin/Tom Stack & Associates 6.2/David R. Frazier 6.3/© L.E. Gilbert, Univ. of Texas at Austin/BPS (ants) © Don and Pat Valenti (bones) 6.4/U.P.I.

CHAPTER 7 Page 96/© Jacques Jangoux/Peter Arnold, Inc. 7.1/© Dave Millert, 1984/Tom Stack & Associates 7.2/S.E. Frederick and E.H. Newcomb, Univ. of Wisconsin—Madison/BPS Page 109/Photo by Dr. W.W. Thomson, Courtesy of R.M. Leech, University of York

CHAPTER 8 Page 114/© John Mitchell/Photo Researchers, Inc. 8.7/© Tom McHugh/Photo Researchers, Inc.

CHAPTER 9 Page 128/© Fritz Goro/*Life Magazine* 9.3/Courtesy of Dr. Henry L. Nadler, Children's Memorial Hospital, Chicago 9.4/Paulson, J.R., and Laemmli, U.K. *Cell* 12:817-828. © 1977 M.I.T. pages 133 & 135 9.6/© C.L. Rieder, New York State Dept. of Health/BPS 9.9/Dr. Andrew S. Bajer

CHAPTER 10 Page 144/© Dr. A.S. Bajer 10.2/Jean-Marie Luciani, Courtesy Pasteur Institute, Paris 10.3/Professor M. Westergaard. In *DNA/Chromatin and Chromosomes* by E.M. Bradbury, N. Maclean and H.C. Matthews. © 1981 by Blackwell Scientific Publications Page 154/© Cathlyn Melloan, 1985, Click/Chicago

CHAPTER 11 Page 158/© Carolina Biological Supply Co. 11.1/Historical Pictures Service, Chicago

CHAPTER 12 Page 173/© G. Ziesler/Peter Arnold Inc. 12.2/© Walter Chandoha 12.3/© Runk/Schoenberger from Grant Heilman 12.5/Courtesy Joiner Associates, Inc. 12.6/© Walter Chandoha 12.7/Keytone Press Agency

CHAPTER 13 Page 185/© Jim Goodwin/Photo Researchers, Inc. Page 190/The Bettmann Archive 13.5/Courtesy of Dr. Murray L. Barr 13.8/© Photo Researchers, Inc.

CHAPTER 14 Page 201/© Erich Hartmann/Magnum Photos 14.2/Omikron Science Source, P.R. 14.3/© Lee D. Simon/Photo Researchers, Inc. 14.5/X-ray diffraction photograph of DNA, B-form, taken by Rosalind Franklin late in 1952. From J.D. Watson, *The Double Helix*, p. 168. New York: Atheneum. © 1968 by J.D. Watson. 14.9/Courtesy Tsuyoshi Kakifuda, National Institutes of Health.

CHAPTER 15 Page 218/Courtesy Tripos Associates Inc. 15.2/Miller, O.L., Jr. and B.R. Beatty, 1969. *Science* 164:955-957 15.4/Lake, J.A. 1981. *Scientific American* 245:84 15.10/Miller, O.L., Jr., B.A. Hamkalo, and C.A. Thomas, Jr. 1970. *Science* 169:392-395. 15.12/Edstrom, J., and W. Beermann. 1962 *J. Cell Biol.* 14:374. Reprinted by copyright permission of The Rockefeller Univ. Press Page 236/NASA

CHAPTER 16 Page 241/© Erich Hartmann/Magnum Photos 16.1/Dr. T.F. Anderson, Institute for Cancer Research, Philadelphia 16.7/Dan McCoy/Rainbow

CHAPTER 17 Page 257/© Robert Lee II Photographer 17.1/"Charles Darwin, Age 30" by George Richmond R.A. Royal College of Surgeons of England 17.3/Historical Pictures Source/Chicago 17.4/© Robert

Rattner Page 262/Wolfgang Kaehler (a,c,d); George H. Harrison (b,e) Page 263/Tui De Roy Moore (i); George H. Harrison 17.6/John Dawson 17.7/© Don and Pat Valenti 17.10/© Don and Pat Valenti

CHAPTER 18   Page 271/© Mark Newman/Tom Stack and Associates 18.1a/Grant Heilman/Grant Heilman Photography 18.1b/Thomas Hovland/Grant Heilman Photography 18.2/Everett C. Johnson 18.4/Wide World 18.6/© M.W.F. Tweedie/Photo Researchers, Inc. 18.10/Jeff Foott 18.12/Milt & Joan Mann/Cameramann International

CHAPTER 19   Page 288/© Brian Parker/Tom Stack and Associates 19.2/M. Phillip Kahl 19.4/Daniel L. Feicht Page 292(l)/Richard Ellis Page 292(c)/Merlin D. Tuttle/Bat Conservation International Page 292(r)/Sonja Bullaty and Angelo Lomeo 19.6/Nadine Orasona/Tom Stack & Associates (Kaibab squirrel); © Grant Heilman/Grant Heilman Photography 19.10/U.S. Department of Agriculture 19.11/Melinda Berge/Photographers, Aspen (cuscus); Edwin & Peggy Bauer (sloth); Douglas Baglin/Animals Animals (rabbit bandicoot); Stephen J. Krasemann/DRK Photo (hare); Gary Milburn/Tom Stack & Associates (glider); Melinda Berge (Tasmanian devil); Hans & Judy Beste/Tom Stack & Associates (numbat); Wayne Lankinen (squirrel); Annie Griffiths (wolverine); Loren McIntyre (anteater); G.R. Roberts (short-nosed bandicoot); Hans & Judy Beste/Animals Animals (long-nosed bandicoot) 19.12/L.E. Gilbert, Univ. of Texas at Austin/BPS 19.13b/Based on data from Sibley and Ahlquist: *Scientific American,* Feb. 1986, p. 87

CHAPTER 20   Page 312/Courtesy Lennart Nilsson/© Boehringer Ingelheim International/GmbH 20.2/© Roger Ressmeyer/Starlight 20.3/Dr. Sidney W. Fox. In Fox and Dose, "Molecular Evolution and the Origins of Life." 20.6/© Rick Smolan 20.8/Dr. R. Wyckoff/National Institutes of Health 20.9/NASA/Ames Research Center 20.10(tl)/Dr. Tony Brain/Science Photo Library 20.10(tc)/The Upjohn Company 20.10(bl)/Armed Forces Institute of Pathology 20.10(bc)/Biophoto Associates 20.11/Drs. Maria Costa and George B. Chapman, Georgetown University 20.12a/© C.C. Brinton, Jr., Univ. of Pittsburgh 20.12b/Centers for Disease Control 20.13a/© Sinclair Stammers/Science Photo Library/Photo Researchers, Inc. 20.13b/J.R. Waaland, Univ. of Washington/BPS 20.13c/© Sherman Thomson/Visuals Unlimited 20.13d/Courtesy of D.L. Findley, P.L. Walne and R.W. Holton, Univ. of Tennessee, Knoxville. From *J. Psychology* 6:182-188, 1970 20.15/© Lee D. Simon/Photo Researchers, Inc.

CHAPTER 21   Page 332/© Biological Photo Service 21.2(l)/Centers for Disease Control 21.2(r)/Dr. J.A.L. Cooke/Animals Animals 21.3a/© John D. Cunningham/Visuals Unlimited 21.3b/© Biophoto Associates/Science Source/Photo Researchers, Inc. 21.3c/© T.E. Adams/Visuals Unlimited 21.3d/© Jan Hinsck/Science Photo Library/Photo Researchers, Inc. 21.5(t)/William Patterson/Tom Stack & Associates 21.5(bl)/Brian Parker/Tom Stack and Associates 21.5(bc)/Manfred Kage/Peter Arnold, Inc. 21.5(br)/Eric V. Grave 21.7/Dr. Paul E. Hargraves 21.8/Biophoto Associates 21.8(cr)/Dr. Paul E. Hargraves 21.9/Frieder Sauer/Bruce Coleman, Ltd. 21.10/© M. Murayama, Murayama Research Lab/BPS 21.11/© Runk/Schoenberger from Grant Heilman 21.12/Howard Hall 21.14/© T.E. Adams/Visuals Unlimited 21.15a/Macmillan Science Co., Inc. 21.15b/© John D. Cunningham/Visuals Unlimited 21.16a/© Runk/Schoenberger from Grant Heilman 21.16b,d/Loomis, William F., *Dictyoslelium discoideum: A Developmental System.* © 1975 by Academic Press, Inc. 21.18c/L. West/Valenti Photo 21.19a/Loren A. McIntyre 21.19b/Runk/Schoenberger from Grant Heilman Photography 21.19c/Robert P. Carr 21.19d/Don and Pat Valenti 21.20/G.R. Roberts 21.21(t)/Eric V. Grave 21.21(b)/Pramer, D. 1964. *Science* 144:382-388 21.22/G.R. Roberts

CHAPTER 22   Page 358/© Donald R. Perry 22.1a/G.R. Roberts 22.1b/© Arnold J. Karpoff/Visuals Unlimited 22.4a/Walter Dawn 22.4b/Robert P. Carr 22.4c/G.R. Roberts 22.5/Steve Lissau 22.6/G.R. Roberts 22.8/A.J. Belling, New York Univ. 22.9/G.R. Roberts 22.9c/Field Museum of Natural History 22.10/Harold Sund 22.12/Biophoto Associates

CHAPTER 23   Page 373/© Rod Planck/Tom Stack and Associates Page 374(l)/Dr. E.S. Ross Page 374(c)/Robert P. Carr Page 374(r)/© Ken Brate/Photo Researchers Page 375(l)/Dr. E.S. Ross Page 375(c)/Oxford Scientific Films/Animals Animals Page 375(r)/Dr. Merlin D. Tuttle, Milwaukee Public Museum 23.2/G.R. Roberts 23.5/J.N.A. Lott, *McMaster U./BPS* Page 382(l)/G.R. Roberts 383/Robert P. Carr Page 384(t,br)/G.R. Roberts Page 384(bl)/John Ebeline Page 385(l)/John Shaw Page 385(r)/© Biological Photo Service

CHAPTER 24   Page 370/© Lynn M. Stone 24.7/© J.R. Waaland/Univ. of Washington/BPS 24.8a/© John D. Cunningham/Visuals Unlimited 24.8b/U.S. Dept. of Agriculture 24.9/© Biological Photo Service 24.12/© John D. Cunningham/Visuals Unlimited 24.13a/© Biological Photo Service 24.13b/© John D. Cunningham/Visuals Unlimited

CHAPTER 25   Page 408/© Kerry T. Givens/Tom Stack and Associates 25.1/Chuck Place 25.2/Grant Heilman/Grant Heilman Photography 25.7/Biophoto Associates 25.9/Paul P. Kormanik, U.S.D.A., F.S.

CHAPTER 26   Page 420/© Kerry T. Givens/Tom Stack and Associates 26.2/Biophoto Associates 26.3/U.S. Department of Agriculture 26.8a/© Runk/Schoenberger from Grant Heilman 26.8b/Zig Leszczynski/Earth Scenes 26.9a,b/Derek Fell 26.9c/Dr. Timothy Plowman

CHAPTER 27   Page 434/© Photo Researchers Inc. 27.5/Jeffrey L. Rotman 27.6/Kim Taylor/Bruce Coleman, Ltd. 27.7/William H. Amos/Bruce Coleman, Inc. 27.8a/© Bob DeGoursey, 1987/Visuals Unlimited 27.8b/Oxford Scientific Films/Animals Animals 27.8c/Douglas Faulkner/Sally Faulkner Collection 27.8d/U.S. Naval Photographic Station, Washington, D.C. 27.10/Ed Reschke 27.11(l)/© Biophoto Associates/Photo Researchers, Inc. 27.13(l)/© T.E. Adams, Click/Chicago 27.13(r)/Tom Adams 27.14/© Larry Jensen, 1987/Visuals Unlimited

CHAPTER 28   Page 452/© Dave Woodward/Tom Stack and Associates Jeff Foott/Tom Stack and Associates (chiton); © Stephen Dalton, 1973/Photo Researchers, Inc. (snail); © H. Wes Pratt/BPS (scallop); © Tom McHugh, Steinhart Aquarium/Photo Researchers, Inc. (squid) 28.3a/© Brian Parker/Tom Stack and Associates 28.3b/© 1981 Martin M. Rotker/Taurus Photos 28.3/© Runk/Schoenberger from Grant Heilman 28.6/M. Philip Kahl (grasshoppers); © D. Murawski, Click/Chicago (centipede); © Stephen Dalton/Photo Researchers, Inc. (millipede); M. Ederegger/DRK Photo (ants & aphids); Maria Zorn/Animals Animals (aphid); John Ebeling (mayflies) 28.7/Robert P. Carr 28.8/Manfred Kage/Peter Arnold, Inc. 28.19/David Scharf 28.12/Douglas Faulkner/Sally Faulkner Collection 28.13(l)/Douglas Faulkner/Sally Faulkner Collection 28.13(r)/Jeffrey L. Rotman 28.15/© Mike Newman, 1984/Photo Researchers.

CHAPTER 29   Page 472/© Donald R. Perry 29.1(t)/Dr. Guiseppe Mazza 29.1(b)/Heather Angel/Biofotos 29.4(t)/© Brian Parker/Tom Stack and Associates 29.4(b)/Wolf H. Fahrenbach 29.5(tl)/© John D. Cunningham/Visuals Unlimited 29.5(tr)/© Ed Robinson/Tom Stack and Associates 29.5(cl)/© Tom McHugh/Photo Researchers, Inc. 29.5(cr)/© Runk/Schoenberger from Grant Heilman 29.5(b)/© S.W. Ross, 1987/Visuals Unlimited 29.7/Peter Scoones/Seaphot 29.9a/C.A. Morgan 29.9b/Dr. E.S. Ross 29.9c/George H. Harris 29.11a/Dr. E.S. Ross 29.11b/Don and Pat Valenti 29.11c/Joe McDonald/Bruce Coleman, Inc. 29.12/James P. Rowan/Click, Chicago, Inc. 29.14a,e/G.R. Roberts 29.14b,c/William Boehm 29.14d/Wolfgang Bayer Productions 29.15/Paläontologisches Museum, Musem für Naturkunde der Humboldt-Universität, Berlin, D.D.R. 29.16/Courtesy of Dr. Carl Welty 29.17/H.R. Duncker

CHAPTER 30   Page 492/© Dan McCoy/Rainbow 30.2a/© Tom McHugh, 1978/Photo Researchers, Inc. 30.2b/David Agee/Anthro Photo 30.3/M. Philip Kahl 30.4/Joy Spurr/Bruce Coleman, Inc. 30.5(l,c)/© Margo Crabtree. Courtesy AAAS 30.5 (r)/Institute for Human Origins

CHAPTER 31   Page 504/© Dan McCoy/Rainbow 31.1/Ed Reschke 31.2/Ed Reschke 31.3b/Ed Reschke 31.4/© Biology Media, 1978, U.C. Berkeley, Dept. of Botany/Photo Researchers, Inc. 31.5/John Watney Photo Library 31.7a/© Eric Grave/Photo Researchers, Inc. 31.7c/© F. Mossler/Visuals Unlimited 31.11/Biophoto Associates

CHAPTER 32   Page 520/© Dan McCoy/Rainbow 32.1/Marty Stouffer/Animals Animals 32.3/Dr. Cedric S. Raine 32.10/Dr. John Heuser

CHAPTER 33 Page 534/© Dan McCoy/Rainbow 33.3/© Dr. C. Chumbley/Photo Researchers, Inc. 33.6b/Museo Cajal, Madrid Page 554/Cea-Orsay/CNRI/Science Photo Library/Photo Researchers, Inc. 33.11/Dan McCoy/Rainbow

CHAPTER 34 Page 551/© Rod Planck/Tom Stack and Associates 34.1/© Stephen Dalton/Photo Researchers, Inc. 34.3/© John D. Cunningham, 1985/Visuals Unlimited 34.7/Courtesy of Dr. Edwin B. Lewis

CHAPTER 35 Page 561/© Manfred Kage/Peter Arnold, Inc. 35.9/Ed Reschke

CHAPTER 36 Page 575/© Dan McCoy/Rainbow 36.1(t)/© Craig Darness, Click/Chicago 36.1(b)/© Barry L. Runk from Grant Heilman 36.1(r)/© Sven-Olof-Linblad/Photo Researchers, Inc.

CHAPTER 37 Page 590/© Joe McDonald/Tom Stack and Associates

CHAPTER 38 Page 605/© Dan McCoy/Rainbow 38.1/Dave Woodward/Taurus Photos (anemone); G.R. Roberts (mud puppy); Douglas Faulkner/Sally Faulkner Collection (fish); D. Wilder (insect); William Boehm (toad); © Thomas Kitchin/Tom Stack and Associates (owl)

CHAPTER 39 Page 619/© Dr. Tony Brain/Science Photo Library 39.4a/McAlpine, W.A. 1975. *Heart and Coronary Arteries.* New York, Heidelberg, Berlin: Springer-Verlag © 1985 39.4b/Nilsson, L. 1974. *Behold Man.* Boston: Little, Brown & Co. 39.6/Richard Stromberg/Chicago Page 627/Dr. Tony Brain/Science Photo Library/Photo Researchers, Inc. 39.8/D.W. Fawcett/Photo Researchers 39.9/Ed Reschke 39.10/Nilsson, Linnart. 1974. *Behold Man.* Boston: Little, Brown & Co. 39.11(tl,cl,cr)/© John D. Cunningham/Visuals Unlimited 39.11(tr)/© Alfred Owczarzak/Taurus Photos 39.11(b)/© Alfred Owczarzak/Science Photo Library International

CHAPTER 40 Page 635/Courtesy Lennart Nilsson © Boehringer Ingelheim International/GmbH 40.1/Bruce Wetzel and Harry Schaefer, NCI 40.2/James D. Hirsch, Rockefeller University 40.3/Zucker-Franklin, D., M.F. Greaves, C.E. Grossi, and A.M. Marmont. 1981. *Atlas of Blood Cells: Function and Pathology,* vol. 2. Philadelphia: Lea & Febiger. © 1981 by Edi. Ermes s.r.l.—Milan, Italy

CHAPTER 41 Page 649/© Fritz Goro/*Life Magazine* 41.1a/© Biophoto Associates/Photo Researchers, Inc. 41.1b/© Tom McHugh, 1973/Photo Researchers, Inc. 41.1c/Neville Coleman/Bruce Coleman, Ltd.

CHAPTER 42 Page 664/© Hans Pfletschinger/Peter Arnold, Inc. 42.1/© Dr. G. Schatten/Photo Researchers, Inc. 42.2/© John Giannicchi/Science Source/Photo Researchers, Inc. 42.3/Anderson, E.J. *J. Cell Biol.* 37:514-539. Reproduced by copyright permission of the Rockefeller University Press. 42.4/Dr. L. M. Beidler 42.7/After Mangold and Tiedemann, from Balinsky, 1975. 42.12/Nilsson, Lennart. 1974. *Behold Man.* Boston: Little, Brown & Co.; Nilsson, Lennart. 1977. *A Child Is Born.* New York: Delacorte Press 42.13/Maternity Center Association

CHAPTER 43 Page 684/© G. Schaller/Bruce Coleman, Inc. 43.1(t)/John Beach/Wildlife Picture Agency 43.1(b)/Brian Parker/Tom Stack & Associates 43.4/BBC Natural History Unit. From Sparks, J. 1982. *The Discovery of Animal Behavior.* London: a Collins Publishers/BBC co-production Page 691(tl)/Erwin and Peggy Bauer Page 691(tr)/Wolfgang Bayer Productions Page 691(b)/Stephen J. Krasemann/DRK Photo Page 693/Thomas McAvoy, *Life Magazine* © 1955 Time, Inc. 43.6/The Bettmann Archive

CHAPTER 44 Page 698/© Brian Parker/Tom Stack and Associates 44.1/John Beach/Wildlife Picture Agency Page 704(tl)/Stephen J. Krasemann/DRK Photo. Page 704(tr)/D. Wilder Page 704(bc)/John Chellman/Animals Animals Page 704(br)/Don and Pat Valenti Page 705/Dr. E.R. Degginger (snakes) Page 705(cl)/J.A.L. Cooke/Oxford Scientific Films/Animals Animals Page 705(bl)/Jeffrey L. Rotman Page 705/Dr. E.S. Ross (wasps) 44.5/George H. Harrison 44.6/© Biological Photo Service Page 709/Jane Burton and Kim Taylor/Bruce Coleman, Ltd. 44.7/Wolfgang Bayer Productions 44.8/Leonard Lee Rue III/Animals Animals 44.9/Stephen J. Krasemann/DRK Photo 44.10/Stephen Dalton/NHPA

CHAPTER 45 Page 717/© Walter H. Hodge/Peter Arnold, Inc. 45.5/James A. Yost 45.6/Loren A. McIntyre 45.7/Dr. E.S. Ross 45.8(l)/John Shaw 45.8(r)/James Tallon/Outdoor Exposures 45.9(tl)/Wymen Meinzer 45.9(tr)/John Gerlach/DRK Photo 45.9(bl)/Bob & Clara Calhoun/Bruce Coleman, Inc. 45.9(br)/William Boehm 45.10/Tom McHugh/Photo Researchers, Inc. 45.11/Loren A. McIntyre 45.12/© Bill Binzer/Photo Researchers, Inc. 45.13(tl)/George J. Sanker/DRK Photo 45.13(tr)/John Ebeling 45.13(bl)/Stephen J. Krasemann/DRK Photo 45.13(br)/Wayne Lankinen/DRK Photo 45.14/Stephen J. Krasemann/DRK Photo 45.14(tr)/Varin-Visage/Jacana 45.17/Phil Degginger 45.18/© Jeff Rotman/Peter Arnold, Inc.

CHAPTER 46 Page 740/© Brian Parker/Tom Stack and Associates Page 743(tl)/Dudley Foster/WHOI Page 743(tr)/Alvin External Camera/WHOI Page 743(b)/James Childress, UC-SB/WHOI 46.9/Muller, C.H. 1966. *Bulletin of the Torrey Botanical Club* 93:332-351 46.11/Bitterroot National Forest, U.S. Forest Service 46.12/John Ebeling

CHAPTER 47 Page 758/© Arthus Bertrand/Peter Arnold, Inc. 47.3/Ann and Myron Sutten/Tom Stack and Associates 47.5(t)/Zig Leszczynski/Animals Animals 47.5(b)/© Warren and Genny Garst/Tom Stack and Associates 47.6/© Frank T. Awbrey, 1986/Visuals Unlimited Page 766(l)/Gary Milburn/Tom Stack and Associates Page 766(r)/Stern/Black Star

CHAPTER 48 Page 770/© Photo Researchers 48.1(l)/© Paolo Koch/Photo Researchers, Inc. 48.1(r)/Wesley Bocxe/Photo Researchers, Inc. 48.3/© Thomas S. England, 1985/Photo Researchers, Inc.

INDEX